2—

Frommer's®

CALIFORNIA
FROM $60 A DAY

Here's what the critics say about Frommer's:

"Packed with places to stay, dine and explore—all at extraordinary low prices. A book to keep on your bookshelf to ensure that you and your friends are not missing a beat."
—*San Francisco Chronicle*

♦

"Amazingly easy to use. Very portable, very complete."
—*Booklist*

♦

"The only mainstream guide to list specific prices. The Walter Cronkite of guidebooks—with all that implies."
—*Travel & Leisure*

♦

"Complete, concise, and filled with useful information."
—*New York Daily News*

Other Great Guides for Your Trip:

Frommer's®

2nd Edition

CALIFORNIA
FROM $60 A DAY

by Erika Lenkert, Matthew R. Poole
& Stephanie Avnet Yates

MACMILLAN • USA

ABOUT THE AUTHORS

Combining the only three things he's good at—eating, sleeping, and criticizing—**Matthew R. Poole** has found a surprisingly prosperous career as a freelance travel writer. He has written and coauthored more than 20 travel guides to California and Hawaii, including *Frommer's San Francisco from $60 a Day* and *Frommer's Portable California Wine Country*. A native northern Californian, he currently lives in San Francisco but spends most of his time on the road.

A native San Franciscan, **Erika Lenkert** spends half her time in Los Angeles and the other half traveling to San Francisco and throughout the state. She's currently a contributing writer for *Los Angeles* magazine, coauthor of dozens of guides to California, the restaurant editor for *California Homes* magazine, and has contributed to *Brides, Cosmopolitan,* and *Time Out*. Erika is pleased that she actually gets paid to force her opinions onto others—something she'd done pro bono for years. Her next challenge? To convince San Franciscans that L.A.'s actually kind of cool.

A native of Los Angeles and an avid traveler, antiques hound, and pop-history enthusiast, **Stephanie Avnet Yates** believes that California is best seen from behind the wheel of a little red convertible. Prior to becoming a travel writer, she worked in the music business, but now prefers to hit the road exploring the Golden State. Stephanie also writes *Frommer's Los Angeles, Frommer's San Diego,* and the getaway guide *Wonderful Weekends from Los Angeles* (Macmillan Travel).

MACMILLAN TRAVEL USA

A Pearson Education Macmillan Company
1633 Broadway
New York, NY 10019

Find us online at **www.frommers.com**.

ISBN 0-02-862577-3
ISSN 1091-5761

Editor: Suzanne Roe Jannetta
Thanks to Vanessa Rosen, Ron Boudreau, and Lisa Renaud
Production Editor: Christy Wagner
Photo Editor: Richard Fox
Design: Michele Laseau
Digital Cartography: John Decamillis and Ortelius Design
Page Creation by Toi Davis, David Faust, Angel Perez
Front Cover Photo: Bodega Bay, Sonoma County
Back Cover Photo: Casa Cody, Palm Spring

SPECIAL SALES

Bulk purchases (10+ copies) of Frommer's and selected Macmillan travel guides are available to corporations, organizations, mail-order catalogs, institutions, and charities at special discounts, and can be customized to suit individual needs. For more information write to Special Sales, Macmillan General Reference, 1633 Broadway, New York, NY 10019.

Manufactured in the United States of America

Contents

8 The Far North: Lake Tahoe, the Shasta Cascades & Lassen Volcanic National Park 219

by Erika Lenkert and Matthew R. Poole

9 The High Sierra: Yosemite, Mammoth Lakes & Sequoia/Kings Canyon 256

by Erika Lenkert and Matthew R. Poole

10 Sacramento, the Gold Country & the Central Valley 287

by Erika Lenkert and Matthew R. Poole

List of Maps

ACKNOWLEDGEMENT

We wish to extend our heartfelt gratitude to Cheryl Farr, whose expertise, guidance, and support enabled us to make all our Frommer's California guidebooks what they are today. Thank you, Cheryl, for your critical eye, abiding humor, unwaivering encouragement, plus that occasional (and needed) kick in the pants. The spirit of your contributions will forever be reflected in subsequent editions.

AN INVITATION TO THE READER

In researching this book, we discovered many wonderful places—hotels, restaurants, shops, and more. We're sure you'll find others. Please tell us about them, so we can share the information with your fellow travelers in upcoming editions. If you were disappointed with a recommendation, we'd love to know that, too. Please write to:

Frommer's California from $60 a Day
Macmillan Travel
1633 Broadway
New York, NY 10019

AN ADDITIONAL NOTE

Please be advised that travel information is subject to change at any time—and this is especially true of prices. We therefore suggest that you write or call ahead for confirmation when making your travel plans. The authors, editors, and publisher cannot be held responsible for the experiences of readers while traveling. Your safety is important to us, however, so we encourage you to stay alert and be aware of your surroundings. Keep a close eye on cameras, purses, and wallets, all favorite targets of thieves and pickpockets.

WHAT THE SYMBOLS MEAN

✪ **Frommer's Favorites**

Our favorite places and experiences—outstanding for quality, value, or both.

The following abbreviations are used for credit cards:

AE	American Express	EU	Eurocard
CB	Carte Blanche	JCB	Japan Credit Bank
DC	Diners Club	MC	MasterCard
DISC	Discover	V	Visa
ER	EnRoute		

FIND FROMMER'S ONLINE

Arthur Frommer's Budget Travel Online (**www.frommers.com**) offers more than 6,000 pages of up-to-the-minute travel information—including the latest bargains and candid, personal articles updated daily by Arthur Frommer himself. No other Web site offers such comprehensive and timely coverage of the world of travel.

The Best of California for the Frugal Traveler

by Erika Lenkert, Matthew R. Poole, and Stephanie Avnet Yates

We know what you're thinking: How could anyone possibly enjoy a vacation in California for as little as $60 a day? After all, the average room rate alone is $123 a night—not including taxes, tipping, and taxi fare.

But if there's one thing we underpaid travel writers know better than anyone, it's how to live large and spend little. So we've pooled our collective wisdom into what we firmly believe is the best budget guide to California. We live here, we know this state, and we know how to have a *lot* of fun without spending mounds of cash—in fact, we do it every day. Some of our advice is obvious (skip the Ritz), even more comes from experience (go for the bargain fixed-priced menus at the hot restaurants)—and all of it is geared to making sure that you will have a fantastic California dreamin' vacation regardless of your tax bracket.

Yes, California has plenty of options for the traveler who wants to stay at ultra-luxurious $300-per-night hotel rooms and dine at blow-your-bank-account restaurants, but that's not how the majority of locals (including us) experience the state—the big cities, the small towns, the natural wonders, and the spaces in between. Traveling on a budget in California means doing what most of its denizens do every day: eating at some of the many affordable restaurants, exploring funky neighborhoods or off-the-beaten-track towns, and taking advantage of the wide variety of free or inexpensive attractions, from spectacular national and state parks to the miles (and miles) of fabulous coastline. Granted, you won't be sleeping on satin sheets or dining on caviar, but you're definitely more likely to experience the real California than those taking limos from their penthouse suite to five-star restaurants and back.

But the best advice we can give you about California is to just *go*. Enjoy the cool blast of salt air as you stroll across the Golden Gate Bridge. Experience the grandeur of Yosemite National Park. Check out the kaleidoscope of humanity at Venice Beach. Hit the slopes, pierce your nose, see a play, spot a celebrity—the list is endless and always affordable. It's all happening in California, and everyone, whether rich or in the red, is invited. All you have to do is arrive with an open mind and a sense of adventure—the rest is waiting for you.

1 The Best of Natural California

- **Point Reyes:** This extraordinarily scenic stretch of undeveloped coast and wetlands is one of the best wildlife-viewing regions in California. Numerous shorebirds, waterfowl, and hawks reside here, as well as elk and sea lions. You might even catch a glimpse of migrating whales from the Point Reyes Lighthouse. See chapter 7.

- **Redwood National Park:** Come see the largest of all living things, the mighty *Sequoia sempervirens.* Within the old-growth redwood forests that line the northern California coast are acres and acres of unbelievably massive and majestic redwood trees, all of which shade a thick, lush canopy of huge ferns, mosses, and wild orchids. It is truly one of the most awe-inspiring natural wonders in the world. See chapter 7.

- **Mt. Shasta:** One of the most spectacular sights in all of northern California is the mighty volcano Mt. Shasta, a solitary tower of rock and snow rising thousands of feet above the valley floor. And if you're in fair shape, it makes for an exhilarating climb as well. See chapter 8.

- **Lake Tahoe:** One of the world's most magnificent bodies of fresh water, Lake Tahoe is famous for its 99.997% pure water and incredible volume. In fact, it's so deep that the water it contains—close to 40 trillion gallons—could cover the entire state of California to a depth of 14½ inches. See chapter 8.

- **Yosemite National Park:** There's no question about it, Yosemite is one of the most amazing places on the entire planet, with its miles of rivers, lakes, peaks, and valleys; 3 out of 10 of the world's tallest waterfalls; the largest single granite monolith in the world; and some of the world's largest trees. It's best seen by making a quick trip through the tourist-laden valley then high-tailing it into the backcountry wilderness for a day or overnight hike. See chapter 9.

- **The Elkhorn Slough Safari:** When you're sick of schlepping your way through Monterey's hordes of tourists, take a 20-minute drive north and embark on a safe and friendly voyage best described as stepping into the pages of *National Geographic.* The tour isn't exactly cheap, but the upclose views of "rafts" of otters, harbor seals, and hundreds of bird species are absolutely priceless. See chapter 11.

- **Point Lobos State Reserve:** Take Calif. 1 about 4 miles south of Carmel to view harbor seals, sea lions, and sea otters at play. From December through May, gray whales pass by on their migration south. The area is filled with nature walks. See chapter 11.

- **Cachuma Lake:** Situated on mountainous and scenic Calif. 154, halfway between Solvang and Santa Barbara, Cachuma Lake is the stunning winter home to dozens of American bald eagles. Loons, white pelicans, and Canada geese are some of the other migratory birds that call this glassy lake home part of the year. See chapter 12.

- **Channel Islands National Park:** This is California in its most natural state. Paddle a kayak into sea caves; camp among indigenous island fox and seabirds; and swim, snorkel, or scuba dive tide pools and kelp forests teeming with wildlife. The channel waters are prime for whale watching, and May brings the elephant-seal mating season, when you'll see them and their sea lion cousins sunbathing on cove beaches. See chapter 12.

- **Antelope Valley Poppy Reserve:** California's state flower, the poppy, blooms between March and May, carpeting the hillsides in brilliant hues of red, orange, and gold. This reserve, in the high desert near Los Angeles, is one of the poppy's most consistent natural growing sites. The fields extend for miles around—it's not uncommon to see motorists along Calif. 14 pull to the side of the road to marvel at the breathtaking spectacle. From Los Angeles, take I-5 north to Calif. 14; you'll know when you've arrived. For driving directions and information, call ☎ **805/724-1180;** for information on the annual California Poppy Festival in Lancaster, call ☎ 805/723-6000. See the "California Calendar of Events" in chapter 2.

- **Joshua Tree National Park:** You'll find awesome rock formations, groves of flowering cacti and stately Joshua trees, ancient Native American petroglyphs, and shifting sand dunes in this desert wonderland—and a brilliant night sky, if you choose to camp here. See chapter 15.
- **Death Valley National Park:** Its inhospitable climate makes it the state's most unlikely tourist attraction. But the same conditions that thwarted settlers create some of the most dramatic landscapes you'll ever see. Mesmerizing rock formations, ever-changing dry lake beds, and often stifling heat provide the setting for relics of hardy 19th-century borax miners and (fool)hardy dwellers from the 1930s. See chapter 15.
- **Torrey Pines State Reserve:** Poised on a majestic cliff overlooking the Pacific Ocean, this reserve is home to the rare torrey pine and numerous hiking trails; hang gliders soaring overhead get a bird's-eye view. At the base of the cliffs you'll find tide pools, and just offshore is a unique Underwater Park for divers. See chapter 16.
- **Anza-Borrego Desert State Park:** The largest state park in the Lower 48 attracts the most visitors during the spring wildflower season, when a kaleidoscopic carpet blankets the desert floor. Others come year-round to hike the more than 100 miles of designated trails. See chapter 16.

2 The Best Beaches

- **The Sonoma Coast State Beaches:** Stretching approximately 10 miles from Bodega Bay to Jenner, these pristine and rarely populated beaches are perfect for exploring tide pools, bird watching, or simply enjoying a quiet day of sunbathing. From March through June, seals giving birth to pups are a common sight, as are migrating gray whales from December through April. See chapter 7.
- **Drake's Beach:** At this massive stretch of white sand at Point Reyes National Seashore, west of Inverness, winds and choppy seas make it rough for swimmers, but sun worshippers can have their Marin County tan for the day. If the rangers say it's all right, beach driftwood can make a romantic campfire in the early evening. See chapter 7.
- **Sand Dollar:** The best Big Sur beach lies beyond Pacific Valley; it's ideal for swimming and surfing, with a panoramic view of Cone Peak, one of the coast's highest mountains. See chapter 11.
- **Pfeiffer Beach:** This is one of Big Sur's best-kept secrets. It can be accessed via an unmarked paved road on the right-hand side of Calif. 1, 1 mile south of Pfeiffer State Park. There are no signs, so you'll have to do some sleuthing, but once you've parked behind the trail of cars on the side of the road and made it to the beach, you'll know why locals want to keep this spot all to themselves. See chapter 11.
- **Santa Barbara's Cabrillo Beach:** This wide swath of clean, white sand hosts beach umbrellas, sand-castle builders, and spirited volleyball games. A grassy, parklike median keeps the happy beachgoers insulated from busy Cabrillo Boulevard. On Sundays local artists display their wares beneath the elegant palm trees. See chapter 12.

- **Malibu's Legendary Beaches:** Zuma and Surfrider beaches are the stretches of sand that were the inspiration for the 1960s surf music that embodies the southern California beach experience. Surfrider, just up from Malibu Pier, is home to Los Angeles's best waves. Zuma is loaded with amenities, including snack bars, rest rooms, and jungle gyms. In addition to some of the state's best sunbathing, you can walk in front of the Malibu Colony, a star-studded enclave of multimillion-dollar homes set in this seductively curving stretch of coast. See chapter 13.
- **Hermosa Beach:** This is one of Los Angeles's top beaches for family outings. It's also popular with the volleyball set. It offers wide sands, a paved boardwalk ("The Strand") that's great for strolling and biking, and loads of amenities, including plenty of parking. See chapter 13.
- **La Jolla's Beaches:** *La Jolla* means "the jewel," and the beaches of La Jolla's cliff-lined coast truly are gems. Each has a distinct personality: Surfers love Windansea's waves; Torrey Pines and La Jolla Shores are popular for swimming and sunbathing; and Black's Beach is San Diego's unofficial (and illegal) nude beach. See chapter 16.
- **Coronado Beach:** On the west side of Coronado extending to the Hotel del Coronado, this beautiful beach is uncrowded and great for watching the sunset. Marilyn Monroe romped in the surf here during the filming of *Some Like It Hot*. See chapter 16.

3 The Best Walks

- **Golden Gate Park:** This walk in the park allows you to escape the bustle of San Francisco and venture through an array of attractions, including the stunning exterior of the 1878 Conservatory of Flowers, splendid museums and a Japanese Tea Garden, a 430-foot-high artificial island (with a great view), Strawberry Hill, and breathtaking flora and fauna along the way. End your walk by renting a row-boat and taking it for a spin. See chapter 4.
- **Point Reyes National Seashore:** If you like day hikes, you'll love Point Reyes National Seashore. In fact, many of the region's best—and least crowded—highlights can only be approached on foot, such as Alamere Falls, a freshwater stream that cascades down a 40-foot bluff onto Wildcat Beach, or Tomales Point Trail, which passes through the Tule Elk Reserve, a protected haven for roaming herds of tule elk that once numbered in the thousands. See chapter 7.
- **Mendocino Headlands State Park:** Between Mendocino and the Pacific is one of the most scenic nature trails in the north. From December through March, the California gray whales pass by on their migration from the Arctic Ocean and Bering Sea to Baja California, and the sunset vistas are incredible. See chapter 7.
- **Yosemite National Park:** It's a relatively short and easy hike to Yosemite Falls, the highest waterfall in North America and the fifth highest in the world (upper falls at 1,430 feet), or to Bridalveil Fall, a ragged 620-foot cascade that can be wind-tossed as much as 20 feet from side to side. A more strenuous option is the 3½-mile Yosemite Fall Trail, which rises to a height of 2,700 feet for one of the most panoramic vistas in the West. See chapter 9.
- **The Beachfront Trails at Big Sur:** Combine towering cliffs, rock-strewn beaches, and a backdrop of redwood forests, and you have one of the most dramatic stretches for coastline hiking in the world. Begin your adventure about 8 miles south of Point Lobos. See chapter 11.

- **Cabrillo Peak:** Morro Bay State Park offers a terrific day hike that culminates with a fantastic 360° view of surrounding hills and the distant ocean. There are hiking trails, but the best way to reach the top is by bushwhacking straight up the gentle slope. See chapter 12.
- **Beverly Hills's "Golden Triangle":** Defined by Wilshire Boulevard, Crescent Drive, and Santa Monica Boulevard, this is a window-shopper's fantasyland of tiny shops with picture-perfect displays and sky-high price tags. It even boasts a cluster of shops built to resemble an Italian plaza, with its own faux cobblestone "streets." Despite what you've heard about Rodeo Drive tariffs (it's all true), don't worry: There are plenty of down-to-earth shops and eateries, plus an elegant Moorish-Mediterranean city hall that's worth a look. See chapter 13.
- **The L.A. Conservancy's Guided Walking Tours of Downtown Los Angeles:** The Conservancy conducts a dozen fascinating, information-packed tours of historic downtown Los Angeles, seed of today's sprawling metropolis. The most popular is "Broadway Theaters," a loving look at movie palaces; other intriguing ones include "Marble Masterpieces," "Art Deco," "Mecca for Merchants," and tours of the landmark Biltmore Hotel and City Hall. See chapter 13.
- **Griffith Park:** This wooded enclave linking Hollywood with the San Fernando Valley has something for everyone. Be on the lookout for golf carts crossing near the picturesque Wilson and Harding golf courses, and for horseback riders from the nearby Equestrian Center. The L.A. Zoo and the Autry Museum lie at the northeast corner near I-5; the hills are loaded with hiking trails and picnic areas, and kids love the merry-go-round and pony rides. See chapter 13.
- **From Crystal Pier (in Pacific Beach) South to the Jetty, and then North Along the Bay Side to the Catamaran Hotel:** During the first part of this walk, you'll share the sidewalk with joggers, cyclists, and in-line skaters, and surfers will be testing their skill on the waves to your right. After you cross over to the Mission Bay side of Mission Boulevard, you'll experience the more subdued side of things: quiet water lapping onto white-sand beaches and the local residents tending their gardens. It's a lovely way to spend the day in San Diego. See chapter 16.
- **From the San Diego Convention Center to Harbor Island:** This delightful stroll takes you around the waterfront of San Diego Bay. Along the way you'll pass Seaport Village, Tuna Bay, the cruise-ship terminal, the Embarcadero, and the Maritime Museum. The foot and cycle path offers a great view of Coronado and the ships plying the harbor. See chapter 16.

4 The Best Budget Golf Courses

- **Lincoln Park Golf Course** (San Francisco): The only problem with playing this course is that the views are so stunning, they may distract your game. For $23 to $27, you can tee off with the Golden Gate Bridge as a backdrop. If you want to play a few holes before sunset, nearby is the casual, but equally beautiful, 9-hole **Golden Gate Park Course,** where you can get 9 in for a mere $10 to $13. See chapter 4.
- **Pacific Grove Municipal Golf Course:** In an area where most golfers cough up $200 to swing their clubs, this course offers golf at a price any duffer can afford. For a mere $25 to $30, you can play 18 holes overlooking the same beautiful ocean landscape that Pebble Beach does. See chapter 11.
- **Santa Barbara Golf Club:** Unlike many municipal courses in California, this 6,009-yard, 18-hole course is well maintained and was designed to present a

moderate challenge for the average golfer. Greens fees are $24 weekdays, $28 on weekends ($17 for seniors). The driving range is an added bonus. See chapter 12.

- **Rancho Park Golf Course** (Los Angeles): Although budget golf is almost an oxymoron in Los Angeles, Rancho Park, located smack-dab in the middle of the west side, offers a private-course atmosphere at public-course prices. Greens fees are $17 Monday through Friday, $22 on weekends. See chapter 13.
- **Palm Springs Country Club:** The oldest public-access golf course within the city limits, this uniquely laid-out course is especially popular with budget-conscious golfers. With greens fees of only $40 to $50 (including cart), this is about as cheap as it gets in the desert. See chapter 15.
- **Torrey Pines Golf Course** (La Jolla): Two gorgeous 18-hole championship courses overlook the ocean and provide players with plenty of challenge. In February, the Buick Invitational Tournament is held here; the rest of the year these popular municipal courses are open to everybody. Greens fees are $48 weekdays and $52 weekends, with twilight fees of only $26. See chapter 16.
- **Coronado Municipal Golf Course** (San Diego): This 18-hole, par-72 municipal course overlooking Glorietta Bay is located to the left of the Coronado Bay Bridge. It's the first thing you see when you arrive in Coronado—a fabulous welcome for duffers. Greens fees are $32 ($20 to walk), with a 50% twilight discount. See chapters 2 and 16.

5 The Best Offbeat Experiences that Won't Cost You a Fortune

- **Taking a Mud Bath in Calistoga:** It's one of the most relaxing experiences in California: getting buck naked and covered in this town's famous volcanic-ash mud (mixed with mineral water). At a dozen or so places you can immerse yourself in the mud bath, followed by a mineral-water shower and a whirlpool bath, then a steam bath. See chapter 6.
- **Panning for Gold in the Gold Country:** In the southern Gold Country, you can dig into living history and pan for gold. Several companies, including **Gold Prospecting Expeditions** (☎ **800/596-0009** or 209/984-4653) in Jamestown, offer dredging lessons and gold-panning tours. You'll quickly learn that this is back-breaking labor, although an adventure. And who knows? You might get lucky and launch a new gold rush. See chapter 10.
- **Riding the Amtrak Rails along the Southern California Coast:** Relive the golden age of train travel and see the natural beauty of California, avoiding the crowded highways at the same time. Spanish-style Union Station, a marble-floored Streamline Moderne masterpiece, is the Los Angeles hub. Trains run between Los Angeles and the romantic mission towns of San Juan Capistrano, San Diego, Santa Barbara, and San Luis Obispo. The scenery includes lush valleys, windswept coastline, and the occasional urban stretch. Call **Amtrak** at ☎ **800/USA-RAIL** (www.amtrak.com) for information.
- **Discovering Downtown Los Angeles's Public Art:** The wealth of public art on display in downtown Los Angeles is one of the city's best-kept secrets. Some works are political or social commentaries (such as the black experience as represented by the life of former slave Biddy Mason in a multimedia exhibit between Broadway and Spring streets just south of 3rd Street, or the provocative evolutionary chronicle installed outside the Central Library). Others are abstract and open to a variety of interpretations. Pershing Square, a formerly untended

eyesore bounded by Fifth, Sixth, Olive, and Hill streets, has been reincarnated as a modern-sculpture garden. See chapter 13.

- **Exploring Forest Lawn Memorial Park:** America's most famous cemetery is a wacky 300-acre park with more stars in the ground than Hollywood's Walk of Fame. In addition to Hollywood's most dearly departed, the cemetery contains 1,000 full-scale reproductions of Renaissance statuary, the enormous Great Mausoleum with its oversized stained-glass reproduction of *The Last Supper,* and the Church of the Recessional, where Ronald Reagan married his first wife, Jane Wyman. See chapter 13.

- **Strolling Venice Beach:** All of humanity, for better and worse, is represented on a boardwalk framed by broad sands, swaying palms, and the sparkling blue Pacific. The day's carnival might include well-tanned body builders, outrageous street performers, scantily clad beach bunnies (bimbos and himbos), roving gangs of teens, psychedelic-era hippies, and much more. Experiment with style at the cheap-sunglass stalls, grab an exotic dog at Jody Maroni's Sausage Kingdom, and make your way to the Santa Monica Pier to check out the historic photo gallery and carousel. See chapter 13.

- **Going to the Movies, San Diego–Style:** Imagine sitting on the deck of the world's oldest merchant ship and watching a film projected on the "screen-sail"; floating on a raft in a huge indoor pool while a movie is shown on the wall; watching a silent movie accompanied by the San Diego Symphony; or sitting on the beach watching a movie that's projected on a floating barge. Only in San Diego! See chapter 16.

- **Experiencing a San Diego Christmas:** Although visions of sugar plums don't dance in most people's heads when they think of San Diego, the area does offer a variety of unusual Christmas traditions. These include Christmas on the Prado in Balboa Park, and the Mission Bay Boat Parade of Lights, where decorated boats of all sizes and types are the focus of attention. And it wouldn't be Christmas without the annual reading of Dr. Seuss's *How the Grinch Stole Christmas* at Loews Coronado Bay Resort. See chapters 2 and 16.

6 The Best Places to Get Away from It All

- **The Mt. Shasta and Mt. Lassen Regions:** The region around Mt. Shasta and Mt. Lassen is a remote yet beautiful swath of northern California, a place where you can wander away from everything and everybody. The best time to come is in the late spring when the wildflowers first burst into bloom and the trout are jumping. See chapter 8.

- **Sequoia and Kings Canyon National Parks:** They have only a fraction of Yosemite's crowds and they're stunningly beautiful. This is a land of grandiose scenery separated by Kings Canyon, the deepest chasm in the continental United States. Virgin forests carpet the parks. Use them for hiking or wilderness camping almost unequaled in America. Autumn is our favorite time to visit. Almost everyone disappears, and you get to experience crisp, fall days and long, lingering Indian summers. See chapter 9.

- **The Ventana Wilderness (Big Sur):** The U.S. Forest Service maintains 167,323 scenic acres straddling the Santa Lucia Mountains. Cascading streams, waterfalls, deep pools, and thermal springs take you back to Eden. Bring your Adam or Eve so you won't get lonely in the midst of all this nature. See chapter 11.

- **Channel Islands National Park:** Just off the coast of Ventura is a world removed from the bustle of southern California. The islands are a wild and storm-blown region of sharp cliffs, curving grasslands, and rocky coves punctuated by the barking of elephant seals and sea lions. Camping among the archipelago's many endemic plant species and fascinating array of animals (including the endangered brown pelican and indigenous fox) is a splendid way to steep yourself in the beauty of this untamed preserve. See chapter 12.

- **The Huntington Library, Art Collections, and Botanical Gardens** (near Pasadena): This Pasadena area getaway is many treats in one. The former estate of railroad baron Henry Huntington is a spectacular botanical garden whose highlights include Japanese and Zen gardens, an oft-filmed statuary lawn, a camellia garden, and tranquil lily ponds. The Italianate main house is a gallery of European paintings, and scholars flock to study at the Huntington Library, one of the world's finest collections of rare manuscripts and first editions (including a Gutenberg Bible). A superb bookstore and delightful tearoom round out this peaceful retreat. See chapter 13.

- **The Pine Hills Area of Julian:** A half-dozen bed-and-breakfast inns are located in this wonderfully quiet small town, where birdsong is the loudest sound you'll hear. Though Main Street is jam-packed during apple harvest season, the surrounding hills never lose their serenity. See chapter 16.

7 The Best Things to Do for Free

- **Beaching It:** It wouldn't be a true California vacation if you didn't hit at least one of the state's beautiful beaches. See each coastal chapter for beach highlights.

- **Walking the Golden Gate Bridge:** Break out your windbreaker and walking shoes and venture across San Francisco's windy Golden Gate Bridge. On a sunny day, every view is spectacular. In dense fog, it can be bone-chilling, but still a mystical experience. See chapter 4.

- **Taking a Wine-Appreciation Class: Goosecross Cellars** (☎ **707/944-1986**), a Napa Valley winery near Yountville, gives a free class each Saturday morning at 11am. In the course of a few hours, they can turn anyone into a budding sommelier. Ignorance being bliss, you even get to taste all kinds of yummy wines while you learn.

- **Discovering Muir Woods and Point Reyes:** If you're in or around the Bay Area and have wheels, indulge in this memorable side trip. Take Calif. 101 to the Stinson Beach exit and spend a few hours gawking at the monolithic redwoods at Muir Woods (this place is amazing); continue on past Stinson Beach, then head up the coast to the spectacular Point Reyes National Seashore. Rain or shine, you won't be disappointed. See chapters 5 and 7.

- **Whale Watching:** Gray whales travel along the California coast from late December to early February, and you don't need to get on a whale-watching boat to enjoy this amazing spectacle. Point Reyes Lighthouse is a particularly good onshore whale-watching spot. See chapter 7.

- **Exploring Shasta Dam and Power Plant:** Located near Mt. Shasta, the Shasta Dam and Power Plant offers one of the best free tours in the state and an entertaining way to beat the summer heat. Explore deep within the dam's many chilly corridors and below the enormous spillway. Call ☎ **530/275-4463** for details. See chapter 8.

- **Exploring Yosemite:** Walk, hike, camp, or just drive in and catch some rays. Whatever you do in Yosemite, bring your camera, because the landscape is nothing less than astounding. If you're the sporting type, you can get up close and personal with some of the largest waterfalls on earth, climb a gargantuan granite monolith, or swim in fresh snowmelt lakes. There's a nominal charge to enter the park, but once you're in, it's yours to explore. See chapter 9.

- **Touring the State Capitol in Sacramento:** Looking very much like a scale model of the U.S. Capitol in Washington, D.C., this domed structure is the city's most distinctive landmark. Free guided tours, offered daily (every hour on the hour), shed light on the building's architecture and the workings of government. For information call ☎ **916/324-0333.** See chapter 10.

- **Cruising Pacific Grove's Ocean View Boulevard:** This coastal stretch, which starts near Monterey's Cannery Row and follows the Pacific Ocean south to Asilomar State Beach, offers views as spectacular as those of 17-Mile Drive, but without the $6.50-per-car entrance fee. See chapter 11.

- **Soaking Up the Sights and Sounds of SLO's Farmers Market:** Spend a Thursday evening at the Farmers Market in San Luis Obispo to get the true flavor of this somewhat earthy, intimate community. There's usually live music, barbecues, demonstrations, discussions, and plenty of places to plop down and watch this small town rejoice. See chapter 12.

- **Checking out the Santa Barbara Crafts Fairs:** Stroll along the promenade of East Beach by Stearns Wharf on a Sunday and you'll get a good dose of ocean air, sunshine, and fabulous art. Here dozens of arts and crafts vendors sell their wares. Don't bother paying $6 to park in the lot; if you continue south on Cabrillo Boulevard, you're likely to find free parking. See chapter 12.

- **Watching the Sunset from a Southern California Pier:** Malibu, Santa Monica, Huntington, Newport, or Oceanside—nothing rivals the sensation of standing suspended over the swirling ocean, watching a glowing sun descend into the horizon. Wispy clouds reflect the reds, oranges, and pinks cast by the receding sun, and behind you waves crash upon meeting the sand. See chapters 13, 14, and 16.

- **Spending an Afternoon at Los Angeles's Central Library:** The city is truly fond of the Central Library, for both its history and its architecture, and for the remarkable effort made by firefighters and philanthropists to save and restore it after a fire in 1986. Behind the familiar facade is a newly designed modern wing housing most of the library's countless volumes and a light-filled atrium with gigantic, whimsical chandeliers. Intriguing outdoor art adorns the front courtyard. Admission is free, of course, and weekend parking in the library's lot is just $2 with validation. See chapter 13.

- **Attending an Organ Concert in Balboa Park** (San Diego): Free 1-hour Sunday concerts are given at the Spreckels Organ Pavilion, home of the world's largest pipe organ; from June through August you can also attend free evening concerts here as part of the city's "Twilight in the Park" festival. See chapter 16.

8 The Best Family Vacation Experiences

- **San Francisco:** Ride the cable cars that "climb halfway to the stars" and visit the Exploratorium, the California Academy of Sciences (which includes the Steinhart Aquarium), the zoo, the ships at the maritime museum, Golden Gate Park, and much more. The City by the Bay is filled with unexpected pleasures for all members of the family and all ages. See chapter 4.

- **San Jose:** You'd be surprised how much fun your family can have in San Jose. The whole gang will enjoy the Children's Discovery Museum, the Tech Museum of Innovation, and especially the architecturally bizarre Winchester Mystery House and Paramount's Great America. See chapter 5.

- **Lake Tahoe:** Lake Tahoe has piles of family-fun things to do. Skiing, snowboarding, hiking, tobogganing, swimming, fishing, boating, waterskiing, mountain biking—the list is nearly endless. Even the casinos cater to kids while Mom and Pop play the slots. See chapter 8.
- **Yosemite National Park:** Camping or staying in a cabin in Yosemite is a premier family activity in California. Sites are scattered over 17 different campgrounds, and the rugged beauty of the Sierra Nevada surrounds you. During the day, the family itinerary is packed with hiking, bicycling, white-water trips, and even mountaineering to rugged, snowy peaks. See chapter 9.
- **Monterey:** It's been called "Disneyland-by-the-Sea" because of all its tourist activities, including those on Cannery Row and Fisherman's Wharf. Check out the state-of-the-art aquarium and have breakfast at the **Bagel Bakery** at 201 Lighthouse Blvd. (the best family bargain in town). See chapter 11.
- **Big Bear Lake:** Families flock year-round to this lake in the San Bernardino Mountains, and not just for the skiing. Horseback riding, miniature golf, water sports, and the Alpine Slide (kind of a snowless bobsled) are fun alternatives, and you can see and learn about native wildlife at the Moonridge Animal Park. The village has a movie theater, arcade, and dozens of cutesy bear-themed businesses. Most of the local lodging consists of clusters of woodsy cabins that are perfect for families. See chapter 14.
- **Disneyland:** The "Happiest Place on Earth" is family entertainment at its best. Whether you're wowed by Disney animation come alive, thrilled by the roller-coaster rides, or interested in the history and hidden secrets of this pop-culture icon, you won't walk away disappointed. Stay at the nearby Disneyland Hotel (connected directly to the park by monorail), a wild attraction unto itself, which offers appealing packages including multiday access to the park that can really save you some money. There's also a terrific extra bonus: On most days, guests of the hotel get to enter the park early and enjoy the major rides with no lines. But if the hotel tariffs are still too rich for your blood, don't worry; we've recommended plenty of comfortable motels nearby. Call ahead for the day's schedule. See chapter 14.
- **San Diego Zoo, Wild Animal Park, and Sea World:** San Diego boasts three of the world's best animal attractions. At the zoo, animals live in creatively designed habitats such as Tiger River and Hippo Beach. At the Wild Animal Park, 3,000 animals roam freely over 2,200 acres. And Sea World, with its ever-changing animal shows and exhibits, is an aquatic wonderland. See chapter 16.

9 The Best of Small-Town California

- **St. Helena:** A small town in the heart of the Napa Valley, St. Helena is known for its Main Street, which is lined with Victorian storefronts featuring intriguing wares. In a horse and buggy, Robert Louis Stevenson and his new bride, the cantankerous Fanny, made their way down this street. But these days it's the thoroughfare for visitors who come for the finest in accommodations, shopping, and dining. See chapter 6.
- **Mendocino:** An artist's colony with a New England flavor, Mendocino served as the backdrop for *Murder, She Wrote*. Perched on the cliff tops above the Pacific Ocean, it's filled with small art galleries, general stores, weathered wooden houses, and elbow-to-elbow tourists. See chapter 7.
- **Arcata:** If you're losing your faith in America, a few days spent at this northern California coastal town will surely restore your patriotism. One of the best small

towns in America, Arcata has it all: its own redwood forest and bird marsh, a charming town square, great family-owned restaurants, and even its own minor-league baseball team, which draws the whole town together for an afternoon of pure camaraderie. See chapter 7.

- **Nevada City:** The whole town is a national historic landmark and the best place to understand gold-rush fever. Settled in 1849, it offers fine dining and shopping and a stock of multigabled Victorian frame houses of the Old West. Relics of the ill-fated Donner Party are on display at the 1861 Firehouse No. 1. See chapter 10.
- **Pacific Grove:** Here you can escape the crowds that descend on Monterey, 2 miles to the west. Pacific Grove is known for its tranquil waterfront location and quiet, unspoiled air. Thousands of monarch butterflies flock here between October and March to make their winter home in Washington Park. See chapter 11.
- **Cambria:** Near Hearst Castle, Cambria benefits from a constant stream of visitors, who bring the right amount of sophistication to this picturesque coastal town. Moonstone Beach holds a string of seaside lodges, while the village itself is filled with charming B&Bs, artists' studios and galleries, and friendly shops. See chapter 12.
- **Ojai:** When Hollywood needed a Shangri-La for the movie *Lost Horizon,* they drove 1½ hours north to idyllic Ojai Valley, an unspoiled hideaway of eucalyptus groves and small ranches warmly nestled among soft, green hills. Ojai is the amiable village at the valley's heart. It's a mecca for artists, free spirits, and weary city folk in need of a restful weekend in the country. See chapter 12.
- **Ventura:** This charming mission town is filled with colorful Victorians. It's also home to a pleasantly eclectic old Main Street lined with thrift and antique shops, used-record stores, friendly diners, and even old-time saloons operating beneath broken-down second-story hotels. Don't miss the historic mission or the deco-era Greek Revival San Buenaventura City Hall looming over the town, bedecked with smiling stone faces of the founding Franciscan friars. See chapter 12.
- **Julian:** This old mining town in the Cuyamaca Mountains near San Diego is well known today for its wildflower fields, the fall apple harvest, and tasty flavored breads from Dudley's Bakery. There's plenty of pioneer history here, too, including a local-history museum, a circa 1888 schoolhouse, and mining demonstrations. A smattering of antique shops, plenty of barbecue, and an old-fashioned soda fountain operating since 1886 round out the experience. See chapter 16.

10 The Best California-Style Americana

- **Mel's Diner** (San Francisco; ☎ **415/921-3039**): Kids from 6 to 60 love this quintessential 1950s diner straight out of *American Graffiti.* Though the fare has advanced to meet today's demands (there's even a veggie burger on the menu), you can still stuff yourself with a big, juicy bacon cheeseburger, a side of "wet fries" (they're smothered in gravy), and a milk shake. There's plenty of chrome, miniature jukeboxes at each table with good ol' American hits on them, and photo memorabilia from the movie that inspired the place. Kids will love the crayons and meal-in-a-car. See chapter 4.
- **Phoenix Hotel** (San Francisco; ☎ **800/248-9466**): Get out your red heart-shaped sunglasses and you'll be ready for the funky Phoenix. An intentionally tacky tropic oasis in the midst of one of the city's most colorful, and shady,

neighborhoods, this 1950s-style retro-chic motel hosts all walks of life, from famous rockers to politicians and movie stars who come for the anonymity, the kidney-shaped pool, and reggae at the adjoining festive restaurant. See chapter 4.

- **Baseball in Arcata:** On Wednesday, Friday, and Saturday evenings between June and July, Arcata's semipro baseball team, the Humboldt Crabs, partakes in America's favorite pastime at Arcata Ballpark at 9th and F streets. For a $3.50 ticket, it's one of the best entertainment bargains on the North Coast. See chapter 7.

- **Samoa Cookhouse** (Samoa; ☎ 707/442-1659): When lumber was king in northern California, cookhouses were the hub of Eureka. Here the mill men and longshoremen came to chow down three hot meals before, during, and after their 12-hour workday. The Samoa is the last of the great cookhouses, and the food is still hearty, served up family style at long red-checkered tables; nobody leaves hungry. See chapter 7.

- **Ponderosa Ranch** (Lake Tahoe; ☎ 702/831-0691): Remember Hoss and Little Joe Cartwright from the popular 1960s television show *Bonanza?* Well, their digs are still kickin', folks, so mosey on over to Tahoe to visit the original 1959 Cartwright Ranch House and Western township, complete with blacksmith's shop and staged gun battles. There are also such activities as breakfast hayrides and pony rides. See chapter 8.

- **Dennis the Menace Playground:** Just north of Monterey, at Camino El Estero and Del Monte Avenue, near Lake Estero, is an expansive, old-fashioned playground created by Pacific Grove resident and famous cartoonist Hank Ketcham. It has a pond, bridges to cross, tunnels to climb through, an authentic Southern Pacific engine car teeming with wanna-be conductors, and plenty of Dennis the Menace motifs. It's a must-see for families. See chapter 11.

- **The Madonna Inn** (San Luis Obispo; ☎ 800/543-9666): No, not that Madonna. This inn is named after Alex and Phyllis Madonna, who, though they have no ties to the pop star, share with her a wild and decidedly unique sense of style. The entire hotel is one giant over-the-top fantasy, done up in Pepto Bismol pink, Flintstone-style rock, and whatever else catches their whim. You've got to see this place for yourself. See chapter 12.

- **The Wheel Inn Restaurant** (Cabazon; ☎ 909/849-7012): What's different about this clean roadside diner and gas station on I-10 near Palm Springs? It's not the food (basic truck stop chow), but rather the looming presence of a four-story brontosaurus and his Tyrannosaurus rex pal. They were built in the 1960s by a sketch artist and sculptor from Knott's Berry Farm with a grandiose dream of an entire dinosaur amusement park. You can climb up into the belly of the larger one, where you'll find a remarkably spacious gift shop selling dinosaur toys, books, and souvenirs. See chapter 15.

- **The Roy Rogers and Dale Evans Museum** (Victorville; ☎ 619/243-4547): Housed in a replica Old West log fort, this tribute to the lives, films, family, and travels of the famous B-movie couple is best known for being the final resting place of Roy's faithful horse, Trigger, who is stuffed, mounted, and prominently displayed. Evoking both Las Vegas tackiness and the jam-packed attic of some wacky, well-traveled relative, the museum is one-of-a-kind, and well worth a 1- or 2-hour stop between Los Angeles and Las Vegas. See chapter 15.

11 The Best Architectural Landmarks

- **The Civic Center** (San Francisco): The creation of designers John Bakewell, Jr., and Arthur Brown, Jr., it is perhaps the most beautiful beaux arts complex in America. See chapter 4.
- **The Painted Ladies** (San Francisco): The so-called "Painted Ladies" are the city's famous, ornately decorated Victorian homes. Check out the brilliant beauties around Alamo Square. Most of the extant 14,000 structures date from the second half of the 19th century. See chapter 4.
- **Winchester Mystery House** (San Jose): The heiress to the Winchester rifle fortune, Sarah Winchester, created one of the major "Believe It or Not?" curiosities of California, a 160-room Victorian mansion. It's been called the "world's strangest monument to a woman's fear." When a fortune teller told her she wouldn't die if she'd continue to build onto her house, her mansion underwent construction day and night from 1884 to 1922. She did die eventually and the hammers were silenced. See chapter 5.
- **The Carson House** (Eureka): This splendidly ornate Victorian is one of the state's most photographed and flamboyant Queen Anne–style structures. It was built in 1885 by the Newsom brothers for William Carson, the local timber baron. Today it's the headquarters of a men's club. See chapter 7.
- **Mission San Carlos Borromeo del Rio Carmelo** (Carmel-by-the-Sea): The second mission founded in California in 1770 by Father Junípero Serra (who is buried there) is perhaps the most beautiful. Its stone church and tower dome have been authentically restored, and a peaceful garden of California poppies adjoins the church. Sights include an early kitchen and the founding father's spartan sleeping quarters. See chapter 11.
- **The Getty Center** (Los Angeles): The imposing headquarters of the J. Paul Getty Trust were part of the L.A. landscape for 14 years of construction; now visitors can fully appreciate architect Richard Meier's grand, postmodern design. Employing giant slabs of travertine marble, sleek edges and bold angles, the sand-colored complex peers down upon the city from its Brentwood perch. See chapter 13.
- **Los Angeles's Central Library:** The city rallied to save the downtown library when an arson fire nearly destroyed it in 1986; the triumphant result has returned much of its original splendor. Working in the early 1920s, architect Bertram G. Goodhue employed the Egyptian motifs and materials popularized by the recent discovery of King Tut's tomb, combined with the more modern use of concrete block. See chapter 13.
- **Tail o' the Pup** (Los Angeles): At first glance, you might not think twice about this hot-dog-shaped bit of kitsch on West Hollywood's San Vicente Boulevard, just across from the Beverly Center. But locals adored this closet-sized wiener dispensary so much that when it was threatened by the developer's bulldozer, they spoke out en masse to save it. One of the last remaining examples of 1950s representational architecture, the "little dog that could" also serves up a great Baseball Special. See chapter 13.
- **The Gamble House** (Pasadena): The Smithsonian Institution calls this Pasadena landmark, built in 1908, "one of the most important houses in the United States." Architects Charles and Henry Greene created a masterpiece of the Japanese-influenced Arts and Crafts movement. Tours are conducted of the spectacular interior, which was designed by the Greenes down to the last piece of teak

furniture and coordinating Tiffany lamp and executed with impeccable crafts-manship. After you're done, stroll the immediate neighborhood to view several more Greene and Greene creations. See chapter 13.

- **Balboa Park** (San Diego): These Spanish/Mayan-style buildings were originally built as temporary structures for the Panama-California Exposition between 1915 and 1916. Although many have been rebuilt over the years, a few of the original buildings still remain and are worth seeking out. See chapter 16.

- **Hotel del Coronado** (Coronado): The "Hotel Del" stands in all its ornate Victorian red-tiled glory on some of the loveliest beach in southern California. Built in 1888, it's one of the largest remaining wooden structures in the world. Even if you're not staying, stop by to take a detailed tour of the splendidly restored interiors, elegant grounds, and fascinating minimuseum of the hotel's spirited history. On your way to Coronado, you can't miss the **Coronado Bay Bridge,** an architectural landmark in its own right. Crossing the bridge by car or bus is an undeniable thrill because you can see Mexico, the San Diego skyline, Coronado, the naval station, and San Diego Bay. See chapter 16.

12 The Best Museums

- **The Exploratorium** (San Francisco): The hands-on, interactive Exploratorium boasts 650 exhibits that help to show how things work. You'll use all your senses and stretch them to a new dimension. Every exhibit is designed to be useful. See chapter 4.

- **The Oakland Museum:** This one might be dubbed the "Museum of California." The colorful people and history of the Golden State, and its sometimes over-powering art and culture, are all on exhibit here—everything from the region's first inhabitants to today's urban violence is depicted. See chapter 5.

- **California State Railroad Museum** (Sacramento): Old Sacramento's biggest attraction, the 100,000-square-foot museum was once the terminus of the transcontinental and Sacramento Valley railways. The largest museum of its type in the United States, it displays 21 locomotives and railroad cars, among other attractions. One sleeping car simulates travel, with all the swaying and flashing lights of lonely towns passed in the night. See chapter 10.

- **Petersen Automotive Museum** (Los Angeles): This museum is a natural for Los Angeles, a city whose personality is so entwined with the popularity of the car. Impeccably restored vintage autos are displayed in life-size dioramas accurate to the last period detail (including an authentic 1930s-era service station). Upstairs galleries house movie-star and motion-picture vehicles, car-related artwork, and visiting exhibits. See chapter 13.

- **J. Paul Getty Museum at the Getty Center** (Los Angeles): Since opening in 1997, the Getty has been deluged by visitors eager to see whether this ambi-tiously conceived (14 years and $1 billion in the making) complex fulfills its promise as new cultural cornerstone of L.A. Besides boasting a superb, international-class art collection, the center is a striking—and starkly futuristic—architectural landmark that also houses the research, educational, and conserva-tion arms of the deep-pocketed Getty Trust. From its picturesque vantage point, the Getty offers panoramic city views and perhaps even a glimpse into the next millennium. See chapter 13.

- **Autry Museum of Western Heritage** (Los Angeles): This is a treat for both young and old. Relive California's historic cowboy past and see how the period has been depicted by Hollywood through the years, from Disney cartoon

re-creations to founder Gene Autry's "singing cowboy" films to popular 1960s TV series. Highlights include a life-size woolly mammoth and a glimmering vault of ornate frontier firearms. See chapter 13.
- **Museum of Contemporary Art** (San Diego): MCA is actually one museum with two locations: one in La Jolla, the other downtown. The museum is known internationally for its permanent collection, focusing primarily on work produced since 1950. The La Jolla location is also noted for the its Irving Gill–designed facade. See chapter 16.
- **The Museums of Balboa Park** (San Diego): Located in a relaxed, verdant setting, the museums here offer unique cultural experiences. Highlights include the Aerospace Historical Center, Museum of Man, Museum of Photographic Arts, Model Railroad Museum, Natural History Museum, and the Lily Pond and Botanical Building. Check in at the Hospitality Center for a map and "Passport to Balboa Park," a low-cost pass to a combination of the museums. See chapter 16.

13 The Best Views

- **Coit Tower** (San Francisco): The round 1933 tower atop Telegraph Hill opens onto a panoramic 360° view of the City by the Bay. In the distance, the Marin Headlands unfold. In a city known for its views and vantage points, Coit Tower is the scenic show-stopper. See chapter 4.
- **From the Top of Mt. Shasta:** If you can make the climb, you'll be rewarded with a view of northern California that few have ever witnessed. The majesty of the rare sight turned fabled naturalist John Muir's "blood to wine." See chapter 8.
- **Glacier Point in Yosemite National Park:** A sweeping 180° panorama of the High Sierra unfolds from 3,200 feet above the valley. Glacier Point looks out over Nevada and Vernal falls, the Merced River, and the snow-covered Sierra peaks of Yosemite's backcountry. See chapter 9.
- **The Coastline at Garrapata State Park:** You'll see 4 miles of California coastline from Garrapata State Park, a 2,879-acre preserve in the Big Sur area. Rock-strewn beaches, towering cliffs, and redwood forests combine to form what may be the world's most dramatic coastal panorama. See chapter 11.
- **The Santa Barbara Mission:** Gazing seaward from the church's majestic steps, you can take in a panoramic view of Santa Barbara's delightful Spanish-style red-tile roofs, plus the California coast and azure Pacific in all their splendor. It is a postcard-worthy vista throughout the day, from the pastel shades of dawn to the midday shimmer of the sea to the fiery brilliance of sunset. See chapter 12.
- **Griffith Observatory and Planetarium** (Los Angeles): For an outlook on urban Los Angeles without compare, head to this spot in the Hollywood Hills. Great ornate bronze doors lead into this 1935 classic Moderne edifice (immortalized in *Rebel Without a Cause*). The view over the city from the hilltop balconies can, on a clear day, stretch to the Pacific. The lights of Hollywood below sparkle seductively at night, and the observatory's telescope can illuminate the myriad moons of Jupiter for you. See chapter 13.
- **Rim of the World Highway** (Lake Arrowhead): This aptly named road winds toward Lake Arrowhead along a mountain ridge above San Bernardino. The view of the vast, flat valley floor beyond the evergreen fringe is breathtaking. At this altitude (about 5,500 feet), where the air is crisp and clean, it's easy to imagine you're floating above the earth. See chapter 14.

- **The Colorado Desert:** If you think the desert is barren and ugly, you'll quickly change your mind here. From the sweeping panorama atop Mt. San Jacinto (accessible by the Palm Springs Aerial Tramway) to the vast, other-worldly wind-turbine fields scattered throughout the valley, the visual splendor of this area mirrors the spirituality felt here by Native Americans and 20th-century spa-goers alike. From sunrise to sunset, natural light and shadow perform magic, transforming the shapes and colors of the arid hills. See chapter 15.
- **Cabrillo National Monument** (near San Diego): From this vantage point, on the tip of Point Loma, you're treated to a spectacular vista of the ocean, San Diego Bay, Los Coronados Islands, and the mountains that ring the city to the east. There's a wind-shielded whale-watching terrace, and kid-friendly tide pools at the base of the cliffs. See chapter 16.
- **Mt. Soledad** (San Diego): For a 360° view of La Jolla, Del Mar, downtown San Diego, inland San Diego, the Pacific Ocean, the mountains, and on a clear day, even Mexico, Mt. Soledad can't be beat. And it can't be missed, either: This La Jolla landmark is topped by a large, white cross. See chapter 16.

14 The Best Moderately Priced Hotels

- **Hotel Bohème** (San Francisco; ☎ 415/433-9111): The rooms may be small and lack extra amenities, but there's no better San Francisco experience than staying at the impeccably stylish Hotel Bohème, in the heart of North Beach. You need only to step outside your door to find some of the city's best cafes, restaurants, and nightlife. See chapter 4.
- **Deer Run Bed & Breakfast** (St. Helena; ☎ 800/843-3408): You may spend the day fighting the crowds at Napa's wineries, but stay here and you'll find respite in Deer Run's romantic rustic hideaway. The four accommodations are upscale-cabin-like and are surrounded by nothing but nature. See chapter 6.
- **St. Orres** (Gualala; ☎ 707/884-3303): Designed in a Russian style—complete with two Kremlinesque onion-domed towers—St. Orres offers secluded accommodations constructed from century-old timbers salvaged from a nearby mill. It's one of the most eye-catching inns on California's north coast. See chapter 7.
- **River Ranch Lodge** (Lake Tahoe; ☎ 800/535-9900): This rustic lodge situated alongside the Truckee River features private balconies that overlook the river, antique furnishings, and a fantastic outdoor patio complete with a small cafe and swimming hole. Better yet, Lake Tahoe is just a short drive away. Prices start as low as $39. See chapter 8.
- **The Jabberwock** (Monterey; ☎ 888/428-7253): This place, only 4 blocks from Cannery Row, was once a convent. Set in its own gardens with waterfalls, it was named after an episode from Lewis Carroll's *Through the Looking Glass.* Each room is individually decorated; one even has a fireplace. See chapter 11.
- **Casa del Mar Inn at the Beach** (Santa Barbara; ☎ 800/433-3097): It may not have ocean views or a pool, but with newly furnished rooms, lovely landscaping, a caring staff, and the beach less than a block away, Casa del Mar is the best in its price range. See chapter 12.
- **Hollywood Roosevelt Hotel** (Los Angeles; ☎ 800/950-7667): This hotel, overlooking the Walk of Fame, is a legendary survivor from Hollywood's golden age. Centrally located for sightseeing, it offers terrific city views, one of the city's most elegant lobbies, and evening entertainment at the popular art-deco Cinegrill. The first Academy Awards ceremony was held here in 1929, and legends

claim the hotel is haunted by the ghosts of Marilyn Monroe and Montgomery Clift. See chapter 13.

- **Casa Malibu** (Malibu; ☎ **800/831-0858**): This beachfront motel will fool you from the front. Its cheesy 1970s entrance, right on noisy Pacific Coast Highway, belies the quiet, restful charm found within. Situated around the courtyard garden are 21 rooms, many with private decks above the Malibu sands; one elegant suite was Lana Turner's favorite. Rooftops and balconies are festooned with bougainvillea vines, creating an effect reminiscent of a Mexican seaside village. There's easy beach access. See chapter 13.
- **Sommerset Suites Hotel** (San Diego; ☎ **800/962-9665**): This terrific bargain is also a good choice for those who find traditional hotels too impersonal. The staff is friendly and helpful, and in the late afternoon they serve complimentary snacks, soda, beer, and wine in the cozy guest lounge. See chapter 16.
- **Ocean Park Inn** (San Diego; ☎ **800/231-7735**): This three-story standout, located right on Pacific Beach's lively beach path, is visually appealing both inside and out. Behind the hotel's modern Spanish-Mediterranean facade is a sharply designed marble lobby that gives way to the less splendid, but completely comfortable, guest rooms. See chapter 16.

15 The Best Places to Stay on a Shoestring

- **Fort Mason Youth Hostel** (San Francisco; ☎ **415/771-7277**): If you don't mind going communal, you'll be hard-pressed to find cheaper accommodations in San Francisco. Throw in the view, the location (near the Marina and Ghirardelli Square), and the free parking, and you've got yourself a deal. See chapter 4.
- **Golden Bear Motel** (Berkeley; ☎ **800/525-6770**): If you're not dying to set up camp at one of the cheap motels on busy University Avenue or entrench yourself in the chaos of UC Berkeley, the Golden Bear is far enough away to make you feel like you're exploring a neighborhood, but close enough to the campus that you can drive there in less than 10 minutes. Added bonuses: It's across from Alice Waters's (of Chez Panisse fame) Cafe Fanny and close to Fourth Street shopping. See chapter 5.
- **Napa Valley Railway Inn** (Yountville; ☎ **707/944-2000**): This is one of our favorite, and most affordable, places to stay in the Wine Country. Guests get their own private caboose or railcar, each sumptuously appointed with comfy love seats, chairs, queen-size brass beds, and full, tiled bathrooms. The coups de grace are the bay windows and skylights, which let in plenty of California sunshine (surely the Pullman cars of yesteryear never had it this good). See chapter 6.
- **Bodega Harbor Inn** (Bodega Bay; ☎ **707/875-3594**): Thank Poseidon for this low-priced accommodation, set on a small bluff overlooking Bodega Bay. There's no better way to enjoy the day than plopping yourself in one of the lawn chairs and watching the fishing boats bring in their daily catches. See chapter 7.
- **Bear Valley Inn** (Point Reyes; ☎ **415/663-1777**): Ron and JoAnne Nowell's venerable two-story 1899 Victorian has survived everything from a major earthquake to a recent forest fire, which is lucky for you because you'll be hard-pressed to find a better B&B for the price in Point Reyes. It's loaded with charm, from the profusion of flowers and vines outside to the comfy chairs fronting a toasty-warm woodstove inside. See chapter 7.

- **Mt. Shasta Ranch B&B** (Mount Shasta; ☎ 530/926-3870): Built in 1923 as a private retreat and thoroughbred horse ranch for one of the country's most famous horse trainers and racing tycoons, this B&B offers one of the best deals anywhere. Rates start at $50 for a room (most with mountain views) and include a big country breakfast. See chapter 8.
- **Tamarack Lodge** (Lake Tahoe; ☎ 888/TAHOEBED): This is one of the oldest lodges on the North Shore—so old it was a favorite haunt of Clark Gable and Gary Cooper. It's now one of the best bets for the cost-conscious traveler. Hidden among a cadre of pines just east of Tahoe City, the Tamarack Lodge consists of a few old cabins, five "poker rooms," and a modern motel unit. The cabins can hold up to four guests, but the most popular rooms are definitely the hokey old poker rooms. See chapter 8.
- **The Miner's Inn** (Nevada City; ☎ 800/977-8884): Located about a mile from Nevada City's historic district, this cabinlike motel is cooled by the shade of a small tree-lined park. Considering all the standard amenities—TV, telephone, air-conditioning—and fantastic price, the cash-conscious traveler could hardly ask for more. See chapter 10.
- **Gunn House Hotel** (Sonora; ☎ 209/532-3421): Built in 1850 by Dr. Lewis C. Gunn, this was the first two-story adobe structure in Sonora, and is now one of the best low-priced hotels in the Gold Country. It's easy to catch the forty-niner spirit here, as the entire hotel and grounds are brimming with quality antiques and turn-of-the-century artifacts. But what really makes the Gunn House one of our favorites is the hotel's beautiful pool and patio, surrounded by lush vegetation and admirable stonework. See chapter 10.
- **Cypress Tree Inn** (Monterey; ☎ 831/372-7586): The rates here are the best in town—and what you get for your money is a clean, spacious, like-new room with a firm bed. Added bonuses include in-room fridges and a shared outdoor hot tub. See chapter 11.
- **The Wilkies Inn** (Pacific Grove; ☎ 800/253-5707): The caring owners who took this old motel and spruced it up with fashionable furnishings and an extra dose of TLC still offer the best deals in town, making the Wilkies our favorite cheap sleep in the area. See chapter 11.
- **Adobe Inn** (San Luis Obispo; ☎ 800/676-1588): The price of a motel combined with the hospitality of a B&B makes this inn a great option for the budget traveler. In addition to its cute and cozy rooms, El Adobe provides a substantial breakfast (with good coffee) and the owners are on hand to help you plan your activities while in town. See chapter 12.
- **The Clamdigger** (Pismo Beach; ☎ 805/773-2342): Take a walk back in time to when a luxury vacation was nothing more than a little shack on the ocean. Stock your fridge in the kitchen, bring a good book, and you'll have no reason to leave your cute little beachfront cabin—except maybe to pick up another bottle of sunscreen. See chapter 12.
- **Banana Bungalow** (Santa Barbara; ☎ 800/3-HOSTEL): Fact is, you can't really find cheap accommodations in Santa Barbara. Unless, of course, you bunk down with the Euro travelers at this bona fide youth hostel. See chapter 12.
- **Sea Shore Motel** (Santa Monica; ☎ 310/392-2787): It may not be on the beach, but this small, family-run motel is only 2 blocks away, and sits amidst stylish boutiques and cafes. Facilities are simple but adequate, cared for by conscientious management. See chapter 13.

- **Best Western Hollywood Motor Hotel** (Los Angeles; ☎ 323/464-5181): If you're longing to stay near all the Hollywood attractions—the Wax Museum, Walk of Fame, Chinese Theater, movie studios, and Universal City—you'll be ideally located at this Best Western just off the U.S. 101 (Hollywood) Freeway and within walking distance of the renowned Hollywood and Vine intersection. Rates start around $70 (quite a bargain in Los Angeles). See chapter 13.
- **Best Western Anaheim Stardust** (Anaheim; ☎ 800/222-3639): Not willing to sacrifice all the comforts in your quest for an affordable Disneyland vacation? Then check out the Stardust, where the entire family can swim, sleep, enjoy a full breakfast, and shuttle to the park (3 blocks away) for as little as $58 a night—even the largest suite is less than $100. See chapter 14.
- **Casa Cody** (Palm Springs; ☎ 760/320-9346): You'll feel more like a private guest than a paying customer at this cozy compound just a couple of blocks from Palm Springs's main drag. Once owned by "Wild" Bill Cody's niece, it was built in the 1920s around two swimming-pool courtyards with large lawns and shady fruit trees. Basic rooms, which come equipped with small kitchens, run $69 to $79, including breakfast and afternoon wine and cheese. See chapter 15.
- **The Cottage** (San Diego; ☎ 619/299-1564): This two-room cottage is a private hideaway tucked away in a secret garden. It comes complete with its own tiny kitchen and a working wood-burning stove. See chapter 16.
- **Hotel La Pensione** (San Diego; ☎ 800/232-4683): This three-story hotel has the sleek, modern feel of a European hostelry, but is situated in the heart of Little Italy's old-world charm. Close to San Diego's downtown, La Pensione offers consistently clean and reliable service—and plenty of great dining just downstairs. See chapter 16.

16 The Best Culinary Experiences

- **Dungeness Crab at Fisherman's Wharf** (San Francisco): Crabs, which are best consumed as soon as possible after being cooked, emerge right from boiling pots onto your plate. You crack the shells and pick the delectable meat out. Gastronomes treasure even the edible organs (crab butter) inside the carapace. See chapter 4.
- **A San Francisco Burrito:** No matter where we go in California, we just can't find a burrito as luscious as those served throughout San Francisco. The tortilla-wrapped meal takes on a gourmet dimension here: flavored tortillas; fresh-grilled meats, fish, and vegetables; three types of beans; a symphony of salsas; guacamole, and sour cream all tidily tucked in the perfect to-go feast. Best of all? They're generally under five bucks. See chapter 4.
- **Hong Kong Flower Lounge** (San Francisco; ☎ 415/668-8998): For an unforgettable dim sum experience, skip the downtown tourist traps and head out to the avenues where real folks go to get their fill of these Chinese delicacies. See chapter 4.
- **An Affordable Decadent Meal in the Wine Country:** Have yours at the incredible new **Oakville Grocery Café** (☎ 707/944-0111), where the locals go when they want to feast. See chapter 6.
- **A Sunset Horseback Ride Through Griffith Park to a Mexican Feast:** This culinary/equine excursion departs Friday evenings from Beachwood Stables in the Hollywood Hills just before dusk, winding up in Burbank at the modest but

tasty—especially coming off the trail!—Viva Restaurant. Tie up your steed outside and saunter in for a steaming plate of enchiladas accompanied by an ice-cold *cerveza* (beer), just like the real *vaqueros* (cowboys). The cost is $35 per person, plus dinner. For information, call the **Sunset Ranch** at ☎ **323/464-9612.** See chapter 13.

- **Grand Central Market** (Los Angeles; ☎ **213/624-2378**): Fresh-produce stands, exotic-spice-and-condiment vendors, butchers and fishmongers, and prepared-food counters create a noisy, fragrant, vaguely comforting atmosphere in this L.A. mainstay. The gem of this airy, cavernous complex is the fresh-juice bar at the southwest corner. A market fixture for many years, it dispenses dozens of fresh varieties from an elaborate system of wall spigots (just like an old-fashioned soda fountain), deftly blending unlikely but heavenly combinations. See chapter 13.

- **Sunday Champagne Brunch Aboard the *Queen Mary*** (Long Beach; ☎ **562/435-3511** or 562/499-1606): This elegant ocean liner was the largest, finest vessel when it was built in 1934, and the grandeur of those Atlantic crossing days remains. A sumptuous buffet-style feast, accompanied by harp soloist and ice sculpture, is presented in the richly wood-furnished first-class dining room. You'll be able to eat all you want for $22.95 ($7.95 for kids), and then walk off your overindulgence on the spectacular teak decks and through the art-deco interiors. See chapter 14.

- **A Date with the Coachella Valley:** Ninety-five percent of the world's dates are farmed here in the desert. While the groves of date palms make evocative scenery, it's their savory fruit that draws visitors to the National Date Festival in Indio each February. Amidst the Arabian Nights parade and dusty camel races, you can feast on an exotic array of plump Medjool, amber Deglet Noor, caramel-like Halawy, and buttery Empress. Throughout the rest of the year, date farms and markets throughout the valley sell dates from the season's harvest, as well as date milk shakes, sticky date coconut rolls, and more. See chapter 15 and the "California Calendar of Events" in chapter 2.

- **Baja-Style Fish Tacos** (San Diego): No one does it better than former surf-bum Ralph Rubio, whose eponymous taco stands have spread across the Southwest, even edging out hot dogs at San Diego's own sports stadium. Batter-dipped fish fillets folded in corn tortillas and garnished with shredded cabbage, salsa, and tangy *crema* sauce; Rubio's recipe is straight from the thatched-roof taco shacks of Mexican fishing villages. Betcha can't eat just one. See chapter 16.

17 The Best Dining Bargains

- **Pasta Pomodoro** (San Francisco; ☎ **415/399-0300**): Join the young, festive crowd for what is perhaps one of the best dinner bargains in town. Pasta Pomodoro's simple, airy dining room offers plenty of atmosphere and counter seating looking onto North Beach action, while the menu offers fresh pasta dishes at cheap prices. See chapter 4.

- **Manora's Thai Cuisine** (San Francisco; ☎ **415/861-6224**): No one can resist the savory sauces topping every mouth-watering dish that comes out of Manora's kitchen. The food here is so good, it almost makes up for the wait and the noise level. See chapter 4.

- **Cha Cha Cha** (San Francisco; ☎ **415/386-5758**): Go with a few friends, share sangria while you wait, and order from the tapas menu when you finally get seated at this eternally popular Haight Street haunt. Beware of overindulgence:

The food is quite rich, and the pitchers of sangria may alter your judgment and break your budget. See chapter 4.

- **Zona Rosa** (San Francisco; ☎ 415/668-7717): It's difficult not to develop an addiction to Zona Rosa's fresh, delicious burritos. But, since they're less than $5, you can afford to eat as many as you want (though you'll be lucky to polish off one of these big suckers). See chapter 4.

- **Cantinetta** (St. Helena; ☎ 707/963-8888): Adjacent to the famed, and expensive, Tra Vigne Restaurant is this rustic little cafe, offering a small selection of inexpensive sandwiches, pizzas, and lighter meals (you've never had a better focaccia in your life). They can also pack your picnic basket for an impromptu lunch at your favorite winery. See chapter 6.

- **Lucas Wharf Deli** (Bodega Bay; ☎ 707/875-3562): This place doles out steaming pints of fresh, tangy crab cioppino for only $5. It's a fabulously messy affair, best devoured at the picnic tables next door. When crab season is over, the cioppino special is replaced by an equally awesome pile of fresh fish-and-chips (easily big enough to feed two). See chapter 7.

- **The Fishwife at Asilomar Beach** (near Pacific Grove; ☎ 831/375-7107): This cozy little shack dating from the early 1800s serves wonderfully fresh fish complemented with hearty side dishes. Its out-of-the-way location and reasonable prices will make you feel like an insider. See chapter 11.

- **Caffè Napoli** (Carmel; ☎ 831/625-4033): Tourists may be eager to throw down big dollars for a dinner out in Carmel, but locals are definitely not. When they hit the town, the most popular spot is Caffè Napoli, a casual family restaurant with traditional Italian decor and reasonably priced, flavorful fare. See chapter 11.

- **Café Kevah** (Big Sur; ☎ 831/667-2344): All the grandeur of the Big Sur coastline will cost you extra if you're seeing it from your table at a restaurant in Big Sur. But Café Kevah offers the same million-dollar view and a variety of tasty international dishes at a fraction of the price. See chapter 11.

- **Farmers Market** (San Luis Obispo): Who would guess that San Luis Obispo residents are big on barbecue? Head to the Thursday-night Farmers Market and taste for yourself—there are plenty of other cheap options, as well. See chapter 12.

- **La Super-Rica Taqueria** (Santa Barbara; ☎ 805/963-4940): Even chefs and restaurateurs from San Francisco and beyond visit this hole-in-the-wall restaurant to get what many consider the best Mexican food this side of the border. See chapter 12.

- **Montecito Cafe** (Santa Barbara; ☎ 805/969-3392): Their prices may not be rock bottom, but if you'd like a special night out, for the money you can't do better than this cafe a few miles south of downtown Santa Barbara. The feeling is California bistro and the fare, California nouveaux. See chapter 12.

- **Grand Central Market** (Los Angeles; ☎ 213/624-2378): A splendid downtown fixture since 1917, this bustling market serves Latino families, enterprising restaurateurs, and home cooks in search of unusual ingredients and bargain fruits and vegetables. Prepared foods of every ethnicity are served up at counters throughout the market, from chile relleno burritos (around $2) to a complete Thai plate for under $5. Visit the fresh-produce sellers for a natural dessert or to stock up for a picnic; we prefer the west end of the market with its fresh-juice bar, where a tropical smoothie with the works is only $2.95. See chapter 13.

- **The Original Pantry Cafe** (Los Angeles; ☎ 213/972-9279): Finicky eaters and snobbish gourmands, skip this listing. L.A. mayor Dick Riordan's round-the-clock downtown diner won't be winning any culinary awards, but still I've never driven past when there weren't a dozen or more folks lined up outside for a table. The reason? Hearty portions of simple American food at bygone-era prices, plus plenty of free munchies. See chapter 13.

- **Bread and Porridge** (Santa Monica; ☎ 310/453-4941): A steady stream of locals will always be found milling outside this neighborhood cafe, reading their newspapers and waiting for a vacant seat. Once inside, you, too, can sample the delicious breakfasts, fresh salads and sandwiches, and super-affordable entrees—almost all are under $10. Menu items range from Mexican omelets to Cajun crab cakes to traditional pasta dishes. You really can't go wrong here. See chapter 13.
- **Belisle's Restaurant** (Anaheim; ☎ 714/750-6560): After you've blown the family budget on Disneyland, haul your hungry brood a couple of miles to this unique diner, where they've been doling out "Texas-size" favorites like omelets and steaks since 1955. Portions are ridiculously enormous—desserts are so large they look like movie props (picture a chocolate eclair the size of a fireplace log). See chapter 14.
- **The Vegetarian Zone** (San Diego; ☎ 619/298-7302): The city's only purely meatless restaurant attracts an equal number of carnivores for its fresh and savory menu, which features delicious ethnic favorites—like Greek spinach and feta pie or spicy Indian turnovers—that just *happen* to be vegetarian. It's a humble place, but always tops our list of must-eats in San Diego. See chapter 16.
- **Point Loma Seafoods** (San Diego; ☎ 619/223-1109): Pick up a fresh-seafood sandwich or salad here and enjoy a view that rivals the best restaurants in town. See chapter 16.
- **Sammy's California Woodfired Pizza** (San Diego; multiple locations): The gourmet-pizza craze rages on at this local favorite, where one salad and personal pizza are enormous enough to feed two—with leftovers! Conveniently located and always crowded, Sammy's serves up creations like duck sausage, potato garlic, or Jamaican jerk shrimp atop their 10-inch rounds. See chapter 16.

18 The Best Deals for Serious Shoppers

- **Aardvark's** (San Francisco; ☎ 415/621-3141): If you have a hot date but nothing to wear, stop by this new- and used-clothing store for everything from hair clips to leather jackets, suits, and ball gowns, all at absurdly low prices. See chapter 4.
- **Catharine Clark Gallery** (San Francisco; ☎ 415/399-1439): Thanks to Catherine Clark, art is no longer a purchase reserved for those who own million-dollar homes in which to exhibit it. This gallery boasts an excellent selection of contemporary artists, many from California, whose works are sold at reasonable prices. There's even an interest-free layaway plan for up to 1 year. See chapter 4.
- **Esprit Outlet** (San Francisco; ☎ 415/957-2550): Shoppers here pile their carts high with sweaters, shoes, bags, accessories, and children's clothes. The bargain bins are especially cheap, with many items priced from $5 to $10. See chapter 4.
- **Jeremys** (San Francisco; ☎ 415/882-4929): Between their own line of merchandise and the array of other designer clothing, shoes, and accessories, you can't help but leave here looking sharp. New shipments come in frequently and prices can be 75% less than those at department stores. See chapter 4.
- **Wine Club San Francisco** (☎ 415/512-9086): Whether you've got $4 or $400 to spend, the Wine Club will direct you toward bargain bottles that are even cheaper than winery prices. See chapter 4.

- **The American Tin Cannery Factory Outlet Center** (Pacific Grove; ☎ **408/372-1442**): Although it's common knowledge now that most "designer" labels produce a cheaper line to sell specifically at outlets, this mall with 45 shops is still a favorite for those who have had enough of neighboring Monterey Bay Aquarium. See chapter 11.
- **Downtown Los Angeles:** During the week, skyscrapers and big business rule downtown Los Angeles, but the weekends illuminate the bustling trade south of the concrete jungle (which actually goes on 7 days a week). Angelenos in the know flock to the Jewelry Mart for wholesale prices on gold, diamonds, watches, and more; the California Mart and Cooper Building for floor upon floor of brand-name clothes and accessories priced way below retail; and Maple Street for bargains on designer yardage. See chapter 13.
- **Ocean Front Walk** (Venice): Whether it's $8 designer-knockoff sunglasses, $5 ethnic-print fanny packs (and $10 backpack purses), Mexican woven huarache sandals, or super-cheap sterling silver jewelry (including rings for a lot more places than earlobes), the colorful vendors crammed together along the board-walk are almost as interesting as the crazy quilt of humanity passing through. See chapter 13.
- **Barneys New York Outlet** (Cabazon; ☎ **909/849-1600**): Even if you detest outlet malls, you can't argue with the classy atmosphere and great deals at Barneys, the most appealing tenant at the Desert Hills Premium Outlets. With a prime location just west of Palm Springs on the much-traveled artery I-10, Desert Hills has all the usual suspects, too: Coach, Eddie Bauer, Joan and David, Old Navy. But Barneys is the true gem, filled with deals on off-the-rack fashions from New York, Paris, and Italy for men and women. See chapter 15.
- **San Diego County Farmers Markets:** The bountiful harvest of San Diego County is sold on various days at movable markets throughout the area. Finds include fresh local fruits, vegetables, and flowers, as well as specialty items such as raw apple cider (in the fall), macadamia nuts, and rhubarb pies. See chapter 16.

2 Planning an Affordable Trip to California

by Stephanie Avnet Yates

California has as many attractions as do some entire countries, and it can be bewildering to plan your trip with so many options vying for your attention. We've made this task easier for you by scouring the entire state from top to bottom. In the pages that follow, we've compiled everything you need to know to handle the practical details of planning your trip in advance—airlines, how to make camping reservations, a calendar of events, driving laws, and more.

But you may still be wondering: How can we see and do everything without going flat broke? You can, using our insider advice, money-saving tips, and recommendations on great places to stay and eat that can keep your basic living costs—a comfortable room and three meals a day—down to as little as $60 a day. (We assume that two adults are traveling together and that between the two of you, you have at least $120 a day to work with.) The costs of sightseeing, transportation, and entertainment are all extras, but don't worry; we'll provide tips on saving money in those areas as well.

1 Visitor Information & Money

VISITOR INFORMATION

For information on the state as a whole, contact the **California Office of Tourism,** 801 K St., Suite 1600, Sacramento, CA 95812 (☎ **800/862-2543;** www.gocalif.ca.gov), and ask for their free information packet. In addition, almost every city and town in the state has a dedicated tourist bureau or chamber of commerce that will be happy to send you information on its particular parcel. These are listed under the appropriate headings in the chapters that follow.

Foreign travelers should also see chapter 3, "For Foreign Visitors," for entry requirements and other pertinent information.

INFORMATION ON CALIFORNIA'S PARKS   To find out more about California's national parks, contact the **Western Region Information Center,** National Park Service, Fort Mason, Building 201, San Francisco, CA 94123 (☎ **415/556-0560**).

For general state park information, contact the **Department of Parks and Recreation,** P.O. Box 942896, Sacramento, CA 94296-0001 (☎ **916/653-6995**). Ten thousand campsites are on the department's reservation system, and can be booked up to 7 months in advance by calling **Park Net** at ☎ **800/444-7275.** Hours for making

What Things Cost in San Francisco	U.S. $
Shuttle from the airport to the city center (tip included)	13.00
Double room at the Grant Plaza (cheap)	59.00
Double room at the Commodore International Hotel (moderate)	99.00
Double room at Petite Auberge (pricey)	160.00
Lunch for one at Mario's Bohemian Cigar Store (cheap)	8.00
Lunch or dinner for one at Cha Cha Cha (affordable)	12.00
Dinner for one, without wine, at Grand Cafe (a splurge)	35.00
Parking ticket (expired meter)	25.00
Alcatraz Island tour, including ferry trip	11.00
Movie ticket	7.50
Theater ticket	8.00 to 50.00

What Things Cost in Santa Barbara	U.S. $
Shuttle bus up State Street	.25
Double room at the Hotel State Street (cheap)	40.00
Double room at the Franciscan Inn (affordable)	65.00
Double room at the Bath Street Inn (pricey)	100.00
Dinner for one at Big Sky Cafe (cheap)	11.00
Dinner for one at Montecito Cafe (affordable)	16.00
Dinner for one at Wine Cask (a splurge)	40.00
Coca-Cola	1.50
Beer (a pint)	3.00
Admission to the Santa Barbara Mission	3.00
Movie ticket	7.50

reservations are 8am to 5pm (Pacific time) 7 days a week; at press time the Parks Department hoped to begin accepting reservations via the Internet by early 1999. Call the numbers above for an update on online parks information.

For information on fishing and hunting licenses, contact the **California Dept. of Fish and Game,** License and Revenue Branch, 3211 S St., Sacramento, CA 95816 (☎ **916/227-2244** for license information, or 916/227-2266 for 24-hour information).

MONEY
Wells Fargo Bank is linked with the Star, Pulse, Cirrus, and GlobalAccess systems. It has hundreds of ATMs at branches and in-store locations throughout the state. To find one near you, call ☎ **800/869-3557,** or visit the bank's Web site at www.wellsfargo. com/findus/. Other statewide banks include Bank of America (accepts PLUS, Star, and Interlink cards), and First Interstate Bank (Cirrus). To locate other **Cirrus** ATMs, call ☎ **800/424-7787** or search online at www.mastercard.com; to find a **PLUS** ATM, call ☎ **800/843-7587** or visit www.visa.com. Most ATMs will also make cash advances against MasterCard and Visa. American Express cardholders can write a

personal check, guaranteed against the card, for up to $1,000 in cash at an American Express office (see "Fast Facts" in the city chapters for locations).

2 50 Money-Saving Tips

While planning your trip, don't get discouraged if you've almost blown your entire vacation budget on hotels before you've even packed your bags. The California coast is one of the most popular destinations in the world, and hotel prices prove that it's no secret. But there's good news, too. Once you get there, pay for your room, and head out to explore, you'll find that many activities and attractions won't cost you a dime. You can hike the Redwood Forest, bodysurf in Malibu, bike 17-Mile Drive, smell the flowers in Golden Gate Park, in-line skate along Venice Beach, or just kick back under a tree with a book.

The following are some tips to help keep your traveling costs to a minimum:

AIR TRAVEL

1. Visit a travel agent before your trip and see what they can arrange in the way of airfares and packages that include hotels or car rentals; agents sometimes know about or arrange deals that you don't have access to independently. There is no charge for their research time and most bookings; all you'll likely pay is a nominal service charge *only* if you purchase airline tickets that aren't part of a package deal. Independent fly/drive packages (no escorted tour groups, just a bulk rate on your airfare, hotel, and possibly your rental car) are also offered directly through many airlines, including **American Airlines Fly AAway Vacations** (☎ 800/321-2121), **Continental Airlines Vacations** (☎ 800/634-5555), **Delta Vacations** (☎ 800/872-7786), **TWA Getaway Vacations** (☎ 800/438-2929), and **United Vacations** (☎ 800/328-6877). See "Getting There," below, for more information.

2. Buy your ticket well in advance. Most airlines offer their best fares on tickets purchased at least 21 days before the departure date; there are also discounts for 14- and 7-day advance purchases. Remember that the cheapest seats always sell out first.

3. *Or,* buy your ticket at the last minute. Sometimes, when a flight is only partially sold 72 hours before takeoff, the airlines kick into high gear to fill those empty seats (and consolidators scramble to sell tickets they've already paid for—see "By Plane" under "Getting There" for more information). The Internet sites listed in "Cyber Deals for Net Surfers," below, are very good sources for finding out about last-minute fares. Be warned, however: There's no guarantee the last-minute approach will work. You run the risk of being stuck with a really expensive ticket—or no ticket at all. This strategy works best in the off-season, when flights are less likely to be full, or when your travel plans are spontaneous or flexible enough.

4. Always ask for the lowest fare, not just the coach fare. Be flexible with your schedule if you can; every route has prime-time and off-time, and you can often save big money by switching to a different day or time of day. Cross-country travelers shouldn't rule out the late-night "red-eye" flights; they're often much cheaper, and airports are a lot less crowded. Always ask about *discounts*—for seniors, children, students, families, military personnel, and any other discounts you might qualify for.

5. Watch the ads in your newspaper's travel section. Airline, consolidators, and charter and tour companies love to advertise package deals and promotions in

weekend travel sections throughout the country. Just remember to use caution when dealing with a new or unknown company; you can always check with the Better Business Bureau to get the lowdown.

6. Flying within California can be expensive, and in doing so you'll miss the sights along the way; in most cases, you're better off driving, especially since rental car rates are relatively low in California. If you do plan to fly from southern California to northern California or vice versa, check first with **Southwest Airlines** (☎ **800/435-9792;** www.iflyswa.com). Southwest usually has the lowest fares and the most flights; they keep prices down with a low-frills service that eliminates assigned seats. However, do note that in the San Francisco area, Southwest only flies into Oakland or San Jose; you'll find additional regional carriers listed below in "By Plane" under "Getting Around."

7. Taxis are the most expensive way to travel to and from the airport. Almost every airport in California has a shuttle or bus that will take you to a central location near your destination for far less money; many hotels have shuttles to and from the airport as well. For further details, see the introductory sections in each chapter.

RENTING A CAR

8. If you're planning to rent a car, call all car-rental companies (use toll-free numbers; see "Getting Around," below, and the Appendix at the end of this book) to compare rates. Even after you've made your reservations, call again and check rates a few days or weeks later—you may stumble upon a cheaper rate.

9. Don't book a rental car through an airline without doing some research. Airlines do not offer the best rental car deals; they merely reserve a car for you.

10. In addition to the big chains, don't forget to research car-rental booking agencies and local or discount rental firms. **Kemwel Holiday Auto (KHA)** (☎ **800/ 678-0678;** www.kemwel.com) is a well-known international agency that works to find you the most favorable rate from amongst all the major rental companies in the area you need—calling them may save you some phone time as well as a few dollars. If you're willing to drive a car that's not brand-spanking new, call **Rent-A-Wreck** (☎ **800/535-1491** for locations), which has been offering dirt-cheap rentals throughout the United States for 26 years. It has dozens of offices throughout California, and most have toll-free numbers; see the separate destination chapters in this book for specific locations.

11. Don't forget to check whether your credit card or personal auto insurance policy covers you when you rent a car. If you're covered by one or the other, you will be able to avoid the cost of collision-damage waivers (usually an additional $10 or $12 a day) that the car-rental agencies are eager to sell you.

12. Whether you're driving or not, it's a good idea to be a member of the **American Automobile Association (AAA).** Members (only those that carry their cards with them) not only receive free roadside assistance, but also have access to a wealth of free travel information (detailed maps and guidebooks). Also, many hotels and attractions throughout California offer discounts to AAA members—always inquire. Call ☎ **800/922-8228** or your local branch for membership information.

13. When renting a car, consider that weekly rates are usually cheaper; but if you return your car before the week is up, you'll be charged the daily (higher) rate. Unless you're *really* going to keep the car a full week (often a 5-day period or longer), keep looking for a better rate.

14. Don't let the car company talk you into a bigger (and more expensive) car than you need. If you can live with manual locks and windows, economy cars are usually just a little smaller than the next step up, and you're likely to save big bucks if you opt for one of them.

15. If you arrive at the rental desk with a valid car reservation and with a confirmation number, the agents are obligated to honor the rate you were quoted—even if they have to give you an upgrade. A ploy some rental companies use when they're all out of the car you booked (economy cars often get booked up first) is to tell you that for a few more dollars a day they'll put you in a "better car." Make them stick to their original quote.

16. Try to find out the going rate for gas locally before you arrive at the car-rental desk (call a local filling station, or ask the visitor bureau); most of the major companies will offer you two choices for refilling the tank. You can prepay for a tank of gas at their per-gallon rate, then try to return the car with as little remaining fuel as possible; or you can take responsibility for refueling yourself and return the car with a full tank. The rate they'll charge for the prepurchased fill-up is usually a little higher than the going local rate, and you lose money for every drop left in the tank when you return it. But you gain the convenience of not having to find a gas station on your way to return the car. If you opt for the second choice, you can save a few dollars, but if you're forced to return a less-than-full tank, the agency will charge nearly triple the going per gallon rate to top it off. Whichever you choose, just remember: Don't bother putting expensive gas in the tank. After all, it is a rental.

17. If you do need to fill up before returning the car to a rental agency at the airport, try to choose a gas station more than a half mile away. The filling stations near the airport *know* that renters are often rushed—and desperate to get their rental returned—so they usually jack up prices in response.

PUBLIC TRANSPORTATION

18. Inquire about money-saving **Amtrak** (☎ **800/USA-RAIL;** www.amtrak.com) packages that include hotel accommodations, car rentals, and tours with your train fare.

19. Discounted train and bus fares, like airfares, are often based on advanced purchase, so make your reservation as far in advance as possible to obtain the lowest rates. Ask Amtrak and **Greyhound** (☎ **800/231-2222**) about discounted fares for children and seniors.

20. If you're planning on using local public transportation to get around, inquire about day or week passes, which could seriously reduce your transportation costs. In San Francisco, a 1-day Passport fare card allows unlimited rides on buses, Metro streetcars, and cable cars for only $6; 3- and 7-day cards are just $10 and $15, respectively. San Diego's Day Tripper passes allow unlimited rides on all MTS bus and trolley routes, plus free passage on the San Diego–Coronado ferry, for just $5 per day (4 days for $12).

ACCOMMODATIONS

21. The sooner you book a room, the better. The cheapest accommodations are always the first to go, so the further in advance you commit, the better your chances of scoring a bargain.

22. Whether you make a reservation or arrive on the spot, ask for the cheapest room. Also, inquire about what makes the room worth less than other options (public versus private bathroom, for example) and be sure that it's acceptable to you.

23. Don't just accept the "rack" (full, published prices) rate—even though this guide lists tariffs that way, in order to aid in comparison between properties, no one ever really pays the published rate (B&Bs are another story—see Tip #28, below). Always ask about promotions, weekly rates (if you're staying a while), and special discounts for students, government employees, military personnel, seniors, and corporate employees. If you belong to AAA or AARP, be sure to ask whether the hotel offers discounts to members; more often than not, they do. Also ask about package deals—sometimes you can get a rental car or daily breakfast included for just a few bucks more.

24. Using toll-free numbers lets you compare hotel rates without spending a lot on long-distance phone calls; and some places, especially the chains, will give you a discount only when you use the toll-free number.

25. Travel in the off-season (winter months in places other than ski areas, plus July through September in the deserts) and you'll save a bundle on room rates. A hotel room on the Monterey peninsula in November can be discounted as much as 50%; and when the mercury tops 100° in Palm Springs, you'll find $300 hotel rooms going for less than $99. You'll find other seasonal tips in "When to Go," below.

26. Bargain at the front desk. A hotel makes zero dollars per night on an empty room. Hence, most hotels are willing to bargain on rates. Haggling probably won't work too well during the high season, when hotels are almost 100% booked, but if you're traveling off-season, go for it. If the front-desk staff says "no" to your request for a better rate, try politely speaking with a manager, with whom you might be able to negotiate a better deal. An especially advantageous time to haggle for lower rates is late afternoon/early evening on the day of your arrival, when a hotel's likelihood of filling up with full-price bookings is remote.

27. Each town's visitor bureau will either be able to provide you with hotel suggestions, or refer you to an accommodations service. But keep in mind that they will only recommend hotels who pay for bureau membership, and the small, cheaper hotels usually aren't members.

28. B&Bs are wonderful places to stay, but can often be more costly than hotels and rarely suited to families with small children. There are, however, many advantages to choosing a B&B: You'll enjoy a full breakfast each morning, which shaves $3 to $10 per person/per day off your budget, and B&Bs with vacancies in the late afternoon are likely to offer you a generous walk-in discount (filling an empty room means a lot more to a small business than a 200-room hotel). You can generally save money at a B&B if you're willing to share a bathroom. Europeans are more comfortable with the idea than Americans, but most establishments take great pains to ensure privacy, cleanliness, and adequate supplies, and a bathroom is rarely shared by more than two rooms.

29. If your heart is set on a bed-and-breakfast, contact **Bed and Breakfast International,** P.O. Box 282910, San Francisco, CA 94128 (☎ **800/872-4500** or 415/696-1690), and let them find affordable accommodations for you. They book hundreds of B&Bs throughout California ranging from $60 to $150 per night. There's a 2-night minimum. Many of the travel-related Web sites listed in "Cyber Deals for Net Surfers," below, have links to sites that list B&Bs nationally, often with photos and very specific descriptions. Some of our favorites

(they're also just plain fun to browse through) are **Bed & Breakfast Inns Online** (www.bbonline.com), **The Bed & Breakfast Channel** (www.bbchannel.com), and **California Bed & Breakfast Travel Directory** (www2.bbtravel.com/ bbtravel). Also, check the hotel listings throughout this book for the destination(s) you want to visit. We recommend lots of great places to stay at low rates, and often list other companies that will help you find a hotel in your price range.

30. When booking your hotel, find out if there's an extra charge for parking. In cities like San Francisco and Los Angeles, stashing your car can cost up to $20 (sometimes more) per day. If there is a charge, be sure to ask about the availability of local street parking or an inexpensive public lot nearby; hotel employees are usually more than happy to give you the lowdown on the local parking situation.

31. If you're traveling with children, try to secure a room at a hotel where they can stay in your room for free. Also, consider a suite accommodation; in some areas, such as Los Angeles, moderately priced suite accommodations abound. At first glance, the rate may seem high, but when you figure in the money you'll save by booking one room instead of two and by preparing some of your own meals (many come with kitchens), the savings start to add up.

32. Camping is one of the best, and cheapest, ways to experience California. California State Parks manages hundreds of campsites throughout the state and offers discounts to seniors, travelers with disabilities, veterans with disabilities, and former prisoners of war. Call **PARK NET** (☎ **800/444-7275**) between 8am and 5pm to reserve a campsite or request a brochure. See each chapter's hotel listings for other camping options.

33. At budget hotels, if the first room you see is disappointing, don't storm out. Politely ask to see other rooms; they often vary considerably.

34. Find out when you check in whether there's a charge for phone calls you make from your room. While it's become more common in recent years for hotels to allow free local and toll-free-number calling, many still charge up to $1 for the service. *Never* dial long distance directly from your room—always use a toll-free access number; if you know you're paying a hotel charge for the call, make sure you get directions from your long-distance company on how to make a string of calls in a row without reconnecting to your access number (usually you press "#" after each call to get another dial tone). You can also save money by making your calls from a hotel lobby or nearby phone booth. If you're planning on making a lot of local calls for business or other reasons, find a hotel that offers free local calls.

DINING

35. Fixed-price menus and early-bird dinners are big money savers. Look for restaurants that offer them. If you're traveling with children, find restaurants that offer reduced-price children's menus.

36. Consider hotels that include breakfast; you'll save money by not heading to a restaurant first thing in the morning. Or opt for a hotel that has rooms with kitchens, and do a little cooking (or a least heating up of leftovers) instead of eating out for every meal.

37. If you want to try out a restaurant that's beyond your budget for dinner, consider visiting at lunch. Often, the lunch menu is served until 4 or 5pm, and main courses, which are duplicated on the dinner menu, cost a few dollars less. You probably won't be hungry for the rest of the day, and will avoid spending a fortune for dinner.

38. Keep an eye out for happy hours. Aside from budget cocktails, many establishments provide a free snack spread that makes a good dinner replacement.

39. California is an outdoor, sporty kind of place. Instead of dining in restaurants,
consider putting together a picnic breakfast, lunch, or dinner. There's an infinite
number of celestial outdoor dining spots, and hundreds of phenomenal take-out
joints that will help you create a cheap feast to go; even a gourmet spread can cost
less than a meal in a restaurant.

40. Check out local alternative and tourist newspapers, many of which regularly run
discounts and two-for-ones for restaurants and activities about town. In San
Francisco, the *Bay Guardian* is a good bet. In Los Angeles, locals know to look
in the *L.A. Weekly* for "twofer" or "free appetizer/dessert" ads; most hotels also
display coupon-filled visitor publications in their lobbies.

SIGHTSEEING

41. The major convention and visitors bureaus usually offer free visitors guides, as
well as information on freebies available in their areas. Some visitor centers, such
as those in San Diego and San Francisco, offer booklets of money-saving coupons
for restaurants, shops, and attractions in the area. Call or stop in to inquire.

42. Most museums are open to the public free 1 day per month (sometimes 1 day a
week). You'll find this information listed in this book next to each museum's
open hours.

43. If you're a senior, student, or active member of the military, be sure to bring identification with you, and inquire before paying full price. Many attractions and
activities offer discounts, but you'll have to have valid ID to qualify.

SHOPPING

44. If you live out of state and make a substantial purchase, it may be wise to have
the store mail it to your home. You will have to pay a shipping charge, but you
won't have to pay California sales tax or lug it around for the rest of your trip.

45. Stock up on groceries and supplies before heading to vast wilderness areas such
as Yosemite, Big Sur, and Death Valley. Stores there tend to be smaller and more
expensive than supermarkets in surrounding metropolitan areas.

46. Don't be afraid to bargain with antique and collectible dealers; they're almost
always prepared to compromise with you. And bring some cash if you see a street
fair or farmers market; artists usually set up booths offering handmade pottery,
jewelry, and clothing at *really* cheap prices—they make great gifts and souvenirs.

NIGHTLIFE

47. In the major cities, avoid clubs with high cover charges. There are plenty of bars
and dance clubs with cover charges of just a couple of dollars, some with no cover
at all; many are recommended in the "After Dark" sections in this book.

48. If you want to see a musical or theatrical performance, contact the box office to
inquire about discounted or matinee shows; some theaters and companies offer
same-day reduced tickets, student discounts, and standing-room rates. In Los
Angeles, there's now a half-price ticket booth called **Times Tix** (☎ **310/
659-3678**); you can also attend morning rehearsals at the Hollywood Bowl
absolutely free—see chapter 13 for details.

49. Inquire about free concerts, films, and other evening programs at museums and
attractions; many regularly offer them.

50. Just hang out. Stroll San Francisco's Chinatown, nurse a Coke or a cocktail in a glitzy L.A. bar, or kick up your feet at an outdoor cafe almost anywhere along the coast and just watch the world go by—in California, there's no better way to spend an evening.

3 When to Go

California's climate is so varied that it's impossible to generalize about the state as a whole. However, the prime tourist areas, along the coast, tend to be mild year-round. This is good news for budget travelers, who can save a bundle by identifying the off-season and taking advantage of reduced rates.

San Francisco's temperate marine climate means relatively mild weather year-round. In summer, temperatures rarely top 70°F (pack sweaters, even in August), and the city's famous fog rolls in most mornings and evenings. In winter, the mercury seldom falls below freezing, and snow is almost unheard of. Because of San Francisco's fog, summer rarely sees more than a few hot days in a row. Head a few miles inland, though, and it's likely to be clear and hot.

The Central Coast shares San Francisco's climate, though it gets warmer as you get farther south; north of the Bay Area, the coast is rainier and foggier; winters tend to be mild but wet.

Summers are refreshingly cool around Lake Tahoe and in the Shasta Cascades—a perfect climate for hiking, camping, and other outdoor activities and a popular escape for residents of California's sweltering deserts and valleys who are looking to beat the heat. Skiers flock to this area for terrific snowfall from late November through early April.

Southern California is usually much warmer than the Bay Area, and it gets significantly more sun. This is the place to hit the beach. Even in winter, daytime thermometer readings regularly reach into the 60s and warmer. Summers can be stifling inland, but southern California's coastal communities are always comfortable. The area's limited rainfall is generally seen between January and mid-April, and is rarely intense enough to be more than a slight inconvenience. It's possible to sunbathe throughout the year, but only die-hard enthusiasts and wet-suited surfers venture into the ocean in winter. The water is warmest in summer and fall, but even then, the Pacific is too chilly for many.

The southern California desert is sizzling hot in summer; temperatures regularly top 100°F. Winter is the time to visit the desert resorts (and remember, it gets surprisingly cold at night in the desert).

TRAVEL SEASONS

As a general rule, summer is the most popular time to visit California. Two exceptions are mountain ski resorts, whose biggest season coincides with snowfall (usually late November through April), and desert destinations, where sweltering summer is the bargain season. Holidays, especially school holidays, are always crowded, particularly in Los Angeles and San Diego, where major family attractions abound. Try to buck the crowds if your schedule is flexible enough. For example, nonskiers will find great deals at the mountain resorts in autumn, after summer's lakefront crowd, but before the first flake of snow falls. Ditto for visitors to the Central and Northern coasts, where in autumn the prime warmest weather is past, but abundant sunshine and crisp temperatures prevail for months before winter's gloom sets in. Springtime is equally lovely here. In the deserts, you can travel dirt-cheap between June and September;

temperatures heat up as the summer progresses, but you won't be alone, since European travelers flock to the Southwest's unique desert climate all summer long. Between October and Christmas is "shoulder season" in the desert; not as popular as springtime, but well past summer's scorching heat.

In areas with less dramatic climate changes, try to avoid holidays and other prime times. It's also worth a call to the local visitor bureau (listed in each destination chapter), to find out if there are any major events (like the Super Bowl) occurring during your trip. Prices will skyrocket around the event, but fall dramatically after everyone leaves and hotels experience a brief lull.

With a little creative thinking and advance planning, you can tailor a California visit to fit any budget.

San Francisco's Average Temperatures (°F)

	Jan	Feb	Mar	Apr	May	June	July	Aug	Sept	Oct	Nov	Dec
Avg. High	56	59	60	61	63	64	64	65	69	68	63	57
Avg. Low	46	48	49	49	51	53	53	54	56	55	52	47

Los Angeles's Average Temperatures (°F)

	Jan	Feb	Mar	Apr	May	June	July	Aug	Sept	Oct	Nov	Dec
Avg. High	65	66	67	69	72	75	81	81	81	77	73	69
Avg. Low	46	48	49	52	54	57	60	60	59	55	51	49

CALIFORNIA CALENDAR OF EVENTS

January

- ✪ **Tournament of Roses,** Pasadena. A spectacular parade down Colorado Boulevard, with lavish floats, music, and extraordinary equestrian entries, followed by the Rose Bowl Game. Call ☎ **626/449-4100** for details, or just stay home and watch it on TV (you'll have a better view). January 1.

- • **Bob Hope Chrysler Classic,** Palm Springs Desert Resorts. Nineteen ninety-nine marks the 40th year of this weeklong PGA golf tournament, which raises money for charity and includes a celebrity-studded Pro-Am. For spectator information and tickets, call ☎ **888/MR-BHOPE** or 760/346-8184. Usually held in the second half of January.

February

- ✪ **Chinese New Year Festival and Parade.** The largest Chinese New Year Festival in the United States is San Francisco's, which includes a Golden Dragon parade with lion-dancing, marching bands, street fair, flower sale, and festive food. Call ☎ **415/982-3000** for more information and exact dates.

    L.A.'s celebration is colorful as well, with dragon dancers parading through the streets of downtown's Chinatown. Chinese opera and other events are scheduled. For this year's schedule, contact the **Chinese Chamber of Commerce** at ☎ **213/617-0396.**

- • **National Date Festival,** Indio. Crowds gather for 2 weeks to celebrate the Coachella Valley desert's most beloved cash crop with appropriately themed events like camel and ostrich races, the Blessing of the Date Garden, and festive Arabian Nights pageants. Plenty of date-sampling booths are set up, along with rides, food vendors, and other county fair trappings. Call ☎ **800/811-3247** or 760/863-8247 for exact dates.

- ✪ **Fresno County Blossom Trail.** A 67-mile driving tour featuring the fruit and nut orchards in full bloom. Call ☎ **209/233-0836.** Late February to late March.

March

- **Return of the Swallows,** San Juan Capistrano. Each St. Joseph's Day (March 19), visitors flock to this charming village for the arrival of the mission's loyal flock of swallows, who'll nest and remain until October. The celebration includes a parade, dances, and special programs. Call ☎ **949/248-2048** for details. March 19 to 21.
- **Snowfest,** Truckee. A 10-day winter carnival with parades, ski challenges, polar-bear swim, children's carnival, and fireworks. Dates vary. Call ☎ **530/583-7625.**
- **Santa Barbara International Film Festival.** For 10 days each March, pretty Santa Barbara does its best impression of Cannes. There's a flurry of foreign- and independent-film premieres, personal appearances by noted actors and directors, and symposia on hot cinematic topics. For a rundown of events and dates, call ☎ 805/963-0023.
- **California Poppy Blooming Season,** Antelope Valley. Less than an hour's drive north of Los Angeles lies the Antelope Valley Poppy Reserve, part of the state park system. In spring, miles of hillside are ablaze with brilliant hues of red and orange, dazzling the senses of motorists who flock to witness the display. For information and directions, call ☎ **805/724-1180.** Mid-March through mid-May. For information on the annual **California Poppy Festival,** held at full bloom (usually in Apr), call ☎ **805/723-6000.**
- **Nabisco Dinah Shore,** Rancho Mirage. This 30-year-old LPGA golf tournament takes place during the last week of March near Palm Springs. After the celebrity Pro-Am early in the week, the best female pros get down to business. For more information, call ☎ **760/324-4546.** Other special-interest events for women usually take place around the Dinah Shore, including the country's largest annual lesbian gathering.
- **Redwood Coast Dixieland Jazz Festival,** Eureka. Three days of jazz featuring 12 of the best Dixieland groups, including a variety of jam sessions. Call ☎ **707/445-3378.** Late March.

April

- ✪ **San Francisco International Film Festival.** One of America's oldest film festivals, featuring more than 100 films and videos from more than 30 countries. Tickets are relatively inexpensive, and screenings are very accessible to the general public during two weeks early in the month. Call ☎ **415/931-FILM.**
- **Toyota Grand Prix,** Long Beach. An exciting weekend of Indy-class auto racing and entertainment in and around downtown Long Beach, drawing world-class drivers from the United States and Europe. Contact the **Grand Prix Association** at ☎ **800/752-9524** or 562/981-2600. Mid-April.
- **Fisherman's Festival,** Bodega Bay. Fishing vessels, decorated with ribbons and banners, sail out for a Blessing of the Fleet, while landlubbers enjoy music, lamb, an oyster barbecue, an arts-and-crafts fair, and a boat parade. For information call ☎ **707/875-3422.** Latter half of April.
- ✪ **Renaissance Pleasure Faire,** San Bernardino. One of America's largest Renaissance festivals, this annual happening is set in Glen Ellen Regional Park in L.A.'s relatively remote countryside. Performers (and many attendees) dress in 16th-century costume and revel in this festive re-creation of a medieval English village. For ticket information, phone ☎ **800/52-FAIRE.** Weekends from late April through Memorial Day.
- **Ramona Pageant,** Hemet. A unique outdoor play that portrays the lives of the southern California Mission Indians. The play was adapted from Helen Hunt

Jackson's 1884 novel *Ramona*. Call ☎ **909/658-3111** for details. Late April to early May.

- **Del Mar National Horse Show.** Horse-and-rider teams compete in national championships. Held at the Del Mar Fairgrounds. Call ☎ **619/792-4288** or 619/755-1161 for more information. Late April to early May.

May

⭕ **Cinco de Mayo.** A weeklong celebration of one of Mexico's most jubilant holidays takes place throughout the city of Los Angeles. The fiesta's Carnival-like atmosphere is created by large crowds, live music, dances, and food. The main festivities are held in El Pueblo de Los Angeles State Historic Park, downtown, with other events around the city. Phone ☎ **213/628-1274** for information.

There's also a Cinco de Mayo celebration in San Diego, featuring folkloric music, dance, food, and historical reenactments. Held in Old Town. Call ☎ **619/296-3161** or 619/220-5422 for more information.

- **Venice Art Walk,** Venice Beach. An annual weekend event that gives visitors a chance to take docent-guided tours, visit five artist's studios, or take a Sunday self-guided art walk through private studios and homes of more than 50 emerging and well-known artists. Call ☎ **310/392-8630,** ext. 342. Mid-May.

⭕ **Calaveras County Fair and Jumping Frog Jubilee,** Angel's Camp. This event was inspired by Mark Twain's story "The Celebrated Jumping Frog of Calaveras County." Entrants from all over the world arrive with their frog participants. There's also a children's parade, livestock competition, rodeo, carnival, and fireworks. Call ☎ **209/736-2561.** Third weekend in May.

- **Bay to Breakers Foot Race,** Golden Gate Park, San Francisco. One of the city's most popular annual events, it's really more fun than run. Thousands of entrants show up dressed in their best Halloween-style costumes for the approximately 7½-mile run across the park. Call ☎ **415/777-7770.** Third Sunday of May.

- **Paso Robles Wine Festival.** What began as a small, neighborly gathering has grown into the largest outdoor wine tasting in California, held on the third weekend in May. The 3-day event features winery open houses and tastings, a golf tournament, a 5K run and a 10K bike ride, concerts, plus a Carnival-like festival in downtown's City Park. For a schedule of events and fees, call ☎ **800/549-WINE.**

⭕ **Carnival,** San Francisco. The Mission District's largest annual event is a 2-day series of festivities that culminates with a parade on Mission Street over Memorial Day weekend. More than a half-million spectators line the route, and the samba musicians and dancers continue to play on 14th Street, near Harrison, at the end of the march. Call the **Mission Economic and Cultural Association** at ☎ **415/826-1401.** Memorial Day weekend.

June

- **Playboy Jazz Festival,** Los Angeles. Bill Cosby is the traditional Master of Ceremonies, presiding over top artists at the Hollywood Bowl. Call ☎ **310/246-4000.** Mid-June.

- **Pony Express Celebration and Re-Ride,** Folsom. Horses and riders follow the same route that the Pony Express took, starting in Missouri and ending with a major celebration in Folsom, about 20 miles east of Sacramento. Much of the route parallels U.S. 50 in El Dorado County. Call ☎ **510/621-5885** or 916/985-2707. Dates vary.

- **Lesbian and Gay Freedom Day Parade.** It's celebrated all over the state, but San Francisco's party draws up to half a million participants. The parade's start and finish has been moved around in recent years to accommodate road construction, but traditionally it begins and ends at Civic Center Plaza, where hundreds of food, art, and information booths are set up around several sound stages. Call ☎ 415/864-3733 for information. Usually the third or last weekend of June.

- **Ojai Music Festival,** Ojai Valley. This 3-day event has been drawing world-class classical and jazz personalities to the open-air Libbey Bowl since 1947. Past events have featured Igor Stravinsky, Aaron Copeland, and the Julliard String Quartet. Seats (and local lodgings) fill up quickly; call ☎ 805/646-2094 for more information. The performance schedule is usually released in November, and tickets go on sale to the general public in January. Early June.
- **Mariachi USA Festival,** Los Angeles. A 2-day family-oriented celebration of Mexican culture and tradition at the Hollywood Bowl, where festival-goers pack their picnic baskets and enjoy music, ballet, folklorico, and related performances by special guests. Call ☎ 213/848-7717. Late June.

July

- ✪ **Festival of Arts and Pageant of the Masters,** Laguna Beach. A fantastic performance-art production in which live actors re-create famous Old Masters paintings. Other festivities include live music, craft sales, art demonstrations and workshops, and the grass-roots Sawdust Festival across the street. Grounds admission is $3; pageant tickets range from $15 to $40. Call ☎ 800/487-FEST or 949/494-1145; there's online info at www.coolsville.com/festival. July through August.
- **Carmel Bach Festival.** A 3-week festival honoring Johann Sebastian Bach and his contemporaries. It culminates in a candlelit concert in the chapel of the Carmel Mission. Call ☎ 408/624-1521 for tickets way in advance (tickets go on sale in Jan). Mid-July.
- **Gilroy Garlic Festival.** A gourmet food fair with more than 85 booths serving garlicky food from almost every ethnic background, plus close to 100 arts, crafts, and entertainment booths. Call ☎ 831/842-1625. Last full weekend in July.
- **Mammoth Lakes Jazz Jubilee.** A 4-day festival featuring 20 bands on 10 different stages, plus food, drinks, and dancing—all under the pine trees and stars. Call ☎ 760/934-2478. Second weekend in July.
- **Shakespeare at the Beach,** Lake Tahoe. A bewitching experience of the Bard at Sand Harbor on the shore beneath the stars. Call ☎ 702/832-1606. Three weeks in late July and August.
- **International Surf Festival,** Los Angeles. Four beachside cities—Hermosa Beach, Manhattan Beach, Redondo Beach, and Torrance—collaborate in the oldest international surf festival in California. Competitions include surfing, boogie boarding, sand-castle building, and other beach-related categories. Contact the International Surf Festival Committee at ☎ 310/376-6911 for information. End of July.

August

- **Old Spanish Days Fiesta,** Santa Barbara. The city's biggest annual event, this 5-day festival features a grand parade with horse-drawn carriages, music and dance performances, *mercados* (marketplaces), and a rodeo. Call ☎ 805/962-8101. Early August.
- **Nisei Week Japanese Festival,** Los Angeles. This weeklong celebration of Japanese culture and heritage is held in Little Tokyo at the Japanese American Cultural and Community Center Plaza. Festivities include parades, food, music, arts, and crafts. Call ☎ 213/687-7193. Mid-August.

- **California State Fair,** Sacramento. At the California Exposition grounds, a gala celebration, with livestock, carnival food, exhibits, entertainment on 10 different stages, plus thoroughbred racing and a 1-mile monorail for panoramic views over the scope of it all. Call ☎ **916/263-3000.** Late August to early September.

September

- **Sausalito Art Festival.** A juried exhibit of more than 180 artists. It is accompanied by music provided by Bay Area jazz, rock, and blues performers and international cuisine enhanced by wines from some 50 different Napa and Sonoma producers. Call ☎ **415/332-3555** for information. Labor Day weekend.

- ✪ **San Diego Street Scene.** The historic Gaslamp Quarter is transformed by this 3-day extravaganza featuring food, dance, international character, and live music on 12 separate stages. Saturday is set aside as an all-ages day; attendees must be 21 and over the other 2 days. Call ☎ **619/557-8487** for more information. First weekend after Labor Day.

- ✪ **Monterey Jazz Festival.** Top names in traditional and modern jazz. One of the oldest annual jazz festivals in the world. Call ☎ **831/373-3366.** Mid-September.

- **San Francisco Blues Festival,** on the grounds of Fort Mason. The largest outdoor blues music event on the West Coast. Local and national musicians perform back-to-back during three marathon days. Call ☎ **415/826-6837.** Usually in mid-September.

- **Los Angeles County Fair.** Horse racing, arts, agricultural displays, celebrity entertainment, and carnival rides are among the attractions of the largest county fair in the world, held at the Los Angeles County Fair and Exposition Center, in Pomona. Call ☎ **909/623-3111** for information. Late September.

- **Danish Days,** Solvang. Since 1936, this 3-day event has been celebrating old-world customs and pageantry with a parade, gymnastics exhibitions by local schoolchildren, demonstrations of traditional Danish arts and crafts, and plenty of *aebleskivers* (Danish fritters) and *medisterpolse* (Danish sausage). Call ☎ **800/GO-SOLVANG** for more information. Dates vary.

- **Watts Towers Day of the Drum Festival,** Los Angeles. Celebrating the historic role of drums and drummers, this event features a variety of unique performance, from Afro-Cuban folkloricos to East Indian tabla players. Call ☎ **213/847-4646.** Late September.

- **Tuolumne County Wild West Film Festival and Rodeo,** Sonora. A gathering of western film stars and rodeo legends, plus arts and crafts, entertainment, rodeo, and an awards dinner. Call ☎ **209/533-4420.** Last weekend in September.

October

- **Oktoberfest,** Big Bear Lake. Don your lederhosen and enjoy a heady beer at this raucous local tradition. The action takes place at the Convention Center on weekends starting in late September and continuing through the end of October; activities range from log-sawing competitions to polka dances to yodeling contests. For information call ☎ **909/585-3000.**

- **Catalina Island Jazz Trax Festival.** Great contemporary jazz artists travel to the island to play in the legendary Avalon Casino Ballroom. The festival is over two consecutive 3-day weekends. Call ☎ **800/866-TRAX** for more information. Early October.

- **Sonoma County Harvest Fair.** A 3-day celebration of the harvest with exhibitions, art shows, and annual judging of the local wines. At the Sonoma County Fairgrounds. Call ☎ **707/545-4203.** Dates vary.

- **The Half Moon Bay Art & Pumpkin Festival,** Half Moon Bay. The festival features a Great Pumpkin Parade, pie-eating contests, a pumpkin-carving competition, arts and crafts, and all manner of squash cuisine. The highlight of the event is the Giant Pumpkin weigh-in contest, won recently by an 875-pound monster. Colorful to the extreme. For exact date and details, call the **Pumpkin Hotline** at ☎ 650/726-9652.
- **Western Regional Final Championship Rodeo,** Lakeside. Top cowboys from 11 western states compete in seven rodeo events including calf roping, barrel racing, bull riding, team roping, and steer wrestling. Held at the Lakeside Rodeo Grounds, Calif. 67 and Mapleview Avenue, Lakeside. Call ☎ 619/561-4331. Mid-October.
- **Halloween,** San Francisco. The City by the Bay celebrates with a fantastical parade organized at Market and Castro streets. A mixed gay-straight crowd revels in costumes of extraordinary imagination. October 31.

November

- **Doo Dah Parade,** Pasadena. An outrageous spoof of the Rose Parade on the Sunday before Thanksgiving, featuring participants such as the Precision Briefcase Drill Team and a kazoo band. Call ☎ 626/449-3689.
- **Hollywood Christmas Parade.** This spectacular star-studded parade marches through the heart of Hollywood the Sunday after Thanksgiving. For information call ☎ 323/469-2337.

December

- *How the Grinch Stole Christmas,* San Diego. In honor of the late Theodore Geisel ("Dr. Seuss," a San Diego resident), the lobby of Loews Coronado Bay Resort is transformed into Whoville, where the Cat in the Hat assembles eager young audiences for regular readings of the beloved Christmas story. Punch and cookies are served at this free event, and carolers also perform following each reading. For more information call ☎ 619/424-4000. December 1 to 24.
- **Christmas Boat Parade of Lights.** Following longstanding tradition, sailors love to decorate their craft with colorful lights for the holidays. Several southern California harbors hold nighttime parades to showcase these creations, which range from tiny dinghies draped with a single strand of lights to showy yachts with entire Nativity scenes twinkling on deck. Call the following for schedules and information: **Ventura Harbor** (☎ 805/642-6746), **Marina Del Rey** (Los Angeles; ☎ 310/821-0555), **Long Beach** (☎ 562/435-4093), **Huntington Harbour** (☎ 714/840-7542), **Mission Bay** (San Diego; ☎ 619/276-8200).
- ✪ **New Year's Eve Torchlight Parade,** Big Bear Lake. Watch dozens of nighttime skiers follow a serpentine path down Snow Summit's ski slopes bearing glowing torches—it's one of the state's loveliest traditions. Afterward, the party continues indoors with live bands and plenty to eat and drink. For more information on this 21-and-over event, call ☎ 909/866-5766.

4 Getting There

BY PLANE

All major U.S. carriers serve the San Francisco, Sacramento, San Jose, Los Angeles, and San Diego airports. Domestic airlines flying in and out of these cities include **Alaska Airlines** (☎ 800/426-0333; www.alaskaair.com), **American Airlines** (☎ 800/433-7300; www.americanair.com), **Continental Airlines** (☎ 800/525-0280; www.flycontinental.com), **Delta Air Lines** (☎ 800/221-1212;

www.delta-air.com), **Northwest Airlines** (☎ 800/225-2525; www.nwa.com),
TWA (☎ 800/221-2000; www.twa.com), **United Airlines** (☎ 800/241-6522;
www.ual.com), and **USAirways** (☎ 800/428-4322; www.usair.com). Foreign travelers should also see "Getting to the U.S." and "Getting Around the U.S." in chapter
3 for a list of airlines offering overseas flights into California. A comprehensive list of
airlines and their Web sites can be found in the Appendix at the back of this book.

The lowest round-trip fares to the West Coast from New York fluctuate between
about $300 and $500; from Chicago they range from $250 to $400. The lowest
round-trip full coach fare between San Francisco and L.A. is about $198—book early,
or during a sale, and you can pay as low as $79 to $89.

You might be able to get a great deal on airfare by calling a consolidator. Our
favorite is the consistently reliable **Cheap Tickets** (☎ 800/377-1000 or 310/
645-5054; www.cheaptickets.com); other choices include **Cheap Seats** (☎ 800/
451-7200 or 213/873-2838; www.cheapseatstravel.com), **1-800-FLY4-LESS, 1-800-
FLY-CHEAP** (www.websrus.com/flycheap), **Travac** (☎ 800/TRAV-800 or 212/
563-3303), and **Unitravel** (☎ 800/325-2222 or 314/569-0900). Also refer to "Cyber
Deals for Net Surfers," below, to learn how to find bargains online.

PACKAGE TOURS

Independent fly/drive packages (no escorted tour groups, just a bulk rate on your airfare, hotel, and possibly your rental car) are offered by **American Airlines Fly AAway
Vacations** (☎ 800/321-2121), **Continental Airlines Vacations** (☎ 800/634-5555),
Delta Vacations (☎ 800/872-7786), **TWA Getaway Vacations** (☎ 800/438-2929),
and **United Vacations** (☎ 800/328-6877). Availability varies widely based upon
season and demand, but it always pays to investigate what these major air carriers are
offering to encourage you to fly with them. The packages are best suited to travelers
who can be flexible in the following ways:

- Try not to be too picky about your hotel. That's not to say packages force you to
  stay in dumps—quite the contrary, they often include some premier hostelries—
  but you'll have a limited selection. Try to pinpoint roughly where you'd like to
  stay (within a region or city), and ask if there's a participating hotel there.
- If you can schedule your departure and arrival so you're not flying on the
  weekend, airfares will usually be at least $25 to $50 lower per person. And it goes
  without saying that the popular season is the most restrictive season—meaning
  winter in the deserts, summer along the coast, holidays and school vacations
  everywhere—though package deals will still save you some money over booking
  separately.
- Engage the reservationist in conversation, mentioning all the activities you're
  considering for your visit. All of the companies have access to various "goodies"
  they can hitch to your package for far less than you'd pay separately. Examples
  include tickets to Universal Studios, Disneyland, or Sea World; passes for city
  tours, harbor cruises, and other excursions; tickets for theater events; rental-car
  upgrades; and other specials.

BY CAR

Here are some handy driving times if you're on one of those see-the-U.S.A. car trips.
From Phoenix, it's about 6 hours to Los Angeles on I-10. Las Vegas is 265 miles northeast of Los Angeles (about a 4-hour drive).

San Francisco is 227 miles southwest of Reno, Nevada, and 577 miles northwest of
Las Vegas. It's a long day's drive 640 miles south from Portland, Oregon, on I-5. The

Cyber Deals for Net Surfers

It's possible to get some great deals on airfare, hotels, and car rentals via the Internet. So go grab your mouse and start surfing—you could save a bundle, and all the sites listed below offer their services free of charge.

Microsoft Expedia (www.expedia.com)   The best part of this multipurpose travel site is the "Fare Tracker": You fill out a form on the screen indicating that you're interested in cheap flights to California from your hometown, and, periodically, they'll e-mail you the best airfare deals. The site's "Travel Agent" will steer you to bargains on hotels and car rentals, and you can book everything, including flights, right online. This site is even useful once you're booked: Before you go, log onto Expedia for oodles of up-to-date travel information, including weather reports and foreign exchange rates.

Preview Travel (www.reservations.com and www.vacations.com)   Another useful travel site, "Reservations.com" has a "Best Fare Finder," which will search the Apollo computer reservations system for the three lowest fares for any route on any days of the year. Just fill out the form on the screen with times, dates, and destinations, and within minutes, Preview will show you the best deals. If you find an airfare you like, you can book your ticket right online—you can even reserve hotels and car rentals on this site. If you're in the preplanning stage, head to Preview's "Vacations.com" site, where you can check out the latest package deals for destinations around the world by clicking on "Hot Deals."

Travelocity (www.travelocity.com)   This is one of the best travel sites out there. In addition to its "Personal Fare Watcher," which notifies you via e-mail of the lowest airfares for up to five different destinations, Travelocity will track the three lowest fares for any routes on any dates in minutes. You can book a flight right then and there, and if you need a rental car or hotel, Travelocity will find you the best deal via the SABRE computer reservations system (a huge database used by travel agents worldwide).

TravelWeb (www.travelweb.com)   If you're obsessed with getting the lowest airfare possible, this Dallas-based reservation service's detachable "Fare Ticker" will run continuously in a corner of your computer screen throughout the day, displaying the lowest fares from your city to various popular destinations. See one you like and, with one click, you're instantly in TravelWeb's reservation system.

drive between San Francisco and L.A. takes about 6 hours on I-5, closer to 8 hours on the more scenic U.S. 101.

Before you set out on a big car trip, you might want to join the **American Automobile Association (AAA)** (☎ **800/922-8228**), which has hundreds of offices nationwide. Members receive excellent maps (AAA will even help you plan an exact itinerary) and emergency road service.

BY TRAIN

Amtrak (☎ **800/USA-RAIL;** www.amtrak.com) connects California with about 500 American cities. Trains bound for both northern and southern California leave daily from New York and pass through Chicago and Denver. The journey takes about 3½ days, and seats fill up quickly. As with plane travel along popular routes, fares fluctuate wildly depending on season, special promotions, etc. As a general rule, heavily restricted advance tickets are competitive with similar airfares. Remember, however,

The Ticker is a great tool to have during fare wars, when prices can fluctuate several times per day (or even per hour). TravelWeb's "Click-It! Weekends" feature guarantees the lowest published rates for the coming weekend at selected hotels worldwide; participating chains include Hilton, Hyatt, ITT Sheraton, Inter-Continental, and La Quinta.

Savvier Traveler (www.savtraveler.com)   Though you won't see their name anywhere on-screen, this multipurpose Web site is the Internet counterpart of the 104-year-old behemoth Rosenbluth Travel agency. In addition to "Air U Control," their sophisticated online reservation system for air, hotel, and car rental bookings, Rosenbluth offers a constantly changing "Hot Deals" feature. Some of the specials even offer further discounts for online purchases. The agency's specialty is cruises.

Internet Travel Network (www.itn.net)   This cyber-only company provides a one-stop shopping destination for air, car, and hotel bookings, and also lets you book packages and cruises. "Fare Mail" keeps you informed of low-cost deals to any of six locations you request; you can eliminate unwanted messages by specifying, for example, that you only want to be notified when flights from New York to Los Angeles drop below $225. ITN will route your booking to your favorite local travel agent for issuance, or will complete any transaction with you online. Air travel options are presented by individual flight, making it convenient to price complex itineraries; they also supply on-time percentages for many specific flights.

Consolidators   Formerly known as "bucket shops," consolidators (wholesalers who buy tickets in bulk at a discount) today are *very* legitimate and offer some of the best deals around. You can get virtually any flight on any airline from them; sometimes their fare is identical to the airline's, often it's discounted between 15% and 50%. The tickets carry the same restrictions imposed by the airline on advance/discount fares. Many consolidators (see "By Plane" under "Getting There," above, for a complete list) have followed the airlines' lead and set up online booking sites, including **1-800-FLY-CHEAP** (www.websrus.com/flycheap), **Cheap Seats** (www.cheapseatstravel.com), and our favorite, **Cheap Tickets** (www.cheaptickets.com).

those low fares are for coach travel in reclining seats; private sleeping accommodations cost substantially more.

The *Sunset Limited* is Amtrak's regularly scheduled transcontinental service, originating in Florida, and making 52 stops along the way as it passes through Alabama, Mississippi, Louisiana, Texas, New Mexico, and Arizona before arriving in Los Angeles 2 days later. The train, which runs three times weekly, features reclining seats, a sightseeing car with large windows, and a full-service dining car. Round-trip coach fares begin at around $300; several varieties of sleeping compartments are also available for an extra charge.

Amtrak's *Coast Starlight* travels along the Pacific Coast between Seattle and Los Angeles. This nostalgic and stylish train—and its scenic route—have been steadily growing in popularity; Amtrak even maintains a dedicated Web site at www.coaststarlight.com. Round-trip adult coach fares between San Francisco and Los Angeles range from $54 to $77; between Seattle and L.A. it's $102 to $170. Kids under 15 travel for half-price. Coach passengers on this overnight trip sleep in surprisingly comfy reclining chairs; there's a substantial surcharge for private sleeping compartments.

Ask about special family plans, tours, and other money-saving promotions Amtrak may be offering. You can call for a brochure outlining routes and prices for the entire system; up-to-date schedules and fares are also available on their comprehensive (but often time-consuming) Web site.

BY BUS

Greyhound/Trailways (☎ **800/231-2222**) can get you here from anywhere cheaply, if not in great comfort. Round-trip fares vary depending on your point of origin, but few, if any, ever exceed $250.

5 Getting Around

BY CAR

California's freeway signs frequently indicate direction by naming a town rather than a point on the compass. If you've never heard of Canoga Park, you might be in trouble, unless you have a map. The best state road guide is the comprehensive **Thomas Bros.** *California Road Atlas,* a 300-plus-page book of maps with schematics of towns and cities statewide. It costs $20 but is a good investment if you plan to do a lot of exploring. Smaller, accordion-style maps are handy for the state as a whole or for individual cities and regions; you'll find a very useful one inserted in the back of this book.

For **road conditions,** call ☎ **916/445-7623** in northern California, ☎ **213/628-7623** in southern California.

If you're heading into the Sierras or Shasta-Cascades for a winter ski trip, stock up on antifreeze and carry snow chains for your tires (chains are mandatory in certain areas).

Here are a few sample distances between key California cities:

San Francisco	
87 miles SW of Sacramento	321 miles NW of Santa Barbara
115 miles NW of Monterey	379 miles NW of Los Angeles
278 miles SE of Eureka	548 miles NW of San Diego

Sacramento	
87 miles NE of San Francisco	383 miles N of Los Angeles
185 miles NE of Monterey	391 miles NE of Santa Barbara
304 miles SE of Eureka	484 miles NW of Palm Springs

Los Angeles	
96 miles SE of Santa Barbara	379 miles SE of San Francisco
103 miles W of Palm Springs	383 miles S of Sacramento
120 miles NW of San Diego	659 miles SE of Eureka
332 miles SE of Monterey	

RENTALS   California is one of the cheapest places in America to rent a car. The best-known firms, with locations throughout the state and at most major airports,

California Driving Times & Distances

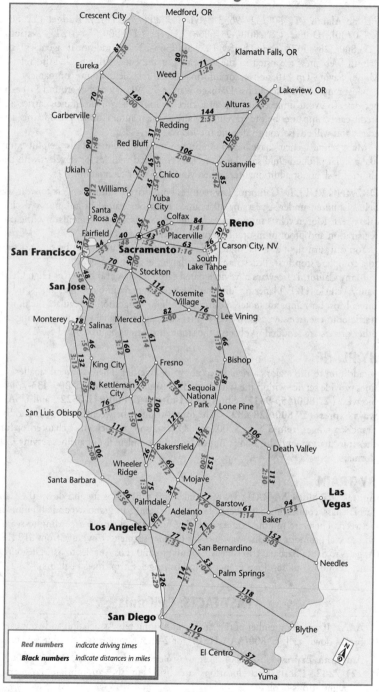

Crescent City

Medford, OR

Klamath Falls, OR

81
1:38

80
1:36

71
1:26

Eureka

Weed

54
1:05

Lakeview, OR

70
1:24

149
3:00

71
1:26

144
2:53

Alturas

Garberville

Redding

105
2:06

90
1:48

31
:38

Red Bluff

106
2:08

Susanville

Ukiah

71
1:26

45
:54

Chico

85
1:42

60
1:12

Williams

45
:54

Yuba
City

Santa
Rosa

45
:56

Colfax

84
1:41

Reno

Fairfield

40
:48

50
1:00

43
:52

Placerville

26
:30

Carson City, NV

San Francisco

53
1:04

44
:53

Sacramento

63
1:16

South
Lake Tahoe

48
:58

70
1:24

50
1:01

Stockton

San Jose

57
1:09

114
2:35

Yosemite
Village

107
2:16

Monterey

18
:25

Salinas

65
1:19

82
2:00

76
1:55

Lee Vining

46
:56

160
3:12

Merced

61
1:14

66
1:19

132
3:15

King City

Fresno

Bishop

82
1:39

54
1:03

84
1:30

58
:58

Kettleman
City

Sequoia
National
Park

Lone Pine

76
1:32

100
2:00

121
2:43

San Luis Obispo

91
1:50

115
2:18

106
2:25

Death Valley

114
2:17

Bakersfield

152
3:00

106
2:08

26
1:12

60

113
2:30

Wheeler
Ridge

75
1:30

34
:46

Mojave

71
1:36

Santa Barbara

96
1:56

Palmdale

Barstow

61
1:14

94
1:53

Las
Vegas

Adelanto

71
1:26

Baker

Los Angeles

60
1:12

41
:50

152
3:03

77
1:33

San Bernardino

Needles

114
2:17

53
1:04

Palm Springs

126
2:29

118
2:20

San Diego

110
2:12

Blythe

57
1:09

El Centro

Yuma

Red numbers *indicate driving times*
Black numbers *indicate distances in miles*

43

include **Alamo** (☎ 800/327-9633), **Avis** (☎ 800/331-1212), **Budget** (☎ 800/527-0700), **Dollar** (☎ 800/421-6868), **Hertz** (☎ 800/654-3131), **National** (☎ 800/328-4567), and **Thrifty** (☎ 800/367-2277). Additional agencies (and helpful Web sites) are listed in the Appendix at the end of this book. Also refer to Money-Saving Tip #10, above, for information on reliable discount companies.

Most rental firms offer a Loss/Damage Waiver (LDW) at a cost of around $10 extra per day. To avoid unnecessary expense, check with both your insurance carrier and credit-card companies before traveling. Many of them automatically provide this coverage, and will advise you to decline the LDW.

Many rental agencies have begun offering a variety of essential or just helpful extras, like cellular phones, child seats, and specially equipped vehicles for travelers with disabilities. Ask about additional fees when you make your reservation.

DRIVING RULES   California law requires both drivers and passengers to wear seat belts. Children under 4 years or 40 pounds must be secured in an approved child safety seat. Motorcyclists must wear a helmet. Auto insurance is mandatory; the car's registration and proof of insurance must be carried in the car.

You can turn right at a red light, unless otherwise indicated—but be sure to come to a complete stop first. Pedestrians always have the right-of-way.

Many California freeways have designated carpool lanes, also known as High Occupancy Vehicle (HOV) lanes or "diamond" lanes. Some require two passengers, others three. Most on-ramps are metered during even light congestion to regulate the flow of traffic onto the freeway; cars in HOV lanes can pass the signal without stopping. All other drivers are required to observe the stoplights—fines begin around $271.

BY PLANE

In addition to the major carriers listed above in "Getting There," several smaller airlines provide service within the state, including **American Eagle** (☎ 800/433-7300), **Skywest** (☎ 800/453-9417), **Shuttle by United** (☎ 800/241-6522), and **USAirways Express** (☎ 800/428-4322). The round-trip fare between Los Angeles and San Francisco ranges from $79 to $200. See "Orientation" in each city's chapter for further information, and this book's Appendix for a complete list of airlines serving California.

BY TRAIN

Amtrak (☎ 800/USA-RAIL; www.amtrak.com) runs trains up and down the California coast, connecting San Diego, Los Angeles, and San Francisco and all points in between. There are multiple trains each day, and rates fluctuate according to season and special promotions. One-way fares for popular segments can range from $18 (Los Angeles to Santa Barbara; trip time: 2½ hours) to $20 (Los Angeles to San Diego; trip time: 2½ hours) to $85 (San Francisco to Los Angeles; trip time: 11 hours).

FAST FACTS: California

AAA   If you're a member of the American Automobile Association and your car breaks down, call ☎ 800/AAA-HELP for 24-hour emergency roadside service.

American Express   To report lost or stolen traveler's checks, call ☎ 800/221-7282. Local office locations are listed in the appropriate chapters throughout this book.

Driving Rules   See "Getting Around," earlier in this chapter.

Earthquakes   In the rare event of an earthquake, you should know about a few simple precautions that every California schoolchild is taught: If you're in a tall building, don't run outside; instead, move away from windows and toward the building's center. Crouch under a desk or table, or stand against a wall or under a doorway. If you're in bed, get under the bed or stand in a doorway, or crouch under a sturdy piece of furniture. When exiting the building, use stairwells, not elevators.

If you're in your car, pull over to the side of the road and stop, but wait until you're away from bridges or overpasses, and telephone or power poles and lines. Stay in your car.

If you're out walking, stay outside and away from trees, power lines, and the sides of buildings. If you're in an area with tall buildings, stand in a doorway.

Emergencies   To reach the police, ambulance service, or fire department, dial ☎ **911** from any telephone. No coins are needed at pay phones.

Liquor Laws   Liquor and grocery stores, as well as some drugstores, can legally sell packaged alcoholic beverages between 6am and 2am. Most restaurants, night-clubs, and bars are licensed to serve alcoholic beverages during the same hours. The legal age for the purchase and consumption of alcoholic beverages is 21; proof of age is strictly enforced.

Maps   Local maps can usually be obtained free from area tourist offices. State and regional maps are sold at gas stations, in drugstores, and in tourist-oriented shops all around the state; the Thomas Bros. maps are the best.

Pets   Many chain hotels and motels accept dogs (though some require a deposit or impose size restrictions). Some good bets include **Best Western** (☎ **800/ 528-1234;** www.bestwestern.com), **Comfort Inns** (☎ **800/228-5150;** www. hotelchoice.com), **Holiday Inns** (☎ **800/HOLIDAY;** www.holiday-inn.com), **La Quinta Inns** (☎ **800/531-5900;** www.laquinta.com), and **Motel 6** (☎ **800/4-MOTEL6**). But remember that managers of individual establishments are free to set or change their pet policy, so it's vital that you contact the hotel itself to confirm your dog's reservation instead of relying solely on these central reservation numbers.

It's not a good idea to bring your dog to any of California's national parks—for your pet's own protection. It's just not safe for dogs to wander in these areas, where they might have dangerous encounters with wildlife.

The *California Dog Lover's Companion* (Foghorn Press) is a huge and incredibly useful resource, with lodging recommendations plus ratings of hundreds of parks and beaches, plus details on where Fido is allowed to romp off-leash. You'll learn that San Francisco is an unusually dog-friendly destination, and that dogs are welcome at Pismo Beach and on the sands at Carmel. *On the Road Again with Man's Best Friend* (Macmillan) is another great reference tool, with detailed reviews of accommodations where dogs are welcome.

Taxes   California's state sales tax is 7.75%. Some municipalities include an additional percentage, so tax varies throughout the state. Hotel taxes are almost always higher than tariffs levied on goods and services.

Time   California and the entire West Coast are in the Pacific standard time zone, 3 hours earlier than the East Coast.

3

For Foreign Visitors

by Erika Lenkert and Matthew R. Poole

The pervasiveness of American culture around the world may make you feel that you know the U.S.A. pretty well, but leaving your own country for the States still requires an additional degree of planning. This chapter will help prepare you for the more common problems (expected and unexpected) that visitors to California may encounter.

1 Preparing for Your Trip

ENTRY REQUIREMENTS

Immigration laws are a hot political issue in the United States these days, and the following requirements may have changed somewhat by the time you plan your trip. Check at any U.S. embassy or consulate for current information and requirements.

DOCUMENT REGULATIONS   The U.S. State Department has a **Visa Waiver Pilot Program** allowing citizens of certain countries to enter the United States without a visa for stays of up to 90 days. At press time these countries included Andorra, Austria, Belgium, Brunei, Denmark, Finland, France, Germany, Iceland, Ireland, Italy, Japan, Liechtenstein, Luxembourg, Monaco, the Netherlands, New Zealand, Norway, San Marino, Spain, Sweden, Switzerland, and the United Kingdom. Citizens of these countries need only a valid passport and a round-trip air or cruise ticket in their possession upon arrival. If they first enter the United States, they may then visit Mexico, Canada, Bermuda, and/or the Caribbean islands and return to the United States without needing a visa. Further information is available from any U.S. embassy or consulate. Canadian citizens may enter the United States without visas; they need only proof of residence.

Citizens of all other countries, including Australia, must have (1) a valid **passport** with an expiration date at least 6 months later than the scheduled end of their visit to the United States; and (2) a **tourist visa,** which may be obtained without charge from the nearest U.S. consulate.

To obtain a visa, the traveler must submit a completed application form (either in person or by mail) with a 1½-inch-square photo, and must demonstrate binding ties to a residence abroad. Usually you can obtain a visa at once or within 24 hours, but it may take longer during the summer rush from June to August. If you cannot go in person, contact the nearest U.S. embassy or consulate for directions on applying by mail. Your travel agent or airline office may also be able to provide you with visa applications and instructions. The U.S. consulate or embassy that issues your visa will determine whether you will be issued a multiple- or single-entry visa and any restrictions regarding the length of your stay.

British subjects can obtain up-to-date passport and visa information by calling the **U.S. Embassy Visa Information Line** (☎ **0891/200-290**) or the **London Passport Office** (☎ **0990/210-410** for recorded information).

Foreign driver's licenses are recognized in California, although you may want to get an international driver's license if your home license is not written in English.

MEDICAL REQUIREMENTS   Unless you're arriving from an area known to be suffering from an epidemic (particularly cholera or yellow fever), no inoculations or vaccinations are required to enter the United States. If you have a disease requiring treatment with medications containing narcotics or drugs requiring a syringe, carry a valid signed prescription from your physician to allay any suspicions that you may be smuggling drugs.

For HIV-positive visitors, requirements for entering the United States are somewhat vague and change frequently. The latest edition of *HIV and Immigrants: A Manual for AIDS Service Providers* states that "although INS doesn't require a medical exam for everyone trying to come into the United States, INS officials may keep out people who they suspect are HIV positive. INS may stop people because they look sick or because they are carrying AIDS/HIV medicine. For this reason, visitors (non-immigrants) should try not to carry their HIV medicine or literature about AIDS in their luggage when they come into the United States." For more information concerning HIV-positive travelers, contact an AIDS center in your area, or call the **Bar Association of San Francisco Immigration Project** at ☎ **415/477-2390.**

CUSTOMS REQUIREMENTS   Every visitor over 21 years of age may bring in, free of duty, the following: (1) 1 liter of wine or hard liquor; (2) 200 cigarettes, 100 cigars (but *not* from Cuba), or 3 pounds of smoking tobacco; and (3) $100 worth of gifts. These exemptions are offered to travelers who spend at least 72 hours in the United States and who have not claimed them within the preceding 6 months. It is altogether forbidden to bring into the country foodstuffs (particularly fruit, cooked meats, and canned goods) and plants (vegetables, seeds, tropical plants, and the like). Foreign tourists may bring in or take out up to $10,000 in U.S. or foreign currency with no formalities; larger sums must be declared to U.S. Customs on entering or leaving, which includes filing Form CM 4790. For more specific information regarding U.S. Customs, call your nearest U.S. embassy or consulate, or the U.S. Customs office at the **San Francisco International Airport** at ☎ **650/876-2816.**

INSURANCE

Unlike many European countries, the United States does not usually offer free or low-cost medical care to its citizens or visitors. Because the cost of medical care is extremely high, health insurance is highly recommended. Comprehensive policies can cover sickness or injury costs; loss or theft of your baggage; trip-cancellation costs; guarantee of bail in case you're arrested; and costs of accident, repatriation, or death. Such packages are sold by automobile clubs as well as by insurance companies and travel agents.

Although lack of health insurance may prevent you from being admitted to a hospital in nonemergencies, don't worry about being left on a street corner to die: The American way is to fix you now and bill the living daylights out of you later.

MONEY

The U.S. monetary system has a decimal base: One American dollar ($1) = 100 cents (100¢). The most common bills (all ugly, all green) are the $1 (colloquially, a "buck"), $5, $10, and $20 denominations. There are also $2 bills (seldom encountered), $50 bills, and $100 bills (the last two are usually not welcome when paying for small purchases). Note that newly redesigned $100, $50, and $20 bills have been introduced (you can spot them easily—they've got really big faces on them). Despite rumors to the contrary, the old-style bills are still legal tender.

There are six denominations of coins: 1¢ (one cent, or a penny); 5¢ (five cents, or a nickel); 10¢ (ten cents, or a dime); 25¢ (twenty-five cents, or a quarter); 50¢ (fifty cents, or a half dollar); and, prized by collectors, the rare $1 piece (the older, large silver dollar and the newer, small Susan B. Anthony coin).

Note: The "foreign-exchange bureaus" so common in Europe are rare even at airports in the United States, and nonexistent outside major cities. It's best not to change foreign money (or traveler's checks denominated in a currency other than U.S. dollars) at a small-town bank, or even a branch in a big city; in fact, leave any currency other than U.S. dollars at home—it may prove a greater nuisance to you than it's worth.

TRAVELER'S CHECKS   Though traveler's checks are widely accepted, make sure they're denominated in U.S. dollars, as foreign-currency checks are often difficult to exchange. The three most widely recognized and readily accepted traveler's checks are Visa, American Express, and Thomas Cook. Be sure to record the numbers of your checks and keep that information in a separate place, should your checks get lost or stolen. California businesses are pretty good about accepting traveler's checks, but you're better off cashing them in at a bank (in small amounts, of course) and paying in cash. *Remember:* You'll need identification, such as a driver's license or passport, to change a traveler's check.

CREDIT CARDS & ATMs   Most major credit and charge cards are accepted at California's larger hotels, and Visa and MasterCard are accepted just about everywhere else. There are, however, a handful of stores and restaurants that do not take credit or charge cards, so be sure to ask in advance. Most businesses display a sticker near their entrance to let you know which cards they accept. (*Note:* Often businesses require a minimum purchase price, usually around $10, to use a credit or charge card.)

We strongly recommend that you bring at least one major credit or charge card. Hotels, car-rental companies, and airlines usually require a credit-card imprint as a deposit against expenses, and in an emergency a credit or charge card can be priceless.

In California's larger cities, you'll find an automated teller machine (ATM) on just about every downtown block. Most accept Visa, MasterCard, and American Express, as well as ATM cards from other U.S. banks. Expect to be charged up to $3 per transaction if you're not using your own bank's ATM.

MONEYGRAMS   If the proverbial poop hits the fan, you can also have someone wire money to you very quickly via **Western Union.** There are numerous offices throughout California; call ☎ **800/325-6000** for the one nearest you.

SAFETY

While most tourist areas in California are generally safe, it's always prudent to exercise common sense when traveling. Follow these basic safety tips and you'll most likely avoid any conflicts:

- Avoid deserted areas, especially at night, and don't go into any of the parks after dusk unless there's a concert or similar occasion that attracts crowds.

- Avoid carrying valuables with you on the street, and don't display expensive cameras or electronic equipment. Hold onto your pocketbook, and place your billfold in an inside pocket. In theaters, restaurants, and other public places, keep your possessions in sight.
- Remember that hotels are open to the public, and in a large hotel, security may not be able to screen everyone entering. Always lock your room door—don't assume that once inside your hotel you are automatically safe and no longer need to be aware of your surroundings.
- Be sure to keep a copy of all your travel papers separate from your wallet or purse, and leave a copy with someone at home should you need it faxed in an emergency.

DRIVING SAFETY   Driving safety is important, too, especially given the highly publicized carjackings of foreign tourists in Florida. Ask your rental agency for advice on traveler safety when you pick up your car. Obtain written directions—or a map with the route clearly marked—from the agency showing how to get to your destination. And, if possible, arrive and depart during daylight hours.

If you drive off a highway into a doubtful neighborhood, leave the area as quickly as possible. If you have an accident, even on the highway, stay in your car with the doors locked until you assess the situation or until the police arrive. If you're bumped from behind on the street or are involved in a minor accident with no injuries and the situation appears to be suspicious, motion to the other driver to follow you. *Never* get out of your car in such situations.

Always try to park in well-lighted and well-traveled areas if possible. If you leave your rental car unlocked and empty of your valuables, you're probably safer than locking your car with valuables in plain view. Never leave any packages or valuables in sight. If someone attempts to rob you or steal your car, don't try to resist the thief/carjacker—report the incident to the police department immediately.

2 Getting to the U.S.

The visitor arriving by air, no matter what the port of entry, should cultivate patience and resignation before setting foot on U.S. soil. Getting through immigration control may take as long as 2 hours on some days, especially on summer weekends, so have this guidebook or something else to read handy. Add the time it takes to clear Customs and you'll see that you should make a very generous allowance for delay in planning connections between international and domestic flights—figure on 2 to 3 hours at least.

In contrast, for the traveler arriving by car or rail from Canada, the border-crossing formalities have been streamlined to the vanishing point. And for the traveler arriving by air from Canada, Bermuda, and some places in the Caribbean, you can sometimes go through Customs and Immigration at the point of departure, which is much quicker.

AIRLINES
FROM THE UNITED KINGDOM & IRELAND   Many airlines offer service from the United Kingdom or Ireland to the United States. If possible, try to book a direct flight. Airlines that offer direct flights from London include British Airways, United, and Virgin. Airlines that do not have direct flights from London to Los Angeles or San Francisco can book you straight through on a connecting flight. You can make reservations by calling the following numbers in London: **American**

Airlines (☎ 0181/572-5555), **British Airways** (☎ 0345/222-111), **Continental Airlines** (☎ 0293/776-464), **Delta Airlines** (☎ 0800/414-767), **United Airlines** (☎ 0181/990-9900), and **Virgin Atlantic** (☎ 01293/747-747).

Residents of Ireland can call **Aer Lingus** (☎ 01/844-4747 in Dublin or 061/415-556 in Shannon).

FROM AUSTRALIA & NEW ZEALAND   **Qantas** (☎ 13 12 11 in Australia) has direct flights from Sydney to Los Angeles and San Francisco. You can also take **United** (☎ 13 17 77 in Australia or 09/379-3800 in New Zealand) from Australia or New Zealand to Los Angeles and San Francisco.

Air New Zealand (☎ 0800/737-000 in Auckland or 643/379-5200 in Christchurch) offers service to Los Angeles International Airport.

FROM CANADA   Canadian readers might also consider **Air Canada** (☎ 800/268-7240 or 800/361-8620 in Canada), which offers direct service from Toronto, Montréal, Calgary, and Vancouver to San Francisco, Sacramento, Los Angeles, and San Diego. Many American carriers also offer similar routes.

3 Getting Around the U.S.

BY PLANE   Some large airlines (for example, Northwest and Delta) offer travelers on their transatlantic or transpacific flights special discount tickets under the name **Visit USA,** allowing travel between any U.S. destinations at minimum rates. These discount tickets are not sold in the United States and must be purchased abroad in conjunction with your international ticket. This system is the best, easiest, and fastest way to see the United States at low cost. You should obtain information well in advance from your travel agent or the office of the airline concerned, since the conditions attached to these discount tickets can be changed without advance notice.

BY TRAIN   International visitors can also buy a **USA Railpass,** good for 15 or 30 days of unlimited travel on Amtrak (☎ 800/USA-RAIL). The pass is available through many foreign travel agents. The latest prices in 1998 for a 15-day pass were $300 off-peak, $400 peak; a 30-day pass costs $450 off-peak, $645 peak. Peak period is roughly June 1 to September 1. (With a foreign passport, you can also buy passes at some Amtrak offices in the United States, including locations in San Francisco, Los Angeles, Chicago, New York, Miami, Boston, and Washington, D.C.) Reservations are generally required and should be made for each part of your trip as early as possible.

BY BUS   Although ticket prices for short hops between cities are often the most economical form of public transit, bus travel in the United States can be both slow and uncomfortable, so this option isn't for everyone (particularly since Amtrak, which is far more luxurious and safe, offers similar rates). **Greyhound/Trailways** (☎ **800/231-2222**), the sole nationwide bus line, offers an **Ameripass** for unlimited travel for 7 days at $179, 15 days at $289, 30 days at $399, and 60 days at $599. Passes must be purchased at a Greyhound terminal.

BY CAR   The most cost-effective, convenient, and comfortable way to travel around the United States—especially California—is by car. The Interstate highway system connects cities and towns all over the country; in addition to these high-speed, limited-access roadways, there's an extensive network of federal, state, and local highways and roads. Some of the national car-rental companies that have offices in California include **Alamo** (☎ 800/327-9633), **Avis** (☎ 800/331-1212), **Budget**

(☎ 800/527-0700), **Dollar** (☎ 800/800-4000), **Hertz** (☎ 800/654-3131), **National** (☎ 800/227-7368), and **Thrifty** (☎ 800/367-2277).

If you plan on renting a car in the United States, you probably won't need the services of an additional automobile organization. If you're planning to buy or borrow a car, automobile association membership is recommended. The country's largest auto club, **American Automobile Association (AAA),** 150 Van Ness Ave., San Francisco, CA 94102 (☎ **800/922-8228**), supplies its members with maps, insurance, and, most important, emergency road service. The cost of joining runs from $63 for singles to $87 for families, but if you're a member of a foreign auto club with reciprocal arrangements, you can enjoy free AAA service in America.

FAST FACTS: For the Foreign Traveler

Business Hours   Offices are usually open weekdays from 9am to 5pm. Banks are open weekdays from 9am to 3pm or later and sometimes on Saturday mornings. Shops, especially those in shopping complexes, tend to stay open late: until about 9pm weekdays and until 6pm on weekends.

Climate   See "When to Go" in chapter 2.

Currency & Exchange   See "Money" under "Preparing for Your Trip," earlier in this chapter.

Drinking Laws   The legal age for purchase and consumption of alcoholic beverages is 21; proof of age is required and often requested at bars, nightclubs, and restaurants, so it's a good idea to bring ID when you go out. In California, liquor is sold in supermarkets and grocery and liquor stores daily from 6am to 2am. Licensed restaurants are permitted to sell alcohol during the same hours. Note that many eateries are licensed only for beer and wine.

A big no-no is having an open container of alcohol in your car or any public area that isn't zoned for alcohol consumption. The police can, and probably will, fine you on the spot. And nothing will ruin your trip faster than getting a citation for DUI ("driving under the influence"), so don't even *think* about driving while intoxicated.

Electricity   U.S. wall outlets give power at 110 to 115 volts, 60 cycles, compared with 220 volts, 50 cycles, in most of Europe. In addition to a 100-volt transformer, small foreign appliances, such as hair dryers and shavers, will require a plug adapter (available at most hardware stores) with two flat, parallel pins.

Embassies & Consulates   All embassies are located in the nation's capital, Washington, D.C. In addition, several of the major English-speaking countries also have consulates in San Francisco or in Los Angeles.

The embassy of **Australia** is at 1601 Massachusetts Ave. NW, Washington, DC 20036 (☎ 202/797-3000); a consulate general is at 1 Bush St., Suite 700, San Francisco, CA 94104 (☎ 415/362-6160). The embassy of **Canada** is at 501 Pennsylvania Ave. NW, Washington, DC 20001 (☎ 202/682-1740); the nearest consulate is at 300 S. Grand Ave., 10th Floor, California Plaza, Los Angeles, CA 90071 (☎ 213/346-2700). The embassy of the **Republic of Ireland** is at 2234 Massachusetts Ave. NW, Washington, DC 20008 (☎ 202/462-3939); a consulate is at 44 Montgomery St., Suite 3830, San Francisco, CA 94104 (☎ 415/392-4214). The embassy of **New Zealand** is at 37 Observatory Circle NW, Washington, DC 20008 (☎ 202/328-4800); the nearest consulate is at

12400 Wilshire Blvd., Suite 1150, Los Angeles, CA 90025 (☎ 310/207-1605). The embassy of the **United Kingdom** is at 3100 Massachusetts Ave. NW, Washington, DC 20008 (☎ 202/462-1340); the nearest consulate is at 1 Sansome St., Suite 850, San Francisco, CA 94104 (☎ 415/981-3030). The embassy of **Japan** is at 2520 Massachusetts Ave. NW, Washington, DC 20008 (☎ 202/939-6700); the consulate general of Japan is located at 50 Fremont St., San Francisco, CA 94105 (☎ 415/777-3533).

If you are from another country, you can get the telephone number of your embassy by calling "Information" (directory assistance) in Washington, D.C. (☎ **202/555-1212**).

Emergencies   You can call the police, an ambulance, or the fire department through the single emergency telephone number, ☎ **911,** from any phone or pay phone (no coins needed). If that doesn't work, another useful way of reporting an emergency is to call the telephone-company operator by dialing 0 (zero, not the letter *O*).

Gasoline (Petrol)   Prices vary, but expect to pay anywhere between $1.25 and $1.65 for 1 U.S. gallon (about 3.8 liters) of "regular" unleaded gasoline (petrol). Higher-octane fuels are also available at most gas stations for slightly higher prices. Taxes are already included in the printed price.

Holidays   On the following legal national holidays, banks, government offices, post offices, and many stores, restaurants, and museums are closed: New Year's Day (Jan 1), Martin Luther King Day (3rd Mon in Jan), Presidents' Day (3rd Mon in Feb), Memorial Day (last Mon in May), Independence Day (July 4), Labor Day (1st Mon in Sept), Columbus Day (2nd Mon in Oct), Veterans Day (Nov 11), Thanksgiving Day (last Thurs in Nov), and Christmas Day (Dec 25). Election Day, for national elections, falls on the Tuesday following the 1st Monday in November. It's a legal national holiday during a presidential election, which occurs every 4th year (next in 2000).

Legal Aid   Happily, foreign tourists rarely come into contact with the American legal system. If you are stopped for a minor driving infraction (speeding, for example), *never* attempt to pay the fine directly to a police officer; fines should be paid to the clerk of the court, and a receipt should be obtained. If you're accused of a more serious offense, it's wise to say and do nothing before consulting a lawyer. Under U.S. law, an arrested person is allowed one telephone call to a party of his or her choice. You may wish to contact your country's embassy or consulate (see above).

Mail   If you want to receive mail, but aren't exactly sure where you'll be, have it sent to you, in your name, ℅ **General Delivery (Poste Restante)** at the main post office of the city or region you're visiting (call ☎ **800/275-8777** for information on the nearest post office). The addressee must pick it up in person and produce proof of identity (driver's license, credit card, passport). Most post offices will hold your mail up to 1 month, and are open Monday through Saturday from 8am to 6pm.

Generally found at street intersections, **mailboxes** are blue and carry the inscription U.S. MAIL. If your mail is addressed to a U.S. destination, don't forget to add the five-digit **zip code** after the two-letter abbreviation of the state to which the mail is addressed (CA for California).

For overseas mail, **postal rates** are as follows: A first-class letter of up to half an ounce costs 60¢ (46¢ to Canada and 40¢ to Mexico); a first-class postcard costs 50¢ (40¢ to Canada and 35¢ to Mexico); and a preprinted postal aerogramme costs 50¢.

Medical Emergencies   To call an ambulance, dial ☎ **911** from any phone—no coins are needed.

Post   See "Mail," above.

Radio & Television   There are five national television networks that are broadcast over the air: ABC (Channel 7), CBS (Channel 5), NBC (Channel 4), PBS (Channel 9), and Fox (Channel 2). Cable television includes the national networks as well as 50 or so other cable stations, including the Cable News Network (CNN), ESPN (sports channel), and MTV. Most hotels offer a dozen cable stations to choose from, as well as pay-per-view movies. You'll also find a wide choice of local radio stations, each broadcasting particular kinds of talk shows and/or music—classical, country, jazz, rock, pop, gospel—punctuated by news broadcasts and frequent commercials.

Smoking   Heavy smokers are in for a tough time in California. There is no smoking allowed in public buildings, sports arenas, elevators, theaters, banks, lobbies, restaurants, offices, stores, bed-and-breakfasts, most small hotels, and bars. Yes, that's right, as of January 1, 1998, you can't even smoke in a bar in California, the only exception being a bar where drinks are served solely by the owner of the establishment.

Taxes   In the United States there is no value-added tax (VAT) or other direct tax at a national level. Every state, as well as every city, is allowed to levy its own local sales tax on all purchases, including hotel and restaurant checks and airline tickets. Taxes are already included in the price of certain services, such as public transportation, cab fares, phone calls, and gasoline. The amount of sales tax varies from 4% to 10%, depending on the state and city, so when you are making major purchases, such as photographic equipment, clothing, or high-fidelity components, it can be a significant part of the cost.

In addition, many cities charge a separate "bed" or room tax on accommodations, above and beyond any sales tax.

Telephone & Fax   Pay phones can be found almost everywhere—at street corners, in bars and restaurants, and in hotels. Outside the metropolitan area, however, public telephones are more difficult to find; stores and gas stations are your best bet.

Phones do not accept pennies and few will take anything larger than a quarter. Some public phones, especially those in airports and large hotels, accept credit/charge cards, such as MasterCard, Visa, and American Express. Credit/charge cards are especially handy for international calls; instructions are printed on the phone.

In California, most **local calls** cost 35¢. To make local calls, dial the seven-digit local number. For domestic long-distance calls or international calls, stock up on a supply of quarters; first dial the number, then a recorded voice will instruct you when and in what quantity you should put the coins into the slot. For **domestic long-distance calls,** first dial 1 (the long-distance access code), the

Travel Tip

Don't mix up the toll-free *800, 888,* or *877* area codes with numbers in area codes *700* or *900,* which are usually attached to chat lines, phone sex, and the like, all charging oodles per minute.

---

area code, and the seven-digit local number. For direct **overseas calls,** dial 011 first (the international access code), then the country code (Australia, 61; Republic of Ireland, 353; New Zealand, 64; United Kingdom, 44), followed by the city code, and then the local number you wish to call. To place a call to Canada or the Caribbean, just dial 1, the area code, and the local number.

Before calling from a hotel room, always ask the hotel phone operator if there are any telephone surcharges. These can sometimes be reduced by calling collect or by using a telephone charge card. Hotel charges, which can be exorbitant, may be avoided altogether by using a pay phone in the lobby.

Note that all calls to phone numbers in area codes 800, 888, and 877 are toll-free.

For **local directory assistance** ("Information"), dial ☎ 411; for **long-distance information** in the United States and Canada, dial 1, then the appropriate area code and ☎ 555-1212.

For collect (reversed-charge) calls and for person-to-person calls, dial 0 (zero, not the letter *O*) followed by the area code and the number you want; an operator or recording will then come on the line, and you should specify that you are calling collect or person-to-person, or both. If your operator-assisted call is international, just dial 0 and wait for the operator.

Like the telephone system, **telegraph** and **telex** services are provided by private corporations, such as ITT, MCI, and above all, Western Union. You can bring your telegram to a **Western Union** office or dictate it over the phone (☎ **800/325-6000**).

You'll find **fax facilities** widely available. They can be found in most hotels and many other establishments. Try Mailboxes, Etc. or any photocopying shop.

Telephone Directory   There are two kinds of telephone directories in the United States. The general directory is the so-called *White Pages,* in which private and business subscribers are listed in alphabetical order. The inside front cover lists the emergency numbers for police, fire, and ambulance, and other vital numbers (like the Coast Guard, poison-control center, crime-victims hot line, and so on). The first few pages are devoted to community-service numbers, including a guide to long-distance and international calling, complete with country codes and area codes.

The second directory, printed on yellow paper (hence its name, *Yellow Pages*), lists all local services, businesses, and industries by type of activity, with an index at the back. The listings cover not only such obvious items as automobile repairs by make of car, or drugstores (pharmacies) often by geographical location, but also restaurants by type of cuisine and geographical location, bookstores by special subject and/or language, places of worship by religious denomination, and other information that the tourist might otherwise not readily find. The *Yellow Pages* also include city plans or detailed maps, often showing postal zip codes and public transportation routes.

Time   The United States is divided into four time zones (six, if Alaska and Hawaii are included). From east to west, these are eastern standard time (EST), central standard time (CST), mountain standard time (MST), and Pacific standard time (PST). There are also Alaska standard time (AST) and Hawaii standard time (HST). California is on Pacific standard time, which is 8 hours behind Greenwich mean time. Noon in New York City (EST) is 11am in Chicago (CST), 10am in Denver (MST), 9am in San Francisco (PST), 8am in Anchorage (AST), and 7am in Honolulu (HST).

Daylight saving time is in effect from the 1st Sunday in April until 2am on the last Sunday in October, except in Arizona, Hawaii, part of Indiana, and Puerto Rico. Daylight saving time moves the clock 1 hour ahead of standard time.

Tipping   Service in America is some of the best in the world, and is rarely included in the price of anything. It's part of the American way of life to tip, on the principle that you must expect to pay for any service you get. Many personnel receive little direct salary and must depend on tips for their main income. In fact, the U.S. federal government imposes income taxes on service personnel based on an estimate of how much they should have earned in tips relative to their employer's total receipts. In other words, they may have to pay taxes on a tip you didn't give them!

Here are some rules of thumb:

In **hotels,** tip bellhops at least $1 per piece of luggage ($2 to $3 if you have a lot of luggage) and tip the chamber staff $1 to $3 per day. Tip the doorman or concierge only if he or she has provided you with some specific service (for example, calling a cab for you or obtaining difficult-to-get theater tickets). Tip the valet parking attendant $1 to $3 every time you get your car.

In **restaurants, bars,** and **nightclubs,** tip service staff 15% to 20% of the check, tip bartenders 10% to 15%, tip checkroom attendants $1 per garment, and tip valet-parking attendants $1 to $3 per vehicle. Tip the doorman only if he has provided you with some specific service (such as calling a cab for you). Tipping is not expected in cafeterias and fast-food restaurants.

Tip **cab drivers** 15% of the fare.

As for **other service personnel,** tip skycaps at airports at least $1 per piece ($2 to $3 if you have a lot of luggage) and tip hairdressers and barbers 15% to 20%.

Tipping gas-station attendants and ushers at movies and theaters is not expected.

Toilets   You can almost always find a public toilet in restaurants and bars; note, however, a growing practice in some establishments of displaying a notice that TOILETS ARE FOR THE USE OF PATRONS ONLY. You can ignore this sign or, better yet, avoid arguments by paying for a cup of coffee or soft drink, which will qualify you as a patron. Large hotels and fast-food restaurants are probably the best bet for good, clean facilities. Museums, department stores, shopping malls, and, in a pinch, gas stations all have public toilets. If possible, avoid the toilets at parks and beaches, which are a real crap shoot (pun intended) when it comes to cleanliness.

4

San Francisco

by Erika Lenkert and Matthew R. Poole

Consistently rated one of the top tourist destinations in the world, San Francisco is awash with multiple dimensions. Its famous, thrilling streets go up, and they go down; its multifarious citizens—and their cultures and cuisines—hail from San Antonio to Singapore; and its politics range from hyper-liberalism to an ever-encroaching wave of conservatism. Even something as mundane as fog takes on a new dimension as it creeps from the ocean and slowly envelops San Francisco in a resplendent blanket of mist.

In a city so multifaceted, so enamored of itself, it's truly hard not to find what you're looking for. Smell the fresh aroma of coffee in North Beach. Stuff yourself on Chinatown dim sum. Browse the Haight for incense and crystals. Walk along the beach, dye your hair, see a symphony, rent a Harley—the list is endless. Like an eternal world's fair, it's all happening in San Francisco, and everyone's invited.

1 Orientation

ARRIVING
BY PLANE

Two major airports serve the Bay Area: San Francisco International and Oakland International. All the major national rental-car companies have offices at these two locations (see "Getting Around," later in this chapter).

SAN FRANCISCO INTERNATIONAL AIRPORT (SFO) San Francisco's major airport (☎ 415/761-0800) is 14 miles south of downtown, directly on U.S. 101. For information on ground transportation to the city, call the airport's toll-free hot line (☎ 800/736-2008).

The **SFO Airporter bus** (☎ 415/495-8404) picks up passengers in front of the baggage claim area every 15 to 30 minutes daily from 6:15am to midnight and stops at several downtown hotels: the Grand Hyatt, San Francisco Hilton, San Francisco Marriott, Westin St. Francis, Parc Fifty-Five, Hyatt Regency, and Sheraton Palace. Reservations are not needed. The cost is $10 each way, and children under 2 ride free.

Other private shuttle companies offer door-to-door airport service, in which you share a van with other passengers. **SuperShuttle** (☎ 415/558-8500) charges $10 per person to a hotel; $12 to a residence or business, plus $8 for each additional person; and $40 to (van for up to seven passengers. **Yellow Airport Shuttle** (☎ 415/282) $10 per person. Each shuttle stops every 20 minutes or so to pick up in the marked areas at the terminals' upper level. Reservations are require~~d for the~~ return trip to SFO only and should be made 1 day before departure. These shuttles usually reach downtown San Francisco in 45 to 60 minutes, but demand they pick you up 2 hours before your flight (3 during holidays).

The San Mateo County Transit system, **SamTrans** (☎ 800/660-4287 or 650/508-6200 within northern California) runs two buses between the airport and the Transbay Terminal at First and Mission streets. The 7B bus costs $1 and takes about 55 minutes. The 7F bus costs $2 and takes only 35 minutes, but permits only one carry-on bag. Both buses run daily, every half hour from about 5:30am to 7pm, then hourly until about midnight.

If you rent a car, it will take you about 40 minutes to get downtown during rush hour; otherwise it's 20 to 25 minutes. A cab will cost $28 to $32, plus tip.

OAKLAND INTERNATIONAL AIRPORT Located about 5 miles south of downtown Oakland, at the Hegenberger Road exit on Calif. 17 (U.S. 880), Oakland International Airport (☎ 510/577-4000) is used primarily by passengers with East Bay destinations. Some San Franciscans, however, prefer this less-crowded airport when flying during busy periods.

Bayporter Express (☎ 415/467-1800) is a shuttle service that charges $20 for the first person and $10 for each additional person to downtown San Francisco (it costs more to outer areas of town). **Easy Way Out** (☎ 510/430-9090) is another option, which charges $20 per person, $10 each additional rider. Both accept advance reservations. To the right of the airport exit there are usually shuttles that will take you to the city for around $20 per person. There are also privately owned shuttle services waiting for passengers at the airport. Fares vary, but are usually around $20 per person (ask before you agree to ride and bargain if you must!).

The cheapest way to get downtown is via **Bay Area Rapid Transit** (**BART;** ☎ 510/464-6000). The **AirBART shuttle bus** leaves about every 15 minutes Monday through Saturday from 6am to 11:30pm and Sunday from 8:30am to 11:30pm from Terminals 1 and 2 near the ground transportation signs. The cost is $2 for the 10-minute ride to BART's Coliseum terminal. BART fares vary, depending on your destination; the trip to downtown San Francisco costs $2.45 and takes 20 minutes once onboard. The entire excursion should take around 45 minutes.

Taxis into the center of San Francisco are expensive. The 1-hour trip will cost about $45, plus tip.

BY CAR

If you're driving in from the north, **U.S. 101** crosses the Golden Gate Bridge at the northernmost tip of the peninsula and runs directly through the city. Approaching from the east, **I-80** crosses the San Francisco–Oakland Bay Bridge and terminates in the city's South of Market (SoMa) district.

Both **I-280** and **U.S. 101** come up the peninsula from the south and drop into the city via several downtown off-ramps.

BY TRAIN

Passengers arriving by train will disembark at Amtrak's Emeryville depot just north of Oakland (east of S.F.). Free shuttles connect the depot with San Francisco's Ferry Building and Cal Train Station; they depart at 40-minute intervals and the trip takes about 45 minutes. For information, call **Amtrak** (☎ 800/872-7245).

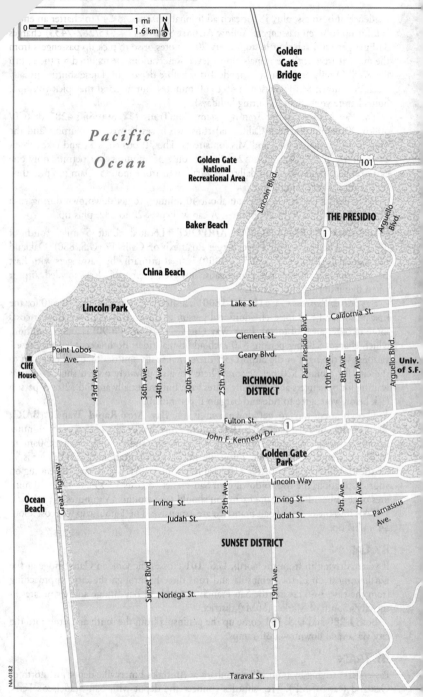

0 | 1 mi | N
1.6 km

Golden Gate Bridge

Pacific Ocean

Golden Gate National Recreational Area

101

THE PRESIDIO

Baker Beach

Lincoln Blvd.

Arguello Blvd.

China Beach

Lincoln Park

Lake St.

California St.

Clement St.

Geary Blvd.

Point Lobos Ave.

Cliff House

Park Presidio Blvd.

10th Ave.

8th Ave.

6th Ave.

Arguello Blvd.

Univ. of S.F.

43rd Ave.

36th Ave.

34th Ave.

30th Ave.

25th Ave.

RICHMOND DISTRICT

Fulton St.

John F. Kennedy Dr.

1

Golden Gate Park

Lincoln Way

Ocean Beach

Great Highway

Irving St.

25th Ave.

Irving St.

9th Ave.

7th Ave.

Parnassus Ave.

Judah St.

Judah St.

SUNSET DISTRICT

Sunset Blvd.

19th Ave.

Noriega St.

1

Taraval St.

N4-0182

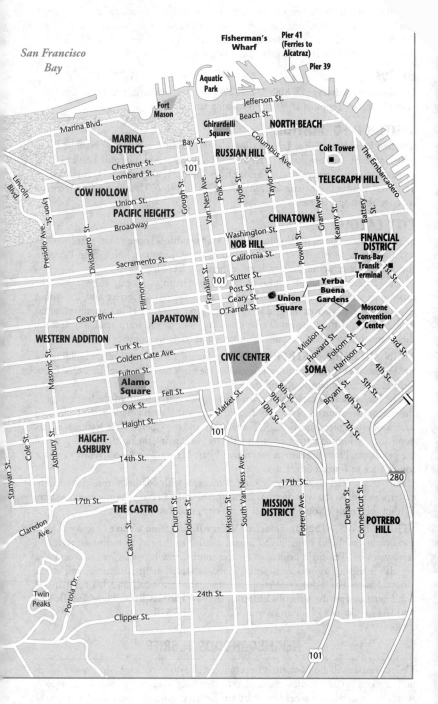

San Francisco
Bay

Fisherman's
Wharf

Pier 41
(Ferries to
Alcatraz)

Pier 39

Aquatic
Park

Fort
Mason

Jefferson St.

Ghirardelli
Square

Beach St.

NORTH BEACH

Marina Blvd.

MARINA
DISTRICT

Bay St.

RUSSIAN HILL

Columbus Ave.

Coit Tower

Chestnut St.

Lombard St.

101

TELEGRAPH HILL

The Embarcadero

COW HOLLOW

Union St.

Lincoln
Blvd.

Lyon St.

Presidio Ave.

PACIFIC HEIGHTS

Broadway

Divisadero St.

Gough St.

Van Ness Ave.

Polk St.

Hyde St.

Taylor St.

CHINATOWN

Grant Ave.

Kearny St.

Battery St.

FINANCIAL
DISTRICT

Washington St.

NOB HILL

California St.

Powell St.

Trans-Bay
Transit
Terminal

1st St.

Sacramento St.

Fillmore St.

Franklin St.

101

Sutter St.

Post St.

Geary St.

Union
Square

Yerba
Buena
Gardens

Moscone
Convention
Center

Geary Blvd.

JAPANTOWN

O'Farrell St.

WESTERN ADDITION

Masonic St.

Turk St.

Golden Gate Ave.

Fulton St.

CIVIC CENTER

Mission St.

Howard St.

Folsom St.

Harrison St.

3rd St.

Alamo
Square

Fell St.

SOMA

4th St.

Oak St.

Market St.

8th St.

9th St.

Bryant St.

5th St.

6th St.

Haight St.

10th St.

7th St.

101

HAIGHT-
ASHBURY

14th St.

Stanyan St.

Cole St.

Ashbury St.

17th St.

280

17th St.

THE CASTRO

Castro St.

Church St.

Dolores St.

Mission St.

South Van Ness Ave.

MISSION
DISTRICT

Potrero Ave.

Deharo St.

Connecticut St.

POTRERO
HILL

Claredon
Ave.

Twin
Peaks

Portola Dr.

24th St.

Clipper St.

101

59

the major car-rental companies has an office at the train station,
ck up your car from downtown Oakland or San Francisco. **Hertz**
31) will reimburse your cab fare (up to $5) from the train station to
e at 1001 Broadway, 2 miles away.

By Bus

Greyhound/Trailways (☎ **800/231-2222**) offers bus service in and out of San Francisco's Transbay Terminal at First and Mission streets.

VISITOR INFORMATION

The **San Francisco Visitor Information Center,** on the lower level of Hallidie Plaza, 900 Market St., at Powell Street (☎ **415/391-2000**), provides information in several languages (open Monday through Friday from 9am to 5:30pm, Saturday from 9am to 3pm, and Sunday from 10am to 2pm). Call ☎ 415/391-2001 any time for a recorded message about special events.

CITY LAYOUT

San Francisco occupies the tip of a 32-mile-long peninsula between San Francisco Bay and the Pacific Ocean. Its land area measures about 46 square miles. Twin Peaks, in the geographic center of the city, is more than 900 feet high.

San Francisco may seem confusing at first, but truth is, it's easy to navigate. The downtown streets are arranged in a grid, except for Market Street and Columbus Avenue, which cut across the grid at right angles to each other. Hills sometimes appear to distort this pattern, which can be confusing. But as you learn your way around, these same hills will become your landmarks and reference points.

MAIN ARTERIES & STREETS   **Market Street,** with the tall office buildings of the Financial District at its northeast end, is the city's main thoroughfare. One block beyond lies the Embarcadero and the bay.

The **Embarcadero** curves along San Francisco Bay from south of the Bay Bridge to the northeast perimeter of the city and terminates at Fisherman's Wharf, the famous tourist-oriented pier. Aquatic Park, Fort Mason, and the Golden Gate National Recreation area are located farther on around the bay, occupying the northernmost point of the peninsula. From the eastern perimeter of Fort Mason, **Van Ness Avenue** runs due south, back to Market Street.

The areas listed above roughly form a triangle, with Market Street as its southeastern boundary, the waterfront as its northern, and Van Ness Avenue as its western. Within this triangle you'll find most of the city's major tourist sites.

STREET MAPS   The **San Francisco Visitor Information Center** (see above) gives away plenty of useful maps; if you intend to stick to the typical tourist areas, they'll serve you well. The maps printed in the free tourist weeklies, *Bay City Guide* and *Key,* are also useful for visitors and can be found at most hotels, attractions, and at the visitor center. For a huge selection of street, topographical, and hiking maps of San Francisco and the state of California, stop by **Thomas Bros. Maps and Books,** 550 Jackson St., at Columbus Avenue (☎ **415/981-7520**).

NEIGHBORHOODS IN BRIEF

Union Square   Union Square is the commercial hub of the city. Most major hotels and department stores are crammed into the area surrounding the actual square, which was named for a series of violent pro-Union demonstrations staged here on the eve of the Civil War. Upscale boutiques, restaurants, and galleries are tucked between the larger buildings.

Civic Center   Although millions of dollars have been expended on brick sidewalks, ornate lampposts, and elaborate street plantings, the southwestern section of Market Street remains downright dilapidated. The Civic Center, at the "bottom" of Market Street, is an exception. This large complex of buildings includes the domed City Hall, the Opera House, Davies Symphony Hall, and the city's main library. The landscaped plaza connecting the buildings is the staging area for San Francisco's frequent demonstrations for or against just about everything.

SoMa   In recent years, high rents have forced residents and businesses into once-desolate South of Market (dubbed "SoMa"). The area still predominantly consists of warehouses and industrial spaces, but now many of them are brimming with art galleries and museums, restaurants, and nightclubs. The area is officially demarcated by the Embarcadero, U.S. 101, and Market Street.

The Financial District   Northeast of Union Square, this area is bordered by the Embarcadero, Market, Third, Kearny, and Washington streets. It's the city's business district and stomping grounds for many major corporations. The TransAmerica Pyramid, at Montgomery and Clay streets, is one of the district's most conspicuous architectural features. To its east stands the sprawling Embarcadero Center, an 8½-acre complex housing offices, shops, and restaurants. Even farther east is the World Trade Center, standing adjacent to the old Ferry Building. Ferries to Sausalito and Larkspur still leave from this point.

Chinatown   The official entrance to Chinatown is marked by a large red-and-green gate on Grant Avenue at Bush Street. Beyond it lies a 24-block labyrinth, bordered by Broadway, Bush, Kearny, and Stockton streets, filled with restaurants, markets, temples, and shops—and, of course, a substantial percentage of San Francisco's Chinese residents. Chinatown is a great place for urban exploration. Stroll along Stockton, Grant, and Portsmouth Square, and the alleys that lead off them, like Ross and Waverly. This area is jam-packed, so don't even *think* about driving around here.

Nob Hill/Russian Hill   Bounded by Bush, Larkin, Pacific, and Stockton streets, Nob Hill is the genteel, well-heeled district of the city, still occupied by the major power brokers and the neighborhood businesses they frequent. Russian Hill extends from Pacific to Bay and from Polk to Mason. It is marked by steep streets, lush gardens, and high-rises, which are home to both the moneyed and the more bohemian.

North Beach   The Italian quarter, which stretches from Montgomery and Jackson to Bay Street, is one of the best places in the city to grab a coffee, pull up a cafe chair, and do some serious people-watching. Nightlife is equally happening; restaurants, bars, and clubs along Columbus and Grant avenues bring folks from all over the Bay Area here to fight for a parking place and romp through the festive neighborhood. Down Columbus toward the Financial District are the remains of the city's Beat-generation landmarks, including Ferlinghetti's City Lights Bookstore and Vesuvio's Bar. Broadway—a short strip of sex joints—cuts through the heart of the district. Telegraph Hill looms over the east side of North Beach, topped by Coit Tower, one of San Francisco's best vantage points.

Fisherman's Wharf   North Beach runs into Fisherman's Wharf, which was once the busy heart of the city's great harbor and waterfront industries. Today, it's a tacky-but-interesting tourist area with little if any authentic waterfront life, except for recreational boating and some friendly sea lions.

The Marina District   Created on landfill for the Pan Pacific Exposition of 1915, the Marina boasts some of the best views of the Golden Gate, as well as plenty of grassy fields alongside the San Francisco Bay. Streets are lined with elegant Mediterranean-style homes and apartments, which are inhabited by the city's well-to-do singles and wealthy families. Here, too, is the Palace of Fine Arts, the Exploratorium, and Fort Mason Center. The main street is Chestnut between Franklin and Lyon, which is lined with shops, cafes, and boutiques. Because of its landfill foundation, the Marina was one of the city's hardest-hit districts in the 1989 quake.

Cow Hollow   Located west of Van Ness Avenue, between Russian Hill and the Presidio, this flat, grazable area supported 30 dairy farms in 1861. Today, Cow Hollow is largely residential and occupied by the city's Young and Yuppie. Its two primary commercial thoroughfares are Lombard Street, known for its many relatively inexpensive motels, and Union Street, a flourishing shopping sector filled with restaurants, pubs, cafes, and shops.

Pacific Heights   The ultra-elite, such as the Gettys and Danielle Steele—and those lucky enough to buy before the real-estate boom—reside in the mansions and homes of Pacific Heights. When the rich meander out of their fortresses, they wander down to Union Street, a long stretch of boutiques, restaurants, cafes, and bars.

Japantown   Bounded by Octavia, Fillmore, California, and Geary, Japantown shelters only about 4% of the city's Japanese population, but it's still a cultural experience to explore these few square blocks and the shops and restaurants within them.

Haight-Ashbury   Part trendy, part nostalgic, part funky, the Haight was the soul of the psychedelic and free-loving 1960s and the center of the counterculture movement. Today, the neighborhood straddling upper Haight Street on the eastern border of Golden Gate Park is more gentrified, but the commercial area still harbors all walks of life. Leftover hippies mingle with grungy street kids outside Ben and Jerry's, probably still reminiscing about Jerry Garcia, and nondescript marijuana dealers whisper offers to sell "buds" as shoppers pass. But you don't need to wear tie-dye or dye your hair chartreuse to enjoy the Haight: The food, shops, and bars cater to all tastes.

Richmond & Sunset Districts   These two districts, which flank the north and south sides of Golden Gate Park from the numbered avenues all the way out to the beach (the western edge of the town and the U.S.) are the bedroom communities of town. Rows and rows of houses are packed along grids, and small neighborhood shopping areas and restaurants are sprinkled throughout. Generally, most tourists don't make it here, except as they breeze by on their way to Ocean Beach.

The Castro   One of the liveliest streets in town, Castro is practically synonymous with San Francisco's gay community, even though technically it is only a street in the Noe Valley district. Located at the very end of Market Street, between 17th and 18th streets, Castro supports dozens of shops, restaurants, and bars catering to the gay community. Open-minded straight people are welcome, too.

The Mission District   The Mexican and Latin American populations, along with their cuisine, traditions, and art, have always made the Mission District vibrant, but the latest crop of restaurants and nightclubs has caused more than one magazine to rank this neighborhood among the hippest in the United States. Because some parts of the area are poor and still plagued with homelessness, gangs, and drugs, many tourists duck into Mission Dolores, cruise by a few of the 200-plus amazing murals, and head back downtown. But there's plenty more to see in the Mission District. There's a substantial community of lesbians around Valencia Street, several alternative

arts organizations, and most recently the ultimate in young hipster
bars, clubs, and incredible budget restaurants surround Mission betv
24th streets and Valencia at 16th Street. Don't be afraid to visit this area, but use
caution at night.

2 Getting Around

BY PUBLIC TRANSPORTATION

The San Francisco Municipal Railway, better known as **Muni** (☎ **415/673-6864**),
operates the city's cable cars, buses, and Metro streetcars. Together, these three public
transportation services crisscross the entire city, making San Francisco fully accessible
to everyone. Buses and Metro streetcars cost $1 for adults, 35¢ for ages 5 to 17, free
for kids under 5, and 35¢ for seniors over 65. Cable cars cost $2 ($1 for seniors from
9pm to midnight and from 6 to 7am). Needless to say, they're packed primarily with
tourists. Exact change is required on all vehicles except cable cars. Fares quoted here
are subject to change.

For detailed route information, phone Muni or consult the bus map at the front of
the *Yellow Pages.* If you plan on making extensive use of public transportation, you
may want to invest in a comprehensive route map ($2), sold at the San Francisco Vis-
itor Information Center (see "Visitor Information" under "Orientation," above) and
in many downtown retail outlets.

BY CABLE CAR   San Francisco's cable cars may not be the most practical means of
transport, but these rolling historic landmarks sure are a fun ride. There are only three
lines in the city, and they're all concentrated in the downtown area. The most scenic,
and exciting, is the **Powell-Hyde line,** which follows a zigzag route from the corner of
Powell and Market streets, over both Nob Hill and Russian Hill, to a turntable at gaslit
Victorian Square in front of Aquatic Park. The **Powell-Mason line** starts at the same
intersection and climbs over Nob Hill before descending to Bay Street, just 3 blocks
from Fisherman's Wharf. The least scenic is the **California Street line,** which begins
at the foot of Market Street and runs a straight course through Chinatown and over
Nob Hill to Van Ness Avenue. All riders must exit at the last stop and wait in line for
the return trip. The cable-car system operates from approximately 6:30am to
12:30am.

BY BUS   Buses reach almost every corner of San Francisco, and travel over the
bridges to Marin County and Oakland. All are numbered and display their destinations on the front. Stops are designated by signs, curb markings, and yellow bands on

Discount Passes

Muni discount passes, called "Passports," entitle holders to unlimited rides on
buses, Metro streetcars, and cable cars. A Passport costs $6 for 1 day, and $10 or
$15 for 3 or 7 consecutive days. As a bonus, your passport also entitles you to
admission discounts at 24 of the city's major attractions, including the M. H.
De Young Memorial Museum, the Asian Art Museum, the California Academy of
Sciences, and the Japanese Tea Garden (all in Golden Gate Park); the Museum of
Modern Art; Coit Tower; the Exploratorium; the zoo; and the National Maritime
Museum and Historic Ships. Among the places where you can purchase a Passport
are the San Francisco Visitor Information Center, the Holiday Inn Civic Center,
and the Tix Bay Area booth at Union Square.

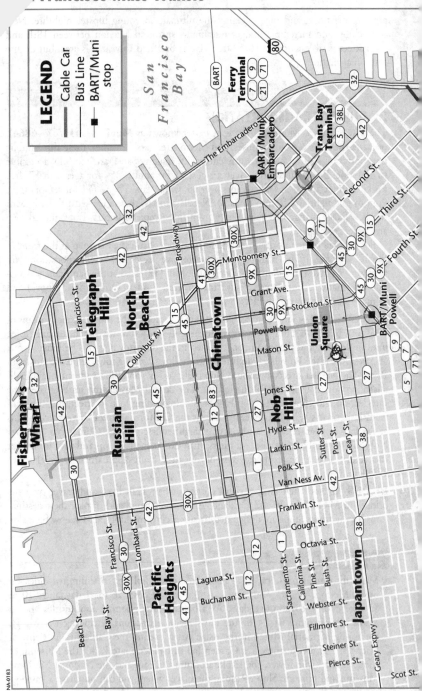

LEGEND

— Cable Car
— Bus Line
■ BART/Muni stop

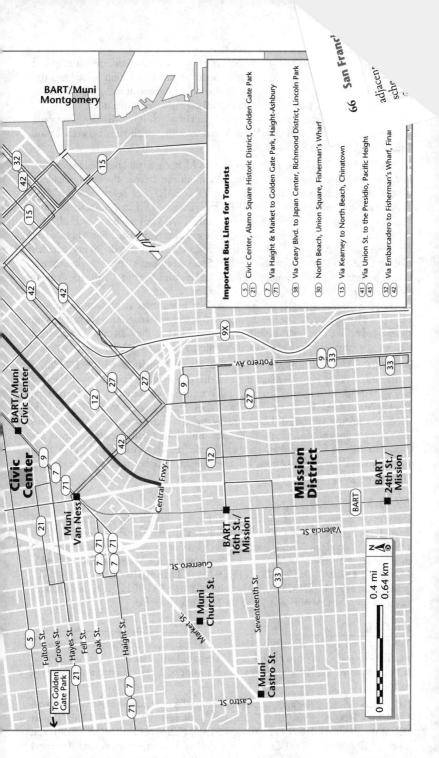

BART/Muni Montgomery

Important Bus Lines for Tourists

- 5 — Civic Center, Alamo Square Historic District, Golden Gate Park
- 21 / 71 — Via Haight & Market to Golden Gate Park, Haight-Ashbury
- 7 / 71
- 38 — Via Geary Blvd. to Japan Center, Richmond District, Lincoln Park
- 30 — North Beach, Union Square, Fisherman's Wharf
- 15 — Via Kearney to North Beach, Chinatown
- 41 / 45 — Via Union St. to the Presidio, Pacific Height
- 32 / 42 — Via Embarcadero to Fisherman's Wharf, Finan

66 — San Franc

adjacent
sche

Civic Center

BART/Muni Civic Center

Muni Van Ness

BART 16th St./ Mission

BART 24th St./ Mission

Mission District

BART

Central Frwy.

Potrero Av.

Valencia St.

Guerrero St.

Seventeenth St.

Market St.

Muni Church St.

Muni Castro St.

Castro St.

Haight St.

Oak St.

Fell St.

Hayes St.

Grove St.

Fulton St.

To Golden Gate Park

N

0   0.4 mi
0   0.64 km

...utility poles, and most bus shelters exhibit Muni's transportation map and ...ule. Many buses travel along Market Street or pass near Union Square and run ...om about 6am to midnight, after which there is infrequent all-night "Owl" service. If you can help it, for safety purposes avoid taking buses late at night.

Popular tourist routes are nos. 5, 7, and 71, all of which run to Golden Gate Park; 41 and 45, which travel along Union Street; and 30, which runs between Union Square and Ghirardelli Square.

BY METRO STREETCAR Five of Muni's six Metro streetcar lines, designated J, K, L, M, and N, run underground downtown and on the street in the outer neighborhoods. The sleek railcars make the same stops as BART (see below) along Market Street, including Embarcadero Station (in the Financial District), Montgomery and Powell streets (both near Union Square), and the Civic Center (near City Hall). Past the Civic Center, the routes branch off in different directions: The J line will take you to Mission Dolores; the K, L, and M lines to Castro Street; and the N line parallels Golden Gate Park. Metros run about every 15 minutes—more frequently during rush hours. Service is offered Monday through Friday from 5am to 12:30am, Saturday from 6am to 12:20am, and Sunday from 8am to 12:20am.

The most recent streetcar additions are not newcomers at all: San Francisco's beloved 1930s streetcars. The beautiful, rejuvenated green-and-cream-colored cars on the F Market line run from downtown Market Street to the Castro and back. It's a quick and charming way to get up and downtown without any hassle.

BY BART BART, an acronym for **Bay Area Rapid Transit** (☎ **650/992-2278**), is a futuristic-looking, high-speed rail network that connects San Francisco with the East Bay—Oakland, Richmond, Concord, and Fremont. Four stations are located along Market Street (see "By Metro Streetcar," above). Fares range from $1 to $3.55, depending on how far you go. Tickets are dispensed from machines in the stations and are magnetically encoded with a dollar amount. Computerized exits automatically deduct the correct fare. Children 4 and under ride free. Trains run every 15 to 20 minutes, Monday through Friday from 4am to midnight, Saturday from 6am to midnight, and Sunday from 8am to midnight.

BY TAXI

If you're downtown or leaving from a major hotel, it shouldn't be too difficult to hail a cab. If the lighted sign on the roof is illuminated, the taxi is available—grab it. Otherwise, it's a good idea to call one of the following companies to arrange a ride in advance, particularly on Friday and Saturday nights: **Veteran's Cab** (☎ 415/552-1300), **Desoto Cab Co.** (☎ 415/673-1414), **Luxor Cabs** (☎ 415/282-4141), **Yellow Cab** (☎ 415/626-2345), and **Pacific** (☎ 415/986-7220). Rates are approximately $2 for the first mile and $1.80 for each mile thereafter.

BY CAR

You don't need a car to explore downtown San Francisco; in fact, in central areas, such as Chinatown, Union Square, and the Financial District, having a car can be your worst nightmare. But if you want to venture outside of the city, driving is the best way to go.

RENTALS Among the major car-rental companies operating in the city are **Alamo** (☎ 800/327-9633), **Avis** (☎ 800/331-1212), **Budget** (☎ 800/527-0700), **Dollar** (☎ 800/800-4000), **Hertz** (☎ 800/654-3131), **National** (☎ 800/227-7368), and **Thrifty** (☎ 800/367-2277). In addition to the big chains, there are dozens of regional rental places in San Francisco, many of which offer lower rates. These include **A-One**

Rent-A-Car, 434 O'Farrell St. (☎ 415/771-3977), and **Bay Area Rentals,** 229 Seventh St. (☎ 415/621-8989).

PARKING   If you want to have a relaxing vacation here, don't even attempt to find street parking in Nob Hill, North Beach, Chinatown, by Fisherman's Wharf, and on Telegraph Hill. Park in a garage or take a cab or a bus. If you do find street parking, pay attention to street signs that will explain when you can park and for how long. Be especially careful not to park in zones that are tow areas during rush hours.

Curb colors also indicate parking regulations. **Red** means no stopping or parking; **blue** is reserved for disabled drivers with a California-issued disabled plate or a placard; **white** means there's a 5-minute limit; **green** indicates a 10-minute limit; and **yellow** and **yellow-black** curbs are for commercial vehicles only. Also, don't park at a bus stop or in front of a fire hydrant; and watch out for street-cleaning signs. If you violate the law, you may get a hefty ticket or your car may be towed. To get your car back, you must obtain a release from the nearest district police department, then go to the towing company to pick up the vehicle.

When parking on a hill, apply the hand brake, put the car in gear, and *curb your wheels*—toward the curb when facing downhill, away from the curb when facing uphill. Curbing your wheels will not only prevent a possible "runaway," but will also keep you from getting a ticket—an expensive fine that is aggressively enforced.

FAST FACTS: San Francisco

American Express   For travel arrangements, traveler's checks, currency exchange, and other member services, American Express has offices in the Financial District at 295 California St., at Battery Street (☎ **415/536-2686**), and at 455 Market St., at First Street (☎ **415/536-2600**), open Monday through Friday from 8:30am to 5:30pm and Saturday from 9am to 2pm. To report lost or stolen traveler's checks, call ☎ **800/221-7282.** For **American Express Global Assist,** call ☎ **800/554-2639.**

Baby-Sitters   Hotels can often recommend a baby-sitter or child-care service. If yours can't, try **Temporary Tot Tending** (☎ 650/355-7377, or 650/871-5790 after 6pm), which offers child care by licensed teachers by the hour for children from 3 weeks to 12 years of age. It's open Monday through Friday from 6am to 7pm (weekend service is available only during convention times).

Dentists   In the event of a dental emergency, see your hotel concierge or contact the **San Francisco Dental Society** (☎ 415/421-1435) for 24-hour referral to a specialist. **The San Francisco Dental Office,** 132 the Embarcadero (☎ 415/777-5115), between Mission and Howard streets, offers emergency service and comprehensive dental care Monday, Tuesday, and Friday from 8am to 4:30pm, and Wednesday and Thursday from 10:30am to 6:30pm.

Doctors   **Saint Francis Memorial Hospital,** 900 Hyde St., between Bush and Pine streets on Nob Hill (☎ 415/353-6000), provides 24-hour emergency-care service. The hospital also operates a **physician-referral service** (☎ 415/353-6566).

Emergencies   Dial ☎ 911 for police, ambulance, or the fire department. Emergency hot lines include the **Poison Control Center** (☎ 800/523-2222) and **Rape Crisis** (☎ 415/647-7273).

Police   For emergencies, dial ☎ 911 from any phone; no coins are needed. For other matters, call ☎ 415/553-0123.

Safety Few locals would recommend walking alone late at night in certain areas, particularly the Tenderloin, between Union Square and the Civic Center. Compared with similar areas in other cities, however, even this section of San Francisco is relatively tranquil. Other areas where you should be particularly alert are the Mission District, around 16th and Mission streets; the lower Fillmore area, around lower Haight Street; and the SoMa area south of Market Street.

Taxes An 8.5% sales tax is added at the register for all goods and services purchased in San Francisco. The city hotel tax is a whopping 14%. There is no airport tax.

Transit Information Call **Muni** at ☎ **415/673-6864** on weekdays between 7am and 5pm and on weekends between 9am and 5pm. At other times, recorded information is available.

Useful Telephone Numbers **Tourist information** (☎ 415/391-2001); **highway conditions** (☎ 415/557-3755); **KFOG Entertainment Line** (☎ 415/777-1045); **MovieFone** (☎ 415/777-FILM).

Weather Call ☎ **415/936-1212** to find out when the next fog bank is rolling in.

3 Accommodations You Can Afford

San Francisco is an outstanding hotel town, especially considering its relatively small size. The bad news is, since hotels are nearly filled to capacity year-round, four walls and a bed can cost a small fortune; around press time the average room rate in the city was hovering at $127. The good news is, with a whole lot of research, we actually managed to find lodgings that are both inexpensive and decent enough that we'd be willing to stay there ourselves.

Of course, there's a catch. Don't expect mints on your pillow; most budget hotels keep their prices down by offering only the essentials—phone, TV, bed, and bathroom (and in the high-rent zones, even a private bathroom is considered an upgrade). San Francisco is probably the most expensive destination in the state; your money won't buy you as much space or as many amenities as it will elsewhere in California.

But you can still find relative bargains if you avoid the heavily concentrated areas such as Union Square and Fisherman's Wharf, and instead park your bags at the city's outlying districts, such as the Marina or the Haight and take a bus into the tourist areas for sightseeing.

You can also save a bundle by reserving well in advance (particular during high season, which runs approximately from Apr through Sept), choosing a place that doesn't charge for local calls and parking, and requesting every possible discount and/or promotion (AAA, AARP, military, etc.).

We've listed our favorite reasonably priced hotels below; if you'd like a larger selection, check out *Frommer's San Francisco from $60 a Day*, which has dozens of other options.

The hotels listed below are classified first by location and then by price. Rates given reflect the price of an average double room—*not including the 14% hotel tax*—during the high season. Read each of the entries carefully: Many hotels also offer rooms at rates above and below the price category that they have been assigned in this guidebook. Also note that prices listed below do not include extras like parking and the sometimes-hefty telephone surcharges. All rooms have private bathrooms unless otherwise noted.

How to Get the Best Room Rate

When reading over your options, keep in mind that prices listed are hotel rack rates (published rates) and you should always ask for special discounts or, even better, vacation packages. You're likely to get the room you want for less than what's quoted here, except in summer when the hotels are mega-packed and bargaining is close to impossible.

If all the hotels in your price range are booked and you don't mind going generic, you can always try **Motel 6** (☎ **800/4-MOTEL6**); **Super 8** (☎ **800/800-8000**); **Best Western** (☎ **800/528-1235**); **Days Inn** (☎ **800/DAYS-INN**); and **Travelodge** (☎ **800/367-2250**). But avoid booking these chains' super-cheap rooms by the airport; the prices may be at their lowest, but there's nothing remotely San Franciscan about the lackluster industrial area, which is about 20 minutes away from the city's center.

If you're having reservations about your reservations, you might want to leave it up to **San Francisco Reservations**, 22 Second St., San Francisco, CA 94105 (☎ **800/667-1550** or 415/227-1500; www.hotelres.com), which has access to more than 200 San Francisco hotels—often at discounted rates.

UNION SQUARE & ENVIRONS
SUPER-CHEAP SLEEPS

✪ **Adelaide Inn.** 5 Isadora Duncan Court (formerly Adelaide Place, off Taylor St., between Post and Geary sts.), San Francisco, CA 94102. ☎ **415/441-2261.** Fax 415/441-0161. 18 units, none with private bathroom. TV. $52–$58 double with shared bathroom. Rates include continental breakfast. AE, MC, V. Bus: 2, 3, 4, 27, 38, or 76.

The last of the true old-style pensiones, this three-level building tucked in a surprisingly quiet cul-de-sac is bright, cheery, and decorated in long-forgotten ornamentation (remember textured wallpaper?). Colors and furniture hark back to the 1960s (not because the owner's gone retro, but probably because he hasn't changed the furnishings since then). But in an inexplicably quaint way, the atmosphere works. Perhaps it's the sunny and funky rooms; the small, bright breakfast room; the stairway skylight; or the shared fridge in the kitchen (it certainly isn't the spongy mattresses or tiny bathrooms and musty showers). Whatever it is, this place does feel a lot like home. Services include complimentary coffee and rolls in the morning, and on-the-premises pay phones. *Note:* This place may not appeal to older travelers and won't work for the disabled—it has steep stairs and no elevators.

Alexander Inn. 415 O'Farrell St. (between Hyde and Taylor sts.), San Francisco, CA 94102. ☎ **800/843-8709** or 415/928-6800. 64 units, 58 with private bathroom. TV TEL. From $45 double without bathroom; $85–$95 double with bathroom. Rates include continental breakfast. AE, DC, DISC, JCB, MC, V. Parking across the street $16. Bus: 2, 3, 4, 28, 37, or 76.

This 75-year-old building has certainly seen better days, but more than the neighboring hotels in its price range, the Alexander has a bit of old-world charm and makes a concerted effort to please its guests. Rooms, which were entirely redecorated in 1998, are tidy and no-nonsense, have coffeemakers and king- or queen-size beds, and seriously worn but clean bathrooms with sweet amenities (bathrooms are next up for remodeling). Perks include access to a snack room with candy and soda machines and a microwave; coin-operated washers and dryers; in-room safes for an extra $1.50; and croissants, Danish, and coffee each morning. The downside is that you have to choose between a snail of an elevator or steep stairs. The most recent renovation means general sprucing

San Francisco Accommodations

Abigail Hotel **31**
Adelaide Inn **33**
Alexander Inn **32**
Amsterdam Hotel **24**
Andrews Hotel **25**
AYH Hostel at Union Square **36**
Beck's Motor Lodge **4**
Beresford Arms **27**
Brady Acres **28**
Castillo Inn **5**
Clarion Bedford Hotel **27**
Commodore International **26**
Cornell Hotel **22**
Cow Hollow Motor Inn & Suites **9**
Edward II Inn & Pub **8**
The Fitzgerald **25**
Fort Mason Youth Hostel **11**
Golden Gate Hotel **21**
Grant Plaza Hotel **20**
Hotel Astoria **20**
Hotel Beresford **23**
Hotel Bohème **18**
Hotel Diva **35**
Hotel Richelieu **29**
Inn on Castro **2**
Lombard Motor Inn **13**
Marina Inn **12**
The Maxwell **37**
The Metro Hotel **6**
Motel Capri **10**
Nob Hill Motel **14**
The Parker House **3**
Petite Auberge **22**
Phoenix Hotel **30**
Queen Anne Hotel **7**
San Remo Hotel **16**
The Sheehan **22**
Stanyan Park Hotel **1**
The Stratford Hotel **38**
Temple Hotel **19**
The Touchstone **34**
Washington Square Inn **17**
The Wharf Inn **15**

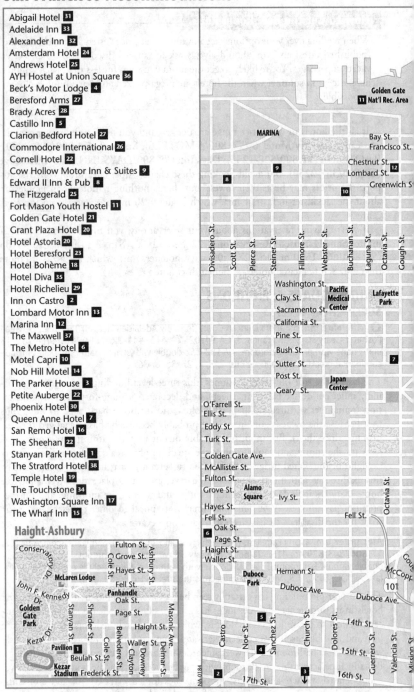

Haight-Ashbury

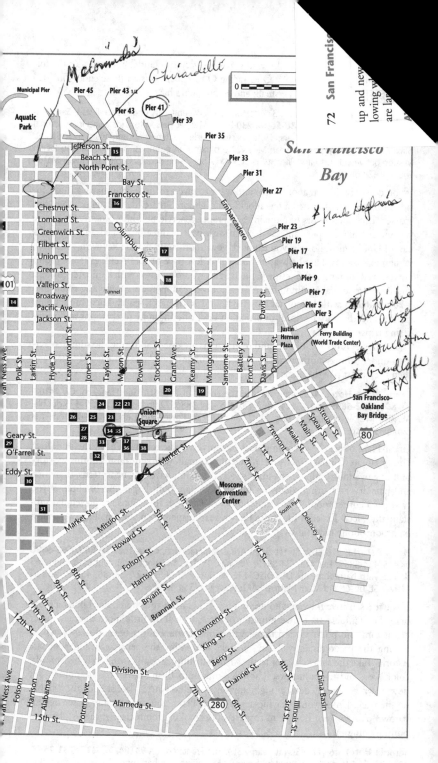

McCormicks'

Ghirardelli

Municipal Pier   **Pier 45**   **Pier 43 ½**   **Pier 43**   **Pier 41**   **Pier 39**

Aquatic Park

Pier 35

Jefferson St. **15**
Beach St.
North Point St.

Pier 33

Bay St.

Pier 31

Francisco St. **16**

Pier 27

San Francisco

Bay

Chestnut St.
Lombard St.
Greenwich St.
Filbert St.
Union St.
Green St.
Vallejo St.
Broadway
Pacific Ave.
Jackson St.

Columbus Ave.

17

18

Tunnel

Embarcadero

Pier 23

✳ Mark Hopkins

Pier 19
Pier 17
Pier 15
Pier 9
Pier 7
Pier 5
Pier 3
Pier 1

Ferry Building (World Trade Center)

Justin Herman Plaza

✳ Nathidies Pologe

✳ Touchstone

✳ Grand Cafe

✳ TIX

San Francisco–Oakland Bay Bridge

80

01

14

Van Ness Ave.
Polk St.
Larkin St.
Hyde St.
Leavenworth St.
Jones St.
Taylor St.
Mason St.
Powell St.
Stockton St.
Grant Ave.
Kearny St.
Montgomery St.
Sansome St.
Battery St.
Front St.
Davis St.
Drumm St.

Davis St.

20   **19**

24 **22** **21**
26 **25** **23**
27
28   **34** **35**
33   **37**
32   **36** **38**

Union Square

Geary St.   **29**
O'Farrell St.

Eddy St.   **30**

Market St.

Steuart St.
Spear St.
Main St.
Beale St.
Fremont St.
1st St.

31

Moscone Convention Center

Market St.

Mission St.
Howard St.
Folsom St.
Harrison St.
Bryant St.
Brannan St.

8th St.
9th St.
10th St.
11th St.
12th St.

4th St.
5th St.

2nd St.

3rd St.

South Park

Delancey St.

Townsend St.
King St.
Berry St.

Division St.

Channel St.

4th St.

China Basin

Van Ness Ave.
Folsom
Harrison
Alabama
Potrero Ave.

15th St.

Alameda St.

7th St.

6th St.

280

3rd St.
Illinois St.

carpeting are in the works. Rooms vary substantially so consider the fol-
...hen you request yours: Ones facing O'Farrell are noisier; those ending in "02"
...ger; "08"s and "04"s are small; and all but "05"s have closets.

...H Hostel at Union Square. 312 Mason St. (between Geary and O'Farrell sts.), San Francisco, CA 94102. ☎ **415/788-5604.** 230 beds. $18 per person for Hostelling International
members, $21 for nonmembers; $9 for persons under 12 when accompanied by a parent.
Maximum stay 14 nights per year. MC, V. No parking on premises. A public parking lot on
Mission between Fourth and Fifth sts. charges $12 per 24-hr. period. Cable car: Powell-Mason
line. Bus: 7B or 38.

If you don't give a darn about decor and want to save a fortune, you may want to consider a room here. Located a few blocks from Union Square, this hostel occupies five
sparsely decorated floors of a quaint San Francisco–style building. Rooms are simple
(we mean really simple!) and clean, each with two or three bunk beds, a sink, and a
closet. Unlike most hostels, you can lock your room and take the key with you. Also,
while most rooms share hallway bathrooms, a few have private facilities (suite rooms
are reserved for families). Freshly painted hallways are adorned with laminated posters,
and there are several common rooms, including a reading room, a smoking room, and
a large kitchen with lots of tables, chairs, and refrigerator space. There are laundry
facilities nearby and a helpful information desk offering tour reservations and sightseeing trips.

The hostel is open 24 hours and reservations are essential during the summer. Persons under 18 may not stay without a parent unless they have a notarized letter, and
then they must pay the adult rate.

Grant Plaza Hotel. 465 Grant Ave. (at the corner of Pine St.), San Francisco, CA 94108.
☎ **800/472-6899** or 415/434-3883. Fax 415/434-3886. 72 units. TV TEL. $59–$75 double.
AE, CB, MC, V. Nearby parking $11.50. Cable car: Powell-Hyde and Powell-Mason lines
(2 blocks west).

Grant Plaza offers cheap accommodations in very basic rooms right in the middle of
Union Square/Chinatown action. Many of the small, well-kept rooms in this six-story
building overlook Chinatown's main street. All rooms have new bedspreads, draperies,
and hair dryers. Corner rooms on higher floors are both larger and brighter. If you
can't get a corner room, try for the top floor—up here, the rooms are newer and substantially nicer. Expect little more than a soap dispenser in the small shower (most
bathrooms don't have tubs).

Hotel Astoria. 510 Bush St. (at Grant Ave.), San Francisco, CA 94108. ☎ **800/666-6696**
or 415/434-8889. Fax 415/434-8919. 70 units. TV TEL. $43 double without bathroom; $63
double with bathroom. AE, DC, DISC, MC, V. Bus: 2, 3, 4, 9X, 27, 30, 38, 45, 76, and all
Market St. buses and Muni Metros. BART: Powell-St. Station.

If you're a sensitive traveler who needs lots of TLC from your hotel, don't book a room
here. The Chinese staff is very matter of fact and will do little more than take your
credit card and point toward the elevator. But if you can get beyond that, you'll be
joining the predominantly Asian clientele who enjoy the very clean and adequate
Astoria. Take the small elevator to the small but simple rooms, with lovely bedspreads,
color TVs, and in-room safes. Those looking onto Bush and Grant are noisier, but
downtown gets pretty quiet at night anyway, so unless you're a late sleeper, they should
do the trick. Unless you're staying at the Grant Plaza, you can't get any closer to Chinatown. *Nonsmokers:* Be sure to request a nonsmoking room clearly; there's plenty of
puffing going on here.

Temple Hotel. 469 Pine St. (at Kearny St.), San Francisco, CA 94104. ☎ **415/781-2565.**
88 units. TV. $45 double without bathroom; $55 double with bathroom. No credit cards. Bus:

2, 3, 4, 9X, 15, 30, 45, and all Market St. buses and Muni Metros. BART: Powell St. Station or Montgomery St. Station.

Ignore the unimpressive entrance and the receptionist behind glass. Prepare yourself for super-funky decor and some of the best ultra-cheap rooms in the entire downtown area. The archaic elevator, the old-fashioned kind with the double doors (the kind you pull yourself), leads to dark rooms with a well-polished dresser and bedside tables, decorative tchotchkes straight out of the 1970s, ancient TVs, and groovy 1960s brown carpeting. Beds are a bit hard and could use new linens, but the claw-foot tubs add charm to the bathrooms. The shared showers are sparse and old, but very, very clean. While you're only a few blocks from Union Square, you're steps away from hoppin' Belden Lane and the martini-and-cigar Occidental Grill restaurant. It ain't heaven, but for $40 it doesn't get much better than this.

For a Few Bucks More

Amsterdam Hotel. 749 Taylor St. (between Sutter and Bush sts.), San Francisco, CA 94108 ☎ **800/637-3444** or 415/673-3277. Fax 415/673-0453. 34 units. TV TEL. $89 double. Rates include continental breakfast. AE, MC, V. Parking $13. Bus: 2, 3, 4, or 76.

The lobby feels like that of a cheap motel, and rooms, though decorated with oak furnishings, are a mixture of old and new, tasteful and cheesy. Still, this place is a remarkably good deal. The owners continue to remodel with Jacuzzi tubs, new drapes and carpet, and marble or black-lacquer bathrooms, even though it's clear there's no interior designer leading the way. Considering all the perks, you can't beat the value. On sunny days, folks head to the small dining patio out back to enjoy their continental breakfasts.

Brady Acres. 649 Jones St. (between Geary and Post sts.), San Francisco, CA 94102. ☎ **800/627-2396** or 415/929-8033. Fax 415/441-8033. www.bradyacres.com. 25 units. TV TEL. $75–$95 double May–Sept. Call for special weekly rates. Available only by the week Oct–Apr; special weekly rates. MC, V. Parking in nearby garage $15. Bus: 2, 3, 4, 27, or 38.

Inside this small, four-story brick building is a penny-pincher's dream come true. Through the black-and-gold front door you'll find everything you need to keep costs to a minimum. The small but very clean rooms have microwaves, small fridges, toasters, and coffeemakers; hair dryers and alarm clocks; direct-dial phones (with free local calls) and answering machines; color TVs and radio/cassette players. Bathrooms are newly renovated, and a coin-operated washer and dryer are located in the basement, along with free laundry soap and irons. Owner Deborah Liane Brady and her staff are usually on hand to offer friendly, personal service, making this option an unbeatable deal. Keep in mind that during the low season you can only rent by the week.

Cornell Hotel. 715 Bush St. (near Mason St.), San Francisco, CA 94108. ☎ **800/232-9698** or 415/421-3154. Fax 415/399-1442. 60 units. TV TEL. $85–$105 double. Rates include full breakfast (except Sun, when it's continental). Weekly room package including 7 breakfasts and 5 dinners, $600 double. AE, CB, DC, MC, V. Parking $12. Cable car: Powell-Hyde and Powell-Mason lines. Bus: 2, 3, 4, 30, or 45.

The quirks make this hotel more charming than many in its price range. Rameau, the resident golden retriever, greets you at the door of this small French-style hotel. Then you embark on a ride in the old-fashioned elevator to get to your room. Each floor is dedicated to a French painter and is decorated with reproductions. Rooms are comfortable and individually decorated in a modest, modern style, with a desk and chairs. No smoking is allowed in any of them. A full breakfast is served in the cavernlike provincial basement dining room.

Golden Gate Hotel. 775 Bush St. (between Powell and Mason sts.), San Francisco, CA 94108. ☎ **800/835-1118** or 415/392-3702. Fax 415/392-6202. 23 units, 14 with private bathroom. TV TEL. $65–$75 double without bathroom; $99–$115 double with bathroom. Rates include continental breakfast. AE, CB, DC, MC, V. Parking $14. Cable car: Powell-Hyde and Powell-Mason lines (1 block east). Bus: 2, 3, 4, 30, 38, or 45.

Among San Francisco's small hotels occupying historic turn-of-the-century buildings are some real gems, and the Golden Gate Hotel is one of them. It's 2 blocks north of Union Square and 2 blocks down (literally) from the crest of Nob Hill, with cable-car stops at the corner for easy access to Fisherman's Wharf and Chinatown (the city's theaters and best restaurants are also within walking distance). But the best thing about the Golden Gate Hotel is that it's family-run: John and Renate Kenaston are hospitable innkeepers who take obvious pleasure in making their guests comfortable. Each individually decorated room has handsome antique furnishings (plenty of wicker) from the early 1900s, quilted bedspreads, and fresh flowers (request a room with a claw-foot tub if you enjoy a good, hot soak). Complimentary afternoon tea is served daily from 4 to 7pm.

The Sheehan. 620 Sutter St. (near Mason St.), San Francisco, CA 94102. ☎ **800/848-1529** or 415/775-6500. Fax 415/775-3271. 68 units, 63 with private bathroom. TV TEL. $55–$75 double without bathroom; $79–$99 double with bathroom. Rates include continental breakfast. AE, CB, DC, MC, V. Parking $16. Cable car: Powell-Hyde and Powell-Mason lines (2 blocks east). Bus: 2, 3, 4, 30, 38, or 45.

Formerly a YWCA hotel, the Sheehan is a lackluster but clean hotel just 2 blocks from Union Square. Rooms are plain and some walls could use a little paint, but the bathrooms are clean and new and rooms have cable color TV. The hotel has a spiffy and pleasant lobby; a comfortable tearoom, open for light lunches and afternoon tea; and an indoor, heated lap-pool and workout facility—a very good value.

✪ **The Stratford Hotel.** 242 Powell St. (between Geary and O'Farrell sts.), San Francisco, CA 94102. ☎ **888/50-HOTEL** or 415/397-7080. Fax 415/397-7087. 105 units, 98 with private bathroom. TV TEL. $69–$75 double without bathroom; $89–$99 double with bathroom. MC, V. Garage parking nearby. Cable car: Powell St. Bus: 2, 3, 4, 27, 30, 38, 76, and all Market St. buses and Muni Metros. BART: Powell-Hyde and Powell-Mason lines.

Renovation fever has hit the ever-touristy downtown, and the Stratford is the latest to get the bug. Until now, the hotels along the noisiest, most densely touristed section of Union Square went unnoticed. But the Stratford's colorful face-lift is turning eyes to the southern corner of the area. The resurrection of this large 1907 building included the addition of colorfully painted hallways and rooms with new carpeting, new TVs, and cheery bedspreads (which currently hide old, scratchy motel blankets). Accommodations vary tremendously, so be sure and request what you want. Some can be small, some dark; those that face Powell have more noise (clanging cable cars are far less cute when you're trying to sleep). Ask for a renovated room, and inquire about ongoing construction—if they're hard at work on your floor, it'll be anything but peaceful.

MODERATELY PRICED OPTIONS

Andrews Hotel. 624 Post St. (between Jones and Taylor sts.), San Francisco, CA 94109. ☎ 800/926-3739 or 415/563-6877. Fax 415/928-6919. 48 units (25 with shower only). MINIBAR TV TEL. $89–$119 double; $129 petite suite. Rates include continental breakfast and evening wine. AE, DC, JCB, MC, V. Self-parking $15. Cable car: Powell-Hyde and Powell-Mason lines (3 blocks east). Bus: 2, 3, 4, 30, 38, or 45.

In this Euro-style hotel, the rooms are small but well maintained and comfortable; lace curtains and fresh flowers in each room add a light touch. Some rooms have shower only, and bathrooms in general tend to be tiny; but for the location and price, the Andrews is a good, safe bet. *An added bonus:* Adjoining Fino Bar and Ristorante offers complimentary wine to hotel guests in the evening.

Beresford Arms. 701 Post St. (at Jones St.), San Francisco, CA 94109. ☎ **800/533-6533** or 415/673-2600. Fax 415/929-1535. 144 units. MINIBAR TV TEL. $129 double; $150 Jacuzzi junior (studio) suite; $190 parlor suite. Rates include mini–continental breakfast. Extra person $10. Children under 12 stay free in parents' room. Senior-citizen and AAA discounts available. AE, CB, DC, DISC, MC, V. Parking $16. Cable car: Powell-Hyde line (3 blocks east). Bus: 2, 3, 4, 27, or 38.

Every time we visit the Beresford Arms, which received a three-diamond rating by AAA, its lobby always seems filled with happy, chatty Europeans. Maybe it's the Jacuzzi whirlpool bathtubs and bidets that keep them smiling, or the "Manager's Social Hour" with free wine and snacks. The price is fair, too: $129 for a reasonably attractive (though a bit old-fashioned) room with TV/VCR, refrigerator/honor bar, and writing desk (video rentals are $5 each). Modest business services are available, as is valet or self-parking. The hotel's location, sandwiched between the Theater District and Union Square in a quieter section of San Francisco, is ideal for visitors without cars.

Clarion Bedford Hotel. 761 Post St. (between Leavenworth and Jones sts.), San Francisco, CA 94109. ☎ **800/227-5642** or 415/673-6040. Fax 415/563-6739. 144 units. MINIBAR TV TEL. $119–$139 double; $139–$179 view room; from $195 suite. Continental breakfast $9.95 extra. AE, CB, DC, JCB, MC, V. Parking $18. Cable car: Powell-Hyde and Powell-Mason lines (4 blocks east). Bus: 2, 3, 4, or 27.

For the price and location (3 blocks from Union Square) the 17-story Bedford offers a darn good deal. Your hard-earned dollars will get you a large, spotless, recently renovated room with flowery decor that's not exactly en vogue but definitely in fine taste, as well as service from an incredibly enthusiastic, attentive, and professional staff. Each accommodation is well furnished with king, queen, or two double beds, a writing desk, an armchair, a VCR, and a well-stocked honor bar with plenty of munchies. Big closets are a trade for the small bathrooms. Most rooms are sunny and bright and have priceless views of the city (the higher the floor, the better the view).

The hotel's bistro, Crushed Tomato's, has a small, beautiful mahogany bar opposite the registration desk. Canvas Café, an enormous restaurant located behind the lobby, is under separate management. Other hotel perks include room service (for breakfast only), dry cleaning, laundry, secretarial services, valet parking, free morning limousine service to the Financial District, and complimentary wine in the lobby each evening from 5 to 6pm.

Commodore International. 825 Sutter St. (at Jones St.), San Francisco, CA 94109. ☎ **800/338-6848** or 415/923-6800. Fax 415/923-6804. 113 units. TV TEL. $99–$119 double or twin. AE, DC, MC, V. Parking $15. Bus: 2, 3, 4, 27, or 76.

If you're looking to pump a little fun and fantasy into your vacation, this is the place to stay. Stealing the show is the Red Room, a Big Apple–style bar and lounge that's ruby red through and through (you gotta see this one). The stylish lobby comes in a close second, followed by Titanic Café, the cute adjoining diner. The first four floors are standard no-frills—though quite clean and comfortable—rooms, while the top two floors are decked out in neo-deco overtones (well worth the extra $10 a night).

The Fitzgerald. 620 Post St., San Francisco, CA 94109. ☎ **800/334-6835** or 415/ 775-8100. Fax 415/775-1278. 47 units. TV TEL. $75–$129 double. Rates include continental breakfast. Extra person $10. Lower rates in winter. AE, DISC, JCB, MC, V. Parking $16. Bus: 2, 3, 4, or 27.

The Fitzgerald is a tasteful and clean boutique hotel 2 blocks off Union Square. A nook of a lobby gives way to the guest rooms, outfitted with generic hotel furniture that's accented with bright bedspreads and patterned carpet. Small rooms and positively tiny closets are a drawback, and some dressers leave only a little over a foot from the bed. Suites, some of which are on nonsmoking floors, include an additional sitting room furnished with a fold-out couch. Breakfasts include home-baked breads, scones, muffins, juice, tea, and coffee. A nearby off-premises swimming pool and fitness center is available for guests at no charge. All in all, a good value.

Hotel Beresford. 635 Sutter St. (near Mason St.), San Francisco, CA 94102. ☎ **800/533-6533** or 415/673-9900. Fax 415/474-0449. 114 units. MINIBAR TV TEL. $129 double. Rates include continental breakfast buffet. Extra person $10. Children under 12 stay free in parents' room. Senior-citizen and AAA discounts available. Ask for special rates. AE, CB, DC, DISC, MC, V. Parking $16. Cable car: Powell-Hyde line (1 block east). Bus: 2, 3, 4, 30, 38, or 45.

Small and friendly, the seven-floor Hotel Beresford is a decent, moderately priced choice near Union Square. Rooms have a mishmash of furniture and a stocked minibar; some even have Jacuzzi tubs. Everything's well kept, but don't expect much more than a clean place to rest. The White Horse restaurant, an attractive replica of an old English pub, serves a complimentary continental breakfast, as well as lunch and dinner.

WORTH A SPLURGE

✪ **Hotel Diva.** 440 Geary St. (between Mason and Taylor sts.), San Francisco, CA 94102. ☎ **800/553-1900** or 415/885-0200. Fax 415/346-6613. 110 units. A/C TV TEL. $169 double; $195 junior suite; $500 villa suite. Rates include continental breakfast. AE, DC, DISC, JCB, MC, V. Parking $17. Cable car: Powell-Mason line. Bus: 38 or 38L.

Appropriately named, the Diva is the prima donna of San Francisco's modern hotels, and one of our favorites. A showbiz darling when it opened in 1985, the Diva won "Best Hotel Design" by *Interiors* magazine for its sleek, ultramodern style. A stunning profusion of curvaceous glass, marble, and steel mark the Euro-tech lobby, while the rooms, each spotless and neat, are softened with fashionable Italian Modern furnishings. Nary a beat is missed with the toys and services either, which range from VCRs (with a discreet video vending machine) and Nintendo to complimentary breakfast delivered to your room. *Insider tip:* Reserve one of the rooms ending in "09," which have extra-large bathrooms with vanity mirrors and makeup tables. Amenities include limited room service, concierge, pay-per-view movies, and same-day laundry. There's also an on-site 24-hour fitness center and a business center.

The Maxwell. 386 Geary St. (at Mason St.), San Francisco, CA 94102. ☎ **800/821-5343** or 415/986-2000. Fax 415/397-2447. 152 units. A/C TV TEL. $135–$165 double; $175–$675 suite. Extra person $10. Corporate discounts available. AE, CB, DC, DISC, MC, V. Parking $17. Cable car: Powell-Hyde and Powell-Mason lines (2 blocks east). Bus: 2, 3, 4, 30, 38, or 45.

The recently renovated Maxwell's chic-boutique atmosphere may be more cosmetic than wholehearted, but fashionable digs a block off Union Square don't come any cheaper. Rooms blend velvets, brocades, stripes, plaids, and handcrafted accents into "Theatre deco fused with Victoriana decor" (think smoking club/study). Though the hotel's age shows in a few nicks and cracks, the lovely new upholstered chairs, hand-painted bedside lamps, luxurious pillows, boldly tiled sinks, and respectable prints inspire most to turn the other cheek. Pluses include writing desks, hair dryers, and two phones. Gracie's Restaurant, which adjoins the hotel, has an oyster bar and live entertainment nightly.

✪ **Petite Auberge.** 863 Bush St. (between Taylor and Mason sts.), S
94108. ☎ **415/928-6000.** Fax 415/775-5717. 26 units. TV TEL. $110–$
petite suite. Rates include full breakfast. AE, DC, MC, V. Parking $19. Cable
and Powell-Mason lines. Bus: 2, 3, 4, 30, 38, or 45.

The Petite Auberge is so cute we can't stand it. We want to say it's overdone, that any
hotel filled with teddy bears is absurd, but we can't. Bribed each year with fresh-baked
cookies from their never-empty platter, we make our rounds through the rooms and
ruefully admit to ourselves that we're just going to have to use that word we loath:
adorable.

Nobody does French country like the Petite Auberge. Handcrafted armoires, delicate lace curtains, cozy little fireplaces, adorable (there's that word again) little antiques
and knickknacks—no hotel in Provence ever had it this good. Honeymooners should
splurge on the Petite suite, which has its own private entrance, deck, spa tub, refrigerator, and coffeemaker. The breakfast room, with its mural of a country market scene,
terra-cotta tile floors, French-country decor, and gold-yellow tablecloths, opens onto
a small garden where California wines and tea are served in the afternoon.

✪ **The Touchstone.** 480 Geary St. (between Taylor and Mason sts.), San Francisco, CA
94102. ☎ **800/524-1888** or 415/771-1600. Fax 415/931-5442. www.hoteldavid.com.
56 units. TV TEL. $119 double. Rates include full breakfast and free airport transportation.
AE, DISC, MC, V. Valet parking $15. BART: Powell St. Bus: 5, 6, 7, 21, 30, 38, 66, and 71.

This place is so well hidden that no one knows it's there. And good thing—if word
gets out about all the hotel's perks, it'll be impossible to get a reservation. Entering this
small, pensionlike hotel via the adjoining large, kosher deli may put you off. But you
can also enter via the street and jump on an elevator to the immaculate, smallish
rooms, with chic-modern decor, streamlined maple furnishings, and colorful accents.
Expect extras like an AM/FM radio, hot towel racks, voice mail, Internet access, in-
room movies, hair dryer, ironing board, and soundproofed walls. And there's more:
free transportation from the S.F. airport (for guests staying 2 nights or more), valet
parking (currently $15 per night), and a free full and hearty breakfast served at David's
Deli (the old-fashioned Jewish kind).

CIVIC CENTER

Abigail Hotel. 246 McAllister St. (between Hyde and Larkin sts.), San Francisco, CA 94102.
☎ **800/243-6510** or 415/861-9728. Fax 415/861-5848. 60 units. TV TEL. $79–$89 double;
$149 suite. Extra person $10. Rates include continental breakfast. AE, CB, DC, MC, V. Parking
$12.50. Muni Metro: All Market St. Metros. Bus: All Market St. buses.

The Abigail is one of the better medium-priced hotels in the city; what it lacks in
luxury it more than makes up for in charm. The rooms, while on the small side, are
clean, cute, and comfortably furnished with cozy antiques and down comforters.
Morning coffee, pastries, and complimentary newspapers greet you in the beautiful
faux-marble lobby, while lunch and dinner are served in the hot "organic" restaurant,
Millennium. There's access to a nearby health club, plus laundry and massage services.

Hotel Richelieu. 1050 Van Ness (at Geary Blvd.), San Francisco, CA 94109. ☎ **800/**
295-RICH or 415/673-4711. Fax 415/673-9362. 168 units. TV TEL. Nov–Mar $109–$119
double; Apr–Oct $129 double. $139–$189 suite. AE, DC, DISC, MC, V. AAA and other dis-
counts available. Parking $13. Bus: 2, 3, 4, 38, 42, 47, 49, or 76.

Considering all the extras, this place offers one heck of a bargain. The 1908 building
has a grand, welcoming lobby and was built with enough rooms to house a small army.
But in modern times its location on Van Ness, the city's street-level U.S. 101 thoroughfare, has made it a less desirable spot. Nonetheless, the Richelieu has all kinds of

ⓘ Affordable Family-Friendly Hotels

Brady Acres *(see p. 73)*   Not only is this one of the city's best budget hotels, it's also a great place for families; rooms come with microwaves, refrigerators, and other lifesaving amenities, and weekly rentals are available.

Hotel Beresford *(see p. 76)*   Ideally located in a quiet neighborhood between Union Square and the Theater District, this cheerful hotel offers spacious suites, some with fully equipped kitchens, at fair prices.

Stanyan Park Hotel *(see p. 82)*   A great moderately priced choice for families, the Stanyan Park is ideally located across from Golden Gate, where kids can let off some steam at the nearby playground and ride on an authentic carousel.

The Wharf Inn *(see p. 79)*   No whining about when you'll get there 'cause you're already there—right smack dab in the middle of Fisherman's Wharf. Parking is free, and there's no charge for packing along an extra pint-sized monster.

things going for it. For starters, with all the discounts the hotel offers, most guests pay far less than $100 per night. Further, the rooms—which are all different—can be quite large and have decent dark-wood furnishings; colorful, newish linens; in-room safes; irons and ironing boards (in most rooms); spotless bathrooms; and hair dryers. An added bonus is the new adjoining restaurant, one of our favorite late-night burger joints—the wonderfully greasy Mel's Diner. Renovations were completed in spring 1998, which means the rooms are even more spiffy and the new lobby, where complimentary coffee and afternoon cookies are served, is looking especially dapper. Its location, 2 blocks from the California Street cable car and near the Opera House, is safer than the cheap hotels that run along Ellis Street in the Tenderloin. *One bummer:* Local calls are 60¢ even if your party doesn't answer the phone. *Tip:* Noisier rooms are facing Van Ness. Request something facing the courtyard for a quieter room.

Phoenix Hotel. 601 Eddy St. (at Larkin St.), San Francisco, CA 94109. ☎ **800/248-9466** or 415/776-1380. Fax 415/885-3109. 44 units. TV TEL. $99–$119 double; $149 suite. Rates include continental breakfast. AE, DC, MC, V. Free parking. Bus: 19, 31, or 38.

If you'd like to tell your friends back home that you've stayed in the same hotel as Linda Rondstadt and the Red Hot Chili Peppers, this is the place for you. Situated on the fringes of the less-than-pleasant Tenderloin District, this retro 1950s-style choice—which has been described by *People* as the hippest hotel in town—is a gathering place for visiting rockers, writers, and filmmakers who crave a dose of southern California on their trips to San Francisco.

The focal point of the pastel-painted Palm Springs–style hotel is a heated, paisley-muraled pool set in a modern-sculpture garden. The rooms, while far from plush, are comfortably outfitted with bamboo furnishings and original local art. Services include on-site massage, concierge, laundry/valet, and—whoo hoo!—free parking. Backflip, a super-swank cocktail lounge, serves mega-martinis and "cocktail fare."

NORTH BEACH/FISHERMAN'S WHARF
SUPER-CHEAP SLEEPS

San Remo Hotel. 2237 Mason St. (at Chestnut St.), San Francisco, CA 94133. ☎ **800/352-REMO** or 415/776-8688. Fax 415/776-2811. E-mail: info@sanremohotel.com. 62 units, none with private bathroom; 1 suite with bathroom. $60–$70 double; $125 suite. AE, DC, JCB, MC, V. Parking $8–$12. Cable car: Powell-Mason line. Bus: 15, 22, 30, or 42.

Located in a quiet North Beach neighborhood and within walking distance of Fisherman's Wharf, this small European-style pensione is one of the best budget hotels in San Francisco. The rooms are small and bathrooms are shared, but all is forgiven when it comes time to pay the bill. Rooms are decorated in a cozy country style with brass and iron beds; oak, maple, or pine armoires; and wicker furnishings; most have ceiling fans. The shared bathrooms, each immaculately clean, feature claw-foot tubs and brass pull-chain toilets with oak tanks and brass fixtures. If the penthouse is available, book it: You won't find a more romantic place to stay in San Francisco for so little money.

MODERATELY PRICED OPTIONS

✪ **Hotel Bohème.** 444 Columbus St. (between Vallejo and Green sts.), San Francisco, CA 94133. ☎ **415/433-9111.** Fax 415/362-6292. 15 units. TV TEL. $125 double. AE, CB, DC, DISC, JCB, MC, V. Parking in nearby public garage $23. Cable car: Powell-Mason line. Bus: 12, 15, 30, 41, 45, or 83.

This hotel, located on the busiest strip in North Beach, is one of our favorite places in the entire city. Its style and demeanor are reminiscent of a prestigious home in upscale Nob Hill. The rooms are small but hopelessly romantic, with gauze-draped canopies and walls accented with lavender, sage green, black, and pumpkin. It's a few steps to some of the greatest cafes, restaurants, bars, and shops in the city, and Chinatown and Union Square are within walking distance. A room in the back equals less street noise.

The Wharf Inn. 2601 Mason St. (at Beach St.), San Francisco, CA 94133. ☎ **800/ 548-9918** or 415/673-7411. Fax 415/776-2181. 51 units. TV TEL. $108–$158 double. AE, CB, DC, DISC, MC, V. Free parking. Cable car: Powell-Mason line. Bus: 15, 32, or 42.

Our top choice for affordable lodging in Fisherman's Wharf, the Wharf Inn offers above-average accommodations smack dab in the middle of the Wharf, 2 blocks away from Pier 39, and the cable-car turnaround. The newly refurbished rooms come with all the standard amenities, including complimentary coffee and tea. The inn is ideal for families with cars; parking's free and there's no charge for packing along an extra person.

WORTH A SPLURGE

Washington Square Inn. 1660 Stockton St. (between Filbert and Union sts.), San Francisco, CA 94133. ☎ **800/388-0220** or 415/981-4220. Fax 415/397-7242. 15 units, all with private bathroom, though 2 units have their bathrooms across from the room. TV TEL. $120–$200 double. Rates include continental breakfast. AE, DISC, MC, V. Valet parking $20. Bus: 15, 30, 41, or 45.

Reminiscent of a traditional English inn, right down to the cucumber sandwiches served during afternoon tea, this small, comely bed-and-breakfast is ideal for those who prefer a more quiet, subdued environment than the commotion of downtown San Francisco. It's located across from Washington Square in North Beach—a coffee-craver's haven—and within walking distance of Fisherman's Wharf and Chinatown. Each room is decorated in English floral fabrics with quality European antique furnishings and plenty of fresh flowers. A continental breakfast is included, as are afternoon tea, wine, and hors d'oeuvres. Fax and VCRs are available upon request.

COW HOLLOW/PACIFIC HEIGHTS
SUPER-CHEAP SLEEPS

✪ **Fort Mason Youth Hostel.** 240 Fort Mason, San Francisco, CA 94123. ☎ **415/ 771-7277.** Fax 415/771-1468. 155 beds. $17 per night. Rates include breakfast. MC, V. Reservations needed well in advance. Bus: 42.

Unbelievable but true: You can get front-row bay views for a mere $17 a night. The hostel is on national-park property, provides dorm-style accommodations for 155 guests, and offers easy access to the Marina's shops and restaurants. Rooms sleep 4 to 12 persons, and communal space includes a fireplace, pool table, kitchen, dining room, coffee bar, complimentary movies, laundry facilities, and free parking. The complimentary breakfast alone practically makes it worth the price.

FOR A FEW BUCKS MORE

Cow Hollow Motor Inn & Suites. 2190 Lombard St. (between Steiner and Fillmore sts.), San Francisco, CA 94123. ☎ **415/921-5800.** Fax 415/922-8515. 130 units. A/C TV TEL. $92 double; from $185 suite. Extra person $10. AE, DC, MC, V. Free parking. Bus: 28, 43, or 76.

If you're less interested in being downtown and more into playing in and around the beautiful bay-front Marina, check out this modest brick hotel smack in the middle of busy Lombard Street. There's no fancy theme here, but each room comes with such amenities as cable TV, free local phone calls, and a coffeemaker. All the rooms were renovated in 1996, so you'll be sure to sleep on a nice firm mattress surrounded by clean, new carpeting and drapes. Families will appreciate the one- and two-bedroom suites, which have full kitchens and dining areas.

Edward II Inn & Pub. 3155 Scott St. (at Lombard St.), San Francisco, CA 94123. ☎ **800/473-2846** or 415/922-3000. Fax 415/931-5784. 32 units, 11 without private bathroom. TV TEL. $75–$79 double with shared bathroom; $99 double with private bathroom; $165–$225 suite. Rates include continental breakfast and evening sherry. AE, DC, MC, V. Bus: 28, 43, or 76.

This three-story, self-styled English-country inn has a room for almost anyone's budget, ranging from pensione rooms with shared bathrooms to luxuriously appointed suites and cottages with living rooms, kitchens, and whirlpool baths. Originally built to house guests who attended the 1915 Pan-Pacific Exposition, it's now run by innkeepers Denise and Bob Holland, who have done a fantastic job maintaining its worldly charm. Regardless of their rate, all rooms are spotlessly clean and comfortably appointed with cozy antique furnishings and plenty of fresh flowers. The only caveat is that its Lombard Street location is usually congested with traffic, but nearby Chestnut and Union streets offer some of the best shopping and dining in the city. Complimentary breakfast and evening drinks are served in the adjoining pub.

Lombard Motor Inn. 1475 Lombard St. (at Franklin St.), San Francisco, CA 94123. ☎ **800/835-3639** or 415/441-6000. Fax 415/441-4291. 48 units. A/C TV TEL. $72–$92 double. Extra person $10. AAA discounts available. AE, CB, DC, MC, V. Free parking. Bus: 42, 47, 49, 76, or 82X.

The Lombard Motor Inn is one of the many big motels along U.S. 101's approach to the Golden Gate Bridge, and a fine option if you're looking for a clean, decent-sized room in the beautiful Marina District. Accommodations are clean, spacious, and a step above standard motel-style ("with three-star AAA ratings" the manager reminds us). The immediate vicinity is not exactly charming, but with Pacific Heights and Cow Hollow as well as the Palace of Fine Arts and the Marina promenade nearby, you'll be one of the lucky few who can park it and meander this crowded and popular area. Extra bonuses include free local calls, in-room coffeemakers (with coffee and tea), and baby cribs on request. Ask for a room in the back to avoid traffic noise, and be forewarned: Large vans won't fit in the covered parking area.

✪ **Marina Inn.** 3110 Octavia St. (at Lombard St.), San Francisco, CA 94123. ☎ **800/274-1420** or 415/928-1000. Fax 415/928-5909. 40 units. TV TEL. Nov 1–Feb 29 $55–$95 double; Mar 1–May 31 $65–$105 double; June 1–Oct 31 $75–$115 double. Rates include continental breakfast, afternoon sherry, and turndown service. AE, MC, V. Bus: 28, 43, or 76.

The Marina Inn is, without question, the best affordable hotel in San Francisco. How they offer so much for so little is mystifying. Each guest room within this 1924 four-story Victorian comes complete with rustic pine furnishings, a four-poster bed with a silky-soft comforter, pretty wallpaper, and soothing tones. There's even high-class touches such as new remote-control TVs discreetly hidden in pine cabinetry, full bathtubs with showers, and nightly turndown service with chocolates on your pillow—all for as little as *$65 a night* ($55 in the winter). Combine that with complimentary continental breakfast, afternoon sherry, friendly service, and an armada of shops and restaurants within easy walking distance, and there you have it: Our #1 choice for best overall value.

Motel Capri. 2015 Greenwich St. (at Buchanan St.), San Francisco, CA 94123. ☎ **415/ 346-4667.** Fax 415/346-3256. 46 units. TV TEL. $70 double; $100 suite. AE, CB, DISC, JCB, MC, V. Free parking. Bus: 22, 41, or 45.

Being 1 block off Lombard (U.S. 101) makes all the difference when it comes to a quiet night's rest. Here the decor is anything but up-to-date (i.e., unintentionally retro 1970s), but the place is squeaky clean and the beds are comfy. Plus you get free parking (a valuable commodity in the crowded Marina District) and complimentary coffee, tea, and hot chocolate in the lobby. A few bucks extra will get you a more modern hotel along Lombard, but if all you require is a quiet crash pad, this is the place. Families should consider a suite, which has four beds and a kitchenette.

✪ **Nob Hill Motel.** 1630 Pacific Ave. (between Van Ness and Polk sts.), San Francisco, CA 94109. ☎ **800/343-6900** or 415/775-8160. Fax 415/673-8842. 29 units. A/C TV TEL. $65–$95 double. Rates include continental breakfast. AE, DISC, MC, V. Free parking. Bus: 12, 42, 47, 49, or 83.

A short walk from decent nightlife and great restaurants and a 20-minute stroll from Fisherman's Wharf is the Nob Hill, a quintessential motel that aims to please. The Astroturf may throw you off at first, but trust us—once you open the shiny wooden door to your room, you'll find it spotless and freshly decorated in lush carpeting, mauves, and florals. Rooms also have large TVs, hair dryers, big closets, and homey touches. Some even have VCRs, microwaves, and fridges. The motel's claim to be one of the quietest in the area is true, and the only drawback we can find is that they charge 40¢ per phone call.

JAPANTOWN & ENVIRONS

Queen Anne Hotel. 1590 Sutter St. (between Gough and Octavia sts.), San Francisco, CA 94109. ☎ **800/227-3970** or 415/441-2828. Fax 415/775-5212. 44 units. TV TEL. $130–$180 double; $185–$295 suite. Extra person $10. Rates include continental breakfast. AE, CB, DC, DISC, MC, V. Parking $12. Bus: 2, 3, or 4.

This majestic 1890 Victorian, located on the outskirts of Pacific Heights, is a stunning hotel that remains true to its heritage and emulates San Francisco's golden days. The lavish "grand salon" greets you with English oak paneling and antiques; rooms follow suit with antique armoires, marble-top dressers, and other period pieces. Some have corner turret bay windows that look out onto tree-lined streets, plus separate parlor areas and wet bars; others have cozy reading nooks and fireplaces. All rooms have phones in the bathroom, computer hookups, and fridges. You can relax in the parlor, with its impressive floor-to-ceiling fireplace, or in the hotel library. Amenities include room service, concierge, morning newspaper, and complimentary afternoon tea and sherry. There's also access to an off-premises health club with a lap pool.

HAIGHT-ASHBURY
SUPER-CHEAP SLEEPS

The Metro Hotel. 319 Divisadero St. (between Oak and Page), San Francisco, CA 94117. ☎ **415/861-5364.** Fax 415/863-1970. 24 units. TV TEL. $55 double; $66 double with queen bed; $80–$104 suite. AE, DC, DISC, MC, V. Bus: 6, 7, or 24.

It's not exactly in the heart of the Haight, but from this remodeled Victorian you can walk to the Castro, Golden Gate Park, or upper or lower Haight in under 30 minutes. Buses stop a block away and blast downtown and to the Haight every few minutes (a 10-min. trip once onboard). The neighborhood isn't the best in town, but it beats Civic Center by a long shot and has plenty of cheap restaurants nearby. The high-ceilinged hotel is reminiscent of a European pensione—smallish rooms, nothing too fancy, but clean and friendly, with everything you need to get by. There's a garden out back, too. *Take note:* Parking is free in the evenings, but you'll have to find your own during the day.

FOR A FEW BUCKS MORE

Stanyan Park Hotel. 750 Stanyan St. (at Waller St.), San Francisco, CA 94117. ☎ **415/751-1000.** Fax 415/668-5454. www.stanyanpark.com. 36 units. TV TEL. $99–$145 double; from $185 suite. Rates include continental breakfast and evening tea. Rollaway bed $20; free cribs. AE, CB, DC, DISC, MC, V. Off-site parking $5. Muni Metro: N line. Bus: 7, 33, 71, or 73.

Considering this small inn is the only real hotel on the east end of Golden Gate Park, it's practically your only option if you want the stay in the Haight. The Victorian has operated as a hotel under a variety of names since 1904, is on the National Register of Historic Places, and is a charming, three-story establishment decorated with antique furnishings, Victorian wallpaper, and pastel quilts, curtains, and carpets. Tub/shower bathrooms come complete with massaging shower head, shampoos, and fancy soaps.

There are one- and two-bedroom suites. Each has a full kitchen and formal dining and living rooms and can sleep up to six comfortably; they're ideal for families. Complimentary tea and cookies are served each afternoon. Continental breakfast is served in a pleasant room off the lobby.

THE CASTRO

Most of the previously recommended hotels are undoubtedly gay- and lesbian-friendly, but San Francisco's Castro also has a number of affordable hotels catering primarily to gay travelers.

SUPER-CHEAP SLEEPS

Castillo Inn. 48 Henry St., San Francisco, CA 94114. ☎ **800/865-5112** or 415/864-5111. Fax 415/641-1321. 4 units, none with private bathroom. $75 double; $160 suite. Suite rate negotiable depending on season and number of guests. Rates include breakfast. MC, V. Muni Metro: F, K, L, or M line. Bus: 8, 22, 24, or 37.

Just 2 minutes from the heart of the Castro, this charming little house provides a safe, quiet, and clean environment. Catering mostly to gay men (though anyone is welcome), the Castillo makes its clientele feel at home. Hardwood floors decorated with throw rugs create warmth. Bedrooms are small yet cozy, and phone messages via voice mail are collected at the front desk. The Castillo also provides the shared usage of a large refrigerator and a microwave oven in the kitchen. One enormous, two-bedroom suite that sleeps four comfortably has a full kitchen, two TVs, VCR, parking, and a deck.

FOR A FEW BUCKS MORE

Beck's Motor Lodge. 2222 Market St. (at 15th St.), San Francisco, CA 94114. ☎ **800/ 227-4360** in the U.S. (except Calif.), or 415/621-8212 in Calif. (call collect to make reservations). Fax 415/241-0435. 57 units. TV TEL. $70–$115 double. AE, CB, DC, DISC, MC, V. Free parking. Muni Metro: F line. Bus: 8 or 37.

You'd think someone would create a gay luxury hotel, or even a moderately priced one, for that matter. But believe it or not, the most commercial and modern accommodation in the ever-touristy Castro district is this run-of-the-mill motel. If you don't like homey B&Bs, this is really your only choice in the area—fortunately, it's very well maintained. Standard but contemporary, the ultra-tidy rooms include coffeemakers, refrigerators, free HBO, and access to coin-operated washing machines and a sundeck overlooking upper Market Street.

MODERATELY PRICED OPTIONS

Inn on Castro. 321 Castro St. (at Market St.), San Francisco, CA 94114. ☎ **415/861-0321.** 8 units, 7 with bathroom. TV TEL. $85–$140 double; from $140 suite. Rates include full breakfast and evening brandy. AE, MC, V. Muni Metro: Castro St.

One of the better choices in the Castro is this Edwardian-style inn, just half a block away from all the action. It's decorated with contemporary furnishings, original modern art, and fresh flowers throughout. TVs are available upon request. Most rooms share a small back patio, and the suite has its own private outdoor sitting area. There's also a two-bedroom apartment available for $140 to $200.

WORTH A SPLURGE

The Parker House. 520 Church St. (between 17th and 18th sts.), San Francisco, CA 94114. ☎ **888/520-PARK** or 415/621-3222. Fax 415/621-4139. members.aol.com/parkerhse/ sf.html or parkerhse@aol.com. 5 units, 2 with shared bathroom. TV TEL. $99 double without bathroom; $119 double with bathroom; $139 double queen with private bathroom; king and junior suite $149–$199 double. Rates include continental breakfast. AE, MC, V. Self-parking $15. Muni Metro: F or J line. Bus: 22 or 33.

This is the best B&B option in the Castro. The area's "newest and grandest guest house" is a 5,000-square-foot 1909 Edwardian located in a cheery neighborhood a few blocks from the heart of the action and half a block from grassy Dolores Park. Along with a well-decorated common library with fireplace and piano, the property includes a breakfast room, formal dining room, and garden with patio, lawn, "fern den," and fountains. Each guest room features voice mail and modem hookups.

4 Great Deals on Dining

As one of the world's cultural crossroads, San Francisco has a bewildering assortment of cuisines, and fortunately for the budget traveler, it doesn't cost a fortune to indulge in them. In fact, most of the city's best dining adventures aren't found in big, fancy dining rooms, but rather in small, affordable neighborhood haunts. And whether you're in the mood for Chinese, Cajun, vegan, Cambodian, or the best burger you've ever tasted, this town serves it up.

To help you decide which restaurants are in your neighborhood and price range, we've categorized the restaurants by area and by price (for a dinner) as follows: **Super-Cheap Eats** (most main courses $10 or less), **For a Few Bucks More** (most main courses $11 to $15), **Moderately Priced Options** (most main courses $16 to $20), and **Worth a Splurge** (most main courses more than $20). These categories reflect the cost per person for a main course and a drink or two—which means you *can* get away with spending that amount, but of course you can easily blow your budget if you go crazy on appetizers, cocktails, coffee, and dessert.

UNION SQUARE
SUPER-CHEAP EATS

Café Claude. 7 Claude Lane. ☎ **415/392-3505.** Main courses $5–$13. AE, MC, V. Mon–Thurs 10am–10pm; Fri–Sat 10am–11pm; Sun noon–4pm. Cable car: Powell-Hyde and Powell-Mason lines. FRENCH.

Euro-transplants love Café Claude, a crowded and lively restaurant tucked into a narrow lane near Union Square. Seemingly everything—every table, every spoon, every saltshaker, and every waiter—is imported from France, and the wine and food follow suit. On most days, diners hang out outdoors at the umbrella-shaded tables that dominate the pedestrians-only street, but at night folks pack inside to check out live jazz (Tuesday and Thursday to Saturday evenings). With prices topping out at about $11 for such main courses as *poussin rôti* or the *poisson du jour* (fish of the day), Café Claude has excellent culinary and entertainment value—and it's worth a visit just to scan the handsome crowd.

Dottie's True Blue Café. In the Pacific Bay Inn, 522 Jones St. (at O'Farrell St.). ☎ **415/885-2767.** Reservations not accepted. Breakfast $4.25–$8; main courses $4–$8. DISC, MC, V. Wed–Mon 7:30am–2pm. Cable car: Powell-Mason line. Bus: 2, 3, 4, 27, or 38. AMERICAN.

This family-owned breakfast restaurant within the Pacific Bay Inn is our favorite downtown diner. It's the humble, low-key kind of place you'd expect to see off Route 66, where most customers are on a first-name basis with the staff and everyone is welcomed with a hearty hello and steaming mug of coffee. Dottie's serves above-average American morning fare (big portions of French toast, pancakes, bacon and eggs, omelets, and the like), which is delivered to blue-and-white checkerboard tablecloths on rugged, diner-quality plates. Delicious homemade bread, muffins, or scones will accompany whatever dish you order. There are also daily specials and vegetarian dishes.

Emporio Armani Cafe. 1 Grant Ave. (at O'Farrell St., off Market St.). ☎ **415/677-9010.** Main courses $6–$13. AE, DC, DISC, MC, V. Mon–Sat 11:30am–4:30pm; Sun noon–4:30pm. Bus: All Union Sq. buses. ITALIAN.

All the hobnobbing of an elite dining club comes cheaply at the counter of the Armani Cafe. It's nothing more than a circular counter located in the middle of Armani's ever-fashionable (and expensive) clothing store. But the fare and upscale/casual atmosphere are enough to lure folks who have just lunch, not a new designer suit, on their minds. Local favorites include a homemade antipasto misto, artichoke-heart salad with baby greens and shaved Parmesan, and penne with smoked salmon, tomato, vodka, mascarpone cheese, and chives. There's also a nice variety of sandwiches—and as always, a large dose of attitude. Although there are a few dishes that cost more than $10, you can easily get by on a 10-spot here. Outside seating is available when weather permits.

Sears Fine Foods. 439 Powell St. (between Post and Sutter sts.). ☎ **415/986-1160.** Reservations accepted only for parties of 6 or more. Breakfast $3–$8; salads and soups $1.80–$8; main courses $5–$10. No credit cards. Daily 6:30am–2:30pm. Cable car: Powell-Hyde and Powell-Mason lines. Bus: 2, 3, 4, or 38. AMERICAN.

Sears would be the perfect place to breakfast on the way to work, but you can't always guarantee you'll get in the door before 9am. It's not just another pink-tabled diner run by motherly matrons; it's an institution famous for its crispy, dark-brown waffles, light sourdough French toast, and Swedish silver-dollar-size pancakes. As the story goes,

Sears was founded in 1938 by Ben Sears, a retired clown.
Hilbur, however, who was responsible for the legendary
whipped up according to her family's secret recipe. Keeping
the menu also offers a "healthy-heart menu."

FOR A FEW BUCKS MORE

Kuleto's. 221 Powell St. (between Geary and O'Farrell sts., in the Villa Florence Hotel.
☎ **415/397-7720.** Reservations recommended. Breakfast $5–$10; main courses $8–$18.
AE, CB, DC, DISC, MC, V. Mon–Fri 7–10:30am; Sat–Sun 8–10:30am; daily 11:30am–11pm.
Cable car: Powell-Hyde and Powell-Mason lines. Muni Metro: Powell St. Station. Bus: 2, 3, 4,
or 38. ITALIAN.

Kuleto's is a beautiful place filled with beautiful people who are here to see and be
seen. The best plan of action is to skip the wait for a table, muscle a seat at the
antipasto bar, and fill up on appetizers—fried calamari, roasted garlic with fresh-baked
bread, smoked salmon on fresh focaccia—which are often better than the entrees. For
a main course, order from the less expensive Bar Menu (same as the lunch menu); the
penne pasta drenched in a tangy lamb-sausage marinara sauce and the clam linguini
(generously overloaded with fresh clams) are both good choices. If you don't arrive by
6pm, expect to wait—this place fills up plenty quick.

WORTH A SPLURGE

✪ **Grand Cafe.** 501 Geary St. (at Taylor St., adjacent to the Hotel Monaco). ☎ **415/
292-0101.** Main courses $13–$24. AE, CB, DC, DISC, MC, V. Daily 7am–2:30pm,
Sun–Thurs 5:30–10pm (cafe menu until 11pm); Fri–Sat 5:30–11pm (cafe menu until
midnight). Valet parking $7 for 3 hr. Bus: 2, 3, 4, 27, or 38. CALIFORNIA/FRENCH.

With the exception of Farallon restaurant, the Grand Cafe has the most stunningly
beautiful dining room in San Francisco, the pièce de résistance being the enormous
turn-of-the-century grand ballroom, a magnificent combination of old Europe inter-
laced with art nouveau and art deco. Until recently, the fare had never quite lived up
to the view, but chef Denis Soriano and his crew have finally worked out the kinks.
During our latest visit we feasted on poached mussels in a savory celery-and-saffron
sauce; a tender, pan-seared duck-leg confit with cabbage-walnut dressing; and a tender
baby spinach salad with sliced pears, feta, walnuts, and fresh raspberry vinaigrette. Service was both friendly and prompt, making the entire dining experience a pleasure.
Budget diners' note: The bar area has its own exhibition kitchen and menu, offering
similar dishes for about half the price. The pizzas from the wood-burning oven are
excellent, as is the grilled marinated skirt steak with whipped potatoes and red-wine
sauce.

✪ **Postrio.** 545 Post St. (between Mason and Taylor sts.). ☎ **415/776-7825.** Reservations required. Main courses $6–$15 breakfast, $14–$15 lunch, $19–$30 dinner.
AE, CB, DC, DISC, MC, V. Mon–Fri 7–10am, 11:30am–2pm, and 5:30–10:30pm; Sat
9am–2pm and 5:30–10:30pm; Sun 9am–2pm and 5:30–10pm; bar daily 11:30am–2am.
Cable car: Powell-Hyde and Powell-Mason lines. Bus: 2, 3, 4, or 38. AMERICAN.

Rumor has it that ever since chefs Anne and David Gingrass left the kitchen to start
their own enterprise, San Francisco's top restaurant isn't what it used to be. If its
owners are crying, however, they're crying all the way to the bank, because it's a rare
night when the kitchen doesn't perform to a full house. Eating, however, is only half
the reason to come to Postrio. After squeezing through the perpetually swinging bar,
which dishes out excellent tapas and pizzas from a wood-burning oven, guests are
forced to make a grand entrance down the antebellum staircase to the cavernous
dining room below (it's everyone's 15 seconds of fame, so make sure your fly is

ou want to dine in high style, but can't afford it? Well, my friend, here's the
side scoop: Both **Postrio** and the **Grand Cafe,** two of the city's primo restaurants
(see listings above), have small open kitchens in their stylish cocktail lounges,
serving cuisine on par with their main menu at about half the price. What's more,
you don't need a reservation.

zipped). The menu combines Italian, Asian, French, and California styles with mixed
results. When we last visited Postrio, the sautéed salmon, for example, was a bit
overcooked, but the accompanying plum glaze, wasabi mashed potatoes, and miso
vinaigrette were outstanding. Despite the prime-time rush, service was friendly and
infallible, as was the presentation.

CIVIC CENTER
SUPER-CHEAP EATS

✪ **Eliza's.** 205 Oak St. (at Gough St.). ☎ **415/621-4819.** Main courses $4.50–$5.15
at lunch, $5.25–$9 at dinner. MC, V ($10 minimum). Mon–Fri 11am–3pm and 5–9pm;
Sat 11am–9pm. Bus: 6, 7, 21, 66, or 71. CHINESE (HUNAN/MANDARIN).

Eliza's serves some of the freshest, best-tasting, cheap Chinese in town. But unlike
most comparable options, here the atmosphere, service, and presentation parallel the
food. The fantastically fresh soups, salads, seafood, pork, chicken, duck, and such specials as spicy eggplant are outstanding and served on beautiful Italian plates. Large
windows flank the front and allow natural light to warm the room, while the modern
colorful decor and art keep the place attractive throughout the evening. We often
come at midday and order the wonderful kung-pao-chicken lunch special: a mixture
of tender chicken, peanuts, chile peppers, a subtly hot sauce, and perfectly crunchy
vegetables. It's only one of 21 main-course choices that come with rice and soup for
around $5. But the place is also jumping at night with the opera- and symphony-
going crowd.

Hard Rock Cafe. 1699 Van Ness Ave. (at Sacramento St.). ☎ **415/885-1699.** Reservations
accepted for groups of 15 or more. Main courses $6–$16. AE, DC, MC, V. Sun–Thurs
11:30am–11pm; Fri–Sat 11:30am–midnight. Valet parking $4.25 for 2 hr. Cable car: California
St. line. Bus: 1. AMERICAN.

Like its affiliated restaurants around the world, this loud, nostalgia-laden place offers
big portions of decent food at moderate prices, rock memorabilia, and plenty of
blaring music to an almost exclusively out-of-town clientele. The menu offers burgers,
fajitas, baby back ribs, grilled fish, chicken, salads, and sandwiches; we usually go for
the chicken sandwich with a side of onion rings, both of which are pretty darn good.
Although it's nothing unique to San Francisco, the Hard Rock is a fine place to bring
the kids and grab a bite.

✪ **Swan Oyster Depot.** 1517 Polk St. (between California and Sacramento sts.).
☎ **415/673-1101.** Reservations not accepted. Seafood cocktails $5–$8, clams and oysters on the half shell $6–$7.50 per half dozen. No credit cards. Mon–Sat 8am–5:30pm.
Bus: 27. SEAFOOD.

Pushing 90 years of faithful service to Bay Area chowderheads, the Swan Oyster Depot
is classic San Francisco, a unique dining experience you shouldn't miss. Opened in
1912, this tiny hole-in-the-wall run by the city's friendliest and most vivacious servers
is little more than a narrow fish market that decided to slap down some bar stools.
There are only 20 or so seats jammed cheek by jowl along a long marble bar. Most

patrons come for a quick cup of chowder or a plate of half-shelled oysters that arrive chilling on crushed ice. The menu is limited to Maine lobster, Boston-style clam chowder, and fresh crab, shrimp, oyster, and clam cocktails, all of which are exceedingly fresh. *Note:* Don't let the lunchtime line dissuade you—it moves fast.

Tommy's Joynt. 1109 Geary St. (at Van Ness Ave.). ☎ **415/775-4216.** Reservations not accepted. Main courses $4–$7. No credit cards. Daily 11am to 2pm. (Bar daily 10am–2am.) Bus: 2, 3, 4, or 38. AMERICAN.

With its colorful mural exterior, it's hard to miss Tommy's Joynt, a late-night favorite for those in search of a cheap and hearty meal. The interior of Tommy's looks like a Buffalo Bill museum that imploded, a wild collage of bamboo poles with attached stuffed birds, a mounted buffalo head, an ancient piano, rusty firearms, fading prints, a beer-guzzling lion, and Santa Claus masks. The Hofbrau-style buffet offers a cornucopia of rib-clinging à la carte dishes such as the signature buffalo stew, ham sandwiches, sloppy joes, oxtails, corned beef, meatballs, and mashed potatoes. There's also a slew of seating and almost 100 varieties of beer.

MODERATELY PRICED OPTIONS

✪ **Zuni Café.** 1658 Market St. (at Franklin St.). ☎ **415/552-2522.** Reservations recommended. Main courses $15–$22.50. AE, MC, V. Tues–Sat 11:30am–midnight; Sun 11am–11pm. Valet parking $5. Muni Metro: All Market St. Metros. Bus: 6, 7, 71, or 75. MEDITERRANEAN.

Even factoring in the sometimes snotty wait staff and ridiculous prices, Zuni Café is still one of our favorite lunch spots in the city. Its expanse of windows and prime Market Street location guarantee good people-watching—a favorite San Francisco pastime—and chef Judy Rodgers's Mediterranean-influenced menu is wonderfully diverse and satisfying. For the full effect, sit at the bustling bar and peruse the foot-long oyster menu (a dozen or so varieties are on hand at all times); you can also sit in the stylish dining room or on the outdoor patio. Though the changing menu always includes meats and fish, the proven winners are Rodgers's brick-oven-roasted chicken for two with Tuscan-style bread salad, the polenta appetizer with mascarpone, and the hamburger on grilled rosemary focaccia (a strong contender for the city's best burger). Whatever you decide, be sure to order a side of the shoestring potatoes.

SOUTH OF MARKET (SOMA)
SUPER-CHEAP EATS

Hamburger Mary's. 1582 Folsom St. (at 12th St.). ☎ **415/626-5767.** Reservations recommended. Breakfast $5–$9; main courses $6–$10. AE, DC, DISC, MC, V. Mon–Thurs 11:30am–1am; Fri 11:30am–2am; Sat 10am–2am; Sun 10am–1am. Bus: 9, 12, 42, or 47. AMERICAN/BURGERS.

Hamburger Mary's is a popular hangout for gays, lesbians, and a funky crowd. The kitschy decor includes thrift-shop floral wallpaper, family photos, garage-sale prints, stained glass, religious drawings, and Oriental screens. You'll get to know the bar well—it's where you'll stand with the tattooed masses while you wait for a table. Sandwiches, salads, and vegetarian dishes provide an alternative to the famous greasy burgers, served on healthful nine-grain bread (like it makes a difference). *Tip:* Go with the home fries over the french fries. In the morning Hamburger Mary's doubles as a breakfast joint—it's a good stop for a three-egg omelet or French toast.

Long Life Noodle Company & Jook Joint. 139 Steuart St. (near Mission St.). ☎ **415/281-3818.** Main courses $5.50–$8.50. MC, V. Mon–Thurs 11am–11pm; Fri 11am–midnight; Sat 5pm–midnight; Sun 5–10pm. Bus: 15, 30, 32, 42, or 45. NOODLES.

Long Life serves a wide range of noodle dishes gleaned from China, Korea, Japan, and other Asian lands in a familiar Westernized setting (in this case, a sleek, supermodern interior with lots of neon and Plexiglas). The problem is choosing from the 30 or so noodle dishes, all of which are wildly different. Do you go with the Buddha's Bliss (ramen noodles in miso broth with smoked trout, tofu, and enoki mushrooms), or the Enchanted Heat (a "Chinese hangover cure" comprised of whole-wheat noodles, lily pods, tree ears, and secret healing ginseng herbs)? One thing we *can* recommend is the Ghengis' Buns, a crisp sesame biscuit filled with Chinese roast beef, cucumber, cilantro, and hoisin sauce. Wash it all down with either the Cool Cucumber Juice or Ginseng Ginger Ale.

Manora's. 1600 Folsom St. (at 12th St.). ☎ **415/861-6224.** Main courses $5.95–$10. MC, V. Mon–Fri 11:30am–2:30pm and 5–10pm; Sat 5:30–10:30pm; Sun 5:30–10pm. Bus: 9, 12, or 47. THAI.

Manora's cranks out some of the best Thai in town and is well worth a jaunt to its SoMa location. But this is no relaxed dining affair: It's perpetually packed (unless you come early), and you'll be seated sardinelike at one of the cramped but well-appointed tables. Start with a Thai iced tea or coffee and one of the tangy soups or the chicken satay, which comes with a decadent peanut sauce. Follow up with any of the wonderful dinner entrees—which should be shared—and a side of rice. There are endless options, including a vast array of vegetarian plates. Every remarkably flavorful dish arrives seemingly seconds after you order it, which is great if you're hungry, a bummer if you were planning a long, leisurely dinner. Come before seven or after nine if you don't want a loud, rushed meal.

Tú Lan. 8 Sixth St. (at Market St.). ☎ **415/626-0927.** All dishes $3.50–$7. No credit cards. Mon–Sat 11am–9pm. Cable car: Powell-Hyde and Powell-Mason lines. Muni Metro: F, J, K, L, M, or N line. Bus: 6, 7, 27, 31, 66, or 71. VIETNAMESE.

If you're brave enough to walk down Sixth Street past the winos, weirdos, and street stench (it's not too scary during lunchtime), you won't find better or cheaper Vietnamese food than what you'll get at this honest-to-goodness dive. Even Julia Child, whose face graces the greasy old menus, has been known to pull up a chair at this shack of a restaurant to feast on such goodies as imperial rolls on a bed of rice noodles, lettuce, peanuts, and mint (less than $5). Take pity on the poor waiter who never seems to bring water no matter how many times you ask; he's been working here forever, he's the only server, and the place is always packed. For the price, this has been one of our all-time favorite restaurants for more than a decade. *Take heed:* Some finicky folks can't handle the down-and-dirty atmosphere.

FOR A FEW BUCKS MORE

South Park Café. 108 S. Park Ave. (between Brannan and Bryant sts.). ☎ **415/495-7275.** Reservations recommended. Main courses $10–$15. AE, MC, V. Mon–Fri 7:30am–10pm; Sat 6–10pm. Bus: 15, 30, 42, 45, or 76. FRENCH.

Whenever we get the urge to chuck it all and fly to Paris, we drive across town to the South Park Café—it's not quite the same thing as a Montparnasse bistro, but it's close. Usually we're content with an espresso and pastry; a splurge involves the saffron mussels or blood sausage served with sautéed apples. For the ultimate romantic intention, bring a blanket and dine *sur l'herbe* at the adorable park across the street. Beware of the midweek lunch rush, though.

✪ **Thirsty Bear Brewing Company.** 661 Howard St. (1 block east of the Moscone Center). ☎ **415/974-0905.** Reservations recommended. Main courses $10–$17. AE, DC, MC, V. Mon–Sun 11:30am–1am. Bus: 12, 15, 30, 45, or 76. SPANISH.

Despite the dumb name, this brew pub has quickly become a favorite of the Financial District/SoMa crowd, who come as much for the excellent house-made brews as they do for chef Daniel Olivella's outstanding Spanish food. A native of Catalonia, Olivella is a master of paella. His paella Valenciana—a sizzling combo of chicken, shrimp, sausage, shellfish, and saffron-laden rice served in a cast-iron skillet—is the best we've had outside of Barcelona. Upscale pub grub includes a variety of hot and cold tapas, a few of our favorites being the *escalivada* (Olivella's mother's version of roasted vegetables served at room temperature) and the *espinacas à la Catalana* (spinach sautéed with garlic, pine nuts, and raisins). Almost as impressive is the costly conversion from a high-ceilinged brick warehouse to a two-level, industrial-chic brew pub complete with pool tables, dartboards, and live music that runs the gamut from flamenco to alternative to classical.

MODERATELY PRICED OPTIONS

✪ **Fringale Restaurant.** 570 Fourth St. (between Brannan and Bryant sts.). ☎ **415/543-0573.** Reservations recommended. Main courses $4–$12 lunch, $14–$18 dinner. AE, MC, V. Mon–Fri 11:30am–2:30pm; Mon–Sat 5:30–10:30pm. Bus: 30 or 45. FRENCH.

One of San Francisco's top restaurants, Fringale has enjoyed a weeklong waiting list since the day chef/co-owner Gerald Hirigoyen first opened this small SoMa bistro in 1991. Sponged, eggshell-blue walls and other muted sand and earth tones provide a serene dining environment, which is all but shattered when the 15-table room inevitably fills with Hirigoyen's fans. For starters, try the steamed mussels with roasted red pepper, basil, and vinaigrette, or the sheep's milk cheese and prosciutto tureen with figs and greens. Among the dozen or so main courses on the seasonal menu, you might find rack of lamb with potato gratin or pork tenderloin confit with onion and apple marmalade. The mostly French waiters provide uncharacteristically charming service, and prices are surprisingly reasonable for such high-quality cuisine.

WORTH A SPLURGE

✪ **Boulevard.** 1 Mission St. (at Embarcadero and Steuart St.). ☎ **415/543-6084.** Reservations recommended. Main courses $19–$27. AE, CB, DC, DISC, MC, V. Mon–Fri 11:30am–2pm; bistro 2:30–5:15pm. Dinner Mon–Wed and Sun 5:30–10pm; Thurs–Sat 5:30–10:30pm. Valet parking $6. Bus: 15, 30, 32, 42, or 45. AMERICAN.

Art-nouveau brick ceilings, floral banquettes, and fluid, tulip-shaped lamps set a dramatic scene for equally impressive dishes. Start with the delicate crab-and-mascarpone ravioli with truffle beurre blanc and tomato cream, then embark on such wonderful concoctions as grilled wild king salmon with leek and sweet corn mashed potatoes, French beans, and herb salad; she makes a mean honey-cured pork loin, too. Vegetarian items, such as wild-mushroom risotto with fresh chanterelles and Parmesan, are also available. Three levels of formality—bar, open kitchen, and main dining room—keep things from getting too snobby.

FINANCIAL DISTRICT

Finding cheap eats, particularly for dinner, in the Financial District can be challenging since most diners in this neighborhood are footing the bill with corporate credit cards or expense accounts. Nevertheless, we've scouted out some affordable options (see "Budget Dining Alfresco at Belden Place," below).

✪ **Yank Sing.** 427 Battery St. (between Clay and Washington sts.). ☎ **415/781-1111.** Dim sum $2.30–$5 for 3 to 4 pieces. AE, DC, MC, V. Mon–Fri 11am–3pm; Sat–Sun 10am–4pm. Cable car: California St. line. Bus: 1 or 42. CHINESE/DIM SUM.

Budget Dining Alfresco at Belden Place

San Francisco is woefully lacking in alfresco dining options, but one pocket of exceptions is Belden Place, an adorable little brick alley in the heart of the Financial District that is pedestrian-only. When the weather is agreeable, the restaurants that line the alley break out the big umbrellas, tables, and chairs à la Boulevard Saint-Michel, and *voilà*—a bit of Paris just off Pine Street. Prices are reasonable, too, with most dinner dishes ranging from $12 to $15.

The four cafes that line Belden Place offer a wide variety of cuisine. From south to north, they are **Cafe Bastille,** 22 Belden Place (☎ **415/986-5673**), your classic French bistro serving excellent crepes, mussels, and French onion soup along with live jazz on weekends; **Cafe Tiramisu,** 28 Belden Place (☎ **415/ 421-7044**), a superb—and stylish—Italian hot spot serving addictive risottos and gnocchi; **Plouf,** 40 Belden Place (☎ **415/986-6491**), which specializes in big bowls of mussels slathered in a choice of seven sauces as well as fresh seafood; and **Fizz Supper Club,** 471 Pine St. (☎ **415/421-3499**), an American-Mediterranean–style bistro serving such entrees as Andouille-stuffed quail with saffron risotto cake and braised rabbit with jalapeno peach chutney. There's also live jazz nightly at Fizz.

Yank Sing does dim sum like almost no other Chinese restaurant we've visited. Poor-quality ingredients have always been the shortcoming of all but the most expensive Chinese restaurants, but not at Yank Sing, which manages to be both affordable and excellent. Confident, experienced servers take the nervousness out of novices—they're good at guessing your gastric threshold. Most dim sum dishes are dumplings, filled with tasty concoctions of pork, beef, fish, or vegetables. Like most good dim sum meals, at Yank Sing you get to choose the small dishes from a cart that's continually wheeled around the dining room. *Tip:* Sit by the kitchen and you're guaranteed to get it while it's hot.

CHINATOWN
SUPER-CHEAP EATS

✪ **House of Nanking.** 919 Kearny St. (at Columbus Ave.). ☎ **415/421-1429.** Reservations accepted for 6 or more. Main courses $4.95–$8.95. No credit cards. Mon–Fri 11am–10pm; Sat noon–10pm; Sun 4–10pm. Bus: 9, 12, 15, or 30. CHINESE.

To the unknowing passerby, the House of Nanking has "greasy dive" written all over it. To its legion of fans, however, it's worth the wait—sometimes up to an hour. Located on the edge of Chinatown, this inconspicuous little diner is one of San Francisco's worst-kept secrets. When the line is reasonable, we drop by for a plate of pot stickers (still the best we've ever tasted) and chef/owner Peter Fang's signature shrimp-and-green-onion pancake served with peanut sauce. Trust the waiter when he recommends a special, or simply point to what looks good on someone else's table. Seating is tight, so prepare to be bumped around a bit, and don't expect good service—it's all part of the Nanking experience.

Royal Jade. 675 Jackson St. (between Kearny St. and Grant Ave.). ☎ **415/392-2929.** Main courses $1.65–$12. MC, V. Daily 9am–10pm. Bus: 15, 30, 41, or 45. CHINESE/DIM SUM.

Dining at Royal Jade is about as relaxing as a train wreck, but the restaurant still packs 'em in with its average-quality dim sum at rock-bottom prices: $1.65 per dim sum plate, served all day. At the lunch hour you'll have to share your table with strangers, most of whom are Chinese and know exactly how to work the service staff for the best dishes, which emerge from the kitchen hidden beneath stainless-steel lids. Waiters shout out the contents, but unless you speak Cantonese it does little good to listen. For non-Chinese they'll reluctantly lift a lid and wait for you to make a move, then look hurt if you shake your head. The dim sum dishes are so inexpensive, though, that you can afford to say yes to everything (except maybe the crispy chicken feet).

Sam Woh. 813 Washington St. (by Grant Ave.). ☎ **415/982-0596.** Reservations not accepted. Main courses $3.50–$6. No credit cards. Mon–Sat 11am–3am. Bus: 15, 30, 41, or 45. CHINESE.

Very handy for late-nighters, Sam's is a total dive that's well known and often packed. The restaurant's two pocket-size dining rooms are located on top of each other, on the second and third floors—take the stairs past the first-floor kitchen. You'll have to share a table, but this place is for mingling almost as much as for eating. The house specialty is *jook* (known as congee in its native Hong Kong)—a thick rice gruel flavored with fish, shrimp, chicken, beef, or pork; the best is Sampan, made with rice and seafood. Try sweet-and-sour pork rice, wonton soup with duck, or a roast-pork/rice-noodle roll. More traditional fried noodles and rice plates are available, too; our favorites are the tomato beef with noodles and the house special chow mein. There's no alcohol served here; most people BYO.

FOR A FEW BUCKS MORE

Brandy Ho's Hunan Food. 217 Columbus Ave. (at Pacific Ave.). ☎ **415/788-7527.** Main courses $8–$13. AE, DC, DISC, MC, V. Sun–Thurs 11:30am–11pm; Fri–Sat 11:30am–midnight. Bus: 15 or 41. CHINESE.

Fancy black-and-white granite tabletops and a large, open kitchen give you the first clue that the food here is a cut above the usual Hunanese fare. Take our advice and start immediately with the fried dumplings (in the sweet-and-sour sauce) or cold chicken salad. Next, move on to the fish-ball soup with spinach, bamboo shoots, noodles, and other goodies. The best main course is Three Delicacies, a combination of scallops, shrimp, and chicken with onion, bell pepper, and bamboo shoots, seasoned with ginger, garlic, and wine, and served with black-bean sauce. Most dishes here are quite hot and spicy, but the kitchen will adjust the level to meet your specifications. There's a small selection of wines and beers, including plum wine and sake.

NORTH BEACH
SUPER-CHEAP EATS

Gira Polli. 659 Union St. (at Columbus Ave.). ☎ **415/434-4472.** Reservations recommended. Main courses $7.50–$12.50. AE, MC, V. Mon–Sun 4:30–9:30pm. Bus: 15, 30, 39, 41, or 45. ITALIAN.

Few places on the planet cook chicken as well as Gira Polli. A favorite of ours is the Gira Polli Special: a foil-lined bag filled with half a wood-fired chicken (scrumptious), Palermo potatoes (the best in the city), a fresh garden salad, perfectly cooked vegetables, and a soft roll—all for under $10. *Tip:* On sunny days, there's no better place in North Beach for a picnic lunch than Washington Square right across the street.

Golden Boy Pizza. 542 Green St. (between Stockton St. and Grant Ave.). ☎ **415/982-9738.** Pizza slice $2–$3. No credit cards. Sun–Thurs 11:30am–11pm; Fri–Sat 11:30am–1am. Bus: 15, 30, 45, 39, or 41. ITALIAN/PIZZA.

Pass by Golden Boy when the bars are hopping in North Beach and you'll find a crowd of inebriated sots savoring steamy slices of darn good pizza. But you don't have to be bombed to enjoy the big, doughy squares of Italian-style pizzas, each enticingly placed in the front windows (the aroma alone is deadly). Locals have flocked here for years to fill up on one of the cheapest and cheesiest meals in town. Expect to take your feast to go on busy nights, as there are only a few bar seats inside.

✪ **L'Osteria del Forno.** 519 Columbus Ave. (between Green and Union sts.). ☎ **415/982-1124.** Sandwiches $5–$6; pizzas $10–$13; main courses $6–$8.25. No credit cards. Mon–Wed 11:30am–10pm; Fri–Sat 11:30am–10:30pm; Sun 1–10pm. Bus: 15 or 41. ITALIAN.

L'Osteria del Forno may be only slightly larger than a walk-in closet, but it's one of the top three Italian restaurants in North Beach. Peer in the window facing Columbus Avenue, and you'll probably see two Italian women with their hair up, sweating from the heat of the brick-lined oven that cranks out the best focaccia and focaccia sandwiches in the city. There's no pomp or circumstance involved: Locals come here strictly to eat. The menu features a variety of superb pizzas and fresh pastas, plus a few daily specials (pray for the roast pork braised in milk). Small baskets of warm focaccia bread keep you going until the entrees arrive, which should always be accompanied by a glass of house red.

Mario's Bohemian Cigar Store. 566 Columbus Ave. ☎ **415/362-0536.** Sandwiches $5–$6.25. No credit cards. Daily 10am–midnight. Closed Dec 24–Jan 1. Bus: 15, 30, 41, or 45. ITALIAN.

Across the street from Washington Square, this is one of North Beach's most popular neighborhood hangouts. The century-old bar—small, well worn, and perpetually busy—is best known for its focaccia sandwiches, including meatball or eggplant. Wash it all down with an excellent cappuccino or a house Campari as you watch the tourists stroll by. And yes, they do sell cigars, though they're overpriced. *Note:* There is a second, larger location at 2209 Polk St., between Green and Vallejo streets (☎ 415/776-8226).

✪ **Pasta Pomodoro.** 655 Union St. (at Columbus Ave.). ☎ **415/399-0300.** Main courses $3.95–$6.50. No credit cards. Mon–Fri 11am–11pm; Sat noon–midnight; Sun noon–11pm. Bus: 15, 30, 41, or 45. ITALIAN.

How cheap is dinner at super-popular Pomodoro? Put it this way: It'd probably cost more to whip up the same meal at home. Atmosphere at this price guarantees a 20-minute wait at dinnertime, but once you order, every heaping plate appears at lightning speed, is fresh, delicious, and—best of all—a third of what you'd pay elsewhere. Winners include the spaghetti *frutti di mare* (with calamari, mussels, scallops, tomato, garlic, and wine) and *cavatappi pollo* (roast chicken with sun-dried tomatoes, cream, mushrooms, and Parmesan)—both less than $7. Avoid the cappellini Pomodoro or ask for extra sauce; it tends to be dry. The other locations, at 2027 Chestnut St., at Fillmore Street (☎ 415/474-3400); 2304 Market St., at 16th Street (☎ 415/558-8123); and 816 Irving St., between 9th and 10th streets (☎ 415/566-0900), are equally good.

MODERATELY PRICED OPTIONS

Enrico's. 504 Broadway (at Kearny St.). ☎ **415/982-6223.** Reservations recommended. Main courses $8–$13 lunch, $13–$19 dinner. AE, DC, DISC, MC, V. Mon–Sun 11:30am–11pm; Fri–Sat 11:30am–midnight; bar daily noon–2am. Bus: 12, 15, 30, or 83. MEDITERRANEAN.

Though it's taking its sweet time, North Beach's bawdy stretch of Broadway is on the road to rehabilitation. Helping things along is Enrico's, a glitzy sidewalk restaurant and supper club that was once the place to hang out before Broadway took its seedy downward spiral. Families may want to skip this one, but anyone with an appreciation

Hog-Heaven Happy Hours

It doesn't matter what your budget is—everybody appreciates happy hour. Low prices, free-flowing drinks, and a lively bar put everyone in the mood to party. And with the money you'll save on free (or super-cheap) food available at the following places, you may even feel sporting enough to buy a round or two. The following are a few of the most popular happy hours in the city that double as early-bird dinner choices:

If a cookout, cold beer, and alternative rock is your kind of Sunday afternoon, wind your way to **Bottom of the Hill,** 1233 17th St., at Missouri (☎ **415/ 626-4455**), and fork over $4 for the all-you-can-eat barbecue. The feast includes chicken, sausages, and a selection of salads. Drinks will cost you a little extra (about $3 to $6) but the music is free. This deal is on Sunday only, from 4 to 7pm.

The wildly festive **Cadillac Bar,** 325 Minna St. at Holland Court (☎ **415/543-8226**), is known for packing in tequila-shooting patrons who are looking to let their hair down. But come early before the suits are let loose, and you can have a somewhat mellow Mexican feast at the all-you-can-eat buffet. The free fare is served Monday through Friday from 4 to 6:30pm and usually includes such fire-starters as buffalo wings, chips and salsa, nachos, and ribs. Cool yourself off with a margarita or well drink for just $2.75.

Thank goodness there's an alternative to the pot of processed pink cheddar cheese and all-you-can-eat Ritz crackers that **Eddie Richenbacker's,** 133 Second St., between Howard and Mission streets (☎ **415/543-3498**), otherwise always has on hand. Show up weekdays between 5 and 7pm (the earlier the better), elbow your way through the crowd of white collars, and indulge in the feast of freebies, which includes a selection of fresh seafood, pâté, sweet-and-sour pork, meatballs, and more. There's also a cool old train set overhead and a bunch of other knickknacks to play with as you munch. Drinks range from $3 to $6.

The party on the patio is always in fashion at **El Rio,** 3158 Mission St., at Army Street (☎ **415/282-3325**), the Mission District's favorite dive. Every Friday from 5 to 7pm the place fills with the young and the thirsty, who come for seriously cheap and *muy fuerte* (strong) margaritas and the free all-you-can-eat oyster bar. Drinks run $2 to $3.50.

The yuppified **Holding Company,** 2 Embarcadero Center (☎ **415/ 986-0797**), offers 21 on-tap beers, as well as barbecued beef, assorted veggies, platters of fruit and cheese, and $4 martinis Monday through Friday from 5 to 7pm. Folks also love the interactive televised trivia games.

Single professionals mingle with free, juicy baby back ribs (quickly clamor for them or miss out) along with an array of vegetables, chips and dip, and chicken wings at **MacArthur Park,** 607 Front St., at Jackson (☎ **415/398-5700**), Monday through Friday from 5 to 7pm. What's the hitch? The food is free, but the drinks aren't, so milk that $5 martini for all it's worth.

The beloved **Tonga Room,** 950 Mason St., at California Street (☎ **415/ 772-5278**), is the venerable Fairmont Hotel's version of an old-fashioned Disneyland attraction, complete with Polynesian theme and fruity cocktails. Happy hour is Monday through Friday from 5 to 7pm and features a $6 all-you-can-eat dim sum spread, as well as barbecued ribs, chicken wings, fruit, cheese, and reduced-price cocktails ($4.50).

nightly), late-night noshing, and weirdo-watching from the out-
be quite content spending an alfresco evening under the heat lamps.

oven pizzas, zesty tapas, and thick steaks are hot items on the monthly
menu. The best part? No cover charge, killer burgers served until midnight
on weekends, and valet parking.

WORTH A SPLURGE

✪ **Rose Pistola.** 532 Columbus Ave. (at Union and Green sts.). ☎ **415/399-0499.**
Reservations highly recommended. Main courses $6.95–$18.50 lunch; most dinner
dishes $9–$21.50. AE, MC, V. Sun–Thurs 11:30am–10:30pm with late-night menu until
midnight; Fri–Sat 11:30am–11:30pm with late-night menu until 1am. Valet parking $5
lunch, $8 dinner. Bus: 15, 30, 41, or 45. ITALIAN.

Still one of the hottest restaurants in San Francisco since it opened in 1997, Rose Pistola is a hit for all the right reasons: It's a great place to be, the food is terrific, and the
menu is varied enough for all tastes and budgets. The atmosphere—like the surrounding North Beach neighborhood—is smart, like a bustling bistro. Although the
dining room is larger than most in the area, it's divided so it doesn't feel impersonal
(though you'll want to avoid the narrow tables next to the bar). Sidewalk seating is
favored on sunny afternoons, but inside there's plenty to see as chefs crank out the
eclectic food from the open kitchen. The fare is meant to be shared, so, aside from
sandwiches, it all comes à la carte. Order one of the five fish dishes (enough for two
and available in five preparations) and a side or two for the best value and culinary
experience.

FISHERMAN'S WHARF
SUPER-CHEAP EATS

Crab Cake Lounge at McCormick and Kuleto's. 900 N. Point St. (at the corner of Beach
and Larkin sts.). ☎ **415/929-1730.** Main courses $6.50–$12. AE, CB, DC, DISC, MC, V.
Mon–Sat 11:30am–11pm; Sun 10:30am–11pm. Cable car: Powell-Hyde line. Bus: 19, 30, or
42. SEAFOOD/ITALIAN.

On the upper level of this glamorous (and expensive) multitiered restaurant is a small
seafood counter called the Crab Cake Lounge, which offers huge selections of shellfish, sandwiches, and light entrees at very reasonable prices. Case in point: the calzone,
made with fresh spinach, mushrooms, tomatoes, and ricotta cheese and baked in their
wood-fired brick oven, goes for a mere $6.50. Twice the price but worth every penny
is the heaping pile of clams, mussels, crayfish, and Dungeness crab in a garlicky broth
that's perfect for dipping the crusty French bread (easily a meal for two). Other menu
items range from fresh oysters on the half shell to salmon sandwiches, blackened catfish, and an array of soups and salads. Just about everything served at the lounge is
under $10, and you still get a slice of the million-dollar view of the bay for free.

FOR A FEW BUCKS MORE

Cafe Pescatore. 2455 Mason St. (at N. Point St.). ☎ **415/561-1111.** Reservations recommended. Main courses $3.95–$7.95 breakfast, $10–$16 lunch or dinner. AE, DC, DISC,
MC, V. Mon–Thurs 11:30am–10pm; Fri 11:30am–11pm; Sat 5–11pm; Sun 5–10pm; Sat–Sun
7am–3pm brunch, 3–5pm cafe menu. Cable car: Powell-Mason line. Bus: 15, 39, or 42.
ITALIAN.

Though San Francisco locals are a rarity at Cafe Pescatore, most agree that if they had
to dine at Fisherman's Wharf, this cozy trattoria would be their first choice. Two walls
of sliding-glass doors offer almost-alfresco seating when the weather's warm, although
heavy traffic can detract from the experience. The general consensus is to order anything that's cooked in the open kitchen's wood-fired oven, such as the pizzas and

roasts. A big hit is the polenta *al forno*—oak-roasted cheese polenta with marinara sauce and fresh pesto. Other safe bets are the verde pizza, with pesto-flavored prawns and spinach, and the huge serving of roast chicken.

THE MARINA DISTRICT/COW HOLLOW/PACIFIC HEIGHTS

If you find yourself in this neck of the woods around lunchtime, you might opt for a picnic in the **Marina Green,** a popular recreational park with fantastic views of the bay. The **Marina Safeway,** 15 Marina Blvd. (☎ **415/563-4946**), is the perfect place to pick up fresh cracked crab (in season), fresh-baked breads, gourmet cheeses, and other foodstuffs.

SUPER-CHEAP EATS

Ace Wasabi's. 3339 Steiner St. (at Chestnut St.). ☎ **415/567-4903.** Main courses $4–$9. AE, MC, V. Mon–Thurs 5:30–10:30pm; Fri–Sat 5:30–11pm; Sun 5–10pm. Bus: 30. JAPANESE/SUSHI.

Here's sushi with a twist. What differentiates this Marina hot spot from the usual sushi places around town are the unique combinations, the varied menu, and the young, hip atmosphere. The innovative rolls are a nice welcome to those bored with the traditional styles, though they may be too adventuresome for some (don't worry, there are plenty of cooked and nonseafood items on the menu). Don't miss the rainbow "Three Amigos" roll, or the "Rock and Roll" with cooked eel, avocado, and cucumber, or the *tako* (octopus) appetizer. The buckwheat-noodle-and-julienne-vegetable salad is also a treat. The service could be improved—you'll wait forever for your server to pour your Sapporo—but the staff is friendly and the atmosphere is fun, so nobody seems to mind.

Home Plate. 2274 Lombard St. (at Pierce St.). ☎ **415/922-HOME.** Main courses $3.75–$6.50. MC, V. Daily 7am–4pm. Bus: 28, 30, 43, or 76. BREAKFAST/AMERICAN.

Dollar for dollar, Home Plate just may be the best breakfast place in San Francisco. Many Marina residents kick off their hectic weekends by carbo-loading at Home Plate on big piles of buttermilk pancakes and waffles smothered with fresh fruit, or hefty omelets stuffed with everything from applewood-smoked ham to spinach. Always the first dish to arrive is a coveted plate of freshly baked scones, best eaten with a bit of butter and dab of jam. Be sure to look over the daily specials scrawled on the little green chalkboard before you order. And as every fan of the this tiny cafe knows, it's best to call ahead and ask them to put your name on the waiting list before you slide into Home Plate.

Mel's Diner. 2165 Lombard St. (at Fillmore St.). ☎ **415/921-3039.** Main courses $4–$5.50 breakfast, $6–$8 lunch, $8–$12 dinner. No credit cards. Sun–Thurs 6am–3am; Fri–Sat 24 hr. (Lombard location only). Bus: 22, 43, or 30. AMERICAN.

Sure, it's contrived, touristy, and nowhere near healthy, but when you get that urge for a chocolate shake and banana cream pie at the stroke of midnight, no other place in the city comes through like Mel's. Modeled after a classic 1950s diner right down to the nickel jukebox at each table, Mel's harks back to the halcyon days when cholesterol and fried foods didn't stroke your guilty conscience with every greasy, wonderful bite. Too bad the prices don't reflect the fifties; a burger with fries and a Coke runs about $8.

There's another Mel's at 3355 Geary St., at Stanyan Street (☎ **415/387-2244**), as well as 1050 Van Ness Ave., at Geary Street (☎ **415/292-6357**).

✪ Pluto's. 3258 Scott St. (at Chestnut St.). ☎ **415/7-PLUTOS.** Main courses $3.50–$5.75. MC, V. Sun–Thurs 11:30am–10pm; Fri–Sat 11:30am–11pm. Bus: 28, 30, 42, or 76. CALIFORNIA.

Pluto's combines assembly-line efficiency with three-star quality. The result is cheap, fresh, high-quality fare ranging from humongous salads with a dozen choices of toppings to oven-roasted poultry and grilled meats (the flank steak is great), sandwiches, and a wide array of sides like crispy garlic potato rings, seasonal veggies, Thanksgiving stuffing, and barbecued chicken wings. There are cappuccinos, teas, sodas, bottled brews, and Napa Valley wines to drink, as well as homemade desserts. The ordering system is bewildering to newcomers; first you grab a checklist and hand it to the food servers, who then check off your order and relay it to the cashier. Odd, yes, but fast and efficient. Seating at the 15 polished-wood tables is limited during the rush, but the turnover is fairly fast.

FOR A FEW BUCKS MORE

Betelnut. 2030 Union St. (at Buchanan St.). ☎ **415/929-8855.** Reservations recommended. Main courses $9–$16. CB, DC, DISC, MC, V. Sun–Thurs 11:30am–11pm; Fri–Sat 11:30am–midnight. Bus: 22, 41, or 45. SOUTHEAST ASIAN.

While San Francisco is teeming with Chinese restaurants, few offer the posh environment of this restaurant on upscale Union Street. As the menu explains, the theme is "Pejui Wu," a traditional Asian beer house offering local brews and savory dishes. But with the bamboo paneling, red Formica, and low-hanging lamps, the place feels more like a set out of Madonna's movie *Shanghai Surprise*. Still, the atmosphere is en vogue, with dimly lit booths, ringside seating overlooking the bustling stir-fry chefs, sidewalk tables, and a cramped but festive bar. Starters include sashimi and tasty salt-and-pepper whole gulf prawns; main courses include orange-glazed beef with asparagus and oyster mushrooms and Singapore chili crab. While prices seem reasonable, it's the incidentals such as white rice ($1.50 per person) and tea ($3.50 per pot) that rack up the bill. In our minds, the main reason to choose this restaurant over others is the atmosphere, plus the heavenly signature dessert: mouth-watering tapioca pudding with sweet red azuki beans.

JAPANTOWN & ENVIRONS
SUPER-CHEAP EATS

Mifune. In the Japan Center, 1737 Post St. ☎ **415/922-0337.** Main courses $4–$16.50. AE, DC, DISC, MC, V. Daily 11am–10pm. Bus: 2, 3, 4, 22, or 38. JAPANESE.

Mifune has been serving traditional Japanese food for 15 years and has a steady clientele of folks who are happy with the fare and ecstatic about the prices. Slide into one of the Japanese-style booths and order the house specialty, a homemade udon and soba noodles dinner. You might go for one of the donburi dishes or a full-blown tempura dinner.

FOR A FEW BUCKS MORE

Isobune. 1737 Post St. (in the Japan Center). ☎ **415/563-1030.** Sushi $1.20–$2.95. MC, V. Daily 11:30am–10pm. Bus: 2, 3, 4, 22, or 38. SUSHI.

Unless you arrive early, there's almost always a short wait to pull up a chair around this enormous oval sushi bar. But once you're seated, the wait is over. Right before your eyes, plates and plates of sushi pass by on a circling sushi tugboat floating in a minuscule canal that encircles the bar. If you see something you like, just grab it (we mean food, of course), enjoy, and the wait person will tally up the damages at the end (they can tell how much you've eaten by the number of empty plates). It's not the best sushi in town, but it's relatively cheap and the atmosphere is fun.

Neecha Thai. 2100 Sutter St. (at Steiner St.). ☎ **415/922-9419.** Reservations accepted only for large parties. Most dishes $5–$8. AE, MC, V. Mon–Fri 11am–3pm; daily 5–10pm. Bus: 2, 4, or 38. THAI.

We've been coming here for many years for very simple reasons: The food's consistently good, the ambiance is homey, and the prices are low. Changes have occurred recently, but not necessarily for the worse; the old, dark, decor was replaced by a brighter but not-quite-harmonious modern style. The original oil paintings on the walls are still by one of the waiters, but apparently he's been "discovered," so while the pieces used to go for a few hundred bucks, they're now several thousand. The fare is standard but well-prepared Thai, with more than 70 choices, including satay, salads, lemongrass soup, coconut-milk curries, and exotic meat, chicken, seafood, and vegetable dishes—and yes, the ever-popular pad Thai, too.

HAIGHT-ASHBURY
SUPER-CHEAP EATS

✪ **Zona Rosa.** 1797 Haight St. (at Shrader St.). ☎ **415/668-7717.** Burritos $3.90–$4.90. No credit cards. Daily 11am–11pm. Muni Metro: N. Bus: 6, 7, 66, 71, or 73. MEXICAN.

This is a great place to stop and get a cheap (and healthful) bite. The most popular items here are the burritos, which are made to order and include your choice of beans (refried, whole pinto, or black), meats, or vegetarian ingredients. You can sit on a stool at the window and watch all the Haight Street freaks strolling by, relax at one of five colorful interior tables, or take it to go and head to Golden Gate Park (it's just 2 blocks away). Zona Rosa is one of the best burrito stores around.

FOR A FEW BUCKS MORE

✪ **Cha Cha Cha.** 1801 Haight St. (at Shrader St.). ☎ **415/386-5758.** Reservations not accepted. Tapas $4.50–$7.75; main courses $9–$13. MC, V. Mon–Sun 11:30am–4pm; Sun–Thurs 5–11pm; Fri–Sat 5–11:30pm. Muni Metro: N. Bus: 6, 7, 66, 71, or 73. CARIBBEAN.

This is one of our all-time favorite places for dinner, but it's not for everybody. Cha Cha Cha is not a meal: It's an *experience.* Put your name on the mile-long list, crowd into the minuscule bar, and drink sangria while you wait. When you do finally get seated (it usually takes at least an hour), you'll dine in a loud—and we mean *loud*—dining room with banana trees and plastic tropical tablecloths. The best thing to do is order from the tapas menu and share the dishes, family-style. The fried calamari, fried new potatoes, Cajun shrimp, and mussels in saffron broth are all bursting with flavor and accompanied by rich, luscious sauces; but whatever you choose, you can't go wrong. This is the kind of place where you take friends in a partying mood, let your hair down, and make an evening of it. If you want all the flavor without the festivities, come at lunch.

✪ **Thep Phanom.** 400 Waller St. (at Fillmore St.). ☎ **415/431-2526.** Reservations recommended. Main courses $5.95–$10.95. AE, CB, DC, DISC, MC, V. Daily 5:30–10:30pm. Bus: 6, 7, 22, 66, or 71. THAI.

By successfully incorporating flavors from India, China, Burma, Malaysia, and more recently the West, Thep Phanom has risen to the heady ranks as one of the best Thai restaurants in San Francisco. Case in point: There's almost always a line out the front door. Start with the signature dish, *ped swan*—a boneless duck in a light honey sauce served on a bed of spinach. The *larb ped* (minced duck salad), velvety basil-spiked seafood curry served on banana leaves, and spicy *yum plamuk* (calamari salad) are also recommended. Its Haight Street location attracts an eclectic crowd and informal atmosphere, though the decor is actually quite tasteful. Reservations are advised, and if you drive, don't leave anything even remotely valuable in your car.

RICHMOND & SUNSET DISTRICTS
SUPER-CHEAP EATS

Ho and Ho Pastry. 309 Sixth Ave. (at Clement St.). ☎ **415/387-5700.** 3 pieces for $1. No credit cards. Thurs–Tues 7am–6pm. Bus: 2, 4, 38, or 44. DIM SUM.

Step inside this tiny take-out shop where fresh-from-the-steamer dim sum is sold by the piece. Prices are ridiculously low, so buy plenty and head a few blocks north for a picnic in Golden Gate Park.

Yum Yum Fish. 2181 Irving St. (between 22nd and 23rd aves.). ☎ **415/566-6433.** Main courses $6–$20. No credit cards. Daily 10:30am–7:30pm. Bus: 71. SUSHI.

Sure, Yum Yum Fish smells like a fish market, but that's only because it *is* a fish market. But those-in-the-know also come here for the freshest cheap sushi in the city, served at a little counter in the back and eaten at a folding table with two garage-sale/give-away chairs. How cheap is cheap? The seven-piece inari combo (California, tofu, and mixed veggie) runs about $12 at most sushi restaurants—here, it's $4. The staff here is super-friendly, and once you get used to the smell, you're bound to stay a while, stuffing yourself on top-notch sushi.

FOR A FEW BUCKS MORE

✪ **Hong Kong Flower Lounge.** 5322 Geary Blvd. (between 17th and 18th aves.). ☎ **415/668-8998.** Most main dishes $7.95–$14.95; dim sum dishes $1.80–$3.50. AE, DC, MC, V. Mon–Fri 11am–2:30pm; Sat–Sun 10am–2:30pm; daily 5–9:30pm. Bus: 1, 2, or 38. CHINESE/DIM SUM.

This has been one of our very favorite restaurants for years. It's not the pink and green decor or the live fish swimming in the tank, or even the beautiful marble bathrooms; it's simply that every little dish that comes our way is so darn good. Don't pass up taro cake, salt-fried shrimp, shark-fin soup, or shrimp or beef crepes. And if you come for dim sum, be prepared to stand in line—you're not the only one who's heard that this is one of the best places for dim sum in the city.

THE CASTRO
SUPER-CHEAP EATS

Firewood Café. 4248 18th St. (at Diamond St.). ☎ **415/252-0999.** Main courses $5.25–$7. MC, V. Sun–Thurs 11am–11pm; Fri–Sat 11am–midnight. Muni Metro: F, K, L, or M line. BART: Castro St. Station. Bus: 8, 33, 35, or 37. MEDITERRANEAN.

One of the sharpest rooms in the neighborhood, this colorful place put its money in the essentials and eliminated extra overhead. There's no waiter or waitress here—everyone orders at the counter and then relaxes at either the long family-style table or one of the small tables facing the huge, street-side windows. There's no skimping, however, on the cozy-chic atmosphere and inspired-but-limited Mediterranean menu: The fresh salads, which are under $5, come with a choice of three "fixings" ranging from caramelized onions to spiced walnuts and three gourmet dressing options. Then there's the pasta—four tortellini selections such as roasted chicken and mortadella, gourmet pizzas, and herb-roasted half chicken with roasted new potatoes for only $5.25. Wines by the glass cost $3.25 and desserts top off at $2.25 (thank goodness *someone* realized that $6 for an after-dinner treat is bordering on ridiculous).

Patio Café. 531 Castro St. (at 18th St.). ☎ **415/621-4640.** Reservations not accepted. Main courses $4.75–$8.95 lunch, $6.95–$12.50 dinner. AE, MC, V. Daily 9am–10:30pm. Bus: 24 or 33. AMERICAN.

Originally established as The Baker's Café, this Castro Street bar and restaurant retains the original ovens that contributed to its early reputation, which are today purely decorative. Ringed with trellises and verdant plants, and set behind a cluster of shops, the patio features a glass roof (whose entertainment value derives from the heft and brawn of the staff, who climb skyward to manually crank it open during clement weather). Menu items include Caesar salad, Chinese chicken salad (laced with fresh ginger), prime rib, and grilled salmon with Cajun hollandaise sauce, plus virtually any drink you can think of; the most popular include the Melon Margarita and Patio Mai-Tai.

MODERATELY PRICED OPTIONS

✪ **Mecca.** 2029 Market St. (between Duboce and Church sts.). ☎ **415/621-7000.** Reservations recommended. Main courses $12.75–$18. AE, DC, MC, V. Sun–Wed 6–11pm; Thurs–Sat 6pm–midnight. Muni Metro: F, K, L, or M line. Bus: 8, 22, 24, or 37. MEDITERRANEAN.

In 1996, Mecca entered the scene in a decadent swirl of chocolate-brown velvet, stainless steel, cement, and brown Naugahyde, unveiling the kind of industrial-chic supper club that makes you want to order a martini just so you'll match the ambiance. A hip, eclectic clientele (with a heavy dash of same-sex couples) mingles at the oval centerpiece bar; a night here promises a dose of live jazz and a tasty, though sometimes unpredictable, California meal. Menu options include such starters as pomegranate-glazed quail on endive and watercress, and herb-skewered prawns with romesco sauce and roasted potatoes. Main courses include the popular mustard-seed-crusted halibut, duck breast with roasted-fig-and-huckleberry sauce and potatoes, and a veal chop with wild-mushroom potato cake. The food is good, but it's that only-in–San Francisco vibe that makes this place a smokin' hot spot in the Castro.

THE MISSION DISTRICT
SUPER-CHEAP EATS

Roosevelt Tamale Parlor. 2817 24th St. (between Bryant and York sts.). ☎ **415/ 550-9213.** Full meals $2.20–$8.25. No credit cards. Tues–Sun 10am–9:45pm. Bus: 9, 27, 33, or 48. MEXICAN.

Open since 1922, Roosevelt's may be the budget traveler's ultimate dream come true. As far as tamales (and other Mexican dishes) go, the food here is nothing fancy, but it's certainly good. Best of all, you can fill yourself to the brim for under $5. The restaurant is dark, a bit of a dive, and filled with an eclectic mix of the young and the groovy, regular folks, and longtime customers.

Taquerias La Cumbre. 515 Valencia St. (between 16th and 17th sts.). ☎ **415/863-8205.** Tacos and burritos $2–$4.25, dinner plates $5–$7. No credit cards. Mon–Sat 11am–10pm; Sun noon–9pm. BART: Mission St. Station. Bus: 14, 22, 33, 49, or 53. MEXICAN.

If San Francisco residents commissioned a flag honoring their favorite food, they would probably all be waving a banner of the Golden Gate Bridge bolstering a giant burrito. And while most restaurants gussy up their gastronomic goods with million-dollar decor and glamorous gimmicks, the well-crafted burrito needs only fresh pork, steak, chicken, or vegetables, plus cheese, beans, rice, salsa, and maybe a dash of guacamole or sour cream—and practically the whole town will drive to the remotest corners to taste it. In this case, the fact that it's served in a cafeterialike brick-lined room with overly shellacked tables and chairs is all the better: There's no mistaking the attraction here.

Ti Couz. 3108 16th St. (at Valencia St.). ☎ **415/252-7373.** Crepes $1.95–$8.25. MC, V. Mon–Fri 11am–11pm; Sat 10am–11pm; Sun 10am–10pm. Bus 14, 22, 33, 49, or 55. CREPES.

With fierce culinary competition around every corner, many places try to invent new gourmet gimmicks to hook the hungry. Not true for Ti Couz (say Tee-*Cooz*), one of the most architecturally stylish and popular restaurants in the Mission. Here the head-liner is simple: a delicate, paper-thin crepe. And while its fillings are not outrageously original, they are well executed and infinite in their combinations. Recommendations are listed, but you can build your own from the 15 main course selections (such as smoked salmon, mushrooms, sausage, ham, scallops, and onions) and 19 dessert options (such as caramel, fruit, chocolate, Nutella). Soups and salads solicit the less adventurous palate, but are equally stellar.

FOR A FEW BUCKS MORE

Pauline's. 260 Valencia St. (between 14th St. and Duboce Ave.). ☎ **415/552-2050.** Reservations recommended. Main courses $10.50–$21.50. MC, V. Tues–Sat 5–10pm. Bus: 14, 26, or 49. PIZZA.

The perfect pizza? Quite possibly. At least it's the best we've ever had. Housed in a cheery double-decker yellow building that stands out like a beacon in a somewhat seedy neighborhood, Pauline's only does two things—pizzas and salads—but does them better than any other restaurant in the city. It's worth navigating the panhandlers for a slice of Pauline's Italian sausage pizza on handmade thin-crust dough. The eclectic toppings range from house-spiced chicken to French goat cheese, roasted egg-plant, Danish fontina cheese, and tasso (spiced pork shoulder). The salads are equally amazing: certified organic, hand-picked by California growers, and topped with fresh and dried herbs (including edible flowers) from Pauline's own gardens in Berkeley. The wine list offers a smart selection of low-priced wines, and service is excellent.

5 The Top Attractions

You've finally made it to San Francisco, checked into your hotel room, and are ready to hit the town. You don't have a ton of cash, so you're pretty much limited to walking and looking around, right? Wrong! San Francisco may be one of the most expensive places in the world to live, but when it comes to seeing the city's sights and playing with all its toys, you can have a ball for mere dollars a day. Listed below and in the next few sections that follow are dozens of cool places and activities that guarantee you an awesome stay without blowing your budget.

✪ **Alcatraz Island.** Pier 41, near Fisherman's Wharf. ☎ **415/773-1188** (for recorded info only; no ferry reservations accepted at this number). Admission (includes ferry trip and audio tour) $11 adults, $9.25 seniors 62 and older, $5.75 children 5–11, free for chil-dren under 5. Winter daily 9:15am–2:30pm; summer daily 9:15am–4:15pm. Advance purchase advised. Ferries depart every half hr., at 15 and 45 min. after the hr. on the weekends, and every 45 min. throughout the week. Arrive at least 20 min. before sailing time.

Visible from Fisherman's Wharf, Alcatraz Island (a.k.a. "The Rock") has seen a check-ered history. It was discovered in 1775 by Juan Manuel Ayala, who named it after the many pelicans that nested on the island. From the 1850s to 1933, when the army vacated the island, it served as a military post protecting the bay shoreline. In 1934, the buildings of the military outpost were converted into a maximum-security prison. Given the sheer cliffs, treacherous tides and currents, and frigid temperatures of the waters, it was believed to be a totally escape-proof prison. Among the famous gang-sters who were penned in cell blocks A through D were Al Capone; Robert Stroud,

Cheap Thrills: What to See & (or Almost) in San Fran

- **Riding the Outdoor Elevators at the Westin St.** St., at Union Square. Your heart may skip a beat as feet per minute. The view, as you'd expect, is dazzlir be a guest at the Westin to take a ride. Almost as thri   ...evator at the **Fairmont Hotel,** 950 Mason St., at California   . The finale is a 360° view—the best in the city—from the Crown Room restaurant and lounge.

- **Skating Golden Gate Park on a Weekend Day.** If you've never tried in-line skating before, there's no better place to learn than on the wide, flat street through Golden Gate Park, which is closed to vehicles on weekends. **Skates on Haight,** 1818 Haight St. (☎ **415/752-8376**), is the best place to rent in-line skates, and it's only 1 block away from the park. Protective wrist guards and knee pads are included in the cost: $8 per hour for in-line or "conventionals," $28 for all-day use. A major credit/charge card and ID are required for rentals.

- **Riding on the Powell-Hyde or Powell-Mason Cable Car.** It's the most fun you can have in San Francisco for only $3. Start on Market Street, then hang on to the brass rail for dear life as you whiz through the city toward Fisherman's Wharf.

- **Climbing the Filbert Street Steps.** San Francisco is a city of stairs, and the crème de la crème of steps is on Filbert Street between Sansome Street and the east side of Telegraph Hill. The terrain is so steep here that Filbert Street becomes Filbert Steps, a 377-step descent that wends its way through verdant flower gardens and some of the city's oldest and most varied housing. It's a beautiful walk down, and great exercise going up.

- **Strolling Haight Street Between Stanyan and Masonic Streets.** The San Francisco Zoo pales in comparison to some of the wildlife you'll see along lower Haight Street (don't worry, they won't bite). You'll also find plenty of colorful characters on Castro Street between Market and 19th streets.

- **Pondering the Mission District Murals.** The Mission is one of the most ethnically colorful parts of the city. You could easily spend a day here seeking out the hundreds of vibrant murals. On Saturday you can take an hour-long tour ($5 for adults, $4 for seniors, and $1 for children under 18), which highlights more than 70 murals. Contact the **Precita Eyes Mural Arts Center,** at 348 Precita Ave., at Folsom Street (☎ **415/285-2287**).

- **Catching Some Air in Your Car.** It's "The Streets of San Francisco" relived as you careen down the center lane of Gough Street between Ellis and Eddy streets, screaming out "*Whooooeee!*" as you feel the pull of gravity leave you momentarily, followed by the requisite thump of the shocks bottoming out. Wimpier folk can settle for the steepest street in San Francisco: Filbert Street, between Leavenworth and Hyde streets.

the so-called Birdman of Alcatraz (because he was an expert in ornithological diseases); Machine Gun Kelly; and Alvin Karpis. It cost a fortune to keep them imprisoned here because all supplies, including water, had to be shipped in. In 1963, after an apparent escape in which no bodies were recovered, the government closed the prison, and in

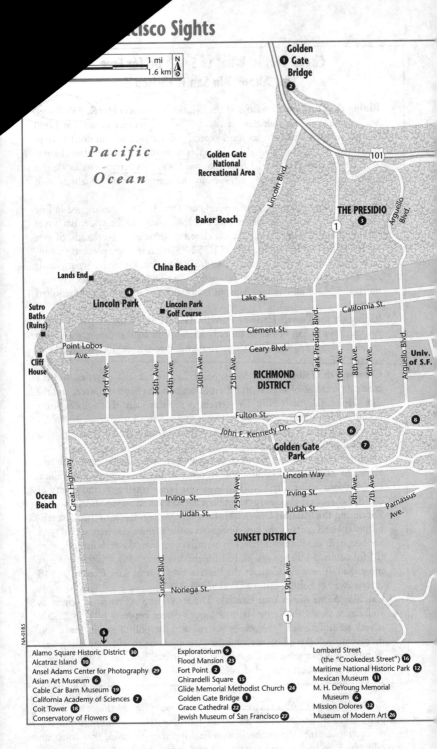

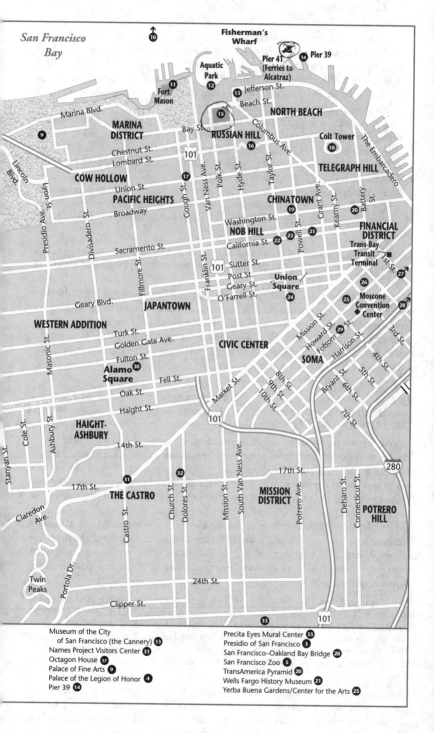

1972 it became part of the Golden Gate National Recreation Area. The wildlife that was driven away during the military and prison years has begun to return—the black-crested night heron and other seabirds are nesting here again—and a new trail has been built that passes through the island's nature areas. Tours, including an audio tour of the prison block and a slide show, are given by the park's rangers, who entertain their guests with interesting anecdotes.

It's a popular excursion and space is limited, so purchase tickets as far in advance as possible. The tour is operated by **Blue & Gold Fleet** and can be charged to a credit card by calling ☎ **415/705-5555** (American Express, MasterCard, and Visa are accepted; $2 per ticket service charge on phone orders). Tickets may also be purchased in advance from the Blue & Gold ticket office on Pier 41.

Wear comfortable shoes and take a heavy sweater or windbreaker because even when the sun's out, it's cold. The National Park Service also notes that there are a lot of steps to climb on the tour. Allow about 2½ hours for the round-trip boat ride and the tour.

✪ **The Cable Cars.** ☎ **415/673-6864.** The Powell-Hyde and Powell-Mason lines begin at Powell and Market sts.; the California St. line begins at the foot of Market St. Fare $3.

Designated official historic landmarks by the National Park Service in 1964, the city's beloved cable cars clank across the hills like mobile museum pieces. Each weighs about 6 tons and is hauled along by a steel cable, enclosed under the street in a center rail. They move at a constant 9½ miles per hour—never more, never less. This may strike you as slow, but it doesn't feel that way when you're cresting an almost perpendicular hill and look down at what seems like a bobsled dive straight into the ocean. But in spite of the thrills, they're perfectly safe.

✪ **Coit Tower.** Atop Telegraph Hill. ☎ **415/362-0808.** Admission to the top of the tower $3 adults, $2 seniors and students, $1 children 6–12, free for children under 6. Daily 10am–6pm. Bus: 39 ("Coit").

In a city known for its panoramic views and vantage points, Coit Tower is "The Peak." If it's a clear day, it's wonderful to get here by walking up the Filbert Steps (thereby avoiding a traffic nightmare) and then taking in the panoramic views of the city and bay at the base of the tower (in fact, we'd recommend not paying the admission and going to the top; the view is just as good from the parking area and you can see the murals for free).

Completed in 1933, the tower is the legacy of Lillie Hitchcock Coit, a wealthy eccentric who left San Francisco a $125,000 bequest. Inside the base of the tower are the impressive WPA murals titled *Life in California, 1934,* which were completed during the New Deal by more than 25 artists, many of whom had studied under master muralist Diego Rivera.

The Exploratorium. In the Palace of Fine Arts, 3601 Lyon St. (at Marina Blvd.). ☎ **415/563-7337,** or 415/561-0360 for recorded information. Admission $9 adults, $7 seniors, $5 children 6–17, $2.50 children 3–5, free for children under 3; free for everyone 1st Wed of each month. Memorial Day to Labor Day and holidays, Mon–Tues and Thurs–Sun 10am–6pm; Wed 10am–9:30pm. The rest of year, Tues and Thurs–Sun 10am–5pm; Wed 10am–9:30pm. Closed Thanksgiving and Christmas. Bus: 30 from Stockton St. to the Marina stop.

This fun, hands-on science fair contains more than 650 permanent exhibits that explore everything from color theory to Einstein's Theory of Relativity. Optics are demonstrated in booths where you can see a bust of a statue in three dimensions—but when you try to touch it, you discover it isn't there! The same surreal experience occurs with an image of yourself: When you stretch your hand forward, a hand comes out to touch you, and the hands pass in midair. Every exhibit is designed to be used. You can whisper into a concave reflector and have a friend hear you 60 feet away, or you can design your own animated abstract art—using sound.

✪ **Golden Gate Bridge.** ☎ **415/921-5858.** Bridge-bound Golden Gate Transit buses (☎ **415/332-6600**) depart every 30–60 min. during the day for Marin County, starting from the Transbay Terminal at Mission and First sts. and making convenient stops at Market and Seventh sts., at the Civic Center, and along Van Ness Ave. and Lombard St. Consult the route map in the *Yellow Pages* of the telephone directory or phone for schedule information.

With its gracefully swung single span, spidery bracing cables, and sky-high twin towers, the bridge looks more like a work of abstract art than one of the greatest practical engineering feats of the 20th century. Construction began in May 1937 and was completed at the then-colossal cost of $35 million. Contrary to pessimistic predictions, the bridge neither collapsed in a gale or earthquake nor proved to be a white elephant. A symbol of hope when the country was afflicted with widespread unemployment, the Golden Gate single-handedly changed the Bay Area's economic life, encouraging the development of areas north of San Francisco.

The mile-long steel link, which reaches a height of 746 feet above the water, is an awesome bridge to cross. You can park in the lot at the foot of the bridge on the city side, then make the crossing by foot. Back in your car, continue to Marin's Vista Point, at the bridge's northern end. Look back and you'll be rewarded with one of the most famous cityscape views in the world.

Millions of pedestrians walk across the bridge each year. You can walk out onto the span from either end. Note that it's usually windy and cold, and the bridge vibrates. Still, walking even a short way is one of the best ways to experience the immense scale of the structure.

Museum of Modern Art. 151 Third St. (2 blocks south of Market St., across from Yerba Buena Gardens). ☎ **415/357-4000.** Admission $8 adults, $5 seniors and students 13–18, free for children 12 and under; half price for everyone Thurs 6–9pm, and free for everyone the 1st Tues of each month. Labor Day to Memorial Day Thurs 11am–9pm; Fri–Tues 11am–6pm. Memorial Day to Labor Day Thurs 10am–9pm; Fri–Tues 10am–6pm. Closed Wed and major holidays. Muni Metro: J, K, L, or M line to Montgomery Station. Bus: 15, 30, or 45.

Swiss architect Mario Botta, in association with Hellmuth, Obata & Kassabaum, designed this $62-million building, which doubled the museum's space when it opened in SoMa in 1995. MOMA's collection consists of more than 15,000 works, including close to 5,000 paintings and sculptures by artists such as Henri Matisse, Jackson Pollock, and Willem de Kooning. Other artists represented include Diego Rivera, Georgia O'Keeffe, Paul Klee, the Fauvists, and exceptional holdings of Richard Diebenkorn. MOMA was also one of the first to recognize photography as a major art form; its extensive collection includes over 9,000 photographs by such notables as Ansel Adams, Alfred Stieglitz, Edward Weston, and Henri Cartier-Bresson.

Free docent-led tours are offered daily. Times are posted at the museum's admission desk. Phone for current details of upcoming special events.

GOLDEN GATE PARK

Everybody loves ✪ **Golden Gate Park:** people, dogs, birds, frogs, turtles, bison, trees, bushes, and flowers. Literally everything feels unified here in San Francisco's enormous arboreal front yard, conveniently located between Fulton Street and Lincoln Way with the main entrance at Fell and Stanyan streets.

Totaling 1,017 acres, Golden Gate Park is a truly magical place. Spend one sunny day stretched out on the grass along J.F.K. Drive, have a good read in Shakespeare Garden, or stroll around Stow Lake and you, too, will understand the allure. It's an interactive botanical symphony—and everyone is invited to play in the orchestra.

The park is made up of hundreds of gardens and attractions attached by wooded paths and paved roads. While many sites worth seeing are clearly visible, the park has infinite hidden treasures, so make your first stop the **McClaren Lodge and Park Headquarters** (☎ **415/831-2700**) if you want detailed information on the park. Enter the park at Kezar Drive, an extension of Fell Street. Bus: 16AX, BX, 5, 6, 7, 66, or 71.

Of the dozens of special gardens in the park, most recognized are the Rhododendron Dell, the Rose Garden, the Strybing Arboretum (see below), and, at the western edge of the park, a springtime array of thousands of tulips and daffodils around the Dutch windmill.

In addition to the highlights discussed below, the park contains several recreational facilities: tennis courts; baseball, soccer, and polo fields; a golf course; riding stables; and fly-casting pools.

If you plan to visit all the park's attractions, consider buying the **Culture Pass,** which enables you to visit the park's three museums and the Japanese Tea Garden for $12. Passes are available at each site and at the Visitor Information Center. For further information, call ☎ **415/391-2000.**

MUSEUMS INSIDE THE PARK

Asian Art Museum. Golden Gate Park, near 10th Ave. and Fulton St. ☎ **415/379-8800,** or 415/752-2635 for the hearing impaired. Admission (including the M. H. De Young Memorial Museum and California Palace of the Legion of Honor) $6 adults, $4 seniors 65 and over, $3 youths 12–17, and free for children 11 and under (fees may be higher for special exhibitions); free for everyone the 1st Wed of each month. Wed–Sun 10am–4:45pm; 1st Wed of each month 10am–8:45pm. Bus: 5, 44, or 71.

This exhibition space can only display about 1,800 of the museum's vast collection of 12,000 pieces. About half the works on exhibit are in the ground-floor Chinese and Korean galleries and include world-class sculptures, paintings, bronzes, ceramics, jades, and decorative objects spanning 6,000 years of history. There's also a wide range of exhibits from more than 40 Asian countries—Pakistan, India, Tibet, Japan, and Southeast Asia—including the world's oldest-known "dated" Chinese Buddha. The museum's free daily guided tours are highly informative and sincerely recommended. Call for times.

✪ **California Academy of Sciences.** On the Music Concourse of Golden Gate Park. ☎ **415/750-7145** for recorded information. Admission (aquarium and Natural History Museum) $8.50 adults, $5.50 students 12–17 and seniors 65 and over, $2 children 4–11, free for children under 4; free for everyone the 1st Wed of each month. Planetarium shows $2.50 adults, $1.25 children under 18 and seniors 65 and over. Labor Day to Memorial Day daily 10am–5pm; Memorial Day to Labor Day daily 9am–6pm; 1st Wed of each month 10am–9pm. Muni Metro: N line to Golden Gate Park. Bus: 5, 71, or 44.

Clustered around the Music Concourse in Golden Gate Park are three outstanding world-class museums and exhibitions that are guaranteed to entertain every member of the family.

The **Steinhart Aquarium** is the most diverse aquarium in the world, housing some 14,000 specimens, including amphibians, reptiles, marine mammals, penguins, and much more. Youngsters will love the California tide pool and a hands-on area where they can touch starfish and sea urchins. The living coral reef is the largest display of

Golden Gate Park

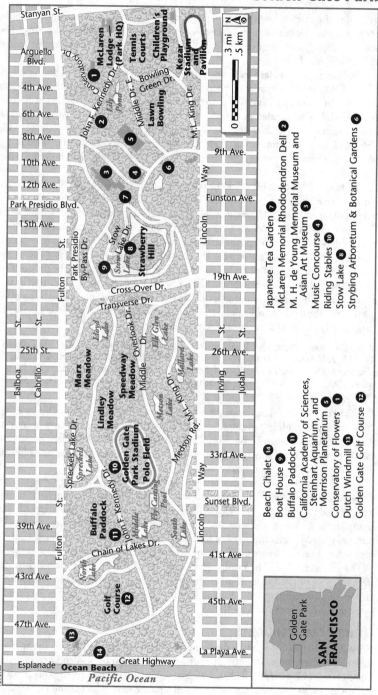

Stanyan St.

Arguello Blvd.

4th Ave.

6th Ave.

8th Ave.

10th Ave.

12th Ave.

Park Presidio Blvd.

15th Ave.

Conservatory Dr.

McLaren Lodge — (Park HQ) ❶

John F. Kennedy Dr.

Lily Pond

Middle Dr. E.

Bowling Green Dr.

Tennis Courts

Children's Playground

Lawn Bowling

M.L. King Dr.

Kezar Stadium and Pavilion

9th Ave.

Funston Ave.

Way

Lincoln

19th Ave.

Park Presidio By-Pass Dr.

Fulton St.

Stow Lake Dr.

Stow Lake

Strawberry Hill

Cross-Over Dr.

Transverse Dr.

Lloyd Lake

Overlook Dr.

Elk Glen Lake

Middle Dr.

St.

St.

25th St.

26th Ave.

Marx Meadow

Speedway Meadow

Lindley Meadow

Metson Lake

M.L. King Dr.

Mallard Lake

Irving

Judah

Balboa

Cabrillo

Spreckels Lake Dr.

Spreckels Lake

St.

Golden Gate Park Stadium Polo Field

Metson Rd.

33rd Ave.

Way

Lincoln

Sunset Blvd.

Buffalo Paddock

John F. Kennedy Dr.

Middle Lake

Fly Casting Pool

South Dr.

39th Ave.

Chain of Lakes Dr.

41st Ave

North Lake

43rd Ave.

Golf Course

45th Ave.

47th Ave.

La Playa Ave.

Esplanade   **Ocean Beach**   Great Highway

Pacific Ocean

N

.3 mi
.5 km

0

Japanese Tea Garden ❼
McLaren Memorial Rhododendron Dell ❷
M. H. de Young Memorial Museum and Asian Art Museum ❸
Music Concourse ❹
Riding Stables ❿
Stow Lake ❽
Strybing Arboretum & Botanical Gardens ❻

California Academy of Sciences, Steinhart Aquarium, and Morrison Planetarium ❺
Conservatory of Flowers ❶
Dutch Windmill ⓭
Golden Gate Golf Course ⓬
Beach Chalet ⓮
Boat House ❾
Buffalo Paddock ⑪

Golden Gate Park

SAN FRANCISCO

NA-0186

107

its kind in the country and the only one in the West. In the Fish Roundabout, visitors are surrounded by fast-swimming schools of fish kept in a 100,000-gallon tank. The seals and dolphins are fed every 2 hours, beginning at 10:30am; the penguins are fed at 11:30am and 4pm.

The **Morrison Planetarium** projects sky shows on its 65-foot domed ceiling as well as laser light shows. Approximately four major exhibits, with titles such as *Star Death: The Birth of Black Holes* and *The Universe Unveiled*, are presented each year. Related cosmos exhibits are located in the adjacent Earth and Space Hall. Sky shows are featured at 2pm on weekdays and hourly every weekend and holiday (call ☎ 415/750-7141 for more information). Laserium laser light shows are also presented in the planetarium Thursday through Sunday nights (call ☎ 415/750-7138 for more information).

The **Natural History Museum** includes several halls displaying classic dioramas of fauna in their habitats. The Wattis Hall of Human Cultures traces the evolution of different human cultures and how they adapted to their natural environment; the *Wild California* exhibition in Meyer Hall includes a 14,000-gallon aquarium and seabird rookery, life-size battling elephant seals, and two larger-than-life views of microscopic life forms; in McBean-Peterson Hall visitors can walk through an exhibit tracing the course of 3½ billion years of evolution, from the earliest life forms to the present day; and in the Hohfeld Earth and Space Hall visitors can experience a simulation of two of San Francisco's biggest earthquakes, determine what their weight would be on other planets, see a real moon rock, and learn about the rotation of the planet at a replica of Foucault's Pendulum (the original one is in Paris).

M. H. De Young Memorial Museum. In Golden Gate Park near 10th Ave. and Fulton St. ☎ **415/750-3600,** or 415/863-3330 for recorded information. Admission $7 adults, $5 seniors over 65, $4 youths 12–17, free for children 11 and under (fees may be higher for special exhibitions); free the 1st Wed of each month. Wed–Sun 9:30am–5pm (1st Wed of the month until 8:45pm). Bus: 44.

The De Young is best known for its American art dating from colonial times to the 20th century, including paintings, sculptures, furniture, and decorative arts by Paul Revere, Winslow Homer, John Singer Sargent, and Georgia O'Keeffe. Special note should be taken of the American landscapes, as well as the fun trompe l'oeil and still-life works from the turn of the century.

Named after the late-19th-century publisher of the *San Francisco Chronicle,* the museum also possesses an important textile collection, with primary emphasis on rugs from central Asia and the Near East. Other collections on view include decorative art from Africa, Oceania, and the Americas. Major traveling exhibitions are equally eclectic, including everything from ancient rugs to great Dutch paintings. Call the museum to find out what's on. Tours are offered daily; call for times.

The museum's **Café De Young** serves daily specials that might include Peruvian stew, Chinese chicken salad, and Italian vegetables in tomato-basil sauce. In summer, visitors can dine among bronze statuary in the garden. The cafe is open Wednesday through Sunday from 10am to 4pm.

OTHER PARK HIGHLIGHTS

BEACH CHALET Listed on the National Register of Historic Places, the Spanish-Colonial Beach Chalet, 1000 Great Hwy., at the west end of Golden Gate Park near Fulton Street (☎ 415/386-8439), was designed by the architect Willis Polk in 1925. Built with a 200-seat restaurant upstairs and a public lounge and changing rooms on the first floor (changing rooms aren't there anymore), it was a popular stopover for generations of beachgoers. In the late 1930s the federal government's Works Progress

Administration (WPA) commissioned Lucien Labaudt (who also painted Coit Tower's frescoes) to create incredible frescoes, mosaics, and wood carvings of San Francisco life. After decades of use the chalet grew old and worn, forcing its closure in 1981; but in December 1996 the historic Beach Chalet reopened its doors, and through the original mosaics and new literature and displays, it continues to celebrate the city's heritage. The upstairs restaurant is far too modern to wax historical, but it's a great place to stop for a house-made brew and a glimpse of the expansive Pacific.

CONSERVATORY OF FLOWERS (1878) This striking assemblage of glass and iron, modeled on the famous glass house at Kew Gardens in London, usually exhibits a rotating display of plants and shrubs. Unfortunately, it's closed until further notice to visitors, but the architecture alone is worth a look.

JAPANESE TEA GARDEN (1894) Developed for the 1894 Midwinter Exposition, this garden would be a quiet place with cherry trees, shrubs, and bonsai crisscrossed by winding paths and high-arched bridges crossing over pools of water—were it not for the hordes of tourists and screaming children who can all but destroy any semblance of peace. Come early to enjoy the focal points and places for contemplation, including the massive bronze Buddha that was cast in Japan in 1790 and donated by the Gump family, the Shinto wooden pagoda, and the Wishing Bridge, which reflected in the water looks as though it completes a circle. The garden is open daily October through February from 8:30am to 6pm (with the teahouse open only until 5:30pm), March through September from 9am to 6:30pm. For information on admissions, call ☎ **415/752-4227**; for the teahouse, call ☎ **415/752-1171**.

STRYBING ARBORETUM & BOTANICAL GARDENS Some 6,000 plant species grow here, among them rare species, very ancient plants in a special "primitive garden," and a grove of California redwoods. Docent tours are given at 1pm daily during operating hours, which are Monday through Friday from 8am to 4:30pm and Saturday and Sunday from 10am to 5pm. For more information, call ☎ **415/ 753-7089**.

✪ STOW LAKE/STRAWBERRY HILL Rent a paddleboat, rowboat, or motorboat here and cruise around the circular lake as painters create still lifes and joggers pass along the grassy shoreline. Ducks waddle around waiting to be fed, and turtles bathe on rocks and logs. Strawberry Hill, the 430-foot-high artificial island that lies at the center of Stow Lake, is a perfect picnic spot and boasts a bird's-eye view of San Francisco and the bay. It also has a waterfall and peace pagoda. To reach the boathouse, call ☎ **415/752-0347**. Boat rentals are available daily from June through September from 9am to 5pm, and the rest of the year from 9am to 4pm. The two-person boats cost $10.50 per hour; four-person boats are $12 per hour.

6 Exploring the City

Mission Dolores. 16th St. (at Dolores St.). ☎ **415/621-8203**. Admission $2 adults, $1 children 5–12. May–Oct daily 9am–4:30pm; Nov–Apr daily 9am–4pm; Good Friday 10am–noon. Closed Thanksgiving and Christmas. Muni Metro: J line to the corner of Church and 16th sts. Bus: 22.

This is the oldest structure in the city, built on order of Franciscan Father Junípero Serra by Father Francisco Palou. It was constructed of 36,000 sunbaked bricks and dedicated in June 1776 at the northern terminus of El Camino Real, the Spanish road from Mexico to California. It's a moving place to visit, with its cool, serene buildings with thick adobe walls and especially the cemetery-gardens where the early settlers are buried.

The NAMES Project AIDS Memorial Quilt Visitors Center & Panelmaking Workshop. 2362-A Market St. ☎ **415/863-1966.** Thurs–Tues noon–7pm; Wed noon–10pm. Muni Metro: J, K, L, or M line to Castro St. Station; F line to Church and Market sts.

The NAMES Project began in 1987 as a memorial to those who have died of AIDS. Sewing machines and fabric were acquired, and the public was invited to make coffin-sized panels for a giant memorial quilt. More than 40,000 individual panels now commemorate the lives of those who have died. Each has been uniquely designed and sewn by the victims' friends, lovers, and family members.

The Quilt, which would cover 24 football fields if laid out end to end, was first displayed on the Capitol Mall in Washington, D.C., during a 1987 national march on Washington for lesbian and gay rights. Although sections of the quilt are often on tour throughout the world, portions of the largest community art project in the world are on display here. A sewing machine and fabrics are also available here, free, for your use.

Lombard Street

Known as the "crookedest street in the world," the whimsically winding block of Lombard Street, between Hyde and Leavenworth streets, puts smiles on the faces of thousands of visitors each year. The elevation is so steep that the road has to snake back and forth to make a descent possible.

ARCHITECTURAL HIGHLIGHTS

The Alamo Square Historic District contains many of the city's 14,000 Victorian **"Painted Ladies,"** homes that have been restored and ornately painted by residents. The small area—bordered by Divisadero Street on the west, Golden Gate Avenue on the north, Webster Street on the east, and Fell Street on the south, about 10 blocks west of the Civic Center—has one of the city's largest concentrations of these. One of the most famous views of San Francisco, which you'll see on postcards and posters all around the city, depicts sharp-edged Financial District skyscrapers behind a row of Victorians. This view can be seen from Alamo Square at Fulton and Steiner streets.

Built in 1881 to a design by Brown and Bakewell, **City Hall** and the **Civic Center** are part of a "City Beautiful" complex done in the beaux arts style. The dome rises to a height of 308 feet on the exterior and is ornamented with occuli and topped by a lantern. The interior rotunda soars 112 feet and is finished in oak, marble, and limestone with a monumental marble staircase leading to the second floor, but you won't be able to see it; City Hall is closed for renovation for the next few years.

The **Flood Mansion,** 1000 California St. at Mason Street, was built between 1885 and 1886 for James Clair Flood, who, thanks to the Comstock Lode, rose from being a bartender to being one of the city's wealthiest men. The house cost $1.5 million (the fence alone carried a price tag of $30,000!). It was designed by Augustus Laver and modified by Willis Polk after the earthquake to accommodate the Pacific Union Club.

The **Octagon House,** 2645 Gough St. at Union Street (☎ **415/441-7512**), is an eight-sided, cupola-topped house dating from 1861. Its features are extraordinary, especially the circular staircase and ceiling medallion. Inside, you'll find furniture, silverware, and American pewter from the colonial and Federal periods. There are also some historic documents, including signatures of 54 of the 56 signers of the Declaration of Independence. Even if you're not able to visit during open hours, this strange structure is worth a look. It's open on the 2nd Sunday and 2nd and 4th Thursdays of each month from noon to 3pm; closed January and holidays.

The **Palace of Fine Arts,** on Baker between Jefferson and Bay streets, is the only building to survive from the Pan Pacific Exhibition of 1915. Constructed by Bernard

Maybeck, it was rebuilt in concrete using molds taken from the original in the 1950s. It now houses the Exploratorium (see "The Top Attractions," above).

The **TransAmerica Pyramid,** 600 Montgomery St. between Clay and Washington streets, is the tallest structure in San Francisco's skyline—48 stories tall and capped by a 212-foot spire.

Although the **San Francisco–Oakland Bay Bridge** is visually less appealing than the Golden Gate Bridge (see "The Top Attractions," above), it is in many ways more spectacular. Opened in 1936, before the Golden Gate, it's 8¼ miles long, one of the world's longest steel bridges. It's not a single bridge at all, but actually a dovetailed series of spans joined in midbay—at Yerba Buena Island—by one of the world's largest (in diameter) tunnels. To the west of Yerba Buena, the bridge is really two separate suspension bridges, joined at a central anchorage. East of the island is a 1,400-foot cantilever span, followed by a succession of truss bridges.

✪ **Yerba Buena Gardens** (☎ **415/978-2787**), between Mission and Howard streets at Third Street, is the city's version of New York's Lincoln Center. The **Center for the Arts** consists of a 755-seat theater designed by James Stewart Polshek and the Galleries and Forum building designed by Fumihiko Maki, which features three galleries and a space for dance. The complex also includes a 5-acre garden featuring several artworks; the most dramatic piece is a mixed-media memorial to Martin Luther King, Jr., created by sculptor Houston Conwill, poet Estella Majoza, and architect Joseph de Pace.

CHURCHES

Glide Memorial United Methodist Church. 330 Ellis St. ☎ **415/771-6300.** Services held Sun 9 and 11am. Muni Metro: Powell. Bus: 37.

There would be nothing special about this plain Tenderloin-area church if it weren't for its exhilarating pastor, Cecil Williams. Williams's enthusiastic and uplifting preaching and singing with the homeless and poor people of the neighborhood crosses all socioeconomic boundaries and has attracted nationwide fame. Go for an uplifting experience.

MUSEUMS

Also see "Golden Gate Park" under "The Top Attractions" above; there you'll find listings for the California Academy of Sciences, the Asian Art Museum, and the M. H. De Young Memorial Museum.

Ansel Adams Center for Photography. 250 Fourth St. ☎ **415/495-7000.** Admission $5 adults, $3 students, $2 seniors and children 13–17. Tues–Sun 11am–5pm; until 8pm the 1st Thurs of each month. Muni Metro: J, K, L, M, or N line to Powell St. Station. Bus: 30, 45, or 9X.

This popular SoMa museum features five separate galleries for changing exhibitions of contemporary and historical photography. One area is dedicated solely to displaying the works and exploring the legacy of Ansel Adams.

Cable Car Barn Museum. Washington and Mason sts. ☎ **415/474-1887.** Free admission. Apr–Oct daily 10am–6pm; Nov–Mar daily 10am–5pm. Cable car: Powell-Hyde and Powell-Mason lines.

If you've ever wondered how cable cars work, this nifty museum will explain (and demonstrate!) it all to you. Yes, this is a museum, but the Cable Car Barn is no stuffed shirt. It's the living powerhouse, repair shop, and storage place of the cable-car system and is in full operation. The exposed machinery, which pulls the cables under San Francisco's streets, looks like a Rube Goldberg invention. Watch the massive groaning and vibrating winches as they thread the cable that hauls the cars through a huge figure eight and back into the system via slack-absorbing tension wheels. In the lower-level viewing room, you can see the cables operating underground. There's also a shop where you can buy a variety of cable-car gifts.

✪ California Palace of the Legion of Honor. In Lincoln Park (at 34th Ave. and Clement St.). ☎ **415/750-3600,** or 415/863-3330 for recorded information. Admission (including the Asian Art Museum and M. H. De Young Memorial Museum) $7 adults, $5 seniors 65 and over, $4 youths 12–17, free for children 11 and under (fees may be higher for special exhibitions); free the 1st Wed of each month when hours are 9:30am–8:45pm. Open Tues–Sun 9:30am–5pm; 1st Sat of each month until 8:45pm. Bus: 38 or 18.

Designed as a memorial to California's World War I casualties, the neoclassical structure is an exact replica of the Legion of Honor Palace in Paris, right down to the inscription *honneur et patrie* above the portal. Reopened after a 2-year, $29-million renovation and seismic upgrading project that was stalled by the discovery of almost 300 turn-of-the-century coffins, the museum's collection contains paintings, sculpture, and decorative arts from Europe, as well as international tapestries, prints, and drawings. The chronological display of more than 800 years of European art includes a fine collection of Rodin sculpture.

The Jewish Museum San Francisco. 121 Steuart St. (between Mission and Howard sts.). ☎ **415/543-8880.** Admission $5 adults, $2.50 students and seniors; free the 1st Mon of each month. Sun–Wed 11am–5pm; Thurs 11am–8pm. Closed Fri–Sat. Bus: 14, 32.

This museum hosts a variety of shows that concentrate on immigration, assimilation, and identity of the Jewish community in the United States and around the world. They are illustrated by paintings, sculptures, photographs, and installation art.

Mexican Museum. Building D, Fort Mason, Marina Blvd. (at Laguna St.). ☎ **415/202-9700.** Admission $3 adults, $2 children; free the 1st Wed of each month. Wed–Fri noon–5pm; Sat–Sun 11am–5pm. Bus: 76 or 28.

The gallery maintains a collection of art covering pre-Hispanic, colonial, folk, and Mexican fine art, plus Chicano/Mexican-American art. A recent show featured religious works by New Mexican women. *Note:* The museum is scheduled to relocate to the Yerba Buena Center at Third and Mission streets in 1999.

San Francisco Maritime National Historical Park. At the foot of Polk St. (near Fisherman's Wharf). ☎ **415/556-3002.** Museum free; ships $2 adults, $1 children 12–17, free for children 11 and under and seniors over 62. Museum daily 10am–5pm. Ships on Hyde St. Pier May 31–Sept 1 daily 10am–6pm; Sept 2–May 30 daily 9:30am–5pm. Closed Thanksgiving, Christmas, and New Year's Day. Cable car: Powell-Hyde line to the last stop. Bus: 19, 30, 32, 42, or 47.

Shaped like an art-deco ship and located near Fisherman's Wharf, the National Maritime Museum is filled with sailing, whaling, and fishing lore. Exhibits include intricate model craft, scrimshaw, and a collection of shipwreck photographs and historic marine scenes, including an 1851 snapshot of hundreds of abandoned ships, deserted en masse by crews dashing off to participate in the gold rush. The museum's walls are lined with finely carved, painted wooden figureheads from old windjammers.

Two blocks east, at Aquatic Park's Hyde Street Pier, are several historic ships that are open to the public. The *Balclutha*, one of the last surviving square-riggers, was built in Glasgow, Scotland, in 1886 and was used to carry grain from California around Cape Horn at a near-record speed of 300 miles a day; it rounded the treacherous Cape 17 times in its career. Visitors are invited to spin the wheel, squint at the compass, and imagine they're weathering a mighty storm. Kids can climb into the bunking quarters, visit the "slop chest" (galley to you, matey), and read the sea chanties (clean ones only) that decorate the walls.

The 1890 *Eureka* still carries a cargo of nostalgia for San Franciscans. It was the last of 50 paddle-wheeled ferries that regularly plied the bay; it made its final trip in 1957. Restored to its original splendor, the side-wheeler is loaded with deck cargo, including antique cars and trucks.

At the pier's small-boat shop, visitors can follow the restoration progress of historic boats from the museum's collection. It's behind the maritime bookstore on your right as you approach the ships.

Wells Fargo History Museum. 420 Montgomery St. (at California St.). ☎ **415/ 396-2619.** Free admission. Mon–Fri 9am–5pm. Closed bank holidays. Muni Metro: J, K, L, or N to Montgomery St. Bus: Any bus to Market St.

Wells Fargo, one of California's largest banks, was founded on the frontier; this museum displays hundreds of frontier relics. In the center of the main room stands a Concord stagecoach, which opened the West as surely as the Winchester rifle and the iron horse locomotive. On the mezzanine, you can take an imaginary ride in a replica stagecoach or send a telegraph message in code using a telegraph key and the code-books, just the way the Wells Fargo agents did more than a century ago.

Yerba Center of the Arts Galleries. 701 Mission St. ☎ **415/978-2700.** Admission $5 adults, $3 seniors and students; Tues–Sun 11am–6pm. Muni Metro: Powell or Montgomery. Bus: 30, 45, or 9X.

Cutting-edge multimedia shows and Bay Area artists works are displayed in the high-tech galleries. The initial exhibition, *The Art of Star Wars,* which featured the special effects created by George Lucas for the film, was a prime example. Performances (like dance) and theater can also be found here, but only during scheduled engagements and for an additional fee. For more information call ☎ **415/978-ARTS.**

NEIGHBORHOODS WORTH SEEKING OUT

THE CASTRO   Castro Street around Market and 18th streets is the center of the city's gay community, which is catered to by the many stores, restaurants, bars, and other institutions here. Among the landmarks are Harvey Milk Plaza, the Quilt Project, and the Castro Theatre, a 1920s movie palace. (See "Organized Tours," below, for details on a walking tour of the area.)

CHINATOWN   California Street to Broadway and Kearny to Stockton Street are the boundaries of today's Chinatown. San Francisco is home to the second-largest community of Chinese in the United States, but the majority of them do not live and work in these 24 blocks, although they do return to shop and dine here on weekends.

The gateway at Grant and Bush marks the entry to Chinatown. Walk up Grant, which has become the tourist face of Chinatown, to California Street and Old St. Mary's.

The **Chinese Historical Society of America,** at 650 Commercial St. (☎ **415/ 391-1188**), has a small but interesting collection relating to the Chinese in San Francisco, which can be viewed for free anytime Tuesday through Friday from 10am to 4pm.

The heart of Chinatown is at **Portsmouth Square,** where you'll find Chinese locals playing board games (often gambling) or just sitting quietly. This square was the center of early San Francisco and the spot where the American flag was first raised on July 9, 1846. From the square, Washington Street leads up to Waverly Place, where you can discover three temples.

Explore the area at your leisure, or see "Organized Tours," below, if you'd like to join a walking tour.

FISHERMAN'S WHARF & THE NORTHERN WATERFRONT   Few cities in America are as adept at wholesaling their historical sites as San Francisco, which has converted Fisherman's Wharf into one of the most popular tourist destinations in the world. Unless you come really early in the morning, you won't find any traces of the traditional waterfront life that once existed here; the only fishing going on around here is for tourist dollars. A small fleet of fewer than 30 boats still operates from here, but basically Fisherman's Wharf has been converted into one long shopping mall stretching from Ghirardelli Square at the west end to Pier 39 at the east. Some people love it, others can't get far enough away from it, but most agree that Fisherman's Wharf, for better or for worse, has to be seen at least once in a lifetime.

Ghirardelli Square, at 900 North Point, between Polk and Larkin streets (☎ 415/775-5500), is best known as the former chocolate-and-spice factory of Domingo Ghirardelli. The factory has been converted into a 10-level mall containing more than 50 stores and 20 dining establishments. Scheduled street performers play regularly in the West Plaza. The stores generally stay open until 8 or 9pm in the summer and 6 or 7pm in the winter.

The Cannery, at 2801 Leavenworth St. (☎ 415/771-3112; www.thecannery. com), was built in 1894 as a fruit-canning plant and converted in the 1960s into a mall containing more than 50 shops and several restaurants and galleries. Vendors' stalls and sidewalk cafes are set up in the courtyard amid a grove of century-old olive trees, and on summer weekends street performers are out in force entertaining tourists. The **Museum of the City of San Francisco** (☎ 415/928-0289), which traces the city's development with displays and artifacts, is on the third floor. The museum is free and is open Wednesday through Sunday from 10am to 4pm.

Pier 39, on the waterfront at Embarcadero and Beach Street (☎ 415/981-8030), is a 4½-acre waterfront complex, a few blocks east of Fisherman's Wharf. Ostensibly a re-creation of a turn-of-the-century street scene, it features walkways of aged and weathered wood salvaged from demolished piers. But don't expect a slice of old-time maritime life. This is the busiest mall of the group, with more than 100 stores. In addition, there are 20 or so restaurants and snack outlets, some with good views of the bay. Two marinas accommodating 350 boats flank the pier and house the Blue & Gold bay sightseeing fleet.

In recent years some 600 California **sea lions** have taken up residence on the adjacent floating docks. They sun themselves and honk and bellow playfully. The latest major addition to Fisherman's Wharf is **Underwater World,** a $38-million,

Amazing Graze

There's no better way to enjoy a bright San Francisco morning than strolling the gourmet **Farmers Market** and snacking your way through breakfast. Every Tuesday and Saturday from 8:30am to 1:30pm, northern California fruit, vegetable, bread, and dairy vendors join local restaurateurs in selling fresh, delicious edibles along the Embarcadero in front of the Ferry Building (at the foot of Market Street, about a 15-min. walk from Fisherman's Wharf). You can also pick up locally made vinegars and oils, which make wonderful gifts. Call ☎ 510/528-6987 for more information. Bus: 2, 7, 8, 9, 14, 21, 31, 32, 66, or 71.

707,000-gallon marine attraction filled with sharks, stingrays, and more, all witnessed via a moving footpath that transports visitors through clear acrylic tunnels.

The shops are open daily from 10:30am to 8:30pm. Cable car: Powell-Mason line to Bay Street.

HAIGHT-ASHBURY   Few of San Francisco's neighborhoods are as varied—or as famous—as the Haight. Walk along Haight Street and you'll encounter everything from drug-dazed drifters begging for change to an armada of the city's most counter-culture (read: cool) shops, clubs, and cafes. Yet turn anywhere off Haight, and instantly you're among the clean-cut, young urban professionals who are the only ones who can afford the steep rents in this hip 'hood. The result is an interesting mix of well-to-do and well-screw-you lifestyles rubbing shoulders with aging flower children, former Deadheads, homeless people, and the throngs of tourists who try not to stare as they wander through this most human of zoos. Some find it depressing, while others find it fascinating, but everyone agrees that it ain't what it used to be back in the free-loving psychedelic Summer of Love. Is it still worth a visit? Absolutely, if only to have a cone of Cherry Garcia at Ben & Jerry's ice-cream shop on the corner of Haight and Ashbury streets. Then wander west and gawk at the exotic people and places that occupy the Haight.

THE MISSION DISTRICT   Once inhabited almost entirely by Irish immigrants, the Mission District is now the center of the city's Latino community, an oblong area stretching roughly from 14th to 30th streets between Potrero Avenue in the east and Dolores on the west. Some of the city's finest Victorians still stand in the outer areas, though many seem strangely out of place in the mostly lower-income neighborhoods. The heart of the community lies along 24th Street between Van Ness and Potrero, where dozens of excellent ethnic restaurants, bakeries, bars, and specialty stores attract people from all over the city. Strolling through the Mission District at night isn't a good idea, but it's usually quite safe during the day and highly recommended.

For even better insight into the community, go to the **Precita Eyes Mural Arts Center,** 348 Precita Ave., at Folsom Street (☎ **415/285-2287**), and take one of the hour-long tours conducted on Saturdays, which cost $5 for adults, $4 for seniors, and $1 for children under 18. You'll see 85 murals in an 8-block walk. Every year they also hold a Mural Awareness Week (usually the 2nd week in May), when tours are given daily. Other signs of cultural life include a number of progressive theaters—Eureka, Theater Rhinoceros, and Theater Artaud, to name only a few.

At 16th and Dolores is the **Mission San Francisco de Assisi** (better known as Mission Dolores), which is the city's oldest surviving building (see the separate listing above) and the district's namesake.

NOB HILL   When the cable car was invented in 1873, this hill became the most exclusive residential area in the city. The Big Four and the Comstock Bonanza kings built their mansions here, but the structures were all destroyed by the 1906 earthquake and fire. Only the Flood Mansion, which serves today as the Pacific Union Club, and the Fairmont (which was under construction when the earthquake struck) were spared. Today the area is home to some of the city's most upscale hotels as well as Grace Cathedral, which stands on the Crocker Mansion site. Stroll around and enjoy the views, and perhaps pay a visit to Huntington Park.

NORTH BEACH   In the late 1800s, an enormous influx of Italian immigrants into North Beach firmly established this aromatic area as San Francisco's "Little Italy." Today, dozens of Italian restaurants and coffeehouses continue to flourish in what is still the center of the city's Italian community. Walk down Columbus Avenue any given morning and you're bound to be bombarded with the wonderful aromas of roasting coffee and savory pasta sauces. Though there are some interesting shops and bookstores in the area, it's the dozens of eclectic little cafes, delis, bakeries, and coffee shops that give North Beach its Italian bohemian character.

For a proper perspective of North Beach, sign up for a guided Javawalk with coffee-nut Elaine Sosa (see "Organized Tours," below).

PARKS, GARDENS & ZOOS

In addition to Golden Gate Park (see "The Top Attractions," above), **Golden Gate National Recreation Area,** and the **Presidio** (see below), San Francisco boasts more than 2,000 additional acres of parkland, most of which are perfect for picnicking.

Lincoln Park, at Clement Street and 34th Avenue, a personal favorite of ours, occupies 270 acres on the northwestern side of the city and contains the California Palace of the Legion of Honor (see "Museums," above) and a scenic 18-hole municipal golf course. But the most dramatic features of the park are the 200-foot cliffs that overlook the Golden Gate Bridge and San Francisco Bay. Take bus no. 38 from Union Square to 33rd and Geary streets, then transfer to bus no. 18 into the park.

✪ **San Francisco Zoo & Children's Zoo.** Sloat Blvd. and 45th Ave. ☎ **415/ 753-7080.** Admission to main zoo $7 adults, $3.50 seniors and youths 12–15, $1.50 children 3–11, and free for children 2 and under if accompanied by an adult; Children's Zoo $1, free for children under 3. Carousel $2. Main zoo daily 10am–5pm. Children's Zoo Mon–Fri 11am–4pm; Sat–Sun 10:30am–4:30pm. Muni Metro: L from downtown Market St. to the end of the line.

Located between the Pacific Ocean and Lake Merced, in the southwest corner of the city, the San Francisco Zoo is among America's highest-rated animal parks. Most of the 1,000-plus inhabitants are contained in landscaped enclosures guarded by concealed moats. The Primate Discovery Center is particularly noteworthy for its many rare and endangered species. Expansive outdoor atriums, sprawling meadows, and a midnight world for exotic nocturnal primates house such species as the ruffed-tailed lemur, black-and-white colobus monkeys, patas monkeys, and emperor tamarins, pint-size primates distinguished by their long, majestic mustaches.

Other highlights include Koala Crossing, housing kangaroos, emus, and wallaroos; Gorilla World, one of the world's largest exhibits of these gentle giants; and Penguin Island, home to a large breeding colony of Magellanic penguins. The Feline Conservation Center is a wooded sanctuary and breeding facility for the zoo's endangered snow leopards, Persian leopards, and other jungle cats. And the Lion House is home to rare Sumatran and Siberian tigers, a rare white Bengal tiger, and the African lions (you can watch them being fed at 2pm Tues through Sun).

At the Children's Zoo, adjacent to the main park, the barnyard is alive with strokable domestic animals such as sheep, goats, ponies, and a llama. Also of interest is the Insect Zoo, which showcases a multitude of insect species, including the hissing cockroach and walking sticks.

A free (with admission), informal walking tour of the zoo is available on weekends at 11am. The Zebra Zephyr train tour takes visitors on a 30-minute "safari" daily (only on weekends in winter). The tour is $2.50 for adults, $1.50 for children 15 and under and seniors.

7 Organized Tours

THE 49-MILE SCENIC DRIVE The self-guided, 49-mile drive is one easy way to orient yourself and to grasp the beauty of San Francisco and its extraordinary location.

Beginning in the city, it follows a rough circle around the bay and passes virtually all the best-known sights, from Chinatown to the Golden Gate Bridge, Ocean Beach, Seal Rocks, Golden Gate Park, and Twin Peaks. Originally designed for the benefit of visitors to San Francisco's 1939 and 1940 Golden Gate International Exposition, the route is marked with blue-and-white seagull signs. Although it makes an excellent half-day tour, this miniexcursion can easily take longer if you decide, for example, to stop to walk across the Golden Gate Bridge or to have tea in Golden Gate Park's Japanese Tea Garden.

The San Francisco Visitor Information Center, at Powell and Market streets, distributes free route maps. Since a few of the Scenic Drive marker signs are missing, the map will come in handy. Try to avoid the downtown area during the weekday rush hours from 7 to 9am and 4 to 6pm.

A BOAT TOUR   One of the best ways to look at San Francisco is from a boat bobbing on the bay. The **Blue & Gold Fleet** tours the bay year-round in a sleek, 400-passenger sightseeing boat, complete with food and beverage facilities. The fully narrated, 1¼-hour cruise passes beneath the Golden Gate and Bay bridges, and comes within yards of Alcatraz Island. Frequent daily departures from Pier 39's West Marina begin at 10am during summer and 11am in winter. Tickets cost $16 for adults, $12 for kids 12 to 18 and seniors over 62, $8 for kids 5 to 11; children under 5 sail free. For recorded information call ☎ **415/773-1188;** for tickets call ☎ **415/705-5555.**

WALKING TOURS   For a totally new insight into the gay community's contribution to the political maturity, growth, and beauty of San Francisco, contact **Cruisin' the Castro** (☎ **415/550-8110**). Tours are personally led by Ms. Trevor Hailey, who was involved in the development of the Castro in the 1970s and knew Harvey Milk— the first openly gay politician elected to office in the United States. Call for tour times, but expect to pay $35 for adults, $30 for seniors 62 and older, and a negotiable price for children 16 and under; the price includes lunch at Castro's popular Luna Piena Caffè.

If you're nostalgic for the 1960s, the **Haight-Ashbury Flower Power Walking Tour** will take you to the city's hippie haunts, including the Grateful Dead's crash pad and Janis Joplin's house. Tours begin at 9:30am Tuesday and Saturday and cost $15 per person. For reservations call ☎ **415/863-1621.**

Self-described "coffeehouse lizard" Elaine Sosa leads **Javawalk,** a 2-hour walking tour. Aside from visiting cafes, Javawalk also serves up a good share of historical and architectural trivia. Sosa keeps the tour interactive and fun, and it's obvious that she knows a dearth of tales and trivia about the history of coffee and its North Beach roots. Tours are Tuesday through Saturday at 10am. The price is $20 for adults and $10 for kids 12 and under. For information and reservations, call ☎ **415/673-9255.**

Founded by author, TV personality, cooking instructor, and restaurant critic Shirley Fong-Torres, **Wok Wiz Chinatown Walking Tours** (☎ **800/281-9255** or 415/ 981-8989) takes you into nooks and crannies not usually seen by tourists. Each of her guides is intimately acquainted with all of Chinatown's backways, alleys, and small businesses. You'll learn about dim sum (a "delight of the heart") and the Chinese tea ceremony; meet a Chinese herbalist; stop at a pastry shop to observe rice noodles being made; watch artist Y. K. Lau do his delicate brush painting; learn about *jook,* a traditional Chinese breakfast; stop in at a fortune-cookie factory; and visit a Chinese produce market and learn to identify the vegetables used in Chinese cuisine. Tours are conducted daily from 10am to 1:30pm and include a Chinese lunch. Groups are generally limited to 12, and reservations are essential. Prices (including lunch) are $37 for adults, $35 for seniors 60 and older, and $30 for children under 12.

8 Golden Gate National Recreation Area & the Presidio

GOLDEN GATE NATIONAL RECREATION AREA

No urban shoreline is as stunning as San Francisco's. Golden Gate National Recreation Area, which wraps around the northern and western edges of the city and is run by the National Park Service, lets visitors fully enjoy it. Along this shoreline are several landmarks, and from its edge visitors have views of the bay and the ocean. Muni provides transportation to most sites, including Aquatic Park, the Cliff House, and Ocean Beach. For more information, contact the **National Park Service** at ☎ **415/556-0560.** For details on outdoor activities in the park, see "Staying Active," later in this chapter.

Here is a brief rundown of the major features of the recreation area, starting at the northern section and moving westward around the coastline:

Aquatic Park, adjacent to the Hyde Street Pier, is a small swimming beach, although it's not that appealing and the water's ridiculously cold.

Fort Mason Center occupies an area from Bay Street to the shoreline and consists of several buildings and piers, which were used during World War II. Today they are occupied by a variety of museums, theaters, organizations, and the renowned (and expensive) **Greens** vegetarian restaurant. For information about Fort Mason events, call ☎ **415/441-5705.** Park headquarters is at upper Fort Mason (☎ **415/561-3000**).

Farther west along the bay at the northern end of Fillmore, **Marina Green** is a favorite spot for flying kites or watching the sailboats on the bay. Next stop along the bay is the St. Francis Yacht Club. From here begins the 3½-mile paved **Golden Gate Promenade,** a favorite biking and hiking path, which sweeps along Crissy Field, leading ultimately to Fort Point under the Golden Gate Bridge. This promenade defines the outer limits of the Presidio (see below).

Fort Point (☎ **415/556-1693**), a National Historic Site sitting directly under the Golden Gate Bridge, was built in 1853 to protect the narrow entrance to the harbor. You might recognize it from Alfred Hitchcock's *Vertigo;* the master of suspense filmed some of the most important scenes here. During the Civil War, the brick Fort Point was manned by 140 men and 90 pieces of artillery to prevent a Confederate takeover of California. Rangers in Civil War regalia lead regular tours and sometimes fire the old cannons.

Lincoln Boulevard sweeps around the western edge of the bay to two of the most popular beaches in San Francisco. **Baker Beach,** a small and beautiful strand just outside the Golden Gate where the waves roll ashore, is a fine spot for sunbathing, walking, or fishing—it's packed on sunny days. Because of the cold water and the roaring currents that pour out of the bay twice a day, swimming is not advised here for any but the most confident. (You'll also see some nude sunbathers here.) Here you can pick up the **Coastal Trail,** which leads through the Presidio (see below). A short distance from Baker, **China Beach** is a small cove where swimming is permitted. Changing rooms, showers, sundeck, and rest rooms are available.

A little farther around the coast appears **Lands End,** looking out to Pyramid Rock. Both a lower and an upper trail provide hiking opportunities amid windswept cypress and pines on the cliffs above the Pacific.

Still farther along the coast lies **Point Lobos,** the **Sutro Baths,** and the **Cliff House.** The latter has been serving refreshments to visitors since 1863. Here you can view the Seal Rocks, home to a colony of sea lions and many marine birds. The visitor center here (☎ **415/556-8642**) is open daily from 10am to 5pm. The kids will enjoy the **Musée Mecanique,** an authentic old-fashioned arcade with 150 coin-operated amusements. Only traces of the Sutro Baths remain today northeast of the Cliff House. This swimming facility was a major summer attraction that could accommodate 24,000 people, but it burned down in 1966. A little farther inland at the western end of California Street is **Lincoln Park,** which contains a golf course and the Palace of the Legion of Honor.

From the Cliff House, the Esplanade continues south along the 4-mile-long **Ocean Beach,** which is not suitable for swimming. At the southern end of Ocean Beach is another area of the park around **Fort Funston** where there's an easy loop trail across the cliffs (for information, call the ranger station at ☎ **415/239-2366**). Here, too, you can watch the hang gliders taking advantage of the high cliffs and strong winds.

Farther south along Route 280, **Sweeney Ridge,** which can only be reached by car, affords sweeping views of the coastline from the many trails that crisscross these 1,000 acres of land. It was from here that the expedition led by Don Gaspar de Portolá first saw San Francisco Bay in 1769. It's located in Pacifica and can be reached via Sneath Lane off Route 35 (Skyline Boulevard) in San Bruno.

THE PRESIDIO

In 1989 the Department of Defense announced what many had long thought impossible: The U.S. Army, which had held the Presidio as a military base since before the Civil War, was pulling out and leaving the most prized piece of real estate in San Francisco to the National Park Service as an example of post–Cold War retrofitting. Now an urban national park, it combines historical, architectural, and natural aspects.

The 1,480-acre area incorporates a variety of terrain—coastal scrub, dunes, and prairie grasslands that shelter many rare plants and more than 150 species of birds, some of which nest here. There are also more than 350 historic buildings, a scenic golf course, a national cemetery, and a variety of terrains and natural habitats. The Park Service offers a number of walking and biking tours around the Presidio; reservations are required.

Walkers and joggers will enjoy the forests of the Presidio. It was once a bleak field of wind-blasted rock, sand, and grass, but in a strangely humanitarian gesture, 60,000 trees were planted in the 1880s to make the place more livable for the troops. Today, on the 2-mile **Ecology Loop Trail,** walkers can see more than 30 different species of those trees, including redwood, spruce, cypress, and acacias. Hikers can follow the 2½-mile **Coastal Trail** from Fort Point along this part of the coastline all the way to Land's End. It follows the bluff top from Baker Beach to the southern base of the Golden Gate Bridge.

Crissy Field is a former airfield that in recent years has become known as one of the see-and-be-seen proving grounds of California's windsurfing culture. Between March and October, hundreds come to try their hand. The beach here provides easy water access and plenty of room to rig up, but is not recommended for the inexperienced. This is also a popular place for joggers en route from the Marina District to Fort Point and back. At the west end of Crissy Field is a pier that can be used for fishing and crabbing.

The Presidio is undergoing major changes so that it may pay for its upkeep. At press time, the old military buildings were to be rented to nonprofit organizations. For schedules, maps, and general information about ongoing developments at the Presidio, the best source is the **Golden Gate National Recreation Area Headquarters** at Fort Mason, Building 102, San Francisco, CA 94123 (☎ **415/556-0560**). The

Golden Gate National Recreation Area & the Presidio

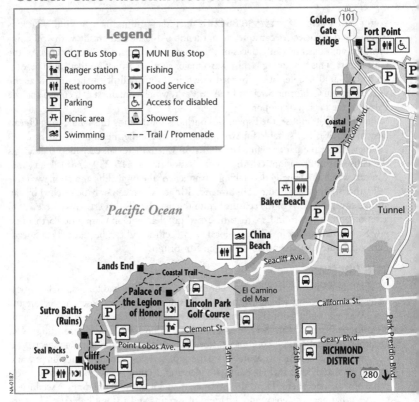

Presidio Visitors Center (☎ **415/561-4323**) is located on the west side of Montgomery Street, in the Presidio on the main parade ground, and is open daily from 10am to 5pm. Bus: 82X, 28, or 76.

9 Staying Active

The prime places to enjoy all kinds of recreational activities in San Francisco have already been described earlier in this chapter. See Section 5, "The Top Attractions," for a complete description of Golden Gate Park; and Section 8, "Golden Gate National Recreation Area and the Presidio," for complete details on Golden Gate National Recreation Area and the Presidio, which comprise most of the city's shoreline.

BEACHES   There are only two beaches in San Francisco that are safe for swimming: **Aquatic Park,** which is adjacent to the Hyde Park Pier and not very memorable, and **China Beach,** a small cove on the western edge of the South Bay (changing rooms, showers, a sundeck, and rest rooms are available).

   Baker Beach, a small, beautiful strand just outside the Golden Gate, isn't the best place for swimming due to strong currents, but it's popular for sunbathing (nude sunbathing in certain sections), walking, picnicking, or fishing. It's wonderful to sit here on a sunny day and take in the view of the bridge. You'll climb down a very long flight of stairs from the street to reach the beach.

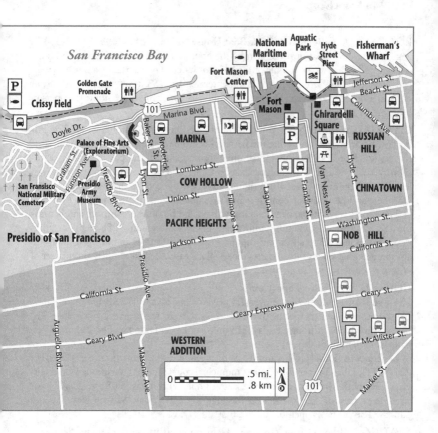

Ocean Beach, at the end of Golden Gate Park, on the westernmost side of the city, is San Francisco's largest beach (4 miles long). Just offshore, at the northern end of the beach in front of Cliff House, are the jagged Seal Rocks, which are inhabited by various shorebirds and a large colony of barking sea lions. Bring binoculars. Ocean Beach is good for strolling or sunning, but don't swim here—tides are tricky, and each year bathers and surfers drown in the rough waters.

BIKING Two city-designated bike routes are maintained by the Recreation and Parks Department. One winds for 7½ miles through Golden Gate Park to Lake Merced; the other traverses the city, starting in the south, and follows a route over the Golden Gate Bridge. A bike map is available from the San Francisco Visitor Information Center and from bicycle shops all around town.

A massive new seawall, constructed to buffer Ocean Beach from storm-driven waves, doubles as a public walk and bikeway along five waterfront blocks of the Great Highway between Noriega and Santiago streets. It's an easy ride from Cliff House or Golden Gate Park.

Park Cyclery, 1749 Waller St. (☎ **415/751-7368**), is a shop in the Haight Street area that rents bikes. Located near Golden Gate Park, the cyclery rents mountain bikes exclusively, along with helmets, locks, and accessories. The charge is $5 per hour or $25 per day, and it's open daily from 10am to 6pm.

There's also great biking in the Presidio. From there you can venture across the Golden Gate Bridge and into the Marin hills.

BOATING At **Golden Gate Park Boat House,** at Stow Lake (☎ 415/752-0347), you can rent a rowboat or pedal boat by the hour and steer over to Strawberry Hill, a large, round island in the middle of the lake, for lunch. There's usually a line on weekends. It's open daily from June through September from 9am to 5pm, and the rest of the year from 9am to 4pm. The two-person boats cost $10.50 per hour; four-person boats are $12 per hour.

CITY STAIR-CLIMBING You don't need a Stairmaster in San Francisco. **The Filbert Street Steps,** 377 steps that run between Sansome Street and Telegraph Hill, scale the eastern face of Telegraph Hill, from Sansome and Filbert past charming 19th-century cottages and lush gardens. Napier Lane, a narrow wooden-plank walkway, leads to Montgomery Street. Turn right, and follow the path to the end of the cul-de-sac where another stairway continues to Telegraph's panoramic summit.

The **Lyon Street Steps,** between Green Street and Broadway, comprise another historic stairway street, containing four steep sets of stairs totaling 288 steps. Begin at Green Street and climb all the way up, past manicured hedges and flower gardens, to an iron gate that opens into the Presidio. A block east, on Baker Street, another set of 369 steps descends to Green Street.

GOLF **Golden Gate Park Course,** 47th Avenue and Fulton Street (☎ 415/751-8987), is a 9-hole course over 1,357 yards and is par 27. All holes are par 3, tightly set, and well trapped with small greens. Greens fees are very reasonable: $10 per person Monday through Friday, $13 on Saturday and Sunday. The course is open daily from 9am to dusk.

✪ **Lincoln Park Golf Course,** 34th Avenue and Clement Street (☎ 415/221-9911), is San Francisco's prettiest municipal course and has terrific views and fairways lined with Monterey cypress trees. Its 18 holes encompass 5,081 yards, for a par 68. Greens fees are $23 per person Monday through Friday, $27 on Saturday and Sunday. The course is open daily from 6:30am to dusk.

SKATING Although people skate in Golden Gate Park all week long, Sunday is best, when John F. Kennedy Drive, between Kezar Drive and Transverse Road, is closed to automobiles. A smooth "skate pad" is located on your right, just past the Conservatory. **Skates on Haight,** 1818 Haight St. (☎ 415/752-8376), is the best place to rent either in-line or conventional skates and is located only a block from the park. Protective wrist guards and knee pads are included free. The cost is $8 per hour for in-line or "conventionals," $28 for all-day use. A major credit card and ID deposit are required.

WALKING & HIKING The **Golden Gate National Recreation Area** offers plenty of opportunities for walking and hiking. One pleasant walk or jog is along the Golden Gate Promenade, from Aquatic Park to the Golden Gate Bridge. The 3½-mile paved trail leads along the northern edge of the Presidio, out to Fort Point. You can also hike along the Coastal Trail all the way from near Fort Point to the Cliff House. The park service maintains several other trails in the city. For more information or to pick up a map of the Golden Gate National Recreation Area, stop by the park service headquarters at Fort Mason at the north end of Laguna Street (☎ 415/556-0560).

Though most drive to this spectacular vantage point, a more rejuvenating way to experience **Twin Peaks** is to walk up from the back roads of UC Medical Center (off Parnassus) or from either of the two roads that lead to the top (off Woodside or Clarendon avenues). Early morning is the best time to trek, when the city is quiet, the air is crisp, and the sightseers haven't crowded the parking lot. Keep an eye out for cars, since there's no real hiking trail and be sure to walk beyond the lot and up to the highest vantage point.

10 The Shopping Scene

Sales tax in San Francisco is 8½%, which is added on at the register for all goods and services purchased. If you live out of state and buy an expensive item, consider having the store ship it home for you. You'll escape paying the sales tax, but will have to pay for its transport.

MAJOR SHOPPING AREAS
UNION SQUARE & ENVIRONS

San Francisco's most congested and popular shopping mecca is centered around Union Square and enclosed by Bush, Taylor, Market, and Montgomery streets. Most of the big department stores and many high-end specialty shops are in this area. Be sure to venture to Grant Avenue, Post and Sutter streets, and Maiden Lane.

One of our favorite galleries is the ✪ **Catharine Clark Gallery,** on the second floor at 49 Geary St., between Kearny and Grant streets (☎ **415/399-1439**). It exhibits up-and-coming contemporary artists mainly from California, and nurtures beginning collectors by offering an unusual interest-free purchasing plan.

Century-old **Gump's,** 135 Post St., between Kearny Street and Grant Avenue (☎ **415/982-1616**), is anything but cheap, but for window-shoppers it's a must. A virtual treasure trove of household items and gifts, they offer a collection of Asian antiquities, contemporary art glass, exquisite jade and pearl jewelry, and more.

Music aficionados will choose to get lost in **Virgin Megastore,** Market Street at Stockton (☎ **415/397-4525**), where thousands of CDs (including an impressive collection of imports), videos, laser discs, and a multimedia department could inspire almost anyone to blow their entire vacation fund. Its literary equivalent is the nearby **Borders Books & Music,** 400 Post, at Powell (☎ **415/399-1633**), which has thousands of titles and a cafe.

SOMA

Though this area isn't suitable for strolling, you'll find almost all the discount shopping in warehouse spaces south of Market. You can pick up a discount shopping guide at most major hotels. Many buses pass through this area, including routes 9, 12, 14, 15, 19, 26, 27, 30, 42, 45, and 76.

One of our favorite gift shops in the city is ✪ **Dandelion,** 55 Potrero Ave., at Alameda Street (☎ **415/436-9500**), which borders on the Mission and offers something for every taste and budget: collectibles, furnishings, and knickknacks, including an excellent collection of teapots, decorative dishes, and gourmet foods as well as books, cards, and picture frames. (Don't miss the Zen-like second floor, with its variety of peaceful furnishings in Indian, Japanese, and Western styles.)

Equally cool is ✪ **SFMOMA MuseumStore,** 151 Third St., 2 blocks south of Market Street, across from Yerba Buena Gardens (☎ **415/357-4035**). Their array of artistic cards, books, jewelry, housewares, knickknacks, and creative tokens of San Francisco makes this one of the locals' favorite shops. It also offers far more tasteful mementos than most Fisherman's Wharf options.

Fashionable bargain hunters head to ✪ **Jeremys,** 2 South Park, at Second Street between Bryant and Brannan streets (☎ **415/882-4929**), where top designer fashions from shoes to suits come at rock-bottom prices.

For the more adventurous thrift-shopper, there's **The North Face** discount outlet, 1325 Howard St., between Ninth and Tenth streets (☎ **415/626-6444**). The sporting, camping, and hiking equipment is still expensive, but the skiwear, boots, sweaters, and goods such as tents, packs, and sleeping bags are far less expensive than if you buy them at a retail shop.

For Art Lovers

If you're into art, pick up *The San Francisco Gallery Guide,* a comprehensive, bimonthly publication listing the city's current shows (most of which are downtown). It's available free by mail; send a self-addressed stamped envelope to San Francisco Bay Area Gallery Guide, 1369 Fulton St., San Francisco, CA 94117 (☎ **415/921-1600**). You can also pick one up at the San Francisco Visitor Information Center at 900 Market St. (at Powell Street).

Burlington Coat Factory, 899 Howard St., at Fifth Street (☎ **415/495-7234**), has hundreds of coats—from cheapies to designer—as well as men's and women's clothing, shoes, and accessories. But the best deal is the home section, where designer bedding, bath, and housewares go for a fraction of their normal retail prices. Open Monday through Saturday from 10am to 8pm and on Sunday from 11am to 7pm.

San Francisco's branch of **Loehmann's,** 222 Sutter St., between Kearny Street and Grant Avenue (☎ **415/982-3215**), caters to a sophisticated white-collar crowd, so you won't find as much tacky fashion as you might at more suburban locations of this discount designer chain. Many women swear this place has the ultimate in professional clothing at bargain prices. Open Monday through Friday from 9am to 8pm, Saturday from 9:30am to 8pm, and Sunday from 11am to 6pm.

Another worthy stop is the ✪ **Wine Club San Francisco,** 953 Harrison St., between Fifth and Sixth streets (☎ **415/512-9086**), which offers bargain prices on more than 1,200 domestic and foreign wines. Bottles cost from $4 to $1,100.

HAYES VALLEY

It may not be the prettiest area in town (with some of the shadier housing projects a few blocks away), but while most neighborhoods cater to more conservative or trendy shoppers, lower Hayes Street, between Octavia and Gough (slightly west of the Civic Center), celebrates anything vintage, artistic, or downright funky. Though still in its developmental stage, it's definitely the most interesting new shopping area in town, with furniture and glass stores, thrift shops, trendy shoe stores, and men's and women's clothiers. There are also lots of great antique shops further south on Octavia and on nearby Market Street. Bus lines include 16AX, 16BX, and 21.

CHINATOWN

When you pass under the gate to Chinatown on Grant Avenue, say good-bye to the world of Union Square fashion and hello to a swarm of cheap tourist shops selling everything from linen and jade to plastic toys and $2 slippers. The real gems are tucked on side streets or in small, one-person shops selling Chinese herbs, original art, and jewelry. Grant Avenue is the area's main thoroughfare, and side streets between Bush Street and Columbus Avenue are full of restaurants, markets, and eclectic shops. Walking is best, since traffic through this area is slow at best and parking next to impossible. Most of the stores in Chinatown are open daily from 10am to 10pm. The area is serviced by bus lines 9X, 15, 30, 41, and 45.

Of the endless array of trinket shops scattered through the compact neighborhood, two worth noting are **Eastwind Books & Arts,** 1435A Stockton St., at Columbus Avenue (☎ **415/772-5877** Chinese department, ☎ 415/772-5899 English department; e-mail: info@eastwindsf.com), which carries an incredible selection of Chinese books, stationery, and stamps, as well as Asian-American and English books covering everything from health and cooking to martial arts and medicine. At the mystical

⭗ **Ten Ren Tea Company,** 949 Grant Ave., between Washington and Jackson streets
(☎ **415/362-0656**), you can enjoy a steaming cup of roselle tea, made of black tea
and hibiscus, while you browse the selection of almost 50 traditional and herbal teas
and related paraphernalia.

NORTH BEACH

Along with a fab cup of coffee, Grant and Columbus streets cater to their hip clientele with a small but worthy selection of boutiques and specialty shops.

Grab a great gift for yourself or anyone else at **Biordi Art Imports,** 412 Columbus
Ave., at Vallejo Street (☎ **415/392-8096**). Most of their exquisite imported Italian
Majolica pottery is expensive, but you can pick up a memento for under $20.

For a dose of local color, join the brooding literary types who browse **City Lights
Booksellers & Publishers,** 261 Columbus Ave., at Broadway (☎ **415/362-8193**),
the famous bookstore owned by renowned Beat-generation poet Lawrence Ferlinghetti. The shelves here are stocked with a comprehensive collection of art, poetry,
and political paperbacks, as well as more mainstream books.

Fun, cheap mementos are for sale at **Quantity Postcards,** 1441 Grant St., at Green
Street (☎ **415/986-8866**), where you'll find the perfect postcard for literally everyone
you know, as well as some depictions of old San Francisco and movie stars, plus Day-
Glo posters featuring concert-poster artist Frank Kozik.

FISHERMAN'S WHARF & ENVIRONS

The tourist-oriented malls—**Ghirardelli Square, Pier 39, the Cannery,** and the
Anchorage—run along Jefferson Street and include hundreds of shops, restaurants,
and attractions.

Locals tend to avoid this part of town, but should they shop here, they're likely to
stop at **Cost Plus Imports,** 2552 Taylor St., between North Point and Bay streets
(☎ **415/928-6200**). Near the Fisherman's Wharf cable-car turntable, Cost Plus is a
vast warehouse crammed to the rafters with Chinese baskets, Indian camel bells,
Malaysian batik scarves, and innumerable other items from Algeria to Zanzibar. More
than 20,000 items from 40 nations are purchased directly from their country of origin
and packed into this well-priced warehouse. They also have a decent wine shop.
Adjoining is a **Barnes & Noble** superstore at 2550 Taylor between Bay and North
Point (☎ **415/292-6762**).

PACIFIC HEIGHTS/COW HOLLOW

UNION STREET   Union Street, from Fillmore to Van Ness, caters to the upper-
middle-class crowd, so there'll be no major bargain-hunting here. It is, however, a great
place to stroll; to window-shop the plethora of boutiques, cafes, and restaurants; and
to watch the beautiful people parade by. Bus lines include nos. 22, 41, 42, and 45.

CHESTNUT STREET   Parallel to and a few blocks north of Union Street,
Chestnut is a younger Union Street, with endless shopping and dining choices, and
the ever-tanned, super-fit population of postgraduate singles who hang around cafes
and scope each other out. The area, which offers few, if any, discounts, is serviced by
bus lines 22, 28, 30, 41, 42, 43, and 76.

FILLMORE STREET   Some of the best (and most expensive) shopping in town is
packed into 5 blocks of Fillmore Street in Pacific Heights. From Jackson to Sutter
streets, Fillmore is the perfect place to grab a bite and at least browse through the high-
priced boutiques, craft shops, and incredible housewares stores. It's serviced by bus
lines 1, 2, 3, 4, 12, 22, and 24.

One of our absolute favorite housewares shops is pricey ❂ **Fillamento,** 2185 Fillmore St., at Sacramento Street (☎ **415/931-2224**), which is always packed with shoppers searching for the most classic, artistic, and refined home items. Whether you're looking to set a good table or revamp your bedroom, you'll find it all here. Head south a few blocks on Fillmore to incredible ❂ **Zinc Details,** 1905 Fillmore St., between Bush and Pine streets (☎ **415/776-2100**), which has an amazing collection of locally handcrafted glass vases, pendant lights, ceramics, and furniture. Each piece is a true work of art created specifically for the store (except vintage items).

HAIGHT STREET

Green hair, spiked hair, no hair, or mohair—even the hippies look conservative next to Haight Street's dramatic fashion freaks. The shopping in the 6 blocks of upper Haight Street, between Central Avenue and Stanyan Street, reflects its clientele and offers everything from incense and European and American street styles to furniture and antique clothing. Bus lines 7, 66, 71, and 73 run down Haight Street. The Muni Metro N line stops at Waller Street and at Cole Street.

In the used-clothing-store mecca of the Haight, one of San Francisco's largest secondhand dealers is ❂ **Aardvark's,** 1501 Haight St., at Ashbury Street (☎ **415/ 621-3141**). Shirts, pants, dresses, skirts, and hats from the last 30 years are packed into the ever-busy shop. Another favorite is **Buffalo Exchange,** 1555 Haight St., between Clayton and Ashbury streets (☎ **415/431-7733**), which is crammed with racks of antique and new fashions from the 1960s, 1970s, and 1990s. A second shop is located at 1800 Polk St., at Washington Street (☎ **415/346-5741**).

Also vintage, but less wearable, are the oldies-but-goodies at **Recycled Records,** 1377 Haight St., between Central and Masonic streets (☎ **415/626-4075**). Easily one of the best used-record stores in the city, this loud shop has a good selection of promotional CDs and cases of used "classic" rock LPs. Sheet music, tour programs, and old *TV Guides* are also sold.

THE CASTRO

You could easily spend all day wandering through the home and men's clothing shops of the Castro. Buses serving this area include nos. 8, 24, 33, 35, and 37.

Our favorite chocolate shop, **Joseph Schmidt Confections,** 3489 16th St., at Sanchez Street (☎ **415/861-8682**), adds a whole new dimension to designer chocolate. Here the sinful sweets take the shape of exquisite sculptural masterpieces that are so beautiful, you'll be hesitant to bite the head off your adorable chocolate panda bear. Prices are also remarkably reasonable (considering).

CHINA BASIN

The only reason to come to the southeastern tip of the city is to dine at one of the shipyard-front restaurants or to shop at the ❂ **Esprit Outlet Store,** 499 Illinois St., at 16th Street (☎ **415/957-2550**). Fashionable bargain hunters will revel in the Esprit collections and Susie Tompkins merchandise, which are available here at 30% or more off regular prices. In addition to clothes, there are accessories, shoes, and assorted other items.

11 San Francisco After Dark

For up-to-date nightlife information, turn to the *San Francisco Weekly* and the *San Francisco Bay Guardian,* both of which contain comprehensive current listings. They're available free at bars and restaurants, and from street-corner boxes all around

Getting Bargain Tickets

Half-price tickets to theater, dance, and music perform...
Bay Area (☎ 415/433-7827) on the day of the show...
Monday events, if available, are sold on Saturday. The...
tickets for most performance halls, sporting events, c...
charge, ranging from $1 to $3, is levied on each ticket...
are accepted for half-price tickets; Visa and MasterCard are accepted for full pri...
tickets. Tix is located on Stockton Street, between Post and Geary streets on the east
side of Union Square (opposite Maiden Lane). It's open Tuesday through Thursday
from 11am to 6pm, Friday and Saturday from 11am to 7pm.

Tickets to most theater and dance events can also be obtained through **City Box
Office,** 153 Kearny St., Suite 402 (☎ 415/392-4400). Visa, MasterCard, and
American Express are accepted.

BASS Ticketmaster (☎ 510/762-2277) sells computer-generated tickets to
concerts, sporting events, plays, and special events, but after all the "processing fees"
are added on you'll probably feel ripped off. Downtown BASS Ticketmaster outlets
can be found at Tix Bay Area (see above) and at **Warehouse** stores throughout the
city. The most convenient location is at 30 Powell St.

the city. **Where,** a free tourist monthly, also has information on programs and performance times; it's available in most of the city's finer hotels. The Sunday edition of the
San Francisco Examiner and Chronicle also features a "Datebook" section, printed
on pink paper, with information and listings on the week's upcoming events.

THE PERFORMING ARTS

✪ **American Conservatory Theater (A.C.T.).** Performing at the Geary Theater, 415
Geary St. (at Mason St.). ☎ **415/749-2228.** Tickets $14–$51.

The American Conservatory Theater (A.C.T.) is the city's premier resident theater
group, so venerated that A.C.T. has been compared to the superb British National
Theatre. The A.C.T. season runs from October through June and features both classical and experimental works.

The Magic Theatre. Performing at Building D, Fort Mason Center, Marina Blvd. (at
Buchanan St.). ☎ **415/441-8822.** Tickets $15–$26. Discounts for students and seniors.

The highly acclaimed Magic Theatre continues to be a major West Coast company
dedicated to presenting the works of new playwrights; over the years it has nurtured
the talents of such luminaries as Sam Shepard and Jon Robin Baitz. Shepard's Pulitzer
Prize–winning play *Buried Child* premiered here. More recent productions have
included works by Athol Fugard, Claire Chafee, and Nilo Cruz. The season usually
runs from September through July; performances are offered Wednesday through
Sunday.

Philharmonia Baroque Orchestra. Performing in the Herbst Theatre, 401 Van Ness Ave.
☎ **415/392-4400** (box office). Tickets $29–$39.

Acclaimed by the *New York Times* as "the country's leading early-music orchestra,"
Philharmonia Baroque performs in San Francisco and all around the Bay Area. The
season lasts from September through April.

✪ **San Francisco Ballet.** Performances at War Memorial Opera House, 301 Van Ness
Ave. (at Grove St.). ☎ **415/865-2000.** Tickets $7–$100.

33, the San Francisco Ballet is the oldest professional ballet company
States and is regarded as one of the country's finest, performing an
pertoire of full-length, neoclassical, and contemporary ballets. Even the *New
mes* proclaimed, "The San Francisco Ballet under Helgi Tomasson's leadership
e of the spectacular success stories of the arts in America." The season runs from
ebruary through June.

San Francisco Opera. Performing at the newly refurbished War Memorial Opera House, 301 Van Ness Ave. (at Grove St.). ☎ **415/864-3330** (box office). Tickets $10–$140.

The San Francisco Opera was the first municipal opera in the United States, and is one of the city's cultural icons. All productions have English super-titles. The season starts in September and lasts just 14 weeks. Performances are held most evenings, except Monday, with matinees on Sundays. Tickets go on sale as early as June, and the best seats quickly sell out. Unless Pavarotti or Domingo is in town, some less-coveted seats are usually available until curtain time.

San Francisco Symphony. Performing at Davies Symphony Hall, 201 Van Ness Ave. (at Grove St.). ☎ **415/864-6000** (box office). Tickets $11–$73.

Founded in 1911, the internationally respected San Francisco Symphony has long been an important part of this city's cultural life under such legendary conductors as Pierre Monteux and Seiji Ozawa. In the last several years, Michael Tilson Thomas has already led the orchestra to new heights, crafting an exciting repertoire of classical and modern music. The season runs from September through June.

COMEDY & CABARET

○ **Beach Blanket Babylon.** At Club Fugazi, 678 Green St./Beach Blanket Babylon Blvd. (between Powell St. and Columbus Ave.). ☎ **415/421-4222.** Tickets $20–$50.

Now a San Francisco tradition, Beach Blanket Babylon is best known for its outrageous costumes and oversize headdresses. It's been playing almost 22 years now, and still almost every performance sells out. Those under 21 are welcome only at Sunday matinees, when no alcohol is served; photo ID is required for evening performances. It's wise to write for tickets at least 3 weeks in advance for weekend performances, or obtain them through Tix Bay Area (see above).

Cobb's Comedy Club. 2801 Beach St. (between Leavenworth and Hyde sts.). ☎ **415/ 928-4320.** Cover $5 Mon–Wed, $10–$13 Fri–Sat, $10 Thurs and Sun (plus a 2-beverage minimum nightly). Validated parking.

Located in the Cannery at Fisherman's Wharf, Cobb's features national headliners. There's comedy every night, including a 15-comedian All-Pro Monday showcase (a 3-hour marathon). Cobb's is open to those 18 and over, and occasionally to kids aged 16 and 17 if they are accompanied by a parent or legal guardian (call ahead first).

Finocchio's. 506 Broadway (at Kearny St.). ☎ **415/982-9388.** Cover $14.50 (no drink minimum, but guests must be 21 and over). Parking available next door at the Flying Dutchman.

For more than 50 years, this family-run cabaret club has showcased the best female impersonators in a funny, kitschy show. Three different revues are presented nightly (usually Thurs through Sat at 8:30, 10, and 11:30pm), and a single cover is good for the entire evening.

THE CLUB & MUSIC SCENE
ROCK & BLUES CLUBS

In addition to the following listings, see "Dance Clubs," below, for (usually) live, danceable rock.

Biscuits and Blues. 401 Mason St. (at Geary St.). ☎ **415/292-2583.** Cover are during performances; no cover during happy hour (Mon–Fri 5–7pm).

With a crisp, blow-your-eardrums-out sound system, a New Orleans–speakeasy (albeit commercial) appeal, and a nightly line-up of live entertainment, there's no better place to muse the blues than at this basement-cum-nightclub.

Blues. 2125 Lombard St. (at Fillmore St.). ☎ **415/771-BLUE.** Cover $3–$6.

This small, dark blues bar is packed most nights with an eclectic ethnic mix of mostly locals. The bands are usually pretty good and easy to dance to. Owner Max Young claims it's "the only real dark, dingy blues club in the city." Gotta love that.

The Fillmore. 1805 Geary Blvd. (at Fillmore St.). ☎ **415/346-6000.** Tickets $9–$25.

Reopened after years of neglect, the Fillmore, made famous by promoter Bill Graham in the 1960s, is once again attracting big names. Check the local listings in magazines or call the theater for information on upcoming events.

Slim's. 333 11th St. (at Folsom St.). ☎ **415/522-0333.** Cover free to $20 (plus a 2-drink minimum when seated at table).

Co-owned by musician Boz Scaggs, who sometimes takes the stage under the name "Presidio Slim," this glitzy restaurant/bar seats 300, serves California cuisine, and specializes in excellent American music—homegrown rock, jazz, blues, and alternative music—almost nightly. Menu items range from $3 to $8.50.

JAZZ & LATIN CLUBS

✪ **Cafe du Nord.** 2170 Market St. (at Sanchez St.). ☎ **415/861-5016.** Nominal cover varies.

Although it's been around since 1907, this basement-cum-supper-club has finally been recognized as a respectable jazz venue. With a younger generation now appreciating the music, the place is often packed from the 40-foot mahogany bar to the back room with a pool table. Du Nord is even putting out its own compilation CDs now, which are definitely worth purchasing.

Jazz at Pearl's. 256 Columbus Ave. (at Broadway). ☎ **415/291-8255.** No cover, but there's a 2-drink minimum. Valet parking $3.

This is one of the best venues for jazz in the city. Ribs and chicken are served with the sounds, too, with prices ranging from $4 to $8.95. The live jams last until 2am nightly.

Up & Down Club. 1151 Folsom St. (between Seventh and Eighth sts.). ☎ **415/626-2388.** Cover varies, usually $5–$10.

One of the original homes for SoMa's now-familiar new-jazz scene, the Up & Down jazz supper club attracts a trendy crowd to both its restaurant and dance floor. Dinner is at 8pm (reservations required), the music starts at 9:30pm, and dancing begins at 10pm.

DANCE CLUBS

Club Ten 15. 1015 Folsom St. (at Sixth St.). ☎ **415/431-1200.** Cover $5–$10.

Get decked out and plan for a late-nighter if you're headed to this enormous party warehouse. Three levels and dance floors offer a variety of settings for a 20- and 30-something gyrating mass who lives for the DJs' pounding house, disco, and acid jazz music. Each night is a different club that attracts its own crowd, ranging from yuppie to hip-hop.

60 Haight St. (between Fillmore and Webster sts.). ☎ **415/**

for dinner; the only hot thing you'll find is the small, crowded
n't let that stop you from checking it out. Nickie's is a sure thing.
here, the old-school disco hits are in full force, casually dressed
happy dan se all inhibitions, and the crowd is mixed with all types of friendly
San Franciscans. This place is perpetually hot, so dress accordingly.

Paradise Lounge. 1501 Folsom St. (at 11th St.). ☎ **415/861-6906.** Cover $3–$15.

Labyrinthine Paradise features three dance floors simultaneously vibrating to different
beats. Smaller, auxiliary spaces include a pool room with a half-dozen tables. Poetry
readings are also given.

SUPPER CLUBS

What exactly is a supper club? Well, if you can eat dinner, listen to live music, and
dance (or at least wiggle in your chair) in the same room, it's a supper club—that's our
criteria.

Coconut Grove Supper Club. 1415 Van Ness Ave. (between Bush and Pine sts.).
☎ **415/776-1616.** Cover $5 Tues–Thurs, $8 Fri–Sat.

Reopened in 1996 after being shunned for outrageous prices, the new—and far less
expensive—Coconut Grove Supper Club is doing a brisk business serving a Cali-
fornia/tropical/Cajun menu and live music to a mostly young, hip audience. Dancing
and chocolate martinis are the main attraction. The dress code is lax, but vintage is
definitely the main attire.

Harry Denton's Starlight Room. At the Sir Francis Drake Hotel, 450 Powell St., 21st floor.
☎ **415/395-8595.** Cover $5 Wed–Thurs after 7pm, $10 Fri–Sat after 8pm.

Come dressed to the nines or in casual attire to this old-fashioned cocktail
lounge/nightclub where tourists and locals sip drinks at sunset and boogie down to
live swing and big-band tunes after dark. The room is classic 1930s San Francisco,
with red-velvet banquettes, chandeliers, and fabulous views. But what really attracts
flocks of all ages is a night of Harry Denton–style fun, which usually includes plenty
of drinking and unrestrained dancing.

330 Ritch. 330 Ritch (between Third and Fourth sts. off Townsend). ☎ **415/541-9574,** or
415/522-9558 for recorded band information. Cover $3–$10.

If you can find the place, you must be cool. It's located on a 2-block alley in SoMa,
and even locals have a hard time remembering how to get here. But once you do,
expect happy-hour cocktails (specials on a few select mixed drinks and draft brews),
pool tables, and a hip, young crowd at play. Fridays, the place really livens up when
bands take center stage and the Latin lovers salsa all night to the spicy beat.

RETRO CLUBS

Bruno's. 2389 Mission St. (at 20th St.). ☎ **415/550-7455.** Cover $3–$7 after 9:30pm.

Before its recognition as a destination restaurant, Mission District hipsters were
already keen on this retro hot spot. Live music is played nightly in the back lounge,
and the long, 1950s-style full bar is almost always crowded with a mixture of wanna-
bes, the cool, and the curious. Appetizers and dessert are served until 1am.

Club Deluxe. 1511 Haight St. (at Ashbury St.). ☎ **415/552-6949.** Cover $4.

Before the recent 1940s trend hit the city, Deluxe and its fedora-wearing clientele
had been celebrating the bygone era for years. And fortunately, even with all the

retro-hype, the vibe here hasn't changed. Expect an eclectic mix of throw-backs and generic San Franciscans in the intimate, smoky bar and adjoining lounge, and live jazz or blues most nights. Although many regulars dress the part, there's no attitude here—so come as you like.

Hi-Ball Lounge. 473 Broadway (between Kearny and Montgomery). ☎ **415/397-9464.** Cover $3–$7.

Retro-jazz is in full swing in the city, and one of the most popular places to hear it—and dance to it—is at this North Beach joint. Harking back to Broadway at its best, the vibe is full-on forties and fifties, from the red banquettes and stage curtains to the small, dark, and smoky room. Live bands perform nightly to a young, swingin' crowd. There's also a swing dance class several nights a week, usually Monday through Thursday from 7 to 9pm (call ahead to confirm, however).

THE BAR SCENE

Albion. 3139 16th St. (between Valencia and Guerrero sts.). ☎ **415/552-8558.**

This Mission District club is a grit-and-leather in-crowd place packed with artistic types and SoMa hipsters. Live music plays Sunday between 5 and 8pm and ranges from ragtime and blues to jazz and swing.

Backflip. 601 Eddy St. (at Larkin St.). ☎ **415/771-FLIP.**

Adjoining the rock 'n' roll Phoenix Hotel, this shimmering aqua-blue cocktail lounge—designed to induce the illusion that you're carousing in the deep end—serves tapas and Caribbean-style appetizers to mostly young, fashionable types, so please don't order a cosmopolitan. On Thursdays the crowd seems to be young and gay/alternative; weekends, wanna-be-cool yuppies tend to pack the place.

Persian Aub Zam Zam. 1633 Haight St. (at Clayton St.). ☎ **415/861-2545.**

If you make it through the forbidding metal doors you'll feel as if you're in *Casablanca,* but the catch is that most people don't even get that far. The owner/bartender, Bruno, who has poured here for over 40 years, opens the place when he wants some company and arbitrarily chooses who's allowed to join him at the bar. If you meet his random requirements, play it safe and order a martini—a drink Bruno likes to serve (we've been banned for ordering a Coors Light).

The Red Room. 825 Sutter St. (at Jones St.). ☎ **415/346-7666.**

At one time the hottest cocktail lounge in town (though it's cooled off a bit), this ultramodern, Big Apple–style bar and lounge reflects no other spectrum but ruby red. Really, you gotta see this one.

Spec's. 12 Saroyan Place (off Columbus Ave.). ☎ **415/421-4112.**

Its incognito locale on Saroyan Place, a tiny alley at 250 Columbus Ave., makes Spec's less of a walk-in bar and more of a lively locals' hangout. Its funky decor—maritime flags that hang from the ceiling, exposed brick walls lined with posters, photos, and various oddities—gives it character that intrigues every visitor. A "museum," displayed under glass, contains memorabilia and items brought back by seamen who drop in between sails, and the clientele is funky enough to keep you preoccupied while you drink a beer.

Vesuvio. 255 Columbus Ave. (at Broadway). ☎ **415/362-3370.**

Situated along Jack Kerouac Alley across from the famed City Lights Bookstore, this renowned literary beatnik hangout isn't just riding its historic coattails. Popular with neighborhood writers, artists, songsters, and wanna-bes, Vesuvio is crowded with self-proclaimed philosophers, along with everyone else ranging from longshoremen and cab drivers to businesspeople.

BREW PUBS

Gordon-Biersch Brewery. 2 Harrison St. (on the Embarcadero). ☎ **415/243-8246.**

Popular with the young Republican crowd (loose ties and tight skirts predominate), this modern, two-tiered brewery and restaurant attracts a more upscale clientele than your typical beer garden. The food—beer-braised lamb shank, baby back ribs, lemon roasted half chicken—is pretty good, but it's the gourmet lagers and ales that account for the line out the door. *One caveat:* When the lower-level bar fills up, you practically have to shout to be heard.

San Francisco Brewing Company. 155 Columbus Ave. (at Pacific St.). ☎ **415/434-3344.** www.sfbrewing.com.

The bar is one of the city's few remaining old saloons, aglow with stained-glass windows, tile floors, skylit-ceiling beveled glass, a mahogany bar, and a massive overhead fan running the full length of the bar—a bizarre contraption crafted from brass and palm fronds. Menu items range from $3.25 to $16. The happy-hour special, a dollar per 10-ounce microbrewed beer (or $1.75 a pint), runs daily from 4 to 6pm and midnight to 1am.

Thirsty Bear Brewing Company. 661 Howard St. (1 block east of the Moscone Center). ☎ **415/974-0905.**

Seven superb, handcrafted varieties of brew, ranging from a fruit-flavored Strawberry Ale to a steak-in-a-cup stout, are always on tap at this stylish high-ceilinged brick edifice. Excellent Spanish food, too (see "Great Deals on Dining," earlier in this chapter, for a complete review). Pool tables and dartboards are upstairs, and live music (jazz, flamenco, blues, alternative, and classical) can be heard most nights.

20 Tank Brewery. 316 11th St. (at Folsom St.). ☎ **415/255-9455.**

Right in the heart of SoMa's popular strip, this huge, come-as-you-are bar is known for serving good beer at fair prices. Pizzas, sandwiches, chilies, and assorted appetizers are also available. Menu items range from $1.95 to $12.95. Pub games include darts, shuffleboard, and dice.

COCKTAILS WITH A VIEW

The Carnelian Room. 555 California St., in the Bank of America Building (between Kearny and Montgomery sts.). ☎ **415/433-7500.** Jacket and tie required for men.

On the 52nd floor of the Bank of America building, the Carnelian Room offers uninterrupted views of the city. From a window-front table you feel as if you can reach out, pluck up the TransAmerica Pyramid, and stir your martini with it. In addition to cocktails, "Discovery Dinners" are offered for $35 per person. *Note:* The restaurant has the most extensive wine list in the city—1,275 selections to be exact.

Cityscape. Atop Hilton Tower I, 333 O'Farrell St. (at Mason St.), 46th floor. ☎ **415/ 923-5002.**

When you sit under the glass roof and sip a drink here, it feels as though you're sitting out under the stars and enjoying views of the bay. There's nightly dancing to a DJ's picks from 10pm. The mirrored columns and floor-to-ceiling draperies help create an elegant and romantic ambiance.

Crown Room. In the Fairmont Hotel, 950 Mason St., 24th floor. ☎ **415/772**

Of all the bars listed here, the Crown Room is definitely the plushest. Reached by an external glass elevator, the panoramic view from the top will encourage you to linger. In addition to drinks (steep at $7 to $9), dinner buffets are served for $34.

Equinox. In the Hyatt Regency Hotel, 5 Embarcadero Center. ☎ **415/788-1234.**

The sales "hook" of the Hyatt's rooftop Equinox is a revolving floor that gives each table a 360° panoramic view of the city every 45 minutes. In addition to cocktails, dinner is served daily.

Harry Denton's Starlight Room. Atop the Sir Francis Drake Hotel, 450 Powell St., 21st floor. ☎ **415/395-8595.**

See "Supper Clubs," above, for a full review.

Top of the Mark. In the Mark Hopkins Intercontinental, 1 Nob Hill (California and Mason sts.). ☎ **415/616-6916.**

This is one of the most famous cocktail lounges in the world. During World War II, it was considered de rigueur for Pacific-bound servicemen to toast their good-byes to the States here. The spectacular glass-walled room features an unparalleled view. Live entertainment is offered at 8:30pm nightly, but there is a $6-to-$10 cover charge these nights, too. Drinks are also pricey, ranging from $6 to $8.

GAY & LESBIAN BARS & CLUBS

✪ **The Café.** 2367 Market St. (at Castro St.). ☎ **415/861-3846.**

When this place first got jumping, it was the only predominantly lesbian dance club on Saturday nights in the city. But once the guys found out how much fun the girls were having, they joined the party. Today it's still a very happening mixed gay and lesbian scene with two bars; a steamy, free-spirited dance floor; and a small patio.

The EndUp. 401 Sixth St. (at Harrison St.). ☎ **415/357-0827.** Cover varies.

It's a different nightclub every night of the week, but regardless of who's throwing the party, the place is always jumping with the DJ's blasting tunes. There are two pool tables, a flaming fireplace, outdoor patio, and a mob of gyrating souls on the dance floor. Some nights are straight, so call for gay nights.

The Stud. 399 Ninth St. (at Harrison St.). ☎ **415/863-6623.** Cover $2–$6 weekends.

The Stud has been around for 30 years, is one of the most successful gay establishments in town, and is mellow enough for straights as well as gays. The interior has an antique-shop look and a miniature train circling over the bar and dance floor. Music here is a balanced mix of old and new, and nights vary from cabaret and oldies to disco. Call in advance for the evening's venue. Drink prices range from $1.25 to $5.75.

Twin Peaks Tavern. 401 Castro St. (at 17th and Market sts.). ☎ **415/864-9470.** No cover.

Right at the intersection of Castro, 17th, and Market streets is one of the Castro's most famous gay hangouts, which caters to an older crowd and is considered the first gay bar in America. Because of its relatively small size and desirable location, the place becomes fairly crowded and convivial by 8pm, earlier than many neighboring bars.

FILM
REPERTORY CINEMAS

Castro Theatre. 429 Castro St. (near Market St.). ☎ **415/621-6120.**

Built in 1922, the beautiful Castro Theatre is known for its screenings of classic cinema and for its Wurlitzer organ, which is played before each show. There's a different feature here almost nightly, and more often than not it's a double feature. Bargain matinees are usually offered on Wednesday, Saturday, Sunday, and holidays. Phone for schedules, prices, and show times.

Red Vic. 1727 Haight St. (between Cole and Shrader sts.). ☎ **415/668-3994.** Tickets $6 adults, $3 seniors 65 and over and children 12 and under.

The worker-owned Red Vic movie collective recently moved from the Victorian building that gave it its name. The theater specializes in independent releases and contemporary cultish hits. Phone for schedules and show times.

Roxie. 3117 16th St. (at Valencia St.). ☎ **415/863-1087.**

The Roxie consistently screens the best new alternative films anywhere. The low-budget contemporary features shown here are largely devoid of Hollywood candy coating; many are West Coast premieres. Films change weekly, sometimes sooner. Phone for schedules, prices, and show times.

Side Trips from San Francisco

5

San Francisco

by Erika Lenkert and Matthew R. Poole

San Francisco may be one of the world's most captivating cities, but don't let it ensnare you to the point of ignoring its environs, which contain a multitude of natural spectacles such as **Mt. Tamalpais** and **Muir Woods;** scenic communities like **Tiburon** and **Sausalito;** and the bustling Bay Area cities **Oakland, Berkeley,** and **San Jose.**

At all of these destinations, most of the fun is either free or very inexpensive: Hiking will cost you no more than a parking pass, and strolling the shorelines and boutique-filled streets doesn't cost a thing (until you slap down your credit card for a bay-side lunch or a special take-home memento). From San Francisco, you can reach any of these points in a few hours or less by car or public transport, and we've scouted out some inexpensive accommodations and dining options for you.

1 Berkeley

10 miles NE of San Francisco

Berkeley would be little more than a sleepy town east of the big city if it weren't for the University of California at Berkeley, which is world-renowned for its first-rate academic standards, 16 Nobel Prize winners, and, of course, the notorious protests that led to the most renowned student riots in U.S. history. Today, there's still hippie idealism in the air, but the radicals have aged; the '60s are only present in tie-dye and paraphernalia shops (which are rapidly being taken over by national chains along Telegraph Avenue), and the students suffer from less angst. The most evident change in recent years is due to the young professionals who are moving into the area to avoid San Francisco's absurdly high housing costs. Still, it's an entertaining town with all types of people, a beautiful campus, vast parks, and some incredible restaurants.

ESSENTIALS

GETTING THERE   The Berkeley **BART** station is 2 blocks from the university. The fare from San Francisco is less than $3. Call BART at ☎ **510/793-2278.**

If you're driving from San Francisco, take I-80 east to the University Avenue exit. Count on walking some distance, because you won't find a parking spot near the university.

VISITOR INFORMATION The **Berkeley Convention and Visitors Bureau,** 2015 Center St., Berkeley, CA 94703 (☎ 800/847-4823 or 510/549-7040), can answer your questions and even find accommodations for you. Call the **Visitor Hotline** (☎ 510/549-8710) for information on events and happenings in Berkeley.

EXPLORING THE UNIVERSITY & ENVIRONS

Hanging out is the preferred Berkeley pastime, and the best place to do it is on **Telegraph Avenue,** the street that leads to the campus's southern entrance. Most of the action lies between Bancroft Way and Ashby Avenue, where coffeehouses, restaurants, shops, great book and record stores, and craft booths swarm with life.

Pretend you're local: Plant yourself at a cafe, sip a latte, and ponder something intellectual while you survey the town's unique population bustling by. Bibliophiles must stop at **Cody's Books,** 2454 Telegraph Ave. (☎ 510/845-7852), to peruse its gargantuan selection of titles, independent-press books, and magazines.

UC Berkeley itself is worth a stroll as well. It's a beautiful old campus with plenty of woodsy paths, architecturally noteworthy buildings, and 31,000 students scurrying to and from classes. Among the architectural highlights of the campus are a number of buildings by Bernard Maybeck, Brown and Bakewell, and John Galen Howard. Contact the **Visitor Information Center** at 101 University Hall, 2200 University Ave., at Oxford Street (☎ 510/642-5215), to join a free, regularly scheduled campus tour (Mon through Sat at 10am; no tours offered from mid-Dec to mid-Jan); or stop by the office and pick up a self-guided walking-tour brochure. If you're interested in notable off-campus buildings, contact the **Berkeley Convention and Visitors Bureau** at ☎ 510/549-7040 for an architectural walking-tour brochure.

You'll find the university's southern entrance at the northern end of Telegraph Avenue, at Bancroft Way. Walk through the main entrance into **Sproul Plaza.** When school is in session, you'll encounter the gamut of Berkeley's inhabitants here as well as the **Student Union,** complete with a bookstore, cafes, and information desk on the second floor, where you can pick up a free map of Berkeley along with the local student newspaper (also found in dispensers throughout campus).

You might be lucky enough to stumble upon some impromptu musicians or a heated—and sometimes absurd—debate. There's always something going on, so stretch out on the grass for a few minutes and take in the Berkeley vibe.

For viewing more traditional art forms, there are some noteworthy museums here, too. The **Lawrence Hall of Science,** Centennial Drive near Grizzly Peak (☎ 510/642-5132), offering hands-on science exploration, is open daily from 10am to 5pm and is also a wonderful place to watch the sunset. Admission is $6 for adults, $4 for seniors and children 7 to 18, and $2 for children 3 to 6. The **University Art Museum,** 2626 Bancroft Way (☎ 510/642-0808), is open Friday through Sunday and Wednesday from 11am to 5pm, Thursday from 11am to 9pm. Admission is $6 for adults, $4 for seniors and children 12 to 17. This museum includes a substantial collection of Hans Hofmann paintings, a sculpture garden, and the Pacific Film Archive, at 2625 Durant Ave. (☎ 510/642-1124).

OFF-CAMPUS ATTRACTIONS

PARKS Unbeknownst to many travelers, Berkeley has some of the most extensive and beautiful parks around. If you enjoy hiking, getting a breath of California air and sniffing a few roses, or just want to wear out the kids, jump in your car and make your way to **Tilden Park** (☎ 510/843-2137), where you'll find plenty of flora and fauna, hiking trails, an old steam train and merry-go-round, a farm and nature area for kids, and a chilly tree-encircled lake. On the way, stop at the colorful terraced **Rose**

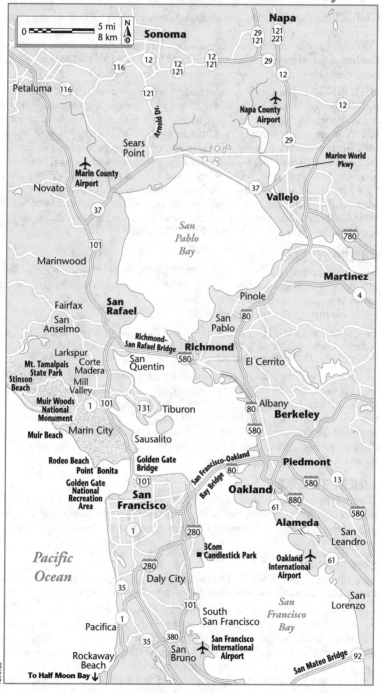

0   5 mi
    8 km

N

Sonoma

Napa

29 121   121 221

12 121   12 121   29

116

Petaluma   116

121

Arnold Dr.

12

Napa County Airport

12

29

Sears Point

Marine World Pkwy

Marin County Airport

37

Vallejo

Novato

37

780

Marinwood

101

San Pablo Bay

Martinez

4

Fairfax

San Rafael

Pinole

San Pablo

80

San Anselmo

Larkspur

Richmond– San Rafael Bridge

Richmond

El Cerrito

580

Mt. Tamalpais State Park

Corte Madera

San Quentin

Stinson Beach

Mill Valley

131

Tiburon

80

Albany

Muir Woods National Monument

1   101

Berkeley

580

Muir Beach

Marin City

Sausalito

Rodeo Beach

Point Bonita

Golden Gate Bridge

San Francisco–Oakland Bay Bridge

80

Piedmont

580

13

Golden Gate National Recreation Area

101

San Francisco

Oakland

880

61

Pacific Ocean

1

280

3Com Candlestick Park

Alameda

San Leandro

580

280

Daly City

Oakland International Airport

61

35

101

South San Francisco

San Francisco Bay

San Lorenzo

Pacifica

1

35

380

San Bruno

San Francisco International Airport

San Mateo Bridge

92

Rockaway Beach

To Half Moon Bay ↓

NA-0188

137

Garden, located in north Berkeley on Euclid Avenue between Bay View and Eunice Street.

Another worthy nature excursion is the **University of California Botanical Garden,** in Strawberry Canyon on Centennial Drive (☎ **510/642-3343**), which features a vast collection of herbage ranging from cacti to redwoods.

SHOPPING   If you're itching to exercise your credit cards, head to one of two places. **College Avenue** from Dwight all the way down to the Oakland border is crammed with eclectic boutiques, antique shops, and restaurants. The other option is **Fourth Street** in west Berkeley, just 2 blocks north of the University Avenue exit off I-80, where you can grab a cup of java, read the paper at a patio table, and then hit the **Crate and Barrel Outlet** (where prices are 30% to 70% off retail). The outlet is located at 1785 Fourth St., between Hearst and Virginia (☎ **510/528-5500**), and is open Monday through Saturday from 10am to 6pm and Sunday from 11am to 6pm. Many of the small, wonderful stores here are crammed with imported and locally made housewares. Nearby is **REI,** the Bay Area's favorite outdoor outfitters, at 1338 San Pablo Ave., near Gilman Street (☎ **510/527-4140**).

WHERE TO STAY

Bed-and-Breakfast California (☎ **800/872-4500** or 650/696-1690; fax 650/696-1699; www.bbintl.com; e-mail: info@bbintl.com), books visitors into private homes and apartments in the Berkeley area. The cost ranges from $70 to $250 per night, and there's a 2-night minimum.

✪ **Golden Bear Motel.** 1620 San Pablo Ave. (between University and Cedar sts.), Berkeley, CA 94702. ☎ **800/525-6770** or 510/525-6770. 42 units. TV TEL. $54–$64 double; $120–$135 cottage. Pets accepted ($5 1-time fee). AE, DC, DISC, MC, V.

The price is right, the rooms are surprisingly attractive and clean, and the staff is congenial at this comfortable, 1950s Spanish-style motor lodge near Cafe Fanny and the hip Fourth Street shops. Each recently renovated room comes with either a queen or two twin beds, a dresser, a nightstand, and a desk. For a few extra dollars you can opt for one of the three cottages, which are perfect for families and have two bedrooms, a living room, and a full kitchen. Guests also enjoy free local calls and voice mail. All in all, an excellent deal.

WHERE TO DINE

Telegraph Avenue has an array of small ethnic restaurants that are priced for student business (that means super-cheap). Walk along, read the posted menus, and take your pick—keep in mind that a crowded restaurant hints that the fare is either especially good or dirt cheap.

SUPER-CHEAP EATS

Blue Nile. 2525 Telegraph Ave. ☎ **510/540-6777.** Reservations required Fri–Sat. Main courses $7.50–$8.95. MC, V. Tues–Sat 11:30am–10pm; Sun 5–10pm. ETHIOPIAN.

Step through the beaded curtains into the Blue Nile, and the African paintings and music will summon your appetite to other parts of the world. But the journey doesn't end there—be prepared to savor the flavorful specialties such as *doro wat* (a spiced stew of beef, lamb, or chicken, served with a fluffy crepe called *injera*) or *gomen wat* (mustard greens sautéed in cream) with no utensils other than your fingers. Sure, you could convince the wait staff to drum up a fork or two, but don't bother. After all, when in Africa . . . No appetizers are served, but meals come with a small salad.

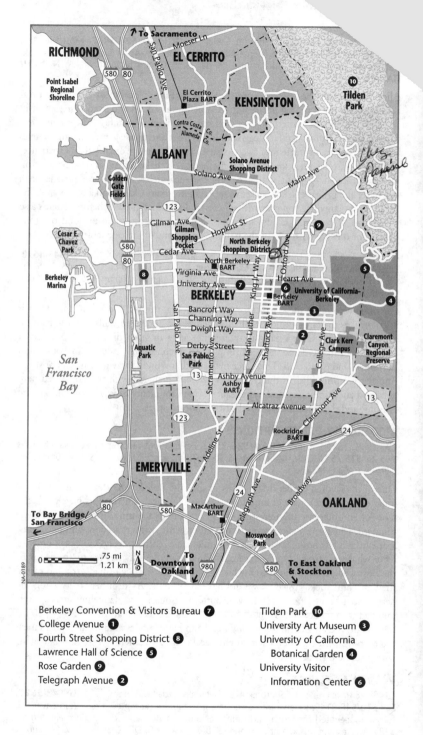

RICHMOND

To Sacramento

Moeser Ln

EL CERRITO

Point Isabel
Regional
Shoreline

El Cerrito
Plaza BART

KENSINGTON

Tilden
Park **10**

Contra Costa Co.
Alameda Co.

ALBANY

Solano Avenue
Shopping District

Marin Ave

Golden
Gate
Fields

Solano Ave

Cesar E.
Chavez
Park

Gilman Ave.
Gilman
Shopping
Pocket
Cedar Ave.

Hopkins St

North Berkeley
Shopping District

Oxford Ave

Rose Garden **9**

Berkeley
Marina

8

Virginia Ave.

North Berkeley
BART

University Ave. **7**

Hearst Ave

University of California–
Berkeley

Berkeley
BART **6**

5

Lawrence Hall of Science

BERKELEY

Bancroft Way
Channing Way
Dwight Way

King Jr. Way

Martin Luther

Shattuck Ave

3

University Art Museum

4

University of California
Botanical Garden

Aquatic
Park

San Pablo Ave

Derby Street
San Pablo
Park

Sacramento Ave

2

College Ave

Clark Kerr
Campus

Claremont
Canyon
Regional
Preserve

San
Francisco
Bay

13

Ashby Avenue
Ashby
BART

Alcatraz Avenue

1

Claremont Ave

13

123

Adeline St

Rockridge
BART

24

EMERYVILLE

24

Telegraph Ave

Broadway

OAKLAND

To Bay Bridge/
San Francisco
←

80

580

MacArthur
BART

Mosswood
Park

To
Downtown
Oakland

980

To East Oakland
& Stockton

0 .75 mi
1.21 km
N

NA-0189

Berkeley Convention & Visitors Bureau **7**
College Avenue **1**
Fourth Street Shopping District **8**
Lawrence Hall of Science **5**
Rose Garden **9**
Telegraph Avenue **2**

Tilden Park **10**
University Art Museum **3**
University of California
   Botanical Garden **4**
University Visitor
   Information Center **6**

San Pablo (at Cedar St.). ☎ **510/524-5447.** Most breakf[...]
MC, V. Mon–Fri 7am–3pm; Sat 8am–4pm; Sun 8am–3pm. Bre[...]
[...]m Mon–Sat and all day Sun. Closed major holidays. FRENC[...]

[...]hez Panisse fame) cafe is one of those local must-do breakfast traditions. Gr[...] morning paper, put on your Birkenstocks, and head here to wait in
line for a simple but masterfully prepared stand-up French breakfast. The menu offers
such items as a soft-boiled farm egg with levain toast and house jam, buckwheat crepes
with jam, and an assortment of sweet pastries. Lunch is more of an Italian experience,
featuring seasonal selections. Sandwiches, such as baked ham and watercress on
focaccia; roasted eggplant with red peppers, mozzarella, aioli, and tapenade on a
baguette; and grilled chicken breast wrapped in prosciutto, sage, and aioli on an Acme
bread might convince you that you've never really had a sandwich before. There's also
a selection of pizzettas, salads, and soup. Eat inside at the stand-up food bar (one
bench), or outside (virtually in the parking lot) at one of the cafe tables.

Cambodiana's. 2156 University Ave. (between Shattuck and Oxford). ☎ **510/843-4630.**
Reservations recommended Fri–Sat. Main courses $7.50–$13; fixed-price dinner $11.25. AE,
CB, DC, JCB, MC, V. Mon–Fri 11:30am–3pm; Sun–Thurs 5–9:30pm; Fri–Sat 5–10:30pm.
CAMBODIAN.

For those who relish the spicy cuisine of Cambodia, this is quite a find. The decor is
as colorful as the fare—amidst brilliant blue, yellow, and green walls, you can feast on
a variety of dishes. Especially tasty are the curry or *naga* dishes with a sauce of
tamarind, turmeric, lemongrass, shrimp paste, coconut-milk galinga, shallot, lemon
leaf, sugar, and green chili. This sauce may smother salmon, prawns, chicken, or steak.
Another tempting dish is the chicken *chaktomuk* prepared with pineapple, red peppers, and zucchini in soy and oyster sauce. There are plenty of vegetarian and low-cal
options, and the three-course, fixed-price dinner is an excellent value.

MODERATELY PRICED OPTIONS

✪ **Rivoli.** 1539 Solano. ☎ **510/526-2542.** Reservations recommended. Main courses
$10.25–$15.75. MC, V. Mon–Thurs 5:30–9:30pm; Fri 5:30–10pm; Sat 5–10pm; Sun
5–9pm. CALIFORNIA.

One of the favored dinner destinations in the East Bay, Rivoli offers a winning combination: top-notch food at amazingly reasonable prices. The owners have made the
most of an otherwise uninteresting space by creating a warm, intimate dining environment, which overlooks a sweet little garden with visiting raccoons and opossums.
Aside from a few house favorites, the menu changes entirely every 3 weeks in order to
serve whatever's freshest and in season. While many love it, we weren't thrilled with
the portobello-mushroom fritter, which in our mind was a glorified variation of the
fried zucchini stick. However, we did have an absolute A+ dish here (very rare): the
hearty oven braised pork ragout with butternut squash and dandelion greens inter-
mingled with tender and crispy semolina gnocchi. Perfection at this price ($13.50 for
the ragout) is enough to put most high-end San Francisco restaurants to shame. Finish
the evening with the Meyer lemon cheesecake; it's a decadent sour-cream-like affair
with a subtle pistachio crust.

WORTH A SPLURGE

✪ **Chez Panisse.** 1517 Shattuck Ave. (between Cedar and Vine). ☎ **510/548-5525.**
Fax 510/548-0140. Reservations essential for restaurant (accepted a month in advance);
for cafe, accepted for lunch and dinner at 9am on the same day. Cafe main courses
$13–$18; restaurant fixed-price dinner $38–$68. AE, CB, DC, DISC, MC, V. Restaurant
dinner seatings Mon–Sat at 6–6:30pm and 8:30–9:15pm. Cafe Mon–Thurs

11:30am–3pm and 5–10:30pm; Fri–Sat 11:30am–4pm and 5–11:30pm. BART: Berkeley. From I-80 N., take the University exit and turn left onto Shattuck Ave. CALIFORNIA.

There's nothing remotely budget about this restaurant, but any true foodie must pay homage to Alice Waters, the mother of California cuisine. You can either put your conscience (and your budget) aside and book in the main dining room, or go for the more affordable choice: the cafe. In the dining room, the menu is fixed (it's cheaper and simpler earlier in the week, more expensive and extensive later in the week and on weekends). In the cafe, you order à la carte, enjoy equally fantastic fare, and will save a few bucks if you don't go overboard on appetizers, wine, and dessert.

The downstairs restaurant and the upstairs cafe both serve Mediterranean-inspired cuisine, most of which is made with organic produce and meat from local farms. The cafe has displays of pastries and fruit, and large bouquets of fresh flowers adorning an oak bar. At lunch or dinner you might find a delicately smoked gravlax or a roasted-eggplant soup with pesto, followed by lamb ragout garnished with apricots, onions, and spices served with couscous. Dinner reservations are not taken for the cafe, so there will be a wait, but it's worth it.

The cozy downstairs restaurant, strewn with blossoming floral bouquets, is an appropriately warm environment to indulge in the ultimate gourmet dinner, which changes daily, and is still regarded as ovation-worthy after all these years. Meals are complemented by an excellent wine list ($20 to $200).

2 Oakland

10 miles E of San Francisco

Though it's less than a dozen miles from San Francisco, Oakland is worlds apart from its sibling across the bay. Originally little more than a cluster of ranches and farms, Oakland exploded practically overnight in size and stature as the last mile of transcontinental railroad track was laid down. Major shipping ports soon followed, and to this day Oakland has retained its hold as one of the busiest industrial ports on the West Coast.

The price for all this economic success, however, is Oakland's reputation for being predominantly a working-class city, forever in the shadow of San Francisco's Euro-chic spotlight. Even the city's NFL football team, the Oakland Raiders, has a proud and longstanding reputation for being mean, tough, and dirty (a cherished antithesis to their mortal enemy, the golden-boy 49ers). But with all its shortcomings and bad press, Oakland still manages to keep a few pleasant surprises up its sleeve for the handful of tourists who venture this way. Rent a sailboat on Lake Merritt, stroll along the waterfront, explore the fantastic Oakland Museum—they're all great reasons to hop the bay and spend a fog-free day exploring one of California's largest and most ethnically diverse cities.

ESSENTIALS

GETTING THERE **Bay Area Rapid Transit (BART)** makes the trip from San Francisco to Oakland through one of the longest underwater transit tunnels in the world. Fares range from $1 to $4, depending on your station of origin; children 4 and under ride free. BART trains operate Monday through Friday from 4am to midnight, Saturday from 6am to midnight, and Sunday from 8am to midnight. Exit at the **12th Street station** for downtown Oakland.

If you're driving from San Francisco, take I-80 across the San Francisco–Oakland Bay Bridge and follow the signs to downtown Oakland. Exit at Grand Avenue South for the Lake Merritt area.

CITY LAYOUT   Downtown Oakland is bordered by Grand Avenue on the north, I-980 on the west, Inner Harbor on the south, and Lake Merritt on the east. Between these landmarks are three BART stations (12th Street, 19th Street, and Lake Merritt), City Hall, the Oakland Museum, Jack London Square, and several other sights.

EXPLORING OAKLAND

Lake Merritt is Oakland's primary tourist attraction along with Jack London Square (see below). Three and a half miles in circumference, the tidal lagoon was bridged and dammed in the 1860s and is now a wildlife refuge that's home to flocks of migrating ducks, herons, and geese. It's surrounded on three sides by the 122-acre **Lakeside Park,** a popular place to picnic, feed the ducks, and escape the fog. At the **Sailboat House** (☎ 510/444-3807), in Lakeside Park along the north shore, you can rent sailboats, rowboats, pedal boats, and canoes for $6 to $12 per hour.

Another site worth visiting is Oakland's **Paramount Theatre** (☎ 510/893-2300), an outstanding example of art-deco architecture and decor. Built in 1931 and authentically restored in 1973, it now functions as the city's main performing-arts center. Guided tours of the 3,000-seat theater are given the 1st and 3rd Saturdays of each month, excluding holidays. No reservations are necessary; just show up at 10am at the box office entrance on 21st Street at Broadway. Cameras are allowed, and admission is $1.

If you take pleasure from strolling around sailboat-filled wharves or are a die-hard fan of Jack London, you might actually enjoy a visit to **Jack London Square,** at Broadway and Embarcadero. Oakland's only patent tourist area, this low-key version of San Francisco's Fisherman's Wharf shamelessly plays up the fact that Jack London spent most of his youth along this waterfront. The square fronts the harbor, housing a tourist-tacky complex of boutiques and eateries that are about as far away from the "call of the wild" as you can get. Most are open Monday through Saturday from 10am to 9pm (some restaurants stay open later). In the center of the square is a small, reconstructed version of the Yukon cabin in which Jack London lived while prospecting in the Klondike during the gold rush of 1897.

In the middle of Jack London Square you'll find a more authentic memorial, **Heinold's First and Last Chance Saloon**—a funky, friendly little bar and historic landmark that's actually worth a visit. This is where London did some of his writing and most of his drinking; the corner table he used has remained exactly as it was nearly a century ago. Also in the square are the mast and nameplate from the **USS** *Oakland,* a ship that saw extensive action in the Pacific during World War II, and a wonderful museum filled with interesting London memorabilia.

To find the square, take I-880 to Broadway, turn south, and go to the end. From the BART 12th Street station, walk south along Broadway (about half a mile) or take bus no. 51a to the foot of Broadway.

The USS *Potomac.* At FDR Pier, Jack London Sq. ☎ **510/839-8256.** Admission $3 adults, $2 seniors, $1 children ages 6–17, free for children 5 and under, $5 for families with children under 18. Dockside tours available Apr–Oct on Wed and Fri 10am–2pm; Sun 11am–3pm. Nov–Mar on Sun 11am–3pm. Hours and days open are subject to change, so be sure to call the 24-hr. information line. Tickets can be purchased in advance by calling the Potomac Association office (☎ **510/839-7533,** ext. 1).

It took the Potomac Association's hundreds of volunteers more than 12 years—at a cost of $5 million dollars—to restore the 165-foot presidential yacht *Potomac,* President Franklin D. Roosevelt's beloved "Floating White House." Now a proud and permanent memorial berthed at the Port of Oakland's FDR Pier at Jack London Square, the revitalized *Potomac* is open to the public for dockside tours, as well as 2-hour public education cruises along the San Francisco waterfront and around Treasure Island. Prior to departure, a 15-minute video, shown at the nearby Potomac Visitor Center, provides background on FDR's presidency and FDR's legacy concerning the Bay Area.

Due to the popularity of the cruises, advance purchase is strongly recommended. The **Potomac Visitor Center** is located at 540 Water St., at the corner of Clay and Water streets adjacent to the FDR pier at the north end of Jack London Square.

Oakland Museum of California. 1000 Oak St. ☎ **510/238-3401,** or 510/238-2200 for recorded information. Admission $8 adults, $6 students and seniors, free for children 5 and under; $3 for everyone 1st Sun of each month. Wed–Sat 10am–5pm; Sun noon–7pm. Closed New Year's Day, July 4, Thanksgiving, and Christmas. BART: Lake Merritt station (1 block south of the museum). From I-880 N., take the Oak St. exit; the museum is 5 blocks east at Oak and 10th sts. Alternatively, take I-580 to I-980 and exit at the Jackson St. ramp.

Located 2 blocks south of the lake, this museum includes just about everything you'd want to know about the state, its people, history, culture, geology, art, environment, and ecology. Inside a low-swept, modern building set down among sweeping gardens and terraces, it's actually three museums in one: exhibitions of works by California artists from Bierstadt to Diebenkorn; collections of artifacts from California's history, from Pomo Indian basketry to Country Joe McDonald's guitar; and re-creations of California habitats from the coast to the White Mountains. The museum holds major shows of California artists, like the recent exhibit of the work of ceramic sculptor Peter Voulkos, or shows dedicated to major California movements, such as arts and crafts from 1890 to 1930. There are 45-minute guided tours leaving the gallery information desks on request or by appointment. There is a fine cafe, a gallery (☎ **510/834-2329**) selling works by California artists, and a book-and-gift shop. The cafe is open Wednesday through Saturday from 10am to 4pm and Sunday from noon to 5pm.

WHERE TO DINE
SUPER-CHEAP EATS

Barney's Gourmet Hamburgers. 4162 Piedmont Ave. (at Pleasant Hill Rd.). ☎ **510/655-7180.** Main courses $4–$7. No credit cards. Mon–Thurs 11am–9:30pm; Fri 11am–10pm; Sat–Sun 10am–10pm. HAMBURGERS.

If you're like us and on a perpetual quest for the best burger in America, a mandatory stop is Barney's Gourmet Hamburgers in Oakland. Beneath a replica of Michelangelo's Sistine Chapel you have a mind-boggling 21 burgers to choose from, any of which can have the beef patty replaced with a chicken breast (at least a dozen are offered with tofu patties, too). The ultimate combo is a humongous basket of fries (enough for a party of three), a one-third-pound burger, and a thick shake. Popular versions are the California Burger with jack cheese, bacon, ortega chilies, and sour cream, or the Popeye Burger made with chicken, sautéed spinach, and feta cheese. You can even dine alfresco in the Roman-style courtyard in back, complete with a fountain and trees.

✪ **Caffe 817.** 817 Washington St. (between Eighth and Ninth sts.). ☎ **510/271-7965.** Main courses $5–$7.50. AE, MC, V. Mon–Fri 7:30am–5pm; Sat 9:30am–4pm. ITALIAN.

After a career as an electrical engineer, Alessandro Rossi decided to go into the restaurant business, and Oakland residents have been ever-so-grateful for his decision. Rossi hired local craftspeople to fashion the avant-garde furnishings for his high-ceilinged space, yet despite its fashionable decor, the menu is very modestly priced (particularly considering the quality of ingredients, all of which are organically grown). Pastries and cappuccino are the mainstays in the morning, and simple salads, Italian sandwiches (favorites are the grilled mozzarella with artichokes and prosciutto with herb butter and pears), and freshly made soups and stews are on the midday menu. Trust us, you'll love this place.

A MODERATELY PRICED OPTION

Citron. 5484 College Ave. (off the northeastern end of Broadway between Taft and Lawton sts.). ☎ **510/653-5484.** Main courses $12–$18. MC, V. Sun–Tues 5–9pm; Wed–Thurs 5:30–9:30pm; Fri–Sat 5:30–10pm. FRENCH/MEDITERRANEAN.

This petite, adorable French bistro was an instant smash when it first opened in 1992, and it continues to draw raves for its small yet enticingly eclectic menu. Chef Chris Rossi draws the flavors of France, Italy, and Spain together with fresh California produce for Chez Panisse–like results. Though the menu changes every few weeks, dishes range from grilled Colorado lamb sirloin with wild-mushroom spoon bread and rosemary jus, to osso buco of lamb on a bed of flageolet bean and sun-dried tomato ragout and sprinkled with a pistachio gremolata garnish. The fresh salads and Citron "40-clove" chicken are also superb.

3 Sausalito

5 miles N of San Francisco

Just off the northern end of the Golden Gate Bridge is the eclectic little town of Sausalito, a slightly bohemian, nonchalant, and studiedly quaint adjunct to San Francisco. With approximately 7,500 residents, Sausalito feels rather like St. Tropez on the French Riviera—minus the starlets and the social rat race. It has its quota of paper millionaires, but they rub their permanently suntanned shoulders with a good number of hard-up artists, struggling authors, shipyard workers, and fishers. Next to the swank restaurants, plush bars, and antique shops and galleries, you'll see hamburger joints, beer parlors, and secondhand bookstores.

Above all, Sausalito has scenery and sunshine, for once you cross the Golden Gate Bridge—or disembark from the ferry, the preferred way to arrive—you're out of the San Francisco fog patch and under blue California sky (we hope). Almost all the tourist action, which is basically limited to window-shopping and eating, takes place at sea level on Bridgeway.

GETTING THERE

The **Golden Gate Ferry Service** fleet, Ferry Building (☎ **415/923-2000**), operates between the San Francisco Ferry Building (at the foot of Market Street) and downtown Sausalito. Service is frequent, departing at reasonable intervals every day of the year except New Year's Day, Thanksgiving Day, and Christmas Day. Phone for exact schedule. The ride takes a half hour; one-way fares are $4.25 for adults and $3.20 for kids 6 to 12. Seniors and passengers with disabilities ride for $2.10; children 5 and under ride free. Family rates are also available.

Ferries of the **Blue & Gold Fleet** (☎ **415/773-1188** for recorded info; ☎ 415/705-5555 for tickets) leave from Pier 41 and cost $11 round-trip, half price for kids 5 to 11, and free for children under 5. Boats run on a seasonal schedule; phone for departure information.

If you're driving from San Francisco, take U.S. 101 north, then the first right after the Golden Gate Bridge (Alexander exit). Alexander becomes Bridgeway in Sausalito.

Sausalito's Cheap Eats

Sausalito may be one of the most expensive places to live in the United States, but that doesn't mean you have a to pay a fortune for good food. One of our favorite things to do in Sausalito is grab a bite to go at any of the cafes listed below and have a picnic in the park fronting the marina. It's a great way to bypass the long wait (and steep prices) at the big bay-side restaurants.

Caledonia Kitchen, 400 Caledonia St. (☎ **415/331-0220**), is the sort of place you wish you had just around the corner from your house—a beautiful little cafe serving a huge assortment of fresh salads, soups, chili, gourmet sandwiches, and inexpensive entrees like herbed roast chicken or vegetarian lasagna for only $4.95. Continental-style breakfast items and good coffee and espresso drinks are also on the menu.

Like the name says, the specialty at tiny, narrow **Hamburgers,** 737 Bridgeway (☎ **415/332-9471**), is juicy flame-broiled burgers, arguably Marin County's best. Look for the rotating grill in the window off Bridgeway, then stand in line and salivate with the rest of the crowd. Chicken burgers are a slightly healthier option. Order a side of fries, grab a bunch of napkins, then head over to the park across the street.

You can get anything at **The Stuffed Croissant,** 43 Caledonia St. (☎ **415/ 332-7103**), from a snack to a meal. There are all sorts of gourmet stuffed croissants, plus bagels, soups, and stews. Hot, cheap meals such as chicken curry with rice are also popular. For dessert there's carrot cake, fudge, peanut brownies, and more.

Small, clean, cute, and cheap, **Café Soleil,** 37 Caledonia St. (☎ **415/ 331-9355**), whips up some good soups, salads, and sandwiches along with killer smoothies. Order to go at the counter, then take your goods a block over to the marina for a dockside lunch.

EXPLORING THE TOWN

Sausalito's main touring strip is **Bridgeway,** which runs along the water, but those in the know make a quick detour to **Caledonia Street** a block inland. Not only is it less congested, but there's also a far better selection of cafes and shops.

Bay Model Visitors Center. 2100 Bridgeway. ☎ **415/332-3871.** Free admission. Winter Tues–Sat 9am–4pm. Summer Tues–Fri 9am–4pm; Sat–Sun 10am–6pm.

The U.S. Army Corps of Engineers uses this high-tech, 1½-acre model of San Francisco's bay and delta to resolve problems and observe what impact any changes in water flow will have. The model indicates trends in sediment movement and reproduces (in scale) the rise and fall of tides, the flows and currents of water, and the mixing of fresh- and saltwater. A tour and a 10-minute film explain it all, but the most interesting time to visit is when it's actually being used, so call ahead.

SHOPPING

Sausalito is a mecca for shoppers seeking handmade, original, and offbeat clothes and footwear, as well as arts and crafts. The town's best shops are found in the alleys, malls, and second-floor boutiques reached by steep, narrow staircases on and off Bridgeway. Additional shops are found on Caledonia Street, which runs parallel to and 1 block inland from Bridgeway.

Village Fair, at 777 Bridgeway, is Sausalito's closest approximation to a mall. It's a complex of 30 shops, souvenir stores, coffee bars, and gardens. Among them, **Quest Gallery** (☎ 415/332-6832) features fine ceramics, functional art, contemporary glass, hand-painted silks, woven clothing, art jewelry, and graphics. The shop specializes in celebrated California artists, many of whom sell exclusively through this store. The complex is open daily from 10am to 6pm; restaurants stay open later.

Burlwood Gallery, 721 Bridgeway (☎ 415/332-6550), sells one-of-a-kind red-wood furniture plus fine jewelry, handblown glass, and other interesting gifts. **Pegasus Leather Company,** 28 Princess St., off Bridgeway (☎ 415/332-5624), specializes in beautiful leather clothing and accessories. The **Sausalito Country Store,** 789 Bridgeway (☎ 415/332-7890), sells oodles of handmade, country-style goods for the home and garden, many by local artists and artisans.

WHERE TO DINE

Horizons. 558 Bridgeway. ☎ **415/331-3232.** Reservations accepted weekdays only. Main courses $9–$21; salads and sandwiches $6–$11. AE, MC, V. Mon–Fri 11am–11pm; Sat–Sun 10am–11pm. 1 hr. free valet parking. SEAFOOD/AMERICAN.

Eventually, every San Franciscan ends up at Horizons to meet a friend for Sunday Bloody Marys. It's not much to look at from the outside, but it gets better as you head past the funky dark-wood interior toward the waterside terrace. On warm days it's worth the wait for alfresco seating, if only to watch dreamy sailboats glide past San Francisco's distant skyline. The food here can't touch the view, but it's well portioned and satisfying enough. Seafood dishes are the main items, including steamed clams and mussels, freshly shucked oysters, and a variety of seafood pastas. In fine Marin tradition, Horizons also has an "herb tea and espresso" bar.

4 Angel Island & Tiburon

8 miles N of San Francisco

A federal and state wildlife refuge, **Angel Island** is the largest of the San Francisco Bay's three islets (the others being Alcatraz and Yerba Buena). The island has been, at various times, a prison, a quarantine station for immigrants, a missile base, and even a favorite site for duels. Nowadays, though, most of the people who visit here are content with picnicking on the large green lawn that fronts the docking area—loaded with the appropriate recreational supplies, these picnickers claim a barbecue, plop their fannies down on the lush green grass, and while away an afternoon free of phones, televisions, and traffic. Hiking, mountain biking, and guided tram tours are also popular options.

Tiburon, situated on a peninsula of the same name, looks like a cross between a fishing village and a Hollywood western set—imagine San Francisco reduced to toy dimensions. This seacoast town rambles over a series of green hills and ends up at a spindly, multicolored pier on the waterfront, like a Fisherman's Wharf in miniature. But in reality it's an extremely plush patch of yacht-club suburbia, as you'll see by both the marine craft and the homes of their owners. **Main Street** is lined with ramshackle, color-splashed old frame houses that shelter chic boutiques, souvenir stores, antique shops, and art galleries. Other roads are narrow, winding, and hilly, leading up to dramatically situated homes. The view of San Francisco's skyline and the islands in the bay is a good enough reason to pay the precious price to live here.

GETTING THERE

Ferries of the **Blue & Gold Fleet** (☎ **415/773-1188** for recorded info; ☎ 415/705-5555 for tickets) leave from San Francisco's Pier 43½ (Fisherman's Wharf) and travel to both Angel Island (trip time: 25 min.) and Tiburon (trip time: 30 min.). Boats run on a seasonal schedule; call for departure information. The round-trip fare is $10 to Angel Island, $11 to Tiburon; half price for kids 5 to 11, and free for children under 5.

By car from San Francisco, take U.S. 101 to the Tiburon/Calif. 131 exit, then follow Tiburon Boulevard all the way into downtown, a 40-minute drive from San Francisco. From Tiburon, you can catch a ferry (☎ **415/435-2131** or 415/388-6770) to Angel Island from the dock located at Tiburon Boulevard and Main Street. The 15-minute round-trip, which only runs on weekends, costs $6 for adults, $4 for children 5 to 11, free for children under 5, and $1 for bikes.

EXPLORING ANGEL ISLAND

Passengers disembark from the ferry at **Ayala Cove,** a small marina abutting a huge lawn area equipped with tables, benches, barbecue pits, and rest rooms. Also at Ayala Cove are a small store, gift shop, cafe (with surprisingly good grub), and overpriced mountain-bike rental shop (helmets included). You can bring your own bike or rented bike at no extra charge.

Among the 12 miles of Angel Island's hiking and mountain-bike trails is the **Perimeter Road,** a partly paved path that circles the island and winds its way past disused troop barracks, former gun emplacements, and other military buildings; several turnoffs lead up to the top of Mt. Livermore, 776 feet above the bay. Sometimes referred to as the "Ellis Island of the West," from 1910 to 1940 Angel Island was used as a holding area for Chinese immigrants awaiting their citizenship papers. You can still see some faded Chinese characters on the walls of the barracks where the immigrants were held. During the warmer months you can camp at a limited number of sites; reservations are required (call ☎ **415/897-0715,** ext. 4).

For recorded information on **Angel Island State Park,** call ☎ **415/435-1915.**

EXPLORING TIBURON

The main thing to do in Tiburon is stroll along the waterfront, pop into the boutique and souvenir stores along Main Street, and enjoy drinks and appetizers at Sam's before heading back to the city.

For a taste of the wine country, stop in at **Windsor Vineyards,** 72 Main St. (☎ **800/214-9463** or 415/435-3113)—their Victorian tasting room dates from 1888. Thirty-five choices are available for a free tasting. Wine accessories and gifts—glasses, cork pullers, gourmet sauces, posters, and maps—are also available. Carry-packs are available (they hold six bottles). Ask about personalized labels for your own selections. The shop is open daily from 10am to 6pm (Friday and Saturday until 7pm).

WHERE TO DINE

✪ **Sam's Anchor Café.** 27 Main St. ☎ **415/435-4527.** Main courses $8–$16. AE, MC, V. Mon–Thurs 11am–10pm; Fri 11am–10:30pm; Sat 10am–10:30pm; Sun 9:30am–10pm. SEAFOOD.

Summer Sundays are liveliest in Tiburon, when weekend boaters tie up to the docks at waterside restaurants like this one, the kind of place where you and your cronies can take off your shoes and have a fun, relaxed time eating burgers and drinking margaritas outside on the pier. The fare is pretty typical—sandwiches, salads, and seafood such as deep-fried oysters—but the quality and selection of the food is inconsequential: beers, burgers, and a designated driver are all you really need.

Sweden House Bakery-Café. 35 Main St. ☎ **415/435-9767.** Reservations not accepted. Omelets $6.50–$7; sandwiches $6–$8. MC, V. Mon–Fri 8am–6pm; Sat–Sun 8am–7pm. SWEDISH/AMERICAN.

This small, cozy cafe with gingham-covered walls adorned with copperware and kitchen utensils is a local favorite. On sunny mornings there's no better seat in the Bay Area than on the bakery's terrace, where you can nurse an espresso and pastry while gazing out over the bay. Full breakfasts are served, too, all accompanied by toasted Swedish limpa bread. Skip the eggs-and-bacon routine and go with the tasty Swedish pancakes: lingonberry, blueberry, and apple. At lunch, there's typical American fare—sandwiches, salads, and such. Beer and wine are also available.

5 Muir Woods & Mount Tamalpais

12 miles N of the Golden Gate Bridge

While the rest of Marin County's redwood forests were being devoured to feed the building spree in San Francisco around the turn of the century, the trees of Muir Woods, in a remote ravine on the flanks of Mt. Tamalpais, escaped destruction in favor of easier pickings.

MUIR WOODS

Although the magnificent California redwoods have been successfully transplanted to five continents, their homeland is a 500-mile strip along the mountainous coast of southwestern Oregon and northern California. The coast redwood, or *Sequoia sempervirens,* is the tallest tree in the immediate region, and the largest-known specimen towers 367.8 feet. It has an even larger relative, the *Sequoiadendron giganteum* of the California Sierra Nevada, but the coastal variety is stunning enough. Soaring toward the sky like a wooden cathedral, it is unlike any other forest in the world, and an experience you won't soon forget.

Granted, Muir Woods is tiny compared to the Redwood National Forest further north, but you can still get a pretty good idea of what it must have been like when these redwood giants dominated the entire coastal region. What is truly amazing is that they exist a mere 6 miles (as the crow flies) from San Francisco; close enough, unfortunately, that tour buses arrive in droves on the weekends. You can, however, avoid the masses by hiking up the **Ocean View Trail** and returning via the **Fern Creek Trail**—a moderately strenuous hike that shows off the woods' best sides and leaves the lazy-butts behind.

To reach Muir Woods from San Francisco, cross the Golden Gate Bridge heading north on U.S. 101, take the Stinson Beach/Calif. 1 exit heading west, and follow the signs (and the traffic). The park is open daily from 8am to sunset, and while there is no charge for admission, a donation box is posted out front to prompt your conscience. There's also a small gift shop, educational displays, and docent-led tours that you're welcome to stand in on. For more information, call the **Muir Woods information line** (☎ **415/388-2595**).

If you don't have a car, you can book a bus trip with the **Red & White Fleet,** which takes you straight to Muir Woods via the Golden Gate Bridge, and on the way back makes a short stop in Sausalito. The 3½-hour tour runs several times daily and costs $30 for adults, $14 for children. Call ☎ **800/229-2784** or 415/447-0597 for more information and specific departure times.

MOUNT TAMALPAIS

The birthplace of mountain biking, Mt. Tam—as the locals call it—is the Bay Area's favorite outdoor playground and the most dominant mountain in the region. Most every local has his or her secret trail and scenic overlook, as well as an opinion on the dilemma between mountain bikers and hikers (a touchy subject around here). The main trails—mostly fire roads—see a lot of foot and bicycle traffic on the weekends, particularly on clear, sunny days when you can see a hundred miles in all directions, from the foothills of the Sierra to the western horizon. It's a great place to escape from the city for a leisurely hike and to soak in the breathtaking views of the bay.

If you're driving from San Francisco, cross the Golden Gate Bridge heading north on U.S. 101 and take the Stinson Beach/Calif. 1 exit. Follow the shoreline highway about 2½ miles and turn onto the Panoramic Highway heading west. After about 5½ miles, turn onto Pantoll Road and continue for about a mile to Ridgecrest Boulevard. Ridgecrest winds to a parking lot below East Peak. From there, it's a 15-minute hike up to the top.

STINSON BEACH

One of the most popular beaches in northern California is Stinson Beach, a 3-mile wide stretch of sand at the western foot of Mount Tamalpais that is packed with Bay Area residents on those rare fog-free summer weekends. Granted, it lacks the hard bodies and soft golden sand found on the fabled beaches of southern California, but it still makes for an enjoyable day-trip via the scenic drive on Calif. 1. Although swimming is allowed and lifeguards are on duty from May to mid-September, notices about riptides usually discourage beachgoers from venturing too far into the water. Adjoining the beach is the small town of Stinson Beach, where you can have an enjoyable alfresco lunch at the numerous cafes along Calif. 1.

To reach Stinson Beach from San Francisco, cross the Golden Gate Bridge heading north on U.S. 101, take the Stinson Beach/Calif. 1 exit heading west, and follow the signs (about a 20-mile trip that's full of curves). The beach is open daily from 9am to 10pm, and there's no charge for admission. For more information, contact the Stinson Beach ranger station at ☎ **415/868-0942.**

6 San Jose

45 miles SE of San Francisco

Some may mourn the San Jose of yesterday, a sleepy small town of orchards, crops, and cattle, but those days are long gone. Founded in 1717 and previously dwelling in the shadows of San Francisco, San Jose is now northern California's largest city. With surveys that declare it one of the safest and sunniest cities in the country and rank it the fifth most popular place to live in America, San Jose is a force to be reckoned with. Today the prosperity of Silicon Valley has transformed what was once an agricultural backwater into a thriving city of restaurants, shops, a state-of-the-art light-rail system, a sports arena (go Sharks!), and a reputable art scene.

ESSENTIALS

GETTING THERE   BART (☎ **510/465-2278**) travels from San Francisco to Fremont in 1¼ hours; you can take a bus from there. **Cal Train** (☎ **800/660-4287**) operates frequently from San Francisco and takes about an hour and 25 minutes. From San Francisco by **car,** take U.S. 101 south, which leads directly to San Jose.

VISITOR INFORMATION   Contact the **San Jose Visitors Information & Business Center,** located in the San Jose McEvery Convention Center, 150 W. San Carlos St., San Jose, CA 95113 (☎ **408/977-0900**).

GETTING AROUND   **Light Rail** (☎ **408/321-2300**) is best for getting around. Tickets cost $1.10 per ride or $2.50 for a day pass and can be purchased at Light Rail stations. Stops include Paramount's Great America, the Convention Center, and downtown museums. Or you can use the historic trolleys, which operate in a loop around downtown (summer only).

MUSEUMS WORTH SEEKING OUT

Children's Discovery Museum. 180 Woz Way. ☎ **408/298-5437.** Admission $6 adults, $5 seniors, $4 children 2 to 18, free for children under 2. Tues–Sat 10am–5pm; Sun noon–5pm (also open Mon 10am–5pm in July and Aug).

Here the kids will find more than 150 interactive exhibits, as well as shows and workshops, which explore science, humanities, arts, and technology. *ZoomZone* consists of science and art activities designed by kids for kids; *Bubbalogna*, an exhibit that explores the whimsical and scientifically intriguing world of bubbles, draws rave reviews. Smaller kids enjoy dressing up in costumes and playing on the fire truck.

San Jose Historical Museum. 1650 Senter Rd. ☎ **408/287-2290.** Admission $4 adults, $3 seniors, $2 children 4 to 17, free for children under 4. Mon–Fri 10am–4:30pm; Sat–Sun noon–4:30pm.

Twenty-six original and replica buildings on 25 acres in Kelley Park have been restored to represent life in 1880s San Jose. The usual cast of characters is here—the doctor, the printer, the postmaster—with an occasional local surprise, such as the 1888 Chinese temple and the original Stevens fruit barn.

San Jose Museum of Art. 110 S. Market St. ☎ **408/294-2787** or 408/271-6840. Admission $7 adults, $4 children 6 to 17 and seniors, free for children under 6. Tues–Sun 10am–5pm; Thurs 10am–8pm.

This museum is collaborating with New York's Whitney Museum for shows that trace the development of 20th-century American art. The 1999 exhibition (starting May 2), *A Century of Landscape,* will include works by Georgia O'Keeffe, Edward Hopper, and Richard Diebenkorn. *The Permanent Collection: Into the 21st Century* includes a variety of works by Bay Area artists such as Christopher Brown, Manuel Neri, and Larry Sultan. The newly renovated Historic Wing now includes a cafe, bookstore, and education center.

✪ **Tech Museum of Innovation.** 201 S. Market St., downtown at the corner of Park and Market sts. ☎ **408/279-7150.** www.thetech.org. Admission $8 adults, $6 children 3 to 12, free for children under 3, $7 seniors 65 and over; additional fee for IMAX shows. Tues–Sun 10am–5pm.

This all-new museum allows visitors to experience the latest in modern technology. You can create your own virtual roller-coaster ride, survive an earthquake on a giant shake table, operate an underwater R.O.V. (remotely operated vehicle) à la *Titanic,* and play with tons of other cool high-tech stuff. There's also an IMAX Dome Theater, Jet Pack simulator, and Virtual Bobsled ride, the same used to train Olympic competitors.

Rosicrucian Egyptian Museum & Planetarium. 1342 Naglee Ave. ☎ **408/947-3636.** Museum admission $7 adults, $5 seniors, $3.50 children 7 to 15, free for children under 7. Daily 10am–5pm. Planetarium admission $4 adults, $3 children; call for show times.

The Winchester Mystery House

Begun in 1884, the Winchester Mystery House, 525 S. Winchester Blvd., at the intersection of I-280 and I-880, San Jose (☎ **408/247-2101**), is a monument to one woman's paranoia. It's the legacy of Sarah L. Winchester, widow of the son of the famous rifle magnate. After the deaths of her husband and baby daughter, Mrs. Winchester consulted with a seer, who proclaimed that the family had been targeted by the evil spirits of those killed with Winchester repeaters, who would only be appeased by perpetual construction on the Winchester mansion. Convinced that she'd live as long as the building continued, the widow used much of her $20-million inheritance to finance the construction, which went on 24 hours a day, 7 days a week, 365 days a year, for 38 years.

As you can probably guess, this is no ordinary home. With 160 rooms, it sprawls across a half-dozen acres. And it's full of disturbing features: a staircase leading nowhere, a Tiffany window with a spider-web design, and doors that open onto blank walls. There are 13 bathrooms, 13 windows and doors in the old sewing room, 13 palms lining the main driveway, 13 hooks in the seance room, and chandeliers with 13 lights. Such schemes were designed to confound the spirits that seemed to plague the heiress.

Touring the house and grounds costs $13.95 for adults, $10.95 for seniors 65 and over, $7.95 for children 6 to 12, and is free for kids 5 and under. Tours leave about every 15 to 30 minutes. The house is open daily from 9am to 8pm in the summer (winter hours vary; call ahead).

The Rosicrucian is associated with an educational organization that traces its origins back to the ancient Egyptians, who strongly believed in the afterlife and reincarnation. On display are human and animal mummies, funerary boats, and canopic jars, as well as jewelry, pottery, and bronze tools. There's also a replica of a noble Egyptian's tomb.

THEME-PARK THRILLS

✪ **Paramount's Great America.** Great America Pkwy. (off U.S. 101), Santa Clara. ☎ **408/988-1776.** Admission $32 adults, $21 seniors, $18.50 children ages 3–6, and free for children under 3. Parking is $6 per vehicle. Mar 20–May 30 Sat–Sun 10am–9pm; Apr 2–Apr 11 daily 10am–9pm (closed Easter); Jun 3–Aug 29 daily 10am–9pm; Sep 4–Oct 17 Sat–Sun 10am–9pm. (The park closes earlier than 9pm on weekdays, and the schedule is subject to change due to weather, so be sure to call ahead.) From San Francisco, take U.S. 101 S. for about 45 miles to the Great America Pkwy. exit.

This amusement park provides 100 acres of family entertainment. A pretty cool place to lose your lunch, the park includes such favorites as the *Top Gun* suspended jet coaster, the *Days of Thunder* auto-racing simulator, a 3-acre Nickelodeon Center for children, "Drop Zone" (the world's tallest free-fall ride), and the new Xtreme Skyflyer, which combines skydiving with hang gliding. Be sure to check for concerts and special events.

WHERE TO STAY

If neither of the lodgings below has a vacancy, San Jose has the usual variety of inexpensive chain motels as well. The best for budget travelers is the **Executive Inn** (☎ **408/280-5300**) at 1215 S. First St., where rates range from $89 to $99 per double.

The Hensley House. 456 N. Third St., San Jose, CA 95112. ☎ **408/298-3537.** 5 units. TV TEL. $79–$175 double. AE, DC, MC, V. In downtown San Jose, between Julian and Jackson sts.

"Location, location, location," is what innkeepers Sharon Layne and Bill Priest will tell you. The Hensley's proximity to museums, theaters, and restaurants certainly hasn't hurt business. This stately Queen Anne is a quiet getaway in a restored landmark building, with beautiful antiques, crystal chandeliers, feather beds—all surrounded by dark wood. If you're up for more luxury and a little superstition, try the Judge's Chambers. Complete with wet bar, whirlpool, hand-painted ceiling and walls, fireplace, VCR, and its very own ghost (previous owner and superior court Judge Perley Gosbey), this room is quite an experience. Guests can also enjoy a complete breakfast, daily afternoon hors d'oeuvres, and high tea on Thursday and Saturday.

Madison Street Inn. 1390 Madison St., Santa Clara, CA 95050. ☎ **408/249-5541.** 6 units. TEL. $75–$115 double. AE, DC, DISC, MC, V. In downtown Santa Clara, at the corner of Lewis and Madison sts.

Located a few miles west of San Jose in the rural South Bay town of Santa Clara, this restored Victorian B&B is nestled among two gigantic pepper trees and ensconced by a white picket fence and rose garden. Each room is distinctively decorated with personal touches from the era. Furnishings range from claw-foot tubs to brass beds, lace coverlets, and more; all come with private bathrooms. Proprietors Ralph and Theresa Wigginton are willing to whip up custom dinners of California cuisine or serve you their hearty breakfast that might feature eggs Benedict, Belgian waffles, omelets, and home-baked muffins and breads.

WHERE TO DINE

Gombei Restaurant. 193 E. Jackson St. (between Fourth and Fifth sts.). ☎ **408/ 279-4311.** Main courses $6–$12. No credit cards. Mon–Sat 11:30am–2:30pm and 5–9:30pm. JAPANESE.

A complete cultural (and nutritional) antithesis to Henry's World Famous Hi-Life (see below) is Gombei, our favorite Japanese restaurant in San Jose. On busy nights the ambiance is akin to controlled chaos, with patrons diving into big bowls of donburi and udon (Gombei's specialty, thick wheat noodles in a chicken broth filled with dried seaweed, green onion, and tender chunks of chicken) while the sprightly staff deftly negotiates around the crowded dining room. *Tip:* Be sure to check the specials board, which often lists some very esoteric Japanese entrees.

Gordon Biersch. 33 E. San Fernando St. ☎ **408/294-6785.** Reservations recommended. Main courses $7.50–$13.95. AE, DC, DISC, MC, V. Sun–Wed 11:30am–11pm; Thurs 11:30am–midnight; Fri–Sat 11:30am–1am. ECLECTIC.

One of the original luxe brew-pub restaurants that are quickly spreading across northern California, this place offers a little of everything. To complement the beer, the menu features some lighter fare, ranging from a Thai satay platter and goat cheese salads to molasses-glazed baby back ribs. Big burgers and filling pub grub is equally popular. A large outdoor patio and live music continues to attract a younger crowd. Four tasty home brews are always on tap, and locals are allowed to keep their own steins in wood lockers.

Henry's World Famous Hi-Life. 301 W. St. John St. (at Almaden Blvd., near Calif. 87). ☎ **408/295-5414.** Main courses $10–$21. AE, MC, V. Mon–Thurs 5–9pm; Fri–Sat 4–10pm; Sun 4–9pm. BARBECUE.

Harking back to the good ol' days before "good" and "bad" cholesterol were invented is Henry's World Famous Hi-Life, one of the last bastions of big-platter barbecue joints. Formica tables lined with paper place mats and little fishnet-covered candles gives you a pretty good indication that you probably won't need that dinner jacket and tie. A bib is more appropriate for tackling the huge servings of barbecued ribs, chicken, and steaks, all cooked in an oak barbecue pit that's big enough to roast a rhino, then slathered in a sweet, tangy barbecue sauce. All platters come with a basket of garlic bread, a big baked potato with all the fixins, and a so-called salad. It's truly a funky place, one that will linger on your mind probably as long the ribs will take to digest.

Il Fornaio. In the Hotel Sainte Claire, 302 S. Market St. ☎ **408/271-3366.** Reservations recommended. Main courses $8–$11. AE, DC, MC, V. Mon–Thurs 11:30am–10pm; Fri and Sun 11:30am–11pm; Sat 11:30am–midnight. Live entertainment Tues–Sat. NORTHERN ITALIAN.

Voted by readers of *San Francisco Focus* magazine as "Best Italian" and "Best Overall Restaurant" 3 years running, this fine establishment is always a sure thing. This location isn't quite as inviting as the one in Palo Alto, but it's still an enjoyable place to dine. The specialties of the house include the mesquite-grilled fresh fish and the veal chop with sage and rosemary, as well as grilled pounded chicken breast with a purée of roasted garlic and rosemary. There are about 10 pizzas to choose from; our favorite comes topped with Maui onions, Gruyère and mozzarella cheese, smoked ham, and sage. For hearty appetites, there's an excellent and tender 22-ounce steak. Salads and appetizers, including a tasty grilled polenta with wild mushrooms and provolone, round out the menu.

6

The Wine Country

by Erika Lenkert and Matthew R. Poole

California's Napa and Sonoma valleys are two of the most famous wine-growing regions in the world, and two of our favorite (and most expensive) places to visit in the state, which would make a cheap visit here impossible were it not for the (relative) bargains and money-saving tips we point out throughout this chapter.

The workaday valleys are a way of life for thousands of vintners, while for wine lovers and romantics they set the scene for the ultimate luxury retreat. You don't need to be a millionaire to enjoy the hundreds of wineries nestled among the vines; the fees at most tasting rooms range from free to $3. You don't need to spend $250 a night to feel as though you're indulging in life's finer things; even if you stayed in a Motel 6 and avoided wine tasting you couldn't help but revel in the fresh country air and beautiful rolling countryside. Heck, the farm-fresh restaurants and affordable spas are reason enough to come. Thus we recommend you spend more than a day here; you'll need a couple of days just to get to know one of the valleys. But no matter how long you stay, you'll probably never get enough of the Wine Country. Believe us, it's that good.

While Napa and Sonoma are close to each other (about a half-hour drive apart), each is packed with attractions, so your best bet is to focus on just one of the valleys, especially if your time is limited. We recommend that you read about each below, then decide which one is right for you—unless, of course, you're lucky enough to have time to explore both. We also recommend that you plan your trip as far in advance as possible (bargains are more scarce than Joseph Phelps' 1994 Insignia cab, and are always snatched up quickly) and consider traveling in the off-season, which is November through May.

1 Exploring Napa Valley

The most obvious distinction between the two valleys is size—Napa Valley dwarfs Sonoma Valley both in population, number of wineries, and sheer volume of tourism (and in summertime, serious traffic). Napa is definitely the more commercial of the two, with dozens more wineries, spas (at far cheaper rates), and a far superior selection of fine restaurants, hotels, and quintessential Wine Country activities like hot-air ballooning, all of which are set amidst rolling, mustard-flower-covered hills and vast stretches of vineyards. And if your goal is to really learn about the wonderful world of wine making,

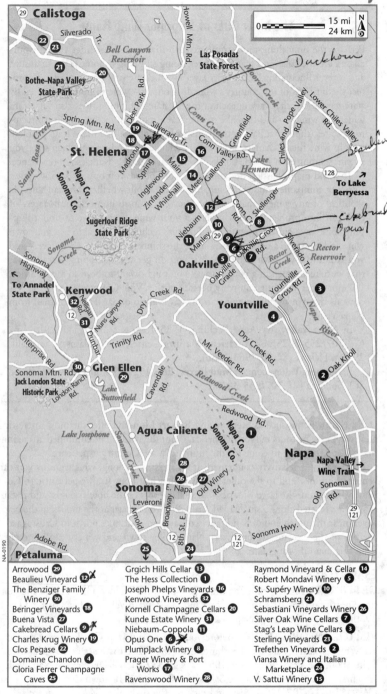

The Wine Country

0 [15 mi] / [24 km] N

Calistoga

Silverado Tr.

⑳ Howell Mtn. Rd.

Las Posadas
State Forest

Duckhorn

Beaulieu

Bell Canyon
Reservoir

⑳ Bothe–Napa Valley
State Park

Spring Mtn. Rd.

Deer Park Rd.

Silverado Tr.

Conn Creek

Greenfield Rd.

Chiles and Pope Valley Rd.

Lower Chiles Valley Rd.

St. Helena

Madrona

Conn Valley Rd.

Lake
Hennessey

128

To Lake
Berryessa

Napa Co.
Sonoma Co.

Sugerloaf Ridge
State Park

Spring Inglewood Zinfandel Whitehall Main Mees Galleron

Conn Cr.

Skellenger

Cakebread
Opus 1

Sonoma Highway

Sonoma Creek

To Annadel
State Park

Niebaum Manley ㉙ ⑥ ⑦

Oakville Cross Rd.

Silverado Tr.

Rector
Reservoir

Rector Creek

Oakville

Oakville Grade

③

Kenwood

Neligan Rd.

Nuns Canyon Rd.

Dry Creek Rd.

Yountville

Yountville Cross Rd.

Napa River

Dunbar

Trinity Rd.

Mt. Veeder Rd.

Dry Creek Rd.

Oak Knoll

②

Enterprise Rd.

Glen Ellen

⑳

Sonoma Mtn. Rd.

Jack London State
Historic Park

London Ranch Rd.

Lake
Suttonfield

Cavendale Rd.

Redwood Creek

Redwood Rd.

Napa Co.
Sonoma Co.

①

Lake Josephone

Agua Caliente

Napa

Napa Valley
Wine Train

Sonoma

E. Napa

Old Winery Rd.

Leveroni

Sonoma Rd.

Arnold

Broadway

8th St. E.

Old Rd.

29 121

Adobe Rd.

12

Sonoma Hwy.

12 121

Petaluma

⑤

⑭

NA-0190

Arrowood ㉙	Grgich Hills Cellar ⑬	Raymond Vineyard & Cellar ⑭
Beaulieu Vineyard ⑫ ✈	The Hess Collection ①	Robert Mondavi Winery ⑤
The Benziger Family Winery ㉚	Joseph Phelps Vineyards ⑯	St. Supéry Winery ⑩
Beringer Vineyards ⑱	Kenwood Vineyards ㉜	Schramsberg ㉑
Buena Vista ㉗	Kornell Champagne Cellars ⑳	Sebastiani Vineyards Winery ㉖
Cakebread Cellars ⑨ ✈	Kunde Estate Winery ㉛	Silver Oak Wine Cellars ⑦
Charles Krug Winery ⑲	Niebaum-Coppola ⑪	Stag's Leap Wine Cellars ③
Clos Pegase ㉒	Opus One ⑥ ✈	Sterling Vineyards ㉓
Domaine Chandon ④	PlumpJack Winery ⑧	Trefethen Vineyards ②
Gloria Ferrer Champagne Caves ㉕	Prager Winery & Port Works ⑰	Viansa Winery and Italian Marketplace ㉔
	Ravenswood Winery ㉘	V. Sattui Winery ⑮

The Ins & Outs of Shipping Wine Home

Perhaps the only thing more complex than that case of cabernet you just purchased are the rules and regulations regarding shipping it home. Due to absurd and forever fluctuating "reciprocity laws"—which are supposedly created to protect the business of the country's wine distributors—wine shipping is limited by state regulations that vary in each of the 50 states. Shipping rules also vary from winery to winery—and to make matters even more confusing, the list of reciprocal states (those that have agreements with California that make it no problem to ship wine there) changes almost daily! Hence, depending on which state you live in, sending even a single bottle of wine can be a truly Kafkaesque experience.

To avoid major hassles, do your homework before you buy. Talk to wineries, shipping companies, and the companies below about whether they can ship. Be skeptical of any winery that tells you they can ship to nonreciprocal states—if they run into problems, you'll never get your wine. If you have to find a shipping company yourself, keep in mind that it's technically illegal to box your own wine and send it to a nonreciprocal state; the shippers could lose their license and you could lose your wine. However, if you do get stuck shipping illegally (not that we're recommending you do that), you might want to head to a post office, UPS, or other shipping company outside of the Wine Country area; it's far less obvious that you're shipping wine from, say, Vallejo or San Francisco than from Napa Valley.

In **Napa Valley,** try **Aero Packing,** 1733 Trancas St. (at Calif. 29), Napa (☎ **707/255-8025**); or **St. Helena Mailing Center,** 1241 Adams St. (at Calif. 29), St. Helena (☎ **707/963-2686**).

In **Sonoma Valley,** contact **Mail Boxes, Etc.,** 19229 Sonoma Hwy. (at Verano St.), Sonoma (☎ **707/935-3438**).

---

world-class wineries such as **Sterling** and **Robert Mondavi** offer the most interesting and edifying wine tours in North America, if not the world. The combined attractions make Napa the place to come for the ultimate Wine Country experience.

Napa Valley is relatively condensed. It's just 25 miles long, which means you can venture from one end to the other in less than a half hour (traffic permitting). Conveniently, most of the large wineries—as well as most of the hotels, shops, and restaurants—are located along a single road, Calif. 29, which starts at the mouth of the Napa River, near the north end of San Francisco Bay, and continues north to Calistoga and the top of the growing region. Every Napa Valley town and winery can be reached from this main thoroughfare.

ESSENTIALS

GETTING THERE From San Francisco, cross the Golden Gate Bridge and continue north on U.S. 101. Turn east on Calif. 37 (toward Vallejo), then north on Calif. 29, the main road through Napa Valley.

VISITOR INFORMATION Before you venture out from San Francisco, you can get Wine Country maps and brochures from the **Wine Institute** at 425 Market St., Suite 1000, San Francisco, CA 94105 (☎ **415/512-0151**). Once in the Napa Valley, stop first at the **Napa Conference & Visitors Bureau,** 1310 Town Center Mall, Napa, CA 94559 (☎ **707/226-7459**), and pick up the slick *Napa Valley Guide,* or call in advance to order their $10 package, which includes the guide plus a bunch of brochures, a map, a *Four Perfect Days in the Wine Country Itinerary,* and hot-air-balloon discount coupons. If you want less to recycle, call **Vintage Publications,** 760 Adobe Dr., Santa Rosa, CA 95404 (☎ **800/651-8953**), to order just the guide ($6, plus $3 for shipping within the U.S.). If you don't want to pay the bucks for the official publications, point your browser to **www.napavalley.com/nvcvb.html**, the NVCVB's official site, which has much of the same information for free.

WHEN TO GO   The beauty of the valley is striking any time of the year, but it's most memorable in September and October when the grapes are being pressed and the wineries are in full production. Another great time to come is the spring, when the mustard flowers are in full bloom and the tourist season hasn't yet begun; you'll find less traffic and fewer crowds at the wineries and restaurants, and better deals on hotel rooms. While winter is beautiful and promises the best budget rates, the vines are dormant and rain is likely, so bring appropriate shoes and an umbrella. Summer? Say hello to hot weather and lots of traffic. This seasonal advice applies to Sonoma Valley as well.

TOURING TIPS   The Napa Valley has more than 250 wineries, each offering distinct wines, atmosphere, and experience—so touring the valley takes a little planning. Decide what you're most interested in and chart your path from there. Ask locals which vintners have the type of experience you're looking for. Whatever you do, plan to visit no more than four or five wineries in one day. Above all, take it slowly. The Wine Country should never be rushed; like a great glass of wine, it should be savored.

Most wineries offer tours daily from 10am to 5pm. Tours usually chart the process of wine making from the grafting and harvesting of the vines to the pressing of the grapes and the blending and aging of the wines in oak casks. They vary in length, detail, and formality, depending on the winery. Most tours are free.

The towns and wineries below are organized geographically, from south to north along Calif. 29, from Napa village to Calistoga. We've included a handful of our favorites below; for a complete list of wineries, be sure to pick up one of the free guides to the valley (see "Visitor Information," above).

THE TOWN OF NAPA

The village of Napa serves as the commercial center of the Wine Country and the gateway to Napa Valley. Most visitors whiz right past it on their way the to the heart of the valley, but if you do veer off the highway, you'll be surprised to discover a small but burgeoning community of 63,000 residents and some of the most affordable accommodations in the area. Unfortunately, any small-town charm Napa may exude is all but squelched by the used-car lots and warehouse superstores surrounding the turn-of-the-century neighborhoods. Just a few minutes north of town, the real Wine Country atmosphere envelops you instantly.

Plan to spend at least an hour if you make a visit to **Red Hen's** co-op collection of antiques. You'll find everything from baseball cards to living-room sets, and prices are remarkably affordable. You can't miss this enormous red barn-style building at 5091 St. Helena Hwy., on Calif. 29 at Oak Knoll Avenue West (☎ **707/257-0822**). It's open daily from 10am to 5:30pm.

✪ **di Rosa Preserve.** 5200 Sonoma Hwy. (Calif. 121/12; look for the blue gate). ☎ **707/226-5991** for reservations. Visits by appointment only; maximum of 25 guests on each guided tour. Tours lasts 2–2½ hr. and cost $10 per person.

Anyone with an appreciation for art absolutely must visit the di Rosa Preserve, which until recently was closed to the public. Rene and Veronica di Rosa, who have been collecting contemporary American art for more than 40 years, converted their 88 acres

---

Fresh from the Farm

Grapes aren't the only thing grown in these verdant valleys. An enormous variety of fresh produce, much of it organically grown, is sold directly to the public at various farmers markets within Napa and Sonoma valleys. Check out the **Napa Downtown Farmers Market,** held every Tuesday from 7:30am to noon at the parking lot on Pearl and West streets off Soscal (☎ **707/252-7142**). A livelier option to the morning markets is Napa's **Chef's Market,** which takes place Friday evenings mid-May through October from 4 to 9pm at the Napa Town Center (take First Street exit off Calif. 29 and head east to First and Coombs streets; ☎ **707/255-8073**). You get all the same farm-fresh produce as the regular farmers markets along with live music, samplings from noted Napa Valley chefs, beer and wine gardens, arts and crafts displays, and a kids' hands-on area.

---

of prime Wine Country property into a monument to northern California's regional art and nature. Their world-renowned collection features 1,500 works in all media by more than 600 greater–Bay Area artists. Their treasures are displayed practically everywhere, from along the shores of their 30-acre lake to each nook and cranny of their 110-year-old winery-turned-residence, adjoining building, two new galleries, and gardens. With hundreds of surrounding acres of rolling hills protected under the Napa County Land Trust, this place is truly a must-see for both art and nature lovers.

THE NAPA WINERIES

✪ **The Hess Collection.** 441 Redwood Rd., Napa. ☎ **707/255-1144.** Daily 10am–4pm. From Calif. 29 N., exit Redwood Rd. west, and follow Redwood Rd. for 6½ miles.

No place in the valley brings together art and wine better than this combination winery/art gallery on the side of Mt. Veeder. Swiss art collector Donald Hess acquired the old Christian Brothers winery in 1978; along with producing wine, he also funded a huge restoration and expansion project to honor wine and the fine arts. The result is a working winery interspersed with gloriously lit rooms that exhibit his truly stunning art collection; the free self-guided tour takes you through these galleries as it introduces you to the wine-making process.

For a $3 fee, you can sample the winery's current cabernet and chardonnay as well as one other featured wine. If you want to take some with you, by-the-bottle prices start at $9.95 for the second-label Hess select brand, while most other selections range from $15 to $35.

Trefethen Vineyards. 1160 Oak Knoll Ave., Napa. ☎ **707/255-7700.** Daily 10am–4:30pm; tours by appointment year-round. To reach Trefethen Vineyards from Calif. 29, take Oak Knoll Ave. E.

Listed on the National Register of Historic Places, the vineyard's main building was constructed in 1886 and remains Napa's only wooden, gravity-powered winery. The bucolic brick courtyard is surrounded by oak and cork trees, and free wine samples are distributed in the brick-floored, wood-beamed tasting room. Although Trefethen is one of the valley's oldest wineries, it did not produce its first chardonnay until 1973—but thank goodness it did. Their whites and reds are both award-winners and a pleasure to the palate.

Stag's Leap Wine Cellars. 5766 Silverado Trail, Napa. ☎ **707/944-2020.** Daily 10am–4pm. Tours by appointment only. From Calif. 29, go east on Trancas St. or Oak Knoll Ave., then north to the cellars.

Founded in 1972, Stag's Leap shocked the oenological world in 1976 when its 1973 cabernet won first place over French wines in a Parisian blind tasting. For $5 per person, you can be the judge of the winery's current releases, or you can fork over another fiver for one of Stag's Leap's best-known wines, Cabernet Sauvignon Cask 23. The 1-hour tour runs through everything from the vineyard to production facilities and ends with a tasting; by the time this book comes out, it could also include their new caves, which are currently under construction.

YOUNTVILLE

The town of Yountville, currently with a population of 3,500, was founded by the first white American to settle in the valley, George Calvert Yount. While it lacks the small-town charm of neighboring St. Helena and Calistoga—primarily because it has no rambunctious main street—it does serve as a good base for exploring the valley, and it's home to a handful of excellent wineries, inns, and restaurants, including James Beard's 1997 top dining spot in the nation, the **French Laundry.**

Domaine Chandon. 1 California Dr. (at Calif. 29), Yountville. ☎ **707/944-2280.** Nov–Apr Wed–Sun 10am–6pm; May–Oct daily 10am–6pm. Free tours every hr. on the hr. from 11am to 5pm; no reservations necessary.

The valley's most renowned sparkling winery was founded in 1973 by French champagne house Moët et Chandon. The grounds suit Domaine Chandon's reputation perfectly, with beautifully manicured gardens, an outdoor patio where visitors can enjoy sips of the famous sparkling wine, and a renowned dining room. Bubbly is sold by the glass ($3 to $6.25) and served with complimentary hors d'oeuvres. The comprehensive tour of the facilities is worth the time. In addition to a shop, there's a small gallery housing artifacts from Moët et Chandon that depict the history of champagnes.

OAKVILLE

Driving farther north on the St. Helena Highway (Calif. 29) brings you to the Oakville Cross Road and the gourmet triangle of the ✪ **Oakville Grocery Café** (see p. 171), **Oakville Grocery Co.** (see p. 175), and **Dean & DeLuca** (see p. 175).

Robert Mondavi Winery. 7801 St. Helena Hwy. (Calif. 29), Oakville. ☎ **800/MONDAVI** or 707/226-1395. May–Oct daily 9:30am–5:30pm; Nov–Apr daily 9:30am–4:30pm. Reservations recommended for the guided tour (book 1 week in advance, especially for weekend tours).

At Mondavi's magnificent mission-style facility, almost every variable in the wine-making process is controlled by computer (fascinating to watch!). After the tour, you can taste the results in selected current wines, free of charge. You can also taste without taking the tour, but it will cost you: The Rose Garden (an outdoor tasting area open in summer) offers an etched Reidel glass and three wines for $10; tastings in the ToKalon Room go from $3 for a 3-ounce taste to $15 for a rare library wine.

The Vineyard Room usually features an art show; in summer, the winery also hosts some great outdoor jazz concerts. Call to learn about upcoming events. There's no picnicking here.

Opus One. 7900 St. Helena Hwy. (Calif. 29), Oakville. ☎ **707/944-9442.** Daily 10:30am–3:30pm. Tours by appointment only (in high season, book 3 weeks in advance).

A visit to Opus One is a serious and stuffy affair. Robert Mondavi and Baroness Phillipe de Rothschild are to thank for this winery, which caters to one ultra-premium wine offered here for a whopping $15 per 4-ounce taste (and a painful $90 per bottle). Architecture buffs in particular will appreciate the tour, which takes in both the impressive Greco-Roman-meets-20th-century building and the no-holds-barred ultra-high-tech production and aging facilities.

Wine lovers should happily fork over the cash for a taste: It's likely to be one of the most memorable reds you'll ever sample. Grab your glass and head to the redwood rooftop deck to enjoy the view.

RUTHERFORD

If you so much as blink after Oakville you're likely to overlook **Rutherford,** the next small town that borders on St. Helena. Still, spectacular wineries exist here, but you probably won't see most of them while driving along Calif. 29.

Silver Oak Wine Cellars. 915 Oakville Cross Rd. (at Money Rd.), Oakville. ☎ **707/ 944-8808.** Tasting room Mon–Sat 9am–4pm. Tours Mon–Thurs at 1:30pm, by appointment only.

Twenty-five years ago, an oil man from Colorado, Ray Duncan, and a former Christian Brothers monk, Justin Meyer, formed a partnership and a mission to create the finest cabernet sauvignon in the world. "We still haven't produced the best bottle of cabernet sauvignon of which Silver Oak is capable," admits Meyer, but this small winery is still the Wine Country's undisputed king of cabernet.

A narrow tree-lined road leads you to the handsome Mediterranean-style winery, where roughly 44,000 cases of 100% varietal cab are produced annually. The elegant tasting room, adorned with redwood panels stripped from old wine tanks and warmed by a wood fire, is quiet and soothing. Tastings and tours are $5, which includes a beautiful German-made burgundy glass. Recently released were a 1993 Alexander Valley and a 1993 Napa Valley. No picnic facilities are available.

✪ **PlumpJack Winery.** 620 Oakville Cross Rd. (just west of Silverado Trail), Oakville. ☎ **707/945-1220.** Daily 10am–4pm.

If most wineries are like a traditional and refined Brooks Brothers suit, PlumpJack stands out as the Todd Oldham of wine tasting—chic, colorful, a little wild, and popular with a young, hip crowd. This playfully medieval winery is a welcome diversion from the same old, same old. But with Getty bucks behind what was once Villa Mt. Eden winery, the budget covers far more than just atmosphere: There's some serious wine making going on here, too, and for $5 you can sample the cabernet, petite sirah, Riesling, and chardonnay—each an impressive product from a winery that's only been open to the public since mid-1997. The few vintages for sale currently range from $15 to $30, and average around $20 per bottle. There are no tours or picnic spots, but this refreshingly stylized and friendly facility will make you want to hang out for a while nonetheless.

Cakebread Cellars. 8300 St. Helena Hwy. (Calif. 29), Rutherford. ☎ **800/588-0298** or 707/963-5221. Daily 10am–4:30pm. Tours by appointment only.

This winery's moniker is actually the owners' surname, but it suits the wines produced here, where the focus is on making wine that pairs well with food. They've done such a good job that 85% of their 65,000 annual cases goes directly to restaurants, which means only a select few wine drinkers get to take home a bottle. Even if you've found their label in your local wine store, your choice has been limited: Just three varieties are distributed nationally. Here you can sample the sauvignon blanc, chardonnay, cabernet, merlot, zinfandel, pinot noir, the Rubaiyat blend wine, and their dry rose Vin de Porche, which are all made from Napa Valley grapes. Prices range from an affordable $14 for a bottle of the 1996 sauvignon blanc to a pricey $53 for the 1994 reserve cab, but the average bottle sells for just a little more than $20. In the tasting room, a large barnlike space, the hospitable hosts pour either a $3 or $6 sampling; both include a keepsake wineglass.

St. Supéry Winery. 8440 St. Helena Hwy. (Calif. 29), Rutherford. ☎ **800/942-0809** or 707/963-4507. Daily 9:30am–4:30pm.

The outside may look like a modern corporate office building, but inside you'll find a functional and welcoming winery that encourages first-time wine tasters to learn more about oenology. On the self-guided tour, you can wander through the demonstration vineyard and learn about growing techniques. Inside, kids gravitate toward "Smella-Vision," an interactive display that teaches you how to identify different wine ingredients. Adjoining is the Atkinson House, which chronicles more than 100 years of wine-making history. For $3 you'll get lifetime tasting privileges, and though they probably won't be pouring their ever-popular Moscato dessert wine, the sauvignon blanc and chardonnay flow freely. Even the prices make visitors feel at home: Many bottles go for around $8, although their 1994 Meritage cabernet will set you back $40.

Niebaum-Coppola. 1991 St. Helena Hwy. (Calif. 29), Rutherford. ☎ **707/963-9099.** Daily 10am–5pm. Tours offered daily.

Hollywood meets Napa Valley at Francis Ford Coppola's historic winery (pronounced *Nee*-bomb *Coh*-pa-la), previously Inglenook Vineyards. Coppola bought and restored the beautiful 1880s ivy-draped stone winery and surrounding property to its historic dimensions, gilding it with the glitz and glamour you'd expect from Tinseltown in the process. On display are Academy Awards and memorabilia from his movies.

In spite of all the Hollywood hullabaloo, wine is not forgotten. Available for tasting are a Rubicon (a blend of estate-grown cabernet, cabernet franc, and merlot, aged for more than 5 years), cabernet franc, merlot, chardonnay, zinfandel, and others, all made from organically grown grapes and ranging from around $10 to more than $50. There's also a wide variety of expensive and affordable gift items. The steep $7.50-per-person tasting fee might make you wonder whether a movie is included in the price—it's not (but you'll at least get to keep the souvenir glass). And at $20 a pop for the château and garden tour, you've gotta wonder whether you're *funding* his next film. But the grounds are indeed spectacular, and the 1½-hour journey includes a private tasting and glass.

Regardless, do visit the grounds—they're absolutely stunning and it costs nothing to stroll. You can also perk yourself up at the cappuccino bar, where you'll get *Godfather*-like atmosphere with your latte. You're welcome to picnic at any of the designated garden sites.

Beaulieu Vineyard. 1960 S. St. Helena Hwy. (Calif. 29), Rutherford. ☎ **707/963-2411.** Daily 10am–5pm. Tours daily 11am–4pm: in summer, roughly every half hr.; call for winter schedule.

Bordeaux native Georges de Latour founded the third-oldest continuously operating winery in Napa Valley in 1900—and, with the help of legendary oenologist André Tchelistcheff, produced world-class, award-winning wines that have been served by every president of the United States since Franklin D. Roosevelt. The brick-and-redwood tasting room isn't much to look at, but with Beaulieu's (pronounced *Bowl*-you) stellar reputation, they have no need to visually impress. They do, however, offer a complimentary glass of chardonnay the minute you walk through the door as well as a variety of bottles under $15. The Private Reserve Tasting Room offers a "flight" of reserve wines to taste for $12.50—but if you want to take a bottle from here to go, it may cost as much as $50. A free tour explains the wine-making process and the vineyard's history. No reservation is necessary.

Grgich Hills Cellar. 1829 St. Helena Hwy. (Calif. 29, north of Rutherford Cross Rd.), Ruther-ford. ☎ **707/963-2784.** Daily 9:30am–4:30pm. Free tours by appointment only, Mon–Fri 11am and 2pm, Sat–Sun 11am and 1:30pm.

Yugoslavian émigré Miljenko (Mike) Grgich made his presence known to the world when his Château Montelena chardonnay bested the top French white burgundies at the famous 1976 Paris tasting. Since then, this master vintner has teamed up with Austin Hills (of the Hills Brothers coffee fortune) and started this extremely successful and respected winery in Rutherford.

The ivy-covered stucco building isn't much to behold, and the tasting room is even less appealing, but people don't come here for the scenery: As you might expect, Grgich's (pronounced *Grr*-gitch) chardonnays are legendary—and priced accordingly. The smart buys, however, are Grgich's outstanding zinfandel and cabernet sauvignon, which are very reasonably priced at around $18 and $25, respectively. The winery also produces a fantastic fumé blanc for as little as $15 a bottle. Before you leave, be sure to poke your head into the barrel-aging room and inhale the divine aroma. Tastings cost $3 on weekends, which includes the glass, and are free on weekdays. No picnic facilities are available.

ST. HELENA

This quiet, attractive little town, located 17 miles north of Napa on Calif. 29, is home to a slew of beautiful old homes as well as first-rate restaurants and accommodations. The former Seventh-Day Adventist village manages to maintain a pseudo–Old West feel while simultaneously catering to upscale shoppers with deep pockets—hence at ✪ **Vanderbilt and Company,** 1429 Main St., between Adams and Pine streets (☎ **707/963-1010**), purveyor of gorgeous cookware and fine housewares, you might be tempted to break out the credit cards. They're open daily from 9:30am to 5:30pm.

Shopaholics won't be able to avoid at least one sharp turn off Calif. 29 for a stop at the **St. Helena Premium Outlets,** located 2 miles north of downtown St. Helena (☎ **707/963-7282**), whose stores include Donna Karan, Coach, Movado, London Fog, and more. It's open daily from 10am to 6pm.

A last favorite stop and one of the best deals around: **Napa Valley Olive Oil Man-ufacturing Company,** 835 Charter Oak Rd., at the end of the road behind Tra Vigne restaurant (☎ **707/963-4173**). This tiny market presses and bottles its own oils and sells them at a fraction of the price you'll pay elsewhere. They also have an extensive selection of Italian cooking ingredients, imported snacks, and the best deals on exotic mushrooms we've ever seen.

If you'd like to go **biking,** the quieter northern end of the valley is an ideal place to rent a bike and ride the Silverado Trail. **St. Helena Cyclery,** 1156 Main St. (☎ **707/963-7736**), rents bikes for $7 per hour or $25 a day, including rear rack and picnic bag.

Raymond Vineyard & Cellar. 849 Zinfandel Lane (off Calif. 29 or the Silverado Trail), St. Helena. ☎ **800/525-2659** or 707/963-3141. Daily 10am–4pm. Tours by appointment only.

As fourth-generation vintners from Napa Valley and relations of the Beringers, brothers Walter and Roy Raymond have had plenty of time to develop terrific wines—and an excellent wine-tasting experience. Passing the heavy-hanging grapes on the way to the tasting room makes you feel you're really in the thick of things before you even get in the door. The spacious, warm room, complete with dining table and chairs, is a perfect setting for sampling the four tiers of wines, most of which are free for the tasting and well priced to appeal to all levels of wine drinkers. The Amber Hill label starts at $9 a bottle for the chardonnay and $13 for the cab; the reserves are priced in the mid-teens, while the "Generations" cab costs $35. Private reserve tastings cost $2.50. Sorry, no picnic facilities.

✪ **V. Sattui Winery.** 1111 White Lane (at Calif. 29), St. Helena. ☎ **707/963-7774.** Winter daily 9am–5pm; summer daily 9am–6pm.

At this combination winery and enormous gourmet deli (pronounced Vee Sa-*too*-ee), you can fill up on wine, pâté, and cheese samples without ever reaching for your pocketbook. The gourmet store stocks more than 200 cheeses, sandwich meats, breads, exotic salads, and delicious desserts such as a white-chocolate cheesecake.

Meanwhile the long wine bar in the back offers everything from chardonnay, sauvignon blanc, Riesling, cabernet, and zinfandel to a tasty Madeira and a muscat dessert wine. Their wines aren't distributed, so if you taste something you simply must have, buy it. (If you buy a case, ask to talk with a manager, who'll give you access to the less crowded, more exclusive private tasting room.) Wine prices start around $9, with many in the $13 range; reserves top out at around $75. V. Sattui's expansive, lively, and grassy picnic facilities make this a favorite for families. *Note:* To use the facilities, food and wine must be purchased here.

✪ **Joseph Phelps Vineyards.** Taplin Rd. (off the Silverado Trail), P.O. Box 1031, St. Helena. ☎ **800/707-5789.** Mon–Sat 9am–5pm; Sun 9am–4pm. Tours and tastings by appointment only.

Joseph Phelps is a favorite stop for serious wine lovers. The winery was founded in 1973 and has since become a major player in both the region and the worldwide wine market. Phelps himself is attributed with a long list of valley firsts, including launching the syrah varietal in the valley and extending the 1970s Berkeley food revolution (led by Alice Waters) up to the Wine Country via his store, the **Oakville Grocery** (see below). The intimate, comprehensive tour and knockout tasting are only available via reservation, and the location—a quick and unmarked turn off the Silverado Trail in Spring Valley—makes it impossible to find unless you're looking for it.

Those in the know come to this modern, state-of-the-art winery and find an air of seriousness that hangs heavier than harvest grapes. Fortunately, the mood lightens as the well-educated tour guide explains the details of what you're tasting while pouring samples of five to six wines, which may include Riesling, sauvignon blanc, gewürztraminer, syrah, merlot, zin, and cab. (Unfortunately, some wines are so popular that they sell out quickly; come late in the season and you may not be able to taste or buy them.) The three excellently located picnic tables, on the terrace overlooking the valley, are available by reservation.

✪ **Prager Winery & Port Works.** 1281 Lewelling Lane (just west of Calif. 29, behind Sutter Home), St. Helena. ☎ **800/969-PORT** or 707/963-7678. Daily 10:30am–4:30pm.

If you want a real down-home, off-the-beaten-track experience, Prager's can't be beat. Turn the corner from Sutter Home and roll into the small gravel parking lot. Pull open the creaky old wooden door, pass the oak barrels, and you'll quickly come upon the clapboard tasting room. Most days, your host will be Jim Prager himself, who's a sort of modern-day Santa Claus in both looks and demeanor. But you won't have to sit on his lap for your wish to come true: Just fork over $5 (refundable with purchase) and he'll pour you samples of his delicious $25 Madeline dessert wine, a late-harvest Johannisberg Riesling, the recently released 10-year-old port (which costs close to $50 per bottle), and a few other yummy selections like chardonnay and cab, which retail in the mid-$30s. Also available is "Prager Chocolate Drizzle," a chocolate liqueur that tops ice creams and other desserts.

Beringer Vineyards. 2000 Main St. (Calif. 29), St. Helena. ☎ **707/963-7115.** Off-season daily 9:30am–5pm (last tour 4pm, last tasting 4:30pm); summer 9:30am–6pm (last tour 5pm, last tasting 5:30pm). Free 45-min. tours offered every hr. between 9:30am–4pm. No reservations necessary.

Follow the line of cars just north of St. Helena's business district to Beringer Vineyards, where everyone stops at the remarkable Rhine House to taste wine and view the hand-dug tunnels carved out of the mountainside. Founded in 1876 by brothers Jacob and Frederick, this is the oldest continuously operating winery in the Napa Valley—it was open even during Prohibition, when Beringer kept afloat by making "sacramental" wines. While their white zinfandel is still the winery's most popular nationwide seller, the 1994 chardonnay is the choice for more discerning palates: It won *Wine Spectator*'s 1996 Wine of the Year award. Free tastings of current vintages are conducted in the upstairs gift shop, where there's also a large selection of bottles for less than $20. Reserve wines are available in the Rhine House for a fee of $2 to $6 per taste.

Charles Krug Winery. 2800 St. Helena Hwy. (just north of the tunnel of trees at the northern end of St. Helena), St. Helena. ☎ **707/963-5057.** Daily 10:30am–5:30pm. Tours daily at 11:30am, 1:30pm, and 3:30pm.

Founded in 1861, Krug was the first winery built in the valley, and is today owned by the family of Peter Mondavi (yes, Robert is his brother). It's worth paying your respects here with a $3 tour, which takes just under an hour and encompasses a walk through the historic redwood Italianate wine cellar, built in 1874, as well as the vineyards, where you'll learn more about grapes and varietals. The tour ends with a tasting in the retail center. But you don't have to tour to taste: Just stop by and fork over $3 to sip current releases, $5 to sample reserves; you'll also get a souvenir glass. On the grounds are picnic facilities with umbrella-shaded tables overlooking vineyards or the historic wine cellar.

CALISTOGA

The last tourist town in Napa Valley was named by Sam Brannan, entrepreneur extraordinaire and California's first millionaire. After making a bundle supplying miners during the gold rush, he went on to take advantage of the natural geothermal springs at the north end of the Napa Valley by building a hotel and spa here in 1859. Flubbing up a speech in which he compared this natural California wonder to New York State's Saratoga Springs resort, he serendipitously coined the name "Calistoga," and it stuck.

Today, this small, simple resort town with 4,400 residents and an old-time main street (no building along the 6-block stretch is more than two stories high) is popular with city folk who come here to unwind. Calistoga is a great place to relax and indulge in mineral waters, mud baths, Jacuzzis, massages, and, of course, wine. The vibe is more casual—and a little more groovy—than you'll find in neighboring towns to the south.

You can rent bikes from **Getaway Adventures BHK** (Biking, Hiking, and Kayaking), 1117 Lincoln Ave. (☎ **800/499-BIKE** or 707/942-0332; www.getawayadventures.com). Full-day tours cost $89 and include lunch and a visit to four or five wineries; downhill cruises ($49) are available for people who hate to pedal. On weekdays they'll even deliver bikes to you. You can also rent a bike and explore on your own for $8 per hour, $18 per half day, and $25 for 24 hours. There are no bike paths, but the roads are fairly flat and easy to pedal.

If you like horses and venturing through cool, misty forests, then $40 will seem like a bargain for a 1½-hour ride with a friendly tour guide from **Napa Valley Trail Rides**

(☎ **707/996-8566;** www.thegridnet/trailrides/). After you've been saddled and schooled in the basics of horse handling at the stable, you'll be led on a leisurely stroll (with the occasional trot thrown in for excitement) through beautiful Bothe–Napa Valley State Park, located off Calif. 29 near Calistoga. They also offer a Western Barbecue Ride, Sunset Ride, Full Moon Ride, and Gourmet Boxed Lunch Ride & Winery Tour. We've taken the trip ourselves and loved every minute of it—sore butts and all.

NATURAL WONDERS

Old Faithful Geyser of California. 1299 Tubbs Lane. ☎ **707/942-6463.** Admission $6 adults, $5 seniors, $2 children 6–12, free for children under 6. Daily 9am–6pm (to 5pm in winter). Follow the signs from downtown Calistoga; it's between Calif. 29 and Calif. 128.

This is one of only three "old faithful" geysers in the world. It's been blowing off steam at regular intervals for as long as anyone can remember. The 350°F water spews out to a height of about 60 feet every 40 minutes, day and night (varying with natural influences such as barometric pressure, the moon, tides, and tectonic stresses). The performance lasts about a minute, and you can watch the show as many times as you wish. Bring along a picnic lunch to munch on between spews. An exhibit hall, gift shop, and snack bar are open daily.

Petrified Forest. 4100 Petrified Forest Rd. ☎ **707/942-6667.** Admission $4 adults, $3 seniors and children 11–17, $1 children 4–10, free for children under 4. Daily 10am–5:30pm (to 4:30pm in winter). Heading north from Calistoga on Calif. 128, turn left onto Petrified Forest Rd., just past Lincoln St.

You won't see thousands of trees turned into stone, but you'll still find many interesting petrified specimens here. Volcanic ash blanketed this area after the eruption of Mt. St. Helena 3 million years ago. As a result, you'll find redwoods that have turned to rock through the slow infiltration of silicas and other minerals, as well as petrified seashells, clams, and marine life indicating that water covered this area even before the redwood forest.

THE CALISTOGA WINERIES

✪ **Kornell Champagne Cellars.** 1091 Larkmead Lane (just off the Silverado Trail), Calistoga. ☎ **707/942-0859.** Daily 10am–4:30pm.

Kornell's wine dudes—Dennis, Bob, Chris, and Rich—will do practically anything to maintain their self-proclaimed reputation as running the "friendliest winery in the valley." They'll serve you all the bubbly you want (four to six varieties: brut, blanc de blanc, blanc de noir, and extra-dry reserve), all ranging from $15 to $20 a bottle. They guarantee that you'll never wait more than 10 minutes to take the 20-minute tour of the oldest champagne cellar in the region, and even offer up a great story about Marie Antoinette's champagne-glass design.

The tasting room is casual-modern, but the stone cellar (listed on the National Register of Historic Places) captures the essence of the Wine Country's history. Meander into the Back Room, where chardonnay, zinfandel, and cabernet are poured. Behind the tasting room is a choice picnic area, situated under the oaks and overlooking the vineyards.

✪ **Schramsberg.** 1400 Schramsberg Rd. (off Calif. 29), Calistoga. ☎ **707/942-4558.** Daily 10am–4pm. Tours and tastings by appointment only.

This 200-acre champagne estate, a landmark once frequented by Robert Louis Stevenson, has a wonderful old-world feel and is one of our all-time favorite places to explore. Schramsberg is the label that presidents serve when toasting dignitaries from around the globe, and there's plenty of historic memorabilia in the front room to

Glorious Calistoga Mud Baths

The one thing you should do while you're in Calistoga is what people have been doing here for the last 150 years: Take a mud bath. The natural baths are composed of local volcanic ash, imported peat, and naturally boiling mineral hot-springs water, all mulled together to produce a thick mud that simmers at a temperature of about 104°F.

Follow your soak in the mud with a warm mineral-water shower, a whirlpool bath, a visit to the steam room, and a relaxing blanket-wrap. The outcome: A rejuvenated, revitalized, squeaky-clean new you. Most places charge about $45 for a 90-minute mud bath; fancier places can charge up to $85.

Indulge yourself at any of these Calistoga spas: **Dr. Wilkinson's Hot Springs,** 1507 Lincoln Ave. (☎ 707/942-4102); **Lincoln Avenue Spa,** 1339 Lincoln Ave. (☎ 707/942-5296); **Golden Haven Hot Springs Spa,** 1713 Lake St. (☎ 707/942-6793); **Calistoga Spa Hot Springs,** 1006 Washington St. (☎ 707/942-6269); **Calistoga Village Inn & Spa,** 1880 Lincoln Ave. (☎ 707/942-0991); **Eurospa & Inn,** 1202 Pine St. (☎ 707/942-6829); **Indian Springs Resort,** 1712 Lincoln Ave. (☎ 707/942-4913); **Lavender Hill Spa,** 1015 Foothill Blvd. (☎ 800/528-4772); **Mount View Spa,** 1457 Lincoln Ave. (☎ 707/942-5789); **Nance's Hot Springs,** 1614 Lincoln Ave. (☎ 707/942-6211); or the **Roman Spa Motel,** 1300 Washington St. (☎ 707/942-4441).

prove it. But the real mystique begins when you enter the champagne caves, which wind 2½ miles (the longest in North America, they say) and were partly hand-carved by Chinese laborers in the 1800s. The caves have an authentic Tom Sawyer ambiance, complete with dangling cobwebs and seemingly endless passageways; you can't help but feel you're on an adventure. The comprehensive, unintimidating tour ends in a charming tasting room, where you'll sit around a big table and sample several surprisingly varied selections of bubbly. Tasting prices are a bit dear at $7.50 per person, but it's money well spent. Note, however, that tastings are only offered to those who take the free tour, and you must reserve a spot in advance.

✪ **Clos Pegase.** 1060 Dunaweal Lane (off Calif. 29 or the Silverado Trail), Calistoga. ☎ **707/942-4981.** Daily 10:30am–5pm. Tours daily at 11am and 2pm.

Renowned architect Michael Graves designed this incredible oasis, which integrates art, 20,000 square feet of aging caves, and a luxurious hilltop private home on its 450 acres. Viewing the art here is as much the point as tasting the wines—which, by the way, don't come cheap: Prices range from $18.50 for the 1995 Mitsuko's chardonnay to as much as $50 for the 1994 Hommage Artist Series Reserve, an extremely limited blend of the winery's finest lots of cabernet sauvignon and merlot. Tasting all the current releases will cost $2.50, and reserves are $2 each. The grounds at Clos Pegase (pronounced *Clo* Pay-*goss*) feature an impressive sculpture garden as well as scenic picnic spots.

Sterling Vineyards. 1111 Dunaweal Lane (off Calif. 29, just south of Calistoga), Calistoga. ☎ **707/942-3300.** Daily 10:30am–4:30pm.

No, you don't need climbing shoes to reach this dazzling white Mediterranean-style winery, perched 300 feet up on a rocky knoll. Just fork over $6 and you'll arrive via aerial tram, which offers dazzling bucolic views along the way. Once on land, follow the self-guided tour (the most comprehensive in the entire Wine Country) of the wine-making process. Currently owned by the Seagram company, the winery produces more than 200,000 cases per year. Samples at the panoramic tasting room are included in the tram fare. Expect to pay anywhere from $8 to $50 for a souvenir bottle ($16 is the average), and if you can find a bottle of their 1995 Napa Valley chardonnay (currently going for about $14), buy it—it's already garnered a septuplet of awards.

2 Accommodations & Dining in Napa Valley

WHERE TO STAY

Accommodations here run the gamut—from motels and B&Bs to world-class luxury retreats—and all are easily accessible from the main highway. While we recommend shacking up in the more romantically pastoral areas such as St. Helena and haven't even bothered mentioning the absurdly priced resorts and inns, there's no question you're going to find better deals in the towns of Napa or laid-back Calistoga.

Keep in mind that during the high season—between June and November—most hotels charge peak rates and sell out completely on weekends; many have a 2-night minimum. If you need help organizing your Wine Country vacation, contact one of the following companies: **Accommodation Referral Bed & Breakfast Exchange** (☎ **800/240-8466,** 800/499-8466 in Calif., or 707/963-8466), which also represents hotels and inns; **Bed & Breakfast Inns of Napa Valley** (☎ **707/944-4444**), an association of 26 Napa Valley B&Bs that provides inn descriptions and makes reservations; or **Napa Valley Reservations Unlimited** (☎ **800/251-NAPA** or 707/252-1985), which is also a source for everything from hot-air-balloon to glider rides.

SUPER-CHEAP SLEEPS

Calistoga Inn. 1250 Lincoln Ave. (at Cedar St.), Calistoga, CA 94515. ☎ **707/942-4101.** 18 units, none with bathroom. $49–$65 double. AE, MC, V.

Would the fact that the Calistoga Inn has its own brewery influence our decision to recommend it? You betcha. Here's the deal: You're probably in town for the spa treatments, but unfortunately, the guest rooms at almost every spa are lacking in the personality-and-warmth department. A better bet for the budget traveler is to book a room at this homey turn-of-the-century inn, then walk a few blocks up the street for your mud bath and massage. You'll have to share the bathrooms, and the rooms above the inn's restaurant can be noisy, but otherwise you get a cozy little room with a double or queen bed, washbasin, and continental breakfast for only $65 on weekends (that's half the average room rate in these parts). What's more, no 2-night minimum is required, and the best beer in town is served downstairs. *Tip:* Request a room as far from the bar/restaurant as possible.

FOR A FEW BUCKS MORE/MODERATELY PRICED OPTIONS

Calistoga Spa Hot Springs. 1006 Washington St. (at Gerrard St.), Calistoga, CA 94515. ☎ **707/942-6269.** 57 units, 1 family unit. A/C TV TEL. Winter $70 double; $95 family unit; $110 suite. Summer $85 double; $110 family unit; $130 suite. MC, V.

Very few hotels in the Wine Country welcome children, which is why we strongly recommend the Calistoga Spa Hot Springs for families. Even if you don't have kids in tow, it's still a great bargain, offering unpretentious yet clean and comfortable rooms with kitchenettes, as well as a plethora of spa facilities ranging from exercise rooms to four naturally heated outdoor mineral pools, aerobic facilities, volcanic-ash mud baths, mineral baths, steam baths, blanket wraps, massage sessions, and more. All of Calistoga's best shops and restaurants are within easy walking distance, and you can even whip up your own grub at the barbecues set up near the large pool and patio area.

Chablis Inn. 3360 Solano Ave., Napa, CA 94558. ☎ **707/257-1944.** Fax 707/226-6862. 34 units. A/C TV TEL. Mid-Nov to Mar $60–$95 double; Apr–Mid-Nov $75–$125 double. AE, DC, DISC, MC, V.

There's no way around it. If you want to sleep cheaply in a town where the *average* room goes for upward of $200 per night in high season, you're going to have to motel it. But look on the bright side: Since your room is likely to be little more than a crashing pad after a day of eating and drinking, a clean bed and a remote control are all you'll really need. But Chablis offers much more than that. Each of the superclean motel-style rooms has a fridge and coffeemaker; some even boast kitchenettes and/or whirlpool tubs. Guests have access to an outdoor heated pool and hot tub, plus a basic continental breakfast. Friendly owner Ken Patel is on hand most of the time and is constantly upgrading his tidy highway-side hostelry; his project in 1998 was to replace all of the mattresses in 1998.

✪ **El Bonita Motel.** 195 Main St. (at El Bonita Ave.), St. Helena, CA 94574. ☎ **800/541-3284** or 707/963-3216. Fax 707/963-8838. 41 units. A/C MINIBAR TV TEL. Dec–Mar $75–$89 double; Apr–May and Nov $89–$115 double; June–Oct $95–$115 double. AE, CB, DC, DISC, MC, V.

This 1930s art-deco motel was built a bit too close to Calif. 29 for comfort, but the 2½ acres of beautifully landscaped gardens behind the place (away from the road) help even the score. The rooms, while small, are spotlessly clean and decorated with new furnishings; all have microwaves and coffeemakers, and some have kitchens or whirlpool baths. Families, attracted to the larger bungalows with kitchenettes, regard El Bonita as one of the best values in Napa Valley—especially considering the heated outdoor pool, Jacuzzi, sauna, and new massage facility.

Napa Valley Budget Inn. 3380 Solano Ave., Napa, CA 94558. ☎ **707/257-6111.** Fax 707/252-2702. 58 units. A/C TV TEL. Mid-Nov to Mar $60–$105 double; Apr to mid-Nov from $90 double. Rates include continental breakfast. AE, DC, DISC, MC, V. From Calif. 29 N., turn left onto the Redwood Rd. turnoff and go 1 block to Solano Ave.; then turn left and go a ½ block to the motel.

This no-frills lodging offers an excellent location—close to Calif. 29—and simple, clean, and comfortable rooms. Local calls are free, and guests can enjoy the complimentary coffee in the lobby and the small pool on the premises (heated in summer only). If you reserve a room here, note that the bathrooms have showers only.

✪ **Napa Valley Railway Inn.** 6503 Washington St. (adjacent to the Vintage 1870 shopping complex), Yountville, CA 94599. ☎ **707/944-2000.** 9 units. A/C TV. $75–$130 double. AE, MC, V.

This is one of our favorite places to stay in the Wine Country. Why? Because it's inexpensive and it's cute as all get out. Looking hokey as heck from the outside, the Railway Inn consists of two rows of sun-bleached cabooses and railcars sitting on a stretch of Yountville's original track and connected by a covered wooden walkway. Things get considerably better, though, as you enter your private caboose or railcar, each sumptuously appointed with comfy love seats, queen-size brass beds, and tiled full bathrooms. The coups de grâce are the bay windows and skylights, which let in plenty of California sunshine. The railcars are all suites, so if you're looking to save your pennies, opt for the cabooses. Adjacent to the inn is Yountville's main shopping complex, which includes wine tastings and some good low-priced restaurants.

✪ **White Sulphur Springs Retreat & Spa.** 3100 White Sulphur Springs Rd., St. Helena, 94574. ☎ **707/963-8588.** Fax 707/963-2890. 28 units, 9 cottages. Carriage House (with shared bathroom) $65–$115 double; The Inn $85–$125 double; small Creekside Cottages $105–$155; large Creekside Cottages $125–$185. Additional person

$15 extra. Discounts available during off-season and midweek. Single-night stays accepted in Carriage House rooms, but cottages require a 2-night minimum weekends from Apr–Oct and all holidays. MC, V.

If your idea of the ultimate vacation is a cozy cabin set among 330 acres of creeks, waterfalls, hot springs, hiking trails, and redwood, madrone, and fir trees, paradise is a short winding drive away from downtown St. Helena. Established in 1852, Sulphur Springs claims to be the oldest resort in California. Guests stay at the inn or in small and large creek-side cabins. Each is decorated with simple but homey furnishings; some have fireplaces or wood-burning stoves and/or kitchenettes. The most upscale are the newly renovated cabins, but the well-worn, wood-paneled ones seem appropriate considering the natural surroundings. From here you can venture off on a hike; take a dip in the natural hot sulphur spring; lounge by the pool; sit under a tree and watch for deer, fox, raccoon, spotted owl, or woodpecker; or schedule a day of massage, aromatherapy, and other spa treatments. *Note:* No RVs are allowed without advance notice.

Wine Valley Lodge. 200 S. Coombs St. (between First and Imola sts.), Napa, CA 94558. ☎ **707/224-7911.** 53 units. A/C TV TEL. $57–$94 double; $77–$154 suite. AE, DISC, MC, V.

Dollar for dollar, the Wine Valley Lodge offers the most for the least in all of Wine Country. Located at the south end of town in a quiet residential neighborhood, the mission-style motel is extremely well kept and accessible—just a short drive from Calif. 29 and the wineries to the north. Soft pastels dominate the color scheme, featured prominently in the matching quilted bedspreads, furniture, and objets d'art. Its decor is reminiscent of Grandma's house, to be sure, but at these prices, who cares? The clincher on the whole deal is a fetching little oasis in the center courtyard, consisting of a sundeck, barbecue, and pool flanked by a cadre of odd teacup-shaped hedges.

WORTH A SPLURGE

Cedar Gables Inn. 486 Coombs St., Napa, CA 94559. ☎ **800/309-7969** or 707/224-7969. Fax 707/224-4838. www.cedargablesinn.com. 6 units. $129–$189 double ($10 less in winter). Rates include breakfast. AE, DISC, MC, V. From Calif. 29 N., exit onto First St. and follow signs to downtown; turn right onto Coombs St.; the house is at the corner of Oak St.

Innkeepers Margaret and Craig Snasdell have developed quite a following with their cozy, romantic B&B in Old Town Napa. The Victorian was built in 1892, and rooms reflect the era with rich tapestries and stunning gilded antiques. Four rooms have fireplaces; four have whirlpool tubs; and all feature queen-size brass, wood, or iron beds. Guests meet each evening in front of the roaring fireplace in the family room for complimentary wine and cheese. At other times, it's a perfect place to cuddle up and watch the large-screen TV.

✪ Cottage Grove Inn. 1711 Lincoln Ave., Calistoga, CA 94515. ☎ **800/799-2284** or 707/942-8400. Fax 707/942-2653. 16 cottages (1 handicapped accessible). A/C TV TEL. $195 double. Rates include continental breakfast and evening wine and cheese. AE, DC, MC, V.

Standing in two parallel rows at the end of the main strip in Calistoga are the perfect couples retreats—brand-spanking-new cottages that, though located on a residential street, seem well-removed from the action once you've stepped across the threshold. Each compact guest house comes complete with a wood-burning fireplace, homey furnishings (perfect for curling up in front of the fire), cozy quilts, and an enormous bathroom with a skylight and a deep, two-person Jacuzzi tub, plus such niceties as gourmet coffee, a stereo with CD player, VCR (a video library is on-site), wet bar, and fridge. Smokers beware—it's not allowed inside, but you can puff all you want on the small front porch. Several major spas are within walking distance. This is our top pick if you want to do the Calistoga spa scene in comfort and style.

✪ **Deer Run Bed & Breakfast.** 3995 Spring Mountain Rd. (P.O. Box 311), St. Helena, CA 94574. ☎ **800/843-3408** or 707/963-3794. Fax 707/963-9026. 4 units, all with shower only. A/C TV. $130–$165 double. AE, MC, V.

Regardless of your budget, if romantic solitude is a big part of your vacation plan, Deer Run had better be on your itinerary. Situated 4½ miles (10 min. by car) from downtown St. Helena along a winding mountain road, this four-room B&B is the ultimate heavenly hideaway. Each of the wood-paneled rooms looks onto owners Tom and Carol Wilson's 4 acres of forest, and all feature gorgeous antiques, feather beds, private entrance, deck, decanter of brandy, fridge, coffee and tea, robes, hair dryer, and access to hiking trails. Deer often meander by the Honeymoon Suite (the most secluded), a sweet split-level cottage with a separate bedroom and gas fireplace; its price includes breakfast delivered to your doorstep. The full breakfast served in the main house may include a frittata or apple crepes with chicken-apple sausage. Outside you'll find Cody, the resident chocolate Lab, hanging out by the very small pool.

Rancho Caymus. 1140 Rutherford Rd. (P.O. Box 78), Rutherford, CA 94573. ☎ **800/845-1777** or 707/963-1777. Fax 707/963-5387. 26 suites. A/C MINIBAR TV TEL. $145–$175 double; from $245 Master Suite; $295 two-bedroom suite. Rates include continental breakfast. AE, DC, MC, V. From Calif. 29 N., turn right onto Rutherford Rd./Calif. 128 E.; the hotel is ahead on your left.

This Spanish-style hacienda, with two floors opening onto wisteria-covered balconies, was the creation of sculptor Mary Tilden Morton (of Morton Salt). Morton wanted each room in the hacienda to be a work of art, thus she hired the most skilled craftspeople of her day. She designed the adobe fireplaces herself, and wandered through Mexico and South America purchasing artifacts for the property.

Guest rooms are situated around a whimsical garden courtyard with an enormous outdoor fireplace. The mix-and-match interior decor is on the funky side, with overly varnished dark-wood furnishings and braided rugs. The inn is cozy, however, and rooms are decent-size, split-level suites with queen beds. Other amenities include wet bars, sofa beds in the sitting areas, and small private patios. Most of the suites have fireplaces, and five have kitchenettes and whirlpool tubs. Breakfast, which includes fresh fruit, granola, orange juice, and breads, is served in the inn's dining room. At press time, there were plans to open a full-service restaurant.

Wine Country Inn. 1152 Lodi Lane, St. Helena, CA 94574. ☎ **707/963-7077.** Fax 707/963-9018. E-mail: romance@winecountryinn.com. 24 units, all with bathroom (12 with shower only). A/C TEL. $130–$258 double. Rates include breakfast. MC, V.

Just off the highway behind Freemark Abbey vineyard, this attractive wood-and-stone inn, complete with a French-style mansard roof and turret, overlooks a pastoral landscape of Napa Valley vineyards. The individually decorated rooms are outfitted with iron or brass beds, antique furnishings, and handmade quilts; most have fireplaces and private terraces overlooking the valley, while others have private hot tubs. One of the inn's best features, besides the absence of TVs, is the outdoor pool (heated year-round), which is attractively landscaped into the hillside.

Another favorite is the selection of suites, which come with stereos, plenty of space, and lots of privacy. Wine and appetizers are served nightly, along with a big dash of hotel-staff hospitality in the inviting living room. A full buffet breakfast is served there, too.

WHERE TO DINE

To best enjoy Napa's restaurant scene, keep a few things in mind: *reserve*—especially for seats in a more renowned room—and eat a late lunch to avoid pricey dinners.

SUPER-CHEAP EATS

Alexis Baking Company. 1517 Third St. (between Main and Jefferson sts.), Napa. ☎ **707/258-1827.** Breakfast items $3.25–$6.25; main courses $6–$8 at lunch, $6.75–$13 dinner. Mon–Fri 6:30am–3pm; Sat 7:30am–3pm; Sun 8am–2pm. BAKERY/CAFE.

This is a great stopover for vegetarians and sweet tooths, a bakery/restaurant so popular that there's almost always a line out the door on weekend mornings. But once you order from the counter and find a seat in the sunny room, you can relax, enjoy the casual coffeehouse atmosphere, and start your day with spectacular pastries, coffee drinks, and breakfast goodies like pumpkin pancakes with sautéed pears. Lunch also bustles with locals who come for the daily specials like fusilli pasta with roasted pumpkin, white beans, ham, and Parmesan in a cream sauce; grilled-chicken Caesar salad; roast lamb sandwich with minted mayo and roasted shallots on rosemary bread; and lentil bulgar orzo salad. Desserts run the gamut and include a moist and magical steamed persimmon pudding during the holiday season.

Bosko's. 1364 Lincoln Ave. (between Cedar and Washington sts.), Calistoga. ☎ **707/942-9088.** Main courses $6.25–$10. MC, V. Daily 11am–10pm. ITALIAN.

It's hard not to like a place that keeps sawdust on its floors, because you immediately know that you won't encounter any snooty waiters or jacked-up prices. Bosko's formula is simple: Serve good, cheap Italian food hot and fast, and make sure nobody leaves hungry. It's a homey place, with red-and-white-checkered tablecloths, an exposed beam ceiling, and a huge U-shaped counter that's always occupied by a least one or two locals. All 16 versions of pasta are cooked to order, as are the 10 or so pizzas and hot sandwiches. Order at the counter, scramble for a table, and then wait for your food to be delivered. The lunch special is a great deal: half a sandwich or plate of pasta, salad, and a darn good bowl of minestrone soup (needs salt, however). Even more brilliant is the method of wine selection: Simply choose a bottle from the wine rack, pay retail for it at the counter, and drink it with your meal. Why don't they all do it this way?

✪ **The Cantinetta.** At Tra Vigne Restaurant, 1050 Charter Oak Ave., St. Helena. ☎ **707/963-8888.** Main courses $4–$8. CB, DC, DISC, MC, V. Daily 11:30am–6pm. ITALIAN.

Regardless of where we dine while in the valley, we always make a point of stopping at the Cantinetta for an espresso and a snack. Part cafe, part shop, it's a casual place with a few tables and a counter. The focaccias (we've never had better in our lives!), pasta salads, and pastries are outstanding, and there's also a selection of cookies and other wonderful treats, flavored oils (free tastings), wines, and an array of gourmet items, many of which were created here. You can also get great picnic grub to go.

✪ **Oakville Grocery Café.** 7848 St. Helena Hwy. (Calif. 29, at the Oakville Cross Rd.), Oakville. ☎ **707/944-0111.** Reservations available for parties of 8 or more. Breakfast $4–$7.50; lunch main courses $5.50–$9. AE, MC, V. Daily 7:30am–11am breakfast; 11am–4pm lunch. CALIFORNIA.

This is one of our favorite places to eat regardless of our budget. The ovation-worthy lunch menu features a melt-in-your-mouth salmon, watercress, and herb-aioli sandwich ($8); soups, such as a hearty vegetable barley; salads (Niçoise, goat cheese with field greens and peach-chardonnay vinaigrette, and hearts of romaine); pizzas, such as wild mushroom; and lasagna. Breakfast is celebrated with "Small Plates" such as granola ($3.75), toasted breads with house preserves ($2), and a breakfast fruit tart; and "Big Plates" of chicken hash ($7), eggs, omelets, and frittatas. Counter service keeps the prices down, thick windows keep traffic noise out, and an absolutely fab meal and sweet ambiance keep the local constituency coming back for more. Our only complaint: They weren't open for dinner yet. (But as of Mar 1998, they are open a few nights a week; call for details.)

Tomatina. At The Inn at Southbridge, 1016 Main St., St. Helena. ☎ **707/967-9999.** Pasta $6–$8; pizza $8–$19. DC, DISC, MC, V. Daily 11:30am–10pm. ITALIAN.

After we've been in the Wine Country for about a week, we usually can't stand the thought of one more decadent wine and foie gras meal. That's when we race to Tomatina for a $3.50 chopped salad, a welcome respite from all the gluttonous excess. Families and locals come here for another reason: Though the menu is limited, it's a total winner for anyone looking for freshly prepared, wholesome food at atypically cheap Wine Country prices. A Caesar salad, for example, costs a mere $4.50. "Apizzas"—pizzas folded like a soft taco—are the house specialty, and come filled with such delights as fresh Maine clams and oregano. Pizzas are of the build-your-own variety with gourmet toppings like sautéed mushrooms, fennel sausage, baby spinach, sun-dried tomatoes, and homemade pepperoni. The 26 respectable local wines are served by the glass at a toast-worthy cost of $3.75, or $18 per bottle. As for dessert, at less than $4 a pop for gelato, biscotti, or pound cake, it's an overall sweet deal. Everything is ordered at the counter and brought to the small or family-style tables in the very casual dining area or the outdoor patio. Kids especially like the pool table and big-screen TV.

FOR A FEW BUCKS MORE

The Diner. 6476 Washington St., Yountville. ☎ **707/944-2626.** Breakfast items $4–$8; main courses $6–$10 at lunch, $8–$13.25 at dinner. No credit cards. Tues–Sun 8am–3pm and 5:30–9pm. From Calif. 29 N., take the Yountville exit and turn left onto Washington St. AMERICAN/MEXICAN.

Funky California meets traditional roadside eatery at this popular diner, decorated with a collection of vintage diner water pitchers and a rotating art exhibit. The Diner's fare is far from that of a regular greasy spoon—the "home-style" menu is extensive, portions are huge, and the food is very good. Breakfasts feature good old-fashioned omelets, French toast, and German potato pancakes. Lunch and dinner dishes include a host of Mexican and American dishes such as chicken picatta with veggies and rice, grilled fresh fish, giant burritos, and thick sandwiches made with house-roasted meats and homemade bread.

Downtown Joe's. 902 Main St. (at Second St.), Napa. ☎ **707/258-2337.** Dinner main courses $8–$14. AE, DC, DISC, MC, V. Mon–Fri 8:30–11am (breakfast) and 11am–10pm; Sat–Sun 8:30am–2pm (brunch) and 3–10pm. AMERICAN BISTRO.

Don't let the name fool you: Downtown Joe's is anything but a greasy diner. Working from a proven formula—good food and lots of it at a fair price—Joe's has capitalized on a prime location in downtown Napa and created what's widely regarded as the best place in town to grub and groove. The menu is all over the place, offering everything from porterhouse steaks to oysters, omelets, pasta, and seafood specials. The beers, such as the tart Lickety Split Lager, are made in-house, as are the breads and desserts. If the sun's out, request a table on the outside patio adjacent to the park. Thursday through Sunday nights, rock, jazz, and blues bands draw in the locals.

Another great reason to visit Joe's is "Hoppy Hour," from 4 to 6pm Monday through Thursday, featuring $2.50 pints and free appetizers plus a drawing every half hour to win free stuff. Every Friday is TGIF, with a giveaway (appetizers, wine, etc.) every 15 minutes.

Wappo Bar & Bistro. 1226B Washington St. (off Lincoln Ave.), Calistoga. ☎ **707/ 942-4712.** Main courses $8.50–$14.50. AE, MC, V. Wed–Mon 11:30am–2:30pm and 6–9:30pm. INTERNATIONAL.

One of the best alfresco dining experiences in the Wine Country is under Wappo's honeysuckle-and-vine-covered arbor, but you'll also be comfortable inside this small bistro at one of the well-spaced, well-polished tables. The menu offers a wide range of choices, from Chilean sea bass with mint chutney to roast rabbit with potato gnocchi. The desserts of choice are the black-bottom coconut cream pie and the strawberry rhubarb pie.

MODERATELY PRICED OPTIONS

All Seasons Café. 1400 Lincoln Ave. (at Washington St.), Calistoga. ☎ **707/942-9111.** Reservations recommended on weekends. Main courses $10.25–$19 at dinner. MC, V. Mon–Tues and Thurs–Fri 11am–3pm; daily 5:30–10pm. Wine shop Thurs–Tues 11am–7pm. CALIFORNIA.

Wine Country devotees often wend their way to the All Seasons Café in downtown Calistoga because of its extensive wine list and knowledgeable staff. The trick here is to buy a bottle of wine from the cafe's wine shop, then bring it to your table; the cafe adds a corkage fee of around $7.50 instead of tripling the price of the bottle (as they do at most restaurants). The diverse menu ranges from pizzas and pastas to such main courses as braised lamb shank osso buco in an orange, Madeira, and tomato sauce. Anything with the house-smoked salmon or spiced sausages is also a safe bet. Chef John Coss saves his guests from any major *faux pas* by matching wines to his dishes on the menu, so you know what's just right for smoked salmon as well as Crescenza cheese pizza.

Bistro Don Giovanni. 4110 St. Helena Hwy. (on Calif. 29, just north of Salvador Ave.), Napa. ☎ **707/224-3300.** Reservations recommended Fri–Sat. Main courses $11–$17. AE, DC, MC, V. Mon–Thurs 11:30am–10pm; Fri–Sun 11:30am–11pm. NORTHERN ITALIAN.

Donna and Giovanni Scala—who also run the fantastic Scala's Bistro in San Francisco—serve refined Italian fare prepared with top-quality ingredients and California flair at this large, lively, Mediterranean-style restaurant. The menu features pastas, risottos, pizzas (baked in a wood-burning oven), and a half dozen other main courses such as braised lamb shank and Niman-Schell bistro burgers. Less traditional appetizers include a grilled pear with a frisée-and-arugula salad with bleu cheese, caramelized walnuts, and bacon. Pasta lovers should go for the farfalle with asparagus, porcini, wild mushrooms, pecorino cheese, and truffle oil. Alfresco dining among the vineyards is available—and highly recommended on a warm, sunny day.

✪ **Catahoula.** 1457 Lincoln Ave. (between Washington and Fairway sts.), Calistoga. ☎ **707/942-2275.** Reservations recommended. Main courses $11–$20. MC, V. Winter Sat–Sun 8:30–10am; summer Fri–Sun 8:30–10am. Year-round Mon and Wed–Fri noon–2:30pm; Sat–Sun noon–3:30pm; daily 5:30–10:30pm. AMERICAN/SOUTHERN.

The domain of chef Jan Birnbaum, formerly of New York's Quilted Giraffe and San Francisco's Campton Place, this restaurant is the current favorite in town. And for good reason—it's the only place in Napa where you can get a decent rooster gumbo. You'd have to travel all over Louisiana to find another pan-fried jalapeño-pecan catfish like this one. Catahoula is funky and fun, and the food that comes out of the wood-burning oven—like the roast duck with chili-cilantro potatoes or the whole roasted fish with lemon broth, orzo, and escarole—is exciting (and usually spicy). Start with the spicy gumbo ya ya with andouille sausage, and finish with what may be a first for many non-Southerners—buttermilk ice cream.

Mustards Grill. 7399 St. Helena Hwy. (Calif. 29), Yountville. ☎ **707/944-2424.** Reservations recommended. Main courses $11–$17. CB, DC, DISC, MC, V. Apr–Oct daily 11:30am–10pm; Nov–Mar daily 11:30am–9pm. CALIFORNIA.

Mustards is a safe bet for anyone in search of a casual atmosphere and quality food that's not overly adventurous. Housed in a convivial, barn-style space, it offers an 11-page wine list and an ambitious chalkboard list of specials. We started out with a wonderfully light seared ahi tuna that melted in our mouths the way ahi should. Although the hoisin quail with apricot sauce and bok choy and the lamb shank braised in syrah with fennel and onions were tempting, we opted for a moist, perfectly flavored grilled chicken breast with mashed potatoes and fresh herbs. The menu includes something for everyone, from gourmands and vegetarians to good old burger lovers.

✪ **Piatti.** 6480 Washington St. (between Mission and Oak sts.), Yountville. ☎ **707/944-2070.** Reservations recommended. Main courses $7–$16. AE, DC, MC, V. Sun–Thurs 11:30am–10pm; Fri–Sat 11:30am–11pm. ITALIAN.

This local favorite—the first (and best) of a swiftly growing northern California chain—is known for serving excellent, reasonably priced food in a rustic Italian-style setting. Chef Peter Hall, a seasoned Napa Valley cook who honed his culinary art at Tra Vigne and Mustards before taking over the helm here, performs to a mostly sold-out crowd nightly. For the perfect meal, start with a salad of morning-cut field greens mixed with white corn and Napa Valley strawberry crostini, accompanied by a bowl of the spaghetti-squash-and-sweet-potato soup. Though Hall offers a wide array of superb pastas and pizzas, it's the wood-oven-roasted duck—basted with a sweet cherry sauce and served over a bed of citrus risotto—that brings back the regulars. There are far fancier and more intimate restaurants in the valley, but we can't think of any that can fill you up on such outstanding fare at these prices. *Note:* Piatti also offers patio dining year-round, weather permitting.

Smokehouse Café. 1458 Lincoln Ave., Calistoga. ☎ **707/942-6060.** Main courses $8–$21. MC, V. Daily 7:30am–10pm. Closed Tues–Wed in Jan–Feb. REGIONAL AMERICAN BBQ.

Who would have guessed that some of the best spareribs and house-smoked meats in northern California would come from this little kitchen in Calistoga? Here's the winning game plan: Start with the Sacramento delta crawfish cakes (better than any wimpy crab cakes you'll find in San Francisco) and husk-roasted Cheyenne corn, then move on to the slow pig sandwich, a half slab of ribs, or homemade sausages—all of which take up to a week to prepare (not while you wait, luckily). The clincher, though, is the fluffy all-you-can-eat cornbread dipped in pure cane syrup, which comes with every full-plate dinner. Kids are especially catered to—a rarity in these parts—and patio dining is available during the summer for breakfast, lunch, and dinner.

Tra Vigne Restaurant. 1050 Charter Oak Ave., St. Helena. ☎ **707/963-4444.** Reservations recommended. Main courses $12.50–$22; Cantinetta $4–$8. CB, DC, DISC, MC, V. Daily 11:30am–10pm; Cantinetta daily 11:30am–6pm. ITALIAN.

Tra Vigne's combination of good food, high-energy atmosphere, and "reasonable" prices (reasonable being a relative term) makes this restaurant a longstanding favorite among visitors. The enormous dining room packs 'em in every night—and whether seated on the veranda (heated on cold nights) or in the center of the bustling scene, diners are usually thrilled just to have a seat. Even though the wonderful bread served with house-made flavored olive oils is tempting, save room for the robust California

Gourmet Picnics, Napa-Style

You could easily plan your whole trip around restaurant reservations. But put together one of the world's best gourmet picnics, and the valley's your oyster.

One of the finest gourmet food stores in the Wine Country, if not all of California, is the **Oakville Grocery Co.,** 7856 St. Helena Hwy. at Oakville Cross Road (☎ 707/944-8802). Here you can put together the provisions for a memorable picnic, or, if you give them at least 24 hours' notice, the staff can prepare a picnic basket for you. The store, with its small-town vibe and claustrophobia-inducing crowds, is crammed with the best breads and the choicest selection of cheeses in the northern Bay Area, as well as pâtés, cold cuts, crackers, top-quality olive oils, fresh foie gras, smoked Norwegian salmon, fresh caviar (Beluga, Sevruga, Osetra), and, of course, an exceptional selection of California wines. The store is open daily from 9am to 6pm; it also has an espresso bar tucked in the corner (open daily from 7am to 3pm), offering breakfast and lunch items, house-baked pastries, and 15 wines available by the glass or for tasting.

Another of our favorite places to fill a picnic basket is New York City's version of a swank European marketplace, **Dean & DeLuca,** 607 S. Main St. (Calif. 29), north of Zinfandel Lane and south of Sulphur Springs Road in St. Helena (☎ 707/967-9980). The ultimate gourmet grocery store is more like a world's fair of foods, where everything is beautifully displayed and often painfully pricey. But even if you choose not to buy, this place is definitely worth a browse. Check out the 200 domestic and imported cheeses; shelves of tapenades, pastas, oils, hand-packed dried herbs and spices, chocolates, sauces, and cookware; an espresso bar; one hell of a bakery section; and more. The wine shop boasts a 1,200-label collection. Hours are Monday through Saturday from 10am to 7pm (the espresso bar opens at 8am) and Sunday from 10am to 6pm.

Of course, if you really want to pack a picnic on the cheap, you can always head to the local Safeway supermarket.

---

dishes, cooked Italian-style, that have made this place everyone's favorite. The menu features about five or so pizzas, including a succulent caramelized onion, thyme, and Gorgonzola version. The dishes of the day might include grilled Sonoma rabbit with teleme-layered potatoes, oven-dried tomatoes, and mustard pan sauce, and a dozen or so antipasti. Equally tempting are the pastas—which include ceppo with sausage, spinach, potatoes, sun-dried tomatoes, and Pecorino—and the delicious desserts. When ordering, plan wisely—most dishes are very rich.

The adjoining Cantinetta offers a small selection of sandwiches, pizzas, and lighter meals (see above).

Wine Spectator Greystone Restaurant. At the Culinary Institute of America at Greystone, 2555 Main St., St. Helena. ☎ **707/967-1010.** Reservations strongly recommended. Tapas $3–7; main courses $14–$19 (same prices at both lunch and dinner). Daily 11:30am–3pm; Mon–Thurs 5:30–9pm; Fri–Sat 5:30–10pm; tapas at the bar 3:30pm–5:30pm. MEDITERRANEAN.

This place offers a visual and culinary feast that's unparalleled in the area, if not the state, so we recommend stopping by for a glass of wine and a few appetizers (skip the main courses—it's more fun, and affordable, to snack). The room is an enormous stone-walled former winery, but the festive decor and heavenly aromas warm the space up. Cooking islands—complete with scurrying chefs, steaming pots, and rotating chicken—provide edible entertainment. The tapas menu focuses on Mediterranean-inspired dishes, including an excellent pork kebab and a grilled calamari that contradicts the sea dweller's rubbery reputation with every moist and peppery bite. Tapas portions are small but affordable; pastas and salads are a bit heftier; main courses will fill you up. If you want to ensure a meal here, reserve far in advance.

3 Sonoma Valley

Sonoma is often thought of as the "other" Wine Country, forever in the shadow of Napa Valley. Truth is, even though there are far fewer wineries here (and far fewer tourists), Sonoma's wines have actually won more awards than Napa's. Sonoma County, which stretches west to the coast, still manages to maintain a backcountry ambiance thanks to its much lower density of wineries, restaurants, and hotels.

The Sonoma Valley is also far less traveled than its neighbor to the east, offering a more genuine escape-from-it-all experience. Small family-owned wineries are its mainstay, just like in the old days of wine making, when everyone started with the intention of going broke and loved every minute of it. Unlike the rigidly structured tours at many of Napa Valley's corporate-owned wineries, tastings and tours on the Sonoma side of the Mayacamas Mountains are usually free and low-key, and come with plenty of friendly banter between the wine makers and their guests.

ESSENTIALS

GETTING THERE   From San Francisco, cross the Golden Gate Bridge and stay on U.S. 101 north. Exit at Calif. 37; after 10 miles, turn north onto Calif. 121. After another 10 miles, turn north onto Calif. 12 (Broadway), which will take you directly into the town of Sonoma.

VISITOR INFORMATION   While you're in Sonoma, stop by the **Sonoma Valley Visitors Bureau,** 10 E. Spain St., Sonoma, CA 95476 (☎ **707/996-1090;** www.sonomavalley.com), right on the plaza next to the Sonoma Cheese Factory. It's open daily from 9am to 7pm in summer, from 9am to 5pm in winter. An additional Visitors Bureau is located a few miles south of the square at 25200 Arnold Dr. (Calif. 121; ☎ **707/996-5793**), at the entrance to Viansa Winery; it's open daily from 9am to 5pm.

If you prefer some advance information, the free pocket-size *Sonoma Valley Visitors Guide* covers most every hotel, winery, and restaurant in the valley. Contact the Sonoma Valley Visitors Bureau to order one.

WHEN TO GO   See "When to Go" in the Napa section, above.

TOURING TIPS   Sonoma Valley is currently home to about 35 wineries (including California's first winery, Buena Vista, founded in 1857) and 13,000 acres of vineyards, which produce roughly 25 types of wines totaling more than five million cases a year. Chardonnay is the varietal for which Sonoma is most noted, and it represents almost a quarter of the valley's vine acreage.

The towns and wineries covered below are organized geographically from south to north, starting at the intersection of Calif. 37 and Calif. 121 in the Carneros District and ending in Kenwood. The wineries here tend to be a little more spread out than they are in Napa, but they're easy to find. Still, it's best to decide which wineries you're most interested in and devise a touring strategy before you set out so you don't find yourself doing a lot of backtracking.

We've reviewed our favorite Sonoma Valley wineries here—more than enough to keep you busy tasting wine for a long weekend. For a complete list of local wineries, pick up one of the free guides to the valley available at the Sonoma Valley Visitors Bureau (see "Visitor Information," above).

THE CARNEROS DISTRICT

As you approach the Wine Country from the south, you must first pass through the Carneros District, a cool, windswept region that borders the San Pablo Bay and marks the entrance to both Napa and Sonoma valleys. Until the latter part of the 20th century, this mixture of marsh, sloughs, and rolling hills was mainly used as sheep pasture (*carneros* means "sheep" in Spanish). After experimental plantings yielded slow-growing yet high-quality grapes—particularly chardonnay and pinot noir—several Napa and Sonoma wineries expanded their plantings here, eventually establishing the Carneros District as an American Viticultural Appellation.

✪ **Viansa Winery and Italian Marketplace.** 25200 Arnold Dr. (Calif. 121), Sonoma. ☎ **800/995-4740** or 707/935-4700. Daily 10am–5pm. Guided tours by appointment only.

The first major winery you'll encounter as you enter Sonoma Valley from the south, this sprawling Tuscany-style villa is perched atop a knoll overlooking the entire lower valley. Viansa is the brainchild of Sam and Vicki Sebastiani, who left the family dynasty to create their own temple to food and wine (*Viansa* being a contraction of "Vicki and Sam"). The marketplace is crammed with a cornucopia of high-quality preserves, mustards, olive oils, pastas, salads, breads, desserts, Italian tableware, cookbooks, and other wine-related gifts. The winery, which does an extensive mail-order business through its Tuscany Club (worth joining if you love getting mail and good wine), has quickly established a favorable reputation for its cabernet, sauvignon blanc, and chardonnay, blended from premium Napa and Sonoma grapes. The vineyard is also experimenting with Italian grape varieties such as muscat canelli, sangiovese, and nebbiolo, most of which are sold exclusively at the winery. Free tastings are poured at the east end of the marketplace, and the self-guided tour includes a trip through the underground barrel-aging cellar adorned with colorful hand-painted murals.

Gloria Ferrer Champagne Caves. 23555 Carneros Hwy. (Calif. 121), Sonoma. ☎ **707/996-7256.** Daily 10am–5:30pm. Tours hourly 11am–4pm.

When you have it up to here with chardonnays and pinots, pay a visit to Gloria Ferrer. (Gloria is the wife of José Ferrer, whose family has been making sparkling wine for the past 5 centuries and whose company, Freixenet, is the largest producer of sparkling wine in the world.) Glimmering like Oz high atop a gently sloping hill, the winery overlooks the verdant Carneros District; on a sunny day, it's impossible not to enjoy a glass of dry Brut while soaking in the magnificent views of the vineyards and valley below.

If you're unfamiliar with the term *méthode champenoise,* be sure to take the free 30-minute tour of the fermenting tanks, bottling line, and caves brimming with racks of yeast-laden bottles. Afterwards, retire to the elegant tasting room for a flute of Brut or Cuvée ($3 to $5.50 a glass, $16 and up per bottle). There are picnic tables, but it's usually too windy up here for comfort—plus you have to purchase a bottle of their sparkling wine to reserve a table.

SONOMA

At the northern boundary of the Carneros District along Calif. 12 is the centerpiece of Sonoma Valley, the midsized town of Sonoma, which owes much of its appeal to Mexican general Mariano Guadalupe Vallejo. It was Vallejo who fashioned this pleasant, slow-paced community after a typical Mexican village—right down to its central plaza, Sonoma's geographical and commercial center. The plaza sits at the top of a T formed by Broadway (Calif. 12) and Napa Street. Most of the surrounding streets form a grid pattern around this axis, making Sonoma easy to negotiate. The plaza's Bear Flag Monument marks the spot where the crude Bear Flag was raised in 1846, signaling the end of Mexican rule; the symbol was later adopted by the state of California and placed on its flag. The 8-acre park at the center of the plaza, complete with two ponds populated with ducks and geese, is perfect for an afternoon siesta in the cool shade. Our favorite attraction, however, is the gaggle of brilliantly feathered chickens that roam unfettered through the streets of Sonoma—a sight you'll definitely never see in Napa.

The best way to see the town of Sonoma is to follow the *Sonoma Walking Tour* map, provided by the Sonoma League for Historic Preservation. Tour highlights include General Vallejo's 1852 Victorian-style home; the Sonoma Barracks, erected in 1836 to house Mexican army troops; and the Blue Wing Inn, an 1840 hostelry built to accommodate travelers—including John Fremont, Kit Carson, and Ulysses S. Grant—and new settlers while they erected homes in Sonoma. You can purchase the $2.75 map at the Vasquez House, located at 414 First St. E., between East Napa and East Spain streets (☎ 707/938-0510), open Wednesday through Sunday from 1:30 to 4pm.

The **Mission San Francisco Solano de Sonoma,** on Sonoma Plaza at the corner of First Street East and Spain Street (☎ 707/938-1519), was founded in 1823. It was the northernmost, and last, mission built in California. It was also the only one established on the northern coast by the Mexican rulers, who wished to protect their territory from expansionist Russian fur traders. It's now part of Sonoma State Historic Park. Admission is $2 for adults, $1 for children 6 to 12, and free for children under 6. It's open daily from 10am to 5pm except Thanksgiving, Christmas, and New Year's Day.

Sebastiani Vineyards Winery. 389 Fourth St. E., Sonoma. ☎ 800/888-5532 or 707/938-5532. Daily 10am–5pm. Tours offered 10:30am–4pm, every ½ hr. in summer, every 45 min. to an hr. in winter; no reservations necessary.

What started in 1904, when Samuele Sebastiani began producing his first wines, has, in three successive generations, now grown into a small empire and Sonoma County's largest winery, producing some six *million* cases a year. The 25-minute tour is interesting, informative, and well worth the time. You can see the winery's original turn-of-the-century crusher and press as well as the world's largest collection of oak-barrel carvings, crafted by local artist Earle Brown. If you don't want to take the tour, head straight for the charmingly rustic tasting room, where you can sample an extensive selection of wines sans tasting fee. Bottle prices are very reasonable, ranging from $5 for a 1996 white zin to $15 for a 1994 cabernet sauvignon. A picnic area is adjacent to the cellars, though a far more scenic spot is located across the parking lot in Sebastiani's Cherryblock Vineyards.

Buena Vista. 18000 Old Winery Rd. (off E. Napa St., slightly northeast of downtown), Sonoma. ☎ 800/926-1266 or 707/938-1266. Daily 10:30am–5pm. Self-guided tours only.

The patriarch of California wineries was founded in 1857 by Count Agoston Haraszthy, the Hungarian émigré who is universally regarded as the father of California's wine industry. A close friend of General Vallejo, Haraszthy returned from Europe in 1861 with 100,000 of the finest vine cuttings, which he made available to all winegrowers. Although Buena Vista's wine making now takes place at an ultra-modern facility in the Carneros District, the winery still maintains a complimentary tasting room inside the restored 1862 Press House—a beautiful stone-crafted room

Sonoma on Two Wheels

Sonoma and its neighboring towns are so small, close together, and relatively flat that it's not difficult to get around on two wheels. In fact, if you're in no great hurry, there's no better way to tour the Sonoma area than via a bicycle. You can rent a bike at the **Goodtime Bicycle Company,** 18503 Sonoma Hwy. (Calif. 12), Sonoma (☎ **888/525-0453** or 707/938-0453). They'll happily point you to easy bike trails, or you can take one of their organized excursions to Kenwood-area wineries or to south Sonoma wineries. Not only do they provide a gourmet lunch featuring local Sonoma products, they'll even carry any wine you purchase for you and help with shipping arrangements to your home. Lunch rides start at 10:30am and end at around 3pm. The cost, including food and equipment, is $55 per person (that's a darn good deal). Rentals cost $25 a day or $5 per hour, and include helmets, locks, and everything else you'll need (delivery is a $25 flat day rate).

Bikes are also available for rent from **Sonoma Valley Cyclery,** 20093 Broadway, Sonoma (☎ **707/935-3377**), for $20 a day, $6 per hour.

brimming with wines, wine-related gifts, and accessories (as well as a small art gallery along the inner balcony).

Tastings are free for most wines, $3 for the really good stuff; bottle prices range from as low as $8.50 for a buttery 1996 sauvignon blanc to $26 for the Carneros Grand Reserve cabernet sauvignon (which was so good that we bought three). There's also a self-guided tour that you can follow any time during operating hours; a "Historical Presentation," offered daily at 2pm, details the life and times of the Count.

Ravenswood Winery. 18701 Gehricke Rd. (off Lovall Valley Rd.), Sonoma. ☎ **800/NO-WIMPY** or 707/938-1960. Daily 10am–4:30pm. Tours by reservation only.

Compared to old heavies like Sebastiani and Buena Vista, Ravenswood is a relative newcomer to the Sonoma wine scene, but it has quickly established itself as the king of zinfandel. In fact, Ravenswood is the first winery in the United States to focus primarily on zins, which make up about three-quarters of its 150,000-case production; it also produces merlot, cabernet sauvignon, and a small amount of chardonnay.

The winery is smartly designed—recessed into the Sonoma hillside to protect its treasures from the simmering summers. Tours follow the wine-making process from grape to glass, and include a visit into the aromatic oak-barrel-aging rooms. A gourmet "Barbecue Overlooking the Vineyards" is held each weekend (11am to 4:40pm, from Memorial Day through the end of Sept; prices about $7 to $12; call for details and reservations), though you're welcome to enjoy your own picnic at any of their tables. Tastings are free and generous, though you may not find some of the pourers to be as witty as they think they are (ours was a jerk, though we've known people who have had great experiences here). Bottle prices range from $8.50 for a light and crisp 1996 French Colombard to $16 for a 1995 cab, but it's the kick-butt zins—priced well in the low- to mid-teens—that you'll want to stock up on.

GLEN ELLEN

About 7 miles north of Sonoma on Calif. 12 is the town of Glen Ellen, which, though just a fraction of the size of Sonoma, is home to several of the valley's finest wineries, restaurants, and inns. Aside from the addition of a few new restaurants, this charming Wine Country town hasn't changed much since the days when Jack London settled on his Beauty Ranch, about a mile west. If you haven't yet decided where you want to set up camp during your visit to the Wine Country, we highly recommend this lovable little town.

Hikers, horseback riders, and picnickers will enjoy **Jack London State Historic Park,** 2400 London Ranch Rd., off Arnold Drive (☎ **707/938-5216**). Within its 800 acres, which were once home to the renowned writer, you'll find 9 miles of trails, the remains of London's burned-down dream house, preserved structures, a museum, and plenty of ideal picnic spots. The park is open daily from 9:30am to 7pm in summer, from 9:30am to 5pm in winter. Admission is $5 per car, $4 per car for seniors 62 and over.

Arrowood. 14347 Sonoma Hwy. (Calif. 12), Glen Ellen. ☎ **707/938-5170.** Daily 10am–4:30pm. Tours by appointment only, Mon–Fri at 10:30am and 2:30pm.

Richard Arrowood had already established a reputation as a master wine maker at Château St. Jean before he and his wife, Alis Demers Arrowood, set out on their own in 1986. Their utterly picturesque winery is perched on a gently rising hillside lined with perfectly manicured vineyards. Tastings take place in the Hospitality House, the newest of Arrowood's two stately gray-and-white buildings that were fashioned after New England farmhouses, complete with wraparound porches. Richard's focus is on making world-class wines with minimal intervention, and his results are impressive: four out of his five current releases have scored over 90 points. Mind you, such excellence doesn't come cheaply: Prices start at $24 for a 1996 chardonnay and quickly climb to the mid- to high $30s. Arrowood is only one of the very few wineries in Sonoma that charge for tastings ($3), but if you're curious what near-perfection tastes like, it's well worth it. No picnic facilities are available.

✪ The Benziger Family Winery. 1883 London Ranch Rd. (off Arnold Dr., on the way to Jack London State Historic Park), Glen Ellen. ☎ **800/989-8890** or 707/935-3000. Tasting room daily 10am–5:30pm. Tram tours daily (weather permitting) at 11:30am, 12:30, 2, and 3:30pm.

A visit here confirms that you are indeed visiting a "family" winery; at any given time three generations of Benzigers (pronounced *Ben*-zigger) may be running around tending to chores, and you're instantly made to feel as if you're part of the clan. The pastoral, user-friendly property features an exceptional self-guided tour ("The most comprehensive tour in the wine industry," exclaims *Wine Spectator*), gardens, an art gallery, and a spacious tasting room manned by an amiable staff. The free 40-minute tram tour, pulled by a beefy tractor, is both informative and fun as it winds through the estate vineyards before making a champagne-tasting pit stop on a scenic bluff. (*Tip:* Tram tickets—a hot item in the summer—are available on a first-come, first-served basis, so either arrive early or stop by in the morning to pick up afternoon tickets.)

Tastings of the standard release wines are free, and bottle prices range from $10 for a 1996 fumé blanc to $18 for a 1995 pinot noir. The best buy, however, is the award-winning 1995 zinfandel (Sonoma County), priced to move at $16 a bottle. You can also purchase a full glass of wine for $5 and tour the estate in style. The winery offers several scenic picnic spots.

KENWOOD

A few miles north of Glen Ellen along Calif. 12 is the tiny town of Kenwood, the northernmost outpost of the Sonoma Valley. The town itself consists of little more than a few restaurants, wineries, and modest homes recessed into the wooded hillsides.

Kunde Estate Winery. 10155 Sonoma Hwy., Kenwood. ☎ **707/833-5501.** Tastings daily 11am–5pm. Cave tours Fri–Sun approximately every ½ hr. from 11am–4pm.

Expect a friendly, unintimidating welcome at this scenic winery, run by four generations of the Kundes since 1904. One of the largest grape suppliers in the area, the Kunde family (pronounced *Kun*-dee) converted 800 acres of their 2,000-acre ranch to growing ultra-premium-quality grapes, which they provide to about 30 Sonoma and Napa wineries. Hence, all their wines are "estate" (made from grapes grown on their own property). The tour includes the details and the winery's history. The free new-release tastings are offered in a spiffy new 17,000-square-foot wine-making facility; bottle prices range from $11 to $24. Private tours are available by appointment, but the picnic tables and man-made pond can be spontaneously enjoyed.

Kenwood Vineyards. 9592 Sonoma Hwy. (Calif. 12), Kenwood. ☎ **707/833-5891.** Daily 10am–4:30pm. Tours by appointment only.

Kenwood's history dates back to 1906, when the Pagani brothers made their living selling wine straight from the barrel and into the jug. In 1970, the Lee family bought the place and converted the aging winery into a modern, high-production facility concealed in the original barnlike buildings. Since then, Kenwood's wines have earned a solid reputation for consistent quality with each of their varietals: cabernet sauvignon, chardonnay, zinfandel, pinot noir, merlot, and their most popular wine, sauvignon blanc—a crisp, light wine with hints of melon.

Though the winery looks rather modest in size, its output is staggering: 275,000 cases of ultra-premium wines fermented in 60 steel tanks and 7,000 French and American oak barrels. Popular with wine collectors is wine maker Michael Lee's Artist Series cabernet sauvignon, a limited production from the winery's best vineyards featuring labels with original artwork by renowned artists. The tasting room, housed in one of the old barns, offers free tastings of most varieties, as well as gift items for sale. Wine prices are moderate, ranging from $7.50 to $20; the Artist Series, on the other hand, runs anywhere from $50 to $250.

4 Accommodations & Dining in Sonoma

WHERE TO STAY

If you have any trouble finding a room, try calling the **Sonoma Valley Visitors Bureau** (☎ 707/996-1090). They'll refer you to a lodging that has a room to spare, but they won't make reservations for you. The **Bed and Breakfast Association of Sonoma Valley** (☎ 800/969-4667) will refer you to one of their member B&Bs, and can make reservations for you as well. Keep in mind, however, that most B&B rates *start* at well over $100.

Best Western Sonoma Valley Inn. 5550 Second St. W., Sonoma, CA 95476. ☎ **800/ 334-5784** or 707/938-9200. Fax 707/938-0935. 75 units. $79–$179 double. Rates include continental breakfast. AE, CB, DC, MC, V.

There are only three reasons to stay at the Sonoma Valley Inn: 1) It's the only place left with a vacancy, 2) you're bringing the kids along, 3) it's the cheapest place you can find. Otherwise, you're probably going to be a little disappointed with a rather drab room with thin walls and a small bathroom. Kids, however, will love the place: There's plenty of room to run around, and a large pool and gazebo-covered spa to play in. The rooms *do* come with a lot of perks, however, such as continental breakfast delivered to your room each morning, a gift bottle of white table wine from Kenwood Vineyards (chillin' in the fridge), cable TV with HBO, and either a balcony or deck overlooking the inner courtyard. It's also in a good location, just a block from Sonoma's plaza.

El Pueblo Inn. 896 W. Napa St., Sonoma, CA 95476. ☎ **800/900-8844** or 707/996-3651. 38 units. A/C TEL. May–Oct $80–$94 double; Mar–Apr and Nov $69–$80 double; Dec–Feb $65–$80 double. AE, DISC, MC, V.

Located on Sonoma's main east-west street 8 blocks from the center of town, this isn't Sonoma's fanciest hotel, but it offers some of the best-priced accommodations around. The rooms here are pleasant enough, with post-and-beam construction, exposed brick walls, light-wood furniture, and geometric prints. A drip coffee machine should be a comfort to early risers, and an outdoor heated pool will cool you off in hot weather. Reservations should be made at least a month in advance for the spring and summer months.

Sonoma Chalet. 18935 Fifth St. W., Sonoma, CA 95476. ☎ **707/938-3129.** 4 units, 1 with private bathroom; 3 cottages. Apr–Oct $85–$160 double; Nov–Mar $85–$150 double. Rates include continental breakfast. AE, MC, V.

This is one of the few accommodations in Sonoma that's truly secluded; it's on the outskirts of town, in a peaceful country setting overlooking a 200-acre ranch. The accommodations, housed in a Swiss-style farmhouse and several cottages, are all delightfully decorated by someone with an eye for color and a concern for comfort. They have claw-foot tubs, beds covered with country quilts, Oriental carpets, comfortable furnishings, and private decks; some have woodstoves or fireplaces. The two least expensive rooms share a bathroom, while the cottages offer the most privacy. A breakfast of fruit, yogurt, pastries, and cereal is served either in the country kitchen or in your room (and the gaggles of ducks, chickens, and ornery geese will be glad to help you finish off the crumbs). If you like country rustic (and farm animals), you'll like the Sonoma Chalet.

Sonoma Hotel. 110 W. Spain St., Sonoma, CA 95476. ☎ **800/468-6016** or 707/ 996-2996. Fax 707/996-7014. 17 units, 5 with private bathroom. Summer $75–$85 double without bathroom; $115–$125 double with bathroom. Winter Sun–Thurs $59 double without bathroom; $90 double with bathroom; Fri–Sat $75 double without bathroom; $115–$125 double with bathroom. Rates include continental breakfast. AE, MC, V.

This cute little historic hotel on Sonoma's tree-lined Town Square still retains the same ambiance it did over a century ago. With an emphasis on European-style elegance and comfort, each room is decorated in an early California style, with antique furnishings, fine woods, and floral-print wallpapers. Some of the rooms feature brass beds, and all are blissfully devoid of phones and TVs. Five of the third-floor rooms share immaculate bathrooms (and significantly reduced rates), while rooms with private bathrooms have deep claw-foot tubs with overhead showers. Perks include continental breakfast and a bottle of wine on arrival. Also within the hotel is Le Bistro, a small restaurant serving Mediterranean cuisine for lunch, dinner, and Sunday brunch.

Victorian Garden Inn. 316 E. Napa St., Sonoma, CA 95476. ☎ **800/543-5339** or 707/996-5339. Fax 707/996-1689. 4 units. $95–$165 double. Rates include breakfast and afternoon wine and sherry. AE, DC, MC, V.

Proprietor Donna Lewis runs what is easily the cutest B&B in Sonoma Valley. A small picket fence and wall of trees enclose an adorable Victorian garden brimming with bowers of violets, roses, camellias, and peonies, all shaded under flowering fruit trees. Four guest rooms—three in the century-old water tower and one in the main house, an 1870s Greek Revival farmhouse—are in keeping with the Victorian theme: white wicker furniture, floral prints, padded armchairs, claw-foot tubs. The most popular rooms are the Top o' the Tower, which has its own entrance and view overlooking the garden, and the Woodcutter's Cottage, which has its own entrance and garden view, plus a sofa and armchairs set in front of the fireplace. A breakfast of croissants, muffins, gourmet coffee, and fruit picked from the garden is served at the dining table, in the garden, or in your room; evening wine and sherry are served in the parlor. Leisure time can be spent in the pool or along the shaded wraparound porch.

WHERE TO DINE
SUPER-CHEAP EATS

Basque Boulangerie Cafe. 460 First St. E., Sonoma. ☎ **707/935-7687.** Menu items $3–$7. MC, V. Daily 7am–6pm. BAKERY/DELI.

If you prefer a lighter morning meal and strong coffee, stand in line with the locals at the Basque Boulangerie Cafe, the most popular gathering spot in the Sonoma Valley. Most everything—sourdough Basque breads, pastries, quiche, soups, salads, desserts, sandwiches, cookies—is made in-house, and made well. Daily lunch specials, such as a grilled veggie sandwich with smoked mozzarella cheese ($4.75), are listed on the chalkboard out front. Seating is scarce, and if you can score a sidewalk table on a sunny day, consider yourself one lucky person. A popular option is ordering to go and eating in the shady plaza across the street. The cafe also sells wine by the glass, as well as a wonderful cinnamon bread by the loaf that's ideal for making French toast.

Café Citti. 9049 Sonoma Hwy., Kenwood. ☎ **707/833-2690.** Main courses $6–$9.50. MC, V. Daily 11am–3:30pm; Sun–Thurs 5–8:30pm; Fri–Sat 5–9pm. ITALIAN.

If you're this far north into the Wine Country, then you're probably doing some serious wine tasting. If that's the case, then you don't want to spend half the day at a fancy, high-priced restaurant. What you need is Café Citti (pronounced *Cheat*-ee), a roadside do-it-yourself Italian trattoria that is both good and cheap. There's no menu; you order from the huge menu board displayed above the open kitchen. Afterwards you scramble for a table (the ones on the patio, shaded by umbrellas, are the best on warm afternoons), and a server will bring your meal. It's all hearty, home-cooked Italian. Standout dishes are the green bean salad, tangy Caesar salad, focaccia sandwiches, and the roasted rotisserie chicken stuffed with rosemary and garlic. The freshly made pastas come with a variety of sauces; our favorite is the zesty marinara. Wine is available by the bottle, and the espresso is plenty strong. Everything on the menu board is available to go, which makes Café Citti and excellent resource for picnic supplies.

The Feed Store Again! 529 First St. W., Sonoma. ☎ **707/939-7147.** Main courses $4.50–$8.25. MC, V. Wed–Mon 7:30am–2:30pm; Sat–Sun 8am–3pm. AMERICAN.

Owners Drake and Madeline Dierkhising tried to retire from the restaurant business, but after seeing how poorly their baby was being run by the new owner, they decided to buy it back. Hence, the "Again!," and once again the locals are back for their daily sustenance. It's a bright, roomy, cheerful place with plenty of windows, high ceilings, an open kitchen, and a tasteful Southwestern color scheme. The wait staff is as nice as can be, and prices are very reasonable. For breakfast try the cheese blintzes or apple crepe, both topped with seasonal fruit, blueberry sauce and yogurt, or the zesty huevos rancheros with guacamole, salsa, and black beans. Best-sellers on the lunch menu are the Jalisco Club (charbroiled chicken, smoked bacon, cheese, avocado, and salsa rolled in a flour tortilla), grilled veggie sandwich, and classic burger. ("Best in town," says Drake, who also says the same about his muffins, made elsewhere at a bakery he also owns.) A small brewery has recently been added to the cafe, but Drake—ever the perfectionist—is still searching for the right brew master for the job, so it may not be in service.

Jack's Village Café. 14301 Arnold Dr., Glen Ellen. ☎ **707/939-6111.** Main courses $5.75–$9.50. AE, DISC, MC, V. Breakfast, lunch daily 8:30am–4pm; dinner Wed–Sun 6–9pm. CALIFORNIA COUNTRY.

Hidden behind the Glen Ellen Tasting Room in Jack London Village is this small cafe run by Debra De Martini, a pretty and vivacious woman who greets guests, waits tables, and works the grill if need be ("All hats" is her job description). Century-old wood beams create a rustic ambiance inside, while the outdoor patio is surrounded by trees, flowers, and soothing sounds from a nearby creek. When the weather is pleasant, there's no better place in Glen Ellen to sit outside with a good glass of wine, a bowl of steamed mussels, and a roasted-eggplant-and-mozzarella sandwich. Other menu items range from a wild-mushroom risotto with braised leeks and sun-dried tomatoes (a bargain at $9.50) to a roasted pork loin sandwich with sautéed onions and Jack's special barbecue sauce. Breakfast is taken seriously here: Chef Jon Brzycki makes his French toast with thick slices of sourdough bread sprinkled with cinnamon and nutmeg. The smoked salmon with toasted bagel and cream cheese is the perfect light breakfast for two, and the hot oatmeal and house-made granola are good choices as well. *Note:* Be sure to check the Daily Specials board above the grill before you order.

✪ **Lo Spuntino.** 400 First St. E., Sonoma. ☎ **707/935-4743.** Deli items $5–$9. AE, CB, DISC, MC, V. Sun–Thurs 10am–6pm; Fri–Sat 10am–9pm. ITALIAN DELI.

Lo Spuntino, Italian for "snack" or a tiny taste, is the sexiest thing going in Sonoma, a suave deli and wine bar owned by Sam and Vicki Sebastiani, who also run Viansa Winery. It's a visual masterpiece, with shiny black-and-white-checkered flooring, long counters of Italian marble, track lighting, and a center deli and wine bar where a crew of young men slice meats, pour wines, and scoop gelato. Start by sampling the preserves and jams near the entrance, then choose among the armada of cured meats, cheeses, fruits, pastas, salads, and breads lining the deli. Popular choices are the hefty sandwiches on herbed focaccia bread or the herb-marinated rotisserie chickens served by the half with your choice of pasta or salad. Roasted turkey, duck, pork, lamb, and rabbit are also available. Opposite the deli is the wine bar, featuring all of Viansa's current releases for both tasting and purchase, as well as a small selection of microbrewed beers on tap. On your way out, stop at the gelateria and treat yourself to some intense Italian ice cream. *Note:* Lo Spuntino also hosts live jazz bands every Friday night from 6 to 9pm.

FOR A FEW BUCKS MORE/MODERATELY PRICED OPTIONS

Della Santina's. 133 E. Napa St. (just east of the square), Sonoma. ☎ **707/935-0576.** Reservations recommended. Main courses $8.95–$14.75. DISC, MC, V. Daily 11:30am–9:30pm. ITALIAN.

Those of you who just can't take another expensive, chichi California meal should follow the locals to this friendly, traditional Italian restaurant. Every classic Tuscan dish we tried was refreshingly authentic and well flavored—without overbearing sauces or one *hint* of California pretentiousness. Start with traditional antipasti, especially the sliced mozzarella and tomatoes or the delicious white beans. The nine pasta dishes are, again, wonderfully authentic (gnocchi lovers, rejoice!). The spit-roasted meat dishes are a local favorite (though we found them a bit overcooked), and for those who can't choose among chicken, pork, turkey, rabbit, or duck, there's a selection that offers a choice of three. Don't worry about breaking your bank on a bottle of wine, as most of the savory choices here go for under $25.

La Casa. 121 E. Spain St., Sonoma. ☎ **707/996-3406.** Reservations recommended on weekends and summer evenings. Main courses $6–$11. AE, CB, DC, DISC, MC, V. Daily 11:30am–10pm (bar appetizers until midnight). MEXICAN.

This no-nonsense Mexican restaurant, on the Sonoma Plaza across from the mission, serves great enchiladas, fajitas, and chimichangas. To start, try the black-bean soup or the ceviche made of fresh snapper, marinated in lime juice with cilantro and salsa, and served on crispy tortillas. Follow that with tamales prepared with corn husks spread with corn masa, stuffed with chicken filling, and topped with a mild red-chili sauce. Or you might opt for the delicious *suiza*—deep-dish chicken enchiladas—or fresh snapper Veracruz if it's available. On a sunny afternoon or a clear night, choose to dine patio-style, where you can sip *cerveza* under the warmth of heat lamps.

Pasta Nostra. 139 E. Napa St., Sonoma. ☎ **707/938-4166.** Main courses $7.50–$16. AE, MC, V. Mon–Sat 11:30am–2:30pm; Mon–Thurs 5–9pm; Fri–Sat 5–10pm; Sun 4:30–9pm. ITALIAN.

Very few restaurants in Sonoma Valley cater to families with children, but Pasta Nostra is the exception. It's not the best restaurant in Sonoma by far, but on a sunny day with kids in tow you won't find a better—and cheaper—place to dine in the sun. Inside the converted Victorian home are semiformal settings with white tablecloths and fine tableware; outside on the ivy-walled patio are a dozen or so additional tables shaded by trees. Expect big portions of hearty Italian-American fare such as freshly made fettuccine carbonara, mostaccioli with house-made Sicilian-style sausage, and roasted lamb loin with a hazelnut-dijon crust and mint balsamic glaze. Kids have their own short menu, featuring all-time favorites such as spaghetti with meatballs and lasagna—at childlike prices. *Tip:* Few people know about the small parking lot in the rear.

7

The Northern Coast

by Erika Lenkert and Matthew R. Poole

Heading north from San Francisco, you'll come upon a California that hardly resembles the southern part of the state. It's an entirely different landscape, in climate as well as flora and fauna. You can forget about California's fabled surfing-and-bikini scene this far north; instead, you'll find miles and miles of rugged coastline with broad beaches and tiny bays harboring dramatic rock formations—from chimney stacks to bridges and blowholes—carved by the ocean waves.

The best time to visit is in the spring or fall. In spring, the headlands are carpeted with wildflowers—golden poppy, iris, and sea foam—and in fall the sun shines clear and bright. Summers are typically cool and windy, with the ubiquitous fog burning off by the afternoon.

You may think you've arrived in Alaska when you hit the beaches of northern California. Take a dip in the sea and you'll soon agree with the locals: When it comes to swimming, the Arctic waters along the north coast are best left to the sea lions. But that doesn't mean you can't enjoy the beaches, whether by strolling along the water or taking in the panoramic views of towering cliffs and seascapes. And unlike their southern counterparts, the beaches along the north coast are not likely to be crowded, even in summer.

The most scenic way to reach Stinson Beach, Gualala, Mendocino, and points north is to drive along the coast via Calif. 1. The larger freeway, U.S. 101, runs inland through Healdsburg and Cloverdale and is much faster, but doesn't provide the spectacular views of coastal cliffs and windswept beaches you will see on Calif. 1. A good compromise if you're headed to, say, Mendocino, is to take U.S. 101 to Cloverdale, then cut over on Calif. 128 to the coast.

Oh, and one last thing: Dress warmly.

1 Point Reyes National Seashore

35 miles N of San Francisco

The National Seashore system was created to protect rural and undeveloped stretches of the coast from the pressures brought on by soaring real-estate values and increasing population. Nowhere is the success of the system more evident than at Point Reyes. Residents of the surrounding towns—**Inverness, Point Reyes Station,** and **Olema**—have steadfastly resisted runaway development. You won't find any strip

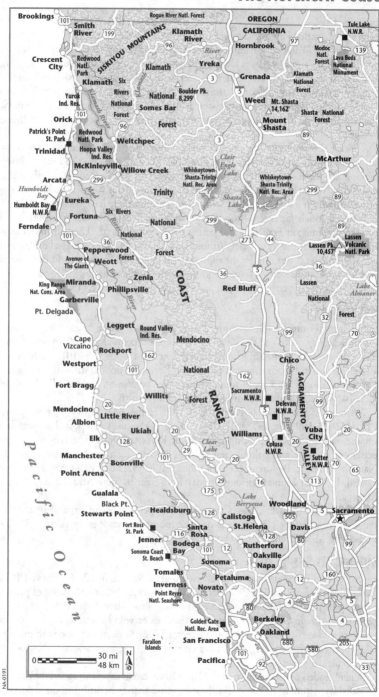

Brookings
Smith River
101
199
Rogue River Natl. Forest
OREGON
CALIFORNIA
Tule Lake N.W.R.

Crescent City
SISKIYOU MOUNTAINS
Klamath River
96
Hornbrook
97
Modoc Natl. Forest
Lava Beds National Monument
139

Redwood Natl. Park
Klamath
Six Rivers National Forest
Somes Bar
Yreka
3
Grenada
5
Weed
Mt. Shasta 14,162'
Klamath National Forest
Shasta National Forest

Klamath
Yurok Ind. Res.
101
Orick
Boulder Pk. 8,299
National
Forest
Mount Shasta
89

Patrick's Point St. Park
Trinidad
Redwood Natl. Park
Hoopa Valley Ind. Res.
Weitchpec
96
3

McKinleyville
Willow Creek
299
Whiskeytown-Shasta-Trinity Natl. Rec. Area
Clair Engle Lake
Whiskeytown-Shasta-Trinity Natl. Rec. Area
299
McArthur
89

Arcata
Humboldt Bay
Eureka
Humboldt Bay N.W.R.
Fortuna
Ferndale
101
Mad River
Six Rivers
National
Trinity
Shasta Lake
299
273
44
89

36
Pepperwood
Weott
Avenue of The Giants
Zenia
Forest
Forest
36
5
Lassen Pk. 10,457'
Lassen Volcanic Natl. Park
Lake Almanor

King Range Nat. Cons. Area
Miranda
Garberville
Pt. Delgada
Phillipsville
Eel River
Red Bluff
COAST
Lassen
National
Forest
32
70

Leggett
Cape Vizcaino
Rockport
162
Round Valley Ind. Res.
Mendocino
National
RANGE
Chico
99
162
Sacramento N.W.R.
SACRAMENTO

Westport
Fort Bragg
101
Willits
Forest
Delevan N.W.R.
5
99
70

Mendocino
Little River
Albion
Elk
20
Ukiah
128
20
Clear Lake
Williams
Colusa N.W.R.
20
Yuba City
VALLEY
Sutter N.W.R.
70
20
65

Manchester
Point Arena
Boonville
101
29
16
29
113

Gualala
Black Pt.
Stewarts Point
175
Lake Berryessa
Woodland
Sacramento River
505
5
Sacramento

Fort Ross St. Park
Jenner
Sonoma Coast St. Beach
Healdsburg
128
Calistoga
St. Helena
128
Davis
80
99

Santa Rosa
116
Bodega Bay
101
12
Rutherford
Oakville
Napa
160

Tomales
Inverness
Point Reyes Natl. Seashore
Sonoma
Petaluma
Novato
12
1

Farallon Islands
Golden Gate Natl. Rec. Area
San Francisco
Berkeley
Oakland
80
4
4
205

Pacifica
101
92
680
580
33

Pacific Ocean

0   30 mi
0   48 km
N

NA-0191

malls or fast-food joints here—just laid-back coastal towns with cafes and country inns where gentle living prevails.

The park, a 71,000-acre hammer-shaped peninsula jutting 10 miles into the Pacific and backed by Tomales Bay, is loaded with wildlife, ranging from tule elk, birds, and bobcats to gray whales, sea lions, and great white sharks. Aside from its beautiful scenery, it also boasts historic treasures that offer a window into California's coastal past, including lighthouses, turn-of-the-century dairies and ranches, the site of Sir Francis Drake's 1579 landing, plus a complete replica of a coastal Miwok Indian village.

Though the peninsula's people and wildlife live in harmony above the ground, the situation beneath the soil is much more volatile. The infamous San Andreas Fault separates Point Reyes—the northernmost landmass on the Pacific Plate—from the rest of California, which rests on the North American Plate. Point Reyes is making its way toward Alaska at a rate of about 2 inches per year, but there have been times when it has moved much faster. In 1906, Point Reyes jumped north almost 20 feet in an instant, leveling San Francisco and jolting the rest of the state. The half-mile **Earthquake Trail,** near the Bear Valley Visitor Center, illustrates this geological drama with a loop through an area torn by the slipping fault. Shattered fences, rifts in the ground, and a barn knocked off its foundation by the quake illustrate how alive the earth is here. If that doesn't convince you, a seismograph in the visitor center will.

ESSENTIALS

Point Reyes is only 30 miles northwest of San Francisco, but it takes at least 90 minutes to reach by car (it's all the small towns, not the topography, that slow you down). The easiest route is via Sir Francis Drake Boulevard from U.S. 101 south of San Rafael; it takes its bloody time getting to Point Reyes, but does so without any detours. For a much longer but more scenic route, take the Stinson Beach/Calif. 1 exit off U.S. 101 just south of Sausalito and follow Calif. 1 north.

As soon as you arrive at Point Reyes, stop at the **Bear Valley Visitor Center** (☎ **415/663-1092**) on Bear Valley Road (look for the small sign posted just north of Olema on Calif. 1) and pick up a free Point Reyes trail map. The rangers here are extremely friendly and helpful, and can answer any questions you have about the National Seashore. Be sure to check out the great natural history and cultural displays as well. It's open Monday through Friday from 9am to 5pm, Saturday and Sunday from 8am to 5pm.

Entrance to the park is free. Camping is $10 per site per night, and permits are required (reservations can be made up to 2 months in advance by calling ☎ **415/663-8054,** Mon through Fri between 9am and 2pm).

WHAT TO SEE & DO

In November 1995, the Bay Area suffered a great loss when 12,354 acres of Point Reyes burned in an uncontrollable brush fire. However, there's still plenty of pristine property in this 65,000-acre park; even the areas that suffered the worst are quickly replenishing themselves with spectacular blankets of wildflowers. The park encompasses several surf-pounded beaches, bird estuaries, open swaths of land with roaming elk, and the Point Reyes Lighthouse—a favorite among visitors who are awestruck by the spectacular views of the coast.

When headed out to any part of the Point Reyes coast, expect to spend the day surrounded by nature at its finest. But bear in mind that as beautiful as the wilderness can be, it's also untamable. Waters in these areas are not only bone-chilling and home to a vast array of sea life, including sharks, but are also unpredictable and dangerous.

Point Reyes National Seashore & Bodega Bay

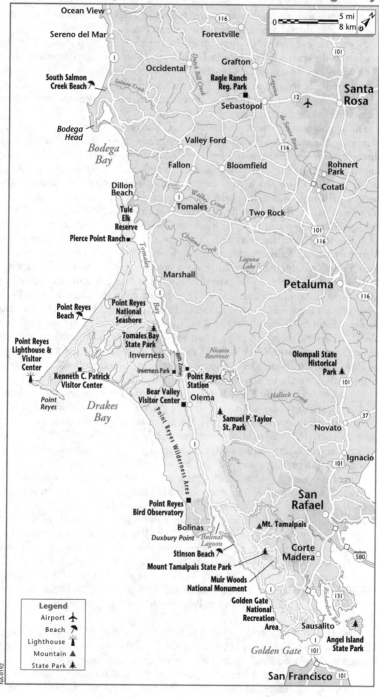

Ocean View

Sereno del Mar

116

Forestville

Occidental

Grafton

Dutch Bill Creek

Ragle Ranch
Reg. Park

**Santa
Rosa**

South Salmon
Creek Beach

Salmon Creek

Sebastopol

12

101

*Bodega
Head*

*Bodega
Bay*

Valley Ford

116

Fallon

Bloomfield

Cotati

**Rohnert
Park**

Dillon
Beach

Tule
Elk
Reserve

Walker Creek

Tomales

Two Rock

101

116

Pierce Point Ranch

Chileno Creek

*Laguna
Lake*

Marshall

Petaluma

116

Tomales Bay

Point Reyes
Beach

Point Reyes
National
Seashore

*Nicasio
Reservoir*

Olompali State
Historical
Park

101

Tomales Bay
State Park

Inverness

**Point Reyes
Lighthouse &
Visitor
Center**

Lagunitas

Inverness Park

Rift Zone

Point Reyes
Station

Kenneth C. Patrick
Visitor Center

Bear Valley
Visitor Center

Olema

Halleck Creek

Novato

37

*Point
Reyes*

*Drakes
Bay*

Samuel P. Taylor
St. Park

101

Ignacio

Point Reyes Wilderness Area

1

Point Reyes
Bird Observatory

**San
Rafael**

Bolinas

Duxbury Point

*Bolinas
Lagoon*

Mt. Tamalpais

**Corte
Madera**

580

Stinson Beach

Mount Tamalpais State Park

Muir Woods
National Monument

131

Richardson Bay

Golden Gate
National
Recreation
Area

Sausalito

Angel Island
State Park

1

Golden Gate

101

San Francisco

101

Legend

✈ Airport
⌐ Beach
☆ Lighthouse
▲ Mountain
🌲 State Park

0 5 mi
   8 km

N

NA-0192

189

There are no lifeguards on duty and waves and riptides make swimming strongly discouraged. Pets are not permitted on any of the area's trails.

By far the most popular—and crowded—attraction at Point Reyes National Seashore is the venerable **Point Reyes Lighthouse,** located at the westernmost tip of Point Reyes (visitor center ☎ 415/669-1534). Even if you plan to forego the 308 steps down to the lighthouse, it's still worth the visit to marvel at the dramatic scenery, which includes thousands of common murres and prides of sea lions that bask on the rocks far below (binoculars come in real handy).

The lighthouse is also the top spot on the California coast to observe gray whales as they make their southward and northward migration along the coast from January through April. The annual round-trip is 10,000 miles—one of the longest mammal migrations known. The whales head south in December and January, and return north in March. *Note:* If you plan to drive out to the lighthouse to whale-watch, arrive early because parking is limited. If possible, come on a weekday. On a weekend or holiday it's wise to park at the Drake's Beach Visitor Center and take the free shuttle bus to the lighthouse. Dress warmly—it's often quite cold and windy—and bring binoculars.

Whale watching is far from being the only activity offered at the Point Reyes National Seashore. Rangers conduct many different free tours: You can walk along the **Bear Valley Trail,** spotting the wildlife at the ocean's edge; see the waterfowl at **Five-brooks Pond;** explore tide pools; view some of North America's most beautiful ducks in the wetlands of **Limantour;** hike to the promontory overlooking **Chimney Rock** to see the sea lions, harbor seals, and seabirds; or take a guided walk along the **San Andreas Fault** to observe the site of the epicenter of the 1906 earthquake and learn about the regional geology. And this is just a sampling. Since tours vary seasonally, you can either call the **Bear Valley Visitor Center** (☎ 415/663-1092) or request a copy of *Park Paper,* which includes a schedule of activities and other useful information. Many of the tours are suitable for travelers with disabilities.

North and South **Point Reyes Beach** face the Pacific and withstand the full brunt of ocean tides and winds—so much so that the water is far too rough for even wading. Until a few years ago, entering the water was actually illegal, but persistent surfers went to court for their right to shred the mighty waves. Today, the park service strongly advises against taking on the tides, so play it safe and stroll the coastline. Along the south coast, the waters of ✪ **Drake's Beach** can be as tranquil and serene as Point Reyes's are turbulent. Locals come here to sun and picnic; occasionally, a hearty soul ventures into the cold waters of Drake's Bay. But keep in mind that storms generally come inland from the south and almost always hit Drake's before moving north or south. A powerful weather front can turn wispy waves into torrential tides.

Some of the park's best—and least crowded—highlights can only be approached on foot, such as **Alamere Falls,** a freshwater stream that cascades down a 40-foot bluff onto Wildcat Beach, or **Tomales Point Trail,** which passes through the Tule Elk Reserve, a protected haven for roaming herds of tule elk that once numbered in the thousands. Hiking most of the trails usually ends up being an all-day outing, however, so it's best to split a 2-day trip within Point Reyes National Seashore into a "by car" day and a "by foot" day.

If you're into bird watching, you definitely want to visit the **Point Reyes Bird Observatory** (☎ 415/868-1221), one of the few full-time ornithological research stations in the United States, located at the southeast end of the park on Mesa Road. This is where ornithologists keep an eye on more than 400 feathered species. Admission to the visitor center and nature trail is free, and visitors are welcome to observe the tricky process of catching and banding the birds. (Open daily from 15 min. after sunrise until sunset. Banding hours vary; call ☎ 415/868-0655 for exact times.)

Johnson's Oyster Farm

If you want to escape the crowds, head to Johnson's Oyster Farm. Granted, it doesn't look like much—a cluster of trailer homes, shacks, and oyster tanks surrounded by huge piles of oyster shells—but that certainly doesn't detract from the taste of fresh-out-of-the-water oysters dipped in Johnson's special sauce. The popular modus operandi is to 1) buy a couple dozen, 2) head for an empty campsite along the bay, 3) fire up the barbecue pit (don't forget the charcoal), 4) split and 'cue the little guys, 5) slather them in Johnson's special sauce, and then 6) slurp 'em down. Johnson's is located off Sir Francis Drake Boulevard, about 6 miles west(ish) of Inverness; open Tuesday through Sunday from 8am to 4pm (☎ 415/669-1149).

One of our favorite things to do in Point Reyes is paddling through placid **Tomales Bay,** a haven for migrating birds and marine mammals. Kayak trips, including 3-hour sunset outings, 3½-hour full-moon paddles, yoga tours, day trips, and longer excursions, are organized by **Tamal Saka Tomales Bay Kayaking.** Instruction, clinics, and boat delivery are available, and all ages and levels are welcome. Prices start at $45 for tours. Rentals begin at $25 for one person, $35 for two. Don't worry—the kayaks are very stable and there are no waves to contend with. The launching point is located on Calif. 1 at the Marshall Boatworks in Marshall, 8 miles north of Point Reyes Station (☎ 415/663-1743; www.tamalsaka.com; open daily from 9am to 6pm).

WHERE TO STAY

Inns of Marin, P.O. Box 547, Point Reyes Station, CA 94956 (☎ 800/887-2880 or 415/663-2000), is a free service that will help you find accommodations in your price range. Keep in mind that many places here have a 2-night minimum, although in slow season they may make an exception. They'll also refer you to restaurants, hiking, and attractions in the area.

✪ **Bear Valley Inn.** 88 Bear Valley Rd., Olema, CA 94950. ☎ 415/663-1777. 3 units, none with private bathroom. $75–$135 double. Rates include breakfast. AE, DISC, MC, V.

Ron and JoAnne Nowell's venerable two-story 1899 Victorian has survived everything from a major earthquake to a recent forest fire, which is lucky for you because you'll be hard-pressed to find a better B&B for the price in Point Reyes. Granted, the Bear Valley Inn isn't perfect—the rooms lack private bathrooms and the main highway is a tad too close—but it's loaded with Victorian charm, right down to the profusion of flowers and vines outside and comfy chairs fronting a toasty-warm woodstove inside. It's in a great location, too, with three good restaurants only a block away, and the entire National Seashore at your doorstep. Ron, who also runs a mountain-bike-rental shop next door, can set you up wheel-wise for about $25 a day and point you in the right direction.

Knob Hill. 40 Knob Hill Rd., Point Reyes Station, CA 94956. ☎ 415/663-1784. 1 unit, 1 cottage. $55–$65 double; $95 cottage. No credit cards.

Shh! It's a secret. Atop a small bluff overlooking beautiful Point Reyes Mesa is Knob Hill, where horse trainer Janet Schlitt rents a small room and private cottage next to her stable. The separate cottage is a bit pricey (about $95 on weekends), but attached to Janet's home is a small room with its own entrance, private bathroom, and garden area that she rents for only $60 a night. Granted, there's barely enough elbow room for a couple to change their minds, but it's simply adorable. Just down the street is a trail leading into Point Reyes. All in all, it's a great deal, particularly for horse lovers.

Motel Inverness. 12718 Sir Francis Drake Blvd., Inverness, CA 94937. ☎ **415/669-1081.** 7 units. TV. $69–$99 double. AE, DISC, MC, V.

Finding an inexpensive place to stay in Point Reyes is next to impossible, as hoity-toity B&Bs reign supreme. There is, however, one exception—Motel Inverness, a homey, well-maintained lodging fronting Tomales Bay. For the outdoor adventurer who plans on spending as little time indoors as possible, it's the perfect place to hole up, as the entire National Seashore awaits outside your door. Each guest room comes with a queen bed, linoleum floors, rosewood blinds, and a color TV; smoking is strictly verboten. Attached to the hotel is a giant rec room, complete with pool table, pinball machine, and big-screen TV to distract the kids, while parents can relax on the back lawn overlooking the bay, bird sanctuary, and rolling green hills beyond.

Point Reyes Country Inn & Stables. 12050 Calif. 1 (P.O. Box 501), Point Reyes Station, CA 94956. ☎ **415/663-9696.** Fax 415/663-8888. 7 units. $85–$160. Extra human guest $25; $10–$15 per horse. Rates include breakfast. MC, V.

Are you and your horsey dreaming of a country getaway? Then book a room at Point Reyes Country Inn & Stables, a five-bedroom, ranch-style home on 4 acres that offers pastoral accommodations for two- and four-legged guests (horses only) plus access to plenty of hiking and riding trails. (The riding trails are only open to guests who bring their own horse.) Each room has a private bathroom and either a balcony or a garden. The innkeepers have also added two new studios (with kitchens) above the stables, and rent out two cottages on Tomales Bay equipped with decks, stocked kitchens, fireplaces, and a shared dock.

Point Reyes Hostel. Off Limantour Rd. (P.O. Box 247), Point Reyes Station, CA 94956. ☎ **415/663-8811.** 44 bunks, 1 private rm. $12 per person. 3-night maximum stay. MC, V. Reception hours 7:30–9:30am and 4:30–9:30pm daily.

Located deep within Point Reyes National Seashore, this beautiful old ranch-style complex has 44 dormitory-style accommodations, including one room that's reserved for families (though at least one child must be 5 years old or younger). There are also two common rooms, each warmed by wood-burning stoves during chilly nights, as well as a fully equipped kitchen, barbecue (BYO charcoal), and patio. If you don't mind sharing your sleeping quarters with strangers, this is a $12-per-person deal that can't be beat. Reservations (and earplugs) are strongly recommended.

WHERE TO DINE

The Gray Whale. 12781 Sir Francis Drake Blvd., Inverness. ☎ **415/669-1244.** Main courses $5–$10. MC, V. Daily 11am–8pm. ITALIAN.

For over a decade, the Gray Whale has been a popular pit stop for Bay Areans heading to the lighthouse at Point Reyes. Why so popular? First off, it's cheap: Sandwiches—such as the roasted eggplant with pesto and mozzarella—are only $5, as are most of the salads and pastas. Second, it's pretty good: Personal favorites are the specialty pizzas, such as the Californian (artichoke hearts, fresh basil, and tomatoes) and the Vegetarian (baked eggplant, roasted onions and romas, broccoli, and piles of freshly grated Parmesan cheese). Veteran hikers and mountain bikers stop by for an espresso booster, sipped on the small patio overlooking the block-long town of Inverness.

Station House Café. Main St., Point Reyes Station. ☎ **415/663-1515.** Reservations recommended. Breakfast $4.45–$7.50; main courses $9–$17.50. DISC, MC, V. Sun–Thurs 8am–9pm; Fri–Sat 8am–10pm. AMERICAN.

This friendly, low-key establishment has been a local favorite for over 2 decades, thanks to its cozy fireplace, open kitchen, outdoor garden dining area (key on sunny days), and live music on weekends. Breakfast dishes range from bread pudding with stewed fruit compote to a frittata with asparagus, goat cheese, and olives. Lunch and dinner specials might include fettuccine with fresh local mussels steamed in white-wine-and-butter sauce, or two-cheese polenta served with fresh spinach sauté and grilled garlic-buttered tomato—all made from local produce, seafood, and organically raised Niman-Schell Farms beef. The cafe has an extensive list of fine California wines, plus local imported beers.

Taqueria La Quinta. 11285 Calif. 1 (at Third and Main sts.), Point Reyes Station. ☎ **415/663-8868.** Main courses $4–$6. No credit cards. Wed–Mon 11:30am–8pm. MEXICAN.

Fresh, good, fast, and cheap: What more could you ask for in a restaurant? Taqueria La Quinta has been one of our favorite lunch stops in downtown Point Reyes for years and years. A huge selection of Mexican-American standards are posted above the counter. Our favorite is chili verde in a spicy tomatillo sauce with a side of handmade corn tortillas. Those in the know inquire about the seafood specials. Since it's all self-serve, you can skip the tip—but watch out for the salsa: That sucker's hot.

2 Along the Sonoma Coast

BODEGA BAY

Beyond the tip of the Point Reyes Peninsula, the road curves around toward the coastal village of Bodega Bay, which supports a fishing fleet of 300 boats. As you drive north, Bodega Bay is a good place to stop for lunch or a stroll around town. There are several interesting shops and galleries, though the best show in town is at **Tides Wharf,** where the fishing boats come in to unload their daily catch, which is promptly gutted and packed in ice.

Bodega Head State Park is a great vantage point for whale watching during the annual migration season from January through April. At **Doran Beach** there's a large bird sanctuary (willets, curlews, godwits, and more), and the **University of California Marine Biology Lab** next door conducts guided tours on Friday afternoons.

One of the bay's major events is the **Fisherman's Festival,** in April. Local fishing boats, decorated with ribbons and banners, sail out for a Blessing of the Fleet, while landlubbers enjoy music, a lamb and oyster barbecue, and an arts-and-crafts fair.

A few miles inland, the tiny town of **Bodega** (pop. 100) is famous as the setting of Alfred Hitchcock's *The Birds.* Fans will want to take a souvenir photo of Potter School House and St. Teresa's Church.

For more information about these festivals and other goings-on in Bodega Bay, call or stop in at the **Bodega Bay Area Visitors Center,** 850 Calif. 1, Bodega Bay, CA 94923 (☎ **707/875-3422**). They have lots of brochures about the town and the surrounding area, including maps of the Sonoma Coast State Beaches and the best local fishing spots.

WHERE TO STAY

✪ **Bodega Harbor Inn.** 1345 Bodega Ave., Bodega Bay, CA 94923. ☎ **707/875-3594.** 14 units. TV. $53–$75 double. MC, V.

Thank Poseidon for the Bodega Harbor Inn, which, besides being the only low-priced accommodation in Bodega Bay, is also one of the best deals for your dollar on the North Coast. Set on a small bluff overlooking the bay, the inn consists of four single-story clapboard buildings surrounded by well-maintained lawns and gardens. The rooms, though small, are impeccably neat and tastefully decorated with unpretentious antique furnishings; double beds, private bathrooms, and cable TV are all standard. (*Insider tip:* The best rooms are nos. 12 and 14, which come with small decks and partial ocean views.) The clincher, though, is the inn's private lawn area overlooking the bay: On sunny days, there's no better way to enjoy the day in Bodega Bay than parking your fanny in one the lawn chairs and watching the fishing boats bring in their daily catch. Families should inquire about the seven vacation homes that the inn rents for as little as $100 per night.

WHERE TO DINE

Breakers Cafe. 1400 Calif. 1, Bodega Bay. ☎ **707/875-2513.** Main courses $6–$16. MC, V. Daily 9am–9pm. CALIFORNIA.

If you're a big breakfast eater, the Breakers Cafe is your best bet in Bodega Bay. Omelets, Belgian waffles, baked polenta, house-baked muffins, and even good ol' biscuits and gravy are served in a pleasant greenhouse-style dining room filled with a profusion of healthy plants and diffused sunlight. The cafe also offers a modest lunch-and-dinner menu, ranging from above-average sandwiches and burgers to fresh pastas, locally caught seafood, and a small selection of vegetarian dishes. Prices run a bit steep for the seafood dishes, but most items are under $10. If the weather's warm, ask for a table on the patio.

✪ **Lucas Wharf Deli.** 595 Calif. 1, Bodega Bay. ☎ **707/875-3562.** Deli items $4–$10. DISC, MC, V. July–Aug daily 10am–7pm; Sept–June daily 10am–6pm. DELI.

We always stop here whenever we pass through Bodega Bay. Most visitors don't even give it a glance as they head into the adjacent restaurant, but that's because they don't know about the big bowls of fresh, tangy crab cioppino they dole out for only $5 a pint—a third of the restaurant price. It's a fabulously messy affair, best devoured at the nearby picnic tables. When crab season is over, the cioppino special is replaced by an equally awesome pile of fresh fish-and-chips (easily big enough for two).

Worth a Splurge

Tides Wharf Restaurant. 835 Calif. 1. ☎ **707/875-3652.** Main courses $12.50–$24.50. AE, DISC, MC, V. Mon–Fri 7:30am–10pm; Sat–Sun 7am–10pm. SEAFOOD.

In summer, as many as 1,000 diners a day pass through the Tides Wharf. Back in the early 1960s, it served as one of the settings for Hitchcock's *The Birds*, but don't expect the weather-beaten, board-and-batten luncheonette you saw in the movie—a recent $6-million renovation has gentrified, enlarged, and redecorated the place beyond recognition. The best tables offer views overlooking the ocean, and the bill of fare is what you might expect at a seaside eatery: oysters on the half shell, clam chowder, and all the fish that the owners (who send their own fishing boat out into the Pacific every day) can dredge up from the cold blue sea. Prime rib, pasta, and poultry dishes are available as well. Adjacent to the restaurant is a fish-processing plant, snack bar, and gift shop.

THE SONOMA COAST STATE BEACHES, JENNER & FORT ROSS STATE HISTORIC PARK

Along 13 winding miles of Calif. 1—from Bodega Bay to Goat Rock Beach in Jenner—stretch the Sonoma Coast State Beaches, which are ideal for walking, tide-pooling, abalone picking, fishing, and bird watching for such species as blue heron, cormorant, osprey, and pelicans. Each beach is clearly marked from the road, and numerous pullouts are provided for parking. Even if you don't stop at any of the beaches, the drive alone is spectacular.

At **Jenner,** the Russian River empties into the ocean. **Penny Island,** in the river's estuary, is home to otters and many species of birds; a colony of harbor seals lives out on the ocean rocks. **Goat Rock Beach** is a popular breeding ground for the seals; pupping season begins in March and lasts until June.

From Jenner, a 12-mile drive along some very dramatic coastline will bring you to **Fort Ross State Historic Park** (☎ **707/847-3286**), a reconstruction of the fort that was established here in 1812 by the Russians as a base for seal and otter hunting (it was abandoned in 1842). At the visitor center you can view the silver samovars and elaborate table services that the Russians used. The fenced compound contains several buildings, including the first Russian Orthodox church ever built on the North American continent outside Alaska. The park also offers beach trails and picnic grounds on more than 1,000 acres. Admission is free, but parking is a hefty $6.

North from Fort Ross the road continues to **Salt Point State Park.** This 3,500-acre expanse contains 30 campsites, 14 miles of hiking trails, dozens of tide pools, a pygmy forest, and old Pomo village sites. Your best bet is to pull off the highway any place that catches your eye and start exploring on foot. At the north end of the park, head inland on Kruse Ranch Road to the 317-acre **Kruse Rhododendron Reserve** (☎ **707/847-3221**), an aesthetic miracle in April and May. Some rhododendrons grow to a height of 18 feet under the redwood-and-fir canopy.

WHERE TO STAY

Jenner Inn & Cottage. 10400 Calif. 1, Jenner, CA 95450. ☎ **800/732-2377** or 707/865-2377. Fax 707/865-0829. www.jennerinn.com. 19 units. $95–$215 double. Rates include extended continental breakfast. AE, MC, V.

The worst-kept secret on the North Coast is Murphy's Jenner Inn, a hodgepodge of individually designed and decorated houses and cottages scattered along the coast and inland along Russian River. Couples from the Bay Area who want to stay along the coast for a night, but dread the long drive to Mendocino, usually wend their way here for an easy weekend getaway. Most of the houses are subdivided into suites, while second honeymooners vie for the ultra-private oceanfront cottages. Wicker furniture, wood paneling, and private bathrooms and entrances are standard, though each lodging has its own distinct personality: Some have kitchens, while others have fireplaces, porches, or private decks. Naturally, the private cottages overlooking the Pacific are the priciest, but for about $95 most couples are content with one of the small suites. A complimentary continental breakfast is served in the main lodge. For a sneak peek at some of the cottages, visit their Web site at www.jennerinn.com.

WHERE TO DINE

River's End. Calif. 1., Jenner. ☎ **707/865-2484.** Reservations recommended. Main courses $13–$33 dinner. MC, V. Fri–Mon 11am–9:30pm (hrs. may change; call ahead). INTERNATIONAL.

Outwardly unpretentious yet deceptively urbane, this small seaside restaurant offers an artfully rustic setting, with big windows overlooking the coast (seals and sea lions might happen to be cavorting offshore). The menu is wonderfully eclectic, ranging from Indonesian *bahmi goreng,* a selection of Indian curries, beef saté, beef Wellington, seafood, and steaks. After dinner, take the remainder of your wine to the outside deck and enjoy the sunset.

Sizzling Tandoor. 9960 Calif. 1, at the south end of the Russian River Bridge, Jenner. ☎ **707/865-0625.** Main courses $8.50–$13.50. AE, DISC, MC, V. Daily 11:30am–3pm; Mon–Thurs 5–9:30pm; Fri–Sun 5–10pm. Closed Mon in winter. INDIAN.

Something of a non sequitur along a rather desolate stretch of Calif. 1 between Bodega Bay and Jenner, the Sizzling Tandoor serves huge, inexpensive plates of classic Indian cuisine. The lonely location, though peculiar for a restaurant, is superb: Perched high atop a windswept hill, the restaurant boasts an exquisite view of the Russian River far below. The large array of curries and kabobs are accompanied by soup, vegetables, pulao rice, and the best naan (Indian bread) on the North Coast. Even if you're not hungry, order some naan to go—it makes the perfect road snack.

GUALALA & POINT ARENA

Back on Calif. 1 going north, you'll pass through Sea Ranch, a series of condominium beach developments, until you reach Gualala (pronounced Wah-*la*-la). To access the beaches along this stretch of coast you'll have to cross private property, and your entrance may therefore be restricted at any time. Still, there are about 10 or so public beaches that are ideal for walking.

The **Gualala River,** adjacent to the town of the same name, is suitable for canoeing, rafting, and kayaking, since all powerboats and jet skis are forbidden. Along its banks you're likely to see osprey, heron, egrets, and ducks; steelhead, salmon, and river otters make their home in the waters. Canoes, kayaks, and bicycles can be rented in Gualala for 2 hours, a half day, or a full day from **Adventure Rents** (☎ **888/881-4386** or 707/884-4386), in downtown Gualala on Calif. 1 north of the Chevron. A bike costs $15 for 2 hours; a double kayak or canoe (which seats 2 to 5 persons) costs $40 for 2 hours, $50 for half a day, or $60 for a whole day (single kayaks cost half as much).

Point Arena lies a few miles north of Gualala. Most folks stop here for the view at the **Point Arena Lighthouse** (☎ **707/882-2777**), which was built in 1870 after 10 ships ran aground here on a single night during a storm. A $2.50 per person fee (50¢ for children under 12) covers parking, entrance to the lighthouse museum, and a surprisingly interesting tour of the six-story, 145-step lighthouse. It's open in the summer from 11am to 3:30pm Monday through Friday, from 10am to 3:30pm Saturday and Sunday; winter hours are daily from 11am to 3:30pm (but closed weekdays in Dec and Jan).

WHERE TO STAY

Old Milano Hotel & Restaurant. 38300 Calif. 1, Gualala, CA 95445. ☎ **707/884-3256.** Fax 707/884-4249. 6 units sharing 2 bathrooms, 1 suite, 6 cottages. $80 double with garden view, $110 double with ocean view; $165 master suite; $140–$215 cottage. Rates include breakfast. MC, V.

This romantic hotel lies just north of Gualala and has a spellbinding view of Castle Rock from the front porch and sloping lawn. The inn was built in 1905 on 3 acres and is listed on the National Register of Historic Places. It has enchanting flower and herb gardens and a superbly situated hot tub, from which you look directly out to the ocean. The rooms are all decorated differently, often with rare antiques. Upstairs, the six lowest-priced rooms share two bathrooms, each with double showers. Our favorite room is the Milano's honest-to-Betsy train caboose, a romantically private space with woodstove and two upstairs brakeman's seats.

A full breakfast is served either in your room or in the parlor. Chef Brain Knutson offers pricey California cuisine—rack of Sonoma lamb, poached salmon, roasted Peking duck—served in an intimate dining room lit by candlelight and, on cool nights, roaring fires in the stone fireplaces.

✪ **St. Orres.** 36601 Calif. 1 (Box 523), Gualala, CA 95445. ☎ **707/884-3303.** Fax 707/884-1840. 8 units (sharing 3 bathrooms), 12 cottages. $60 double without ocean view; $75 double with ocean view; $85–$220 double occupancy of cottage, depending on the size. MC, V.

An extraordinary Russian-style building—complete with two onion-domed towers—St. Orres lies 1½ miles north of Gualala. The complex was built in 1972 with century-old timbers salvaged from a nearby mill. It offers secluded cottage-style accommodations on 42 acres, but the best deal for your dollar are the eight beautifully handcrafted rooms in the main building, which share three bathrooms decorated in brilliant colors. Possibly worth a splurge is one of the seven cottages that border St. Orres Creek, which all have exclusive use of a spa facility that includes hot tub, sauna, and sundeck (the most luxurious is Pine Haven, with two bedrooms, two redwood decks, two bathrooms, a tiled breakfast area, beach stone fireplace, and wet bar).

The hotel is especially well known for its intimate restaurant, The St. Orres, a 17-seat charmer set below one of the main building's onion domes. Light filters through stained-glass windows onto strands of ivy that cascade down from the upper balcony. Unfortunately, the only offering is a pricey $30 three-course fixed-price meal, but what a meal it is: Dishes are inspired by Pacific Northwest cuisine and include wild boar, pheasant, venison, quail, and rack of lamb. Reservations are essential. It's open daily for dinner only and is closed Tuesday and Wednesday from January through May. MasterCard and Visa are accepted for hotel guests only; otherwise, no credit cards.

WHERE TO DINE

The Food Company. 38411 Calif. 1 at Robinsons Reef Rd., Gualala. ☎ **707/884-1800.** Deli items $3–$9. MC, V. Daily 8–10:30am; Sun–Thurs 11am–8pm; Fri–Sat 11am–9pm. DELI.

If the St. Orres restaurant (see above) is out of your price range, you'll be happy to know that you can have an equally romantic lunch or dinner just down the road for a fraction of the price. Place your order at the deli counter, grab a bottle of wine from the rack, then head to the adjacent garden and plop your collective fannies at one of the picnic tables. The menu offers a dizzying array of specials from around the globe—corn tamales, Greek moussaka, lamb curry, quiche lorraine, pasta puttanesca—as well as fresh-baked breads, pastries, and sandwiches. Better yet, order it all to go and head for the beach.

NORTH FROM POINT ARENA

Driving north from Point Arena, you'll pass the small towns of **Elk, Manchester, Albion,** and **Little River** on your way to Mendocino. This stretch of Calif. 1 also has some of the most dramatic and beautiful coastline in California, so be sure to plan on frequent stops along the way.

Though most of these coastal communities have existed for more than a century in relative obscurity, the recent tourism boom in California (in addition to the fact that there's not enough realty left in Mendocino to build an outhouse) has resulted in an explosion of new restaurants and B&Bs; unfortunately, almost all of them are out of the price range of this guide. If you don't mind the long, wayward drive to get here, it's worth skipping the Mendocino masses for some true small-town R&R along the coast.

WHERE TO STAY

✪ **KOA Kamping Kabins.** 44300 Kinney Rd. (P.O. Box 266; off Calif. 1, 1.6 miles north of Point Arena), Manchester, CA 95459. ☎ **800/562-4188** or 707/882-2375. 18 cabins. $41–$49 cabin. AE, DISC, MC, V.

What? You expect *me* to stay at a Kampgrounds of America?!? You bet. Once you see these adorable little log cabins, you can't help but admit that, rich or poor, this is one great way to spend the weekend on the coast. The cabins have one or two bedrooms with log-frame double beds or bunk beds for the kids and sleep four to six people, respectively. Rustic is the key word here: mattresses, a heater, and a light bulb are your standard amenities. Beyond that, you're on your own, but basically all you need is some bedding or a sleeping bag, cooking and eating utensils, and a bag of charcoal for the barbecue out on the front porch (next to the log porch swing). Hot showers, bathrooms, laundry facilities, a small store, and a swimming pool are a short walk away, as is Manchester Beach.

WHERE TO DINE

✪ **Pangaea.** 250 Main St., Point Arena. ☎ **707/882-3001.** Reservations recommended. Main courses $8–$20. No credit cards. Wed–Sun 6–9pm. ECLECTIC.

North Coast locals have been raving about this place since the day it opened. Chef/owner Shannon Hughes, an expatriate of the St. Orres and Old Milano Hotel restaurants, decided it was time to do her own thing, and boy is she doing it well. Everything that comes out of her kitchen is wondrously fresh, inventive, and organically grown and/or raised, such as the succulent pork confit, served on a potato tart with homemade apricot chutney. And how's this for a $4.50 salad: organic greens in a vinaigrette of toasted shallots, sherry vinegar, and Italian mountain Gorgonzola. Hughes has become famous for her Thai-style crab cakes made with ginger scallions and served with a Thai green-curry coconut sauce. Even her burgers are beyond reproach, made with Niman-Schell beef, organic cheese and greens, caramelized onions and Thai chili sauce, garlic roasted red potatoes, and homemade ketchup. Desserts—strawberry rhubarb crisp à la mode, lemon-curd tart with a blood-orange sauce—are equally impressive, as is the hip decor. Highly recommended.

3 Mendocino

Mendocino is, to our minds, *the* premier destination on California's north coast. Despite (or because of) its relative isolation, it emerged as one of northern California's major centers for the arts in the 1950s. It's easy to see why artists were—and still are—attracted to this idyllic community, a cluster of New England–style sea captain's homes and small stores set on headlands overlooking the ocean.

At the height of the logging boom, Mendocino became an important and active port. Its population was about 3,500, and eight hotels were built along with 17 saloons and more than a dozen bordellos. Today, it has only about 1,000 residents, most of whom reside on the north end of town. On summer weekends the population seems more like 10,000, as hordes of tourists drive up from the Bay Area—but despite the crowds, Mendocino still manages to retain its small-town charm.

ESSENTIALS

GETTING THERE The fastest route from San Francisco is via U.S. 101 north to Cloverdale. From there, take Calif. 128 west to Calif. 1, then go north along the coast. It's about a 4-hour drive. (You could also take U.S. 101 all the way to Ukiah or Willits, and cut over to the west from there.) The most scenic route from the Bay Area, if you have the time and your stomach doesn't mind the twists and turns, is to take Calif. 1 north along the coast the entire way; it's at least a 5- to 6-hour drive.

VISITOR INFORMATION You can stock up on lots of free brochures and maps at the **Fort Bragg/Mendocino Coast Chamber of Commerce,** 332 N. Main St. (P.O. Box 1141), Fort Bragg, CA 95437 (☎ **800/726-2780** or 707/961-6300; www. mendocinocoast.com). Pick up a copy of the center's monthly magazine, *Arts and Entertainment,* which lists upcoming events throughout Mendocino. It's available at numerous stores and cafes, including the Mendocino Bakery, Gallery Bookshop, and the Mendocino Art Center.

EXPLORING THE TOWN

Stroll through town, enjoy the architecture, and browse through the dozens of galleries and shops. Our favorites include the **Highlight Gallery,** 45052 Main St. (☎ 707/937-3132), for its handmade furniture, pottery, and other craft work; **Old Gold,** 6 Albion St. (☎ 707/937-5005), which carries a great selection of antique and contemporary jewelry and watches; and the **Gallery Bookshop & Bookwinkle's Children's Books,** at Main and Kasten streets (☎ 707/937-2665), one of the best independent bookstores in northern California, with a wonderful selection of books for children and adults. Another popular stop is **Mendocino Jams & Preserves,** 440 Main St. (☎ 800/708-1196 or 707/937-1037), which offers free tastings of their natural, locally made gourmet wares on little bread chips.

After exploring the town, walk out on the headlands that wrap around the town and constitute ✪ **Mendocino Headlands State Park.** (The visitor center for the park is in Ford House on Main Street.) Three miles of trails wind through the park, giving visitors panoramic views of sea arches and hidden grottoes. If you're here in the fall, the area will be blanketed with wildflowers, and when we last stopped by, you could pick fresh blackberries beside the trails. The headlands are home to many unique species of birds, including black oystercatchers. Behind the Mendocino Presbyterian Church on Main Street is a trail leading to stairs that take you down to the beach, a small but picturesque stretch of sand where driftwood formations have washed ashore.

On the south side of town, **Big River Beach** is accessible from Calif. 1; it's good for picnicking, walking, and sunbathing.

In town, stop by the **Mendocino Art Center,** 45200 Little Lake Rd. (☎ 707/937-5818), the town's unofficial cultural headquarters. It's also known for its gardens, three galleries, and shops that display and sell local fine arts and crafts. Admission is free; open daily from 10am to 5pm.

For a special treat, go to **Sweetwater Gardens,** 955 Ukiah St. (☎ 800/300-4140 or 707/937-4140), which offers group and private saunas and hot-tub soaks by the hour. Additional services include Swedish or deep-tissue massages. Reservations are recommended. Private tub prices are $8 per person per half hour, $11 per person per hour. Group tub prices are $7.50 per person with no time limit. Special discounts are available on Wednesdays. Open Monday through Thursday from 2 to 10pm, Friday through Sunday from noon to 11pm.

OUTDOOR PURSUITS

Explore the Big River by renting a canoe, sea cycle, kayak, or outrigger from **Catch a Canoe & Bicycles Too** (☎ 707/937-0273), located on the grounds of the Stanford Inn by the Sea, just south of town on Calif. 1. If you're lucky, you'll see some osprey, blue herons, harbor seals, deer, and wood ducks. These same folks will also rent you a mountain bike (much better quality than your usual bike rental), so you can head up Calif. 1 and explore the nearby state parks on two wheels.

Horseback riding (both English and Western) on the beach and into the redwoods is offered by **Ricochet Ridge Ranch,** 24201 N. Calif. 1, Fort Bragg (☎ 888/873-5777 or 707/964-PONY). Prices range from $35 for a 2-hour beach ride to $195 for an all-day private beach/redwoods trail ride with lunch.

In addition to Mendocino Headlands State Park (see "Exploring the Town," above), there are several other state parks near Mendocino; all are within an easy drive or bike ride and make for a good day's outing. Information on all the parks' features, including maps of each one, is found in a brochure called *Mendocino Coast State Parks,* available from the visitor center in Fort Bragg. These areas include **Manchester State Park,** located where the San Andreas Fault sweeps to the sea; **Jughandle State Reserve;** and **Van Damme State Park,** with a sheltered, easily accessible beach.

Our favorite of these parks, located directly on Calif. 1 just north of Mendocino, is **Russian Gulch State Park** (☎ **707/937-5804**). It's one of the region's most spectacular parks, where roaring waves crash against the cliffs that protect the park's California coastal redwoods. The most popular attraction is the **Punch Bowl,** a collapsed sea cave that forms a tunnel through which waves crash, creating throaty echoes. Inland, there's a scenic paved bike path, and visitors can also hike along miles of trails, including a gentle, well-marked 3-mile **Waterfall Loop** that winds past tall redwoods and damp green foliage to a 36-foot-high waterfall. Admission is $5. Thirty camping sites enjoy a beautiful setting and are available from April to mid-October ($14 to $16 per night). Call ☎ **800/444-7275** for reservations.

Fort Bragg is just a short distance up the coast; deep-sea fishing charters are available from its harbor.

WHERE TO STAY

The trick to living large on a small budget in these parts is to spend your days in Mendocino and your nights in Fort Bragg, which is only about a 10-minute drive away. Why? Because Fort Bragg is full of cheap motels, most charging a *third* less than what you'll fork out for an average B&B. See "Fort Bragg," below, for details.

Mendocino Hotel & Garden Suites. 45080 Main St., Mendocino, CA 95460. ☎ **800/ 548-0513** or 707/937-0511. Fax 707/937-0513. 57 units, 43 with private bathroom. TEL. $85 double without bathroom; $120–$185 double with bathroom; $190–$250 suite. Extra person $20. AE, MC, V.

Right in the heart of town, this 1878 hotel evokes California's gold-rush days. Beveled-glass doors open into a Victorian-style lobby and parlor where it would be easy to imagine Mae West in all her glory. The hotel's decor combines antiques and reproductions, like the oak reception desk from a demolished Kansas bank. Remington paintings, stained-glass lamps, and Persian carpets contribute to the Wild West aura. Guest rooms feature hand-painted French porcelain sinks with floral designs, quaint wallpaper, old-fashioned beds and armoires, and photographs and memorabilia of historic Mendocino. About half the rooms are located in four handsome small buildings behind the main house; the most affordable rooms, of course, share a common bathroom, but it's a minor inconvenience for such regal digs. Breakfast and lunch are served daily in the Garden Room, while dinner is offered daily in the Victorian-style dining room.

✪ **Mendocino Village Inn.** 44860 Main St. (P.O. Box 626), Mendocino, CA 95460. ☎ **800/882-7029** or 707/937-0246. 11 units, 9 with bathroom. $75 double with shared bathroom; $95–$175 double with bathroom; $175 suite. Rates include full breakfast and evening refreshments. No credit cards.

A garden of flowers, plants, and frog ponds fronts the large blue-and-white guest house, which was built in 1882 by a local doctor and later occupied by famed local

Deluxe Dining Tip

Tuesday through Thursday, the nationally acclaimed Café Beaujolais offers a prix-fixe country menu for only $25. That's a pretty darn good deal, wouldn't you say?

Great Deals on Mendocino Meals

You'd be surprised what $5 will get you for lunch in Mendocino if you know where to go.

Tote Fete Bakery (☎ **707/937-3383**) has a wonderful little carry-out booth at the corner of Albion and Lansing streets. If it's on the specials menu, be sure to order the delicious foil-wrapped barbecue chicken sandwiches; the pizza, focaccia bread, and twice-baked potatoes are also good choices. Dine at the stand-up counter, or opt for a picnic at the headlands down the street.

Regardless of preference—beef, chicken, turkey, or veggie—burger lovers won't be let down at **Mendo Burgers** (☎ **707/937-1111**), arguably the best burger joint on the North Coast. A side of thick, fresh-cut fries is mandatory, as is a pile of napkins. Hidden behind the Mendocino Bakery and Café at 10483 Lansing St., it's a little hard to find, but well worth searching out.

On the opposite spectrum of Mendo Burgers is **Lu's Kitchen** (☎ **707/937-4939**), which uses only organically grown produce for their vegetarian burritos, salads, tacos, and quesadillas. The restaurant is little more than a small shack hidden at 45013 Ukiah St., between Lansing and Ford streets (look for the white plastic tables and chairs on the south side of the street), and can be hard to find.

In the back of the **Little River Market** (☎ **707/937-5133**), located directly across from the Little River Inn on Calif. 1, is a trio of small tables overlooking the Mendocino coastline. All you need to procure a seat is to order a tamale, sandwich, or whatever else is on the menu at the tiny deli inside the market. On the way out, be sure to buy a loaf of the legendary Café Beaujolais bread sold at the front counter. It's open daily 8am to 7pm.

---

artist Emmy Lou Packard. Innkeepers Bill and Kathleen Erwin have decorated each room differently. The Queen Anne Room features a four-poster canopy bed, and the sentimental Maggie's Room is named for a child who etched her name in the window glass almost a century ago (you can still see it). The least expensive rooms are the two attic units, which share a bathroom. The rest all have private bathrooms, and four rooms have private outside entrances. Complimentary beverages are served in the evening.

WHERE TO DINE

Bay View Café. 45040 Main St. ☎ **707/937-4197.** Reservations not accepted. Main courses $6–$15. No credit cards. Summer daily 8am–9pm. Winter Mon–Thurs 8am–3pm; Fri–Sun 8am–9pm. AMERICAN.

This reasonably priced cafe is one of the most popular in town and the only place around besides the Mendocino Hotel that serves breakfast ("And we're way better," says the owner). From the second-floor dining area of the cafe, there's a sweeping view of the Pacific and faraway headlands; to reach it, climb a flight of stairs running up the outside of the town's antique water tower, then detour sideways. Surrounded by dozens of ferns suspended from the ceiling, you'll find a menu with Southwestern selections (the marinated chicken breast is very popular), a good array of sandwiches (our favorite is the hot crabmeat with avocado slices), fish-and-chips, and the fresh catch of the day. Breakfast ranges from the basic bacon 'n' eggs to eggs Florentine and honey-wheat pancakes.

✪ **Café Beaujolais.** 961 Ukiah St. ☎ **707/937-5614.** Reservations recommended. Main courses $16–$25. DISC, MC, V. Daily 5:45–9pm. AMERICAN/FRENCH.

This is one of Mendocino's—if not northern California's—top dining choices, owned and managed since 1977 by chef and entrepreneur Margaret Fox, and worth a splurge. The venerable French-country-style tavern is set in a turn-of-the-century house; rose-colored carnival-glass chandeliers add a burnish to the oak floors and the heavy oak tables adorned with flowers. On warm summer nights, request a table at the enclosed deck overlooking the "designer" gardens.

Though Café Beaujolais started out as a breakfast and lunch place, it's strictly a dinner house now (yes, their famed weekend brunch has been discontinued). The menu changes weekly and usually lists about five main courses, such as wild sturgeon fillet pan-roasted with truffle emulsion sauce, roast free-range duck with wild huckleberry sauce, or broiled Wildwood Ranch pork loin chop with yam purée. Sure, it's expensive, but if you've budgeted for one dining blowout, this is where you'll want to indulge.

The Mousse Cafe. 390 Kasten St. (at Albion St.). ☎ **707/937-4323.** Reservations recommended for dinner. Main courses $11–$17. No credit cards. Mon–Thurs 11:30am–9pm; Fri–Sat 11:30am–10:30pm; Sun 9am–9pm. CONTINENTAL/CALIFORNIA.

The setting is a turn-of-the-century clapboard-sided house inspired by a New England architecture and set in a pleasant garden. In 1995, the place was gutted and redone, resulting in a brand-new, bright, streamlined interior. The menu utilizes many local items such as organic herbs and vegetables, as in the kick-butt Caesar salad. We also enjoyed the roast chicken with garlic mashed potatoes and the swordfish special, which came with a pile of fresh vegetables. The Blackout cake is a chocoholic's fantasy. Service is friendly; our only complaint is that the tables are a bit too close together, especially if it's crowded.

4 Fort Bragg

As Mendocino Coast's commercial center—hence the site of the region's only fast-food restaurants and supermarkets—Fort Bragg is far more down-to-earth than Mendocino. Inexpensive motels and cheap eats used to be its only attraction, but over the past few years gentrification has quickly spread throughout the town as the logging and fishing industries have continued to decline. With no room left to open new shops in Mendocino, many gallery, boutique, and restaurant owners have moved up the road. The result is a huge increase in Fort Bragg's tourist trade, particularly during the annual Whale Festival in March and Paul Bunyan Days over Labor Day weekend.

To explore the town properly, make your first stop at the **Fort Bragg/Mendocino Coast Chamber of Commerce,** 332 N. Main St. (P.O. Box 1141), Fort Bragg, CA 95437 (☎ **800/726-2780** or 707/961-6300), and pick up a free walking map. The friendly staff can answer any questions about Mendocino, Fort Bragg, and the surrounding region.

SHOPPING & EXPLORING THE AREA

The town doesn't boast as many well-coiffed stores and galleries as its dainty cousin to the south, but it does have some worthwhile shopping spots. **Antique shops** line the 300 block of North Franklin Street, 1 block east of Main Street, while an old car dealership, at 401 N. Main St. (☎ **707/964-8324**), has been turned into a shopping center and historical museum with logging equipment and restored steam trains.

For the Shell of It, 344 N. Main St. (☎ **707/961-0461**), stocks handmade jewelry, baskets, and collectibles made of shells or designed around a nautical theme, as well as rocks, gems, minerals, and fossils. The **Hot Pepper Jelly Company,** 330 N. Main St. (☎ **707/961-1422**), is famous for its assortment of Mendocino food products—dozens of varieties of pepper jelly, plus local mustards, syrups, and biscotti along with hand-painted porcelain bowls, unusual baskets, and more. The **Mendocino Chocolate Company,** 542 N. Main St. (☎ **707/964-8800**), makes and sells homemade chocolates and truffles, which it ships all over the world. Painters, jewelers, sculptors, weavers, potters, and other local artists display their works at **Northcoast Artists,** 362 N. Main St. (☎ **707/964-8266**). At **Windsong,** 324 N. Main St. (☎ **707/964-2050**), you'll find a clutter of colorful kites, cards, candles, and other gifts.

Fort Bragg is also the home of the **Mendocino Coast Botanical Gardens,** 18220 N. Calif. 1 (☎ **707/964-4352**), about 8 miles north of Mendocino. This cliff-top public garden, set among the pines along the rugged coast, nurtures rhododendrons, fuchsias, azaleas, and a multitude of flowering shrubs. The area contains bridges, streams, canyons, dells, picnic areas, and trails for easy walking. Children under 12 must be accompanied by their parents. Admission is $5 for adults, $4 for seniors 60 and over, $3 for children 13 to 17, $1 for children 6 to 12, and free for children 5 and under. Open April 1 through September 30 daily from 9am to 5pm, October 1 through March 31 daily from 9am to 4pm.

From Fort Bragg, the **Skunk Train** (☎ **800/77-SKUNK** or 707/964-6371) gives riders a fine tour of the area's redwoods. Locals have always said of the logging trains, "You can smell 'em before you can see 'em," which explains the nickname. The trains, which can be boarded at the Fort Bragg Depot at the foot of Laurel Avenue in Fort Bragg (2 blocks from the Grey Whale Inn), travel 40 miles inland along the Redwood Highway (U.S. 101) to Willits. It's a scenic route through the redwood forest, crossing 31 bridges and trestles and cutting through two deep tunnels. The round-trip takes 6 to 7 hours, allowing plenty of time for lunch in Willits before you return on the afternoon train. Half-day trips are offered on weekends throughout the year, and daily in summer from mid-June to early September. In summer call for reservations. The trains run year-round, but call for exact times as schedules vary. Tickets cost $35 for a full-day trip, $25 half-day; children ages 3 to 11 board for $18 full-day, $13 half-day; free for children under 3. Serious train buffs can ride in the locomotive cab with the engineer for $100. Family packages are also available.

Also worth checking out is the **North Coast Brewing Company** (☎ **707/964-2739**), which offers free tours of the brewery daily at 1:30pm. Since the tours are limited to 12 persons, be sure to sign up in advance at the gift store downstairs at 445 N. Main St. Across the street is the Brewing Company's pub, open for lunch and dinner (see "Where to Dine," below).

OUTDOOR PURSUITS

Fort Bragg is the county's sportfishing center. Just south of town, **Noyo Fishing Center,** 32450 N. Harbor, Noyo (☎ **707/964-7609**), is a good place to buy or rent tackle and the best source of information on local fishing boats. Lots of party boats leave from the town's harbor, as do whale-watching tours.

Lost Coast Kayaking, located in Van Damme State Park (☎ **707/937-2434**), offers kayak tours of the coastline's numerous sea caves. All the necessary equipment is provided; all you need to bring is a bathing suit and $45 for the 2-hour tour.

Three miles north of Fort Bragg off Calif. 1 lies **Mackerricher State Park** (☎ **707/937-5804**), a popular place for biking, hiking, and horseback riding. This enormous 1,700-acre park has 142 campsites and 8 miles of shoreline. For a true biking or hiking venture, travel the 8-mile-long "Haul Road," an old logging road that provides fine ocean vistas all the way to Ten-Mile River. Harbor seals make their home at the park's Laguna Point Seal-Watching Station, reached via an elevated wooden gangway (truly a pleasant walk).

CUTTING-EDGE THEATER

Living proof that poor, maligned ol' Fort Bragg is on the road to respect is its upstart new theatrical company, ✪ **Warehouse Repertory Theatre**, 18791 N. Calif. 1. Determined to make Fort Bragg the Ashland of California, this cadre of highly talented professional actors from around the country has finally answered the age-old Mendocino County question of "So, what is there to do around here at night?" From Shakespeare to Shepard, no play is too shocking or sultry for artistic director Meg Patterson and her crew, who have received kudos for the fresh, significant interpretations they have brought to the north coast. The Warehouse's season runs from late February through December, Thursday through Saturday (and the occasional Mon) at 8pm, with the occasional Sunday matinee at 2pm. For information about current shows and future plays, or to reserve tickets (which range from $10 to $15), call the box office at ☎ 707/961-2940 or visit their Web site at www.theatre@warerep.org.

WHERE TO STAY

Coast Motel. 18661 Calif. 1, Fort Bragg, CA 95437. ☎ **707/964-2852.** 28 units. TV TEL. $46–$52 double. MC, V.

Located 6 miles north of Mendocino on a rural stretch of Calif. 1, the Coast Motel is the most convenient budget accommodation for those who want to be as near to Mendocino as possible. Though it lacks any sort of charm, the motel does come with all the standard amenities, such as a heated pool, and even a fish-cleaning facility (oh boy!). Most rooms have refrigerators, and a few have kitchenettes. The only caveat is that it's not within walking distance of any restaurants or shops, but it certainly offers quieter surroundings than the motels in downtown Fort Bragg.

Columbi Motel. 647 Oak St., Fort Bragg, CA 95437. ☎ **707/964-5773.** 21 units. A/C TV TEL. $50–$55 double. MC, V.

The Columbi Motel is what we budget travelers call a real score. For only 50 bones you get a plethora of lodging perks at this humble little motel just off Fort Bragg's main strip: cable TV; queen-size bed; a minikitchen complete with full-size fridge, sink, and stove; and even your own covered carport. Families will want to reserve one of the two-bedroom units that sleep up to six. Across the street is a Laundromat, a small cafe serving good Mexican food, and the Columbi Market, which is where the motel's guests check in.

Fort Bragg Motel. 763 N. Main St., Fort Bragg, CA 95437. ☎ **707/964-4787.** 48 units. TV TEL. $40–$90 double. AE, MC, V.

The Fort Bragg Motel has two things going for it: 1) It's very clean, and 2) it's within staggering distance of the North Coast Brewing Company (see "Where to Dine," below). Okay, so it's also as glamorous as Al Gore, but if you just need a safe and sanitary place to crash for the night, with perhaps a television, phone, queen-size bed, and your own bathroom, then you'll be quite content here.

WHERE TO DINE

North Coast Brewing Company. 444 N. Main St. ☎ **707/964-3400.** Reservations accepted for large parties only. Main courses $6–$17. DISC, MC, V. Tues–Sun noon–11pm. AMERICAN.

This homey brew pub is the most happening place in town, especially during happy hour, when the bar and dark-wood tables are occupied by boisterous locals. The building that houses the pub is a dignified, century-old redwood structure, which in previous lives has functioned as a mortuary, an annex to the local Presbyterian church, an art studio, and administration offices for the College of the Redwoods. Beer is brewed on the premises in large copper vats that are displayed behind plate glass. A pale ale, a pilsner, a stout, and a fourth seasonal brew are always available. Standard fare such as burgers and barbecued-chicken sandwiches are supplemented by more substantial dishes, ranging from linguini with smoked mushrooms to a hefty pile of country-style Carolina barbecued pork. After lunch, browse the retail shop or take a free tour of the brewery (see "Shopping & Exploring the Area," above).

The Restaurant. 418 Main St. ☎ **707/964-9800.** Reservations recommended. Lunch $6.50–$8.50; dinner $12.50–$19.50. MC, V. Thurs–Fri 11:30am–2pm; Sun brunch 10am–1pm; Thurs–Tues 5–9pm. PACIFIC NORTHWEST/CALIFORNIA.

One of the oldest family-run restaurants on the coast, this small, unpretentious Fort Bragg landmark is known for its good dinners and Sunday brunches. The eclectic menu offers dishes from just about every corner of the planet: blackened New York strip steak, sweet-and-sour stir-fry, Livorno-style shellfish stew, and even shrimp rellenos. There are also a few vegetarian specialties, including grilled polenta with melted mozzarella and sautéed mushrooms, topped with tomato-herb sauce and Parmesan cheese. The comfortable booth section is the best place to sit if you want to keep an eye on the entertainment—courtesy of ebullient chef Jim Larsen—in the kitchen. On weekends, additional entertainment comes in the form of live music.

✪ **Viraporn's Thai Café.** 500 S. Main St. (across from PayLess off Calif. 1). ☎ **707/ 964-7931.** Main courses $5.50–$7.50. No credit cards. Wed–Mon 11:30am–2:30pm and 5–9pm. THAI.

Born in northern Thailand, Viraporn Lobell attended cooking school and apprenticed in restaurants in her homeland before coming to the United States. After working at Mendocino's premier restaurant, Café Beaujolais, she opened her own restaurant in Fort Bragg in 1991, giving local Thai-food fans good reason to cheer. Viraporn works wonders with Thai mainstays such as pad Thai, lemongrass soup, spring rolls, and satays, all of which have a pleasant balance of the five traditional Thai flavors of tart, bitter, hot, sweet, and salty. Viraporn also whips up some wonderful curry dishes, best washed down with a cool, super-sweet Thai iced tea.

5 The Avenue of the Giants & Ferndale

From Fort Bragg, Calif. 1 continues north along the shoreline for about 30 miles before turning inland to Leggett and U.S. 101, a.k.a. the "Redwood Highway," which runs north to Garberville.

Six miles beyond Garberville, the **Avenue of the Giants** begins around Phillipsville; it's an alternative route that roughly parallels U.S. 101, and there are about a half dozen interchanges between U.S. 101 and the Avenue of the Giants if you don't want to drive the whole thing. It's one of the most spectacular scenic routes in the west (Calif. 254), cutting along the Eel River through the 51,000-acre Humboldt Redwoods State Park. The avenue ends just south of Scotia; from here, it's only about 10 miles to the turnoff to Ferndale, about 5 miles west of U.S. 101.

For more information or a detailed map of the area, go to the **Humboldt Redwood State Park Visitor Center,** P.O. Box 276, Weott, CA 95571 (☎ **707/946-2263**), just north of Hidden Springs State Campground, 2 miles south of Weott, in the center of the Avenue of the Giants.

Thirty-three miles long, the Avenue of the Giants was left intact for sightseers when the freeway was built. The giants, of course, are the majestic coast redwoods (*Sequoia sempervirens*); more than 50,000 acres of them make up the most outstanding display in the redwood belt. Their rough-bark columns climb 100 feet or more without a branch and soar to a total height of more than 340 feet. With their immunity to insects and fire-resistant bark, they have survived for thousands of years. The oldest dated coast redwood is more than 2,200 years old.

The state park has three **campgrounds** with 248 campsites: Hidden Springs, half a mile south of Myers Flat; Burlington, 2 miles south of Weott, near park headquarters; and Albee Creek State Campground, 5 miles west of U.S. 101 on the Mattole Road north of Weott. You'll also come across picnic and swimming facilities, motels, resorts, restaurants, and numerous resting and parking areas.

Sadly, the route has several tacky attractions that attempt to turn the trees into some kind of freak show. Our suggestion is to skip these and appreciate the trees by taking advantage of the trails and the campgrounds off the beaten path. As you drive along, you'll see numerous parking areas with short loop trails leading into the forest. From south to north the first of these "attractions" is the **Chimney Tree** (☎ 707/ 923-2265), where J. R. R. Tolkien's Hobbit is rumored to reside. This living, hollow redwood is more than 1,500 years old. Nearby is a gift shop and a burger place. Then there's the **One-Log House,** a small apartmentlike house built inside a log. At Myers Flat midway along the avenue, you can also drive your car through a living redwood at the **Shrine Drive-Thru Tree.**

A few miles north of Weott is **Founders Grove,** named in honor of those who established the Save the Redwoods League in 1918. Farther north, close to the end of the avenue, stands the 950-year-old **Immortal Tree,** just north of Redcrest. Near Pepperwood at the end of the avenue, the **Drury Trail** and the **Percy French Trail** are two good short hikes. The park itself is also good for mountain biking. Ask the rangers for details. For more information, contact Humboldt Redwoods State Park, P.O. Box 100, Weott, CA 95571 (☎ **707/946-2409**).

The village of **Ferndale,** beyond the Avenue of the Giants and west of U.S. 101, has been declared a historic landmark because of its many Victorian homes and storefronts (which include a smithy and a saddlery). About 5 miles inland from the coast and close to the redwood belt, Ferndale is one of the best-preserved Victorian hamlets in northern California. Despite its collection of unbearably cute shops, it is nonetheless a vital part of the northern coastal tourist circuit (the budget traveler, however, will have to continue north to Eureka to find affordable lodging). The small town has a number of artists in residence and is also home to one of California's oddest events, the **World Championship Great Arcata to Ferndale Cross-Country Kinetic Sculpture Race,** a bizarre 3-day event run every Memorial Day weekend. The race, which draws more than 10,000 spectators, is run over land and water in whimsically designed human-powered vehicles. Stop in at the museum at 780 Main St. if you want to see some recent race entries.

WHERE TO DINE

Curley's Grill. 460 Main St., Ferndale. ☎ **707/786-9696.** Main courses $6–$18. DISC, MC, V. Daily 11:30am–9pm; breakfast Sat–Sun 8–11am. CALIFORNIA GRILL.

Set in what looks like a clapboard-sided Victorian farmhouse, across the street from Ferndale's Repertory Theater, this bright and lively restaurant specializes exclusively in California-inspired grilled foods. Don't think for a moment that the menu is limited to steaks, prime rib, and lamb, however. Owner Curley Tait also grills up such items as polenta with a sausage-tomato sauce, a medley of Pacific sea fish, crab cakes, and some of the freshest vegetables on the California coast. If money is a concern, you can always opt for Curley's tasty Garden Burger, a mere $6. Curley has added house-made breads and desserts to the menu as well. The interior decor is vaguely art deco and showcases local artists' works, but the best seating is behind the kitchen in the secluded back patio. Curley's also offers a small but interesting selection of California wines.

6 Eureka & Environs

EUREKA

On first glance, Eureka (pop. 27,000) doesn't look very appealing: Fast-food restaurants, cheap motels, and shopping malls predominate on the main thoroughfare. But if you turn west off U.S. 101 anywhere between A and M streets, you'll discover Old Town Eureka along the waterfront, which is worth exploring. It has a large number of Victorian buildings, a museum, and some good-quality stores and restaurants.

The **Clarke Memorial Museum,** 240 E St. (☎ **707/443-1947**), has a fine collection of Native American baskets and other historic artifacts. The other popular attraction is the extraordinary architectural gem, the ◐ **Carson House,** built from 1884 to 1886 for lumber baron William Carson. A three-story conglomeration of ornamentation, it's designed in a mélange of styles—Queen Anne, Italianate, Stick, and Eastlake. It took 100 men more than 2 years to build. Today it's a private club, so you can only marvel at the exterior of this 18-room mansion—said to be the most photographed Victorian home in the U.S.—from the sidewalk. Across the street stands the **"Pink Lady,"** designed for William Carson as a wedding present for his son. Both testify to the wealth that was once made in Eureka's lumber trade. As early as 1856, there were already seven sawmills producing 2 million board feet of lumber every month.

Humboldt Bay, where the town stands, was discovered by whites in 1850. In 1853 Fort Humboldt was established to protect settlers from local Native American tribes. Ulysses S. Grant was stationed here for 5 months until he resigned after serious disputes with his commanding officer about his drinking. The fort was abandoned in 1870. Today the fort offers a self-guided trail past a series of logging exhibits, plus a reconstructed surgeon's quarters and a restored fort hospital, used today as a museum housing Native American artifacts and military and pioneer paraphernalia. **Fort Humboldt State Historic Park** is located at 3431 Fort Ave. (☎ **707/445-6567**). Admission is free; it's open daily from 9am to 5pm.

Humboldt Bay supplies a large portion of California's fish, and Eureka has a fishing fleet of about 200 boats. To get a better view (and perspective) of the bay and surrounding waters, you can board skipper Leroy Zerlang's *Madaket*—said to be the oldest passenger-carrying vessel in operation in the United States—for a 75-minute **Humboldt Bay Harbor Cruise** (☎ **707/445-1910**), departing daily from the foot of C Street in downtown Eureka. The price is $9.50 for adults, $8.50 for ages 12 to 17 and 65 and older, $6.50 for ages 4 to 11, and free for kids under 4.

You can also do some fishing for halibut, king salmon, steelhead, and even shark, depending on the season. A license is required and can be secured for 1 day. For information, contact **Larry's Guide Service,** 3380 Utah St. (☎ **707/444-0250**). Fishing information can also be obtained from the **Eureka Fly Shop,** 505 H St. (☎ **707/444-2000**), and kayaks and sailboats can be rented from **Hum Boats,** on F Street (☎ **707/443-5157**), which also provides tours and lessons.

Humboldt County is also suitable for biking because it's relatively uncongested. Bikes can be rented from **Pro Sport Center,** 508 Myrtle Ave. (☎ **707/443-6328**). Fishing, diving, biking, and hiking information are also available.

Humboldt Bay is an important stopover point along the Pacific Flyway and is the winter home for thousands of migratory birds. South of town, the **Humboldt Bay National Wildlife Refuge,** 1020 Ranch Rd., Loleta (☎ **707/733-5406**), provides an opportunity to see many of the 200 or so species that live in the marshes and willow groves—including Pacific black brant, western sandpiper, northern harrier, great blue heron, and green-winged teal. The egret rookery on the bay, best viewed from Woodley Island Marina across the bay en route to Samoa, is spectacular. Peak viewing for most species of waterbirds and raptors is between September and March. The refuge's entrance is off U.S. 101 north at the Hookton Road exit. Cross the overpass and turn right onto Ranch Road.

For information, contact the **Eureka/Humboldt County Convention and Visitors Bureau,** 1034 Second St., Eureka, CA 95501 (☎ **800/346-3482** or 707/443-5097; fax 707/443-5115), or the **Eureka Chamber of Commerce,** 2112 Broadway, Eureka, CA 95501 (☎ **800/356-6381** or 707/442-3738).

WHERE TO STAY

In addition to the more-inspiring choices below, the **Downtowner Motel,** 424 Eighth St., at F Street, Eureka (☎ **707/443-5061**), and the **Fireside Inn,** 1716 Fifth St., at R Street, Eureka (☎ **707/443-6312**), offer comfortable accommodations at very reasonable prices.

✪ **An Elegant Victorian Mansion Bed & Breakfast Experience.** 14th and C sts., Eureka, CA 95501. ☎ **707/444-3144.** Fax 707/442-5594. 5 units. $85–$185 double. Rates include breakfast. MC, V.

For anyone interested in Victorian history and design, this is a special experience; those who just want comfort, service, a true gourmet breakfast, and a lovely garden will also find this lodging ideal. The 1888 house is the labor of love of owners Doug and Lily Vieyra, who have combed the country for the fabrics and designs that now provide the most authentic Victorian atmosphere we have ever encountered in the United States. The wallpapers are extraordinary—brilliant blues, golds, jades, and reds in intricate patterns that feature peacocks and mythological figures. Doug has paid attention to every detail, from the butler who greets you in morning dress to the silent movies and period music on the phonograph. Each unit is individually furnished: The Van Gogh room contains the Belgian bedroom suite of Lily's mother. The Lily Langtry room, named after the actress and king's mistress who stayed here when she performed locally, features a four-poster bed and Langtry memorabilia. Bikes and a sauna are available, and croquet is played on the manicured lawn, where ice-cream sodas and lemonade are served in the afternoon.

Bayview Motel. 2844 Fairfield St. (corner of Calif. 1 and Henderson St.), Eureka, CA 95501. ☎ **707/442-1673.** 17 units. A/C TV TEL. $75–$85 double. AE, DISC, MC, V.

While nowhere near the caliber of the Victorian Mansion, the Bayview Motel has it soundly beat in the price and privacy category. This is, without a doubt, one of the cleanest and most meticulously landscaped motels we have ever seen. Indeed, what it lacks in character it makes up for in cost and cleanliness. Poised on the top of a small knoll on the south side of Eureka, it *does* have a bay view, but you have to peer through a seedy industrial area to see it (a better view, actually, is of the gardens). All rooms are minisuites and come with the standard motel amenities, including queen-size beds. If you feel like splurging, request a room with a Jacuzzi or fireplace. Family units are also available.

WHERE TO DINE

Ramone's Bakery & Cafe. 209 E St. (in Old Town). ☎ **707/445-2923.** Main courses $4–$6. No credit cards. Cafe Mon–Sat 7am–6pm; Sun 8am–4pm. BAKERY.

Ramone's combines a bakery on one side with a small cafe on the other. The baked items are extraordinary—try any one of the croissants, Danish, or muffins, and you won't be disappointed. Alas, the once-popular restaurant has closed down, but you can still find a few lunch specials to choose from among the breads and pastries, such as soups, salads, burgers, and more. At any time of the day, it's a great place to stop in for a light, inexpensive meal and cup of coffee.

There's a second bakery location at 2223 Harrison St. in Eureka, as well as one in Arcata at 747 13th St., at Wildberries Marketplace.

✪ **Samoa Cookhouse.** Cookhouse Rd., Samoa. ☎ **707/442-1659.** Reservations accepted for large groups only. Main courses $11.95. AE, DISC, MC, V. Mon–Sat 6am–3:30pm and 5–10pm; Sun 6am–10pm (closes an hr. earlier in winter). From U.S. 101, take Samoa Bridge to the end and turn left on Samoa Rd.; then take the first left. AMERICAN.

When lumber was king, cookhouses (like this one dating from 1885) were common, serving as community hubs. Here the mill men and longshoremen at the Hammond Lumber Company came to chow down on three hot meals before, during, and after their 12-hour work day. The food at the Samoa Cookhouse is still hearty—though not particularly healthy—and served family-style at long tables covered with red-checkered cloths. In fact, the not-so-lean cuisine keeps on comin' until you howl "Uncle." Is the food fantastic? Not particularly, but the God Bless America experience sure is priceless. Speaking of prices, the $12 cover includes beverages, soup, salad, fresh-baked bread, the main course, and dessert (usually pie). The lunch-and-dinner menu still features a different dish each day—roast beef, fried chicken, or pork chops. Breakfast typically includes eggs, sausages, bacon, pancakes, and all the orange juice and coffee you can drink. Adjacent to the dining room is a small museum featuring memorabilia from the lumbering era.

ARCATA

From Eureka it's only 7 miles to Arcata, one of our favorite towns on the northern coast. Sort of a cross between Mayberry and Berkeley, it has an undeniable small-town flavor—right down to the bucolic town square—yet possesses that intellectual and environmentally conscious esprit de corps so characteristic of university towns (Arcata is the home of Humboldt State University).

There are loads of things to do here. On Wednesday, Friday, and Saturday evenings between June and July, Arcata's semipro baseball team, the Humboldt Crabs, partake in America's favorite pastime at **Arcata Ballpark,** at Ninth and F streets. Also worth a stop: the **Humboldt State University Natural History Museum,** 1315 G St. (☎ 707/826-4479), which is open Tuesday through Saturday from 10am to 4pm; **Tin Can Mailman,** at 10th and H streets (☎ 707/822-1307), a wonderful used-book store with more than 130,000 titles; **Redwood Park** (east end of 11th Street), which has an outstanding playground for kids and miles of forested hiking trails; and the **Humboldt Brewing Company,** 10th and I streets (☎ 707/826-BREW), creators of the heavenly Red Nectar Ale (call for tour information).

The **Arcata Marsh and Wildlife Sanctuary,** at the foot of South I Street (☎ 707/826-2359), is another worthwhile excursion. The 154-acre

Arcata on $30 a Day

You don't need much money to have a great day in Arcata. For example, you can start your morning off with a big three-course breakfast at **TJ's Classic Café,** 1057 H St., at 11th Street (☎ **707/822-4650**), for under $5. Next, catch a $3.75 matinee at the **Arcata Theatre,** 1039 G St., at 10th Street (☎ **707/ 822-5171**), which shows some classic college flicks as well as first-run movies. If you're the bookish type, pick up a 50¢ used paperback at **Tin Can Mailman,** 1000 H St., at 10th Street (☎ **707/822-1307**), an incredible bookstore whose shelves hold more than 130,000 titles. Then head for the **Humboldt Brewing Company** (see above) for a free tour, followed by a fresh pitcher of their oh-so-sweet Red Nectar Ale and a burger.

If it's baseball season, $3.50 will buy you nine innings of America's favorite pastime at **Arcata Ballpark** (see above), home of the Humboldt Crabs. After a hike through Arcata's **Redwood Park** and **Marsh and Wildlife Sanctuary** (see above), end the day with a big plate of organic mushroom stroganoff and all the trimmings for a mere $8.50 at **Wildflower Café,** 1604 G St., at 16th Street (☎ **707/822-0360**).

That's a full-day's food and fun for under $30. Not bad, Arcata, not bad.

sanctuary—which doubles as Arcata's integrated wetland wastewater treatment plant—is a popular stopover for march wrens, egrets, and other waterfowl, including the rare Arctic loon. Each Saturday at 8:30am (rain or shine), the Audubon Society gives free 1-hour guided tours at the cul-de-sac at the foot of South I Street.

Heading east from Arcata, Calif. 299 leads to the Trinity River in the heart of **Six Rivers National Forest.** Willow Creek and Somes Bar are the prime recreational centers for the area. Here visitors can sign up for canoeing, rafting, and kayaking trips with such outfitters as **Aurora River Adventures,** in Willow Creek (☎ **800/ 562-8475** or 530/629-3843), which offers some offbeat, educationally oriented adventures that are great for kids, as well as gnarly Class V trips for the more daring.

A few miles north of Willow Creek lies the Hoopa Indian Reservation. In the Hoopa Shopping Center, the **Hoopa Tribal Museum** (☎ **530/625-4110**) archives the culture and history of the native people of northern California—their ceremonial regalia, basketry, canoes, and tools. Hours are Monday through Friday from 8am to 5pm (closed noon to 1pm for lunch).

WHERE TO STAY

Fairwinds Motel. 1674 G St. (at 17th St.), Arcata, CA 95521. ☎ **707/822-4824.** 27 units. TV TEL. $50–$60 double. AE, DISC, MC, V.

If you can afford it, stay at The Lady Anne (see below). If you can't, stay here. This is your classic American freeway-side AAA-rated motel, right down to the cheap framed prints and wall-to-wall carpeting, but the rates are low, HBO is free, and it's only a short walk from the town square and Humboldt campus (the only other lodgings in the area are miles down the road). The Fairwinds offers a choice of queen, king, and family units, as well as nonsmoking rooms.

Hotel Arcata. 708 Ninth St., Arcata, CA 95521. ☎ **800/344-1221** or 707/826-0217. Fax 707/826-1737. 32 units. TV TEL. $65–$110 double. Rates include continental breakfast. AE, CB, DC, DISC, MC, V.

This is the town's most prominent hotel, and many guests are parents visiting their ungrateful offspring at Humboldt State University. Located at the northeast corner of the town plaza, its handsome turn-of-the-century brick facade belies a rather bland, modern interior; few of its original furnishings remain. The bedrooms have a rather characterless decor, but they're safe and comfortable lodgings nonetheless. On the premises, under different management, is a Japanese restaurant called Tomo. The hotel also offers its guests free passes to the health club and indoor pool just a few blocks down the street.

✪ **The Lady Anne.** 902 14th St., Arcata, CA 95521. ☎ **707/822-2797.** 5 units. $90–$110 double. Rates include breakfast. MC, V.

Easily Arcata's finest lodging, this Queen Anne–style bed-and-breakfast is kept in top-notch condition by innkeepers Sharon Ferrett and Sam Pennisi, who also served a term as Arcata's mayor. The large, cozy guest rooms are individually decorated with period antiques, lace curtains, Oriental rugs, and English stained glass. For second honeymooners there's the Lady Sarah Angela Room with its four-poster bed and pleasant bay view. The Cinnamon Bear Room sleeps up to four on its king-size trundle beds, which makes it an obvious choice for parents with kids in tow. Breakfast is served in the grand dining room, warmed on winter mornings by a toasty fire. On summer afternoons, you can lounge on the veranda with a book or play a game of croquet on the front lawn. Several good dining options are only a few blocks away at Arcata Plaza.

WHERE TO DINE

The best way to review your dining options in Arcata is to stroll around the downtown area and compare cafes. For a quick, cheap lunch, we prefer a juicy hot dog and ice cold cola á la the hot dog cart, which is usually stationed at one of the corners of Arcata Plaza. Otherwise, we invariably head to Jacoby's Storehouse (a deftly converted mid-19th-century warehouse located at the southwest corner of the Plaza) and situate ourselves at one of the restaurants there—either Abruzzi or the Plaza Grill.

Abruzzi. Jacoby's Storehouse (at the corner of Eighth and H sts.). ☎ **707/826-2345.** Reservations recommended. Main courses $9–$22. AE, DISC, MC, V. Sun–Thurs 5:30–8:30pm; Fri–Sat 5:30–9pm. ITALIAN.

Abruzzi, on the street level of Jacoby's Storehouse, is generally acknowledged as the best restaurant in town. Specialties include a roasted lamb loin served with three-cheese polenta and ratatouille and baked halibut in a white-wine/butter sauce served over fettuccine. Chicken, pastas, veal dishes, and well-seasoned fillet steaks are available as well.

Plaza Grill. Jacoby's Storehouse (at the corner of Eighth and H sts.). ☎ **707/826-0860.** Appetizers and dinners $5–$15. AE, DISC, MC, V. Sun–Thurs 5:30–8:30pm; Fri–Sat 5:30–9pm. AMERICAN.

Less formal (and expensive) than its haute cuisine cousin downstairs, the Plaza Grill is more in line with patrons who want a substantial meal without the fuss. The menu offers everything from salads and sandwiches to fish platters, hamburgers, and hearty pasta dishes.

TRINIDAD & PATRICK'S POINT STATE PARK

Back on U.S. 101 north of Arcata, you'll come to Trinidad, a tiny coastal fishing village of some 400 people. One of the smallest incorporated cities in California, it occupies a peninsula 25 miles north of Eureka. If you're not into fishing, there's little to do in town expect poke around at the handful of shops, walk along the busy pier, and wish you owned a house here.

Five miles north of Trinidad takes you to the 640-acre **Patrick's Point State Park,** 4150 Patrick's Point Dr. (☎ **707/677-3570**), which has one of the finest ocean access points in the north at sandy **Agate Beach.** It's suitable for driftwood picking, rock-hounding, and camping on a sheltered bluff. The park contains a re-creation of a Sumeg Village, which is actively used by the Yurok people and neighboring tribes. A self-guided tour takes you to replicas of family homes and sweat houses.

WHERE TO DINE

The Seascape Restaurant. Beside the pier at the foot of Bay St. ☎ **707/677-3762.** Full dinners $9–$20. MC, V. Daily 7am–9pm. CALIFORNIA.

Established in the 1940s, this is an unpretentious cross between a cafe and a diner, with three dining rooms, overworked but cheerful waitresses, and a nostalgic aura. Folks pop in for coffee or snacks from early morning until after sundown, but by far the biggest seller here is the Trinidad bay platter ($17.95). Heaped with halibut, scallops, and shrimp, and accompanied by salad and rice pilaf, it's even more popular than the prawn brochette, which draws a close second.

ORICK

From Trinidad it's about another 15 miles to Orick. You can't miss it: Just look for the dozens of burl stands alongside the road. Carved with chisels and chain saws, these former redwood logs have been transformed into just about every creature you can imagine—perhaps a gift for your mother-in-law?

At the south end of Orick is the town's only saving grace, the sleek **Redwood National Park Information Center** (☎ **707/464-6101,** ext. 5265). If you plan to spend any amount of time exploring the park, stop here first and pick up a free map; the displays of fauna and wildlife aren't too bad, either. It's open daily from 9am to 5pm.

The first of the parks that make up Redwood National Park, **Prairie Creek,** is 6 miles north of Orick. About 14 miles farther on is the mouth of the **Klamath River,** famous for its salmon, trout, and steelhead. Tours aboard a jet boat take visitors upriver from the estuary to view bear, deer, elk, osprey hawks, otters, and more along the riverbanks. Rates for the 30-mile scenic trip are $20 for adults, $10 for children 4 to 11, and free for kids under 4. For more information and reservations, contact **Klamath River Jet Boat Tours,** Klamath (☎ **800/887-JETS** or 707/482-7775).

A more serene alternative to exploring the Klamath is taking a ranger-led **kayak tour.** Offered only during the summer months (and only if they have enough money in their budget), the half-day trip costs only $20 and includes all the requisite kayak gear. For more information, call the Redwood National Park Information Center at ☎ **707/464-6101,** ext. 5265.

From Klamath it's another 20 miles to Crescent City, gateway to the other parks that make up Redwood National Park.

7 Crescent City: Gateway to Redwood National Park

Crescent City itself has little to offer, but it makes a good base for exploring Redwood National Park and the Smith River, one of the great recreational rivers of the West. The **Battery Point Lighthouse,** at the foot of A Street (☎ **707/464-3089**), which is accessible on foot only at low tide, houses a museum with exhibits on the coast's history. Tours of the lighthouse ($2 for adults, 50¢ for children) are offered Wednesday through Sunday from 10am to 4pm, tides and weather permitting (so call ahead in questionable weather), April through September.

Another draw is the **Smith River National Recreation Area,** east of Jedediah Smith State Park and part of Six Rivers National Forest. The Area Headquarters is at 10600 U.S. 199, Gasquet, CA 95543 (☎ 707/457-3131), which is reached via U.S. 199 from Crescent City (19 miles, about a 30-min. drive). Maps of the forest can be obtained here, at the Supervisor's Office in Eureka, or at either of the Redwood National Park centers in Orick and Crescent City.

The 300,000-plus acres of wilderness offer camping at five modest-sized camp-grounds (all with fewer than 50 sites) along the Smith River. Sixteen trails attract hikers from across the country. The easiest short trail is the **McClendon Ford,** which is 2 miles long and drops from 1,000 to 800 feet in elevation to the south fork of the river. Other activities include mountain biking, white-water rafting, kayaking, and fishing for salmon and trout.

For information, contact the **Crescent City–Del Norte County Chamber of Commerce,** 1001 Front St., Crescent City, CA 95531 (☎ **800/343-8300** or 707/464-3174).

WHERE TO STAY

Crescent Beach Motel. 1455 Redwood Hwy. S. (U.S. 101), Crescent City, CA 95531. ☎ **707/464-5436.** 27 units. TV. Summer $65–$72 double; winter $49–$55 double. AE, DISC, MC, V.

Crescent City has the dubious distinction of being the only city along the coast without a fancy hotel or bed-and-breakfast. There is, however, an armada of cheap motels, the best of which is the Crescent Beach Motel. Near the highway, about 1 mile south of town, this single-story structure is the only local motel set directly on the beach. The newly remodeled and refurbished rooms are clean and simple. Four of the units face the highway; try to get one of the others, all of which have sliding-glass doors to decks and a small lawn area overlooking the bay. There's no restaurant or bar on the premises, but one of the city's most popular restaurants, the Beachcomber (see "Where to Dine," below), is located next door.

Curly Redwood Lodge. 701 Redwood Hwy. S. (U.S. 101), Crescent City, CA 95531. ☎ **707/464-2137.** 36 units. TV TEL. Summer $60–$65 double; winter $37–$39 double. AE, CB, DC, MC, V.

This is a blast from the past, the kind of place where you might have stayed as a kid during one of those cross-country vacations in the family station wagon. It was built in 1959 on grasslands across from the town's harbor and completely trimmed with lumber from a single ancient redwood. Although they're not full of the latest high-tech gadgets, the bedrooms are among the largest and best-soundproofed in town, and cer-tainly the most evocative of a bygone, more innocent age. In winter, about a third of the rooms (the ones upstairs) are locked and sealed. Overall, the aura is more akin to Oregon than anything you might imagine in California.

WHERE TO DINE

Beachcomber. 1400 U.S. 101. ☎ **707/464-2205.** Reservations recommended. Main courses $6–$15. MC, V. Thurs–Tues 5–9pm (call ahead Nov–Jan). SEAFOOD.

The decor is as predictably nautical as the name implies: rough-cut planking, a scat-tering of artfully arranged driftwood, fishnets, and buoys dangling above a dimly lit space. The restaurant lies beside the beach, 2 miles south of Crescent City's center. The cuisine is a joy to fish lovers who prefer not to mask the flavor of their seafood with complicated sauces. Most of the dishes are grilled over madrone-wood barbecue pits, a technique perfected since this place was established in 1975. Pacific salmon, halibut, lincod, shark, sturgeon, Pacific snapper, oysters, and steamer clams are house specialties that have visitors lining up, especially on Friday and Saturday nights.

Harbor View Grotto Restaurant & Lounge. 150 Starfish Way. ☎ **707/464-3815.** Reservations recommended. Main courses $6–$9 lunch; $4.25–$49.90 dinner. MC, V. Daily 11:30am–10pm. SEAFOOD/STEAKS.

This is the best-established nonchain restaurant in town, specializing in fresh seafood at market prices since 1961. Completely renovated in December 1995, it has pleasant views of the ocean and harbor from both the dining room and lounge. It's capped with a miniature lighthouse inspired by Crescent City's Battery Point Lighthouse. The "light eaters" menu includes a cup of white chowder (made fresh daily), salad, a main course, and vegetables; heartier appetites can choose from among three different cuts of prime rib. Menu items include fresh, locally caught fish like Pacific snapper or salmon. Crab or shrimp Louis, as well as crabmeat or shrimp sandwiches, are popular in season.

8 Redwood National & State Parks

It's impossible to explain the feeling you get in the old-growth forests of Redwood National and State Parks without resorting to Alice-in-Wonderland comparisons. Like a tropical rain forest, the redwood forest is a multistoried affair, the tall trees being only the top layer. Everything is so big, misty, and primeval—flowering bushes cover the ground, 10-foot-tall ferns line the creeks, and the smells are rich and musty. It's so *Jurassic Park* that you can't help but half expect to turn the corner and see a dinosaur.

When Archibald Menzies first noted the botanical existence of the coast redwood in 1794, more than 2 million acres of redwood forest carpeted California and Oregon. By 1965 heavy logging had reduced that to 300,000 acres, and it was obvious something had to be done if any redwoods were to survive. The state created several parks around individual groves in the 1920s, and in 1968 the federal government created Redwood National Park. In May 1994, the National Park Service and the California Department of Parks and Recreation signed an agreement to manage these four redwood parks cooperatively, hence the Redwood National *and* State Parks.

Although logging of old-growth redwoods in the region is still a major bone of contention between the government, private landowners, and environmentalists, it's an auspicious sign that contention even exists, a sign that perhaps we have all learned to see the forest *and* the trees for what they are—the undisputed monarchs of all living things, a thriving link to the age of dinosaurs, and a humble reminder that the age of mankind is but a hiccup in time to the venerable *Sequoia sempervirens.*

JUST THE FACTS

The southern gateway to the Redwood National and State Parks is the town of Orick (see section 6, earlier in this chapter), which you can identify by the dozens of burl stands alongside the road. Here you'll find the sleek **Redwood Information Center,** P.O. Box 7, Orick, CA 95555 (☎ **707/464-6101,** ext. 5265), one of California's rare examples of well-placed tax dollars (though some may dispute this since it's located near a floodplain and within a tsunami zone). Stop here and pick up a free map; it's open daily from 9am to 5pm.

If you missed the Orick center, don't worry: About 10 miles further north on U.S. 101 is the **Prairie Creek Visitor Center** (☎ **707/464-6101,** ext. 5300), which

Redwood National & State Parks

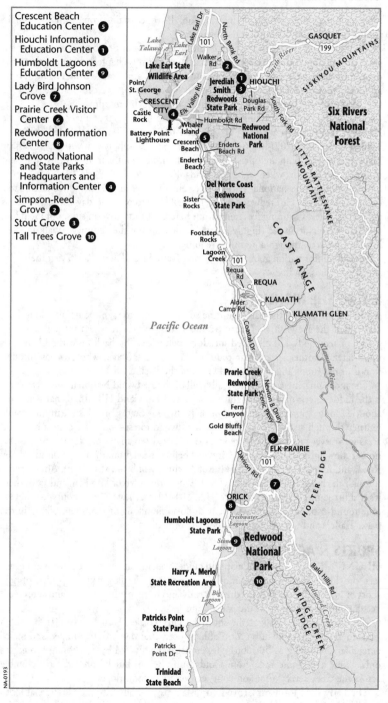

Lake Earl Dr

Lake
Talawa

Lake
Earl

North Bank Rd

101

Walker
Rd

GASQUET

199

Smith River

SISKIYOU MOUNTAINS

Lake Earl State
Wildlife Area

Point
St. George

Jerediah
Smith
Redwoods
State Park

1 HIOUCHI

3

Douglas
Park Rd

South Fork Rd

Six Rivers
National
Forest

CRESCENT
CITY

Castle
Rock

Elk Valley Rd

Humboldt Rd

Whaler
Island

4

5

Redwood
National
Park

LITTLE RATTLESNAKE MOUNTAIN

Battery Point
Lighthouse

Crescent
Beach

Enderts
Beach Rd

Enderts
Beach

Del Norte Coast
Redwoods
State Park

Sister
Rocks

COAST RANGE

Footstep
Rocks

Lagoon
Creek

101

Requa
Rd

REQUA

Alder
Camp Rd

KLAMATH

KLAMATH GLEN

Klamath River

Pacific Ocean

Coastal Dr

Prairie Creek
Redwoods
State Park

Newton B. Drury Scenic Pkwy

Fern
Canyon

Gold Bluffs
Beach

6

ELK PRAIRIE

101

Davison Rd

7

HOLTER RIDGE

ORICK

8

*Freshwater
Lagoon*

Humboldt Lagoons
State Park

*Stone
Lagoon*

9

Redwood
National
Park

Bald Hills Rd

Harry A. Merlo
State Recreation Area

*Big
Lagoon*

10

Redwood Creek

BRIDGE CREEK RIDGE

Patricks Point
State Park

101

Patricks
Point Dr

Trinidad
State Beach

NA-0193

carries all the same maps and information. It's open daily from 9am to 5pm in summer, daily from 10am to 2pm in winter.

The northern gateway to the park is Crescent City, your best bet for a cheap motel, gas, fast food, and outdoor supplies (see section 7 of this chapter). Before touring the park, pick up a free guide at the **Redwood National and State Parks Headquarters and Information Center,** 1111 Second St. (at K Street), Crescent City, CA 95531 (☎ **707/464-6101,** ext. 5064). It's open daily from 8am to 5pm.

If you happen to be arriving via U.S. 199 from Oregon, the rangers manning the **Hiouchi Information Station** (☎ **707/464-6101,** ext. 5067) and **Jedediah Smith Visitor Center** (☎ **707/464-6101,** ext. 5113) can also supply you with the necessary maps and advice. Both are open daily in the summer months from 9am to 5pm, and in the winter months when staffing is available.

Admission to the national park is free, but to enter any of the three state parks (which contain the best redwood groves), you'll have to pay a $6 day-use fee, which is good at all three. Camping fees range from $10 to $14 for drive-in sites, not including the $6.75 reservation fee (highly recommended during the summer). Walk-in sites, however, are free, though a permit is required.

For more information about the Redwood National and State Parks, visit their Web site at www.nps.gov/redw.

SEEING THE HIGHLIGHTS

If you're approaching the park from the south, be sure to take the detour along U.S. 101 called the **Newton B. Drury Scenic Parkway,** which passes through dazzling groves of redwoods and elk-filled meadows before leading back onto the highway 8 miles later. Another spectacular route is the **Coastal Drive,** which winds through stands of redwoods and offers grand views of the Pacific.

The most amazing car-friendly trail in all of the Redwood National and State Parks is the hidden, well-maintained gravel road called **Howland Hill Road** that winds for about 12 miles through Jedediah Smith Redwoods State Park. It's an unforgettable journey through a spectacular old-growth redwood forest—one of the most beautiful areas we've ever seen. To get there from U.S. 101, keep an eye out for the BP gas station at the south end of Crescent City; just before the station, turn right on Elk Valley Road, and follow it to Howland Hill Road, which will be on your right. After driving through the park, you'll end up at U.S. 199 near the town of Hiouchi, and from there it's a short jaunt west to get back to U.S. 101. Plan at least 2 to 3 hours for the 45-mile round-trip, or all day if you want to do some hiking or mountain biking in the park. Trailers and motor homes are not recommended.

SPORTS & ACTIVITIES

HIKING The parks' official map and guide, available at any of the information centers, provides a fairly good layout of hiking trails within the parks. Regardless of how short or long your hike may be, dress warmly and bring plenty of water and sunscreen. Pets are prohibited on all of the parks' trails.

The most popular walk is the short, heavily traveled **Fern Canyon Trail,** which leads to an unbelievably lush grotto of lady, deer, chain, sword, five-finger, and maidenhair ferns clinging to 50-foot-high vertical walls divided by a babbling brook. It's only about a 1½-mile walk from Gold Bluffs Beach, but be prepared to scramble across the creek several times on your way via small footbridges.

The **Lady Bird Johnson Grove Loop** is an easy, 1-hour self-guided tour that loops 1 mile around a glorious lush grove of mature redwoods. It's the site at which the national park was dedicated by Lady Bird Johnson in 1968. Also an easy trek is the

Yurok Loop Nature Trail at Lagoon Creek. The 1-mile self-guided trail gradually climbs to the top of a rugged sea bluff (with wonderful panoramic views of the Pacific) before looping back to the parking lot. If someone's willing to act as shuttle driver, have him or her meet you at the Requa Trailhead and take the 4-mile coastal trail to the mouth of the Klamath. And for the whiner in your group, there's **Big Tree Trail,** a quarter-mile paved trail leading to a really big tree.

Tall Trees Trail leads to the world's tallest tree—some 365½ feet tall, 14 feet in diameter, and over 600 years old—but first you'll have to go to the Redwood Information Center near Orick (see "Just the Facts," above) to obtain a free map and permit to drive to the trailhead of Tall Trees Grove. (*Note:* Only 50 permits are issued per day on a first-come, first-served basis.) After driving to the trailhead, you have to walk a steep 1⅓ miles down into the grove, but what a small price to see the tallest tree in the world.

WILDLIFE VIEWING   One of the most striking aspects of Prairie Creek Redwoods State Park is its 200- to 300-strong herd of Roosevelt elk, usually found in the appropriately named Elk Prairie in the southern end of the park. These gigantic beasts can weigh 1,000 pounds, and the bulls carry huge antlers from spring to fall. Elk are also sometimes found at Gold Bluffs Beach—it's an incredible rush to suddenly come upon them out of the fog or after a turn in the trail. Nearly a hundred black bears also call the park home, but are seldom seen. Unlike those at Yosemite and Yellowstone, these bears are still afraid of people. Keep them that way by giving them a wide berth, observing food storage etiquette while camping, and disposing of garbage properly.

BEACHES, WHALE WATCHING & BIRD WATCHING   The park's beaches vary from long white-sand strands to cobblestone pocket coves. The water temperature is in the high 40s to low 50s year-round; it's often rough out there, so swimmers and surfers should be prepared for adverse conditions.

Crescent Beach is a long sandy beach just 2 miles south of Crescent City that's popular with beachcombers, surf fishermen, and surfers.

Just south of Crescent Beach is **Endert's Beach,** a protected spot with a hike-in campground and tide pools at the southern end of the beach.

High coastal overlooks (like Klamath overlook and Crescent Beach overlook) make great whale-watching outposts during the southern migration in December and January and the return migration in March and April. The northern sea cliffs also provide valuable nesting sites for marine birds like auklets, puffins, murres, and cormorants. Birders will thrill at the park's freshwater lagoons as well. These coastal lagoons are some of the most pristine shorebird and waterfowl habitat left and are chock-full of hundreds of different species.

MOUNTAIN BIKING   Unfortunately, most of the hiking trails throughout the Redwood National and State Parks are off-limits to mountain bikers. However, Prairie Creek Redwoods State Park has a fantastic 19-mile mountain-bike trail through dense forest, elk-filled meadows, and glorious mud holes. Parts of it are a real thigh burner, though, so beginners should sit this one out. Pick up a 25¢ trail map at the Elk Prairie campground ranger station.

There are a few other mountain-bike loops in the 20-mile range, but they are *serious* thigh burners and make the one above look easy. These loops are the Holter Ridge Trail and Little Bald Hills. Mountain biking is also available on the old U.S. 101 road, now the coastal trail within Del Norte Coast Redwoods State Park.

JET-BOAT TOURS   Tours aboard a jet boat take visitors upriver from the Klamath River estuary to view bear, deer, elk, osprey hawks, otters, and more along the riverbanks. It's about $20 for a 30-mile trip, $28 for a 45-mile lunch or dinner cruise;

offered May 1 to October 30. For more information, contact **Klamath River Jet Boat Tours,** Klamath (☎ **800/887-JETS** or 707/482-7775).

RANGER PROGRAMS   The park service runs interpretive programs—from trees to tide pools, legends to landforms—at the Hiouchi, Crescent Beach, and Redwood information centers during summer months, as well as year-round at the park head-quarters in Crescent City. State rangers lead campfire programs (usually free) and numerous other activities throughout the year as well. Call the Parks Information Service for both the national and state parks (☎ **707/464-6101,** ext. 5265) to get current schedules and events.

CAMPING & ACCOMMODATIONS

Five small campgrounds are located in the national park proper. Four of the walk-in (more like backpack-in) camps—Little Bald Hills, Nickel Creek, Flint Ridge, and Butler Creek—are free, and only one (the Redwood Creek Gravel Bar) requires a permit from the visitor center in advance.

Most car campsites are in the **Prairie Creek** and **Jedediah Smith State Parks,** which lie entirely inside the national park. Prairie Creek contains two campgrounds, at Elk Prairie and Gold Bluffs Beach. Sites are $14 per night and can be reserved by calling the state's **Park Net reservation system** (☎ **800/444-7275**), which requires an additional $7.50 reservation fee. Be prepared to deal with a truly annoying computer before you call, and know exactly what campground, and if possible which site you would like. (The state park service has promised improvements in this system, but we'll see.)

If the camping areas above are all filled, try the **Mill Creek Campground,** in Del Norte Coast Redwoods State Park (part of RNSP), located 7 miles south of Crescent City on U.S. 101, which has 145 tent or RV sites. The walk-in tent sites are actually quite nice, situated amidst the forest. Fees range from $14 to $16 per night. For reservations, call the Park Net reservation system at ☎ **800/444-7275.**

A number of bed-and-breakfasts and funky roadside motels are available in the surrounding communities of Crescent City, Orick, and Klamath (see sections 6 and 7 of this chapter for some recommendations). The **Crescent City/Del Norte Chamber of Commerce** (☎ **800/343-8300**) can probably steer you toward a proper match.

Redwood AYH Hostel—Demartin House. 14480 U.S. 101 (off U.S. 101 across from Wilson Creek Beach, about 7 miles north of Klamath), Klamath, CA 95548. ☎ **707/ 482-8265.** 30 bunks, 1 family rm. $12 per bed, per night. MC, V.

The only lodging actually within the park, this turn-of-the-century logger's mansion was remodeled in 1987 to accommodate 30 guests, dormitory-style (i.e., bunks and shared bathrooms). What it lacks in creature comforts it makes up for in location—a mere 100 yards from the beach, and surrounded by hiking trails leading along the Redwood Coast (the staff leads nature walks and is well versed in local history). Family rooms are available with advance notice, and the hostel even takes reservations by credit card (strongly recommended in the summer). The $12 nightly rate includes use of the showers, common room, redwood deck, country kitchen, dining room, wood-stove, and bicycle storage.

The Far North: Lake Tahoe, the Shasta Cascades & Lassen Volcanic National Park

by Erika Lenkert and Matthew R. Poole

Dominated by the eternally snowcapped Mt. Shasta—visible for 100 miles around on a clear day—California's upper northern territory is among the least visited sections of the state. Often referred to as "The Far North," this vast region stretches from the rice fields north of Sacramento all the way to the Oregon border. In fact, the area is so immense that the state of Ohio would fit comfortably within its borders.

The Far North is a virtual outdoor playground for the adventurous traveler on a limited budget, offering myriad inexpensive recreational activities such as hiking, climbing, fishing, cross-country skiing, and mountain biking. Other attractions, both artificial and natural, range from the amazing Shasta Dam to Lava Beds National Monument, which has dozens of caves to explore, and Lassen Volcanic National Park, a towering laboratory of volcanic phenomena.

Directly south of the Cascade Range is one of the most popular recreational regions in the Golden State: Lake Tahoe. Situated at 6,225 feet above sea level in the Sierra Nevada mountains, it straddles the border between Nevada and California. Although parts of the lakeshore have been marred by overdevelopment—particularly along the casino-riddled southern shore—the western and eastern coastlines still provide quiet havens for hiking and mountain biking, and the surrounding mountains offer some of the best skiing in the United States at more than a dozen resorts.

1 Lava Beds National Monument

324 miles NE of San Francisco; 50 miles NE of Mount Shasta

Lava Beds takes a while to grow on you. It's a seemingly desolate, windy place with high plateaus, cinder cones, and rolling hills covered with lava cinders, sagebrush, and tortured-looking junipers. Miles of land just like it cover most of this corner of California. So why, asks the first-time visitor, is this a national monument? The answer lies underground.

The earth here is like Swiss cheese, so porous in places that it actually makes a hollow sound. When lava pours from a shield volcano, it doesn't cool all at once; the outer edges cool first and the core keeps flowing, forming underground tunnels, like a giant pipeline system.

More than 330 lava-tube caves lace the earth at Lava Beds, caves that are open to the public to explore on its own or with park rangers. Where most caves lend themselves to a fear of getting lost with their huge chambers, multiple entrances, and bizarre topography, these are simple, relatively easy-to-follow tunnels with little room to go wrong. Once inside, you'll feel that this would be a great place for a game of hide-and-seek.

JUST THE FACTS

Park elevations range from 4,000 to 5,700 feet, and this part of California can get cold any time of year. Summer is the best time to visit, with average temperatures in the 70s; winter temperatures plunge down to about 40°F in the day and as low as 20°F by night. Summer is also the best time to participate in ranger-led hikes, cave trips, and campfire programs. Check at the visitor center in the **Lava Beds National Monument** headquarters for schedules or call the headquarters at ☎ **530/667-2282.** The visitor center is located in the south-central portion of the monument, along the main Park Road.

SEEING THE HIGHLIGHTS

A hike to **Schonchin Butte** (three-quarters of a mile, each way) will give you a good perspective on the wildly stark beauty of the monument and nearby Tule Lake Valley. Wildlife lovers should keep their eyes peeled for terrestrial animals like mule deer, coyote, marmots, and squirrels, while watching overhead for bald eagles, 24 species of hawks, and enormous flocks of ducks and geese headed to the Klamath Basin, one of the largest waterfowl wintering grounds in the Lower 48. Sometimes the sky goes dark with ducks and geese during the peak migrations.

The caves at **Lava Beds** are open to the public with very little restriction or hassle. All you need to see most of them is a good flashlight or headlamp, sturdy walking shoes, and a sense of adventure. Many of the caves are entered by ladders or stairs, others still by holes in the side of a hill. Once inside, walk far enough to round a corner, and then shut off your light—a chilling experience, to say the least.

One-way **Cave Loop Road,** just southwest of the visitor center, is where you'll find many of the best cave hikes. About 15 lava tubes have been marked and made accessible. Two are ice caves, where the air temperature remains below freezing all year and ice crystals form on the walls. If exploring on your own gives you the creeps, check out **Mushpot Cave.** Almost adjacent to the visitor center, this cave has been outfitted with lights and a smooth walkway; you'll have plenty of company.

Hardened spelunkers will find enough remote and relatively unexplored caves in the monument, many requiring specialized climbing gear, to keep themselves busy.

Above ground, several trails crisscross the monument. The longest of these, the 8.2-mile (one-way) **Lyons Trail,** spans the wildest part of the monument, where you are likely to see plenty of animals. The 3.4-mile (one-way) **Whitney Butte Trail** leads from Merill Cave along the shoulder of 5,000-foot Whitney Butte to the edge of the Callahan Lava Flow and the monument boundary.

PICNICKING, CAMPING & ACCOMMODATIONS

The 40-unit **Indian Well Campground** near the visitor center has spaces for tents and small RVs year-round, with water available only during the summer. The rest of the year, you'll have to carry water from the nearby visitor center.

Two **picnic grounds,** Fleener Chimneys and Captain Jacks Stronghold, have tables but no water; open fires are prohibited.

There are no hotels or lodges in the monument, but numerous services are available in nearby Tulelake and Klamath Falls. For more information, call or write **Lava Beds National Monument,** P.O. Box 867, Tulelake, CA 96134 (☎ **530/ 667-2282**).

2 Mt. Shasta & the Cascades

274 miles N of San Francisco

Chances are, your first glimpse of Mt. Shasta's majestic, snowcapped peak will result in a twang of awe. A dormant volcano with a 17-mile-diameter base, it stands in virtual isolation 14,162 feet above the sea. When John Muir first saw Shasta from 50 miles away in 1874, he wrote: "[I] was alone and weary. Yet my blood turned to wine, and I have not been weary since." He went on to describe it as "the pole star of the landscape," which indeed it is.

For the budget traveler, Mt. Shasta and the Cascades offer a gold mine of opportunities. Dining and lodging here are the cheapest in the state, and most activities simply require an adventurous soul and a few outdoor toys (most of which can be rented for dollars a day). Don't forget to pack your binoculars—the endangered bald eagle is a common sight in these parts—and a pair of broken-in hiking boots.

ESSENTIALS

GETTING THERE   From San Francisco, take I-80 to I-505 to I-5 to Redding. From the coast, pick up Calif. 299 east a few miles north of Arcata to Redding.

Redding Municipal Airport, 6751 Woodrum Circle (☎ 530/224-4320), is serviced by **United Express** (☎ 800/241-6522) and **Horizon Air** (☎ 800/547-9308). **Amtrak** (☎ 800/USA-RAIL) stops in Dunsmuir and Redding.

VISITOR INFORMATION   Regional information can be obtained from the following organizations: **Shasta Cascade Wonderland Association,** 1699 Calif. 273, Anderson, CA 96007 (☎ 800/474-2782 or 530/365-7500); **Mt. Shasta Visitors Bureau,** 300 Pine St., Mount Shasta, CA 96067 (☎ 800/926-4865 or 530/ 926-4865); **Redding Convention and Visitors Bureau,** 777 Auditorium Dr., Redding, CA 96001 (☎ 800/874-7562 or 530/225-4100); **Trinity County Chamber of Commerce,** 210 N. Main St., P.O. Box 517, Weaverville, CA 96093 (☎ 800/ 487-4648 or 530/623-6101).

A HISTORIC STOP EN ROUTE

En route to Mt. Shasta from the south, you may want to stop near Red Bluff at **William B. Ide Adobe State Historic Park,** 21659 Adobe Rd. (☎ **530/529-8599**), for a picnic along the Sacramento River. The 4-acre park commemorates William B. Ide, the Republic of California's first and only president, proclaimed on June 14, 1846, by those who led the Bear Flag Rebellion against the Mexicans who were excluding the Americans from California. The republic lasted only 3 weeks before the American victory in the Mexican–American War made California a state in the Union. The adobe home dates from 1852. Some historians claim it was not Ide's home, but it does give visitors an idea of frontier life. In summer, the park is open from 8am to sunset, and the house is open from noon to 4pm; call ahead in winter. Parking is $3 per vehicle.

REDDING & SHASTA

Note to reader: Don't confuse the old mining town, Shasta, located a few miles west of Redding, with the much larger community, Mount Shasta, a major tourist destination located on I-5 near the base of Mt. Shasta.

The largest town and gateway to the region is Redding, the hub of the panoramic Shasta-Cascade region, lying at the top of the Sacramento Valley. From here you can either turn westward into the wilderness forest of Trinity and the Klamath Mountains, or north and east into the Cascades and Shasta Trinity National Forest.

In Redding, with its fast-food joints, gas stations, and cheap motels, summer heat generally hovers around 100°F. A city of some 60,000, Redding is the transportation hub of the upper reaches of northern California. It has little of interest; it's mainly useful as a base for exploring the natural wonders nearby. Information is available from the **Redding Convention and Visitors Bureau,** 777 Auditorium Dr., Redding, CA 96001 (☎ **800/874-7562** or 530/225-4100), west of I-5 on Calif. 299. It's open Monday through Friday from 8am to 5pm, Saturday and Sunday from 9am to 5pm.

To the northeast of Redding, Mt. Shasta rises to a height of more than 14,000 feet. From Redding, I-5 cuts north over the Pit River Bridge, crossing Lake Shasta and leading eventually to the mount itself. Before striking north, however, you may want to explore **Lake Shasta** and see **Shasta Dam.** Another option is to take a detour west of Redding to Weaverville, Whiskeytown–Shasta Trinity National Recreation Area, and Trinity Lake (see below).

About 3 miles west of Redding on Calif. 299 is the old mining town of **Shasta,** which has been converted into a State Historic Park (☎ **530/243-8194**). Shasta was founded on gold and was the "Queen City" of the northern mines in the Klamath Range. Its life was short, and the town expired in 1872 when the Central Pacific Railroad bypassed it in favor of Redding. Today the business district is a ghost town, complete with a restored general store and a Masonic hall. The 1861 courthouse has been converted into a museum where you can view the jail and a gallows out back, as well as a remarkable collection of California art assembled by Mae Helen Bacon Boggs. The collection includes works by Maynard Dixon, Grace Hudson, and many others. It's open Wednesday through Sunday from 10am to 5pm. Admission is $2 for adults, $1 for children 6 to 12, and free for children 5 and under.

Continue along Calif. 299 west to Calif. 3 north, which will take you to Weaverville (see below) and then to the west side of Trinity Lake (officially known as Clair Engle Lake) and to Trinity Center.

WHERE TO STAY

Tiffany House Bed and Breakfast Inn. 1510 Barbara Rd., Redding, CA 96003. ☎ **530/244-3225.** 4 units. $75–$95 double; $125 cottage. Rates include breakfast. AE, DISC, MC, V.

If this B&B was located on the coast, a room here would easily cost twice as much, but in Redding a little money can buy a lot of luxury. Despite the fact that this two-story gray-and-white house wasn't built until 1939, everyone in town refers to it as a Victorian. A sweeping view of the Lassen Mountain Range is visible from every guest room and cottage, as well as from the oversize deck, which seems to float above a garden in back. There's also a Music Room with piano, Victorian Parlor with fireplace, games and puzzles, and even a swimming pool. Each guest room is furnished with a queen-size bed and antique furnishings, and all have private bathrooms and soft robes. If you're in the mood to splurge, the secluded Lavinia's Cottage has a 7-foot spa tub, sitting area, and magnificent laurel-wreath iron bed.

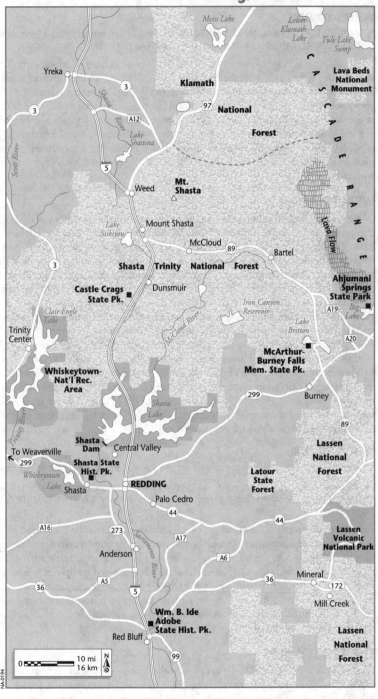

Meiss Lake

Lower Klamath Lake

Tule Lake Sump

Lava Beds National Monument

Yreka

3

Klamath

A12

97

National

C A S C A D E

Scott River

Lake Shastina

5

Forest

R A N G E

Weed

Mt. Shasta
△

Lava Flow

Lake Siskiyou

Mount Shasta

McCloud

89

Bartel

3

Shasta Trinity National Forest

Dunsmuir

Iron Canyon Reservoir

Ahjumani Springs State Park

A19

Big Lake

Castle Crags State Pk.

Clair Engle Lake

McCloud River

Lake Britton

A20

Trinity Center

Whiskeytown-Nat'l Rec. Area

McArthur-Burney Falls Mem. State Pk.

299

Burney

89

Shasta Lake

Lassen National Forest

To Weaverville

299

Shasta Dam

Central Valley

Shasta State Hist. Pk.

Whiskeytown Lake

Shasta

REDDING

Palo Cedro

44

Latour State Forest

44

A16

273

Sacramento River

A17

A6

Lassen Volcanic National Park

Anderson

A5

36

5

36

Mineral

172

Mill Creek

Wm. B. Ide Adobe State Hist. Pk.

Red Bluff

99

Lassen National Forest

0   10 mi
     16 km

N

NA-0194

WHERE TO DINE

Jack's Grill. 1743 California St. ☎ **530/241-9705.** Reservations not accepted. Main courses $8.25–$18.95. AE, DISC, MC, V. Mon–Sat 4–11pm. STEAK HOUSE.

This building was originally constructed in 1835 as a secondhand-clothing store. The second floor served as a whorehouse in the late 1930s, and an entrepreneur named Jack Young set up the main floor as a steak house (his establishment serviced all of a body's needs, you might say). Today, it's a local favorite. Waiting for a table over drinks in the bar is part of the fun. Good old-fashioned red meat is supplemented by a couple of seafood dishes such as deep-fried jumbo prawns and ocean scallops. Prices include salad, hot garlic bread, and baked or french-fried potatoes. It's a very fetching spot, with good, honest tavern food and a jovial crowd. Be prepared for a long wait on weekends.

WEAVERVILLE

Weaverville was a gold-mining town in the 1850s, and part of the history of the place is captured at the **Jake Jackson Memorial Museum–Trinity County Historical Park,** 508 Main St. (☎ **530/623-5211**). The collection of memorabilia, from firearms to household items, is interesting for what it reveals about the residents of the town—Native Americans, miners, pioneers, and especially the Chinese. In the gold-rush era, the town was half Chinese, with a Chinatown of about 2,500 residents. Admission is free, although a $1 donation is suggested. It's open in April and November daily from noon to 4pm; May 1 to October 31 daily from 10am to 5pm; and December through March, Tuesday and Saturday from noon to 4pm.

Across the parking lot, you can view the oldest continuously used Taoist temple in California at the **Joss House State Historic Park** (☎ **530/623-5284**). This well-preserved temple was built by immigrant Chinese miners in 1874. It's open June through August daily from 10am to 5pm; September through November, Wednesday through Sunday from 10am to 5pm; December through March, Saturday from 10am to 5pm; and April through May, Wednesday through Sunday from 10am to 5pm. Admission is $2 for adults, $1 for children 6 to 12, and free for children 5 and under.

WHERE TO DINE

Weaverville isn't exactly a star in the culinary firmament, but there is one bright spot.

La Grange Café. 315 N. Main St. ☎ **530/623-5325.** Main courses $6.95–$18.95. AE, DISC, MC, V. Mon–Fri 11am–9:30pm; Sat–Sun 7am–9:30pm. CREATIVE TRADITIONAL CUISINE.

This is far and away the best food in town. Heck, it would even be considered good in Redding, Sacramento, or Tahoe. The decor may be unprepossessing, but the friendly small-town ambiance makes up for it. Owner Sharon Heryford's menu includes the local favorite—chicken enchiladas with marinated tri-tip—plus seasonal items such as the local rabbit, which is braised with mushrooms, fresh herbs, and white wine. The 135-plus selections on the wine list makes it one of the strongest in northern California. Desserts, like a sinfully rich banana cream pie and that quintessential comfort food, bread pudding, are all made on the premises.

THE TRINITY ALPS

West of Weaverville stretch the Trinity Alps, with Thompson Peak rising to more than 9,000 feet. The second-largest wilderness area in the state lies between the Trinity and Salmon rivers and contains more than 55 lakes and streams. Its alpine scenery makes it popular with hikers and backpackers. You can access the **Pacific Crest Trail** west of

Mt. Shasta at Parks Creek, South Fork Road, Whalen Road, and also from Castle Crags State Park. For trail and other information, contact the Forest Service at Weaverville (☎ **530/623-2121**).

The Fifth Season, 300 N. Mt. Shasta Blvd. (☎ **530/926-3606**), offers mountaineering and backpack rentals and will provide trail maps and other information concerning Shasta's outdoor activities.

Living Waters Recreation, 706 Carmen Ave., Mount Shasta, CA 96067 (☎ **530/926-5446**), offers half-day to 2-day rafting trips on the Upper Sacramento, Klamath, Trinity, and Salmon rivers. **Trinity River Rafting Company,** on Calif. 299W in Big Flat (☎ **800/30-RIVER** or 530/623-3033), also operates local whitewater trips.

For additional outfitters and information, contact the **Trinity County Chamber of Commerce,** 210 N. Main St., P.O. Box 517, Weaverville, CA 96093 (☎ **800/ 487-4648** or 530/623-6101).

WHISKEYTOWN NATIONAL RECREATION AREA

In adjacent Shasta County, Whiskeytown National Recreation Area is on the eastern shore of Trinity Lake, a quiet and relatively uncrowded lake with 157 miles of shoreline. When this reservoir was created, it was officially named Clair Engle, after the politician who created it. But locals insist on calling it Trinity after the name of the river that used to rush through the region past the towns of Minersville, Stringtown, and an earlier Whiskeytown. All of these were destroyed when the river was dammed. They now lie submerged under the lake's glassy surface.

Both Trinity Lake and the Whiskeytown National Recreation Area are in the Shasta Trinity National Forest, 1.3 million acres of wilderness with 1,269 miles of hiking trails. For information on trails, contact **Shasta Trinity National Forest** (☎ **530/246-5222**).

LAKE SHASTA

Heading north on I-5 from Redding, travel about 12 miles and take the Shasta Dam Boulevard exit to the ✪ **Shasta Dam and Power Plant** (☎ **530/275-4463**), which has an overflow spillway that is three times higher than Niagara Falls. The huge dam—3,460 feet long, 602 feet high, and 883 feet thick at its base—holds back the waters of the Sacramento, Pit, and McCloud rivers. A dramatic sight indeed, it is a vital component of the Central Valley water project. At the visitor center is a series of photographs and displays covering the dam's construction period. You can either walk or drive over the dam, but far more interesting are the free 1-hour tours given daily from 9am to 5pm on the hour in the summer, and at 10am, noon, and 2pm from Labor Day to Memorial Day. The guided tour takes you deep within the dam's many chilly corridors (not a good place for claustrophobes) and below the spillway. It's an entertaining way to beat the summer heat.

Lake Shasta has 370 miles of shoreline and attracts anglers (bass, trout, and king salmon), water-skiers, and other boating enthusiasts—two million, in fact, in summer. The best way to enjoy the lake is aboard a houseboat; they can be rented from several companies, including **Antlers Resort & Marina,** P.O. Box 140, Antlers Rd., Lakehead, CA 96051 (☎ **800/238-3924**); and **Packers Bay Marina,** 16814 Packers Bay Rd., Lakehead, CA 96051 (☎ **800/331-3137** or 530/275-5570). Prices range from $150 to $300 a day, but if you split it up among five friends, that's only $30 a pop for a full day of fun.

While you're here, you can visit **Lake Shasta Caverns** (☎ **530/238-2341**). These caves contain 20-foot-high stalactite and stalagmite formations—60-foot-wide curtains of them in the great Cathedral Room. To see the caves, drive about 15 miles north of Redding on I-5 to the O'Brien/Shasta Caverns exit. A ferry will take you across the lake and a short bus ride will follow to the cave entrance for a 2-hour-long tour. Admission is $14 for adults, $7 for children, and free for kids 3 and under. The caverns are open daily year-round, with tours every half hour from 9am to 4pm Memorial Day through Labor Day; every hour from 9am to 3pm in April, May, and September; and at 10am, noon, and 2pm October through March.

Farther north, off I-5 about 50 miles north of Redding, you'll reach **Castle Crags State Park** (☎ 530/235-2684), a 4,300-acre park with 64 campsites and 28 miles of hiking trails. Here granite crags that were formed 225 million years ago tower more than 6,500 feet above the Sacramento River. The park is filled with dogwood, oak, cedar, and pine as well as tiger lilies, azaleas, and orchids in summer. You can walk the 1-mile Indian Creek nature trail or take the easy 1-mile Root Creek Trail. The entrance fee is $5 per vehicle per day.

For information about the Lake Shasta region, contact the **Redding Convention and Visitors Bureau,** 777 Auditorium Dr., Redding, CA 96001 (☎ **800/874-7562** or 530/225-4100), west of I-5 on Calif. 299. It's open Monday through Friday from 8am to 5pm, Saturday and Sunday from 9am to 5pm.

✪ MT. SHASTA

A volcanic mountain with eight glaciers, **Mt. Shasta** is a towering peak of legend and lore. It stands alone, always snowcapped, unshadowed by other mountains—visible from 125 miles away. Although it's been dormant since 1786, eruptions cannot be ruled out, and indeed, hot sulfur springs bubble at the summit. The springs saved John Muir on his third ascent of the mountain in 1875. Caught in a severe snowstorm, he and his partner took turns submersing themselves in the hot mud to survive.

Many New Agers are convinced that Mt. Shasta is the center of an incredible energy vortex. These devotees flock to the foot of the mountain. In 1987 the foothills were host to the worldwide Harmonic Convergence, calling for a planetary union and a new phase of universal harmony. Yoga, massage, meditation, and metaphysics are all the rage here. These New Agers seem to coexist harmoniously with those whose metaphysical leanings begin and end with Dolly Parton song lyrics.

Those who don't want to climb can drive up to about 7,900 feet. From Mount Shasta City, drive 14 miles up the Everitt Memorial Highway to the end of the road near Panther Meadow. At the **Everitt Vista Turnout,** you'll be able to stop and see the Sacramento River Canyon, the Eddy Mountains to the west, and glimpses of Mount Lassen to the south. You can also take the short hike through the forests to a lava outcrop overlooking the McCloud area.

Continue on to **Bunny Flat,** a major access point for climbing in summer and also for cross-country skiing and sledding in winter. The highway ends at the Old Ski Bowl Vista, providing panoramic views of Mount Lassen, Castle Crags, and the Trinity Mountains.

While in Mount Shasta, visit the **Fish Hatchery** at 1 N. Old State Rd. (☎ **530/926-2215**), which was built in 1888. Here you can observe rainbow and brown trout being hatched to stock rivers and streams statewide—millions are born here annually. You can feed them via coin-operated food dispensers, and observe the spawning process on every Tuesday during fall and winter. Admission is free, and it's open daily from 8am to sunset. Adjacent to the hatchery is the **Sisson Museum** (☎ **530/926-5508**), which displays a smattering of local-history exhibits. It's open

Picture Perfect

Lake Siskiyou, at Shasta's base, is a great spot from which to photograph Mt. Shasta and its reflection. See "Enjoying the Great Outdoors," below, for more on Lake Siskiyou.

daily year-round, from 10am to 4pm in summer, from 1 to 4pm in winter; admission is free.

ENJOYING THE GREAT OUTDOORS

MOUNTAIN CLIMBING   Mt. Shasta attracts thousands of hikers from around the world each year, from timid first-timers to serious mountaineers who search for the most difficult paths up. The hike isn't technically difficult, but it's a demanding ascent that takes about 8 hours of continuous exertion, particularly when the snow softens up. (*Tip:* Start real early, while the snow is still firm.) Before setting out, hikers must secure a permit by signing in at the trailhead or at the Mt. Shasta Ranger District office, which also gives out plenty of good advice for amateur climbers. The office is at 204 W. Alma St., off North Mount Shasta Boulevard in Mount Shasta (☎ **530/926-4511**). Be sure to wear good hiking shoes and carry crampons and an ice ax, a first-aid kit, a quart of water per person, and a flashlight in case it takes longer than anticipated. Sunblock is an absolute necessity. All the requisite equipment can be rented at **The Fifth Season,** 300 N. Mount Shasta Blvd. (☎ **530/926-3606**).

Weather can be extremely unpredictable, and every year hikers die on this dormant volcano, usually from making stupid mistakes. For weather and climbing conditions, call ☎ **530/926-5555.** Traditionally climbers make the ascent from the Sierra Lodge at Horse Camp, which can be reached from the town of Mount Shasta via Alma Street and the Everitt Memorial Highway or from Bunny Flat.

For more information as well as supervised trips, contact **Shasta Mountain Guides,** 1938 Hill Rd. (☎ **530/926-3117**). This outfitter offers a 2-day climb that follows the traditional John Muir route and costs about $240. They also offer a glacier climb and rock climbing in Castle Crags State Park, plus cross-country and telemark skiing.

SKIING   In winter, visitors can ski at **Mt. Shasta Ski Park,** 104 Siskiyou Ave., Mount Shasta (☎ **530/926-8610**), which has 25 runs with 80% snowmaking, three triple-seat chairlifts, and a surface lift. A day pass costs less than $30 (a bargain compared to Tahoe resorts). There's also a Nordic Ski center with 15½ miles of groomed trails, as well as a Terrain Park that's geared toward snowboarders. In summer you can ride the chairlifts to scenic views, mountain-bike down the trails (an all-day pass is $10), or practice on the two-story climbing wall. Access to the chairlifts is 10 miles east of Mount Shasta (the town) on its southern slopes via Calif. 89 from McCloud. For information call ☎ **530/926-8600.** The ski lodge's number is ☎ **530/926-8612.**

WATER SPORTS   The source of the headwaters of the Sacramento River accumulates in **Lake Siskiyou,** a popular spot for boating, swimming, and fishing—and a great vantage point for photographs of Mt. Shasta and its reflection. Waterskiing and jet-skiing are not allowed, but windsurfing is, and boat rentals are offered at **Lake Siskiyou Camp Resort,** 4239 W. A. Barr Rd., Mount Shasta (☎ **530/926-2618**).

GOLF & TENNIS   Golfers should head for the 27-hole Robert Trent Jones, Jr., golf course at **Lake Shastina Golf Resort,** 5925 Country Club Dr., Weed (☎ **530/938-3201**), where greens fees are $35 Monday through Thursday and $40 Friday through Sunday; or the 18-hole course at **Mount Shasta Resort,** 1000 Siskiyou Lake

Blvd., Mount Shasta (☎ **530/926-3030**), where the greens fees are $51 with cart daily until 2pm and $39 with cart after 2pm. Mount Shasta Resort also has tennis courts.

OTHER WARM-WEATHER ACTIVITIES   Mt. Shasta offers some excellent **mountain biking.** In the summer, ride the chairlifts to the top of Mt. Shasta Ski Park and bike down the trails. An all-day chairlift pass is only $10 (☎ **530/926-8610**). Another good source for renting mountain bikes and getting trail information is **Shasta Cycling** (☎ **530/938-3002**).

For fishing information or guided trips, call **Jack Trout Flyfishing Guide** (☎ 530/926-4540). Two other recommended sources are **Mt. Shasta Fly Fishing** (☎ 530/926-6648) and **Hart's Guide Service** (☎ 530/926-2431).

For an really offbeat experience, contact **Rainbow Ridge Ranch** (☎ 530/ 926-5794) and join one of their **llama-trekking** trips. Trips last from 3 to 5 days and cost from $400.

WHERE TO STAY

Best Western Tree House. 111 Morgan Way (at I-5 and Lake St.), Mount Shasta, CA 96067. ☎ **800/545-7164** or 530/926-3101. Fax 530/926-3542. 95 units. A/C TV TEL. $79–$160 double. AE, CB, DC, MC, V.

Just off the main highway, this motor inn offers rooms with standard Scandinavian-style furnishings. Some accommodations have decks and fridges, making them family favorites. Facilities include a rustic dining room and lounge with a stone fireplace. There's also a huge indoor pool that's usually deserted, as well as an exercise room. This is the best place to stay in the town of Mount Shasta, and it keeps its prices low. Downhill and cross-country ski areas are 10 miles away.

✪ **McCloud Guest House.** 606 W. Colombero Dr. (P.O. Box 1510), McCloud, CA 96057. ☎ **530/964-3160.** 5 units, all with bathroom (2 with shower only). $80–$95 double. Rates include continental breakfast. MC, V.

Off Calif. 89, west of McCloud, and set among the oak and pine trees of Mt. Shasta's lower slopes, this bungalow-style house has a wraparound veranda and dormer windows. Built in 1907, the house was nicely restored in 1984 by innkeepers Bill and Patti Leigh and Dennis and Pat Abreu. Upstairs there's a large comfortable parlor with a pool table for guests. Off the parlor are five individually decorated rooms with white iron beds. Three of the rooms have claw-foot tubs; the other two have shower only.

On the ground floor, there's an atmospheric dining room with leaded- and stained-glass interior decoration. The menu offers a fine selection of Italian chicken, veal, pasta, and seafood dishes.

✪ **Mt. Shasta Ranch B&B.** 1008 W. A. Barr Rd., Mount Shasta, CA 96067. ☎ **530/926-3870.** Fax 530/926-6882. 9 units, 4 with bathroom; 1 cottage. TV. $50–$70 double without bathroom; $95 double with bathroom; $95 cottage for 2. Rates include breakfast. AE, DISC, MC, V. Take Central Mt. Shasta exit off I-5 to W. A. Barr Rd.

Mt. Shasta Ranch was conceived and built in 1923 by one of the country's most famous horse trainers and racing tycoons, H. D. ("Curley") Brown, as the centerpiece of a private retreat and thoroughbred-horse ranch. Despite the encroachment of nearby buildings, the main house and its annex are still available as a cozy B&B with touches of nostalgia, the occasional antique, and spectacular views of Mt. Shasta. Four bedrooms (the ones with private bathrooms) lie in the main house; the remaining five share two bathrooms in the carriage house. It's a 3-minute trek to the shores of nearby Lake Siskiyou (15 min. to the ski slopes), or you could stay here to enjoy the hot tub, Ping-Pong tables, pool table, darts, and horseshoes.

Railroad Park Resort. 100 Railroad Park Rd., Dunsmuir, CA 96025. ☎ **800/974-RAIL** or 530/235-4440. Fax 530/235-4470. 23 units, 4 cabins. A/C TV TEL. $60–$85 double. Extra person/pets $8. AE, DISC, MC, V. Take Railroad Park exit off I-5, 1 mile south of Dunsmuir.

Lying a quarter of a mile from the Sacramento River, this is an offbeat place that kids enjoy. It's located at the foot of Castle Crags and contains several facilities—a restaurant and lounge, campground and RV park, rustic cabins, and the Caboose Motel. The railroad cabooses have been converted into rooms, leaving their pipes, ladders, and lofts in place. They're furnished with modern brass beds, table and chairs, dressers, and TVs; they're located around the fenced-in kidney-shaped pool and whirlpool. The restaurant and lounge are also in vintage railroad cars.

✪ **Stewart Mineral Springs Resort.** 4617 Stewart Springs Rd., Weed, CA 96094. ☎ **530/938-2222.** 2 teepees (suitable for up to 4 persons), 4 dorm units (suitable for up to 5 persons), 6 motel units (suitable for up to 6 persons), 5 cabins with kitchens (suitable for 1 or 2 persons), 1 large A-frame house (suitable for 10–15 persons). $15 teepee for 1, $5 for each additional person; $30 dorm unit for 1, $10 for each additional person; $40 motel unit double; $45 cabin double; $300 A-frame house for up to 15. MC, V. Closed Dec 1–Mar 1 or even later depending on snow.

Stewart Mineral Springs is one of the most unusual health spas in California, loaded with lore and legends. It lies above cold-water springs that Native Americans valued for their healing powers. Don't expect anything approaching a European spa or big-city luxury here. Everything is deliberately rustic, with as few intrusions from the urban world as possible (no phones or TVs). Designed in a somewhat haphazard compound of about a dozen buildings, 4 miles west of the town of Weed, it occupies a 37-acre site of sloping, forested land accented with ponds, gazebos, and decorative bridges and riddled with hiking and nature trails, freshwater streams, and a swimming hole. There are no restaurants on-site, and the spa facilities are often beside campers and RVs.

Activities revolve around hiking, nature-watching, and taking the healing waters of the legendary springs. The bathhouse is the curative headquarters of the resort and contains 13 private rooms where water from the springs is heated and run into tubs for soaking. A staff member will describe the rituals for you: A 20-minute soak is followed by a visit to a nearby sauna and an immersion in the chilly waters of Parks Creek, just outside the bathhouse. Other feel-good options include massages ($30 per half-hour session). On Saturdays, medicine man Walking Eagle guides guests on a spiritual journey within the Native American Purification Sweat Lodge.

If you opt for treatment and R&R here, you won't be alone. Despite its rusticity, the place often caters to celebrities, including soap actors, San Francisco 49ers football players, and local newscasters.

Wagon Creek Inn. 1239 Woodland Park Dr., Mount Shasta, CA 96067. ☎ **530/926-0838.** 3 units, 1 with bathroom. $65–$75 double without bathroom; $85 double with bathroom. Rates include buffet breakfast. AE, DC, DISC, MC, V. From I-5 take the Central Mt. Shasta exit to Old Stage Rd. Go 1½ miles and turn right at Woodland Park Dr.

Loretta Lynn would feel at home in one of the rustic Southwestern-style rooms within this log-cabin home, located about 2½ miles from Mt. Shasta. The King Room has its own bathroom; the other two share. Guests can use the living room with fireplace, TV, and VCR. It's a homey, inexpensive place where pets and kids are welcome.

WHERE TO DINE

The Bagel Cafe and Bakery. 105 E. Alma St., Mount Shasta. ☎ **530/926-1414.** Main courses $4–$6. No credit cards. Mon–Sat 6am–4pm; Sun 7am–2pm. AMERICAN.

This is the hands-down winner for a low-cost meal in Mount Shasta. Packed daily with locals, the lively little cafe serves the best coffee in the region, as well as wonderful vegetarian pizzas, soups, salads, sandwiches and healthy entrees such as wok-fried veggies with tofu served over brown rice. If you're planning on spending the day out in the great outdoors, stop by here first for a large coffee and sandwich to go.

✪ **Café Maddalena.** 5801 Sacramento Ave., Dunsmuir. ☎ **530/235-2725.** Main courses $8.50–$16.50. MC, V. Thurs–Sun 5:30–9:30pm. SARDINIAN/MEDITERRANEAN COUNTRY COOKING.

Owner/chef Maddalena Serra has created a wonderful restaurant in the refurbished old railroad quarter of Dunsmuir. The smells wafting from this small place will literally draw you in. Maddalena cooks in full sight of the happy, satisfied (and stuffed) customers, preparing dishes like pasta Marco—fresh fettuccine with shrimp, tomatoes, cream, and herbs all wrapped in a flaky dough and baked in a pizza oven. Everything is made fresh daily, including the breads and desserts. Try the deceptively simple yet utterly scrumptious panna cotta, a cream flan with lemon, vanilla, and caramelized sugar. A memorable and special place.

Lily's. 1013 S. Mt. Shasta Blvd., Mount Shasta. ☎ **530/926-3372.** Reservations recommended. Main courses $5–$18.95. AE, DISC, MC, V. Mon–Fri 7am–9pm; Sat–Sun 7am–9:30pm. AMERICAN.

Set within a white-clapboard, turn-of-the-century house in a residential neighborhood south of the town center, this friendly little restaurant has a front porch, a picket fence, a back garden, and dining in two rooms inside and two patios out. It's popular for breakfast, when chunky breads and omelets ($5 to $6) start the morning off right. Lunch and dinner dishes—polenta, enchiladas, scampi al Roma, kung pao shrimp salad—span the globe.

A WORTHWHILE STOP EN ROUTE
TO LASSEN VOLCANIC NATIONAL PARK

On its way to Lassen Volcanic National Park (see below) from Mt. Shasta, Calif. 89 east loops back south to ✪ **McArthur–Burney Falls Memorial State Park** (☎ **530/335-2777**). One of the spectacular features of this 875-acre park is a waterfall that cascades over a 129-foot cliff. Theodore Roosevelt once called the falls "the eighth wonder of the world." Giant springs lying a few hundred yards upstream feed the falls and keep them flowing, even during California's legendary dry spells.

The half-mile **Headwater Trail** will take you to a good vantage point above the falls. If you're lucky, you can observe the black swift that nest in the mossy crevices behind the cascade. Other birds to look for include barn and great horned owls, the belted kingfisher, the common flicker, and even the Oregon junco. The year-round park also has a mile-long nature trail, 128 campsites, picnicking grounds, and good fishing for bass, brown trout, rainbow trout, and brook trout. For **camping reservations** call ☎ **800/444-PARK** (7275).

From here, Lassen Volcanic National Park lies about 40 miles south.

3 Lassen Volcanic National Park

45 miles E of Redding; 255 miles NE of San Francisco

Stashed away in the far northeastern corner of California, Lassen Volcanic National Park is a remarkable reminder that North America is still forming, and that the ground below is alive with the forces of creation and, sometimes, destruction. Lassen Peak is

Lassen Volcanic National Park

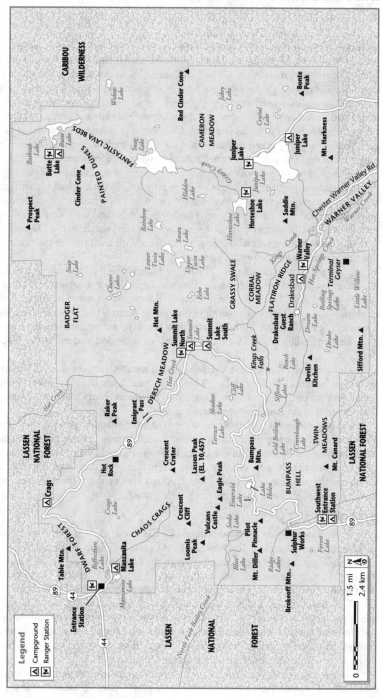

Legend

◮ Campground
☗ Ranger Station

0   1.5 mi
0   2.4 km

N

the southernmost peak in a chain of volcanoes (including Mt. Saint Helens) that stretches all the way from British Columbia.

Although it's dormant, 10,457-foot Lassen Peak is still very much alive. It last awakened in May 1914, beginning a cycle of eruptions that spit lava, steam, and ash until 1921. The eruption climaxed in 1915 when Lassen blew its top, sending a mushroom cloud of ash 7 miles high that was seen from hundreds of miles away. The peak itself has been dormant for nearly three-quarters of a century now, but the area still boils with a ferocious intensity: Hot springs, fumaroles, geysers, and mud pots are all indicators that Lassen hasn't had its last word. Monitoring of geothermal features in the park shows that they are getting hotter, not cooler, and some scientists take this as a sign that the next big eruption in the Cascades is likely to happen here.

Until then, the park gives visitors an interesting chance to watch a landscape recover from the massive destruction brought on by an eruption. To the north of Lassen Peak is the aptly named Devastated Area, a huge swath of volcanic destruction steadily repopulating with conifer forests. Forest botanists have revised their earlier theories that forests must be preceded by herbaceous growth after watching the Devastated Area immediately revegetate with a diverse mix of eight different conifer species, four more than were present before the blast.

The 108,000-acre park is a place of dazzling beauty. The flora and fauna here are an interesting mix of species from the Cascade Range, which stretches north from Lassen, and species from the Sierra Nevada Range, which stretches south. The resulting blend accounts for an enormous diversity of plants: 715 distinct species have been identified in the park. Although it is snowbound in winter, Lassen is an important summer feeding ground for transient herds of mule deer and numerous black bears.

In addition to the volcano and all its geothermal features, Lassen Volcanic National Park includes miles of hiking trails, 50 beautiful alpine lakes, large meadows, cinder cones, lush forests, cross-country skiing, and great backcountry camping. In fact, three-quarters of the park is designated wilderness.

And crowds? Forget it. Lassen is one of the least-visited national parks in the lower 48 states, so crowd control isn't as big a consideration here as in other places. Unless you're here on the Fourth of July or Labor Day weekend, you won't encounter anything that could rightly be called a crowd. Even then, you can escape the hordes simply by skipping the popular sites like Bumpass Hell or the Sulphur Works and heading a few miles down any of the backcountry trails.

JUST THE FACTS

Part of the reason Lassen Volcanic National Park is one of the least visited national parks is its remote location. The most foolproof route here is to take Calif. 44 east from Redding (via I-5), which leads directly to the northern gateway to the park. A shortcut if you're coming from the south along I-5 is Calif. 36 in Red Bluff, which leads to the park's southern gateway. If you're arriving from the east via I-80, take the U.S. 395 turnoff at Reno and head to Susanville. Depending on which end of the park you're shooting for, take either Calif. 44 (to the northwest entrance) or Calif. 36 (to the southwest entrance) from Susanville. The $5-per-car entrance fee, valid for a week, comes with a copy of the *Lassen Park Guide,* a handy little newsletter listing activities, hikes, and points of interest. Camping fees range from $8 to $12.

Only one major road, Calif. 89 (a.k.a. the Park Road), crosses the park in a 39-mile half circle with entrances and visitor centers at either end. Calif. 89 closes due to snow from November through June.

Most visitors enter the park at the southwest entrance station, drive through the park, and leave through the northwest entrance, or vice versa. Two other entrances

Park Safety

Because of the dangers posed by the park's thermal features, rangers ask that you remain on trails at all times. Fires are allowed in campgrounds only; please make sure they are dead before leaving them. Mountain bikes are prohibited on all trails.

Another concern is the weather: Lassen Volcanic National Park resides in one of the coldest places in California. Winter begins in late October and doesn't release its grip until June. Even in the summer you should plan for possible rain and snow. Temperatures at night can drop below freezing at any time. Winter, however, shows a different and beautiful side of Lassen that more people are starting to appreciate. Since most of the park is over a mile high and the highest point is 10,457 feet, snow accumulates in incredible quantities. Don't be surprised to find snowbanks lining the Park Road into July.

---

lead to remote portions of the park. Warner Valley is reached from the south on the road from Chester. Butte Lake entrance is reached by a cut-off road from Calif. 44 between Calif. 89 and Susanville.

Ranger stations are clustered near each entrance and provide the full spectrum of interpretive displays, ranger-led walks, informational leaflets, and emergency help. The largest **visitor center** is located just inside the northwest entrance station at the Loomis Museum. The park information number for all requests is ☎ **530/595-4444,** or write **Lassen Volcanic National Park,** P.O. Box 100, Mineral, CA 96063-0100.

SEEING THE HIGHLIGHTS

The highlight of Lassen is, of course, the volcano and all of its offshoots: boiling springs, fumaroles, mud pots, and more. You can see many of the most interesting sites in a day, making it possible to visit Lassen as a short detour from I-5 or U.S. 395 on the way to or from Oregon. Available at park visitor centers, the *Road Guide to Lassen Park* is a great traveling companion that will explain a lot of the features you'll see as you traverse the park.

Bumpass Hell, a 1½-mile walk off the Park Road in the southern part of the park, is the largest single geothermal site in the park—16 acres of bubbling mud pots cloaked in a stench of rotten-egg-smelling sulfur. The name comes from an early Lassen traveler, Bumpass, who lost a leg after he took a shortcut through the area while hunting and plunged into a boiling pool. Don't make the same error.

Sulphur Works is another stinky, steamy example of Lassen's residual heat. Two miles from the southwest park entrance, the ground roars with seething gases escaping from the ground.

Boiling Springs Lake and **Devil's Kitchen** are two of the more remote geothermal sites; they're located in the Warner Valley section of the park, which can be reached by hiking from the main road or entering the park through Warner Valley Road from the small town of Chester.

ACTIVE ENDEAVORS

In addition to the activities below, free naturalist programs are offered daily in the summer, highlighting everything from flora and fauna to geologic history and volcanic processes. For more information, call the park headquarters at ☎ **530/595-4444.**

HIKING   Most Lassen visitors drive through in a day or two, see the geothermal hot spots, and move on. That leaves 150 miles of trails and expanses of backcountry to the few who take the time to get off-road. The *Lassen Trails* booklet available at the visitor centers gives good descriptions of some of the most popular hikes and backpacking destinations. Anyone spending the night in the backcountry must have a wilderness permit issued at the ranger stations. And don't forget to bring plenty of water, sunscreen, and warm clothing.

The most popular hike in the park is the **Lassen Peak Trail,** a 2½-mile climb from the Park Road to the top of the peak. The trail may sound short, but it's steep and generally covered with snow until late summer. At an elevation of 10,457 feet, though, you'll get a view of the surrounding wilderness that's worth every step of the way. On clear days you can see south all the way to Sutter Buttes near Yuba City and north into the Cascades. The round-trip takes about 4 to 5 hours.

Running a close second in popularity is **Bumpass Hell Trail.** This 1½-mile walk off the Park Road in the southern part of the park leads you through a quiet and peaceful meadow of wildflowers and chirping birds before depositing you right in the middle of the largest single geothermal site in the park. Stay on the wooden catwalks that safely guide visitors past the pyrite pools, steam vents, and noisy fumaroles.

The 4-mile **Cinder Cone Trail,** located in the northeast corner of the park, is another worthy hike, best reached from Butte Lake Campground at the far northeast corner of the park. If 4 miles seems too short, you can extend the hike (and shorten the drive) by walking in about 8 miles from Summit Lake on the Park Road. Now dormant, Cinder Cone is generally accepted as the source of mysterious flashing lights that were seen by early settlers to the area in the 1850s. Black and charred-looking, Cinder Cone is bare of any sort of life and surrounded by dunes of multihued volcanic ash.

CANOEING & KAYAKING   Paddlers can take canoes, rowboats, or kayaks on any of the park lakes except Reflection, Emerald, Helen, and Boiling Springs. Motors, including electric motors, are strictly prohibited on all park waters. Park lakes are full of trout and fishing is popular. You must have a current California fishing license (see "Visitor Information & Money," in chapter 2, for information on getting a license). You'll have to bring your own canoe, kayak, or rowboat, as there is no place to rent these in the region; you can buy fishing poles and other fishing gear at the Lassen Mineral Lodge, on Calif. 36 in Mineral (☎ **530/595-4422**).

CROSS-COUNTRY SKIING   The park road usually closes due to snow in November, and most years it doesn't open until June, so cross-country skiers have their run of the park. Snowmobiles were once allowed but are now forbidden. Marked trails of all skill levels leave from Manzanita Lake at the north end of the park and Lassen Chalet at the south. Most visitors come to the southwest entrance, where the ski chalet offers lessons, rental gear, and a warm place to stay. Popular trips are the beginners' trails to Lake Helen or Summit Lake. More advanced skiers can make the trek into Bumpass Hell, a steaming valley of sulfuric mud pots and fumaroles.

You can also ski the popular 30-mile course of the Park Road in an overnight trek, but doing this involves a long car shuttle. For safety reasons the park requires all skiers to register at the ranger stations before heading into the backcountry, whether for an overnight or just the day. For more information, call **Lassen Ski Touring** at ☎ **530/595-3376.**

SNOWSHOEING   From January through March, a park naturalist gives a free 2-hour eco-adventure snowshoe hikes across Lassen's snowpacked hills. The tours take place on Saturday afternoons at 1:30pm at the Lassen Chalet, located at the park's southwestern entrance. You must be at least 8 years old, be warmly dressed, and be wearing boots. Snowshoes are provided free of charge on a first-come, first-served basis, although a $1 donation is requested for upkeep. For more details, call park head-quarters at ☎ **530/595-4444,** ext. 5133.

CAMPING

Car campers have their choice of seven park campgrounds with a total of 375 sites, more than enough to handle the trickle of visitors who come to Lassen every summer. In fact, so few people camp in Lassen that there is no reservations system except for at the **Lost Creek Group Campground,** and stays are granted a generous 14-day limit. Sites do fill up on weekends, so your best bet is to get to the park early on Friday to secure a place to stay. If the park is packed, there are 43 campgrounds in surrounding Lassen National Forest, so you're bound to find a site somewhere.

By far the most "civilized" campground in the park is at **Manzanita Lake,** where you can find hot showers, electrical hookups, flush toilets, and a camper store. When Manzanita fills up, rangers open the **Crags Campground** overflow camp, about 5 miles away and much more basic. Further within the park along Calif. 89 are **Summit Lake Campgrounds,** located on the north and south ends of Summit Lake. It's a pretty spot, often frequented by deer, and is a launching point for some excellent day hikes.

On the southern end of the park you'll find **Southwest Campground,** a walk-in camp directly adjacent to the Lassen Chalet parking lot.

The two remote entrances to Lassen and Warner Valley have their own primitive campgrounds with pit toilets and no water, but the price is right—it's free.

Backcountry camping is allowed almost everywhere, and traffic is light. Ask about closed areas when you get your wilderness permit, which are issued at the ranger stations and are required for anyone spending the night in the backcountry.

WHERE TO STAY NEAR THE PARK

✪ **The Bidwell House.** 1 Main St. (P.O. Box 1790), Chester, CA 96020. ☎ **530/258-3338.** 14 units, 12 with bathroom; 1 cottage with kitchenette. $82 double without bathroom; $103 double with bathroom; cottage $163 (sleeps up to 6). Rates include full breakfast. MC, V.

In 1901, General John Bidwell, a California senator who made three unsuccessful bids for the U.S. presidency, built a country retreat and summer home for his beloved young wife, Annie. The house, with its farmhouse-style design and spacious veranda, sits at the extreme eastern end of Chester, adjacent to a rolling meadow. The lake is visible across the road, and inside, Ian and Kim James maintain one of the most charming B&Bs in the region. Seven of the rooms have Jacuzzi tubs, and three offer wood-burning stoves. Breakfast is presented with fanfare and incorporates many gourmet touches, including home-baked breads and mouth-watering omelets. The Jameses also serve dinner Thursday through Saturday in the summer.

Lassen Mineral Lodge. On Calif. 36 (P.O. Box 160), Mineral, CA 96063. ☎ **530/595-4422.** Fax 530/595-4452. 20 units. $60–$75 double. MC, V.

A mere 9 miles south of Lassen Volcanic National Park's southern entrance, the Lassen Mineral Lodge offers 20 motel-style accommodations in a forested setting. In summer, the lodge is almost always bustling with guests and customers who venture in to the gift shop, ski shop, general store, and full-service restaurant and bar. Also on the grounds are a pool and tennis court that are available during the summer months. For families, this is probably your best lodging option in the Lassen area.

Mill Creek Resort. On Calif. 172 (3 miles south of Calif. 36), Mill Creek, CA 96061. ☎ **530/595-4449.** 9 units. $50–$70 per cabin. No credit cards. Pets are welcome.

Set deep within the forest, the Mill Creek Resort is that rustic mountain retreat you've always dreamed of while slaving away in the office. A homey country general store and coffee shop serve as the resort's center, a good place to stock up on food while exploring Lassen Volcanic National Park. Nine housekeeping cabins, available on a daily or weekly basis, are clean, cute, and outfitted with vintage 1930s and 1940s furniture, including kitchens (a good thing, since restaurants are scarce in this region).

WHERE TO DINE

INSIDE THE PARK   The only restaurant within Lassen Volcanic National Park is the **Summer Chalet Café** (☎ **530/595-3376**), which serves inexpensive, basic breakfasts, as well as sandwiches and burgers for lunch. Located at the park's south entrance, it's open daily from 8am to 6pm (grill closes at 4pm, however) May to mid-October, weather permitting.

NEAR THE PARK   When you're this far into the wilderness, the question isn't *which* restaurant to choose, but *if* there even is a restaurant to choose. If bacon and eggs, sandwiches, steaks, chicken, burgers, pizza, and salads aren't part of your diet, you're in big trouble unless you packed your own grub.

Deciding where you're going to eat near Lassen Volcanic National Park depends mostly on which side you're on, north or south. Near the north entrance to the park in the town of Old Station is **Uncle Runt's Place** (☎ **530/335-7177**), which serves your standard steaks, chicken, burgers, and sandwiches for lunch and dinner. At the south entrance to the park, the closest restaurant is the **Lassen Mineral Lodge** (see "Where to Stay Near the Park," above) in the town of Mineral, which serves the usual American fare.

The best approach, however, is to stay at a B&B or lodge that offers meals to its guests—such as **The Bidwell House**—or at least provides a kitchen to cook your own meals, such as the **Mill Creek Resort** (see above). Food and camping supplies are available at the **Manzanita Lake Camper Store** (☎ **530/335-7557**; closed in winter), located at the north entrance to the park; or **Lassen Mineral Lodge,** on Calif. 36 in Mineral at the southern end of the park (☎ **530/595-4422**). They also sell or rent just about every outdoor toy you'd ever want to play with in Lassen Park, including cross-country and ski equipment.

4 Lake Tahoe

107 miles E of Sacramento; 192 miles E of San Francisco

Lake Tahoe has long been California's most popular recreational playground. In summer you can enjoy boating and water sports, plus in-line skating, bungee jumping, camping, ballooning, horseback riding, bicycling, parasailing—the list is endless. In winter Lake Tahoe becomes one of the nation's premier ski destinations with its 14 downhill resorts and 11 cross-country skiing centers. There's also sleigh riding, ice-skating, snowmobiling, and snowshoeing. Year-round activities include tennis, fishing, Vegas-style gambling, and big-name entertainment on the Nevada border.

Then there's the lake. It's disputable whether Lake Tahoe is the most beautiful lake in the world, but it's certainly near the top of the list. It's famous for its 99.997% pure water (a white dinner plate at a depth of 75 feet would be clearly visible from the surface), and its size: The lake is so immense that the water it contains—close to 40 trillion gallons—could cover the entire state of California to a depth of 14½ inches. Its average depth is 989 feet, although it reaches 1,645 feet in places, making it the second-deepest lake in the United States (after Crater Lake, Oregon) and the eighth-deepest in the world.

A Tale of Two Shores

You wouldn't think the people and places on one end of Lake Tahoe would be much different from the other, but ask any local: North Shore and South Shore—Tahoe's two main destinations—have about as much in common as snow cones and sand castles.

Don't let the "City" in North Shore's "Tahoe City" fool you: The entire town can be driven through in about 40 seconds, whereas South Lake Tahoe is brimming with high-rise casinos, condominiums, and minimalls. Which side you choose to stay on is important because driving from one end of the lake to the other is a 3-hour affair on summer weekends and downright treacherous during snowstorms, so don't make the common mistake of thinking you can sleep for cheap on the South Shore and party all day on the North.

So which side is for you? If you're here to gamble, stay south: The selection of casinos is better and the lodging more abundant. If it's the great outdoors you're after, or simply a little R&R in the shade of a Douglas fir, head north. The North Shore offers a far better selection of quality lodgings, restaurants, and scenery, whereas the South Shore shoots for quantity, offering three times as many lodgings and restaurants at better rates.

More important to the visitor, however, is this region's pristine beauty: the play of light during the day, which transforms the color of the lake from a dazzling emerald to blues and rich purples; the snowy mountaintops reflecting off the water; the fresh, crisp air; and the deep green of the trees carpeting the expanse of the valley. It's a sight that no one should miss, and that nobody ever forgets.

Though the private homes surrounding the lake are reserved for the wealthy—the price tag of most lakefront abodes starts in the millions—Lake Tahoe is by no means solely a rich person's retreat. Droves of college students on extended sabbatical account for a healthy portion of the population. As a result, cheap cafes and coffeehouses catering to underpaid "lifties" (ski lift operators) and rafting guides line both ends of the lake, and a slew of inexpensive hotels continues to be built for the thousands of gamblers who make the pilgrimage here year-round.

In short, you don't need a bundle of cash to have a good time in Tahoe. What's more, some of the best things to see and do around the lake—hiking, mountain biking, cross-country skiing—are free. The trick is to know where to stay, eat, and play.

ESSENTIALS

GETTING THERE   It's a 4-hour drive from San Francisco; take I-80 east to Sacramento, then U.S. 50 to the lake's south shore, or I-80 east to Calif. 89 south to reach the lake's north shore.

From Los Angeles, it's a grueling 9-hour drive; take I-5 through the Central Valley to I-80 east at Sacramento, then U.S. 50 east. If the weather's good and you can spare a few additional hours, it's really worth avoiding the interstate for the scenic drive on U.S. 395 and U.S. 50, which lie along the corridor between the towering peaks of the eastern Sierra and the Inyo Mountain Range.

Reno/Tahoe International Airport, 40 miles northeast of Lake Tahoe (about a 50-min. drive), offers regularly scheduled service from 13 national airlines, including **American** (☎ 800/433-7300), **Delta** (☎ 800/221-1212), and **United/United Express** (☎ 800/241-6522).

Lake Tahoe & Environs

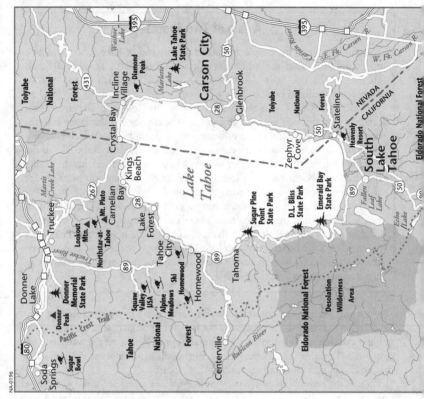

Amtrak (☎ 800/USA-RAIL) services Truckee, 10 miles north of the lake; shuttle service is available to North Lake Tahoe from the station. Trains connect with the rest of the state through Sacramento.

VISITOR INFORMATION   Call the **North Lake Tahoe Resort Association** in Tahoe City (☎ **800/824-6348** or 530/583-3494), or stop by the Resort Association's **Visitor Service Center** at 245 N. Lake Blvd., Tahoe City (☎ **800/824-6348**). It's open Monday through Friday from 9am to 5pm, Saturday and Sunday from 9am to 4pm.

In South Lake Tahoe, there's the **Lake Tahoe Visitors Authority,** 1156 Ski Run Blvd. (☎ **800/AT-TAHOE,** 800/288-2463, or 530/544-5050), which is open Monday through Friday 9am to 5pm, and the **South Lake Tahoe Chamber of Commerce,** 3066 Lake Tahoe Blvd. (☎ **530/541-5255**), which is open Monday through Friday from 8:30am to 5pm and Saturday from 9am to 4pm (closed on major holidays).

HITTING THE SLOPES

Tahoe offers California's best skiing, with 14 downhill-ski resorts and 11 cross-country centers. The ski season usually lasts from November through May, but frequently extends into the early summer (in 1995 there was skiing until July 4th!). Lift tickets are expensive, unfortunately, usually costing about $40 to $45 per day, $30 per half day, and $6 for children under 13.

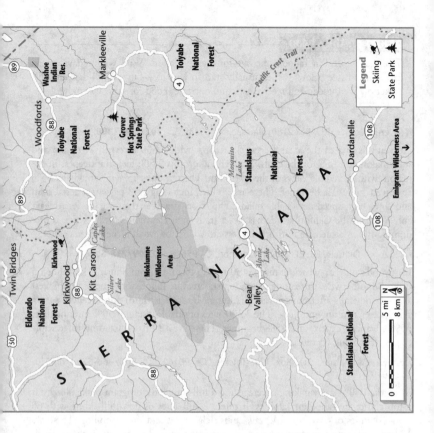

If you've come to ski, contact both visitor offices (see above) for information about the ski packages offered by almost every hotel and resort on the lake—you're likely to save a bundle. The following are some of Tahoe's most popular resorts.

✪ **Alpine Meadows.** P.O. Box 5279, Tahoe City, CA 96145. ☎ **800/441-4423** or 530/583-4232.

Six miles from Tahoe City, Alpine has a high elevation (8,637 ft.) that gives it a long skiing season, often lasting until Memorial Day. The midsize resort—ranked by readers of *Snow Country* magazine as their favorite resort in California—is a great all-around performer, with 40% of the terrain groomed for intermediate skiers, 35% for advanced, and 25% for beginners. Recent additions include Tahoe's only six-passenger high-speed chair and a new terrain park and half-pipe for snowboarders.

Diamond Peak. 1210 Ski Way, Incline Village, NV 89451. ☎ **702/832-1177** or 702/831-3249.

One of Tahoe's smaller—and less crowded, less expensive—ski resorts, Diamond Peak plugs itself as the "premier family ski resort." It's primarily a mountain for intermediates (49%), with 33% of the mountain groomed for advanced, and 18% for beginners. Kids love the new snowboard park and sledding area. There's also cross-country skiing and snowshoeing, as well as dining and lodging in nearby Incline Village.

Skiing on the Cheap

The best ski deal in Tahoe is the two-for-one special on "Wild Wednesdays" at Ski Homewood (see below), which usually start in January—buy one all-day adult lift ticket on Wednesday and receive a second one free (good for same day only).

Heavenly Resort. P.O. Box 2180, Stateline, NV 89449. ☎ **702/586-7000.**

Heavenly is one of the area's largest ski resorts, with 4,800 acres of ski terrain and snowmaking on 66% of the trails. The vertical drop is 3,500 feet, the steepest in the region, with incredible views of the lake basin. The terrain is 45% intermediate, 35% advanced, and 20% beginner. There are 25 lifts, including a 50-passenger aerial tram and three high-speed detachable quads. The resort straddles the state borders; Heavenly West on the California side has easier trails than Heavenly North, which is predominantly intermediate territory. It's less crowded, however, on the Nevada side.

Kirkwood. Off Calif. 88, P.O. Box 1, Kirkwood, CA 95646. ☎ **209/258-6000.**

Kirkwood's only drawback is that it's 30 miles (45 min.) from South Lake Tahoe on Calif. 88; otherwise, this is one of the top ski areas in Tahoe, with one of the highest average snowfalls after Squaw Valley (Alpine Meadows is third) and excellent spring skiing often running into June. The 2,300 acres of skiable terrain is 50% intermediate, 35% advanced/expert, and 15% beginner. There are 12 lifts—including three triple chairs—accessing 65 trails.

Northstar-at-Tahoe. P.O. Box 129, Truckee, CA 96160. ☎ **800/466-6784** or 530/562-1010.

More than 50% snowmaking coverage and a full-time kids' program make Northstar a top choice in Tahoe for families. It offers 2,000 acres of downhill skiing with 60 runs, 37 miles of cross-country trails, plus sleigh rides and snowmobiling. There are 12 lifts, including a six-passenger express gondola and four express quad chairs. Facilities include on-site lodging and five restaurants. It's only 45 minutes from the Reno-Tahoe airport.

Ski Homewood. 5145 W. Lake Blvd. (P.O. Box 165), Homewood, CA 96141. ☎ **530/525-2992.**

Homewood is one of our favorite small ski areas, a homey little resort with lean lift lines and gorgeous views of the lake. The ski area covers 1,260 acres and offers 57 trails and 18 lifts. It's a good family resort, with child care for 2- to 6-year-olds and a special Snow Stars program for kids 6 to 12. It's located 6 miles south of Tahoe City and 19 miles north of South Lake Tahoe.

✪ **Squaw Valley USA.** Squaw Valley, CA 96146. ☎ **800/545-4350** or 530/583-6985.

Site of the 1960 Olympic Winter Games, Squaw is almost every serious skier's favorite resort, simply because it offers the most challenging array of runs. Squaw's terrain is 25% for beginners, 45% intermediate, and 30% advanced/expert/insane. There are 33 chairlifts, including a 120-passenger tram. It's famous for the chutes called the Palisades and the acrobatic skiing that they inspire. Skiing is spread across six mountains.

The **Squaw Creek Cross-Country Ski Center** at the Resort at Squaw Creek (☎ **530/583-6300**) has 400 acres for touring and 28 miles of groomed trails.

Sugar Bowl. P.O. Box 5, Norden, CA 95724. ☎ **530/426-4000.**

Although it was ranked by *Ski* magazine in 1994 as one of the top 30 resorts in the nation, Sugar Bowl's best attribute is its location: If you're driving to Tahoe from the

Tips for Saving Money on Your Ski Vacation

Yeah, we know, $45 for a ski lift ticket is awfully steep, but there are ways around it if you do a little advance planning. The number one money saver is to buy one of the ski packages offered by most hotels—you're likely to cut the lift ticket price in half. Other options are to ski midweek, buy a multiday pass, or wait until the spring ski season, when rates are usually 20% less. Half-day passes are another option; they're usually sold only for afternoons, but some resorts will let you ski the first half of the day and refund the difference if you turn your pass in before 1pm (a good idea during the spring season when the slopes get too slushy in the afternoon anyway). Another option is to ski the smaller, cheaper resorts: Boreal, Tahoe Donner, Soda Springs, Mt. Rose, and Diamond Peak are all about $10 to $20 less than the big resorts. And don't forget about Ski Homewood's two-for-one Wednesdays (see "Skiing on the Cheap," above).

Bay Area via I-80, it's about an hour's drive closer than Squaw Valley. Known for its deep snowpack (does "powder skiing" mean anything to you?), the midsize resort has 58 runs serviced by eight lifts. Whether it's worth the drive from the lake is questionable, but anyone coming up from the valley should seriously consider this one. Should you choose to stay, lodging is available at the base of the resort.

CROSS-COUNTRY SKIING & OTHER WINTERTIME FUN

CROSS-COUNTRY SKIING   Lakeview Cross Country (☎ 530/583-9353) has 37 miles of groomed trails, a full-service day lodge, and three warming huts. It's only 2 miles from Tahoe City off Calif. 28 at Dollar Point Shell, making it very accessible.

The **Royal Gorge Cross-Country Ski Resort,** Soda Springs (☎ **800/500-3871** or 530/426-3871), is one of the largest cross-country facilities anywhere, with 88 trails (203 miles), including 28 novice trails and four ski lifts. Facilities include a day lodge, wilderness lodge, ski school, 10 warming huts, and four trailside cafes. It's 1 mile off I-80 at the Soda Springs exit.

Sugar Pine Point State Park (☎ 530/525-7982) also has cross-country skiing on well-maintained trails. The park is located on the west side of the lake, halfway between North and South Lake Tahoe on Calif. 89. You can't miss it—just look for the big sign on the side of the road.

ICE-SKATING   One of the world's most unusual ice rinks is at Squaw Valley's **High Camp** (☎ 530/583-6985). The ice is accessible only by tram—a scenic ride that's included with admission. Skating costs $19 for adults and $10 for children, including cable-car ride and skate rentals. After 4pm the prices drop to $11 for adults and $8 for children. The rink is open year-round daily from 11am to 9pm. Call first, as the rink closes a few days in the spring and fall for maintenance.

SNOWMOBILING   Snowmobiles are available for rent at several locations in the Lake Tahoe area. The **Zephyr Cove Snowmobile Center** (☎ 702/882-0788) is about 4 miles north of Stateline, Nevada, on the lake's east side. It offers 2-hour guided snowmobile tours from November 26 to April 15 (weather permitting). Tours are scheduled usually three times daily—at 10am, 12:15pm, and 2:30pm—and cost $74 for a single rider and $99 for two people on one snowmobile (limit 400 lbs.). Special moonlight tours are also offered.

High Sierra Snowmobiling, Calif. 267 and Calif. 28, Kings Beach (☎ **530/546-9909**), is open from November 15 to April 1 (again, weather permitting). It

Cheap Thrills: What to See & Do for Free (or Almost) in Tahoe

Nothing beats a cheap thrill, and Tahoe is loaded with them. Your most affordable adventures will inevitably involve getting outside and taking in the area's natural wonders. Take a drive around the lake, hike to a scenic vista and have a picnic lunch, soak up some rays on the beach. Whatever you choose to do, if it's a sunny day (and it probably will be), we promise you won't be disappointed. Here's some other inexpensive and offbeat things to do in and around Tahoe:

If you visit in winter and skiing just isn't in the budget, revisit the childhood thrill of **sledding.** On the South Shore the best place to go is directly across from the tiny South Lake Tahoe Airport, which is about a 15-minute drive south of town on U.S. 50. Park in the lot, cross the street, and start lugging your sled up the hill. The slope is small, but it's fast, fun, and free of trees.

Now that the lake is full again, tourists can partake in Tahoe's cheapest and most popular thrill of all: feeding the trout that hang out below **Fanny Bridge** (located at the intersection of Calif. 28 and Calif. 89 in Tahoe City). Bring bread or crackers and join the others leaning over the rail. If you step back and take a look, you'll know how the bridge got its name.

At some point during your visit you should get out on the water. We recommend trolling along the shores on a sit-on-top sea kayak. They're almost uncapsizable and require no previous experience; you'll discover places you'd never see otherwise. On the North Shore, **Tahoe Paddle and Oar,** 7860 N. Lake Blvd., Kings Beach (☎ **530/581-3029**), rents kayaks for about $10 an hour, and on the South Shore **Kayak Tahoe,** 3411 Lake Tahoe Blvd. at Timber Cove Marina (☎ **530/544-2011**), rents kayaks for about $14 an hour. Two-seater kayaks are also available at both locations.

For the ultimate sunset experience, you can ride the **Squaw Valley cable car** (☎ **530/583-6985**) after 5pm for only $5 (that's $9 off the regular price) and

offers no trail tours, just a manicured track, for which it charges $30 per half hour. High Sierra is open daily from 9am to 5pm.

BIKING, HIKING & OTHER SUMMERTIME FUN

BIKING   There are miles of excellent paved bike paths around the lake. The 3.4-mile **Pope-Baldwin Bike Path** on the south shore runs parallel to Calif. 89 and through Camp Richardson and the Tallac Historic Site. In South Lake Tahoe, another paved path runs from El Dorado Beach along the lake, paralleling U.S. 50. Along the west shore there are 15 miles of paved pathways, extending from Tahoe City in three directions. On the northeast shore, Incline Village has a 2½-mile trail from Gateway Park on Calif. 28.

You can rent bikes in Tahoe City at **Porter's Ski and Sport,** 501 N. Lake Blvd. (☎ **530/583-2314**), and in Incline Village at another Porter's location, 885 Tahoe Blvd. (☎ 702/831-3500). In South Lake Tahoe, go to **Anderson's Bike Rental** on the lake side of Calif. 89 at 13th Street (☎ **530/541-0500**). Bike rentals usually cost $7 per hour, $20 for 4 hours, and $25 per day.

BOAT RENTALS   Several companies rent a variety of boats—canoes, powerboats, and pedal boats. Among them are: **Zephyr Cove Resort Marina** (☎ 702/588-3833), which rents all three; **Paradise Watercraft** at Camp Richardson Resort (☎ 530/ 541-1801); **Tahoe Keys Boat Rentals** at Tahoe Keys Marina (☎ 530/544-8888 or

hang out at the High Camp, a miniresort—complete with a restaurant, bar, and ice rink—near the top of the mountain that sports a gorgeous view of the lake basin. The 8-minute ride also offers incredible vistas as you rise 2,000 feet above the valley floor. The last ride up departs at 8:40pm. Open daily year-round.

If you feel the urge for golf but don't have the time or the money, consider miniature golf. The Putt-Putt season in Tahoe runs from mid-May through September (depending on the weather). On the North Shore head for **Magic Carpet Golf** at Carnelian Bay, 5167 N. Lake Blvd. (☎ **530/546-4279**); on the South Shore, there's **Fantasy Kingdom Miniature Golf,** 4046 Lake Tahoe Blvd. (☎ **530/544-3833**).

At the **Headwall Cafe and Climbing** (☎ **530/583-ROPE**), at the base of the Squaw Valley Tram off Calif. 89 in Squaw Valley, you can test your strength on an artificial 30-foot climbing wall for $12. A sturdy harness prevents you from falling, which makes it perfectly safe for kids (who usually out-climb the adults). It's an exhilarating challenge, and the best part is that absolutely no experience is necessary. Open daily year-round.

At the end of the day, soak yourself at the **North Tahoe Beach Center,** 7860 N. Lake Blvd., Kings Beach (☎ **530/546-2566**). Besides offering a full line of exercise equipment, the center also boasts the largest spa on the lake, some 26 feet in diameter—all this for $7. It's open daily from 10am to 10pm.

Another spa that's popular with the locals is **Walley's Hot Springs Resort** (☎ **702/782-8155**). You'll need wheels to get there (it's located 2 miles north of the east end of Kingsbury Grade at 2001 Foothill Blvd. in Nevada), but it's worth the drive to indulge in their six open-air pools (each a bit warmer than the next) and massage center. Last we checked, admission was only $12.

530/541-8405), which only rents powerboats; and **North Tahoe Marina,** Calif. 28, 1 mile west of Calif. 267, Tahoe Vista (☎ 530/546-8248), which rents skis and tow lines along with 18- to 21-foot motorboats. Canoes and kayaks can be rented from **Tahoe Paddle & Oar** in Tahoe City (☎ 530/581-3029).

FISHING   Fishing in the crystal-clear waters of the lake presents a special challenge to anglers. Deep-water fishing for mackinaw trout is good year-round. Surface fishing for kokanee salmon is best in May and June, whereas fishing for rainbow trout is ideal in the fall and winter months.

There are dozens of charter companies offering daily excursions on Lake Tahoe year-round. **Mickey's Big Mack Charters,** Tahoe City (☎ 800/877-1462 after 6pm, or 530/546-4444), is a well-respected outfit, led by experienced guide Mickey Daniels. All the fishing gear is provided, but you'll need a license, which can be purchased on the boat. Call for requirements and reservations. Mickey's boats depart from Sierra Boat Co., in Carnelian Bay, about 5 miles north of Tahoe City. Five-hour trips cost $65 per person (or 3 hr. for $45) and depart daily year-round, in the early morning and late afternoon; exact times vary according to season. Other fishing specialists include **Blue Ribbon Fishing Charters,** South Lake Tahoe (☎ 530/541-8801); and **Tahoe Sportfishing,** Ski Run Marina, 900 Ski Run Blvd., South Lake Tahoe (☎ 530/541-5448).

FITNESS CENTERS/SPAS   At the end of the day, soak your sore bones at the **North Tahoe Beach Center,** 7860 N. Lake Blvd., at Kings Beach (☎ **530/ 546-2566**). Besides offering a full line of exercise equipment, the center also boasts the largest spa on the lake, some 26 feet in diameter. It's all yours for $7 for adults and $3 for kids under 12; kids under 4 are free. It's open daily from 10am to 10pm (on Mon, Wed, and Fri it opens at 7am). Another spa that's popular with the locals is **Walley's Hot Springs Resort** (☎ **702/782-8155**), located 2 miles north of the east end of Kingsbury Grade at 2001 Foothill Blvd. in Nevada. It's worth the drive to indulge in their six open-air pools (each a bit warmer than the next) and massage center. Admission is $12.

HIKING   The mountains surrounding Lake Tahoe are crisscrossed with hiking trails graded for all levels of experience. Before setting out, you may wish to contact the local visitor bureau for a map and more in-depth information on particular trails, or hire a guide. From $25 to $60 per person—depending on the hike, group size, and transportation—an experienced mountaineer from **Tahoe Trips & Trails** (☎ **800/ 581-HIKE** or 530/583-4506) will take anyone, from Grandpa to Rambo, on a guided hike specifically suited to each person's ability, ranging from super-easy to hard-core hoofin' it. Everything is provided, including a gourmet vegetarian-friendly lunch, drinks, transportation, and answers to any questions you have about the history and geology of Lake Tahoe. It's truly a great outfit that guarantees a good time at a fair price.

Some of the most popular trails in the area are:

Eagle Falls/Eagle Lake: One of the best trails for novice hikers, the Eagle Falls walk offers a cascading reward. The trail begins at Eagle Picnic Area, directly on Calif. 89 across from Emerald Bay.

Emerald Bay/Vikingsholm: From the parking area, 1½ miles above Tahoe's prettiest inlet, you can hike down to Vikingsholm, a 38-room replica of a medieval Scandinavian castle. The trail begins at the parking area on the north side of Emerald Bay, on Calif. 89.

Loch Levon Lakes: An easy but beautiful walk to three lakes, the Loch Levon trail is perfect for hikers who wish to stay on the beaten path. To reach the trailhead, take I-80 to the Big Bend exit and look for the sign PRIVATE ROAD PUBLIC TRAIL across from the Big Bend ranger station.

Shirley Lake: In Squaw Valley, near the tram line, this excellent hike has the advantage of a one-way adventure: You can take the tram up and hike down, or vice versa. The trail begins at the end of Squaw Peak Road, next to the cable-car building.

HORSEBACK RIDING   Camp Richardson Corral, South Lake Tahoe (☎ **530/ 541-3113**), offers a variety of trail rides and pack trips. A 2-hour trail ride is $35, whereas pack trips cost $150 per day, including packer, livestock, food, boat, and tackle. From December through March, sleigh rides are offered.

Northstar Stables, 2499 Northstar Dr. and Calif. 267 (☎ **530/562-2267**), at the resort of the same name, offers a variety of trail rides, lessons, and pack trips. Special breakfast and dinner rides are also available. Children under the age of 7 are not allowed on trail rides. Northstar is on the north side of Lake Tahoe, between Kings Beach and Truckee. Prices range from $5 for pony rides to $28 for 1½ hours, $50 for half-day rides, and $100 for a full day. Call for pack-trip information. Open year-round, daily from 9am to 5pm; when winter prohibits trail rides, sleigh rides are available.

Squaw Valley Stables, 1525 Squaw Valley Rd. (☎ **530/583-7433**), offers trail rides and lessons for all ages and riding levels. Squaw Valley is about 5 miles north of

Tahoe City. Prices range from $19 for a 1-hour guided ride to $55 for a half-day ride. Pony rides are $6 per half hour. Open mid-May to early September daily from 8:30am to 4:30pm.

Sunset Ranch, U.S. 50, South Lake Tahoe (☎ 530/541-9001), is the only stable to allow unescorted riding. A quarter of a mile west of the Lake Tahoe Airport, Sunset Ranch offers rides to both children and adults along the open meadows that abut the Truckee River. Prices are $21 per hour, or $31 per hour for two people on a single horse; children 12 and under are $16. Open year-round, daily from 9am to 6pm.

IN-LINE SKATING   Although there are trails all around Lake Tahoe, the best ones for blading are the well-paved BICYCLE AND PEDESTRIANS ONLY paths that hug the Truckee River and Calif. 89, between Tahoe City and Squaw Valley. In-line skates can be rented from the nearby **Squaw Valley Sport Shop,** Tahoe City (☎ 530/583-6278). The shop charges $12 for a half day, $18 for a full day (the price covers wrist guards and other protective gear). The shop is open Sunday through Thursday from 9am to 6pm, Friday and Saturday from 9am to 7pm.

JET-SKIING   The **Lighthouse Watersports Center,** 950 N. Lake Blvd., Tahoe City (☎ 530/583-7245), rents jet skis, paddleboats, and canoes during summer months only. Reservations are recommended for jet-ski rentals. Jet skis cost $35 per half hour and $60 per hour; paddleboats and canoes go for $15 per half hour and $20 for 2 hours. The water-sports center is open June through September, daily from 9am to 6pm.

In South Lake Tahoe, the place to rent is **Lakeview Sports,** 3131 U.S. 50, across from the El Dorado Campground (☎ 530/544-0183 or 530/541-8405). They also rent mountain bikes, in-line skates, and boats.

MOUNTAIN BIKING   At both **Northstar** (☎ 530/562-1010) and **Squaw Valley** (☎ 530/583-6985), you can ride the cable car (Squaw) or lift chair (Northstar) with your bike and ride the trails all the way down (call for complete information), but a far more rewarding experience can be had by setting up a guided off-road tour with **Cyclepaths Mountain Bike Adventures** (☎ 800/780-BIKE or 530/581-1171). Whether you're into hard-core downhill single-track or easy-going scenic outings, the expert guides will provide you will all the necessary equipment, food, and transportation. Cyclepaths is located at 1785 W. Lake Blvd. in Tahoe Park, a few miles south of Tahoe City. Check out their Web site at www.tahoecountry.com/cyclepaths.

If you would rather to go it on your own, the numerous sports stores in Tahoe City and South Lake Tahoe all carry books and maps to the mountain-biking trails around the lake. Be sure to carry plenty of water and wear strong sunscreen.

RIVER RAFTING   The Truckee River—Lake Tahoe's only outlet—dumps plenty of water for a swift but gentle ride. Rafts seat anywhere from 2 to 14 people and cost about $25 per person for adults and $20 per person for kids (no kids under 5); the season runs from Memorial Day weekend to Labor Day. Rafting outfits include **Truckee River Raft Rental** (☎ 530/583-0123), **Fanny Bridge Rafts** (☎ 530/581-0123), and **Truckee River Rafting/Mountain Air Sports** (☎ 530/583-7238).

TENNIS   All the major resorts have tennis courts open to the public on a fee basis. Call the **Resort at Squaw Creek** (☎ 530/583-6300) or **Northstar** (☎ 530/562-0321) for information and reservations.

Budget-minded players looking for good local courts should visit Tahoe Lake School, Grove Street, Tahoe City, where two lighted courts are available free on a first-come, first-served basis. South Tahoe Intermediate School, Lyons Avenue off U.S. 50, has eight lighted courts. It charges a manageable $3 per hour.

WINDSURFING Easy winds and relatively calm conditions make Lake Tahoe an ideal place to learn. **Lakeside Chalets,** 5240 N. Lake Blvd., Carnelian Bay (☎ 530/546-5857), rents boards and offers lessons by appointment, June through September. Windsurfers cost $20 per initial hour and $10 per hour thereafter ($50 to $60 a day).

LAKE CRUISES

The best way to experience the lake is to get out on it. **MS *Dixie II,*** Zephyr Cove Marina, Nevada (☎ 702/588-3508), a 570-passenger vessel with bars, a dance floor, and a full dining room, offers daily cruises year-round, which may include breakfast, champagne brunch, or dinner. Zephyr Cove Marina is on U.S. 50, 4 miles north of Stateline in South Lake Tahoe. Bay cruises cost $16 for adults and $5 for children 11 and under; breakfast and brunch cruises, $18 for adults and $9 for children; dinner cruises, $28 to $38 for adults and $12 for children. Call for schedules.

The ***Tahoe Queen*** (☎ 800/238-2463 or 530/541-3364), a 500-passenger stern-wheeler, operates year-round, offering daily Emerald Bay cruises, sunset dinner-dance cruises, and shuttle service between the lake's north and south shores during the ski season. There are large outdoor and indoor viewing decks and a glass bottom for peering deep into the lake. The Emerald Bay Cruise costs $14 for adults and $5 for children 11 and under; dinner cruise, $18 for adults and $9.50 for children (dinner optional, menu selections from $15); round-trip North/South Shore Ski Shuttle, $18 for adults and $9 for children. The *Tahoe Queen* departs from Ski Run Marina, just west of Stateline. Call to confirm rates and schedules.

The North Shore version of *Tahoe Queen* is the ***Tahoe Gal*** (☎ 800/218-2464 or 530/583-0141), a Mississippi River paddle wheeler that departs from the Lighthouse Marina in Tahoe City (behind Safeway). Cruises include Emerald Bay ($20 for adults and $8 for children) and Scenic Shoreline ($15 for adults and $5 for children). Dinner is available for an additional $15 for adults and $5 for children.

Woodwind **Sailing Cruises,** in the Zephyr Cove Resort, on U.S. 50, Zephyr Cove, Nevada (☎ 702/588-3000), offers daily sailing trips aboard a 41-foot trihull craft that takes up to 30 passengers, as well as a new 55-foot catamaran. Both boats have glass bottoms that allow for good underwater viewing. Reservations are recommended. Trips are $18 for adults, $9 for children under 12, and free for children under 2. Trips start daily at 11:30am, 1, 2:30, and 4pm from April through October. There's also a sunset champagne cruise for $26 (adults only).

A DRIVE AROUND THE LAKE

Other than cruising over it, the next best way to contemplate the lake is to drive the 72 miles around it, although at times the route can be completely clogged with traffic. And while the lake has never frozen over, the roads that surround it do; many are closed in winter, making this trip possible during summer only. If your car sports a tape deck, consider buying *Drive Around the Lake,* a drive-along audio cassette that contains facts, tales and legends, places of interest, and just about everything else you could possibly want to know about the lake. It's available at numerous gift shops or at the **South Lake Tahoe Chamber of Commerce,** 3066 Lake Tahoe Blvd. (☎ 530/541-5255), which is open Monday through Friday from 8:30am to 5pm and Saturday from 9am to 4pm (closed on major holidays).

We'll start at the California/Nevada border in South Lake Tahoe and loop around the western shore on Calif. 89 to Tahoe City and beyond. U.S. 50, which runs along the south shore, is an ugly, overdeveloped strip that obliterates any view of the lake unless you're staying at one of these motels. Keep heading west and you'll soon be free of this ugly zone.

First stop is the **Tallac Historic Site,** a cluster of rustic mansions that were built 100 years ago and are currently being restored by the Forest Service. A little farther on you'll find the Forest Service's **Lake Tahoe Visitors Center** located along Taylor Creek, which offers nature trails and as well as an opportunity to view kokanee salmon making their way upstream to spawn.

From here Calif. 89 climbs northward. Soon you'll be peering down into beautiful **Emerald Bay,** a 3-mile-long inlet containing tiny Fanette Island, which has an old stone teahouse clearly situated at its peak. It was built by Lora Knight, who also built Vikingsholm (see below).

Across Calif. 89 from Emerald Bay, there's another parking area. From here it's a short, steep, quarter-mile hike to a footbridge above Eagle Falls. Then it's about 1 mile to Eagle Lake. Register at the trailhead. **Emerald Bay State Park** (☎ 530/988-0205) offers 100 camping sites on the south side of the bay.

It's not surprising that someone chose to build a mansion right here overlooking the bay—**Vikingsholm,** Emerald Bay, Calif. 89 (☎ **530/525-7277** or 530/525-7232). Constructed in 1929, this 38-room mansion is a replica of a medieval Viking castle. It is so striking that a paved parking area on the highway had to be built for all the gawkers. Tree branches shaped like spears jut out from the gutters to ward off evil spirits. Inside, carved dragon heads decorate the ceiling beams. A layer of sod blankets the roof, which sprouts wildflowers in the spring. You can visit Vikingsholm by hiking down a steep 1-mile trail (but remember, you have to come back up, too). The mansion is open for tours, every half hour on the hour and half hour, during summer only. Admission is $3 for adults, $2 for children 6 to 12, and free for kids under 6. It's open June 3 to Labor Day daily from 10am to 4pm.

From here it's only about 2 miles to **D. L. Bliss State Park** (☎ **530/525-7277**), where you'll find one of the lake's best beaches. It gets very crowded in summer, so arrive early before all the parking places are occupied. The park also contains 168 campsites and several trails, including one along the shoreline.

About 7 miles farther on, **Sugar Pine Point State Park** (☎ **530/525-7982**) is the largest (2,000 acres) of the lake's parks and also the only one that has year-round camping. In summer, you can visit one of several beaches in the park plus a nature trail; in winter, there's cross-country skiing on well-maintained trails.

It's a clear drive through the small town of Homewood (site of the ski resort of the same name) to **Tahoe City,** which is smaller and much more appealing than South Lake Tahoe, although it, too, has its share of strip development.

At Tahoe City, Calif. 89 turns off to **Truckee** and to Alpine Meadows and Squaw Valley ski resorts. Squaw Valley is only 5 miles out, and a ride on the **Squaw Valley cable car** (☎ **530/583-6985**) rewards visitors with incredible vistas from 2,000 feet above the valley floor. The cable car operates year-round, daily from 8am to 8:40pm (the last ride up). A ticket is $14 for adults, $12 for seniors 65 and over, $5 for children 4 to 12, and free for children under 3. From Squaw Valley, it's another 5 or so miles to the railroad town of Truckee and **Donner State Park,** with its museum and monument to the Donner Party Expedition of 1846.

If you continue around the lake on Calif. 28, you'll reach Carnelian Bay, Tahoe Vista, and Kings Beach before crossing the state line into Nevada to Crystal Bay, Incline Village, the Ponderosa Ranch, and Sand Harbor Beach. **Kings Beach State Recreation Area** (☎ **530/546-7248**), 12 miles east of Tahoe City, is jammed in summer with sunbathers and swimmers. From Incline Village, a 4-mile side trip up the Mount Rose Highway leads to an overlook of the entire Tahoe Basin.

Remember Hoss and Little Joe Cartwright? The ✪ **Ponderosa Ranch,** Calif. 28, Incline Village (☎ **702/831-0691**), is a theme park inspired by the popular 1960s television show *Bonanza*. The original 1959 Cartwright Ranch House can be visited

along with a western township complete with blacksmith's shop and staged gun battles. There are also such activities as pony rides and a petting farm. The barbecue grill
is almost always fired up, and breakfast hayrides on tractor-pulled wagons are offered
for an extra $2. Admission is $9.50 for adults, $5.50 for children 5 to 11, and free for
children under 5. It's open mid-April through October only, daily from 9:30am
to 5pm.

Also at Incline Village is **Sand Harbor,** one of the best beaches on the lake (though
it can get incredibly crowded in summer).

South of Sand Harbor, if you wish, you can then turn inland to Spooner Lake and
Carson City, capital of Nevada, or continue south along Calif. 28 to an outcropping
called **Cave Rock,** where the highway passes through 25 yards of solid stone. Farther
along is **Zephyr Cove,** from which the tour boats depart. You'll then return to Stateline and South Lake Tahoe, your original starting point.

WHERE TO STAY
SOUTH SHORE/SOUTH LAKE TAHOE
Super-Cheap Sleeps
Chamonix Inn. 913 Friday Ave. (at Manzanita Ave.), South Lake Tahoe, CA 96150. ☎ **800/
447-5353** or 530/544-5274. 32 units. TV TEL. $35–$125 double. AE, DISC, MC, V.

Although it invokes about as much French atmosphere as a fillet-o-fish sandwich, the
Chamonix Inn is a budget skier's paradise. Start the day fueling up at the on-premises
coffee shop, then walk 20 yards to the free ski shuttle stop. After a hard day of skiing,
relax in the toasty spa, then gear up for a night of gambling, courtesy of another free
shuttle. Summer seductions include a heated pool and access to a private beach where
you can rent paddle boats. The rooms aren't anything fancy, but they are all tidy and
come with phones, remote control TVs with HBO, and big, firm beds. Skiers should
definitely inquire about the Chamonix's ski packages.

Emerald Motel. 515 Emerald Bay Rd./Calif. 89, South Lake Tahoe, CA 96150. ☎ **530/
544-5515.** 9 units. TV TEL. $45–$59 double. MC, V.

If you prefer to stay on the South Shore but want to distance yourself from the hustle
and bustle of the casinos, this small green-and-white motel on the west side of town
is the budget-minded traveler's best option. The rooms are rather ordinary, but they
are all clean and come with the basics—queen beds, cable TV, microwaves, and coffeemakers. For a few dollars more you can get a room with a kitchenette or fireplace,
a real deal for Lake Tahoe. Although the downtown area is out of walking range, there
are a handful of good, inexpensive restaurants just down the street, including Cantina
Bar & Grill, a local favorite. Also within hoofing distance are all the major ski shuttle
stops, a supermarket, and a movie theater.

Lamplighter Motel. 4143 Cedar Ave., South Lake Tahoe, CA 96159. ☎ **888/544-4055** or
530/544-2936. Fax 530/544-5249. 28 units, all with bathroom (25 with shower only). TV TEL.
$36–$55 double. AE, DISC, JCB, MC, V.

A diamond in the rough, this family-run motel is everything the budget traveler could
hope for: clean, cozy, and loaded with perks such as cable TV, in-room coffeemaker,
and a ceiling fan (a few also have bathtubs). It's in a great spot, only 3 blocks from the
beach and 50 yards from the casinos, but why you would ever want to leave the open-
air spa and sundeck is beyond us. Be sure to inquire about the terrific ski packages,
and request the room with air-conditioning in summer.

For a Few Bucks More/Moderately Priced Options
Lakeland Village Beach & Ski Resort. 3535 Lake Tahoe Blvd., South Lake Tahoe, CA
96150. ☎ **800/822-5969** or 530/544-1685. Fax 530/541-6278. 210 condo units. A/C
(except in town house) TV TEL. $90–$175 double. AE, MC, V.

Off-Season Deals

Spring and **fall** are Tahoe's slowest seasons, when the snow hasn't quite melted (or fallen) and the summer's heat has yet to arrive (or leave). It's the lull every Tahoe business owner dreads, but a boon for visitors looking to save a bundle. To drum up some business, the **North Lake Tahoe Resort Association** (☎ 800/824-6348 or 530/583-3494) has put together two fantastic packages: **Spring Fling** and **Tahoe Autumn Package.** Spring Fling offers two-for-one skiing at Alpine Meadows (consecutive days), two-for-one lodging, two-for-one dining, and even two-for-one coupons for bicycle, ski, snowboard, and in-line-skate rentals, sightseeing tours, massages, and lake cruises—all starting at $70 per person from April 15 to June 14.

Available from October 1 to December 17 and starting at $100, Fall in Tahoe includes 2-night lodging at economy inns, B&Bs, or gaming resorts; one dinner (from a selection of great restaurants); one breakfast or lunch; and one activity of choice per person, which ranges from horseback riding to lake cruises and cable-car rides.

The Lakeland Village is a good choice for families or a group of friends who want to room together and split the cost. Clustered on 19 lightly forested acres of prime shoreline property is this half-residential-apartment-half-holiday-resort complex, built in the 1970s as one of South Lake Tahoe's most ambitious developments. The layout is a complicated labyrinth of buildings whose wood sides blend into the surrounding landscape. The only drawback is the proximity to traffic headed into Lake Tahoe, although some units, placed out among the grounds, are quieter than those in the main lodge, which lies adjacent to the road. When you check in, be prepared for a baffling choice of layouts; the staff will present an array of floor plans. The units, ranging from studios to four-bedroom lakeside apartments, are streamlined California architecture, and many have upstairs sleeping lofts.

There are no restaurants on the premises, although complimentary shuttle buses carry gamblers to the nearby casinos, a grocery store is within walking distance, and all suites have fully equipped kitchens. Perks include two outdoor pools, three saunas, tennis and volleyball courts, a large private beach opening directly onto the lake, and access to a boat dock.

✪ **Richardson's Resort.** Calif. 89 at Jamison Beach, South Lake Tahoe, CA 96158. ☎ **800/544-1801** or 530/541-1801. Fax 530/541-1802. 29 units, 39 cabins. $69–$90 double; $550–$1,400 cabin, per week. AE, DISC, MC, V.

Rich or poor, this is one of the most enjoyable places to stay in Lake Tahoe. The resort is a collection of real log cabins, condominiums, hotel rooms, and tent/RV sites spread out over several acres of wooded grounds adjacent to the beach. If you're staying only a few nights, book a room in the classic old lodge, but for stays of a week or more (particularly with families or groups) the homey little cabins are the only way to go. Activities on the premises include volleyball, hiking, biking, horseback riding, cross-country skiing, and swimming and sunbathing. Nearby facilities include a bike-rental shop, general store, ice-cream parlor, boat/jet-ski/kayak-rental shop, full-service marina, casino shuttle service, and one of the best restaurants on the lake, The Beacon.

NORTH SHORE/TAHOE CITY
Super-Cheap Sleeps
Lake of the Sky Motor Inn. 955 N. Lake Blvd. (P.O. Box 227), Tahoe City, CA 96145. ☎ **530/583-3305.** 23 units. Apr 30–June 13 $50–$65 double; June 14–Sept 21 $75–$90 double; Sept 22–Apr 29 $50–$90 double; holidays $99–$105 double. AE, DC, DISC, MC, V.

Not much more than a 1960s-style A-frame motel in the heart of Tahoe City, the Lake of the Sky Motor Inn offers decent accommodations in a central location, only steps away from shops and restaurants. The place is popular with budget travelers and skiers, some of whom can be seen grabbing a very early morning cup of coffee and obviously itching to get out and tackle the wilderness. Rooms throughout have almost no style, but the housekeeping is good and the comfort level is in tiptop motor-inn tradition. There's a heated pool as well as a barbecue area.

Mother Nature's Inn. 551 N. Lake Blvd., P.O. Box 7075, Tahoe City, CA 96145. ☎ **530/583-0287.** 9 units. TV TEL. $55–$65 double. AE, MC, V.

Smack dab in the middle of Tahoe City, the Mother Nature's Inn (formerly the Family Tree Restaurant and Motel) is one of the best lodging deals in Tahoe. The rooms, located behind an art gallery and gift shop, are individually decorated with various wildlife themes (prints of bears, raccoons, and deer abound) and cute log furniture. You're offered a choice of a queen bed or two doubles, and most have air-conditioning. The best part, of course, is the location, with the entire town at your doorstep. Make reservations as early as possible, folks, because this place fills up fast.

North Lake Lodge. 8716 N. Lake Blvd. (P.O. Box 955), Kings Beach, CA 96143. ☎ **888/923-5253** or 530/546-2731. 21 units, 8 bungalows, 5 cabins. TV TEL. $50–$70 double; $50–$75 bungalow; $50–$80 cabin. AE, DISC, MC, V. Pets are welcome.

Sure, the private lakeside cabins at North Lake Lodge are a little on the funky side, but for as little as $50 a night most people are willing to put up with a few blemishes here and there. This is truly a great deal: Each unit, some dating from the 1920s, has its own bathroom, deck, and picnic facilities, and many have fully equipped kitchens and views of the lake (units without kitchens have refrigerators, coffeemakers, and microwaves). If the cabins are all booked, go for the bungalows next, and as a last resort the rooms in the lodge. There's a public beach nearby (as well as a boat ramp), and in the winter free shuttle buses from Alpine Meadows, Squaw, and Northstar swing by. Be sure to bring a bag of charcoal for the lodge's barbecue pits, and some chump change for the nearby casinos.

✪ **Tamarack Lodge.** 2311 N. Lake Blvd. (P.O. Box 859), Tahoe City, CA 96145. ☎ **888/TAHOEBED** or 530/583-3350. 17 units, 4 cabins. TV TEL. $36–$66 unit; $46–$111 cabin. DISC, MC, V.

One of the oldest lodges on the North Shore—so old it was a favorite haunt of Clark Gable and Gary Cooper—is now one of the best bets for the cost-conscious traveler. Hidden among a 4-acre cadre of pines just east of Tahoe City, the Tamarack Lodge consists of a few old cabins, five "poker rooms," and a modern (and far less nostalgic) motel unit. The rooms in the motel unit are the least appealing, but are certainly clean and comfortable. The cabins all have kitchenettes and can hold up to four guests, but the most popular rooms by far are the original poker rooms (where Gable and Cooper used to play cards) lined with gleaming knotty pine. Complimentary coffee and tea are served in the lobby, and rollaway beds are available for only $5 extra. Though the beach is within walking distance, you'll need a car to make forays into town.

For a Few Bucks More/Moderately Priced Options

Meeks Bay Resort. P.O. Box 411, Tahoma, CA 96142 (summer); P.O. Box 70248, Reno, NV 89570 (winter). ☎ **530/525-7242** (summer) or 702/829-1977 (winter). 21 units. $75 double per night; $600–$3,000 per week. No credit cards. Closed Sept 16–June 14.

Lying 10 miles south of Tahoe City on Calif. 89, Meeks Bay Resort is one of the oldest hostelries on the lake and something of a historical landmark. This wide, sweeping lakefront boasts the best fine-sand beach in Tahoe. Known centuries ago to the Washoe Indians, Meeks Bay was opened as a public campground in 1920. During the next 50 years the resort grew to include cabins and other improvements, and attracted many celebrities from southern California. Acquired by the U.S. Forest Service in 1974 under a special-use year-round permit, the property is open from June 15 to September 15 only. Most rentals are on a weekly basis and consist of cabins perched near the lake. Units vary in size, sleeping 2 to 12, and are modest without being austere. Each has a full kitchen, and some have fireplaces. Facilities include a beachfront cafe.

Pepper Tree Inn. 645 N. Lake Blvd. (P.O. Box 29), Tahoe City, CA 96145. ☎ **800/ 624-8590** or 530/583-3711. 50 units. TV TEL. $74–$89 double. AE, DC, DISC, MC, V.

If you're a Holiday Inn kind of person (no frills, no surprises) traveling on a Motel 6 kind of budget, the Pepper Tree Inn is for you. Two people can share a perfectly comfortable room for about $35 each (considerably less in the off-season), which includes access to a hot tub, heated outdoor pool with sundeck, free shuttle service to the major ski resorts, and all the cable channels you could want (okay, maybe not *all* the ones you want). Formerly the Rodeway Inn, the new owners did a complete renovation, adding new beds, furnishings, paint, and big 27-inch TVs. The location, right in the middle of Tahoe City, is great, but where the Pepper Tree Inn really shines is with its generous ski packages: For about $150 you and a friend can score a room and two all-day lift tickets to Alpine Meadows, Northstar, or Squaw Valley (Sun through Thurs only).

✪ **River Ranch Lodge & Restaurant.** On Calif. 89, at Alpine Meadows Rd. (P.O. Box 197), Tahoe City, CA 96145. ☎ **800/535-9900** or 530/583-4264. 19 units. TV TEL. Winter $55–$125 double; summer $55–$110 double; spring and fall $39–$75 double. Rates include continental breakfast. AE, MC, V.

The River Ranch Lodge has long been one of our favorite places to stay in Lake Tahoe. Situated alongside the Truckee River, the lodge is mere minutes away from Alpine Meadows and Squaw Valley ski resorts, and a short drive (or ride along the bike path) into Tahoe City. The best rooms in this rustic lodge feature private balconies that overlook the river. All have antique furnishings. Rooms 9 and 10, the farthest from the road, are our top choices.

   In the summer, guests relax under umbrellas on the huge patio overlooking the river, munching on barbecued chicken while watching the rafters float by. During the ski season, the River Ranch's spectacular circular cocktail lounge, which cantilevers over the river, is an immensely popular après-ski hangout. Also a big hit is the handsome River Ranch Lodge Restaurant, which serves fresh seafood, steaks, rack of lamb, and more exotic meats such as wood-oven-roasted Montana elk loin with a dried-cherry-port sauce.

✪ **Tahoma Meadows Bed & Breakfast.** 6821 W. Lake Blvd., on Calif. 89, 8½ miles from Tahoe City (P.O. Box 810), Homewood, CA 96141. ☎ **800/355-1596** or 530/525-1553. 11 units. TV. $75–$145 double. Rates include breakfast. AE, DISC, MC, V.

Owners/innkeepers Bill and Missy Sanderman—two of the friendliest folks you'll ever meet—offer one of Tahoe's best B&B bargains: 11 private cabins perched on a gentle forest slope amongst a cadre of sugar pines and flowers. Missy, a talented watercolorist, has individually decorated each cabin in a decidedly warm and cozy style. All rooms have comfy king-, queen-, or twin-size beds; most have gas-log fireplaces. Favorites are the cheery Sunflower and Fox Glove cabins, both equipped with claw-foot tubs. The largest cabin, Columbine, sleeps six and is ideal for families.

   A full breakfast is served at the main lodge upstairs, by the independently owned (and highly recommended) Stoneyridge Cafe. Nearby activities include skiing at Ski Homewood (including shuttle service), fly-fishing at the Sandermans' friend's private trout-stocked lake, and sunbathing at the lakeshore just across the street.

WHERE TO DINE
SOUTH SHORE/SOUTH LAKE TAHOE
Super-Cheap Eats
Ernie's Coffee Shop. 1146 Emerald Bay Rd./Calif. 89. ☎ **530/541-2161.** Main dishes $5–$8. No credit cards. Daily 6am–2pm. DINER.

The undisputed king of coffee shops in South Lake Tahoe is Ernie's, which has been serving huge plates of good old American grub to cholesterol-be-damned locals since the Nixon administration. Since the food is far from original (omelets, bacon and eggs, pancakes), it must be the perpetually friendly service, low prices, and huge portions that attracts the steady stream of customers. Another good reason to come here is that Ernie's is located next to the cheapest gas station in town, so you can top off your tummy and your tank in one stop.

✪ **Sprouts Natural Foods Cafe.** 3123 Harrison Ave. (at U.S. 50 and Alameda St. next to Lakeview Sports). ☎ **530/541-6969.** Meals $3.75–$6.50. No credit cards. Daily 8am–10pm. HEALTH FOOD/JUICES.

Sprouts owner Tyler Cannon has filled a much-needed niche in South Lake, serving wholesome food that looks good, tastes good, and *is* good. Most everything is made in-house, including the soups, smoothies, and fresh-squeezed juices. Menu items range from rice bowls to sandwiches (try the Real Tahoe Turkey), huge burritos, coffee drinks, muffins, fresh-fruit smoothies, and a marvelous mayo-free tuna sandwich made with yogurt and packed with fresh veggies. Order from the counter, then scramble for a vacant seat (outdoor tables are coveted), and listen for your name as Tyler's buff and beautiful servers bring out your tray of earthy delights. This is also an excellent place to pack a picnic lunch, whether skiing, hiking, or mountain biking.

Yellow Sub. 983 Tallac Ave. (at U.S. 50). ☎ **530/541-8808.** Sandwiches $3–$6. No credit cards. Daily 10:30am–10pm. SANDWICHES.

When it comes to picnic supplies, there's stiff competition in South Lake Tahoe: three sandwich shops on this single block alone. Still, our favorite is Yellow Sub, voted Best Deli Sandwich Shop by readers of the *Tahoe Daily Tribune*. They offer a whopping 21 versions of overstuffed subs—made in 6-inch and 12-inch varieties—as well as four kinds of wraps. The shop is hidden in a small shopping center across from the El Dorado Campground.

For a Few Bucks More/Moderately Priced Options
Cantina Bar & Grill. 765 Emerald Bay Rd. ☎ **530/544-1233.** Main courses $7–$13. MC, V. Daily 11:30am–10:30pm (bar open until midnight). MEXICAN.

Sporting a new Southwestern look, the Cantina Bar & Grill (formerly Cantina Los Tres Hombres) serves the best Mexican food in South Lake. The bar and adjacent dining area are two of the busiest rooms in South Lake Tahoe. The menu is well priced and extensive, offering tried-and-true Cal-Mex specialties such as tacos, burritos, and enchiladas along with a half-dozen Southwestern dishes such as Texas crab cakes, smoked chicken polenta, and grilled pork chops with jalapeño mashed potatoes. The steak fajitas (with shrimp, sweet peppers, and onions) get a thumbs-up, as does the half chicken smothered in rich mole sauce, served with rice, black beans, and tortillas. A few vegetarian selections are offered as well. Service is brisk but not unfriendly, and some patrons may have had more than their share of tequila.

Scusa! 1142 Ski Run Blvd. ☎ **530/542-0100.** Main courses $9–$18. AE, DISC, MC, V. Daily 5–10pm. ITALIAN.

Located on the trail to the Heavenly Ski Resort, this cozy Italian spot may have a decor that errs a little garishly on the neon side, but the food more than compensates. Dishes are interspersed with enough surprises to keep the locals happy. The place is civilized, basic but clean, and the staff is usually cheerful and knowledgeable unless they're rushed or having bad hair days. Among the specialties are a smoked chicken and ravioli made with cheese ravioli, sun-dried tomatoes, capers, black olives, and sage butter; and a savory baked penne with smoked mozzarella, prosciutto, roasted garlic, and focaccia crust

The Swiss House. 787 Emerald Bay Rd. ☎ **530/542-1717.** Main courses $10–$17. AE, MC, V. Daily 11:30am–2pm and 5–9pm. SWISS/CONTINENTAL.

The ambiance of this South Lake Tahoe spot is genuine enough and warmly appreciated by diners, especially those arriving from the ski slopes in winter to find a fire blazing away. Despite its name, the place is not exactly into yodeling and cowbells, but the dishes are often alpine. The operation seems to run like Swiss clockwork, and, although we've had better Wiener schnitzel, the one served here is perfectly adequate. There's also cheese fondue and raclette to take you back to the old country; it's warmly flavored but so filling you might not be able to finish.

NORTH SHORE/TAHOE CITY
Super-Cheap Eats
Bridgetender Tavern and Grill. 30 W. Lake Blvd. (at Fanny Bridge), Tahoe City. ☎ **530/583-3342.** Burgers, salads, and ribs $5–$7. MC, V. Daily 11am–2am. PUB FARE.

Although it's located in one of the most popular tourist areas in North Lake, the Bridgetender is a local's hangout through and through. Still, they're surprisingly tolerant of out-of-towners, who come for the cheap grub and huge selection of draft beers. The tavern is built around a trio of Ponderosa pines that meld in with the decor so well you hardly notice. Big burly burgers, salads, pork ribs, and such round out the menu, and the daily beer specials—posted on the wall in Day-Glo colors—are definitely worth going over. During the summer months, dine outside among the pines.

✪ **Fire Sign Café.** 1785 W. Lake Blvd., Tahoe City. ☎ **530/583-0871.** Breakfast and lunch $4–$9. MC, V. Daily 7am–3pm. AMERICAN.

Choosing a place to have breakfast in North Tahoe is a no-brainer. Since the late 1970s, the Fire Sign Café has been the locals' choice—which explains the lines out the door on weekends. Just about everything is made from scratch, such as the delicious coffee cake that accompanies the big ol' plates of bacon and eggs or blackberry-buckwheat pancakes. Even the salmon for chef/owner Bob Young's legendary salmon omelet is smoked in-house. Lunch—burgers, salads, sandwiches, burritos, and more—is also quite popular, particularly when the outdoor patio is open.

Izzy's Burger Spa. 100 W. Lake Blvd. (at Fanny Bridge), Tahoe City. ☎ **530/583-4111.** Burgers $3.50–$6. No credit cards. Daily 11am–7pm. BURGERS.

It's just a simple, wooden A-frame building containing a small short-order grill, but Izzy's Burger Spa flips an unusually hefty and tasty burger and an equally enticing grilled chicken-breast sandwich. On a sunny day, the best seats are at the picnic tables set out front. The restaurant is directly across from the Tahoe Yogurt Factory.

Tahoe Yogurt Factory. 125 W. Lake Blvd., Tahoe City. ☎ **530/581-5253.** Coffee/espresso $1–$2.60; yogurt $1.50–$3.25; sandwiches $2–$4. No credit cards. Daily 6am–6pm (until 9pm in summer). YOGURT/SANDWICHES.

This small coffee shack, located near Fanny Bridge in Tahoe City, is frequently mentioned as "the best little cafe in Tahoe," and we have to agree. Whenever we're in town, we always start our mornings here with a cappuccino or fruit smoothie fortified with some sort of energy powder. If we're feeling entirely too healthy, we wolf down an egg and croissant sandwich topped with plenty of salt. The cafe also sells an armada of bagels, muffins, sandwiches and such, as well as excellent java. Small tables are placed outdoors in the summer, where locals and visitors vie for a free table.

✪ **Za's.** 395 N. Lake Blvd. (across from the fire station), Tahoe City. ☎ **530/583-1812.** Main courses $6–$10. MC, V. Daily 4:30–9:30pm. ITALIAN.

The sign used to say PIZZA'S until half of it fell off, which is just as well because there's a whole lot more to Za's than just pizza. One of the most popular restaurants in North Tahoe, this little gem serves great Italian food at bargain prices. Example: A hefty plate of smoked chicken fettuccine in a garlic-cream sauce with roasted bell peppers, fresh artichoke hearts, and mushrooms is under $10. Start with Pudge's Plate—a pleasing platter of fresh-roasted veggies doused in a balsamic vinaigrette—and a tumbler or two of Chianti, then pick from the wide range of pasta, calzone, and pizza. Za's is a bit hard to find (look behind Pete-n-Peter's Saloon), but *mama mia*, is it worth the search.

For a Few Bucks More/Moderately Priced Options

Tahoe House Restaurant and Bäckerei. 625 W. Lake Blvd., Tahoe City. ☎ **530/583-1377.** Main courses $9–$19.50. AE, DISC, MC, V. Bakery daily 6am–10pm. Deli lunch 11am–4pm; dinner 5–10pm. SWISS/CALIFORNIA.

Serving Tahoe's skiers, boaters, and sunbathers for nearly 2 decades, Tahoe House is one of the oldest Swiss restaurants on the lake, located at the "Y" in Tahoe City. Although not a trendsetter, it is known locally as a reliable venue for good food at reasonable prices. Chef/owner Barbara Vogt's menu features some Swiss-German dishes such as Wiener schnitzel, Rahmschnitzel (veal with creamy mushroom sauce), grilled Bratwurst, and pork Cordon Bleu. Steaks and fresh seafood also satisfy, as do several house-made pastas and vegetarian choices. The full-service European-style bakery items and desserts are wonderful. Dishes are based on the seasonal availability of ingredients, and usually only the freshest and best are used. Vogt has added a selection of lighter choices, including vegetarian dishes straight from the family farm.

Worth a Splurge

Sunnyside Restaurant. At the Sunnyside Lodge, 1850 W. Lake Blvd., Tahoe City. ☎ **530/583-7200.** Main courses $13–$19. AE, MC, V. Oct–June Sun–Thurs 4–9:30pm; Fri–Sat 4–10:30pm. July–Sept daily 11am–10:30pm; Sun brunch 9am–2pm. SEAFOOD/AMERICAN.

Located about 2 miles south of Tahoe City on Calif. 89, the Sunnyside Restaurant is worth blowing your budget for. In summer, when the sun is shining, there's no more highly coveted table in Tahoe than one on Sunnyside's lakeside veranda. Guests can also dine in the lodge's more traditional dining room with its 1930s aura. Nothing out of the ordinary here menu-wise: Lunch items range from fresh pastas and burgers to chicken and fish sandwiches and a variety of soups and salads. Dinners are fancier, with such main courses as Australian lobster tail, lamb chops with roasted-garlic chutney butter, and fresh salmon oven-baked on a cedar plank. All dinners come with San Francisco–style sourdough bread, the chef's starch of the day, and a Caesar salad or cup of creamy chowder.

TAHOE AFTER DARK

Tahoe is not known particularly for its nightlife, although there's always something going on in the showrooms of the major casino hotels located in Stateline, just east of South Lake Tahoe. Call **Harrah's** (☎ 702/588-6611), **Harvey's** (☎ 702/588-2411), **Caesar's** (☎ 702/588-3515), and the Lake Tahoe **Horizon** (☎ 702/588-6211) for current show schedules and prices. Most cocktail shows cost $12 to $40, and headliners are likely to include the likes of Jay Leno or Johnny Mathis.

There's usually live music nightly in **Bullwhackers Pub,** at the Resort at Squaw Creek (☎ 530/583-6300), 5 miles west of Tahoe City. The **Pierce Street Annex,** 850 N. Lake Blvd. (☎ 530/583-5800), behind the Safeway in Tahoe City, has pool tables, shuffleboard, and DJ dancing every night. It's one of the livelier places around.

The college crowd will feel at home at **Elevation,** 877 N. Lake Blvd., across from Safeway in Tahoe City (☎ 530/583-4867), which has the cheapest drinks in town and live rock music most nights.

If it's just a casual cocktail you're after, our favorite spot is the handsome fireside lounge at **River Ranch Lodge,** which cantilevers over a turbulent stretch of the Truckee River, on Calif. 89 at the entrance to Alpine Meadows, about 10 miles northwest of Tahoe City (☎ **530/583-4264**).

9

The High Sierra: Yosemite, Mammoth Lakes & Sequoia/Kings Canyon

by Erika Lenkert and Matthew R. Poole

The national parks of California's Sierra are a mecca for travelers across the globe. The big attraction is Yosemite, of course, but the entire region is the stuff from which postcards are made.

It was in Yosemite that naturalist John Muir found "the most songful streams in the world . . . the noblest forests, the loftiest granite domes, the deepest ice sculptured canyons." Even today, few visitors would disagree with Muir's early impressions as they explore this land of waterfalls, towering cliffs, wilderness, snowfields, alpine lakes, river beaches, and waterfalls. The waterfalls, one of the most stunning sights, reach their peak in mid-May. Yosemite Valley is riddled with waterfalls, sheer walls, and domes and peaks reaching toward the sky. The valley is the most central and accessible part of the park, stretching for some 20 miles, all the way from Wawona Tunnel in the west to Curry Village in the east. If you visit during spring or early fall, you'll encounter fewer problems with crowds.

Across the heart of the Sierra Nevada in east-central California sprawl Sequoia and Kings Canyon national parks, administered as one entity. Their peaks stretch across some 1,300 square miles, taking in the giant sequoias for which they are fabled. It's a land of alpine lakes, granite peaks, and deep canyons. At 14,495 feet, Mt. Whitney is the highest point in the Lower 48.

Another big attraction in the area is Mammoth Lakes, one of the major playgrounds of California, with dozens of recreational activities in a setting of lakes, streams, waterfalls, and rugged meadows evocative of Austria. As if they had giant knives, glaciers in unrecorded times carved out much of this panoramic region, as did volcanic activity.

Because of the vast popularity of the parks, facilities can be strained at peak visiting times. Always secure your reservations in advance if possible (and that definitely includes camping). You'll be glad you did.

1 Yosemite's Gateways

Yosemite could not accommodate its 4.1 million annual guests even before a severe storm and flood struck Yosemite Valley in January

Area Code Change

Please note that, effective November 14, 1998, portions of the High Sierra, specifically areas south of the Mariposa-Madera county line and south of the Merced-Madera county line, changed from the 209 area code to the **559** area code. You will be able to dial 209 until May 14, 1999, after which you will be required to use 559 for affected numbers.

1997, eliminating 400 campsites and at least 250 guest rooms. (Reservations are usually booked up to a year in advance.) The good news: Towns on each gateway's periphery are virtually built around the tourism industry. They offer plenty of places to stay and eat (though the food up here is hardly a gourmet experience) and have natural wonders of their own. The bad news: If you stay here, reaching any point within the park requires at least a half-hour drive (usually closer to an hour), which is especially frustrating during high season, when motor homes and overall congestion cause traffic to move at a snail's pace.

Should you need to reserve outside the park, choose based on which gate offers you easiest access. Our selections below are grouped by the three most popular entrances: The west entrances are Big Oak Flat (via Calif. 120), which is 88 miles east of Manteca and accommodates traffic from San Francisco, and Arch Rock (via Calif. 140), which is 75 miles northeast of Merced and is the easiest route from central California. The South Entrance is Wawona (via Calif. 41), which is 64 miles north of Fresno and the passage leading from southern California.

BIG OAK FLAT ENTRANCE

This is our favorite entrance to the park. It's 150 miles east of San Francisco and 130 miles southeast of Sacramento. Among the string of small communities along the way is charming **Groveland** (23 miles from the park's entrance), a throwback to gold-mining days complete with rednecks, the oldest saloon in the state, and at least some semblance of a real town. It'll take about an hour to reach the park entrance from Groveland, but at least there are some activities in town to keep you occupied should you choose to base yourself here. Big Oak Flat has a few hotels as well, but no town. Call the visitor information number below for details.

GETTING THERE   If you're driving from San Francisco, take I-580 (which turns into I-205) to Manteca, then Calif. 120 east.

VISITOR INFORMATION   Contact the Calif. 120 **Chamber of Commerce** (☎ **800/449-9120**) for information on lodging.

WHERE TO STAY & DINE

Besides the places mentioned below, there are only a few other dining options—none of which are worth writing home about. Ask anyone in town and they'll point you to the offerings. A few super-cheapies are **PJ's Café and Pizzeria,** 18986 Main St., Groveland (☎ **209/962-7501**), and **Two Guys Pizza Pies,** 18955 Ferretti Rd., Groveland (☎ **209/962-GUYS**).

✪ **Evergreen Lodge.** 33160 Evergreen Rd. (at Calif. 120), Groveland, CA 95321. ☎ **800/935-6343** or 209/379-2607. www.evergreenlodge.com. 22 units. TV. Apr–Oct $69 double; $79–$85 cabin (with 1 queen and 2 single beds); $89–$95 two-bedroom cottage. DISC, MC, V. Closed in winter. From San Francisco, take I-580 E. (which turns into I-205) to Manteca; take Calif. 120 E. through Groveland; turn left at Hetch Hetchy/ Evergreen Rd.

The Flood of 1997

A severe storm in January 1997 flooded Yosemite Valley, stranding visitors and wreaking havoc on campsites, cabins, and trails. The raging Merced River eroded 1½ miles of riverbank, washed over 550 acres of meadow, moved building-size boulders, and chewed up huge portions of highway.

The storm ruined hundreds of campsites, flooded over 350 motel and lodge units, and left 440 employees homeless. Throughout the park, the storm damaged 800 miles of trails, destroyed nine road bridges, and washed out 33 trail bridges. When the water receded, much of the valley floor was covered with a fine layer of silt more than a foot deep. Picnic tables, bear-proof storage boxes, garbage cans, and fire grates were found miles downstream.

Over a year later, the trails and bridges have long been repaired and the valley shows few signs of nature's wrath. However, restoration of the park's lost amenities is far from complete. Construction began in 1998 and is scheduled to continue through 2001. Accommodations and campgrounds are still severely limited.

This has been a favorite rustic retreat for everyone from families to bikers for over 75 years. The 22 cabins, which look very cheap-motel-like on the inside, offer the basic necessities and are well dispersed along a wooded grove. But what's great about this place is its surroundings: It's only 8 miles away from Yosemite's entrance and has a fun log-cabin lodge/bar where dinner is served and where dudes in 10-gallon hats shoot pool. (On warm nights, it's best to enjoy a pitcher of beer and some barbecue on the outdoor patio.) There are endless hiking trails and, during summer, access to Camp Mather's tennis courts, pool (major family action), and horseback riding. Though officially in Groveland, the lodge is 40 minutes east of downtown.

The Groveland Hotel. 18767 Main St., Groveland, CA 95321. ☎ **800/273-3314** or 209/962-4000. Fax 209/962-6674. 18 units, all with bath (4 with shower only). A/C TEL. $105–$125 double; $185 suite. Rates include extended continental breakfast. AE, DC, DISC, MC, V.

Constructed around 1850, this adorable historic hotel complements the surroundings of the Wild West–like town. Rooms are sweetly appointed with antiques as well as modern amenities like hair dryers and coffeemakers; the suite has a spa tub and fireplace. The staff is both friendly and accommodating. The most expensive and fanciest (a far cry from big-city fancy, mind you) restaurant in town is on the premises, and the supercool Iron Door Saloon (the other place to eat well) is across the street. This is a nonsmoking hotel.

Hotel Charlotte. Calif. 120 (P.O. Box 787), Groveland, CA 95321. ☎ **209/962-6455.** 12 units, 8 with bathroom. $52.50 double without bathroom; $62.50 double with bathroom. Rates include continental breakfast. Extra person $10. AE, MC, V.

Far funkier than the Groveland Hotel (and half the price!), the two-story Hotel Charlotte was built in 1918, and from the looks of things, decorating started around then and was completed in the early 1960s (think moose head meets macramé). The lounge features a quirky smattering of antiques. Further down the hall a Ping-Pong table is tucked into a very modest game room; and there's a TV room, too, in case you can't bare the slow country living. Guest quarters are upstairs (more macramé plus shag) and have a homey, albeit antiquated, rather 1960s and lived-in vibe; many are adjoining, which is a plus for families. Pay telephones are outside. The staff is not as

---

Driving Warning

If you plan on entering or exiting the park via Calif. 140 (the Merced route), be forewarned that due to damage from the 1997 storms, repairs began on that road in October 1998 and will continue for the next 2 years. Driving will be restricted to certain times of the day, and you should expect delays. For complete details contact the **National Park Service Road & Weather Recording** at ☎ **209/372-0200.**

---

accommodating as across the street at the Groveland, but on the bright side, prices are a flashback, too, and you didn't come here to hang in your room anyway. Another plus: The in-house restaurant offers fish, chicken, or beef dinners (including soup, salad, and side dishes) for $13 to $17.

ARCH ROCK ENTRANCE

Arch Rock is 75 miles northeast of Merced. If you're driving from central California, take I-5 to Calif. 99 to Merced, then Calif. 140 east. If driving this route, make sure you bring along the necessary provisions; after passing through the small town of Mariposa, which is east of Merced en route to the entrance, there's virtually nothing but nature until you're in the center of the valley.

WHERE TO STAY

Yosemite View Lodge. 11136 Calif. 140 (P.O. Box D), El Portal, CA 95318. ☎ **800/ 321-5261** or 209/379-2681. Fax 209/379-2704. www.yosemite-motels.com. 308 units. TV TEL. Apr–Oct $99–$139 double; Nov–Mar $82–$104 double. 2-night minimum during holidays. MC, V.

Once you've come this far, you're practically at the gate, so it's literally shocking to drive upon this gargantuan pink compound amidst the otherwise awesome natural surroundings. But the crowds need to stay somewhere, and with the ongoing construction, this mega-motel is scheduled to offer around 500 rooms within the coming year. The attractively decorated units include fridges, microwaves, and HBO; some offer river views, balconies, and fireplaces. There's also a general store, two well-priced restaurants, two pools, three hot tubs, laundry facilities, and more public areas in the works. If this place is booked, the lodge also represents three other properties in the vicinity, although they're not nearly as close to the entrance. Call the number above for information.

SOUTH ENTRANCE

The South Entrance is 332 miles north of Los Angeles, 190 miles east of San Francisco, 59 miles north of Fresno, and 33 miles south of Yosemite Valley. Fish Camp and Oakhurst are the closest towns to the south entrance at Wawona.

If you're driving from Los Angeles, take I-5 to Calif. 99 north, then Calif. 41 north.

WHERE TO STAY

For more options, contact the **Yosemite Sierra Visitors Center,** 41729 Calif. 41, Oakhurst, CA 93644 (☎ **209/683-4636;** www.yosemite-sierra.org). They'll send you a helpful brochure on the area.

The Narrow Gauge Inn. 48571 Calif. 41, Fish Camp, CA 93623. ☎ **209/683-7720.** Fax 209/683-2139. www.narrowgaugeinn.com. 25 units (all but 1 with shower only). TV TEL. Memorial Day to Labor Day $85–$95 Nelder Ridge double; $95 Courtyard double; $120 Creekside double; $120–$130 Clover Hill double. Labor Day to Memorial Day $70–$80 Nelder Ridge double; $85 Courtyard double; $100 Creekside double; $80–$130 Clover Hill double. Extra person $5; children under 3 stay free. AE, DISC, MC, V.

If you want to stay in a place that celebrates the mountain atmosphere, book a room at this very friendly inn, just 4 miles south of the park entrance. All of the superclean motel-style rooms have a rustic cabin feel to them, complete with A-frame ceilings, little balconies or decks, antiques, quilts, lace curtains, and coffeemakers; some have wood-paneled walls. The higher the price of the room, the cuter they get (rooms 16 through 26 are the best and most secluded; they look directly into forest). A pool, hot tub, and hiking trails are on the property. A wonderfully old-fashioned, lodge-style restaurant/buffalo bar serves "Old California Rancho Cuisine." *One downside:* Some of the mattresses are soft. *Note:* The inn closes during winter; the restaurant is closed on Tuesday and Wednesday even during high season.

Tenaya Lodge. 1122 Calif. 41, Fish Camp, CA 93623. ☎ **800/635-5807** or 209/683-6555. Fax 209/683-8684. 244 units. A/C MINIBAR TV TEL. Summer from $229 double. Winter from $109 double Sun–Thurs; from $149 double Fri–Sat. Add $20–$80 for suite. Buffet breakfast $12.50 per person. Children 17 and under stay free in parents' room. AE, DC, DISC, MC, V.

Tenaya Lodge is the best resort outside the southern entrance to Yosemite; it's particularly idyllic for families. The three- and four-story complex, which is run by the Marriott chain, is set on a 35-acre tract of forested land a few miles outside of the national park. Inside, the decor is a cross between an Adirondack hunting lodge and a Southwestern pueblo, with a lobby dominated by a massive river-rock fireplace rising three stories. There's an indoor pool and three restaurants (which leave much to be desired). The ultramodern rooms, however, definitely do the trick, with three phones; roomy, well-appointed bathrooms; and other amenities like in-room safes.

   Amenities: Room service, indoor and outdoor pools, health club, on-site massage, game room, sleigh and hay rides (depending on the season).

2 Yosemite National Park

Yosemite is a place of record-setting statistics: the highest waterfall in North America and three of the world's 10 tallest (Upper Yosemite Fall, Ribbon Fall, and Sentinel Falls); the tallest and largest single granite monolith in the world (El Capitan); the most recognizable mountain (Half Dome); one of the world's largest trees (the Grizzly Giant in the Mariposa Grove); and literally thousands of rare plant and animal species. But trying to explain its majesty is impossible: This is a place you simply must experience firsthand. Even after extensive world travel, it's still one of the most awe-inspiring places we've ever been—every single time we visit.

   What sets the valley apart is its incredible geology. The Sierra Nevada was formed between 10 and 80 million years ago, when a tremendous geological uplift pushed layers of granite lying under the ocean up into an impressive mountain range. Cracks and rifts in the rock gave erosion a start at carving canyons and valleys. Then, during the last ice age, at least three glaciers flowed through the valley, shearing vertical faces of stone and hauling away the rubble. The last glacier retreated 10,000 to 15,000 years ago, but left its legacy in the incredible number and size of the waterfalls pouring into the valley from hanging side canyons. From the 4,000-foot-high valley floor, the 8,000-foot tops of El Capitan, Half Dome, and Glacier Point look like the top of the world, but they're small in comparison to the highest mountains in the park, some of which reach over 13,000 feet. The 7-square-mile valley is really a huge bathtub drain for the combined runoff of hundreds of square miles of snow-covered peaks (which explains why the valley flooded during the great storm of 1997).

   High country creeks flush with snowmelt catapult over the abyss left by the glaciers and form an outrageous variety of falls, from tiny ribbons that never reach the ground to the torrents of Nevada and Vernal falls. Combined with the shadows and lighting of the deep valley, the effect of all this falling water is mesmerizing. All that vertical stone gets put to use by hundreds who flock to the park for some of the finest climbing anywhere.

The valley is also home to beautiful meadows and the Merced River. When the last glacier retreated, its debris dammed the Merced and formed a lake. Eventually sediment from the river filled the lake and created the rich and level valley floor we see today. Tiny Mirror Lake was created later by rockfall that dammed up Tenya Creek; the addition of a man-made dam in 1890 made it more of a lake than a pond. Rafters and inner-tubers enjoy the slow-moving Merced during the heat of summer.

Deer and coyote frequent the valley, often causing vehicular mayhem as one heavy-footed tourist slams on the brakes to whip out the camcorder while another rubber-necker, also mesmerized, drives right into him. Metal crunches, tempers flare, and the deer daintily hops away.

Bears, too, are at home in the valley. Grizzlies are gone from the park now, but black bears are plentiful—and hungry for your "pic-a-nic" baskets. They don't actually come begging by daylight, but they make their presence known through late-night ransacking of ice chests, and have even been known to rip into cars that have treats inside.

Right in the middle of the valley's thickest urban cluster is the **Valley Visitor Center** (☎ **209/372-0200**), with exhibits that will teach you about glacial geology, history, and the park's flora and fauna. Check out the **Indian Cultural Museum** next door for insight into what life in the park was once like. Excellent exhibits highlight the Miwok and Paiute cultures that thrived here. The Ansel Adams Gallery displays the famous photographer's prints as well as other artists' works. You'll also find much history and memorabilia from the career of nature writer John Muir, one of the founders of the conservation movement.

While it's easy to let the tremendous beauty of the valley monopolize your attention, remember that 95% of Yosemite is wilderness. Of the four million visitors who come to the park each year, very few ever venture more than a mile from their cars. That leaves most of Yosemite's 750,000 acres open for anyone adventurous enough to hike a few miles. Even though the valley is a hands-down winner for dramatic freak-of-nature displays, the high country offers a more subtle kind of beauty: glacial lakes, roaring rivers, and miles of granite spires and domes. In the park's southwest corner, the Mariposa Grove is a striking forest of rare sequoias, which are the world's largest trees, as well as several meadows and the rushing south fork of the Merced River.

Tenaya Lake and Tuolumne Meadows are two of the most popular high-country destinations, as well as starting points for many great trails to the backcountry. Since this area of the park is under snow from November through June, the short season we call summer is really more like spring. From snowmelt to the first snowfall, the high country explodes with wildflowers and long-dormant wildlife trying to make the most of the short season.

JUST THE FACTS

ENTRY POINTS   There are four main entrances to the park. Most valley visitors enter through the **Arch Rock Entrance** on Calif. 140. The best entrance for Wawona is the **South Entrance** on Calif. 41 from Oakhurst. If you're going to the high country, you'll save a lot of time by coming in through the **Big Oak Flat Entrance,** which puts you straight onto Tioga Road without forcing you to deal with the congested valley. The **Tioga Pass Entrance** is only open in summer and is only really relevant if you're coming from the east side of the Sierra (in which case it's your only choice). A fifth, little-used entrance is the **Hetch Hetchy Entrance,** in the euphonious Poopenaut Valley, on a dead-end road.

FEES   It costs $20 per car per week to enter the park or $10 per person per week. Annual Yosemite Passes are a steal at only $40. Wilderness permits are free, but reserving them requires a $3 fee per person.

GAS   There are no gas stations in Yosemite Valley, so be sure to fill up at a gas station before entering the park.

VISITOR CENTERS & INFORMATION   There's a central, 24-hour recorded information line for the park (☎ **209/372-0200**). All visitor-related service lines, including hotels and information, can be accessed by touch-tone phone at ☎ **209/372-1000.**

By far the biggest visitor center is the **Valley Visitor Center** (☎ 209/372-0200). The **Wawona Information Station** (☎ 209/375-9501) and the **Big Oak Flat Information Center** (☎ 209/372-0615) give general park information. For interesting biological and geological displays about the High Sierra, as well as trail advice, the **Tuolumne Meadows Visitor Center** (☎ 209/372-0263) is great. All can provide you with maps, plus more newspapers, books, and photocopied leaflets than you'll ever read.

REGULATIONS   Rangers in the Yosemite Valley spend more time being cops than being rangers. They even have their own jail, so don't do anything here you wouldn't do in your hometown. Despite the pressure, park regulations are pretty simple. Wilderness permits are required for all overnight backpacking trips. Fishing licenses are required. Utilize proper food-storage methods in bear country. Don't collect firewood in the valley. No off-road bicycle riding. Dogs are allowed in the park but must be leashed and are forbidden from trails. Don't feed the animals.

SEASONS   Winter is one of the nicest times to visit the valley. It isn't crowded, as it is during summer, and a dusting of snow provides a stark contrast to all that granite. To see the waterfalls at their best, come in spring when snowmelt is at its peak. Fall can be cool, but it's beautiful and much less crowded than summer. Sunshine seekers will love summer—if they can tolerate the crowds.

The high country is under about 20 feet of snow from November through May, so unless you're snow camping, summer is pretty much the only season to pitch a tent. Even in summer, thundershowers are a frequent occurrence, sometimes with a magnificent lightning show. Mosquitoes can be a plague during the peak of summer but get better after the first freeze.

RANGER PROGRAMS   Even though they're overworked just trying to keep the peace, Yosemite's wonderful rangers also take time to lead a number of educational and interpretive programs ranging from backcountry hikes to fireside talks to snow-country survival clinics. Call the main park-information number with specific requests for the season and park area you'll be visiting. Also a great service are the free painting, drawing, and photography classes offered spring to fall at the Art Activity Center next to the Museum Gallery in the valley.

AVOIDING THE CROWDS   Unfortunately, popularity isn't always the greatest thing for wild places. Over the last 20 years, tourist-magnet Yosemite Valley has set records for the worst crowding, noise, crime, and traffic in any California national park. More than 4.1 million visitors came in 1997.

The park covers more than 1,000 square miles, but most visitors flock to the floor of Yosemite Valley, a 1-mile-wide, 7-mile-long freak of glacial scouring that tore a deep and steep valley from the solid granite of the Sierra Nevada. It's still one of the most beautiful places on earth, but the Yosemite Valley becomes a total zoo between Memorial Day and Labor Day.

Yosemite National Park

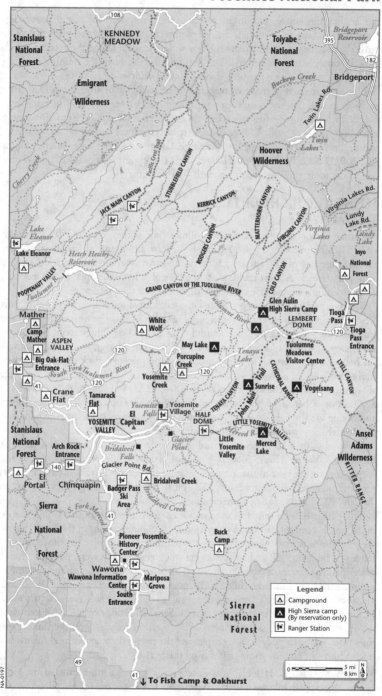

Stanislaus National Forest

KENNEDY MEADOW

108

Toiyabe National Forest

395

182

Bridgeport Reservoir

Bridgeport

Buckeye Creek

Emigrant Wilderness

Twin Lakes Rd.

Twin Lakes

Cherry Creek

Pacific Crest Trail

JACK MAIN CANYON

STUBBLEFIELD CANYON

KERRICK CANYON

Hoover Wilderness

MATTERHORN CANYON

RODGERS CANYON

VIRGINIA CANYON

Virginia Lakes

Virginia Lakes Rd.

Lundy Lake Rd.

Lundy Lake

Lake Eleanor

Lake Eleanor

Hetch Hetchy Reservoir

COLD CANYON

Inyo National Forest

POOPENAUT VALLEY

Tuolumne R.

GRAND CANYON OF THE TUOLUMNE RIVER

Tuolumne River

Glen Aulin High Sierra Camp

LEMBERT DOME

Tioga Pass

Tioga Pass Entrance

120

LYELL CANYON

Mather

Camp Mather

ASPEN VALLEY

120

White Wolf

May Lake

Porcupine Creek

Tenaya Lake

Tuolumne Meadows Visitor Center

Big Oak-Flat Entrance

South Fork Tuolumne River

120

Yosemite Creek

Sunrise

CATHEDRAL RANGE

Vogelsang

41

Crane Flat

Tamarack Flat

Yosemite Falls

Yosemite Village

JOHN MUIR TENAYA CANYON

John Muir Trail

Ansel Adams Wilderness

YOSEMITE VALLEY

El Capitan

HALF DOME

LITTLE YOSEMITE VALLEY

Merced R.

RITTER RANGE

Stanislaus National Forest

Arch Rock Entrance

Bridalveil Falls

Glacier Point

Little Yosemite Valley

Merced Lake

El Portal

140

Chinquapin

Glacier Point Rd.

Bridalveil Creek

Bridalveil Creek

Sierra

S. Fork Merced R.

41

Badger Pass Ski Area

National

Buck Camp

Forest

Pioneer Yosemite History Center

Wawona

Wawona Information Center

South Entrance

Mariposa Grove

Sierra National Forest

Legend

△	Campground
▲	High Sierra camp (By reservation only)
🛉	Ranger Station

0 ——— 5 mi
0 ——— 8 km

N

49

41

↓ To Fish Camp & Oakhurst

NA-0197

263

Cars line up bumper to bumper on almost any busy weekend. Until now, federal authorities did not show enough courage to implement one of several plans that would reduce traffic. But in 1995, Yosemite's new superintendent closed the entrances to the park 11 times between Memorial Day and mid-August when the number of visitors reached the park's quota; she turned away 10,000 vehicles.

Our best advice is to try to come before Memorial Day or after Labor Day. If you must go in summer, try to do your part to help out. It's not so much the numbers of people that are ruining the valley, but their insistence on driving from attraction to attraction within the valley. Once you're here, park your car and bike, hike, or ride the shuttle buses. **Curry Village** and **Yosemite Lodge** both rent bikes in the summer (☎ 209/372-1240). It may take longer to get from point A to point B, but you're in one of the most gorgeous places on earth—so why hurry?

SEEING THE HIGHLIGHTS
THE VALLEY

First-time visitors are often completely dumbstruck as they enter the valley from the west. The first two things you'll see are the delicate and beautiful **Bridalveil Fall** and the immense face of **El Capitan,** a stunning and anything-but-delicate 3,593-foot-tall solid-granite rock. A short trail leads to the base of Bridalveil, which at 620 feet tall is only a medium-size fall by park standards, but one of the prettiest.

This is a perfect chance to get those knee-jerk tourist impulses under control early: Resist the temptation to rush around bagging sights like they're feathers for your cap. Instead, take your time and look around. One of the best things about the valley is that many of its most famous features are visible from all over. Instead of rushing to the base of every waterfall or famous rock face and getting a crick in your neck from staring straight up, go to the visitor center and spend a half hour learning something about the features of the valley. Buy the excellent *Map and Guide to Yosemite Valley* for $2.50; it describes many hikes and short nature walks. Then go take a look. Walking and biking are the best ways to get around. To cover longer distances, the park shuttles run frequently around the east end of the valley.

If you absolutely must see it all and want to have someone tell you what you're seeing, the **Valley Floor Tour** is a 2-hour narrated bus or open-air tram tour (depending on the season) that provides an introduction to the valley's natural history, geology, and human culture for $17. Purchase tickets at valley hotels or call ☎ 209/372-1240 for advance reservations.

Three-quarters of a mile from the visitor center is the **Ahwahnee.** Unlike the rest of the hotel accommodations in the park (see "Accommodations in the Park," below), the Ahwahnee actually lives up to its surroundings. The native granite-and-timber lodge was built in 1927 and reflects an era when grand hotels were, well, grand. Fireplaces bigger than most Manhattan studio apartments warm the immense common rooms. Parlors and halls are filled with antique Native American rugs. Don't worry about what you're wearing unless you're going to dinner—this is Yosemite, after all.

The best single view in the valley is from **Sentinel Bridge** over the Merced River. At sunset, Half Dome's face functions as a projection screen for all the sinking sun's hues from yellow to pink to dark purple, and the river reflects it all. Ansel Adams took one of his most famous photographs from this very spot.

VALLEY WALKS & HIKES   Yosemite Falls is within a short stroll of the visitor center. You can actually see it better elsewhere in the valley, but it's really impressive to stand at the base of all that falling water. The wind, noise, and blowing spray generated when millions of gallons catapult 2,425 feet through space onto the rocks below are sometimes so overwhelming you can barely stand on the bridge.

If you want more, the **Upper Yosemite Fall Trail** zigzags 3½ miles from Sunnyside Campground to the top of Upper Yosemite Fall. This trail gives you an inkling of the weird, vertically oriented world climbers enter when they head up Yosemite's sheer walls. As you climb this narrow switchback trail, the valley floor drops away until people below look like ants, but the top doesn't appear any closer. It's a little unnerving at first, but braving it promises indescribable rewards. Plan on spending all day on this 7-mile round-trip because of the incredibly steep climb.

A mile-long trail leads from the Valley Stables (shuttle bus stop 17; no car parking) to **Mirror Lake.** The already-tiny lake is gradually becoming a meadow as it fills with silt, but the reflections of the valley walls and sky on its surface remain one of the park's most introspective sights.

Also accessible from the Valley Stables or nearby Happy Isles is the best valley hike of all—the **John Muir Trail** to Vernal and Nevada falls. It follows the Sierra crest 200 miles south to Mount Whitney, but you only need go 1½ miles round-trip to get a great view of 317-foot Vernal Fall. Add another 1½ miles and 1,000 vertical feet for the climb to the top of Vernal Fall on the **Mist Trail,** where you'll get wet as you climb directly alongside the falls. On top of Vernal and before the base of Nevada Fall is a beautiful little valley and deep pool. For a truly outrageous view of the valley and one heck of a workout, continue on up the Mist Trail to the top of Nevada Fall. From 2,000 feet above Happy Isles where you began, it's a dizzying view straight down the face of the fall. To the east is an interesting profile perspective of Half Dome. Return either by the Mist Trail or the slightly easier John Muir Trail for a 7-mile round-trip hike.

Half Dome may look insurmountable to anyone but an expert rock climber, but thousands every year take the popular cable route up the backside. It's almost 17 miles round-trip and a 4,900-foot elevation gain from Happy Isle on the John Muir Trail. Many do it in a day, starting at first light and rushing home to beat nightfall. A more relaxed strategy is to camp in the backpacking campground in Little Yosemite Valley just past Nevada Fall. From here the summit is an easy striking distance to the base of Half Dome. If you plan to spend the night, you must have a Wilderness Pass (see "Camping in Yosemite," below). You must climb up a very steep granite face using steel cables installed by the park service. During summer, boards are installed as crossbeams, but they're still far apart. Wear shoes with lots of traction and bring your own leather gloves for the cables (your hands will thank you). The view from the top is an unbeatable vista of the high country, Tenaya Canyon, Glacier Point, and the awe-inspiring abyss of the valley below. When you shuffle up to the overhanging lip for a look down the face, be extremely careful not to kick rocks or anything else onto the climbers below, who are earning this view the hard way.

THE SOUTHWEST CORNER

This corner of the park is densely forested and gently sculpted in comparison to the stark granite that makes up so much of Yosemite. Coming from the valley, Calif. 41 passes through a long tunnel. Just prior to the entrance is **Tunnel View,** site of another famous Ansel Adams photograph, and the best scenic outlook of the valley accessible by automobile. Virtually the whole valley is laid out below: Half Dome and Yosemite Falls straight ahead in the distance, Bridalveil to the right, and El Capitan to the left.

A few miles past the tunnel, Glacier Point Road turns off to the east. Closed in winter, this winding road leads to a picnic area at ✪ **Glacier Point,** site of another fabulous view of the valley, this time 3,000 feet below. Schedule at least an hour to drive here from the valley and an hour or two to absorb the view. This is a good place to study the glacial scouring of the valley below; the Glacier Point perspective makes it easy to picture the valley filled with sheets of ice.

Some 30 miles south of the valley on Calif. 41 is the **Wawona Hotel** and the **Pioneer Yosemite History Center.** The Wawona was built in 1879 and is the oldest hotel in the park. Its Victorian architecture evokes a time when travelers spent several days in horse-drawn wagons to get here. The Pioneer Center is a collection of early homesteading log buildings across the river from the Wawona.

One of the primary reasons Yosemite was first set aside as a park was the **Mariposa Grove** of giant sequoias. (Many good trails lead through the grove.) These huge trees have personalities that match their gargantuan size. Single limbs on the biggest tree in the grove, the Grizzly Giant, are 10 feet thick. The tree itself is 209 feet tall, 32 feet in diameter, and more than 2,700 years old. Totally out of proportion with the size of the trees are the tiny cones of the sequoia. Smaller than a baseball and tightly closed, the cones won't release their cargo of seeds until opened by fire.

THE HIGH COUNTRY

The high country of Yosemite has the most grandiose landscape in the entire Sierra Nevada. Dome after dome of beautifully crystalline granite reflects the sunlight above deep-green meadows and icy-cold rivers.

Tioga Pass is the gateway to the high country. At times it clings to the side of steep rock faces; in other places it weaves through canyon bottoms. Several good campgrounds make it a pleasing overnight alternative to fighting summertime crowds in the valley, although use is increasing here, too. Unlike in the valley, a car is vital to getting around here, as the only public transportation is the once-a-day Tuolumne Shuttle. This bus travels to and from Tenaya Lake and Tioga Pass, leaving the valley at 8am and letting you off anywhere along the way. The driver waits 2 hours at Tuolumne Meadows, which isn't much time to see anything, then heads back down to the valley, returning around 4pm. The one-way fare is $13, slightly less to intermediate destinations.

Tenaya Lake is a popular windsurfing, fishing, canoeing, sailing, and swimming spot. The water is very chilly. Many good hikes lead into the high country from here, and the granite domes surrounding the lake are popular with climbers. Fishing here varies greatly from year to year.

Near the top of Tioga Pass is stunning **Tuolumne Meadows.** This enormous meadow covering several square miles is bordered by the Tuolumne River on one side and spectacular granite peaks on the other. The meadow is cut by many stream channels full of trout, and herds of mule deer are almost always present. The **Tuolumne Meadows Lodge** and store is a welcome counterpoint to the overdeveloped valley. In winter the canvas roofs are removed and the buildings fill with snow. You can buy last-minute backpacking supplies here, and there's a basic burgers-and-fries cafe.

TUOLUMNE MEADOWS HIKES & WALKS   So many hikes lead from here into the backcountry that it's impossible to do them justice. A good trail passes an icy-cold spring and traverses several meadows.

On the far bank of the Tuolumne from the meadow, a trail leads downriver, eventually passing through the grand canyon of the Tuolumne and exiting at Hetch Hetchy. Shorter hikes will take you downriver past rapids and cascades.

An interesting geological quirk is the **Soda Spring** on the far side of Tuolumne Meadow from the road. This bubbling spring gushes carbonated water from a hole in the ground; a small log cabin marks its site.

For a great selection of Yosemite high-country hikes and backpacking trips, consult some of the specialized guidebooks to the area. Two of the best are published by Wilderness Press: *Tuolumne Meadows,* a hiking guide by Jeffrey B. Shaffer and Thomas Winnett, and *Yosemite National Park,* by Thomas Winnett and Jason Winnett.

ROCK CLIMBING & OTHER ACTIVE ENDEAVORS IN YOSEMITE

BICYCLING   With 10 miles of bike paths in addition to the valley roads, biking is the perfect way to go. You can rent one-speeds at the **Yosemite Lodge** or **Curry Village** for $5.25 per hour or $20 per day (☎ **209/372-1240**). Six-speed bikes with trailers for kids are also available. If you want a fancier bike, you'll have to bring it from home. All trails in the park are closed to mountain bikes.

FISHING   The Merced River in the valley is catch-and-release only, and barbless hooks are required. High-country lakes and streams are literally leaping with trout. A California license is required and available in the park at the Yosemite Village Sport Shop.

HORSEBACK RIDING   Three stables offer scenic day rides and multiday pack excursions in the park. **Yosemite Valley Stables** (☎ 209/372-8348) is open spring through fall. The other two—**Wawona** (☎ 209/375-6502) and **Tuolumne Stables** (☎ 209/372-8427)—operate only in summer. Day rides run from $30 to $60, depending on length. Multiday backcountry trips cost roughly $100 per day and must be booked almost a year in advance. The park wranglers can also be hired to make supply drops at any of the backcountry High Sierra camps if you want to arrange for a food drop while on an extended trip.

ICE-SKATING   In winter the **Curry Village Ice Rink** is a lot of fun. It's outdoors and melts quickly when the weather warms up. Rates are $5 for adults and $4.50 for children. Skate rentals are available.

ROCK CLIMBING   Much of the most important technical advancement in rock climbing came out of the highly competitive Yosemite Valley climbing scene of the 1970s and 1980s. Though other places have taken some of the limelight, Yosemite is still one of the most desirable climbing destinations in the world.

The **Yosemite Mountaineering School** runs classes for beginners through advanced climbers (☎ **209/372-8444** in the valley or 209/372-8435 at Tuolumne Meadows). Considered one of the best climbing schools in the world, it offers a basic lesson for $100 per person per day that will teach you basic body moves and rappelling, and will take you on a single pitch climb. Classes run from early spring to early October in the valley, during summer in Tuolumne Meadows.

SKIING   Yes, there is an alpine ski area in Yosemite, but it isn't much of one. Opened in 1935, **Badger Pass** (☎ **209/372-8430**) is the oldest operating ski area in California. Four chairs and two T-bars cover a compact mountain of beginner and intermediate runs. At $28 per day for adults and $13 for children on weekends (about 20% cheaper midweek), it's a great place to learn how to ski or snowboard. If you're a good skier or boarder already, don't bother.

Yosemite is a better destination for cross-country skiers and snowshoers. Both the Badger Pass ski school and the mountaineering school run trips and lessons for all abilities, ranging from basic technique to trans-Sierra crossings. If you're on your own, Crane Flat is a good place to go, as is the groomed track up to Glacier Point, a 20-mile round-trip.

CAMPING IN YOSEMITE

Campgrounds in Yosemite can be reserved up to 3 months in advance through the **National Park Reservation Service (NPRS)** (☎ **800/436-7275**). During the busy season, all valley campsites sell out within hours of becoming available on the service.

Backpacking into the wilderness and camping is always the least crowded option and takes less planning than reserving a campground. If you plan to backpack and camp in the wilderness, you must get a free Wilderness Pass (and still pay the park entrance fee). Half of the passes are allocated up to 24 hours in advance; the other half are available through the mail. Write to **Wilderness Center,** P.O. Box 545, Yosemite, CA 95389, and specify the dates and trailheads of entry and exit, principal destination, number of people, and any accompanying animals; include a $3 advance-registration fee. You may also secure a pass by calling ☎ **209/372-0740.**

VALLEY CAMPGROUNDS

Until January 1997, the park had five car campgrounds that were always full except in the dead of winter. Now the park has half the number of campsites available, and getting a reservation on short notice takes a minor miracle. (Yosemite Valley lost almost half of its 900 camping spaces in a freak winter storm that washed several campsites downstream and buried hundreds more beneath a foot of silt.)

The two and a half campgrounds that remain—**North Pines, Upper Pines,** and half of **Lower Pines**—charge $15 per night. All have drinking water, flush toilets, pay phones, fire pits, and a heavy ranger presence. Showers are available for a small fee at Curry Village. Upper Pines, North Pines, and Lower Pines allow small RVs (less than 40 feet long).

Sunnyside Campground is the only walk-in campground in the valley and fills up with climbers since it only costs $3 per night. Hard-core climbers used to live here for months at a time, but the park service has cracked down on that. It still has a much more bohemian atmosphere than at any of the other campgrounds.

ELSEWHERE IN THE PARK

Outside the valley things start looking up for campers. Two car campgrounds near the South Entrance of the park, **Wawona** and **Bridalveil Creek,** offer a total of 210 sites with all the amenities. Wawona is open year-round; reservations are required May through October, otherwise it's first-come, first-served (call the National Park Reservation Service at ☎ **800/436-7275**). Because it sits well above snow line at more than 7,000 feet, Bridalveil is open in summer only. Both campgrounds cost $10 per night.

Crane Flat, Hodgdon Meadow, and Tamarack Flat are all in the western corner of the park near the Big Oak Flat Entrance.

Crane Flat is the nearest to the valley, about a half-hour drive, with 166 sites, water, flush toilets, and fire pits. Its rates are $15 per night, and it's open from June through October. **Hodgdon Meadow** is directly adjacent to the Big Oak Flat entrance at 4,800 feet elevation. It's open year-round, charges $15 per night, and requires reservations May through October through NPRS (☎ **800/436-7275**). Facilities include flush toilets, running water, a ranger station, and pay phones. It's one of the least crowded low-elevation car campgrounds, but there's not a lot to do here. **Tamarack Flat** is a waterless, 52-site car campground with pit toilets, open June through October. It's a bargain at $6 per night.

Tuolumne Meadows, White Wolf, Yosemite Creek, and Porcupine Flat are all above 8,000 feet and open in summer only.

Tuolumne Meadows is the largest campground in the park, with more than 300 spaces, but it absorbs the crowd well and has all the amenities, including campfire programs and slide shows in the outdoor amphitheater. You will, however, feel

Crowd Alert

If you're expecting a real nature experience, skip camping in the valley unless you like doing so with 4,000 strangers.

Tips for Getting a Room

All hotel reservations can be made exactly 366 days in advance. Call ☎ **209/252-4848** in the morning 366 days before your intended arrival for the best chance of securing your reservation. If you don't plan far in advance, it's good to call anyway—cancellations may leave new openings. Winter reservations may also be booked through the Yosemite Concession Services at **www.yosemitepark.com**. Keep in mind that reservations held without deposit must be confirmed on the scheduled day of arrival by 4pm. Otherwise, you'll lose your reservation.

---

sardine-packed between hundreds of other visitors. Half of the sites are reserved in advance; the rest are set aside on a first-come, first-served basis. Rates are $15 per night.

White Wolf, west of Tuolumne Meadows, is the other full-service campground in the high country, with 87 sites available for $10 per night. It offers a drier climate than the meadow and doesn't fill up as quickly.

Two primitive camps, **Porcupine Flat** and **Yosemite Creek,** are the last to fill up in the park. Both have pit toilets but no running water, and charge $6 per night.

ACCOMMODATIONS IN THE PARK

The grandest (and most expensive) accommodations in the park are found at the **Ahwahnee** (☎ 209/252-4848), one of the most romantic and beautiful hotels in California. It's a special-occasion (doubles go for $250 a night) sort of affair.

The next best thing (and more moderately priced) is the **Wawona Hotel** (☎ 209/252-4848), near the South Entrance. Now a National Historic Landmark, the Wawona is a romantic throwback to another century. That has its pros and cons. Private bathrooms were not a big hit in the 19th century, rooms were small to hold in heat, and there are no TVs or phones. Still, the Wawona is charming, less commercial than the accommodations on the valley floor, and offers a restaurant, pool, stables, and a lounge. Doubles are $112 with bathroom and $87 without.

Yosemite Lodge (☎ 209/252-4848) is the next step down in Yosemite Valley accommodations. It's actually not a lodge but a huge complex, with an array of accommodations including luxurious suites with outdoor balconies and striking views of Yosemite Falls. Since the 1997 flood, the lodge has had only 249 of its 495 rooms in use. In addition to a pool and bar, the lodge has two restaurants and a cafeteria that serve mediocre meals. Doubles go for $92.

Curry Village (☎ 209/252-4848) is the valley's low-rent district. This compound of almost 200 cabins and 400 tent cabins varies widely in quality. Some have private bathrooms; others share campground-style facilities. Ironically, the oldest cabins are the nicest. Shoddy construction gives the others a slapped-together appearance, not to mention making them cold and drafty in winter. The tent cabins have wood floors and canvas walls; without real walls to stop noise, they lack any sort of privacy, but they're fun in that summer-camp way. You'll have to sustain yourself with fast food from the Curry Village shopping center, as no cooking is allowed in the rooms. A standard room is $92, a cabin is $75.25 with bathroom and $60 without, and a canvas tent cabin is $40.

An intriguing option bridging the gap between backpacking and staying in a hotel are Yosemite's five backcountry **High Sierra camps.** These wilderness lodges are simple tent cabins and cafeteria tents located in some of the most beautiful, remote parts of the park. The five camps—Glen Aulin, May Lake, Sunrise, Merced Lake, and

Vogelsang—make for good individual destinations. Or you can link several together, since they're arranged in a loose loop about a 10-mile hike from one another—a nice wilderness circuit. Overnight rates are $93 per person and include a tent cabin, breakfast, dinner, bathrooms, and showers. High Sierra camp reservations are accepted beginning in December for the following summer; they're usually booked solid by January. Contact High Sierra Reservations, Yosemite Concession Services, 5410 E. Home Ave., Fresno, CA 93727 (☎ **209/253-5674**).

3 Mammoth Lakes

40 miles E of Yosemite; 319 miles E of San Francisco; 325 miles NE of Los Angeles

High in the Sierra, just southeast of Yosemite, Mammoth Lakes is surrounded by glacier-carved, pine-covered peaks that soar up from flower-filled meadows. It's an alpine region of sweeping beauty and one of California's favorite playgrounds for hiking, biking, horseback riding, skiing, and more. It's also home to one of the top-rated ski resorts in the world, which makes it a great place to play any time of year.

ESSENTIALS

GETTING THERE   It's a 6-hour drive from San Francisco via Calif. 120 over the Tioga Pass in Yosemite (closed in winter); 5 hours north of Los Angeles via Calif. 14 and U.S. 395; and 3 hours south of Reno, Nevada, via U.S. 395. In winter, Mammoth is accessible via U.S. 395 from the north or the south.

VISITOR INFORMATION   For information, contact the **Mammoth Lakes Visitors Bureau,** Calif. 203 (P.O. Box 48), Mammoth Lakes, CA 93546 (☎ **800/ 367-6572** or 760/934-2712).

ENJOYING THE GREAT OUTDOORS

Mammoth Lakes is at the heart of several wilderness areas and is cut through by the San Joaquin and Owens rivers. Mammoth Mountain overlooks the Ansel Adams Wilderness Area to the west and the John Muir Wilderness Area to the southeast, and beyond to the Inyo National Forest and the Sierra National Forest.

The **Mammoth Mountain Ski Area** (☎ **888/462-6668** or 760/934-2571) is the central focus for both summer and winter activities. Visitors can ride the lifts to see panoramic vistas; those who want an active adventure have a world of options. If you do hit the slopes in winter, you may want to contact **Mammoth Area Shuttle (MAS)** (☎ **760/934-0687**) for transportation to and from town and the ski area. The shuttle is free, makes many stops throughout town, and eliminates the long wait in traffic you might encounter if you take your own car.

DOWNHILL SKIING, CROSS-COUNTRY SKIING & SNOWBOARDING In winter Mammoth Mountain has more than 3,500 skiable acres, a 3,100-foot vertical drop, 150 trails (22 with snowmaking), and 31 lifts, including seven high-speed quads. The terrain is 30% beginner, 40% intermediate, and 30% advanced. It's known for power sun, ideal spring skiing conditions, and anywhere from 8 to 12 feet of snow. Lift tickets are around $50.

Cross-country ski centers are at **Tamarack Lodge** (☎ 800/237-6879) (see "Where to Stay," below) and **Sierra Meadows Ski Touring Center** (☎ 760/934-6161). There's also snowmobiling, dogsledding, snowshoeing, and sleigh rides.

If you're renting equipment, you'll save money if you do it in town instead of at the resort. Try **Sandy's Ski & Sports** (☎ 760/934-7518), on Calif. 203 next to Schat's Bakery, for all types of winter equipment, and **Wave Rave Snowboard Shop,** on Main Street (Calif. 203; ☎ 760/934-2471), for snowboards and accessories.

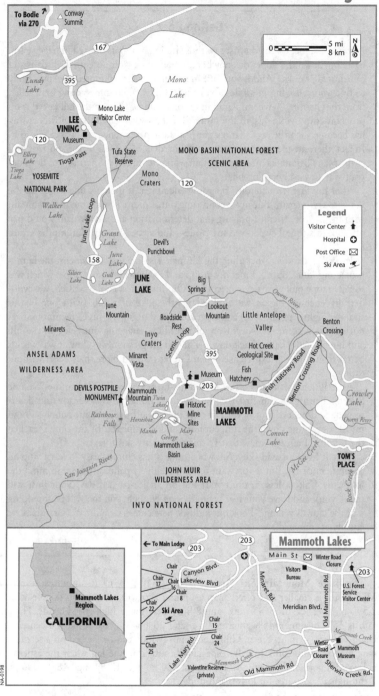

Mammoth Lakes Region

To Bodie via 270
Conway Summit
167
Lundy Lake
395
Mono Lake
Mono Lake Visitor Center
LEE VINING
120
Museum
Ellery Lake
Tioga Pass
Tioga Lake
YOSEMITE NATIONAL PARK
Walker Lake
Tufa State Reserve
MONO BASIN NATIONAL FOREST SCENIC AREA
Mono Craters
120

June Lake Loop
Grant Lake
June Lake
158
Silver Lake
Gull Lake
JUNE LAKE
Devil's Punchbowl

June Mountain

Minarets

ANSEL ADAMS WILDERNESS AREA

Inyo Craters
Minaret Vista

Roadside Rest
Scenic Loop

Big Springs
Lookout Mountain

Little Antelope Valley

Owens River
Benton Crossing

Hot Creek Geological Site

395
Museum
203
Fish Hatchery

Benton Crossing Road
Fish Hatchery Road

DEVILS POSTPILE MONUMENT
Mammoth Mountain
Twin Lakes

Historic Mine Sites
MAMMOTH LAKES

Crowley Lake
Owens River

Rainbow Falls
Horseshoe
Mamie
George
Mary

Convict Lake

TOM'S PLACE

McGee Creek

San Joaquin River
Mammoth Lakes Basin

JOHN MUIR WILDERNESS AREA

Rock Creek

INYO NATIONAL FOREST

Legend

Visitor Center	🛉
Hospital	✚
Post Office	✉
Ski Area	🎿

0   5 mi   8 km

CALIFORNIA

Mammoth Lakes Region

Mammoth Lakes

← To Main Lodge
203
203
Main St   Winter Road Closure
Visitors Bureau
203
U.S. Forest Service Visitor Center

Chair 7
Chair 17
Chair 16
Chair 8
Chair 22
Ski Area
Chair 15
Chair 24
Chair 25

Canyon Blvd.
Lakeview Blvd.
Minaret Rd.
Meridian Blvd.
Old Mammoth Rd.

Mammoth Creek

Lake Mary Rd.
Mammoth Creek
Old Mammoth Rd.
Valentine Reserve (private)

Winter Road Closure
Mammoth Museum
Sherwin Creek Rd.

NA-0198

Get on Board

If you're like me, when you first saw those junior skate-rats dressed in baggy garb, barreling down the slopes on snowboards, you stuck your nose up in disdain and murmured "Punks." And if you, like me, in all fairness attempted the sport, only to find yourself lying in a pile of your own limbs while some young brat yelled from the chairlift, "Give it up grandma; you could *walk* down the hill faster!" you probably loved your skis all the more. But that was then. Today snowboarding has become such the rage that it's not just those pesky renegades who are into it. In fact, there are plenty of polite, mature boarders who swear by the sport, as well as the many beginners on the mountain who offer moral support as you flounder your way toward boarding bliss.

After my first (treacherous) boarding encounter, it took a while to get up the nerve to try it again. But my second time out, I didn't just charge the mountain with my boarder friends, praying that determination and masochism would pay off. No, this time I swallowed my pride—and signed up for Mammoth's group lesson.

Packed in padding (including the ultimate fashion embarrassment, the fanny-protecting "duck butt"), I met my group at the wimpiest bunny slope, which was so flat, a rope pull wasn't even necessary. Our instructor, cool-guy Rich, was wonderfully encouraging as we hobbled up the joke of a hill (with our boards strapped tightly to one foot) and then attempted to imitate his elementary moves during our descent. This went on all morning—dragging ourselves up the hill and intentionally falling back down. Though progression was slow, it was worlds better than my prior experience, when I never traveled more than 2 feet without eating it.

After lunch break (and a few loosen-me-up beers) we headed to the "Sesame Street" chairlift for our first true bunny-slope bonanza. I was ready and determined. And believe it or not, I not only made it off the chairlift, but also found myself zigzagging down the run, euphoric and triumphant. By the time I reached the bottom, I already knew that I'd abandoned my skis forever.

Take it from an avid skier: Snowboarding is less clumsy, easy to learn, and an absolute must-try. But if you want to do it relatively painlessly, keep in mind the following: Take a lesson, don't start out on an ice-packed day (your butt will thank you), and leave your fear behind. Soon enough, you too will be shredding past the crowds yelling, "Look out kiddies, here comes Grandma!" (Grandpas are equally encouraged.)

—*Erika Lenkert*

The **June Mountain Ski Area** (☎ 760/648-7733), 20 minutes north of Mammoth, is smaller and offers many summer activities. It has 500 skiable acres, a 2,590-foot vertical drop, 35 trails, and 8 lifts, including 2 high-speed quads. The terrain is 35% beginner, 45% intermediate, and 20% advanced. It's at the center of a chain of lakes—Grant, Silver, Gull, and June—which can be viewed on a scenic driving loop around Calif. 158. It's especially beautiful in the fall when the aspens are ablaze with gold. Lift tickets $40 for adults, $30 for ages 13 through 18, $20 for ages 7 through 12, and free for kids 6 and under.

MOUNTAIN BIKING   In summer Mammoth Mountain becomes one huge bike park and climbing playground. The **Bike Center** at the base of the mountain has rentals and accessories. The bike park is famous for its **Kamikaze Downhill Trail,** an obstacle arena and slalom course where riders can test their balance and skill. There's also an area designed for kids. A pass granting unlimited access to the gondola and trail systems is $23 for adults, $12 for children 12 and under; with limited uphill access it's $18 for adults, $10 for children. The park operates daily from 9am to 6pm, from about July 1 to September 29 and then weekends-only to October 13.

In town, mountain bikes can also be rented from the **Footloose Sports Center,** at the corner of Canyon and Minaret (☎ 760/934-2400). The **NORBA National Mountain Bike Championships** are held here in the summer. Regular bikes go for $28 per day; fancy ones with high suspension (for mountain biking) go for $33; and top-of-the-line bikes go for $38.

CLIMBING   Climbing and orienteering courses are offered by **Mammoth Mountain Adventure Connection** (☎ 760/934-0606).

TROUT FISHING   Mammoth Lakes Basin sits in a canyon a couple of miles west of town. Here are the lakes—Mary, Mamie, Horseshoe, George, and Twin—that have made the region known for trout fishing. Southeast of town, Crowley Lake is also famous for trout fishing, as are the San Joaquin and Owens rivers. In addition, there are plenty of other lakes in which to spin your reel.

For fishing information and guides, contact **Rick's Sport Center,** at Calif. 203 and Center Street (☎ 760/934-3416); **The Trout Fitter,** in the Shell Mart Center at Main Street and Old Mammoth Road (☎ 760/924-3676); and **Kittredge Sports,** Main Street and Forest Trail (☎ 760/934-7566), which rents equipment, supplies guides, teaches fly-fishing, and offers backcountry trips and packages.

KAYAKING   Kayaks are available at Crowley Lake from **Caldera Kayaks** (☎ 760/935-4942) from $30 a day. This outfitter also offers half- and full-day trips on Crowley and Mono lakes and provides instruction as well.

PACK TRIPS   The region is also an equestrian's paradise, and numerous outfitters offer pack trips. Among them are **Red's Meadows Pack Station,** Red's Meadows, past Minaret Vista (☎ 800/292-7758 or 760/934-2345); **Mammoth Lakes Pack Outfit,** Lake Mary Road, past Twin Lakes (☎ 760/934-2434), which offers 1- to 6-day riding trips and semiannual horse drives, plus other wilderness workshops; and **McGee Creek Pack Station,** McGee Creek Road, Crowley Lake (☎ 760/935-4324).

HIKING   Trails abound in the Mammoth Lakes Basin area. They include the half-mile-long **Panorama Dome Trail,** located just past the turnoff to Twin Lakes on Lake Mary Road. The trail leads to the top of a plateau that provides a view of the Owens Valley and Lakes Basin. Another trail of interest is the 5-mile-long **Duck Lake Trail,** which starts at the end of the Coldwater Creek parking lot with switchbacks across Duck Pass past several lakes to Duck Lake. The head of the **Inyo Craters Trail** is reached via a gravel road, off the Mammoth Scenic Loop Road. This trail takes you to the edge of these craters and a sign that explains how they were created.

For additional trail information and maps, contact the **Mammoth Ranger Station** (☎ 760/924-5500). For equipment and maps, go to **Footloose Sports Center,** at the corner of Canyon Boulevard and Minaret Road (☎ 760/934-2400), which also rents in-line skates and mountain bikes.

EXPLORING THE SURROUNDING AREA

Bodie, one of the most authentic ghost towns in the West, lies about an hour's drive north of Mammoth, past the Tioga Pass entrance to Yosemite. In 1870 more than 10,000 people lived in Bodie; today it's an eerie shell. En route to Bodie, you'll pass **Mono Lake,** near Lee Vining, which has startling tufa towers arising from its

Winter Driving in the Sierra

Winter driving in the Sierra Nevada Range can be dangerous. While the most hazardous roads are often closed, others are negotiable by vehicles with four-wheel drive or with tire chains. Be prepared for sudden blizzards, and protect yourself by taking these important pretrip precautions:

• Check road conditions before setting out by calling ☎ **800/427-7623.**
• If you're driving a rental car, let the rental company know you're planning to drive in snow, and ask whether the antifreeze is prepared for cold climates.
• Make sure your heater and defroster work.
• Always carry chains. If there's a blizzard, the police will not allow vehicles without chains on certain highways. You'll have to pay about $40 to "chain up" at the side of the road.
• Recommended items include an ice scraper, a small shovel, sand or burlap for traction if you get stuck, warm blankets—and an extra car key (it's surprisingly common for motorists to lock their keys in the car while putting on tire chains).
• Don't think winter ends in March. At the end of April 1998, snow was up to 7 feet high on the sides of the roads leading to the valley, and cold temperatures made more snowfall a very real possibility.

surface—limestone deposits formed by underground springs. It's a major bird-watching area—about 300 species nest or stop here during their migrations.

WHERE TO STAY

The mountain's resort is expensive, so your best bet is to opt for accommodations in the town; besides, you'll be closer to the restaurants and nightlife. Regardless, the mountain and town are within a 5-minute drive from each other, so you're never too far from the action.

CAMPING   There are more than 700 **campsites** available in the area. These sites open on varying dates in June, depending on the weather. The largest campgrounds are at Convict Lake, Twin Lakes and Cold Water (both in the Mammoth Lakes Basin), and Red's Meadow. For additional information call the **Mammoth Ranger Station** at ☎ 760/924-5500.

SUPER-CHEAP SLEEPS

Fern Creek Lodge. Rte. 3, Box 7, June Lake, CA 93529. ☎ **760/648-7722.** 10 cabins, 4 apts. TV. Cabin for 2 Sept–July $47.50, Aug $52.50; 4-bedroom cabin (sleep up to 14) Sept–July $200, Aug $225. DISC, MC, V. "Certain pets" allowed ($10 extra).

June Mountain skiing is less than a mile away and Mammoth is 25 miles from this fully furnished budget lodge. Up until a few years ago, the place was a complete dump (it was built in 1927 and has definitely weathered with age), but thanks to the new owners, the lodge is slowly but surely coming back to life. Cabins are small and more popular in summer when a fireplace isn't needed. They've got just enough room for a bed, a table and chairs, and small kitchen and bathroom, and come complete with linens and kitchen appliances. There are no phones in rooms, but there is a pay phone on the premises.

✪ **Motel 6.** 3372 Main St. (P.O. Box 1260), Mammoth Lakes, CA 93546. ☎ **800/4-MOTEL-6** or 760/934-6660. Fax 760/934-6989. 151 units. A/C TV TEL. Winter

$45–$60 double; summer from $58 double. Extra person $5. AARP discounts. AE, DC, DISC, MC, V.

The rooms may be small, but after a $1.5-million renovation in 1997, accommodations here are the newest—and nicest—around in this price range. Although quarters are a bit more cramped than at some other options, factor in the heated pool (summer only), vending machines, and free coffee in the lobby, and you've got all you really need to set up camp.

ULLR Lodge. On Minaret Rd., near Main St. (Calif. 203; P.O. Box 53), Mammoth Lakes, CA 93546. ☎ **760/934-2454.** Fax 760/934-3353. 17 units, 4 with bathroom; 8 dorm beds. Summer double with bathroom and TV $39–$59; double without bathroom $32–$61; dorm bed $14. Winter double with bathroom and TV $39–$49; double without bathroom $30–$48; dorm bed $18–$21. MC, V.

If you're planning to plunk down all your money on play, you may want to cut corners by staying here. ULLR Lodge is the closest thing around to a hostel (expect plenty of young folks), but does offer private rooms and bonuses like use of the fireplace lounge (with TV), community kitchen, and sauna. For $20 don't expect the Ritz, but rather older, rustic accommodations run by a kindhearted staff. A few nice bonuses: Everyone gets keys to their rooms (even dorm rooms, which also have a private locker for each person). Pay phones are on the property and the desk takes messages. Reserve well in advance in winter.

FOR A FEW BUCKS MORE

Sherwin Villas. P.O. Box 2249, Mammoth Lakes, CA 93546. ☎ **800/228-5291** or 760/934-4773. 70 condos. TV. One-bedroom unit for up to 4 people $95–$110 winter, $70 summer. Two-bedroom loft for up to 6 people $130–$180 winter, $85 summer. Extra person $10. MC, V.

Just outside the center of town on Old Mammoth Road is this cluster of woodsy condos, perfect for larger families or groups of friends traveling together. Here you'll find one-, two-, three-, and four-bedroom units, each with a fully stocked kitchen, fireplace, linens, and access to the sauna, Jacuzzi, pool, tennis courts, and free ski shuttle that will take you to the slopes (a 5-min. drive away). Considering how many people you can pack into these apartments—and that if you stay 4 weekday nights, the 5th night is free—it's a good deal. When making reservations, make sure you specify exactly what you're looking for; each condo is independently owned and varies dramatically in both decor and quality. You can also request a phone.

Snow Goose Inn. 57 Forest Trail (P.O. Box 387), Mammoth Lakes, CA 93546. ☎ **800/ 874-7368** or 760/934-5655. www.mammothweb.com/snowgoose/ snowgoose.html. 19 units. TV TEL. Winter Sun–Thurs $78 double, $148 suite; Fri–Sat $98 double, $168 suite. Summer $68 double; $98 suite. Rates include breakfast, evening wine, and appetizers. Doubles with kitchens $10 extra. Special packages available. DISC, MC, V.

The owners here run this place as if it were a B&B rather than a traditional hotel. Set half a block off the main street near a number of restaurants, the Snow Goose consists of two separate two-story buildings. Rooms are comfortably and attractively furnished, and two come with kitchens. The two-bedroom suites can accommodate four in a two-story space with dinette, kitchen, and living room complete with fireplace. Antiques add a graceful note to some of the public rooms, and the helpful staff can direct you to cross-country and downhill skiing possibilities 3 miles away.

MODERATELY PRICED OPTIONS

Sierra Lodge. 3540 Main St. (Calif. 203), Mammoth Lakes, CA 93546. ☎ **800/356-5711** or 760/934-8881. Fax 760/934-7231. 36 units. TV TEL. Winter Sun–Thurs $95–$110 double; Fri–Sat $110–$130 double. Summer Sun–Thurs $75 double; Fri–Sat $85 double. MC, V.

In the heart of the resort town near a resort shuttle stop, this two-story inn offers clean, modern surroundings; rock-built fireplaces in the public areas; and a sincere effort to please its guests. Rooms are large and equipped with a kitchenette and utensils, but are unfortunately decorated in upscale-motel style. Still, everything is spotless, rooms have small patios or balconies, and although there's no proper closet, there is a nook to hang your things as well as a few drawers. Facilities include an outdoor Jacuzzi and a fireside room for relaxing. Continental breakfast is the only meal served, but many restaurants are nearby. Smoking is not permitted.

Tamarack Lodge. Twin Lakes Rd., off Lake Mary Rd. (P.O. Box 69), Mammoth Lakes, CA 93546. ☎ **800/237-6879** or 760/934-2442. Fax 760/934-2281. 11 units, 6 with bathroom; 25 cabins. TEL. Winter $80 double without bathroom; $95–$140 double with bathroom; $110–$300 cabin. Summer $70 double without bathroom; $85–$105 double with bathroom; $85–$260 cabin. Special packages available. DISC, MC, V.

The lodge and cabin accommodations at this rustic lakeside retreat are nothing fancy, but that's exactly what's kept guests coming here since the 1920s. Folks relax in front of the fire in the sitting room or hang out in their rooms, which are intentionally rustic with knotty-pine walls and modern furnishings. The cabins, which can accommodate two to nine people, are dotted around the property and offer a variety of configurations, from studios with wood-burning stove and shower to two-bedroom/two-bathroom accommodations with fireplace. Each cabin has a fully equipped kitchen, but there's no daily maid service (fresh towels are provided at the front desk). In the main lodge, there are rooms with private bathrooms and with shared bathrooms.

The lodge has a very popular cross-country ski center with more than 25 miles of trails and skating lanes, ski rentals, and a ski school. Boat and canoe rentals are also available. The dining room, overlooking Twin Lakes, offers California and continental fare.

White Horse Inn. 2180 Old Mammoth Rd. (P.O. Box 2326), Mammoth Lakes, CA 93546. ☎ **800/982-5657** or 760/924-3656. 5 units. Winter $105–$135 double; summer $75–$95 double. Rates include breakfast. DISC, MC, V.

Set about a mile southwest of the resort's center, this gray-and-white gabled house was built in the 1950s. Unlike its competitors, there's no flowery Laura Ashley decor here. Accommodations are furnished eclectically and wittily, each with a distinct theme carried out by, say, all Chinese antiques or a furniture ensemble from Austria and Mexico. A country breakfast is included as part of the price, and in nice weather you can enjoy it on an outdoor deck. Wine and cheese are served near a billiard table during the early evening. There's a hot tub on the premises and a communal kitchen reserved for the use of guests.

WORTH A SPLURGE

Mammoth Mountain Inn. Minaret Rd. (P.O. Box 353), Mammoth Lakes, CA 93546. ☎ **800/228-4947** or 760/934-2581. Fax 760/934-0701. 173 units, 40 condos (some suitable for up to 13 people). TV TEL. Winter $110–$210 double; from $425 condo. Summer $99–$130 double; from $195 condo. Special ski and mountain-biking packages available. AE, MC, V.

Located opposite the ski lodge at the base of the ski resort, the inn started out in 1954 as only one building, but was expanded a decade later into a larger, glossier complex. Though it was remodeled in the early 1990s, it still retains the rustic charm you'd expect from a mountain resort. Rooms are well equipped and pleasantly furnished, but not exactly inspired. Families love this place because of its day-care activities, cribs ($10 one-time charge), playground, box lunches for picnics, game room, and even picnic tables. There's also an array of sports facilities, including bicycles, fishing or hiking guides, downhill or cross-country skiing, sleighing, horseback riding, and hay-wagon rides. The hotel has a snack bar and offers barbecues and room service. The rather standard restaurant serves breakfast, lunch, and dinner. Extras include free airport transportation and occasional entertainment. A whirlpool spa is also on the property.

WHERE TO DINE
SUPER-CHEAP EATS

Roberto's Cafe. 271 Old Mammoth Rd. ☎ **760/934-3667.** Main courses $6.75–$9.75. DC, DISC, MC, V. Daily 11am–10pm. MEXICAN.

Plunk down on a wooden bench and table at this small restaurant for the best Mexican food in town. The decor features hand-painted tiles and original Mexican art, and the menu is pretty simple. Just choose one of the combination plates of chicken or beef tacos, burritos, chimichangas, or enchiladas; all, of course, come with rice and beans. You can also order à la carte ($3.75 to $4.95). Wednesday night is "Locos Night," when draft beers go for a measly 75¢, margarita specials $2, and you can order a whole pitcher for $3.75.

FOR A FEW BUCKS MORE

Berger's Restaurant. 6118 Minaret Rd. ☎ **760/934-6622.** Reservations recommended. Main courses $8.25–$14.95. MC, V. Daily 11am–9:30pm. AMERICAN.

If after all that slope swishing you're looking to fill your tummy with a big slab of meat, head to Berger's, the best in American cuisine. Its cabinlike interior, with local photographs on the wooden walls, fits its surroundings. Portions are huge and include an array of burgers, steak, ribs, chicken, and sandwiches. There are even a few hefty salads to satisfy a more health-conscious hunger. Entrees include salad, garlic bread, and either fries or a baked potato. Sandwiches, which cost up to $7 and come with salad and fries, will also easily fill you up without emptying your wallet. The children's menu is the ultimate bargain, offering a selection of kid-friendly feasts for under $6. The daily lunch specials are most coveted by locals, but if you want to try one, come early—they almost always sell out.

Grumpy's Saloon and Eatery. 37 Mammoth Rd. ☎ **760/934-8587.** Main courses $6.25–$15.95. AE, MC, V. Mon–Thurs 11:30am–11pm; Fri 11:30am–midnight; Sat 11am–midnight, Sun 11am–11pm; bar stays open until 2am. AMERICAN.

Don't let the name fool you, Grumpy's is actually a fun-loving saloon with an Old West feel (minus the big-screen TVs, pool tables, and video games). The bar serves a great selection of beers on tap, and the hearty and affordable grub features burgers (go for the Grumpy Burger), tasty barbecued ribs, homemade chili, a handful of Mexican items, and the famous quarter-pound Dogger, an unbelievably enormous hot dog. Everything on the menu comes with a choice of fries, coleslaw, or barbecued baked beans, so trust us when we say you won't leave hungry. Stop by for happy hour when there's usually a free buffet of hors d'oeuvres that may include Buffalo wings, cheese and crackers, or mini-quesadillas.

MODERATELY PRICED OPTIONS

Whiskey Creek. 18 Main St. (at Minaret Rd.). ☎ **760/934-2555.** Reservations recommended. Main courses $11–$22. AE, DC, DISC, MC, V. Daily 5:30–10pm; bar stays open until 2am. AMERICAN.

If you favor surf-and-turf fare combined with alpine atmosphere, you've found your dining spot. The building's wraparound windows encompass a view of the snow-clad mountains, and the menu is known for its beef, baby back ribs, tequila shrimp, and lemon-garlic chicken. While this is better than many options in town, it's our least favorite of those listed.

Although the dining room may offer a peaceful experience, the upstairs brew pub is a whole different world. The recently added Mammoth Brewing Company and its live music (every night from 9pm until at least 1am) make this place the number one spot to mingle, slam suds, and get happy. (Think very crowded, postcollegiate frat party.) The cover charge ranges from free to $5.

WORTH A SPLURGE

✪ **Nevados.** Main St. (at Minaret Rd.). ☎ **760/934-4466.** Reservations recommended. Main courses $14–$23; fixed-price meal $27. AE, CB, DC, DISC, MC, V. Daily 5:30–9:30pm. EUROPEAN/CALIFORNIA.

If you want seriously good food and cheery atmosphere, reserve a table here. The innovative cuisine is fresh and homemade, and the tasty bread is house-baked. The real clincher here, however, is the $27 fixed-price meal: a first course such as potato-crusted crab cake, salad of duck confit and baby lettuces, or seared-tuna sashimi; a main course featuring the likes of rosemary rack of lamb or grilled New York steak; and dessert (love that warm pear-and-almond tart). Throw in the casual-but-sweet ambiance (white tablecloths, candles, and French country murals) and the extensive selection of wines, single-malt scotches, and single-batch bourbons, and it's no wonder this is the hangout for ski instructors and race coaches.

✪ **Skadi.** 587 Old Mammoth Rd. (in the Sherwin Plaza III Shopping Mall). ☎ **760/934-3902.** Reservations recommended. Main courses $9.50–$20. AE, MC, V. Wed–Mon 5:30–10pm. ECLECTIC.

The minimall where this restaurant is located (a half mile south of Mammoth Lake's center) may not be the home of the Viking goddess of skiing and hunting whose name this restaurant bears, but she wouldn't have cared once she saw the view—it encompasses most of the mountains for miles around. This universal favorite is perfect for an après-ski cocktail at the 14-seat bar, a snack from the substantial selection of appetizers and desserts, or a full-blown dinner on the town.

The decor evokes a big-city postmodern aura that's a welcome change after all that local alpine rusticity. Main courses are self-proclaimed "Alpine cuisine" and include such dishes as smoked trout Napoleon or grilled venison with lingonberries and a game sauce. Finish the evening with crème brûlée or the frozen macadamia-nut parfait.

4 Devils Postpile National Monument

10 miles W of Mammoth; 50 miles E of Yosemite's eastern boundary

by Andrew Rice

Just a few miles outside the town of Mammoth Lakes, Devils Postpile National Monument is home to one of nature's most curious geological spectacles. Formed when molten lava cracked as it cooled, the 60-foot-high, blue-gray basalt columns that form the postpile look more like some sort of enormous eerie pipe organ or a jumble of giant pencil leads than anything you'd expect to see made from stone. The mostly six-sided columns formed underground and were exposed when glaciers scoured this valley in the last ice age, some 10,000 years ago. Similar examples of columnar basalt are found in Ireland and Scotland.

Because of its high elevation (7,900 ft.) and heavy snowfall, the monument is open only from summer until early fall. The weather in the summer is usually clear and warm, but afternoon thundershowers can soak the unprepared. Nights are still cold, so bring good tents and sleeping bags if you'll be camping. The Mammoth Lakes region is famous for its beautiful lakes—but unfortunately all that water also means lots of mosquitoes. Plan for them.

From late June until early September, cars are prohibited in the monument between 7:30am and 5:30pm because of the small roads' inability to handle the traffic. Visitors must take a shuttle bus from the Mammoth Mountain Inn to and from locations in the monument. While it takes some planning, the resulting peace and quiet is well worth the trouble and makes you wonder why the park service hasn't implemented similar programs at Yosemite Valley and other traffic hot spots.

HIKING   There's more to Devils Postpile than a bunch of rocks, no matter how impressive they might be. Located on the banks of the San Joaquin River in the heart of a landscape of granite peaks and crystalline mountain lakes, the 800-acre park is a gateway to a hiker's paradise. Short paths lead to the top of the postpile and to Soda Springs, a spring of cold carbonated water.

A longer hike (about 1¼ miles) from the separate Rainbow Falls trailhead will take you to **spectacular Rainbow Falls,** where the entire middle fork of the San Joaquin plunges 101 feet from a lava cliff. From the trail, a stairway and short trail lead to the base of the falls and swimming holes below.

The **John Muir Trail,** which connects Yosemite National Park with Kings Canyon and Sequoia national parks, and the **Pacific Crest Trail** both run through here. Named after the famous conservationist and author who is largely credited with saving Yosemite and popularizing the Sierra Nevada as a place worth preserving, the 211-mile John Muir Trail traverses some of the most rugged and remote parts of the Sierra. There are two accesses to it in Devils Postpile, one via the ranger station, and the other from Rainbow Falls Trailhead. From here you can hike as far as your feet will take you, north or south.

Note that mountain bikes are not permitted on trails.

CAMPING   While most visitors stay in or around Mammoth Lakes, the monument does maintain a 21-site campground with piped water, flush toilets, fire pits, and picnic tables on a first-come, first-served basis. Rates are $8 per night. Bears are common in the park, so proper food-storage measures must be taken. Leashed pets are permitted on trails and in camp. Call the **National Park Service** (☎ **760/934-2289**) for details, but don't expect an answer during winter—the park is closed. There are several other U.S. Forest Service campgrounds nearby, including **Red's Meadow** and **Upper Soda Springs.**

5 En Route to Sequoia & Kings Canyon

Though Visalia is the official "gateway" and the city closest to Sequoia and Kings Canyon national parks, it's still 40 minutes to the park entrance. Much closer to the entrance is the small town of **Three Rivers,** which has little more than some coffee shops, motels, and a restaurant. However, we've included information on both areas, should you decide to make Visalia your home base.

ESSENTIALS
GETTING THERE   If you're driving from San Francisco, take I-580 east to I-5 south to Calif. 198 east.

The **Visalia Municipal Airport,** 9500 Airport Dr. No. 1 (☎ 209/651-1131), is served by **Shuttle by United** (☎ 800/241-6522). **Amtrak** (☎ 800/USA-RAIL) stops at nearby Hanford, and there's a shuttle from there to Visalia.

VISITOR INFORMATION   For information, contact the **Visalia Convention and Visitors Bureau,** 301 E. Acequia St., Visalia, CA 93291 (☎ **800/524-0303** or 209/738-3435; www.cvbvasilia.com). Since Three Rivers has no tourist office, you should call here for information on the town.

VISALIA
WHERE TO STAY

Ben Maddox House. 601 N. Encina St., Visalia, CA 93291. ☎ **800/401-9800** or 209/739-0721. Fax 209/625-0420. www.placetostay.com/visalia-benmaddox/. 4 units. A/C TV TEL. $75–$90 double. Rates include breakfast. AE, DISC, MC, V.

Set in a residential street of Victorian homes, 4 blocks from the town's main street, the Ben Maddox House is an impressive sight. Its triangular gable is punctuated with a round window and two extremely tall palm trees looming over the front yard. The house, built in 1876, is constructed of redwood, and its rooms retain their original dark-oak trim and white-oak floors. The guest rooms contain fridges and 18th- and 19th-century furnishings, and the two front rooms have French doors leading to two small porch sitting areas. A pool and hot tub in the back are open to guests, and a full made-to-order breakfast is served.

Radisson Hotel. 300 S. Court St., Visalia, CA 93291. ☎ **800/333-3333** or 209/636-1111. Fax 209/636-8224. 208 units. A/C MINIBAR TV TEL. $100–$138 double; $225–$450 suite. Extra person $15. Cribs provided free. AE, CB, DC, MC, V.

Seven blocks from the town center, the eight-story Radisson is the finest hotel in Visalia and a family favorite for those en route to Sequoia and Kings Canyon national parks. Some of the attractively furnished rooms open onto balconies. This is certainly not the most glamorous Radisson in California, but it's serviceable in every way, offering a whirlpool, exercise equipment, pool with poolside service, a fleet of bikes, room service until 2am, and free airport transfers. The restaurant serves breakfast, lunch, and dinner, with last seating at 10pm. You can also patronize the local bar, which provides entertainment on Friday and Saturday nights.

A GOOD PLACE TO SPLURGE ON A MEAL

✪ **The Vintage Press.** 216 N. Willis St. ☎ **209/733-3033.** Reservations recommended. Main courses $13–$26. AE, CB, DC, MC, V. Mon–Thurs 11:30am–2pm and 6–10:30pm; Fri–Sat 11:30am–2pm and 6–11pm; Sun 10am–2pm and 5–9pm. AMERICAN/CONTINENTAL.

This is the best restaurant within a surrounding 100-mile radius, a culinary stopover of widely acknowledged merit. The design is reminiscent of a fin de siècle gin mill in gold-rush San Francisco, with a bar imported from that city manufactured by the Brunswick Company (of bowling-alley fame), lots of antiques bought at local auctions, and glittering panels of leaded glass and mirrors. The place is big enough (250 seats) to feed a boatload of gold-rush hopefuls, and has a bustling bar/lounge where a piano player presents live music Thursday through Saturday from 5:30 to 9pm.

The menu is supplemented by daily specials—a zesty rack of lamb roasted in a cabernet sauce with rosemary and pistachios, for example. The regular menu offers about a dozen meat and fish dishes, with steaks as well as such dishes as red snapper with lemon, almonds, and capers, or pork tenderloin with Dijon mustard, red chili, and honey. To start, we recommend farm-raised fresh oysters on the half shell or the wild mushrooms with cognac in puff pastry.

WHERE TO STAY IN THREE RIVERS

The **Holiday Inn Express,** 40820 Sierra Dr. (Calif. 198), Three Rivers, CA 93271 (☎ **800/HOLIDAY** or 209/561-9000), has an outpost here. Rates range from $69 to $109. For other options, contact **The Reservation Centre** (☎ **209/561-0410;** www.sequoiapark.com).

6 Sequoia & Kings Canyon National Parks

30 miles E of Visalia

by Andrew Rice

Only 200 road miles separate Yosemite from Sequoia and Kings Canyon national parks, but they're worlds apart. While the National Park Service has taken every opportunity to modernize, accessorize, and urbanize Yosemite, resulting in a frenetic tourist scene much like the cities so many of us strive to escape, at Sequoia and Kings Canyon they've treated the wilderness beauty of the park with respect and care. Only one road loops through the park, the Generals Highway, and no road traverses the Sierra here. The park service recommends that vehicles over 22 feet long avoid the steep and windy stretch between Potwisha Campground and the Giant Forest in Sequoia National Park. Generally speaking, the park is much less accessible by car than most, but spectacular for those willing to head out on foot.

The Sierra Nevada tilts upward as it runs south. **Mount Whitney,** at 14,494 feet the highest point in the lower 48 states, is just one of many high peaks in Sequoia and Kings Canyon. The **Pacific Crest Trail** also reaches its highest point here, crossing north to south through both parks. In addition to rocky, snow-covered peaks, Sequoia and Kings Canyon are home to the largest groves of giant sequoias in the Sierra Nevada, as well as the headwaters of the Kern, Kaweah, and Kings rivers. A few small, high-country lakes are home to some of the only remaining pure-strain golden trout. Bear, deer, and numerous smaller animals and birds depend on the park's miles of wild habitat for year-round breeding and feeding grounds.

Technically two separate parks, Sequoia and Kings Canyon are contiguous and managed jointly from the park headquarters at Ash Mountain, just past the entrance on Calif. 198 east of Visalia.

JUST THE FACTS

Most visitors make a loop through the parks by entering at Grant Grove and leaving through Ash Mountain, or vice versa.

ENTRANCE FEES   A $10-per-car fee is good for 7 days' entry at any park entrance. An annual pass costs $20; the Golden Age pass offers lifetime access for seniors 62 and over for $10; and blind visitors or visitors with permanent disabilities get free entry with the Golden Access pass.

VISITOR CENTERS & INFORMATION   The **Lodgepole** and **Grant Grove** visitor centers are the largest, with a full selection of park information and displays about the history, biology, and geology of this incredible place. Some time spent here will pay off by letting you decide which parts of the park you most want to concentrate on. For visitor information before you go, call ☎ **209/565-3341.**

AVOIDING THE CROWDS   To escape the crowds and see less-used areas of the park, enter on one of the dead-end roads to Mineral King or Cedar Grove (only open in summer), or South Fork. The lack of through-traffic makes these parts of the park incredibly peaceful even at full capacity, and they're gateways to some of the best hiking.

RANGER PROGRAMS   Park rangers offer hikes, campfire talks, and slide shows at several campgrounds and visitor centers during the summer.

Fill'er Up

There are no gas stations in the park, so be sure to fill up your gas tank before you enter.

REGULATIONS Mountain bikes and dogs are forbidden on all park trails (dogs are only permitted in developed areas, but must be leashed). The park service allows firewood gathering at campgrounds, although supplies can be scarce. Removing wood from living or standing trees is forbidden.

RESERVATIONS FOR CAMPING Wilderness permits are required for all overnight trips in the park. You can reserve the $10 permits in advance by writing the Wilderness Office, Superintendent, Sequoia and Kings Canyon National Parks, HCR 89 Box 60, Three Rivers, CA 93271. You must reserve backpacking permits for climbing Mt. Whitney via the Inyo National Forest. Reservations can be made by phone, fax, or mail through **Wilderness Reservations,** P.O. Box 430, Big Pine, CA 93513 (☎ **888/374-3773** or 760/938-1136; fax 760/938-1137).

THE SEASONS In the high altitudes, where most Sequoia and Kings Canyon visitors are headed, summer is short and the winters are cold. Snow, although rare, is not unheard of in July and August. At mid-elevations, where the sequoias grow, spring can come as early as April and as late as June. Afternoon showers are occasional. During winter months, only the main roads into the parks are usually open; the climate can range from bitter cold to pleasant and can change minute by minute. The Generals Highway between Sequoia and Kings Canyon closes for plowing during and after snowstorms. Be ready for anything if you head into the backcountry on skis. During summer, poison oak and rattlesnakes are common in lower elevations, and mosquitoes are plentiful in all wet areas.

SEEING THE HIGHLIGHTS

There are some 75 groves of giant sequoias in the park, but the most convenient places to see the trees are **Grant Grove,** in Kings Canyon near the park entrance on Calif. 180 from Fresno, and **Giant Forest,** a huge grove of trees containing 40 miles of footpaths, located 16 miles from the entrance to Sequoia National Park on Calif. 198. Saving the sequoias was one of the reasons Sequoia National Park was created in 1890 at the request of San Joaquin Valley residents; it's the second-oldest national park in the United States.

The 2-mile **Congress Trail** loop in the Giant Forest starts at the base of the **General Sherman Tree,** the largest living thing in the world. Single branches of this monster are more than 7 feet thick. Each year it grows enough wood to make a 60-foot-tall tree of normal dimensions. Other trees in the grove are nearly as large, and many of the peaceful-looking trees have also been saddled with strangely militaristic and political monikers like General Lee and Lincoln. Longer trails lead to remote reaches of the grove and nearby meadows.

Unlike the coast redwoods, which reproduce by sprouting or by seeds, giant sequoias only reproduce by seed. Adult sequoias rarely die of diseases and are protected from most fires by thick bark. The huge trees have surprisingly shallow roots, and most die from toppling when their roots are damaged for some reason and can no longer support them. These groves, like the ones in Yosemite, were explored by conservationist and nature writer John Muir, who named the Giant Forest.

Besides the sequoia groves, Sequoia and Kings Canyon are home to the most pristine wilderness in the Sierra Nevada. At **Road's End** on the Kings Canyon Highway

Sequoia & Kings Canyon National Parks

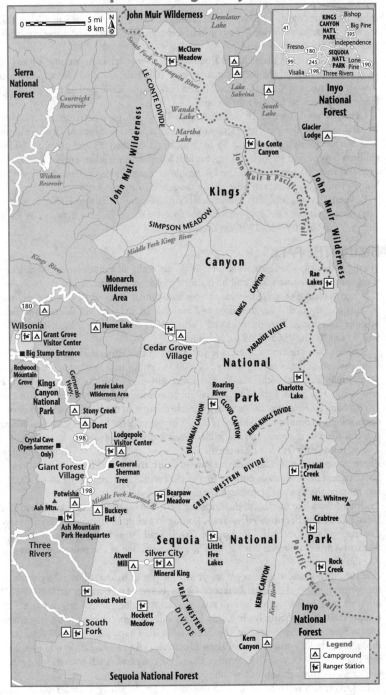

John Muir Wilderness

Desolator Lake

McClure Meadow

KINGS CANYON NAT'L PARK   Bishop
Big Pine
41
Fresno   180   Independence
SEQUOIA NAT'L PARK   Lone Pine
99   245
Visalia   198   Three Rivers   190

Lake Sabrina

South Lake

LE CONTE DIVIDE

South Fork San Joaquin River

Wanda Lake

Martha Lake

Sierra National Forest

Courtright Reservoir

John Muir Wilderness

Wishon Reservoir

Le Conte Canyon

Glacier Lodge

Inyo National Forest

John Muir & Pacific Crest Trail

John Muir Wilderness

Kings

SIMPSON MEADOW

Middle Fork Kings River

Kings River

Canyon

Monarch Wilderness Area

Rae Lakes

KINGS CANYON

180

Wilsonia

Grant Grove Visitor Center

Big Stump Entrance

Hume Lake

Cedar Grove Village

PARADISE VALLEY

National

Redwood Mountain Grove

Kings Canyon National Park

Generals Hwy.

Jennie Lakes Wilderness Area

Roaring River

Charlotte Lake

Crystal Cave (Open Summer Only)

Stony Creek

Dorst

Lodgepole Visitor Center

DEADMAN CANYON

CLOUD CANYON

Park

KERN-KINGS DIVIDE

198

Giant Forest Village

General Sherman Tree

Tyndall Creek

Potwisha

Bearpaw Meadow

Mt. Whitney

Ash Mtn.

198

Middle Fork Kaweah R.

Buckeye Flat

GREAT WESTERN DIVIDE

Crabtree

Ash Mountain Park Headquartes

Three Rivers

Atwell Mill

Silver City

Little Five Lakes

Sequoia

National

Park

Rock Creek

Mineral King

KERN CANYON

Pacific Crest Trail

Lookout Point

Hockett Meadow

GREAT WESTERN DIVIDE

Kern River

Inyo National Forest

South Fork

Kern Canyon

Sequoia National Forest

Legend

⚑ Campground

☗ Ranger Station

(open from late May to early Nov), you can stand by the banks of the Kings River and stare up at granite walls rising thousands of feet above the river, the deepest canyon in the United States.

Near Giant Forest Village, **Moro Rock** is a 6,725-foot-tall granite dome formed by exfoliation of layers of the rock. A quarter-mile trail scales the dome for a spectacular view of the adjacent Canyon of the Middle Fork of the Kaweah. The trail gains 300 feet in 400 yards, so be ready for a climb.

Crystal Cave is located 15 miles from the Calif. 198 park entrance and an additional 7 miles to cave parking. Here you can take a 50-minute tour of Crystal's beautiful marble interior. The tour is $5 for adults and children 12 and older, $2.50 for children 6 to 11 and seniors, and free for kids 5 and under. Tickets are not sold at the cave and must be purchased at the Lodgepole or Foothills visitor centers at least 1½ hours in advance. Be sure to wear sturdy shoes and bring a jacket.

Boyden Cavern, on Calif. 180 in neighboring Sequoia National Forest, is a large cave where you can take a 45-minute tour to see stalactites and stalagmites. A fee is charged; call ☎ **209/736-2708** for details.

HIKING THE PARKS

Hiking and backpacking are what these parks are really all about. Some 700 miles of trails connect canyons, lakes, and high alpine meadows and snowfields.

When traveling overnight inside the parks' boundaries, overnight and/or day-use permits are required. They're limited and available by writing to **Wilderness Office,** Sequoia and Kings Canyon National Parks, HCR 89 Box 60, Three Rivers, CA 93271; call ☎ **209/565-3708** for information.

Some of the parks' most impressive hikes start in the **Mineral King** section in the southern end of Sequoia. Beginning at 7,800 feet, trails lead onward and upward to destinations like Sawtooth Pass, Crystal Lake, and the old White Chief Trail to the now-defunct White Chief Mine. Once an unsuccessful silver-mining town in the 1870s, Mineral King was the center of a pitched battle in the late 1970s when developers sought to build a huge ski resort here. They were defeated when Congress added Mineral King to the park, and the wilderness remains unspoiled.

The **John Muir Trail,** which begins in Yosemite Valley, ends at Mount Whitney. For many miles it coincides with the **Pacific Crest Trail** as it skirts the highest peaks in the park. This is the most difficult part of the Pacific Crest, remaining above 10,000 feet most of the time and crossing 12,000-foot-tall passes.

Other hikers like to explore the northern part of the park from **Cedar Grove** and **Road's End.** The **Paradise Valley Trail,** leading to beautiful Mist Falls, is a fairly easy day trip by park standards. The **Copper Creek Trail** immediately rises into the high wilderness around Granite Pass at 10,673 feet and is one of the most strenuous day hikes in the park.

If the altitude and steepness are too much for you at these trailheads, try some of the longer hikes in the **Giant Forest** or **Grant Grove.** These forests are woven with interlocking loops that allow you to take as short or as long a hike as you want. The 6-mile **Trail of the Sequoias** in Giant Forest will take you to the grove's far-eastern end, where you'll find some of the finest trees. In Grant Grove, a 100-foot walk through the hollow trunk of the **Fallen Monarch** makes a fascinating side trip. The tree has been used for shelter for more than 100 years and is tall enough inside that you can walk through without bending over.

Perhaps the most traversed trail to the park is the **Whitney Portal Trail.** It runs from east of the park near Lone Pine, through Inyo National Forest, to the park's boundary, the summit of Mount Whitney. Though it's a straightforward walk to the summit and it's possible to bag it in a very long day hike, you'd better be in really good shape before attempting it. Almost half the people who attempt Whitney, including those who camp part-way up, don't reach the summit. Weather, altitude, and fatigue can conspire to stop even the most prepared party. If you're interested in an overnight trip into the backcountry, contact Whitney Portal reservations (☎ **888/374-3730**) 6 months in advance.

The official park map and guide has good road maps for the parks, but for serious hiking you'll want to check out *Sierra South: 100 Back-Country Trips* by Thomas Winnett and Jason Winnett (Wilderness Press). Another good guide is *Kings Canyon Country,* a hiking handbook by Ginny and Lew Clark. The Grant Grove, Lodgepole, Cedar Grove, Foothills, and Mineral King visitor centers all sell a complete selection of maps and guidebooks to the park. Books and maps are also available by mail through the **Sequoia Natural History Association** (☎ **209/565-3768**).

OTHER OUTDOOR ACTIVITIES

FISHING   Trout fishing in the lower altitudes is fairly limited; most fishing takes place along the banks of the Kings and Kaweah rivers. A few high-country lakes are refuges for trout and are not stocked with hatchery fish. Before venturing into the high country, inquire at a ranger station about the area you'll be visiting to find out about closures or specific regulations. A California fishing license is required for everyone over 16 years old. Tackle and licenses are available at several park stores.

RAFTING & KAYAKING   Only recently have professional outfitters begun taking experienced rafters and kayakers down the Class IV and V Kaweah and Upper Kings rivers outside the parks. Contact **Sequoia National Forest** at ☎ **209/784-1500** for a current listing of companies running trips. This is only for the very adventurous.

SKIING & SNOWSHOEING   In Kings Canyon, **Sequoia Ski Touring** (☎ **209/335-2314**) in Grant Grove offers complete rentals and trail maps for 35 miles of Sequoia backcountry trails. People with their own equipment are welcome on all trails in the park at no cost. Trail maps are available at the visitor centers. On winter weekends, park rangers lead introductory snowshoe hikes at Giant Forest and Grant Grove. The roads to Cedar Grove and Mineral King are closed in winter.

CAMPING & ACCOMMODATIONS

There are 13 campgrounds in the park, offering the most convenient and economical accommodations here, although none have hookups. Only two accept reservations: **Lodgepole Campground** and **Dorst Campground** in Sequoia (☎ **800/365-2267**). Others are first-come, first-served, and often fill up on weekends. Three campgrounds—Azalea, Lodgepole, and Potwisha—are open year-round. The rest are open from snowmelt to September. Call ☎ **209/565-3341** for camping information. Even in summer, campers should prepare for rain and cold temperatures. Bring a good tent and warm sleeping bags. Also note that due to bears, proper food storage is required.

Two large campgrounds in Sequoia are **Dorst** and **Lodgepole.** Both are close to the Giant Forest. Lodgepole is within a short stroll of a restaurant, market, showers, laundry, and a visitor center. With more than 200 sites each, these tend to be the noisiest campgrounds in Sequoia. Lodgepole and Dorst each charge $14 per night.

Smaller and more peaceful are **South Fork, Potwisha, Buckeye Flat, Atwell Mill,** and **Cold Springs.** South Fork, Atwell Mill, and Cold Springs have pit toilets and are $6 per night. The others, with flush toilets and sinks, charge $12.

Campers in the remote Cedar Grove area of Kings Canyon National Park in the Kings River gorge can choose from **Moraine, Sentinel, Sheep Creek,** and **Canyon**

View, which also has a group camp. All four have flush toilets and are convenient to some of the park's best hiking. The small **Cedar Grove Village** offers a restaurant, motel, showers, and store. Sites are $12.

Three campgrounds in the Grant Grove area will put you near the sequoias without the noise and crowds of Giant Forest Village. All three—**Sunset, Azalea,** and **Crystal Springs**—have flush toilets and phones. The area has an RV disposal site, a visitor center, and showers nearby. The charge is $12 per site.

Lodging in the parks ranges from rustic one-room cabins (with no bathrooms or heat) to a luxury motel. None of the complexes are very big. Lodging in Kings Canyon is operated by the park concessionaire, **Kings Canyon Park Services Co.,** P.O. Box 909, Kings Canyon National Park, CA 93633 (☎ **209/335-5500** for information and reservations).

Grant Grove offers a variety of cabins with private or shared bathrooms. **Cedar Grove** is the site of an 18-room motel. Each room has its own bathroom and two queen-size beds.

Sequoia National Park is in the process of eliminating the old lodgings at Giant Forest and replacing them with a new development. Delaware North Parks Services also plans to open a new lodge, restaurant, and shop in Wuksachi Village in late 1999.

Sacramento, the Gold Country & the Central Valley

10

by Erika Lenkert and Matthew R. Poole

On the morning of January 24, 1848, a carpenter named James Marshall was working on John Sutter's mill in Coloma when he made an exciting discovery: He stumbled upon a gold nugget on the south fork of the American River. Despite Sutter's wishes to keep the find a secret, word leaked out—a word that would change the fate of California almost overnight: Gold!

The news spread like wildfire, and a frenzy seized the nation; the gold rush was on. Within 3 years, the population of the state grew from a meager 15,000 to more than 265,000. Most of these newcomers were single men under the age of 40, and not far behind were the thousands of merchants, bankers, and women who made their fortunes catering to the miners, most of whom went bust in their search for instant wealth.

Sacramento grew quickly as a supply town at the base of the surrounding goldfields. The Gold Country boom lasted less than a decade; the gold supply was quickly exhausted and many towns shrank or disappeared. Sacramento, however, continued to grow as the fertile Central Valley south of it exploited another source of wealth, becoming the vegetable-and-fruit garden of the nation.

A trip along Calif. 49 from the northern mines to the southern mines will give visitors a sense of what life might have been like on the rough mining frontier. The towns along this route seem frozen in time, with the main streets boasting raised wooden sidewalks, double-porched buildings, ornate saloons, and Victorian storefronts. Each town tells a similar story of sudden wealth and explosive growth, yet each has also left behind its own unique imprint. Any fan of movie westerns will recognize the setting—hundreds, perhaps even thousands, of films have been shot in these parts.

For the budget traveler, the Gold Country offers a wealth of inexpensive hotels and restaurants. Most towns along Calif. 49 depend on tourism as their main source of income (the gold-mining business has pretty much run dry), and hotel rates are fairly competitive. As long as you avoid the higher-end B&Bs, which charge up to $150 a night, you can easily keep expenses down to about $70 a day and still live like a Comstock king.

At the base of the Gold Country's rolling hills is the sprawling and decidedly flat Central Valley. Some 240 miles long and 50 miles wide, it's California's agricultural bread basket, the source of much of the bounty that is shipped across the nation and overseas. Much of the history of California has revolved around the struggle for control of the water used to irrigate the valley (it receives less than 10 inches of rainfall per year) and make this inland desert bloom. Despite the scarcity of water, a breathtaking panorama of orange and pistachio groves, grape vines, and strawberry fields stretches uninterrupted for miles.

1 Sacramento

90 miles E of San Francisco

Sacramento, with a metropolitan population of 1,782,000, is one of the state's fastest-growing areas. In addition to being the state capital, it is a thriving shipping and processing center for the fruit, vegetables, rice, wheat, and dairy goods that are produced in the fertile Central Valley. In the past decade, it's also become an area of high-tech spillover from Silicon Valley. This prosperous and politically charged city has broad, tree-shaded streets lined with some impressive Victorians and well-crafted bungalows. At its heart sits the capitol building—Sacramento's main attraction—in a well-maintained park replete with flower gardens and curious squirrels. It's far from a tourist town, but it does have its share of touristy activities. Visitors and locals alike enjoy spending the day walking through Old Sacramento or floating down the American River.

ESSENTIALS

GETTING THERE If you're driving from San Francisco, Sacramento is located about 90 miles east on I-80. From Los Angeles, take I-5 through the Central Valley directly into Sacramento. From North Lake Tahoe, get on I-80 west, and from South Lake Tahoe take U.S. 50.

Sacramento Metropolitan Airport (☎ 916/929-5411), 12 miles northwest of downtown Sacramento, is served by about a dozen airlines, including **American** (☎ 800/433-7300), **Delta** (☎ 800/221-1212), **Northwest** (☎ 800/225-2525), **Southwest** (☎ 800/435-9792), and **United** (☎ 800/241-6522).

AAA Taxi and Shuttle Service (☎ 916/362-5525) will get you from the airport to downtown; they charge a flat rate of $15 to the capital, a bargain compared to the $30 a conventional taxi would cost.

Amtrak (☎ 800/USA-RAIL) trains serve Sacramento daily.

VISITOR INFORMATION The **Sacramento Convention and Visitors Bureau,** 1421 K St., Sacramento, CA 95814 (☎ **916/264-7777;** fax 916/264-7788), provides plenty of helpful information for tourists. Once in the city, visitors can also stop by the **Sacramento Visitor Center,** 1101 Second St. (☎ **916/442-7644**), in Old Sacramento; it's usually open daily from 9am to 5pm.

ORIENTATION Suburbia sprawls around Sacramento, but its downtown area is relatively compact. Getting around the city is made easy by a gridlike pattern of streets that are designated by numbers or letters. The **capitol building,** on 10th Street between N and L streets, is the key landmark. From the front of the capitol, M Street—which is at this point called **Capitol Mall**—runs 10 straight blocks to **Old Sacramento,** the oldest section of the city.

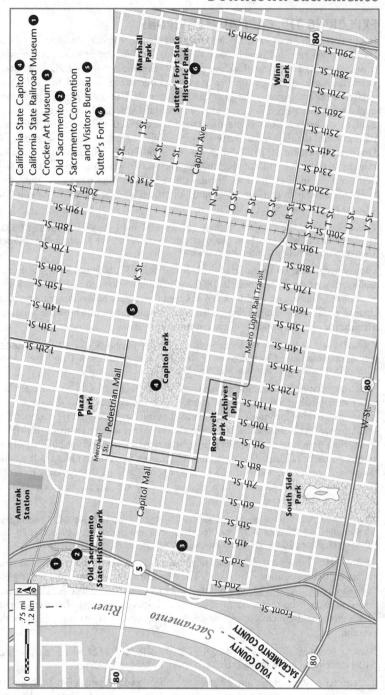

Downtown Sacramento

1. California State Capitol
2. California State Railroad Museum
3. Crocker Art Museum
4. Old Sacramento
5. Sacramento Convention and Visitors Bureau
6. Sutter's Fort

EXPLORING THE CAPITAL & ENVIRONS

In town, you'll want to stroll around **Old Sacramento,** 4 square blocks at the foot of the downtown area that have become a major attraction. These blocks contain more than 100 restored buildings (California's largest restoration project), including restaurants and shops. Although the area has cobblestone streets, wooden sidewalks, and gold-rush-era architecture, the high concentration of T-shirt shops and other gimmicky stores has turned it into a sort of historical Disneyland. Nonetheless, there's a lot to see here, such as where the Pony Express ended and the transcontinental railroad—and the Republican Party—began. While you're at it, be sure to stop at the **Discovery Museum** at 101 I Street (☎ **916/264-7057**), which houses hands-on exhibits of California's history, highlighting the valley's agricultural gold rush as well as the real one in 1849. It's open Tuesday through Friday from noon to 4:30pm, Saturday and Sunday from 10am to 4:30pm. Admission is $4 for adults, $2 for kids 6 to 12, and free for kids 5 and under.

✪ **California State Capitol.** 10th St. (between N and L sts.). ☎ **916/324-0333.** Free admission. Daily 9am–5pm. Tours offered every hr. on the hr. until 4pm. Closed Thanksgiving, Christmas, and New Year's Day.

Closely resembling a scale model of the U.S. Capitol in Washington, D.C., the domed California state capitol was built in 1869 and massively renovated in 1976. It is Sacramento's most distinctive landmark and has been the stage of many important political dramas in California history. The guided tours provide insight into both the building's architecture and the workings of the government it houses.

✪ **California State Railroad Museum.** 125 I St. (at Second St.). ☎ **916/445-6645.** Admission $6 adults, $3 children 6–12, free for children under 6. Daily 10am–5pm. Closed Thanksgiving, Christmas, and New Year's Day.

Well worth visiting, this museum is one of the highlights of Old Sacramento. You won't miss much if you bypass the memorabilia displays and head straight for the museum's 21 shiny locomotives and rail cars, beautiful antiques that are true works of art. Afterward, you can watch a film on the history of the western railroads that's quite good, then peruse related exhibits that tell the amazing story of the building of the transcontinental railroad. This museum is not just for train buffs: Over a half million people visit each year, and even the hordes of schoolchildren that typically mob this place shouldn't dissuade you from visiting one of the largest and best railroad museums in the country.

✪ **Crocker Art Museum.** 216 O St. (at Third St.) ☎ **916/264-5423.** Admission $4.50 adults, $2 children 7–17, free for children 6 and under. Tues–Wed and Fri–Sun 10am–5pm; Thurs 10am–9pm. Closed major holidays.

This museum houses a truly outstanding collection of California art, as well as temporary exhibits from around the world. The museum itself is an imposing century-old Italianate building, with an ornate interior of carved and inlaid woods. The Crocker Mansion Wing, the museum's most recent addition, is modeled after the Crocker family home and contains works by northern Californian artists from 1945 to the present.

Sutter's Fort State Historic Park. 2701 L St. ☎ **916/445-4422.** Admission $3 adults, $1.50 children 6–12, free for children 5 and under. Daily 10am–5pm.

John Sutter established this outpost in 1839, and the park, restored to its 1846 appearance, aims to recapture the pioneering spirit of 19th-century California. The usual exhibits are on hand—a blacksmith's forge, cooperage, bakery, and jail—and a self-guided audio tour is available. Historic demonstrations and live reenactments in

---

All Aboard!

April through September, on weekends and holidays from 11am to 5pm, steam locomotive rides carry passengers 6 miles along the Sacramento River. Trains depart on the hour from the Central Pacific Freight Depot in Old Sacramento, at K and Front streets. Fares are $6 for adults, $3 for children 6 to 12, and free for children under 6.

---

costume are staged daily from Memorial Day to Labor Day, when admissions are bumped to $5 for adults and $2 for children.

ENJOYING THE GREAT OUTDOORS

BICYCLING   One good thing about a town that's as flat as a tortilla: It's perfect for exploring on a bike. One of the best places to ride is through Old Sacramento and along the 22-mile American River Parkway, which runs right through it. If you didn't bring your own wheels, the friendly guys at **City Bicycle Works,** 2419 K St., at 24th Street (☎ **916/447-2453**), will rent you one for about $15 a day and point you in the right direction.

RIVER RAFTING   Sacramento lies nestled at the confluence of the American and Sacramento rivers, and rafting on the clear blue water of the American is immensely popular, especially on warm weekends. Several Sacramento area outfitters rent rafts for 4 to 15 persons, along with life jackets and paddles. Their shuttles drop you and your entourage upstream and meet you 3 to 4 hours later at a predetermined point downstream. Recommended outfitters include **River Rat,** 9840 Fair Oaks Blvd., Fair Oaks (☎ **916/966-6777**), and **American River Raft Rentals,** 11257 S. Bridge St., Rancho Cordova (☎ **916/635-6400**).

FOR KIDS: WHERE THE WILD THINGS ARE

The best place to take your kid on a sunny afternoon in Sacramento is **Fairytale Town,** at William Land Park, Land Park Drive and Sutterville Road (☎ **916/264-5233**). I can still remember dragging my poor parents through the stone archway, guarded by a perilously perched Humpty Dumpty. After riding all the rides and climbing everything in sight, we would cross the street to the **Sacramento Zoo** (☎ **916/264-5885**), buy a big spool of cotton candy, and see *all* the animals.

WHERE TO STAY

Best Western Sutter House. 1100 H St., Sacramento, CA 95814. ☎ **800/830-1314** or 916/441-1314. Fax 916/441-5961. 98 units. A/C TV TEL. $85–$160 double. Rates include continental breakfast. AE, CB, DC, DISC, MC, V.

You would never know from the plain, motel-like exterior that this is one of the best values in Sacramento. Rooms here are as up-to-date as any offered by upscale hotels such as the Hilton or the Sheraton; they include well-coordinated furnishings, cable TV, phone with voice mail, and valet and laundry service. There's also a swimming pool in the courtyard, and complimentary coffee and pastries are served each morning in the lobby.

Quality Inn. 818 15th St. (at I St.), Sacramento, CA 95814. ☎ **916/444-3980.** 40 units. A/C TV TEL. $59–$79 double. AE, DC, DISC, MC, V.

Formerly the Americana Lodge, the new Quality Inn has been freshly remodeled and modernized. All rooms now have data ports, coffeemakers, and that oh-so-necessary Sacramento summer prerequisite—air-conditioning. The inn also has a swimming pool and is within walking distance of just about everything worth seeing in town. Granted, the Quality Inn is no architectural masterpiece, but for rates starting at $60 a night at a prime location, nobody's complaining.

Sacramento International Hostel. 900 H St. (at Ninth St.), Sacramento, CA 95814. ☎ **916/443-1691.** 60 bunk beds. $13 for HI-AYH members, $16 for nonmembers. MC, V. Family and couple rooms available. Check-in 7:30–9:30am and 5–10pm.

Housed in a 12,000-square-foot Victorian mansion, this hostel is a real beauty (in fact, it's regarded as one of the finest hostels in the country). Yeah, yeah, we know: You don't want to share a room with snoring strangers. But if you happen to be towing a family along, you'd be hard-pressed to find a better place for your money than the private rooms reserved for cash-conscious clans. There are four "couples" rooms: one with a double bed and private bathroom, two with a double and twin bed, and one with two twins—all of which go for about $36 a night. There are also "family" rooms available with basic bunk beds. As for amenities, there are none: just a light and the beds—that's it. Everything else—men's and women's bathroom, kitchen, dining room, lounge, rec room, laundry room, TV room—is scattered throughout the Victorian. Naturally, the private rooms are a hot item, so make reservations as far in advance as possible.

The Sacramento Vagabond Inn. 909 Third St., Sacramento, CA 95814. ☎ **800/ 522-1555** or 916/446-1481. Fax 916/448-0364. 108 units. A/C TV TEL. $83 double. Extra person $5. Children under 19 stay free in parents' room. Rates include continental breakfast. AE, DC, DISC, MC, V.

A reliable choice within walking distance of the state capitol, the Vagabond Inn has a heated pool and a host of free features, including local phone calls, weekday newspapers, and continental breakfast. Bedrooms are clean and comfortable, but not exceptional—it's the economical rates and the convenient location that make it worth your while. There's an adjoining 24-hour coffee shop as well.

WHERE TO DINE

Fox & Goose Public House. 1001 R St. (at 10th St.). ☎ **916/443-8825.** Main courses $4–$7. AE, MC, V. Mon–Fri 7am–2pm; Sat–Sun 8am–1pm. Bar stays open until midnight Mon–Sat. ENGLISH PUB.

The Fox is a popular English pub complete with darts, a giant picture of the queen, and 13 varieties of beer on tap. The soups at lunch are excellent, and the specials often include bangers and mash, Welsh rarebit, and Cornish pasties. The burnt cream dessert is a local legend. Either arrive early for lunch or be prepared for a wait, as locals love this place. Equally popular breakfasts include kippers, grilled tomatoes, and crumpets, as well as the ubiquitous waffles and French toast. There's live entertainment by local bands six nights a week, as well as serve-yourself pub grub Monday through Friday from 5:30 to 9:30pm.

Jammin' Salmon. 1801 Garden Hwy. (north of downtown on the Sacramento River). ☎ **916/929-6232.** Reservations recommended. Main courses $9–18. AE, DC, DISC, MC, V. Mon–Thurs 11:30am–9pm; Fri–Sat 10am–10pm; Sun 9am–9pm. CALIFORNIA.

The Jammin' Salmon, a small restaurant built on a barge right on the Sacramento River, offers some of the best food—and riverside views—in River City (as the locals call Sacramento). Part of the experience is rocking gently while dining on locally grown produce, fresh fish, and imaginatively prepared entrees. Try the grilled salmon fillet with a red curry sauce or the macadamia-crusted chicken breast topped with a fresh strawberry balsamic vinaigrette. Desserts include a seasonal fresh-fruit crisp with house-made vanilla ice cream or a silky chocolate crème brûlée.

Sacramento's Best Budget Dining

- **Best Artery Clogger: Willie's Burgers,** 2415 16th St., between Broadway and X Street (☎ 916/444-2006), a takeoff on L.A.'s Tommy Burgers, slathers everything in so much chili and cheese that heavy-duty paper towel dispensers are mandatory equipment. Open late most nights.
- **Best Vegetarian: Greta's Cafe,** 1831 Capital Ave., at 19th St. (☎ 916/442-7382), is silly with salads, offering a dozen choices along with fresh baked pastries and mondo sandwiches for under $4.
- **Best Coffee Joint:** A tough one, since there are so many great new coffee joints springing up, but one that's been popular forever and will probably remain that way is **Java City** (☎ 916/444-5282), at the corner of Capitol Avenue and 18th Street. Sure, there are plenty of bums around, but at least they keep the yuppies at bay.
- **Best Mexican: Taco Loco Taqueria,** 2326 J St., at 24th Street (☎ 916/447-0711). Try the charbroiled black-tip shark taco, big ole shrimp burrito, or snapper ceviche tostado, all so fresh the restaurant doesn't even own a freezer. Wash it all down with a Los Cabos Margarita while soaking up the sun on the front patio. There's another location at 1122 11th St. at L Street (☎ 916/447-TACO).
- **Best Breakfast:** Whenever we tell our friends about **Cornerstone Restaurant,** 2330 J. St., at 24th Street (☎ 916/441-0948), they always come back for more. The choices are all standard American, but the servings are huge, the service is friendly, and the price is right. A four-egg omelet with home fries, toast, and fruit costs less than $5.
- **Best Brewery:** Breweries seem to be popping up like weeds these days, but the **Rubicon Brewing Company,** 2004 Capitol Ave., at 20th Street (☎ 916/448-7032), still remains our favorite hangout. A pitcher of India Pale and a side of fries is guaranteed to do the trick.

Paragary's Bar and Oven. 1401 28th St. ☎ **916/452-3335.** Reservations recommended for parties of 6 or more. Main courses $10–$17. AE, DC, DISC, MC, V. Mon–Thurs 11:30am–11pm; Fri 11:30am–midnight; Sat 4:30pm–midnight; Sun 4:30–10pm. ITALIAN/CALIFORNIA.

Paragary's is widely considered the best moderately priced restaurant in Sacramento's downtown area. During good weather, the best seats are outside amid the gorgeous fountains and plantings of the courtyard; other seating options include the formal fireplace room and the brightly lit cafe. The same menu is served no matter where you sit, with some of the best dishes coming from the kitchen's wood-burning pizza oven. But this is more than a gourmet pizza parlor, as evidenced by the grilled rib-eye steak with mashed potatoes, portobello mushrooms, and grilled leeks, or the hand-cut rosemary noodles with seared chicken, pancetta, artichokes, leeks, and garlic.

✪ **33rd Street Bistro.** 3301 Folsom Blvd. (at 33rd St.). ☎ **916/455-2282.** Main courses $8–$15. AE, MC, V. Mon–Thurs 7am–10pm; Fri 7am–11pm; Sat 8am–11pm; Sun 8am–9pm. BISTRO.

Seattle transplants Fred Haynes (chef) and his brother Matt (manager) have taken an old brick building and transformed it into a bistro that's been a raging success from the day it opened. And it's popular for all the right reasons—the food is wonderful (and priced right), the staff is friendly and helpful, and the ambiance is warm and cheerful. Selections include a variety of Italian grilled sandwiches and house favorites such as wood-roasted vegetables with sun-dried tomatoes and goat cheese crostini; Uncle Bum's jerk ribs with Jamaican barbecue sauce and key-lime crème fraîche; and wood-roasted pork loin with ancho-chili butter and linguisa risotto.

Tower Café. 1518 Broadway. ☎ **916/441-0222.** Main courses $7–$12. AE, MC, V. Mon–Fri 7–11am and 11:30am–4pm; Sun–Thurs 4:30–10pm; Fri–Sat 4:30–11pm; Sat 8am–4pm; Sun 8am–2pm. Open later for dessert and drinks only. INTERNATIONAL.

The Tower Café gets its name from the building in which it's located: a grand old 1939 movie house with a tall art-deco spire. The restaurant occupies the same space in which a small mom-and-pop music store once stood. This former resident, Tower Records, has since grown into America's second-largest record retailer. While it's unlikely that Tower Café will share the phenomenal success of its predecessor, it's not for the lack of effort. Both the food and the ambiance are pleasant, and even with its perpetually sluggish service, this restaurant remains our favorite Sacramento lunch spot. On warm days, it seems as if everyone in the city is lunching here (in fact, recent patrons included the president and his staff), and people-watching can be a real treat. Dishes reflect a variety of international flavors, from the Jamaican jerk chicken to Brazilian chicken salad.

2 The Gold Country

Cutting a serpentine swath for nearly 350 miles along aptly numbered Calif. 49, the Gold Country stretches from Sierra City to the foothills of Yosemite. Much of this rugged region still retains its forty-niner ambiance: Mining sites, horse ranches, Wild West saloons, and ghost towns are common sights in these parts.

The town of Placerville, 44 miles east of Sacramento at the intersection of U.S. 50 and Calif. 49, is in the approximate center of the Gold Country. To the north are the classic old mining towns of Grass Valley and Nevada City, while in the central and southern Gold Country are such well-preserved towns as Amador City, Sutter Creek, Columbia, and Jamestown, to name just a few.

In fact, the Gold Country is so immense that it would take weeks to thoroughly explore. But rather than provide an exhaustive list of each and every town, we have instead narrowed our coverage to include three of our favorite regions, each of which can be thoroughly explored in just 2 or 3 days: the utterly charming side-by-side towns of Grass Valley and Nevada City to the north; the well-preserved gold-rush communities of Amador City, Jackson, and Sutter Creek in the central Gold Country; and at the southern end of Gold Country, the wonderfully authentic neighboring mining towns of Angels Camp, Murphys, Columbia, Sonora, and Jamestown.

Any of these three regions will provide an excellent base for exploring and experiencing the Gold Country, whether you're intent on panning for gold, exploring old mines and caverns, or rafting the area's many white-water rivers. In fact, the Gold Country is one of the most underrated, inexpensive, and least congested tourist destinations in California, a winning combination of Old West ambiance, adorable (and affordable) bed-and-breakfasts, and outdoor adventures galore.

THE NORTHERN GOLD COUNTRY: NEVADA CITY & GRASS VALLEY

Lying about 60 miles northeast of Sacramento, Nevada City and Grass Valley are far and away the top tourist destinations of the northern Gold Country.

These two historic towns were at the center of the hard-rock mining fields of northern California. Grass Valley, in fact, was California's richest mining town, producing more than a billion dollars worth of gold. Both are attractive, although we usually spend most of our time traipsing through Nevada City. Its wealth of Victorian homes and storefronts makes it one of the most appealing small towns in California, particularly in the fall when the maple trees are ablaze with color (in fact, its entire downtown has been designated a National Historic Landmark).

It's easy to get here. If you're driving from San Francisco, take I-80 to the Calif. 49 turnoff in Auburn and follow the signs. For information about the area, go to—or call in advance—the **Grass Valley/Nevada County Chamber of Commerce,** 248 Mill St., Grass Valley, CA 95945 (☎ **530/273-4667**), or the **Nevada City Chamber of Commerce,** 132 Main St., Nevada City, CA 95959 (☎ **800/655-NJOY** or 530/ 265-2692). You can also visit their Web site at www.ncgold.com.

✪ **NEVADA CITY** Rumors of miners pulling a pound of gold a day out of Deer Creek brought thousands of fortune seekers to the area in 1849. Within a year, Nevada City was a boisterous town of 10,000, the third largest city in California. In its heyday, everyone who was anyone visited this rollicking western outpost with its busy red-light district. Mark Twain lectured here in 1866, telling the audience about his trips to the Sandwich Islands (Hawaii). Former president Herbert Hoover also lived and worked here as a gold miner.

Pick up a walking-tour map at the **Chamber of Commerce,** 132 Main St., and stroll the streets lined with impressive Victorian buildings, including the **Firehouse Number 1 Museum,** 214 Main St. (☎ **530/265-5468**), complete with bell tower, gingerbread decoration, a small museum that displays mementos from the Donner Party, a Maidu Indian basket collection, and an altar from a temple originally located in the Chinese section of Grass Valley. It's open in summer daily from 11am to 4pm; winter hours (from Nov 1 to Apr 1) are Thursday through Sunday from 11am to 4pm. The **National Hotel** (1854–56) is here (we always stop in at the handsome gold-rush-era bar for a refresher), as is the **Nevada Theatre** (1865), one of the oldest theaters in the nation and still operating as such, today home to the Foothill Theatre Company.

If you want to see the source of much of the city's wealth, visit **Malakoff Diggins State Historic Park,** 23579 N. Bloomfield Rd. (☎ **530/265-2740**), 28 miles northeast of Nevada City. Once the world's largest hydraulic gold mine, it's an awesome (some might say disturbing) spectacle of hydraulic mining—nearly half a mountain has been washed away by powerful jets of water, leaving behind a 600-foot-deep canyon of exposed rock. In the 1870s, North Bloomfield, then located in the middle of this park, had a population of 1,500. Some of the buildings have been reconstructed and refurnished to show what life was like then. The 3,000-acre park also offers several hiking trails, swimming at Blair Lake, and 30 **campsites** that can be reserved through Park Net by calling ☎ **800/444-7275.** The museum is open daily in summer from 10am to 5pm, but only on weekends from 10am to 4pm in the winter. To reach the park, take Calif. 49 toward Downieville for 11 miles. Turn right onto Tyler-Foote Crossing Road for 17 miles. The name will change to Curzon Grade and then to Backbone. Turn right onto Derbec Road and into the park. The fee is $5 per car.

Another 6 miles up Calif. 49 from the Malakoff Diggins turnoff will bring you to Pleasant Valley Road, the exit that will take you (in about 7 miles) to one of the most impressive **covered bridges** in the country. Built in 1862, it's 225 feet long and was crossed by many a stagecoach (during the fall it makes for a spectacular photo opportunity).

GRASS VALLEY In contrast to Nevada City's "tourist town" image, Grass Valley is the commercial/retail center of the region (and, ergo, has the most inexpensive motels). The **Empire Mine State Historic Park,** 10791 E. Empire St., Grass Valley (☎ **530/273-8522**), the largest and richest gold mine in California, is just outside of town. This mine, which once had 367 miles of underground shafts, produced an estimated 5.8 million ounces of gold between 1850 and 1956, when it closed. Here you can look down the shaft of the mine, walk around the mine yard, and stroll through the gardens of the mine owner. March through November, tours are given daily and a mining movie is shown. You can also enjoy picnicking, cycling, mountain biking, or hiking in the 784-acre park. It's open year-round except for Thanksgiving, Christmas, and New Year's Day. Admission to the park, tour, and museum is $3 for adults and $1 for children and dogs.

In town, visitors can pick up a walking-tour map at the **Chamber of Commerce** and explore the historic downtown area along Mill and Main streets. There are also a few museums that California history and gold-mining buffs will want to visit: the **Grass Valley Museum,** 410 S. Church St., adjacent to St. Joseph's Cultural Center (☎ 530/273-5509); the **North Star Mining Museum,** at the south end of Mill Street at McCourtney Road (☎ 530/273-4255); and the **Video History Museum,** in the center of Memorial Park off Calif. 174 (☎ 530/274-1126), which houses a collection of old films of the region from the 1920s.

Grass Valley was, for a time, the home of Lola Montez, singer, dancer, and paramour of the rich and famous. A fully restored home that she bought and occupied in 1853 can be viewed at 248 Mill St., now the site of Grass Valley's Chamber of Commerce. Lotta Crabtree, Montez's famous protégé, lived down the street at 238 Mill St., now an apartment house. Also pop into the **Holbrooke Hotel,** 212 Main St., to see the signature of Mark Twain, who stayed here, as did five U.S. presidents. The saloon has been in continuous use since 1852, and it's the place to meet the locals and have a tall cold one.

The surrounding region offers many recreational opportunities on its rivers and lakes and in the Tahoe National Forest. You can enjoy fishing, swimming, and boating at **Scotts Flat Lake** near Nevada City (east on Calif. 20) and at **Rollins Lake** on Calif. 174, between Grass Valley and Colfax. White-water rafting is available on several rivers. **Tributary Whitewater Tours,** 20480 Woodbury Dr., Grass Valley, CA 95949 (☎ **800/672-3846** or 530/346-6812), offers half- to 3-day trips from March through October. The region is also ideal for **mountain biking.** The chambers of commerce publish a trail guide, but there's nowhere to rent a bike in either Nevada City or Grass Valley, so bring your own wheels. For regional **hiking** information, contact Tahoe National Forest headquarters at Coyote Street and Calif. 49 in Nevada City (☎ **530/265-4531**).

WHERE TO STAY
Nevada City
✪ **Miner's Inn.** 760 Zion St., Nevada City, CA 95959. ☎ **800/977-8884** or 530/265-2253. Fax 530/265-3310. 20 units. A/C TV TEL. $60–$75 double. Cabins also available. AE, DC, DISC, MC, V.

Surely no forty-niner miner had it this good: his own cabinlike motel room cooled by the shade of a small tree-lined park equipped with barbecues, picnic tables, and a horseshoe pit. Granted, the rooms are a bit small and simple, but considering all the standard amenities—TV, telephone, air-conditioning—and the price, the cash-conscious traveler could hardly ask for more. Heck, there's even access to a fitness and racquetball club and fax and dry cleaning service. The inn also rents three fully furnished cabins, popular with families and groups, that cost $110 to $145 a night, which is a good deal for such a prime location—about a mile from Nevada City's historic district. After a hard day's touring, rest your dry, weary bones at the restaurant and cocktail lounge next door.

National Hotel. 211 Broad St., Nevada City, CA 95959. ☎ **530/265-4551.** 42 units, 30 with private bathroom. A/C TV TEL. $42 double with shared bathroom; $68 with private bathroom; from $124 suite with bathroom. AE, MC, V.

You can't miss this classic three-story Victorian, the oldest hotel in continuous operation west of the Rocky Mountains. It's located near what was once the center of the town's red-light district. The lobby is full of mementos from that era, hence the grandfather clock and early square piano. The suites are replete with gold-rush-era antiques and large, cozy beds. Most rooms have private bathrooms, and some come with canopy beds and romantic love seats. A definite bonus during typically sweltering summers is the secluded swimming pool filled with cool mountain water. *Note:* The hotel doesn't take reservations for the rooms with shared bathroom; they're available on a walk-in basis only.

The hotel's Victorian dining room, which serves traditional items such as prime rib, steaks, lobster tail, and homemade desserts, also has a gold-rush atmosphere; tables, for example, are lit with coal oil lamps. The hotel provides live entertainment on Friday and Saturday nights. There's also a popular Sunday brunch, one of the best in the county.

Red Castle Historic Lodgings. 109 Prospect St., Nevada City, CA 95959. ☎ **800/ 761-4766** or 530/265-5135. 7 units. $70–$155 double. Rates include breakfast. MC, V.

This elegant, comfortable hillside inn occupies a four-story Gothic Revival brick house built in 1860; it's situated in a secluded spot with a panoramic view of the town. The highlight of the week is the Sunday afternoon "Conversations with Mark Twain," in which guests can engage the great author (or at least a reasonable facsimile thereof) in conversation while enjoying such specialties as lemon tarts and a choice cup of tea. The house has retained its original woodwork, plaster moldings, ceiling medallions, and much of the handmade glass; it lacks any modern intrusions, such as TVs and phones. Guests enjoy bountiful five-course buffet breakfasts and relax on the verandas that encircle the first two floors of the house and overlook the rose gardens.

Grass Valley

If none of the hotels below pan out (pun intended), try calling the modern, fully equipped **Best Western Gold Country Inn,** 11972 Sutton Way, Grass Valley (☎ **800/274-6590** or 530/273-1393).

Coach & Four Motel. 628 S. Auburn St., Grass Valley, CA 95945. ☎ **530/273-8009.** 17 units. A/C TV TEL. $55–$65 double. Rates include continental breakfast. AE, MC, V.

If you're short on greenbacks and are not terribly finicky about where you stay while your touring the northern Gold Country, then the homey Coach & Four Motel will suffice. The rooms have all the standard amenities—TV, telephone, refrigerator, and private bathrooms—and though they're lacking in even the vaguest form of style, you have to admit that $55 is a real bargain for a clean, comfortable room for two (heck, you even get a free continental breakfast thrown in). It's about a 15-minute walk to Grass Valley's Old Town, or you can hop on a Nevada City/Grass Valley shuttle that stops in front of the motel.

Holbrooke Hotel. 212 W. Main St., Grass Valley, CA 95945. ☎ **800/933-7077** or 530/273-1353. Fax 530/273-0434. 30 units. A/C TV TEL. $66–$106 double; $120–$145 suite. AE, DC, DISC, MC, V.

This Victorian-era white-clapboard building was a rollicking saloon during the gold-rush days, and then evolved into a place for exhausted miners to "rack out." The oldest and most historic hotel in town, it has hosted a number of legendary figures since opening its doors: Ulysses Grant, Mark Twain, Benjamin Harrison, and Grover Cleveland, among others. Seventeen of the rooms lie within the main building. The remainder are in an adjacent annex, a house occupied long ago by the hotel's owner. Each guest room is decorated with an eclectic collection of gold-rush-era furniture and antiques. All have cable TVs tucked away in armoires, and most bathrooms have claw-foot tubs. If you can, reserve one of the larger "Veranda" rooms, which face Main Street and have access to the balconies; it's well worth the few extra dollars.

Holiday Lodge. 1221 E. Main St., Grass Valley, CA 95945. ☎ **800/742-7125** or 530/ 273-4406. 36 units. A/C TV TEL. $50–$85 double. AE, DC, DISC, MC, V.

Anyone who loves to lounge poolside with a good book will appreciate the Holiday Lodge. Located just outside downtown Grass Valley, the motel is a short drive away from the historic Old Town of Nevada City and Grass Valley, and across the street from a 9-hole golf course. The rooms are your typical ordinary motel style, with the ubiquitous queen beds, televisions, and blazing air conditioner. The real bonus, however, is the central sauna and swimming pool, the perfect place to rest your tired, sweaty bones after a hard day's shopping. And for all you prospective prospectors, the Holiday Lodge offers a Goldpanning Vacation package, where an "expert guide leads the way through the wilds of the Sierra to the most promising gold-panning location." Who knows? One promising nugget might even pay for your vacation.

WHERE TO DINE
Nevada City
Circino's. 309 Broad St. ☎ **530/265-2246.** Main courses $8.95–$19.95. AE, DISC, MC, V. Fri–Sun 11am–4pm; Sun–Thurs 5–9pm; Fri–Sat 5–10pm. ITALIAN.

If a heaping plate of pasta with spicy marinara sauce sounds good to you, head to Circino's, the de facto Italian restaurant in Nevada City. It's a lively place that's hugely popular with the locals. Entrees range from a savory penne pasta with salmon, leeks, and dill to veal picatta prepared with tangy lemon caper sauce. Despite the fact that you'll be challenged to finish your main entree, every order also comes with garlic focaccia, soup or salad, *and* a choice of spaghetti with marinara sauce, fettuccine Alfredo, or spaghetti with garlic and olive oil (the last mentioned is the best).

Cowboy Pizza. 315 Spring St. ☎ **530/265-2334.** Pizzas $15–$20. No credit cards. Sun–Tues 4–8pm; Wed–Sat 4–9pm PIZZA.

Garlic lovers will find a slice of heaven here, usually in the form of a Gilroy Pizza (garlic stuffed with garlic), or our favorite, the Greek Vegetarian—artichoke-heart pizza with fresh tomatoes, feta cheese, black olives, and, of course, garlic. Founder Cowboy Wallie has gussied up his pizza joint with plenty of cowboy knickknacks, our favorite being the *Singer Cowboy* poster of Gene Autry. The pizzas, each made to order and baked in an old stone-floor oven, are wickedly good (the aroma alone will lead you here), as is the selection of microbrewed beer. If you have the opportunity, order in advance; otherwise you may be a bit stewed on beer by the time your pie arrives.

Friar Tucks. 111 N. Pine St. ☎ **530/265-9093.** Main courses $14–$20. AE, DISC, MC, V. Sun–Thurs 5–9:30pm; Fri–Sat 5–10pm. INTERNATIONAL.

A local favorite for nearly a quarter of a century, this restaurant consists of a series of rustic, dimly lit rooms furnished with high-backed oak booths. The eclectic menu changes weekly, offering everything from French fondues and Swiss meatballs to teriyaki steak, Tuck's bouillabaisse, fresh seafood, filet mignon, and roast duck. The accompanying wine list is surprisingly impressive. The bar has the flavor and ambiance of a British pub and is a popular local hangout. A guitar player entertains nightly from

7pm. A recent expansion has added a new dining room overlooking Nevada City's historic district.

Grass Valley

Mrs. Dubblebee's Pasties. 251-C South Auburn St., Grass Valley. ☎ **530/272-7700.** Pasties $2.75–$3.95. No credit cards. Daily 10:30am–6pm. PASTIES.

Miners who emigrated from Cornwall, England, didn't think much of the local grub, so between digging for gold dust they baked their own. Hence, the Cornish pasty, a belly-filling mix of beef and veggies topped with a buttery crust. William Brooks, founder of Mrs. Dubblebee's Pasties, patented Billy Brooks Pie Machine, used to make pasties worldwide. Now his granddaughter, Janine Clark, continues the tradition using hallowed family recipes. Varieties range from the Traditional British beef (well done, of course) to the spicy Olé pasty or spinach pasty with mushroom and three cheeses. Our usual routine is to order a few to go—along with a few squares of Scottish shortbread—and have a picnic lunch.

The Old California. 341 E. Main St. ☎ **530/273-7341.** Main courses $8–$14.95. MC, V. Mon–Fri 11:30am–2pm; Sun–Thurs 5–9:30pm; Fri–Sat 5–10pm. PRIME RIB/AMERICAN.

Set about a half mile east of the commercial center of town, this restaurant has a very loyal clientele that swears by the prime rib. It occupies a sprawling, turn-of-the-century building that once housed a bordello that thrived for a while beginning around 1901. Inside, you'll find lots of old-time memorabilia and photos of earlier and lustier eras. A platter of prime rib (6 oz.), with salad and vegetables, is a bargain at $7.95, although other choices include boneless breast of chicken, vegetarian pastas, prawns, calamari steak, and such fish platters of the day as herbed and grilled fillets of red snapper. The most expensive item on the menu, priced at $14.95, is a heaping platter with 16 ounces of prime rib cooked any way you like it.

Pasta Luigi. 760 S. Auburn St. (at McNight St.). ☎ **530/477-0455.** Reservations recommended. Main courses $8–$14.95. AE, MC, V. Tues–Sun 5–9pm. ITALIAN.

This is the closest thing to a neighborhood Italian restaurant in town. It's a thoroughly charming, unpretentious spot, packed most nights with happy locals who couldn't care less about the less-than-trendy location. Menu items include a zesty cioppino; linguine *zingarella*, a "gypsy sauté" of Italian sausages, peppers, garlic, and onions; a classic veal scallopini; and *cappellini alla contadina*, with diced chicken, fresh basil, olive oil, and tomatoes.

Tofanelli's. 302 W. Main St. ☎ **530/272-1468.** Main courses $7–$12. AE, MC, V. Mon–Fri 8am–9pm; Sat–Sat 8am–3pm (brunch) and 5–9pm. INTERNATIONAL.

If a diet of meat and potatoes isn't your cup of tea, head to Tofanelli's, which specializes in good—and good for you—entrees for brunch, lunch, and dinner. You'll like the setting, three bright, cheery dining areas (outdoor patio, atrium room, and dining room) separated by exposed brick walls and decorated with beautiful prints and paintings. Specials on the menu, such as Gorgonzola ravioli topped with garlic cream sauce or mu shu vegetables with baked tofu, change weekly, but you can always rely on Tofanelli classics like Linda's famous vegetarian lasagna and the popular veggie burger. And yes, they serve good ol' New York steak, too. Don't you dare depart without a slice of Katherine's chocolate cake.

THE CENTRAL GOLD COUNTRY: AMADOR CITY, SUTTER CREEK & JACKSON

Though Placerville is technically the center of the Gold Country, it's the small trio of towns a few miles to the south—Amador City, Sutter Creek, and Jackson—that are

Coloma: Where the Gold Rush Began

Located on Calif. 49 between Auburn and Placerville, the town of Coloma is so small, placid, and unpretentious that it's hard to imagine the significant role it played in the rapid development of California and the West. For it was here that James Marshall, working on John Sutter's mill, first discovered that there was gold aplenty in the foothills of California. Over the next 50 years, 125 *million* ounces of gold were taken from the Sierra foothills, an amount worth a staggering $50 billion today.

Although Marshall and Sutter tried to keep the discovery secret, word soon leaked out. Sam Brannan, who ran a general store at Fort Sutter, secured some gold samples himself—as well as significant amounts of choice Coloma real estate—and then headed for San Francisco, where he ran through the streets shouting, "Gold! Gold! Gold! From the American River!" San Francisco rapidly emptied as men rushed off to seek their fortunes at the mines (and make Sam Brannan's as well).

Coloma was quickly mined out, but its boom brought 10,000 people to the settlement and lasted long enough for residents to build a schoolhouse, a gunsmith, a general store, and a tiny, tin-roofed post office. The miners also planted oak and mimosa trees that shade the street during hot summers. About 70% of this quiet, pretty town lies in the **Marshall Gold Discovery State Historic Park** (☎ **530/622-3470**), which preserves the spot where James Wilson Marshall discovered gold along the banks of the south fork of the American River.

Farther up Main Street is a huge replica of the mill Marshall was building when he made his discovery. The largest building in town, the mill is powered by electricity during the summer months. Other attractions in the park include the **Gold Discovery Museum,** which relates the story of the gold rush, and a number of Chinese stores, all that remain of the once sizable local Chinese community. The park also has three picnic areas, four trails, recreational gold panning, and a number of buildings and exhibits relating the way of life that prevailed here in the 19th century. Admission is $5 per vehicle; hours are daily from 10am to 5pm, except on major holidays.

Folks also come here for white-water thrills on the American River (Coloma is a popular launching point). **White Water Connection** in Coloma (☎ **530/622-6446**), offers half- to 2-day trips down the frothy forks of the American River. It's great fun and one of the Gold Country's best outdoor attractions.

far and away the most appealing destination in this beautiful region of rolling hills, dotted with solitary oaks and granite outcroppings. When the mining boom went bust, most of the towns were abandoned; nowadays, most of these restored gold-rush towns rely solely on tourism (hence the rapid conversion of many Victorian homes into B&Bs), though a few mines have reopened recently and are reportedly making a profit.

One of the advantages of staying in this area is that both the northern and southern regions of the Gold Country are only a few hours' drive away (via very winding roads, however). If you're intent on seeing as much of the Gold Country as possible in a few days' time, any one of these three towns will suffice as a good home base.

To reach Amador City, Sutter Creek, or Jackson from Placerville, head south along Calif. 49 past Plymouth and Drytown. If you're coming straight here from Sacramento, take U.S. 50 to Placerville and head south on Calif. 49; Calif. 16 from

The Central & Southern Gold Country

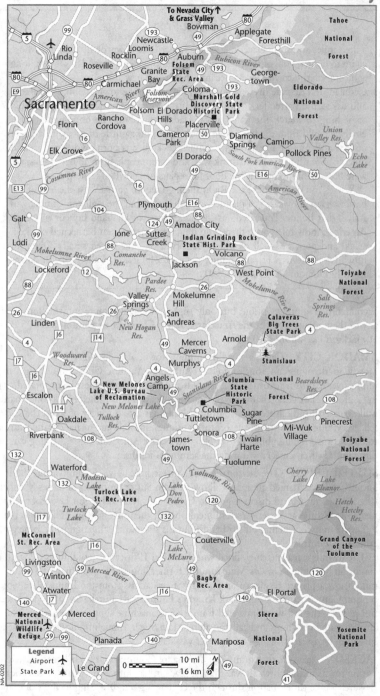

To Nevada City↑
& Grass Valley

Bowman

Tahoe

National

Forest

Newcastle
Loomis
Applegate   Foresthill

99
Rio
Linda
Rocklin

193
Auburn
Folsom
State
Rec. Area

Georgetown

Eldorado

Carmichael
Granite
Bay

Coloma
Marshall Gold
Discovery State
Park

National

Sacramento
Folsom El Dorado
Hills

Historic

Forest

American River   Folsom
Reservoir

Placerville

Union
Valley Res.

Florin
Rancho
Cordova

Cameron
Park

Diamond
Springs   Camino
Pollock Pines

Echo
Lake

Elk Grove

El Dorado

South Fork American River

American River

Cosumnes River

Galt

Plymouth

E16

Lodi

Ione
Sutter
Creek

Amador City

Indian Grinding Rocks
State Hist. Park

Mokelumne River

Comanche
Res.

Jackson

Volcano

West Point

Toiyabe

Lockeford

Pardee
Res.

Valley
Springs

Mokelumne
Hill

Mokelumne River

National

Forest

Salt
Spring
Res.

Linden

New Hogan
Res.

San
Andreas

Arnold

Calaveras
Big Trees
State Park

Woodward
Res.

Mercer
Caverns

Stanislaus

Escalon

Angels
Camp
New Melones
Lake U.S. Bureau
of Reclamation

Murphys

Columbia
State
Historic
Park

National

Beardsleys
Res.

New Melones Lake

Stanislaus River

Forest

Oakdale

Tullock
Res.

Columbia
Tuttletown

Sugar
Pine

Mi-Wuk
Village

Pinecrest

Riverbank

Sonora

Jamestown

Twain
Harte

Toiyabe

National

Forest

Waterford

Modesto
Lake

Tuolumne

Tuolumne River

Cherry
Lake

Lake
Eleanor

Turlock Lake
St. Rec. Area

Turlock
Lake

Lake
Don
Pedro

Hetch
Hetchy
Res.

McConnell
St. Rec. Area

Couterville

Grand Canyon
of the
Tuolumne

Livingston

Lake
McLure

Winton

Merced River

Bagby
Rec. Area

El Portal

Atwater

Merced
National
Wildlife
Refuge

Merced

Sierra

Yosemite
National
Park

Planada

Mariposa

National

Le Grand

Legend
Airport ✈
State Park 🌲

0   10 mi
0   16 km

N

Forest

301

Poor but Proud

Three miles south of Placerville is the funky little town of El Dorado, whose claim to fame is gold of another kind—Galliano liqueur. Legend has it that, long ago, one of the town's locals became the proud new owner of a gold-colored Cadillac. To celebrate his new purchase, he went to the town saloon, Poor Red's, and asked the bartender to whip him up a commemorative drink, preferably something to match the color of his Caddy. Grabbing the only golden-hued elixir he could find, the bartender proceeded to mix a little of this with a jigger of that and presto! The Golden Cadillac cocktail was born. Word got around quickly about how great the drink was, and soon people from all over the *world* were literally lining up out the door for a glass of Poor Red's finest.

What? You don't believe us? Right then, go see for yourself. At the end of the bar in a glass showcase is a plaque—sent directly from the Galliano company in Italy—that honors Poor Red's as the largest user of Galliano liqueur in North America. And while you're there, you might as well try their barbecued chicken, steak, and pork ribs—all of which are served big and priced small. (Open for lunch Mon through Fri and dinner daily; 6221 Pleasant Valley Rd., in downtown El Dorado; ☎ 530/622-2901.)

Sacramento is another option, but only slightly faster. For more information about any of these towns, contact the **Amador County Chamber of Commerce,** 125 Peek St., Jackson (☎ 209/223-0350).

AMADOR CITY   Once a bustling mining town, Amador City is now devoted mostly to dredging up tourist dollars. Although Amador City sounds large and impressive, it is in fact so tiny that it holds the title as the smallest incorporated city in California. Local merchants have made the most of a refurbished block-long boardwalk, converting the historic false-fronted buildings into a gallery of sorts; the stores sell everything from turn-of-the-century antiques and folk art to handcrafted furniture, gold-rush memorabilia, rare books, and Native American crafts. Parking can be difficult, however, especially during the summer months.

SUTTER CREEK   The self-proclaimed "nicest little town in the Mother Lode," Sutter Creek was named after sawmill owner John Sutter, employer of James Marshall (the first white man to discover gold in California). Railroad baron Leland Stanford made his fortune at Sutter Creek's Lincoln Mine, then invested his millions to both build the transcontinental railroad and fund his successful campaign to become governor of California.

The town is a real charmer, lined with beautiful 19th-century buildings in pristine condition, including **Downs Mansion,** the former home of the foreman at Stanford's mine (now a private residence on Spanish Street, across from the Immaculate Conception Church), and the landmark **Knight's Foundry,** 81 Eureka St., off Main Street (no phone), the last water-powered foundry and machine shop in the nation. There are also numerous shops and galleries along Main Street, though finding a free parking space can be a real challenge on summer weekends.

JACKSON   Jackson, the county seat of Amador County, is far livelier than its neighboring towns to the north (it was the last place in California to outlaw prostitution). Be sure to take time to stroll through the center of town, browsing in the stores and admiring the Victorian architecture. Although the Kennedy and Argonaut mines ultimately produced more than $140 million in gold, Jackson initially earned its place in the gold rush as a supply center. That history is apparent in the town's wide Main Street, lined by tall buildings adorned with intricate iron railings.

Make no mistake: This is not a ghost town, but rather a modern minicity that has worked to preserve its pre-Victorian influence. At the southern end of the street is the famous **National Hotel,** 2 Water St., at Main Street (☎ **209/223-0500**), rumored to be California's oldest continuously operating hotel since it opened its doors in 1862. Will Rogers, John Wayne, Leland Stanford, and many other celebrities and big-time politicos of the previous century stayed here. Today, the hotel's **Louisiana House Bar**—a cool, dark establishment where weary travelers can rest while a honky-tonk pianist beats out ragtime tunes and classic oldies—does a brisk business (alas, the guest rooms aren't nearly as enjoyable).

Also worth a look is the **Wells Fargo Club and Charcoal Broiler,** located diagonally across the street from the hotel. This two-story brick structure with its wooden balcony and awning is an original 1851 Wells Fargo building. The **Amador County Museum,** a huge brick building at 225 Church St., is where Will Rogers filmed *Boys Will Be Boys* in 1920. Today, the former home of Armstead Calvin Brown and his 11 children is filled with mining memorabilia and information on two local mines, the Kennedy and the Argonaut, that were among the deepest and richest in the nation. Within the museum is a working large-scale model of the Kennedy. The museum (☎ **209/223-6386**) is open Wednesday through Sunday from 10am to 4pm; requested donation is $2. Tours of the museum cost $1 and are offered Saturday and Sunday on the hour from 11am to 3pm.

If you would rather see the real thing, head to the **Kennedy Tailing Wheels Park** (no phone), site of the famous Kennedy and Argonaut mines, the deepest in the Mother Lode. The mines have been closed for decades, but the huge tailing wheels and head frames, used to convey mine debris over the hills to a settling pond, remain. To reach the park, take Main Street to Jackson Gate Road, just north of Jackson.

A few miles south of Jackson on Calif. 49 is one of the most evocative mining towns of the region, **Mokelumne Hill.** The town basically consists of one street overlooking a valley with a few old buildings, and somehow its sad, abandoned air has the mark of authenticity. At one time, the hill was dotted with tents and wood-and-tar-paper shacks and the town boasted a population of 15,000, including an old French quarter and a Chinatown. But now many of its former residents are merely memorialized in the town's Protestant, Jewish, and Catholic cemeteries.

A SIDE TRIP TO VOLCANO   About a dozen miles east of Jackson on Calif. 88 is the enchantingly decrepit town of Volcano—one of the most authentic ghost towns in the central Sierra. The town got its name in 1848, after miners mistook the origins of the enormous craggy boulders that lie in the center of town. The dark rock and blind window frames of a few backless, ivy-covered buildings give the town's main thoroughfare a haunted look. Sprinkled between boarded-up buildings, about a hundred residents do business in the same sagging storefronts that a population of 8,000 frequented nearly 150 years ago.

One thing you'll notice about Volcano is the overwhelming silence of its streets. But the tiny, now-quiet burg has a rich history: Not only was this boomtown once home to 17 hotels, courts of quick justice, and the state's first lending library and astronomical observatory, but Volcano gold also supported the Union during the Civil War. Residents even smuggled a huge cannon to the front line in a hearse (it was never used). The story goes that had the enthusiastic blues fired it, "Old Abe" would have exploded, it was so overcharged. The cannon sits in the town center today, under a rusting weather vane.

Looming over the small buildings is the stately **St. George Hotel** (☎ 209/296-4458), a three-story, balconied building that testifies to the $90 million in gold mined in and around the town. Its ivy-covered brick and shuttered windows will remind you of colonial New England. The 20-room hotel is still in operation (though not particularly recommended), as is the restaurant, which serves breakfast Saturday and Sunday and dinner Wednesday through Sunday. Even if you're not hungry, stop in for a libation at the classic old bar.

In the summer the **Volcano Theatre Company** performs at the town's outdoor amphitheater, hidden behind stone facades on Main Street, a block north of the St. George Hotel. It's a wonderful Gold Country experience. For information on upcoming performances, call ☎ **209/296-2525.** And in early spring, hundreds of people come from all around to picnic amid the nearly half million daffodils in bloom on **Daffodil Hill,** a 4-acre ranch 3 miles north of Volcano (follow the sign on Ram's Horn Grade; no phone).

WHERE TO STAY
Amador City

Imperial Hotel. Main St. (Calif. 49; P.O. Box 195), Amador City, CA 95601. ☎ **800/242-5594** or 209/267-9172. 6 units. A/C. $80–$100 double. AE, DISC, MC, V. The hotel is on Calif. 49, in an 1879 brick Victorian building.

Proprietors Bruce Sherrill and Dale Martin did a brilliant job restoring this stately century-old brick hotel and restaurant, located at the foot of Main Street overlooking Amador City. The individually decorated rooms—all with private bathrooms—are furnished with brass, iron, or pine beds and numerous antiques; two come with private balconies. Our favorite room features hand-painted furnishings by local artist John Johannsen. Amenities include hair dryers and heated towel bars, as well as newspaper delivery and in-room massage upon request. The restaurant, serving Mediterranean/California cuisine, has a sterling reputation, and hotel guests can take advantage of room service when it's open.

Drytown

Old Well Motel. 15947 Calif. 49 (P.O. Box 187), Drytown, CA 95699. ☎ **209/245-6467.** 11 units. A/C TV. $40–$65 double. MC, V.

Just up the road from Amador City is the don't-blink-or-you'll-miss-it community of Drytown, which, oddly enough, was built next to a swiftly moving creek. There's only a handful of buildings here, one of which is this small, 11-room motel that surprisingly few people know about. If it's Old West ambiance you're after, you'll be happier at the Imperial Hotel down the street. But if all you need is a cheap, clean place to hang your hat for the night, the Old Well Motel will do. Next to the motel is a small diner and swimming pool, and you can even test your panning skills along the creek that ambles past your room.

Sutter Creek

Gold Quartz Inn. 15 Bryson Dr., Sutter Creek, CA 95685. ☎ **800/752-8738** or 209/267-9155. Fax 209/267-9170. 24 units. A/C TV TEL. $80–$150 double. AE, DISC, MC, V.

Just off Calif. 49 outside Sutter Creek is one of the town's premier B&Bs, a modern establishment designed in Queen Anne style. Its amenities and first-class bedrooms make it comparable to a deluxe small hotel. The rooms are decorated with antique reproductions and iron or brass beds, and all have private bathrooms. Some units have their own porches, the only place where smoking is allowed. Afternoon tea and a full breakfast are served daily in the dining rooms; the adjacent parlor offers an array of sofas and a VCR with a movie library. Services include a courtesy laundry.

Jackson

Jackson Holiday Lodge. 850 Calif. 49 (P.O. Box 1147), Jackson, CA 95642. ☎ **209/ 223-0486.** A/C TV TEL. $50–$80 double. Rates include continental breakfast. AE, DC, DISC, MC, V.

If you're willing to forgo even the slightest hint of Old West ambiance, the Jackson Holiday Lodge offers all the familiar trappings of a modern motel at a third of the cost of most B&Bs. We recommend it for the swimming pool alone, which comes in real handy on those sweltering Gold Country summer days. The price includes a continental breakfast (served in the lobby), in-room coffeemakers, and free local calls. Dollar for dollar, it's one of the best deals around.

WHERE TO DINE

Sutter Creek

Ron and Nancy's Palace Restaurant & Saloon. 76 Main St. ☎ **209/267-1355.** Reservations recommended on weekends. Main courses $9–$14. AE, CB, DC, DISC, MC, V. Daily 11:30am–3pm and 5–9pm (last order). AMERICAN/CONTINENTAL.

Ron and Nancy Gottheiner are the first to agree that they don't run the fanciest restaurant in the Gold Country, and that's just the way they like it. Where else can you get a prime rib served with hot bread, potato, and sautéed vegetables for under $10? Decent food at a fair price is the catch at this converted 1853 stable. Many visitors come just for the two-fisted drinks served in the bar/lounge, where a battle for your attention will rage between the Elvis memorabilia favored by Nancy and the Oakland Raiders memorabilia prized by Ron. (The bar, incidentally, remains open through the afternoon, even when the restaurant area is closed.) One of the most popular lunchtime dishes is the $5.95 steak croissant sautéed in Marsala and flavored with onions and herbs. Dinner items—all priced to move—range from the charbroiled rib eye for $12 to R&N's signature veal-and-scampi picatta for a mere $13. On Friday and Saturday nights, live entertainment starts at 8pm.

✪ **Zinfandels.** 51 Hanford St. ☎ **209/267-5008.** Reservations recommended. Main courses $12.95–$19.95. AE, DC, DISC, MC, V. Thurs–Sun 5:30–9:30pm. CALIFORNIA.

Greg and Kelley West's Zinfandels has received nothing but kudos since it first opened in July 1996. Greg, a 6-year veteran of Greens (a highly respected vegetarian restaurant in San Francisco), is responsible for the entrees, while his wife, Kelley, bakes the breads and pastries. Though the emphasis is on low-fat vegetarian fare such as butternut-squash risotto with pancetta, leeks, crimini mushrooms, and spinach, West also offers a trio of fresh fish, chicken, and beef dishes ranging from cannelloni filled with lamb sausage, chard, and smoked mozzarella to Patrale sole with a citrus-ginger beurre blanc. The menu changes weekly to take advantage of seasonal produce from local farms, and even the wines—paired with each dish—are provided by local wineries such as Stevenot and Ironstone. A recent addition is a wine tasting/appetizer/ dessert/espresso room downstairs, an appealing alternative to a full sit-down dinner.

Jackson

Mel and Faye's Diner. 205 Calif. 49 (at Main St.). ☎ **209/223-0853.** Menu items $3–$6. No credit cards. Daily 4:45am–10pm. AMERICAN.

How can anybody not love a classic old diner? In business since 1956, Mel and Faye have been cranking out the best diner food in the Gold Country for so long that it's okay to not feel guilty for salivating over the thought of a sloppy double cheeseburger smothered with onions and special sauce and washed down with a large chocolate shake and could you please add a large side of fries with that and how much is a slice of pie? It's a time-honored Jackson tradition.

Upstairs Restaurant & Streetside Bistro. 164 Main St. ☎ **209/223-3342.** Reservations recommended. Main courses $12–$20. DISC, MC, V. Tues–Fri 11:30am–2:30pm; Sat–Sun 11:30am–3:30pm; daily 5:30–9pm. INTERNATIONAL.

This adorable little restaurant offers a limited, often changing menu, but you might stumble on some true culinary gems, such as pasta puttanesca with tomato-basil fettuccine and fresh Roma tomatoes, or duck julienned and served with a blackberry-ginger port sauce. Layne McCollum, a graduate of California's Culinary Institute, is known as the town's finest and most sophisticated chef, with a reputation for imaginative and innovative cuisine. Crisp white linens, bowls of fresh flowers, and background music provide a romantic backdrop to the restaurant's 12 tables. Lunch—quiche, soups, salads, and gourmet sandwiches such as smoked pork loin with red-chili pesto on chipotle—is served until about 3pm in the bright, cheery Streetside Bistro. Tastefully outfitted with wrought-iron furniture, tile flooring, and colorful oil paintings, the Bistro remains open after lunch for wine, house-roasted espresso drinks, and appetizers.

THE SOUTHERN GOLD COUNTRY: ANGELS CAMP, MURPHYS, COLUMBIA, SONORA & JAMESTOWN

No other region in the Gold Country offers more to see and do than these towns in the south, 86 miles southeast of Sacramento. From exploring enormous caverns to riding in the stagecoach and panning for real gold, the neighboring towns of Angels Camp, Murphys, Columbia, Sonora, and Jamestown offer a cornucopia of gold-rush-related sites, museums, and activities. It's a great place to bring the family (kids love roaming around the dusty car-free streets of Columbia), and the region offers some of the best lodgings and restaurants in the Gold Country. In short, if you're the Type-A sort who needs to stay active, the southern Gold Country is for you.

To reach any of these towns from Sacramento, head south on Calif. 99 to Stockton, then take Calif. 4 east directly into Angels Camp (from here it's a short, scenic drive to all the other towns). For a much longer but more scenic route, take U.S. 50 east to Placerville and head south on Calif. 49, which also takes you directly to Angels Camp.

ANGELS CAMP You've probably heard of Angels Camp, the town that inspired Mark Twain to pen "The Celebrated Jumping Frog of Calaveras County." This pretty, peaceful Gold Country community is built on hills that are honeycombed with mine tunnels. In the 1880s and 1890s, five mines were located along Main Street—Sultana, Angel's, Lightner, Utica, and Stickle—and the town echoed with noise as more than 200 stamps crushed the ore. Between 1886 and 1910 the five mines generated close to $20 million.

But a far more lasting legacy than the town's gold production is the **Jumping Frog Jubilee,** started in 1928 to mark the paving of the town's streets. To this day, the ribiting competition takes place every 3rd weekend in May. The record, 21 feet, 5¾ inches, was jumped in 1986 by "Rosie the Ribiter," beating the old record by 4½ inches. Livestock exhibitions, pageants, cook-offs, arm-wrestling tournaments, live music, carnival rides, a rodeo, and plenty of beer and wine keep the thousands of spectators entertained between jump-offs (heck, you can even rent a frog if you forget to pack one). For more information and entry forms ($5 per frog), call the Jumping Frog Jubilee headquarters at ☎ **209/736-2561.**

MURPHYS From Angels Camp, a 20-minute drive east along Calif. 4 takes you to Murphys, one of our favorite Gold Country towns. Legend has it Murphys started as a former trading post set up by brothers Dan and John Murphy in cooperation with local Indians (John married the chief's daughter). These days, its peaceful community is made up of gingerbread Victorians shaded by tall locust trees bordering narrow streets. Be sure to take a stroll down Main Street, stopping in **Grounds** for a bite to eat (see "Where to Dine," below) and perhaps a cool draft of Murphys Red—direct from **Murphys Brewing Company**—at the rustic saloon within Murphys Historic Hotel and Lodge.

While you're here, you might also want to check out **Ironstone Vineyards,** 1894 Six Mile Rd., 1 mile south of downtown Murphys (☎ **209/728-1251**), a veritable wine theme park built by the Kautz family. It boasts an enormous tasting room, jewelry shop, museum housing the largest crystalline gold piece in existence, gallery, amphitheater, music room, caverns, park and gardens, and even a culinary academy.

Also in the vicinity—just off Calif. 4, 1 mile north of Murphys off Sheep Ranch Road—are the **Mercer Caverns** (☎ **209/728-2101**). These caverns, discovered in 1885 by Walter Mercer, contain a variety of geological formations—crystalline stalactites and stalagmites—in a series of descending chambers. Tours of the well-lit caverns take about 55 minutes. From Memorial Day through September, hours are Sunday through Thursday from 9am to 6pm, Friday and Saturday from 9am to 8pm; October through May, Sunday through Thursday from 10am to 4:30pm, Friday and Saturday from 10am to 6pm. Admission is $7 for adults, $3.50 for children 5 to 11, and free for children 4 and under.

Fifteen miles east of Murphys up Calif. 4 is **Calaveras Big Trees State Park** (☎ **209/795-2334**), where you can witness giant sequoias that are among the biggest and oldest living things on earth. It's a popular summer retreat that offers camping, swimming, hiking, and fishing along the Stanislaus River. (It's open daily; admission is $5 per car for day use.)

COLUMBIA   Though somewhat hokey and contrived, **Columbia State Historic Park** (☎ **209/532-4301** for museum) is the best maintained gold-rush town in the Mother Lode (as well as one of the most popular, so expect crowds in the summer). At one point this boisterous mining town was the state's second-largest city (and only two votes shy of becoming the state capital over Sacramento). When gold mining no longer panned out in the late 1850s, most of the town's 15,000 residents departed, leaving much of the mining equipment and buildings in place. In 1945 the entire town was turned into a Historic Park.

As a result, Columbia has been preserved and functions much as it did in the 1850s, with stagecoach rides, western-style Victorian hotels and saloons, a newspaper office, a working blacksmith's forge, a Wells Fargo express office, and numerous other relics of California's early mining days. Cars are banned from its dusty streets, giving the shady town an authentic and uncommercial feel. Merchants still do business behind some storefronts, as horse, stagecoach, and pedestrian traffic wanders by.

If Columbia's heat and dust get to you, pull up a stool at the **Jack Douglass Saloon** (☎ **209/533-2355**) on Main Street, open from 10am to 5pm daily. Inside the swinging doors of the classic Western bar, you can sample homemade sarsaparilla and wild cherry, drinks the saloon has been serving since 1857. The storefront's large shuttered windows open onto a dusty main street, so put up your boots, relax awhile, and watch the stagecoach go by.

SONORA   Located a few miles south of Columbia, Sonora is the largest town in the southern Gold Country (you'll know you've arrived when traffic starts to crawl). Back in the gold-rush days, Sonora and Columbia were the two richest towns in the Mother Lode. Dozens of stores and small cafes line the main thoroughfare. If you can find a parking space, it's worth your while to spend an hour or two checking out the sites, including the 19th-century **St. James Episcopal Church,** at the top of Washington

Street, and the **Tuolumne County Museum and History Center,** 158 W. Bradford Ave. (☎ 209/532-1317), located in the 1857 County Jail. Admission is free, and it's open daily year-round: Sunday, Monday, and Wednesday from 9am to 4pm; Tuesday and Thursday from 10am to 4pm; and Saturday from 10am to 3:30pm.

JAMESTOWN About 4 miles southwest of Sonora on Calif. 49 is Jamestown, a 4-block-long town of old-fashioned storefronts and two charming turn-of-the-century hotels. Yes, there's gold in these parts, too, as the marker commemorating the discovery of a 75-pound nugget will attest (panning nearby Woods Creek is a popular pastime among both locals and tourists). If Jamestown looks eerily familiar to you, that's probably because you've seen it in the movies or on television. It's one of Hollywood's favorite western movie sets; scenes from such films as *Butch Cassidy and the Sundance Kid* were shot here.

Jamestown's most popular attraction is the **Railtown 1897 State Historic Park,** a train buff's paradise featuring three original Sierra steam locomotives. These great machines were used in many a movie and television show, including *High Noon, Little House on the Prairie, Bonanza,* and *My Little Chickadee.* Rides are given April through January on Saturday and Sunday, from 11am to 3pm on the hour (in Nov and Dec on Sat only); the trains at the roundhouse are on display daily year-round. There's also guided tours on weekends, and self-guided tours daily. The Depot Store and Museum are open daily from 9:30am to 4:30pm. The park is located near the center of town, on Fifth Avenue at Reservoir Road (☎ 209/984-3953).

WHERE TO STAY
Angels Camp
Cooper House Bed & Breakfast Inn. 1184 Church St. (P.O. Box 1388), Angels Camp, CA 95222. ☎ **800/225-3764,** ext. 326, or 209/736-2145. 3 units. A/C. $90 double. Rates include breakfast. DISC, MC, V.

Once the home and office of a prominent community physician, Dr. George P. Cooper, the Cooper House is now Angels Camp's only B&B. This small Arts and Crafts home is mercifully positioned well away from the hustle and bustle of the town's Main Street. Owner/innkeeper Kathy Reese maintains three units, all with private bathrooms. The Zinfandel Suite has its own private entrance and deck, and the Chardonnay Suite has a king-size bed, antique claw-foot bathtub, and a private deck. The third bedroom, the Cabernet Suite, is midsize, with a queen bed, adjoining sunroom, and splendid garden view.

Columbia
City Hotel. Main St., Columbia State Park (P.O. Box 1870), CA 95310. ☎ **800/532-1479** or 209/532-1479. Fax 209/532-7027. 10 units, all with shared bathroom. A/C. $85–$105 double. Rates include breakfast. AE, DISC, MC, V.

Established in 1856, the historic City Hotel was fully restored in 1975 by the State of California, the nonprofit City Hotel Corporation, and Columbia College, and is now run as a sort of on-the-job training center for hospitality management students (hence, the eager-to-please staff). It's a big, beautiful building, complete with a stately parlor furnished with Victorian sofas, antiques, and Oriental rugs. The largest guest rooms have two balconies overlooking Main Street; the units off the parlor are also spacious. The hallway rooms are smaller, but still nicely furnished with Renaissance Revival beds and antiques. Each room has a sink and toilet. A large buffet breakfast is served in the dining room, and the hotel also runs a fine-dining restaurant serving classic continental cuisine (roast rack of lamb, grilled salmon, smoked duck breast) and the What Cheer saloon, which boasts its original cherry-wood bar, shipped around the Horn from New England.

How to Pan for Gold

Find a gold pan, ideally a 12- to 15-inch steel pan. Place the pan over an oven burner, or better yet, in a campfire. This will darken the pan, making it easier to see any flakes of placer gold (many gold pans come already blackened). Find some gravel, sand, or dirt in a stream that looks promising or feels lucky. Scoop dirt into the pan until it's nearly full, then place it under water and keep it there while you break up the clumps of mud and clay and toss out any stones. Then grasp the pan with both hands. Holding it level, rotate it in swirling motions. This will cause the heavier gold to loosen and settle to the bottom of the pan. Drain off the dirty water and loose stuff. Keep doing this until gold and heavier minerals called "black sand" are left in the pan. Carefully inspect the black sand for nuggets or speck traces of gold. Who knows? You just might get lucky.

If this all seems too much to try on your own, you can sign up for a gold-panning lesson with Jamestown's **Gold Prospecting Expeditions** (☎ **800/596-0009** or 209/984-4653). The hour-long instruction costs about $15 and yes, you get to keep any gold you might find.

Fallon Hotel. Washington St. (P.O. Box 1870), Columbia State Park, CA 95310. ☎ **800/532-1479** or 209/532-1470. 14 units, 13 with shared bathroom. A/C. $55–$105 double. Rates include breakfast. AE, DISC, MC, V.

This hotel, which opened in 1857, has been restored and decorated to evoke the 1890s. The classic two-story building has retained many of its original antiques and furniture. The largest rooms are those along the front upper balcony. Only one unit has a full bathroom; the rest have a private sink and toilet, and showers are down the hall. The rooms are furnished with high-backed Victorian beds, marble-topped dressers, rockers, and similar oak pieces. A full breakfast is served in the downstairs parlor.

Sonora

✪ **Gunn House Hotel.** 286 S. Washington St., Sonora, CA 95370. ☎ **209/532-3421.** 20 units. A/C TV. $45–$75 double. Rates include continental breakfast. AE, DISC, MC, V.

Built in 1850 by Dr. Lewis C. Gunn, the Gunn House was the first two-story adobe structure in Sonora, built to house his family, who sailed around Cape Horn from the East Coast to join him in the gold rush. Painstakingly restored by its present owners, Margaret Dienelt and her daughter Peggy, it's now one of the best low-priced hotels in the Gold Country. It's easy to catch the forty-niner spirit here, as the entire hotel and grounds are brimming with quality antiques and turn-of-the-century artifacts. Rare for a building this old, each guest room has a private bathroom and air-conditioning. What really makes the Gunn House one of our favorites, though, is the hotel's beautiful pool and patio, surrounded by lush vegetation and admirable stonework. Also within the hotel is the Josephine Room, a small, elegant Italian restaurant and bar where guests are served their complimentary continental breakfast.

Jamestown

Jamestown Hotel. Main St. (P.O. Box 539), Jamestown, CA 95327. ☎ **800/205-4901** or 209/984-3902. Fax 209/984-4149. 10 units. A/C. $70–$135 double; $125 suite. Rates include continental breakfast. AE, DC, DISC, MC, V.

The most worked-over building in town, the Jamestown was originally built in 1858; it burned down and was rebuilt twice before 1915. To achieve the old-fashioned, brick-fronted Victorian look it sports today, its current owners ripped out a lot of stucco and Spanish-revival paraphernalia. Much of the lower floor is devoted to the front office, bar, and restaurant (see "Where to Dine," below). The second floor contains a cadre of cozy bedrooms outfitted with antiques acquired along both coasts of North America. All of the spacious rooms are loaded with nostalgic charm; a few have sitting rooms, and all have private bathrooms (some with claw-foot tubs). The street-level rooms are the most luxurious, outfitted with whirlpool tubs, TV/VCR, private patios, and separate heat/air-conditioning controls.

National Hotel. 77 Main St. (P.O. Box 502), Jamestown, CA 95327. ☎ **800/894-3446** or 209/984-3446. Fax 209/984-5620. 9 units. A/C. $80–$100 double. Rates include continental breakfast. AE, CB, DC, DISC, MC, V.

Located in the center of town, this two-story classic Western hotel has been operating since 1859, making it 1 of the 10 oldest continuously operating hotels in the state. The saloon has its original 19th-century redwood bar, and you can imagine what it must have been like when miners traded gold dust for drinks. New this year is a "Soaking Room," a sort of 1800s Jacuzzi for two. The rooms above are outfitted with numerous period antiques, as well as oak furnishings and brass beds made up with quilts. All units have private bathrooms. The restaurant on the main floor serves continental cuisine with a California influence, such as brandy-apple pork, ruby trout amandine, and blackened prime rib with sautéed prawns.

WHERE TO DINE
Angels Camp
B of A Cafe. 1262 S. Main St. ☎ **209/736-0765.** Main courses $9–$15. MC, V. Daily 11am–3pm; Thurs and Sun 5:30–8pm; Fri–Sat 5:30–9pm. Cafe opens daily at 8am. AMERICAN.

Katherine Reese, who also runs the Cooper House Bed & Breakfast Inn, has done a marvelous job restoring and converting this 1936 Bank of America building into a bright, cheerful cafe. Using leftover banking curios, she decorated the walls with polished teller windows and converted the vault into a wine-tasting room. Lunch items range from country-style quiche du jour to roasted eggplant sandwiches on multigrain bread and gourmet baby-green salad. Dinners include sliced pork loin marinated with Australian maple wood, lemon rosemary chicken, prime rib, and mesquite-marinated baby back ribs. Daily specials include fresh fish, pasta, and vegetables, and all entrees come with fresh bread, soup or salad, and Kathy's Famous Herbed Roasted Red Potatoes. Basque-style dinners (steak, chicken, or lamb with tureens of soup, salad, and pasta for $15 per person) are served Sunday between 5 and 8pm, but be sure to make a reservation—tables fill up fast.

Murphys
○ Grounds. 402 Main St. ☎ **209/728-8663.** Reservations recommended on weekends. Main courses $7.50–$15.50. DISC, MC, V. Wed 7am–4pm; Thurs–Mon 7am–3pm and 5–9pm. ECLECTIC.

When River Klass moved here from the East Coast to open his own place, Murphys's restaurant-challenged residents heaved a collective sigh of relief. Its nickname is the "Rude Boy Cafe," but you'll find only happy smiles and friendly service from the energetic staff. The majority of Klass's business is with the locals, who have become addicted to the potato pancakes that come with every made-to-order omelet. For lunch, try the sausage sandwich on house-baked bread or the grilled eggplant sandwich stuffed with smoked mozzarella and fresh basil. Although the menus change twice a week, typical dinner choices include fettuccine topped with sautéed shrimp, halibut, and mussels in a garlic cream sauce; oven-roasted sweetheart ham with glazed yams; and a New York steak with caramelized onions and half-mashed red potatoes. Monday is Mexican night. The long, narrow dining rooms are bright and airy with pinewood furnishings, wood floors, and an open kitchen. On sunny days, request a table on the back patio.

Sonora

Diamondback Grill. 110 S. Washington St. ☎ **209/532-6661.** Main courses $5–$10. No credit cards. Mon–Sat 6am–9pm; Sun 8am–3pm. AMERICAN.

This modest little family-owned diner whips up one doozy of a burger: the Diamondback. The mesquite-grilled half-pounder comes with all the works, including fries, for only five bucks. There's about a dozen other burgers to choose from, as well as gourmet sandwiches (go for the grilled eggplant with fresh tomato and mozzarella); house-made soups and pecan pies; a zesty black-bean-and-steak chili; and great specials listed daily on the board, most of which cost well under $10.

But wait, it gets better: They also do breakfast. Their three-egg artichoke-heart-and-mushroom omelet is only $4.95, and a full stack of whole-wheat honey hotcakes costs just $3.25. There's also a good selection of beer and wine by the glass, but we prefer to finish our feast with a thick chocolate shake from Jim Town Frosty, located at the north end of Main Street in Jamestown.

Good Heavens. 49 N. Washington St. ☎ **209/532-3663.** Main courses $5–$10 lunch, $10–$15 dinner. DISC, MC, V. Daily year-round 11am–3pm; summer Thurs–Sun 5–9pm; winter Fri–Sat 5–9pm. AMERICAN.

This small, homey cafe is one of our favorite places to eat in the Gold Country. The lunch menu features a variety of unusual yet wonderful sandwiches—cucumber and pesto cream, turkey and cranberry orange—plus an array of delicious soups, salads, and desserts. There are several daily lunch specials as well, ranging from chile rellenos to crepes and pastas. Just recently they've added a dinner menu, featuring such dishes as a hearty beef-loin pot roast with potatoes, carrots, and gravy; Cornish game hen with fresh cornbread and vegetables; and a wonderful honey-fried chicken with a crispy buttermilk crust. Each meal starts with fresh herb-and-cheese biscuits and a choice of freshly made jams, such as the decadent raspberry-chocolate or the tart orange marmalade. Don't leave without purchasing a jar or two; they're sold at the counter.

North Beach Cafe. 14317 Mono Way/Calif. 108 (from central Sonora, go 3 miles east on Calif. 108 to John's Sierra Market, turn right into parking lot). ☎ **209/536-1852.** Main courses $7.50–$12.50. Sun–Thurs 11am–9pm; Fri–Sat 11am–10pm. No credit cards. ITALIAN.

Chef/owner Terry La Torre has turned this former auto-parts store into one of the most popular restaurants in Sonora. A longtime local and progeny of San Francisco restaurateurs, the well-rounded, mustachioed La Torre can usually be found draped in chef's whites, barking orders to his amiable staff as he deftly flips a New York on his blazing mesquite grill. The place is almost always abuzz with customers who come to eat La Torre's cooking and to bask in his infectious pomposity. The menu is predominantly Italian, including a dozen or so pastas, fresh fish, veal, chicken, and steaks. The lunch menu is less complex, ranging from chicken or steak sandwiches to burgers, soups, and salads. La Torre tends to be a bit heavy-handed with the sauces; we usually request that he halves the regular amount. Otherwise, the combination of fair prices, good food, and classic La Torre histrionics makes North Beach Cafe worth searching out.

Jamestown

Jenny Lind Room at the Jamestown Hotel. Main St. ☎ **800/205-4901** or 209/ 984-3902. Reservations recommended. Main courses $10–$17. AE, DC, DISC, MC, V. Mon– Sat 11am–3pm; Sun brunch 10am–3pm; daily 5–9pm. AMERICAN/INTERNATIONAL.

The Jenny Lind Room may not be the top restaurant in the Gold Country, but it's certainly the most authentic looking, a dark-wood affair with stuffed wingback chairs, a fireplace, and dozens of old photos. There are about 15 tables inside, plus another 13 on an outdoor deck. Menu items from chef Brian Johnson's menu include escargot in mushroom caps cooked in garlic butter; breast of chicken "Jerusalem," with artichokes, mushrooms, and lemon-scented cream sauce; and a hugely popular filet mignon stuffed with Gorgonzola cheese and topped with a portobello-mushroom wine sauce. There's also a Sunday champagne brunch served until 3pm.

3 The Central Valley & Sierra National Forest

The Central Valley (also known as the San Joaquin Valley) is about as far as you can get from California's glamorous movie-stars-in-stretch-limos image. This hot, flat strip of farms, dairies, fast-food joints, cheap motels, and truck stops stretches for some 225 miles from Bakersfield to Redding. The 18,000-square-mile valley is central to the economy of the Golden State, in part because of its cultivated and irrigated fields, orchards, pastures, and vineyards.

The major traffic arteries through the valley are Calif. 99 and Interstate 5. Calif. 99 links the agricultural communities, while I-5 provides access routes to the roadside attractions in the valley. Rivers cutting through the valley offer fishing, boating, houseboating on the delta, and white-water rafting on the rapids. And the valley's spectacular landscapes provide unrivaled natural beauty; many visitors drive through in spring just to view the orchards in bloom.

The Central Valley also stands on the doorstep of some of America's greatest attractions, the most well-known being Yosemite National Park (see chapter 9).

Fresno, although not much in itself, is on the doorstep of the Sierra National Forest and nearby natural attractions like the Millerton Lake State Recreation Area.

FRESNO

The running joke in California is that Fresno is the "gateway to Bakersfield." For most visitors, Fresno, located 185 miles southeast of San Francisco, is just a place to pass through en route to the state parks; it can, however, be a good place to stop for food and lodging, and it makes a good base for exploring the Sierra National Forest (see below). But be careful if you're looking for a bargain at one of the cheap motels along the highway—security may be questionable (in other words, don't leave anything valuable in your car).

Founded in 1874 in the geographic center of the state, Fresno lies in the heart of the Central Valley and has experienced incredible growth in recent years. Like most growing cities, it has been plagued by an increase in crime, drugs, and urban sprawl.

As the seat of Fresno County, the city handles more than $3 billion annually in agricultural production. It also contains Sun Maid, the world's largest dried-fruit-packing plant, and Guild, one of the country's largest wineries.

If you have any reason at all to be in Fresno, try to visit between late February and late March so you can drive the **Fresno County Blossom Trail.** This 62-mile, self-guided tour takes in the beauty of California's agrarian bounty at its peak. The trail

courses through fruit orchards in full bloom and citrus groves with lovely orange blos-
soms and a heady natural perfume. The **Fresno Convention and Visitors Bureau,**
808 M St. in Fresno (☎ **800/788-0836** or 209/233-0836), supplies full details,
including a map.

A PLACE TO STAY

San Joaquin. 1309 W. Shaw Ave., Fresno, CA 93711. ☎ **800/775-1309** or 209/225-1309.
Fax 209/225-6021. 68 units. A/C TV TEL. $82–$89 junior suite; $125 one-bedroom suite with
kitchen; $165 two-bedroom suite with kitchen; $185 three-bedroom suite with kitchen. Rates
include breakfast. AE, CB, DC, DISC, MC, V.

Set on the northern edge of Fresno, this hotel was conceived as an apartment complex
in the 1970s. Around 1985, a lobby was added, the floor plans were adjusted, and the
place was reconfigured as an all-suite hotel. Each suite is outfitted in a slightly different
style, with light, contemporary colors and furniture. Room service is available from an
independently managed restaurant down the street.

SIERRA NATIONAL FOREST

Leaving Fresno's taco joints, used-car lots, and tract houses behind, an hour's drive 45
miles northeast gets you to the Sierra National Forest, a land of lakes and coniferous
forests lying between Yosemite and Sequoia and Kings Canyon National Parks. The
entire eastern portion of the park is still unspoiled wilderness protected by the
government. Development—some of it, unfortunately, beside the bigger lakes and
reservoirs—is confined to the western side.

The 1.3-million-acre forest contains 528,000 acres of wilderness. The Sierra's five
wilderness areas include Ansel Adams, Dinkey Lakes, John Muir, Kaiser, and Monarch
(see below). The forest offers plenty of opportunities for fishing, swimming, sailing,
boating, camping, waterskiing, white-water rafting, kayaking, and horseback riding,
all regulated by certain guidelines. Downhill and cross-country skiing, as well as
hunting, are also available, depending on the season. Backpackers looking to retreat to
the wilderness will find solace here, as the park is traversed by some 1,100 miles of
forest hiking trails.

In the lower elevations, summer temperatures can frequently reach 100°F, but in
the higher elevations, more comfortable temperatures in the 70s and 80s are the norm.

After visiting the ranger station at Oakhurst (see below), take Calif. 41 to Calif. 49,
the major road into the northern part of the national forest. This is more convenient
for visitors approaching the park from northern California. Calif. 168 via Clovis is the
primary route from Fresno if you're headed for Shaver Lake. There is no approach road
from the eastern Sierras, only from the west.

To learn about hiking, camping, or other activities, or to obtain the fire and wilderness permits needed for backcountry jaunts, visit one of the ranger stations in the
park's western section. These include: **Mariposa Ranger District,** 43060 Calif. 41,
Oakhurst (☎ 209/683-4665); **Minarets Ranger Station,** 57003 North Fork
(☎ 209/877-2218); **Kings River Ranger District,** 34849 Maxon Rd., Sanger, near
the Pine Flat Reservoir (☎ 209/855-8321); and the **Pineridge Ranger Station,**
29688 Auberry Rd., Prather (☎ 209/855-5360).

Shaver Lake is one place where you can stock up on goods and supplies if you're
going into the wilderness, but stores in Fresno carry much of the same stuff at lower
prices. Cheaper supplies are also available in the town of **Clovis** outside Fresno (which
you must pass through en route to the forest), especially at the Peacock Market, at
Tollhouse Road (Third Street) and Sunnyside Avenue (☎ **209/299-6627**).

THE MAJOR WILDERNESS & RECREATION AREAS

ANSEL ADAMS WILDERNESS   Divided between the Sierra and Inyo national forests, this wilderness area covers 228,500 acres. Elevations range from 3,500 to 13,157 feet. The frost-free period extends from mid-July through August, the best time for a visit to the park's upper altitudes.

Ansel Adams is dotted with scenic alpine vistas, including steep-walled gorges and barren granite peaks. There are several small glaciers in the north and some fairly large lakes on the eastern slope of the precipitous Ritter Range. This vast wilderness has excellent stream and lake fishing, especially for rainbow, golden, and brook trout, and offers challenging mountain climbing on the Minarets Range. The wilderness is accessed by the Tioga Pass Road in the north, U.S. 395 and Reds Meadow Road in the east, the Minarets Highway in the west, and Calif. 168 to High Sierra in the south.

DINKEY LAKES WILDERNESS   The 30,000-acre Dinkey Lakes area was created in 1984 and occupies the western slope of the Sierra Nevada, southeast of Huntington Lake and just northwest of Courtright Reservoir. Most of the timbered, rolling terrain here is 8,000 feet above sea level, reaching its highest point (10,619 ft.) at Three Sisters Peak. Sixteen lakes are clustered in the west-central region. You can reach the area on Kaiser Pass Road (north), Red/Coyote Jeep Road (west), Rock Creek Road (southwest), or Courtright Reservoir (southeast), generally from mid-June to late October. The frost-free period is July through August.

JOHN MUIR WILDERNESS   Occupying 584,000 acres in the Sierra and Inyo national forests, John Muir Wilderness—named after the turn-of-the-century naturalist—extends southeast from Mammoth Lakes along the crest of the Sierra Nevada for 30 miles before forking around the boundary of Kings Canyon National Park to Crown Valley and Mount Whitney. Elevations range from 4,000 to 14,496 feet at Mount Whitney, with many of the area's peaks surpassing 12,000 feet.

Split by deep canyons, the wilderness is also a land of meadows (especially beautiful when wildflowers bloom), lakes, and streams. The South and Middle Forks of the San Joaquin River, the North Fork of Kings River, and many creeks draining into Owens Valley originate in the John Muir Wilderness. Mountain hemlock, red and white fir, white-bark, and western pine dot the park's landscape. Temperatures vary wildly throughout any 24-hour period: Summer temperatures range from 25°F to 85°F, and the only really frost-free period is between mid-July and August. The higher elevations are marked by barren expanses of granite splashed with many glacially carved lakes.

KAISER WILDERNESS   Immediately north of Huntington Lake and some 70 miles northeast of Fresno, Kaiser is a 22,700-acre forest tract commanding a view of the central Sierra Nevada. It was named after Kaiser Ridge, which divides the area into two different regions. Four trailheads provide easy access to the wilderness, but the northern half is much more open than the forested southern half; the primary point of entry is the Sample Meadow Campground. All other lakes are approached cross-country. Winter storms begin to blow in late October, and the grounds are generally snow-covered until early June.

MONARCH WILDERNESS   This area extends across 45,000 acres in the Sierra and Sequoia national forests. The Sierra National portion of the region—about 21,000 acres—is very rugged and hard to traverse. Steep slopes climb from the Middle and Main Forks of Kings River, with elevations increasing from 2,400 to more than 10,000 feet. Rock outcroppings are found throughout Monarch, and most of the lower elevations are mainly chaparral covered with pine stands near the tops of the higher peaks. The frost-free period is July through August.

HUNTINGTON LAKE RECREATION AREA   At 7,000 feet, this area is a 2-hour drive east of Fresno via Calif. 168. The lake is one of the reservoirs in the Big Creek Hydroelectric System and has 14 miles of shoreline. It's a popular recreational area, offering camping, hiking, picnicking, sailing, swimming, windsurfing, fishing, and horseback riding—or you can just appreciate the beauty. The main summer season stretches from Memorial Day to Labor Day. There are seven campgrounds and four picnic areas in the Huntington Lake Basin, plus numerous hiking and riding trails. For information, stop in at the **Easterwood Visitor Center** (☎ **209/893-6611**), open from May through September.

✪ **NEIDER GROVE OF GIANT SEQUOIAS**   This 1,540-acre tract in the Sierra National Forest contains 101 mature giant sequoias in the center of the Sequoia range, south of Yosemite National Park. A visitor center stands near the Neider Grove Campground, with historical relics and displays, including two restored log cabins. The Bull Buck Tree—at one time thought to be the largest in the world—is 246 feet high and has a circumference at ground level of 99 feet. There's a mile-long, self-guided walk along the "Shadow of the Giants" National Recreational Trail in the southwest corner of the grove.

OUTDOOR ACTIVITIES

CAMPING   The Sierra National Forest seems like one vast campsite. Options range from unembellished, primitive wilderness camps to developed and often crowded campgrounds with snack bars, flush toilets, bathhouses, and hookups for RVs. For information and reservations, call the National Forest Reservation Center at ☎ **800/280-CAMP.**

   The major campgrounds are the Shaver Lake area; the Huntington Lake area (which has seven family campgrounds open from the end of June to Labor Day that must be reserved in advance); the Florence and Edison Lake area (first-come, first-served); the Dinkey Creek area (family and group camping); the Wishon and Courtright area (four campgrounds; first-come, first-served); the Pine Flat Reservoir (in the Sierra foothills, with two first-come, first-served campgrounds); and Upper Kings River, east of Pine Flat Reservoir (family campgrounds, first-come, first-served).

FISHING   The many streams of the Sierra are home to rainbow, golden, brown, and brook trout. The best freshwater angling is in the Pineridge and Kings River Rangers District. At the lower elevations, Shaver Lake, Bass Lake, and Pine Flat Reservoirs are known for their black-bass fishing. Questions about fishing in the national forest can be directed to the **California Department of Fish and Game,** 1234 E. Shaw Ave., Fresno, CA 93710 (☎ **209/222-3761**).

SKIING   Lying 65 miles northeast of Fresno on Calif. 168 in the Sierra National Forest, the **Sierra Summit Ski Area** offers mildly challenging alpine skiing, as well as marked trails for cross-country skiing and snowmobiling. The resort area has two triple and three double chairlifts, plus four surface lifts and 30 runs, the longest of which extends for 2¼ miles. There's a vertical drop-off at 1,600 feet. Other facilities include a lodge, snack bar, cafeteria, restaurant, and bar, all open daily from mid-November until mid-April. For resort information or a ski report, call ☎ **209/893-3311.**

   The **Pineridge Ranger Station** (☎ **209/855-5360**) also maintains several marked cross-country trails along Calif. 168, ranging from a 1-mile tour for beginners to a 6-mile trail for more advanced skiers.

WHITE-WATER RAFTING   The Upper Kings River, east of Pine Flat Reservoir, offers a 10-mile rafting run through Garnet Dike to Kirch Flat Campground. Rafting season is from late April to mid-July, with the highest waters in late May and early June. To get there, take Belmont Avenue in Fresno east (toward Pine Flat Reservoir) for about 63 miles.

Two commercial rafting companies that offer guided rafting trips on the Kings River are **Kings River Expeditions** (☎ 209/233-4881) and **Zephyr Whitewater Expeditions** at (☎ 209/532-6249).

The Monterey Peninsula & the Big Sur Coast

11

by Erika Lenkert and Matthew R. Poole

The Monterey Peninsula and the Big Sur coast comprise one of the world's most spectacular shorelines, skirted with cypress, rugged shores, and crescent-shaped bays. Monterey reels in visitors with its world-class aquarium and array of outdoor activities. Pacific Grove is so peaceful and quaint that the butterflies choose it as their yearly mating ground. Pebble Beach attracts the world's golfing elite. Although packed with tourists who come for the beaches, shops, and restaurants, tiny Carmel-by-the-Sea somehow remains romantic and sweet. Big Sur's dramatic and majestic coast, backed by pristine redwood forests and rolling hills, is one of the most breathtaking and tranquil environments on earth. And if you're traveling on Calif. 1 (which you should be), the magnificent coastline will guide you all the way through the region.

Although Santa Cruz isn't really part of the Monterey Peninsula, we've included it at the beginning of this chapter since you'll pass it on the drive down from San Francisco (or up from L.A. on your way to San Francisco).

Monterey and Pacific Grove occupy the northern half of the peninsula overlooking Monterey Bay, while Pebble Beach and Carmel-by-the-Sea look out over Carmel Bay and hug the peninsula's south coast. Between the north and south coasts, which are only about 5 miles apart, are at least eight golf courses, some of the state's most stunning (read: expensive) homes and hotels, and 17-Mile Drive, one of the most scenic coastal roads in the world. Inland lies Carmel Valley, with its elegant inns and resorts, golf courses, and guaranteed sunshine, even when the coast is socked in with fog.

Farther down the coast is Big Sur, a stunning 90-mile stretch of coast south of the Monterey Peninsula and west of the Santa Lucia Mountains.

1 Santa Cruz

77 miles SE of San Francisco

For a small bay-side city, Santa Cruz has a lot to offer. The main show, of course, is the Beach Boardwalk, the West Coast's only seaside amusement park, which attracts millions of visitors each year. But past the arcades and cotton candy is a surprisingly diverse and energetic city that has a little something for everyone. Shopping, hiking, mountain biking, sailing, fishing, kayaking, surfing, wine tasting, golfing, whale watching—the list of things to do here is almost endless, making Santa Cruz one of the premier family destinations on the California coast.

ESSENTIALS

GETTING THERE   Santa Cruz is 77 miles southeast of San Francisco. The most scenic route to Santa Cruz is along Calif. 1 from San Francisco, which, aside from the "you fall, you die" stretch called Devil's Slide, allows you to cruise at a steady 50 miles per hour along the coast. Faster but far less romantic is Calif. 17, which is accessed near San Jose from I-280, I-880, or U.S. 101, and literally ends at the foot of the boardwalk. The exception to this rule is weekend mornings, when Calif. 17 tends to logjam with Bay Area beachgoers while Calif. 1 remains relatively uncrowded.

VISITOR INFORMATION   For information, contact the **Santa Cruz County Conference and Visitors Council,** 701 Front St., Santa Cruz, CA 95060 (☎ **800/ 833-3494** or 831/425-1234). It's open Monday through Saturday from 9am to 5pm and Sunday from 10am to 4pm.

SPECIAL EVENTS   Special events include the Santa Cruz Hot and Cool Jazz Festival (☎ **831/662-1912;** July), Shakespeare Santa Cruz (☎ **831/459-2121;** July/Aug), and the Cabrillo Music Festival (☎ **831/426-6966;** Aug).

WHAT TO SEE & DO: BEACHES, HIKING, FISHING & MORE

One of the top amusement parks in the nation, the privately owned **Santa Cruz Beach Boardwalk** draws more than 3 million visitors a year to its 28 rides and multitudes of arcades, shops, and restaurants. The park has two national landmarks— a 1924 wooden Giant Dipper roller coaster and a 1911 carousel complete with hand-carved wooden horses and a 342-pipe band organ. It's open daily in the summer (from Memorial Day weekend through Labor Day) from 11am to 11pm, and on weekends and holidays throughout the spring and fall from 11am to 10pm. Admission to the boardwalk is free, but an all-day "unlimited rides" pass will set you back about $19. For more information call ☎ **831/426-7433.**

Here, too, at 400 Beach St. is **Neptune's Kingdom** (☎ **831/426-7433**), an enormous indoor family recreation center where the main feature is a two-story miniature golf course. Also on Beach Street is the **Municipal Wharf** (☎ **831/429-3628**) and pier, lined with shops and restaurants—a beachfront strip that is serenaded by the sea lions below. You can also crab and fish from here. Most shops are open daily from 7am to 9am, the wharf daily from 5am to 2am. Stagnaro's (☎ **831/427-2334**) operates **fishing and whale-watching trips** from the pier from November through April.

Farther down on West Cliff Drive, you'll come to a favorite **surfing** spot, **Steamers Lane,** where you can watch the surfers coasting onto the beach. If you want to find out more about this local sport that's been practiced here for 100 years, then go to the memorial lighthouse, which contains the **Santa Cruz Surfing Museum** (☎ **831/ 429-3429**), open Thursday through Monday from noon to 4pm in winter, and Wednesday through Monday from noon to 5pm in summer.

Continue along West Cliff and you'll eventually reach **Natural Bridges State Beach,** 2531 West Cliff Dr. (☎ **831/423-4609**), a large sandy beach with nearby tide pools and hiking trails. It's also home to a large colony of monarch butterflies that roost and mate in the nearby eucalyptus grove.

Other **Santa Cruz beaches** worth noting are: Bonny Doon, at Bonny Doon Road and Calif. 1, an uncrowded sandy beach and a major surfing spot accessible by a steep walkway; Pleasure Point Beach, East Cliff Drive at Pleasure Point Drive; and Twin Lakes State Beach, which is ideal for sunning and also provides access to Schwann Lagoon, a bird sanctuary.

Santa Cruz on the Cheap

Tireless researchers that we are, we've compiled a list of the best money-saving tips Santa Cruz has to offer, everything from lodging and dining to beaches and the Boardwalk. If you do the math, it adds up to an awesome day of sightseeing, partying, and lodging for under 50 bucks.

- On Friday summer nights, head to the Santa Cruz Beach Boardwalk and check out the free concerts at 6:30 and 8:30pm.
- Every summer after 5pm on Monday and Tuesday, the Santa Cruz Beach Boardwalk holds **1907 Nights,** celebrating the year it opened by reducing prices to 50¢ a ride (that's $2.50 off). Hot dogs, sodas, and cotton candy are all marked down, too.
- Great **Mexican food and cocktails** at cheap prices are served daily at the **El Palomar Restaurant's** taco bar, attached to the main restaurant at 1336 Pacific Ave. (☎ **831/425-7575**). As of press time, killer specials were offered Monday through Thursday between 5 and 8pm (Mon: $2 burritos; Tues: $1.50 tacos/$2 margaritas; Wed: $1.50 tacos/$2 draft beers; Thurs: $2 burritos/$2 draft beers and margaritas).
- To skip the $5 entrance fee to **Henry Cowell Redwoods State Park,** drive 1½ miles south of the main entrance on Calif. 9 to the Ox Road parking lot. Park for free, then follow the trail into the park, which takes you past a popular swimming hole called the Garden of Eden.
- A far better walk than the boardwalk is along the 2-mile ocean-side paved path on **West Cliff Drive** (west of the wharf). The scenery is spectacular, particularly at sunset, and it won't cost you a penny.
- Parking at the **Santa Cruz Wharf** is free for the first 30 minutes, which is plenty of time to cruise the armada of schlocky shops and cafes.
- The **Carmelita Cottages,** 321 Main St. (☎ **831/423-8304**), is a hostel in Santa Cruz that will rent you one of their bunk beds for a mere $13. The gaggle of white-washed Victorian cottages is located a few blocks north of the Boardwalk in a quiet residential neighborhood. The hostel also reserves a few rooms just for couples and families. (Okay, so it's not exactly Romance Central, but for less than $40 a night for your own room at such a prime location, it's hard to complain.)
- Don't you dare pay for parking in downtown Santa Cruz. Along Cedar and Front streets there are three parking garages and 16 surface lots that offer 3 hours of **free parking.**

In addition to many cultural and sporting events, the University of California at Santa Cruz also has the **Long Marine Laboratory and Aquarium,** 100 Shaffer Rd. at the northwest end of Delaware Avenue (☎ 831/459-4308), where you can observe (and sometimes touch) the various marine creatures kept in tide-pool touch tanks and aquariums. Open Tuesday through Sunday from 1 to 4pm.

The Santa Cruz Harbor, 135 Fifth Ave. (☎ **831/475-6161**), is the place to head for **boat rentals,** open boat **fishing** (cod, shark, and salmon), and **whale-watching trips.** Operators include **Santa Cruz Sportfishing Inc.** (☎ **831/426-4690**) and **Shamrock Charters,** 2210 East Cliff Dr. (☎ **831/476-2648**). Fishing trips cost about $60, which includes bait and rig, and whale watching costs about $20 to $25 for a 2-hour cruise.

There's a great bike route along the 2-mile cliff walk. Bikes—mountain, kids', tandem, hybrid—are available by the hour, day, or week from the **Bicycle Rental and Tour Center,** 131 Center St., 2 blocks from the Municipal Wharf (☎ **831/ 426-8687;** open 10am to 6pm in summer). Figure on paying $25 a day, which includes helmets, locks, and packs.

There are several public golf courses, the best being the **Pasatiempo Golf Club,** at 18 Clubhouse Rd. (☎ **831/459-9155**), which is rated among the top 100 courses in the United States.

Hikers, bikers, and birders in need of some direction can call **The Tour Center,** where experienced local guides will provide free information on trails in the area. They also rent bikes for about $25 a day. Contact them at ☎ **831/426-8687.**

Sea kayaking is also available. Outfitters include **Kayak Connection,** 413 Lake Ave. No. 4 (☎ **831/479-1121**), and **Venture Quest Kayaking** (☎ **831/425-8445** or 831/427-2267), which rents single, double, and triple kayaks at Building No. 2 on the wharf and at 125 Beach St. across from the wharf. Classes, wildlife tours, and moonlight paddles are also available. Single kayaks rent for $27 for half a day; double kayaks go for $30 to $35 for half a day.

Surfing equipment can be rented at the **Cowell Beach 'n' Bikini Surf Shop,** 109 Beach St. (☎ **831/427-2355**), and also from the **Club Ed Surf School,** on Cowell Beach in front of the Dream Inn (☎ **831/459-9283**). Surfboard rental is $6 for 1 hour or $10 for 2 hours.

In the redwood-forested mountains behind Santa Cruz, there are quite a few **wineries,** although visitors may not be familiar with the labels because the output is small and consumed locally. Most wineries are clustered around Boulder Creek and Felton or around Capitola. All offer tours by appointment; some feature regular tasting, including the **Bargetto Winery,** 3535 N. Main, Soquel (☎ **831/475-2258**), which has a courtyard wine-tasting area overlooking the creek. For additional information, contact the **Santa Cruz Mountains Winegrowers Association** at ☎ **831/ 479-WINE.**

WHERE TO STAY

Two Travelodges (☎ **800/578-7878**), two Best Westerns (☎ **800/528-1234**), two Super 8s (☎ **800/800-8000**), and an Econolodge (☎ **800/553-2666**) provide moderate- and budget-priced accommodations in addition to the more inspiring choices below. Keep in mind, however, that $100 for a decent room is a bargain along this stretch of the California coast.

Casa Blanca Inn. 101 Main St. (at the corner of Beach), Santa Cruz, CA 95060. ☎ **831/ 423-1570.** Fax 831/423-0235. 34 units. TV TEL. High season (summer) $105–$300 double; low season $68–$195 double. AE, CB, DC, MC, V.

Across from the wharf in a heavily trafficked area, this motel along the waterfront was once the Mediterranean-style Cerf Mansion, dating from 1918. Other motel-style accommodations have grown up around the main building. It offers individually decorated bedrooms, some with brass beds and velvet draperies. Some units contain fireplaces and terraces, and all are equipped with microwaves and coffeemakers. Most of the rooms have views of the water. There's a restaurant on the premises that serves good seafood in a romantic ocean-view setting.

Darling House. 314 West Cliff Dr., Santa Cruz, CA 95060. ☎ **831/458-1958.** 8 units, 2 with private bathroom. TEL. $95 double without bathroom; $225 double with bathroom. Rates include breakfast. AE, DISC, MC, V.

This stately Spanish-style house, designed in 1910 by William Weeks, architect of Santa Cruz's Coconut Grove, has a panoramic view of the Pacific Ocean and is situated in a quiet residential area within walking distance of the Boardwalk and Lighthouse. The gardens are fragrant with citrus and orchids, and contain some stately palms, too. From the tiled front veranda, guests enter an elegant interior, the focal point of which is the dining room, handcrafted from tiger oak. The house boasts fine architectural features throughout, such as beveled glass, antiques, and handsome fireplaces. Each of the eight rooms is individually decorated, and though all have sinks, only two come with private bathrooms. The Pacific Ocean room, decorated like a sea captain's quarters, features a fireplace, telescope, and one of the finest ocean views in Santa Cruz. A backyard hot tub is available for guests. Breakfast includes oven-fresh breads and pastries, fruit, and homemade granola made with walnuts from Darling's own farm.

Edgewater Beach Motel. 525 Second St., Santa Cruz, CA 95060. ☎ **831/423-0440.** 17 units. TV TEL. $105–$185 double. AE, DC, DISC, MC, V.

If the other two inns listed here are booked, consider the Edgewater Beach Motel. It looks like a time capsule from the 1960s, which, oddly enough, makes it all the more appealing (how they kept the furnishings in such prime condition is a mystery). The motel offers a range of accommodations, from family suites with kitchens to nonsmoking rooms and rooms with fireplaces; most have microwaves and all have refrigerators. The Edgewater also sports a heated pool, sundeck, and barbecue area, but the real bonus is the location—the Santa Cruz Beach Boardwalk is only a block away. *Tip:* Inquire about the Edgewater's off-season minivacation packages, which can save you a bundle on room rates.

WHERE TO DINE

Cafe Bittersweet. 787 Rio Del Mar Blvd. (about 10 miles SE of Santa Cruz on Calif. 1), Rio Del Mar. ☎ **831/662-9799.** Reservations recommended. Main courses $12–$18. AE, MC, V. Tues–Sun 5–10pm. MEDITERRANEAN.

What started out as a tiny operation within a small strip development has grown into one of the most popular restaurants in the Santa Cruz region. The relocation to bigger digs in Rio Del Mar hasn't tarnished chef/owner Thomas Vinolus's reputation for serving exceptional cuisine. The menu features only five main dishes, which ensures quality. Start with the grilled shrimp over greens with garlic, sage, and white beans, or one of the fresh salads. Follow with the richly flavored veal medaillons with a brandied wild-mushroom sauce. We also enjoyed the old-fashioned lasagna with three cheeses, basil, spinach, and marinara sauce.

Café El Palomar. 2222 East Cliff Dr. (at the Santa Cruz Harbor). ☎ **831/462-4248.** Main courses $4–$6. MC, V. Mon–Wed; Sat–Sun 7am–7pm; Thurs 7am–8:30pm. MEXICAN.

If both O'Mei and Cafe Bittersweet are out of your price range, then head to the Santa Cruz Harbor and plop your poor butt down on one of seven tables at Café El Palomar. An offshoot of the far fancier El Palomar restaurant in the Pacific Garden Mall, the cafe serves the standard Mexican fare—chimichangas, burritos, tacos, chorizo, etc.— for breakfast, lunch, and dinner. For the money, it's *mucho bueno* grub.

✪ **O'Mei.** 2316 Mission St. ☎ **831/425-8458.** Reservations recommended Fri–Sat. Main courses $7–$12. AE, MC, V. Mon–Fri 11:30am–2pm; Mon–Thurs 5–9:30pm; Fri–Sun 5–10pm. SZECHUAN.

O'Mei's (pronounced Oh-*may*) minimall location may not be very inviting, but the fantastic food served here more than makes up for it. The menu features some unusual specialties such as apricot-almond chicken and wine-braised chicken livers, along with more familiar dishes such as chicken with cashews or Szechuan shrimp. Dinner starts with a dim sum–style tray of exotic offerings such as sesame-cilantro-eggplant salad or pan-roasted peppers with feta cheese. A recommended dish is the sliced rock cod in black-bean-and-sweet-pepper sauce.

A SIDE TRIP TO MISSION SAN JUAN BAUTISTA

On U.S. 101, San Juan Bautista is an authentic mission town that works hard to honor its pioneer heritage by retaining the flavor of a 19th-century village. The mission complex is perched in a picturesque farming valley, surrounded by the restored buildings of the original city plaza.

From U.S. 101, take Calif. 156 east (south) to the center of town to the mission itself, which was founded in 1797. Here you'll see the largest church in the mission chain and the only one in unbroken service since its founding. The padres here inspired many Native Americans to convert, creating one of the largest congregations in all of California. The small museum contains many musical instruments and transcriptions, evidence of the mission's musical focus—it once boasted a formidable Native American boys' choir.

Mission San Juan Bautista is open daily from 9:30am to 5pm from May through October; it closes at 4:30pm the rest of the year. Admission is $2 per person. For more information call ☎ **831/623-4528.**

East of the church, perched at the edge of an abrupt drop created by the movement of the San Andreas Fault, is a marker pointing out the path of the old **El Camino Real.** Accompanying the marker are seismographic measuring equipment and an earthquake science exhibit.

There's much to see on the restored city plaza in addition to the mission. Be sure to visit the **San Juan Bautista State Historic Park.** The park is comprised of not only the old Plaza Hotel with its classic frontier barroom and furnished rooms, but also the Plaza Hall, its adjoining stables and blacksmith shop, and the Castro House, where the Breen family lived after traveling here with the ill-fated Donner Party in 1846.

Allow 1½ to 2 hours to see the entire plaza. Admission to the park buildings is $2 per person (separate from your charge to the mission).

For more information (including events schedules), call ☎ **831/623-4881.**

2 Monterey

45 miles S of Santa Cruz; 116 miles S of San Francisco; 335 miles N of Los Angeles

While its neighbors are romantic coastal hideaways, Monterey is the antithesis. A harbor-town-cum-tourist-trap, it's big enough that you have to drive from downtown to Cannery Row, and affected enough that chain hotels and restaurants have put the squeeze on boutique establishments. Plenty of history and heritage remain, but you'll have to weed though minimalls to find them. Its saving grace is the fantastic aquarium and beautiful Monterey Bay, where sea lions and otters still frolic in abundance.

It's easy to blow money in this area: Hotels aren't exactly cheap—especially come summertime, and aquarium tickets, restaurant meals, and silly souvenirs add up. You can, however, save major bucks by staying in an inexpensive motel in Monterey and easily driving into pricier Carmel-by-the-Sea to shop and go to the beach, and by following our restaurant recommendations. If you can afford the full charm of the area or are traveling in winter (when discounted room rates are easily negotiated), we recommend you set up camp in Pacific Grove or Carmel-by-the-Sea and make Monterey a day trip.

Originally settled in 1770, Monterey was one of the West Coast's first European settlements. The town was the capital of California under the Spanish, Mexican, and American flags. California's state constitution was drafted here in 1849, paving the way for admission to the Union a year later. Many buildings from the early colonial era still stand. A major whaling center in the 1800s, it also became a sardine center when the first packing plant was built in 1900. By 1913 the boats were bringing in 25 tons of sardines a night. The lives of the residents, who thronged down to the 18 canneries, were captured by John Steinbeck in his 1945 novel *Cannery Row*. After the sardines disappeared, the town and the peninsula went after tourist dollars instead.

ESSENTIALS

GETTING THERE   The region's most convenient runway, at the **Monterey Peninsula Airport** (☎ 831/373-1704), is 3 miles east of Monterey on Calif. 68. **American Eagle** (☎ 800/433-7300), **Northwest** (☎ 800/225-2525), **Skywest** (☎ 800/453-9417), **United** (☎ 800/241-6522), and **US Airways** (☎ 800/428-4322) have daily flights in and out of Monterey.

Many area hotels offer free airport shuttle service. If you take a taxi, it will cost about $20 to $25 to get to a peninsula hotel. Several national car-rental companies have airport locations, including **Dollar** (☎ 800/800-4000) and **Hertz** (☎ 800/654-3131).

VISITOR INFORMATION   The **Monterey Peninsula Visitors and Convention Bureau,** 380 Alvarado St., near the intersection of Pacific Street and Del Monte Avenue (☎ 831/649-1770), has good maps and free pamphlets and publications, including an excellent visitors guide and the magazine *Coast Weekly.*

GETTING AROUND   The **Waterfront Area Visitor Express (WAVE)** operates each year from Memorial Day weekend through Labor Day and takes passengers to and from the aquarium and other waterfront attractions. Stops are located at many hotels and motels in Monterey and Pacific Grove. The cost of $1 for adults and 50¢ for kids and seniors gets you unlimited rides all day between 9am and 6pm and eliminates the stress of parking in crowded downtown. Call **Monterey Salinas Transit** for more information (☎ **831/899-2555**).

SEEING THE SIGHTS

✪ **Monterey Bay Aquarium.** 886 Cannery Row. ☎ **800/756-3737,** 800/225-2277, or 831/648-4888. Admission $15.95 adults, $12.95 students and seniors 65 and over, $7.95 disabled visitors and children 3–12, free for children 2 and under. Avoid lines at the gate by calling the above numbers and ordering tickets in advance. AE, MC, V. Daily 10am–6pm (opens at 9:30am in summer and holidays).

The site of one of the world's most spectacular aquariums was not chosen at random. It sits on the border of one of the largest underwater canyons on earth (wider and deeper than even the Grand Canyon) and is surrounded by incredibly diverse local marine life.

The Monterey Bay Aquarium is one of the best exhibit aquariums in the world, and one of the largest, too—home to more than 350,000 marine animals and plants. One of the living museum's main exhibits is a three-story, 335,000-gallon tank, with clear acrylic walls that give visitors an unmatched look at local sea life. A towering kelp forest, which rises from the floor of this oceanic zoo, gently waves with the water as hundreds of leopard sharks, sardines, anchovies, and other fish swim back and forth in an endless game of hide-and-seek.

In 1996 the outstanding *Outer Bay* exhibit opened, which features creatures that inhabit the open ocean. This tank—holding a million gallons of water—houses

The Monterey Peninsula

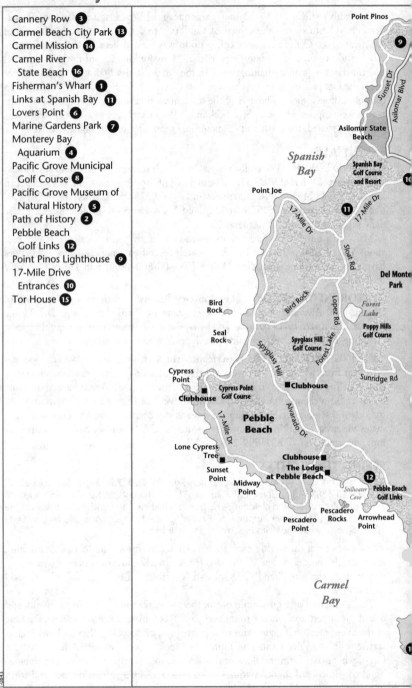

L0843

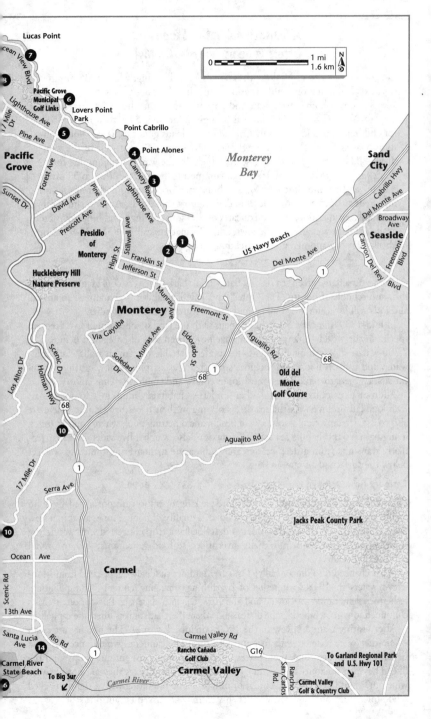

Lucas Point

7

8

Ocean View Blvd

Lighthouse Ave

Pacific Grove
Municipal
Golf Links

6

Lovers Point
Park

5

Point Cabrillo

Pine Ave

4 Point Alones

**Pacific
Grove**

Forest Ave

Pine St

Cannery Row

3

Sunset Dr

David Ave

Prescott Ave

Lighthouse Ave

*Monterey
Bay*

**Sand
City**

Cabrillo Hwy

Del Monte Ave

Broadway
Ave

Seaside

Presidio
of
Monterey

High St

Stillwell Ave

Franklin St

1

2

Jefferson St

US Navy Beach

Del Monte Ave

1

Canyon Del Rey

Freemont Blvd

**Huckleberry Hill
Nature Preserve**

Munras Ave

Monterey

Freemont St

Via Gayuba

Munras Ave

Eldorado St

Aguajito Rd

68

Scenic Dr

Holman Hwy

Soledad Dr

1

68

**Old del
Monte
Golf Course**

68

Los Altos Dr

68

10

Aguajito Rd

1

Serra Ave

17 Mile Dr

10

Jacks Peak County Park

Ocean Ave

Carmel

Scenic Rd

13th Ave

Santa Lucia
Ave

Rio Rd

Carmel Valley Rd

14

**Carmel River
State Beach**

6

1

To Big Sur

Carmel River

Rancho Cañada
Golf Club

G16

Carmel Valley

San Carlos
Rd

Rancho

To Garland Regional Park
and U.S. Hwy 101

Carmel Valley
Golf & Country Club

0   1 mi
           1.6 km

N

A Sensational Safari Stopover:
Otters & Seals & Birds, Oh My!

One of our favorite stops along the coast is Moss Landing, which is 25 minutes north of Monterey on Calif. 1. Along the virtually one-street town are a few adorable down-home restaurants and antique shops. But the main attraction is Captain Yohn Gideon's ✪ **Elkhorn Slough Safari.** For $24 (so worth it!; $18 for children under 15), friendly Cap'n Gideon loads guests onto a 27-foot pontoon boat (safe for old and young) and embarks on a 2-hour tour of the wondrous Elkhorn Slough wildlife reserve, which, by the way, is like jumping into a *National Geographic* special. It's not uncommon to see a "raft" of up to 50 otters toes-up and sunning themselves, an abundance of lounging harbor seals, and hundreds of species of waterfowl and migratory shorebirds. An onboard naturalist answers questions, Cap'n educates on the surroundings, and binoculars are available. For reservations, schedules, and information, call ☎ **831/633-5555** or check out www.monterey-bay.net/elkhornslough/.

---

yellowfin tuna, large green sea turtles, barracuda, sharks, the very cool giant ocean sunfish, and schools of bonito. The Outer Bay's jellyfish exhibit is guaranteed to amaze, and kids will love Flippers, Flukes, and Fun, a learning area for families.

In mid-1999, the *Deep Sea* exhibit opens with the largest collection of live deep-sea species in the world—many of which have never been part of an exhibit before. The 7,000-square-foot exhibit highlights the underwater life of canyon walls, dark midwater, and canyon floors and includes such creatures as spider crabs, ratfish, file-tail cat-sharks, predatory tunicates, mushroom corals, and California king crabs.

Additional exhibits re-create other undersea habitats found in Monterey Bay. Everyone falls in love with the sea otters playing in their two-story exhibit. There are also coastal streams, tidal pools, a sand beach, and a petting pool, where you can touch living bat rays and handle sea stars. Visitors can also watch a live video link that regularly transmits from a deep-sea research submarine maneuvering thousands of feet below the surface of Monterey Bay.

Cannery Row. Between David and Drake aves. ☎ **831/649-6690.**

Once the center for an industrial sardine-packing operation immortalized by John Steinbeck as "a poem, a stink, a grating noise, a quality of light, a tone, a habit, a nostalgia, a dream," this area today is better described as a strip congested with wandering tourists, tacky gift shops, minimalls, overpriced seafood restaurants, and an overall parking nightmare.

What changed it so dramatically? The silver sardines suddenly disappeared from Monterey's waters in 1948 as a result of overfishing, changing currents, and pollution. Fishermen left, canneries closed, and the Row fell into disrepair. But curious tourists continued to visit Steinbeck's fabled area, and where there are tourists, there are capitalists.

After visiting Cannery Row in the 1960s, Steinbeck wrote, "The beaches are clean where they once festered with fish guts and flies. The canneries which once put up a sickening stench are gone, their places filled with restaurants, antique shops, and the like. They fish for tourists now, not pilchards, and that species they are not likely to wipe out." Not likely indeed. Like it or not, you'll be migrating with a tightly-packed school of visitors anytime you wander this entirely contrived oceanfront strip.

For Steinbeck Fans

The **National Steinbeck Center** is not in town, but if you're a fan you'll want to make the 20-mile trek northeast from Monterey on Calif. 68 to 371 Main St. in Salinas (☎ **831/753-6411;** www.steinbeck.org). A new $10.3-million, 37,000-square-foot museum opened in mid-1998, offering walk-through interactive exhibits, a changing exhibition gallery, an orientation theater presenting a 10-minute video on Steinbeck's life, educational programs, a gift shop, and cafe. Admission is $7 for adults, $6 for seniors over 62, $4 for ages 11 to 17, and free for kids 10 and under. Hours are daily from 10am to 5pm.

Fisherman's Wharf. 99 Pacific St. ☎ **831/373-0600.**

Just like San Francisco's Fisherman's Wharf, this wooden pier is jam-packed with craft and gift shops, boating and fishing operations, fish markets, and seafood restaurants all baiting tourist dollars. But Monterey's wharf does have redeeming qualities. The natural surroundings are so beautiful that if you cast your view toward the bobbing boats and surfacing sea lions, you might not even notice the hordes of tourists around you. Grab some clam chowder in a sourdough bread bowl and find a seaside perch along the pier. Or when the wind picks up, find a bay-front seat at one of the seafood restaurants (see "Where to Dine," below).

If the seaside sights have got you itching to set sail, boats depart regularly from Fisherman's Wharf and will lead you on a number of ocean adventures. See "Outdoor Pursuits," below, for details on some of the offerings.

FOLLOWING THE PATH OF HISTORY

The dozen or so historic buildings clustered around Fisherman's Wharf and the adjacent town collectively comprise the "Path of History," a tour that examines 1800s architecture and lifestyle. Many of the buildings are a part of the **Monterey State Historic Park,** 20 Custom House Plaza (☎ **831/649-7118**). Highlights include the **Custom House,** which was constructed around 1827 and is the oldest government building in California, and the **Monterey Maritime Museum and History Center,** 5 Custom House Plaza (☎ **831/373-2469**), which showcases ship models and other collections that relate the area's seafaring history (admission is $5 for adults, $4 for seniors and military, $3 for youths 13 to 18, $2 for children 6 to 12, and free for kids 5 and under; open daily from 10am to 5pm).

You can go the self-guided route by picking up a free tour booklet at the Monterey Peninsula Visitors and Convention Bureau, 380 Alvarado St., Monterey (☎ **831/649-1770**), the Cooper-Molera Adobe (at the corner of Polk and Munras streets), and various other locations. You may also opt to take the 80-minute guided tour, which departs from Cooper-Molera Adobe and includes interiors not accessible by the self-guided tour. (The price is $5 for adults, $3 for youths 13 to 18, and $2 for children 6 to 12.) Call ☎ **831/649-7118** for complete details or visit the **State Park Visitor Center** at Stanton Center, 5 Custom House Plaza. A free film on the history of Monterey is shown here every 20 minutes.

FARMERS MARKET   If you're in town on a Tuesday afternoon, check out the street market on **Alvarado Street** (from Pearl to Del Monte streets) from 4 to 7pm. More than 100 vendors participate, bringing food, music, crafts, and entertainment together for an afternoon of flavorful festivities.

EXPLORING THE MONTEREY WINE COUNTRY

The congestion and price of Napa and Sonoma vineyards has encouraged industry newcomers to plant their grapes south of the big boys. Nowadays, if you visit any area between Monterey and Santa Barbara, there's easy access to new appellations and a variety of boutique vintners making respectable wines. Stop by **A Taste of Monterey,** 700 Cannery Row (☎ **831/646-5446**), between 11am and 6pm to learn about and taste locally produced wines in front of huge bay-front windows. This is also the place to get a map and winery touring information.

OUTDOOR PURSUITS

Cast your hook on a deep-sea-fishing expedition. Among the operators are **Chris' Fishing Trips,** 48 Fisherman's Wharf (☎ **831/375-5951**), which offers large party boats. Cod and salmon are the main catches, with separate boats leaving daily. Call for a complete price list and sailing schedule. Full-day excursions cost $32 to $40 per person.

Sam's Fishing Fleet, 84 Fisherman's Wharf (☎ **831/372-0577**), offers fishing excursions for cod, salmon, and whatever else is running, as well as seasonal whale-watching tours. Make reservations and bring lunch. Departures are at 7:30am Monday through Friday (salmon-fishing boats leave earlier) and at 7am on Saturday and Sunday. Check-in is 45 minutes prior to departure. Weekday prices are $30 for adults, $17 for children 11 and under; weekend and holiday rates are $34 for adults, $20 for children. Equipment rental costs a bit extra.

Kayaks can be rented from several outfitters for a spin around the bay. Contact **Monterey Bay Kayaks,** 693 Del Monte Ave. (☎ **800/649-5357** or 831/373-5357; montereykayaks.com), on Del Monte Beach north of Fisherman's Wharf, which offers instruction as well as natural-history tours that introduce visitors to the Monterey Bay National Marine Sanctuary. Prices start at $45 for the tours, $25 for rentals.

For bikes and in-line skates as well as kayak tours and rentals, contact **Adventures by the Sea,** 299 Cannery Row (☎ **831/372-1807**). Bikes cost $6 per hour or $24 a day; kayaks are $25 per person; and skates are $12 for 2 hours, $24 for a day. Adventures also has other locations at 201 Alvarado Mall (☎ **831/648-7235**) at the Doubletree Hotel (☎ **831/648-7235**), and on the beach at Lovers Point in Pacific Grove.

Experienced scuba divers wishing to go out on an excursion can contact **Monterey Bay Dive Center,** 225 Cannery Row (☎ **831/656-0454**), which arranges personal dives with a dive master and has scheduled weekend dives. **Aquarius Dive Shop,** 2040 Del Monte Ave. (☎ **831/375-1933**), also has regularly scheduled trips and dive masters. Certification cards are essential.

KID STUFF

Feeling playful? The ✪ **Dennis the Menace Playground** at Camino El Estero and Del Monte Avenue (☎ **831/646-3866**), near Lake Estero, is an old-fashioned playground created by Pacific Grove resident and famous cartoonist Hank Ketcham. It has bridges to cross, tunnels to climb through, and an authentic Southern Pacific engine car teeming with wanna-be conductors. There's also a hot-dog and burger stand, and a big lake where you can rent paddleboats or feed the ducks. The park is open daily from 10am to sunset.

WHERE TO STAY

For the most part there are only three types of choices for accommodations in Monterey: lace-and-flowers B&Bs; large corporate-cum-beachy hotels; or run-of-the-mill motel digs. If you're on a strict budget or come during summertime, your choices pretty much stop with the run-of-the-mill variety. The two things you should consider when making your reservations are how much you want to spend and which area you'd like to be in (beach, Cannery Row, wharf, secluded, central). For the most part, budget accommodations are scarce and are located on the periphery of town (and even these are hardly a bargain during high season). But don't let that discourage you: The entire area from north Monterey to Carmel is within a 15-minute drive. For more scenic budget options, check out what's available in adjoining Pacific Grove before booking in north Monterey. Monterey's Munras and northern Fremont avenues are lined with inexpensive family-style motels, some independently owned and some chains. They are not as central as downtown options, but if transportation is not an issue, you can save a bundle staying in one of these areas. If the selection below is full, try calling **Best Western** (☎ 800/528-1234), **Motel 6** (☎ 800/4-MOTEL6), **Comfort Inn** (☎ 800/221-2222), or **Super 8** (☎ 800/800-8000) for several other options. There's also the **Cypress Gardens Inn,** 1150 Munras Ave. (☎ 831/373-2761), which offers a pool, hot tub, free movie channel, and continental breakfast, and welcomes dogs.

You may also want to contact **Time to Coast** reservation service, which represents about 40 lodging facilities in Monterey and Pacific Grove (☎ **800/555-WAVE;** www.timetocoast.com).

SUPER-CHEAP SLEEPS

Carmel Hill Lodge. 1374 Munras Ave. (near Soledad Dr.), Monterey, CA 93940. ☎ **888/ 551-4455** or 831/373-3252. Fax 831/655-2420. 38 units. TV TEL. Sun–Thurs $39–$59 double; Fri–Sat $59–$129 double. AE, DISC, MC, V.

Very clean and very basic, the Carmel Hill Lodge is a decent motel option along the cheap-sleeps strip on the outskirts of downtown Monterey. Accommodations, again basic, but with new textiles, are arranged in a rather old two-story building, which has been gussied with flower boxes. Extra perks include a heated swimming pool, free HBO, free local calls, and easy access to the lil' Del Monte Shopping Center across the street. Hair dryers are available on request.

Del Monte Beach Inn. 1110 Del Monte Ave. (at Park), Monterey, CA 93940. ☎ **831/ 649-4410.** 19 units, 17 with shared bathrooms. Winter $55–$66 double; summer $66–$99 double. Rates include breakfast. Discounts for divers and AAA members (except during special events). AE, DISC, MC, V.

Less than a mile away from all the action of downtown Monterey, 6 blocks from the wharf, and a block away from the beach, you'll find one of the cheapest places to stay in the entire area (if you're willing to share a bathroom). This hotel was built in the late 1800s as a private residence, and though it's on a busy street, many tourists will still appreciate it as a respite from the hordes of tourists crowding up and down the even busier Cannery Row. The inn models itself after European B&Bs, with period reproductions and other homey furnishings, as well as an extended continental breakfast included in the price. There are no phones or TVs in your room, but there is a pay phone inside the inn and a TV in the library. Another plus is the sunny balcony out back that overlooks the garden. Three rooms have wharf and ocean views. Parking is free.

FOR A FEW BUCKS MORE

✪ **Cypress Tree Inn.** 2227 N. Fremont St., Monterey, CA 93940. ☎ **831/372-7586.** Fax 831/372-2940. 55 units. TV TEL. $62–$102 double. MC, V.

Although it's not centrally located (2 miles from downtown), if you're on a budget and have transportation, you won't be sorry if you stay here. The large rooms are spotless, and all but one has a combination tub/shower. Nine also have hot tubs. There's no shampoo, hair dryer, or in-room treats other than the taffy left by the maid, but the hostelry does have a hot tub, sauna, and coin-op laundry. RV spaces are also available.

MODERATELY PRICED OPTIONS

Best Western DeAnza Inn. 2141 N. Fremont St., Monterey, CA 93940. ☎ **800/ 858-8775** or 831/646-8300. Fax 831/646-8130. 43 units. TV TEL. $65–$129 double; $100–$199 suite. Rates include continental breakfast. Extra person $8. Senior discounts available. AE, DC, DISC, MC, V.

The common areas of this north Monterey motel are more modern and elaborate than most Best Westerns we've seen, but the rooms, though newly decorated, don't venture far beyond your generic motel style. They are clean and newish, however, which always makes for better accommodations. Amenities include in-room coffee; microwaves and refrigerators are available upon request ($5 extra for each). There's also a heated pool and Jacuzzi on the premises. The only drawback is the motel's location a few miles north of all of Monterey's action; downtown's a quick and easy drive, but if you prefer great strolling grounds outside your door, opt for one of Best Western's other more centrally located properties. (There are 10 Best Westerns in the area. Call the toll-free number provided above for details.)

Casa Munras Garden Hotel. 700 Munras Ave., Monterey, CA 93940. ☎ **800/222-2558** in the U.S., 800/222-2446 in Calif., or 831/375-2411. Fax 831/375-1365. 150 units. TV TEL. $79–$129 double (queen); $129–$149 double (king). AAA, Entertainment discounts available. AE, DC, DISC, MC, V.

Casa Munras is one hotel on Monterey's motel strip that knows how to make the most of old-fashioned digs. Accommodations are scattered among one- and two-story buildings along the landscaped property. Each is ornamented with an armoire, newish furnishings, and sweet window shutters. All guests have access to the outdoor pool, greenhouse, on-site trinket shops, and Casa Café & Bar. Refrigerators are available on request, and local calls will run you only 25¢ each. A few extra bucks will get you a room with a gas fireplace.

El Adobe Inn. 936 Munras (at El Dorado), Monterey, CA 93940. ☎ **831/372-5409.** Fax 831/375-7236. 26 units. TV TEL. Winter $39–$129 double; summer $129 double. Rates include continental breakfast. AARP, AAA, senior, and corporate discounts available. AE, DISC, MC, V. Pets allowed.

A far cry from an authentic adobe, this basic motor lodge close to downtown is simple and clean, not too tacky, and offers perks that make it an overall good deal. Many rooms have ocean views (distant though they may be), and all have alarm clocks and a free movie channel. "Deluxe" rooms have coffeemakers and refrigerators. There's a small Jacuzzi on the premises.

Fireside Lodge. 1131 10th St., Monterey, CA 93940. ☎ **831/373-4172.** Fax 831/ 655-5640. 24 units. TV TEL. $69–$149 double. Rates include continental breakfast. AE, CB, DC, DISC, MC, V.

Location is the primary advantage of this hotel near Fisherman's Wharf and downtown. The room furnishings are relatively standard but make an attempt at coziness with wicker chairs set around the gas-heated brick fireplace; six have kitchenettes, which go for an extra $10 per night. Amenities include an in-room tea/coffeemaker, a hot tub on the premises, and a continental breakfast served daily in the hotel's lobby.

Travelodge, Downtown Monterey. 675 Munras Ave., Monterey, CA 93940. ☎ **831/ 373-1876.** Fax 831/373-8693. 51 units, all with bathroom (45 with shower only). TV TEL. $49–$139 double. AARP, AAA, and corporate discounts available. AE, DC, DISC, MC, V.

You already know what to expect from Travelodge, so if you're hankering for lace window curtains and fresh flowers by the bed, you'd better bring 'em yourself. What you will find here are recently redecorated rooms (very clean!) with tidy bedspreads, a table and chairs, a vanity, and shower bathrooms (six have tubs). Extra perks such as hair dryers, free HBO, in-room coffeemakers, free local calls, free parking, and free newspapers in the lobby make this Travelodge a good deal (comparatively). There's even a small swimming pool (which unfortunately overlooks the street). This hotel is closer to downtown than the North Fremont options.

WORTH A SPLURGE

✪ The Jabberwock Bed & Breakfast. 598 Laine St., Monterey, CA 93940. ☎ **888/ 428-7253** or 831/372-4777. Fax 831/655-2946. 7 units, 5 with bathroom. $110 double without bathroom; $200 double with bathroom. Rates include full breakfast, afternoon aperitifs, and bedtime cookies. MC, V.

One of the better B&Bs in the area, the Jabberwock (named after an episode in Lewis Carroll's *Through the Looking Glass*) is four short blocks from Cannery Row. Although centrally located, the property is tranquil, and its half-acre garden with waterfalls offers a welcome respite from the downtown crowds. The seven rooms are individually furnished, some more elegantly than others, but all with goose-down comforters and pillows. The Toves Room has a huge walnut Victorian bed; the Borogrove has a fireplace and a view of Monterey Bay; the Mimsey has a fine ocean view from its window seat; and the Wabe has an Austrian carved bed. A full breakfast is served in the dining room or in your own room. Evening hors d'oeuvres are also offered on the veranda, and a Vorpal rabbit tucks each guest in with cookies and milk.

✪ Old Monterey Inn. 500 Martin St. (off Pacific Ave.), Monterey, CA 93940. ☎ **800/ 350-2344** or 831/375-8284. Fax 831/375-6730. 9 units, 1 cottage. $200–$300 double; from $350 cottage. Rates include American breakfast and wine and hors d'oeuvres in the evening. MC, V. Free parking. From Calif. 1, take the Soledad Dr. exit and turn right onto Pacific Ave., then left onto Martin St.

Though this comfortable vine-covered, three-story-Tudor-style country inn is away from the surf, it's a perfect choice for romantics, with rose gardens, a bubbling brook, and brick-and-flagstone walkways shaded by a panoply of oaks. Almost every guest room enjoys peaceful garden views and all are charmingly furnished in Laura Ashley or Ralph Lauren with cozy beds with goose-down comforters and pillows. Most units also have feather beds and wood-burning fireplaces, and two open onto private patios. Special touches are evident throughout, including fresh fruit, flowers, and candies; books and magazines; and bathrooms complete with hair dryers and toiletry packages.

A stellar breakfast, consisting of perhaps orange French toast, soufflé, or Belgian waffles, is served either en suite, or in the dining room or rose garden. Beach blankets and towels are available, as are passes to a nearby health club. At 5pm guests meet for wine and hors d'oeuvres in front of a blazing fire.

WHERE TO DINE

If you're going cheap in Monterey, you'll almost invariably have to give up atmosphere. We recommend you join the locals, who head to Pacific Grove for a pleasant, affordable evening.

SUPER-CHEAP EATS

Papá Chano's Taquería. 462 Alvarado St. (at Bonifaceo Place near Franklin). ☎ **831/ 646-9587.** Mexican plates $2.80–$7. No credit cards. Daily 10am–midnight. MEXICAN.

Don't expect cloth napkins, a formal waiter (or any waiter for that matter), or quiet music surrounding your ears, but rather kick-ass burritos and other Mexican specialties made from fresh ingredients and served quickly and at dirt-cheap prices. Forget about atmosphere—the cavernous ceilings, unadorned walls, and plain wooden tables and brick floors are anything but cozy. But who cares? The burritos, quesadillas, tacos, nachos, and *platillos especiales* (steak, pork, chicken, or chile relleno plates served with rice, beans, cheese, lettuce, tomato, salsa, sour cream, guacamole, and tortillas) are under six bucks and are good enough to bring us back every time we come to town.

Rosine's. 434 Alvarado St. (at Franklin). ☎ **831/375-1400.** Breakfast $3.50–$8.25; lunch $5.50–$7.95; most dinner dishes $5.75–$8.50. AE, DC, DISC, MC, V. Mon–Thurs 7:30am–9pm; Fri 7:30am–10pm; Sat 8am–10pm; Sun 8am–9pm. AMERICAN.

Everything about this place is straightforward and fair priced, which is why the place is always busy. Aside from the large, airy window seats, the place has an upscale cafeteria feel, but its menu, filled with standard entrees, aims to please all tastes. Lunch features an extensive list of salads and sandwiches, and dinner offers an array of pastas, burgers, and more expensive items such as prime rib ($16.95). Other than steak and seafood, most entrees hover around $8 and include side salads and/or potatoes. Sugar fiends will appreciate the huge cakes behind glass as you walk in the front door (yes, you can buy them by the slice).

MODERATELY PRICED OPTIONS

Cafe Fina. 47 Fisherman's Wharf. ☎ **831/372-5200.** Reservations recommended. Main courses $13–$17. AE, CB, DC, DISC, MC, V. Mon–Fri 11:30am–2:30pm; Sat–Sun 11:30am–3pm; daily 5–10pm. ITALIAN/SEAFOOD.

While other pier-side restaurants lure in tourists with little more than an outstanding view, Cafe Fina's mesquite-grilled meats, well-prepared fresh fish, brick-oven pizzas, and array of delicious salads and pastas give even locals a reason to head to the wharf. Combine the food with a million-dollar vista and a casual atmosphere, and Cafe Fina ranks hands-down as the best choice on the pier.

Tarpy's Roadhouse. 2999 Monterey-Salinas Hwy. (at Calif. 68 and Canyon del Rey near the Monterey Airport). ☎ **831/647-1444.** Reservations recommended for dinner. Most main courses $12–$20. AE, DISC, MC, V. Daily 11:30am–10pm. CALIFORNIA/AMERICAN.

Always a mandatory stop when we're passing through Monterey is this lively Southwestern-style restaurant located a few miles east of downtown (and definitely worth the detour). The very handsome dining room has a stylish yet soothingly rustic decor. On sunny afternoons, patrons relax under market umbrellas on the huge outdoor patio, sipping margaritas and munching on Tarpy's legendary Caesar salad. Come nightfall, the place fills quickly with tourists and locals who pile in for the hefty plate of bourbon-molasses pork chops or Dijon-crusted lamb loin. There's also a modest selection of fresh fish, shellfish, and vegetable dishes, but it's the good ol' meat 'n' potato mainstays that sell the best. (The thick, juicy meat loaf with garlic mashers and fresh veggies is a bargain at $12.)

Wharfside Restaurant & Lounge. 60 Fisherman's Wharf. ☎ **831/375-3956.** Reservations recommended. Main courses $11–$20. AE, DC, DISC, MC, V. Daily 11am–9:30pm. Closed the 1st 2 weeks of Dec. SEAFOOD.

While the fresh seafood is okay, the real attraction is the Wharfside's casual upstairs dining room, which offers a nautical decor and a great view from the end of Fisherman's Wharf (there's also downstairs and upper-deck outdoor seating). Choose from six different varieties of ravioli (made on the premises), such specialties as a combination bouillabaisse, and any of the house-made desserts. Daily specials usually include fresh seasonal fish, beef, and pasta. Clam chowder, sandwiches (including hot crab), and pizzas are on the regular menu.

WORTH A SPLURGE

✪ **Montrio.** 414 Calle Principal (at Franklin). ☎ **831/648-8880.** Reservations recommended. Main courses $14–$19. AE, DISC, MC, V. Mon–Thurs 11:30am–10pm; Fri–Sat 11:30am–11pm; Sun 11am–10pm. AMERICAN BISTRO.

Big-city sophistication met old Monterey when Montrio hit the ground running here in March 1995. The enormous dining room is definitely the sharpest in town, mixing chic style with a playful canopied vineyard of modern light fixtures, clouds hanging from the ceiling, and the buzz of well-dressed diners. You can watch chefs scurry around in the open kitchen, but you're more likely to keep your eyes on the tasty dishes, such as the crispy Dungeness crab cakes with spicy rémoulade; succulent grilled pork chops with apple, pear, and currant compôte; or an oven-roasted portobello mushroom with polenta and ragoût of vegetables. Finish the evening with passion-fruit gratin with wild-berry coulis.

3 Pacific Grove

42 miles S of Santa Cruz; 113 miles S of San Francisco; 338 miles N of Los Angeles

Some compare 2.6-square-mile Pacific Grove—the locals call it "P.G."—to Carmel as it was 20 years ago. Although tourists wind their way through here on oceanfront trails and dining excursions, the town remains quaint and peaceful—amazing considering that Monterey is a stone's throw away (a quarter of the Monterey Bay Aquarium is actually in Pacific Grove). While neighboring Monterey is comparatively congested and cosmopolitan, Pacific Grove is a community sprinkled with historic homes, blooming flowers, and the kind of tranquillity that inspires butterflies to flutter and deer to meander fearlessly across the road in search of another garden to graze.

ESSENTIALS

VISITOR INFORMATION   Although the town is small, there is the **Pacific Grove Chamber of Commerce,** at the corner of Forest and Central avenues (☎ 831/373-3304).

ORIENTATION   **Lighthouse Avenue** is the Grove's principal thoroughfare, running from Monterey to the lighthouse at the very point of the peninsula. Lighthouse Avenue is bisected by **Forest Avenue,** which runs from Calif. 1 (where it's called Holman Highway, or Calif. 68) to Lover's Point, an extension of land that sticks out into the bay in the middle of Pacific Grove.

EXPLORING THE TOWN

Pacific Grove is a town to be strolled, so park the car, put on your walking shoes, and make an afternoon of it. Meander around **George Washington Park** and along the waterfront around the point.

The **Point Pinos Lighthouse,** at the tip of the peninsula on Ocean View Boulevard (☎ 831/648-3116), is the oldest working lighthouse on the West Coast. It dates from 1855, when Pacific Grove was little more than a pine forest. The museum and grounds are open free to visitors Thursday through Sunday from 1 to 4pm.

Marine Gardens Park, a stretch of shoreline along Ocean View Boulevard on Monterey Bay and the Pacific, is renowned not only for its ocean views and colorful flowers, but also for its fascinating tide-pool seaweed beds. Walk out to **Lover's Point**

(named after Lovers of Jesus, not groping teenagers) and watch the sea otters playing in the kelp beds and cracking open an occasional abalone for lunch.

An excellent shorter alternative, or complement, to the 17-Mile Drive (see section 4, "The 17-Mile Drive," below) is the scenic drive or bike ride along Pacific Grove's ✪ **Ocean View Boulevard.** This coastal stretch starts near Monterey's Cannery Row and follows the Pacific around to the lighthouse point. There it turns into Sunset Drive, which runs along secluded **Asilomar State Beach.** Park on Sunset and explore the trails, dunes, and tide pools of this sandy stretch of shore. You might find purple shore crabs, green anemone, sea bats, starfish, and limpets, as well as all kinds of kelp and algae. The 11 buildings of the conference center established here by the YWCA in 1913 are historic landmarks that were designed by noted architect Julia Morgan. If you follow this route during winter months, a furious sea rages and crashes against the rocks.

To learn more about the marine and other natural life of the region, stop in at the **Pacific Grove Museum of Natural History,** 165 Forest Ave. (☎ **831/648-3116**). It has displays about the monarch butterflies and their migration, plus stuffed examples of the local birds and mammals. Admission is free; hours are Tuesday through Sunday from 10am to 5pm.

Pacific Grove is widely known as "Butterfly Town, U.S.A.," a reference to the thousands of **monarch butterflies** that migrate here from November through February, traveling from as far away as Alaska. Many settle in the **Monarch Grove** sanctuary, a eucalyptus stand on Grove Acre Avenue off Lighthouse Avenue. **George Washington Park,** at Pine Avenue and Alder Street, is also famous for its "butterfly trees." To reach these sites, the butterflies may travel as far as 2,000 miles, covering 100 miles a day at an altitude of 10,000 feet. Collectors beware: The town imposes strict fines for molesting butterflies.

Just as Ocean View Boulevard serves as an alternative to the 17-Mile Drive, the ✪ **Pacific Grove Municipal Golf Course,** 77 Asilomar Ave. (☎ **831/648-3177**), serves as a reasonably priced alternative to the high-priced courses at Pebble Beach. The back 9 holes of this 5,500-yard, par-70 course overlook the sea and offer the added challenge of coping with the winds. Views are panoramic, and the fairways and greens are better maintained than most semiprivate courses. There's a restaurant, pro shop, and driving range. Greens fees are $25 Monday through Thursday and $30 Friday through Sunday; optional carts cost $25 and twilight rates are available. Visa and MasterCard are accepted for greens fees and equipment rental.

The **American Tin Cannery Factory Premium Outlets,** 125 Ocean View Blvd. (☎ **831/372-1442**), is a warehouse of 40 factory-outlet shops. Labels represented here include Anne Klein, Joan & David, Bass Shoes, Reebok, Carter's Childrenswear, Royal Doulton, Jones New York, Maidenform, London Fog, and Carole Little.

WHERE TO STAY

Keeping with Pacific Grove's country town atmosphere, accommodations here are either of the B&B or old-style motel variety. Hate making decisions? **Resort II Me** (☎ **800/449-1499**) will help you choose a hotel and make a reservation.

FOR A FEW BUCKS MORE

Bide-A-Wee. 221 Asilomar Blvd., Pacific Grove, CA 93950. ☎ **831/372-2330.** Fax 831/372-3947. 17 units. TV. Oct–June $59–$98 double; July–Sept $89–$129 double. Weekly rates available. AE, MC, V. Pets allowed.

Bide-A-Wee's accommodations may be a little worn, but the price and its location (a block from the beach along a quiet wooded street) makes this a charming out-of-the-way hotel option. Rooms are comfortable and individually decorated in country-rustic style and come with coffeemakers and coffee. Some have ocean views and/or a refrigerator. For a few extra bucks you can rent one of the nine family units, which come with kitchenettes (one has a fireplace). *Note:* New owners took over in mid-1998, and they plan to do some upgrading in the next year or so.

Butterfly Grove Inn. 1073 Lighthouse Ave., Pacific Grove, CA 93950. ☎ **831/373-4921.** Fax 831/373-7596. 22 units. TV TEL. Summer $99–$159 double; winter $65–$95 double. AE, DC, DISC, MC, V.

More like a motor lodge than an inn, accommodations here are run-of-the-mill, but the amenities are not; some rooms come with refrigerators, kitchenettes, and/or fireplaces, and guests have access to the property's pool, spa, Jacuzzi, and shuffleboard, croquet, and volleyball courts. (Don't get too excited: This is no California spa, but it is in one of the sweeter, and quieter, parts of Pacific Grove, and a pool is a pool after all.) Folks traveling with the family opt for one of the six family units tucked into a Victorian house. If you tire of the sporting life, just meander out your door and you're likely to see a soiree of butterflies (during winter), who migrate here each year, as well as deer who frequently wander the streets.

✪ **The Wilkies Inn.** 1038 Lighthouse Ave., Pacific Grove, CA 93950. ☎ **800/253-5707** or 831/372-5960. Fax 831/655-1681. 24 units. $55–$105 double. Extra person $8. 2-night minimum stay on weekends. AE, DISC, JCB, MC, V.

This motel is a great value: It consistently charges less than the other hotels in town, gets an "A+" for service, and is located on a quiet tree-lined street with a resident deer who often drops by for breakfast. (Apparently since we announced the animal in this guide, arriving guests always ask, "So, where's the deer." Ironically, it usually tends to appear.) The motel recently added new furnishings and carpet, stylish bedspreads, and special amenities for divers. All the squeaky-clean rooms come with coffeemakers and free movies and local calls. Some have VCRs (free movies!), microwaves, and partial ocean views; two have full kitchens; and you can have a fridge for a few extra dollars.

MODERATELY PRICED OPTIONS

Centrella Inn. 612 Central Ave., Pacific Grove, CA 93950. ☎ **800/233-3372** or 831/372-3372. Fax 831/372-2036. 27 units. $109–$179 double; from $179 cottage or suite. Rates include buffet breakfast and hors d'oeuvres in the evening. MC, V.

A couple of blocks from the waterfront and from Lover's Point Beach, the two-story Centrella is an old turreted Victorian that was built as a boardinghouse in 1889. Today the rooms are decorated in Victorian style, but they're somewhat plain—iron beds, side table, floor lamp, and armoire—although the bathrooms do have claw-foot tubs. In the back, connected to the house by brick walkways, are several newly remodeled private cottages and suites with fireplaces, wet bars, TVs, and separate bedrooms and bathrooms. Two have private decks; the others offer decks facing the rose garden and patio, which is set with umbrella tables and chairs. Cheese and hors d'oeuvres are served in the evening.

Gosby House. 643 Lighthouse Ave., Pacific Grove, CA 93950. ☎ **800/527-8828** or 831/375-1287. Fax 831/655-9621. 22 units, 20 with bathroom. $105 double without bathroom; $90–$160 double with bathroom. Rates include full breakfast and afternoon wine and snacks. AE, DC, MC, V. From Calif. 1, take Calif. 68 to Pacific Grove, where it turns into Forest Ave.; continue on Forest to Lighthouse Ave., turn left, and go 3 blocks.

Originally a boardinghouse for Methodist ministers, this Victorian was built in 1887, 3 blocks from the bay. It's still one of the most charming Victorians in town, with individually decorated rooms, floral-print wallpapers, lacy pillows, and antique furnishings. Twelve guest rooms have fireplaces, and all come with the inn's trademark teddy bears. Especially noteworthy are the two Carriage House rooms, which have a fireplace, deck, and extra-large bathroom with spa tub.

The house has a separate dining room and parlor, where guests gather for breakfast and complimentary wine and snacks in the afternoon. Other amenities include complimentary newspaper, twice-daily maid service, and bicycles. Smoking is not permitted.

Green Gables Inn. 104 Fifth St., Pacific Grove, CA 93950. ☎ **800/722-1774** or 831/ 375-2095. Fax 831/375-5437. 12 units, 7 with bathroom. $110–$135 double without bathroom; $145–$160 double with bathroom; $170 suite. Rates include buffet breakfast and afternoon wine, tea, and hors d'oeuvres. AE, DC, MC, V. From Calif. 1, take the Pacific Grove exit (Calif. 68) and continue to the Pacific Ocean; turn right on Ocean View Blvd. and drive half a mile to Fifth St.

This 1888 Queen Anne–style mansion, which is decorated like an English country inn, forgoes opulence (and in some cases private bathrooms) to allow for reasonable rates and more homey accommodations. The rooms are divided between the main building and the carriage houses behind it. Carriage House rooms, which are better for families, were recently remodeled and have large private bathrooms with Jacuzzi tubs. All accommodations are individually decorated with dainty furnishings, including some antiques and an occasional poster bed. Most rooms in the original home have ocean views and share two immaculate bathrooms. There's an antique carousel horse in the comfortable parlor, where complimentary wine, tea, and hors d'oeuvres are served each afternoon. Teddy bears populate every nook and cranny. Smoking is not permitted.

WORTH A SPLURGE

✪ **Martine Inn.** 255 Ocean View Blvd., Pacific Grove, CA 93950. ☎ **800/852-5588** or 831/373-3388. Fax 831/373-3896. 20 units. $135–$245 double; $295 suite. Rates include full breakfast and evening hors d'oeuvres. AE, DISC, MC, V.

One glance at the lavish Victorian interior and the incredible bay views and you'll know why this Mediterranean-style inn is one of the best B&Bs in the area. Enjoy the vista via binoculars that the management leaves out for guests, or stroll the bay-front promenade. Always above par, the rooms have been recently redecorated but still maintain their Victorian style. You'll pay more if you want a fireplace and ocean view. Request a room with a bathtub if it matters to you; some have only a shower. The inn recently purchased an adjacent Victorian cottage, which is now a luxury suite. A full breakfast is served at lace-covered tables in the large front room; hors d'oeuvres are served in the evening. Guests also have access to two additional sitting quarters: a small room downstairs overlooking the ocean and a larger room with shelves of books. Amenities include newspaper delivery, free coffee and refreshments, Jacuzzi, and a billiards table. *Note:* This is a popular spot for wedding parties in summertime.

WHERE TO DINE
SUPER-CHEAP EATS

First Awakenings. In the American Tin Cannery, 125 Ocean View Blvd. ☎ 831/372-1125. Reservations not accepted. Breakfast $4–$7; lunch $5–$7. AE, DISC, MC, V. Daily 7am– 2:30pm. From Calif. 1, take the Pacific Grove exit (Calif. 68) and turn right onto Lighthouse Ave.; after a mile turn left onto Eardley Ave., and take it to the corner of Ocean View. AMERICAN.

This huge, open restaurant offers one of the cheapest and healthiest breakfasts in the area. Eye-openers include eight varieties of omelets; granola with nuts, fruit, and yogurt; walnut and wheat pancakes; "gourmet" pancakes; and raisin French toast. At lunch there's a fine choice of salads and a slew of sandwiches ranging from albacore to zucchini. Sunny days are best celebrated at the outdoor patio tables.

Thai Bistro. 159 Central Ave. (between David Ave. and Eardley St.), Pacific Grove. ☎ **408/372-8700.** Reservations recommended on weekends. Most main courses $8–$12. AE, MC, V. Daily 11:30am–9:30pm. THAI.

This restaurant has been voted "Best Thai" by readers of *Monterey Weekly* for the past 4 years running. The menu is a mini manifesto, with over 60 options ranging from fresh chili and sweet basil sauce, the very popular and delicious Panang curry, and hot-and-sour coconut soup to the ever-requested pad Thai and a full vegetarian menu. All are served in a modern, congenial dining room—usually filled with locals—and accompanied by Carmel Valley wines and French desserts.

Tilly Gort's Café. 111 Central Ave. (between David Ave. and Eardley St.), Pacific Grove. ☎ **831/373-0335.** Most main courses $5–$8. AE, DISC, MC, V. Daily 11am–10:30pm. CAFE/VEGETARIAN.

Down the street from Thai Bistro is Tilly Gort's, the "best vegetarian" option in town with the least appetizing name. This place is about as vegan-friendly and California casual as it gets; order at the counter, kick back in a dining room split by wood-plank walls, and enjoy low-fat, healthy cuisine covering all the meatless bases (with the exception of a few turkey and chicken options). Mexican (soft tacos with a veggie patty are a fave), pastas (spinach ravioli), plenty o' salads, sandwiches, and veggie burgers are under $7 and for about $3 more you can kick in the calories with a black-bottom cup-cake or slice of fruit pie. Nibblers get happy with the side dishes—baked potatoes, steamed veggies, black beans, and more—for under $3.

Toastie's Cafe. 702 Lighthouse Dr. ☎ **831/373-7543.** Breakfast and lunch dishes $5.95–$7.25; dinner main courses $9–$11.50. MC, V. Mon–Sat 6am–3pm; Sun 7am–2pm; Tues–Sat 5–9pm. AMERICAN.

While most restaurants' success depends not only on food but also on clever decor and elaborate presentation, Toastie's shrugs its traditional-style shoulders and continues to pack 'em in. What's the attraction? A good old-fashioned meal served in a no-frills casual dining room. Some rave about the eggs Benedict (with roasted potatoes) or the hefty, sinful waffles. Others indulge in one of the many other expected options. Regardless, one thing's for sure: This place serves up what everyone wants from breakfast—lots of selections, good service, endless coffee refills, and a heaping plate of food. Dinner is an equally homey affair and includes chicken and prawn Marsala, teriyaki steak, seafood pasta, stuffed chicken.

FOR A FEW BUCKS MORE

✪ **The Fishwife at Asilomar Beach.** 1996½ Sunset Dr. (at Asilomar Beach). ☎ **831/375-7107.** Main courses $8.75–$13. AE, DC, DISC, MC, V. Mon and Wed–Sat 11am–10pm; Sun 10am–10pm. From Calif. 1, take the Pacific Grove exit (Calif. 68) and stay left until it becomes Sunset Dr.; the restaurant will be on your left about 1 mile ahead, as you approach Asilomar Beach. SEAFOOD.

The Fishwife is the ideal dining spot for anyone looking for a casual, affordable, and quality meal. The restaurant dates from the 1830s, when a sailor's wife started a small food market that became famous for its Boston clam chowder. Today locals still return for the savory soup as well as some of the finest seafood in Pacific Grove. Two best-sellers at dinner are calamari steak sautéed with shallots, garlic, tomatoes, and white wine; and prawns Belize, presented sizzling with red onions, tomatoes, fresh serrano chilies, jicama, lime juice, and cashews. Steak and pasta dishes are also available, and

Readers Recommend

Red House Café, 662 Lighthouse Ave. (at 19th), Pacific Grove. ☎ **831/643-1060.** *There's no sign, no business cards, and no menus. This restaurant is a rustic turn-of-the-century cottage painted a delightful shade of red. In the backyard is Mrs. Trawick's Garden Shop, a wonderful collection of garden ornaments, tools, and whimsies. The neighborhood birds seem very pleased to stay and add a bit of local color. Inside the restaurant, an eclectic mix of clients are served a wonderful changing menu for break-fast, lunch, or pastries. We sampled a pork loin sandwich on focaccia bread, café au lait served in its traditional bowl, and an exquisite pear tart. The young couple, Laura and Chris, opened this jewel in 1997, but you can tell from the crowd that they have won over the hearts and tummies of the town.*

—Karla Baer Cohen and Jim Cohen, Huntington Beach, Calif.

Authors' Note: Main courses are $6.25 to $8.25; hours are Tuesday through Friday from 7:30am to 3pm and Saturday and Sunday from 8am to 3pm.

---

all main courses come with vegetables, bread, black beans, and rice or potatoes. Kids get their own color-in menu, which has smaller portions for less than $6.

Peppers Mexicali Cafe. 170 Forest Ave. ☎ **831/373-6892.** Reservations recommended. Main courses $6–$13. AE, CB, DC, DISC, MC, V. Mon and Wed–Thurs 11:30am–10pm; Fri–Sat 11:30am–10:30pm; Sun 4–10pm. MEXICAN/LATIN AMERICAN.

Peppers is a casual, festive place with good food at excellent prices. The inviting dining room has wooden floors and tables, pepper art visible from every viewpoint, and a per-petual crowd of diners who come to suck up beers and savor spicy specialties such as well-balanced seafood tacos and fajitas or house-made tamales and chile rellenos. Other fire-starters include the snapper Yucatán, which is cooked with chilies, citrus cilantro, and tomatoes; and grilled prawns with lime-cilantro dressing. Add a sub-stantial selection of suds, an addicting compilation of chips and salsa, and a friendly service staff, and your taste buds are bound to bellow "Olé!"

MODERATELY PRICED OPTIONS

✪ **Joe Rombi's.** 208 17th St. (at Lighthouse Ave.). ☎ **831/373-2416.** Reservations recommended. Main courses $12–$19. AE, MC, V. Wed–Sun 5–10pm. ITALIAN.

Joe Rombi's serves enjoyable Italian fare in a refreshingly intimate dining room warmed with dim lighting and enormous French antique posters. The food here is very fresh (lasagnas and pastas are made each day) and enjoyed at one of 11 tables. The basket of fresh house-made focaccia is munch-worthy, as is the limited menu of appe-tizers, soups, salads, pizzas, pastas, and four main courses (some of which come with soup and salad, which makes them an especially good deal). Go with the fish of the day—we had a halibut dish that any upscale San Francisco restaurant would be proud to present.

WORTH A SPLURGE

Cypress Grove. 663 Lighthouse Ave. (at 19th St.). ☎ **408/375-1743.** Reservations rec-ommended. Main courses $15–$29. AE, MC, V. Tues–Fri 11:30am–2:30pm; Sat–Sun 11am–3pm; Tues–Sat 5–9:30pm. CALIFORNIA/FRENCH.

This area has few seriously gourmet restaurants, so when chef/proprietor Kurt Steeber opened Cypress Grove in early 1998, gourmands breathed a collective sigh of relief. Steeber, who hails from S.F.'s Campton Place and Zuni and N.Y.'s Tapastry, is a creative chef who knows how to make a dish work. The sophisticated menu, which is California-farm-fresh French, offers sautéed foie gras with port-poached pear and Maytag blue cheese; onion and fennel tart; roasted quail with morels, mango, and leeks; and oxtail ragout with orzo. With a romantic dining room and an enthusiastic start, we're guessing Cypress Grove will continue to be worth a visit.

Fandango. 223 17th St. ☎ **831/372-3456.** Reservations recommended. Main courses $11–$24. AE, CB, DC, DISC, MC, V. Mon–Sat 11am–3:30pm; Sun 10am–2:30pm; daily 5–9:30pm. From Calif. 1, take the Pacific Grove exit (Calif. 68), turn left on Lighthouse Ave., and continue a block to 17th St. MEDITERRANEAN.

Provincial Mediterranean specialties from Spain to Greece to North Africa spice up the menu with such offerings as seafood paella with North African couscous (the recipe has been in the owner's family for almost 200 years), cassoulet maison, cannelloni niçoise, and a Greek-style lamb shank. You'll feel transported straight to Europe in one of the five upstairs and downstairs dining rooms, cozied by roaring fires, wood tables, and antiqued walls. There's an award-winning international wine list with 450 options and a dessert menu that includes a Grand Marnier soufflé with fresh raspberry purée sauce and profiteroles. In winter, ask to be seated in the fireplace dining room, and in summer, request the terrace room—but whenever you come, expect everything here to be lively and colorful, from the regional decor to the owner himself.

4 The 17-Mile Drive

The $7.25 you'll have to fork over to drive through this coastal area buys you great ocean views and a gander at some of the most exclusive coastal real estate in California. (You can skip the drive altogether and see the same beautiful landscape just south of the gates.) The drive can be entered from of any of five gates: two from Pacific Grove to the north, one from Carmel to the south, or two from Monterey to the east. The most convenient entrance from Calif. 1 is just off the main road at the Holman Highway exit. Admission to the drive includes an informative map that points out 26 points of interest along the way. (You may beat traffic by entering at the Carmel Gate and doing the tour backwards.) Aside from the homes of the ultrarich and the pristine greens of that elite golfer's paradise **Pebble Beach,** highlights include **Seal and Bird Rocks,** where you can see countless gulls, cormorants, and other offshore birds as well as seals and sea lions; and **Cypress Point Lookout,** which on a clear day affords a 20-mile view all the way to the Big Sur lighthouse. Also visible is the famous **Lone Cypress tree,** an inspiration to so many artists and photographers, which you can stop and admire from afar but can no longer approach. The drive also traverses Del Monte Forest, thick with tame black-tailed deer, and often compared to some "billionaire's private game preserve." One of the best ways to see the 17-Mile Drive is by bike, but the ride toward Carmel is all downhill, so unless you're in great shape, arrange for a ride back or simply do it by car. If you're planning to make a day of it, bring a picnic lunch or you're doomed to blow your budget at one of the resort restaurants.

If you prefer to avoid the $7.25 fee, either ride a bike (you must enter from Pacific Grove) or walk in to 17-Mile Drive.

5 Carmel-by-the-Sea

5 miles S of Monterey; 121 miles S of San Francisco; 33 miles N of Big Sur

If you visited the town officially known as Carmel-by-the-Sea dozens of years ago, you're likely to be of the school that criticizes its present-day overcommercialization.

Carmel began as an artists' colony that attracted such luminaries as Robinson Jeffers, Sinclair Lewis, Robert Louis Stevenson, Ansel Adams, William Rose Benet, and Mary Austin. It was a nonconformist enclave where residents resisted assigned street numbers and lighting (they carried lanterns, which they considered more romantic).

Today Carmel may not be the bohemian artists' village of seasoned travelers' memories, but it's still an adorable (albeit touristy) town that knows how to celebrate its surroundings. Vibrant wildflower gardens flourish along each residential street, gnarled cypress trees reach up from white sandy beaches, and at the end of each day tourists magically disappear and the town—for a split second—feels undiscovered.

It's still intimate enough that there's no need for street numbers. Carmel's inns, restaurants, boutiques, and art galleries all identify their locations only by cross streets. A few hints such as Saks Fifth Avenue, convertible roadsters cruising through town, intolerable traffic, and the price tags on B&Bs indicate we're not in Kansas anymore, but rather a well-preserved upscale tourist haven.

If you're interested in saving money, we recommend staying in quaint Pacific Grove (see section 3, above). It's only a few miles away, has better rates, and you can easily day-trip into crowded Carmel.

ESSENTIALS

The **Carmel Business Association,** P.O. Box 4444, Carmel, CA 93921 (☎ **831/ 624-2522**), is above the Hog's Breath Inn on San Carlos between Fifth and Sixth streets. It distributes local maps, brochures, and publications. Pick up a copy of the *Carmel Gallery Guide* and a schedule of local events. Hours are Monday through Friday from 9am to 5pm. On weekends, they have a booth set up from 11am to 3pm at Carmel Plaza, on Ocean Avenue between Junipero and San Carlos streets.

EXPLORING THE TOWN

A wonderful stretch of white sand backed by cypress trees, **Carmel Beach City Park** is a wee bit o' heaven on earth (though the jammed parking lot can feel more like a visit to hell). There's plenty of room for families, surfers, and dogs with their owners (yes, pooches are allowed to run off-leash here). If the parking lot is full, there are some spaces on Ocean Avenue, but take heed: They're generally good for 90-minute parking only, and you will get a ticket if you park for the day.

Farther south around the promontory, **Carmel River State Beach** is a less crowded option, with white sand and dunes, plus a bird sanctuary where brown pelicans, black oystercatchers, cormorants, gulls, curlews, godwits, and sanderlings make their home.

The ✪ **Mission San Carlos Borromeo del Rio Carmelo,** on Basilica Rio Road at Lasuen Drive, off Calif. 1 (☎ **831/624-3600**), is the burial ground of Father Junípero Serra and the second-oldest of the 21 Spanish missions he established. Founded in 1771 on a scenic site overlooking the Carmel River, it remains one of the largest and most interesting of California's missions. The stone church, with its gracefully curving walls and Moorish bell tower, was begun in 1793. Its walls are covered with a lime plaster made of burnt seashells. The old mission kitchen, the first library in California, the high altar, and the flower gardens are all worth visiting. More than 3,000 Native Americans are buried in the adjacent cemetery; their graves are decorated with seashells. The mission is open June through August, Monday through Saturday from 9:30am to 7:30pm, Sunday from 10:30am to 7:30pm; in other months, Monday through Saturday from 9:30am to 4:30pm, Sunday from 10:30am to 4:30pm. A $2 donation is requested.

One of Carmel's prettiest homes and gardens is **Tor House,** 26304 Oceanview Ave. (☎ **831/624-1813,** or 831/624-1840 on Fridays and Saturdays only), built by

California poet Robinson Jeffers. Situated on Carmel Point, the house dates from 1918 and includes a 40-foot tower containing stones from around the world, which are embedded in the walls (there's even one from the Great Wall of China). Inside, an old porthole is reputed to have come from the ship on which Napoléan escaped from Elba in 1815. No photography is allowed. Admission is by guided tour only, and reservations are requested. It's $7 for adults, $4 for college students, and $2 for high-school students (no children under 12). Open on Friday and Saturday from 10am to 3pm.

If **shopping** is more your bag, leave the car at the hotel or park and check out the town on foot. You'll be surprised at the number of (expensive) shops packed into this small town—more than 500 boutiques offering unique fashions, baskets, housewares, imported goods, and a veritable cornucopia of art galleries. All the commercial action is packed along the small stretch of Ocean Avenue between Junipero and San Antonio avenues.

If you want to tour the galleries, pick up a copy of the *Carmel Gallery Guide* from the Carmel Business Association (see "Essentials," above).

Serious shoppers (who are ready to blow some cash) should head south a few miles to the **Crossroads Shopping Center** (from Calif. 1 south, take the Rio Road exit west for 1 block and turn right onto Crossroads Boulevard). As far as malls go, this is a great one with oodles of shopping and a few good restaurants.

WHERE TO STAY

You're not going to find a room for much less than $100 in Carmel-by-the-Sea unless it's off-season. It doesn't hurt to give the hotels here a try, but you'll be just as happy staying in cozy Pacific Grove and cruising down to Carmel (a 10-minute drive, traffic permitting) for daytime visits.

If you'd like some guidance in finding a room, contact the **Tourist Information Center** at Mission Street (between Fifth and Sixth; ☎ **800/847-8066** or 831/624-1711).

SUPER-CHEAP SLEEPS

The Homestead. Lincoln St. (at Eighth Ave.), Carmel, CA 93921. ☎ **831/624-4119.** 8 units, 4 cottages. TV. $65–$100 double (some with shower only); $85 to $95 cottage. 2-night minimum during high season. MC, V.

This remodeled home with private entrances and private bathrooms is most likely the cheapest place to stay in Carmel. Rooms are individually decorated in "Old Carmel" (classic country) style and come with either a tub/shower or just a shower bathroom. The four nearby cottages have kitchens and fireplaces. All guests have access to the peaceful gardens, a pay phone, and the beach, which is just 6 blocks away. Smoking is allowed on the patio only.

MODERATELY PRICED OPTIONS

Traveling with Fido? Your best bet is the pet-friendly **Cypress Inn,** Lincoln and Seventh (P.O. Box Y), Carmel, CA 93921 (☎ **800/443-7443** or 831/624-3871; www.cypress-inn.com), which is a moderately priced option run by owner/actress Doris Day.

Carmel Village Inn. Ocean Ave. and Junipero St. (P.O. Box 5275), Carmel, CA 93921. ☎ **800/346-3864** in Calif. or 831/624-3864. Fax 831/626-6763. 34 units. TV TEL. $69–$155 double; $89–$300 triple or quad; from $89 suite. Rates include continental breakfast. AE, MC, V. From Calif. 1, exit onto Ocean Ave. and continue straight to Junipero St.

Well run and centrally located, the Village Inn is nothing more than a motor lodge. The rooms, arranged around a courtyard/parking lot lined with potted geraniums, are outfitted with bland but functional decor. The guest rooms come equipped with fridges. Breakfast, accompanied by the morning newspaper, is served in the downstairs lounge.

Normandy Inn. Ocean Ave., between Monte Verde and Casanova sts. (P.O. Box 1706), Carmel, CA 93921. ☎ **800/343-3825** in Calif. or 831/624-3825. Fax 831/624-4614. 48 units. TV TEL. $98–$200 double; $165–$400 suite or cottage. Rates include continental breakfast. Extra person $10. AE, MC, V. From Calif. 1, exit onto Ocean Ave. and continue straight for 5 blocks past Junipero St.

Three blocks from the beach, this Tudor-style hotel is like something out of a storybook, especially with the array of colorful flowers that brighten up the property. The guest rooms show their age a little, but are well appointed with French country decor, down comforters, and coffeemakers; some also have fireplaces and/or kitchenettes. The tiny heated pool is banked by a sweet flower garden. Other perks include a self-service laundry and newspapers delivered to your room daily.

The three large family-style cottages are an especially good deal and accommodate up to eight; each one has three bedrooms, two bathrooms, a fully equipped kitchen, a dining room, a living room with a fireplace, and a back porch. Be sure to reserve far in advance, especially in summer.

Pine Inn Hotel. Ocean Ave. (between Monte Verde and Lincoln; P.O. Box 250), Carmel-by-the-Sea, CA 93921. ☎ **800/228-3851** or 831/624-3851. Fax 831/624-3030. www.pine-inn.com. E-mail: info@pine-inn.com. 49 units. TV TEL. $95–$140 double. AE, DC, DISC, JCB, MC, V.

The three-story historic Pine Inn, which was built in 1889 and claims to be the oldest hotel in Carmel, looks like a set out of "Wild, Wild West." The ornate deep-red and mahogany lobby and library (with fireplace) is a fun departure from the beachy alternatives (think turn-of-the-century bordello). Unfortunately, rooms are less impressive and are clearly in need of a fashion makeover. The most affordable (doubles) are also very small; pay more and you might secure a larger room with a half-canopy. The good news is, the hotel is a few blocks from the beach on Carmel's main strolling street, room service hails from adjoining Il Fornaio from 7am to 10:30pm, and the place is quite clean and atmospheric. One big bummer: There are no elevators.

✪ **Vagabond House.** Fourth and Dolores (P.O. Box 2747), Carmel-by-the-Sea, CA 93921. ☎ **800/262-1262,** 800/221-1262 in Canada, or 831/624-7738. Fax 831/626-1243. 12 units. TV TEL. $85–$95 double; $125 double with fireplace; $145–$165 double with kitchen and/or fireplace; $165 cottage. 2-night minimum. 20% discount weeknights between Thanksgiving and Christmas. AE, MC, V. Pets allowed.

This place is so ridiculously cute and cozy that even the ultrafriendly woman at the front desk will remind you of your long lost grandmother. Attention is paid to every element of this place, from the lobby adorned with knickknack antiques and a welcoming decanter of sherry to the wonderfully lush garden courtyard that's draped with greenery and dotted with bloom. Each room is warm and homey, decorated in country decor, and has a private entrance and a refrigerator; all have fireplaces except two, which means the $85 rooms book quickly, so call ahead if you want one. Guests are welcomed with a basket of fruit and the extended continental breakfast is delivered to your room, but you'll most likely prefer to enjoy it on the garden patio.

WORTH A SPLURGE

✪ **La Playa.** Camino Real and Eighth Ave. (P.O. Box 900), Carmel, CA 93921. ☎ **800/582-8900** or 831/624-6476. Fax 831/624-7966. 80 units. MINIBAR TV TEL. $135–$235 double; $235–$525 suite or cottage. AE, DC, MC, V. Complimentary valet parking.

Only 2 blocks from the beach and yet within walking distance of town, the four-story La Playa is a romantic Mediterranean-style villa built in 1904. Norwegian artist Christopher Jorgensen ordered its construction for his bride, an heiress of the Ghirardelli chocolate dynasty. The stylish lobby sets the elegant tone with its terra-cotta floors, Oriental rugs, and white marble fireplace. The charming and cozy rooms, which were renovated in 1997, are arranged around a lawn and garden with a pool at the center. The cottages have full kitchens, wet bars, and garden patios, and most have wood-burning fireplaces.

Amenities include room service (limited to breakfast and lunch in cottages), dry cleaning, newspaper delivery, twice-daily maid service, and nightly turndown (excluding cottages). The moderately priced Terrace Grill serves California cuisine; for a very relaxing summertime meal, dine out on the alfresco terrace overlooking the gardens.

✪ **Mission Ranch.** 26270 Dolores St., Carmel, CA 93923. ☎ **800/538-8221** or 831/624-6436. Fax 831/626-4163. 31 units. TV TEL. $85–$225 double. Rates include continental breakfast. MC, V.

If you want to stay a bit off the beaten track, consider this converted 1850s dairy farm, which was purchased and restored by Clint Eastwood to preserve the vista of the nearby wetlands stretching out to the bay.

Guest units are spaciously scattered amid different structures, both old and new, and surrounded by wetlands and grazing sheep. As befits a ranch, rooms are decorated in a provincial style, with high-carved wooden beds bedecked with handmade quilts.

Accommodations range from "regulars" in the main barn (which are less desirable) to meadow-view units, each with a vista across the fields to the bay. Most are equipped with whirlpool baths, fireplaces, and decks or patios. The Martin family farmhouse contains six units, all arranged around a central parlor, while the Bunkhouse (the oldest structure on the property) contains separate living and dining areas, bedrooms, and a fridge. On the grounds are tennis courts, an exercise room, a putting green, and a pro shop. Even if you're not staying here, call for a table at the The Restaurant at Mission Ranch (see "Where to Dine," below).

WHERE TO DINE
SUPER-CHEAP EATS

Carmel Bakery. Ocean (between Dolores and Lincoln). ☎ **831/626-8885.** Sandwiches $3.50–$5.25. No credit cards. Daily 6:30am–9pm. BAKERY/DELI.

The fanciest of the few bakeries along this main street leading down to the beach serves espresso, soup, sandwiches, and pastries. It's also the most festive and well decorated, with a few tables and chairs, and music playing from speakers overhead. Most patrons grab their grub and go. For a more formal (and a mite more expensive) encounter with espresso and the like, head down the block to Il Fornaio (see below).

Little Swiss Cafe. Sixth (between Lincoln and Mission). ☎ **831/624-5007.** Reservations not accepted. $4.75–$8. No credit cards. Mon–Sat 7:30am–3pm; Sun 8am–2pm. CONTINENTAL.

Locals led us to this quirky little eatery designed to look like a Swiss cottage. Kids may love the decor (old-fashion Grandma cute) but the grown-ups come for what they consider the best homemade blintzes and pancakes in town. Late risers rejoice: Breakfast is served all day. Lunch is pleasantly affordable and features sandwiches, which are served with potato salad, mixed green salad, or soup ($5 to $7); salads; and an array of unusual entrees such as Swiss sausage with smothered onions, calves' liver sauté, and fillet of red snapper with a rémoulade sauce.

Neilsen Brothers. San Carlos (at Seventh). ☎ **831/624-6263** (deli) or 831/624-6441 (market). Picnic items $3–$5. MC, V. Mon–Sat 8am–8pm; Sun 10am–7pm. DELI.

Why bother burning away precious midday vacation minutes indoors when you can dine alfresco at Carmel Beach? Duck a few blocks off the main drag to Neilsen Brothers market and you'll find everything you could want to fill your picnic basket, including sandwiches, barbecued chicken and ribs, pasta salads, and a vast selection of cheeses. You can even get french fries and veggie and meat burgers (from noon to 6pm), but expect a 10-minute wait—they cook to order. Call and order over the phone or drop in.

FOR A FEW BUCKS MORE

✪ **Caffè Napoli.** Ocean Ave. (between Dolores and Lincoln). ☎ **831/625-4033.** Reservations recommended. Main courses $8–$15. MC, V. Daily 11:30am–10pm. ITALIAN.

The decor here is so quintessentially Italiana, with flags, gingham tablecloths, garlic, and baskets overhead, that we expected a flour-coated pot-bellied Padrino Napoli to emerge from the kitchen, embrace us wholeheartedly, and exclaim "Mangia! Mangia!" as he slapped down a bowl overflowing with sauce-drenched pasta. Of course there is no Padrino here, and we received no welcoming hug, but we did indulge in the fine Italian fare that keeps locals coming back for more.

MODERATELY PRICED OPTIONS

Flying Fish Grill. In Carmel Plaza, Mission St. (between Ocean and Seventh aves.). ☎ **831/625-1962.** Reservations recommended. Main courses $13.75–$19.75. AE, DISC, MC, V. Daily 5–10pm. Closed Tues in winter. PACIFIC RIM/SEAFOOD.

Chef/proprietor Kenny Fukumoto presides over this dark, romantic, and Asian-influenced dining room serving fresh seafood with exquisite Japanese accents. Start with sushi, tempura, or any of the other exotic and tantalizing taste teasers. Then prepare your tongue for splendid main courses. House favorites include a savory rare peppered ahi, blackened and served with mustard/sesame-soy vinaigrette and angel-hair pasta, and a pan-fried almond sea bass with whipped potatoes, Chinese cabbage, and rock shrimp stir-fry.

The Hog's Breath Inn. San Carlos St. (between Fifth and Sixth aves.). ☎ **831/625-1044.** Reservations not accepted. Main courses $9.50–$23. AE, DC, MC, V. Mon–Sat 11:30am–3pm; Sun 11am–3pm; daily 5–10pm. From Calif. 1, take the Ocean Ave. exit and turn right onto San Carlos St. AMERICAN.

Clint Eastwood's involvement with this restaurant has made it famous, but we have to admit the patio with tree-trunk tables and plastic chairs is ideal for drinking a pint or two and chowing down on good ol' American standbys—that is, if you don't mind the usual wait. (Tables in the wood-paneled dark-and-rustic dining room decorated with farm implements fill up, too, though they're not as lively as outdoor seats.) The food (burgers, nachos, etc.) here isn't remotely as legendary as the owner (whom you're not likely to see), but the small dark bar with sports on the tube is the best place to pull up a stool and get drunk on a rainy day (or a sunny one for that matter). Come for lunch—it's more affordable.

Il Fornaio. Ocean Ave. (at Monte Verde). ☎ **831/622-5100,** or 831/622-5115 for the bakery. Main courses $8.50–$21.50. AE, DC, MC, V. Mon–Thurs 7am–10pm; Fri 7am–11pm; Sat 8am–11pm; Sun 8am–10pm. ITALIAN.

We don't care if it is a chain—Il Fornaio is still one of our favorite restaurants because we're guaranteed a well-prepared mocha and thick chocolate-dipped biscotti at every outpost. There's also a great selection of salads (go with the simple house salad with shaved Parmesan, croutons, and a tangy light dressing), pastas, pizzas, and rotisserie chicken, duck, and rabbit fresh from the brick oven. The house-made breads and seeded breadsticks alone are reason enough to come. We must admit the tasty-but-measly $11 lasagna is disappointing, so skip it and start with the seared swordfish antipasto with roast pepper and Dijon mustard, or decadent grilled polenta with sautéed wild mushrooms, provolone, and Italian truffle oil. Follow it up with a gourmet pizza or pasta. The large airy dining room and sunny terrace offer charming and diverse atmosphere. The Panetteria, a retail bakery, is the perfect place to pick up a gourmet picnic or have a breakfast snack.

La Bohème. Dolores St. and Seventh Ave. ☎ **831/624-7500.** Reservations not accepted. Fixed-price, 3-course dinner $21.75. MC, V. Daily 5:30–10pm. Closed 2 weeks before Christmas. From Calif. 1, exit onto Ocean Ave. and turn left onto Dolores St. FRENCH COUNTRY.

Like a set from Disney's "It's a Small World," La Bohème mimics a French street with cartoony asymmetrical shingled house facades and a painted blue sky overhead. Thankfully, the similarity stops with the decor, and there are no dolls singing anywhere—in French or English. Dinner here is utterly romantic French, served at cramped tables set with floral-print cloths in bright colors, hand-painted dinnerware, and vibrant bouquets. Dinner is a three-course, fixed-price feast consisting of a large salad, a tureen of soup, and a main dish (perhaps roast breast of duckling with green peppercorn, plums, and red-wine sauce or filet mignon with cognac-cream sauce). Vegetarian specials are available nightly. Homemade desserts and fresh coffee are sold separately, and are usually worth the extra expense. Dress is casual. Curious online folks can learn more at www.laboheme.com.

WORTH A SPLURGE

Casanova. Fifth Ave. (between San Carlos and Mission sts.). ☎ **831/625-0501.** Reservations recommended. 3-course dinner $21.75–$35.75. MC, V. Mon–Sat 11:30am–3pm; Sun 9am–3pm; Sun–Thurs 5–10pm; Fri–Sat 5–10:30pm. From Calif. 1, take the Ocean Ave. exit and turn right on Mission, then left onto Fifth Ave. NORTHERN ITALIAN/SOUTHERN FRENCH.

It's the European ambiance that makes this place special. The building, which once belonged to Charlie Chaplin's cook, is divided into three Belgian-chalet-style dining rooms that serve as the perfect setting for leaning over a bottle of red wine and creating vacation memories. More festive folk step back to the old-world-style covered patio where it's bustling and crowded. Since all dinner entrees include antipasto and a choice of appetizers (such as baked stuffed eggplant with rice, herbs, cheese, and tomatoes), $30 is not such a bad deal (at least in overpriced Carmel). The menu features typical Mediterranean cuisine: paella, homemade pastas, meats, and fish. Casanova also boasts an award-winning wine cellar featuring more than 1,600 French, California, German, and Italian wines.

✪ **The Restaurant at Mission Ranch.** At Mission Ranch, 26270 Dolores St. ☎ **831/625-9040.** Reservations recommended. Most main courses $13–$23.75. AE, DC, MC, V. Mon–Fri 4–9:45pm; Sat 11am–9:45pm; Sun 9am–9:45pm; bar stays open until midnight. AMERICAN.

Clint Eastwood bought this rustic out-of-the-way property in 1986 and restored the ranch-style building to its original integrity, and although the chance of seeing him brings in some folks, the views, quality food, and merry atmosphere are what really make the place pop. The wooden building is encased with large windows that accentuate the wonderful view of the marshlands, grazing sheep, and bay beyond. Warm days make patio dining the prime choice, but the key time to come is at sunset, when the sky is transforming and happy hour is in full swing (you'll find some of the cheapest drinks around, and Clint often stops by when he's in town). As you'd expect from the ranch motif, meat is king here: Burgers are freshly ground on-site, and prime rib with twice-baked potato and vegetables is the favored dish. There are, of course, wonderful seafood and vegetarian options as well, and all dinners include soup or salad. Entertainment is provided at the piano bar, where locals and tourists have been known to croon their favorites.

6 Carmel Valley

3 miles SE of Carmel-by-the-Sea

Inland from Carmel stretches Carmel Valley, where wealthy folks retreat beyond the reach of the coastal fog and mist. It's a scenic and perpetually sunny valley of rolling hills dotted with manicured golf courses and many a horse ranch.

Hike the trails in **Garland Regional Park,** 8 miles east of Carmel on Carmel Valley Road (dogs are welcome off-leash). The sun really bakes you out here, so bring lots of water. If you're a horse lover, you can also sign up for a pricey $30-per-hour trail ride at **The Holman Ranch,** 60 Holman Rd. (☎ **831/659-6054**), 12 miles east of Calif. 1. While you're in the valley, taste the wines (for free) at the **Château Julien Winery,** 8940 Carmel Valley Rd. (☎ **831/624-2600**), which is open daily.

WHERE TO STAY

Accommodations don't come cheaply in these wealth-ridden woods, but it makes no difference since the only reason tourists stay here is to visit the superluxurious retreats. The rest of us just would end up driving north to Carmel-by-the-Sea and into Monterey for the day anyway.

CAMPING

Saddle Mountain. 27625 Schulte Rd., Carmel, CA 93923. ☎ **831/624-1617.** 50 sites. Basic sites $25 for 2 ($3 extra per person); full hookup and tent-cabins $35. MC, V.

The cheapest way to stay in exorbitant Carmel is to camp at Saddle Mountain. It may not be ocean-side (it's 4½ miles east of Calif. 1 in Carmel Valley), but its sites are surrounded by natural beauty, offer a cornucopia of free activities, and are especially good for families. Twenty-five sites come complete with full hookups (water, sewer, electric, and even cable, if you brought the TV). Bring your own tent and you'll save 10 bucks a night, or pay extra for a teepee or tent-cabin (canvas tent cabin on wooden platform). Amenities include bath and shower facilities; a 24-yard heated pool; plenty of ocean-view hiking trails; a clubhouse with TV, couches, and video games; a natural redwood children's playground; and volleyball and basketball courts. Call a month in advance to reserve in summer.

WHERE TO DINE
SUPER-CHEAP EATS

Carmen's Place Restaurant & Gallery. 211 Crossroads Blvd., at Crossroads Shopping Center. ☎ **408/625-3030.** Lunch sandwiches and main courses $5.45–$10; dinner main courses $7–$15. MC, V. Daily 5am–3pm; Mon–Sat 5–8:30pm. ECLECTIC.

If you want a full meal and don't want to pay Carmel prices, head to this very casual restaurant at the Crossroads Shopping Center. Carmen's offers "Brazilian hospitality and European cooking," which in this case translates into an easily navigable menu of salads (Caesar for $4!), pastas, quesadillas, grilled salmon, lemon chicken (with pesto, pine nuts, and penne), and classic burgers and sandwiches for under $6. You can choose the light and airy inside or dine on the courtyard patio.

WORTH A SPLURGE

✪ **Rio Grill.** Crossroads Shopping Center, 101 Crossroads Blvd. ☎ **831/625-5436.** www.riogrill.com. Reservations recommended. Most main courses $10–$18. AE, DISC, MC, V. Sun–Thurs 11:30am–10pm; Fri–Sat 11:30am–11pm. From Calif. 1, take the Rio Rd. exit west for 1 block and turn right onto Crossroads Blvd. AMERICAN.

The food or the festive atmosphere (walls decorated with a cartoon mural of famous locals such as Clint Eastwood and the late Bing Crosby, playful sculpture, cacti, and other vibrant art) have kept this place popular with the locals for the past several years. The whimsical nature of the modern Santa Fe–style dining room belies the kitchen's serious preparations, which include homemade soups, barbecued baby back ribs from a wood-burning oven ($14), fresh fish from an open oak grill, and an awesome half chicken ($16). The restaurant's good selection of wines includes some rare Californian vintages and covers a broad price range. As usual in this town, dress is casual.

Robert Kincaid's Bistro on the Boulevard. In Crossroads Shopping Center, 217 Crossroads Blvd. ☎ **831/624-9626.** Reservations recommended for dinner. Fixed-price lunch $15; dinner main courses $18–$27. AE, DISC, MC, V. Mon–Fri 11:30am–2pm; daily 5:30–10pm. From Calif. 1, take the Rio Rd. exit west for 1 block and turn right onto Crossroads Blvd. FRENCH.

Unless you're prepared to break the bank, make a point of coming here for the killer three-course lunch deal. Chef/owner Robert Kincaid was at renowned Fresh Cream before he went solo and wowed locals with hard-to-beat ambiance and quality food, which you can experience for $15 during the price-fixed lunch. The three-courser goes something like this: Start with either a country sausage in a puff pastry or some other tantalizing treat, pick one of four main courses such as spicy blackened swordfish, then finish off with dessert). The decor—sophisticated country French with antiqued walls, dried flowers, and divided dining rooms—is cozy and romantic (especially if you grab a booth). There are no deals at dinner, only delightful offerings such as crab dumplings, award-winning crisp roast duck, roast rack of lamb with a mustard crust, and serious desserts that may almost be worth the $7 price tag.

7 The Big Sur Coast

3 miles S of Carmel-by-the-Sea; 123 miles S of San Francisco; 87 miles N of Hearst Castle

Big Sur is more than a drive along one of the most dramatic coastlines on earth or a peaceful evening amid a forest of towering California redwoods. It's a stretch of vast wilderness so overwhelmingly beautiful—especially when the fog glows in the moonlight—that it enchants all who walk its majestic paths. It's also home to a particular breed of nature lovers who prefer a rustic lifestyle over the rest of California's offerings. When the 1997 and 1998 El Niño storms caused landslides and major road damage, cutting the area off from civilization for months, reports from Big Sur were unusual: Some residents fled, vowing never to return; others were loving it even though their incomes were temporarily all but eliminated. The remaining residents rejoiced in the temporary solitude, while Post Ranch, the state's ultimate luxury getaway, shared the impromptu intimacy with deep-pocketed guests by flying them in via helicopter (for an extra fee, of course). Such is the price paid for living among the untamable California wilderness. Since the roads reopened, they're packed again, and driving through the region is painfully slow; rubber-neckers admire the view (drive at night and miss the whole point) and nervous Nellys inch around the cliffs and can't seem to help driving with their feet on the brakes.

Although there is an actual Big Sur Village approximately 25 miles south of Carmel, "Big Sur" refers to the entire 90-mile stretch of coastline between Carmel and San Simeon, blessed on one side by the majestic Santa Lucia Range and on the other by the rocky Pacific coastline. It's one of the most romantic and relaxing places on earth, and if you need respite from the rat race, we can recommend no better place to find it (although Yosemite, if you hike past the crowds, is equally rejuvenating).

Vacationing in Big Sur can be both exorbitantly expensive and remarkably cheap at the same time. Unless you're camping, you aren't going to find ultra-cheap lodgings here, and since there are only a handful of restaurants, there's little alternative to paying hand-over-fist for a romantic night out. However, the good news is that the only thing to do here is enjoy the land and sea, so once you've forked over a few bucks for a good book and some sunblock (if the fog's not looming), the majority of your time here won't cost you a dime.

ESSENTIALS

VISITOR INFORMATION   The **Monterey Peninsula Visitors and Convention Bureau,** 380 Alvarado St., Monterey (☎ **831/649-1770**), also has specialized information on places and events in Big Sur.

ORIENTATION   Most of this stretch is state park, and Calif. 1 runs its entire length, hugging the ocean the whole way. Restaurants, hotels, and sights are easy to spot—most are situated directly on the highway—but without major towns as reference points, their addresses can be obscure. For the purposes of orientation, we'll use the River Inn as our mileage guide. Located 29 miles south of Monterey on Calif. 1, the inn is generally considered to mark the northern end of Big Sur.

EXPLORING THE COAST

Big Sur offers visitors tranquillity and wild natural beauty—ideal for hiking, picnicking, camping, fishing, and beachcombing.

The first settlers arrived here only a century ago, and the present highway was built in 1937, making the area accessible. (Electricity arrived only in the 1950s, and it's still not available in the remote inland mountains.) Big Sur's mysterious, misty beauty has inspired several modern spiritual movements, the most famous being Esalen, the birthplace of the human potential movement. Even the tourist bureau bills the area as a place in which "to slow down . . . to meditate . . . to catch up with your soul." Take the board's advice and take your time—nothing better lies ahead.

The region affords a bounty of wilderness adventure opportunities. The inland ✪ **Ventana Wilderness,** which is maintained by the U.S. Forest Service, contains 167,323 acres straddling the Santa Lucia mountains and is characterized by steep-sided ridges separated by V-shaped valleys. The streams that cascade through the area are marked by waterfalls, deep pools, and thermal springs. The wilderness offers 237 miles of hiking trails that lead to 55 designated trail camps—a backpacker's paradise. One of the easiest trails to access is the **Pine Ridge Trail** at Big Sur station (☎ **831/ 667-2315**). However, if you go beyond the first few miles, you're likely to encounter obstacles on the path resulting from the 1998 storms.

From Carmel, the first stop along Calif. 1 is ✪ **Point Lobos State Reserve** (☎ **831/624-4909**), 3 miles south of Carmel. Sea lions, harbor seals, sea otters, and thousands of seabirds reside in this 456-acre reserve. You can see whales in season, too.

Trails follow the shoreline and lead to hidden coves. Note that parking is limited; on weekends especially, you need to arrive early to secure a place.

From here, cross the Soberanes Creek, passing **Garrapata State Park,** a 2,879-acre preserve with 4 miles of coastline. It's unmarked and undeveloped, though the trails are maintained. To explore them, you'll need to park at one of the turnouts on Calif. 1 near Soberanes Point and hike in.

Ten miles south of Carmel, you'll arrive at North Abalone Cove. From here, Palo Colorado Road leads back into the wilderness to the first of the Forest Service camping areas at **Bottchers Gap** ($10 to camp, $5 to park overnight).

Continuing south, you'll cross two dramatic bridges at Rocky Creek and Bixby Creek, which will bring you to the **Point Sur Lighthouse,** at the 18½-mile marker. The **Bixby Bridge,** 13 miles south of Carmel, towers nearly 260 feet above Bixby Creek Canyon. It offers canyon and ocean views and several observation alcoves at regular intervals along the bridge. The lighthouse, which sits 361 feet above the surf on a volcanic rock promontory, was built in 1887 and 1889, when only a horse trail provided access to this part of the world. Tours, which take 2 to 3 hours and involve a steep half-mile hike each way, are scheduled on most weekends. For information call ☎ **831/625-4419.** Admission is $5 for adults, $3 for youths 13 to 17, $2 for children 5 to 12, and free for kids 4 and under.

About 3 miles south of the lighthouse is **Andrew Molera State Park** (☎ **831/ 667-2315**), the largest state park on the Big Sur Coast at 4,800 acres. It's much less crowded than Pfeiffer–Big Sur (see below). Miles of trails meander through meadows and along beaches and bluffs. Hikers and cyclists use the primitive trail camp about a third of a mile from the parking area. **Molera Big Sur Trail Rides** (☎ **800/942-5486** or 831/625-5486) offers coastal trail rides for riders of all levels of experience; rates range from $25 for a 1-hour ride to $59 for a 2½-hour ride. The 2½-mile-long beach, which is sheltered from the wind by a bluff, is accessible via a mile-long path flanked in spring by wildflowers. You can walk the entire length of the beach at low tide; otherwise take the bluff trail above the beach. The park also has campgrounds.

Back on Calif. 1, you'll soon reach the village of Big Sur, where commercial services are available.

About 26 miles south of Carmel you'll come to **Big Sur Station** (☎ **831/ 667-2315**), where you can pick up maps and other information about the region. It's located a quarter mile past the entrance to **Pfeiffer–Big Sur State Park** (☎ **831/ 667-2315**), an 800-acre park that offers 218 camping sites along the Big Sur River, picnicking, fishing, and hiking. It's a scenic park of redwoods, conifers, oaks, and open meadows. For this reason it gets very crowded. The Lodge in the park has cabins with fireplaces and other facilities (see "Where to Stay," below). Sycamore Canyon Road (unmarked; it's the only public paved road west of Calif. 1 between the Big Sur post office and the state park entrance) will take you 2 miles to sandy ✪ **Pfeiffer Beach,** which has an arch-shaped rock formation just offshore. It's open for day use only and is the only beach accessible by car. Admission to the park is $5, and it's open daily from dawn to dusk.

Back on Calif. 1, the road travels 11 miles past Sea Lion Cove to Julia Pfeiffer Burns State Park. High above the ocean is the famous **Nepenthe** restaurant (see "Where to Dine," below), the retreat bought by Orson Welles for Rita Hayworth in 1944. A few miles farther south is the **Coast Gallery,** the premier local art gallery, which shows lithographs of works by Henry Miller. Miller fans will also want to stop at the **Henry Miller Memorial Library** (☎ **831/667-2574**) on Calif. 1, 30 miles south of Carmel and a quarter mile south of Nepenthe restaurant. The library displays and sells books and artwork by Miller and houses a permanent collection of first editions. It also serves as a community art center, hosting concerts, poetry readings, and art exhibitions. The rear gallery room is a video-viewing space where films about Henry Miller can be seen. There's a sculpture garden, plus tables on the adjacent lawn where visitors can rest and enjoy the surroundings. Admission is free, and it's open Tuesday through Sunday from 11am to 5pm.

Julia Pfeiffer Burns State Park (☎ **831/667-2315**) encompasses some of Big Sur's most spectacular coastline. To get a closer look, take the trail from the parking area at McWay Canyon, which leads under the highway to a bluff overlooking an 80-foot-high waterfall dropping directly into the ocean. It's less crowded here than at Pfeiffer–Big Sur, and there are miles of trails to explore in the 3,580-acre park. Scuba divers can apply for permits to explore the 1,680-acre underwater reserve.

From here, the road skirts the Ventana Wilderness, passing Anderson and Marble peaks and the Esalen Institute, before crossing the Big Creek Bridge to Lucia and several campgrounds farther south. **Kirk Creek Campground,** about 3 miles north of Pacific Valley, offers camping with ocean views and beach access. Beyond Pacific Valley, the ✪ **Sand Dollar Beach** picnic area is a good place to stop and enjoy the coastal view and take a stroll. A half-mile trail leads down to the sheltered beach, from which there's a fine view of Cone Peak, one of the coast's highest mountains. Two miles south of Sand Dollar is **Jade Cove,** a popular spot for rock hounds. From here, it's about another 27 miles past the Piedras Blancas Light Station to San Simeon.

WHERE TO STAY

Want to stay within your budget? Well, break out the tent and sleeping bag, because the only affordable walls surrounding you here will be the towering redwood trees around your campsite. But hey, if you're not into the wilderness, there's no real reason to be here anyway. So either drum up a few of your favorite campfire songs or dig deep into your pockets and pay premium prices for rustic accommodations. Whichever you choose, Big Sur is especially busy in summer, so make reservations well in advance.

CAMPING

If you plan to camp, be sure to stock up on food before you enter Big Sur. There are no supermarkets here (the closest is around 30 miles out) and small stores have limited supplies and high prices.

Big Sur Campground and Cabins. Calif. 1, 26 miles south of Carmel (half a mile south of the River Inn). ☎ 831/667-2322. 81 tent sites (30 with electricity and water hookup), 13 cabins (all with shower). $24 tent site for 2; $24 RV hookup, plus $3 extra for electricity and water; $45 tent cabin (bed, but no heat or plumbing); $82–$165 all-wood cabin for 2. Rates include entrance for car. MC, V. Pets $3 for tent site, $12 for tent cabin; pets not allowed in all-wood cabins. Open year-round.

The sites are cramped, so the feel is more like a camping village than an intimate retreat. However, it's very well maintained and perfect for families, who love the playground, river swimming, and inner-tube rentals. Each campsite has its own wood-burning fire pit, picnic table, and freshwater faucet within 25 feet of the pitching area. There are also RV water and electric hookups available. Facilities include bathhouses with hot showers, laundry facilities, an aged volleyball/basketball court, and a grocery store. The all-wood cabins are absolutely adorable, with stylish country furnishings, wood-burning ovens, patios, and full kitchens.

Fernwood. Calif. 1, 31 miles south of Carmel (2 miles south of the River Inn). ☎ 831/667-2422. 86 sites (39 with electricity). $24 double without electricity; $27 double with electricity. Additional person $3. RV hookup $27 for 2. Car entrance $5 extra. MC, V.

This campground on 23 woodland acres has 86 sites, each of which has running water and a fire pit. About half the sites overlook the river. The restaurant on the premises is open daily from 11:30am to 10pm and serves burgers, ribs, and other summer camp fare. An adjacent bar/cocktail lounge features live music on the weekends, and a grocery store sells wood, ice, beer, and other essentials.

Ventana Campground. Calif. 1, 28 miles south of Carmel (4¼ miles south of the River Inn). ☎ 831/667-2688. 75 sites. $25 tent site for 2 with 1 vehicle; $30 per night with a 3-night minimum holiday weekends. Additional person $5. Pets $5. Rates include entrance fee for your car. MC, V.

The entrance is adjacent to the entrance of the resort of the same name, but the comparison stops there. This is pure rusticity. The 75 campsites, on 40 acres of a redwood canyon, are set along a hillside and spaced well apart for privacy. Each is shaded by towering trees and has a picnic table and fire ring, but offers no electricity, RV hookups, or river access. There are, however, three bathhouses with hot showers (25¢ fee), which are conveniently located. To reserve a space, call and charge on a credit card (MasterCard or Visa) 1 night's deposit. You can also write a check for the deposit, mail it along with the dates you'd like to stay and a stamped, self-addressed envelope at least 2 weeks in advance (earlier during peak months).

FOR A FEW BUCKS MORE

Deetjen's Big Sur Inn. Calif. 1, Big Sur, CA 93920. ☎ **831/667-2377.** 20 units, 15 with bathroom. Sun–Thurs from $75 double without bathroom; from $100 double with bathroom. Fri–Sat from $85 double without bathroom; from $180 double with bathroom. MC, V.

Man, is this place cute. In the 1930s, before Calif. 1 was built, this homestead was an overnight stopping place on the coastal wagon road. It was begun by Norwegian homesteader Helmuth Deetjen, who over the years built several units constructed from hand-hewn logs and lumber. Folks either love or hate the accommodations, which are set in a redwood canyon. They're rustic, cozy, and adorable with their old-fashioned furnishings and down-home feel. But those who want extensive creature comforts should go elsewhere. Single-wall construction means that the rooms are far from soundproof, so children under 12 are allowed only if families reserve both rooms of a two-room building. There's no insulation, so prepare to crank up the fire or wood-burning stove.

The restaurant is a local favorite and consists of four intimate, English country-inn-style rooms lit by candlelight (see "Where to Dine," below).

MODERATELY PRICED OPTIONS

✪ **Big Sur Lodge.** In Pfeiffer–Big Sur State Park, Calif. 1 (P.O. Box 190), Big Sur, CA 93920. ☎ **800/424-4787** or 831/667-3100. Fax 831/667-3110. www.bigsurlodge. com. 61 cabins. $79–$139 cabin for 2; $99–$159 cabin with kitchen or fireplace; $109–$179 cabin with kitchen and fireplace. Rates include park entrance fees. AE, MC, V. From Carmel, take Calif. 1 south 26 miles.

A family-friendly place, the Big Sur Lodge—sheltered by towering redwoods, sycamores, and broad-leafed maples—is situated in the enormous state park. The rustic motel-style cabins are huge, with high peaked cedar- and redwood-beamed ceilings. They're clean and heated and have private bathrooms and reserved parking spaces. Some have fireplaces and/or kitchenettes (bring your own cooking utensils, though). All offer porches or decks with views of the redwoods or the Santa Lucia Range. Cabins 34 to 50 will put you in Siberia.

An advantage to staying here is that you're entitled to free use of all the facilities of the park, including hiking, barbecue pits, and picnic areas. In addition, the lodge has its own outdoor heated pool, gift shop, grocery stores, and laundry facilities.

The lodge dining room is open for breakfast, lunch, and dinner, but it doesn't have the ambiance of other nearby options. Evening menus feature fresh seafood, steaks, and pasta dishes.

WHERE TO DINE
MODERATELY PRICED OPTIONS

Big Sur River Inn. On Calif. 1. ☎ **831/667-2700.** Main courses $7.95–$12.25 lunch, $8.25–$20 dinner. AE, DC, DISC, MC, V. Daily 8am–9pm. CALIFORNIA/AMERICAN.

Popular with everyone from families to bikers, the River Inn is an unpretentious, rustic, down-home restaurant that's got something for all tastes. Trying to seat a small army? No problem. Want to watch sports on TV at a local bar? Pull up a stool. Looking to snag a few rays from a deck right beside the Big Sur River? Break out the suntan lotion. In winter, the wooden dining room is the prime spot; on summer days, some folks grab their patio chair and a cocktail and hang out literally midstream. Along with the local color, attractions include a full bar, good ol' American breakfasts (steak and eggs, omelets, pancakes, etc., plus espresso with most dishes for around $6), lunch (an array of salads, sandwiches, and baby back ribs, or fish-and-chips), and dinner (which features a few selections: fresh catch, pasta, burger, or ribs).

✪ **Café Kevah.** Calif. 1, 28 miles south of Carmel (5 miles south of the River Inn). ☎ **831/667-2344.** Main courses $5.75–$10.75. Daily 9am–3pm. AE, MC, V. SOUTH-WEST/CALIFORNIA.

Located one level below Nepenthe (see below), Café Kevah offers the same celestial view (at a fraction of the price), a more casual environment, and—depending on your taste—better food. Seating is entirely outdoors—a downside when the biting fog rolls in, but perfect on a clear day. You can order breakfast or lunch from the small shack of a kitchen, then grab an umbrella-shaded table, and enjoy the feast for your eyes and taste buds. Fare here is more eclectic than Nepenthe's, with such choices as homemade granola, pastries, baby greens with broiled salmon and papaya, chicken brochettes, omelets, and new potato hash. It ain't cheap, but innovative cuisine, the view, and a surprisingly decent mocha make it a worthwhile stopover. Don't forget to bring a coat.

WORTH A SPLURGE

Deetjen's Restaurant. On Calif. 1. ☎ **831/667-2377.** Reservations recommended. Main courses $7–$9.50 breakfast, $14.50–$24 dinner. MC, V. Mon–Sun 8am–noon; daily 6–8:30pm. AMERICAN.

With the feel of an English farmhouse, this cozy, country setting is the perfect venue for the delicious comfort food and friendly service that you'll find here. Mornings start off with a jump after a cup of the delicious and strong coffee, and breakfast offers all the basics: omelets, eggs Benedict, pancakes, and granola, most of which come piled high with breakfast potatoes. Dinner is highly regarded by locals, and might include lamb with au jus and twice-baked potato; grilled chicken with mushrooms and a garlic Marsala sauce; and roast duckling with brandy, peppercorn, and molasses sauce.

Nepenthe. Calif. 1, 28 miles south of Carmel (5 miles south of the River Inn). ☎ **831/667-2345.** Reservations accepted only for parties of 5 or more. Main courses $9–$25. AE, MC, V. Daily 11:30am–10pm. AMERICAN.

This is a must-stop for two reasons: The views are outrageous and the atmosphere rocks. Sitting 808 feet above sea level along the cliffs overlooking the ocean, Nepenthe is naturally celestial—especially when fog lingers above the water below. On a warm day, join the crowds on the terrace. On colder days, go the indoor route—the redwood-and-adobe structure offers a warmer and equally magical view, and with its big wood-burning fireplace, redwood ceilings, and large bay-front windows, the atmosphere is something you can't find anywhere else.

Unfortunately, that's not been our experience with the fare. We would scoff at a $10 burger (without fries!) and a $4 draft beer anywhere else—but we'd cough up the cash all over again for an afternoon here (think of it as nominal admission to dine at heights only angels usually enjoy). Lunch is adequate and basic: burgers, sandwiches, and salads. Dinner main courses include steak, broiled chicken, and fresh fish prepared any number of ways, though we suggest you come only for lunch and spend big dinner bucks elsewhere.

WHERE TO STOCK UP FOR A PICNIC

Can't stand another night of high-priced dining? Don't worry, there are plenty of little stores throughout Big Sur where you can pick up some goodies for a picnic. You'll pay a little more for your Pepperidge Farm cookies, baguette, salami, and cheese than you would at a supermarket, but you'll still save a fortune if you avoid dining out. Your best budget bet, however, is to stock up on edibles before you head to this neck of the woods.

Big Sur Deli. Calif. 1, 26½ miles south of Carmel. ☎ **831/667-2225.** Sandwiches $4. AE, DISC, MC, V. Daily 8am–8pm.

Sandwiches, a selection of pasta and chicken salad, rice, and other picnic necessities join basic grocery-store and gift-shop items here, at one of the cheaper stores around.

The Center Deli. Calif. 1, next to the Big Sur Post Office. ☎ **831/667-2225.** Sandwiches $2.50–$3.95. AE, DC, DISC, MC, V. Summer Sun–Thurs 7:30am–8pm; Fri–Sat 7:30am–9pm; winter hours vary.

Talk about one-stop shopping. This full-service deli not only sells fresh baked goods; a variety of salads, wine, and beer; and a slew of more substantial options (such as fet-tuccine, calzones, enchiladas, and barbecue chicken), it also rents videos and has a gro-cery store. Sandwiches are made to order, or you can grab a ready-made hoagie or vegetarian portobello mushroom on a roll. Treats and coffee drinks are available, as well. Everything from the deli is made on the premises.

8 Pinnacles National Monument

58 miles SE of Monterey

by Andrew Rice

Once a little-known outpost of the national park system, Pinnacles National Monu-ment has become one of the most popular weekend climbing destinations in central California over the past decade. The mild winter climate and plentiful routes make this a perfect off-season training ground for climbers (with the exception of 1997–1998's El Niño winter, which hit the area hard). It's also a popular haven for campers, hikers, and nature lovers. One of the unique chaparral ecosystems in the world supports a large community of plant and animal life here, including one of California's largest breeding populations of raptors.

The Pinnacles themselves—hundreds of towering crags, spires, and hoodoos—are seemingly out of place in the voluptuously rolling hills of the coast range. And they are, in fact, out of place, part of the eroded remains of a volcano formed 23 million years ago 195 miles south in the middle of the Mojave Desert. The volcano was car-ried here by the movement of the San Andreas Fault, which runs just east of the park (the other half of the volcano remains in the Mojave).

You could spend days here without getting bored, but it's possible to cover the most interesting features in a weekend. With a single hike you can go from the lush oak woodland around the Bear Gulch Visitor Center to the dry and desolate crags of the high peaks, then back down through a half-mile-long cave complete with under-ground waterfalls.

JUST THE FACTS

ACCESS POINTS   Two entrances lead to the park. The **West Entrance** from Soledad and U.S. 101 is a dry, dusty, winding single-lane road (not suitable for trailers) with the best drive-up view of the park. It doesn't connect with the east side.

The alternative route is via the **East Entrance.** Unless you're coming from nearby, take the longer drive on Calif. 25 to enter through the east. Because most of the peaks of the Pinnacles face east and the watershed drains east, most of the interesting hikes and geologic features are on this side. No road crosses the park.

FEES   Park entrance fees, which are good for 7 days, are $2 per person or $5 per car.

VISITOR CENTER   The first place you should go upon entering the park from the east is the **Bear Gulch Visitor Center** (☎ 831/389-4485). This small center is rich with exhibits about the park's history, wildlife, and geology, and also has a great selection of nature handbooks and climbing guides for the Pinnacles. Climbers should check with rangers about closures and other information before heading out: Many routes are closed during hawk- and falcon-nesting season, and rangers like to know how many climbers are in the park.

Adjacent to the visitor center, the Bear Gulch picnic ground is a great place to fuel up before setting out on a hike or, if you're not planning on leaving your car, one of the best places to gaze up at dramatic spires of the high peaks (the ultimate spot is from the west side).

REGULATIONS & WARNINGS   Beware of poison oak, particularly in Bear Gulch. Rattlesnakes are common throughout the park but rarely seen. Bikes and dogs are prohibited on all trails, and no backcountry camping is allowed anywhere in the park.

Hiking through this variety of landscapes demands versatility. Come prepared with a good pair of hiking shoes, snacks, lots of water, and a flashlight.

Daytime temperatures often exceed 100°F in summer, so the best time of year to visit is spring, when the wildflowers are blooming, followed by fall. Crowds are common during spring weekends.

HIKING/SEEING THE HIGHLIGHTS

To see most of the park in a single, moderately strenuous morning, take the **Condor Gulch Trail** from the visitor center. As you climb quickly out of the parking area, the Pinnacles' wind-sculpted spires seem to grow taller. In less than 2 miles you're among them, and Condor Gulch intersects with the **High Peaks Trail.** The view from the top spans miles: the Salinas Valley to your west, the Pinnacles below, and miles of coast to the east. After traversing the high peaks (including stretches of footholds carved in steep rock faces) for about a mile, the trail drops back toward the visitor center via a valley filled with eerie-looking hoodoos.

In another 1½ miles, you'll reach the reservoir marking the top of **Bear Gulch Cave** (which closes occasionally: in 1998 both due to storm damage and to accommodate migrating townsend bats, who in the past 2 years have come here to have their babies). It's usually open, but if you want to explore you'll need your own flashlight and you might get wet, but this .6-mile-long talus cave is a thrill. From the end of the cave you're just a short walk (through the most popular climbing area of the park) away from the visitor center. It's also possible to hike just Bear Gulch and the cave, then return via the **Moses Spring Trail.** It's about 2 miles round-trip, but you'll miss the view from the top.

If you're coming from the west entrance, the **Juniper Canyon Trail** is a short (1.2 miles), but very steep, blast to the top of the high peaks. You'll definitely earn the view. Otherwise, try the short **Balconies Trail** to the monument's other talus cave, **Balconies Cave.** Flashlights are required here, too.

CAMPING

The park's campground on the west side was demolished by El Niño storms in 1997 and 1998 and is not scheduled for repair. Now the only campground is the privately run **Pinnacles Campground, Inc.,** on the east side (☎ 831/389-4462; $6 per person). It's just outside the park (off Calif. 25, 32 miles south of Hollister) and offers lots of privacy and space between sites, plus showers, a store, and a pool. It's close enough so you can hike into the park from the campground, though it will add a few miles to your outing. Though private campgrounds are often overdeveloped, the management here saw the benefits of leaving the surroundings natural. Dogs are not recommended, but you can bring them for $10 extra per night. *Note:* No animals are allowed at Pinnacles.

The Central Coast 12

by Erika Lenkert and Matthew R. Poole

California's Central Coast—a spectacular amalgam of beaches, lakes, and mountains—is the state's most diverse region. The narrow strip of coast that runs for more than 100 miles from San Simeon to Ventura spans several climate zones and is home to an eclectic mixture of students, middle-class families, retirees, farmers, wineries, computer techies, and fishermen. The ride along Calif. 1 (usually known around these parts as Highway 1), which follows the ocean cliffs, is almost always packed with rental cars, recreational vehicles, and bicyclists. Traffic may give your brakes a workout, but it also allows you to take longer looks at one of the most spectacular vistas in the world.

Whether you're driving from Los Angeles or San Francisco, Calif. 1 is the most scenic, leisurely, and popular tourist route (U.S. 101 gets you there faster, but is less picturesque). It's this drive that reminds Californians why they're thrilled to live in the state—each and every time they make the trip.

Equally thrilling to the budget traveler is that whether you're headed out of Los Angeles or south from Carmel-by-the-Sea, the Central Coast is one of the most affordable seaside tourist destinations in the entire state. But there is a catch (or two). The ocean's too cold for swimming, there are fewer expansive beaches than there are to the north or the south, and the atmosphere in these parts is more laid-back California country living (read: slow). Additionally, the climate's generally cooler than southern California. Still, this shoreline makes this the best route for traveling north or south in the state, and the seemingly untainted country towns are quaint and hospitable, giving you plenty of reasons to break out the ol' camera and play *touristus maximus*.

1 San Simeon: Hearst Castle

205 miles S of San Francisco (via Calif. 1); 94 miles S of Monterey (via Calif. 1); 9 miles N of Cambria; 254 miles NW of Los Angeles

If you continue south along the rugged cliffs beyond Big Sur, you'll wind your way to calmer shores and the more populated area of San Simeon and Cambria. But even after you've left the mountains behind you, the terrain is still predominantly natural, except, that is, for what's got to be the ultimate fabrication in the entire state: Hearst Castle.

Few places on earth compare to Hearst Castle. This 165-room estate of publishing magnate William Randolph Hearst, situated high above the coastal village of San Simeon atop a hill he called *La Cuesta Encantada* ("the Enchanted Hill"), is an ego trip par excellence. One of the last great estates of America's Gilded Age, it's an astounding, completely over-the-top monument to wealth and to the power that money brings with it.

Hearst Castle is a sprawling compound of structures, constructed over 28 years in a Mediterranean Revival architectural style, set in undeniably magical surroundings. The focal point of the estate is the you-have-to-see-it-to-believe-it **Casa Grande,** a 100-plus-room mansion brimming with priceless art and antiques. Hearst bought the majority of his vast European Collection via New York auction houses, where he bought entire rooms (including walls, ceilings, and floors) and shipped them here. The result is an old-world castle done in a priceless mix-and-match style. You'll see fantastic 400-year-old Spanish and Italian ceilings, enormous 500-year-old fireplace mantels, 16th-century Florentine bedsteads, Renaissance paintings, Flemish tapestries, and innumerable other treasures. And then there are the swimming pools: The Roman-inspired indoor pool has intricate mosaic work, Carrara marble replicas of Greek gods and goddesses, and alabaster globe lamps that create the illusion of moonlight. The breathtaking outdoor Greco-Roman Neptune pool, flanked by marble colonnades that frame the distant sea, is one of the mansion's most memorable features.

In 1957, in exchange for a massive tax write-off, the Hearst Corporation donated the estate to the state of California (while retaining ownership of approximately 80,000 acres); the California Department of Parks and Recreation now administers it as a State Historic Monument.

TOURING THE ESTATE

✪ **Hearst Castle** can be visited only by guided tour. Four distinct daytime tours are offered on a daily basis, each lasting almost 2 hours.

Tour 1 is usually recommended for first-time visitors and is the first to get booked up. In addition to the swimming pools, this tour visits several rooms on the ground floor of the main house (Casa Grande), including Hearst's private theater where you'll see some home movies taken during the castle's heyday. A formal esplanade and gardens feature sculptures and flowers, and you'll also get to see the largest guest house, Casa del Sol.

Tour 2 focuses on Casa Grande's upper floors, including Hearst's opulent library, private suite of rooms, and lots of fabulous bathrooms. Ongoing efforts are made to lend a lived-in look to the house; examples are the lifelike food displayed in the kitchen and pantry, and vintage sewing equipment in Marion Davies's suite. Although Tour 1 is commonly recommended for first-timers, Tour 2 is a perfectly fine choice if you're only planning to take one, particularly if your interest lies more in the home's private areas.

Tour 3 delves into the complex construction and subsequent alterations of Hearst Castle. You'll visit Casa del Monte, a guest house unaltered from its original design, then head to the North Wing of Casa Grande, the last portion of the property to be completed, to contrast the different styles. A video called *The Building of a Dream,* which uses film and photographs from the 1920s and 1930s to go behind the scenes of the construction process, is shown on this tour. Tour 3 is especially fascinating for architecture buffs and detail hounds, but shouldn't be the first and only tour you take if you've never visited the castle before.

Tour 4 is dedicated to the estate's gardens, terraces, and walkways, and is only offered from April through October. You'll also tour the Casa del Mar guest house, the wine cellar of Casa Grande, and the colorful dressing rooms at the Neptune Pool. Like Tour 3, this one is best taken after you've seen some of the more essential areas of the estate.

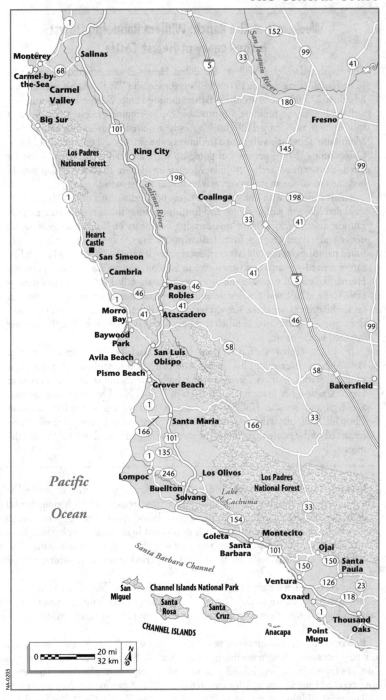

The Central Coast

Weekends at the Ranch: William Randolph Hearst & the Legacy of Hearst Castle

The lavish palace that William Randolph Hearst always referred to simply as "The Ranch" took root in 1919. William Randolph ("W. R." to his friends) had inherited 275,000 acres from his father, mining baron George Hearst, and was well on his way to building a formidable media empire. He often escaped to a spot known as "Camp Hill" on his newly acquired lands in the Santa Lucia Mountains above the village of San Simeon, the site of boyhood family outings. Complaining that "I get tired of going up there and camping in tents," Hearst hired Paris-trained architect Julia Morgan to design the retreat that would become one of the most famous private homes in the world.

An art collector with indiscriminate taste and inexhaustible funds, Hearst overwhelmed Morgan with interiors and furnishings from the ancestral collections of Europe. Each week, railroad cars carrying fragments of Roman temples, lavish doors and carved ceilings from Italian monasteries, Flemish tapestries, hastily rolled paintings by the Old Masters, ancient Persian rugs, and antique French furniture arrived—5 tons at a time—in San Simeon. *Citizen Kane,* which depicts a Hearst-like mogul with a similarly excessive estate called Xanadu, has a memorable scene of hoarded priceless treasures warehoused in dusty piles, stretching as far as the eye can see. Like Kane, Hearst, once described as a man with an "edifice complex," purchased so much that only a fraction of what he bought was ever installed in the estate.

In 1925, Hearst separated from his wife and began to spend time in Los Angeles overseeing his movie company, Cosmopolitan Pictures. His principal starlet, Marion Davies, became his constant companion and hostess at Hearst Castle—her main role for the rest of W. R.'s life. The ranch soon became a playground for the Hollywood crowd as well as dignitaries like Winston Churchill and playwright George Bernard Shaw, who is said to have wryly remarked of the estate that "this is the way God would have done it if He had the money."

Evening Tours are held most Friday and Saturday nights during spring and fall. These last about 30 minutes longer than the daytime tours, and visit highlights of the main house, the largest and most elaborate guest house, and the estate's pools and gardens, which are illuminated by hundreds of restored light fixtures. The pools, in particular, are most breathtaking when you see them this way. The entire living-history experience is enhanced by docents dressed in period costume assuming a variety of roles.

Tours are conducted daily beginning at 8:20am, except on New Year's Day, Thanksgiving Day, and Christmas Day. Two to six tours leave every hour, depending on the season. Allow 2 hours between starting times if you plan on taking more than one tour.

Reservations are recommended and can be made up to 8 weeks in advance. Tickets can be purchased by telephone through **Park Net** (☎ **800/444-7275**). Daytime tours cost $14 for adults, $8 for children 6 to 12, and free for children under 6. The evening tour costs $25 for adults, $13 for children 6 to 12, and free for children under 6.

The latest addition to the estate is the giant-screen **Hearst Castle National Geographic Theatre,** which you can visit regardless of whether you take a tour. Films include *Hearst Castle: Building the Dream,* a movie about Hearst, his castle, and—you

Despite its opulence, Hearst promoted "The Ranch" as a casual weekend home. He regularly laid the massive refectory table in the dining room with paper napkins and bottled ketchup and pickles to invoke a rustic, camplike atmosphere. Folklore has it that the only formal dinner held here was in honor of Calvin Coolidge. In Hearst's beautiful library, his priceless collection of ancient Greek pottery—one of the greatest collections of its kind in the world—is arranged casually among the rare volumes, like knickknacks.

The Hollywood crowd would take Hearst's private railway car from Los Angeles to San Luis Obispo, where a fleet of limousines waited to transport them to San Simeon. Those who didn't come by train were treated to a flight on Hearst's private plane from the Burbank Airport (MGM head Irving Thalberg and wife Norma Shearer preferred this mode of transportation). Hearst, an avid aviator, had a sizable landing strip built; Charles Lindbergh used it when he flew up for a visit in the summer of 1928.

Oh, if the walls could talk. Atop one of the castle's looming towers are the hexagonal Celestial Suites. One was a favorite of Clark Gable and Carole Lombard, who would be startled out of their romantic slumber by the clamor of 18 carillon bells directly overhead. David Niven, a frequent guest, was one of the unknown number who defied teetotaler Hearst's edict against liquor in private rooms. Niven was called upon more than once to explain the several "empties" under the bed (which Cardinal Richelieu once owned and slept in) in his customary suite.

W. R. and Marion Davies hosted frequent costume parties at the ranch, which were as intricately planned as a movie production. The most legendary, the Circus Party, was held to celebrate W. R.'s 75th birthday on April 29, 1938. Much of Hollywood attended to honor the tycoon, including grand dame Bette Davis—dressed as a bearded lady.

—*Stephanie Avnet Yates*

guessed it—his dreams. There are also additional movies shown, so call ☎ **805/ 927-6811** or visit their Web site at www.ngthe.com for current information. The Hearst film shows hourly at half past the hour, and tickets cost $6 for adults and $4 for children 12 and under.

GETTING THERE & GETTING AROUND   Hearst Castle is located directly on Calif. 1, about 42 miles north of San Luis Obispo and 94 miles south of Monterey. From San Francisco or Monterey, take U.S. 101 south to Paso Robles, then Calif. 46 west to Calif. 1, and Calif. 1 north to the castle. From Los Angeles, take U.S. 101 north to San Luis Obispo, then Calif. 1 north to the castle. Park in the visitor-center parking lot; a bus will take you the 5 miles up the hill to the estate. The movie theater and visitor center are adjoining the parking lot and are easily accessible without heading up to the actual estate.

A NEARBY TOWN WORTH A STOP: CAMBRIA

After driving from either Big Sur or along Highway 101 without passing anything but lush green hills and nature at its most glorious (especially from Calif. 46 off U.S. 101), it's a quaint surprise to roll into the adorable coastal minitown of Cambria just inland of San Simeon. Cambria, originally known as an artist colony, is so charming that the

Hearst Castle Touring Tip

Because these are walking tours, be sure to wear comfortable shoes—you'll be walking about a half mile per tour, which includes between 150 and 400 steps to climb or descend. (Wheelchair tours are available by calling ☎ **805/927-2020** at least 10 days in advance.)

town itself is reason enough to make the drive. With little more than 3 blocks worth of boutiques, restaurants, and a handful of B&Bs, Cambria is the perfect place to escape the everyday, enjoy the endless expanses of pristine coastal terrain, and meander through little shops selling local artwork.

Gray whales pass through the area from late December to early February, and for the past few years hundreds of **elephant seals** have made the shore just north of the Hearst Castle entrance their year-round playground—much to the delight of locals and nature enthusiasts. There is a parking lot, and docents are usually on-hand to answer questions. Regardless, keep your distance from these mammoth mammals: They're a protected species and can be dangerous if molested. The beaches and coves are also wonderful places for humans to frolic as well. For more information on Cambria, check out **www.cambria-online.com**.

Aside from eating and lounging, the most popular pastime in Cambria is browsing the **boutique shops.** If you're on a serious budget, you probably won't want to make many purchases here. But window-shopping is a free and mellow pursuit. In the West Village is **Maison de Marie** (768 Main St.; ☎ **805/927-7234**), which offers one-stop shopping for French imports ranging from Provincial fabric to herbs d' Provence. Another good stop is **Home Arts** (707 Main St.; ☎ **805/927-2781**), which has an eclectic mix of furnishings and gifts. After blocks of antique shops and country collectibles, this place renews your faith that someone hip might actually live in Cambria. In the East Village is **Seekers Collection and Gallery** (4090 Burton Dr.; ☎ **800/841-5250** or 805/927-4352), which has one of the finest collections of museum-quality art glass to be found anywhere. Seekers represents more than 200 leading artists from the American art-glass movement. You can also visit their virtual gallery online at www.seekersglass.com. ☉ **Heart's Ease,** 4101 Burton Dr. (☎ **800/266-4372** or 805/927-5224), is located inside a quaint historic cottage and is packed with an abundance of garden delights, apothecary herbs, and custom blended potpourris.

WHERE TO STAY
CAMPING

San Simeon Creek Campgrounds/Washburn Campgrounds. 750 Hearst Castle Rd., San Simeon, CA 93452 (Attn: campground). Calif. 1, 2 miles north of Cambria. ☎ **805/927-2035** for information, or call **Park Net** (☎ **800/444-7275**) for reservations. San Simeon Creek has 132 sites, Washburn 70 sites. San Simeon sites up to $18 (high season); Washburn sites up to $11 (high season). MC, V.

Not far from the beach are more than 200 of California State Parks' camping sites in two open areas (read: not wooded). The San Simeon Creek grounds are "developed" with coin-op showers (25¢ for 3 min.); they're also closer to the beach and a little more sheltered than the Washburn Campgrounds. Washburn has chemical flush toilets and no showers, but does offer a good view of the ocean and hills. There's about a mile between the two campgrounds. Sites can be reserved from 1 day up to 7 months in advance through Park Net.

SUPER-CHEAP SLEEPS

Cambria Palms Motel. 2662 Main St., Cambria, CA 93428. ☎ **805/927-4485.** 18 units. TV. $30–$62 double. AE, DISC, MC, V.

When heading into Cambria, you'll know you've arrived at this motel when you see the British flag and a sign reading BEST DEAL IN TOWN—and indeed it is, depending on your idea of a deal. You'll be paying substantially less to stay here than anywhere else in the vicinity, but saving $20 means you're a few blocks outside of the nook of shops and B&Bs that constitutes the center of town. You'll be subjected to downright tacky decor (vinyl-covered lamps, old lackluster desks), and there are no phones in the rooms. A queen- or king-size bed will cost extra, as do any of the four rooms with kitchenettes ($5 to $8 more). Some rooms have TV and/or coolers, and all have coffeemakers. Ask for a room with a creek-side and pasture view—it will help divert your attention from your boring room.

Cambria Pines Lodge. 2905 Burton Dr., Cambria, CA 93428. ☎ **800/445-6868** or 805/927-4200. Fax 805/927-4016. 125 units. $65–$120 cabin or suite. Rates include buffet breakfast. AE, CB, DC, DISC, MC, V.

On a mountain just above town on 25 acres of mostly landscaped grounds dotted with Monterey pines, this lodge offers a variety of accommodations, of which the rustic cabins are most appealing for the budget traveler. The nine oldest cabins are the most charming of all the selections as well as the cheapest at $65 per night. The bathrooms are small and have showers, but no tubs. Amenities increase with the price of the room; $20 extra and you can get a cabin with a fireplace or a kitchenette. The main lodge is where the full complimentary buffet breakfast and reasonably priced dinner are served. Other communal benefits include an indoor pool, spa, sauna, and nature trails.

FOR A FEW BUCKS MORE

Creekside Inn. 2618 Main St., Cambria, CA 93428. ☎ **800/269-5212** or 805/927-4021. 21 units. $45–$85 double. Extra person $5. DISC, MC, V.

Of the bare-bones accommodation choices in the area, Creekside's newer rooms are one of the safest bets. The motel style and decor aren't nearly as charming as many of the authentic inns in the neighborhood, but ask for a room that faces the hills and has a small deck, and you're liable to forget all about the concrete promenade out front.

San Simeon Pines. Moonstone Beach Dr. and Calif. 1 (no street address), P.O. Box 117, San Simeon, CA 93452. ☎ 805/927-4648. 58 units, all with bathroom (33 with showers only). TV TEL. $74–$98 double. Rates include continental breakfast. AE, MC, V.

This 8-acre mini "resort" near Moonstone Beach is a cute, rustic-contemporary alternative to a generic motel and appeals especially to families. Rooms are arranged in clusters and vary from a standard motel variety to a cottage-style unit with a fireplace. Most considerate are the separate adult and family sections; that way kidless travelers aren't subjected to screaming babes, and families have easy access to the children's play area and solar-heated pool. Unfortunately, trees block any ocean scenery here. The property has a par-3 golf course and trail leading to Moonstone Beach and San Simeon Beach State Park (good otter and whale spotting). Complimentary coffee and continental breakfast are served in the lobby.

MODERATELY PRICED OPTIONS

Best Western Cavalier Oceanfront Resort. 9415 Hearst Dr. (Calif. 1), San Simeon, CA 93452. ☎ **800/826-8168** or 805/927-4688. Fax 805/927-6472. 90 units. TV TEL. $74–$185 double. AE, CB, DC, DISC, MC, V.

"Oceanfront" and "budget" are generally a contradiction, but this family-friendly hotel offers the best of both. Aside from the basics, the rooms are all outfitted with VCRs (video rentals are available next door), refrigerators, computer jacks, and hair dryers; some even have fireplaces. Other bonuses include two outdoor heated pools, an exercise room, two restaurants, a launderette, a shopping center, video arcade, and three oceanfront fire pits lit daily by the resort. This also happens to be the only true "oceanfront" resort in the area.

WORTH A SPLURGE

✪ **Olallieberry Inn.** 2476 Main St., Cambria, CA 93428. ☎ **888/927-3222** or 805/927-3222. Fax 805/927-0202. www.olallieberry.com. 8 units. $90–$150 double; $175 cottage suite. Rates include full breakfast and evening wine and hors d'oeuvres. MC, V.

This 1873 Greek Revival house is our favorite B&B in the area. The grounds are perfectly manicured but whimsically blooming, in the afternoon wafts of baked brie and homemade bread served during wine hour blows through the main house, and the staff does everything imaginable to make your stay special. They have a passion for cooking and gardening, but the decor doesn't fall by the wayside: Victorian floral-and-lace reigns, and the guest rooms are lovingly and individually appointed. Each has its own private bathroom, although some are across or down the hall. Rooms in a newer adjoining building overlook a creek; they're remarkably charming and have a fireplace and private deck. The delicious full breakfast—accompanied by olallieberry jam, of course—is gourmet all the way.

WHERE TO DINE
SUPER-CHEAP EATS

JBJ Round-up Pizza N Grub. 815 Main St. (in the West Village), Cambria. ☎ **805/927-4115.** Sandwiches and grub $4.95–$6.95; pizza $4.15–$22.70. MC, V. Mon–Fri 9:30am–9pm; Fri–Sat 9:30am–10pm; extended hours during summer. Delivery available after 5pm. AMERICAN.

The exterior may look like your average pizza joint, but this is actually a virtual gold mine of budget grub. Saunter on in and saddle yourself a chair amidst the over-the-top Western decor (their tables are branded JBJ and there's a covered-wagon buffet area if that gives you any idea). Read the menu and hear your wallet yell "Yee ha!"; nothin' on the menu is over $7, except for pizzas, which you can lasso for anywhere from $4.15 (8-in. nibbler) to $22.70 (16-in. jumbo with fancy toppings). That's right, partner: appetizers like buffalo wings ($5.50), potato skins ($4.95), and zucchini wedges ($3.95); a herd of sandwiches such as home-roasted turkey or roast beef, which come with ortega chili strips and sharp cheddar piled high on French rolls for $5.95; a trip to the salad bar for under $5; half a rotisserie chicken with all the fixin's for $6.95; and a Kids Corner menu with $3.50 selections. Don't pass up the cinnamon rolls; served hot in the morning with coffee, this is a key traveler's breakfast. The day-old rolls comprise a darn good bread pudding, which comes with homemade caramel sauce and is topped with whipped cream.

Soto's Market and Deli. 2244 Main St. ☎ **805/927-4411.** Sandwiches $3.95. DISC, MC, V. DELI. Mon–Thurs 7am–8pm; Fri–Sat 7am–9pm; Sun 8am–6pm.

When the sun is shining down on the mountainous coast of Cambria, there's no better way to "do lunch" than to grab a picnic and head for the hills (or the ocean). This small-town supermarket's deli will help you fill your basket with made-to-order sandwiches for $3.95, meat loaf, and a good selection of cheeses and salads. They're also knowledgeable about local wines and can tell you how to get to a scenic luncheon spot.

MODERATELY PRICED OPTIONS

Bistro Sole. 1980 Main St., Cambria. ☎ **805-927-0887.** Reservations recommended. Main courses $7–$10 at lunch, $8–$18 at dinner. MC, V. Daily 11am–10pm. ECLECTIC.

"Quaint" is the best word to describe Cambria, and the same goes for this restaurant located in an old house in the town's east village. The cozy California bungalow and the tree-filled back garden are the ideal settings for to-die-for oysters Rockefeller, tasty wontons with baked yam and goat cheese, lobster bisque, one of five lovely salads, and a selection of Italian-influenced dinner main courses. When we dined here, the nut-crusted pork loin was a bit dry, but the filet mignon was on the money. The 20 or so main courses include a handful of pastas (chicken artichoke linguini and cannelloni, for example) balanced with a selection of chicken and seafood dishes. Lunch heads south of the border with enchiladas, fish tacos, chicken mole, and a selection of gourmet sandwiches. This is one of the most contemporary places to eat in town—in both decor and cuisine.

Robin's. 4095 Burton Dr., Cambria. ☎ **805/927-5007.** www.robinsrestaurant.com. Reservations recommended. Main courses $9–$17. MC, V. Daily 11am–9pm. ECLECTIC.

Robin's is a restaurant with something for everyone, from exotic dishes from Mexico, Thailand, India (try the fragrant Tandoori prawns and vegetables), and beyond to more straightforward preparations like a tasty salad or juicy steak and an array of vegetarian dishes. Offerings include a salmon-bisque appetizer; porcini raviolis with roasted-pepper/cream sauce, fresh spinach, basil, and Parmesan; and other flavorful combinations such as Thai prawns in green curry with basmati brown rice, fruit chutney, and chapati. Don't miss dessert—try the tiramisu or vanilla-custard bread pudding.

WORTH A SPLURGE

✪ **McPhee's Grill.** 416 Main St., Templeton. ☎ **805/434-3204.** Reservations recommended. Main courses $6–$12 at lunch, $12–$24 at dinner; brunch $12.95 adults, $5.95 kids under 10. MC, V. Daily 11:30am–2pm and 5–9pm. CALIFORNIA GRILL.

When Ian McPhee left Ian's restaurant (Cambria) and launched this one, it didn't take long for word to get out: McPhee's is worth the 15-minute drive to the historic town of Templeton. This converted old saloon has contemporary country decor and an open kitchen and indoor and outdoor dining. The half-dozen appetizers include such options as duck quesadilla, artichoke fritters, and a zingy greens-and-grapefruit salad with Maytag bleu cheese and spiced nuts. Gourmet pizza, pasta, an amazing macadamia-crusted salmon, and four varieties of tender, juicy steaks cooked to perfection round out the Americana-with-a-twist-style menu. Especially impressive are the prices; it's rare that a restaurant "Dedicated to great food & great service" offers the majority of their dishes for under $16; it's the steaks and rack of lamb that hover closer to $20. The menu is accompanied by a fine selection of local wines. There's a champagne buffet brunch on Sunday. This is one of the very best restaurants in the region.

2 Morro Bay

235 miles S of San Francisco (via Hwy. 1); 124 miles S of Monterey; 100 miles N of Santa Barbara; 220 miles N of Los Angeles

Morro Bay is separated from the ocean by a long peninsula of towering sand dunes. It's best known for dramatic Morro Rock, an enormous egg-shaped monolith that juts out of the water just offshore. Part of a chain of long-extinct volcanoes, the huge domed rock is a winter and fall sanctuary for thousands of migrating birds, including cormorants, pelicans, sandpipers, and the rare peregrine falcon.

But other than gawking at the amazing "Gibraltar of the Pacific," there's little reason to visit the town itself. The motel strip and the horrific, gigantic, absurdly placed oceanfront electrical plant (directly blocking the view of the rock) mar the appeal. If you do stay for more than a quick stop to snap a few photos, you'll find a touristy and unimpressive bay-front strip of stores and the pathetic **Morro Bay Aquarium** (☎ 805/772-7647), which makes you want to free the seals and fish jailed within it. (It's only redeeming quality is that it takes injured and abandoned sea otters and seals and nurses them back to health, eventually releasing the recovered animals back into the sea; open daily from 9am to 6pm in summer and to 5pm in winter.) The town's saving grace is its natural surroundings; the beaches and wildlife sanctuaries can be quite peaceful and wondrous.

The **Morro Bay Chamber of Commerce,** 880 Main St., Morro Bay, CA 93442 (☎ **800/231-0592** or 805/772-4467), offers armfuls of area information. It's open Monday through Friday from 8:30am to 5pm and on Saturday from 10am to 3pm.

EXPLORING THE AREA

Most visitors come to Morro Bay to ogle **Morro Rock,** the much-photographed Central Coast icon known as the "Gibraltar of the Pacific." It's definitely worth a gander (actually you couldn't miss it if you wanted to) and a few snapshots, but there's more to do in the area beyond this morro, or miniature volcanic peak.

BEACHES   Popular **Atascadero State Beach,** just north of Morro Rock, has gentle waves and lovely views. Rest rooms, showers, and dressing rooms are available. Just north of Atascadero is **Morro Strand State Beach,** a long, sandy stretch with normally gentle surf. Rest rooms and picnic tables are available here. Morro Strand has its own campgrounds; for information, call ☎ 805/772-2560, or reserve a spot through **Park Net** (☎ 800/444-7275).

NEARBY STATE PARKS   Cabrillo Peak, a morro located in the lovely **Morro Bay State Park** (☎ 805/772-7434), makes for a terrific day hike and offers fantastic 360° views from its summit. There is a faint zigzagging trail, but the best way to reach the top is by bushwhacking straight up the gentle slope—a hike that takes about 2 hours round-trip. To reach the trailhead, take Calif. 1 south and turn left at the Morro Bay State Park/Montana de Oro State Park exit. Follow South Bay Boulevard for ¾ mile, then take the left fork another ½ mile to the dirt parking lot, located on your left. This park also has a campground (reserve through **Park Net** at ☎ 800/444-7275) and a decent public **golf course** (green fees $22 to $28; reserve a tee-time by calling ☎ 805/782-8060).

Montana de Oro State Park ("Mountain of Gold") is fondly known as "petite Big Sur" because of its stony cliffs and rugged terrain. There's great swimming at Spooner's Cove (warm enough, perhaps, only to those visiting from the North Pole) and lots of easy hiking trails here, including a number that lead to spectacular coastal vistas or hidden forest streams. The Hazard Reef trail will take you up on the Morro Bay Sandspit dunes. The park's campground is in the trees, across from the beach. For information, call the park rangers at ☎ 805/528-0513 or 805/772-7434, or reserve a spot through **Park Net** (☎ 800/444-7275).

You can escape being landlocked by renting a kayak through Kayak Horizons (☎ 805/772-6444), which is located at 551 Embarcadero at the end of Marina Street in Morro Bay. Rentals range from $8 to $35 depending on the kind of boat you want and length of time you use it.

WHERE TO STAY

Ascot Inn. 845 Morro Ave. (at Morro Bay Blvd.), Morro Bay, CA 93442. ☎ **800/887-6454** or 805/772-4437. Fax 805/772-8860. www.ascotinn.com. 57 units. TV TEL. $38–$95 double; $85–$295 suite. Rates include continental breakfast. AE, MC, V. From Calif. 1, take Morro Bay Blvd. exit and head straight for the water.

There's no beach out front, but this hotel has a close-up view of looming Morro Rock and a key location (you can walk down the steps to the waterfront Embarcadero). The clean and newly remodeled rooms with English country decor and complimentary continental breakfast make this place a good value. Perks include direct-dial phones, coffee and tea, and HBO in each room. The hotel recently constructed a brand new building across the street that harbors 34 suites complete with minibars, fireplaces, Jacuzzis, VCRs, refrigerators, and microwaves.

Baywood Bed & Breakfast Inn. 1370 Second St., Baywood Park, CA 93042. ☎ **805/528-8888.** Fax 805/528-8887. www.baywoodinn.com. 15 units. TV TEL. $80–$110 double; $110–$160 suite. Additional person $15 extra. Rates include breakfast and wine and cheese in the evening. MC, V.

Rarely will you find such affordable accommodations with so many extras. Each room at the two-story bay-front inn, located in Baywood Park just south of Morro Bay, is decorated with a distinct (over-the-top) theme and grandma-style flair. Guests can cuddle in a floral and light-wood country cottage, stretch out in a 19th-century English affair, or saddle down in a Southwestern suite. Every room has a private entrance, gas fireplace, microwave, coffeemaker, and a refrigerator stocked with complimentary sodas and snacks; all but a few have ocean views. Breakfast is brought to your room, wine and cheese are served each evening, and turndown service includes cookies.

A GOOD PLACE TO SPLURGE ON DINNER

Hoppe's at Marina Square. 699 Embarcadero (at Pacific). ☎ **805/772-9012.** Reservations recommended. Main courses $12–$22. AE, DC, DISC, MC, V. Sun–Thurs 5–9pm; Fri–Sat 5–10pm; Sun 11am–2pm. CALIFORNIA.

Ask locals where to go for the best meal in Morro Bay and they're likely to send you to Hoppe's. Here you get a stellar view of Morro Rock, as well as such dishes as potato-crusted free-range chicken with mushroom sauce, rack of lamb with white beans and homemade curry sausage, and a variety of fresh seafood. The service can be slow, but the atmosphere is surprisingly upscale, and the food respectable. Considering the neighboring options, Hoppe's is as good as it gets.

3 San Luis Obispo

226 miles S of San Francisco; 38 miles S of Cambria; 13 miles N of Pismo Beach; 106 miles N of Santa Barbara; 198 miles N of Los Angeles

Because the actual town of San Luis Obispo is not visible from U.S. 101, even many Californians don't know that it's more than a McDonald's-and-gasoline stopover on the way to southern California. But its secret location is exactly what keeps San Luis Obispo a quaint little Central Coast jewel that also happens to be very affordable for budget travelers.

San Luis Obispo is neatly tucked into the mountains about halfway between San Francisco and Los Angeles. It's surrounded by green pristine mountain ranges and filled with college kids (hence plenty of cheap stuff to do and eat) and friendly locals. The atmosphere is small-town casual, making it the perfect place to meander and ponder a simpler, more carefree existence.

The town grew up around an 18th-century mission, and its dozens of historical landmarks, quaint Victorian homes, shops, and restaurants are the primary tourist attractions. Today, it's still quaint and best explored on foot. It also makes a good base for an extensive survey of the region as a whole. To the west of town, a short drive away, are some of the state's prettiest swimming beaches; turning east, you enter the Central Coast's wine country, home to dozens of respectable wineries (see "The Central Coast Wine Country: Paso Robles & the Santa Ynez Valley," below).

ESSENTIALS

GETTING THERE   U.S. 101, one of the state's primary north-south roadways, runs right through San Luis Obispo; it's the fastest land route here from anywhere. If you're driving down along the coast, Calif. 1 is the way to go for its natural beauty and oceanfront cliffs. If you're entering the city from the east, take Calif. 46 or 41 to 101, then go south.

VISITOR INFORMATION   The **San Luis Obispo Visitors Center,** 1039 Chorro St., Suite E, San Luis Obispo, CA 93401 (☎ 805/781-2777; fax 805/543-1255), is located downtown, between Monterey and Higuera streets. This helpful office is one of the best-run visitors bureaus we've ever come across. Drop in to ask questions and to pick up maps, a calendar of events, or specialized information on local sights. Ask for a "Path of History" map, which details many of the sights listed below. The center is open Sunday and Monday from 10am to 5pm, Tuesday and Wednesday from 8am to 5pm, Thursday and Friday from 8am to 8pm, and Saturday from 10am to 8pm.

ORIENTATION   San Luis Obispo is about 10 miles inland, at the junction of Calif. 1 and U.S. 101. The downtown is laid out in a grid, roughly centered around the historic mission and its Mission Plaza (see below). Most of the main tourist sights are around the mission, within the small triangle created by U.S. 101 and Santa Rosa and Marsh streets.

EXPLORING THE TOWN

Before heading downtown, definitely make a pit stop at the perpetually pink **Madonna Inn,** 100 Madonna Rd. (off U.S. 101; ☎ **805/543-3000**), if for no other reason than to use its unique public rest rooms (see "Where to Stay," below).

Once downtown you can check out the minitown via the free trolley that does a repeat loop through the downtown area daily from noon to 5pm. (Stops are well marked.)

Ah Louis Store. 800 Palm St. (at Chorro St.). ☎ **805/543-4332.** Hours are whenever the owner feels like opening, which is rarely.

Mr. Ah Louis was a Cantonese immigrant who was lured to California by gold fever in 1856. Emerging from the mines empty-handed, he soon began a lucrative career as a labor contractor, hiring and organizing Chinese crews that would build the railroad. In 1874 he opened this store.

Today the store is rarely open, but if it is you can chat with Ah Louis's only living heir, 90-year-old Howard, while you browse the clutter of Asian merchandise.

✪ **Farmers Market.** Higuera St. (between Osos and Nipomo sts.). Thurs 6:30–9pm.

If you're lucky enough to be in town on a Thursday, take an evening stroll down Higuera Street, when the county's largest weekly street fair fills four downtown city blocks. You'll find much more here than fresh-picked produce—there's an ever-changing array of street entertainment, open-pit barbecues, food stands, and market stalls selling fresh flowers, cider, and other seasonal goodies. Surrounding stores stay open until 9pm.

Mission San Luis Obispo de Tolosa. 751 Palm St. ☎ **805/543-6850.** www.thegrid. net/slomission. Free admission ($2 donation requested). Summer daily 9am–5pm (sometimes later); winter daily 9am–4pm.

Founded by Father Junípero Serra in 1772, California's fifth mission was built with adobe bricks by Native American Chumash people. It remains one of the prettiest and most interesting structures in the Franciscan chain.

Serra chose this valley for the site of his fifth mission based on tales told to him of friendly natives and bountiful food (including grizzly bears). It was here that the traditional red-tile roof was first used atop a California mission, after the original thatched tule roofs repeatedly fell to hostile Native Americans' burning arrows. The former padres' quarters are an excellent museum chronicling both Native American and missionary life through all eras of the mission's use. Allow about 30 to 45 minutes to tour the mission and its grounds.

Mission Plaza, a pretty garden with brick paths and park benches fronting a meandering creek in which children love to wade, still functions as San Luis Obispo's town square. It's the focal point for local festivities and activities, from live concerts to poetry readings and dance and theater productions. Check at the visitor center (see "Essentials," above) to find out what's on when you're in town.

At the south end of Mission Plaza you'll also find the **San Luis Obispo Art Center** (☎ **805/543-8562**), whose three galleries display and sell an array of California-made art. Admission is free, and hours are Tuesday through Sunday from 11am to 5pm.

San Luis Obispo Children's Museum. 1010 Nipomo St. (at Monterey St.) ☎ **805/544-KIDS.** Admission $4 adults and children 2 and older, free for kids under 2. Mid-June to Sept Mon–Tues and Thurs–Sat 10am–5pm; Sun 1–5pm (closed Wed). Oct to mid-June Mon and Sat 10am–5pm; Tues, Thurs–Fri, and Sun 1–5pm (closed Wed).

This terrific children's museum features a playhouse of interesting manipulatives for toddlers, an authentic reproduction of a Native American Chumash cave dwelling, a music room, a computer corner, a pint-sized bank and post office, and over 20 interactive exhibits rotated on a regular basis. Special events like mask making, sing-alongs, and stage-makeup classes are scheduled regularly; call for a list of events.

San Luis Obispo County Historical Museum. Mission Plaza, 696 Monterey St. ☎ **805/543-0638.** Free admission. Wed–Sun 10am–4pm.

This little museum, run by the San Luis Obispo County Historical Society in a Carnegie library, houses an extensive research library and historical photograph collection. The permanent exhibit includes artifacts from Native American Chumash and early European settlers.

SHOPPING
Don't expect New York's Fifth Avenue here, but rather a few charming boutiques (and many uninteresting ones) scattered throughout town. The best place to exercise your credit cards is on the downtown streets surrounding the mission, specifically the 5

Chew on This

Follow the alley fronting Higuera between Garden and Broad streets for a local curiosity called Gum Alley. What is it? Its name says it all—it's basically an alley covered with gum.

blocks of Higuera Street from Nipomo to Osos streets as well as a short stretch of Monterey Street between Chorro and Osos streets. On Higuera Street, check out **Hands Gallery** at 777 Higuera St. (☎ **805/543-1921**), which has a bright and playful collection of local and international art. Trinkets range from glass candies to vases, jewelry, and ceramics.

You might also want to check out **The Creamery,** 570 Higuera St., at Nipomo Street (☎ **805/541-0106**), which functioned as one of the state's most important milk-producing centers for more than 40 years. Restored, remodeled, and opened as a shopping and restaurant mall, the complex is centered around the creamery's old cooling tower. Antique freezer doors, overhead workhouse lights, and milk-can lamps pointedly remind visitors of the structure's original function.

OUTSIDE OF TOWN

There are dozens of wineries in the area, which offer tastings and tours daily and make for a fun country diversion. See section 5, "The Central Coast Wine Country: Paso Robles & the Santa Ynez Valley," later in chapter, for more details. If you don't have time to tour the wineries, you can visit the **Central Coast Wine Room,** 10 Old Creamery Rd., Harmony (around 8 miles south of Cambria; ☎ 805/927-7337), which offers excellent selections from Paso Robles and the Edna Valley. The tasting room is open daily from 10am to 5pm (closed Tues in winter); tastings cost $2.

If you're into history and architecture, another worthy side trip is the **Mission San Miguel Arcangel,** 775 Mission St., in San Miguel (7 miles north of Paso Robles on U.S. 101) (☎ **805/467-3256**). Founded in 1824, this mission is less spoiled by restoration than many others in the state and is still run by the Franciscan order and inhabited by brown-robed friars. The modest exterior belies one of the most elaborate and best-preserved interiors of the entire central California chain. Painted and decorated by area Native Americans under the supervision of Spanish designer Estevan Munras, the walls and woodwork glow with luminous colors untouched since their original application. Behind the altar and its statue of San Miguel (St. Michael) is splendid tile work featuring a radiant Eye of God.

Mission San Miguel is open to the public daily from 9:30am to 4:30pm; the church remains open until 5pm. The requested donation is $1 per family, 50¢ per person; allow 30 minutes to see the sights. For more information, call ☎ **805/467-3256.**

WHERE TO STAY

In addition to what's listed below, there's a pristine branch of **Holiday Inn Express** (☎ **800/465-4329** or 805/544-8600) and two reliable **Motel 6** locations (☎ **800/4-MOTEL-6** or 805/541-6992); the south location is the newer and better of the two and a great deal at $45 for a double on the weekend.

If you'd like free help making reservations in the area, contact the **Accommodations Reservation Service** (☎ **800/292-2222**).

SUPER-CHEAP SLEEPS

Lamp Lighter Inn. 1604 Monterey St. (at Grove St.), San Luis Obispo, CA 93401. ☎ **800/547-7787** or 805/547-7777. Fax 805/547-7787. 40 units. A/C TV TEL. $49–$80 double; from $69 suite. Rates include continental breakfast. AE, DISC, MC, V.

Even if you're not looking for a bargain, you'll be pleasantly surprised with the value you get at this motel. The rooms boast traditional motel style and colors, but look brand new, are squeaky clean, and have firm mattresses. Other bonuses are coffeemakers, refrigerators (except in three rooms), and a heated pool and whirlpool. Breakfast is served in the lobby by an amazingly enthusiastic staff.

Travelodge. 345 Marsh St., San Luis Obispo, CA 93401. ☎ **805/543-6443.** Fax 805/545-0951. 53 units. 39 with shower only. TV TEL (A/C in some rooms). $48–$56 double; $68–$76 suite. Senior discounts available. Rates include continental breakfast. AE, CB, DC, DISC, MC, V.

This recently remodeled Travelodge offers decent accommodations 2 miles from the downtown area and includes free cable TV. The cheapest rooms have no tubs, but are clean and have a vanity and credenza. A small bump up in price promises newer rooms with plush carpeting, better-fashioned motel furnishings, and a tub.

For a Few Bucks More

✪ **Adobe Inn.** 1473 Monterey St., San Luis Obispo, CA 93401. ☎ **800/676-1588** or 805/549-0321. Fax 805/549-0383. 15 units. TV TEL. $55–$105 double. Additional person $6 extra in winter, $10 in summer. Rates include breakfast. Seasonal discounts available. AE, DISC, MC, V.

Okay, it's not actually adobe, or even remotely close for that matter, but Michael and Ann Dinshaw have taken this old motor inn and given it a creatively homey atmosphere at unbeatable prices. Each spotless room is individually decorated in Southwestern style with quirky additions such as playfully painted cupboards or a window-side reading nook. Eight rooms have kitchenettes (but no stove). Breakfast is served in a clean dining area that unfortunately faces the street, but coffee snobs will delight in the strong, locally roasted blend. The owners go out of their way to make guests happy and offer a slew of packages that explore the surrounding areas and attractions.

Moderately Priced Options

✪ **Apple Farm Trellis Court, at the Apple Farm Inn.** 2015 Monterey St., San Luis Obispo, CA 93401. ☎ **800/255-2040** or 805/544-2040. Fax 805/546-9495. Trellis Court 35 units; Apple Farm 69 units. A/C TV TEL. Trellis Court $59–$149 double; Apple Farm $119–$210 double. AE, DISC, MC, V.

The ultra-popular Apple Farm Inn is a pricey and peaceful getaway in an expensive Disney plantation kind of way. If you're into cheek-pinchingly cute style, it's definitely worth a splurge. But you can get all the bang without the bucks if you book a room at the property's motel, the Trellis Court. Rooms are smaller than those in the inn's immaculate Victorian-style farmhouse, but each is well decorated with gas fireplaces, comes with a continental breakfast, and shares the inn's wonderful grounds. Rooms at the pricier inn have floral wallpaper, fresh flowers, and sugar-sweet colorful touches. No two are alike, although all have a gas fireplaces, large well-equipped bathrooms, pine antiques, lavish country decor, and either a canopy four-poster or brass bed. San Luis Creek runs along the property where a working mill spins its huge wheel to power an apple press. There's an on-site restaurant. Cider is always on hand in the inn's lobby and Trellis Court guests are welcome to it. An outdoor heated swimming pool and Jacuzzi are open year-round.

✪ **Madonna Inn.** 100 Madonna Rd. (off U.S. 101), San Luis Obispo, CA 93405. ☎ **800/543-9666** or 805/543-3000. Fax 805/543-1800. http://www.madonnainn. com. 134 units. TV TEL. $97–$198 double; from $145 suite. MC, V.

If the Apple Farm sounds too cutesy for you, consider going to the other end of the spectrum—a total Americana kitsch experience at Madonna Inn, the ideal spot for the person who loves velvet Elvis posters and Vegas-style decor. It is here that the creative imaginations of owners Alex and Phyllis Madonna gave birth to the wildest—and most superfluously garish—fantasy world this side of Graceland. The only decor consistency throughout the hotel is its color scheme, which is perpetual pink. Beyond that, it's a free-for-all. Every nook and cranny has been built to delight—even the men's room has a rock-waterfall urinal and clam-shell sinks. Each room offers a different thematic fantasy far beyond a creative paint job. One room features a trapezoidal bed—it's 5 feet long on one side and 6 feet long on the other. "Rock" rooms with zebra- or tiger-patterned bedspreads and stonelike showers and fireplaces conjure up thoughts of a Flintstones' Playboy palace. There are also blue rooms, red rooms, and over-the-top Spanish, Italian, Irish, Alps, Currier and Ives, Native American, Swiss, and hunting rooms. The coffee shop, dining room, and two cocktail lounges are also outlandishly ornate. If you're booking a room, always ask about discounts; this place can be overpriced for what it is. Even if you don't stay here, stop by and check it out. One major bummer: There's no pool here, and there definitely should be.

WHERE TO DINE

Like the town itself, San Luis's restaurants are modest and affordable, which means you can basically eat anywhere you like while you're here. Don't hesitate to stop and ask locals their favorite places to eat, and keep an eye out for public barbecues, especially at the Thursday night farmers market. SLO folks love their barbecues, and they're liable to make you a fan, too.

SUPER-CHEAP EATS

Big Sky Cafe. 1121 Broad St. ☎ **805/545-5401.** Main courses $5–$11; salads and sandwiches $5–$8; breakfast $4–$8. AE, MC, V. Mon–Sat 7am–10pm; Sun 8am–8pm. AMERICAN.

The folk-artsy fervor of San Luis really shines at this Southwestern mirage, where local art and a blue, star-studded ceiling surround diners who come for fresh, healthy food in a very casual atmosphere. Most everything on the menu, like shrimp tacos and herb-infused roasted chicken, is created with local ingredients. Lighter meals, such as black-bean vegetarian chili, charcoal-broiled eggplant sandwich, and the chilled sesame ginger noodles with shrimp, chicken, or veggies, are local favorites. Breakfasts include buttermilk pancakes, a jambalaya omelet, turkey hash, and black-bean huevos rancheros.

Linnaea's Cafe. 1110 Garden St. (near Marsh St.). ☎ **805/541-5888.** Reservations not accepted. Main courses $3–$5.75 at lunch, $4.75–$7 at dinner. No credit cards. Daily 7am–midnight. VEGETARIAN.

Linnaea's is the reigning champ among budget breakfast and lunching folk. Morning meals include waffles and French toast, plus breakfast burritos, delicious pastries, and more. In the afternoon, the most coveted dishes are soup, main-course salads, and SLO roll sandwiches. Lunch is served until it's gone (it doesn't last long) and guest chefs prepare dinner Sunday through Friday (call for details); the rest of the evening is devoted to coffee drinks and delectable desserts. Food for the soul is always available in the form of local art, and acoustic music and poetry join in on the weekends.

Mondéo Pronto. 893 Hugeura St., #D4. ☎ **805/544-2956.** Wraps and "fusion bowls" $5.25–$6.25. MC, V. Sun–Wed 11am–9pm; Thurs–Sat 11am–10pm. INTERNATIONAL.

Mondéo Pronto provides patrons an affordable bite of international fillings in a burrito-type wrap. But unlike most "wrap" restaurants in California, this place goes a step beyond by paying attention to detail with presentation and freshness. Choices range from Americana versions like the "Mardi gras," which comes in a tomato tortilla packed with Cajun sausage, rock shrimp, Creole veggies, and jambalaya sauce; to

Mediterranean selections like "the Sicilian," with grilled portobello mushrooms, herb polenta, veggies, goat cheese, olives, capers, and sun-dried-tomato pesto. "Fusion bowls" satisfy non-wrappers with such combinations as basil scampi, a lovely shrimp dish over bow-tie pasta with pesto, marinara, pine nuts, and herbs. Big bonuses: Everything on the kids' menu is under $2.25, and as the menu announces, "Substitutions and sides are no problem."

Mo's Smokehouse BBQ. 970 Higuera St. (at Osos St.). ☎ **805/544-6193.** Sandwiches and combo meals $5–$13. AE, MC, V. Sun–Wed 11am–9pm; Thurs–Sat 11am–10pm. BARBECUE.

Friends of ours who moved from San Francisco to San Luis Obispo insisted we dine at Mo's, the town's top choice for great barbecue. It's not fancy, but you name it, it's here—pork or baby back ribs, BBQ beef, tri-tip and chicken in either a mild or hot sauce, all accompanied by baked beans, bread, potato salad, or coleslaw. To top off this delectable deal, practically everything on the menu is under $10.

SLO Brewing Company. 1119 Garden St. ☎ **805/543-1843.** Main courses $6–$9. DISC, MC, V. Mon–Wed 11:30am–10pm; Thurs–Sat 11:30am–12:30am; Sun 11:30am–9pm. AMERICAN.

Anyone who loves pub-style suds and snacks will love SLO Brewing Co. Here the focus is homemade beer: Pale Ale, Amber Ale, and Porter are brewed from all-natural ingredients, which help wash down the burger-and-fried-food menu. Join the festive collegiate crowd at night for live music and the action at the downstairs pool hall, stop by for lunch, or check the place out on the Web at www.slobrew.com.

Thai Classic. 1101 Higuera St. (at Osos St.). ☎ **805/541-2025.** Reservations recommended on weekends. Most dishes $6–$11. DISC, MC, V. Sun–Thurs 11am–10pm; Fri–Sat 11am–11pm. THAI.

It's not much to look at, but if you ignore the cheesy white booths and plain walls and focus on the Thai food coming out of the kitchen, you won't be sorry you came. There's an extensive vegetarian selection and trademark Thai appetizers such as satay with peanut and cucumber sauces, pad Thai, and spring rolls. Locals favor the pineapple fried rice with shrimp, chicken, and cashews as well as the curry plates, all of which should be eaten family-style. Lunch specials on weekdays are a real bargain at $4.50 to $5.50 for soup, salad, spring roll, fried wonton, steamed rice, and one of 21 main courses.

WORTH A SPLURGE

✪ **Buona Tavola.** 1037 Monterey St. ☎ **805/545-8000.** Reservations recommended. Main courses $8.25–$17. AE, DISC, MC, V. Mon–Fri 11:30am–2:30pm; Sun–Thurs 5:30–9:30pm; Fri–Sat 5:30–10pm. NORTHERN ITALIAN.

While most choices in town are burger-and-sandwich casual, Buona Tavola offers well-prepared Italian food in a more upscale setting. You can stroll in wearing jeans, but the dining room, with checkerboard floors and original artwork, is warmer and more intimate than other spots in town. There's also backyard-terrace seating where you can enjoy your meal surrounded by magnolias, ficus, and grapevines. The menu boasts a number of salads on the antipasti list. Favorite pastas include *agnolotti de scampi allo zafferand*, which is homemade, filled with scampi, and served in a cream-saffron sauce. The *spaghettini scoglio d'oro* comes with lobster, sea scallops, clams, mussels, shrimp, and diced tomatoes in a saffron sauce. Don't worry—once you've gotten past trying to pronounce your desired dish, the rest of the evening should be both relaxing and satisfying.

4 Pismo Beach

13 miles S of San Luis Obispo

Just outside San Luis Obispo, on Pismo's 23-mile-stretch of prime beachfront, flip-flops are the shoes of choice and surf wear is the dominant fashion. It's all about beach life here, so bring your bathing suit, your board, and a good book.

If building sand castles or tanning isn't your idea of a tantalizing time, you can explore isolated dunes, cliff-sheltered tide pools, and old pirate coves. Bring your dog (Fido's welcome here) and play an endless game of fetch, or go fishing—it's permitted from Pismo Beach Pier, which also offers arcade entertainment, bowling, and billiards. Pismo is also the only beach in the area that allows all-terrain vehicles on the dunes.

Since the town itself consists of little more than tourist shops and surf-and-turf restaurants, nearby San Luis Obispo is a far more charming place to stay. But if all you want are a few lazy days on a beautiful beach at half the price of an oceanfront room in Santa Barbara, Pismo is a perfect choice.

The **Pismo Beach Chamber of Commerce and Visitors Bureau,** 581 Dolliver St., Pismo Beach, CA 93449 (☎ **800/443-7778** in Calif. or 805/773-4382), offers free brochures and information on local attractions, lodging, and dining. The office is open Monday through Saturday from 9am to 5pm and Sunday from 10am to 4pm. You can peruse their information on the Internet at www.pismobeach.org.

WHAT TO SEE & DO

Beaches in Pismo are exceptionally wide, making them some of the best in the state for sunning and playing. The beach north of Grand Avenue is popular with families and joggers. North of Wadsworth Street, the coast becomes dramatically rugged as it rambles northward to Shell Beach and Pirates Cove.

Pismo Beach was once one of the most famous places in America for clamming, but the clam population was depleted almost to extinction. Government intervention has saved the "Pismo clam," and if you have a fishing license you're now permitted to pick them in limited numbers directly from the sand. If you're into it, clam forks can be rented from a number of locations around the pier. You can get a fishing license at the pier, as well.

If fishing is more your style, you'll be pleased to know no license is required to fish from Pismo Beach Pier. Catches here are largely bottom fish like red snapper and ling cod. There's a bait-and-tackle shop on the pier.

Livery Stables, 1207 Silver Spur Place (☎ **805/489-8100**), in Oceano (about 5 minutes south of Pismo Beach), is one of the very few places in the state that rents horses for riding on the beach. Horses go for $15 to $20 per hour and can be ridden at your own pace or you can opt for a guided ride.

You can hike along the **Guadalupe-Nipomo Dunes** year-round. This 18-mile strip of coastline, 20 minutes south of Pismo, has the highest beach dunes in the West. It's a great place for observing native plants and birds, including the California brown pelican, one of 200 species that migrates here each year.

From late November through February, tens of thousands of migrating **monarch butterflies** take up residence in the area's eucalyptus and Monterey pine tree groves. The colorful butterflies form dense clusters on the trees, each hanging with its wings over the one below it, providing warmth and shelter for the entire group. During the monarchs' stay, naturalists at **Pismo State Beach** conduct 45-minute narrative walks every Saturday and Sunday at 11am and 2pm (call ☎ **805/772-2694** for tour information). Most of the "butterfly trees" are located on Calif. 1, between Pismo Beach and Grover Beach, to the south.

WHERE TO STAY
SUPER-CHEAP SLEEPS

✪ **The Clamdigger.** 150 Hinds Ave., Pismo Beach, CA 93449. ☎ **805/773-2342.** 12 units. TV. $60–$75 cabin; $75–$90 suite. 7th night free. AE, DC, DISC, MC, V.

Just south of the pier, this cluster of cabins and the adjoining motel offer a true old-style California beach vacation. Little more than a one-room shack on the beach (it does have a bathroom), each cabin welcomes you with a stained-glass ship on the door, a queen-size bed, cable TV, a kitchenette with microwave, a coffeemaker (bring your own ground beans), and basic furniture. The few adjoining motel suites sleep up to six. The place has some history, too—Valentino stayed here when he filmed on location in the 1920s. *Note:* Bedding can be a bit scratchy, so you may want to bring your own sheets.

Surf Motel. 250 Main St., Pismo Beach, CA 93449. ☎ **800/472-7873** or 805/773-2070. 33 units. TV TEL. $65–$85 double (lower on off-season weekends). Rates include continental breakfast. AE, MC, V.

Strategically located just half a block from the beach, the Surf Motel is a good bet if you want basic, clean accommodations. All rooms have refrigerators; some have fully stocked kitchenettes. The indoor swimming pool is open year-round. Unless you prefer modernity and new motel amenities, however, you'll get more of Pismo's true flavor at the rustic oceanfront cottages of The Clamdigger.

WORTH A SPLURGE

SeaVenture Resort. 100 Ocean View Ave., Pismo Beach, CA 93449. ☎ **800/662-5545** or 805/773-4994. Fax 805/773-0924. www.seaventure.com. 50 units. MINIBAR TV TEL. $119–$349 double (rates vary according to view, season, and special promotions). Rates include continental breakfast. AE, CB, DC, DISC, MC, V. Take U.S. 101 to the Price St. exit and turn west onto Ocean View (at the beach).

If luxury accommodations overlooking the beach and an outdoor spa on your private deck sound like heaven to you, head for SeaVenture, a 3-year-old resort providing the most luxurious accommodations in Pismo. Once in your room, you need only drag your tired traveling feet through the thick forest-green carpeting, past the white country furnishings and feather bed, and turn on your gas fireplace to begin what promises to be a relaxing stay. Then rent a movie from the video library, schedule a massage, or simply bathe your weary bones in your own outdoor hydrotherapy spa tub. With the beach right outside your door, there's not much more you could ask for—although there is, in fact, more provided: plush robes, a wet bar, refrigerator, coffeemaker, continental breakfast delivered to your room, and a restaurant on the premises with a lovely brunch. Most rooms have ocean views and many have a private balcony overlooking the beach. Services include room service from 4 to 9pm, laundry, and massage, and there's also a swimming pool.

WHERE TO DINE

Giuseppe's. 891 Price St. ☎ **805/773-2870.** Reservations not accepted. Main courses $6–$10 at lunch, $9–$22 at dinner. AE, DISC, MC, V. Daily 11:30am–3pm; Sun–Thurs 4:30–10pm; Fri–Sat 4:30–10:30pm. SOUTHERN ITALIAN.

This is the region's best southern Italian restaurant. Along with the fresh homemade bread baked in the wood-burning oven imported from Italy, the classic fare comes with a clutter of Italian culinary accoutrements and an atmosphere reminiscent of a busy Columbus Avenue restaurant in San Francisco's North Beach. The long, extensive menu of antipasti, salads, pizzas, pastas, fish, and steak makes it virtually impossible not to find something to your liking.

Splash Cafe. 197 Pomeroy St. (near Pismo Beach Pier). ☎ **805/773-4653.** Most items $2.50–$5.75. No credit cards. Daily 10am–8pm. AMERICAN.

This beachy burger stand, with a short menu and just a few tables, gets high marks each year at the Pismo Beach Clam Fest for its award-winning clam chowder, served in a sourdough bread bowl. Fish-and-chips, burgers, hot dogs, and grilled-ahi sandwiches are also available and you can even have frozen chowder shipped via mail order to your home.

5　The Central Coast Wine Country: Paso Robles & the Santa Ynez Valley

Paso Robles: 29 miles N of San Luis Obispo; Solvang: 60 miles S of San Luis Obispo

by Stephanie Avnet Yates

When people talk about California wines, you can normally assume they mean those from the Napa/Sonoma regions north of San Francisco. But locally here in California, and increasingly across the country, wine lovers are becoming more aware of vintages coming from California's Central Coast wineries, located in the dewy green hills and sun-kissed valleys of San Luis Obispo and Santa Barbara counties. Closer and more convenient than the Napa Valley, the Central Coast is coming into its own as a respected wine region, and offers another excuse to visit some of the state's most beautifully scenic countryside. Wine snobs might tell you that Central Coast wines cannot compare to those from the northern appellations, where precious vintages can age to sublime flavor and astronomical price, but if you're in the market for bottles in the $10-to-$18 range that are ready to drink within 5 years—trust me, you'll love what this up-and-comer has to offer. And, unless you go overboard in purchasing wines to take home, the pleasures of wine touring are largely free. Many wineries offer complimentary tours and tastings; others have a nominal charge for pouring tastes, which can easily be shared by two people. Factor in a self-assembled picnic lunch, and you've planned one of the most affordable days of your whole vacation!

PASO ROBLES

Welcome to Paso Robles—"pass through the oaks"—so named for the clusters of oak trees liberally scattered throughout the rolling hills of this inland region. The town has a faintly checkered past: it was established in 1870 by Drury James, uncle of outlaw Jesse James (who reportedly hid out in tunnels under the original Paso Robles Inn). In 1913, pianist Ignace Paderewski came to live in Paso Robles, where he brought Zinfandel vines for his ranch (zinfandel is now the most successful varietal among area wineries) and played often in the Paso Robles Inn, which today maintains a small exhibit in his honor in the lobby. Paderewski really wasn't here for long, returning to Poland after World War I, but the town today treats him like a native son, and fans gather each year at the Paderewski Festival in March.

ESSENTIALS

GETTING THERE/ORIENTATION　　Paso Robles lies along U.S. 101; there's an exit for the town's main business thoroughfare, Spring Street. Calif. 46 intersects, and briefly joins, U.S. 101. Many wineries are located on the winding roads off Calif. 46

The Paso Robles Wine Country

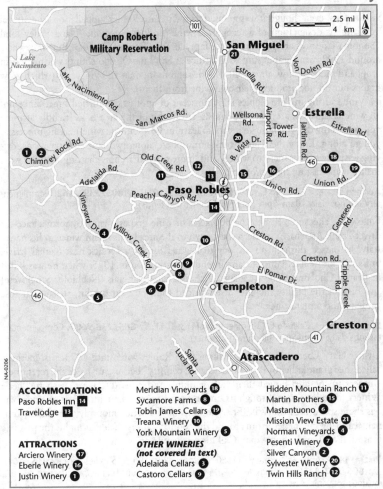

ACCOMMODATIONS
Paso Robles Inn 14
Travelodge 13

ATTRACTIONS
Arciero Winery 17
Eberle Winery 16
Justin Winery 1

Meridian Vineyards 18
Sycamore Farms 8
Tobin James Cellars 19
Treana Winery 10
York Mountain Winery 5

OTHER WINERIES
(not covered in text)
Adelaida Cellars 3
Castoro Cellars 9

Hidden Mountain Ranch 11
Martin Brothers 15
Mastantuono 6
Mission View Estate 21
Norman Vineyards 4
Pesenti Winery 7
Silver Canyon 2
Sylvester Winery 20
Twin Hills Ranch 12

on either side—try to cluster your visit according to this designation, visiting one side and then the other. You'll be able to feel how the weather on the western side, which is cooler due to higher elevations and frequent coastal fog, differs from the hotter east side, which is on a flat plain leading inland; wine makers bicker constantly over which conditions are "better" for wine grapes.

VISITOR INFORMATION   For a complete list of area wineries, tasting rooms, and seasonal events, contact the **Paso Robles Vintners and Growers Association,** 1940 Spring St. (P.O. Box 324), Paso Robles, CA 93447 (☎ **800/549-WINE** or 805/ 239-8463; fax 805/237-6439; www.pasowine.com). Additional information on the area is offered by the **Paso Robles Chamber of Commerce,** 1225 Park St., Paso Robles, CA 93446 (☎ **800/406-4040** or 805/238-0506; fax 805/238-0527; www.pasorobleschamber.com).

TOURING THE LOCAL WINERIES

They've been tending vines in Paso Robles's fertile foothills since the turn of the century—the 19th century, that is. For decades, the area was overlooked by wine aficionados, even though it was granted its own "Paso Robles" appellation (the official government designation of a recognized wine-producing region; "Napa Valley" and "Sonoma County" are probably more familiar appellations) in 1983. But somewhere around 1992, wine grapes surpassed lettuce as San Luis Obispo county's primary cash crop, and there are now almost 40 wineries and more than 100 vineyards (which grow grapes but do not produce their own wine from them).

Wine touring in Paso Robles is reminiscent of another, unhurried time. Since not all wine enthusiasts are wine experts, an advantage of the area is its friendly attitude and small crowds, which make it easy to learn more about the wine-making process as you go along. Enjoy the relaxed rural atmosphere along two-lane country roads, driving leisurely from winery to winery and, more often than not, chatting with the wine maker while tasting their product.

Arciero Winery. Calif. 46 East (6 miles east of U.S. 101). ☎ **805/239-2562.** Complimentary tastings daily 10am–5pm (till 6pm summer weekends).

Follow the checkered flag to the 800 acres of wine grapes owned by former race-car driver Frank Arciero, Sr. Arciero was drawn to the area by its resemblance to his native Italy; he passed through on his way to Laguna Seca, a racetrack near Salinas (trivia buffs will know it as James Dean's intended destination in 1955, when he was killed in nearby Cholame). The label specializes in Italian varietals (Nebbiolo, Sangiovese) and blends; the facility includes a self-guided tour, race-car exhibit, spectacular rose gardens, and a picnic area.

Eberle Winery. Calif. 46 E. (3.5 miles east of U.S. 101). ☎ **805/238-9607.** Complimentary tastings daily 10am–5pm (till 6pm in summer).

Owner Gary Eberle, who's been making Paso Robles wine since 1973, is sometimes called the "grandfather of Paso Robles's wine country" because many of the recent new vintners in the area honed their craft working under his tutelage. A visit to Eberle Winery includes a tour through its underground caves, where hundreds of aging barrels share space with the Wild Boar Room, site of Eberle's monthly wine-maker dinners featuring guest chefs from around the country (always held Sat night; the prix fixe is around $80, including wine). Call for a schedule of events.

Justin Vineyards & Winery. 11680 Chimney Rock Rd. (15 miles east of U.S. 101). ☎ **805/237-4150.** Tastings Mon–Fri 11am–4pm; Sat–Sun 10am–5pm. Tasting fee $3; includes souvenir glass.

At the end of a scenic country road lies Justin and Deborah Baldwin's boutique winery, and even a casual glance shows how much love and dedication the ex–Los Angelenos have put into their operation. The tasting room, dining room, offices, and even wine-making barns have a stylish Tuscan flair. Justin's flagship wine is Isosceles, a Bordeaux-style blend that's pricier than most area wines, but exudes both sophistication and superior aging potential. Also worth a try is their port-style dessert wine, called Obtuse. Since 1987 the Baldwins have commissioned a different artist each year to interpret their property for the label; you can see the framed results throughout the complex.

Meridian Vineyards. Calif. 46 E. (7 miles east of U.S. 101). ☎ **805/237-6000.** Complimentary tastings daily 10am–5:30pm.

The local vintner with the largest profile is also the Central Coast's best-known label, producing more cases each year than all the other Paso wineries *combined*. Veteran wine maker Chuck Ortman brought a respected Napa Valley pedigree to Meridian; as a result, here's where you'll get the most Napa-like tasting experience. In addition to a grand tasting room, there's a man-made lake surrounded by rolling lawns, where picnicking is encouraged.

Tobin James Cellars. 8950 Union Rd. (at Calif. 46 E., 8 miles east of U.S. 101). ☎ 800/543-0256 or 805/239-2204. Complimentary tastings daily 10am–6pm.

Wine maker Tobin James is a walking contradiction. A life-long wine expert who claims to still wear the same pair of khaki shorts every day, Toby has patterned his winery in the spirit of local bad boys the James Gang. The tasting room has a Wild West theme, a 100-year old saloon bar, and blaring country music, all serving to dispel the wine-snob atmosphere that prevails at so many wineries. Tobin James's particular expertise lies in the production of a "user-friendly" zinfandel; the late-harvest dessert wine from zinfandel grapes is smooth and spicy.

Treana Winery. 2175 Arbor Rd. (at Calif. 46 W., 1 mile west of U.S. 101). ☎ 805/238-6979. Complimentary tastings daily 10am–5pm.

There's a spit and polish about this sleek player in the Paso wine game. The Hope family's elegant tasting room now features a gourmet deli for picnickers, an adjacent cigar gazebo (a relaxed room of tropical palms and wicker invoking 1950s Cuba), and the luxurious Arbor Inn Bed & Breakfast set amongst the vines. With the help of a Napa-alumnus wine maker, Treana is turning out some of the best reds around, including cabernets rich in character, and a portlike late-harvest merlot that's sweet, smooth, and complex.

York Mountain Winery. 7505 York Mountain Rd. (off Calif. 46 W., 7 miles west of U.S. 101). ☎ 805/238-3925. Tastings daily 10am–5pm; tasting fee $1.

If you're impressed by superlatives, don't miss York Mountain. It's the *first* winery established in the area (in 1882 by Andrew York, on land originally deeded by President Ulysses S. Grant), the *oldest* continuously operating vintner, and the *only* producer in the "York Mountain" viticulture appellation. In the 100-year-old stone tasting room, look for a dry chardonnay with a complex, spicy aroma, and award-winning cabernet sauvignons, the best of which are the "Reserve" bottlings from hand-chosen grapes.

WHERE TO PACK A PICNIC LUNCH

You'll find everything you need for a casual snack or sophisticated picnic at Paso Robles's new **Odyssey Culinary Provisions,** 1214 Pine St. (☎ 805/237-7516). A sandwich board features gourmet deli selections on focaccia and other fresh-baked breads, and refrigerator cases yield up inventive salads, cheeses, salami, olives, and other delicacies. Mustards, crackers, chocolates, and pastries line the shelves, along with baskets and knapsacks to hold your feast. Odyssey is also the place to come for fresh-brewed coffee and espresso drinks. It's open Sunday through Thursday from 7am to 7pm, Friday and Saturday from 7am to 11pm.

OTHER DIVERSIONS IN THE PASO ROBLES AREA

The fragrance emanating from **Sycamore Farms,** Calif. 46 West, 3 miles west of U.S. 101 (☎ 800/576-5288 or 805/238-5288), is that of hundreds of herbs, grown for culinary, medicinal, and decorative purposes. Learn about them at the farm's walk-through garden; they also sell fresh-cut and dried herbs; nursery seedlings to transplant at home; and a bevy of herbal vinegars, olive oils, mustards, herbal soaps, and potpourri. They're open daily from 10:30am to 5:30pm, except Christmas Day and January 4 through 14.

For a special splurge, nothing beats the exhilaration of seeing the wine country at sunrise from the serenity of a hot-air balloon. **Seventh Heaven Balloons** (☎ **805/687-8459**) offers two flights daily followed by champagne brunch on select weekends throughout the year. The price is $139 per person, and reservations are suggested at least 4 weeks in advance.

WHERE TO STAY

Adelaide Inn. 1215 Ysabel Ave., Paso Robles, CA 93446. ☎ **800/549-PASO** or 805/238-2770. Fax 805/238-3497. www.centralcoast.com/AdelaideInn/. 67 units. A/C TV TEL. $45–$59 double. Extra person $5. AE, DC, DISC, MC, V. From U.S. 101, exit Calif. 46 E. Turn west at 24th St.; the hotel is just west of the freeway.

Tended with loving care rare among lower-priced accommodations, the Adelaide Inn stands out from other motels. Although it's situated adjacent to freeway gas stations and coffee shops, special attention has been given to isolating this quiet, lushly landscaped property from its bustling surroundings. The rooms are clean and comfortable, and the motel has a safe, welcoming ambiance. Unexpected comforts include refrigerators; coffeemakers; hair dryers; complimentary newspaper, fruit, and muffins; and in-room amenities for the business traveler. There's a heated outdoor pool, spa, sauna, and even a putting green.

Paso Robles Inn. 1103 Spring St., Paso Robles, CA 93446. ☎ **805/238-2660**. 68 units. A/C TV TEL. $70–$75 double. Extra person $5. AE, CB, DC, DISC, JCB, MC, V.

This Mission Revival–style inn was built to replace the 1891 Stanford White masterpiece El Paso de Robles Hotel that burned to the ground in 1940. Photos of the grand landmark in its heyday line the Spanish-tiled lobby and adjacent dining room and cocktail lounge. A creek meanders through this oak-shaded property, and bungalow-style motel units are scattered across the tranquil and lovely grounds. Rooms are simple and well shielded from street noise; many will find them charming and nostalgic, but if you demand modern amenities and appointments, you'll be disappointed. There's a large heated swimming pool near the creek and convenient carports located behind each building. *Tip:* Avoid room numbers beginning with 1 or 2—they're too close to the street.

Travelodge Paso Robles. 2710 Spring St., Paso Robles, CA 93446. ☎ **800/578-7878** or 805/238-0078. Fax 805/238-0822. 31 units. A/C TV TEL. $48–$68 double. Extra person $5. Off-season rates available. AE, CB, DC, DISC, MC, V. Pets allowed for $5 per night.

Clean, friendly, and reliable, this 1950s-era motel (renovated in 1995) lies a few blocks north of the commercial section of town. There's no food available within walking distance, but Paso Robles is small, and everything is just a short drive away. Arranged around a small, outdoor pool, the Travelodge's rooms are basically what you'd expect; all come with coffeemakers, though, and the motel provides free local calls and daily newspaper. The Adelaide (see above), in the same price range, is a more attractive option, but can sometimes fill up unexpectedly; this Travelodge is a perfectly reasonable option.

WHERE TO DINE

Bistro Laurent. 1202 Pine St., Paso Robles. ☎ **805/226-8191**. Reservations recommended. Main courses $14–$19. AE, MC, V. Mon–Sat 4:30–10pm. FRENCH/CALIFORNIA.

Executive chef Laurent Grangien's sophisticated bistro initially caused quite a stir in this town unaccustomed to such innovations as a chef's tasting menu. But once the dust settled, everyone kept returning for the unpretentious neighborhood atmosphere, delicious recipes, and reasonable (by L.A. or San Francisco standards) prices. Whet your appetite with a complimentary teaser hors d'oeuvre (goat-cheese toasts, for example) before plunging into dishes like rosemary garlic chicken, pork loin bathed in peppercorn sauce, or ahi tuna in a red-wine reduction. Bargain "twilight dinners" are served nightly until 6:30pm.

Busi's on the Park. 1122 Pine St., Paso Robles. ☎ **805/238-1390.** Main courses $7–$9. AE, MC, V. Tues–Fri 11:30am–2pm; Tues–Sun 5–9pm. CALIFORNIA ECLECTIC.

The name may sound snooty and scenic, but Busi's is neither. It's just a comfortable, tavernlike joint downtown across the street from City Park. The capable kitchen, however, draws a big local crowd. The brief seasonal menu highlights fresh local ingredients; eclectic offerings range from Southwestern chicken salad with refreshing cilantro-lime crema or Chinese stir-fry beef tinged with orange and sesame to a superior cannelloni rolled in freshly made basil-egg pasta, ladled with roasted tomato sauce and accompanied by sautéed spinach.

THE SANTA YNEZ VALLEY

Welcome to the Santa Ynez Valley, an idyllic domain of oak-covered hills and uncrowded roads set against a mountain backdrop. This is beautiful country, where the clear blue sky achieves a brilliance unheard of in California's smog-clogged cities. In the Santa Ynez Valley, the pace is a little slower, the locals a little friendlier. Don't expect to find yokels gnawing on hay, though—this is gentleman-farmer country, where some of the nicest ranches are gated and have video surveillance. This balance of old-fashioned living and modern sophistication is what makes the area pleasurable; you can wallow in simple pleasures one day and go wine-tasting the next.

Los Olivos is a good ol'-fashioned country town right in the middle of wine country. There's a big flagpole in the center of the town's intersection, and stretches of boardwalk stand in for sidewalk here and there, giving the town a Wild West air. If you saw TV's *Return to Mayberry,* that was Los Olivos standing in for Andy Griffith's sentimental Southern hamlet. But these days the town's storefronts feature art galleries, stylish cafes, and wine-tasting rooms; you'll see more Land Rovers than John Deeres in this upscale retreat. Just minutes away from one another, the towns of Los Olivos, Santa Ynez, Ballard, Solvang, and Buellton each make an excellent base for touring the wineries of this fertile area.

ESSENTIALS

GETTING THERE/ORIENTATION   From U.S. 101, take Calif. 246 east 4 miles to reach Solvang, Santa Ynez, and Ballard. Los Olivos is located on Calif. 154 about 2 miles from U.S. 101. Lake Cachuma is also on Calif. 154, traveling southeast toward Santa Barbara.

U.S. 101, Calif. 246, and Calif. 154 form a triangle enclosing the towns of the Santa Ynez Valley. Calif. 246 becomes Mission Drive within Solvang city limits, then continues east past the mission toward Santa Ynez. Alamo Pintado Road connects Solvang with Los Olivos, whose commercial stretch is located along 3 blocks of Grand Avenue. Foxen Canyon Road continues north from downtown Los Olivos.

VISITOR INFORMATION   Contact the **Santa Barbara County Vintners Association,** 3669 Sagunto St., Unit 101 (P.O. Box 1558), Santa Ynez, CA 93460 (☎ **800/218-0881** or 805/688-0881), to request a copy of their *Winery Touring Map.* It's open Monday through Friday from 9am to 5pm. The **Solvang Visitor Bureau,** 1511 Mission Dr., at Fifth St. (P.O. Box 70), Solvang, CA 93464 (☎ **800/ GO-SOLVANG** or 805/688-6144; www.geninc.com/solvang), has additional information on the Santa Ynez Valley; it's open daily from 10am to 4pm.

TOURING THE LOCAL WINERIES

Santa Barbara County has a 200-year tradition of growing grapes and making wine—an art originally practiced by Franciscan friars at the area's missions—but only in the past 20 to 30 years have wine-grape fields begun to approach the size of many other crops that do so well in these fertile inland valleys.

Geography makes the area well-suited for successful vineyards: The Santa Ynez and San Rafael mountain ranges are *transverse* (east-west) ranges, which allow ocean breezes to flow through, keeping the climate temperate. Variations in temperature and humidity within the valley create many microclimates, and vintners have learned how to cultivate nearly all the classic grape varietals. Today you'll find about 25 vintners in the Santa Ynez Valley area, most of which have tasting rooms; a few offer tours of their operations. If you'd like to start with a winery tour to acquaint yourself with viticulture, Gainey Vineyard or Firestone Vineyard are good bets (see below).

The Brander Vineyard. 2401 Refugio Rd., Los Olivos. ☎ **805/688-2455.** Tastings daily 10am–5pm. Tasting fee of $2.50 includes souvenir glass and is applied toward any purchase.

Wine maker Fred Brander has been making a name for himself since 1976; although the winery's production is small, his is a name you'll see frequently on local wine lists. Brander is among the valley's most pleasant wineries; their tasting room is small, with a friendly family of staff. Brander's best are Cuvee Nicolas, a 100% sauvignon blanc from low-yielding vines, and a high-density cabernet to cellar for full-bodied perfection.

Fess Parker Winery & Vineyard. 6200 Foxen Canyon Rd., Los Olivos. ☎ **800/841-1104** or 805/688-1545. Tastings daily 10am–5pm; tours daily 11am, 1pm, and 3pm. Reservations not required for tours. Tasting fee $3.

You loved him as a child, now see what Hollywood's Davy Crockett/Daniel Boone is up to. Fess Parker has made a big name for himself in Santa Barbara County, with an ocean-side resort, cattle ranches, and now an eponymous winery that's turning out some critically acclaimed syrahs, among other varietals. Look for the syrah and chardonnay American Tradition Reserve vintages in the tasting room. Parker's grandiose complex, shaded by the largest oak tree I've ever seen, also features picnic tables on a breezy terrace and an extensive gift shop where you can buy—you guessed it—coonskin caps!

Firestone Vineyard. 5017 Zaca Station Rd., Los Olivos. ☎ **805/688-3940.** Complimentary tastings daily 10am–5pm; tours hourly Sat–Sun. Reservations not required for tours.

Probably the largest producer in Santa Barbara County, this operation, started by Brooks Firestone (of tire manufacturing fame), now includes two "second" labels. The wines are affordable and reasonably good, and they've started experimenting with Chilean-grown grapes, some of which can be excellent. Firestone's tasting room and gift shop are a three-ring circus of merchandise, but they have a quick, worthwhile tour and free tastings.

The Gainey Vineyard. 3950 E. Calif. 246, Santa Ynez. ☎ **805/688-0558.** Tastings daily 10am–5pm; tours daily 11am, 1, 2, and 3pm. Reservations not required for tours. Tasting fee $3; includes souvenir glass.

This slick operation is one of the most-visited wineries in the valley, thanks to its prime location on Calif. 246 and its in-depth tours, offered 7 days a week. It's got every hallmark of a visitor-oriented winery: a terra-cotta-tiled tasting room, plenty of logo merchandise, and a deli case for impromptu lunches at the picnic tables situated in a secluded vineyard garden. They bottle the most popular varietals—chardonnay, cabernet sauvignon, pinot noir, sauvignon blanc—and offer them at moderate prices.

Sunstone Vineyards and Winery. 125 Refugio Rd., Santa Ynez. ☎ **800/313-WINE** or 805/688-WINE. Tastings daily 10am–4pm. Tasting fee $3–$5; includes souvenir glass.

Take a rambling drive down to this locally well known winery, whose gracious wisteria-wrapped stone tasting room belies the dirt road you take to reach it. Sunstone is nestled in an oak grove overlooking the river and boasts a splendid view from its lavender-fringed picnic courtyard. Inside, try their flagship merlot or treasured reserve vintages; there's also a fine selection of gourmet foods, logo ware, and cigars.

Zaca Mesa Winery. 6905 Foxen Canyon Rd., Los Olivos. ☎ **800/350-7972** or 805/688-9339. Complimentary tastings daily 10am–4pm; call for tour schedule.

One of the region's old-timers, Zaca Mesa has been in business since 1972, so I can forgive them the hippie/New Age mumbo-jumbo pleasantly interwoven with their well-honed vintages. Situated on a unique plateau that the Spanish named *la zaca mesa* (the restful place), this winery's 750 acres are uniquely beautiful—a fact they celebrate with two easy nature trails for visitors; you'll also find picnic tables and a giant lawn chessboard. Inside, look for the usual syrah and chardonnay offerings jazzed up with experimental Rhône varietals like grenache, roussanne, and voignier.

WHERE TO PACK A PICNIC LUNCH

You can assemble a picnic lunch at **Solvang Market and Deli,** at Mission Road and Fifth Street (☎ **805/688-6117**), where a fresh deli counter prepares simple sandwiches and side salads, plus buckets of fried chicken. With a little advance notice, they'll prepare box lunches that include a sandwich, chips, a piece of fruit, and a cookie, for $7.50 per box. The market is open daily from 7am to 10pm. Their sister location, **Santa Ynez Valley Market,** on Calif. 154 about a mile east of Los Olivos (☎ **805/688-5115**), offers the same services and is open daily from 7am to 8pm.

Los Olivos offers easy-to-carry, eat-at-room-temperature goodies packed up with all the necessary utensils. At **Panino,** 2900 Grand Ave. (☎ **805/688-9304**), choose from 31 gourmet sandwiches priced from $5 to $7. All are served on Panino's fresh-baked Italian-style bread; varieties include grilled chicken with sun-dried tomatoes, fresh basil, and provolone cheese (#10), or English Stilton with Asian pear on fresh walnut bread (#31). It's open Monday through Friday from 10am to 4pm and Saturday and Sunday from 9am to 5pm.

OTHER DIVERSIONS IN THE SANTA YNEZ VALLEY

SOLVANG: A TASTE OF DENMARK   The valley's largest town is also one of the state's most popular tourist stops, and Solvang takes a lot of flack for being a Disneyfied version of its founders' vision. Everything here that *can* be Danish *is* Danish: You've never seen so many windmills, cobblestone streets, wooden shoes, and so much gingerbread trim—even the sidewalk trash cans look like little Danish farmhouses with pitched-roof lids. One way to find a little authentic history amid the unabashed tourism is to visit the **Elverhøj Museum,** 1624 Elverhoy Way (☎ 805/686-1211), a warm and welcoming place devoted to Danish culture and Solvang history. Set in a traditional handcrafted Scandinavian-style home, and featuring many original old-world furnishings, this little museum can be fully appreciated in 30 minutes or less. It's open Wednesday through Sunday from 1 to 4pm; a $2 donation is suggested.

Solvang has always been renowned for its traditional and delectable pastries, and the oldest and best bakery in town is **Birkholm's Bakery,** 1555 Mission Dr. (☎ 805/688-3872). It opened in 1951 and is still family-run. In addition to sticky pastries, sweet rolls, fresh bread, and fresh-brewed coffee, Birkholm's sells its trademark blue-and-white waxed tub of Danish butter cookies ($7.95 each). Open daily from 8am to 5:30pm.

Old Mission Santa Ines. 1760 Mission Dr., Solvang. ☎ **805/688-4815.** $3 donation requested; free for children under 16. Summer Mon–Fri 9am–7pm; Sat 9am–4pm; Sun 1:30–5:30pm. Winter Mon–Fri 9am–5:30pm; Sat 9am–4pm; Sun 1:30–5:30pm. From downtown Solvang, take Calif. 246 1 mile east to Mission Dr.

Just on the edge of town, and one of few buildings minus a windmill or other Scandinavian fanfare, this Spanish mission was founded by Franciscan friars in 1804 and is still in use for daily services. Most of the original structure, painstakingly constructed of adobe by Native Americans, has been destroyed; the reconstruction features the ornately tiled and painted chapel typical of the Spanish missions, and an extensive museum display of mission artifacts and Franciscan vestment robes.

CACHUMA LAKE: A BALD-EAGLE HABITAT Created in 1953 by damming the Santa Ynez River, this picturesque reservoir running along Calif. 154 is the primary water source for Santa Barbara County. It's also the centerpiece of a 6,600-acre county park with a flourishing wildlife population and well-developed recreational facilities. Cachuma has, through both agreeable climate and diligent ranger efforts, become a notable habitat for resident and migratory birds, including rarely sighted bald eagles, which migrate south from as far as Alaska in search of food.

One of the best ways to appreciate this fine-feathered bounty is to take one of the naturalist-led **Eagle Cruises** of the lake, offered between November and February. The 48-foot *Osprey* was specially designed for wildlife observation, with unobstructed views from nearly every seat. During the rest of the year, rangers lead **Wildlife Cruises** around the lake, helping you spot resident waterfowl, grazing deer, and the elusive bobcats and mountain lions that live here. Eagle Cruises depart Wednesday through Sunday at 10am, with additional cruises Friday and Saturday at 2pm. Wildlife Cruises take place Friday and Saturday at 3pm, Saturday and Sunday at 10am; all cruises are 2 hours long. In addition to the park day-use fee of $5 per car, the cruise fare is $10 for adults and $5 for children 12 and under. Reservations are recommended for all cruises; call the **Santa Barbara County Parks Dept.** (☎ **805/686-5050**).

The recreational opportunities at Cachuma don't stop there; campers, boaters, and fishermen will find abundant facilities. Contact the **Lake Cachuma Recreation Area** (☎ **805/686-5054**) for more information.

WHERE TO STAY
Moderately Priced Options

Inn at Petersen Village. 1576 Mission Dr., Solvang, CA 93465. ☎ **800/321-8985** or 805/688-3121. Fax 805/688-5732. 42 units. A/C TV TEL. $105–$175 double. Extra person $15. Rates include generous buffet breakfast, evening wine and hors d'oeuvres, and dessert buffet. Midweek and auto-club discounts available. AE, MC, V.

If you think every hotel in Solvang has a kitschy, Danish theme, then step off the street right into this quiet, tasteful, and affordable hotel. Rooms are decorated in a European country motif, with print wallpaper, canopy beds, and mahogany-hued furniture. But it's the little touches that impress the most, like lighted magnifying mirrors, dimmable bathroom lights, free coffee/tea service to your room, and the complimentary food nearly always laid out in the hotel's friendly piano lounge. Some rooms overlook a bustling courtyard of shops, while others face Solvang's scenic hills. All are designed so everyone's happy: Smaller rooms have private balconies, those with noisier views are more spacious, and so on.

Royal Scandinavian Inn. 400 Alisal Rd. (P.O. Box 30), Solvang, CA 93464. ☎ **800/624-5572** or 805/688-8000. Fax 805/688-0761. E-mail: sroyal@silcom.com. 133 units. A/C TV TEL. Mar–Nov $91–$141 double; from $136 suite. Dec–Feb $61–$121 double; from $126 suite. Extra person $10. AE, CB, DC, DISC, JCB, MC, V.

If you're looking for a traditional, full-service hotel, this attractive and comfortable mainstay in Solvang is nicely located away from the congested main drag. Popular with business conventions and leisure groups, the inn has an all-day restaurant and a cocktail lounge, and is within walking distance of downtown Solvang. The championship Alisal River golf course is next door. Rooms are furnished in a vaguely Danish country decor, but are otherwise unremarkable; bathrooms are up-to-date. Ask for a room overlooking the courtyard, with its heated pool and spa; the view extends to the foothills beyond.

Worth a Splurge

Fess Parker's Wine Country Inn. 2860 Grand Ave. (P.O. Box 526), Los Olivos, CA 93441. ☎ 800/446-2455 or 805/688-7788. Fax 805/688-1942. 21 units. A/C TV TEL. $175–$270 double; $315–$340 suite. Rates include full breakfast and afternoon wine and hors d'oeuvres. Ask about packages and off-season discounts. "Grape Escape" package includes 2 nights' lodging, dinner for 2 at the Vintage Room, and gourmet picnic lunch for 2 for $380–$480. AE, DC, DISC, MC, V.

Local entrepeneur—and former actor—Fess Parker took over this popular country inn in late 1998 and is continuing its tradition of pampering. Each of its spacious rooms has a gas fireplace, wet bar, and a turndown fairy who leaves Godiva chocolates on your pillow. There's a heated outdoor swimming pool, whirlpool, and fleet of bicycles for guests' use. Room service is available from the hotel's chichi dining room, the Vintage Room, which serves pricey American/California cuisine in an almost stuffy formal setting.

WHERE TO DINE

If you're looking for traditional Danish fare in Solvang, head for **Bit O' Denmark,** 473 Alisal Rd. (☎ 805/688-5426). Their smorgasbord may not be the largest in town, but it's the freshest and highest quality; you can also order from the regular menu. Open daily from 9am to 9pm; the smorgasbord goes for $8.95 at lunch and $12.95 at dinner.

Brothers Restaurant. 409 First St. (in the Storybook Inn), Solvang. ☎ 805/688-9934. Reservations recommended. Main courses $11–$22. AE, MC, V. Wed–Sun 5–9pm. CALIFORNIA.

Jeff and Matt Nichols are the brothers; though young, these two chefs nevertheless bring 28 combined years of culinary experience to this intimate parlor of only nine tables. Since opening in 1996, Brothers has quickly won the hearts of smorgasbord-weary Solvangites with a California/international menu that changes seasonally according to Matt and Jeff's whims. You can always count on selections from the grill, such as swordfish resting on vegetable rice, splashed with Thai curry sauce and accented with mango salsa. A tender rack of lamb is fanned over mashed potatoes studded with tangy black olives on a rich rosemary sauce. And I always like a restaurant with as many dessert offerings as entrees; two to try are the fudge brownie with homemade roasted banana ice cream and the passion-fruit cheesecake. A carefully chosen, moderately priced list of Central Coast wines complements the menu.

Mattei's Tavern. Calif. 154, Los Olivos. ☎ 805/688-4820. Reservations recommended on weekends. Meals, including main course, soup or salad, and side dishes, $15–$35; menu items $8–$15. AE, DISC, MC, V. Daily 5:30–9pm; Sat–Sun noon–2:30pm. AMERICAN/ CONTINENTAL.

Mattei's is proud of its stagecoach past, and this rambling white Victorian submerged in climbing wisteria has successfully retained its historic charm and is well known throughout the county for fun and good food. Rumors abound of high-stakes poker games in Mattei's back room, where many an early rancher literally "lost the farm."

You'll find fine steaks on the menu, along with chicken picatta, Marsala, or teriyaki; Australian lobster tail, rainbow trout, burgers, prime-rib chili, and a dill-tinged tomato bisque soup all appear at both lunch and dinner.

Paula's Pancake House. 1531 Mission Dr., Solvang. ☎ **805/688-2867.** Most menu items under $7. AE, DISC, MC, V. Daily 6am–3pm. AMERICAN/DANISH.

Morning means one thing in Solvang, and that's Paula's three-page menu of *just breakfast!* There are wafer-thin Danish pancakes, served plain and simple, sweet and fruity, or with sausage and eggs; buttermilk pancakes; whole-wheat/honey pancakes; fresh-baked waffles; sourdough French toast; plus every omelet and egg dish imaginable, including some south-of-the-border salsa-fied specials. Paula's is friendly and casual, plunked in the heart of town so patio diners can watch the whole wacky world go by.

6 Santa Barbara

332 miles SE of San Francisco; 239 miles S of Monterey; 105 miles S of San Luis Obispo; 45 miles S of Solvang (via U.S. 101); 92 miles NW of Los Angeles

Between the Santa Ynez Mountains and the Pacific, charming, spoiled Santa Barbara is coddled by wooded mountains, caressed by baby breakers, and sheltered from tempestuous seas by rocky offshore islands. And it's just far enough from Los Angeles to make the Big City seem at once remote and accessible. There are few employment opportunities and real estate is expensive, so demographics have favored college students and rich retirees, thought of by the locals as the "almost wed and almost dead."

Downtown Santa Barbara is distinctive for its Spanish-Mediterranean architecture; all the structures sport matching red-tile roofs. But it wasn't always this way. Santa Barbara had a thriving Native American Chumash population for hundreds, if not thousands, of years. The European era began in the late 18th century, around a presidio (fort) that's been reconstructed in its original spot. The earliest architectural hodgepodge was destroyed in 1925 by a powerful earthquake that leveled the business district. Out of the rubble rose the Spanish-Mediterranean town of today, a stylish planned community that continues to rigidly enforce its strict building codes.

ESSENTIALS

GETTING THERE   U.S. 101 runs right through Santa Barbara; it's the fastest and most direct route from north or south (2 hr. from Los Angeles and 6 hr. from San Francisco).

The **Santa Barbara Municipal Airport** (☎ 805/967-7111) is located in Goleta, about 10 minutes north of downtown Santa Barbara. Airlines serving Santa Barbara include **American Eagle** (☎ 800/433-7300), **Skywest/Delta** (☎ 800/453-9417), **United** (☎ 800/241-6522), and **USAirways Express** (☎ 800/428-4322). **Yellow Cab** (☎ 805/965-5111) and other metered taxis line up outside the terminal; the fare is about $22 to downtown.

Amtrak (☎ 800/USA-RAIL) offers daily service to Santa Barbara. Trains arrive and depart from the **Santa Barbara Rail Station,** 209 State St. (☎ 805/963-1015); fares can be as low as $16 from Los Angeles.

VISITOR INFORMATION   The **Santa Barbara Visitor Information Center,** 1 Santa Barbara St., Santa Barbara, CA 93101 (☎ 800/927-4688 or 805/965-3021 to order a free destination guide), is on the ocean, at the corner of Cabrillo Street. The staff distributes maps, literature, an events calendar, and excellent advice. The office is open Monday through Saturday from 9am to 5pm and on Sunday from 10am to 5pm.

Downtown Santa Barbara

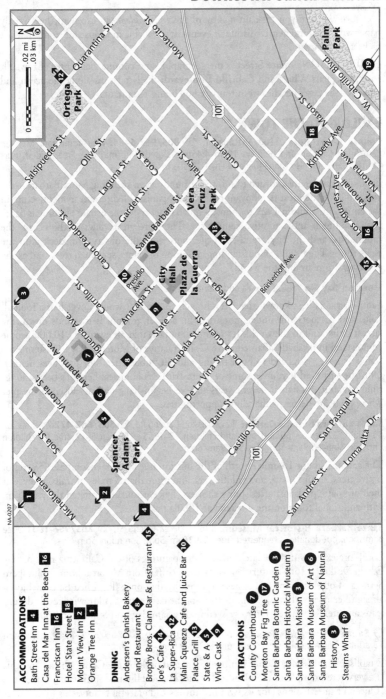

ACCOMMODATIONS
Bath Street Inn **4**
Casa del Mar Inn at the Beach **16**
Franciscan Inn **16**
Hotel State Street **18**
Mount View Inn **2**
Orange Tree Inn **1**

DINING
Andersen's Danish Bakery
and Restaurant **8**
Brophy Bros. Clam Bar & Restaurant **15**
Joe's Cafe **14**
La Super-Rica **12**
Main Squeeze Cafe and Juice Bar **10**
Palace Grill **13**
State & A **5**
Wine Cask **9**

ATTRACTIONS
County Courthouse **7**
Moreton Bay Fig Tree **17**
Santa Barbara Botanic Garden **3**
Santa Barbara Historical Museum **11**
Santa Barbara Mission **3**
Santa Barbara Museum of Art **6**
Santa Barbara Museum of Natural
History **3**
Stearns Wharf **19**

NA-0207

387

Also make sure you pick up a copy of the *Independent,* an excellent, free weekly paper with a comprehensive listing of events. It's available in shops and from sidewalk racks around town.

ORIENTATION **State Street** is the geographic and commercial center of town. It ends at **Stearns Wharf** and **Cabrillo Boulevard;** the latter runs along the ocean and separates the city's beaches from touristy hotels and restaurants.

EXPLORING THE TOWN

County Courthouse. 1100 Anacapa St. ☎ **805/962-6464.** Free admission. Mon–Fri 8am–5pm; Sat–Sun and holidays 10am–4:45pm; closed Christmas day. Free guided tours Mon–Sat at 2pm; also Mon, Tue, and Fri at 10:30am.

Even the accused are afforded exquisite surroundings in stunning Santa Barbara—the courthouse is the most flamboyant example of Spanish-Mediterranean architecture in the entire city. Built in 1929 to mimic a much older style, the ornate building is Santa Barbara's literal and figurative centerpiece. There are great views of the ocean, the mountains, and the city's terra-cotta-tile roofs from the observation deck atop the clock tower. There's also an outstanding collection of palms, specimen trees, and exotic plantings from around the world.

Moreton Bay Fig Tree. Chapala and Montecito sts.

Santa Barbara's best-known tree has a branch spread that would cover half a football field, and its roots run under more than an acre of ground. It is, hands down, the largest of its kind in the world. It's so broad, in fact, that an estimated 10,000 people could stand in its shade. Planted in 1877, it's a native of Moreton Bay in eastern Australia. The tree is related to both the fig and the rubber tree, but produces neither. Don't be surprised if you see some of Santa Barbara's homeless here; it's been a long-time hangout, though in recent years they've begun hanging out closer to the pier where there are better panhandling opportunities.

Santa Barbara Botanic Garden. 1212 Mission Canyon Rd. ☎ **805/682-4726.** Admission $3 adults, $2 seniors 60 and over and children 13–19, $1 children 5–12, free for children under 5. Mon–Fri 9am–5pm; Sat–Sun 9am–6pm.

The gardens, about 1½ miles north of the mission (see below), encompass 65 acres of native trees, shrubs, cacti, and wildflowers, and more than 5 miles of trails. They're at their aromatic peak just after spring showers. Docent tours are offered daily at 2pm, with additional tours on the weekend at 10:30am.

Santa Barbara Historical Museum. 136 E. De La Guerra St. ☎ **805/966-1601.** Free admission, but donations requested. Tues–Sat 10am–5pm; Sun noon–5pm.

Local-lore exhibits include late 19th-century paintings of the California missions by Edwin Deakin; a 16th-century carved Spanish coffer from Majorca, home of Junípero Serra; and objects from the Chinese community that once flourished here, including a magnificent carved shrine from the turn of the last century. A knowledgeable docent leads an interesting free tour every Wednesday, Saturday, and Sunday at 1:30pm.

✪ **Santa Barbara Mission.** Laguna and Los Olivos sts. ☎ **805/682-4149.** Admission $3 adults, free for children 16 and under. Daily 9am–5pm.

Established in 1786 by Father Junípero Serra and built by the Chumash Indians, this is a very rare example of the blending of Indian and Hispanic spirituality. Called the "Queen of the Missions" for its twin bell towers and graceful beauty, this hilltop mission overlooks the town and the Channel Islands beyond. The design of the imposing church incorporates many Moorish and classical elements. Santa Barbara's residents embraced the church's distinctive look as the town grew during the 1920s and 1930s, utilizing red-roof tiles, thick stucco walls, arches, and outdoor arcades.

Brochures are available in six languages, and docent-guided tours can be arranged in advance. It's worthwhile to tour the museum and gift shop, established in the restored padres' quarters. A highlight of the museum is the collection of historical photographs of the buildings and the surrounding area, some dating from the 1850s, featuring brown-robed friars tending the old orchards and gardens. The gift shop has an extensive collection of crucifixes, religious statuary, and pottery crafted by local artisans.

Don't miss the cemetery outside the church, its yard populated with centuries of headstones, vaults, and mausoleums. Shaded by a majestic Australian fig tree, it's still in use to this day. While you're in the cemetery, take a minute to study the exterior of the church. Over the door are three sets of skulls and crossbones. Upon careful observation, you'll see that only one is carved in stone—two sets are real bones embedded in the plaster.

Santa Barbara Museum of Art. 1130 State St. ☎ **805/963-4364.** Admission $5 adults, $3 seniors 65 and over, $1.50 students and children 6–16, free for children 5 and under, free for everyone Thurs and the 1st Sun of each month. Mon–Thurs and Sat 10am–5pm; Fri 10am–8pm; Sun noon–5pm.

A trip here feels like visiting the private galleries of a wealthy art collector. Works by Monet and other midquality oils by Dali, Picasso, Matisse, Chagall, and Rousseau are displayed on a rotating basis in rooms that, for the most part, are ample, airy, and well lit. Quantitatively, the museum's strengths lie in early-20th-century western American paintings and 19th- and 20th-century Asian art. Qualitatively, the best are the antiquities and the Chinese ceramics collections. Many pieces are often on loan to other museums, but good temporary exhibits show a high degree of reciprocity. Some awkward arrangements don't always make sense, and lighting could be improved on the placards. For the most part, though, Santa Barbara Museum of Art is a jewel of a museum. Free docent-led tours are given Tuesday through Sunday at 1pm. Focus tours are held on Wednesday and Saturday at noon. The new Peck Wing completed in 1998 includes more galleries, a larger gift shop, and a cafe, which is operated by the Wine Cask folks (see "Where to Dine," below).

Santa Barbara Museum of Natural History. 2559 Puesta del Sol Rd. (2 blocks uphill from the mission). ☎ **805/682-4711.** Admission $5 adults, $4 seniors and teens, $3 children. Mon–Sat 9am–5pm; Sun and holidays 10am–5pm.

This museum focuses on the study and interpretation of Pacific Coast natural history, which includes mammals, birds, marine life, plants, and insects; displays range from fossil ferns to the complete skeleton of a blue whale. Native American history is emphasized in basketry and textile exhibits, among others, and a full-size replica of a Chumash canoe. Recent additions include a replica of a pygmy mammoth skeleton and the "Lizard Lounge," featuring live reptiles and amphibians. An adjacent planetarium projects sky shows every Saturday and Sunday.

Santa Barbara Zoological Gardens. 500 Ninos Dr. ☎ **805/962-5339** or 805/962-6310 for a recording. Admission $6 adults, $4 seniors and children 2–12, free for children under 2. Daily 10am–5pm (last admission is 1 hr. before closing). Closed Thanksgiving Day and Christmas Day.

This is a thoroughly charming, pint-sized place, where all 600 animals can be seen in about 30 minutes. Most of the animals live in natural, open settings. The zoo has a children's Discovery Area, a miniature train ride, and a small carousel. The picnic areas (complete with barbecue pits) are underutilized and especially recommended.

Stearns Wharf. At the end of State St.

In addition to a small collection of second-rate shops, attractions, and restaurants, the city's 1872 vintage pier offers terrific inland views and good drop-line fishing. The Dolphin Fountain at the foot of the wharf was created by local artist Bud Bottoms for the city's 1982 bicentennial.

HITTING THE BEACH & OTHER OUTDOOR PURSUITS

BEACHING IT Santa Barbara has an array of beaches perfect for stretching out on a towel, playing volleyball (a very popular sport around here), or frolicking seaside. Two good choices are **Hendry's Beach,** located at the end of Cliff Drive and popular with families, boogie-boarders, and sunset strollers; and ✪ **Cabrillo Beach,** a wide swath of clean, white sand that hosts beach umbrellas, sand-castle builders, and spirited volleyball games. A grassy, parklike median buffers the noise of busy Cabrillo Boulevard. On Sundays, local artists set up shop beneath the palms. **East Beach,** by Stearns Wharf, is not incredibly interesting, and you'll have to pay $6 to park your car unless you find parking on the street. It is, however, a great place to stroll on Sundays when dozens of arts and crafts vendors exhibit their wares.

Note: A tragic oil spill off the coast of Santa Barbara in 1969 left surfers and sea critters dodging gobs of floating tar for the next 20 years. Although the area has finally cleared up, the staining brown substance still finds its way onto clothes and skin from time to time even if you don't go in the water.

BICYCLING A relatively flat, palm-lined 2-mile coastal pathway runs along the beach and is perfect for biking. More-adventurous riders can peddle through town, up to the mission, or to Montecito, the next town over. The best mountain-bike trail begins at the end of Tunnel Road and climbs up along a paved fire road before turning into a dirt trail to the mountaintop.

Beach Rentals, 22 State St. (☎ **805/966-6733**), rents well-maintained one-speeds. They also have tandem bikes and surrey cycles that can hold as many as four adults and two children. Rates vary depending on equipment; one-speeds rent for $6 per hour or $24 per day, and tandems go for $9 per hour or $24 per day. Bring an ID (driver's license or passport) to expedite your rental. It's open daily from 8am to dusk.

GOLF At the ✪ **Santa Barbara Golf Club,** 3500 McCaw Ave., at Las Positas Road (☎ **805/687-7087**), there's a great, affordable (relatively speaking) 6,009-yard, 18-hole course and driving range. Unlike many municipal courses, the Santa Barbara Golf Course is well maintained and was designed to present a moderate challenge for the average golfer. Greens fees are $24 Monday through Friday and $28 on weekends (discounts are offered to residents and seniors). Optional carts rent for $22 for 18 holes, $12 for 9 holes.

HIKING The hills and mountains surrounding Santa Barbara have excellent hiking trails. One of my favorites begins at the end of Tunnel Road. Take Mission Canyon Road past the mission, turn right onto Foothill Road, and take the first left onto Mission Canyon Drive. Bear left onto Tunnel Road and park at the end (where all the other cars are). You can buy a trail map at the Santa Barbara Visitor Information Center.

HORSEBACK RIDING Several area stables rent horses, including **Circle Bar B Ranch,** 1800 Refugio Rd. (☎ 805/968-3901), and **Rancho Oso,** Paradise Road, off Calif. 154 (☎ 805/964-8985), which offers a $20 (ouch!) 1-hour trail ride.

IN-LINE SKATING The paved beach path that runs along Santa Barbara's waterfront is perfect for skating. **Beach Rentals,** 22 State St. (☎ **805/966-6733**), located nearby, rents in-line skates. The $5 per-hour fee includes wrist and knee pads.

SPORTFISHING, DIVE CRUISES & WHALE WATCHING   It won't be cheap, but think of it this way: If you spend all day at sea, you won't be blowing money at State Street shops. **Sea Landing,** at the foot of Bath Street and Cabrillo Boulevard (☎ 805/963-3564), makes regular sportfishing runs with specialized boats. They also offer a wide variety of other fishing and diving cruises and camping trips to the Channel Islands. Food and drink are served onboard, and rental rods and tackle are available. Rates vary according to the excursion; call for reservations. Whale-watching cruise rates range from $24 for 2½ hours to $65 for all day. A 4-day scuba trip costs $455.

Whale-watching cruises are offered from February through April, when California gray whales make their migratory journey from Baja California to Alaska. Tours are $24 for adults and $14 for children; sightings of large marine mammals (though perhaps only dolphins) are guaranteed.

SHOPPING

There's no way around it; this is simply not a budget town. If you don't mind paying top dollar for a few trinkets, **State Street** from the beach to Victoria Street has the largest concentration of shops. Many specialize in T-shirts and postcards, but there are a number of boutiques and antique shops (where you should haggle over prices) as well. If you get tired of strolling, hop on one of the electric shuttle buses (25¢) that run up and down State Street at regular intervals.

Also check out **Brinkerhoff Avenue** (off Cota Street, between Chapala and De La Vina streets), Santa Barbara's "antique alley"; most shops are open Tuesday through Sunday from 11am to 5pm (again, no real bargains). **El Paseo,** 814 State St., is a picturesque shopping arcade reminiscent of an old Spanish street. Built around an 1827 adobe home, the mall is lined with charming shops and art galleries. Sadly, there are no great steals here either.

WHERE TO STAY

Before you even begin calling around for reservations, keep in mind that Santa Barbara accommodations are expensive, especially during summer. Then decide whether you'd like to stay beachside (even more expensive) or downtown; the town is small, but not small enough to happily stroll between the two areas. There is, however, a shuttle that will cart you back and forth.

Hot Spots Accommodations, 36 State St., Santa Barbara, CA 93101 (☎ 800/793-7666 or 805/564-1637), is a one-stop shop for hotel and B&B rooms. They'll help you find a room in your price range, and there's no charge for their services. Significantly discounted rates are often available at the last minute, when hotels need to fill their rooms—usually in January and February (although Santa Barbara's tourist season seems to be getting longer and longer each year, which means you'll be lucky to find an affordable room regardless of the time of year).

Another option is **Accommodations Reservations Service** (☎ 800/292-2222; www.coastalescapes@linkline.com), a company that books rooms along California's coast from Oxnard to Monterey. The service is free and has information on accommodations in all price ranges.

In addition to the hotels listed below, Santa Barbara also has a ✪ **Banana Bungalow International Hostel** (☎ 800/3-HOSTEL or 805/963-0154; sBres@Bananabunglaow.com), which offers dorm-style accommodations for $12 to $18 per person near the beach and downtown.

Other highly recommendable, moderately priced accommodations are offered at the **Best Western Encina Lodge and Suites** (☎ 800/526-2282 or 805/682-7277) and **Tropicana Inn and Suites** (☎ 800/468-1988 or 805/966-2219).

SUPER-CHEAP SLEEPS

Hotel State Street. 121 State St. (1 block from the beach), Santa Barbara, CA 93101 ☎ **805/966-6586.** Fax 805/962-8459. 54 units, 51 without bathroom (2 with toilet only, 1 with full bathroom). TV TEL. Summer $40–$70 double; winter $30–$50 double. Rates include continental breakfast. AE, MC, V. Free parking.

Young travelers and Europeans fill this hotel in the summer, but it's clean and well kept enough to make any budget traveler rest easy. The hotel makes an effort to be homey and stylish while maintaining its cheap rates. Rooms come with firm mattresses, a sink and hand towels, and prints on the walls. The feel here is slightly reminiscent of a boarding house, but that's half the fun—imagine the worldly people you'll meet on your way to the shower. Bonuses include a continental breakfast of sweet rolls, coffee, tea, and fruit, as well as free parking. Plus, the hotel is just a 1-block stroll from East Beach. A drawback is that trains pass nearby and blow their whistles (it can be quite loud); they usually quiet down after 10pm, but have been known to wake folks from time to time, and can start up again as early as 7am. Call if you're checking in late; you'll need a code to get in after-hours.

FOR A FEW BUCKS MORE/MODERATELY PRICED OPTIONS

All the best buys fill up fast in the summer months, so be sure to reserve your room well in advance. This is true even if you're just planning to stay at the nice, reliable **Motel 6** (☎ 800/466-8356 or 805/564-1392) near the beach or the good-value **Sandpiper Lodge** (☎ 800/40-LODGE or 805/687-5326) just a little farther away.

✪ **Casa del Mar Inn at the Beach.** 18 Bath St., Santa Barbara, CA 93101. ☎ **800/433-3097** or 805/963-4418. Fax 805/966-4240. www.casadelmar.com. 21 units. TV TEL. $64–$159 double; from $114 suite. Rates include continental breakfast and wine-and-cheese social. Extra person $10. Midweek discounts available. AE, DISC, DC, MC, V. From northbound U.S. 101, exit at Cabrillo, turn left onto Cabrillo and head toward the beach; Bath is the 2nd street on the right after the wharf. From southbound U.S. 101, take the Castillo exit, turn right on Castillo, left on Cabrillo, and left on Bath. Free parking. Pets allowed for $10 extra per pet.

A half block from the beach (sorry, no views), Casa del Mar is an excellent-value motel with one- and two-room suites. The largish rooms have brand-new furnishings, with plenty of pastels. The flower-sprinkled grounds are well maintained, and the staff is eager to please. Many rooms have kitchenettes, fridges, and stoves. The Jacuzzi here stays open half an hour later than the neighboring Franciscan's. Considering the prices of hotels in this town, Casa del Mar is a great bargain.

✪ **Franciscan Inn.** 109 Bath St. (at Mason St.), Santa Barbara, CA 93101. ☎ **805/963-8845.** Fax 805/564-3295. 53 units. TV TEL. $65–$99 double; from $85 suite. Rates include continental breakfast and afternoon cookies and drinks. Extra person $8. AE, CB, DC, MC, V. Free parking.

One of the best bargains beachside can be found a block from the shore at the Franciscan Inn. The exterior is motel-like. Inside, the rooms are looking dapper, especially since the motel poured $400,000 into redecorating in 1997. Several rooms have fully equipped kitchenettes and/or balconies, and most bathrooms come with a tub. All rooms have coffeemakers, computer jacks, and VCRs; hair dryers are available upon request. The suites come complete with living rooms, separate kitchens, and sleeping quarters for up to four adults; one has a fireplace. Breakfast, afternoon appetizers, and a complimentary newspaper are included in the price, as is the use of the heated outdoor pool, Jacuzzi, video library, and coin-operated laundry. Reserve well in advance, especially for May through September.

Mount View Inn. 3055 De La Vina St. (at State St.), Santa Barbara, CA 93105. ☎ **805/ 687-6636.** 34 units. A/C TV TEL. Mid-Sept to May $60–$99 double. June to mid-Sept $75–$129 double. 2-night minimum on weekends. Rates include continental breakfast. AE, DISC, MC, V. Free parking.

It may be over a mile from the downtown action and on a busy street corner, but Mount View's price and amenities make it worth considering. The very clean rooms are arranged motel-style, decorated in an attempt at brightness (some lace curtains), and have firm mattresses, a refrigerator, and a table and chairs. Bathrooms are small, and some of the furniture looks a little weathered; but there is a pool, and rates include a continental breakfast, which is served in the lobby.

Orange Tree Inn. 1920 State St. (at Alamar St.), Santa Barbara, CA 93101. ☎ **800/ LEM-ORNG** or 805/569-1521. 46 units. A/C TV TEL. $70–$145 double; from $125 suite. AE, DISC, MC, V. Free parking.

We'd personally prefer to stay by the beach, but if you want cheap downtown accommodations, you're safe with the Orange Tree. Don't get too excited, though—it's a motel. Still, the rooms were recently renovated and have nice carpets and bedspreads. Most have a balcony or patio, and some have bathtubs. Guests also get free local calls and use of the pool.

WORTH A SPLURGE

✪ **Bath Street Inn.** 1720 Bath St. (north of Valerio St.), Santa Barbara, CA 93101. ☎ **800/341-BATH,** 800/549-BATH in Calif., or 805/682-9680. 12 units. TV TEL. $100– $200 double. Rates include breakfast and afternoon tea, wine, and cookies. Midweek rates up to 20% off. Street parking available. AE, MC, V.

This is one of the cutest, most meticulously cared-for B&Bs we've ever seen. The minute we walked in, a gracious innkeeper guided us to the redwood patio to see an amazing wisteria canopy in bloom (lucky guests can have breakfast beneath it). We were then treated to fresh-baked cookies, which are served with tea and wine each afternoon. After our snack, we wandered from room to room, astonished by the exquisite details of each nook and cranny throughout the three-story Victorian. Each adorable (and immaculate) room is intimately and individually decorated with antiques, colorful wallpaper, and fresh flowers. Some include a Jacuzzi and/or a VCR. The common areas are equally attractive and include a third-floor reading nook with a VCR (there's a video library downstairs). No smoking.

WHERE TO DINE
SUPER-CHEAP EATS

Andersen's Danish Bakery and Restaurant. 1106 State St. (near Figueroa St.). ☎ **805/ 962-5085.** Reservations recommended for larger parties. Breakfast $5–$12; lunch $5–$12. MC, V. Daily 8am–8pm. EUROPEAN.

Remember how ice-cream parlors used to look? Well, pink and frilly does not describe this bakery's sweets, but rather the old-style decor of this family restaurant. Grandma will feel at home here, and kids won't have a problem finding something they like on the menu (especially when it comes to dessert). Authentically Danish Ms. Andersen greets you herself (when she's not baking) and offers substantial (and cheap!) portions of New York steak, chicken or crab salad, and an array of other edibles (including an honest-to-goodness smorgasbord). Seating provides great State Street people-watching from both indoor and outdoor tables.

✪ **La Super-Rica Taquería.** 622 N. Milpas St. (between Cota and Ortega sts.). ☎ **805/963-4940.** Reservations not accepted. Main courses $3–$6. No credit cards. Daily 11am–9:30pm. MEXICAN.

Following celebrity chef Julia Child's lead, aficionados have deemed this place the state's best Mexican restaurant, or to be more specific, taco stand. Excellent soft tacos are the shack's real forte. Unfortunately, portions can be quite small—you have to order two or three items in order to satisfy an average hunger, which can easily turn a meal for two into a $20 excursion. Still, there's no denying this place is darn good.

✪ **Main Squeeze Cafe and Juice Bar.** 138 E. Canon Perdido St. ☎ **805/966-5365.** $4.35–$11.50. MC, V. Summer Mon–Fri 11am–10pm; Sat–Sun 10am–10pm. Winter Mon–Fri 11am–9pm; Sat–Sun 10am–10pm. DELI/CAFE.

Health food has come a long way since wheat-grass juice and alfalfa sprouts, and you can experience its evolution here at this quintessential no-nonsense, health-conscious California cafe. The fare goes far beyond rabbit food to include a variety of substantial sandwiches and soups, soft tacos, and special plates, as well as excellent budget brunch items and a good selection of smoothies. Hard-core carnivores beware: The only burgers you'll find on the menu are of the soy or garden variety. This place is less hippielike than many other cafes in town. Diners order at the counter and then grab a table inside or out.

State & A Bar and Grill. Corner of State St. and Anapamu. ☎ **805/966-1010.** Reservations accepted for large parties only. Main courses $4.95–$12.95. AE, DISC, MC, V. Daily 11am–midnight; bar open until 2am. AMERICAN.

Perfect for families or young folks in search of a cheap brew, State & A is a casual joint that's infamous for its huge portions and festive glass-encased street-front patio (there's indoor seating, as well). The menu includes an array of appetizers (nachos, chicken strips, hot wings), hefty salads (including grilled mahi, Indonesian, and classic Caesar), Southwestern fare, burgers, steak, and pasta. The cocktail crowd will appreciate happy hour, Monday through Friday from 3:30 to 6:30pm, when pints pour for $1.50 and well drinks, $2.50.

FOR A FEW BUCKS MORE

Brophy Bros. Clam Bar & Restaurant. Yacht Basin and Marina (at Harbor Way). ☎ **805/966-4418.** Reservations not accepted. Main courses $9–$16. AE, MC, V. Sun–Thurs 11am–10pm; Fri–Sat 11am–11pm. SEAFOOD.

This place is most known for its unbeatable view of the marina, but the dependable fresh seafood keeps tourists and locals coming back. Dress is casual, portions are huge, and favorites include New England clam chowder, cioppino, and any one of an assortment of seafood salads. The scampi is consistently good, as is all the fresh fish, which come with soup or salad, coleslaw, and pilaf or french fries. A nice assortment of beers and wines is available. *Be forewarned:* The wait at this small place can be up to 2 hours on a weekend night.

Joe's Cafe. 536 State St. (at Cota St.). ☎ **805/966-4638.** Reservations recommended. Pasta $5–$6.75; most main courses $9.25–$12; steaks $14–$20. AE, DISC, MC, V. Mon–Thurs 11am–11:30pm; Fri–Sat 11am–12:30am; Sun 4–11pm. AMERICAN.

Joe's has been around so long (since 1928), it seems that coming here is a generationally inherited habit with locals and college students alike. Maybe it's because Joe's is dependable and reasonably priced, or perhaps it's the strong drinks served at the full bar. Whatever the reason, folks seem to love the hunting-lodge-cum-picnic ambiance and the fare you'd expect from such an old-school establishment. There are plenty of red-meat dishes on the menu (five different steak options), Southern fried chicken, and a fried-shrimp dish and garden burger thrown in for good measure. Meals come with a barrage of side dishes. Steaks will cost you, but all the other main courses are closer to $10—and talk about a real bargain, how about a big plate of pasta for $6? Weekends here are especially popular with partying students.

✪ **Montecito Cafe.** 1295 Coast Village Rd. (off Olive Mill Rd.). ☎ **805/969-3392.** Reservations recommended for dinner. Main courses $7–$13. AE, MC, V. Daily 11:30am–2:30pm and 5:30–10pm. CALIFORNIA NOUVEAU.

Overlooking Montecito's shopping street, the light and airy Montecito Cafe provides diners a high-quality culinary experience at an affordable price (some say it's the best value in the area). Menu items include a watercress salad with sesame vinaigrette and broiled oysters; an Emmenthal-cheese-filled pork chop with lemon-wine-herb sauce; and capellini with mushrooms, tomato, basil, olive oil, and wine. The petite dining room itself is pleasantly simple, with well-set tables, a wall of windows, plants, a small fountain, and original art—it's the perfect place to impress a date.

✪ **Palazzio.** 1151 Coast Village Rd., Montecito. ☎ **805/969-8565.** Main courses: half orders $7.95–$10.95, full orders $11.95–$14.95. MC, V. Mon–Sat 11:30am–2:30pm; Sun–Thurs 5:30–10pm; Fri–Sat 5:30–11pm. ITALIAN.

Cheap tasty Italian, a bottomless basket of yummy garlic rolls, and one of the most festive atmospheres in town can all be yours—if you don't mind waiting awhile to mange. Palazzio, a noisy and fun restaurant whose menu reads like an encyclopedia of pasta (25 choices!) with a few antipasti, salads, and specials (chicken, lasagna, and cannelloni), is arranged so you can go for the huge full portions or the hearty half orders, which are generally enough for a main course. The happy atmosphere could be due to the prices, but its more likely attributed to the vats of Italian merlot ($2.95 per glass!), to which diners help themselves while they wait (often an hour) to be seated as well as during the meal. The waiter tallies the damage at the end of the evening, but it always seems like a deal. Besides, it's almost impossible not to leave with mammoth amounts of leftovers.

Pan e Vino. 1482 E. Valley Rd., Montecito. ☎ **805/969-9274.** Reservations required. Pastas $8–$10; meat and fish dishes $11–$19. AE, MC, V. Mon–Sat 11:30am–10pm; Sun 5:30–9pm. ITALIAN.

The perfect Italian trattoria, Pan e Vino offers food as authentic as you'd find in Rome. The simplest dish, spaghetti topped with basil-tomato sauce, is so delicious it's hard to understand why diners would want to occupy their taste buds with more complicated concoctions. But this kitchen is capable of almost anything. Pasta puttenesca, with tomatoes, anchovies, black olives, and capers, is always tops. Pan e Vino also gets high marks for its reasonable prices, attentive service, and casual atmosphere. Although many diners prefer to eat outside on the intimate patio, some of the best tables are in the charming, cluttered dining room.

Your Place. 22-A N. Milpas St. (at Mason St.). ☎ **805/966-5151.** Reservations recommended. Main courses $7–$13. AE, MC, V. Tues–Thurs and Sun 11am–10pm; Fri–Sat 11am–11pm. THAI.

There are lots of Thai restaurants in Santa Barbara, but when locals argue about which one is best, Your Place invariably ranks high on the list. Traditional dishes are prepared with the freshest ingredients and represent a wide cross-section of Thai cuisine. It's best to begin with *tom kah kai,* a hot-and-sour chicken soup with coconut milk and mushrooms, ladled out of a hot pot tableside—it's enough for two or more. Siamese duckling, a top main dish, is prepared with sautéed vegetables, mushrooms, and ginger sauce. Like other dishes, it can be made mild, medium, hot, or very hot.

WORTH A SPLURGE

✪ **The Palace Grill.** 8 E. Cota St. (at State St.). ☎ **805/963-5000.** www.palacegrill. com. Reservations limited: Sun–Thurs, and Fri–Sat from 5:30–6pm only. Main courses $9–$25. AE, MC, V. Sun–Thurs 5:30–10pm; Fri–Sat 5:30–11pm. CAJUN/CREOLE/ ITALIAN.

If you're looking for a festive scene, great food, and an all-around fun evening, this is the place to find it. Even when there's a line out the door (always the case on weekends), The Palace makes the wait enjoyable with free appetizers and live entertainment (weekends only) by a local magician. Inside the divided dining room, amidst the jazz memorabilia and lively music, the staff pampers you silly as they provide you with an overflow of Cajun, Creole, and recently added Italian favorites (i.e., pasta dishes). We tried a knockout rum punch, splendid oysters Rockefeller, an outstanding blackened filet mignon, an absolutely divine blackened salmon, and tasty crispy Louisiana softshell crabs. Portions are large, but we did manage to squeeze in a few bites of the key lime pie and bread pudding soufflé—both very tasty.

✪ **Wine Cask.** 813 Anacapa St. (in El Paseo Center). ☎ **805/966-9463.** Reservations recommended. Main courses $8–$12 at lunch, $17–$23 at dinner. AE, DC, MC, V. Mon–Fri 11:30am–3pm; Sat–Sun 10am–3pm; Sun–Thurs 5:30–9pm; Fri–Sat 5:30–10pm. Valet parking $4. ITALIAN.

One of Santa Barbara's most popular upscale restaurants, the Wine Cask evolved from the adjoining 17-year-old wine shop. The large dining room—with a hand-stenciled, gold-leaf, 1920s historic-landmark ceiling—is the backdrop for fine Italian fare served amid a bustling atmosphere. Whether you opt for the dining room (request fireside for romance) or the patio (yes, there are heat lamps), you'll be treated to such creations as lamb sirloin with red-wine and wild-mushroom risotto or porcini-crusted salmon with toasted pearl couscous. The wine list reads like a novel, with more than 1,000 wines (ranging from $14 to $1,400), and has deservedly received a *Wine Spectator* award for excellence. There's also a happy hour at the adjoining Intermezzo from 4 to 6pm daily.

SANTA BARBARA AFTER DARK

To find out what's going on while you're in town, check the free weekly *Independent*, or call the following venues: the **Center Stage Theater**, upstairs at the Paseo Nuevo Shopping Center, Chapala and De La Guerra streets (☎ 805/963-0408); the **Lobero Theater**, 33 E. Canon Perdido St. (☎ 805/963-0761); **the Arlington Theater**, 1317 State St. (☎ 805/963-4408); or the **Earl Warren Showgrounds**, at Las Positas Road and U.S. 101 (☎ 805/687-0766).

At night a young crowd spills out of the bars on lower State Street. Unless you're aching to relive your college days, it isn't likely to be your bag.

7 The Ojai Valley

35 miles E of Santa Barbara; 88 miles NW of Los Angeles

by Stephanie Avnet Yates

In a crescent-shaped valley between Santa Barbara and Ventura, surrounded by mountain peaks, lies Ojai (pronounced "*O*-hi"). It's a magical place, selected by Frank Capra as Shangri-La, the legendary utopia of his 1936 classic *Lost Horizon*. The spectacularly tranquil setting has made Ojai a mecca for artists and a particularly large population of New Age spiritualists, both drawn by the area's mystical beauty.

Life is low-key in the peaceful Ojai Valley. Perhaps the most excitement generated all year happens during the 1st week of June, when the **Ojai Music Festival** draws world-renowned contemporary jazz artists to perform in the Libbey Bowl amphitheater.

While in Ojai, you're bound to hear folks wax poetic about something called the "pink moment." It's a phenomenon first noticed by the earliest Native American valley dwellers, when the brilliant sunset over the nearby Pacific is reflected onto the mountainside, creating an eerie and beautiful pink glow.

ESSENTIALS

GETTING THERE   The 45-minute drive south from Santa Barbara to Ojai is along two-lane Calif. 150, a beautiful road that's as curvaceous as it is stunning. From Los Angeles, take U.S. 101 north to Calif. 33, which winds through eucalyptus groves to meet Calif. 150—the trip takes about 90 minutes. Calif. 150 is called Ojai Avenue in the town center and is the village's primary thoroughfare.

VISITOR INFORMATION   The **Ojai Valley Chamber of Commerce,** 150 W. Ojai Ave., Ojai, CA 93023 (☎ 805/646-8126), distributes free area maps, brochures, and a *Visitor's Guide to the Ojai Valley,* which lists galleries and current events. It's open Monday through Friday from 9:30am to 4:30pm, Saturday and Sunday from 10am to 4pm. For information on the Ojai Music Festival, call ☎ **805/646-2094.**

EXPLORING THE TOWN & VALLEY

Small Ojai is home to more than 35 artists working in a variety of media; most have home studios and are represented in one of several galleries in town. The best for jewelry and smaller pieces is HumanArts, 310 E. Ojai Ave. (☎ 805/646-1525); a home-accessories annex, HumanArts Home, is located at 246 E. Ojai Ave. (☎ **805/646-8245**). Artisans band together each October for an organized Artists' Studio Tour (for information call ☎ 805/646-8126); it's fun to drive from studio to studio at your own pace, meeting various artists and perhaps purchasing some of their work. There is a $15 to $20 fee for the tour. Ojai's most famous resident is world-renowned Beatrice Wood, who worked up until her death in 1998 at the age of 104. Her whimsical sculpture and luminous pottery are internationally acclaimed, and her spirit is still a driving force in Ojai.

Strolling the Spanish arcade shops downtown and the surrounding area will yield a treasure trove, including open-air **Bart's Books,** Matilija St. at Canada St. (☎ 805/646-3755), an Ojai fixture for many years. Antique hounds head for **The Antique Collection,** 236 W. Ojai Ave. (☎ 805/646-6688), an indoor antique mall packed to the rafters with treasures, trash, and everything in between.

Residents of the Ojai Valley *love* their equine companions—miles of bridle paths are painstakingly maintained, and horse-crossing signs are everywhere. If you'd like to explore the equestrian way, call the **Ojai Valley Inn's Ranch & Stables** (☎ 805/646-5511, ext. 456). One-hour trail rides cost $40 per person.

Ojai has long been a haven for several esoteric sects of metaphysical and philosophical beliefs. **The Krotona Institute and School of Theosophy,** Calif. 33 and Calif. 150 at Hermosa Road (☎ 805/646-2653), has been in the valley since moving from Hollywood in 1926, and visitors are welcome at their library and bookstore.

When Ronald Coleman saw Shangri-La in *Lost Horizon,* he was really admiring the Ojai Valley. To visit the breathtakingly beautiful spot where Coleman stood for his view of **Shangri-La,** drive east on Ojai Avenue, up the hill, and stop at the stone bench near the top; the view is spectacular.

Incredibly beautiful **Lake Casitas Recreation Area** boasts nearly 32 miles of shoreline and is just minutes from downtown Ojai. Boating and fishing are popular activities; you can rent rowboats and small powerboats year-round from the **boathouse** (☎ 805/649-2043), enjoy picnicking by the lakeside (a year-round snack bar serves breakfast and lunch), or bike around the lake to the sound of chirping birds. Bicycle rentals are available at the lake from **Cycles 4 Rent** (☎ 805/652-0462); prices start at $4 per hour or $12 per half-day. Because the lake serves as a domestic water supply, swimming is not allowed. More than 450 campsites have picnic tables, fire pits, and available drinking water; to make reservations, call ☎ **805/649-1122.** To get there from Calif. 150, turn left onto Santa Ana Road, and follow the signs to the recreation area.

WHERE TO STAY
SUPER-CHEAP SLEEPS

Ojai Rancho Motel. 615 W. Ojai Ave. (at Country Club Dr.), Ojai, CA 93023. ☎ **800/ 362-1434** or 805/646-1434. 12 units. A/C TV TEL. $80–$135 double. AE, DISC, MC, V.

This classic ranch-style motel has been well maintained and presents an attractively rustic alternative to the pricey country club around the corner, but don't expect the same gracious service from the cranky front office here. The rooms all come with microwaves, refrigerators, and coffeemakers, and there's a heated outdoor pool, sauna, and Jacuzzi; two rooms have fireplaces. The rooms in back look out on ranch land and tend to be quieter than the front rooms near the street.

FOR A FEW BUCKS MORE

Best Western Casa Ojai. 1302 E. Ojai Ave., Ojai, CA 93023. ☎ **800/255-8175** or 805/646-8175. Fax 805/640-8247. 45 units. A/C TV TEL. $91–$117 double. Rates include continental breakfast. Midweek and off-season rates available. Extra person $10. Children under 12 stay free in parents' room. AE, DISC, MC, V.

This pleasant-enough two-story motel is on the main road through town; although it's a mile or so from the hubbub, street traffic can get a little noisy at times. The rooms are light and airy, however, and come with coffeemakers; some have refrigerators as well. There's a heated pool and whirlpool, plus a wooded public golf course across the street. This hotel's rack rates are misleading; AAA members, for example, can get rates as low as $60 midweek. Free stays for kids 12 and under also make the Casa Ojai a good family option.

The Moon's Nest Inn. 210 E. Matilija, Ojai, CA 93023. ☎ **805/646-6635.** 7 units, 5 with bathroom. A/C. $95–$135 double. Rates include breakfast and evening wine and spirits. Midweek discounts available. MC, V.

Conveniently located a block off Ojai Avenue, this comfortable clapboard B&B was built as a schoolhouse in 1874 and is Ojai's oldest building. At press time, new owners were renovating the inn, adding private bathrooms to most rooms, building some private balconies, and planning warm-weather breakfasts on the new garden deck. The cozy parlor remains unchanged, and guest rooms still sport antique iron beds and a simple mix of vintage and contemporary decor. A cottage on the grounds houses a friendly beauty-and-massage salon, and guests enjoy full privileges at the Ojai Valley Athletic Club for a nominal day-use fee.

WORTH A SPLURGE

Ojai Valley Inn and Spa. Country Club Dr. (off Calif. 33), Ojai, CA 93023. ☎ **800/ 422-OJAI** or 805/646-5511. Fax 805/646-7969. www.ojairesort.com. 222 units. A/C

Money-Saving Tip

One look at the rack rates at the **Ojai Valley Inn and Spa** and you may flip. Don't automatically assume this place is out of your price range, however. At press time they were offering a midweek, AAA-member rate of just $99. Other packages are available, too. Don't be shy about asking about discounted rates.

MINIBAR TV TEL. $195–$260 double; from $345 suite. Packages available. AE, DC, MC, V. Pets permitted for $25 per night with advance notice.

In 1923, famous Hollywood architect Wallace Neff designed the clubhouse that's now the focal point of this quintessentially Californian, Spanish colonial–style resort. The inn has carefully kept a sprawling ranch ambiance while providing gracious, elegant service and amenities, along with a beautiful, oak-studded Senior PGA Tour golf course (greens fees for guests are a steep $95, including cart). Many of the unusually spacious guest rooms have fireplaces; most have sofas, writing desks, and secluded terraces or balconies that open onto expansive views of the valley and the magnificent Sierra Madre. Added comforts include coffeemakers, plush terry robes, and hair dryers.

In 1998 the resort unveiled ✪ **Spa Ojai,** where pampering spa treatments—many modeled after Native American traditions—are administered inside a beautifully designed and exquisitely tiled Spanish-Moorish complex. Mind/body fitness classes, art classes, nifty workout machines, and a sparkling outdoor pool complete the relaxation choices. For the price of one treatment (many start at around $50), you can stretch out a whole splendid day at this rejuvenating spot. The resort also has two outdoor heated pools (including a 60-ft. lap pool); eight hard-court tennis courts (four lit for night play) for $12 per hour, a state-of-the-art fitness center with exercise room, Jacuzzi, sauna, and steam room; jogging trails; complimentary bicycles; and horseback riding. "Camp Ojai" offers special children's programs including a supervised play area and activities during peak holiday periods.

The hotel's newly revamped dining room, Maravilla, offers Mediterranean fare at very expensive prices; a more economical choice is the Oak Cafe and Terrace, which serves breakfast, lunch, and dinner overlooking the oak-lined golf course. Main courses are $9 to $16 at lunch and $10 to $24 at dinner.

WHERE TO DINE
SUPER-CHEAP EATS

Boccali's. 3277 Ojai–Santa Paula Rd. ☎ **805/646-6116.** Reservations not accepted. Pizza $9–$19; pasta $6–$12. No credit cards. Mon–Tues 4–9pm; Wed–Sun noon–9pm. ITALIAN.

This small, wood-frame restaurant, set among citrus groves, is a pastoral pleasure spot where patrons eat outside at picnic tables under umbrellas and twisted oak trees, or inside at tables covered with red-and-white-checked oilcloths. Pizza is the main dish served here, topped California-style with the likes of crab, garlic, shrimp, and chicken. Fresh lemonade, squeezed from fruit plucked from local trees, is the usual drink of choice.

Oak Pit BBQ. 820 N. Ventura Ave. (Calif. 33), Oak View. ☎ **805/649-9903.** Reservations not accepted. Sandwiches $4; main courses $8–$12. Tues–Thurs and Sun 11:30am–8:30pm; Fri–Sat 11am–9pm. BARBECUE.

This stick-to-your-ribs joint on the road between Ojai and Ventura is worth building up an appetite for. The rust-colored shack doesn't have much going for it looks-wise—just some gingham curtains, a few tables indoors and out, and stacks of wood for firing up the BBQ—but generous portions of slowly oak-smoked meats will have dedicated carnivores coming back for more. BBQ tri-tip brisket, ham, pork, Cajun sausage, chicken—they're all served up in sandwiches or full dinners, with available sides of coleslaw, potato salad, french fries, baked beans, and corn-on-the-cob.

FOR A FEW BUCKS MORE

Blue Moon Cafe. 401 E. Ojai Ave. ☎ **805/646-1766.** Reservations not accepted. Main courses $4–$9 at breakfast/lunch, $9–$15 at dinner. AE, MC, V. Daily 7am–10pm (subject to seasonal Mon closure). AMERICAN.

This casual and tasty cafe is perfectly situated at the heart of Ojai, within walking distance of the Arcade and all downtown. Recently opened in an awkward little building with more tables on the patio than indoors, its not much to look at. But their convenient hours—from early breakfast through late dinner—and hearty, affordable menu, make the Blue Moon one to watch. They serve a typical American breakfast of pancakes, omelets, roast-beef hash, etc.; lunch features some burgers, sandwiches, and lunchroom-style salads; at dinnertime they fire up the grill for steaks and chops plus a home-style meat loaf and a cheese-fondue appetizer. Call it coffee-shop fare raised to Ojai's rigorous culinary standards.

A MODERATELY PRICED OPTION

Suzanne's Cuisine. 502 W. Ojai Ave. ☎ **805/640-1961.** Reservations recommended for dinner. Main courses $7–$12 lunch, $10–$22 dinner. AE, CB, DC, DISC, MC, V. Wed–Mon 11:30am–8:30pm. CONTEMPORARY EUROPEAN.

Enjoy a great meal in a comfortably sophisticated setting at this local fave, which smartly stays open throughout the afternoon. Favorites from a seasonally changing menu include the lunch-only Southwest salad (wild, brown, and jasmine rice tossed with smoked turkey, feta cheese, veggies, and green chiles), and pepper-and-sesame crusted ahi, served at dinner either sautéed or seared (your choice). From seafood specialties to Italian recipes from chef-owner Suzanne Roll's family, everything is fresh and natural; veggies are crisply al dente, and even the occasional cream sauce tastes light and healthy. Don't skip dessert.

WORTH A SPLURGE

✪ **The Ranch House.** S. Lomita Ave. ☎ **805/646-2360.** Reservations recommended. Main courses $19–$25. AE, CB, DC, DISC, MC, V. Wed–Sat 6–8:30pm; Sun 11am–7:30pm. CALIFORNIA.

This restaurant has been placing emphasis on the freshest vegetables, fruits, and herbs in its cuisine since opening its doors in 1965, long before this practice became a national craze. Freshly snipped sprigs from the restaurant's lush herb garden will aromatically transform your simple meat, fish, or game dish into a work of art. From an appetizer of cognac-laced liver pâté served with its own chewy rye bread to leave-room-for desserts like fresh raspberries with sweet Chambord cream, the ingredients always shine through. And you'll dine in a magical setting, for The Ranch House offers alfresco dining year-round on the wooden porch facing the scenic valley, as well as in the romantic garden amid twinkling lights and stone fountains.

8 En Route to Los Angeles: Ventura

15 miles SW of Ojai; 74 miles NW of Los Angeles

by Stephanie Avnet Yates

Nestled between gently rolling foothills and the sparkling blue Pacific Ocean, Ventura may not have the cultural and gastronomic appeal of Los Angeles or even nearby Santa

Barbara, but it does boast the picturesque setting and clean sea breezes typical of California coastal towns. Southland antique hounds know about Ventura's quirky collectible shops, and time-pressed vacationers zip up to charming bed-and-breakfast inns just an hour from Los Angeles. Ventura is also the headquarters and main point of embarkation for Channel Islands National Park (see below).

Most travelers don't bother exiting U.S. 101 for a closer look. But think about stopping to while away a couple of hours around lunchtime; sleepy Ventura's charm might even convince you to spend a night.

ESSENTIALS

GETTING THERE   If you're traveling northbound on U.S. 101, exit at California Street; southbound, take the Main Street exit. If you are coming west on Calif. 33 from Ojai, there's also a convenient Main Street exit. By the way, don't let the directions throw you off; because of the curve of the coastline, the ocean is not always to the west, but often southward.

VISITOR INFORMATION   For a visitor's guide and genial answers to any questions you might have, stop in at the **Ventura Visitors & Convention Bureau,** 89-C S. California St., Ventura, CA 93001 (☎ **800/333-2989** or 805/648-2075; www.ventura-usa.com).

EXPLORING THE TOWN

Much of Ventura's recent development has taken place inland and to the south, so many folks overlook the charming seaside **Main Street,** the town's historic center, which grew outward from the Spanish Mission of San Buenaventura (see below). The best section for strolling is between the mission (to the north) and Fir Street (to the south). Both sides of the street are lined almost entirely with antique stores, used-book stores, and charity thrift stores, making it perfect for browsing.

Although Ventura stretches south to one of California's most picturesque little harbors (the jumping-off point for the Channel Islands; see below), the town has its own simple **pier** at the end of California Street. Exceptionally well maintained and favored by area fishers, the charming wooden pier is the longest of its kind in California.

Mission San Buenaventura. 225 E. Main St. ☎ **805/643-4318.** Free admission but donations appreciated. Mon–Sat 10am–5pm; Sun 10am–4pm.

Founded in 1782 (current buildings date from 1815) and still in use for daily services, this whitewashed and red-tile church lent its style to the contemporary civic buildings across the street. Step back into time by touring the mission's inside garden, where you can examine the antique water pump and olive press once essential to daily life here. Good for a quick history fix, the mission is small and near the rest of Ventura's action. Pick up a self-guided-tour brochure in the adjacent gift shop for the modest donation of $1 per adult, 50¢ per child.

San Buenaventura City Hall. 501 Poli St. ☎ **805/658-4726.** Guided tours $4 adults, $3 seniors, free for children 6 and under. 1-hr. tours given May–Sept Sat 11am–1pm.

This majestic neoclassical building was built in 1912 to serve as the Ventura County Courthouse. It sits on the hillside, regally overlooking old downtown and the ocean. To either side on Poli Street are some of Ventura's best-preserved and most ornate late-19th- and early-20th-century houses. Full of architectural detail (like the carved heads of Franciscan friars adorning the facade) inside and out, City Hall can be fully explored by escorted tour.

Ventura County Museum of History & Art. 100 E. Main St. ☎ **805/653-0323.** Admission $3 adults, free for children 16 and under. Tues–Sun 10am–5pm.

This museum is worth visiting for its rich Native American Room, filled with Chumash treasures, and its Pioneer Room, which contains a collection of artifacts from the Mexican-American War (1846–48). The art gallery features revolving exhibits of local painters and photographers, and the museum has an enormous archive (20,000 and counting) of photos depicting Ventura County from its origin to the present. There is also a small archaeological museum across Main Street from the main building.

WHERE TO STAY

Bella Maggiore Inn. 67 S. California St. (½ block south of Main St.), Ventura, CA 93001. ☎ **800/523-8479** or 805/652-0277. 24 units. TV TEL. $75–$150 double; $100–$130 suite. Extra adult $10, extra child (under 12) $5. Rates include full breakfast and afternoon refreshments and appetizers. Ask about midweek specials. AE, DISC, MC, V.

The Bella Maggiore is an intimate Italian-style inn whose simply furnished rooms (some with fireplaces, balconies, or bay window seats) overlook a romantic courtyard or roof garden. Complimentary breakfast is served each morning around the patio fountain, an intimate spot known to nonguests as Nona's Courtyard Cafe. Nona's also serves dinner on Friday and Saturday nights. A kind of European elegance pervades all but the reasonable rates here.

The Country Inn at Ventura by the Sea. 298 Chestnut St. (½ block south of Thompson), Ventura, CA 93001. ☎ **800/44-RELAX** or 805/653-1434. 122 units. A/C TV TEL. $74–$99 double; $129–$199 suite. Extra adult $10, extra child (under 12) free. Rates include full breakfast and afternoon cocktails and appetizers. AE, DISC, MC, V.

Set within walking distance of the beach and Ventura pier, the Country Inn is a good choice for families. It blends the convenience of a chain hotel (the Country Inns are operated by the Comfort Inn chain) with the perks of a bed-and-breakfast. All rooms come with microwaves and refrigerators, and for an additional $10 you can add a canopy bed and fireplace. Try to get a room facing away from the highway—the traffic can get pretty loud.

Holiday Inn Beach Resort. 450 E. Harbor Blvd. (at California St.), Ventura, CA 93001. ☎ **800-HOLIDAY** or 805/648-7731. Fax 805/653-6202. 260 units. A/C TV TEL. $100–$110 double. Midweek and off-season rates available. AE, CB, DC, DISC, JCB, MC, V.

One of the nicer Holiday Inns we've seen, this waterfront high-rise enjoys some spectacular views courtesy of its 12 stories. Because there's little else around as tall, nearly every room has a panoramic view of the sea or Ventura's pretty foothills—or both! Situated on the boardwalk that runs between the pier and the fairgrounds, the hotel is also within easy walking distance of historic downtown Ventura. There's excellent beach access, a heated outdoor pool facing the ocean, a couple of nearby restaurants in addition to the hotel's coffee shop, plus bike and surrey rentals right outside the front door. Ride up to the top floor and check out the hotel's circular ballroom; its adjacent cocktail lounge is oh-so-perfect for sunset gazing. Rooms are decent, thoroughly renovated, but otherwise unremarkable. As with most Holiday Inns, their published rates are misleading, and terrific deals can be had by asking for packages, promotions, and discounts for seniors.

WHERE TO DINE

Eric Ericsson's. Harbor Blvd. at the Ventura pier. ☎ **805/643-4783.** Reservations recommended on weekends. Main courses $7–$12 lunch, most full dinners $9–$15. AE, MC, V. Sun–Thurs 11am–10pm; Fri–Sat 11am–11pm. SEAFOOD/AMERICAN.

Having already established a reputation in Ventura for crowd-pleasing seafood, Ericsson's moved to this pier-top spot in 1997. Here scruffy beachgoers mingle with suited business folk at lunch, sports fans and 20-somethings scarf down appetizers at cocktail hour, families come early for generous dinners, and dating couples linger at window tables until closing. The staggering array of seafood includes clams, oysters, mussels, shrimp, scallops, cod, halibut, lobster, and calamari. Add specialties like Mexican cioppino or traditional clambake, plus plenty of nonfish and vegetarian dishes, and it's impossible to imagine anyone being stumped by this menu.

Rosarito Beach Cafe. 692 E. Main St. (at Fir St.). ☎ **805/653-7343.** Main courses $10–$19. AE, DISC, MC, V. Tues–Sat 11:30am–2pm; Tues–Thurs and Sun 5:30–9pm; Fri–Sat 5–10pm. MEXICAN.

The Rosarito Beach Cafe really packs them into this 1938 Aztec Revival Moderne building and its welcoming outdoor patio. Diners in-the-know bring their palates for superb Baja-style cuisine whose tangy elements are borrowed from the Caribbean, delicious handmade tortillas, and a culinary sophistication rare in modest Ventura.

The Sportsman. 53 California St. (½ block south of Main). ☎ **805/643-2851.** Main courses $4–$14. AE, MC, V. Mon–Fri 11am–10pm; Sat–Sun 9am–2pm; Sat 5–10pm; Sun 4–10pm. AMERICAN.

You might walk right by the inconspicuous facade of Ventura's oldest (since 1950) restaurant. Like the intriguingly retro lettering on its awning, the interior hasn't changed a lick since then: plush leather booths, brass lamps, wood-paneled bar, giant trophy swordfish on the back wall, and light kept at dimness levels normally reserved for planetariums. The Sportsman looks fancy but is quite affordable (especially at breakfast and lunch), and they serve up fine hearty breakfasts, burgers, steaks, and other grilled items. Or you can wet your whistle with $2.50 well drinks from the bar.

9 Channel Islands National Park

by Andrew Rice and Stephanie Avnet Yates

There's nothing like a visit to the Channel Islands for discovering the sense of awe the explorers must have felt over 400 years ago. It's miraculous what 25 miles of ocean can do, for compared to the mainland, this is wild and empty land. Whether you approach the islands by sea or air, you'll be bowled over by how untrammeled they remain despite neighboring southern California's teeming masses.

Channel Islands National Park encompasses the five northernmost islands of the eight-island chain: Santa Barbara, Anacapa, Santa Cruz, Santa Rosa, and San Miguel. The park also protects the ocean 1 nautical mile offshore from each island, thereby prohibiting oil drilling, shipping, and other industrial uses.

The islands are the meeting point of two distinct marine ecosystems: The cold waters of northern California and the warmer currents of southern California swirl together here, creating an awesome array of marine life. On land, the relative isolation from mainland influences has allowed distinct species, like the island fox and the night lizard, to develop and survive here. The islands are also the most important seabird nesting area in California and home to the biggest seal and sea-lion breeding colonies in the United States.

JUST THE FACTS

GETTING THERE   Each of the five islands is relatively distinct and difficult to reach. Odds are you're only going to visit one island on a given trip, so it's a good idea to study your options before going.

Visit the **Channel Islands National Park Headquarters and Visitor Center,** 1901 Spinnaker Dr., Ventura, CA 93001 (☎ 805/658-5700), to get acquainted with the various programs and individual personalities of the islands through maps and displays. Rangers run interpretive programs both on the islands and at the center year-round.

Island Packers, next door to the visitor center at 1867 Spinnaker Dr. (recorded information ☎ 805/642-7688, reservations 805/642-1393), is the park's concessionaire for boat transportation to and from the islands. It's another great source of information.

There are no park fees, but getting to the islands is expensive—anywhere from $32 to $120 per person—since you must go by boat or plane. Island Packers will take you on one of a range of regularly scheduled boat excursions, from 3½-hour nonlanding tours of the islands ($21 per person) or full-day tours of individual islands led by naturalists ($49 per person) to 2-day excursions to two islands ($245). Private yachts and commercial dive and tour boats from all over southern California also visit the park on a regular basis.

If you want to get to Santa Rosa in a hurry, **Channel Islands Aviation,** 305 Durley Ave., Camarillo (☎ 805/987-1678), will fly you there in one of their small, fixed-wing aircraft. If you just want a quick overflight and maybe a picnic stop with a short hike, **Heli-Tours, Inc.** at the Santa Barbara Airport (☎ 805/964-0684), offers 3- to 4-hour flights to Santa Cruz Island.

THE WEATHER   While the climate is mild, with little variation in temperature year-round, the weather in the islands is always unpredictable. Thirty-mile-an-hour winds can blow for days, or sometimes a fog bank will settle in and smother the islands for weeks at a time. Winter rains can turn island trails into mud baths. In general, plan on wind, lots of sun (bring sunscreen), cool nights, and the possibility of hot days. Water temperatures are in the 50s and 60s year-round. If you're camping, bring a good tent—if you don't know the difference between a good and a bad tent, the island wind will gladly demonstrate it for you.

CAMPING   Camping is permitted on all the park-owned islands, but is limited to a certain number of campers per night, depending on the island. Fires and pets are prohibited on all the islands. You must bring everything you'll need; there are no supplies on any of the islands. To reserve free camping permits for any of the islands, schedule your transportation, then call the visitor center (see "Getting There," above) no more than 90 days in advance (no more than 30 days in advance for San Miguel).

EXPLORING THE ISLANDS

SANTA BARBARA   As you come upon Santa Barbara Island after a typical 3-hour crossing, you'll think that someone took a single, medium-sized, grassy hill, ringed it with cliffs, and plunked it down in the middle of the ocean. When you drop anchor, you'll realize that your initial perception is basically on target. Land-wise, there's just not a lot here. But the upside is that, of all the islands, Santa Barbara gives you the best sense of what it's like to be stranded on a desert isle. Being on Santa Barbara, far enough out to sea that the mainland is almost invisible, gives you an idea of just how immense the Pacific really is.

Other than the landing cove, there's no access to the water's edge. The snorkeling in the chilly cove is great. You can hike the entire 640-acre island in a few hours; then, it's time to stare out to sea. You won't be let down. The cliffs and rocks are home to elephant seals, sea lions, and swarms of seabirds such as you'll never see on the mainland. There's also a small campground, pit toilets, and a tiny museum chronicling island history. Camping is available year-round. Island Packers schedules boats to Santa Barbara in summer and fall only (see "Getting There," above).

ANACAPA   Most people who visit the park come to Anacapa. It's only 14½ nautical miles from Ventura, an easy half-day trip. At only 1.1 square miles, Anacapa—actually three small islets divided by narrow stretches of ocean—is only marginally larger than Santa Barbara and, consequently, not a place for those who need a lot of space to roam around. Only East Anacapa is open to visitors, as the other two islets are important brown-pelican breeding areas. Several trails on the island will take you to beautiful overlooks of clear-watered coves and wild ocean. **Arch Rock,** a natural land bridge, is visible from the landing cove, where you'll clamber up 154 stairs to the island's flat top.

Camping is allowed on East Anacapa year-round, but don't bring more than you can carry the half mile from the landing cove. Bring earplugs and steer clear of the foghorn, which can leave permanent hearing damage. Most of the waters around the island, including the landing cove, are protected as a National Marine Preserve, where divers can look but not take anything. Pack a good wet suit, mask, fins, and snorkel; you can dive right off the landing cove dock.

SANTA CRUZ   By far the biggest of the islands—nearly 100 square miles—Santa Cruz is also the most diverse. It has huge canyons, year-round streams, beaches, cliffs, the highest mountain in the Channel Islands (2,400 ft.), now-defunct early cattle and sheep ranches, and Native American Chumash village sites—2,000 Chumash were probably living on the island when Spanish explorer Juan Rodriguez Cabrillo first visited in 1542. The island also hosts seemingly endless displays of flora and fauna, including 650 species of plants, nine of which are endemic; 140 land bird species; and a small group of other land animals, including the island fox.

Most of the island is still privately owned: The Nature Conservancy holds the western nine-tenths. On February 10, 1997, the park service took over the eastern end from the Gherini family who had owned a sheep ranch here. While this eliminated the island's formerly exorbitant landing and camping fees, it also eliminated the Channel Islands' only noncamping overnight options—lodges that are being converted to interpretive centers.

Valdez Cave (also known as Painted Cave for its colorful rock types, lichens, and algaes) is the largest and deepest known sea cave in the world. The huge cave stretches nearly a quarter-mile into the island and is nearly 100 feet wide. The entrance ceiling rises 160 feet, and in the spring, a waterfall tumbles over the opening. Located on the northwest end of the island, the cave can only be entered via dinghy or kayak.

Island Packers (see "Getting There," above) runs day trips as well as overnight trips to Santa Cruz. Camping is allowed in the park-owned portion of the island year-round; apply for a free permit at the visitor center.

SANTA ROSA   Windy Santa Rosa was California's only singly owned, private island until it was purchased by the park service for $30 million in the 1980s from the Vail and Vickers ranching company. As part of the purchase agreement, the Vails are allowed to ranch the island until 2011. Close to 6,500 cattle still call the 54,000-acre island home. You can camp in the old ranch compound on the island's northeast end, where you might be lucky enough to see the Vail and Vickers cowboys working the herd, just as they have for more than 100 years.

Santa Rosa is also home to a large concentration of endangered plant species, 34 of which occur only on the islands. And like Santa Cruz, Santa Rosa is home to the diminutive island fox, a tiny cousin of the gray fox that has become nearly fearless as it has evolved in the predator-free island environment. Santa Rosa also has great beaches, a benefit somewhat outweighed by the nearly constant winds.

SAN MIGUEL People often argue about what's the wildest place left in the Lower 48 states. They bat around names like Montana, Colorado, and Idaho. Curiously, no one ever thinks to consider San Miguel. They should, for this 9,500-acre island is a wild, wild place. The wind blows constantly, and the island can be shrouded in fog for days at a time. Human presence is definitely not the status quo here.

Visitors land at Cuyler Harbor, a half-moon-shaped cove on the island's east end. Arriving here is like arriving on earth the day it was made: perfect, outrageously blue water; perfect sand. Seals bask on the offshore rocks. The island's two most interesting features are the **Caliche Forest,** a sort of petrified forest left when the wind exposed sandstone casts of a forest that once stood on the island; and **Point Bennett,** the outrageous-sounding (and smelling) breeding ground of six separate species of seals and sea lions. During the winter, thousands carpet the beach; their barking is deafening.

The waters around san Miguel are the richest and most dangerous of all the island.

Island Packers's schedule to San Miguel is sporadic in summer and almost nonexistent in winter, so call ahead. Primitive camping is allowed near the ranger's residence, but no potable water is available, and fires are prohibited.

THE EXTRA MILE: EXPLORING THE COASTLINE & WATERS OFF THE CHANNEL ISLANDS

DIVING A good portion of Channel Islands National Park is underwater. In fact, twice as many visitors come annually to dive the waters than ever set foot on the islands. Scuba divers come here from all over the globe for the chance to explore stunning kelp forests, shipwrecks, and underwater caves, all with the best visibility in California. Everything from sea snails and urchins to orcas and great white sharks call these waters home. **Truth Aquatics** in Santa Barbara (☎ 805/962-1127) is the best provider of single- and multiday dive trips to all the islands. **Ventura Dive & Sport** (☎ 805/650-6500) also leads trips, including their "Discover Program," which allows novice and uncertified divers to explore the waters accompanied by an instructor. **Channel Islands Scuba** (☎ 805/644-3483) and **Pacific Scuba** (☎ 805/984-2566) also lead regular trips, as do boats from San Pedro and other southern California ports.

SEA KAYAKING One of the best ways to explore the fascinating coastline of the islands is by kayak. Warren Glaser of **OAARS** (Outdoor and Aquatic Recreation Specialist) based in Ventura (☎ 805/642-2912), leads small-group tours by sea kayak to all five Channel Islands. The trips allow you to explore sea caves and rock gardens. Channel crossing by charter boat, brief lessons, and lunch are included. Fares generally run $125 per person. Three-day adventures to Santa Rosa, with meals, campsite, and guide included are $295. **Aqua Sports** (☎ 805/968-7231) and **Paddle Sports** (☎ 805/899-4925) also lead similar trips, or trips can be arranged through **Island Packers** (recorded information ☎ 805/642-7688, reservations ☎ 805/642-1393).

Los Angeles 13

by Stephanie Avnet Yates

The entire world knows what Los Angeles looks like. It's a real-life version of one of those souvenir postcard folders that spills out images accordion-style: tall palm trees sweeping an azure sky, the gleaming white HOLLYWOOD sign, freeways flowing like concrete rivers, a lone surfer riding the day's last wave silhouetted against the sunset's glow. These seductive images are just a few of many that bring to mind the city everyone loves to hate—and to experience, at least once.

Los Angelenos know their city will never have the sophisticated style of Paris or the historical riches of London—but we cheerfully lay claim to being the most fun city in the United States, maybe the world. Home to the planet's first amusement park, L.A. kind of feels like one, as the line between fantasy and reality is so often obscured. The colors of the city seem just a little bit brighter—and more sur-real—than those in other cities, the angles just a little sharper. Every-thing seems larger than life. Drive down Sunset Boulevard and you'll see what I mean: The billboards are just a little bit taller, the wacky folks just a touch wackier.

Part of the spontaneity and excitement of L.A. comes from the fact that it's constantly redefining itself. Just like the movies and TV shows that come to life here, the physical landscape, social doctrines, and popular pastimes of the city are fluid and unreliable. L.A. gleefully embraces individuality and weirdness and change. Collectively, the city is like a theatrical actor projecting to the very back row: We want everyone else to sit up and take notice—and we're constantly rein-venting ourselves so they will. We'd never want our city to be Paris or London for all the Mona Lisas in the world.

1 Orientation

ARRIVING
BY PLANE

LOS ANGELES INTERNATIONAL AIRPORT (LAX)   Most vis-itors to the area fly into Los Angeles International Airport, better known as **LAX** (☎ **310/646-5252**). Situated ocean-side just off I-405, south of Santa Monica, LAX is a convenient place to land; it's minutes away from all the city's beach communities and about a half-hour drive from the Westside, Hollywood, or downtown.

Transportation from LAX You'll probably be renting a car from LAX—you'll need one (see "Getting Around," below). All the major car-rental firms provide shuttles from the terminals to their off-site branches. To reach **Santa Monica** and other **northern beach communities,** exit the airport, take Sepulveda Boulevard north, then follow the signs to Calif. 1 (Pacific Coast Highway, or PCH) north. To reach **the southern beach communities,** take Sepulveda Boulevard south, then follow the signs to Calif. 1 (PCH) south. To reach **Beverly Hills** or **Hollywood,** exit the airport via Century Boulevard, then take I-405 north to Santa Monica Boulevard east. To reach **downtown,** exit the airport, turn right onto Sepulveda Boulevard south, then take I-105 east to I-110 north. To reach **Pasadena,** drive through downtown (following the directions above) and continue north on Calif. 110 (the Pasadena Freeway).

Many city hotels provide **free shuttles** for their guests; ask about transportation when you make reservations. You can also catch a **taxi** from your terminal. Taxis line up outside each terminal, and rides are metered. Expect to pay about $30 to Hollywood and downtown, $25 to Beverly Hills, $20 to Santa Monica, and $45 to Pasadena, including a $2.50 service charge for rides originating at LAX.

The **SuperShuttle** (☎ 800/554-3146 from LAX, or 310/782-6600) offers regularly scheduled minivans from LAX (and the other area airports) to any location in the city. The set fare can range from $10 to $50 per person, depending on your destination (you're unlikely to pay more than $35, which will get you as far as Burbank or Universal City). The vans are infinitely more comfortable than cabs, but you might have to wait while other passengers are dropped off. Groups of three or more, though, will end up paying less by cabbing it.

When you arrive at LAX, you can call SuperShuttle from a pay phone in baggage claim at the toll-free number provided above or at the courtesy phones at the services information board. If you call during a very busy time, however, expect a wait. Reservations for SuperShuttle aren't required, but I strongly advise them, even if you just make them the day before you arrive; call the 310 number given above to book. When traveling to the airport for your trip home, reserve your shuttle at least a day in advance.

City buses also go between LAX and many parts of the city; for schedules and fares, phone **MTA Airport Information** at ☎ 800/252-7433 or 213/626-4455.

OTHER AREA AIRPORTS One of the area's smaller airports might be more convenient for you, landing you closer to your destination and allowing you to avoid the traffic and bustle of LAX. **Burbank-Glendale-Pasadena Airport** (☎ 818/840-8840) is the best place to land if you're locating in Hollywood or the valleys. This small airport has especially good links to Las Vegas and other southwestern cities. **Long Beach Municipal Airport** (☎ 562/421-8293), south of LAX, is the best place to land if you're visiting Long Beach or northern Orange County and want to avoid L.A. entirely. **The Orange County/John Wayne International Airport** in Anaheim (☎ 714/252-5200) is closest to Disneyland, Knott's Berry Farm, and other Anaheim-area attractions (see chapter 14).

BY CAR

If you're driving in **from the north,** you have two choices: the quick route, along I-5 through the middle of the state; or the scenic route along the coast.

Heading south along I-5, you'll pass a small town called Grapevine. This marks the start of a mountain pass known as the Grapevine. Once you've reached the southern end of the mountain pass, you'll be in the San Fernando Valley, and you've arrived in Los Angeles County. To reach the beach communities and L.A.'s Westside, take I-405 south; to get to Hollywood, take Calif. 170 south to U.S. 101 south (this route is called the Hollywood Freeway the entire way); I-5 will take you through downtown and into Orange County.

If you're taking the scenic coastal route in from the north, take U.S. 101 to I-405 or I-5 or stay on U.S. 101, following the instructions as listed above to your final destination.

If you're approaching **from the east,** you'll be driving in on I-10. For Orange County, take Calif. 57 south. I-10 continues through downtown and terminates at the beach. If you're heading to Hollywood, take U.S. 101 north; if you're heading to the Westside, take I-405 north. To get to the beaches, take Calif. 1 (PCH) north or south, depending on your destination.

From the south, head north on I-5. At the southern end of Orange County, I-405 splits off to the west; take this road to the Westside and beach communities. Stay on I-5 to reach downtown.

BY TRAIN

Passengers arriving via **Amtrak** (☎ **800/USA-RAIL;** www.amtrak.com) will disembark at **Union Station,** on downtown's northern edge. From the station, you can take one of the many taxis that line up outside the station.

BY BUS

The main Los Angeles bus station for arriving **Greyhound/Trailways** (☎ **800/ 231-2222**) buses is downtown at 1716 E. Seventh St., east of Alameda (☎ **213/ 262-1514**). For additional area terminal locations, call their toll-free number.

VISITOR INFORMATION

The **Los Angeles Convention and Visitors Bureau,** 633 W. Fifth St., Suite 600, Los Angeles, CA 90071 (☎ **213/624-7300**), is the city's main source for information. Call or write for a free visitors kit containing a book of coupons for discounts on various attractions, accommodations, and restaurants. The bureau staffs a Visitors' Information Center at 685 S. Figueroa St., between Wilshire Boulevard and Seventh Street; it's open Monday to Friday from 8am to 5:30pm and Saturday from 8:30am to 5pm.

Many Los Angeles–area communities also have their own tourist offices: **Visitor Information Center Hollywood** (☎ 323/236-2331); **Beverly Hills Visitors Bureau** (☎ 800/345-2210 or 310/271-8174; www.bhvb.org); **Marina del Rey Chamber of Commerce** (☎ 800/919-0555 or 310/821-0555; www.itlnet.com/marina); **Pasadena Convention and Visitors Bureau** (☎ 626/795-9311; www. pasadenavisitor.org); **Santa Monica Convention and Visitors Bureau** (☎ 310/ 393-7593; www.santamonica.com); **West Hollywood Convention & Visitors Bureau** (☎ 800/368-6020 or 310/289-2525; www.ci.west-hollywood.ca.us). Call for information, hours, and locations.

OTHER INFORMATION SOURCES   Several city-oriented newspapers and magazines offer up-to-date information on current happenings. *L.A. Weekly* (www.laweekly.com), a free weekly listings newspaper, is packed with information on current events around town. It's available from sidewalk news racks and in many stores and restaurants around the city and often offers discount or two-for-one coupons at area restaurants. The *Los Angeles Times*'s **"Calendar"** section of the Sunday paper is an excellent guide to the world of entertainment in and around Los Angeles and includes listings of what's doing and where to do it. The *Times* also maintains a comprehensive Web site at **www.calendarlive.com**; once there, you'll find departments like

"Southland Scenes," "Tourist Tips," "Family & Kids," and "Recreation & Fitness." Information is culled from the newspaper's many departments and is always up-to-date. If you'd like to check out L.A.'s most immediate news, the *Times*'s main Web site is **www.latimes.com**.

Los Angeles magazine (**www.lamag.com**) is a stylish city-based monthly full of real news and pure gossip, plus guides to L.A.'s art, music, and food scenes, spotlighting different trends each month. Serious cyber-hounds should visit **At L.A.'s** Web site at **www.at-la.com**; one of my favorite tools, their exceptionally precise search engine provides links to over 23,000 sites in thousands of categories relating to the L.A. area.

CITY LAYOUT

Los Angeles isn't a single compact city but a sprawling suburbia comprising dozens of disparate communities. Most of the city's communities are located between mountains and ocean, on the flatlands of a huge basin. Even if you've never visited Los Angeles before, you'll recognize the names of many of these areas: Hollywood, Beverly Hills, Santa Monica, and Malibu. Ocean breezes push the city's infamous smog inland, toward dozens of less well known communities and through mountain passes into the suburban sprawl of the San Fernando and San Gabriel valleys.

Downtown Los Angeles, which isn't where most visitors will stay, is in the center of the basin, about 12 miles east of the Pacific Ocean. You'll probably spend the bulk of your time either on the coast or on the city's Westside (see "Neighborhoods in Brief," below, for complete details on all the city's sectors).

THE MAJOR FREEWAYS & BOULEVARDS   L.A.'s extensive freeway system connects the city's patchwork of communities; they work well together to get you where you need to be, though rush-hour traffic can sometimes be bumper-to-bumper. You might drive on only a couple of L.A's freeways, but here's an overview of the entire system:

U.S. 101, called the "Ventura Freeway" in the San Fernando Valley and the "Hollywood Freeway" in the city, runs across L.A. roughly northwest-southeast, from the San Fernando Valley to the center of downtown.

Calif. 134 continues as the Ventura Freeway after U.S. 101 turns into the city and becomes the Hollywood Freeway. The Calif. 134 branch of the Ventura Freeway continues directly east, through the valley towns of Burbank and Glendale, to I-210 (the "Foothill Freeway"), which takes you through Pasadena and out toward the eastern edge of Los Angeles County.

I-5, otherwise known as the "Golden State Freeway" north of I-10 and the "Santa Ana Freeway" south of I-10, bisects downtown on its way from San Francisco to San Diego.

I-10, labeled the "Santa Monica Freeway" west of I-5 and the "San Bernardino Freeway" east of I-5, is the city's major east-west freeway, connecting the San Gabriel Valley to downtown and Santa Monica.

I-405, also known as the "San Diego Freeway," runs north-south through L.A's Westside, connecting the San Fernando Valley with LAX and the southern beach areas.

I-105, Los Angeles's newest freeway—called the "Century Freeway"—extends from LAX east to I-605.

I-110, commonly known as the "Harbor Freeway," starts in Pasadena as **Calif. 110** (the "Pasadena Freeway"); it turns into the interstate in downtown Los Angeles and runs directly south, where it dead-ends in San Pedro. The section that's now the Pasadena Freeway is Los Angeles's historic first freeway, known as the Arroyo Seco when it opened in 1940.

I-710, also called the "Long Beach Freeway," runs north-south through East Los Angeles and dead-ends at Long Beach.

I-605, the "San Gabriel River Freeway," runs roughly parallel to I-710 farther east, through the cities of Hawthorne and Lynwood and into the San Gabriel Valley.

Calif. 1—called "Highway 1," the "Pacific Coast Highway," or simply "PCH"—is really a highway (more like a surface thruway) rather than a freeway. It skirts the ocean, linking all of L.A.'s beach communities, from Malibu to the Orange Coast.

The freeways are complemented by a complex web of **surface streets.** The major east-west thoroughfares connecting downtown to the beaches (listed from north to south) are Sunset Boulevard, Santa Monica Boulevard, Wilshire Boulevard, and Olympic, Pico, and Venice boulevards. The section of Sunset Boulevard that runs between Crescent Heights Boulevard and Doheny Drive is the famed Sunset Strip.

STREET MAPS   Because Los Angeles is so spread out, a good map of the area is essential. Fold-out maps are available at gas stations, hotels, bookshops, and tourist-oriented shops around the city. Members of **AAA** should stock up on L.A. maps before they arrive; they're free to members and are the most precise and helpful area maps I've seen. For locations, call ☎ **800/922-8228** or check www.aaa-calif.com on the Web; the Hollywood/Wilshire branch is at 5550 Wilshire Blvd., Suite 101 (☎ 323/525-0018).

NEIGHBORHOODS IN BRIEF

Los Angeles is a very confusing city, with fluid neighborhood lines and equally elastic labels. I've found the best way to grasp the city is to break it into six regions—Santa Monica and the beaches, Westside L.A. and Beverly Hills, Hollywood, downtown, the San Fernando Valley, and Pasadena and environs—each of which encompasses a more-or-less distinctive patchwork of city neighborhoods and independently incorporated communities.

Santa Monica & the Beaches   These are my favorite L.A. communities. The 60-mile beachfront stretching south from Malibu to the Palos Verdes Peninsula has milder weather and less smog than the inland communities, and traffic is nominally lighter—except on summer weekends, of course. The towns along the coast each have their own mood and charm. I've listed them below from north to south:

Malibu, at the northern border of Los Angeles County, is 25 miles from downtown. Its particularly wide beaches, sparsely populated hills, and relative remoteness from the inner city make it extremely popular with rich recluses. With plenty of green space and dramatic rocky outcroppings, Malibu's rural beauty is unsurpassed in L.A.

Pretty **Santa Monica,** Los Angeles's premier beach community, is known for its long ocean pier, artsy atmosphere, and somewhat wacky residents. The Third Street Promenade, a pedestrians-only thoroughfare lined with great shops and restaurants, is one of the country's most successful revitalization projects.

Venice, a planned community in the spirit of its Italian forebear, was constructed with a series of narrow canals connected by quaint one-lane bridges. The area has been infested with grime and crime, but gentrification is in full swing. Some of L.A.'s most innovative and interesting architecture lines funky Main Street. Without question, Venice is best known for its Ocean Front Walk, a nonstop circus of skaters, sellers, and posers of all ages, colors, and sizes.

Marina del Rey, just south of Venice, is a somewhat quieter, more upscale community best known for its small-craft harbor, one of the largest of its kind in the world.

The Los Angeles Area at a Glance

(1)	Lincoln Blvd. Sepulveda Blvd. Pacific Coast Hwy.	(91)	Artesia Blvd. & Fwy. Gardena Fwy. Riverside Fwy.
(2)	Santa Monica Blvd. Glendale Fwy.	(101)	Ventura Fwy. Hollywood Fwy.
(5)	Golden State Fwy. Santa Ana Fwy.	(105)	Glenn Anderson- Century Fwy.
(10)	Santa Monica Fwy. San Bernardino Fwy.	(110)	Pasadena Fwy.
(22)	Garden Grove Fwy.	(110)	Harbor Fwy.
(27)	Topanga Canyon Blvd.	(134)	Ventura Fwy.
(39)	Beach Blvd. San Gabriel Canyon Rd.	(170)	Hollywood Fwy.
(47)	Terminal Fwy. Ocean Blvd.	(210)	Foothill Fwy.
(55)	Newport Fwy. and Blvd.	(405)	San Diego Fwy.
(57)	Orange Fwy.	(605)	San Gabriel River Fwy.
(60)	Pomona Fwy.	(710)	Long Beach Fwy.
(90)	Marina Fwy.		

LEGEND

(22)	**State Highway**
(101)	**U.S. Highway**
(210)	**Interstate Highway**

NA-0241

412

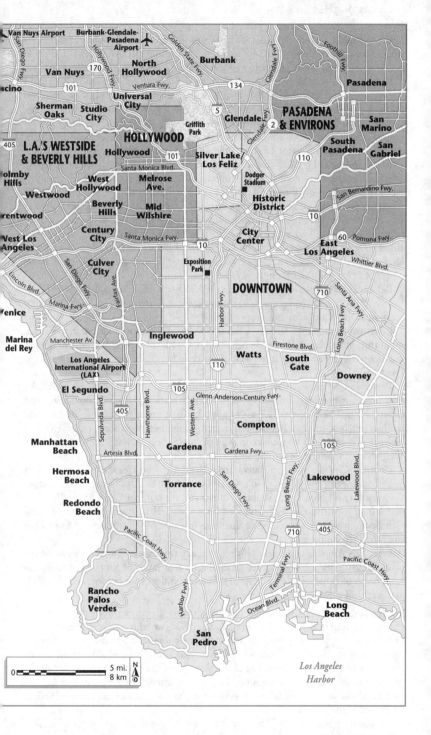

L.A.'s Westside & Beverly Hills   The Westside, an imprecise, misshapen L sandwiched between Hollywood and the city's coastal communities, includes some of the Los Angeles's most prestigious neighborhoods, all with names you're sure to recognize:

Beverly Hills is roughly bounded by Olympic Boulevard on the south, Robertson Boulevard on the east, and Westwood and Century City on the west; it extends into the hills to the north. Politically distinct from the rest of Los Angeles, this famous enclave is best known for its palm-tree-lined streets of palatial homes and high-priced shops (does Rodeo Drive ring a bell?), but it's the healthy mix of the filthy rich, tourists, and wanna-bes that creates a unique—and sometimes bizarre—atmosphere.

West Hollywood is a key-shaped community (go ahead, look at your map) whose epicenter is the intersection of Santa Monica and La Cienega boulevards. It's bounded on the west by Doheny Drive and on the south roughly by Melrose Avenue; the tip of the key extends east for several blocks north and south of Santa Monica Boulevard as far as La Brea Avenue, but it's primarily located to the west of Fairfax Avenue. Nestled between Beverly Hills and Hollywood, this politically independent town can feel either tony or tawdry, depending on which end of it you're in. In addition to being home to the city's best restaurants, shops, and art galleries, West Hollywood is the center of L.A.'s gay community.

Bel Air and **Holmby Hills,** located in the hills north of Westwood and west of the Beverly Hills city limits, comprise a wealthy residential area and feature prominently on most maps to the stars' homes.

Brentwood, the world-famous backdrop for the O. J. Simpson melodrama, is really just a tiny, quiet, relatively upscale neighborhood with the typical L.A. mix of homes, restaurants, and strip malls. It lies west of I-405 and north of Santa Monica and West Los Angeles.

Westwood, an urban village that the University of California, Los Angeles (UCLA), calls home, is bounded by I-405, Santa Monica Boulevard, Sunset Boulevard, and Beverly Hills. The village, which used to be a hot destination for a night on the town, has lost much of its appeal because of overcrowding, lack of parking, and even street violence. There's still a high concentration of movie theaters, but we're all waiting for Westwood to regain the charm it once had.

Century City is a compact, busy, rather bland high-rise area sandwiched between West Los Angeles and Beverly Hills. Once the back lot of 20th Century Fox studios, Century City is home to the Shubert Theatre and the outdoor Century City Marketplace. Its three main thoroughfares are Century Park East, Avenue of the Stars, and Century Park West; it's bounded on the north by Santa Monica Boulevard and on the south by Pico Boulevard.

West Los Angeles is a label applying basically to everything that isn't one of the other Westside neighborhoods. It's generally the area south of Santa Monica Boulevard, north of Venice Boulevard, east of the communities of Santa Monica and Venice, and west and south of Century City.

Hollywood   Yes, they still come. Young aspirants are attracted to this town like moths fluttering in the glare of neon lights. But Hollywood is now much more a state of mind than a glamour center. Many of the neighborhood's former movie studios have moved to less expensive, more spacious venues. **Hollywood Boulevard** is now one of the city's seediest strips. The area is now just a less-than-admirable part of the whole of Los Angeles, but the legend of the neighborhood as the movie capital of the world endures, and it's still home to several important attractions, such as the Walk of Fame and Mann's Chinese Theatre.

For our purposes, the label "Hollywood" extends beyond seedy Hollywood itself—centered around Hollywood and Sunset boulevards—to surrounding neighborhoods.

It generally encompasses everything between Western Avenue to the east and Fairfax Avenue to the west and from the Hollywood Hills (with its dazzling homes and million-dollar views) south.

Melrose Avenue, a scruffy but fun neighborhood, is the city's funkiest shopping district.

The stretch of Wilshire Boulevard running through the southern part of Hollywood is known as the **Mid-Wilshire District,** or **Miracle Mile.** It's lined with contemporary apartment houses and office buildings; the stretch just east of Fairfax Avenue, now known as **Museum Row,** is home to almost a dozen museums, including the Los Angeles County Museum of Art, the La Brea Tar Pits, and that shrine to L.A. car culture, the Petersen Automotive Museum.

Griffith Park, up Western Avenue in the northernmost reaches of Hollywood, is one of the country's largest urban parks and home to the Los Angeles Zoo and the famous Griffith Observatory.

Downtown   Roughly bounded by U.S. 101, I-110, I-10, and I-5, L.A.'s downtown is home to a tight cluster of high-rise offices, the El Pueblo de Los Angeles Historic District, and the neighborhoods of **Koreatown, Chinatown,** and **Little Tokyo.** For our purposes, the residential neighborhoods of **Los Feliz** and **Silver Lake** (a grungy burgeoning artistic community that has been called the "West Coast SoHo"), **Exposition Park** (home to Los Angeles Memorial Coliseum, the L.A. Sports Arena, and several downtown museums), and **East and South-Central L.A.,** the city's famous barrios, all fall under the downtown umbrella.

The construction of skyscrapers—facilitated by earthquake-proof technology—transformed downtown Los Angeles into the business center of the city. Despite the relatively recent construction of numerous cultural centers—including the Music Center and the Museum of Contemporary Art—and a few smart restaurants, downtown isn't the hub it would be in most cities; the Westside, Hollywood, and the beach communities are all more popular.

The San Fernando Valley   The San Fernando Valley, known locally as "the Valley," was nationally popularized in the 1980s by the notorious mall-loving "Valley Girl" stereotype. Snuggled between the Santa Monica and the San Gabriel mountain ranges, most of the Valley is residential and commercial and off the beaten tourist track. But there are some attractions bound to draw you over the hill: **Universal City,** located west of Griffith Park between U.S. 101 and Calif. 134, is home to Universal Studios and CityWalk, a vast shopping-and-entertainment complex. And you may make a trip to **Burbank,** just north of Universal City, to see one of your favorite TV shows being filmed at the NBC or Warner Bros. studios. There are also many good restaurants and shops along Ventura Boulevard in and around **Studio City.**

Pasadena & Environs   Best known to the world as the site of the Tournament of Roses Parade each New Year's Day, **Pasadena** was mercifully spared from the teardown epidemic that swept L.A., so it has a refreshing old-time feel. Once upon a time, Pasadena was every Angeleno's best-kept secret—a quiet community whose slow and careful regentrification meant excellent, unique restaurants and boutique shopping without the crowds in a revitalized downtown respectful of its old brick and stone commercial buildings. Though the area's natural and architectural beauty still shines through—so much so that Pasadena remains Hollywood's favorite backyard location for countless movies and TV shows—Old Town has become a pedestrian mall similar to Santa Monica's Third Street Promenade, complete with huge crowds, predictable midrange chain eateries, and standard mall-issue stores. It still gets my vote as a scenic alternative to the congestion of central L.A., but it has lost much of its small-town charm.

The residential neighborhoods in Pasadena and its adjacent communities—Arcadia, La Cañada, San Marino, and South Pasadena—are renowned for well-preserved historic homes, ranging from humble bungalows to lavish mansions. Some present-day uses include public gardens, designated historic neighborhoods, house museums, and B&Bs. See "Accommodations You Can Afford," "The Top Attractions," and "Exploring the City," below.

2 Getting Around

BY CAR

Despite its hassles, driving is the way to get around Los Angeles. The golden rule is this: Always allow more time to get to your destination than you reasonably think it'll take, especially during morning and evening rush hours.

RENTALS   Los Angeles is one of the cheapest places in America to rent a car. Among the national firms operating in L.A. are **Alamo** (☎ 800/327-9633), **Avis** (☎ 800/331-1212), **Budget** (☎ 800/527-0700), **Dollar** (☎ 800/800-4000), **Hertz** (☎ 800/654-3131), **National** (☎ 800/328-4567), and **Thrifty** (☎ 800/367-2277). Be sure to check out the "50 Money-Saving Tips" in chapter 2; tips 8 to 17 offer valuable information for getting the best possible car-rental rate.

PARKING   Parking in Los Angeles is usually ample, but in some sections—most notably downtown and in Santa Monica, West Hollywood, and Hollywood—finding a space can be fraught with frustration. In most places, you'll be able to find metered street parking, but carry plenty of quarters. When you can't, expect to valet or garage your car for between $4 and $10. Many restaurants and nightclubs, and even some shopping centers, offer valet parking; they usually charge $3 to $5. Most of the hotels listed in this chapter offer off-street parking; it's often complimentary but can cost as much as $20 per day in high-density areas.

DRIVING TIPS   Many southern California freeways have designated carpool lanes, also known as high-occupancy-vehicle (HOV) lanes. Some require two passengers, others three. The minimum fine for an HOV violation is $271. Most on-ramps are metered to control the traffic flow; carpools are exempt and pass in their own lane.

On surface roads, you may turn right at a red light (unless otherwise indicated) after making a complete stop and yielding to traffic and pedestrians. Pedestrians have the right-of-way at intersections and crosswalks.

BY PUBLIC TRANSPORTATION

I've heard rumors about visitors to Los Angeles who have toured the city entirely by public transportation, but they can't be more than that: rumors. It's hard to believe anyone can comprehensively tour this "Auto Land" without a car of their own. Still, if you're in the city for only a short time, are on a very tight budget, or don't expect to be moving around a lot, public transport might be for you. The city's trains and buses are operated by the **Los Angeles County Metropolitan Transit Authority (MTA),** 425 S. Main St., Los Angeles, CA 90013 (☎ **213/626-4455**).

LOCAL SHUTTLES   Some of L.A.'s more popular (read: more congested) neighborhoods offer the opportunity to park once and take advantage of shuttle service. These include **downtown,** where Downtown Area Short Hop (**DASH**) buses run every 5 to 15 minutes and cost only 25¢. DASH also runs shuttles in **Hollywood** (along Sunset and Hollywood boulevards), and between **Fairfax Avenue** and the

---

Hot Deals on Low-Cost Wheels

If the major chains just can't come up with a rental in your price range, consider going to a discount rental company. By eliminating some of the service frills of the majors (for example, don't expect a waiting shuttle from baggage claim) and using a fleet of late-model but not brand-new cars, these companies are able to shave dollars off your bill. Remember that most operate only during regular business hours, so if you're arriving late at night, you may have to make other plans until the morning.

   There are dozens and dozens of these operations around; before using an unfamiliar company, check with the Better Business Bureau—or stick with these agencies: **A-One Rent A Car,** 6502 Arizona Ave., Los Angeles, near LAX (☎ **310/410-1414**); **Costless Car Rental,** 4831 W. Century Blvd., Inglewood, near LAX (☎ **310/673-9899**); or **Rent-A-Wreck,** 12333 W. Pico Blvd., Los Angeles, near Santa Monica (☎ **800/423-2158** or 310/478-0676).

Beverly Center (via Melrose Avenue and 3rd Street). Call the MTA for schedules and route information.

In **Pasadena,** free **Arts Buses** run between Old Town and the Lake Avenue shopping district. Shuttles come every 20 minutes (12 min. during lunchtime) Monday through Saturday from 11am to 8pm; stops are marked with ARTS BUS signs. The visitor center can provide additional information, including route maps.

FAST FACTS: Los Angeles

American Express   In addition to those at 327 N. Beverly Dr., Beverly Hills (☎ 310/274-8277), and at 8493 W. 3rd St., Los Angeles (☎ **310/659-1682**), offices are located throughout the city. To locate one nearest you, call ☎ **800/221-7282.**

Area Codes   Within the past 20 years, L.A. has gone from having a single (213) area code to, by the end of 1998, a whopping six. Even residents can't keep up with the changes. As of press time, here's the basic layout: Those areas west of La Cienega Boulevard, including Beverly Hills and the city's beach communities, use the **310** area code. Portions of Los Angeles county east and south of the city, including Long Beach, are in the **562** area. The San Fernando Valley has the **818** area code, while points east—including parts of Burbank, Glendale, and Pasadena—use the newly created **626** code. What happened to 213, you ask? Only the downtown business area still uses **213.** All other numbers, including Griffith Park, Hollywood, and parts of West Hollywood (east of La Cienega) now use the new area code **323.** If it's all too much to remember, just call ☎ **411.**

Baby-Sitters   If you're staying at one of the larger hotels, the concierge can usually recommend a reliable baby-sitter. If not, contact the **Baby-Sitters Guild** in Glendale (☎ 818/552-2229) or **Sitters Unlimited** (☎ 800/328-1191).

Dentists   For a recommendation in the area, call the **Dental Referral Service** (☎ 800/422-8338).

Doctors   Contact the **Uni-Health Information and Referral Hot Line** (☎ 800/922-0000) for a free confidential physician referral.

Emergencies For police, fire, highway patrol, or in case of life-threatening medical emergencies, dial ☎ **911.**

Liquor Laws Liquor and grocery stores can sell packaged alcoholic beverages 6am to 2am. Most restaurants, nightclubs, and bars are licensed to serve alcoholic beverages during the same hours. The legal age for purchase and consumption is 21; proof of age is required.

Newspapers/Magazines See "Other Information Sources" under "Orientation," above.

Police See "Emergencies," above. For nonemergency police matters, phone ☎ **213/485-2121** or 310/550-4951 in Beverly Hills.

Post Office Call ☎ **213/586-1467** to find the one closest to you.

Taxes The combined L.A. County and California state **sales taxes** amount to 8.25%; **hotel taxes** range 12% to 17%, depending on the municipality you're in.

Taxis You can order a taxi in advance from **Checker Cab** (☎ 213/221-2355), **L.A. Taxi** (☎ 213/627-7000), or **United Independent Taxi** (☎ 213/483-7604).

Time For the correct time, call ☎ **853-1212** (good for all area codes).

Weather Call **L.A. Weather Information** (☎ 213/554-1212) for the daily forecast. For beach conditions, call the **Zuma Beach Lifeguard** recorded information (☎ 310/457-9701).

3 Accommodations You Can Afford

In sprawling Los Angeles, location is everything. Choosing the right neighborhood as a base can make or break your vacation; if you plan to while away a few days at the beach but base yourself downtown, for example, you're going to lose a lot of valuable relaxation time on the freeway. Take into consideration where you'll be wanting to spend your time before you commit yourself to a base. But, wherever you stay, count on doing a good deal of driving—no hotel in Los Angeles is convenient to everything.

Several hotel reservations services offer one-stop shopping; they'll tell you what's available at many of L.A.'s hotels and book you into the one of your choice, at no extra charge. These services are particularly helpful for last-minute reservations, when rooms are often scarce or discounted. The following companies serve the L.A. area: **Central Reservation Service,** 505 Maitland Ave., Suite 100, Altamonte Springs, FL 32701 (☎ **800/548-3311** or 417/339-4116; fax 407/339-4736); and **Hotel Reservations Network,** 8140 Walnut Hill Lane, Suite 203, Dallas, TX 75231 (☎ **800/96-HOTEL** or 214/361-7311; fax 214/361-7299).

In a pinch, you can avail yourself of one of the profusion of chain hotels around town that are generally a reliable source of cheap, clean sleeps. Chain hotels are listed under the appropriate neighborhood headings below. My advice with these properties is to get the best discounted rate you can, since none is worth paying full price for. Some of the more noteworthy chain options are reviewed in full below. **Best Western** has dozens of properties in the greater L.A. area, most at bargain-basement prices. Call ☎ **800/528-1234** or browse their online listings at www.bestwestern.com/best.html. Other options include **Travelodge** (☎ **800/255-3050**; www.travelodge.com), **Holiday Inn** (☎ **800/HOLIDAY;** www.holiday-inn.com), and **Days Inn** (☎ **800/325-2525;** www.daysinn.com).

How to Get the Best Room Rate

The hotels below are categorized first by area, then by price. While some of the listings drop as low as $50 a night, remember that L.A. is one of the nation's most expensive destinations; any room under $100 is considered a bargain. Rates given are the regular rack rates (published rates) for a standard room for two with private bathroom (unless otherwise noted). I list the rack rates in order to help you compare—it wouldn't be fair to list maximum rates for one property and a discount rate for another—but you can nearly always do better. Before you book, turn to "Money-Saving Tips" in chapter 2; tips 21 to 34 offer valuable information on getting the very best hotel rates. Prices given don't include Los Angeles's hotel tax, which runs 12% to 17%.

SANTA MONICA & THE BEACHES

A few more chain-hotel options in Santa Monica are **Holiday Inn Santa Monica Beach,** 120 Colorado Blvd. (☎ 310/451-0676); **Comfort Inn,** 2815 Santa Monica Blvd. (☎ 310/828-5517); and **Days Inn Santa Monica,** 3007 Santa Monica Blvd. (☎ 310/829-6333).

SUPER-CHEAP SLEEPS

✪ **Sea Shore Motel.** 2637 Main St. (south of Ocean Park Blvd.), Santa Monica, CA 90405. ☎ **310/392-2787.** Fax 310/392-5167. www.seashoremotel.com. 20 units. TV TEL. $65–$70 double; $85 suite. Extra person $5; children under 12 stay free in parents' room. AE, CB, DC, DISC, MC, V. Free parking.

Most denizens of Santa Monica's trendy Main Street area don't even know about this small family-run motel in the heart of dining and shopping action. A recent total upgrade of the property (furnishings, fixtures, exterior) has brought it up to standard; the rooms are unremarkable, arranged around a parking courtyard, but the management is caring and conscientious, installing conveniences like refrigerators, voice mail, and attractive terra-cotta floor tiles. An attached little deli is attached, providing morning muffins and sandwiches and homemade soup at lunchtime. The beach is a short walk away, and the businesses on Main Street are among the city's chicest; the Sea Shore makes a terrific bargain base for exploring this part of town.

Travelodge at LAX. 5547 W. Century Blvd., Los Angeles, CA 90045. ☎ **800/421-3939** or 310/649-4000. Fax 310/649-0311. 147 units. A/C TV TEL. $69–$89 double. Extra person $8; children under 18 stay free in parents' room. Lower rates off-season. AE, CB, DC, DISC, JCB, MC, V. Free parking.

The lobby is nondescript and the rooms standard at this chain motel, but there's a surprisingly beautiful tropical garden surrounding the pool area. Some units have terraces. Services include free airport transportation, baby-sitting, 24-hour room service (a rarity for a hotel in this price range), and a car-rental desk. A Denny's is attached to the hotel.

FOR A FEW BUCKS MORE

Bayside Hotel. 2001 Ocean Ave., Santa Monica, CA 90405. ☎ **800/525-4447** or 310/396-6000. Fax 310/451-1111. 44 units. TV TEL. Summer $109–$124 double; winter $84–$109 double. Midweek discounts available. Full kitchen $10 extra. AE, DISC, JCB, MC, V. Free parking.

With a splendid ocean view, easy access to the beach, and free parking, this plain-Jane motel several blocks from downtown Santa Monica shapes up as a bargain-hunter's gem. Though the rooms are small, the furnishings simple (perhaps even ugly), and the

Los Angeles Area Accommodations

Bayside Hotel **9**
Belle Bleu Inn **7**
Best Western Hollywood
   Motor Hotel **33**
Best Western Mikado Hotel **41**
Best Western Ocean View **5**
Best Western Sunset Plaza **23**
Beverly Garland Holiday Inn **40**
Beverly Hills Inn **25**
Beverly House Hotel **26**
Beverly Laurel Motor Hotel **27**
Cal Mar Hotel Suites **3**
Carlyle Inn **28**
Casa Malibu **1**
Courtyard by Marriott **15**
Gateway Hotel
   Los Angeles Airport **16**
The Georgian **4**
Holiday Inn Hollywood **31**
Hollywood Celebrity Hotel **29**
Hollywood Hills Magic Hotel **32**
Hollywood Roosevelt **30**
Hotel Carmel by The Sea **6**
Hotel Del Capri **20**
Hotel Shangri-La **2**
Hotel Stillwell **35**
Hyatt West Hollywood **22**
Kawada Hotel **37**
La Maida House **39**
Le Montrose Suite Hotel **24**
Los Angeles West Travelodge **18**
Mansion Inn **13**
Marina International **14**
Omni Los Angeles Hotel **36**
Pacific Shore Hotel **8**
Park Sunset Hotel **21**
Ramada Limited Hotel **19**
Sea Shore Motel **11**
Sportsmen's Lodge **42**
Travelodge at LAX **17**
Universal City Hilton & Towers **38**
Venice Beach House Inn **12**
Westin Bonaventure **34**

Pacific Ocean

(1)	Lincoln Blvd. Sepulveda Blvd. Pacific Coast Hwy.	(91)	Artesia Blvd. & Fwy. Gardena Fwy. Riverside Fwy.
(2)	Santa Monica Blvd. Glendale Fwy.	(101)	Ventura Fwy. Hollywood Fwy.
(5)	Golden State Fwy. Santa Ana Fwy.	(105)	Glenn Anderson-Century Fwy.
(10)	Santa Monica Fwy. San Bernardino Fwy.	(110)	Pasadena Fwy.
(22)	Garden Grove Fwy.	(110)	Harbor Fwy.
(27)	Topanga Canyon Blvd.	(134)	Ventura Fwy.
(39)	Beach Blvd. San Gabriel Canyon Rd.	(170)	Hollywood Fwy.
(47)	Terminal Fwy. Ocean Blvd.	(210)	Foothill Fwy.
(55)	Newport Fwy. and Blvd.	(405)	San Diego Fwy.
(57)	Orange Fwy.	(605)	San Gabriel River Fwy.
(60)	Pomona Fwy.	(710)	Long Beach Fwy.
(90)	Marina Fwy.		

LEGEND

(22) **State Highway**
(101) **U.S. Highway**
(210) **Interstate Highway**

NA-0241

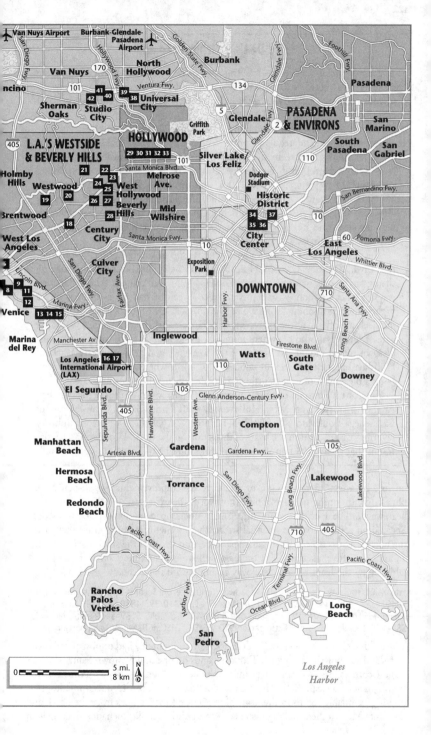

Suite Deals & Other Bargains

There's no getting around it—Los Angeles is an expensive city. However, there are some terrific deals to be had out there—even on rooms you thought were way out of your price range. The key to finding all these bargains is being flexible—and knowing where to look.

Low occupancy, the winter months (excluding holidays), and even just the onset of the weekend regularly bring sky-high rates down to earth all around town. Just look at the scene in downtown L.A.: At such renowned places as the **New Otani Hotel and Gardens,** 120 S. Los Angeles St., at First Street (☎ **800/421-8795** or 213/629-1200), and the **Hyatt Regency Los Angeles,** 711 S. Hope St., at Seventh Street (☎ **800/233-1234** or 213/683-1234), regular rates start at around $170 on most nights. On weekends, however, when the business travelers who normally fill these towers have gone home, rates plummet, often to bargain-basement levels of $95 or $100 a night.

The same holds true in the Valley. At the **Radisson Valley Center,** 15443 Ventura Blvd., Sherman Oaks (☎ **800/333-3333** or 818/981-5400), conveniently sitting at the crossroads of the San Diego (I-405) and Ventura (U.S. 101) freeways, a spacious room with a private balcony can be had for as little as $99 a night—quite a discount from the regular room rates, which start at $160. Similar deals are offered at the **Universal City Hilton and Towers** (see p. 434), at the gate of Universal Studios, where rooms go for as little as $110 once all the out-of-town movie moguls go home for the weekend; and at the **Beverly Garland Holiday Inn** in North Hollywood (see p. 433), where off-season visitors can book a pleasant room for as little as $69—less than half the regular rate.

You don't have to go downtown or to the Valley to get deals like these, either. At the 13-story **Hyatt West Hollywood,** 8401 Sunset Blvd., 2 blocks east of La Cienega Boulevard (☎ **800/233-1234** or 323/656-1234), a record-industry favorite situated right in the heart of the action on the world-famous Sunset Strip, rooms that go for $180 on weekdays go for around $100 once the weekend rolls

---

linens a bit worn, there are signs of care in recent improvements like all-new carpet, plus air-conditioning in some rooms (not worth the extra cost unless there's a record heat wave). The bathrooms are surprisingly uncramped, and the place is spotless. Located on a safe, mostly residential street (that's sometimes noisy with beachgoers), the hotel is across from a small grassy park, beyond which is the sand. Each room has an ancient coffeemaker and TV; there's a well-landscaped inner courtyard and some tables along the front balcony walkway gazing toward the ocean.

Hotel Carmel by the Sea. 210 Broadway (entrance on Second St.), Santa Monica, CA 90401. ☎ **800/445-8695** or 310/451-2469. Fax 310/393-4810. E-mail: Hotlcarmel@ aol.com. 110 units. A/C TV TEL. June–Oct $119–$129 double; $139–$169 suite. Nov–May $85–$95 double; $125 suite. Extra person $10. AE, DC, DISC, JCB, MC, V. Valet parking $7.70.

When this eight-story hotel was built in 1924, it undoubtedly had unobstructed ocean views and state-of-the-art luxury. Today it stands on one of downtown Santa Monica's busiest corners, and—despite a glamorous remodeled lobby—boasts rooms that are simply basic and clean. What the Carmel does have going for it is location and price, offering affordable rooms in the heart of the action (just 3 blocks from the beach and the Santa Monica Pier, walking distance to the Third Street Promenade), making it an

around. At the historic **Hollywood Roosevelt,** in the heart of Tinseltown (see p. 431), there's no need to pay the $129 to $169 rack rate; off-season and weekend specials start at $89!

Just across the street from the beach in Santa Monica is **Hotel Oceana,** 849 Ocean Ave. (☎ **800/777-0758** or 310/393-0486), a recently renovated, wonderfully hip all-suite hotel where you can book you and your family a $200 suite for as little as $125 in winter. Since the suites come with fully equipped kitchens, you can save even more by cooking for yourself. Another great all-suite option worth checking out is **Le Montrose Suite Hotel,** 900 Hammond St., West Hollywood (☎ **800/776-0666** or 310/855-1115). These upscale condolike one-bedroom apartments, which come complete with gas fireplace, fax machine, and Nintendo games, normally start at a budget-crushing $180; however, they've often got a deal going on, so call and inquire.

If you need a comfortable place to stay at the airport, try the **Sheraton Gateway Hotel–Los Angeles Airport,** 6101 W. Century Blvd., near Sepulveda Boulevard (☎ **800/325-3535** or 310/642-1111), where rooms that officially start at $135 and go as high as $300 can be booked for as little as $89 on weekends—with breakfast! Auto-club members can get a rate of $101 anytime; if you're smart enough to ask for the corporate rate, you can get a room for $119 just about any day of the week. Not bad for a hotel with an outdoor pool, a Jacuzzi, and 24-hour room service.

Wherever you book, always ask about package deals (some include breakfast or bargain tickets to local attractions), corporate rates, family plans, auto-club member discounts—many L.A. hotels offer sizable discounts every day to AAA members—and military and senior discounts. Also check out "50 Money-Saving Tips" in chapter 2; tips 21 to 34 will help you make the most of your hotel dollars.

ideal choice for the carless visitor. The hotel's tour desk can arrange guided excursions to the rest of L.A. Renovation, though slow, is improving the facilities; new carpets and air-conditioning were installed in 1998—now I hope work is planned for some of the ancient bathrooms.

The Mansion Inn. 327 Washington Blvd., Marina del Rey, CA 90291. ☎ **800/828-0688** or 310/821-2557. Fax 310/827-0289. 43 units. A/C TV. $95–$105 double; $135 suite. Extra person $10; children under 12 stay free in parents' room. AE, CB, DC, DISC, EU, JCB, MC, V. No cash or checks accepted. Rates include breakfast. Free parking.

A charming, friendly, well-located inn with affordable rates that even include breakfast—it sounds too good to be true, but the Mansion Inn is all that and more. Each room has a small balcony and a refrigerator and features such thoughtful touches as hair dryers, complimentary weekday newspapers, free movies, and separate vanity areas. Since the hotel is just 3 blocks from the ocean on the border between Venice and Marina del Rey, there's an endless parade of people out front exploring the marina, the beach, or the nearby canals on foot, bike, or in-line skates (rentals are 2 blocks away; inquire at the front desk). Breakfast is served in a cobblestone outdoor courtyard shielded from the noisy boulevard. About the only thing missing is a pool, but the staff will cheerfully lend you beach towels for an ocean dip. Suites, which have high-ceilinged living rooms and spacious sleeping lofts with queen-size beds, are the best deals. AAA members enjoy a sizable discount.

MODERATELY PRICED OPTIONS

Belle Bleu Inn. 1670 Ocean Ave. (south of Colorado Ave.), Santa Monica, CA 90401. ☎ **310/393-2363.** Fax 310/393-1063. www.smweb.com/bbi. 25 units. TV TEL. Summer $150 double; $220 suite. Off-season $100 double; $140 suite. AE, MC, V. Free parking.

I was so pleased to discover new owners have completely revamped this former back-packers' flophouse into a clean and welcoming beachfront inn; after all, the location has always been a potential gold mine. Literally next door to the behemoth Loews, the Belle Bleu offers small but comfortable rooms with brand-new furnishings—the interior and exterior of this 1948 motel have been spruced up with fresh woodwork on doors, floors, and decks; retiled bathrooms; all-new fixtures; and lovingly tended landscaping. Private cottages line the path to the beach. Enjoy a partially obstructed ocean view from the suites and some rooms; all have a coffee machine and small refrigerator. Here's the clincher: For a $10 daily fee, guests can stroll over and use Loews's exceptional fitness center and ocean-view pool. The Belle Bleu is a nonsmoking facility.

Best Western Ocean View Hotel. 1447 Ocean Ave., Santa Monica, CA 90401. ☎ **800/452-4888** or 310/458-4888. Fax 310/458-0848. 65 units. A/C TV TEL. Summer $159–$219 double. Off-season and midweek discounts available. AE, CB, DC, DISC, JCB, MC, V. Parking $7.

Yes, there are oceanfront bargains to be found, even in high-rent Santa Monica, and this gem is one of them. Clean and modern, the Ocean View boasts the detail-minded touch of Best Western and offers terrific bargains to those willing to forego an ocean view. Even the view rooms, all with private balconies looking across noisy Ocean Avenue, are a steal for this area. Use their rack rates as a guideline; rooms can go as low as $89 off-season and $99 in summer. All rooms feature refrigerators, coffeemakers, and hair dryers; microwaves are available on request. Within walking distance of many fine restaurants, the hotel offers room service from La Luna Mare, an Italian cafe around the corner.

Cal Mar Hotel Suites. 220 California Ave., Santa Monica, CA 90403. ☎ **800/776-6007** or 310/395-5555. Fax 310/451-1111. 36 units. TV TEL. June–Aug and holidays $154–$169 double. Rest of the year $104–$119 double. Extra person $10; children under 10 stay free in parents' room. AE, MC, V. Free parking.

Tucked away in a beautiful residential neighborhood 2 blocks from the ocean, these former garden apartments are lovingly cared for and deliver a lot of bang for your vacation buck. Each is a suite with separate bedroom, living room, and full-size kitchen; most are spacious enough to accommodate three to four people in comfort. Built in the 1950s with an eye for quality (attractive tile work, large closets), the building wraps around a garden courtyard with heated pool and plenty of chaise lounges. There's also a laundry room on premises. While the furnishings aren't luxurious—they may remind you of a college dorm or apartment—every need is provided for, and it's easy to imagine being content to stay here for a week or more. The staff is attentive and courteous, which helps account for the high rate of return.

✪ **Casa Malibu.** 22752 Pacific Coast Hwy. (about ¼ mile south of Malibu Pier), Malibu, CA 90265. ☎ **800/831-0858** or 310/456-2219. Fax 310/456-5418. E-mail: casamalibu@earthlink.net. 21 units. TV TEL. $99–$139 double with garden view; $159 double with ocean view; $189–$199 beachfront double; from $189 suite. Room with

ⓘ Affordable Family-Friendly Hotels

In addition to these affordable family options, L.A. has some terrific all-suite hotels that bring their rates down to manageable levels on occasion, particularly on weekends and during winter. See "Suite Deals & Other Bargains" on p. 422 for details.

Cal Mar Hotel Suites *(see p. 424)*   There's a homey feel to these spacious suites—former garden apartments—in a prime Santa Monica location. Children under 10 stay free in their parents' room; older kids are $10 extra. Rates drop as low as $104 (higher in summer) and include free parking; all suites have fully equipped kitchens to help save dollars feeding the family.

The Mansion Inn *(see p. 423)*   Families can save a bundle at this charming inn 3 blocks from Venice Beach and across from Marina del Rey. Breakfast is included in the already excellent rates, the rooms are spacious and comfortable, and kids under 12 stay (and eat) free. Two parents and two children can easily share a $95 two-double-bed room or a $135 ($105 for AAA members) bi-level suite. Plus, bicycles, in-line skates, and other recreational equipment can be rented nearby.

Sportsmen's Lodge *(see p. 433)*   Ideally located for families visiting Universal Studios and other San Fernando Valley attractions, the Lodge is near affordable restaurants and offers a number of discounts if you take the time to inquire. The first thing kids gravitate to here is the Olympic-size pool (fenced in for safety), but there's also a nice lawn and garden area near the pool for rambunctious youngsters to let off a little steam. You can also take them down the street to the popular Sports Center bowling alley and arcade.

kitchen $12 extra. Rates include continental breakfast. Midweek discounts available off-season. AE, MC, V. Free parking.

I'm hesitant to crow too loudly about Casa Malibu—one of my favorite L.A. hotels—for fear that it'll be even harder to get a room here. The modest two-story motel wraps around a palm-studded inner courtyard with well-tended flower beds and cuppa d'oro vines climbing the facade. Just past the garden is the blue Pacific and a large swath of private Malibu beach for the exclusive use of guests. The rooms are surprisingly contemporary and cheerful, with top-quality mattresses, bathrobes, coffeemakers, and refrigerators; some have fireplaces and/or air-conditioning. The king-size-bedded oceanfront rooms have balconies directly over the sand—they're a great place to watch the pelicans dive for fish in the late afternoon. If you've got a room without a view, you can see the ocean only from the communal balcony; but since the sound of the waves will put you soundly to sleep in any of the rooms, that criticism seems like complaining the caviar is too cold.

Courtyard by Marriott. 13480 Maxella Ave., Marina del Rey, CA 90292. ☎ **800/ 628-0908** or 310/822-8555. Fax 310/823-2996. 276 units. A/C TV TEL. $114–$124 double. Children under 10 stay free in parents' room. AE, DC, DISC, MC, V. Free parking.

This resortlike hotel is conveniently located only a few blocks from the marina and the Villa Marina Center, where you'll find good dining options and shopping. The rooms have been recently renovated and feature two phones, coffeemakers, hair dryers, and irons and ironing boards; many have patios or balconies. Take advantage of the spa, pool, sauna, steam room, and whirlpool; you'll also have free use of a nearby fitness center. Your AAA membership brings the weekend rate to $80, while nonmembers pay $89; $95 buys a bonus breakfast for two on the weekends.

Hotel Shangri-La. 1301 Ocean Ave., Santa Monica, CA 90401. ☎ **800/345-STAY** or 310/394-2791. Fax 310/451-3351. 55 units. A/C TV TEL. $125 studio; from $165 suite. Rates include continental breakfast and afternoon tea. AE, CB, DC, DISC, MC, V. Free parking.

Perched right on Ocean Avenue overlooking the Pacific and just 2 blocks from the Third Street Promenade, the Shangri-La has a great location. The small lobby opens to a large plant-filled courtyard (surprisingly lacking a pool) bordered on two sides by the hotel. The rooms—which are accessed motel-style, from outside balconies overlooking the courtyard—are spacious, and almost all offer ocean views. The overall art-deco feel of the hotel carries through into the rooms—the lamps and mirrors, even the faucets and doorknobs evoke the early part of the century. The large Formica-covered furniture, however, evokes the Starship *Enterprise* more than the golden age of Hollywood. There's a small ocean-view exercise room. AAA member discounts bring the rate down to around $100.

Marina International. 4200 Admiralty Way (west of Lincoln Blvd.), Marina del Rey, CA 90292. ☎ **800/529-2525** or 310/301-2000. Fax 310/301-6687. 110 units, 25 bungalows. A/C TV TEL. $125–$300 double; from $150 bungalow. AE, CB, DC, EU, MC, V. Free parking.

This hotel's lovely rooms are bright, contemporary, and very private. Most rooms are decorated in a casual California style; all have balconies or patios. The bungalows are plush and absolutely huge—some are even split-level duplexes—with sitting areas and sofa beds. The Crystal Fountain serves continental fare indoors or out, and the hotel offers a concierge, room service, and a complimentary airport shuttle. There's an outdoor heated pool, a whirlpool, a sundeck, nearby golf and tennis, a business center, and a tour desk. AAA member rates, when available, bring the tariff down to $89.

✪ **Pacific Shore Hotel.** 1819 Ocean Ave. (at Pico Blvd.), Santa Monica, CA 90401. ☎ **800/622-8711** or 310/451-8711. Fax 310/394-6657. 168 units. A/C TV TEL. Summer $135–$200 double. Off-season and midweek discounts available. AE, CB, DC, DISC, JCB, MC, V. Parking $5.

This eight-story glass-and-concrete monolith, about a block from the beach, is a good choice for those who want to be in the heart of Santa Monica. The rooms are decent and well priced, and the hotel provides extras like a minigym and complimentary shuttle service to/from anywhere nearby. The remodeled lobby is classically chic, but every standard-issue hotel room is identical; you'll pay at least $30 more for an ocean view, albeit slightly marred by busy Ocean Avenue and nearby Shutters on the Beach. Consider the discounted city-view rooms, which have an unspoiled vista toward downtown L.A. and gaze out over the hotel's charming tropical-themed garden, complete with a heated pool, a whirlpool, and plenty of chaises. There's a bar and full-service restaurant downstairs. Auto-club membership earns a discount rate of $115 in summer, making this a surprising bargain if you simply must be by the sea.

Venice Beach House. 15 30th Ave. (off Pacific Ave.), Venice, CA 90291. ☎ **310/823-1966.** Fax 310/823-1842. 9 units, 5 with bathroom. TV TEL. $95–$165 double. Extra person $10. Rates include continental breakfast. AE, EU, MC, V. Free parking.

This 1911 Victorian house is now a homey B&B on one of funky Venice's unique sidewalk streets, just a block from the beach. The interiors bear witness to years of family life: well-worn hardwood floors, faded Oriental rugs, and shelves of vintage hardbound books. Ask innkeeper Elaine Alexander to recount the home's colorful history, including its many notable house guests. My favorite room is the Pier Suite—light and airy, with a fireplace and sunny sitting room, this is as romantic as it gets. An expanded continental breakfast is served in the sunroom overlooking a splendid garden; afternoon tea or cool lemonade is served with fresh-baked cookies every day. The inn lends bicycles and can prepare picnic baskets for day excursions. *Beware:* The inn hums noisily with activity when there's a full house; seekers of absolute quiet and pristine appointments won't be comfortable here. Smoking isn't permitted.

WORTH A SPLURGE

The Georgian Hotel. 1415 Ocean Ave. (between Santa Monica Blvd. and Broadway), Santa Monica, CA 90401. ☎ **800/538-8147** or 310/395-9945. Fax 310/451-3374. www. georgianhotel.com. E-mail: sales@georgianhotel.com. 84 units. MINIBAR TV TEL. Summer $190–$225 double; off-season $175–$210 double. From $295 suite. Packages available. AE, CB, DC, MC, V. Parking $12. Small pets accepted with $200 refundable deposit and $100 fee.

This gracious eight-story art-deco grande dame opened in 1933 as the Lady Windermere, frequented by Hollywood elite who often patronized the infamous nightclubs lining PCH below. In fact, the "Lady" had its own speakeasy, rumored to have been established by mobster Bugsy Siegel—today guests enjoy breakfast in the historic room. The Georgian was used as a retirement home until 1994, when an elegantly tasteful and historically sensitive renovation uncovered the hotel you see today. The juxtaposition of classical-revival architecture with bold pastels (à la Miami Beach's hotels of the same era) works splendidly, and every comfort is considered, from in-room robes and Starbucks coffee to comfy wicker chaises on the front veranda. Most rooms have a partial or full ocean view; the hotel is perched with an unobstructed coastal vista. Always inquire about available packages; at press time, the combo of oceanfront room and convertible rental car (with parking!) was only $224 per night in high season.

L.A.'S WESTSIDE & BEVERLY HILLS

A couple more chain hotel options on the Westside are **Holiday Inn Express,** 10330 W. Olympic Blvd. (☎ 310/553-1000), and **Holiday Inn Select,** 1150 S. Beverly Dr. (☎ 310/553-6561).

SUPER-CHEAP SLEEPS

Beverly Laurel Motor Hotel. 8018 Beverly Blvd. (west of Fairfax), Los Angeles, CA 90048. ☎ **800/962-3824** or 323/651-2441. Fax 323/651-5225. 62 units. A/C TV TEL. $69 double, $79 double with kitchen. Extra person $5. Senior and AAA 10% discount. AE, CB, DC, MC, V. Free parking. Pets accepted for $5 extra per day.

I admit it: This slightly dingy motel wouldn't rate a mention without the enormously popular Swingers coffee shop downstairs (see "Great Deals on Dining," below). After taking a look, though, I have to concede that its location is ideal for exploring most of Los Angeles. Beverly Hills, downtown, Universal Studios, and the beaches are all equidistant from this little dive near the Farmers Market and the Orthodox Jewish Fairfax district. The Beverly Laurel does offer clean, safe rooms; most boast better-than-they-have-to-be brand-new and stylish furnishings, and you'll appreciate the ample closet space and almost full-size kitchens. The postage-stamp-sized outdoor pool is a little public for carefree sunbathing but does the job on hot summer days. This place is cheap, cheap, cheap—and did I mention the great coffee shop?

Los Angeles West Travelodge. 10740 Santa Monica Blvd. (at Overland Ave.), Los Angeles, CA 90025. ☎ **310/474-4576.** Fax 310/470-3117. 55 units (47 with shower only). A/C TV TEL. $69–$79 double. Rates include continental breakfast. AE, CB, DC, EU, MC, V. Free parking.

This clean and friendly motel offers good value in a high-priced area. The pleasant, modern rooms have been renovated. They come with coffeemakers and refrigerators, though most rooms have only a shower stall (no tub). There's an enclosed heated pool with a sundeck.

Park Sunset Hotel. 8462 Sunset Blvd., West Hollywood, CA 90069. ☎ **800/821-3660** or 323/654-6470. Fax 323/654-5918. 82 units. A/C TV TEL. $79–$89 double; $159 suite. AE, CB, DC, DISC, EU, MC, V. Parking $5.

You'd think that the Park Sunset's location—right on the Strip—would make this one of the noisiest places to sleep in L.A. But all the guest rooms are in the back of the modest three-story hotel, away from the cars and cacophony. The rooms are well kept and surprisingly well decorated, though the carpets are a bit worn and the bathroom color schemes a tad dated. Some rooms have balconies and/or kitchens, and corner rooms feature panoramic city views. There's a small heated pool in a lush courtyard and a continental restaurant on the lobby level that also provides room service. Tours can be arranged at the front desk, and many of the Strip's hot spots are within easy walking distance.

Ramada Limited Hotel. 1052 Tiverton Ave. (near Glendon Ave.), Los Angeles, CA 90024. ☎ **800/631-0100** or 310/208-6677. Fax 310/824-3732. 36 units. A/C TV TEL. $76–$85 double; from $85 suite. Rates include continental breakfast. AE, CB, DC, DISC, EU, MC, V. Free parking.

This isn't a fancy place by any stretch of the imagination, but the rooms are comfortable and have recently been updated—they're in better condition than those in many hotels that cost more. Some have stoves, refrigerators, and stainless-steel countertops; others have microwaves. The bathrooms have marble vanities and hair dryers. Facilities include an exercise room, a lounge, and an activities desk.

FOR A FEW BUCKS MORE

Beverly House Hotel. 140 S. Lasky Dr., Beverly Hills, CA 90212. ☎ **800/432-5444** or 310/271-2145. Fax 310/276-8431. 45 units. A/C TV TEL. $99–$109 double; $150 suite. Rates include continental breakfast. AE, CB, DC, JCB, MC, V. Free parking.

Tucked discreetly away on a quiet tree-shaded residential street, this European-style small hotel is a half block from the well-heeled streets of Beverly Hills's "Golden Triangle" shopping district. Location and value are the main draws, but the smallish rooms are nicer than you'd expect: sparsely but comfortably furnished, with brand-new carpeting, upholstery, and wallpaper. Though there's no view to speak of, plenty of sunlight streams in. More than half the little bathrooms have only a stall shower; if you prefer a tub/shower, specify when you reserve. The plush spacious lobby is furnished with antiques and a checkers/backgammon table; it's a nice place to enjoy your morning coffee. The hotel also provides complimentary morning newspapers, in-room minifridges, and free parking (an amenity virtually unheard of in these parts). *Tip:* Ask for one of the four front rooms—they're larger and have a lovely street view.

✪ **Hotel Del Capri.** 10587 Wilshire Blvd. (at Westholme Ave.), Los Angeles, CA 90024. ☎ **800/444-6835** or 310/474-3511. Fax 310/470-9999. 79 units. A/C TV TEL. $95–$115 double; from $115 suite. Extra person $10. Rates include continental breakfast. AE, CB, DC, EU, MC, V. Free parking. Pets accepted for additional fee equal to 1 night's stay.

The Del Capri is one of the best values in trendy Westwood. This well-located and fairly priced hotel is popular with tourists, business travelers, and parents visiting their UCLA offspring. There are two parts to the property: a four-story building on the boulevard and a quieter two-story motel surrounding a kidney-shaped pool. Though the rooms are beginning to show wear and tear, all are of good quality and have electrically adjustable beds—a decidedly novel touch. The more expensive rooms are slightly larger and have whirlpool baths and an extra phone in the bathroom. Most of the suites have kitchenettes. The hotel provides free shuttle service to nearby shopping and attractions in Westwood, Beverly Hills, and Century City.

MODERATELY PRICED OPTIONS

Best Western Sunset Plaza Hotel. 8400 Sunset Blvd., West Hollywood, CA 90069. ☎ **800/421-3652** or 323/654-0750. Fax 323/650-6146. 94 units. A/C TV TEL. $99–$119 double; $139–$199 suite. Extra person $10. Off-season and AAA discounts available. Rates include continental breakfast. AE, CB, DC, DISC, JCB, MC, V. Free parking.

Located on the Sunset Strip—and just as central as pricier options like the Hyatt or Mondrian—this three-story Best Western just emerged from a total overhaul that updated the facade and installed brand-new (but equally boring) guest-room furnishings. Expect classy, courteous service and extras like hair dryers, refrigerators, tiled (rather than fiberglass) showers, free newspapers, and a pretty-decent continental breakfast. Most rooms enjoy a partial city view, as does the heated pool that's well shielded from street noise. Many rooms have small but well-equipped kitchens, and the suites have terraces overlooking the city. There's a tour desk in the lobby; free parking adds to this hotel's value.

WORTH A SPLURGE

Beverly Hills Inn. 125 S. Spalding Dr., Beverly Hills, CA 90212. ☎ **800/463-4466** or 310/278-0303. Fax 310/278-1728. 49 units. A/C TV TEL. $145–$160 double; from $190 suite. Rates include full breakfast, plus afternoon fruit and cheese. AE, DC, EU, MC, V. Free parking.

The secret to a Beverly Hills lifestyle is knowing how to put on a good appearance—any face-lifted, tummy-tucked socialite will tell you that. So go ahead and brag about your Beverly Hills address to your friends—they'll never know about the bargain you're really enjoying. You can honestly say you've got a newly decorated room with cable TV, a refrigerator, a hair dryer, and other thoughtful touches (like a bathrobe for strolling down to the small but lushly landscaped garden pool). Popular with Asian business travelers, the hotel is impeccably furnished in a bland but vaguely tropical motif. Most rooms have a view of either the pool or the quiet tree-lined street out front. When you're ready to face the world, you'll find yourself ideally located a block from Rodeo Drive shopping and dining, plus an easy walk from Century City. Breakfast and afternoon snacks are served in the aptly named Garden Hideaway Room (which doubles as a full bar). The free breakfast/snacks and free parking make this an extra-good deal in the most expensive part of town.

✪ **Carlyle Inn.** 1119 S. Robertson Blvd. (south of Olympic Blvd.), Los Angeles, CA 90035. ☎ **800/322-7595** or 310/275-4445. Fax 310/859-0496. 32 units. A/C TV TEL. $168–$198 double; $218 suite. Rates include full breakfast and weekday hors d'oeuvres. AE, DC, DISC, JCB, MC, V. Parking $8.

Hidden on an uneventful stretch of Robertson Boulevard just south of Beverly Hills, this four-story inn is one of the best-priced finds in L.A. An exceedingly clever design has transformed an ordinary square lot in a high-density district into a delightfully airy hotel. Despite the hotel's small size and unlikely location, the architects have managed to create a multistory interior courtyard, which almost every room faces. Well-planned contemporary interiors are fitted with recessed lighting, deco wall lamps, pine furnishings, and well-framed classical architectural monoprints. Amenities include coffeemakers and VCRs. The hotel's primary drawback is that it lacks views; curtains must remain drawn at all times to maintain any sense of privacy. The suites are only slightly larger than the standard rooms.

Hyatt West Hollywood. 8401 Sunset Blvd. (2 blocks east of La Cienega Blvd.), West Holly-wood, CA 90069. ☎ **800/233-1234** or 323/656-1234. Fax 323/650-7024. 262 units. A/C TV TEL. $185–$220 double; $235–$400 suite. Special weekend and AAA rates available. AE, CB, DC, DISC, EU, MC, V. Parking $10.

In 1997, this 13-story Sunset Strip hotel completed extensive renovations that erased any last remnants of its former debauched life as the rock 'n' roll "Riot Hyatt." It doesn't even look like other Hyatts, since the management eschewed the corporate standard decor and contracted locally; the end result is a stylish cross between the clean black-and-white geometrics of a 1930s movie set and a Scandinavian birch-and-ebony aesthetic. While not as haute couture as the Mondrian across the street, neither is it as haute attitude. The rooms have beautiful city or hillside views (about half have balconies), but stay away from front-facing rooms on the lower floors—too close to noisy Sunset. The Hyatt woos both business and leisure travelers, providing secure access to guest floors and ergonomic desk chairs in each room; in-room minifridges are an extra $5 a day. You'll love the view from the rooftop heated pool. Special AAA rates are as low as $139.

HOLLYWOOD

A couple more chain hotel options in Hollywood are **Ramada Limited,** 1160 N. Ver-mont Ave. (☎ 323/660-1788), and **Days Inn Hollywood,** 7023 Sunset Blvd. (☎ 323/464-8344).

SUPER-CHEAP SLEEPS

✪ **Best Western Hollywood Motor Hotel.** 6141 Franklin Ave. (between Vine and Gower sts.), Hollywood, CA 90028. ☎ **800/287-1700** (in Calif. only) or 323/464-5181. Fax 323/962-0536. 82 units. $79–$89 double. Senior and AAA discounts available. DC, DISC, MC, V. Free parking.

Location is a big selling point for this chain representative, just off U.S. 101 and within walking distance of the famed Hollywood and Vine intersection. They know it too: The walls showcase images from the golden age of movies, and the front desk offers an endless variety of arranged tours, ranging from the Hollywood Walk of Fame to Six Flags Magic Mountain. Check out their package deals for extra value. The rooms are plain and clean but lack much warmth—the outer walls are painted cinder block, and the closets are hidden behind institutional metal accordion doors. On the plus side, however, all come with refrigerators and free movies and cable TV. The rooms in back have an attractive view of the neighboring hillside. There's a gleaming blue-tiled heated outdoor pool, plus one of the city's most trendy retro-eateries, the Hollywood Hills Coffee Shop (see "Great Deals on Dining," below) off the lobby.

Hollywood Celebrity Hotel. 1775 Orchid Ave. (north of Hollywood Blvd.), Hollywood, CA 90028. ☎ **800/222-7017,** 800/222-7090 in Calif., or 323/850-6464. Fax 323/850-7667. 38 units. A/C TV TEL. $60–$70 double; from $75 suite. Rates include continental breakfast. AE, CB, DC, DISC, EU, JCB, MC, V. Free parking. Small pets allowed with $50 deposit.

This small but centrally located hotel is one of the best budget buys in Hollywood. Located just half a block behind Mann's Chinese Theatre, it offers spacious and comfortable art-deco-style units. Breakfast is delivered to your door along with the newspaper every morning.

FOR A FEW BUCKS MORE

Hollywood Hills Magic Hotel. 7025 Franklin Ave. (between La Brea and Highland), Holly-wood, CA 90028. ☎ **800/741-4915** or 323/851-0800. Fax 323/851-4926. www.netpage.com/magichotel. 40 units. A/C TV TEL. $75 double; $99–$115 suite. Extra person $5. Off-season and other discounts available. AE, DC, DISC, JCB, MC, V. Free secured under-ground parking.

You'll love being centrally located to visit all of Hollywood Boulevard's tourist attractions, and I think you'll be surprised by the spacious comfort afforded by this bargain nestled up against the Hollywood Hills. Named for the landmark illusionist club The Magic Castle just uphill, the hotel was once an apartment building and hasn't lost that private feeling of being insulated from the street's frenzy. Situated around a pool courtyard, most of the rooms are apartment-style suites, but all are roomy and boast kitchens with a microwave and coffeemaker; several units have balconies overlooking the large heated pool. It's ideal for families or long-term stays; they offer self-service laundry, and extras like hair dryers and irons/ironing boards are free for the asking.

MODERATELY PRICED OPTIONS

Holiday Inn Hollywood. 1755 N. Highland Ave. (between Franklin and Hollywood blvds.), Hollywood, CA 90028. ☎ **800/465-4329** or 323/462-7181. Fax 323/466-9072. 470 units. A/C TV TEL. $120–$150 double; from $170 suite. AE, DC, DISC, EU, MC, V. Parking $6.50.

This 23-story hotel in the heart of Hollywood offers perfectly acceptable rooms that are both pleasant and comfortable—as long as you don't mind being on a busy thoroughfare and sharing the pavement with bikers, wanna-be rockers, and the other colorful characters that make up the neighborhood mélange. Once you're inside, you'll see this is Holiday Inn standard-issue, but they do offer some terrific discounts, often as low as $80 to $100. The suites, with small kitchenettes, are particularly good buys. There's a pool, a sundeck, and a revolving rooftop restaurant.

✪ **Hollywood Roosevelt Hotel.** 7000 Hollywood Blvd., Hollywood, CA 90028. ☎ **800/950-7667** or 323/466-7000. Fax 323/469-7006. 330 units. $129–$169 double; from $269 suite. Terrific AAA discount rates available. AE, CB, DC, DISC, EU, MC, V. Valet parking $10.

This 12-story movie-city landmark is on a slightly seedy, very touristy part of Hollywood Boulevard, across from Mann's Chinese Theatre and down the street from the Walk of Fame. The Roosevelt was one of the city's grandest hotels when it opened in 1927 and was home to the first Academy Awards ceremony. The exquisitely restored two-story lobby features a Hollywood minimuseum. The rooms, however, are typical of chain hotels, far less appealing—in both size and decor—than the public areas; but a few are charmed with their original 1920s-style bathrooms. The suites are named after stars who stayed in them during the glory days; some have grand verandas, while others are rumored to be haunted by the ghosts of Marilyn Monroe and Montgomery Clift. High floors feature unbeatable skyline views. David Hockney decorated the famous Olympic-size pool. The Cinegrill supper club draws locals with a zany cabaret show and guest chanteuses from Eartha Kitt to Cybill Shepherd.

DOWNTOWN

A couple decent chain-hotel options downtown are **Holiday Inn City Center,** 1020 S. Figueroa St. (☎ 213/748-1291), and **Ramada Inn–L.A. Downtown,** 611 S. Westlake Ave., near Sixth and Alvarado streets (☎ 213/483-6363). My advice with these properties is to get the best discounted rate you can; none is worth paying full price for.

SUPER-CHEAP SLEEPS

Hotel Stillwell. 838 S. Grand Ave. (between Eighth and Ninth sts.), Los Angeles, CA 90017. ☎ **800/553-4774** or 213/627-1151. Fax 213/622-8940. 250 units. A/C TV TEL. $49 double; $75–$95 suite. AE, DC, EU, MC, V. Parking $3.

It's far from fancy, but the Stillwell's modestly priced rooms are a good option in an otherwise expensive neighborhood. This relatively clean, basic hotel is conveniently located, close to the Civic Center, the Museum of Contemporary Art, and Union

Station. The rooms are simply decorated; some are large enough for families. The hotel is a safe haven in downtown, as is the lobby-level Indian restaurant that's a popular lunch spot for downtown office workers. There's a business center and a tour desk.

FOR A FEW BUCKS MORE

Kawada Hotel. 200 S. Hill St. (at Second St.), Los Angeles, CA 90012. ☎ **800/752-9232** or 213/621-4455. Fax 213/687-4455. 116 units. A/C TV TEL. $79–$119 double; $145 suite. AE, DC, DISC, EU, MC, V. Parking $6.60.

This pretty, well-kept, and efficiently managed hotel is a pleasant oasis in the otherwise gritty heart of downtown, conveniently near the Civic Center, the Museum of Contemporary Art, and Union Station. Behind the clean redbrick exterior are over a hundred pristine rooms, all with handy kitchenettes and simple furnishings. The rooms aren't large but are extremely functional, each with a VCR (movies are available free) and two phones. Nonsmoking rooms are available. The hotel's lobby-level restaurant features an eclectic international menu all day.

A MODERATELY PRICED OPTION

Omni Los Angeles Hotel. 930 Wilshire Blvd. (at Figueroa St.), Los Angeles, CA 90071. ☎ **800/843-6664** or 213/688-7777. 900 units. A/C TV TEL. $129–$199 double; from $425 suite. AE, CB, DC, DISC, EU, MC, V. Valet parking $18.

After taking over this huge hotel from the Hilton chain in 1995, Omni began a 3-year course of renovations that altered little from the utilitarian feel of the old Hilton, which seems to assume that all business travelers are strictly right-brained. The best rooms have city views or overlook the oval heated pool. The hotel is centrally located, near many downtown attractions. The premium Towers rooms (on the 15th and 16th floors) offer separate check-in facilities, a dedicated concierge, and complimentary continental breakfast and afternoon cocktails. Of the hotel's three restaurants, Cardini, serving northern Italian cuisine, is the only one worth staying in for. Amenities at the Omni include a small cardio and weight room, a concierge, room service (6am to 11pm), dry cleaning, laundry service, and a car-rental desk.

WORTH A SPLURGE

Westin Bonaventure. 404 S. Figueroa St. (between Fourth and Fifth sts.), Los Angeles, CA 90071. ☎ **800/228-3000** or 213/624-1000. Fax 213/612-4800. 1,523 units. A/C TV TEL. $175–$215 double; from $190 suite. AE, CB, DC, EU, MC, V. Parking $18.50.

The 35-story Bonaventure is architecturally unique: The hotel's five gleaming glass silos—like giant mirrored rolls of paper towels—constitute one of downtown's most distinctive landmarks. This is an enormous convention hotel, designed on the scale of a minicity. The six-story skylit lobby houses splashing fountains, gardens, trees, and even a large lake. There's a tangle of concrete ramps and 12 glass-enclosed, high-speed elevators that appear to rise from the reflecting pools. Five lower levels are filled with shops and boutiques. The guest rooms begin on the 10th floor; each has a wall of windows offering good views, but they're generally small due to the cylindrical shape of the building. The two best ways to get a room: Take advantage of bargain weekend rates or stay as part of a package deal (the hotel hosts a lot of discount travelers).

THE SAN FERNANDO VALLEY

Universal City is on this side of the hill, and most hotels do a booming business with travelers visiting Universal Studios and other showbiz attractions in the area. You can often find great off-season hotel deals, and the Valley is a more peaceful setting than other Los Angeles neighborhoods.

FOR A FEW BUCKS MORE

Best Western Mikado Hotel. 12600 Riverside Dr. (between Whitsett and Coldwater Canyon), North Hollywood, CA 91607. ☎ **800/826-2759,** 800/433-2239 in Calif., or 818/763-9141. Fax 818/752-1045. 58 units. A/C TV TEL. $89–$99 double; $100–$125 double with kitchenette. Extra person $10; children under 12 stay free in parents' room. Rates include full breakfast. AE, CB, DC, DISC, JCB, MC, V. Free parking.

The Mikado has been a Valley feature for 40-plus years. The 1998 renovation muted but didn't obliterate the motel's kitsch, which extends from the pagoda-style exterior to the sushi bar (the Valley's oldest) across the driveway. Two-story motel buildings face onto well-maintained courtyards, one with a koi pond and wooden footbridge, the other with a shimmering blue-tiled pool and spa. The recent face-lift stripped most of the Asian vibe from room interiors, which are nevertheless comfortable and provide extras like hair dryers and free cable and movies. American-style breakfast is served in the spacious lobby, and room service is available for lunch and dinner (Japanese dishes only).

La Maida House. 11159 La Maida St. (west of Lankershim Blvd.), North Hollywood, CA 91601. ☎ **818/769-3857.** Fax 818/753-9363. 11 units. A/C TV TEL. $85–$125 double; $155–$210 suite. Discounts on stays over 7 days. Rates include breakfast and evening aperitif. MC, V. Free parking.

Comprised of four converted homes on the same quiet residential street in North Hollywood, this B&B is elegant and discreet, with a carefully assembled decor of antiques and treasures from the owners' many travels. Without ever advertising, they've stayed full for 15 years with mostly entertainment-industry folks working at nearby NBC, Warner Bros., and Universal studios. You'll feel like an honored houseguest, particularly in the main house, a lovingly restored Italianate with a sunlit dining room. Behind one of the bungalows is a pool and an exercise room for use by all guests. Answering machines are available on request. In addition to prohibiting smoking, the owners—animal-rights activists—refuse to allow furs on the premises.

A MODERATELY PRICED OPTION

Sportsmen's Lodge. 12825 Ventura Blvd. (east of Coldwater Canyon), Studio City, CA 91604. ☎ **800/821-8511** or 818/769-4700. Fax 213/877-3898. www.slhotel.com. E-mail: Information@slhotel.com. 191 units. A/C TV TEL. $117–$156 double; from $180 suite. AE, DC, DISC, EU, MC, V. Free parking.

It's been a long time since this part of Studio City was wilderness enough to justify the lodge's name. This sprawling motel has been enlarged and upgraded since those days, the most recent improvements—sprucing up the worn room furnishings—made within the last 3 years. Relaxing around the heated Olympic-size pool surrounded by chaise lounges, you might take advantage of the new pool cabana bar and forget all about busy Ventura Boulevard beyond this garden setting. The guest rooms are large and comfortable but not luxurious; all have balconies or patios, and refrigerators are available. There's a well-equipped exercise room and a variety of shops and service desks, and both golf and bowling are nearby. A hunting-lodge motif bar and grill is on the property, adjoining a fine-dining room that serves only weekend dinner and brunch in stunning glass-enclosed surroundings. Don't miss the beautiful black and white swans frolicking out back in the koi-filled ponds.

WORTH A SPLURGE

Beverly Garland Holiday Inn. 4222 Vineland Ave., North Hollywood, CA 91602. ☎ **800/BEVERLY** or 818/980-8000. Fax 818/766-5230. 270 units. A/C TV TEL. $149–$159 double; from $199 suite. Off-season and other discounts available. AE, JCB, MC, V. Free parking.

Don't get confused by the name—this hotel is named for its owner, actress Beverly Garland (of *My Three Sons* fame), not Beverly Hills. Grassy areas and greenery abound at this North Hollywood Holiday Inn, a virtual oasis in the concrete jungle that is most of L.A. The southern California mission–style buildings that make up the hotel are a bit dated, but if you grew up with "Brady Bunch" reruns, this only adds to the charm—it looks like something Mike Brady would've designed. Southwestern-themed fabrics complement the natural-pine furnishings in the recently renovated rooms; unfortunately, the painted cinderblock walls give something of a college-dorm feel. There are a pool, sauna, and two tennis courts, and all rooms feature balconies. The Paradise Restaurant serves Polynesian-influenced cuisine throughout the day. A complimentary shuttle to Universal Studios is available. It's easy to stay here for around $100 per night.

Universal City Hilton and Towers. 555 Universal Terrace Pkwy., Universal City, CA 91608. ☎ **800/HILTONS** or 818/506-2500. Fax 818/509-2031. 472 units. A/C TV TEL. $130–$212 double; from $175 suite. Weekend rates start at $110. AE, DC, DISC, EU, MC, V. Valet parking $13.

Though this 24-story hotel sits right outside the Universal Studios theme park, there's more of a conservative business-traveler feel than the raucous family-with-young-children feel you might expect. The large lobby is built almost entirely of glass, giving it an openness that doesn't feel hollow or empty. The rooms are tastefully decorated in light earth tones with English-style furniture. Cafe Sierra serves California cuisine and is open for breakfast, lunch, dinner, and Sunday brunch.

PASADENA & ENVIRONS

Pretty Pasadena is on the east side of downtown and a fine choice for charming historic hotels situated to enjoy this well-preserved and architecturally rich area. Although close via freeway to both Hollywood and the valleys, Pasadena is quite a distance from the beach communities and the Westside. Plenty of visitors here for events at Pasadena's Rose Bowl find little reason to leave, since the dining and shopping scene stands on its own.

A few decent chain-hotel options in the Pasadena area are **Holiday Inn Convention Center,** 303 E. Cordova St., south of Colorado Boulevard via Marengo Avenue (☎ 626/449-4000); **Comfort Inn,** 2462 E. Colorado Blvd. (☎ 626/405-0811); and **Vagabond Inn,** 1203 E. Colorado Blvd. (☎ 626/449-3170). My advice with these properties is to get the best discounted rate you can; none is worth paying full price for.

SUPER-CHEAP SLEEPS

Saga Motor Hotel. 1633 E. Colorado Blvd. (between Allen and Sierra Bonita aves.), Pasadena, CA 91106. ☎ **800/793-7242** or 626/795-0431. Fax 626/792-0559. 72 units. A/C TV TEL. $62–$69 double; $75 suite. Rates include continental breakfast. AE, CB, DC, MC, V. Free parking.

This 1950s relic of old Route 66 is a little bland by modern standards but has far more character than most others in its price range. The rooms are small, clean, and simply furnished with just the basics. The best ones are in the front building surrounding the gated pool, which is shielded from the street and inviting in warm weather. The grounds are attractive and surprisingly well kept, if you don't count the Astroturf "lawn" around the pool. The motel is about a mile from the Huntington Library and within 10 minutes of both the Rose Bowl and Old Pasadena.

FOR A FEW BUCKS MORE

Pasadena Hotel Bed & Breakfast. 76 N. Fair Oaks Ave. (between Union and Holly sts.), Pasadena, CA 91103. ☎ **800/653-8886** or 626/568-8172. Fax 626/793-6409. 12 units, 11 with shared bathroom, 1 with half-bathroom. A/C TV TEL. $80–$165 double. Rates include continental breakfast. AE, MC, V. Parking $5.

This old-style hostelry is definitely not for everyone. In true turn-of-the-century rooming-house style, the guest rooms all have washbasins, but all but one must share hall bathrooms (three full, two half). Part of the attraction here is the well-restored National Historic Register building, and part is the hotel's flawless location: It's the only accommodation literally in the heart of lively—and noisy—Old Pasadena. The guest rooms are small but comfortable. The central sitting room/lounge is elegant and welcoming, and there's a spirited coffeehouse in the courtyard behind the hotel where you can enjoy your breakfast and complimentary afternoon teas. Shuttle buses to the Rose Bowl depart 1 block away during major events.

MODERATELY PRICED OPTIONS

The Artists' Inn Bed-and-Breakfast. 1038 Magnolia St., South Pasadena, CA 91030. ☎ **888/799-5668** or 626/799-5668. Fax 626/799-3678. 9 units. A/C. $110–$150 double. Rates include full breakfast and afternoon tea. Extra person $20. AE, MC, V.

This Victorian-style inn, an unpretentious yellow-shingled home pleasantly furnished with wicker throughout, was built in 1895 as a farmhouse and recently expanded to include a neighboring 1909 home. Each room is decorated to reflect the style of a particular artist or period, including impressionist, Fauve, and van Gogh. While the three annex suites have deluxe amenities (whirlpool tubs, minibars, coffeemakers, phones, and TVs), every room is thoughtfully arranged with fresh roses from the front garden, hair dryers, port wine, and chocolates. The inn is on a quiet residential street 5 minutes from the heart of downtown.

Bissell House. 201 Orange Grove Ave. (at Columbia St.), South Pasadena, CA 91030. ☎ **626/441-3535.** Fax 626/441-3671. 5 units. A/C. $115–$160 double. Rates include full breakfast on weekends, expanded continental breakfast weekdays, plus afternoon snacks and all-day beverages. AE, MC, V.

Hidden behind tall hedges that carefully isolate it from busy Orange Grove Avenue, this 1887 gingerbread Victorian is furnished with antiques and offers a delightful taste of life on what was once Pasadena's "Millionaire's Row." All rooms have private bathrooms with both shower and tub (one an antique claw-foot, one a private whirlpool). There's a pool and Jacuzzi on the beautifully landscaped grounds, and a downstairs library offers a telephone and fax machine for guests' use.

4 Great Deals on Dining

Any way you look at it—food, decor, service—Los Angeles is one of the world's great dining cities. When it comes to culinary innovation and architectural design, L.A.'s restaurants are tops. Dining out is a recreational activity here, and an experience that shouldn't be passed up. Though budget-minded coffee shops, cafes, and ethnic dives (especially those serving Mexican fare) abound, I recommend splurging at least once at one of L.A.'s top-notch restaurants, as much for the people-watching as for the food.

Here are some tips on approaching L.A.'s finer restaurants with a budget:

- See if the restaurant serves lunch. Many finer eateries have a moderately priced lunch menu offering smaller portions of their signature dishes. Some of my favorites are Joe's, Röckenwagner, Joss, Campanile (also good for breakfast), and The Raymond.

- Consider keeping the meal tab down by skipping alcoholic beverages, which can add as much as $10 to $15 per person in the blink of an eye (or the bend of an elbow!). Alternately, you might want to visit the bar for *just* cocktails and hors d'oeuvres, which is another excellent way to experience the ambiance and cuisine without breaking the bank. The tapas bar at Cava, for example, lends itself perfectly to this ploy.
- Check out L.A.'s newest downsize trend: the upscale coffee shops like Swingers and Hollywood Hills Coffee Shop, where you can get gourmet- and ethnic-tinged versions of comfort food at old-fashioned blue-plate prices.

The restaurants below are categorized first by geographic area, then by price. Our limited space forced us to make tough choices; for a greater selection of reviews, see *Frommer's Los Angeles.*

Reservations are recommended almost everywhere in Los Angeles, particularly on weekends and during peak lunch (noon to 1:30pm) and dinner (7 to 8:30pm) times.

SANTA MONICA & THE BEACHES
SUPER-CHEAP EATS

✪ **Blueberry.** 510 Santa Monica Blvd. (at Fifth St.), Santa Monica. ☎ **310/394-7766.** Reservations not accepted. Main courses $4.50–$8. AE, MC, V. Daily 8am–3pm. AMERICAN.

Serving only breakfast and lunch—Blueberry's owner devotes the dinner hour to the über-trendy Rix around the corner—this Santa Monica cafe is popular among shoppers and locals from the surrounding beach community. The setting is 1930s American farmhouse: From the blue bandanna seat cushions to the vintage music and print ads, from the picket-fence railings to the wait staff dressed in overalls, it truly does evoke a depression-era small-town diner. The food is a "square deal" too, starting with a basket of crispy-edged minimuffins (blueberry, of course) when you're seated and including hearty egg dishes, waffles, pancakes, and generous lunch salads and sandwiches. But I'll bet Ma Kettle never used goat cheese or pancetta in *her* omelets—the menu is up-to-date and served with plenty of fresh-brewed gourmet-roasted coffee. Blueberry is tiny, with just a few tables on the main floor and cozy loft, so expect a wait during peak times.

✪ **Bread & Porridge.** 2315 Wilshire Blvd. (3 blocks west of 26th St.), Santa Monica. ☎ **310/453-4941.** Main courses $4.50–$9. No credit cards. Tues–Sun 7am–3pm. INTERNATIONAL.

A dozen tables are all that comprise this neighborhood cafe, but a steady stream of locals mills outside, reading newspapers and waiting for a seat. Once inside, surrounded by the vintage fruit-crate labels adorning the walls and tabletops, you can sample the delicious breakfasts, fresh salads and sandwiches, and super-affordable entrees. There's a vaguely international twist to the menu, which leaps from breakfast quesadillas and omelets—all served with black beans and salsa—to the Southern comfort of Cajun crab cakes and coleslaw to typical Italian pastas adorned with Roma tomatoes and plenty of garlic. All menu items are cheap (truck-stop cheap) but with an inventive elegance that truly makes this a best-kept secret. Get a short stack of one of five varieties of pancakes with any meal; they thoughtfully serve breakfast all day.

Gallegos Mexican Deli. 1424 Broadway (corner of 15th St.), Santa Monica. ☎ **310/ 395-0162.** Most items under $4. No credit cards. Mon–Fri 7:30am–6pm; Sat 7:30am–4pm. MEXICAN.

California Themes

If you're looking for theme restaurants, you'll find the **Hard Rock Cafe** at two locations: at the Beverly Center, 8600 Beverly Blvd., at San Vicente Boulevard, Los Angeles (☎ 310/276-7605), and at Universal CityWalk, the Universal Center Drive exit off U.S. 101 (☎ 818/622-7625). **Planet Hollywood** is at 9560 Wilshire Blvd., west of Rodeo Drive, Beverly Hills (☎ 310/275-7828).

The main order of business at Gallegos is catering, but they'll sell you a single home-made tamale as happily as a tray of 50! Choose from six varieties of the corn-husk-wrapped delicacies (plus a "dessert" tamale made with vanilla, raisins, and sugar) and from eight fresh salsas to top it off. Tacos, burritos, chile rellenos, and enchiladas are prepared with the freshest of ingredients, and the chips (can't eat just one) are made from Gallegos's homemade yellow- and blue-corn tortillas. Office workers, car mechanics, and art-gallery curators from the surrounding light industrial/residential neighborhood all converge on the outdoor patio, where simple plastic furniture, vine-covered fences, and a communal copy of today's paper provide a simple setting for a cheap, quick, and enormously satisfying meal.

✪ **Jody Maroni's Sausage Kingdom.** 2011 Ocean Front Walk (north of Venice Blvd.), Venice. ☎ **310/822-JODY.** Sandwiches $4–$6. No credit cards. Daily 10am–sunset. SANDWICHES/SAUSAGES.

Your cardiologist might not approve, but Jody Maroni's all-natural, preservative-free "haute dogs" are some of the best wieners served anywhere. The grungy walk-up (or in-line skate-up) counter looks fairly foreboding—you wouldn't know there was gourmet fare behind that aging hot-dog-stand facade, from which at least 14 different grilled sausage sandwiches are served up. Bypass the traditional hot Italian and try the Toulouse garlic, Bombay curried lamb, all-chicken apple, or orange-garlic-cumin. Each is served on a freshly baked onion roll and smothered with onions and peppers. Burgers, BLTs, and rotisserie chicken are also served, but why bother?

Other locations include the Valley's Universal CityWalk (☎ **818/622-JODY**), and inside LAX Terminals 3, 4, and 6, where you can pick up some last-minute vacuum-packed sausages for home. Having elevated sausage worship to an art form, Jody's now boasts a helpful and humorous cookbook, plus its own Web site at **www.maroni.com**.

Kay 'n Dave's Cantina. 262 26th St. (south of San Vicente Blvd.), Santa Monica. ☎ **310/260-1355.** Main courses $5–$10. MC, V. Mon–Thurs 11am–9:30pm; Fri 11am–10pm; Sat 8:30am–10pm; Sun 8:30am–9:30pm. HEALTHY MEXICAN.

A beach community favorite for "really big portions of really good food at really low prices," Kay 'n Dave's cooks with no lard and has a vegetarian-friendly menu with plenty of meat items too. Come early (and be prepared to wait) for breakfast, as local devotees line up for five kinds of fluffy pancakes, zesty omelets, or one of the best breakfast burritos in town. Grilled tuna Veracruz, spinach-and-chicken enchiladas in tomatillo salsa, seafood fajitas tostada, vegetable-filled corn tamales, and other Mexican specialties are served in huge portions, making this mostly-locals minichain a great choice to energize for (or reenergize after) an action-packed day of beach sightseeing. Bring the family—there's a kids' menu and crayons on every table.

Sidewalk Cafe. 1401 Ocean Front Walk (between Horizon Ave. and Market St.), Venice. ☎ **310/399-5547.** Reservations not accepted. Main courses $6–$13. MC, V. Sun–Thurs 8am–11pm; Fri–Sat 8am–midnight. AMERICAN.

Nowhere in L.A. is the people-watching better than along Ocean Front Walk. The constantly bustling Sidewalk Cafe is ensconced in one of Venice's few remaining early-20th-century buildings. The best seats, of course, are out front, around overcrowded open-air tables, all with a perfect view of the crowd, which provides nonstop entertainment. The menu is extensive and the food a whole lot better than it has to be at a location like this. Choose from the seriously overstuffed sandwiches or other oversize American favorites: omelets, salads, burgers.

FOR A FEW BUCKS MORE

Aunt Kizzy's Back Porch. 4325 Glencove Ave. (in the Villa Marina Shopping Center), Marina del Rey. ☎ **310/578-1005.** Reservations not accepted. Main courses $8–$13. AE. Mon–Thurs 11am–11pm; Fri–Sat 11am–midnight; Sun 11am–3pm and 4–11pm. SOUTHERN.

This is a real Southern restaurant, owned by genuine Southerners from Texas and Oklahoma. Kizzy's chicken Creole, jambalaya, and smothered pork chops are just about as good as it gets in this city. Almost everything comes with vegetables, red beans and rice, and corn muffins. Fresh-squeezed lemonade is served by the mason jar. These are huge meals that, as corny as it sounds, are as delicious as they are filling. Sunday brunches are all-you-can-eat buffets. The biggest problem with Aunt Kizzy's is its location, hidden in a shopping center that has too few parking spaces to accommodate its customers. Look for the restaurant to the right of Vons supermarket.

Montego Bay. 1031 Abbot Kinney Blvd., Venice. ☎ **310/450-1933.** Reservations recommended for dinner. Main courses $9–$15; lunch/brunch $7–$9. AE, MC, V. Tues–Fri noon–3pm; Sat–Sun 10am–3:30pm; Tues–Thurs and Sun 6–10pm; Fri–Sat 6–11:30pm. CARIBBEAN.

Within 5 minutes of entering Montego Bay's vibrant indoor/outdoor atmosphere, you'll think you're on a Caribbean vacation isle. Awash with color and the festive strains of steel drum music (live on weekends), the dining patio sits under a flower-laden trellis and canopy of trees. The short menu blends elements of Jamaican, Cuban, and Spanish cooking to create specialties like guava-glazed salmon, eggplant terrine with red-pepper sauce, curried goat with rice and crispy sweet potatoes, and the old Jamaican standby, jerk chicken with plantain fritters. The full bar dispenses cool tropical concoctions. The restaurant is in a funky artist-infested Venice neighborhood that's perfect for a pre- or postmeal stroll.

MODERATELY PRICED OPTIONS

✪ **Border Grill.** 1445 Fourth St. (between Broadway and Santa Monica Blvd.), Santa Monica. ☎ **310/451-1655.** Reservations recommended. Main courses $10–$20. AE, DC, DISC, MC, V. Mon 5–10pm; Tues–Sat 11:30am–11pm; Sun 11:30am–10pm. MEXICAN.

Before Mary Sue Milliken and Susan Feniger spiced up cable TV with their cooking shows "Too Hot Tamales" and "Tamales World Tour," they started this restaurant over in West Hollywood. Now Border Grill has moved to a boldly painted, cavernous (read: loud) space in Santa Monica, and the gals aren't in the kitchen very much at all (though cookbooks and paraphernalia from their Food Network shows are displayed prominently for sale). But their influence on the inspired menu is enough to maintain the cantina's enormous popularity with folks who swear by the authentic flavor of Yucatán fish tacos, rock shrimp with ancho chiles, and meaty *ropa vieja,* the traditional Latin stew. The best meatless dish is *mulitas de hongos,* a layering of portobello mushrooms, poblano chiles, black beans, cheese, and guacamole spiced up with roasted garlic and seared red chard. Distracting desserts are displayed near the entrance, so you may spend the meal fantasizing about the yummy coconut flan or key lime pie.

JiRaffe. 502 Santa Monica Blvd. (corner of Fifth St.), Santa Monica. ☎ **310/917-6671.** Reservations recommended. Main courses $14–$20. AE, DC, MC, V. Tues–Fri noon–2pm and 6–11pm; Sat 5:30–11pm; Sun 5:30–9pm. AMERICAN/FRENCH.

"JiRaffe"—it isn't a quirky long-necked zoo creature but a blending of names from the two chefs responsible for this overnight sensation. Always popular at West Hollywood's Jackson's, friends-since-cooking-school Josiah Citrin and Raphael Lunetta defected in late 1996 to open an instantly crowded upscale bistro in restaurant-hungry Santa Monica. The deafening din of conversation is usually praise for JiRaffe's artistic treatment of whitefish (spiced and served with sugar snap peas, glazed carrots, and ginger-carrot sauce), roasted rabbit, crispy salmon, or pork chop (grilled with wild rice, smoked bacon, apple chutney, and cider sauce). JiRaffe also wins culinary points for highlighting oft-ignored vegetables like salsify, Swiss chard, and fennel, as well as complex appetizers that are more like miniature main dishes.

Joe's. 1023 Abbot Kinney Blvd., Venice. ☎ **310/399-5811.** Reservations recommended. Main courses $8–$10 at lunch, $15–$18 at dinner. AE, MC, V. Tues–Fri 11:30am–2:30pm; Sat–Sun 11am–3pm; Tues–Sun 6–11pm. AMERICAN ECLECTIC.

This is one of West L.A.'s best dining bargains. Chef/owner Joe Miller excels in simple New American cuisine, particularly grilled fish and roasted meats accented with piquant herbs. Set in a tiny quirky storefront, the humble room is a blank palette that belies Joe's popularity; the best tables are tucked away on the enclosed back patio. Lunch is a hidden treasure for those with a champagne palate but seltzer budget: Topping out at $10, all include salad, one of Miller's exquisite soups, and especially prompt service. Beer and wine are served, except during weekday lunchtime (regulation, due to the elementary school across the street).

There's a nearly identical (but more spacious) sister restaurant in Sherman Oaks, called **Joe Joe's,** 13355 Ventura Blvd. (☎ **818/990-8280**).

WORTH A SPLURGE

Röckenwagner. 2435 Main St. (north of Ocean Park Blvd.), Santa Monica. ☎ **310/399-6504.** Reservations recommended. Main courses $8–$13 at lunch, $18–$22 at dinner. AE, CB, DC, MC, V. Tues–Fri 11:30am–2:30pm; Sat–Sun 9am–2:30pm; daily 6–9:45pm. CALIFORNIA.

Set in Frank Gehry's starkly modern Edgemar complex (itself a work of art), chef Hans Röckenwagner's eponymous restaurant continues the motif by presenting edible sculpture amid a gallerylike decor. Though in the midst of a popular shopping area, the space manages to be refreshingly quiet. Röckenwagner takes his art—and his food—very seriously, once orchestrating an entire menu around German white asparagus at the height of its short season. The delightfully unpretentious staff carries out deliciously pretentious dishes fusing Pacific Rim ingredients with traditional European preparations; a good example is the langostine ravioli with mangoes in port-wine reduction and curry oil. The menu tastes as good as it reads, and the desserts are to die for. Don't overlook the lunch bargains or the unique European-style breakfast of bread and cheese.

Valentino. 3115 Pico Blvd. (west of Bundy Dr.), Santa Monica. ☎ **310/829-4313.** Reservations required. Pasta $14–$18; meat and fish dishes $22–$28. AE, CB, DC, DISC, MC, V. Mon–Thurs 5:30–10:30pm; Fri 11:30am–2:30pm; Fri–Sat 5:30–11pm. ITALIAN.

Charming owner Piero Selvaggio oversees two other restaurants, but his distinctive touch still pervades this 25-year-old flagship. Elegant Valentino continues to maintain its position as *Wine Spectator* magazine's top wine cellar, and *New York Times* food critic Ruth Reichl calls this the best Italian restaurant in America. The creations of

Selvaggio and his brilliant young chef, Angelo Auriana, make dinners lengthy multi-course affairs (often involving several bottles of wine). You might begin with a crisp pinot grigio paired with caviar-filled cannoli or crespelle, thin little pancakes with fresh porcini mushrooms and a rich melt of fontina cheese. A rich Barolo is the perfect accompaniment to rosemary-infused roasted rabbit; the fantastically fragrant risotto with white truffles is one of the most magnificent dishes I've ever had. Jackets are all but required in the elegant dining room. Valentino is a good choice if you're splurging on just one special dinner.

L.A.'S WESTSIDE & BEVERLY HILLS
SUPER-CHEAP EATS

✪ **The Apple Pan.** 10801 Pico Blvd. (east of Westwood Blvd.). ☎ **310/475-3585.** Main courses $6–$7. No credit cards. Tues–Thurs and Sun 11am–midnight; Fri–Sat 11am–1am. SANDWICHES/AMERICAN.

There are no tables, just a U-shaped counter, at this classic American burger shack and L.A. landmark. Open since 1947, The Apple Pan is a diner that looks—and acts—the part. It's famous for juicy burgers, bullet-speed service, and authentic frills-free atmosphere. The hickory burger is best, though the tuna sandwich also has its huge share of fans. Ham, egg-salad, and Swiss-cheese sandwiches round out the menu. Definitely order fries, if you're in the mood, the home-baked apple pie.

Cadillac Cafe. 359 N. La Cienega Blvd. (1 block north of Beverly Blvd.), Los Angeles. ☎ **310/657-6591.** Reservations recommended for dinner. Main courses $7–$11. AE, MC, V. Mon–Thurs 11am–11pm; Fri 11am–midnight; Sat 10am–midnight; Sun 10am–11pm. AMERICAN ECLECTIC.

The buzz around town is all about the Cadillac Cafe—at least this month. It's smaller and friendlier than you'd expect from an ultra-trendy hipster hang less than a block from the Beverly Center. The attitude here says "coffeehouse." Vinyl booths and 1950s-style dinette tables are offset by brightly colored geometrics and artwork as edgy as the new wave and punk soundtrack; the menu has a split-personality too. New twists on comfort-food basics, like the light Waldorf salad redux or turkey "sundae" (my fave: turkey and mashed potatoes with gravy and cranberry toppings sprinkled with pecans), share space with stuffed grape leaves, Chinese chicken salad (another winner), and other ethnic surprises. *Helpful hint:* There's a free parking lot in back.

Skewers'. 8939 Santa Monica Blvd. (between Robertson and San Vicente blvds.), West Hollywood. ☎ **310/271-0555.** Main courses $7–$9; salads and pitas $4–$7. AE, MC, V. Daily 11am–midnight. MIDDLE EASTERN.

Santa Monica Boulevard is the heart of West Hollywood's commercial strip, and Skewers's sidewalk tables are a great place to see all kinds of neighborhood activity (and audacity). Inside is a New York–like narrow space with changing artwork adorning bare brick walls. From the zesty marinated carrot sticks you get the moment you're seated to the sweet, sticky squares of baklava for dessert, this Mediterranean grill is sure to please. The cuisine features baskets of warm pita bread for scooping up traditional salads like babaghanoush (grilled eggplant with tahini and lemon) and tabbouleh (cracked wheat, parsley, and tomatoes). Try marinated chicken and lamb off the grill or dolmades (rice- and meat-stuffed grape leaves) seared with a tangy tomato glaze.

Versailles. 1415 S. La Cienega Blvd. (south of Pico Blvd.). ☎ **310/289-0392.** Main courses $5–$11. AE, MC, V. Daily 11am–10pm. CUBAN.

Outfitted with Formica tabletops and looking something like an ethnic IHOP, Versailles feels very much like any number of Miami restaurants that cater to the exiled

Cuban community. The menu reads like a veritable survey of Havana-style cookery and includes specialties like "Moors and Christians" (flavorful black beans with white rice), *ropa vieja* (a stringy beef stew), *eastin lechón* (suckling pig with sliced onions), and fried whole fish (usually sea bass). Shredded roast pork is particularly recommendable, especially when tossed with the restaurant's trademark garlic-citrus sauce. But what everyone comes for is the chicken—succulent, slow roasted, and smothered in onions and either garlic-citrus sauce or barbecue sauce. Most everything is served with black beans and rice; wine and beer are available. Because meals are good, bountiful, and cheap, there's often a wait.

Another Versailles restaurant is in Culver City at 10319 Venice Blvd. (☎ **310/558-3168**).

FOR A FEW BUCKS MORE

✪ **Bombay Cafe.** 12021 W. Pico Blvd. (at Bundy).   ☎ **310/473-3388.** Reservations recommended on weekends. Main courses $9–$15. MC, V. Mon–Thurs 11:30am–10pm; Fri–Sat 11:30am–11pm; Sun 11:30am–4pm. INDIAN.

This friendly sleeper may well be L.A.'s best Indian restaurant, serving excellent curries and kurmas typical of south Indian street food. In 1999, its loyal clientele (and L.A. foodies in-the-know) followed Bombay Cafe to this new, larger location, a much-needed improvement. Once seated, immediately order *sev puri* for the table—these crispy little chips topped with chopped potatoes, onions, cilantro, and chutneys are the perfect accompaniment to what's sure to be an extended menu-reading session. Also recommended are the burritolike "frankies," juicy little bread rolls stuffed with lamb, chicken, or cauliflower. The best dishes come from the tandoor and include spicy yogurt-marinated swordfish, lamb, and chicken. While some dishes are authentically spicy, plenty of others have a mellow flavor for less incendiary palates. The restaurant is phenomenally popular and gets its share of celebrities: Meg Ryan and Dennis Quaid hired the Bombay Cafe to cater an affair at their Montana ranch.

Cava. 8384 W. 3rd St. (at Orlando Ave., in the Beverly Plaza Hotel). ☎ **323/658-8898.** Reservations recommended on weekends. Main courses $8–$17; breakfast $3–$9; lunch $4–$14. AE, CB, DC, DISC, MC, V. Daily 6:30am–midnight. SPANISH.

Trendy types in the mood for some fun are attracted to Cava's great mambo atmosphere; the tapas bar is made festive with flamboyant colors, and the loud flamenco really is live on weekends. The dining room is less raucous, with velvet drapes and tassels adorning the walls and comfortable booths. The cuisine is Spanish livened up with Caribbean touches, an influence reflected in dishes like black-bean tamales with tomatillo salsa and golden caviar; thick, dark tortilla soup; jerk chicken with sweet yams; and pan-seared shrimp in spicy peppercorn sauce. Spanish paella is stewed up three ways—seafood, chicken and sausage, or all-vegetable—and is featured in Monday's all-you-can-eat Paella Festival. If you have room for dessert, try the ruby-colored pears poached in port, rice pudding, or flan.

Kate Mantilini. 9101 Wilshire Blvd. (at Doheny Dr.), Beverly Hills. ☎ **310/278-3699.** Reservations recommended. Main courses $7–$16. AE, MC, V. Mon–Thurs 7:30am–1am; Fri 7:30am–2am; Sat noon–2am; Sun 10am–midnight. AMERICAN.

It's rare to find a restaurant that feels comfortably familiar yet cutting-edge trendy at the same time—and also happens to be one of L.A.'s few late-night eateries. Kate Mantilini fits the bill perfectly. One of the first to bring meat loaf back into fashion, Kate's offers a huge menu of upscale truck-stop favorites like "white" chili (with chicken, white beans, and Jack cheese), grilled steaks and fish, a few token pastas, and just about anything you could crave. If you get the munchies late at night, nothing quite beats a steaming bowl of lentil-vegetable soup and some garlic-cheese toast, unless your taste runs to fresh oysters and a dry martini—Kate has it all. The huge mural of the Hagler-Hearns boxing match that dominates the stark open interior provides the only clue to the namesake's identity: Mantilini was an early female-boxing promoter, around 1947.

✪ **La Serenata Gourmet.** 10924 W. Pico Blvd., West Los Angeles. ☎ **310/441-9667.** Reservations not accepted. Main courses $8–$13. AE, MC, V. Daily 11am–3:30pm and 5–10pm (Fri–Sat to 10:30pm). MEXICAN.

Westsiders rejoiced when this branch of Boyle Heights's award-winning La Serenata de Girabaldi began serving their authentic but innovative Mexican cuisine just a block away from the Westside Pavilion shopping center. It's casual, fun, and intensely delicious; specialties like shrimp enchiladas, fish tacos, and pork *gorditas* are all accented with hand-patted corn tortillas, fresh chips dusted with añejo cheese, and flavorful fresh salsas. Always packed to capacity, the restaurant finally expanded in 1998, but try to avoid the prime lunch and dinner hours nevertheless.

There's also a brand-new **La Serenata** in Santa Monica at 1416 Fourth St. (☎ **310/656-7017**) that boasts an upscale atmosphere and a full bar.

Nate & Al's. 414 N. Beverly Dr. (at Brighton Way), Beverly Hills. ☎ **310/274-0101.** Main courses $8–$13. AE, DISC, MC, V. Daily 7:30am–9pm. DELI.

Despite its location in the center of Beverly Hills's "Golden Triangle," Nate & Al's has remained unchanged since it opened in 1945, from the Naugahyde booths to the motherly waitresses who treat you the same whether you're a house-account celebrity regular or just a visitor stopping in for an overstuffed pastrami on rye. Their too-salty chicken soup keeps Nate & Al's from being the best L.A. deli (actually, I'd be hard-pressed to choose any one deli as the city's best), but staples like chopped liver, dense potato pancakes, blintzes, borscht, and well-dilled pickles more than make up for it. If you want to know where old-money rich-and-famous types go for comfort food, look no further.

Replay Country Store Cafe. 8607 Melrose Ave. (between San Vicente and La Cienega blvds.), West Hollywood. ☎ **310/657-6404.** Reservations suggested on weekends. Main courses $6–$13. AE, DISC, MC, V. Mon–Fri 11am–11pm; Sat–Sun 11am–midnight. ITALIAN/CONTINENTAL.

The two things to remember at Replay are don't buy the clothes and always order the soup. Most of the cafe's tables are on the wraparound wood porch of the overpriced boutique it's attached to. This faux country general store on trendy Melrose Avenue near the Pacific Design Center won't fool anyone into plunking down $150 for denim overalls, but the restaurant is one of West Hollywood's hidden treasures. Everything on the casual, vaguely Italian menu is outstanding, from gourmet pizzas and pasta with delicately puréed tomato-basil sauce to warm chicken salad (a surprise combination of bleu cheese, walnuts, and mandarin-orange wedges) and exquisite pastries for dessert. Each day a different soup, always a simple purée allowing the fresh ingredients to shine through, is ladled into wide bowls at your table from heavy copper saucepans.

MODERATELY PRICED OPTIONS

Joss. 9255 Sunset Blvd. (west of Doheny Dr.), West Hollywood. ☎ **310/276-1886.** Reservations suggested. Main courses $8–$18; dim sum $4 per order. AE, DC, DISC, MC, V. Mon–Fri noon–3pm; Sun–Thurs 6–10:30pm; Fri–Sat 6pm to midnight. HAUTE CHINESE.

On the fringe between Beverly Hills and the Sunset Strip, Joss has a minimalist yet welcoming decor of beige linen chairs, white tablecloths, and tiny halogen lights suspended over each table. The entryway's ever-present sherry decanter hints at the surprisingly well-chosen and affordable wine list, compiled by owner Cecile Tang Shu

Shuen, whose inventive menu takes Chinese essentials beyond your expectations—not by creating fussy "fusion" dishes but by subtly manipulating ingredients and preparations according to her superb artist's palate. Fried rice is spiked with the tang of dried black beans and ginger; velvety curry sauce is creamed with coconut milk and tossed with chicken; and tender beef is marinated with spicy red chiles but mellowed with tangerine liqueur. You could make a meal of the dozen dim sum varieties, like delicately steamed dumplings (spinach and chicken, shrimp with bamboo shoots, or vegetable and black mushrooms) served in stacked bamboo steaming trays, crisp-bottom pot stickers filled with Peking duck or lamb and leeks, and crispy wonton or spring rolls. The desserts, never overly sweet, complement Joss's sublime meals perfectly. The location draws many celebrities and Industry honchos—but gawking is definitely uncool.

✪ **Pastis.** 8114 Beverly Blvd. (west of Crescent Heights), Los Angeles. ☎ **323/ 655-8822.** Reservations recommended. Main courses $13–$17. AE, MC, V. Daily 5:30– 10pm. FRENCH PROVENÇALE.

Of the new wave of country French bistros in town, Pastis usually takes a back seat to the ultrahip celebrity-frequented Mimosa, which happens to be just a block away. But locals and regulars often prefer this rustic yet civilized spot, named for the licorice-flavored liqueur imbibed throughout the south of France. Intimate and friendly, with sidewalk tables and a warmly ochre-toned dining room, Pastis manages to be elegant and also the kind of place you can scrape your chair, raise your voice, or drink a little too much wine. Distinctive menu selections include curly endive salad with bacon and poached-egg garnish, wine-braised rabbit, and Marseilles-style seafood bouillabaisse. For chocolate lovers: The *chocolat pot au crème* is a beautiful thick custard served in a rustic glazed pot.

WORTH A SPLURGE

✪ **Jozu.** 8360 Melrose Ave. (at Kings Rd.), West Hollywood. ☎ **323/655-5600.** Reservations recommended. Main courses $16–$27. AE, MC, V. Daily 5:30–10:30pm. ASIAN/ CALIFORNIA.

Jozu means "excellent" in Japanese, and it perfectly describes everything about this tranquil restaurant where everyone's meal begins with a complimentary sake from Jozu's premium sake list. Chef Suzanne Tracht honed her art at Campanile, and the menu presents Asian flavors interpreted with an international inventiveness. Outstanding dishes include pork *charsui*-style, caramelized with tart kumquat sauce and laid on a bed of celery root purée; delicately roasted sea bass on crunchy cabbage; and scallops grilled with lemongrass and other Thai flavorings. There's a heavenly tofu-and-daikon-salad appetizer lightly dressed with mustard, soy, and scallion oil; the dessert of choice is banana tart, lightly caramelized fruit laid in a buttery crust. The interior is warmly comfortable and subtly lit; plenty of beautiful Hollywood types dine here, including celebs as diverse as Kareem Abdul-Jabbar and *Simpsons* creator Matt Groening, but it's quiet enough for real dinner conversation.

HOLLYWOOD
SUPER-CHEAP EATS

Flora Kitchen. 460 S. La Brea Ave. (at Sixth St.). ☎ **323/931-9900.** Reservations not accepted. Main courses $8–$10. MC, V. Sun–Thurs 8am–10pm; Fri–Sat 8am–11pm. AMERICAN.

Picture an upscale, funky Carrow's or Denny's and you've imagined Flora Kitchen. Known for its tuna and chicken salads served on exalted La Brea Bakery breads, the restaurant is equally comfortable dishing out more eclectic fare like cayenne-spiced

ⓘ Affordable Family-Friendly Restaurants

✪ **Grand Central Market** *(see p. 454)*   No, this isn't a restaurant per se, but this downtown venue is a great dining bargain for families. You'll have to keep smaller hands from grabbing at the displayed produce and other wares, but the sights, smells, and flavors of this bustling food market are sure to thrill both grown-ups and kids. If the little ones want tacos while you'd prefer a salad or maybe some stir-fry, try assembling a mix-and-match lunch from the many prepared-food counters inside the market (tables are set up at either end for eating). You've never had such good eats at such cheap prices!

✪ **Jerry's Famous Deli** *(see p. 452)*   This Studio City delicatessen is frequented mostly by industry types who populate this Valley community; their kids often sport baseball caps or production T-shirts from Mom or Dad's latest project. With the most extensive deli menu in town and a casual coffee shop atmosphere, families flock to Jerry's for lunch, early dinner, and (crowded) weekend breakfast.

Pink's Hot Dogs *(see p. 445)*   Pink's is an institution in its own right; they've been serving franks here for what seems like forever. Everyone loves Pink's chili dogs, but you may never get the orange stains out of your kid's clothes.

Here are some other family-friendly spots. The upscale **Cafe Pinot,** in the L.A. Public Library, 700 W. Fifth St., between Grand and Flower streets, downtown (☎ **213/239-6500**); **Pinot Bistro,** 12969 Ventura Ave., west of Coldwater Canyon Avenue, Studio City (☎ **818/990-0500**); and **Pinot at the Chronicle,** 897 Granite Dr., behind Lake Avenue, Pasadena (☎ **626/792-1179**), don't often come to mind when you're searching for family eats, and many kids are certainly too antsy to behave during an entire bistro meal. But the Pinot dynasty welcomes little ones with a special child-friendly menu, and kids under 10 eat free. It's a great way to enjoy L.A.'s finest and stay close to your budget.

Dive!, in the Century City Marketplace, 10250 Santa Monica Blvd., Century City (☎ **310/788-3483**), is more a theme park than a restaurant, a festive submarine-theme eatery that's packed with child-pleasing special-effects gadgetry of all kinds.

potato soup, poached salmon with dill sauce, and seared ahi with roast vegetables. Flora is popular with art-gallery strollers by day and with music lovers (who take the restaurant's dinners, boxed, to the Hollywood Bowl) on warm summer nights. Unfortunately, the service at Denny's is better.

Hollywood Hills Coffee Shop. 6145 Franklin Ave. (between Gower and Vine sts.). ☎ **323/467-7678.** Most items under $10. AE, DISC, MC, V. Tues–Sat 7am–10pm; Sun–Mon 7am–4pm. DINER.

Having for years served as the run-of-the-mill coffee shop for the attached freewayside Best Western, this place took on a life of its own when chef Susan Fine commandeered the kitchen and spiked the menu with quirky Mexican and Asian touches. Hotel guests spill in from the lobby to rub noses with the actors, screenwriters, and other artistic types who converge from nearby canyons while awaiting that sitcom casting call or feature-film deal—a community immortalized in the 1996 film *Swingers,* which was filmed in the restaurant. Prices have gone up (to pay for the industrial-strength cappuccino-maker visible behind the counter?), and the dinner menu features surprisingly sophisticated entrees. But breakfast and lunch are still bargains, and the comfy Americana atmosphere is a nice break from the bright lights of nearby Hollywood Boulevard.

Pink's Hot Dogs. 709 N. La Brea Ave. (at Melrose Ave.). ☎ **323/931-4223.** Hot dogs $2.10. No credit cards. Sun–Thurs 9:30am–2am; Fri–Sat 9:30am–3am. HOT DOGS.

Pink's isn't your usual guidebook recommendation, but then again, this crusty corner stand isn't your usual doggery either. The heartburn-inducing chili dogs are so decadent that otherwise-upstanding, health-conscious Angelenos crave them. Bruce Willis reportedly proposed to Demi Moore at the 59-year-old shack that grew around the late Paul Pink's 10¢ wiener cart. Pray the bulldozers stay away from this little nugget of a place.

Roscoe's House of Chicken 'n' Waffles. 1514 N. Gower St. (at Sunset Blvd.). ☎ **323/466-7453.** Main courses $4–$11. No credit cards. Sun–Thurs 9am–midnight; Fri–Sat 9am–4am. AMERICAN.

It sounds like a bad joke: Only chicken and waffle dishes are served here, a rubric that also encompasses eggs and chicken livers. Its close proximity to CBS Television City has turned this simple restaurant into a kind of de facto commissary for the network. A chicken-and-cheese omelet isn't everyone's ideal way to begin the day, but it's de rigueur at Roscoe's. At lunch, few calorie-unconscious diners can resist the chicken smothered in gravy and onions—a house specialty served with waffles or grits and biscuits. Large chicken-salad bowls and chicken sandwiches also provide plenty of cluck for the buck. Homemade cornbread, sweet-potato pie, homemade potato salad, and corn on the cob are available as side orders, and wine and beer are sold.

Roscoe's can also be found at 4907 W. Washington Blvd., at La Brea Avenue (☎ **323/936-3730**), and 5006 W. Pico Blvd. (☎ **323/934-4405**).

Swingers. Attached to the Beverly Laurel Motor Hotel, 8020 Beverly Blvd. (west of Fairfax Ave.). ☎ **323/653-5858.** Most items less than $8. AE, DISC, MC, V. Sun–Thurs 6am–2am; Fri–Sat 9am–4am. DINER/AMERICAN.

Resurrected from a motel coffee shop so dismal I can't even remember it, Swingers was transformed by a couple of L.A. hipster nightclub owners into a 1990s version of comfy Americana. The interior seems like a slice of the 1950s until you notice the plaid upholstery and Warhol-esque graphics, which contrast nicely with the retro red-white-and-blue "Swingers" logo adorning everything. Guests at the Beverly Laurel chow down alongside body-pierced industry hounds from nearby record companies, while a soundtrack that runs the gamut from punk to Schoolhouse Rock plays in the background. It's not all attitude here, though—you'll enjoy a menu of high-quality diner favorites spiked with trendy crowd-pleasers: Steel-cut Irish oatmeal, challah French toast, grilled Jamaican jerk chicken, and a nice selection of tofu-enhanced vegetarian dishes are just a few of the eclectic offerings. Sometimes I just "swing" by (ha ha) for a malt or milk shake to go—theirs are among the best in town.

✪ Toi on Sunset. 7505½ Sunset Blvd. (at Gardner). ☎ **323/874-8062.** Reservations accepted only for parties of 6 or more. Main courses $6–$11. AE, DISC, MC, V. Daily 11am–4am. THAI.

Because it's open *really* late, Toi has become an instant fave of Hollywood hipsters like Sean Penn and Woody Harrelson, who make postclubbing excursions to this rock 'n' roll eatery a few blocks from the Sunset Strip. After all the hype, I was surprised to find possibly L.A.'s best bargain Thai food, authentically prepared and served in portions so generous the word *enormous* seems inadequate. Menu highlights include hot-and-sour chicken, coconut soup, and the house specialty—chicken curry somen, a spicy dish with green curry and mint sauce spooned over thin Japanese rice noodles. Vegetarians will be pleased with the vast selection of meat-free items like *pad kee mao,* rice noodles served spicy with tofu, mint, onions, peppers, and chili; another standout is eggplant, pumpkin, and tofu in a piquant soy-and-ginger sauce. The interior is a noisy amalgam of cultish movie posters, rock memorabilia, and haphazardly placed industrial-issue dinette sets; the plates, flatware, and drinking glasses are cheap coffee-shop issue. In other words, it's all about the food and the scene—neither will disappoint.

Westsiders can opt for **Toi on Wilshire,** 1120 Wilshire Blvd., Santa Monica (☎ **310/394-7804**), open daily from 11am to 3am.

FOR A FEW BUCKS MORE

✪ **El Cholo.** 1121 S. Western Ave. (south of Olympic Blvd.). ☎ **213/734-2773.** Reservations recommended. Main courses $7–$13. AE, DC, MC, V. Mon–Thurs 11am–10pm; Fri–Sat 11am–11pm; Sun 11am–9pm. MEXICAN.

There's authentic Mexican and then there's traditional Mexican—El Cholo is comfort food of the latter variety, south-of-the-border cuisine regularly craved by Angelenos. They've been serving it up in this pink adobe hacienda since 1927, though the once-outlying mid-Wilshire neighborhood around them has turned into Koreatown. El Cholo's expertly blended margaritas, invitingly messy nachos, and classic combination dinners don't break new culinary ground, but the kitchen has perfected these standards over 70 years. I wish they bottled their rich enchilada sauce! Other specialties are seasonally available green-corn tamales and creative sizzling vegetarian fajitas that go way beyond just eliminating the meat. The atmosphere is festive, as people from all parts of town dine happily in the many rambling rooms. There's valet parking as well as a free self-park lot directly across the street.

Westsiders head to El Cholo's new Santa Monica branch at 1025 Wilshire Blvd. (☎ **310/899-1106**).

Lumpy Gravy. 7311 Beverly Blvd. ☎ **323/934-9400.** Reservations recommended on weekends. Main courses $6–$13. AE, MC, V. Mon–Fri 11:30am–2:30pm; Mon–Thurs 6–11pm; Fri–Sat 6pm to midnight. INTERNATIONAL ECLECTIC.

Frank Zappa fans will recognize the name of this quirky avant-garde restaurant/gallery, where everything from the menu to the artwork (including several framed Zappa record jackets) to the bizarro gift/music shop upstairs pays homage to the late art-rocker. Amidst a dark surreal decor featuring twisted industrial metal suspended from the ceiling and a bank of attention-grabbing TV monitors, you'll find a surprisingly friendly atmosphere and food that's distractingly good. One of the owners is animator Gabor Csupo, who personally contributes an old-world Hungarian flavor to much of the menu—the rest is equal parts Pacific Rim and American Heartland. Where else can diners share "Waka Jawaka" ahi tuna with wasabi mashed potatoes, "Uncle Meat" ground New York steak burger, and creamy chicken paprikas over *galuska* dumplings? The signature dessert is the Bananagasm, a wonton-wrapped banana deep-fried and served over ice cream with rich fudgy sauce. It gets this dessertaholic's highest recommendation. A small stage features poetry readings and live avant-garde or ethnic music Friday and Saturday nights (no cover); atmospheric dinner music is piped in the rest of the week.

Sofi. 8030¾ W. 3rd St. (between Fairfax Ave. and Crescent Heights Blvd.). ☎ **323/651-0346.** Reservations recommended. Main courses $7–$14. AE, DC, MC, V. Mon–Sat noon–3pm; daily 5:30–11pm. GREEK.

Look for the simple black awning over the narrow passageway leading from the street to this hidden Aegean treasure. Be sure to ask for a table on the romantic patio amid twinkling lights and immediately order a plate of the thick, satisfying *tsatziki* (yogurt-cucumber-garlic spread) accompanied by a basket of warm pitas for dipping. Other specialties (recipes courtesy of Sofi's old-world grand-mother) are herbed rack of lamb with rice, fried calamari salad, *saganaki* (kasseri cheese flamed with ouzo), and other hearty taverna favorites. Near the Farmers Market in a popular part of town, Sofi's odd off-street setting has made it an insiders' secret.

MODERATELY PRICED OPTIONS

Boxer. 7615 Beverly Blvd. (east of Fairfax), Los Angeles. ☎ **323/932-6178.** Reservations suggested. Main courses $11–$20. AE, MC, V. Tues–Fri 11:30am–2:30pm; Tues–Sun 6–11pm; Sat–Sun 10:30am–2:30pm. CALIFORNIA.

This minimally furnished space on ever-developing Beverly Boulevard has been a favorite of L.A. foodies since opening in 1996. Recently, chef Michael Plapp assumed the toque; his style is similar to that of former star chef Neal Fraser, whose career was launched by the success of Boxer. That style weaves elements of Italian, Moroccan, Mexican, and French cuisine into an eclectic "New American" mélange, producing selections like rack of lamb glazed with pomegranate and paired with couscous and roasted eggplant. Thankfully he still prepares the Boxer salad, a cool mix of ripe tomatoes, beets, avocado, crisp green beans, and curried onions splashed with vinaigrette and pressed into a multilayered square with a fluffy hat of greens. The crowd ranges from suited yuppies to Chanel-ed socialites to chunky-shoed 20-somethings—all of whom blend inside as well as the menu's varied ingredients. You might even catch a glimpse of members of the *Friends* cast. Every plate is artistically arranged, including the splendid desserts. Eschew the valet for always-plentiful street parking and bring your own wine; Boxer sells no liquor and charges no corkage fee.

✪ **Lola's.** 945 N. Fairfax Ave. (south of Santa Monica Blvd.), Los Angeles. ☎ **323/736-5652.** Reservations recommended. Main courses $10–$18. AE, MC, V. Daily 5:30pm–2am. NEW AMERICAN.

As the song goes, "Whatever Lola wants, Lola gets," and Lola must've wanted to open a stylish restaurant/martini bar that'd instantly become the in crowd's darling. This centrally located place has a lot going for it: Not only is this circa 1935 Hollywood building a perfect foil for Lola's semi-Gothic decor, but the menu is reasonably priced (and better than it reads). Then there's the famed martini bar: All the several dozen colorful concoctions are available table-side, served in individual stainless-steel cock-tail shakers with chilled conical glasses. Menu selections are unfussy and flavorful, fea-turing mesquite-grilled meats, simple pastas, and internationally flavored appetizers. Be sure to try Domenick's Mashed Potatoes, a creamy dollop of mash atop a nest of crispy shoestring potatoes. The star dessert is Lola's Chocolate Kiss Cake, a dense and rich treat.

Tahiti. 7910 W. 3rd St. (at Fairfax), Los Angeles. ☎ **323/651-1213.** Reservations recom-mended on weekends. Main courses $10–$16. AE, MC, V. Mon–Fri 11:30am–2:30pm; Mon–Thurs 6–10pm; Fri–Sat 6–11pm. PACIFIC RIM/CALIFORNIA.

With a rapidly growing fan base of showbiz types and artists who inhabit the eclectic neighborhood, Tahiti may have only recently joined the L.A. dining scene but will be instantly familiar to the scores who frequented chef/owner Tony DiLembo's late, great Indigo restaurant nearby. DiLembo has imported his distinctive "world cuisine," a provocative mix of zesty influences that create diverse specialties like rare ahi tuna

Sea Breezes & Sunsets: Ocean-View Dining in Malibu

Despite fires, mud slides, and high rents, Malibu residents are steadfast in protecting their precious parcel of beachfront paradise. There really is a beautifully calm on-vacation vibe to this upscale stretch of coast; one way you can sample a slice of the happiness pie is to (literally) turn your back on the frenzy of L.A. and gaze on the sparkling Pacific—at least for the duration of a meal.

From south to north, numerous eateries dot the coastline, all exploiting as much ocean view as their property line allows. Here are my favorites:

A local tradition, **Gladstone's 4 Fish,** 17300 Pacific Coast Hwy., at Sunset Boulevard (☎ **310/454-3474**), is perfectly immersed in the Malibu scene. It shares a parking lot with a public beach, so the restaurant's wood deck has a constant view of surfers, bikini-clad sunbathers, and other frolicking beachgoers. When they're busy, Gladstone's even sets up picnic-style tables right out on the sand. The prices are moderate, but the atmosphere is casual anything-goes. The menu boasts several pages of fresh fish and seafood, augmented by a few salads and other meals for landlubbers. It's popular for afternoon/evening drinking, offering nearly 20 seafood appetizer platters; it's also known for decadent chocolatey desserts large enough for the whole table. Gladstone's is open Monday through Thursday from 11am to 11pm, Friday from 11am to midnight, Saturday from 7am to midnight, and Sunday from 7am to 11pm. Parking costs $3.50.

Lovers of Hawaii and all things Polynesian will thrive at **Duke's Malibu,** 21150 Pacific Coast Hwy., at Las Flores Canyon (☎ **310/317-0777**), a Cali outpost of the Hawaiian chain. Imagine a South Pacific TGI Fridays, where the food is secondary to the decor—add a prestigious rocky perch atop breaking waves and you have this surfing-themed crowd-pleaser. Worth a visit for the impressive memorabilia alone (the place is named for Hawaiian surf legend "Duke" Kahanamoku), Duke's offers up pretty good food at inflated but not outrageous prices. There's plenty of good-quality fresh fish prepared in the Hawaiian regional style, hearty surf 'n' turf, a smattering of chicken and pasta dishes, and plenty of

drizzled with lime-ginger butter, sprinkled with toasted sesame seeds, and served with wasabi horseradish and papaya garnish; Argentinean-style T-bone with chimichurri dipping sauce; sherry-sautéed chicken-and-spinach pot stickers accented with mint; and perennial standout rosemary chicken strips with fettuccine in sun-dried tomato cream sauce. The relaxing decor is sophisticated South Seas with a modern twist, incorporating thatch, batik, rattan, and palm fronds. If the weather is nice, try to sit on the patio. Be sure to save room for Tahiti's tropical-tinged desserts.

WORTH A SPLURGE

✪ **Campanile.** 624 S. La Brea Ave. (north of Wilshire Blvd.). ☎ **323/938-1447.** Reservations required. Main courses $18–$32. AE, MC, V. Mon–Fri 7:30am–2:30pm; Sat–Sun 8am–1:30pm; Mon–Thurs 6–10pm; Fri–Sat 5:30–11pm. CALIFORNIA/MEDITERRANEAN.

Built as Charlie Chaplin's private offices in 1928, this lovely building has a multilevel layout with flower-bedecked interior balconies, a bubbling fountain, and a skylight through which you can see the campanile (bell tower). The kitchen, headed by Spago alumnus chef/owner Mark Peel, gets a giant leg up from baker (and wife) Nancy Silverton, who runs the now-legendary La Brea Bakery next door. Meals might begin

finger-lickin' appetizers to accompany Duke's Day-Glo tropical cocktails. It's open Monday through Thursday from 11:30am to 10pm, Friday and Saturday from 11:30am to 10:30pm, and Sunday from 10am to 10pm. Valet parking is $2 (dinner and weekends only, otherwise there's free self-parking).

The appropriately named **Pier View Cafe & Cantina,** 22718 Pacific Coast Hwy. (☎ **310/456-6962**), sits on the beach about half a mile south of the pier and offers huge portions of inexpensive food in an ultracasual ("shirts and shoes required") setting. Inside there's sawdust on the floor and surfboards in the rafters; sun lovers get the wind in their hair at tables along Pier View's clunky wooden deck. The comprehensive menu has something for everyone, including giant farm-style breakfasts, Baja-style fish tacos, burgers with a mound of curly fries, and a terrifically meaty chili. In addition to fresh seafood and enormous main-course salads, they have a long list of appetizer platters for the lingering cocktail crowd. An added bonus is patrons-only direct beach access from the deck. Pier View is open Sunday through Thursday from 7am to midnight and Friday and Saturday from 7am to 1am. Valet parking is $3 (Fri through Sun only, otherwise there's free self-parking).

The **Paradise Cove Beach Cafe,** 28128 Pacific Coast Hwy. (☎ **310/457-2503**), sits on a delightful crescent beach complete with a short fishing pier and critter-filled tide pools. Recently updated by veteran restaurateur Bob Morris (of Gladstone's fame), this light-filled wooden clubhouse features enormous portions, reasonable prices, and better-than-expected food. Nearly every table has a view of the water, and black-and-white photo blow-ups of historic Malibu line the walls. The menu skips from freshly shucked oysters and clam chowder to terrific burgers and meal-sized salads—heartier appetites can pig out on ribs and meats off the grill. Breakfast is also a big local draw. Diners can park free for a couple hours with validation; regular Cove parking is $15. The Beach Cafe is open daily 6am to 11pm, and gets pretty crowded at peak mealtimes; reservations are highly recommended.

with fried zucchini flowers drizzled with melted mozzarella or lamb carpaccio surrounded by artichoke leaves—a dish that arrives looking like one of van Gogh's sunflowers. Chef Peel is particularly known for his grills and roasts; try the grilled prime rib smeared with black-olive tapenade or papardelle with braised rabbit, roasted tomato, and collard greens. And don't skip dessert—the restaurant's many enthusiastic sweets fans have turned Nancy's dessert book into a best-seller. Breakfast is a surprising crowd-pleaser and a terrific way to appreciate this beautiful space on a budget.

DOWNTOWN
SUPER-CHEAP EATS

Fred 62. 1850 N. Vermont Ave., Los Feliz. ☎ **323/667-0062.** Main courses $3–$10. MC, V. Daily 24 hr. AMERICAN.

Opened in the heart of trendy Los Feliz by chef Fred Eric—whose overly contrived Vida restaurant is just a couple of blocks away—this slightly skewed coffee shop comes by its retro kitsch honestly. Eric remodeled the formerly tiny corner diner with spiffy 1950s car-culture icons, including hood ornament sconces and blue service-station smocks for the wait staff. He then named it after himself and his birth year (1962) and peppered the menu with puns and inside jokes: There's a daily "cream of what Fred wants" soup, plus sandwiches, burgers, salads, and a handful of Asian noodle bowls, including "SEOUL-FULL NOO*DEL +I," a cryptic name for Korean potato noodles, vegetables, and sesame dressing in hot broth. You might feel like you've stepped into a circa "Route 66" beatnik diner in TV land, but the clientele is very real and the food is comforting yet stylish. Don't miss the homemade potato chips and the fresh lemonade dispensed from a spacey churning tank on the counter.

Original Pantry Cafe. 877 S. Figueroa St. (at Ninth St.). ☎ **213/972-9279.** Main courses $6–$11. No credit cards. Daily 24 hr. AMERICAN.

An L.A. institution if there ever was one, this place has been serving huge portions of comfort food around the clock for more than 60 years. In fact, they don't even have a key to the front door. Owned by L.A. mayor Richard Riordan, the Pantry is especially popular with politicos who come for weekday lunches and conference-goers en route to the nearby L.A. Convention Center. The well-worn restaurant is also a welcoming beacon to clubbers after hours, when downtown becomes a virtual ghost town. A bowl of celery stalks, carrot sticks, and whole radishes greets you at your Formica table, and creamy coleslaw and sourdough bread come free with every meal. Famous for quantity rather than quality, the Pantry serves huge T-bone steaks, densely packed meat loaf, macaroni and cheese, and other favorites. A typical breakfast (served all day) might consist of a huge stack of hotcakes, a big slab of sweet cured ham, home fries, and coffee.

Philippe the Original. 1001 N. Alameda St. (at Ord St.). ☎ **213/628-3781.** Reservations not accepted. Main courses $3–$7. No credit cards. Daily 6am–10pm. SANDWICHES/ AMERICAN.

Good old-fashioned value is what this legendary landmark cafeteria is all about. Popular with both South-Central project dwellers and Beverly Hills elite, Philippe's decidedly unspectacular dining room is a microcosm of the entire city; it's one of the few places, it seems, where everyone can get along. Philippe's claims to have invented the French-dipped sandwich at this location in 1908; these remain the most popular menu items. Patrons push trays along the counter and watch while their choice of beef, pork, ham, turkey, or lamb is sliced and layered onto crusty French bread that's been dipped in meat juices. Other menu items include homemade beef stew, chili, and pickled pigs' feet. A hearty breakfast, served daily until 10:30am, is worth attending if only for Philippe's uncommonly good cinnamon-dipped French toast. Beer and wine are available.

FOR A FEW BUCKS MORE

Cha Cha Cha. 656 N. Virgil Ave. (at Melrose Ave.), Silver Lake. ☎ **323/664-7723.** Reservations recommended. Main courses $8–$15. AE, DC, DISC, MC, V. Sun–Thurs 8am–10:30pm; Fri–Sat 8am–11:30pm. CARIBBEAN.

Cha Cha Cha serves the West Coast's best Caribbean food in a fun and funky space on the seedy fringe of downtown. The restaurant is a festival of flavors and colors that are both upbeat and offbeat. It's impossible to feel down when you're part of this eclectic hodgepodge of pulsating Caribbean music, wild decor, and kaleidoscopic clutter; still, the intimate dining rooms cater to lively romantics, not obnoxious frat boys. Claustrophobes should choose seats in the airy covered courtyard. The very spicy black-pepper jumbo shrimp gets top marks, as does the paella, a generous mix of chicken, sausage, and seafood blended with saffron rice. Other Jamaican-, Haitian-, Cuban-, and Puerto Rican–inspired recommendations include jerk pork and mambo gumbo, a zesty soup of okra, shredded chicken, and spices. Hard-core Caribbeanites might visit for breakfast, when the fare ranges from plantain, yucca, onion, and herb omelets to scrambled eggs with fresh tomatillos served on hot grilled tortillas.

Langer's. 704 S. Alvarado St. (at Seventh St.). ☎ **213/483-8050.** Main courses $6–$14. MC, V. Mon–Sat 8am–4pm. DELI.

A leader in L.A.'s long-running deli war, Langer's makes some of the best stuffed kishka and matzoh-ball soup this side of the Hudson. For many, however, it's the fresh chopped liver and lean and spicy hot pastrami sandwiches that make Langer's L.A.'s best deli. Langer's has been serving the business community and displaced New Yorkers for almost 50 years. After the riots, when things got dicey around this neighborhood, the restaurant began a curbside delivery service: Phone in your order with an ETA, and they'll be waiting for you at the curb—with change.

Yang Chow Restaurant. 819 N. Broadway (at Alpine St.), Chinatown. ☎ **213/625-0811.** Reservations recommended on weekends. Main courses $8–$12. AE, MC, V. Daily 11:30am–2:30pm; Sun–Thurs 5–9:30pm; Fri–Sat 5–10:30pm. MANDARIN/SZECHUAN.

Open for more then 30 years, family-operated Yang Chow is one of downtown's more popular Chinese restaurants. It's not the dining room's bland and functional decor that accrues accolades, however; what makes Yang Chow so popular is an interesting menu of seafood specialties complementing well-done Chinese standards. After covering the Mandarin and Szechuan basics—sweet-and-sour pork, shrimp with broccoli, moo shu chicken—the kitchen leaps into high gear, concocting dishes like spicy Dungeness crab; a tangy and hot sautéed squid; and sautéed shellfish with a pungent hoisin-based dipping sauce. The key to having a terrific meal is to first order the house speciality—steamed dumplings served on a bed of spinach—then respectfully ask for recommendations from your server.

THE SAN FERNANDO VALLEY
SUPER-CHEAP EATS

Casa Vega. 13371 Ventura Blvd. (at Fulton Ave.), Sherman Oaks. ☎ **818/788-4868.** Reservations recommended. Main courses $5–$11. AE, CB, DC, MC, V. Mon–Fri 11am–2am; Sat–Sun 4pm–2am. MEXICAN.

I believe everyone loves a friendly dive, and Casa Vega is one of my local favorites. A faux-weathered adobe exterior conceals red Naugahyde booths lurking among fake potted plants and 1960s amateur oil paintings of dark-eyed Mexican children and red-cape-waving bullfighters. (The decor achieves critical mass at Christmas, when everything drips with tinsel.) Locals love it for its good, cheap margaritas (order on the rocks), bottomless baskets of hot and salty chips, and traditional combination dinners, which all come with Casa Vega's patented tostada-style dinner salad. Street parking is so plentiful you should use the valet only as a last resort.

Du-par's Restaurant & Bakery. 12036 Ventura Blvd. (1 block east of Laurel Canyon Blvd.), Studio City. ☎ **818/766-4437.** All items under $10. AE, DC, DISC, MC, V. Sun–Thurs 6am–1am; Fri–Sat 6am–4am. AMERICAN/DINER.

It's been called a "culinary wax museum," the last of a dying breed, the kind of coffee shop Donna Reed took the family to for blue-plate specials. This isn't a trendy new theme place, it's the real deal—and that motherly waitress who calls everyone under 60 "hon" has probably been slinging hash here for 20 or 30 years. It's popular among old-timers who made it part of their daily routine decades ago, showbiz denizens who eschew the industry watering holes, a new generation who appreciates a tasty, cheap meal . . . well, everyone. It's common knowledge that Du-par's makes the best buttermilk pancakes in town, though some prefer the eggy, perfect French toast (extra-crispy around the edges, please). Mouth-watering pies (blueberry cream cheese, coconut cream) line the front display case and can be had for a song.

There's another Du-par's in Los Angeles at the Farmers Market, 6333 W. 3rd St. (☎ 323/933-8446), but it doesn't stay open as late.

FOR A FEW BUCKS MORE

Iroha Sushi. 12953 Ventura Blvd. (west of Coldwater Canyon Ave.), Studio City. ☎ **818/ 990-9559.** Reservations recommended. Main courses $7–$12; sushi $3–$7. AE, DC, MC, V. Mon–Sat 5:30–10:15pm. JAPANESE.

You can't help feeling special at this tiny Japanese cottage hidden behind an ethnic art gallery; there are only about a dozen tables and a short sushi bar. Enter from a Zen-garden-like gravel courtyard to the demure welcome of kimono-clad waitresses and bowing waiters. The service is discreetly efficient, and everything on the simple menu is excellent, from the airy tempura to tangy teriyaki, and especially the sushi. Dinner ends with an artistically carved orange to sweetly cleanse the palate . . . then it's back to the reality of busy Ventura Boulevard.

✪ **Jerry's Famous Deli.** 12655 Ventura Ave. (just east of Coldwater Canyon Ave.), Studio City. ☎ **818/980-4245.** Dinner main courses $9–$14; breakfast $2–$11; sandwiches and salads $4–$12. AE, MC, V. Daily 24 hr. DELI.

Here's a simple yet sizable deli where all the Valley's hipsters go to relieve their late-night munchies. This place probably has one of the largest menus in America—a tome spanning cultures and continents, from Central America to China to New York. From salads to sandwiches to steak-and-seafood platters, everything—including breakfast—is served all day. Jerry's is consistently good at lox and eggs, pastrami sandwiches, potato pancakes, and all the deli staples. It's also an integral part of L.A.'s cultural landscape and a favorite of the showbiz types who populate the adjacent foothill neighborhoods. It also has a full bar.

Miceli's. 3655 Cahuenga Blvd. (east of Lankershim), Los Angeles. ☎ **818/508-1221.** Main courses $7–$12; pizza $9–$15. AE, DC, MC, V. Mon–Thurs 5pm–midnight; Fri 5pm–1am; Sat 4pm–1am; Sun 4–11pm. ITALIAN.

Mostaccioli marinara, lasagna, thin-crust pizza, and eggplant parmigiana are indicative of the Sicilian-style fare at this cavernous stained-glass-windowed Italian restaurant adjacent to Universal City. The wait staff sings show tunes or opera favorites in between serving dinner (and sometimes instead of); make sure you have enough Chianti to get into the spirit of it all. This is a great place for kids, but way too rollicking for romance.

If you're near Hollywood Boulevard, visit the original (since 1949) Miceli's at 1646 N. Las Palmas (☎ 323/466-3438).

PASADENA & ENVIRONS
SUPER-CHEAP EATS

Goldstein's Bagel Bakery. 86 W. Colorado Blvd. (at Delacey Ave.), Old Pasadena. ☎ **626/ 79-BAGEL.** Most items under $3. AE, MC, V. Sun–Thurs 6am–9pm; Fri–Sat 6am–10:30pm. BAKERY/DELI.

Join the locals who storm Goldstein's each morning for freshly baked bagels (in the authentic New York style, they'll assure you)—the reliable plain and onion are as good as exotic honey oat raisin or banana nut. In addition to six flavored cream cheeses, you can choose a bagel sandwich prepared with your choice of any deli ingredient under the sun. Centrally located in the heart of Old Pasadena, this is a good choice for snacks and light meals without interrupting the rhythm of your day.

Old Town Bakery & Restaurant. 166 W. Colorado Blvd. (at Pasadena Ave.), Pasadena. ☎ **626/792-7943.** Main courses $5–$11. DISC, MC, V. Sun–Thurs 7:30am–10pm; Fri–Sat 7:30am–midnight. CALIFORNIA/BAKERY.

Set back from the street in a quaint fountain courtyard, this cheery bakery is an especially popular place to read the morning paper over one of the tasty breakfasts, like pumpkin pancakes or zesty omelets. The display counters are packed with cakes, muffins, scones, and other confections, all baked expressly for this shop. The rest of the menu is a mishmash of pastas, salads, and the like, borrowing heavily from Latin and Mediterranean cuisines. A great place to spy on local Pasadenans in their natural habitat.

FOR A FEW BUCKS MORE

Pasadena Baking Company/Mi Piace. 25-29 E. Colorado Blvd. (east of Fair Oaks Ave.), Old Pasadena. ☎ **626/796-9966** or 626/795-3131. Main courses $6–$15; bakery items under $3. AE, MC, V. Mon–Thurs 7am–11pm; Fri 7am–midnight; Sat 8am–midnight; Sun 8am–11pm. BAKERY/ITALIAN CAFE.

This little cafe holds just a handful of small tables, which spill out onto the sidewalk during nice weather (about 90% of the time). The large and sweet-smelling selection of fresh pastries, tarts, truffles, cakes, and candies are all proudly displayed. There's also an assortment of fresh breads and a fresh-fruit stand to accompany the breakfast and lunch menu.

Mi Piace is the adjoining casual trattoria, offering the usual pastas and northern Italian dishes done unusually well. The Baking Company commandeers the sidewalk tables at breakfast, but starting around 11:30am it's not unusual to see Pasadena locals enjoying an espresso with their dogs tethered to a table leg.

MODERATELY PRICED OPTIONS

Cafe Santorini. 64 W. Union St. (west of Fair Oaks Ave.), Pasadena. ☎ **626/564-4200.** Reservations recommended on weekends. Main courses $9–$17. AE, MC, V. Sun–Thurs 11am–11pm; Fri–Sat 11am–midnight. Parking in area structures $3. GREEK.

Located at ground zero of Pasadena's crowded Old Town shopping mecca, this second-story gem has a secluded Mediterranean ambiance, due in part to its historic brick building with splendid patio tables overlooking, but insulated from, the busy plaza below. In the evening, the lighting is subdued and romantic but the ambiance casual; many diners are coming or going from an adjacent movie-theater complex. The food is outstanding and affordable, featuring expertly grilled meats and kebobs, fresh tangy hummus, plenty of warm pitas, and other staples of Greek cuisine. A few pizzas round out the menu, featuring regional flavors like lamb, feta cheese, spinach, or Armenian sausage; the vegetarian baked butternut squash is filled with fluffy rice and smokey roast vegetables. The back door is on Union Street, but the main entrance is from the shopping plaza at the corner of Fair Oaks and Colorado.

✪ **Shiro.** 1505 Mission St. (at Fair Oaks Ave.), Pasadena. ☎ **626/799-4774.** Reservations required. Main courses $15–$20. AE, MC, V. Tues–Sun 6pm–closing (usually 9:30–10:30pm). FRANCO-JAPANESE.

Ever since chef/owner Shiro defected from the late, great Cafe Jacoulet, his eponymous restaurant has been consistently ranked at the top of Zagat's lists. Though the menu changes nightly at this minimalist bento box, certain favorites are always among the half-dozen selections. Look first for the whole sizzling catfish in cilantro-tangy ponzu sauce; many devotees insist you should stop reading right there, but you'll also find Canadian scallops in saffron sauce and often chicken or lamb charbroiled with inventive herb sauces. Shiro's careful attention to detail extends to desserts like fruit-filled wontons with ginger custard—the perfect sweet follow-up to the savory catfish.

Yujean Kang's Gourmet Chinese Cuisine. 67 N. Raymond Ave. (between Walnut St. and Colorado Blvd.), Pasadena. ☎ **626/585-0855.** Reservations recommended. Main courses $8–$19. AE, MC, V. Daily 11:30am–2:30pm and 5–10pm. CONTEMPORARY CHINESE.

Many Chinese restaurants put the word *gourmet* in their name, but few really mean— or deserve—it. Not so at Yujean Kang's, where Chinese cuisine is taken to an entirely new level. A master of "fusion" cuisine, the eponymous chef/owner snatches bits of techniques and flavors from both China and the West, commingling them in an entirely fresh way. Can you resist such provocative dishes as "Ants on Tree" (beef sautéed with glass noodles in chili and black sesame seeds), lobster with caviar and fava beans, and Chilean sea bass in passion fruit sauce? Kang is a wine aficionado and has assembled a magnificent cellar of California, French, and particularly German vintages. Try pairing a German Spätlese with tea-smoked duck salad. The red-wrapped dining room is less subtle than the food, but just as elegant.

There's a second Yujean Kang's in West Hollywood, at 8826 Melrose Ave. (☎ 310/288-0806). Even though Kang consulted with a *feng shui* master on the location and layout of the new space, some Angelenos grumble about the less adventurous menu and higher prices. Others are merely grateful they don't have to trek to Pasadena anymore.

WORTH A SPLURGE

✪ **The Raymond.** 1250 S. Fair Oaks Ave. (at Columbia St.), Pasadena. ☎ **626/441-3136.** Reservations required. Main courses $10–$17 at lunch, $27–$32 at dinner; 4-course dinner $40–$45; prix-fixe 3-course dinner $28 (including wine). AE, MC, V. Tues–Thurs 11:30am–2:30pm and 6–9:30pm; Fri 11:30am–2:30pm and 5:45–10pm; Sat 11am–2:30pm and 5:45–10pm; Sun 10am–2:30pm and 4:40–8pm; afternoon tea Tues–Sun noon–4pm. AMERICAN/CONTINENTAL.

Easy-to-miss and tucked away in a sleepy part of Pasadena, The Raymond is a jewel even few locals know about. This Craftsman cottage was once the caretaker's house for a grand Victorian hotel called The Raymond, and, though the city has grown to surround it, the place maintains an enchanting air of seclusion and serenity. Chef/owner Suzanne Bourg brings a romantic sensibility and impeccable culinary instincts to a menu of mostly haute American—with an occasional European flair—dishes. The menu changes weekly: One night a grilled rack of lamb is sauced with orange, Grand Marnier, and peppercorns; another night it boasts a creamy white-wine-and-chèvre sauce punctuated with dried cherries. Bourg's soups are always heavenly (the restaurant gladly gives out their recipes), the desserts are inspired, and they often showcase a seasonal treat like Dutch white asparagus. The tables are scattered throughout the house and in the lush English garden, and there's plenty of free nonvalet parking (you wouldn't find *that* on the Westside!)

FRUIT SHAKES & PRODUCE

✪ **Grand Central Market.** 317 S. Broadway (between 3rd and 4th sts.), downtown. ☎ 213/624-2378.

This bustling market, opened in 1917, has watched the face of downtown Los Angeles change, but has changed little itself. Today it serves Latino families as well as enterprising restaurateurs and home cooks in search of unusual ingredients and bargain fruits and vegetables. On weekends you'll be greeted by a lively mariachi band at the Hill Street entrance, near my favorite market feature: the fruit-juice counter that dispenses 20 fresh varieties from wall spigots and blends up the tastiest, healthiest "shakes" in town. Farther into the market you'll find produce sellers and prepared-food counters, plus spice vendors straight out of a Turkish alley and a grain and bean seller who'll scoop out dozens of exotic rices and dried legumes.

5 The Top Attractions

SANTA MONICA & THE BEACHES

Venice Ocean Front Walk. On the beach, between Venice Blvd. and Rose Ave.

Venice is one of the world's most engaging bohemias. It's not an exaggeration to say that no visit to L.A. would be complete without a stroll along the famous beach path, an almost surreal assemblage of every L.A. stereotype—and then some. Among stalls and stands selling cheap sunglasses, Mexican blankets, and "herbal ecstasy" pills, swirls a carnival of humanity that includes bikinied roller-skaters, tattooed bikers, muscle-bound pretty boys, panhandling vets, beautiful wanna-bes, and plenty of tourists and gawkers. On any given day you're bound to come across all kinds of performers: white-faced mimes, break-dancers, buskers, chain-saw jugglers, talking parrots, even an occasional apocalyptic evangelist. Last time I was there, a man stood behind a table and railed against the evils of circumcision: "It's too late for us, guys, but we can save the next generation." But a chubby guy singing "Kokomo"—out of tune but with all his heart—cheered me up.

L.A.'S WESTSIDE & BEVERLY HILLS

✪ **J. Paul Getty Museum at the Getty Center.** 1200 Getty Center Dr., Los Angeles. ☎ **310/440-7300.** Free admission. Tues–Wed 11am–7pm; Thurs–Fri 11am–9pm; Sat–Sun 10am–6pm. Parking $5; advance reservations required.

After 14 years of planning, construction, and endless delays, the über-wealthy Getty Trust finally opened its dramatic Richard Meier–designed center overlooking Brentwood. In the months after its front-page-news opening in December 1997, the Getty Center quickly began assuming its place in the L.A. landscape (literally and figuratively) as a cultural cornerstone and international mecca. Headquarters for the Getty Trust's research, education, and conservation concerns, the complex is most frequently visited for the museum galleries displaying collector J. Paul Getty's enormous collection of important art.

Always known for antiquities, the expanded galleries now allow the display of impressionist paintings, French decorative arts, fine illuminated manuscripts, and contemporary photography and graphic arts that were previously overlooked. A sophisticated system of programmable window louvers allows many outstanding works to be displayed in natural light for the first time in the modern era. One of these is van Gogh's *Irises,* one of the museum's finest holdings. Trivia buffs will enjoy knowing the museum spent $53.9 million to acquire the painting; it's displayed in a complex costing roughly $1 billion to construct. Visitors to the center park at the base of the hill and ascend via a cable-driven electric tram. On clear days, the sensation is of being in the clouds, gazing across Los Angeles and the Pacific Ocean (and into a few chic Brentwood backyards). In addition to a casual cafe and several espresso/snack carts, the complex has a bona fide restaurant, complete with a panoramic view.

Rancho La Brea Tar Pits/George C. Page Museum. 5801 Wilshire Blvd. (east of Fairfax Ave.), Los Angeles. ☎ **323/934-PAGE.** www.tarpits.org. Admission $6 adults, $3.50 seniors 62 and older and students with ID, $2 children 5–12, free for kids 4 and under; free for everyone the 1st Tues of each month. Museum Tues–Sun 10am–5pm.

A Getty Center Tip

At press time, parking reservations were in high demand, particularly on weekends. If you're planning a trip to Los Angeles, make your Getty Center reservations as early as possible. Even visitors without cars—who arrive by taxi, tour bus, bicycle, whatever—aren't guaranteed admittance during high-volume periods.

Avoid the crowds at the Getty Center by visiting in the late afternoon or evening; the center is open until 9pm Thursday and Friday, the nighttime view is breathtaking, and you can finish with a late dinner on the Westside.

An odorous, murky swamp of congealed oil continuously oozes to the earth's surface in the middle of Los Angeles. No, it's not a low-budget horror-movie set: It's the La Brea Tar Pits, an awesome primal pool right on Museum Row, where hot tar has been bubbling from the earth for over 40,000 years. The glistening pools, which look like murky water, have enticed thirsty animals throughout history. Thousands of mammals, birds, amphibians, and insects—many of which are now extinct—mistakenly crawled into the sticky sludge and stayed forever. In 1906, scientists began a systematic removal and classification of entombed specimens, including ground sloths, giant vultures, mastodons, camels, bears, lizards, and even prehistoric relatives of today's beloved super-rats. The best finds are on display in the adjacent George C. Page Museum of La Brea Discoveries, where an excellent 15-minute film documenting the recoveries is shown. Archaeological work is ongoing; you can watch as scientists clean, identify, and catalog new finds in the Paleontology Laboratory.

HOLLYWOOD

HOLLYWOOD Sign. At the top of Beachwood Dr., Hollywood.

These 50-foot-high white sheet-metal letters have come to symbolize both the movie industry and the city itself. Erected in 1923 as an advertisement for a fledgling real-estate development, the full text originally read "Hollywoodland." The recent installation of motion detectors around the sign just made this graffiti tagger's coup a target even more worth boasting about. A thorny hiking trail leads to it from Durand Drive near Beachwood Drive, but the best view is from down below, at the corner of Sunset Boulevard and Bronson Avenue.

Hollywood Walk of Fame. Hollywood Blvd., between Gower St. and La Brea Ave.; and Vine St., between Yucca St. and Sunset Blvd. ☎ **323/469-8311.**

More than 2,500 celebrities are honored along the world's most famous sidewalk. Each bronze medallion, set into the center of a granite star, pays homage to a famous TV, film, radio, theater, or recording personality. Though about a third of them are just about as obscure as Andromeda—their fame simply hasn't withstood the test of time—millions of visitors are thrilled by the sight of famous names like **James Dean** (1719 Vine St.), **John Lennon** (1750 Vine St.), **Marlon Brando** (1765 Vine St.), **Rudolph Valentino** (6164 Hollywood Blvd.), **Greta Garbo** (6901 Hollywood Blvd.), **Louis Armstrong** (7000 Hollywood Blvd.), and **Barbra Streisand** (6925 Hollywood Blvd.).

The sight of bikers, metalheads, druggies, hookers, and hordes of disoriented tourists all treading on memorials to Hollywood's greats makes for quite a bizarre tribute indeed. But the Hollywood Chamber of Commerce has been doing a terrific job sprucing up the pedestrian experience with filmstrip crosswalks, swaying palms, and more. And at least one weekend a month a privately organized group of fans calling themselves Star Polishers busy themselves scrubbing tarnished medallions.

Recent subway digging under the boulevard has caused the street to sink several inches. When John Forsythe's star cracked, authorities removed many others to prevent further damage. In the next few years, up to 250 stars, including those of **Marilyn Monroe** (6744 Hollywood Blvd.) and **Elvis Presley** (6777 Hollywood Blvd.) will be temporarily removed as the subway project expands.

The legendary sidewalk is continually adding new names. The public is invited to attend dedication ceremonies; the honoree is usually in attendance. Contact the **Hollywood Chamber of Commerce,** 6255 Sunset Blvd., Suite 911, Hollywood, CA 90028 (☎ **323/469-8311**), for information on who's being honored while you're in town.

Mann's Chinese Theatre. 6925 Hollywood Blvd. (3 blocks west of Highland Ave.). ☎ **323/464-8111** or 323/461-3331. Movie tickets $8. Call for show times.

This is one of the world's great movie palaces and one of Hollywood's finest landmarks. The Chinese Theatre was opened in 1927 by entertainment impresario Sid Grauman, a brilliant promoter who's credited with originating the idea of the paparazzi-packed movie "premiere." Outrageously conceived, with both authentic and simulated Chinese embellishments, gaudy Grauman's theater was designed to impress. Original Chinese heaven doves top the facade, and two of the theater's exterior columns once propped up a Ming Dynasty temple.

Visitors flock to the theater by the millions for its world-famous entry court, where stars like Elizabeth Taylor, Paul Newman, Ginger Rogers, Humphrey Bogart, Frank Sinatra, Marilyn Monroe, John Wayne (remember the *I Love Lucy* episode?), and about 160 others set their signatures and hand- and footprints in concrete. It's not always hands and feet, though: Betty Grable made an impression with her shapely leg; Gene Autry with the hoofprints of his horse, Champion; and Jimmy Durante and Bob Hope used their trademark noses.

Farmers Market. 6333 W. 3rd St. (corner of Fairfax Ave.). ☎ **323/933-9211.** Mon–Sat 9am–6:30pm; Sun 10am–5pm.

The original market was little more than a field clustered with stands set up by farmers during the depression so they could sell directly to city dwellers. It slowly grew into permanent buildings recognizable by the trademark shingled 10-story clock tower and has evolved into a sprawling food marketplace with a carnival atmosphere, a kind of "turf" version of San Francisco's surfy Fisherman's Wharf. About 100 restaurants, shops, and grocers cater to a mix of workers from the adjacent CBS Television City complex, locals, and tourists, who are brought here by the busload. Retailers sell greeting cards, kitchen implements, candles, and souvenirs; but everyone comes for the food stands offering oysters, Cajun gumbo, fresh-squeezed orange juice, roast-beef sandwiches, fresh-pressed peanut butter, and all kinds of international fast foods. You can still buy produce—no longer a farm-fresh bargain but a better selection than the grocery stores offer. Don't miss **Kokomo,** a "gourmet" outdoor coffee shop that has become a power-breakfast spot for showbiz types. Red turkey hash and sweet-potato fries are the dishes that keep them coming back.

✪ **Griffith Observatory.** 2800 E. Observatory Rd. (in Griffith Park, at the end of Vermont Ave.). ☎ **323/664-1191,** or 323/663-8171 for the Sky Report, a recorded message on current planet positions and celestial events. Free admission; planetarium show tickets $4 adults, $3 seniors, $2 children. June–Aug daily 12:30–10pm. Sept–May Tues–Fri 2–10pm; Sat–Sun 12:30–10pm.

Made world-famous in the film *Rebel Without a Cause,* Griffith Observatory and its bronze domes have been Hollywood Hills landmarks since 1935. Most visitors never

Hollywood Area Attractions

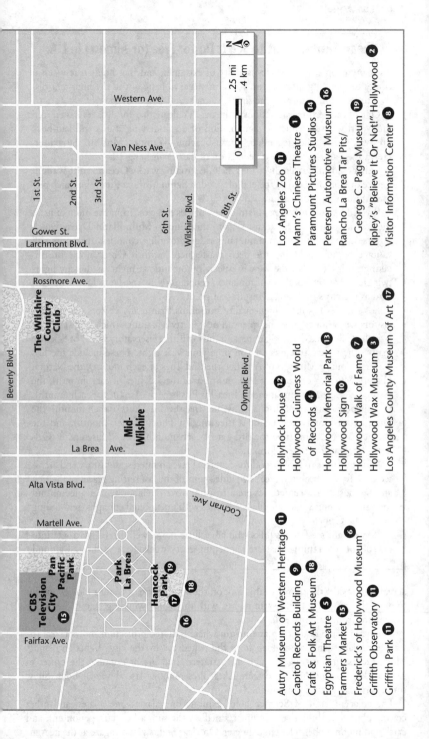

Autry Museum of Western Heritage ⑪

Capitol Records Building ⑨

Craft & Folk Art Museum ⑱

Egyptian Theatre ⑤

Farmers Market ⑮

Frederick's of Hollywood Museum ⑥

Griffith Observatory ⑪

Griffith Park ⑪

Hollyhock House ⑫

Hollywood Guinness World of Records ④

Hollywood Memorial Park ⑬

Hollywood Sign ⑩

Hollywood Walk of Fame ⑦

Hollywood Wax Museum ③

Los Angeles County Museum of Art ⑰

Los Angeles Zoo ①

Mann's Chinese Theatre ①

Paramount Pictures Studios ⑭

Petersen Automotive Museum ⑯

Rancho La Brea Tar Pits/
George C. Page Museum ⑲

Ripley's "Believe It Or Not!" Hollywood ②

Visitor Information Center ⑧

Cheap Thrills: What to See & Do for Free (or Almost) in L.A.

To many people, Los Angeles is a city of extremes, and that holds true when it comes to spending money. But, you don't have to hang out in the high-rent district to have fun absorbing the sights, sounds, and flavors of the city.

One of the best free attractions is the beach culture that for decades has enticed the world with its seductive combination of death-defying stunts and laid-back lifestyle. Visit the legendary surf beaches—**Zuma, Malibu Surfrider, Hermosa**—and watch a new generation of daredevils hang-10.

Other colorful coastal diversions include strolling wacky **Ocean Front Walk** in Venice or clomping out to the end of wooden **Santa Monica Pier** for a quick pictorial history of the coastline.

If you'd like to enjoy a panoramic view of Los Angeles "from the mountains to the sea" (a local news broadcast slogan), head up to **Mulholland Drive,** which traverses the Santa Monica mountains ridge providing countless turn-outs and vantage points, including the deco masterpiece Griffith Observatory. Breathtaking during the day, the view is especially romantic at night, as the city lights twinkle alluringly. Speaking of romance, generations of Angelenos know Mulholland as the city's traditional "inspiration point."

Los Angeles has more high-quality **museums** than many visitors expect. Few visitors will want to miss the splendid new Getty Museum, which is always free, as is the California Science Center and the Griffith Observatory's Hall of Science; many others have **free days** if you time your visit right. These include the Los Angeles County Museum of Art (free the 2nd Tues of each month), the Natural History Museum of Los Angeles County (free the 1st Tues of each month), the George C. Page Museum at the La Brea Tar Pits (free the 1st Tues of each month), the Japanese American National Museum (free the 3rd Thurs of each month), the Huntington Library and Gardens (free the 1st Thurs of each month), and the Pacific Asia Museum (free the 3rd Sat of each month). See "Museums & Galleries," below, for more information.

Did you come to Hollywood to see stars? Have an interest in history and architecture? Try an absolutely free self-guided tour of the last resting places of the rich and famous. **L.A.'s cemeteries** are a treasure trove of elaborate mausoleums and monuments, plus some humble headstones with unexpected epitaphs (see "Seeing Stars: The Cemetery Set," below).

If you want see famous folks who are a little more, well, lively, try to get into one of the **TV tapings** that are happening every weekday at studios all around

---

actually go inside; they come to this spot on the south slope of Mount Hollywood for unparalleled city views. On warm nights, with the lights twinkling below, this is one of the most romantic places in L.A.

The main dome houses a **planetarium** where narrated projection shows reveal the stars and planets that are hidden from the naked eye by the city's lights and smog. Mock excursions into space search for extraterrestrial life or examine the causes of earthquakes, moonquakes, and starquakes. Presentations last about an hour. Show times vary, so call for information.

The adjacent **Hall of Science** holds exhibits on galaxies, meteorites, and other cosmic objects, including a telescope trained on the sun, a Foucault pendulum, and earth and moon globes 6 feet in diameter. On clear nights you can gaze at the heavens through the powerful 12-inch telescope.

town. It's a time-consuming but very intimate experience as you watch sitcom friends like Tim Allen and Fran Drescher do their day's work, bloopers and all (see "TV Tapings," below).

If you don't have the time—or the patience—to sit through a TV taping, not to worry: Stargazing is a good do-it-yourself activity. Often, the best places to see members of the A-list aren't as obvious as a back-alley stage door or the front room of Spago. Shops along Sunset Boulevard, like **Tower Records** and the **Virgin Megastore,** are often star-heavy. **Book Soup,** that browser's paradise across the street from Tower, is usually good for a star or two. You'll often find them casually browsing the international newsstand (if they're not there to sign their latest tell-all autobiography). You might even pop into **Sunset Strip Tattoo,** where Cher, Charlie Sheen, Lenny Kravitz, and members of Guns 'N' Roses all got inked.

And don't forget that celebs keep their larders stocked just like the rest of us. You haven't lived until you've stumbled on Paul Reiser or Rosanna Arquette sifting for unbruised tomatoes in the supermarket. Good bets are **Gelson's,** at Sunset Boulevard and Swarthmore Avenue in Pacific Palisades; and **Mayfair Market,** at Franklin and Bronson avenues in Hollywood Hills.

Window-shopping doesn't get much better than in ✪ **Beverly Hills's "Golden Triangle,"** a tony few blocks that includes legendary Rodeo Drive. If Prada handbags, Hermès scarves, or Cartier watches don't catch your fancy, turn your attention to the Beverly Hills denizens strolling alongside and actually shopping—they're a different kind of sight altogether.

Downtown Los Angeles, an area often bypassed by tourists who remember its all-too-recent gritty past, is an ongoing regentrification project with hours (or days) worth of cost-free activities for the entire family. Check out the spectacular architecture of the **Bradbury Building** and the **Central Library.** If the library's courtyard art installations inspire you, venture on to **Pershing Square** and beyond to take advantage of the city's largest free gallery. **Grand Central Market** is another feast for the senses, where you might be tempted to part with a few dollars in exchange for an authentic food treat.

Even prime evening entertainment can be had for a song. While L.A.'s elite dine in $75-a-head box seats at the **Hollywood Bowl,** the venue's excellent acoustics guarantee an enjoyable time even if you're in "the trees" ($3 bench seats at the very top). Baseball fans visiting in season can take in a game at **Dodger Stadium** for as little as $3—but remember, Dodger dogs are extra!

DOWNTOWN

El Pueblo de Los Angeles Historic District. Enter on Alameda St. across from Union Station. ☎ 213/628-1274.

This historic district was built in the 1930s on the site where the city was founded, as an alternative to the wholesale razing of a particularly unsightly slum. The result is a contrived nostalgic fantasy of the city's beginnings, a kitschy theme park portraying Latino culture in a Disneyesque fashion. Nevertheless, El Pueblo has proven wildly successful, as L.A.'s Latinos have adopted it as an important cultural monument.

El Pueblo isn't entirely without authenticity. Some of L.A.'s oldest extant buildings are here, and the area really does exude the ambiance of Old Mexico. At its core is a Mexican-style marketplace on Olvera Street. The carnival of sights and sounds is heightened by mariachis, colorful piñatas, and more than occasional folkloric dancing.

Olvera Street, the district's primary pedestrian thoroughfare, and adjacent Main Street are home to about two dozen 19th-century buildings; one houses an authentic Mexican restaurant, **La Golondrina** (☎ 213/628-4349). Stop in at the **visitor center,** 622 N. Main St. (☎ 213/628-1274), open Monday through Saturday from 10am to 3pm. Don't miss the **Avila Adobe,** at E-10 Olvera St. (open Mon through Sat 10am to 5pm); built in 1818, it's the oldest building in the city.

THE SAN FERNANDO VALLEY

Universal Studios. Hollywood Fwy. (Lankershim Blvd. exit), Universal City. ☎ **818/ 508-9600.** Admission $38 adults, $33 seniors 60 and older, $28 children 3–11; free for kids under 3. Parking $6. Summer daily 7am–11pm; the rest of the year daily 9am–7pm.

Believing that filmmaking itself was a bona fide attraction, Universal Studios began offering tours to the public in 1964. The concept worked. Today Universal is more than just one of the largest movie studios in the world—it's one of the biggest amusement parks.

The main attraction continues to be the **Studio Tour,** a 1-hour guided tram ride around the company's 420 acres. You pass stars' dressing rooms and production offices before visiting famous back-lot sets that include an eerily familiar Old West town, a clean New York City street, and the famous town square from the *Back to the Future* films. Along the way the tram encounters several staged "disasters," which I won't divulge here lest I ruin the surprise.

Other attractions are more typical of high-tech theme-park fare, but all have a film-oriented slant. On **Back to the Future—The Ride,** you're seated in a mock time-traveling DeLorean and thrust into a fantastic multimedia roller-coasting extravaganza—it's far and away Universal's best ride. The **Backdraft** ride surrounds you with brilliant balls of very real fire spewing from imitation ruptured fuel lines. Kids love it. A **Waterworld** live-action stunt show is thrilling to watch (and more successful than the film that inspired it), while the latest special-effects showcase, **Jurassic Park—The Ride,** is short in duration but long on dinosaur illusions and computer magic lifted from the Universal blockbuster. **Totally Nickelodeon** is an interactive live show from the kids' TV network, providing adventure and gallons of green slime.

PASADENA & ENVIRONS

✪ **Huntington Library, Art Collections, and Botanical Gardens.** 1151 Oxford Rd., San Marino. ☎ **626/405-2141.** www.huntington.org. Admission $8.50 adults, $7 seniors 65 and over, $5 students and children 12 and over, free for children under 12; free for everyone the 1st Thurs of each month. June–Aug daily 10:30am–4:30pm. Sept–May Tues–Fri noon–4:30pm; Sat–Sun 10:30am–4:30pm. Closed major holidays.

The **Huntington Library** is the jewel in Pasadena's crown. The 207-acre hilltop estate was once home to industrialist/railroad magnate Henry E. Huntington (1850–1927), who bought books on the same massive scale that he acquired businesses. The continually expanding collection includes dozens of Shakespeare's original works, Benjamin Franklin's handwritten autobiography, a Gutenberg Bible from the 1450s, and the earliest known manuscript of Chaucer's *Canterbury Tales.* Though some rarer works are available only to visiting scholars, the library has a regularly changing (and always excellent) exhibit showcasing different items in the collection.

If you prefer canvas to parchment, Huntington also put together a terrific 18th-century British and French art collection. His most celebrated paintings are Gainsborough's *The Blue Boy,* and *Pinkie,* a companion piece by Sir Thomas Lawrence depicting the youthful aunt of Elizabeth Barrett Browning. These and other works are displayed in the stately Italianate mansion on the crest of this hillside estate, so you can also get a glimpse of its splendid furnishings.

A Universal Studios Tip

Universal Studios is really a fun place. But just as in any theme park, lines can be long; the wait for a 5-minute ride can sometimes last more than an hour. In summer, the stifling Valley heat can dog you all day. To avoid the crowds, skip weekends, school vacations, and Japanese holidays.

But the **botanical gardens** are what draw most locals to the Huntington. The Japanese Garden is complete with a traditional open-air Japanese house, koi-filled stream, and serene Zen garden; the cactus garden is exotic, the jungle garden intriguing, the lily ponds soothing—and there are benches scattered about encouraging you to sit and enjoy.

Because the Huntington surprises many with its size and the wealth of activities to choose from, first-timers might want to start by attending one of the regularly scheduled 12-minute introductory slide shows or take the more in-depth 1-hour garden tour, given each day at 1pm.

I also recommend you tailor your visit to include the popular English tea served Tuesday through Sunday from 1:30 to 3:30pm. The charming tearoom overlooks the Rose Garden (home to 1,000 varieties displayed in chronological order of their breeding), and since the finger sandwiches and desserts are served buffet-style, it's a genteel bargain (even for hearty appetites) at $11 per person. Phone ☎ **626/683-8131** for reservations.

6 TV Tapings

Being part of the audience for the taping of a TV show might be the quintessential L.A. experience. This is a great way to see Hollywood at work, to find out how your favorite sitcom or talk show is made, and to catch a glimpse of your favorite TV personalities. Timing is important: Remember that most series productions go on hiatus between March and July. Tickets to the top shows, like *Friends* and *Home Improvement,* are in greater demand than others, and getting your hands on them usually takes advance planning—and possibly some time waiting in line.

Request tickets as far in advance as possible. Several episodes may be shot on a single day, so you may be required to remain in the theater for up to 4 hours (in addition to the recommended 1-hr. early check-in). If you phone at the last moment, you may luck into tickets for your top choice. More likely, however, you'll be given a list of shows that are currently filming and won't recognize many of the titles; studios are always taping pilots, few of which end up on the air. But you never know who may be starring in them—look at all the famous faces that've launched new sitcoms in the past couple of years. Tickets are always free, usually limited to two per person, and are distributed on a first-come, first-served basis. Many shows don't admit children under 10; in some cases no one under 18 is admitted.

In addition to the suppliers below, tickets are sometimes given away to the public outside popular tourist sites like Mann's Chinese Theatre in Hollywood and Universal Studios in the Valley; L.A.'s visitor information centers in downtown and Hollywood often have tickets as well (see "Orientation," above). But if you're determined to see a particular show, contact the following sources:

Audiences Unlimited (☎ **818/506-0043** or 818/506-0067; www.tvtickets.com) is a good place to start. They distribute tickets for most of the top sitcoms, like *Friends, Saved by the Bell, Caroline in the City, Suddenly Susan, Home Improvement, Everybody Loves Raymond,* and many more. Their service is organized and informative and fully

Seeing Stars: The Cemetery Set

Almost everybody who visits Los Angeles hopes to see a celebrity—they are, after all, our most common export item. Celebs usually don't cooperate, failing to gather in readily viewable herds. There's a much better alternative. An absolutely guaranteed method of being within 6 feet of your favorite star: Visit a cemetery. Cemeteries are *the* place for star (or at least headstone) gazing: The star is always available, and you're going to get a lot more up close and personal than you probably would to anyone who's actually alive. What follows is a guide to the most fruitful cemeteries, listed in order (more or less) of their friendliness to stargazers.

Weathered Victorian and art-deco memorials add to the decaying charm of **Hollywood Forever** (formerly Hollywood Memorial Park), 6000 Santa Monica Blvd., Hollywood (☎ 323/469-1181). Fittingly, there's a terrific view of the HOLLYWOOD sign over the graves, as many of the founders of the community rest here. You'll see their names on the nearby street signs: the Gowers, the Wilcoxes, the Coles. The most notable tenant is Rudolph Valentino, who rests in an interior crypt. And there's silent-film director William Desmond Taylor (under his real name, William Deane Tanner), whose 1922 murder was an enormous scandal, ruining the careers of silent stars Mary Miles Minter and Mabel Normand, who were considered guilty by association. (Sidney Kirkpatrick's excellent *A Cast of Killers* delves into this decades-old mystery in great detail, even solving the crime at last.) Outside are Tyrone Power, Jr.; Douglas Fairbanks; *Shiek* co-star Agnes Ayres; Cecil B. DeMille (facing Paramount, his old studio); Alfalfa from *The Little Rascals* (contrary to what you might think, the dog on his grave isn't Petey); Hearst mistress Marion Davies; Charlie Chaplin's mother, Hannah, and son Charlie; John Huston; and a headstone for Jayne Mansfield (she's really buried in Pennsylvania with family). In other mausoleums are the Talmadge Sisters and Bugsy Siegel.

Catholic **Holy Cross Cemetery,** 5835 W. Slauson Ave., Culver City (☎ 310/670-7697), hands out maps to the stars' graves. Religion makes for strange gravefellows: In one area, within feet of one another, lie Bing Crosby, Bela Lugosi (buried in his Dracula cape), and Sharon Tate (the name of her unborn son, Richard, is also on her marker—she was more than 8 months pregnant when the Manson family murdered her); not far away are Rita Hayworth and Jimmy Durante. Also here are Tin Man Jack Haley and Scarecrow Ray Bolger; Mary Astor; John Ford; Spike Jones; gossip queen Louella Parsons; Mack Sennett; Elizabeth Taylor's first husband, Conrad "Nicky" Hilton; Rosalind Russell; and even Gloria Morgan Vanderbilt (whose namesake daughter is quite well known for her jeans hawking).

The front office at **Hillside Memorial Park,** 6001 Centinela Ave., Baldwin Hills (☎ 310/641-0707), can provide a guide to this Jewish cemetery, which has an L.A. landmark: the behemoth tomb of Al Jolson, another humble star. His rotunda, complete with bronze reproduction of Jolson in his Mammy pose and cascading fountain, is visible from I-405. Also on hand are Georgie Jessel, Jack Benny, Eddie Cantor, Vic Morrow, comic Dick Shawn, and *Fugitive* star David Janssen.

You just know developers get stomachaches looking at **Westwood Memorial Park,** 1218 Glendon Ave., Westwood (☎ 310/474-1579; the staff can direct you around), smack-dab in the middle of some of L.A.'s priciest real estate. But it's not going anywhere. Especially when you consider its most famous resident: Marilyn Monroe. It also boasts Truman Capote; John Cassavetes; Armand

Hammer; Donna Reed; Edith Massey (John Waters's Egg Lady); Natalie Wood; *Playboy* playmate Dorothy Stratten (who was murdered by her husband; remember *Star 80?*); Darryl Zanuck; and Will and Ariel Durant, the husband-and-wife historian/writer team (most notably, the 11-volume *Story of Civilization*), who died within days of each other after a nearly 70-year romance. Peter Lawford was here, but he got evicted for nonpayment of rent and his ashes were scattered.

✪ **Forest Lawn Glendale,** 1712 S. Glendale Ave. (☎ **323/254-3131**), likes to pretend it has no celebrities. The most prominent of L.A. cemeteries, it's also the most humorless, which is pretty silly when you realize it has done its darndest to turn its graveyard into an amusement park. What else would you call its regular "dramatic" (read: cheesy) unveilings (complete with music and narration) of such works of "art" as a reproduction of Leonardo da Vinci's *Last Supper* in stained glass? The place is full of bad art, all part of the continuing vision of founder Hubert Eaton, bane of cemetery buffs everywhere. Eaton thought cemeteries—excuse me, *memorial parks*—should be happy places, uninterrupted by nasty thoughts of, ick, death. So he banished all those gloomy upright tombstones and monuments in favor of flat, pleasant, character-free, flush-to-the-ground slabs. Voilà! A rolling parklike vista, easy on the eyes and easy to mow.

Contrary to what you've heard, Walt Disney was *not* frozen and placed under Cinderella's castle at Disneyland. He was cremated and resides in a little garden to the left of the Freedom Mausoleum. Turn around and just behind you are Errol Flynn (in the Garden of Everlasting Peace) and Spencer Tracy (to right of the George Washington statue). In the Freedom Mausoleum are Alan Ladd, Clara Bow, Nat "King" Cole, Chico and Gummo Marx, Larry Fine (of the Three Stooges), and Gracie Allen, finally joined by George Burns. In a columbarium near the Mystery of Life is Humphrey Bogart. Keep moving to your left and you should find Mary Pickford. Alas, some of the best celebs, like Clark Gable and Carole Lombard, W. C. Fields, and Jean Harlow, are in the Great Mausoleum, which you often can't get into unless you're visiting a relative.

You'd think a place that encourages people just to visit for fun would understand what the real attraction is. But no, Forest Lawn Glendale won't tell you where any of its illustrious guests are, so don't even bother asking. And this place is immense and, frankly, dull in comparison to the previous cemeteries, unless you appreciate the kitsch value of the Forest Lawn approach to art.

Forest Lawn Hollywood Hills, 6300 Forest Lawn Dr. (☎ **800/204-3131**), is slightly less anal than the Glendale branch, but the same basic attitude prevails. On the right lawn, beside the wall near the statue of George Washington, is Buster Keaton. Marty Feldman is in front of the next garden, over on the left. From Buster's grave, go up several flights of stairs to the last wall on the right: There's Stan Laurel. In the Courts of Remembrance are Lucille Ball, Charles Laughton, Freddie Prinze, George Raft, Forrest Tucker, and the not-quite-gaudy-enough tomb of Liberace, with his mother, Frances, and brother, George. Outside, in a vault on the Ascension Road side, is Andy Gibb. Bette Davis's sarcophagus is in front of the wall, to the left of the entrance to the Courts. Also on the grounds are Ozzie and Ricky Nelson, Sammy Davis, Jr., Ernie Kovacs, Jack Soo, Jack Webb, and John Travolta's mother Helen.

—Mary Susan Herczog

sanctioned by production companies and networks. ABC, for example, no longer handles ticket distribution directly but refers all inquiries to Audiences Unlimited. **Television Tickets** (☎ 323/467-4697) distributes tickets for talk and game shows, including the popular *Jeopardy!* You may want to contact the networks directly for information on a specific show, including some whose tickets aren't available at the above agencies:

At **ABC,** all ticket inquiries are referred to Audiences Unlimited (see above), but you may want to check out their Web site at **www.abc.com** for a colorful look at their line-up and links to specific show's sites. For tickets to *Politically Incorrect with Bill Maher,* call the show's ticket line at ☎ 323/852-2655 to make a reservation (taken on a first-come, first-served basis), or order them online at **www.abc.com/pi**.

For **CBS,** 7800 Beverly Blvd., Los Angeles, CA 90036 (☎ 323/852-2458), call to see what's being filmed while you're in town. Tickets for tapings are distributed on a first-come, first-served basis; you can write in advance to reserve them or pick them up directly at the studio up to an hour before taping. Tickets for many CBS sitcoms, including *The Nanny* and *Everybody Loves Raymond,* are also available from Audiences Unlimited (see above). Tickets for *The Price Is Right* must be requested by mail; allow 4 to 6 weeks. For a virtual visit to CBS's shows, check out their Web site at **www.cbs.com**.

For **NBC,** 3000 W. Alameda Ave., Burbank, CA 91523 (☎ 818/840-4444 or 818/840-3537), call to see what's on while you're in L.A. Tickets for NBC tapings, including *The Tonight Show with Jay Leno,* can be obtained in two ways: Pick them up at the NBC ticket counter on the day of the show you want to see (they're distributed on a first-come, first-served basis at the ticket counter off California Avenue); or at least 3 weeks before your visit, send a self-addressed stamped envelope with your ticket request to the address above. All the NBC shows are represented online at **www.nbc.com**.

7 Exploring the City
ARCHITECTURAL HIGHLIGHTS

Los Angeles is a veritable Disneyland of architecture. The city is home to an amalgam of distinctive styles, from art deco to Spanish revival to coffee-shop kitsch to suburban ranch to postmodern—and much more. Cutting-edge, over-the-top styles that would be out of place in other cities, from the oversize hot dog that's Tail o' the Pup to the mansions lining the streets of Beverly Hills, are perfectly at home in movie city.

SANTA MONICA & THE BEACHES

When you're strolling the historic canals and streets of Venice, be sure to check out the **Chiat/Day** offices at 340 Main St. What would otherwise be an unspectacular contemporary office building is made fantastic by a three-story pair of binoculars framing the entrance to this advertising agency. The sculpture is modeled after a design created by Claes Oldenburg and Coosje van Bruggen.

When you're flying in or out of LAX, be sure to stop for a moment to admire the **Control Tower and Theme Building.** The spacey *Jetsons*-style Theme Building, which has always loomed over LAX, has been joined by a brand-new silhouette. The main control tower, designed by local architect Kate Diamond to evoke a stylized palm tree, is tailored to present southern California in its best light. You can go inside to enjoy the view from the Theme Building's observation deck or have a space-age cocktail at the Technicolor bachelor-pad that's Encounter restaurant.

L.A.'s Westside & Beverly Hills

The **Rudolph M. Schindler House,** 835 N. Kings Rd. (☎ **310/651-1510**), is distinguished by the intermingling of indoors and out, daring modern (1921–22) design, and technological innovations. A protégé of Frank Lloyd Wright and contemporary of Richard Neutra, the Austrian architect was very active in Los Angeles; little survives of his work, and his own home barely escaped the wrecking ball. But Austria's Museum of Applied Arts (MAK) now maintains the restored house as a mini-MAK, and also offers guided tours on weekends.

Lovers of postmodern architecture should check out the **Pacific Design Center** (☎ **310/657-0800**), 8687 Melrose Ave. Designed by Argentinean Cesar Pelli, the bold architecture and overwhelming scale of the center aroused plenty of controversy when it was erected in 1975. The seven-story building, sheathed in gently curving cobalt-blue glass and housing over 750,000 square feet of wholesale interior-design showrooms, is known to locals as "the blue whale." Nearby on San Vicente Boulevard—on a totally different scale—is the iconic ✪ **Tail o' the Pup.** This is roadside art, and the wiener, at its best.

Hollywood

In addition to the **Griffith Observatory** and **Mann's Chinese Theatre** (see "The Top Attractions," above), and the **Hollywood Roosevelt Hotel** (see "Accommodations You Can Afford," above), check out the old **Egyptian Theatre,** 6712 Hollywood Blvd. Conceived by grandiose Sid Grauman, it's just down the street from Grauman's better-known Chinese Theatre but remains less altered from its 1922 design based on the then-headline news discovery of hidden treasures in Pharaohs' tombs. It's undergoing a (hopefully) sensitive restoration by American Cinematheque—planned reopening is by early 1999 for public screenings.

Farther east is the **Capitol Records Building.** This 12-story tower just north of the legendary intersection of Hollywood and Vine is one of the city's most recognizable buildings. Often, but incorrectly, rumored to have been made to resemble a stack of 45s on a turntable (it kinda does, really), this circular tower is nevertheless unmistakable. Nat "King" Cole, songwriter Johnny Mercer, and other 1950s Capitol artists populate a giant exterior mural.

Built between 1917 and 1920, **Hollyhock House** was the first Frank Lloyd Wright residence to be constructed in Los Angeles. The centerpiece of art-filled Barnsdall Park, the house, at 4800 Hollywood Blvd. (☎ **323/485-4581**), is now owned by the city and operates as a small gallery and house museum, though it's still undergoing extensive repairs for structural damage from the 1994 earthquake.

Downtown

Built in 1928, the 27-story **City Hall,** 200 N. Spring St., remained the tallest building in the city for over 30 years. The structure's distinctive ziggurat roof was featured in the film *War of the Worlds* but is probably best known as the headquarters of the *Daily Planet* in the original *Superman* TV series. On a clear day the top-floor observation deck (open Mon through Fri 10am to 4pm) offers views of Mt. Wilson, 15 miles away.

On West Fifth Street, between Flower Street and Grand Avenue, is one of L.A.'s early architectural achievements, the carefully restored **Central Library** (the majestic main entrance is actually on Flower). Working in the 1920s, architect Bertram G. Goodhue played on the Egyptian motifs and materials popularized by the discovery of King Tut's tomb, combining them with modern concrete block to great effect.

The 1893 **Bradbury Building,** at South Broadway and 3rd Street, is Los Angeles's oldest commercial building and one of the city's most revered architectural landmarks. You've got to go inside to appreciate it. The glass-topped atrium is often used as a movie and TV set; you've seen it in *Chinatown* and *Blade Runner.*

Union Station, at Macy and Alameda streets, is one of the finest examples of California-mission-style architecture, built with the opulence and attention to detail that characterize 1930s WPA projects. The richly paneled cathedral-size ticket lobby and waiting area of this fantastic cream-colored structure stand sadly empty most of the time, but the MTA does use Union Station for Blue Line commuter trains.

For a taste of what downtown's Bunker Hill was like before the bulldozers tore through, visit the residential neighborhood of **Angelino Heights,** near Echo Park. Entire streets are still filled with stately gingerbread Victorian homes; most still enjoy the splendid views that led early L.A.'s elite to build here. The 1300 block of Carroll Avenue is the best preserved. Don't be surprised if a film crew is scouting locations while you're there—these blocks often appear on the silver screen.

The **Watts Towers,** at 1765 E. 107th St. (☎ **323/847-4646**), are more than a bit off the beaten track, but they warrant a visit. The fantastically colorful 99-foot-tall concrete-and-steel sculptures are ornamented with mosaics of bottles, seashells, cups, plates, generic pottery, and ceramic tiles. They were completed in 1954 by folk artist Simon Rodia, an immigrant Italian tile setter who worked on them for 33 years. Call for a tour schedule.

THE SAN FERNANDO VALLEY

At first glance, Burbank's **Walt Disney Corporate Office,** 500 S. Buena Vista St. (at Alameda Avenue), is just another neoclassical building. But wait a minute: Those aren't Ionic columns holding up the building's pediment . . . they're the Seven Dwarfs—giant-size, of course.

PASADENA & ENVIRONS

For a quick but profound architectural fix, stroll past Pasadena's grandiose and baroque **City Hall,** 100 N. Garfield Ave., 2 blocks north of Colorado; closer inspection will reveal its classical colonnaded courtyard, formal gardens, and spectacular tiled dome.

Architects Charles and Henry Greene built prolifically in Pasadena's Arroyo Seco area (overlooking the Rose Bowl) in the early 1900s, their masterpiece being ✪ **Gamble House,** 4 Westmoreland Place (off Orange Grove, north of the Ventura Freeway). Intricately crafted teakwood interiors, custom furnishings, and California-specific features like a sleeping porch make this a one-stop primer in Craftsman design. One-hour tours are given Thursday through Sunday afternoons; call ☎ **626/793-3334** for more information. Additional elegant Greene & Greene creations (still privately owned) abound 2 blocks away along **Arroyo Terrace,** including nos. **368, 370, 400, 408, 424,** and **440;** the Gamble House bookshop can give you a walking-tour map and conducts guided neighborhood tours by appointment.

While the Greenes were building retreats for the wealthy, scaled-down Craftsman bungalows were becoming the standard in affordable housing nearby. An exceptionally well-preserved neighborhood of around 900 predepression homes is the Landmark District **Bungalow Heaven,** between Lake and Hill avenues north of Orange Grove Boulevard. The Bungalow Heaven Neighborhood Association (☎ **626/585-2172**) conducts a house tour each April, or they can give you information on taking a self-guided walking tour of this charming enclave.

BOTANICAL GARDENS

These Pasadena-area gardens are in addition to Pasadena's splendid **Huntington Library, Art Collections, and Botanical Gardens** (see "The Top Attractions," above).

Arboretum of Los Angeles County. 301 N. Baldwin Ave., Arcadia. ☎ **626/821-3222.** Admission $5 adults, $3 students and seniors 62 and over, $1 children 5–12, free for kids 4 and under. Daily 9am–5pm. Closed Christmas Day.

This horticultural and botanical center was formerly the estate of silver magnate "Lucky" Baldwin—the man responsible for bringing horse racing to southern California. He lived until 1909 on these lushly planted 127 acres overlooking the Santa Anita Racetrack. You might recognize Baldwin's red-and-white Queen Anne cottage from the opening sequence of the original *Fantasy Island* ("de plane, boss, de plane"); the gardens are also a favorite location for movie filming and local weddings. In addition to spectacular flora, the arboretum boasts a bevy of resident peafowl who seem unafraid of humans—one of the best treats is being up close when the peacocks, attempting to impress passing peahens, unfold their brilliant rainbow plumage. Avid gardeners will want to visit the nurserylike gift shop on the way out.

Descanso Gardens. 1418 Descanso Dr., La Cañada. ☎ **818/952-4402** or 818/952-4401. Admission $5 adults, $3 students and seniors 62 and over, $1 children 5–12, free for kids 4 and under. Daily 9am–4:30pm.

Camellias—evergreen flowering shrubs from China and Japan—were the passion of amateur gardener E. Manchester Boddy, who began planting them here in 1941. Today his Descanso Gardens contain more than 100,000 camellias in over 600 varieties, blooming under a 30-acre canopy of California oaks. The shrubs now share the limelight with a 5-acre Rose Garden, home to hundreds of varieties. This is really a magical place, with paths and streams that wind through the towering forest, bordering a lake and bird sanctuary. Each season features different plants: daffodils, azaleas, tulips, and lilacs in spring; chrysanthemums in fall; and so on. Monthly art exhibits are held in the garden's hospitality house.

There's also a beautifully landscaped Japanese-style teahouse serving tea and cookies on Saturday and Sunday from 11am to 4pm. Free docent-guided walking tours are offered every Sunday at 1pm; guided tram tours, costing $1.50, run Tuesday through Friday at 1, 2, and 3pm and Saturday and Sunday at 11am and 1, 2, and 3pm. Picnicking is allowed in specified areas.

MISSIONS

Two of the 21 missions built by Franciscan missionaries in the late 18th century along the California coast from San Diego to Sonoma are in the Los Angeles area. The valleys in which they're nestled eventually took their names.

THE SAN FERNANDO VALLEY

Mission San Fernando. 15151 San Fernando Mission Blvd., Mission Hills. ☎ **818/361-0186.** Admission $4 adults, $3 seniors and children 12 and under. Daily 9am–5pm. From I-5, exit at San Fernando Mission Blvd. east and drive 5 blocks to the mission.

Established in 1797, Mission San Fernando once controlled more than 1.5 million acres, employed 1,500 Native Americans, and boasted over 22,000 head of cattle and extensive orchards. The mission complex was destroyed several times but always faithfully rebuilt with low buildings surrounding grassy courtyards. The aging church was replaced in the 1940s and again in the 1970s after a particularly destructive

Downtown Area Attractions

 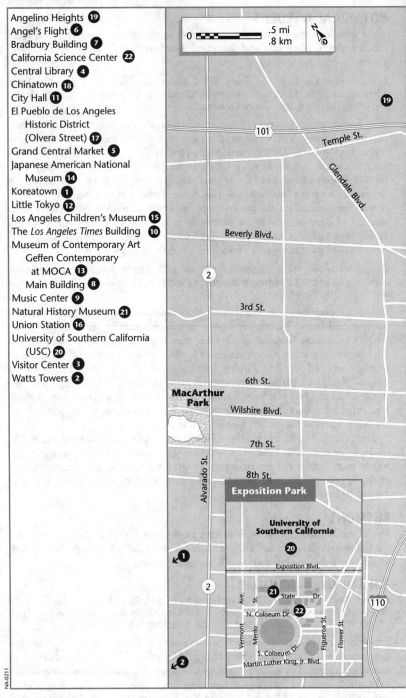
0   .5 mi
    .8 km

⑲

101

Temple St.

Glendale Blvd.

Beverly Blvd.

2

3rd St.

6th St.

MacArthur
Park

Wilshire Blvd.

7th St.

Alvarado St.

8th St.

Exposition Park

**University of
Southern California**
⑳

Exposition Blvd.

2

㉑ State   Dr.

Vermont   Ave.

Menlo   St.

N. Coliseum Dr.

㉒

Figueroa St.

Flower St.

110

S. Coliseum Dr.

Martin Luther King, Jr. Blvd.

①

②

NA-0211

earthquake. The Convento, a 250-foot-long colonnaded structure dating from 1810, is the compound's oldest remaining part. Some of the mission's rooms, including the old library and the private salon of the first bishop of California, have been restored to their late-18th-century appearance. A half-dozen padres and many hundreds of Shoshone Indians are buried in the adjacent cemetery.

PASADENA & ENVIRONS

Mission San Gabriel Arcangel. 537 W. Mission Dr., San Gabriel. ☎ **626/457-3048.** Admission $4 adults, $1 children 6–12, free for kids 5 and under. Daily 9am–5pm. Closed Christmas Day, Good Friday, Easter, and Thanksgiving Day.

Founded in 1771, Mission San Gabriel Arcangel still retains its original facade, notable for its high oblong windows and large capped buttresses that are said to have been influenced by the cathedral in Cordova, Spain. The mission's self-contained compound encompasses an aqueduct, a cemetery, a tannery, and a working winery. In the church stands a copper font with the dubious distinction of being the first one used to baptize a native Californian. The most notable contents of the mission's museum are Native American paintings depicting the Stations of the Cross, painted on sailcloth, with colors made from crushed desert-flower petals. The mission is about 15 minutes south of Pasadena.

MUSEUMS & GALLERIES

SANTA MONICA & THE BEACHES

Museum of Flying. Santa Monica Airport, 2772 Donald Douglas Loop N., Santa Monica. ☎ **310/392-8822.** Admission $7 adults, $5 seniors, $3 children. Wed–Sun 10am–5pm.

Once headquarters of the McDonnell Douglas corporation, the Santa Monica Airport is the birthplace of the DC-3 and other pioneers of commercial aviation. The museum celebrates this bit of local history with 24 authentic aircraft displays and some interactive exhibits. In addition to antique Spitfires and Sopwith Camels, there's a new kid-oriented learning area where hands-on exhibits detail airplane parts, pilot procedures, and the properties of air and aircraft design. The shop is full of scale models of World War II birds; the coffee-table book *The Best of the Past* beautifully illustrates 50 years of aviation history.

L.A.'S WESTSIDE & BEVERLY HILLS

Museum of Tolerance. 9786 W. Pico Blvd. (at Roxbury Dr.). ☎ **310/553-8403.** www.wiesenthal.com. Admission $8 adults, $6 seniors, $5 students, $3 children 3–12, free for children 2 and under. Tickets are issued for specific entry times. Tickets can be purchased with a credit card, and advance purchase is recommended. Mon–Thurs 10am–5pm; Fri 10am–3pm (to 1pm Nov–Mar); Sun 11am–5pm. Closed many Jewish and secular holidays; call for schedule.

The Museum of Tolerance is designed to expose prejudices and teach racial and cultural tolerance. It's located in the Simon Wiesenthal Center, an institute founded by the legendary Nazi-hunter. While the Holocaust figures prominently, this isn't just a Jewish museum—it's an academy that broadly campaigns for a live-and-let-live world. Tolerance is an abstract idea that's hard to display, so most of this $50-million museum's exhibits are high-tech and conceptual in nature. Fast-paced interactive displays are designed to touch the heart as well as the mind and engage both serious investigators and the MTV crowd. One of three major museums in America that deals with the Holocaust, the Museum of Tolerance is considered by some to be inferior to its Washington, D.C., counterpart, and visitors can be frustrated by the museum's policy of insisting you follow a prescribed 2½-hour route through the exhibits.

Pasadena & Environs

NA-0212

ACCOMMODATIONS

The Artists' Inn Bed-and-Breakfast **8**
Bissell House **5**
Pasadena Hotel Bed-and-Breakfast **10**
The Ritz-Carlton Huntington Hotel **6**
Saga Motor Hotel **16**

ATTRACTIONS

Arboretum of L.A. County **17**
Bungalow Heaven **15**
City Hall **11**
Descanso Gardens **1**
Gamble House **3**
Green Street Antique Row **14**
Huntington Library, Art Collections
& Botanical Gardens **18**
Mission San Gabriel Arcangel **7**
Norton Simon Museum of Art **4**
Old Pasadena **12**
Pacific Asia Museum **13**
Pasadena Antiques Center **9**
Rose Bowl **2**

473

Museum of Television and Radio. 465 N. Beverly Dr. (at Santa Monica Blvd.), Beverly Hills.
☎ **310/786-1000.** www.mtr.org/camsm. Admission $6 adults, $4 students and seniors, $3 kids 12 and under. Wed and Fri–Sun noon–5pm; Thurs noon–9pm. Closed New Year's Day, July 4, Thanksgiving Day, and Christmas Day.

Want to see the Beatles on *The Ed Sullivan Show* (1964) or Edward R. Murrow's examination of Joseph McCarthy (1954), watch Arnold Palmer win the 1958 Masters Tournament, or listen to radio excerpts like FDR's first "Fireside Chat" (1933) and Orson Welles's famous *War of the Worlds* UFO hoax (1938)? All these, plus a gazillion episodes of *The Twilight Zone, I Love Lucy,* and other beloved series, can be viewed within the starkly white walls of architect Richard Meier's neutral, contemporary museum building. Like the ritzy Beverly Hills shopping district surrounding it, the museum is more flash than substance. Once you gawk at the celebrity and industry-honcho names adorning every hall, room, and miscellaneous area, it becomes quickly apparent that "library" would be a more fitting name for this collection, since the main attractions are requested via sophisticated computer catalogs and viewed in private consoles. Though no one sets out to spend a vacation watching TV, it can be tempting once you start browsing the archives. The West Coast branch of the 20-year-old New York City facility succeeds in treating our favorite pastime as a legitimate art form, with the respect history will prove it deserves.

HOLLYWOOD

✪ **Autry Museum of Western Heritage.** 4700 Western Heritage Way (in Griffith Park). ☎ **323/667-2000.** www.autry-museum.org. Admission $7.50 adults, $5 seniors 60 and over and students 13–18, $3 children 2–12, free for kids under 2. Tues–Sun 10am–5pm.

If you're under 45, you might not be familiar with the late Gene Autry, a Texas-born actor who starred in 82 westerns and became known as the "Singing Cowboy." Opened in 1988, Autry's museum is one of L.A.'s best. It's located north of downtown in Griffith Park. This collection of art and artifacts of the European conquest of the West is remarkably comprehensive and intelligently displayed. Evocative exhibits illustrate the everyday lives of early pioneers, not only with antique firearms, tools, saddles, and the like but also with many hands-on exhibits that successfully stir the imagination and the heart. There's footage from Buffalo Bill's Wild West Show, movie clips from the silent days, contemporary films, the works of Wild West artists, and plenty of memorabilia from Autry's own film and TV projects. The "Hall of Merchandising" displays Roy Rogers bedspreads, Hopalong Cassidy radios, and other items from the collective consciousness—and material collections—of baby boomers.

Craft & Folk Art Museum. 5800 Wilshire Blvd. (at Curson Ave.). ☎ **323/937-5544.** Admission $4 adults, $2.50 seniors and students, free for children under 12. Tues–Sun 11am–5pm.

This gallery has grown into one of the city's largest, opening in a prominent Museum Row building in 1995. "Craft and folk art" is quite a large rubric encompassing everything from clothing, tools, religious artifacts, and other everyday objects to wood carvings, papier-mâché, weaving, and metalwork. The museum displays folk objects from around the world, but its strongest collection is masks from India, America, Mexico, Japan, and China. Special recent exhibits included a retrospective of California woodworker Sam Maloof (whose custom-made chairs grace many a celebrity home) and a collection examining parallels between Italy's rich textile heritage and traditional bread shapes and textures. The museum is well known for its annual International Festival of Masks, a colorful ethnic celebration held each October in Hancock Park, across the street.

✪ **Los Angeles County Museum of Art.** 5905 Wilshire Blvd. ☎ **323/857-6000.** www.lacma.org. Admission $6 adults, $4 students and seniors 62 and over, $1 children 6–17, free for kids 5 and under; regular exhibits free for everyone the 2nd Tues of each month. Mon, Tues, and Thurs noon–8pm; Fri noon–9pm; Sat–Sun 11am–8pm.

This is one of the finest art museums in the United States. The huge complex was designed by three very different architects over a span of 30 years. The architectural fusion can be migraine inducing, but this city landmark is well worth delving into.

The newest wing is the **Japanese Pavilion,** which has exterior walls made of Kalwall, a translucent material that, like shoji screens, permits the entry of soft natural light. Inside is a collection of Japanese Edo paintings that's rivaled only by the holdings of the emperor of Japan.

The **Anderson Building,** the museum's contemporary wing, is home to 20th-century painting and sculpture. Here you'll find works by Matisse, Magritte, and a good number of Dada artists.

The **Ahmanson Building** houses the rest of the museum's permanent collections. Here you'll find everything from 2,000-year-old pre-Columbian Mexican ceramics to a unique glass collection spanning the centuries to 19th-century portraiture. There's also one of the nation's largest holdings of costumes and textiles and an important Indian and Southeast Asian art collection.

The **Hammer Building** is primarily used for major special loan exhibitions. Free guided tours covering the museum's highlights depart on a regular basis from here.

✪ **Petersen Automotive Museum.** 6060 Wilshire Blvd. (at Fairfax Ave.). ☎ **323/ 930-CARS.** www.lam.mus.ca.us/petersen. Admission $7 adults, $5 seniors and students, $3 children 5–12, free for kids 4 and under. Tues–Sun 10am–6pm.

When the Petersen opened in 1994, many locals were surprised it had taken this long for the City of Freeways to salute its most important shaper. Indeed, this museum says more about the city than probably any other one in L.A. Named for Robert Petersen, the publisher responsible for *Hot Rod* and *Motor Trend* magazines, the four-story museum displays over 200 cars and motorcycles, from the historic to the futuristic. Cars on the first floor are depicted chronologically, in period settings. Other floors are devoted to frequently changing shows of race cars, early motorcycles, and famous movie vehicles. Recent exhibits have included the Flintstones' fiberglass-and-cotton movie car; a customized dune buggy with seats made from surfboards, created for the Elvis Presley movie *Easy Come, Easy Go;* and a three-wheeled scooter that folds into a Samsonite briefcase, created in competition by a Mazda engineer.

DOWNTOWN

California ScienCenter. 700 State Dr., Exposition Park. ☎ **213/SCIENCE** or 213/744-7400; IMAX theater ☎ 213/744-2014. www.casciencectr.org. Museum free; IMAX theater $7 adults, $4.75 ages 18–21, $4 seniors and children. Multishow discounts available. Parking $5. Daily 10am–5pm. Closed New Year's Day, Thanksgiving Day, and Christmas Day.

A $130-million reinvention has turned the former Museum of Science and Industry into Exposition Park's newest attraction. Using high-tech sleight-of-hand, the center stimulates kids of all ages with questions, answers, and lessons about the world. One of the museum's educational highlights is Tess, a 50-foot animatronic woman whose muscles, bones, organs, and blood vessels are revealed, demonstrating how the body reacts to a variety of external conditions and activities. There are nominal fees to enjoy the Science Center's more thrilling attractions: a 43-foot high-wire bicycle ride or the zero-gravity Space Docking Simulator. The newly expanded IMAX theater screens breathtaking surround-sound movies in 2D and 3D throughout the day until 9pm.

Japanese American National Museum. 369 E. First St. (at Central Ave.). ☎ **213/ 625-0414.** Admission $4 adults, $3 seniors and children 6–17, $2 students; free for everyone the 3rd Thurs of each month. Tues–Wed and Fri–Sun 10am–5pm; Thurs 10am–8pm.

Located in a beautifully restored historic building in Little Tokyo, this museum is a private nonprofit institute created to document and celebrate the history of the Japanese in America. Its fantastic permanent exhibition chronicles Japanese life in America, while temporary exhibits highlight distinctive aspects of Japanese-American culture.

Los Angeles Children's Museum. 310 N. Main St. (at Los Angeles St.). ☎ **213/ 687-8800.** Admission $5 adults, free for kids under 2. Late June to early Sept Mon–Fri 11:30am–5pm; Sat–Sun 10am–5pm. The rest of the year Sat–Sun 10am–5pm.

This thoroughly enchanting museum is a place where children learn by doing. Everyday experiences are demystified by interesting interactive exhibits displayed in a playlike atmosphere. In the Art Studio, kids are encouraged to make finger puppets from a variety of media and shiny rockets out of Mylar. Turn the corner and you're in the unrealistically clean and safe City Street, where kids can sit on a police officer's motorcycle or pretend to drive a bus or a fire truck. Kids (and adults) can see their shadows freeze in the Shadow Box and play with giant foam-filled, Velcro-edged building blocks in Sticky City. Because this is Hollywood, the museum wouldn't be complete without its own recording and TV studios, where kids can become "stars."

Museum of Contemporary Art/Geffen Contemporary at MOCA. 250 S. Grand Ave. and 152 N. Central Ave. ☎ **213/626-6222** or 213/621-2766. Admission $6 adults, $4 seniors and students, free for children 11 and under. Tues–Wed and Fri–Sun 11am–5pm; Thurs 11am–8pm.

MOCA is Los Angeles's only institution exclusively devoted to art from 1940 to the present. Displaying works in a variety of media, it's particularly strong in works by Cy Twombly, Jasper Johns, and Mark Rothko, and shows are often superb. For many experts, MOCA's collections are too spotty to be considered world-class, and the conservative museum board blushes when offered controversial shows (they passed on a Whitney exhibit that included photographs by Robert Mapplethorpe). Nevertheless, I've seen some excellent exhibitions here.

MOCA is one museum housed in two buildings that are close to each other but not within walking distance. The Grand Avenue main building is a contemporary red sandstone structure by renowned Japanese architect Arata Isozaki. Located here, the museum restaurant, **Patinette** (☎ 213/626-1178), is the casual dining creation of celebrity chef Joachim Splichal.

The museum's second space, on Central Avenue in Little Tokyo, was the "temporary" Contemporary while the Grand structure was being built and now houses a superior permanent collection in a fittingly neutral warehouse-type space recently renamed for entertainment mogul and passionate art collector David Geffen. An added feature here is a detailed timeline corresponding to the progression of works. Unless there's a visiting exhibit of great interest at the main museum, I recommend you start at the Geffen building—where it's also easier to park.

Natural History Museum of Los Angeles County. 900 Exposition Blvd., Exposition Park. ☎ 213/743-3466. www.nhm.org. Admission $8 adults; $5.50 children 12–17, seniors, and students with ID; $2 children 5–11; free for kids 4 and under; free for everyone the 1st Tues of each month. Tues–Sun 10am–5pm. Free docent-led tours daily at 1pm.

The "Fighting Dinosaurs"—they're not a high-school football team but the trademark symbol of this massive museum, Tyrannosaurus rex and triceratops skeletons poised in a stance so realistic that every kid feels inspired to imitate their *Jurassic Park* bellows. Opened in 1913 in a beautiful columned and domed Spanish Renaissance building, the museum is a 35-hall warehouse of the earth's history, chronicling the planet and its inhabitants from 600 million years ago to the present. There's a mind-numbing number of exhibits of prehistoric fossils, bird and marine life, rocks and minerals, and North American mammals. The best permanent displays include the world's rarest shark, a walk-through vault of priceless gems, and an insect zoo.

PASADENA & ENVIRONS

✪ **Norton Simon Museum of Art.** 411 W. Colorado Blvd., Pasadena. ☎ **626/ 449-6840.** Admission $4 adults, $2 students and seniors, free for children 12 and under. Museum Thurs–Sun noon–6pm; bookshop Thurs–Sun noon–5:30pm.

Named for a food-packing king/financier who reorganized the failing Pasadena Museum of Modern Art, the Norton Simon Museum has become one of California's most important museums. Comprehensive collections of masterpieces by Degas, Picasso, Rembrandt, and Goya are augmented by sculptures by Henry Moore and Auguste Rodin, including *The Burghers of Calais,* which greets you at the gates. The "Blue Four" collection of works by Kandinsky, Jawlensky, Klee, and Feininger is particularly impressive, as is a superb collection of Southeast Asian sculpture. *Still Life with Lemons, Oranges, and a Rose* (1633), an oil by Francisco de Zurbarán, is one of the museum's most important holdings. One of the most popular pieces is Mexican artist Diego Rivera's *The Flower Vendor/Girl with Lilies.* Also look for recent Frank Gehry–designed enhanced galleries.

Pacific Asia Museum. 46 N. Los Robles Ave., Pasadena. ☎ **626/449-2742.** Admission $5 adults, $3 students and seniors, free for children under 12; free for everyone the 3rd Sat of each month. Wed–Sun 10am–5pm.

The most striking aspect of this museum is the building itself. Designed in the 1920s in Chinese Imperial Palace style, it's rivaled in flamboyance only by Mann's Chinese Theatre in Hollywood (see "The Top Attractions," above). Rotating exhibits of Asian art span the centuries from 100 B.C. to the present. This manageably sized museum is usually worth a peek, since its curators usually assemble intriguing and unusual exhibits.

PARKS
SANTA MONICA & THE BEACHES

Will Rogers State Historic Park. 1501 Will Rogers State Park Rd., Pacific Palisades. ☎ **310/454-8212.** Park entrance $6 per vehicle, including all passengers. Daily 8am–sunset. The house opens daily at 10am; guided tours can be arranged for groups of 10 or more. From Santa Monica, take the Pacific Coast Hwy. (Calif. 1) north, turn right onto Sunset Blvd., and continue to the park entrance.

Will Rogers (1879–1935) was born in Oklahoma and became a cowboy in the Texas Panhandle before drifting into a Wild West show as a folksy, humorous roper. The "cracker-barrel philosopher" performed lariat tricks while carrying on a deadpan monologue on current events. In 1919, the showman moved to Los Angeles, where he become a movie actor as well as the author of numerous books detailing his down-home "cowboy philosophy."

Between Santa Monica and Malibu, Will Rogers State Historic Park was once Rogers's private ranch and grounds. The 168-acre estate is now both a park and a historic site. You can explore the grounds, the former stables, and the 31-room house filled with the original furnishings, including a porch swing in the living room and many Native American rugs and baskets. Charles and Anne Morrow Lindbergh hid out here in the 1930s during part of the craze that followed the kidnap and murder of their first son. There are picnic tables, but no food is sold.

HOLLYWOOD

✪ **Griffith Park.** Entrances along Los Feliz Blvd. at Riverside Dr., Vermont Ave., and Western Ave. ☎ **323/665-5188.** Park and museum free; zoo $8.25 adults, $5.25 seniors, $3.25 children 2–12, free for kids under 2. Park daily 24 hr. Zoo daily 10am–5pm. Museum Mon–Fri 10am–4pm; Sat–Sun 10am–5pm.

Mining tycoon Griffith J. Griffith donated these 4,000 acres of parkland to the city in 1896. Today Griffith Park is one of the largest city parks in America. There's a lot to do here, including hiking, horseback riding, golfing, swimming, biking, and picnicking (see "Staying Active," below). For a general overview, drive the mountainous loop road winding from the top of Western Avenue, past Griffith Observatory, and down to Vermont Avenue. For a more extensive foray, turn north at the loop road's midsection, onto Mount Hollywood Drive. To reach the golf courses or Los Angeles Zoo, take Los Feliz Boulevard to Riverside Drive, which runs along the park's western edge.

L.A.'s medium-sized **Los Angeles Zoo** (see "The L.A. Zoo," below) is an easy place to tote the kids around. Animal habitats are divided by continent. The best features are the brand-new Chimpanzees of the Mahale Mountains habitat and the interactive Adventure Island children's zoo.

Near the zoo, in a particularly dusty corner of the park, you'll find the **Travel Town Museum,** 5200 Zoo Dr. (☎ **323/662-5874**), a little-known outdoor museum with a small collection of vintage locomotives and old airplanes. Kids love it. It's open Monday through Friday from 10am to 5pm and Saturday, Sunday, and holidays from 10am to 6pm (closed Christmas); admission is free.

THE SANTA MONICA PIER

Santa Monica Pier. Ocean Ave. at Colorado Ave., Santa Monica.

This famous pier is doing a pretty good job of recapturing the glory days of southern California piers. Built in 1909 for passenger and cargo ships, the wooden wharf is now home to seafood restaurants and snack shacks, a touristy Mexican cantina at the far end, and a gaily colored turn-of-the-century indoor wooden carousel (which Paul Newman operated in *The Sting*). Summer evening concerts, which are free and range from Big Band to Miami-style Latin, draw huge crowds, as does the new fun-zone perched halfway down. Its name, Pacific Park, hearkens back to the granddaddy pier amusement park in California, Pacific Ocean Park; this new version has a roller coaster and other rides, plus a high-tech arcade shoot-out. But fishermen still head to the end to angle, and nostalgia buffs to view the photographic display of the pier's history. This is the last of the great pleasure piers, offering rides, romance, and perfect panoramic views of the bay and mountains.

The pier is about a mile up Ocean Front Walk from Venice; it's a great round-trip stroll. For information on twilight concerts (generally held Thurs mid-June to the end of Aug), call ☎ **310/393-7593.**

THE L.A. ZOO

Los Angeles Zoo. Zoo Dr., Griffith Park. ☎ **323/664-1100.** www.lazoo.org. Admission $8.25 adults, $3.25 kids 2–12, $5.25 seniors 65 and over, free for children under 2. Discount for AAA members. Daily 10am–5pm. Closed Christmas Day. Free parking.

Nestled in the foothills of Griffith Park and sharing a parking lot with the Autry Museum (see above), the L.A. Zoo has been welcoming visitors and busloads of school kids since 1966. In 1982, the zoo welcomed a display of cuddly koalas, still one of the biggest attractions, and Chinese pandas, who stayed for only 3 months during the 1984 Olympics. While mature shade trees now help cool the once-barren grounds and new habitats are light-years ahead of the cruel concrete roundhouses originally used to exhibit animals, there are still some depressing remnants of the humble old zoo—like a polar bear whose enclosure looks as much like the Arctic as the average suburban pool. Stick with the newer, more humane and authentic exhibits, like the interactive and educational Adventure Island (promoted as the Children's Zoo, it's actually just as cool for grown-ups), and the brand-new Chimpanzees of the Mahale Mountains habitat that manages to simulate a forest environment where you can still see plenty of primate activity. Renowned in zoo circles for the successful breeding and releasing of California condors, the zoo occasionally has some of the majestic and endangered birds of prey on exhibit.

TOURIST TRAPS

You've heard of all of the following attractions, of course, but you should know exactly what you're in for before you part with your dollars.

Hollywood Guinness World of Records. 6746 Hollywood Blvd., Hollywood. ☎ **323/ 63-6433.** Admission $8.95 adults, $7.50 seniors, $6.95 children 6–11. Sun–Thurs 10am–midnight; Fri–Sat 10am–2am.

Scale models, photographs, and push-button displays of the world's fattest man, biggest plant, smallest woman, fastest animal, and other superlatives don't make for a superlative experience.

Hollywood Wax Museum. 6767 Hollywood Blvd., Hollywood. ☎ **323/462-8860.** Admission $8.95 adults, $7.50 seniors, $6.95 children 6–12, free for kids 5 and under. Sun–Thurs 10am–midnight; Fri–Sat 10am–2am.

Cast in the Madame Tussaud mold, the Hollywood Wax Museum features dozens of lifelike figures of famous movie stars and events. The "museum" isn't great, but it can be good for a cheeky laugh or two. A "Chamber of Horrors" exhibit includes the coffin used in *The Raven*, as well as a diorama from the Vincent Price classic *The House of Wax*. The "Movie Awards Theatre" exhibit is a short film highlighting Academy Award presentations from the last 4 decades.

Ripley's "Believe It Or Not!" Hollywood. 6780 Hollywood Blvd. ☎ **323/466-6335.** Admission $8.50 adults, $7 students and seniors, $5.50 children 5–11. Daily 10am–midnight.

Believe it or not, this amazing and silly "museum" is still open. A bizarre collection of wax figures, photos, and models depicts unnatural oddities from Robert Leroy Ripley's infamous arsenal. My favorites are the skeleton of a two-headed baby, a statue of Marilyn Monroe sculpted with shredded money, and a portrait of John Wayne made from laundry lint.

8 Studio Tours & Other Organized Sightseeing

STUDIO TOURS
HOLLYWOOD

Paramount Pictures. 5555 Melrose Ave. ☎ **323/956-1777.** Tours $15 per person. Mon–Fri 9am–2pm.

Paramount's 2-hour walking tour around its Hollywood headquarters is both a historical ode to filmmaking and a real-life look at a working studio. Tours depart hourly; the itinerary varies, depending on what productions are in progress. Visits might include a walk through the sound stages of TV shows or feature films, though you can't enter while taping is taking place. Cameras, recording equipment, and children under 10 aren't allowed.

THE SAN FERNANDO VALLEY

NBC Studios. 3000 W. Alameda Ave., Burbank. ☎ **818/840-3537.** Tours $6 adults, $5.50 seniors, $3.75 children 6–12. Mon–Fri 9am–3pm.

According to a security guard, John Wayne and Redd Foxx once got into a fight here after Wayne refused to ride in the same limousine as Foxx, who called the movie star a "redneck." Well, your NBC tour will probably be a bit more docile than that. The guided 1-hour tour includes a behind-the-scenes look at *The Tonight Show with Jay Leno* set; wardrobe, makeup, and set-building departments; and several sound studios. The tour includes some cool video demonstrations of high-tech special effects.

✪ **Warner Bros. Studios.** Olive Ave. (at Hollywood Way), Burbank. ☎ **818/972-TOUR.** Reservations required 2–4 weeks in advance. Admission $30 per person. Mon–Fri 9am–4pm.

This is the most comprehensive (and the least theme park–like) of the studio tours. The tour takes you on a 2-hour informational drive-and-walk jaunt around the studio's faux streets. After a brief introductory film, you'll pile into glorified golf carts and cruise past parking spaces marked "Clint Eastwood," "Michael Douglas," and "Sharon Stone," then walk through active film and TV sets. Whether it's an orchestra scoring a film or a TV show being taped or edited, you'll get a glimpse of how it's done. Stops may include the wardrobe department or the mills where sets are made. Whenever possible, you can visit working sets to watch actors filming actual productions. Children under 8 aren't admitted.

SIGHTSEEING TOURS

Oskar J's Tours (☎ 818/501-2217) operates regularly scheduled panoramic motorcoach tours of the city. Buses (or plush minivans) pick up passengers from major hotels for morning or afternoon tours of the Sunset Strip, the movie studios, Farmers Market, Hollywood, homes of the stars, and other attractions. Tours vary from 2 to 5 hours and cost $25 to $50. Call for details and to make reservations.

Next Stage Tour Company offers a unique Insomniacs' Tour of L.A. (☎ 213/939-2688), a 3am tour of the predawn city that usually includes trips to the *Los Angeles Times;* the flower, produce, and fish markets; and the top of a skyscraper to watch the sun rise over the city. The fact-filled tour lasts about 6½ hours and includes breakfast. Tours depart twice monthly and cost $47 per person. Phone for information and reservations.

Grave Line Tours (☎ 323/469-4149) is a terrific journey through Hollywood's darker side. You're picked up in a renovated hearse and taken to the murder sites and final residences of the stars. You'll see the Hollywood Boulevard hotel where female impersonator/actor Divine died, the liquor store where John Belushi threw a temper tantrum shortly before his overdose, and more. Tours are $44 per person and last about 2½ hours. They depart at 9:30am daily from the corner of Orchid Street and Hollywood Boulevard, by Mann's Chinese Theatre. Reservations are required.

The ✪ **L.A. Conservancy** (☎ 213/623-2489) conducts a dozen fascinating information-packed walking tours of historic downtown L.A., seed of today's sprawling metropolis. The most popular is "Broadway Theaters," a loving look at movie palaces. Other intriguing ones are "Marble Masterpieces," "Art Deco," "Mecca for Merchants," "Terra-Cotta," and tours of the landmark Biltmore Hotel and City Hall.

They're usually held Saturday mornings and cost $5. Call Monday through Friday between 9am and 5pm for exact schedule and information.

In Pasadena, various tours spotlighting architecture or neighborhoods are lots of fun, given this area's history of wealthy estates and ardent preservation. Call **Pasadena Heritage** at ☎ **626/793-0617** for a schedule of guided tours or pick up *Ten Tours of Pasadena,* self-guided walking or driving maps available at the **Pasadena Convention and Visitors Bureau,** 171 S. Los Robles Ave. (☎ **626/795-9311**).

9   L.A.'s Best Beaches

Los Angeles County's 72-mile coastline sports over 30 miles of beaches, most of which are operated by the **Department of Beaches & Harbors,** 13837 Fiji Way, Marina del Rey (☎ **310/305-9503**). County-run beaches usually charge for parking ($4 to $8). Alcohol, bonfires, and pets are prohibited, so you'll have to leave Fido at home. For recorded surf conditions (and coastal weather forecast), call ☎ **310/457-9701.**

The following are the county's best beaches, listed from north to south:

EL PESCADOR, LA PIEDRA & EL MATADOR BEACHES   These relatively rugged and isolated beaches front a 2-mile stretch of the Pacific Coast Highway (Calif. 1) between Broad Beach and Decker Canyon roads, about 10 minutes' driving from the Malibu Pier. Picturesque coves with unusual rock formations are perfect for sunbathing and picnicking, but swim with caution as there are no lifeguards or other facilities. These beaches can be difficult to find, marked only by small signs on the highway. Visitors are limited by the small number of parking spots atop the bluffs. Descend to the beach via stairs that cling to the cliffs.

✪ **ZUMA BEACH COUNTY PARK**   Jam-packed on warm weekends, L.A. County's largest beach park is located off the Pacific Coast Highway (Calif. 1) a mile past Kanan Dume Road. While it can't claim to be the most lovely beach in the Southland, Zuma has the most comprehensive facilities: plenty of rest rooms, lifeguards, playgrounds, volleyball courts, and snack bars. The southern stretch, toward Point Dume, is Westward Beach, separated from the noisy highway by sandstone cliffs. A trail leads over the point's headlands to Pirate's Cove, once a popular nude beach.

PARADISE COVE   This private beach in the 28000 block of the Pacific Coast Highway (Calif. 1) charges $15 to park and $5 per person if you walk in. Changing rooms and showers are included in the price. The beach is often full by noon on weekends.

✪ **MALIBU LAGOON STATE BEACH**   Not just a pretty white-sand beach but an estuary and wetlands area as well, Malibu Lagoon is the historic home of the Chumash Indians. The entrance is on the Pacific Coast Highway (Calif. 1) south of Cross Creek Road, and there's a small admission charge. Marine life and shorebirds teem where the creek empties into the sea, and the waves are always mild. The historic Adamson House is here, a showplace of Malibu tile now operating as a museum.

✪ **SURFRIDER BEACH**   Without a doubt, L.A.'s best waves roll ashore here. One of the city's most popular surfing spots, this beach is between the Malibu Pier and the lagoon. In surf lingo, few "locals only" wave wars are ever fought here—surfing isn't as territorial as it can be in other areas, where out-of-towners can be made to feel unwelcome. As the beach is surrounded by all of Malibu's hustle and bustle, don't come to Surfrider for peace and quiet.

TOPANGA STATE BEACH   Noise from the highway prevents solitude at this short narrow strip of sand located where Topanga Canyon Boulevard emerges from the

Beaches & Coastal Attractions

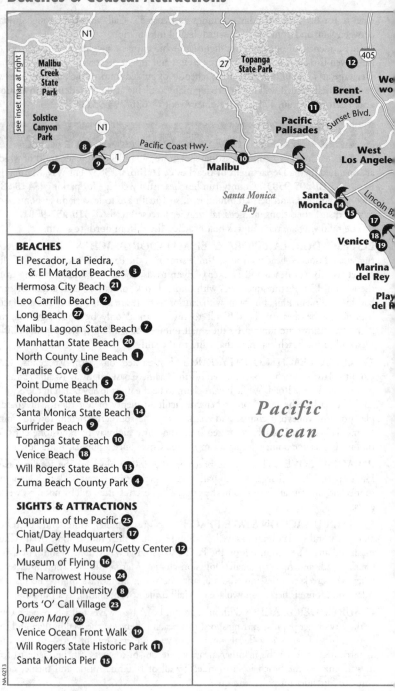

see inset map at right

N1

Malibu
Creek
State
Park

Solstice
Canyon
Park

N1

Topanga
State Park

27

405

12

Brent-
wood

We
wo

11

Pacific
Palisades

Sunset Blvd.

Pacific Coast Hwy.

8

1

9

7

10

Malibu

13

West
Los Angele

Santa Monica
Bay

Santa
Monica

14

15

Lincoln B

17

18

19

Venice

Marina
del Rey

Play
del R

Pacific
Ocean

BEACHES
El Pescador, La Piedra,
  & El Matador Beaches ③
Hermosa City Beach ㉑
Leo Carrillo Beach ②
Long Beach ㉗
Malibu Lagoon State Beach ⑦
Manhattan State Beach ⑳
North County Line Beach ①
Paradise Cove ⑥
Point Dume Beach ⑤
Redondo State Beach ㉒
Santa Monica State Beach ⑭
Surfrider Beach ⑨
Topanga State Beach ⑩
Venice Beach ⑱
Will Rogers State Beach ⑬
Zuma Beach County Park ④

SIGHTS & ATTRACTIONS
Aquarium of the Pacific ㉕
Chiat/Day Headquarters ⑰
J. Paul Getty Museum/Getty Center ⑫
Museum of Flying ⑯
The Narrowest House ㉔
Pepperdine University ⑧
Ports 'O' Call Village ㉓
Queen Mary ㉖
Venice Ocean Front Walk ⑲
Will Rogers State Historic Park ⑪
Santa Monica Pier ⑮

NA-0213

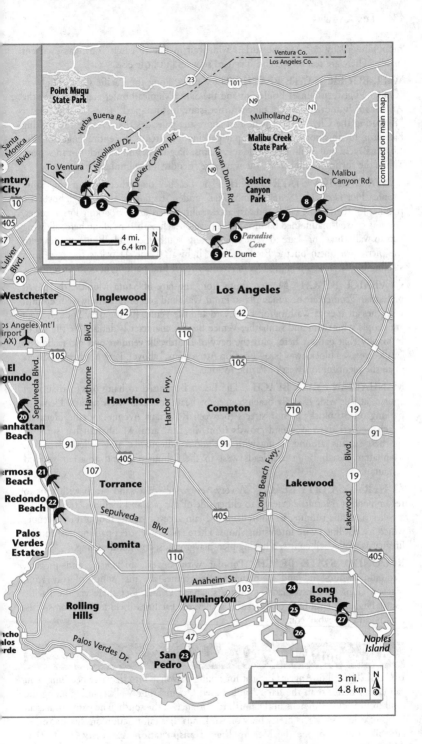

continued on main map

Ventura Co.
Los Angeles Co.

Point Mugu
State Park

Yerba Buena Rd.

Mulholland Dr.

Decker Canyon Rd.

To Ventura

Santa
Monica
Blvd.

entury
City

Mulholland Dr.

Malibu Creek
State Park

N9

N1

Kanan Dume Rd.

Solstice
Canyon
Park

Malibu
Canyon Rd.

N1

1 **2** **3** **4** **6** **7** **8** **9**

*Paradise
Cove*

5 Pt. Dume

0 | 4 mi.
6.4 km

N

Westchester

Inglewood

Los Angeles

42

42

os Angeles Int'l
irport
LAX)

1

105

El
gundo

Sepulveda Blvd.

Hawthorne Blvd.

Harbor Fwy.

110

105

20

anhattan
Beach

Hawthorne

Compton

710

19

91

91

91

405

Long Beach Fwy.

Lakewood

19

Lakewood Blvd.

rmosa **21**
Beach

107

Redondo **22**
Beach

Sepulveda
Blvd.

405

Palos
Verdes
Estates

Lomita

110

405

Anaheim St.

ncho
alos
rde

Rolling
Hills

Palos Verdes Dr.

103

24

Wilmington

47

San
Pedro **23**

25

26

27

Long
Beach

Naples
Island

0 | 3 mi.
4.8 km

N

mountains. Why go? Ask the surfers who wait in line to catch Topanga's excellent breaks. There are rest rooms and lifeguard services but little else.

WILL ROGERS STATE BEACH Three miles along the Pacific Coast Highway (Calif. 1) between Sunset Boulevard and the Santa Monica border are named for the American humorist whose ranch-turned-state-historic-park (see "Parks" under "Exploring the City," above) is nestled above the palisades that provide the striking backdrop for this popular beach. A pay parking lot extends the entire length of Will Rogers Beach, and facilities include rest rooms, lifeguards, and a snack hut in season. While the surfing is only so-so, the waves are friendly for swimmers of all ages.

SANTA MONICA STATE BEACH The beaches on either side of the Santa Monica Pier (see "The Santa Monica Pier" under "Exploring the City," above) are popular for their white sands and easy accessibility. There are big parking lots, eateries, and lots of well-maintained bathrooms. A paved beach path runs along here, allowing you to walk, bike, or skate to Venice and points south. Colorado Boulevard leads to the pier; turn north on the Pacific Coast Highway (Calif. 1) below the coastline's striking bluffs, or south along Ocean Avenue; you'll find parking in both directions.

✪ VENICE BEACH Moving south from the city of Santa Monica, the paved pedestrian Promenade becomes Ocean Front Walk and gets progressively weirder until it reaches an apex at Washington Boulevard and the Venice fishing pier. Though there are people who swim and sunbathe, Venice Beach's character is defined by the sea of humanity that gathers here, plus the bevy of boardwalk vendors and old-fashioned "walk-streets" a block away (see "The Top Attractions," above). Park on the side streets or in the plentiful lots west of Pacific Avenue.

MANHATTAN STATE BEACH The Beach Boys used to hang out (and surf, of course) at this wide friendly beach backed by beautiful ocean-view homes. Plenty of parking on 36 blocks of side streets (between Rosecrans Avenue and the Hermosa Beach border) draw weekend crowds from the L.A. area. Manhattan has some of the best surfing around, along with rest rooms, lifeguards, and volleyball courts. Manhattan Beach Boulevard leads west to the fishing pier and adjacent seafood restaurants.

✪ HERMOSA CITY BEACH A very, very wide white-sand beach with tons to recommend it, Hermosa extends to either side of the pier and includes "the Strand," a pedestrian lane running its entire length. Main access is at the foot of Pier Avenue, which itself is lined with interesting shops. There's plenty of street parking, rest rooms, lifeguards, volleyball courts, a fishing pier, playgrounds, and good surfing.

REDONDO STATE BEACH Popular with surfers, bicyclists, and joggers, Redondo's white-sand and ice-plant-carpeted dunes are just south of tiny King Harbor, along "the Esplanade" (South Esplanade Drive). Get there via the Pacific Coast Highway (Calif. 1) or Torrance Boulevard. Facilities include rest rooms, lifeguards, and volleyball courts.

10 Staying Active

BICYCLING Los Angeles is great for biking. If you're into distance peddling, you can do no better than the flat 22-mile paved Ocean Front Walk running along the sand from Pacific Palisades in the north to Torrance in the south. The path attracts all levels of riders, so it gets pretty busy on weekends. For information on this and other city bike routes, phone the **Metropolitan Transportation Authority** at ☎ 213/244-6539.

The best place to mountain-bike is along the trails of **Malibu Creek State Park** (☎ **800/533-7275** or 818/880-0350), in the Santa Monica Mountains between Malibu and the San Fernando Valley. Fifteen miles of trails rise to a maximum of 3,000 feet and are appropriate for intermediate to advanced bikers. Pick up a trail map at the park entrance, 4 miles south of U.S. 101 off Las Virgenes Road, just north of Mulholland Highway. Park admission is $5 per car.

Sea Mist Rental, 1619 Ocean Front Walk, Santa Monica (☎ **310/395-7076**), rents 10-speed cruisers for $5 per hour and $14 per day; 15-speed mountain bikes rent for $6 per hour and $20 per day.

FISHING   **Marina del Rey Sports Fishing,** 13759 Fiji Way (☎ **310/822-3625**), known locally as "Captain Frenchy's," has four deep-sea boats departing daily on half- and full-day ocean fishing trips. Of course, it depends on what's running when you're out, but bass, barracuda halibut, and yellowtail tuna are the most common catches on these party boats. Excursions run $20 to $25 and include bait and tackle. Phone for reservations.

No permit is required to cast from shore or to drop a line from a pier.

GOLF   Most of the city's public courses are administered by the Department of Recreation and Parks, which follows a complicated registration/reservation system for tee times. While visitors can't reserve start times in advance, you're welcome to play any of the courses by showing up and getting on the call sheet. Expect to wait for the most popular tee times, but try to use your flexible vacationer status to your advantage by avoiding the early-morning rush.

Of the city's seven 18-hole and three 9-hole courses, you can't get more central than the ✪ **Rancho Park Golf Course,** 10460 W. Pico Blvd. (☎ **310/838-7373**), smackdab in the middle of L.A.'s Westside. The par-71 course has lots of tall trees but not enough to blot out the towering Century City buildings next door. Rancho also has a 9-hole, par-3 course.

For a genuinely woodsy experience, try one of the three courses inside Griffith Park, northeast of Hollywood (see "Parks," above; ☎ **323/664-1191**). All named for presidents, the courses are extremely well maintained, challenging without being frustrating, and (despite some holes alongside I-5) a great way to leave the city behind. Bucolic pleasures abound, particularly on 9-hole **Roosevelt,** on Vermont Avenue across from the Greek Theatre; early morning wildlife often includes deer, rabbits, skunks, and raccoons (fore!). **Wilson** and **Harding** are each 18 holes and start from the main clubhouse off Riverside Drive, the park's main entrance.

Greens fees on all city courses are $17 Monday through Friday and $22 weekends and holidays; 9-hole courses charge $8.50 weekdays and $11.50 weekends and holidays. For details on other city courses or to contact the starter directly by phone, call the **Department of Recreation and Parks** at ☎ **213/485-5566.**

HIKING   L.A.'s mountains peak at 3,111 feet and are part of the **Santa Monica Mountains National Recreation Area,** a contiguous conglomeration of 350 public parks and 65,000 acres. Many animals make their homes in this area, including deer, coyote, rabbit, skunk, rattlesnake, fox, hawk, and quail. The hills are also home to almost 1,000 drought-resistant plant species, like live oak and coastal sage.

Hiking is best after spring rains, when the hills are green, the flowers are in bloom, and the air is clear. Summers can be very hot; hikers should always carry fresh water.

Santa Ynez Canyon, in Pacific Palisades, is a long and difficult climb that rises steadily for about 3 miles. At the top, hikers are rewarded with fantastic views over the Pacific. Also at the top is Trippet Ranch, a public facility providing water, rest rooms, and picnic tables. From Santa Monica, take the Pacific Coast Highway (Calif. 1) north. Turn right onto Sunset Boulevard, then left onto Palisades Drive. Continue for 2½ miles, turn left onto Verenda de la Montura, and park at the cul-de-sac at the end of the street, where you'll find the trailhead.

Temescal Canyon, in Pacific Palisades, is far easier than the Santa Ynez Trail and, predictably, far more popular with locals. It's one of the quickest routes into the wilderness. Hikes here are anywhere from 1 to 5 miles. From Santa Monica, take the Pacific Coast Highway (Calif. 1) north; turn right onto Temescal Canyon Road and follow it to the end. Sign in with the gatekeeper, who can also answer your questions.

Will Rogers State Historic Park, Pacific Palisades, is also a terrific place for hiking. An intermediate-level hike from the park's entrance ends at Inspiration Point, a plateau from which you can see a good portion of L.A.'s Westside. See "Parks" under "Exploring the City," above, for complete information.

Griffith Park (see "Parks," above) is an urban hiker's paradise. Explore this 100-year-old park and find spectacular vistas or privately tended little gardens; you can get a map of both paved roads and hiking trails at the ranger center 1 mile inside the Riverside Drive main entrance.

SKATING   The 22-mile-long Ocean Front Walk running from Pacific Palisades to Torrance is one of the premier skating spots in the country. In-line skating is especially popular, but conventionals are often seen here too. Roller skating is allowed just about everywhere bicycling is, but be aware that cyclists have the right-of-way. **Spokes 'n' Stuff,** 4175 Admiralty Way, Marina del Rey (☎ 310/306-3332), is just one of many places to rent wheels near the Venice portion of Ocean Front Walk. Skates cost $5 per hour; kneepads and wrist guards come with every rental.

TENNIS   You'll find mostly hard-surface courts in California. If your hotel doesn't have a court and can't suggest any courts nearby, try the well-maintained, well-lit **Griffith Park Tennis Courts,** on Commonwealth Road, just east of Vermont Avenue. Or call the **City of Los Angeles Department of Recreation and Parks** at ☎ 213/485-5555 to make a reservation at a municipal court near you.

11 The Shopping Scene

Here's a rundown of the primary shopping areas, along with descriptions of a few of their best stores. For a more complete guide to shopping, see *Frommer's Los Angeles.*

The **sales tax** in Los Angeles is 8¼%, but savvy out-of-state shoppers know to have more expensive items shipped directly home and save the tax.

SANTA MONICA & THE BEACHES

THIRD STREET PROMENADE (3RD STREET, FROM BROADWAY TO WILSHIRE BOULEVARD, SANTA MONICA)   Packed with chain stores and boutiques as well as dozens of restaurants and a large movie theater, Santa Monica's pedestrians-only section of 3rd Street is one of the most popular shopping areas in the city. The promenade bustles on into the evening with a seemingly endless assortment of street performers. Stores stay open late (often until 1 or 2am on the weekends) for the movie-going crowds. There's plenty of metered parking in structures on the adjacent streets, so bring lots of quarters! Highlights include **Hennessey & Ingalls,** 1254 Third Street Promenade (☎ 310/458-9074), a bookstore devoted to art and architecture, from magnificent coffee-table photography books to graphic-arts titles and obscure biographies of artists and art movements; **Midnight Special Bookstore,** 1318 Third Street Promenade (☎ 310/393-2923), a medium-size general bookshop known for its good small-press selection and regular poetry readings; **Na Na,** 1245

Third Street Promenade (☎ 310/394-9690), a funky clothing store featuring clunky shoes, knit hats, narrow-striped shirts, and baggy street wear; and **Puzzle Zoo,** 1413 Third Street Promenade (☎ 310/393-9201), voted "Best in L.A." by *Los Angeles* magazine. You'll find the double-sided World's Most Difficult Puzzle, the Puzzle in a Bottle, and collector's serial-numbered Ravensburger series, among others. Book lovers may also want to stop by the local **Barnes & Noble,** 1201 Third Street Promenade (☎ 310/260-9110), which carries thousands of titles.

MAIN STREET IN SANTA MONICA & VENICE (BETWEEN PICO BOULEVARD & ROSE AVENUE)   Another good strip for strolling, Main Street boasts a healthy combination of mall standards as well as upscale left-of-center boutiques. You'll also find plenty of casually hip cafes and restaurants. The primary strip connecting Santa Monica and Venice, Main Street has a relaxed beach-community vibe that sets it apart from similar strips. The stores straddle the fashion fence between upscale trendy and beach-bum edgy. A couple of highlights are **C. P. Shades,** 2925 Main St. (☎ 310/392-0949), a San Francisco ladies' clothier whose loose and comfy cotton and linen line is carried by many department stores and boutiques. Their trademark monochromatic neutrals are meticulously arranged in an airy well-lit store. **Horizons West,** 2011 Main St., south of Pico Boulevard (☎ 310/392-1122), sells brand-name surfboards, wet suits, leashes, magazines, waxes, lotions, and everything else you need to catch the perfect wave. Stop in and say "hi" to Randy and pick up a free tide table.

If you're looking for some truly sophisticated, finely crafted eye ware, friendly **Pepper's Eyeware,** 2904 Main St., between Ashland and Pier streets (☎ 310/ 392-0633), is for you. Ask for frames by cutting-edge L.A. designers Bada and Koh Sakai. If you're lucky enough to have perfect vision, consider some stylish shades. Outdoor types will get lost in 5,600-square-foot **Patagonia,** 2936 Main St. (☎ 310/ 314-1776), where climbers, surfers, skiers, and hikers can gear up in the functional colorful duds that put this environmentally friendly firm on the map.

MONTANA AVENUE IN SANTA MONICA (BETWEEN 7TH & 17TH STREETS)   This breezy stretch of slow-traffic Montana is one of my favorite regentrified parts of the city. OK, so it's gotten a lot more pricey than in the late 1970s, when tailors and Laundromats ruled the roost, but I'm just happy the specialty shops still outnumber the chains. Look around and you'll see upscale moms with strollers and cell phones shopping for designer fashions, country home decor, and gourmet takeout. Montana's biggest selling point is that it's still original enough for residents from across town to make a special trip to shop here, seeking out distinctive shops like **Shabby Chic,** 1013 Montana Ave. (☎ 310/394-1975), much-copied purveyor of slipcovered sofas and flea-market furnishings. Vintage-jewelry buffs keep coming back to **Brenda Cain,** 1211 Montana Ave. (☎ 310/395-1559), for platinum rings, bracelets, earrings, and brooches from the 1920s, while clotheshorses shop for designer wear at minimalist **Savannah,** 706 Montana Ave. (☎ 310/458-2095), ultrahip **Jill Roberts,** 920 Montana Ave. (☎ 310/260-1966), and sleekly professional **Weathervane,** 1209 Montana Ave. (☎ 310/393-5344).

Upscale moms can find tiny fashions at **Real Threads,** 1527 Montana Ave. (☎ 310/393-3175), and kid-sized bedroom furnishings at **Little Folk Art,** 1120 Montana Ave. (☎ 310/576-0909). For more grown-up style, head to **Ponte Vecchio,** 702 Montana Ave. (☎ 310/394-0989), for Italian hand-painted dishes and urns, or to **Cinzia,** 1129 Montana Ave. (☎ 310/393-7751), which features a smattering of both Tuscan and English home accessories. The stylish choice for lunch is **Wolfgang Puck Cafe,** 1323 Montana Ave. (☎ 310/393-0290). Main courses $8 to $12.

Dressing the Part—for Less

Admit it: You've dreamed of being a glamorous movie or TV star—everyone has. Well, you shouldn't expect to be "discovered" during your L.A. vacation, but you can live out your fantasy by dressing the part. Costumes from famous movies, TV-show wardrobes, castoffs from celebrity closets—they're easier to find (and more affordable to own) than you might think.

A good place to start is **Star Wares,** 2817 Main St., Santa Monica (☎ **310/399-0224;** open daily noon to 6pm). This deceptively small shop regularly has leftovers from Cher's closet, as well as celebrity-worn apparel from the likes of Joan Rivers, Tim Curry, and Kathleen Turner. It also stocks movie production wardrobes and genuine collector's items. If the $5,000 *Star Trek: The Next Generation* uniform or *Planet of the Apes* military regalia you covet is out of your price range, don't worry: You can still pick up one of Johnny Depp's *Benny and Joon* outfits, dresses from the closets of Lucille Ball and Greer Garson, or ET's bathrobe, all of which are surprisingly affordable. Many pieces have accompanying photos or movie stills, so you'll know exactly who donned your piece before you.

For sheer volume, you can't beat **It's a Wrap,** 3315 W. Magnolia Blvd., Burbank (☎ **818/567-7366;** open Mon through Sat 11am to 6pm, Sun 11am to 4pm). Every item is marked with its place of origin, and the list is staggering: *Beverly Hills, 90210; Melrose Place; Seinfeld; Baywatch; All My Children; Forrest Gump; The Brady Bunch Movie;* and so on. Many of these wardrobes (which include shoes and accessories) aren't outstanding but for their Hollywood origins: Jerry Seinfeld's trademark polo shirts, for instance, are standard mall issue. Some collectible pieces, like Sylvester Stallone's *Rocky* stars-and-stripes boxers, are framed and on display.

When you're done at It's a Wrap, stop in across the street at **Junk for Joy,** 3314 W. Magnolia Blvd., Burbank (☎ **818/569-4903;** open Tuesday through Friday 10am to 6pm, Saturday 11am to 6pm). A Hollywood wardrobe coordinator or two will probably be hunting through this wacky little store right beside you. The emphasis is on funky items more suitable as costumes than everyday wear (the store is mobbed each year around Halloween). At press time, they were loaded with 1970s polyester shirts and tacky slacks, but you never know what you'll find when you get there.

The grande dame of all wardrobe and costume outlets is **Western Costume,** 11041 Vanowen St., North Hollywood (☎ **818/760-0900;** open for rentals Monday through Friday 8am to 5:30pm, for sales Tuesday through to Friday 10am to 5pm). In business since 1912, Western Costume still designs and executes entire wardrobes for major motion pictures; when filming is finished, the garments are added to their staggering rental inventory. This place is perhaps best known for outfitting Vivien Leigh in *Gone with the Wind.* Several of Scarlett O'Hara's memorable gowns were even available for rent until they were recently auctioned off at a charity event. Western maintains an "outlet store" on the premises, where damaged garments are sold at rock-bottom (nothing over $15) prices. If you're willing to do some rescue work, there are definitely some hidden treasures here.

BERGAMOT STATION (2525 MICHIGAN AVE., SANTA MONICA)   Once a station for the Red Car trolley line, the industrial space of Bergamot Station (☎ 310/829-5854) is now home to the **Santa Monica Museum of Art,** plus two dozen art galleries, a cafe, a bookstore, and offices. Most of the galleries are closed Monday; the train yard is at the terminus of Michigan Avenue west of Cloverfield Boulevard.

Exhibits change often and vary widely, ranging from a Julius Shulman black-and-white photo retrospective of L.A.'s Case Study Houses, to a provocative exhibit of Vietnam War propaganda posters from the United States and Vietnam, to whimsical furniture constructed entirely of corrugated cardboard. A sampling of offerings includes the **Gallery of Functional Art** (☎ 310/829-6990), featuring one-of-a-kind and limited-edition furniture, lighting, bathroom fixtures, and other functional art pieces, as well as smaller items like jewelry, flatware, ceramics, and glass. The **Rosamund Felson Gallery** (☎ 310/828-8488) is well known for showcasing L.A.–based contemporary artists; this is a good place to get a taste of current trends. And **Track 16 Gallery** (☎ 310/264-4678) has exhibits ranging from pop art to avant-garde inventiveness—try to see what's going on here.

L.A.'S WESTSIDE & BEVERLY HILLS

WEST 3RD STREET (BETWEEN FAIRFAX AVENUE & ROBERTSON BOULEVARD)   You can shop 'till you drop on this trendy strip, anchored on the east end by the Farmers Market (see "The Top Attractions," above). Many of Melrose Avenue's shops have relocated here, alongside some terrific up-and-comers and several cafes. *Fun* is more the catchword here than *funky,* and the shops (including the vintage-clothing stores) tend a bit more to the refined than do those along Melrose; you'd never find upscale bookshops dedicated to travel tomes and cookbooks in that neck of the woods—but you will here. The **Cook's Library,** 8373 W. 3rd St. (☎ 323/655-3141), is where the city's top chefs find both classic and deliciously offbeat cookbooks and other food-oriented tomes. Browsing is welcomed, even encouraged, with tea, tasty treats, and rocking chairs. **Traveler's Bookcase,** 8375 W. 3rd St. (☎ 323/655-0575), is truly one of the best travel-book shops in the West, stocking a huge selection of guidebooks and travel literature, as well as maps and travel accessories. A quarterly newsletter chronicles the travel adventures of the genial owners, who know firsthand the most helpful items to carry. Borders Books & Music has a branch at 330 S. La Cienga Blvd., at Third Street (☎ 310/659-4045).

There's lot's more to see along this always-growing street, enough to take up several hours. Refuel at ✪ **Chado Tea Room,** 8422 W. 3rd St. (☎ 323/655-2056), a temple for tea lovers. Chado is designed with a nod to Paris's renowned Mariage Frères purveyor; one wall is lined with nooks whose recognizable brown tins are filled with over 250 varieties of tea from around the world. Among the choices are 15 kinds of Darjeeling, Indian teas blended with rose petals, and ceremonial Chinese and Japanese blends. They also serve tea meals featuring delightful sandwiches and individual pots of any loose tea in the store.

SUNSET STRIP (BETWEEN LA CIENEGA BOULEVARD & DOHENY DRIVE, WEST HOLLYWOOD)   The monster-size billboards advertising the latest rock god make it clear this is rock 'n' roll territory. So it makes sense you'll find legendary **Tower Records,** 8801 W. Sunset Blvd. (☎ 310/657-7300), in the heart of the action. Tower insists it has L.A.'s largest selection of CDs—over 125,000 titles—despite the Virgin Megastore's contrary claim. Even if Virgin has more, Tower's collection tends to be more interesting and browser friendly. And the shop's enormous blues, jazz, and classical selections are definitely greater than the competition's. At the east end of the strip sits the gigantic **Virgin Megastore,** 8000 Sunset Blvd., at Crescent Heights (☎ 323/650-8666). Some 100 CD "listening posts" and an in-store "radio station" make this a music lover's paradise. Virgin claims to stock 150,000 titles, including an extensive collection of hard-to-find artists.

The "Strip" is lined with trendy restaurants, industry-oriented hotels, and dozens of shops offering outrageous fashions and chunky stage accessories. One anomaly is **Sunset Plaza,** an upscale cluster of Georgian-style shops resembling Beverly Hills at its snootiest. Here's where you'll find **Billy Martin's,** 8605 Sunset Blvd. (☎ 310/289-5000), founded by the legendary Yankee manager in 1978. This chic men's Western shop—complete with fireplace and leather sofa—stocks hand-forged silver and gold belt buckles, Lucchese and Liberty boots, and stable staples like flannel shirts. **Book Soup,** 8818 Sunset Blvd. (☎ 310/659-3110), has long been one of L.A.'s most celebrated bookshops, selling both mainstream and small-press books and hosting regular book signings and author nights. A great browsing shop, it has a large selection of showbiz books and an extensive outdoor news-and-magazine stand on one side. The Book Soup Bistro offers an appealing bar, a charming outdoor patio, and an extensive traditional bistro menu catering to hungry intellectuals.

LA BREA AVENUE (NORTH OF WILSHIRE BOULEVARD)   This is L.A.'s artsiest shopping strip. Anchored by the giant **American Rag, Cie.** alterna-complex, 150 S. La Brea Ave. (☎ 323/935-3157), La Brea is home to lots of great urban antique stores dealing in deco, arts and crafts, 1950s modern, and the like. You'll also find vintage clothiers, furniture galleries, and other warehouse-size stores, as well as some of the city's hippest restaurants, such as Campanile.

Bargain hunters can find flea-market furnishings at **Nick Metropolis,** 100 S. La Brea Ave. (☎ 323/934-3700), while the more upscale seeker of home decor should head to **Mortise & Tenon,** 446 S. La Brea Ave. (☎ 323/937-7654), where handcrafted heavy wood pieces sit next to overstuffed velvet-upholstered sofas and even vintage steel desks. The best place for a snack is Nancy Silverton's **La Brea Bakery,** 624 S. La Brea Ave. (☎ 323/939-6813), which foodies know from gourmet markets and the attached Campanile restaurant (see "Great Deals on Dining," above). Though the art of millinery often seems to have gone the way of white afternoon gloves for ladies, inventive ✪ **Drea Kadilak,** 463 S. La Brea Ave., at Sixth Street (☎ 323/931-2051), charms with her tiny hat shop. Designing in straw, cotton duck, wool felt, and a number of more unusual fabrics, she does her own blocking, will cheerfully take measurements for ladies' custom head wear, is reasonably priced, and gives away signature hatboxes with your purchase.

Stuffed to the rafters with hardware and fixtures of the last 100 years, **Liz's Antique Hardware,** 453 S. La Brea Ave. (☎ 323/939-4403), thoughtfully keeps a canister of wet-wipes at the register—believe me, you'll need one after sifting through bags and crates of doorknobs, latches, finials, and any other home hardware you can imagine needing. Perfect sets of Bakelite drawer pulls and antique ceramic bathroom fixtures are some of the more intriguing items. Be prepared to browse for hours, whether you're redecorating or not! They might be single-handedly responsible for bringing back Hush Puppies, and **The Swell Store,** 126 N. La Brea Ave. (☎ 323/937-2096), stocks every configuration and shade of these hip-again suede retro loafers. There's also a respectable collection of coordinatingly trendy clothing for men and women.

RODEO DRIVE & BEVERLY HILLS'S GOLDEN TRIANGLE (SANTA MONICA BOULEVARD, WILSHIRE BOULEVARD & CRESCENT DRIVE)
Everyone knows about Rodeo Drive, the city's most famous shopping street. Couture shops from high fashion's Old Guard are located along these three hallowed blocks,

along with plenty of newer high-end labels. And there are two examples of the Beverly Hills version of minimalls, albeit more insular and attractive—the **Rodeo Collection,** 421 N. Rodeo Dr., and **Two Rodeo,** at Wilshire Boulevard. The 16-square-block area surrounding Rodeo Drive is known as the "Golden Triangle." Shops off Rodeo are generally not as name-conscious as those on the strip (you might actually be able to buy something!), but they're nevertheless plenty upscale. Little Santa Monica Boulevard has a particularly colorful line of specialty stores, and Brighton Way is as young and hip as relatively staid Beverly Hills gets.

The big names to look for here are **Giorgio Beverly Hills,** 327 N. Rodeo Dr. (☎ 800/GIORGIO or 310/274-0200); **Gucci,** 347 N. Rodeo Dr. (☎ 310/278-3451); **Hermès,** 343 N. Rodeo Dr. (☎ 310/278-6440); **Louis Vuitton,** 307 N. Rodeo Dr. (☎ 310/859-0457); **Polo/Ralph Lauren,** 444 N. Rodeo Dr. (☎ 310/281-7200); and **Tiffany & Co.,** 210 N. Rodeo Dr. (☎ 310/273-8880). The newest arrival is **Tommy Hilfiger,** 468 N. Rodeo Dr. (☎ 310/888-0132). **Niketown,** at the corner of Wilshire Boulevard and Rodeo Drive (☎ 310/275-9998), is a behemoth shrine to the reigning athletic-gear king.

BEVERLY BOULEVARD (FROM ROBERTSON BOULEVARD TO LA BREA AVENUE)   Though these businesses are too far apart to be considered adjacent, they're representative of the variety you'll find along this stylish street.

Every Picture Tells a Story, 7525 Beverly Blvd., between Fairfax and La Brea avenues (☎ 323/932-6070), is a gallery devoted to the art of children's literature, displaying antique children's books as well as the works of over 100 illustrators, including lithos of *Curious George, Eloise,* and *Charlotte's Web.* Whether you're indulging your inner child or introducing your kids to their first "art gallery," you'll also enjoy the story readings and interactive workshops. Across from Cedars-Sinai Medical Center, the **Mysterious Bookshop,** 8763 Beverly Blvd. (☎ 310/659-2959), carries over 20,000 used, rare, and out-of-print titles in the field of mystery, espionage, detective stories, and thrillers. Author appearances and other special events are regularly hosted. If you can name more than three tenors, then pleasantly cluttered **Opera Shop of Los Angeles,** 8384 Beverly Blvd., 3 blocks east of La Cienega Boulevard (☎ 323/658-5811), is for you. Everything imaginable is available with an opera theme: musical motif jewelry, stationery, T-shirts, opera glasses (of course!), plus tapes, videos, and CDs of your favorite productions.

If you complain they just don't make 'em like they used to . . . well, they do at **Re-Mix,** 7605½ Beverly Blvd., between Fairfax and La Brea avenues (☎ 323/936-6210). Selling only vintage (1940s to 1970s) but brand-new (as in unworn) shoes for men and women, it's more like a shoe-store museum featuring wing tips, Hush Puppies, Joan Crawford pumps, and 1970s platforms. A rackful of unworn vintage socks all display their original tags and stickers, and the prices are downright reasonable. Celebrity hipsters and hep cats from Madonna to Roseanne are often spotted here. Other vintage wares are found at **Second Time Around Watch Co.,** 8840 Beverly Blvd., west of Robertson Boulevard (☎ 310/271-6615): The city's best selection of collectible timepieces includes dozens of classic Tiffanys, Cartiers, Piagets, and Rolexes, plus rare pocket watches. Priced for collectors, but a fascinating browse for the Swatch crowd too.

HOLLYWOOD

MELROSE AVENUE (BETWEEN FAIRFAX & LA BREA AVENUES)   It's showing some wear—some stretches have become downright ugly—but this is still one of the most exciting shopping streets in the country for cutting-edge fashions—and some eye-popping people-watching to boot. There are scores of shops selling the latest in clothes, gifts, jewelry, and accessories. Melrose is a playful stroll, dotted with plenty of hip restaurants and funky shops that are sure to shock. Where else could you find green patent-leather cowboy boots, a working 19th-century pocket watch, an inflatable girlfriend, and glow-in-the-dark condoms in the same shopping spree? From east to west, here are some highlights:

Condomania, 7306 Melrose Ave. (☎ 323/933-7865), is quintessentially 1990s: A vast selection of condoms, lubricants, and kits creatively encourage safe sex. Curious? Check out their Internet site at www.condomania.com. **Retail Slut,** 7308 Melrose Ave. (☎ 323/934-1339), is a famous rock shop carrying new clothing and accessories for men and women. The unique designs are for a select crowd (the name says it all), so don't expect to find anything for your next PTA meeting here. **Betsey Johnson Boutique,** 7311 Melrose Ave. (☎ 323/931-4490), is a favorite among the young and pencil-thin; the New York–based designer has brought her brand of fashion—trendy, cutesy, body-conscious women's wear in colorful prints and faddish fabrics—to L.A. Also in Santa Monica at 2929 Main St. (☎ 310/452-7911).

Across the street, **Off the Wall,** 7325 Melrose Ave. (☎ 323/930-1185), is filled with neon-flashing, bells-and-whistles kitsch collectibles, from vintage Wurlitzer jukeboxes to life-size fiberglass cows. The L.A. branch of a Bay Area hipster hangout, **Wasteland,** 7428 Melrose Ave. (☎ 323/653-3028), has an enormous steel-sculpted facade. There's a lot of leather, denim, and some classic vintage—but mostly funky 1970s garb, both vintage and contemporary. This ultra-trendy store is packed with the flamboyantly colorful polyester halters and bell-bottoms from the decade some of us would rather forget. More racks of vintage treasures (and trash) are found at **Aardvark's Odd Ark,** 7579 Melrose Ave. (☎ 323/655-6769). They stock everything, from suits and dresses to neckties, hats, handbags, and jewelry. And they manage to anticipate some of the hottest new street fashions. There's another Aardvark's at 85 Market St., Venice (☎ 310/392-2996).

HOLLYWOOD BOULEVARD (BETWEEN GOWER STREET & LA BREA AVENUE)   One of Los Angeles's most famous streets is, for the most part, a sleazy strip. But along the Walk of Fame, between the T-shirt shops and greasy pizza parlors, you'll find some excellent poster shops, souvenir stores, and Hollywood-memorabilia dealers that are worth getting out of your car for—especially if there's a chance of getting your hands on that long-sought-after Ethel Merman autograph or 200 Motels poster. Some longstanding purveyors of memorabilia are **Book City Collectibles,** 6631 Hollywood Blvd. (☎ 323/466-0120), which has more than 70,000 color prints of past and present stars available, along with a good selection of autographs from the likes of Lucille Ball ($175), Anthony Hopkins ($35), and Grace Kelly ($750); and **Hollywood Book and Poster Company,** 6349 Hollywood Blvd. (☎ 323/465-8764), whose excellent collection of movie posters (from about $15 each) is particularly strong in horror and exploitation flicks. Photocopies of about 5,000 movie and TV scripts are also sold for $10 to $15 each, and the store also carries music posters and photos; and **The Last Moving Picture Company,** 6307 Hollywood Blvd., near Vine Street (☎ 323/467-0838), which sells movie-related merchandise of all kinds, including stills from 1950s movies and authentic production notes from a variety of films.

SILVER LAKE & LOS FELIZ   Located at the eastern end of Hollywood and technically part of just plain Los Angeles, these two communities have been steadily rising on the hipness meter. Silver Lake, named for the manmade Silver Lake reservoir at its center, is a bohemian community of artists and ethnic families that's popular for nightclubbing and bar-hopping. Los Feliz is northwest of Silver Lake, centered on Vermont and Hillhurst avenues between Sunset Boulevard and Los Feliz Boulevard; it's slightly tamer and filled with 1920s and 1930s buildings. You'll find tons of unique businesses of all sorts, including artsy boutiques, music stores, and furniture dealers that've inspired some to compare the area with New York's SoHo.

Many alternative bands call Silver Lake home, so it's not surprising to find cutting-edge music stores around every corner. A neighborhood mainstay with tons of used CDs, collectible discs, and new releases is **Rockaway Records,** 2395 Glendale Blvd., south of Silver Lake Boulevard (☎ **323/664-3232**); **Destroy All Music,** 3818 Sunset Blvd., south of Santa Monica Boulevard (☎ **323/663-9300**), covers all punk bases, from hard-core to ska, indie, and lo-fi. Vintage clothing is another big draw in these parts: The most reliable yet eclectic selections to browse through are at **Ozzie Dots,** 4637 Hollywood Blvd., west of Hillhurst (☎ **323/663-2867**); **Pull My Daisy,** 3908 Sunset Blvd., at Griffith Park Boulevard (☎ **323/663-0608**); and **Squaresville,** 1800 N. Vermont Ave., south of Franklin (☎ **323/669-8464**).

Hollywood set designers know to prowl the vintage-furniture stores of Silver Lake: The best for midcentury modern gems are **Edna Hart,** 2945 Rowena Ave., south of Hyperion (☎ **323/661-4070**), and **Rubbish,** 1630 Silver Lake Blvd., north of Sunset (☎ **323/661-5575**). Plastic decorative items from the 1950s on reign at the aptly named **Plastica,** 4685 Hollywood Blvd., east of Hillhurst (☎ **323/644-1212**), while ethnic and international furniture, gifts, and clothing blend in the browsers' paradise of **Sol e Luna,** 2910 Rowena Ave., south of Hyperion (☎ **323/664-7254**). One not-to-be-missed neighborhood highlight is the wacky and eclectic **Soap Plant/Wacko/ La Luz de Jesus Art Gallery,** 4633 Hollywood Blvd., west of Hillhurst (☎ **323/ 663-0122**), a three-in-one business with candles, art books, erotic toys, soap and bath items, and a large selection of lava lamps.

DOWNTOWN

Since the lamented grande dame department store Bullock's closed in 1993 (its deco masterpiece salons were rescued to house the Southwestern Law School's library), downtown has become even less of a shopping destination than ever. Though many of the once-splendid streets are lined with cut-rate-luggage and cheap-electronics storefronts, shopping downtown can be a rewarding if gritty experience for the adventuresome. Savvy Angelenos still go for bargains in the garment and fabric districts, florists and bargain hunters arrive at the vast Flower Mart before dawn for the city's best selection of fresh blooms, and families of all ethnicities stroll the ✪ **Grand Central Market,** 317 S. Broadway, between 3rd and 4th streets (☎ **213/624-2378**). Opened in 1917, this bustling market has watched the face of downtown L.A. change while changing little itself. Today it serves Latino families, enterprising restaurateurs, and home cooks in search of unusual ingredients and bargain-priced fruits and vegetables. On weekends you'll be greeted by a lively mariachi band at the Hill Street entrance, near my favorite market feature—the fruit-juice counter, which dispenses 20 fresh varieties from wall spigots and blends up the tastiest, healthiest "shakes" in town. Farther into the market you'll find produce sellers and prepared-food counters, plus spice vendors who seem straight out of a Turkish alley and a grain-and-bean seller who'll scoop out dozens of exotic rices and dried legumes.

THE SAN FERNANDO VALLEY

Technically an outdoor mall rather than a shopping area, **Universal CityWalk** (☎ **818/622-4455**) gets mention here because it's so utterly unique. A pedestrian promenade next door to Universal Studios, CityWalk is dominated by brightly colored, outrageously surreal, oversize storefronts. The heavily touristed faux street is home to an inordinate number of restaurants, including B. B. King's Blues Club, the newest Hard Rock Cafe, and a branch of the Hollywood Athletic Club featuring a restaurant and pool hall. This is consumer culture gone haywire, an egotistical eyesore not worth a special visit unless you have the kids in tow—they'll love it.

PASADENA & ENVIRONS

Compared to L.A.'s behemoth shopping malls, the streets of pretty, compact Pasadena are a true pleasure to stroll. As a general rule, stores are open daily from about 10am, and while some close at the standard 5 or 6pm, many stay open until 8 or 9pm to accommodate the before- and after-dinner/movie crowd.

OLD PASADENA (CENTERED AROUND THE INTERSECTION OF COLORADO BOULEVARD & FAIR OAKS AVENUE)   In my opinion, Old Pasadena is some of the best shopping in L.A., but I hope they retain more of the mom-and-pop businesses currently being pushed out by the likes of Banana Republic and Crate & Barrel. As you move east, the mix begins to include more eclectic shops and galleries commingling with dusty pre-yuppie relics.

At the contemporary craft gallery **Del Mano,** 33 E. Colorado Blvd. (☎ **626/ 793-6648**), it's a whole lot of fun to see the creations—some whimsical, some exquisite—of American artists working with glass, wood, ceramics, or jewelry. Across the street, **Penny Lane,** 12 W. Colorado Blvd. (☎ **626/564-0161**), carries new and used CDs, plus a great selection of music magazines and kitschy postcards. The stock is less picked-over here than at many record stores in Hollywood. Travelers always seem to find something they need at **Distant Lands Bookstore and Outfitters,** 54 and 62 S. Raymond Ave. (☎ **626/449-3220**), a duo of related stores. The bookstore has a terrific selection of maps, guides, and travel-related literature, while the recently opened outfitters two doors away offers everything from luggage and pith helmets to space-saving and convenient travel accessories. An Old Town mainstay is **Rebecca's Dream,** 16 S. Fair Oaks Ave. (☎ **626/796-1200**), where men and women can find vintage-clothing treasures. The store is small and meticulously organized (by color scheme); be sure to look up at the vintage hats adorning the walls.

OTHER PASADENA SHOPPING   In addition to Old Town Pasadena, there are numerous good hunting grounds in the surrounding area. Antique hounds might want to head to the **Green Street Antique Row,** 985–1005 E. Green St., east of Lake Avenue; or the **Pasadena Antique Center,** on South Fair Oaks Boulevard south of Del Mar. Each has a rich concentration of collectibles that can captivate for hours.

You never know what you'll find at the **Rose Bowl Flea Market,** at the Rose Bowl, 991 Rosemont Ave., Pasadena (☎ **626/577-3100**). Built in 1922, the horseshoe-shaped Rose Bowl is one of the world's most famous stadiums, home to UCLA's football Bruins, the annual Rose Bowl Game, and an occasional Super Bowl. California's largest monthly swap meet, on the 2nd Sunday of every month from 9am to 3pm, is a favorite of L.A. antique hounds (who know to arrive as early as 6am for the best finds). Antique furnishings, clothing, jewelry, and other collectibles are assembled in the parking area to the left of the entrance, while the rest of the flea market surrounds the exterior of the Bowl. Expect everything from used surfboards and car stereos to one-of-a-kind lawn statuary and bargain athletic shoes. Admission is $5 after 9am (early-bird admission $10 to $15).

STORES WORTH SEEKING OUT ELSEWHERE IN THE CITY

There's a great selection of recorded music at ✪ **Rhino Records,** 1720 Westwood Blvd., Westwood (☎ **310/474-8685**), L.A.'s premier alternative shop; it specializes in new artists and independent-label releases. In addition to new releases, there's a terrific used selection; this is where record-industry types come to trade in the records they don't want for the records they do, so you'll be able to find never-played promotional copies of brand-new releases at half the retail price. You'll also find the definitive collection of records on the Rhino label. If you're feeling wanderlust—or just plain lost— check out **California Map and Travel Center,** 3312 Pico Blvd., Santa Monica (☎ **310/396-6277**). As the name says, this store carries a good selection of domestic and international maps and travel accessories, including guides for hiking, biking, and touring. Globes and atlases are also sold. Visit them online at **www.mapper.com.**

12 Los Angeles After Dark

With additional research by Bryan Yates

The *L.A. Weekly* (www.laweekly.com), a free weekly paper available at sidewalk stands, shops, and restaurants, is the best place to find out what's going on about town, especially for club happenings. The "Calendar" section of the *Los Angeles Times* (www.calendarlive.com) is also a good place to find out what's going on after dark.

For weekly updates on music, art, dance, theater, special events, and festivals, call the **Cultural Affairs Hotline** at ☎ **323/688-ARTS,** a 24-hour directory listing a wide variety of events, most of which are free.

Ticketmaster (☎ **323/480-3232**) and **Telecharge** (☎ **800/447-7400**) are the major charge-by-phone agencies in the city, selling tickets to concerts, sporting events, plays, and special events.

THEATER

MAJOR THEATERS & COMPANIES   The Ahmanson Theater and Mark Taper Forum, the city's top two playhouses, are both part of the all-purpose **Music Center,** 135 N. Grand Ave., downtown. The **Ahmanson Theater** (☎ **213/972-7401**) reopened in 1995 after a $71-million renovation that improved acoustics and seating. This theater is active year-round, with shows produced by the in-house Center Theater Group or with traveling Broadway productions. Each season has a guaranteed handful of high-profile shows, ranging from a musical about the *Titanic* to the Pulitzer- and Tony-winning *Rent.* A recent highlight was the Olivier Award–winning (and slightly controversial) Mathew Bourne production of *Swan Lake,* which featured contemporary settings and *male* swans. The Ahmanson is so huge you'll want seats in the front third or half of the theater.

The **Mark Taper Forum** (☎ **213/972-0700**) is a more intimate circular theater staging contemporary works by international and local playwrights. Kenneth Branagh's Renaissance Theatre Company staged their only American productions of *King Lear* and *A Midsummer Night's Dream* at the Mark Taper, to give you an idea of the quality of the shows. I also saw a respectable production of Tom Stoppard's complex and highbrow comedy *Arcadia.* Productions are usually excellent, run with plenty of spirit and no shortage of controversy.

Ticket prices vary depending on the performance. Discounted tickets are usually available on the day of performance for students and seniors.

Big-time traveling troupes and Broadway-bound musicals that don't go to the Ahmanson head instead for the **Shubert Theater,** in the ABC Entertainment Center, 2020 Avenue of the Stars, Century City (☎ **800/233-3123**). This plush playhouse presents major musicals on the scale of *Sunset Boulevard* and *Les Misérables.* Highlights from 1998 included the musical adaptation of E. L. Doctorow's *Ragtime* and the West Coast premiere of the Bob Fosse tribute *Chicago.*

Getting Half-Price Theater Tickets

Tickets for most plays usually cost $10 to $35, though performances of big-name shows at the major theaters can fetch up to $50 to $60 for the best seats. **Theatre LA,** an association of live theaters and producers in Los Angeles (and the organization that puts on the L.A. version of Broadway's Tony Awards), operates a half-price ticket booth in the Beverly Center. Modeled after New York's successful TKTS, **Times Tix** (☎ **310/659-3678**) is open Monday through Friday from 10am to 9pm, Saturday from 10am to 8pm, and Sunday from 11am to 6pm; tickets are sold on a walk-up basis only. You can get more information online at **www. TheatreLA.org.**

Across town, the moderately sized **Geffen Playhouse,** 10886 Le Conte Ave., Westwood (☎ **310/208-5454;** www.geffen.ucla.edu), presents dramatic and comedic productions by prominent and always cutting-edge writers. Formerly the Westwood Playhouse but renamed for philanthropic entertainment mogul David Geffen, this charming theater is often the West Coast choice of many acclaimed off-Broadway shows; the theater also attracts locally based TV and movie actors eager for the immediacy of stage work. A recent highlight featured Sam Shepard in *Cruising Paradise,* a one-man evening of readings from Shepard's plays and books. Always audience-friendly, the Playhouse prices tickets around $25 to $38.

For a current schedule at any of the above theaters, check the listings in *Los Angeles* magazine or the "Calendar" section of the Sunday *Los Angeles Times,* or call the box offices directly at the numbers listed above.

SMALLER PLAYHOUSES   Like New York's off-Broadway or London's fringe, Los Angeles's small-scale theaters often outdo the slick high-budget shows. Because this is Tinseltown, movie and TV stars sometimes headline, but more often than not, the talent is up-and-coming. Who knows—the unknown on stage today might be the next David Duchovny tomorrow.

The **Colony Studio Theatre,** 1944 Riverside Dr., Silver Lake (☎ **323/665-3011;** www.colonytheatre.org), boasts an excellent resident company that has played in this air-conditioned, 99-seat, converted silent-movie house for over 20 years; **Actors Circle Theater,** 7313 Santa Monica Blvd., West Hollywood (☎ **323/882-8043**), is a 47-seater that's as acclaimed as it is tiny; and the **Los Angeles Theater,** 615 S. Broadway (☎ **213/629-2939**), is a grand movie palace recently converted to live theater.

One of the most highly acclaimed professional theaters in L.A., the **Pasadena Playhouse,** 35 S. El Molino Ave., near Colorado Boulevard, Pasadena (☎ **626/356-7529**), is a registered historic landmark that's served as the training ground for many theatrical, film, and TV stars, including William Holden and Gene Hackman. Productions are staged on the main theater's elaborate Spanish-colonial-revival stage.

CLASSICAL MUSIC & OPERA

Beyond the pop realms, music in Los Angeles generally falls short of that found in other cities. For the most part, Angelenos rely on visiting orchestras and companies to fulfill their classical-music appetites; scan the papers to find out who's playing and dancing while you're in the city.

The **Los Angeles Philharmonic** (☎ **323/850-2000**) isn't just the city's top symphony; it's the only major classical-music company in Los Angeles. Finnish-born music director Esa-Pekka Salonen concentrates on contemporary compositions;

despite complaints from traditionalists, he does an excellent job attracting younger audiences. Tickets can be hard to come by when celebrity players like Itzak Perlman, Isaac Stern, Emanuel Ax, or Yo-Yo Ma are in town. In addition to regular performances at the Music Center's **Dorothy Chandler Pavilion,** 135 N. Grand Ave., downtown, the Philharmonic also plays a popular summer season at the **Hollywood Bowl** (see "Concerts Under the Stars," below). Tickets, which regularly run $10 to $60, are discounted 50% at the box office on the day of the show when a large number go unsold. Call after 10am the day of the performance to check on availability.

Slowly but surely, the **L.A. Opera** (☎ 213/972-8001) is gaining both respect and popularity with inventive stagings of classic operas, usually with guest divas. The Opera, which also calls the Music Center home, offers "rush" tickets at $15 (regularly $23 to $130) for students and seniors 65 and over. They can be purchased at the box office (cash only), beginning an hour before the performance.

CONCERTS UNDER THE STARS
✪ **Hollywood Bowl.** 2301 N. Highland Ave. (at Odin St.), Hollywood. ☎ **323/850-2000.**

Built in the early 1920s, the Hollywood Bowl is an elegant Greek-style natural outdoor amphitheater cradled in a small mountain canyon. This is the summer home of the Los Angeles Philharmonic Orchestra; internationally known conductors and soloists often sit in on Tuesday and Thursday nights. Friday and Saturday concerts often feature orchestral swing or pops. The summer season also includes a jazz series; past performers have included Natalie Cole, Mel Torme, Dionne Warwick, and Chick Corea. Other events, from Tom Petty concerts to an annual Mariachi Festival, are often on the season's schedule. Ticket prices vary widely; while prime box seats (which are usually filled with season subscribers anyway) can be as high as $90, seats on the farthest benches are often only $3; there are numerous price levels in between.

LIVE-MUSIC CLUBS
Let's face it: Los Angeles is more or less the center of the entertainment industry. So finding something to satisfy any musical fancy on any given night can be a snap. From acoustic rock to jazz fusion, from Judas Priest cover bands to Latin funk, from the up-and-coming to the already gone, L.A. has it all. The best way to see what's up with the music scene, of course, is to check *LA Weekly* or the "Calendar" in Sunday's *Los Angeles Times.*

In addition to the venues below, which are popular as attractions in their own right, there are several distinctly L.A. concert venues worth visiting if someone on the bill appeals to you: The alfresco **John Anson Ford Theatre,** 2580 Cahuenga Blvd. E., Hollywood (☎ 323/461-3673), is across the Cahuenga pass from the more highbrow Hollywood Bowl but features an eclectic mix of jazz, folk, and international music plus dance and family events; numerous significant alternative rock shows—including key appearances by Smashing Pumpkins and Garbage—take place at the vaudeville-era **Palace,** 1735 N. Vine St., Hollywood (☎ 323/467-4571), which doubles as a late-night dance club; the carefully restored **Wiltern Theatre,** 3790 Wilshire Blvd., Los Angeles (☎ 323/380-5005), is a WPA-era art-deco showplace that has hosted countless national and international acts, from Penn and Teller to Radiohead.

Bar Deluxe. 1710 N. Las Palmas Ave., Hollywood. ☎ **323/469-1991.** Cover $5–$7.

This is the club to go to when you're looking for a hassle-free, no-lines affair. This dimly lit, black and red, voodoo-meets-hoodoo haven specializes in surf, blues, and rockabilly bands and is as comfortable as an old pair of Doc Martens.

Hollywood Bowl Tip

It's not widely known, but the Bowl's morning rehearsals are open to the public and absolutely free. On Tuesday, Thursday, and Friday from 9:30am to 12:30pm, you can see the program scheduled for that evening. So grab some coffee and donuts (it's strictly bring-your-own) and enjoy the best seats in the house!

B. B. King's Blues Club. CityWalk, Universal City. ☎ **818/622-5464.** Ticket prices vary.

B. B. King's is a bit more "real" than the House of Blues (below). Its three-floor seating area (resembling an old Southern club) is tastefully decorated, the music stays closer to authentic blues, and the ribs are terrific.

Doug Weston's Troubadour. 9081 Santa Monica Blvd., West Hollywood. ☎ **310/276-6168.** Cover varies.

The Troubadour has worked long and hard to shed its creepy 1980s spandex-'n'-big-hair image, and it's emerged vibrant and vigorous once again. Turning 42 in 1999, the club counts the Byrds and the Eagles among the bands that virtually formed here, and even in the metal years saw Mötley Crüe and others rise to the big time. Today the Troub can be counted on for excellent sound and a wide array of up-and-coming break-out bands and already made-its.

House of Blues. 8430 Sunset Blvd., West Hollywood. ☎ **323/848-5100.** Ticket prices vary.

Despite its Disneyland-ish decor, this club—co-owned by some really strange bedfellows, including Hard Rock–founder Isaac Tigrett, Jim Belushi, Dan Ackroyd, Aerosmith, and Harvard University—does earnestly honor its namesake music with informative displays and a wealth of colorful folk art. Still, it's permeated with Industry types more interested in being seen than seeing and hearing the music. Even so, there's enough top-notch music here to keep many who routinely bad-mouth the place coming back, and the food in the upstairs restaurant can be superb (reservations are a must).

Jack's Sugar Shack. 1707 Vine St., Hollywood. ☎ **323/466-7005.** Cover varies.

Jack doesn't mess around. The *Gilligan's Island* meets *Love Boat* decor combined with a select booking policy makes this nightclub a tasty treat. Less interested in trends than in quality music, Jack's books national and local blues, country-and-western, and alternative music and is the current host to Ronnie Mack's Barndance, an always free Tuesday affair of alternative country music.

Jazz Bakery. 3233 Helms Ave., Los Angeles. ☎ **310/271-9039.** Cover $10–$20.

Ruth Price's nonprofit venue is renowned for attracting some of the most important names in jazz—and for the restored Helms bakery factory that houses the club and inspires its name. Hers is a no-frills, all-about-the-music affair, and the place is pretty much B.Y.O. in the drinks department.

Lava Lounge. 1533 La Brea Ave., Hollywood. ☎ **323/876-6612.** Cover varies.

Described by its lovely owner, a former set decorator, as a "Vegas in hell" motif, the interior of this small bar/performance space, located in a très-ugly strip mall, is very inventive. Think ticky-tacky coupled with big-city chic. Live music includes jazz and surfabilly, and live regulars include Quentin Tarantino.

LunaPark. 665 N. Robertson Blvd., West Hollywood. ☎ **310/652-0611.** Cover varies, usually around $10.

Late-Night Bites

After-hours snacking is getting easier in L.A., as each year sees more 24-hour eateries join the culinary landscape. There are also plenty of places serving past midnight, and here's a rundown of my favorites:

The Apple Pan, 10801 W. Pico Blvd., West Los Angeles (☎ 310/475-3585), is a classic American burger shack, an L.A. landmark that hasn't changed much since opening in 1947—and the burgers and pie still hit the spot. See "Great Deals on Dining," above, for more information. A 24-hour Jewish deli that's been a hit with late-nighters since it opened more than 65 years ago, **Canter's Restaurant & Bakery,** 419 N. Fairfax Ave., Los Angeles (☎ 323/651-2030), feeds the need after the clubs close. You're sure to spot a bleary-eyed celebrity or two alongside the rest of the after-hours crowd, chowing down on a giant pastrami sandwich, matzoh-ball soup, potato pancakes, or another deli favorite. Try a potato knish with a side of brown gravy—trust me, you'll love it.

During the week, **Du-par's Coffee Shop,** 12036 Ventura Blvd., 1 block east of Laurel Canyon, Studio City (☎ 818/766-4437), probably isn't the place to go; they serve blue-plate specials only until 1am. However, come the weekend, they sling hash until 4am. See "Great Deals on Dining," above. **Jerry's Famous Deli,** 12655 Ventura Blvd., at Coldwater Canyon Boulevard, Studio City (☎ 818/980-4245), is where Valley hipsters go to relieve their late-night munchies. See "Great Deals on Dining," above.

Kate Mantilini, 9101 Wilshire Blvd., at Doheny Drive, Beverly Hills (☎ 310/278-3699), serves stylish nouveau comfort food in a striking setting. See "Great Deals on Dining," above. Straight from an episode of *Happy Days,* **Mel's Drive-In,** 8585 Sunset Blvd., west of La Cienega, West Hollywood (☎ 310/854-7200), is a 24-hour 1950s diner on the Sunset Strip, attracting customers ranging from chic shoppers during the day to rock-'n'-rollers at night; the fries and shakes are among the best in town.

✪ **Operetta,** 8223 W. 3rd St., near Harper Street, Los Angeles (☎ 323/852-7000), is a 24-hour French bakery/cafe that's a welcome sight to L.A. night owls; even though the kitchen stops serving sandwiches and other light fare at midnight, Operetta's mouthwatering pastries and breads are available around the clock. At the ✪ **Original Pantry Cafe,** 877 S. Figueroa St., at Ninth Street (☎ 213/972-9279), owner and Los Angeles Mayor Richard Riordan has been serving huge portions of comfort food around the clock for more than 60 years; in fact, they don't even have a key to the front door. See "Great Deals on Dining," above.

The hip coffee shop **Swingers,** attached to the Beverly Laurel Motor Hotel, 8020 Beverly Blvd., west of Fairfax Avenue (☎ 323/653-5858), keeps L.A. hipsters happy with its retro comfort food. See "Great Deals on Dining," above.

For those requiring a little more *oomph* from their late-night snack, there's ✪ **Toi on Sunset,** 7505½ Sunset Blvd., at Gardner, Hollywood (☎ 323/874-8062). At this colorful and *loud* hangout, garbled pop-culture metaphors mingle with the tastes and aromas of "rockin' Thai" cuisine in delicious ways. See "Great Deals on Dining," above.

Proprietor Jean-Pierre Boccarra has turned this bi-level restaurant/performance space into one of the most unpredictable yet reliable venues in the area—not just for music, which ranges from up-and-coming sensations (Ani DiFranco played her first L.A. show here) to global music stars (Cape Verde's "barefoot diva" Cesaria Evora), but also for performance art, cabaret, and comedy. Insiders know to come hungry, because LunaPark's kitchen rivals those of the hottest restaurants in West Hollywood.

McCabe's. 3101 Pico Blvd., Santa Monica. ☎ **310/828-8037.** Cover varies.

Since the early 1970s, the back room of this earthy guitar shop has been the leading folk club in L.A., and possibly west of the Mississippi. Bonnie Raitt, Jackson Browne, and Linda Ronstadt are among those who played here early in their careers, and top-flight folk, country, and even rock musicians still return regularly to perform in an unbeatable, low-key, almost living-room-esque setting. It's an all-ages venue, serving no alcohol.

The Opium Den. 1605 Ivar St., Hollywood. ☎ **323/466-7800.** Cover varies.

Brent Bolthouse, an über-promoter on the Hollywood nightlife circuit, opened this club so his friends would have a comfortable quality venue to perform in. With pals who appear in nearly every issue of *People*, the plan works in everyone's favor. Live alternative music is scheduled 7 nights a week, with late-night dance parties occurring on Thursday, Friday, and Saturday. Stand-out performances include the Geraldine Fibbers, Rickie Lee Jones, Spain, and X.

Roxy. 9009 Sunset Blvd., West Hollywood. ☎ **323/276-2222.** Ticket prices vary.

Veteran record producer/executive Lou Adler opened this Sunset Strip club in the mid-1970s with concerts by Neil Young and a lengthy run of the pre-movie *Rocky Horror Show*. Since, it has remained among the top showcase venues in Hollywood—though it's lost its unchallenged preeminence among cozy clubs to increased competition from the revitalized Troubadour and such new entries as the House of Blues.

Spaceland at Dreams. 1717 Silver Lake Blvd., Silver Lake. ☎ **323/413-4442.** Cover varies.

In less than a year, promoter Mitchell Frank took over a spacious dowdy bar on the eastern edge of Hollywood and turned it into one of the most happening nightspots in Los Angeles. With his eclectic booking (everyone from the Foo Fighters and the Beasties to hometown faves Extra Fancy), Frank built a scene from scratch; Spaceland now rivals such Hollywood fixtures as the Whisky and Roxy as a place to see and be seen.

✪ **Viper Room.** 8852 Sunset Blvd., West Hollywood. ☎ **310/358-1880.** Cover varies.

Yes, Johnny Depp owns it (with partner Sal Jenco) and yes, River Phoenix overdosed here, and the combo either attracts or repulses clubgoers. The advertised line-up ranges from smokin' to snorin', but it's still a great place for celebrity spotting; huge stars like Johnny Cash, Iggy Pop, and David Bowie often perform unannounced late-night sets when they're in town playing the 6,000-seaters. Situated at ground zero of the Sunset Strip, the Viper Room will always have a "scene."

✪ **Whisky A Go-Go.** 8901 Sunset Blvd., West Hollywood. ☎ **310/652-4202.** Cover varies.

If you don't go to any other club in L.A., you must a go-go to the Whisky. The bi-level venue personifies L.A. rock, from Jim Morrison to X to Guns 'N' Roses. Every trend has passed through this club, and it continues to be the most vital venue of its kind. Recently, an in-house booker was hired to bring more local music to the club, so call ahead for an up-to-date schedule.

DANCE CLUBS

There's some good news to the city's dance scene; in short, there's plenty of it. The momentous popularity of Latin dance and swing has resulted in the opening of new clubs dedicated to both, taking some of the pressure off the old standbys. DJ club culture is also on the rise locally, featuring some pretty noteworthy shows at some enjoyable clubs; such dance clubs, however, can come and go as quickly as you can say "jungle-hip hop-drum and bass-rave." Mere whispers of a happening thing practically relegate a club to been-there-done-that status. Check *LA Weekly* for listings on specific club information.

Cherry. Fridays at the Love Lounge, 657 N. Robertson Blvd., West Hollywood. ☎ **310/659-0472.** Cover $10.

DJ Mike Messex's Friday gig finds him digging deep into the 1980s for loads of glam rock, new wave, and disco, keeping the dance floor packed all evening. Promoter Bryan Rabin knows how to keep the energy level high, with selective live performances—often with a homoerotic edge—as well as theme nights. The celebration of *Showgirls* was a must-see.

Congo Room. 5364 Wilshire Blvd., Los Angeles. ☎ **323/938-1696.** Cover varies.

Recently opened in a former Jack LaLanne health club on the Miracle Mile, the Congo Room is fast becoming the new nightspot to sway to the sounds of live salsa. Early highlights included Jose Feliciano, Celia Cruz, and Albita. This is the place to shake yourself to some sexy Latin grooves while feeling transported back to Cuba's pre-Castro era.

The Derby. 4500 Los Feliz Blvd., Los Feliz. ☎ **323/663-8979.** Cover $5.

Located at a former Brown Derby restaurant site, this class-A swing club was restored to its original luster and detailed with a heavy 1940s edge. This would explain the inordinate number of guests who come decked out in garb from that era to swing the night away to such musical acts as Big Bad Voodoo Daddy and the Royal Crown Revue (whose popularity soared after weekly bookings at the club). The club offers dance lessons but can be impossibly crowded on weekends.

Dragstrip 66. The 2nd Sat of each month at Rudolpho's, 2500 Riverside Dr., Silver Lake. ☎ **323/969-2596.** Cover $10–$20.

Note the cover disparity: If you ain't in drag, prepare to pay for it (and wait in line a wee bit longer than the more fashionably hip). This all-time great drag club, located in a Mexican restaurant, switches themes each month ("Chicks with Dicks" was a standout) and offers up every type of music—except disco and Liza. That's entertainment.

El Floridita. 1253 N. Vine St., Hollywood. ☎ **323/871-8612.** Cover varies.

This Cuban restaurant-cum-salsa joint is hot, hot, hot. Despite its modest strip lot locale, the tiny club attracts the likes of Jennifer Lopez, Sandra Bullock, Jimmy Smits, and Jack Nicholson, and the hippest nights continue to be Monday and Thursday, when Johnny Polanco and his swinging New York–flavored salsa band get the dance floor jumpin'.

Hollywood Athletic Club. 6525 Sunset Blvd., Hollywood. ☎ **323/962-6600.** Cover $10–$20.

Quickly gaining a reputation as one of L.A.'s best dance spots, this behemoth entertainment facility is home to some groovin' dance clubs. Club EO on Tuesdays has weekly guest DJs spinning a mixture of drum 'n' bass and house sounds; Saturdays feature a lively mix of progressive house music spun by deejays Drew Down and Dave Audé.

The Pink. 2810 Main St., Santa Monica. ☎ **310/392-1077.** Cover $10.

Thursday is the most popular night here, when DJs and label execs Jason Bentley and Bruno Guez spin an eclectic collection, and noteworthy guest DJs round out the mood, which includes electronic, acid jazz, and more. During the rest of the week, musical fare ranges from drum 'n' bass to progressive house.

The Gate. 643 N. La Cienega Blvd., West Hollywood. ☎ **310/289-8808.** Cover varies.

This is one despicable club, but folks seem to migrate here anyway. The Gate attracts chemically altered, surgically enhanced Eurotrash bimbos and himbos, who enjoy its elaborate decor and gargoyles a-plenty. Dancing is scheduled Wednesday through Saturday—and don't wear shorts if you want to get in.

BARS & COCKTAIL LOUNGES

El Carmen. 8138 W. 3rd St., Los Angeles. ☎ **323/852-1552.** No cover.

Opened by L.A. restaurant/bar wunderkind Sean Macpherson, the man with the mezcal touch, El Carmen conjures the feel of a back-alley Mexican cantina from a bygone era. Vintage Mexican movie posters, vibrant Latin American colors, and oil paintings of masked Mexican wrestlers decorate the Quonset hut interior, while an eclectic jukebox offers an array of tunes from Desi Arnaz to Tool. The busy bar boasts a gargantuan list of more than 100 tequilas and a small menu of tacos and light fare.

Good Luck Bar. 1514 Hillhurst Ave. (between Hollywood and Sunset blvds.), Los Angeles. ☎ **323/666-3524.** No cover.

Until they installed a flashing neon sign outside, only locals and hipsters knew about this Kung Fu–themed room in the Los Feliz/Silver Lake area. The dark-red windowless interior boasts Oriental ceiling tiles, fringed Chinese paper lanterns, sweet-but-deadly drinks like the "Yee Mee Loo" (translated as "blue drink"), and a jukebox with selections from Thelonius Monk to Cher's "Half Breed." The spacious sitting room, furnished with mismatched sofas, armchairs, and banquettes, provide a great atmosphere for conversation or romance. Arrive early to avoid the throngs of L.A. scenesters.

Kane. 5574 Melrose Ave., Hollywood. ☎ **323/466-6263.** No cover.

The classic spirit of American lounge is the mainstay at Kane, where sounds from recent decades—ranging from Bobby Darin to the Jackson 5—are spun by a DJ flanked by a duo of go-go dancers in hot pants. Kitsch notwithstanding, owner Ivan Kane has created an atmosphere reminiscent of 1960s Vegas and 1970s funk that's warm, friendly, and inviting to its 20-something crowd.

Lola's. 945 N. Fairfax Ave. (south of Santa Monica Blvd.), Los Angeles. ☎ **323/736-5652.** No cover.

The swimming-pool-sized martinis oughtta be enough reason to trek over to Lola's. From the classic gin or vodka martini for the purist to the chocolate- or apple-flavored concoctions for the adventurous, this place has a little something for everyone. Two bars, a billiards table, and plush couches hidden in dark, romantic corners make for an enjoyable setting and plenty of celeb spotting. For a full listing, see "Great Deals on Dining," above.

Lucky Seven. 1610 N. Vine St., Hollywood. ☎ **323/463-7777.** No cover.

Lucky Seven is a swank and old-school supper club/lounge, minus the kitschy sentimentality affected by so many other places. From the original sea-green interior to the burgundy banquettes in the dining room to the shiny bar, the timeless spirit of the Rat Pack lives and breathes in every dimly lit nook. There's live music during the week, including an occasional performance by Jeff Goldblum on keys and Peter Weller on horn, a duo the staff has fondly dubbed "RoboFly."

360. 6290 Sunset Blvd., Hollywood. ☎ **323/871-2995.** No cover.

From the 19th story, this penthouse-perched restaurant/lounge, a relative newcomer to the L.A. scene, is a perfect place to romance that special someone. It's all about the view—all 360° of it—the understated and softly lit interior emphasizes the scene *outside* the plentiful windows, including a spectacular vista of the famed HOLLYWOOD sign.

Windows on Hollywood. In the Holiday Inn, 1755 N. Highland Ave., Hollywood. ☎ **323/462-7181.** No cover.

There's nothing like a revolving bar/restaurant to enjoy a panoramic view of the city; this one is 23 floors above the heart of Hollywood. While it scores low on the hipness scale, I'm glad trendy bar-hoppers have taken their scene elsewhere, freeing up the prime window tables for you and me. The slowly revolving outer circle will show you downtown's skyline, the lights of Hollywood, and the hills to the north; the noncirculating center offers entertainment and dancing. If you're lucky, there'll be some young Sinatra wanna-be providing a schmaltzy soundtrack for your cocktail hour.

COMEDY & CABARET

Except for the Cinegrill, which is in its own league, each of the following venues claims—and justly so—to have launched the careers of the comics who are now household names. The funniest up-and-comers are playing all the clubs (except for the Groundlings, which is an improvisation group), so you're probably best off choosing a club for its location.

The Cinegrill. 7000 Hollywood Blvd., in the Hollywood Roosevelt Hotel, Hollywood. ☎ **323/466-7000.** Cover varies.

There's something going on every night of the week here, at one of L.A.'s most historic hotels. Some of the country's best cabaret singers pop up regularly. The Cinegrill draws locals with a zany cabaret show and guest chanteuses from Eartha Kitt to Cybill Shepherd.

Comedy Store. 8433 Sunset Blvd., West Hollywood. ☎ **323/656-6225.** Cover varies, usually $5–$10.

You can't go wrong here: New comics develop their material, and established ones work out the kinks from theirs, at owner Mitzi Shore's (Pauly's mom) landmark venue. The talent is always first-rate and includes comics who regularly appear on *The Tonight Show* and other high-profile TV.

Groundling Theater. 7307 Melrose Ave., Los Angeles. ☎ **323/934-9700.** Tickets $10–$18.

L.A.'s answer to Chicago's Second City has been around for over 20 years yet remains the most innovative and funny group in town. Their collection of skits changes every year or so, but they take new improvisational twists every night, and the satire is often savage. The Groundlings were the springboard to fame for Pee-Wee Herman, Lisa Kudrow from *Friends,* and former *Saturday Night Live* stars Jon Lovitz, Phil Hartman, and Julia Sweeney. Trust me—you haven't laughed this hard in ages.

The Improvisation. 8162 Melrose Ave., West Hollywood. ☎ **323/651-2583.** Cover varies.

A showcase for top stand-ups since 1975, the Improv offers something different each night. Owner Budd Freedman's buddies—like Jay Leno, Billy Crystal, and Robin Williams—hone their skills here more often than you'd expect. But even if the comedians on the bill the night you go are all unknowns, they won't be for long.

COFFEEHOUSES

The Abbey. 692 N. Robertson Blvd., West Hollywood. ☎ **310/289-8410.**

This coffeehouse in the heart of West Hollywood is really a cafe, offering full meals. But it's also perhaps the best casual hangout in this heavily gay neighborhood, with desserts galore. Lingering over an iced mocha on the patio with a few friends makes for a perfect evening time-waster.

Bourgeois Pig. 5931 Franklin Ave., Hollywood. ☎ **323/962-6366.**

With a bit more of a bar atmosphere than the usual coffeehouse, this veteran, on a hot business strip at the Hollywood/Los Feliz border, is a youth and showbiz drone favorite. An added draw is the terrific newsstand next door.

Equator. 22 Mills Place, Pasadena. ☎ **626/564-8656.**

Airy and comfy, this brick room on a busy alleyway in the heart of resurgent Old Town Pasadena has withstood the challenge of a Starbucks that moved in a block away. The menu—with smoothies, soup, and desserts in addition to a wide variety of coffee drinks—and the friendly service keep people coming back. The post-Haring art on the walls contributes to the distinctive character of the place, which has been used for scenes in such films and TV shows as *Beverly Hills, 90210* and *A Very Brady Sequel.*

Highland Grounds. 742 N. Highland Ave., Hollywood. ☎ **323/466-1507.**

Predating the coffeehouse explosion, this comfortable, relatively unpretentious place set the L.A. standard with a vast assortment of food and drink—not just coffee—and often first-rate live music, ranging from nationally known locals, such as Victoria Williams, to open-mike Wednesdays for all-comers. The ample patio is often used for readings and record-release parties.

Onyx/Sequel. 1804 N. Vermont Ave., Hollywood. No phone.

These two cozy adjacent rooms in the Los Feliz district offer generally friendly service, as well as a decent line-up of soup, sandwiches, and desserts to go with the beverages. Owner John has long supported local performers and visual artists, giving a home to spoken word and music nights that've drawn such luminaries as Ann Magnuson and Beck. But if you're looking for something fancy, go elsewhere.

OUT & ABOUT IN LOS ANGELES: THE GAY SCENE

Though West Hollywood, often affectionately referred to as "Boys Town," has the densest gay population in Los Angeles, there are several other noteworthy enclaves. Silver Lake, in particular, has a longstanding gay community; Santa Monica and Venice also enjoy a prevalent gay and lesbian presence.

There's plenty to do in the city, so if you're looking for specific info on gay culture in L.A. beyond what I've included here, there are several options: *4-Front* (☎ 323/650-7772), *Edge* (☎ 323/962-6994), and *Frontiers* (☎ 323/848-2222). For women, there's *Female FYI* (☎ 323/938-5969), *LA Girl Guide* (☎ 310/ 391-8877), and *Lesbian News* (☎ 310/392-8224). *Edge* and *Frontiers* are the most prominently featured free biweekly gay mags, readily available in coffeehouses and newsstands citywide. If you're having a difficult time locating any of these magazines, give the good people at **A Different Light Bookstore,** 8853 Santa Monica, West Hollywood (☎ 310/854-6601), a call or visit for some assistance. Also, *LA Weekly* and *New Times Los Angeles* have lesbian and gay articles and listings.

Also check out the entry for **Dragstrip 66** under "Dance Clubs," above.

✪ **The Abbey.** 692 N. Robertson Blvd., West Hollywood. ☎ **310/289-8410.** No cover.

By all accounts, this is *the* gay coffee bar. Sitting inside or out, this is the place to come for a latte and watch the passing parade of WeHo boys in muscle shirts. Most of West Hollywood seems to end up here on Saturday nights—even k.d. lang occasionally makes an appearance. See listing under "Coffeehouses" above.

Club 7969. 7969 Santa Monica Blvd., West Hollywood. ☎ **323/654-0280.** Cover varies.

Fashionable of late, Club 7969 is the kind of place in which male and female strippers bare it all while mingling with the gay, lesbian, and straight crowd. Each night has a different theme, ranging from drag burlesques to techno parties. On Tuesdays, Michelle's CC revue—with its legion of topless female dancers—attracts a largely lesbian crowd.

Cobalt Cantina. 4326 Sunset Blvd., Silver Lake. ☎ **323/953-9991.** Also at 616 N. Robertson Blvd., West Hollywood. ☎ **310/659-8961.** No cover.

For years, the "Martini Lounge" located in the Silver Lake restaurant has been one of the hottest gay cocktail bars in town. Around the long bar and zinc-colored cocktail tables, gargantuan margaritas and strong martinis are sipped by the ethnically mixed crowd of buffed-out locals. There's a largely gay crowd but Cobalt is definitely straight-friendly. The WeHo location's "Bluebar" is a quiet alternative to the nearby wild party-oriented clubs.

Micky's. 8857 Santa Monica Blvd., West Hollywood. ☎ **310/657-1176.** Cover varies.

A diverse, outgoing, and mostly older crowd cruises back and forth between the front-room bar and the dance floor in back. More women—probably looking to party with the friendly crowd and enjoy the great drink specials—are drawn to Micky's than to some of the neighboring bars.

Rage. 8911 Santa Monica Blvd., West Hollywood. ☎ **310/652-7055.** Cover varies.

For 15 years this high-energy, high-attitude disco has been the preferred mainstay on WeHo's gay dance-club circuit. Between turns around the dance floor, shirtless muscle boys self-consciously strut about—like peacocks flashing their plumage—looking to exchange vital statistics.

Side Trips from Los Angeles

by Stephanie Avnet Yates

The area within a 100-mile radius of Los Angeles is one of the most diverse regions in the world: There are arid deserts, rugged mountains, industrial cities, historic towns, alpine lakes, rolling hillsides, and sophisticated seaside resorts. You'll also find an offshore island that's been transformed into the ultimate city-dweller's hideaway, not to mention the Happiest Place on Earth.

1 Long Beach & the *Queen Mary*

21 miles S of downtown Los Angeles

The fifth-largest incorporated city in California, Long Beach is best known as the permanent home of the former cruise liner *Queen Mary* and for the annual Long Beach Grand Prix in mid-April, whose star-studded warm-up race sends the likes of young hipster Jason Priestly (*Beverly Hills, 90210*) and perennial racer Paul Newman burning rubber through the streets of the city. In 1998, a sleek new aquarium joined the waterfront attractions.

ESSENTIALS

GETTING THERE   From Los Angeles, take I-5 or I-405 to I-710 south; it follows the Los Angeles River on its path to the ocean and leads directly to both downtown Long Beach and the *Queen Mary* Seaport.

ORIENTATION   Downtown Long Beach is at the eastern end of the vast Port of Los Angeles; Pine Avenue is the central restaurant and shopping street, extending south to Shoreline Park and the Aquarium of the Pacific. The *Queen Mary* is docked just across the waterway, gazing south toward tiny Long Beach marina and Naples Island.

VISITOR INFORMATION   Contact the **Long Beach Area Convention & Visitors Bureau,** One World Trade Center, Suite 300 (☎ **800/4LB-STAY** or 562/436-3645; www.golongbeach.org). For more information on the **Long Beach Grand Prix,** call ☎ **562/981-2600** or check out www.longbeachgp.com.

THE *QUEEN MARY* & OTHER PORT ATTRACTIONS

Queen Mary. Pier J (at the end of I-710), Long Beach. ☎ **562/435-3511.** Admission $12 adults, $10 seniors 55 and over and military, $7 children

4–11, free for kids 3 and under. Daily 10am–6pm (last entry at 5:30pm), with extended summer hours. Parking $6 for up to 5 hr. or $8 for up to 24 hr.

It's easy to dismiss the *Queen Mary* as a barnacle-laden tourist trap, but it's the only surviving example of this particular kind of 20th-century elegance and excess. From the staterooms paneled lavishly in now-extinct tropical hardwoods to the miles of hallway handrails made of once-pedestrian Bakelite and the perfectly preserved crew quarters, wonders never cease aboard this deco luxury liner. Stroll the teakwood decks with just a bit of imagination and you'll be back in 1936 on the maiden voyage from Southampton, England. Don't miss the Streamline Moderne observation lounge, featured often in period films. Kiosk displays of photographs and memorabilia are everywhere; following the success of *Titanic*, the *Queen Mary* even hosted an exhibit of artifacts from her less fortunate sister. Regular admission includes a self-guided tour. For an additional $6 for adults or $3 for kids, you can take a behind-the-scenes guided tour, peppered with worthwhile anecdotes and details.

Aquarium of the Pacific. 100 Aquarium Way, off Shoreline Dr., Long Beach. ☎ **562/ 590-3100.** www.aquariumofpacific.org. Admission $13.95 adults, $11.95 seniors 60 and over, $6.95 ages 3–11, free for kids under 3. Daily 10am–6pm. Closed Christmas. Parking $6 max.

Opened in summer 1998 to much local scrutiny, this enormous facility is the cornerstone of Long Beach's new waterfront, designed to stimulate the city's flagging economy. Figuring that what worked in Monterey and Baltimore would work in Long Beach, planners gave their all to this project, creating a crowd-pleasing attraction just across the harbor from Long Beach's other mainstay, the *Queen Mary*. With enough exhibit space to fill three football fields, the aquarium re-creates three areas of the Pacific—the warm Baja and southern California regions, the Bering Sea and chilly northern Pacific, and faraway tropical climes, including a stunning coral lagoon and barrier reef. There are over 12,000 animals, from sharks and sea lions to delicate sea horses and moon jellies. Learn little-known aquatic facts at the many educational exhibits or thrill to come nose-to-nose with sea lions, eels, sharks, and other inhabitants of three-story-high tanks.

Gondola Getaway. Naples Island, Long Beach. ☎ **562/433-9595.** http://clever.net/ gondolas. 1-hr. cruise $55 for 2. Daily 11am–11pm.

Since 1982, these authentic Venetian gondolas have been snaking around the manmade canals of Naples Island, under gracefully arched bridges and past the gardens of resort cottages. Feel free to bring your beverage of choice, for they send you out with a nice basket of bread, cheese, and salami, plus wineglasses and a full ice bucket. Perhaps your traditionally clad oarsman will sing an Italian aria or relate the many tales of marriage proposals by romance-minded passengers (some not so successful).

Tall Ship *Californian*. ☎ **800/432-2201** for reservations. 4-hr. day sail $75 per person or $113 for 2; 2-, 3-, or 4-day cruise to Catalina or the Channel Islands $140 per person per day. Sailings late Aug to mid-Apr.

The flagship of the Nautical Heritage Society, the *Californian* sails from Long Beach between late August and mid-April (it's based in northern California in summer). At 145 feet long, this two-masted wooden cutter-class vessel offers barefooters the opportunity to help raise and lower eight sails, steer by compass, and generally experience the "romance of the high seas." Landlubbers will want to choose the 4-hour day sail, including lunch, while old salts can take the 2-, 3-, or 4-day cruises. Overnight sails should be booked well in advance.

WHERE TO STAY

✪ **Hotel Queen Mary.** 1126 Queen's Hwy. (end of I-710), Long Beach, CA 90802-6390. ☎**800/437-2934,** 562/435-3511, or 562/432-6964. Fax 562/437-4531. 382 units. A/C TV TEL. $75–$160 double; from $350 suite. AE, DC, EU, MC, V. Parking $6 for up to 5 hr., $8 for up to 24 hr.

If you're too young and/or too poor to have traveled on the old luxury liners, this is the perfect opportunity to experience the romance of an Atlantic crossing—and with no seasickness, cabin fever, or week of dull formal dinners. Since the ship is now permanently docked in Long Beach, its staterooms—once occupied by royalty and wealthy transatlantic voyagers—can be yours for a night or longer. But be advised that though the *Queen Mary* is considered the most luxurious ocean liner ever to sail the Atlantic, with the largest rooms ever built aboard a ship, the quarters aren't exceptional when compared to those on terra firma today, nor are the amenities. The idea is to enjoy the novelty and charm of features like the original bathtub watercocks ("cold salt," "cold fresh," "hot salt," "hot fresh"). The beautifully carved interior is a feast for the eye and fun to explore, and the weekday rates are hard to beat. The three restaurants are overpriced but convenient, and the shopping arcade has a decidedly British feel (one shop sells great *Queen Mary* souvenirs). An elegant Sunday champagne brunch—complete with an ice sculpture and a harpist—is served in the Grand Salon, and it's always worth having a cocktail in the art-deco Observation Bar.

WHERE TO DINE

The Long Beach dining scene gets better every year, especially along hip, redeveloped Pine Avenue downtown. Choice picks are **Alegria,** 115 Pine Ave. (☎ 562/436-3388), a colorful Spanish/Latin American hot spot with tapas and flamenco dancing; **L'Opera,** 101 Pine Ave. (☎ 562/491-0066), high-style elegance with classic Italian cuisine; and **Mum's,** 144 Pine Ave. (☎ 562/437-7700), a pioneer of downtown revival, offering eclectic California cuisine, plus billiards and cigars at Cohiba, its upstairs club. A few minutes away, at the Belmont Pier, grab a harbor-view seat at **Belmont Brewing Company,** 25 39th Place (☎ 562/433-3891), whose casual pub menu complements the five fine house brews.

Papadakis Taverna. 301 W. Sixth St. (at Centre St.), San Pedro. ☎ **310/548-1186.** Reservations recommended. Main courses $12–$35. CB, DC, MC, V. Daily 5–10pm. GREEK.

The food here rates higher than the ambiance—even genial host John Papadakis's hand-kissing greeting doesn't soften the blunt lines and bright lights of this banquet-room-like space decorated with equal parts Aegean murals and football art (in deference to Papadakis's glory days as a University of Southern California football legend). The waiters dance and sing loudly when they're not bringing plates of *spanikopita* (spinach-filled phyllo pastry) or thick, satisfying *tsatziki* (garlic-laced cucumber-and-yogurt spread) to your table. Servings are very generous, and the wine list has something for everyone.

Parker's Lighthouse. 435 Shoreline Village Dr., Long Beach. ☎ **562/432-6500.** Reservations recommended on weekends. Lunch $7–$15; dinner $13–$28. AE, DC, DISC, MC, V. Mon–Thurs 11am–10pm; Fri 11am–11pm; Sat 3–11pm; Sun 3:30–9:30pm. SEAFOOD GRILL.

Built to look like a giant Cape Cod lighthouse, Parker's fits right into the Shoreline Village motif. It's actually kind of fun to wind upstairs to one of three dining levels, including the circular bar on the top floor, which looks out over the harbor and the behemoth *Queen Mary.* The main dining room specializes in mesquite-fired fresh seafood but also offers steaks and chicken.

2 Santa Catalina Island

22 miles W of mainland Los Angeles

Santa Catalina—which everyone calls simply Catalina—is a small cove-fringed island famous for its laid-back inns, largely unspoiled landscape, and crystal-clear waters. Many devotees consider it southern California's alternative to Capri or Malta. Because of the island's relative isolation, out-of-state tourists tend to ignore it; but those who do show up have plenty of elbow room to boat, fish, swim, scuba, and snorkel. There are miles of hiking and biking trails, plus golf, tennis, and horseback riding.

Catalina is so different from the mainland it almost seems like a different country, remote and unspoiled. In 1915, the island was purchased by William Wrigley, Jr., the chewing-gum manufacturer, in order to develop a fashionable pleasure resort. To publicize the new vacation land, Wrigley brought big-name bands to the Avalon Ballroom and moved the Chicago Cubs, which he owned, to the island for spring training. His marketing efforts succeeded, and this charming and tranquil retreat became—and still is—a favorite vacation resort for mainlanders.

Today about 86% of the island remains undeveloped, owned and preserved by the Santa Catalina Island Conservancy. Some of the spectacular outlying areas can be reached only by arranged tour (see "Exploring the Island," below).

ESSENTIALS

GETTING THERE The most common way to get to/from the island is via the **Catalina Express** (☎ **800/464-4228** or 562/519-1212), operating up to 22 daily departures year-round from San Pedro and Long Beach. The trip takes about an hour. Round-trip fares are $36 for adults, $32.50 for seniors 55 and over, $27 for children 2 to 11, and $2 for infants. In San Pedro, the Catalina Express departs from the **Sea/Air Terminal,** Berth 95; take the Harbor Freeway (I-110) south to the Harbor Boulevard exit, then follow the signs to the terminal. In Long Beach, boats leave from the *Queen Mary* **Landing;** take the Long Beach Freeway (I-710) south, following the QUEEN MARY signs to the Catalina Express port. Call ahead for reservations. *Note:* Luggage is limited to 50 pounds per person; reservations are necessary for bikes, surfboards, and dive tanks; and there are restrictions on transporting pets.

Catalina Cruises (☎ **800/CATALINA**) also ferries passengers from Long Beach to Avalon Harbor. It has the best rates going (about $10 cheaper than above) because it runs monstrous 700-passenger boats, which take longer to make the crossing (about 2 hours). If you want to save money, particularly if you're staying overnight and don't have to maximize your island time, Catalina Cruises is the choice for you.

Parking is available at each departure terminal; rates are around $7 per 24-hour period.

VISITOR INFORMATION The **Catalina Island Chamber of Commerce and Visitor's Bureau,** P.O. Box 217, Avalon, CA 90704 (☎ **310/510-1520;** fax 310/510-7606), located on the Green Pleasure Pier, distributes brochures and information on activities, hotels, and transportation. Call for a free 100-page visitor's guide. Their colorful Internet site at **www.catalina.com** offers current news from the *Catalina Islander* newspaper in addition to updated activities, events, and general information.

ORIENTATION The picturesque town of **Avalon** is the island's only city and the port of entry. From the ferry dock you can wander along Crescent Avenue, the main road along the beachfront, and easily explore adjacent side streets.

Northwest of Avalon is the village of **Two Harbors,** accessible by boat or shuttle bus. Its twin bays are favored by pleasure yachts from L.A.'s various marinas, so there's more camaraderie and a less touristy ambiance overall.

GETTING AROUND   Visitors aren't allowed to drive cars on the island. There are only a limited number of autos permitted; most residents motor around in golf carts (many of the homes have only golf-cart-size driveways). But don't worry—you'll be able to get everywhere you want to go by renting a cart yourself or just hoofing it, which is what most visitors do.

If you want to explore the area around Avalon beyond where your feet can comfortably carry you, try renting a mountain bike or tandem from **Brown's Bikes,** 107 Pebbly Beach Rd. (☎ **310/510-0986**), or even a gas-powered golf cart from **Cartopia,** on Crescent Avenue at Pebbly Beach Road (☎ **310/510-2493**), where rates are about $30 per hour.

EXPLORING THE ISLAND

ORGANIZED TOURS   The Santa Catalina Island Company's **Discovery Tours** (☎ **800/626-7489** or 310/510-TOUR) has a ticket-and-information office on Crescent Avenue across from the pier. It offers the greatest variety of excursions from Avalon; many last just a couple of hours, so you don't have to tie up your whole day. In addition to day and night scenic tram tours of Avalon, glass-bottomed-boat cruises, and bus trips along Skyline Drive to the Airport in the Sky, Discovery conducts some worthwhile outings none of the other operators offers. Tours are available in *money-saving combo packs;* inquire when you call.

Noteworthy excursions are the **Undersea Tour,** a slow cruise of Lover's Cove Marine Preserve in a semisubmerged boat (1 hour; adults $21/kids $13); the ✪ **Casino Tour,** a fascinating look at the style and inventive engineering of this elegant ballroom (1 hour; adults $8.50/kids $4.25); nighttime **Flying Fish Boat Trips,** a Catalina tradition in searchlight-equipped open boats (70 minutes; adults $8.50/kids $4.25); and the ✪ **Inland Motor Tour,** a half-day jaunt through the island's rugged interior, including an Arabian horse show and refreshments at Wrigley's Rancho Escondido (4 hours; adults $30/kids $15).

VISITING TWO HARBORS   If you want to get a better look at the rugged natural beauty of Catalina and escape the throngs of beachgoers, head over to Two Harbors, the quarter-mile "neck" at the island's northwest end that gets its name from the "twin harbors" on each side, known as the Isthmus and Cat Harbor. An excellent starting point for campers and hikers, Two Harbors also offers just enough civilization for the less intrepid traveler.

The **Banning House Lodge** (☎ **310/510-2800**) is an 11-room B&B overlooking the Isthmus. The clapboard house was built in 1910 for Catalina's pre-Wrigley owners and has seen duty as on-location lodging for movie stars like Errol Flynn and Dorothy Lamour. Peaceful and isolated, the simply furnished but comfortable lodge has spectacular views of both isthmus harbors. Rates range from $88 to $165 (Apr through Nov, with substantial midweek and winter discounts available), and they'll even give you a lift from the pier.

Everyone eats at **Doug's Harbor Reef** (☎ **310/510-7265**), down on the beach. This nautical/tropical-themed saloon/restaurant serves breakfast, lunch, and dinner, the latter being hearty steaks, ribs, swordfish, chicken teriyaki, and buffalo burgers in summer. The house drink is sweet "buffalo milk," a potent concoction of vodka, crème de cacao, banana liqueur, milk, and whipped cream.

WHAT TO SEE & DO IN AVALON Walk along horseshoe-shaped Crescent Avenue, past **private yachting and fishing clubs,** toward the landmark **Casino** building. You can see the art-deco **theater** for the price of a movie ticket any night; also on the ground floor is the **Catalina Island Museum** (☎ 310/510-2414), which features exhibits on island history, archaeology, and natural history. The museum has a **contour relief map** of the island that's helpful to hikers. Admission is $1.50 for adults and 50¢ for kids; it's included in the price of Discovery's Casino Tour (see above).

Around the point from the Casino lies **Descanso Beach Club** (☎ 310/510-7410), a mini–Club Med in a private cove. While you can get on the beach year-round, the club's facilities (including showers, a restaurant/bar, volleyball lawns, and thatched beach umbrellas) are open only from Easter to September 30. Admission is $1.50.

About 1½ miles from downtown Avalon is the **Wrigley Memorial and Botanical Garden** (☎ 310/510-2288), an invigorating walk or a short taxi ride. The specialized gardens, a project of Ada Wrigley, showcase plants endemic to California's coastal islands. It's open daily from 8am to 5pm, and admission is $1.

SNORKELING, DIVING & KAYAKING

Snorkeling, scuba diving, and sea kayaking are among the main reasons mainlanders head to Catalina. Purists will prefer the less-spoiled waters of Two Harbors, but Avalon's many coves have plenty to offer as well, especially the protected marine life in Casino Point Underwater Park. **Banana Boat Riders,** 107 Pebbly Beach Rd., Avalon (☎ 800/708-2262 or 310/510-1774), offers snorkel gear and sea-kayak rentals, as well as half- and full-day excursions to Two Harbors and other island coves. **Scuba Luv** (☎ 800/262-DIVE or 310/510-2350) offers guided snorkel and scuba tours with certified instructors, ranging from half-day to 2-day excursions. **Descanso Beach Ocean Sports** (☎ 310/510-1226) offers sea-kayak and snorkel rentals with instruction, plus specialty expeditions and kids' programs.

At Two Harbors, stop by the **West End Dive Center** (☎ 310/510-2800). Excursions range from half-day introductory dives to complete certification courses to multiday dive packages. They also rent snorkel gear and offer kayak rental, instruction, and excursions.

WHERE TO STAY

If you plan to stay overnight, be sure to reserve a room in advance, since most places fill up pretty quickly during summer and holiday seasons. **Catalina Island Accommodations** (☎ 310/510-3000) might be able to help you out in a pinch; it's a reservations service with updated information on the whole island.

In addition to the choices below, I recommend the **Hotel Metropole,** at Metropole and Crescent avenues (☎ 800/300-8528 or 310/510-1884), a contemporary, polished choice overlooking a quaint shopping plaza and the harbor beyond. The rates are moderate (from $109 summer, from $89 winter) and include continental breakfast. Or, for a European ambiance, try the waterfront **Vista del Mar,** 417 Crescent Ave. (☎ 310/510-1452), above the boardwalk and featuring plenty of lounge chairs and thoughtful amenities. The rates are moderate (from $105 summer, from $75 winter) and include breakfast as well as afternoon cookies and milk. If you'd like to stay on the less-visited side of the island, see "Visiting Two Harbors" under "Exploring the Island," above.

Catalina Island Inn. 125 Metropole Ave. (P.O. Box 467), Avalon, CA 90704. ☎ **800/246-8134** or 310/510-1623. Fax 310/510-7218. 36 units. TV TEL. May–Sept and

A Catalina Accommodations Tip

Catalina Island is one of the few places in southern California with vastly differing rates depending on the season (others are the Palm Springs area and the Big Bear/Arrowhead mountain resorts). Watch your budget by watching the calendar; avoid the pricey summer months and opt instead for the fall or spring "shoulder season," when the weather is temperate and the crowds are . . . well, somewhere else.

holidays/weekends year-round, $99–$189 double. Oct–Apr weekdays $49–$99 double. Boat/hotel/tour combo packages available. Rates include continental breakfast. AE, DISC, MC, V. Closed Dec 24–25.

It's not fancy, mind you, but this venerable 1930s boarding-house-style hotel is doing well for its age and just underwent some modernizing cosmetic improvements. The inn is about a block from the bay, and some rooms have balconies and harbor views.

Pavilion Lodge. 513 Crescent Ave. (P.O. Box 737), Avalon, CA 90704. ☎ **800/851-0217** or 310/510-1788. Fax 310/510-2073. 73 units. A/C TV TEL. Summer $139–$219 double; spring/fall $89–$149 double; winter $59–$119 double. AE, DC, DISC, JCB, MC, V.

The shuffleboard courts only serve to reinforce the cruise-ship atmosphere at this complex of economical motel-style rooms with tropical shutters clustered around a grassy courtyard filled with lounge chairs. It's across from Avalon's beach, so it's a mecca for families and party animals. When it's quiet, you might be reminded of modest 1950s Waikiki hotels; when it's not, you'll think "Palm Springs Weekend." Some advantages of staying at the lodge are the complimentary coffee, tea, and pastries; the refrigerators in every room; the courtesy beach towels; the free baggage service to/from the boat terminal; and a bevy of money-saving package deals available through the Catalina Island Company (operator of Discovery Tours). Nearly everyone avoids the rack rates by staying here on a package: For example, a fall (Sept 21 to Nov 1) weekend, including round-trip boat, 2 nights' lodging, Undersea Tour, and Inland Motor Tour, is around $170 per person. Not bad.

Zane Grey Pueblo Hotel. Off Chimes Tower Rd. (north of Hill St.; P.O. Box 216), Avalon, CA 90704. ☎ **800/3-PUEBLO** or 310/510-0966. 17 units. Apr–Oct $75–$125 double; Nov–Mar $59 double. Rates include continental breakfast. AE, MC, V.

Author and avid fisherman Zane Grey spent his later years in Avalon and wrote many books here, including *Tales of Swordfish and Tuna,* which tells of his local fishing adventures. Perched atop a steep road overlooking the bay, this welcome unfancy house still sports many of the ethnic decor—Tahitian teak, Hopi elements—Grey enjoyed. The simply furnished rooms have ceiling fans; a comfortable living room features a fireplace, grand piano, and TV. The house is one of only two Avalon hotels with its own pool, and they offer shuttle service to/from town.

WHERE TO DINE

In addition to the listings below, recommended Avalon options are **The Channel House,** 205 Crescent Ave. (☎ **310/510-1617**), where continental fare is served with elegance—but without pretension—on a romantic outdoor patio or in a quiet dining room. For a special treat, head to the recently reopened **Clubhouse Bar & Grille** at the historic Catalina Island Country Club (☎ **310/510-7404**), open daily. The California/Pacific Rim menu is peppered with abundant anecdotes from the club's star-studded history, and the restaurant is open from 11am to 9pm. On the Two Harbors side of the island, **Doug's Harbor Reef** is the place to eat (see "Exploring the Island," above).

The Busy Bee. 306 Crescent Ave. (north of the Pleasure Pier). ☎ **310/510-1983.** Reservations not accepted. Main courses $7–$15. AE, CB, DC, DISC, MC, V. Summer daily 8am–10pm; winter daily 10am–8pm. AMERICAN.

An Avalon institution occupying this prime waterfront spot since 1923, this casual deli/diner serves throughout the day; it has a heated and wind-protected patio as well as full bar service. While the food is unremarkable, it's reliable home-style good stuff; the place is always crowded in season because it's right in the middle of the action.

El Galleon. 411 Crescent Ave. ☎ **310/510-1188.** Reservations recommended on weekends. Main courses $6–$12 at lunch, $11–$37 at dinner. AE, DISC, MC, V. Daily 11am–2:30pm and 5–10pm. (Bar daily 10am–1:30am.) AMERICAN.

It's Catalina's answer to Disney's Pirates of the Caribbean. Red-leather booths, brass portholes, ship's rigging, and wrought-iron conquistador decor are the perfect setting for a hearty menu of steaks and seafood. You can also make a respectable repast from the many appetizer selections, each of which is like a meal. My favorites are the zesty BBQ pork ribs, Cajun crab cakes with Creole sauce, and warm spinach-artichoke dip with chewy sourdough bread.

3 Big Bear Lake & Lake Arrowhead

100 miles NE of Los Angeles

These two deep blue lakes lie close to each other in the San Bernardino Mountains and have long been a favorite year-round alpine playground for city-weary Angelenos.

Big Bear Lake has always been popular with skiers as well as avid boaters (it's much larger than Arrowhead, and equipment rentals abound). In the past decade the area has been given a much-needed face-lift. Big Bear Boulevard was substantially widened to handle high-season traffic and downtown Big Bear Lake (the "Village") spiffed up without losing its woodsy charm. In addition to two excellent ski slopes less than 5 minutes from town (see "Winter Fun," below), you can enjoy the comforts of a real supermarket (there's even a K-mart now) and several video-rental shops, all especially convenient when staying in a cabin. Most people choose Big Bear over Arrowhead because there's so much more to do, from boating, fishing, and hiking to snow sports, mountain biking, and horseback riding. The weather is nearly always perfect at this 7,000-foot-plus elevation: If you want proof, ask Caltech, which operates a solar observatory here to take advantage of nearly 300 days of sunshine per year.

Lake Arrowhead has always been privately owned, as is immediately apparent from the affluence of the surrounding homes, many of which are gated estates rather than rustic mountain cabins. The lake and the private docks lining its shores are reserved for the exclusive use of homeowners, but visitors can enjoy Lake Arrowhead by boat tour (see "Organized Tours," below) or use of the summer-season beach clubs, a privilege included in nearly all private-home rentals (see "Where to Stay," below). Reasons to choose a vacation at Lake Arrowhead? The roads up are less grueling than the winding ascent to Big Bear Lake, and, at a lower elevation, Arrowhead gets little snow (you can forget those pesky tire chains). It's very easy and cost-effective to rent a luxurious house from which to enjoy the spectacular scenery, crisp mountain air, and relaxed resort atmosphere—and if you do ski, the slopes are only half an hour away.

ESSENTIALS

GETTING THERE   Lake Arrowhead is reached by taking Calif. 18 from San Bernardino. The last segment of this route takes you along the aptly named ✪ **Rim**

of the World Highway, offering a breathtaking panoramic view out over the valley below on clear days. Calif. 18 then continues east to Big Bear Lake, but to get to Big Bear Lake it's quicker to bypass Arrowhead by taking Calif. 330 from Redlands, which meets Calif. 18 in Running Springs. During heavy-traffic periods it can be worthwhile to take scenic Calif. 38, which winds up from Redlands through mountain passes and valleys to approach Big Bear from the other side.

VISITOR INFORMATION   National ski tours, mountain-bike races, and one of southern California's longest running Oktoberfest gatherings are just some of the many year-round events that may entice or discourage you from visiting at the same time. Contact the **Big Bear Lake Resort Association,** 630 Bartlett Rd., Big Bear Lake Village (☎ **909/866-7000;** www.bigbear.com), for schedules and details. They also provide information on sightseeing and lodging and will send you a free visitor's guide.

In Lake Arrowhead, contact the **Lake Arrowhead Communities Chamber of Commerce** (☎ **800/337-3716** for the Lodging Information Line or 909/337-3715; fax 909/336-1548; www.lakearrowhead.com). The visitor center is in the Lake Arrowhead Village lower shopping center.

ORIENTATION   The south shore of Big Bear Lake was the first resort area to be developed and remains the most densely populated. Calif. 18 passes first through the city of **Big Bear Lake** and its downtown **Village;** then, as Big Bear Boulevard, it continues east to **Big Bear City,** which is more residential and suburban. Calif. 38 traverses the north shore, home to pristine national forest and great hiking trails, as well as a couple of small marinas (see "Water Sports," below) and a lakefront B&B inn (see "Where to Stay," below).

Arrowhead's main town is **Lake Arrowhead Village,** on the south shore at the end of Calif. 173. The village's commercial center is home to factory-outlet stores, about 40 chain and specialty shops, and the Lake Arrowhead Resort Hotel. Minutes away is the town of **Blue Jay** (along Calif. 189), where the Ice Castle Skating Rink is located (see "Winter Fun," below).

ENJOYING THE OUTDOORS

In addition to the activities below, there's a great recreation spot for families near the heart of Big Bear Lake: **Magic Mountain,** on Calif. 18/Big Bear Boulevard (☎ **909/866-4626**), has a year-round bobsled-style Alpine Slide, a splashy double water slide open mid-June to mid-September, and bunny slopes for snow tubing November to Easter. The dry Alpine Slide is $3 a ride, the water slide is $1 (or $10 for a day pass), and snow play costs $10 per day, including tube and rope tow.

WATER SPORTS

BOATING   You can rent all kinds of boats—including speedboats, rowboats, paddleboats, pontoons, sailboats, and canoes—at a number of Big Bear Lake marinas. Rates vary only slightly from place to place: A 14-foot dinghy with an outboard runs around $10 per hour or $30 for a half day; pontoon (patio) boats, which can hold large groups, range in size and price from $25 to $45 per hour or $80 to $150 for a half day. **Pine Knot Landing** (☎ **909/866-BOAT**) is the most central marina, behind the post office at the foot of Pine Knot Boulevard in Big Bear Lake. **Gray's Landing** (☎ **909/866-2443**) is just across the dam on the north shore and offers the best prices and the least attitude. **Big Bear Marina,** Paine Road at Lakeview (☎ **909/866-3218**), is also close to Big Bear Lake Village and provides take-along chicken dinners when you rent a pontoon boat for a sunset cruise ($75 for 3 hours).

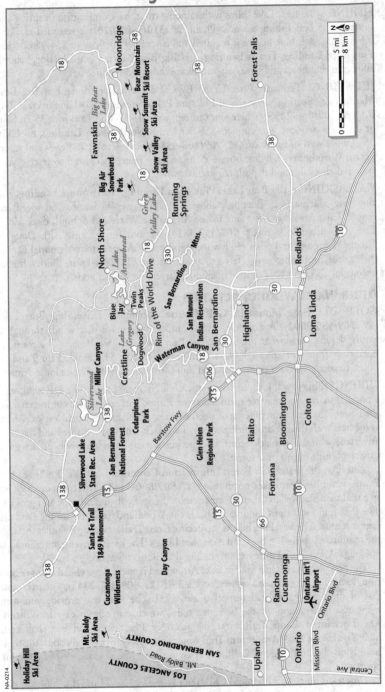

FISHING   Big Bear Lake brims with rainbow trout, bass, and catfish in spring and summer, the best fishing seasons. Phone ☎ **310/590-5020** for recorded stocking information. A fishing license is required and costs $8.95 per day or $24.95 per year. **Pine Knot Landing, Gray's Landing,** and **Big Bear Marina** (see "Boating," above) all rent fishing boats and have bait-and-tackle shops that sell licenses.

JET SKIING   Personal Water Craft (PWCs) are available for rent at **Big Bear Marina** (see "Boating," above) and **Pleasure Point Landing,** 603 Landlock Landing Rd. (☎ **909/866-2455**), where you can rent a single-rider SeaDoo for $35 an hour or opt for a two-seat Waverunner ($55 per hour). **North Shore Landing,** on Calif. 38, 2 miles west of Fawnskin (☎ **909/868-4386**), rents jet skis and two- and three-person Waverunners ranging from $55 to $65 per hour. Call ahead to reserve your craft and check age and deposit requirements.

WATERSKIING   Big Bear Lake, Pine Knot Landing, North Shore Landing, and **Big Bear Marina** (see "Boating," above) all offer water-ski lessons and speedboat rentals. Lake Arrowhead is home to the **McKenzie Water Ski School,** dockside in Lake Arrowhead Village (☎ **909/337-3814**), famous for teaching Kirk Douglas, George Hamilton, and other Hollywood stars to ski. It's open from Memorial Day to the end of September and offers group lessons for $115 per hour, short refresher lessons for $35, and boat charter (including driver) for $95 an hour.

OTHER WARM-WEATHER ACTIVITIES

GOLF   The **Bear Mountain Golf Course,** Goldmine Drive, Big Bear Lake (☎ **909/585-8002**), is a 9-hole, par-35, links-style course that winds through a gently sloping meadow at the base of the Bear Mountain Ski Resort. The course is open daily from April through November. Greens fees are $17 and $23 for 9 and 18 holes, respectively. Both riding carts and pull carts are available. Phone for tee times.

HIKING   Hikers will love the San Bernardino National Forest. The gray squirrel is a popular native; you may see them scurrying around gathering acorns or material for their nest. You can sometimes spot deer, coyotes, and American bald eagles, which come here with their young during winter. The black-crowned stellar jay and the talkative red, white, and black acorn woodpecker are the most common of the great variety of birds in this pine forest.

Stop in at the brand-new **Forest Information Center** on Calif. 38, 3 miles east of Fawnskin on Big Bear Lake's north shore (☎ **909/866-3437**). There you can pick up free trail maps, as well as other information on the area's plants, animals, and geology. The best trail for a short mountain hike is the **Woodland Trail,** beginning near the ranger station. The best long hike is the **Pacific Crest Trail,** traveling 39 miles through the mountains above Big Bear and Arrowhead lakes. The most convenient trailhead is at Cougar Crest, half a mile west of the Big Bear Ranger Station.

The best place to begin a hike in Lake Arrowhead is at the **Arrowhead Ranger Station,** located in the town of Skyforest on Calif. 18 (☎ **909/337-2444**), a quarter-mile east of the Lake Arrowhead turnoff (Calif. 173). The staff will provide you with maps and information on the best area trails, which range from easy to difficult. The **Enchanted Loop Trail,** near the town of Blue Jay, is an easy half-hour hike. The **Heaps Peak Arboretum Trail** winds through a grove of redwoods; the trailhead is on the north side of Calif. 18, at an auxiliary ranger kiosk west of Running Springs.

The area is home to a **National Children's Forest,** a 20-acre area developed so that children, the wheelchair-bound, and the visually impaired could enjoy nature. To get to the Children's Forest from Lake Arrowhead, take Calif. 330 to Calif. 18 east, past

Deer Lick Station; when you reach a road marked IN96 (only open in summer), turn right and go 3 miles.

HORSEBACK RIDING   Horses are permitted on all the mountain trails through the national forest. **Bear Mountain Stables,** at Bear Mountain Ski Resort, City of Big Bear Lake (☎ **909/878-HORSE**), offers 1- and 2-hour guided rides for $20 per hour and sunset hay rides for $45. The stables are open daily from May through December; phone for reservations. **Baldwin Lake Stables,** southeast of Big Bear City (☎ **909/ 585-6482**), also conducts hourly, lunch, and sunset rides in addition to offering lessons.

MOUNTAIN BIKING   Big Bear Lake has become a mountain-bicycling center, with most of the action around the **Snow Summit ski area** (see "Winter Fun," below), where a $7 lift ticket will take you and your bike to a scenic web of trails, fire roads, and meadows at about 8,000 feet. Call its **Summer Activities Hotline** at ☎ **909/866-4621.** The lake's north shore is also a popular biking destination; the brand-new Forest Information Center (see "Hiking," above) and the Old Big Bear Ranger Station (about ¼ mile from the Forest Information Center) have maps to the historic gold-rush-era Holcomb Valley and the 2-mile Alpine Pedal Path (an easy lake-side ride).

   Big Bear Bikes, 41810 Big Bear Blvd. (☎ **909/866-4565**), rents mountain bikes for $6 per hour or $21 for 4 hours. **Bear Valley Bikes,** 40298 Big Bear Blvd. (☎ **909/ 866-8000**), rents bikes at roughly the same rates and offers free lessons on Sunday. **Team Big Bear,** at the base of Snow Summit (☎ **909/866-4565**), rents bicycles at roughly the same rates and provides detailed maps and guides for all Big Bear–area trails.

   At Lake Arrowhead, bikes are permitted on all hiking trails and back roads except the Pacific Crest Trail. See the local ranger station for an area map. Gear can be rented from the **Lake Arrowhead Resort,** 27984 Calif. 189 (☎ **909/336-1511**), or **Above & Beyond Sports,** 32877 Calif. 18, Running Springs (☎ **909/867-5517**).

WINTER FUN

SKIING & SNOWBOARDING   When the L.A. basin gets wintertime rain, skiers everywhere rejoice, for they know snow is falling up in the mountains. The last few seasons have seen abundant natural snowfall at Big Bear, augmented by sophisticated snowmaking equipment, which also compensates during drier years. While the slopes can't compare with those in Utah or Colorado, they do offer diversity, difficulty, and convenience.

   Snow Summit at Big Bear Lake (☎ **909/866-5766;** www.bigbear.com/summit) is the skier's choice, especially since they installed their second high-speed quad express from the 7,000-foot base to the 8,200-foot summit. Another nice feature is green (easy) runs even from the summit, so beginners can enjoy the Summit Haus lodge and breathtaking lake views from the top. Advanced risk-takers will appreciate three double-black-diamond runs. Lift tickets range from $30 to $42. The resort offers mid-week, beginner, half-day, night, and family specials, as well as ski and snowboard instruction. Hey, you can even ski free on your birthday! Other helpful Snow Summit phone numbers include advance lift-ticket sales (☎ **909/866-5841**), the ski school (☎ **909/866-4546**), and a snow report (☎ **310/390-1498** in L.A. County).

   The **Bear Mountain Ski Resort** at Big Bear Lake (☎ **909/585-2519;** 213/ 683-8100 for a snow report; www.bearmtn.com) is the smallest of the area's three major resorts, but experts flock to the double-black-diamond "Geronimo" run from the 8,805-foot Bear Peak. Natural terrain skiers and snowboarders will enjoy legal access to off-trail canyons, but the limited beginner slopes and kids' areas get pretty crowded in season. One high-speed quad express rises from the 7,140-foot base to 8,440-foot Goldmine Mountain; most runs from there are intermediate. Bear Mountain has a ski school, abundant dining facilities, and a well-stocked ski shop.

The **Snow Valley Ski Resort** in Arrowbear, midway between Arrowhead and Big Bear (☎ **800/680-SNOW** or 909/867-2751; www.aminews.com/snowvalley), has improved its snowmaking and facilities to be competitive with the other two major ski areas and is the primary choice of skiers staying at Arrowhead. From a base elevation of 6,800 feet, Snow Valley's 13 chairlifts (including five triples) can take you from the beginner runs all the way up to black-diamond challenges at the 7,898-foot peak. Lift tickets cost $35 to $40 for adults; children's programs, night skiing, and lesson packages are available.

The **Big Air Snowboard Park** in Green Valley (☎ **909/867-2338**)—take Green Valley Lake Road from Arrowbear—is the answer to a snowboarder's dream. No skiers are allowed on Big Air's 50 rideable acres full of hits, bonks, spines, and more. Use the rope tow or take the high-speed chair to untouched forest full of natural hits. It offers equipment rentals, lessons, and package deals. All-day passes are $24 for adults, $18 for kids 12 and under; half-day passes are $20 and $14, respectively.

ICE-SKATING The **Blue Jay Ice Castle,** at North Bay Road and Calif. 189 (☎ **909/33-SKATE;** www.ice-castle.com), near Lake Arrowhead Village, is a training site for world champion Michelle Kwan and boasts Olympic gold medalist Robin Cousins on its staff. Several public sessions each day—as well as hockey, broomball, group lessons, and book-in-advance private parties—give nonpros a chance to enjoy this impeccably groomed "outdoor" rink (it's open on three sides to the scenery and fresh air).

ORGANIZED TOURS

LAKE TOURS The *Big Bear Queen* (☎ **909/866-3218**), a midget Mississippi-style paddle wheeler, cruises Big Bear Lake on 90-minute tours daily from late April through November. The boat departs from Big Bear Marina (at the end of Paine Avenue). Tours are $9.50 for adults, $8 for seniors 65 and older, and $5 for children 3 to 12. Call for reservations and details on the special Sunday brunch, champagne sunset, and dinner cruises. Fifty-minute tours of Lake Arrowhead are offered year-round on the *Arrowhead Queen* (☎ **909/336-6992**), a sister ship that departs hourly each day from 10am to 6pm from Lake Arrowhead Village. Tours are $9.50 for adults, $8.50 for seniors, and $6.50 for children 2 to 12. This is about the only way to really see this alpine jewel, unless you know a resident with a boat.

FOREST TOURS **Big Bear Jeep Tours** (☎ **909/878-JEEP**) journeys into Big Bear Lake's backcountry, including historic Holcomb Valley, relic of the gold rush, plus the panoramic viewpoint Butler Peak. These off-road adventures range from 2 to 4½ hours and cost $38 to $80 per person. Bring your own snack; though the guide carries ample water, the longer excursions have short but appetite-building hikes scheduled into the itinerary. Phone for reservations, particularly on weekends and holidays.

WHERE TO STAY
BIG BEAR LAKE

Vacation rentals are plentiful in the area, from cabins to condos to private homes. Some can accommodate up to 20 people and can be rented on a weekly or monthly basis. The oldest Realtor, with seven area offices and a wide range of rental properties, is **Spencer Real Estate** (☎ **800/237-3725** or 909/866-7591). The **Village**

Reservation Service (☎ **909/866-8583** or 909/585-5850) can arrange for everything from Jacuzzi condos to lakefront homes, or call the **Big Bear Lake Resort Association** (☎ **909/866-7000**) for information and referrals on all types of lodging.

In addition to those below, I recommend **Apples Bed & Breakfast Inn,** 42430 Moonridge Rd. (☎ **909/866-0903**), a crabapple-red New England–style clapboard that blends hotel-like professionalism with B&B amenities—and lots of cute frilly touches. Rates are $125 to $185.

Gold Mountain Manor. 1117 Anita Ave. (P.O. Box 2027), Big Bear City, CA 92314. ☎ **909/585-6997.** 6 units. $125–$149 double; $180–$190 suite. Midweek and off-season discounts available. Rate includes full breakfast and afternoon hors d'oeuvres. MC, V.

If your taste runs to log-cabin style, you can't do much better than this B&B in a woodsy neighborhood a couple of minutes east of the lake. From the broad front lawn dotted with Adirondack chairs to the rough-hewn rock fireplace in the parlor, this place screams "photo shoot"—it's been used for a variety of layouts, including an Eddie Bauer catalog. The 1920s house is furnished with well-worn antiques accented with memorabilia from the days when lovebirds like Clark Gable and Carole Lombard visited. Each of the cute 'n' cozy bedrooms has either a fireplace or a wood-burning stove, and all have puffy down comforters. The game room features a giant TV with VCR and tapes, a pool table, a player piano, and board games and books, and there are always complimentary snacks and beverages available.

Grey Squirrel Resort. 39372 Big Bear Blvd., Big Bear Lake, CA 92315. ☎ **909/866-4335.** Fax 909/866-6271. 18 cabins. TV TEL. $75–$95 one-bedroom cabin; $99–$125 two-bedroom cabin; $125–$275 three-bedroom cabin. Value rates available; higher rates on holidays. AE, DISC, MC, V. Pets are welcome for a $5 daily surcharge.

This is the most attractive of the many cabin-cluster-type motels near the city of Big Bear Lake, offering a wide range of rustic cabins, most with fireplace and kitchen. They're adequately, if not attractively, furnished—the appeal here is the flexibility and privacy it gives long-term or large parties. A heated pool is enclosed in winter, and there's an indoor spa, a fire pit and barbecues, volleyball and basketball courts, laundry facilities, and completely equipped kitchens.

Holiday Inn Big Bear Chateau. 42200 Moonridge Rd. (P.O. Box 1814), Big Bear Lake, CA 92315. ☎ **800/BEAR-INN** or 909/866-6666. Fax 909/866-8988. 76 units. A/C TV TEL. $120–$180 double; $180–$250 suite. Winter-ski and summer-fun packages available. AE, DISC, MC, V.

One of only two traditional full-service hotels in Big Bear, this European-flavored property underwent a complete renovation in 1997. Its highly visible location—just off Big Bear Boulevard at the base of the road to Bear Mountain—makes the Chateau a popular choice for skiers and families. The rooms are modern but more charming than your average Holiday Inn, with tapestries, brass beds, antique furniture, gas fireplaces, and lavish marble baths, many with whirlpool tubs. There's a heated outdoor pool and spa, and the entire compound is surrounded by tall forest. The restaurant (which also provides room service) is advertised as "casually elegant"—which means you can enjoy upscale continental/American cuisine even in après-ski duds.

LAKE ARROWHEAD

There are far more private homes than tourist accommodations in Arrowhead, but rental properties abound, from cozy cottages to palatial mansions; and many can be surprisingly economical for families or other groups. Two of the largest agencies are **Arrowhead Cabin Rentals** (☎ **800/244-5138** or 909/337-2403) and **Arrowhead Mountain Resorts Rentals** (☎ **800/743-0865** or 909/337-4413).

Overnight guests in rental properties enjoy some resident lake privileges—be sure to ask when you reserve.

Another option is the **Saddleback Inn,** 300 S. Calif. 173 (☎ **800/858-3334** or 909/336-3571), an inn/restaurant that still boasts historic charm while offering up-to-date in-room amenities, a prime location in the center of the village, and terrific midweek and seasonal discount rates.

Bracken Fern Manor. 815 Arrowhead Villas Rd. (P.O. Box 1006), Lake Arrowhead, CA 92352. ☎ **909/37-8557.** Fax 909/337-3323. 10 units. $85–$185 double. Rates include full breakfast. AE, DISC, MC, V. Located ½ mile north of Calif. 18.

Billing itself as a "House of Now Fine Repute," this off-the-beaten-path inn boasts a registered historical marker as well as a checkered past. The present owners work hard at evoking its 1930s heyday: They've preserved the downstairs public rooms, along with many well-maintained antiques, and named each guest room (decorated in a fresh country style) for one of the "girls." There are many quiet corners for relaxing, including a game room, hidden library, whirlpool gazebo, and wood-lined sauna.

Lake Arrowhead Resort. 27984 Calif. 189, Lake Arrowhead, CA 92352. ☎ **800/ 800-6792** or 909/336-1511. Fax 909/336-1378. 177 units. A/C MINIBAR TV TEL. $119–$229 double; $299–$399 suite. Inquire about AAA discounts. AE, CB, DC, DISC, MC, V.

This sprawling resort has been upgraded somewhat since it was part of the Hilton chain, but location is still its most outstanding feature, coupled with unparalleled service and facilities. On the lakeshore adjacent to Lake Arrowhead Village, the hotel has its own beach, plus docks that are ideal for fishing. The rooms are fitted with good-quality, bulk-purchased contemporary furnishings, and most have balconies, king-size beds, and fireplaces. The suites, some in private cottages, are equipped with full kitchens and whirlpool tubs.

The hotel offers a casual restaurant serving all meals (and room service), plus the elegant Seasons, which serves dinner but is open only limited days off-season. Facilities include a fully equipped health club, a heated outdoor pool and whirlpool, racquetball courts, massage, and a video arcade. A full program of supervised children's activities, ranging from nature hikes to T-shirt painting, is offered on weekends year-round.

Pine Rose Cabins. 25994 Calif. 189 (P.O. Box 31), Twin Peaks, CA 92391. ☎ **800/ 429-PINE** or 909/337-2341. Fax 909/337-0258. 16 units. TV. $69–$179 cabin for up to 4; $350 five-bedroom lodge. Ski packages offered in season. AE, DISC, MC, V. Pets accepted with $5 fee per night and $100 refundable deposit.

The only place of its kind in Lake Arrowhead, Pine Rose Cabins is a good choice for families. Situated on five forested acres about 3 miles from the lake, the wonderful freestanding cabins offer lots of privacy. Innkeepers Tricia and David Dufour have 15 cabins, ranging in size from romantic studios to a large five-bedroom lodge, each decorated in a different theme: The Indian cabin has a tepeelike bed; the bed in Wild Bill's cabin is covered like a wagon. One- and two-bedroom units have a fully stocked kitchen and a separate living area. There's a large heated pool, plus swing sets, croquet, tetherball, and Ping-Pong.

WHERE TO DINE
Big Bear Lake

The Captain's Anchorage. Moonridge Way at Big Bear Blvd., Big Bear Lake. ☎ **909/ 866-3997.** Reservations recommended. Full dinners $10–$25. AE, MC, V. Sun–Thurs 4:30–9pm; Fri–Sat 4:30–10pm. STEAK/SEAFOOD.

Historic and rustic, this knotty-pine restaurant has been serving fine steaks, prime rib, seafood, and lobster since 1947. Inside, the dark nautical decor and fire-warmed bar will hit the spot on blustery winter nights. It's got one of those mile-long soup-and-salad bars, plus some great early-bird and weeknight specials.

Ché Faccia. 607 Pine Knot Ave., Big Bear Lake. ☎ **909/878-3222.** Reservations recommended for dinner. Main courses $6–$8 at lunch, $8–$16 at dinner. AE, MC, V. Mon–Thurs 5–9pm; Fri–Sat 11:30am–10pm; Sun 11:30am–9pm. ITALIAN.

It's pronounced "Kay *Fah*-cha" and means "What a face!"—a nod to owner Steve Earley's old-world grandmother, whose recipes live on at this popular newcomer. Specialties include rigatoni with porcinis in creamy marsala sauce and veal saltimbocca rolled with spinach and prosciutto. The menu rounds out with individual gourmet pizzas, a decadent tiramisu, and a pretty good house wine. The decor is casual and pleasant, and the walls are adorned with doodles from diners, including many of professional quality from vacationing cartoonists and artists.

Madlon's. 829 W. Big Bear Blvd., Big Bear City. ☎ **909/585-3762.** Reservations required. Main courses $8–$16. AE, MC, V. Daily 5–9pm; Sat–Sun 8am–2:30pm (year-round); Wed–Fri 11am–2:30pm (summer only). AMERICAN/CONTINENTAL.

One of the few nonretro-fare dining rooms at the mountain resorts, Madlon's brings a bit of European flair to this fairy-tale cottage. A variety of creative croissant sandwiches at lunch are complemented by dinner selections like black-pepper filet mignon with mushroom-and-brandy sauce and lemon-pepper-marinated chicken breast over pasta, all of which are prepared with a sophisticated touch.

Old Country Inn. 41126 Big Bear Blvd., Big Bear Lake. ☎ **909/866-5600.** Main courses $5–$14. AE, CB, DC, DISC, MC, V. Sun–Thurs 7am–9pm; Fri–Sat 7am–10pm. DINER/GERMAN.

The Old Country Inn has long been a favorite for hearty pre-ski breakfasts and stick-to-your-ribs old-world dinners. The restaurant is casual and welcoming and the adjacent cocktail lounge is raucous on weekends. At breakfast, enjoy German apple pancakes or colossal omelets, while salads, sandwiches, and burgers are lunch choices. At lunch or dinner, feast on Wiener schnitzel, sauerbraten, and other gravy-topped German standards, along with grilled steaks and chicken.

LAKE ARROWHEAD

Surprisingly for an affluent residential community, there aren't many dining options around Lake Arrowhead. But not surprisingly, what there is tends to run to pricey elegance—elegant for a rustic mountain resort, that is.

Though there's a California/continental restaurant and a casual family eatery in the Lake Arrowhead Resort (see "Where to Stay," above), you might want to venture out to some of the locals' choices. These include the **Chef's Inn & Tavern,** 29020 Oak Terrace, Cedar Glen (☎ **909/336-4488**), a moderate-to-expensive continental restaurant in a turn-of-the-century former bordello; the **Antler's Inn,** 26125 Calif. 189, Twin Peaks (☎ **909/337-4020**), serving prime rib, seafood, and buffalo in a historic log lodge; the **Royal Oak,** 27187 Calif. 189, Blue Jay Village (☎ **909/337-6018**), an expensive American/continental steak house with a pub; and **Belgian Waffle Works,** dockside at Lake Arrowhead Village (☎ **909/337-5222**), an inexpensive coffee shop with Victorian decor, known for its generous crispy waffles with tasty toppings.

4 Disneyland & Other Anaheim-Area Attractions

27 miles SE of downtown Los Angeles

The sleepy Orange County town of Anaheim grew up around Disneyland, the West's most famous theme park. Now, even beyond this Happiest Place on Earth, the city and its neighboring communities are kid central: Otherwise unspectacular, sprawling suburbs have become a playground of family-oriented hotels, restaurants, and unabashedly tourist-oriented attractions. Among the nearby draws are Knott's Berry Farm, another family-oriented theme park, in nearby Buena Park. At the other end of the scale is the Richard Nixon Library and Birthplace, a surprisingly compelling presidential library and museum, just 7 miles northeast of Disneyland in Yorba Linda.

ESSENTIALS

GETTING THERE   **Los Angeles International Airport (LAX)** is about 30 minutes from Anaheim via I-5 south (see chapter 13). If you're heading directly to Anaheim and want to avoid L.A. altogether, try to land at the **John Wayne International Airport in Irvine** (☎ **714/252-5200**), Orange County's largest airport, about 15 miles from Disneyland. Check to see if your hotel has a free shuttle to/from either airport or call one of the following commercial shuttle services (fares are generally $10 one-way from John Wayne): **L.A. Xpress** (☎ 800/I-ARRIVE); **Prime Time** (☎ 800/262-7433); or **SuperShuttle** (☎ 714/517-6600). Car-rental agencies at the John Wayne Airport include **Budget** (☎ 800/221-1203) and **Hertz** (☎ 800/654-3131).

VISITOR INFORMATION   The **Anaheim/Orange County Visitor and Convention Bureau,** 800 W. Katella Ave. (P.O. Box 4270), Anaheim, CA 92803 (☎ **714/999-8999**), can fill you in on area activities and shopping shuttles. It's just inside the Convention Center (across from Disneyland), next to the dramatic cantilevered arena, and welcomes visitors Monday through Friday from 8am to 5pm. The **Buena Park Convention and Visitors Office,** 6280 Manchester Blvd., Suite 103, Buena Park, CA 90621 (☎ **800/541-3953** or 714/562-3560), will provide specialized information on its area, including Knott's Berry Farm.

DISNEYLAND

Walt Disney was the originator of the mega–theme park. Opened in 1955, Disneyland remains unsurpassed. Despite constant threats from pretenders to the crown, Disneyland and its sibling park, Walt Disney World outside Orlando, Florida, remain the kings of the theme parks. At no other park is fantasy elevated to an art form. Nowhere else is as fresh and fantastic every time you walk through the gates, whether you're 6 or 60—and no matter how many times you've done it before. There's nothing like Disney magic.

ESSENTIALS

GETTING THERE   Disneyland is at 1313 Harbor Blvd. in Anaheim, about an hour's drive from downtown Los Angeles. Take I-5 south; while construction is being completed on the new Disneyland exit, orange signs will direct you off the freeway at either Harbor or Katella boulevard.

ADMISSION, HOURS & INFORMATION   Admission to the park, including unlimited rides and all festivities and entertainment, is $39 for adults and children 12 and over, $37 for seniors 60 and over, and $29 for children 3 to 11; children under 3 enter free. Parking is $6. Passes for 2 or 3 days are available; in addition, some

New & Noteworthy

Disneyland stays on the cutting edge by continually updating and expanding, while still maintaining the hallmarks that make it the world's top amusement park (a term coined by Walt Disney himself). Look for the most recent Disney additions during your visit—1995's **Indiana Jones Adventure** is a high-tech thrill that's not to be missed, no matter how long the wait. It was lights out in 1996 for the beloved **Main Street Electrical Parade's** 24-year run; in its place, a changing series of **nighttime parades** feature larger-than-life fiber-optic and video light displays. At press time, the parade showcased characters and themes from *Mulan,* Disney's latest animated feature. In 1998, **Tomorrowland** blasted off with a bunch of new attractions to replace dated and closed features; I'm predicting long lines for the superhigh-speed outer-space **Rocket Rods.**

And keep your eyes open as Disney prepares to round the century mark—work has already begun on **California Adventure,** a new sister park and great big hotel/resort that'll debut in 2001 adjacent to Disneyland. Until then, related construction obstructions are likely to add time and frustration to your park experience, so be prepared.

area accommodations offer lodging packages that include 1 or more days' park admission.

Disneyland is open every day of the year, but operating hours vary, so I recommend you call for information that applies to the specific day(s) of your visit (☎ 714/781-4565 or 213/626-8605, ext. 4565). Generally speaking, the park is open 9 or 10am to 6 or 7pm on weekdays, fall to spring, and 8 or 9am to midnight or 1am on weekends, holidays, and during winter, spring, or summer vacation periods.

If you've never been to Disneyland before and would like to get a copy of their *Vacation Planner* brochure to orient yourself to the park before you go, call their **automated request line** at ☎ 800/225-2057. Or pick up a copy of *The Unofficial Guide to Disneyland* (Macmillan Travel) at your local bookstore.

DISNEY TIPS   Disneyland is busiest from mid-June to mid-September and on weekends and school holidays year-round. Peak hours are noon to 5pm; visit the most popular rides before and after these hours and you'll cut your waiting times substantially. If you plan on arriving during a busy time, purchase your tickets in advance and get a jump on the crowds at the ticket counters.

Many visitors tackle Disneyland systematically, beginning at the entrance and working their way clockwise around the park. But a better **plan of attack** is to arrive early and run to the most popular rides first—Rocket Rods, the Indiana Jones Adventure, Star Tours, Space Mountain, Big Thunder Mountain Railroad, Splash Mountain, the Haunted Mansion, and Pirates of the Caribbean. Lines for these rides can last an hour or more in the middle of the day.

If you're going to stay in Anaheim, you might want to consider staying at the **Disneyland Hotel** (see "Where to Stay," below). Hotel guests get to enter the park early almost every day and enjoy the major rides before the lines form. The amount of time varies from day to day, but usually you can enter 1½ hours early. Call ahead to check the schedule for your specific day.

Disneyland's attendance falls dramatically late fall to early spring, so the park offers **discounted admission** (about 25% off) to southern California residents who may purchase up to six tickets by showing proof of their zip code. If you'll be visiting the park with someone who lives here, be sure to take advantage of this money-saving opportunity.

Disneyland

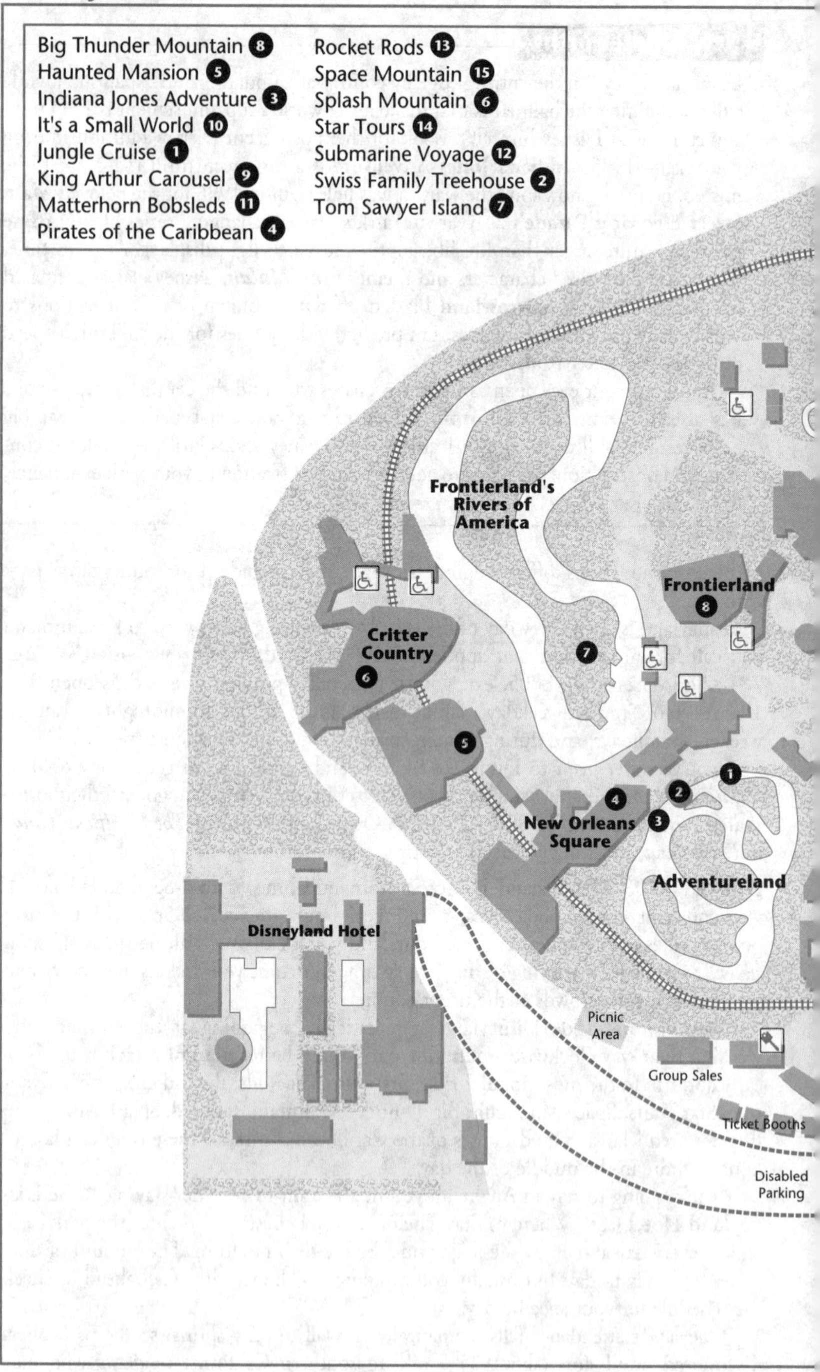

Frontierland's
Rivers of
America

Frontierland
8

Critter
Country
6

7

5

4   **2**   **1**
3

New Orleans
Square

Adventureland

Disneyland Hotel

Picnic
Area

Group Sales

Ticket Booths

Disabled
Parking

1-0853

524

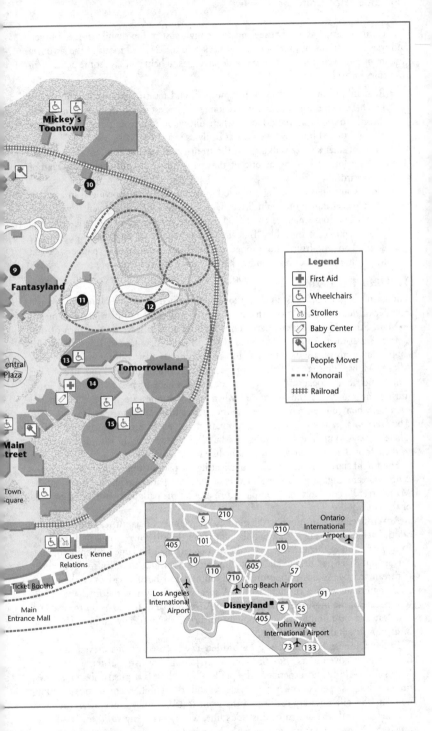

Mickey's
Toontown

10

9
Fantasyland

11

12

Central
Plaza

13

Tomorrowland

14

15

Main
Street

Town
Square

Guest
Relations   Kennel

Ticket Booths

Main
Entrance Mall

Legend
- ✚ First Aid
- ♿ Wheelchairs
- Strollers
- Baby Center
- 🔍 Lockers
- —— People Mover
- ---- Monorail
- ▥▥▥ Railroad

5   210

210

Ontario
International
Airport ✈

405   101   10

10

1

110   710   605

57

Long Beach Airport ✈

Los Angeles
International
Airport ✈

Disneyland ■

5   55

91

405

John Wayne
International Airport

73 ✈ 133

525

A common gripe about Disneyland is the high cost of food while inside: Burgers and fries for a family of four can set you back $20 to $25, and meals at the sit-down restaurants are even pricier. Here are some strategies to help you save some pennies for souvenirs instead:

- Remember how easy it is to exit the park and return again—you'll also get a much-needed break if lines are very long. The easiest way is to take the monorail directly to the Disneyland Hotel, where dining options from dressy to casual are also overpriced but nowhere near as badly as inside the park.
- Also consider simply walking out the front gates, leaving your car safely in the parking lot, and eating at one of the many coffee shop/diners along Harbor Boulevard.
- Do-it-yourselfers can bring a picnic lunch into the park, stowing it in a locker (near the entrance on Main Street U.S.A.) until lunchtime. Even if you don't have access to a small ice chest, you can store perishables in a plastic-lined bag with a couple of freezable "Blue Ice" packs (about $2 each). Or simply pack chips, cookies, fruit, and canned or bottled beverages in a paper sack—at lunchtime purchase fresh sandwiches and some cups of ice.

TOURING THE PARK

The Disneyland complex is divided into several themed "lands," each of which has a number of rides and attractions that are, more or less, related to that land's theme.

Main Street U.S.A., at the park's entrance, is a cinematic version of turn-of-the-century small-town America. This whitewashed Rockwellian fantasy is lined with gift shops, candy stores, a soda fountain, and a silent theater that continuously runs early Mickey Mouse films. You'll find the practical things you might need too, like stroller rentals and storage lockers. Because there are no rides here, it's best to tour Main Street during the middle of the afternoon, when lines for rides are longest, and in the evening, when you can rest your feet in the theater that features *Great Moments with Mr. Lincoln,* a patriotic (and Audio-Animatronic) look at America's 16th president. There's always something happening on Main Street; stop in at the information booth to the left of the main entrance for a schedule of the day's events.

You might start your day by circumnavigating the park by train. An authentic 19th-century steam engine pulls open-air cars around the park's perimeter. Board at the Main Street Depot and take a complete turn around the park or disembark at any one of the lands.

Adventureland is inspired by the most exotic regions of Asia, Africa, India, and the South Pacific. There are several popular rides here. This is where you'll find the Swiss Family Treehouse. On the Jungle Cruise, passengers board a large authentic-looking Mississippi River paddleboat and float along an Amazon-like river. En route, the boat is threatened by Audio-Animatronic wild animals and hostile natives, while a tour guide entertains with a running patter. A spear's-throw away is the Enchanted Tiki Room, one of the most sedate attractions in Adventureland. Inside, you can sit down and watch a 20-minute musical comedy featuring electronically animated tropical birds, flowers, and "tiki gods."

Indiana Jones: Temple of the Forbidden Eye is based on the Steven Spielberg films, taking adventurers into the temple in joltingly realistic all-terrain vehicles. Riders follow Indy and experience the perils of bubbling lava pits, whizzing arrows, fire-breathing serpents, collapsing bridges, and the familiar cinematic tumbling boulder (this effect is very realistic in the front seats!). Disney "Imagineers" reached new heights with the design of this ride's line, which—take my word for it—has so much detail throughout its twisting path that a half hour or more simply flies by.

Disney Dossier

Believe it or not, the Happiest Place on Earth keeps more than a few skeletons—as well as some just plain interesting facts—in its closet. Did you know the following?

- Disneyland was carved out of orange groves, and the original plans called for carefully chosen individual trees to be left standing and included in the park's landscaping. On groundbreaking day, July 21, 1954, each tree in the orchard was marked with a ribbon—red to be cut and green to be spared. But the bulldozer operator went through and mowed down *every* tree indiscriminately . . . no one had foreseen his color-blindness.

- Disneyland designers utilized forced perspective in the construction of many of the park's structures to give the illusion of height and dramatic proportions while keeping the park a manageable size. The buildings on **Main Street U.S.A.,** for example, are actually 90% scale on the first floor, 80% on the second, and so forth. The stones on **Sleeping Beauty Castle** are carved in diminishing scale from the bottom to the top, giving it the illusion of towering height.

- The faces of the **Pirates of the Caribbean** were modeled after some of the early staff of Walt Disney Imagineering, who also lent their names to the second-floor "businesses" along **Main Street U.S.A.**

- Walt Disney maintained two apartments inside Disneyland. His private apartment above the **Town Square Fire Station** has been kept just as it was when he lived there.

- The elaborately carved horses on Fantasyland's **King Arthur Carousel** are between 100 and 120 years old; Walt Disney found them lying neglected in storage at Coney Island in New York and brought them home to be carefully cleaned and restored.

- **It's a Small World** was touted at its opening as "mingling the waters of the oceans and seas around the world with Small World's Seven Seaways." This was more than a publicity hoax—records from that time show such charges as $21.86 for a shipment of seawater from the Caribbean.

- The peaceful demeanor of Disneyland was broken during the summer of 1970 by a group of radical Vietnam protesters who invaded the park. They seized **Tom Sawyer Island** and raised the Viet Cong flag over the fort before being expelled by riot specialists.

- **Indiana Jones: Temple of the Forbidden Eye,** Disneyland's subterranean thrill ride, won't be experienced the same way by any two groups of riders. Like a sophisticated computer game, the course is programmed with so many variables in the action that there are 160,000 possible combinations of events.

- After the 24-year run of the enormously popular **Main Street Electrical Parade** ended in 1996, 700,000 of the floats' light bulbs were sold, at $10 a piece, with the benefits going to several local charities.

New Orleans Square, a large gas-lamp-dotted green, is home to the Haunted Mansion, the most high-tech ghost house ever. The spookiness has been toned down so kids won't get nightmares anymore, so the events are as funny as they are scary. Even more fanciful is Pirates of the Caribbean, one of Disneyland's most popular rides. Here visitors float on boats through mock underground caves, entering an enchanting world of swashbuckling, rum-running, and buried treasure. Even in the middle of the afternoon you can dine by the cool moonlight and to the sound of crickets in the Blue Bayou Restaurant, the best eatery in the land.

Critter Country is supposed to be an ode to the backwoods—a sort of Frontierland without those pesky settlers. Little kids like to sing along with the Audio-Animatronic critters in the musical Country Bear Jamboree show. Older kids and grown-ups head straight for Splash Mountain, one of the largest water flume rides in the world. Loosely based on the Disney movie *Song of the South,* the ride is lined with about 100 characters that won't stop singing "Zip-A-Dee-Doo-Dah." Be prepared to get wet, especially if someone sizable is in the front seat of your log-shaped boat.

Frontierland gets its inspiration from 19th-century America. It's full of dense "forests" and broad "rivers" inhabited by hearty-looking (but, luckily, not smelling) "pioneers." You can take a raft to Tom Sawyer's Island, a do-it-yourself play island with balancing rocks, caves, and a rope bridge, and board the Big Thunder Mountain Railroad, a runaway roller coaster that races through a deserted 1870s gold mine. You'll also find a petting zoo and an Abe Lincoln–style log cabin; both are great for exploring with the little ones.

On Saturdays, Sundays, holidays, and vacation periods, head to Frontierland's Rivers of America after dark to see the FANTASMIC! show—a mix of magic, music, live performers, and sensational special effects. Just as he did in *The Sorcerer's Apprentice,* Mickey Mouse appears and uses his magical powers to create giant water fountains, enormous flowers, and fantasy creatures. There's plenty of pyrotechnics, lasers, and fog, as well as a 45-foot-tall dragon that breathes fire and sets the water of the Rivers of America aflame. Cool!

Mickey's Toontown is a colorful, wacky, whimsical world inspired by the *Roger Rabbit* films. This is a gag-filled land populated by toons. There are several rides, including Roger Rabbit's CarToonSpin, but these take a back seat to Toontown itself—a trippy smile-inducing world without a straight line or right angle in sight. This is a great place to talk with Mickey, Minnie, Goofy, Roger Rabbit, and the rest of your favorite toons. You can even visit their "houses." Mickey's red-shingled house and movie barn is filled with props from some of his greatest cartoons.

Fantasyland has a storybook theme and is the catchall "land" for all the stuff that doesn't quite seem to fit anywhere else. Most of the rides are geared to the under-6 set, including the King Arthur Carousel, Dumbo the Flying Elephant ride, and the Casey Jr. Circus Train, but some, like Mr. Toad's Wild Ride and Peter Pan's Flight, grown-ups have an irrational attachment to as well. You'll also find Alice in Wonderland, Snow White's Scary Adventures, Pinocchio's Daring Journey, and more. The most lauded attraction is It's a Small World, a slow-moving indoor river ride through a saccharine nightmare of all the world's children singing the song everybody loves to hate. For a different kind of thrill, try the Matterhorn Bobsleds, a zippy roller coaster through chilled caverns and drifting fog banks. It's one of the park's most popular rides. An indoor live-action theater features a musical extravaganza called "Classic Disney Characters."

Tomorrowland, conceived as an optimistic look at the future, has always had a hard time keeping a jump on real advances. Nineteen fifty-five's Rocket to the Moon became Mission to Mars in 1975, only to be a dated laughingstock by the early 1980s. In 1998, Disney architects unveiled a redesigned Tomorrowland that employs an angular metallic look popularized by futurists like Jules Verne. The high-speed ride Rocket Rods will join Tomorrowland favorites Space Mountain, a pitch-black indoor roller coaster that assaults your equilibrium and ears, and Star Tours, the original Disney/George Lucas joint venture; it's a 40-passenger StarSpeeder that encounters a spaceload of misadventures on the way to the Moon of Endor, achieved with wired seats and video effects (not for the queasy). Other new attractions are a 3-D adventure called "Honey, I Shrunk the Audience," which uses a variety of theatrical effects to impart the sensation that you've shrunk to thumbnail size; and an interactive pavilion of near-future technology called Innoventions—a feature close to what old Walt originally envisioned for Tomorrowland, when he created exhibits like the House of the Future and Bathroom of Tomorrow to showcase imaginative technology of the day.

The "lands" themselves are only half the adventure. Other joys include roaming Disney characters, penny arcades, restaurants and snack bars galore, summer fireworks, mariachi and ragtime bands, parades, shops, marching bands, and much more. Oh, yeah—there's also that storybook Sleeping Beauty Castle . . . can you spot the evil witch peering from one of the top windows?

KNOTT'S BERRY FARM

Cynics say Knott's Berry Farm is for people who aren't smart enough to find Disneyland. Well, there's no doubt that visitors should tour Disney first, but it's worth staying in a hotel nearby so you can play at Knott's during your stay.

Like Disneyland, Knott's Berry Farm isn't without its historical merit. Rudolph Boysen crossed a loganberry with a raspberry, calling the resulting hybrid the boysenberry. In 1933, Buena Park farmer Walter Knott planted the boysenberry, thus launching Knott's berry farm on 10 acres of leased land. When things got tough during the Great Depression, Mrs. Knott set up a roadside stand, selling pies, preserves, and home-cooked chicken dinners. Within a year she was selling 90 meals a day. Lines became so long that Walter decided to create an Old West Ghost Town as a diversion for waiting customers.

The Knott family now owns the farm surrounding the world-famous Chicken Dinner Restaurant, an eatery serving over a million fried meals a year. And Knott's Berry Farm is the nation's third-most-attended family entertainment complex (after the two Disney parks, of course).

During the last half of October, locals flock to Knott's Berry Farm. Why? Because the entire park is revamped as "Knott's *Scary* Farm"—the ordinary attractions are made spooky and haunted, every grassy area is transformed into a graveyard or gallows, and even the already-scary rides get special surprise extras, like costumed ghouls who grab your arm in the middle of a roller-coaster ride!

ESSENTIALS

GETTING THERE   Knott's Berry Farm is at 8039 Beach Blvd. in Buena Park, about a 5-minute ride north on I-5 from Disneyland. From I-5 or Calif. 91, exit south onto Beach Boulevard. The park is about half a mile south of Calif. 91.

ADMISSION, HOURS & INFORMATION   Admission to the park, including unlimited access to all rides, shows, and attractions, is $35 for adults and children 12 and over, $25 for seniors 60 and over and children 3 to 11, and free for children under 3. Admission is $15 for everyone after 4pm. Parking is $6. Like Disneyland, Knott's offers discounted admission during off-season for southern California residents, so if you're bringing local friends or family members along, be sure to take advantage of the bargain. Also like Disneyland, Knott's Berry Farm's hours vary from week to week, so you should call about the day you plan to visit. Generally speaking, the park is open during summer every day from 9am to midnight. The rest of the year, it opens at 10am and closes at 6 or 8pm, except Friday and Saturday, when it stays open to 10pm or midnight. Knott's is closed Christmas Day. Special hours and prices are in effect during Knott's Scary Farm in late October. For recorded information, call ☎ 714/220-5200.

TOURING THE PARK

Knott's Berry Farm still maintains its original Old West motif. It's divided into seven "Old Time Adventures" areas:

Old West Ghost Town, the original attraction, is a collection of refurbished 19th-century buildings that have been relocated from actual deserted Old West towns. You can pan for gold, ride aboard an authentic stagecoach, ride rickety train cars through the Calico Mine, get held up aboard the Denver and Rio Grande Calico Railroad, and hiss at the villain during a melodrama in the Birdcage Theater.

Fiesta Village has a south-of-the-border theme that means festive markets, strolling mariachis, and wild rides like Montezooma's Revenge and Jaguar!, a roller coaster that includes two heart-in-the-mouth drops and a loop that turns you upside down.

The **Roaring '20s Amusement Area** contains Sky Tower, a parachute jump/drop with a 20-story free fall. Other white-knuckle rides are XK-1, an excellent flight simulator "piloted" by the riders; and Boomerang, a state-of-the-art roller coaster that turns riders upside down six times in less than a minute. Kingdom of the Dinosaurs features extremely realistic *Jurassic Park*–like creatures. It's quite a thrill but may scare the little kids.

Wild Water Wilderness is a $10-million, 3½-acre attraction styled like a turn-of-the-century California wilderness park. The top ride is a white-water adventure called Bigfoot Rapids, featuring a long stretch of artificial rapids; it's the longest ride of its kind in the world.

Camp Snoopy, meant to re-create a wilderness camp in the picturesque High Sierra, will probably be the youngsters' favorite area. Its 6 rustic acres are the playgrounds of Charles Schulz's beloved beagle and his pals, Charlie Brown and Lucy, who greet guests and pose for pictures. The rides, including Beary Tales Playhouse, are tailor-made for the 6-and-under set.

Thunder Falls contains Mystery Lodge, a truly amazing high-tech, trick-of-the-eye attraction based on the legends of local Native Americans. Don't miss this wonderful theater piece.

The **Boardwalk** is Knott's newest themed area, presented as a salute to southern California's beach culture—it's main attraction is Windjammer, a wind-whipping dual roller coaster originally intended to evoke the flips and glides of windsurfing but often advertised as a twister tornado.

Stage shows and special activities are scheduled throughout the day. Pick up a schedule at the ticket booth.

A NEARBY PRESIDENTIAL LIBRARY

Richard Nixon Library and Birthplace. 18001 Yorba Linda Blvd., Yorba Linda. ☎ **714/ 993-5075.** Fax 714/993-3393. Admission $5.95 adults, $3.95 seniors, $2 children 8–11, free for children 7 and under. Mon–Sat 10am–5pm; Sun 11am–5pm.

Though he was the most vilified U.S. president in modern history, there has always been a warm place in the hearts of Orange County locals for Richard Nixon. This presidential library, located in Nixon's boyhood town, celebrates the roots, life, and legacy of America's 37th president. The 9-acre site contains the modest farmhouse where Nixon was born, manicured flower gardens, a modern museum containing presidential archives, and the final resting place of both Nixon and his wife, Pat.

Displays include videos of the famous Nixon-Kennedy TV debates, an impressive life-size statuary summit of world leaders, gifts of state (including a gun from Elvis), and exhibits on China and Russia. There's also an exhibit of Pat Nixon's sparkling First Lady gowns and a 12-foot-high graffiti-covered chunk of the Berlin Wall, symbolizing the defeat of Communism, but hardly a mention of Nixon's leading role in the anti-Communist witch hunts of the 1950s. There are exhibits on Vietnam, yet no mention of Nixon's illegal expansion of that war into neighboring Cambodia. Only the Watergate Gallery is relatively forthright, where you can listen to actual White House tapes and view a montage of the president's last day in the White House.

WHERE TO STAY
SUPER-CHEAP SLEEPS

✪ **Best Western Anaheim Stardust.** 1057 W. Ball Rd., Anaheim, CA 92802. ☎ **800/222-3639** or 714/774-7600. Fax 714/535-6953. 121 units. A/C TV TEL. $70–$85 double; $105 family room. Rates include full breakfast. AE, DC, DISC, MC, V. Free parking; shuttle to Disneyland.

On the back side of Disneyland, this modest hotel will appeal to the budget-conscious traveler who isn't willing to sacrifice everything. All the rooms have a refrigerator and microwave, breakfast is served in a refurbished train dining car, and you can relax by the large outdoor heated pool and spa while doing wash in the laundry room. The extra-large family rooms will accommodate virtually any brood.

Candy Cane Inn. 1747 S. Harbor Blvd., Anaheim, CA 92802. ☎ **800/345-7057** or 714/774-5284. Fax 714/772-5462. 173 units. A/C TV TEL. $74–$95 double. Rates include expanded continental breakfast. AE, DC, DISC, MC, V. Free parking; shuttle to Disneyland.

Take your standard U-shaped motel court with outdoor corridors, spruce it up with cobblestone drive- and walkways, old-time street lamps, and flowering vines engulfing the balconies of attractively painted rooms, and you have the Candy Cane. The face-lift worked, making this motel near Disneyland's main gate a real treat for the stylish bargain hunter. The rooms are decorated in bright floral motifs with comfortable furnishings, including queen beds and a separate dressing/vanity area. Breakfast is served in the courtyard, where you can also splash around in a heated pool, spa, or kids' wading pool.

Colony Inn. 7800 Crescent Ave. (west of Beach Blvd.), Buena Park, CA 90620. ☎ **800/98-COLONY** or 714/527-2201. Fax 714/826-3826. 130 units. A/C TV TEL. $49–$98 double or suite. AE, MC, V. Free parking.

Though it's composed of two modest U-shaped motels, the recently refurbished Colony has a lot to offer. It's the closest lodging to Knott's Berry Farm's south entrance and just 10 minutes from Disneyland. They cheerfully offer discount coupons for Knott's and other nearby attractions, as well as complimentary coffee and doughnuts to jump-start your morning. The rooms are spacious (doubles sleep up to four, suites up to eight) and comfortably outfitted with conservatively styled furnishings. There are two pools, two wading pools for kids, two saunas, and a coin-operated laundry.

Howard Johnson Hotel. 1380 S. Harbor Blvd., Anaheim, CA 92802. ☎ **800/422-4228** or 714/776-6120. Fax 714/533-3578. 320 units. A/C TV TEL. $74–$94 double. AE, CB, DC, DISC, MC, V. Free parking; trolley to Disneyland.

This hotel occupies an enviable location opposite Disneyland, and a cute San Francisco trolley car runs to and from the park every 30 minutes. The rooms are divided among several low-profile buildings, all with balconies opening onto a central garden with two heated pools for adults and one for children. Garden paths lead under eucalyptus and olive trees to a splashing circular fountain. During summer you can see the nightly fireworks display at Disneyland from the upper balconies of the park-side rooms. Try to avoid the rooms in the back buildings, for they get some freeway noise. Services and facilities include in-room movies and cable, room service from the attached Coco's Restaurant, a gift shop, a game room, laundry service plus a coin-laundry room, an airport shuttle, and family lodging/Disney admission packages. It's pretty classy for a HoJo's.

FOR A FEW BUCKS MORE

Anaheim Plaza Hotel. 1700 S. Harbor Blvd., Anaheim, CA 92802. ☎ **800/228-1357** or 714/772-5900. Fax 714/772-8386. 300 units. A/C TV TEL. $79–$119 double; from $175 suite. AE, DC, DISC, MC, V. Free parking; shuttle to Disneyland.

You can easily cross the street to Disneyland's main gate or can take advantage of the Anaheim Plaza's free shuttle. Once you return, you'll appreciate the way this 30-year-old hotel's clever design shuts out the noisy world. In fact, the seven two-story garden buildings remind me of 1960s Waikiki more than busy Anaheim. The Olympic-size heated outdoor pool and whirlpool are unfortunately surrounded by Astroturf, a retro feature left intact despite a total room renovation in 1997. Thankfully, the new management didn't change a thing about the light-filled modern lobby or the friendly rates, which can often drop as low as $49. There's room service from the casual cafe in the lobby, plus valet service and coin-operated laundry.

MODERATELY PRICED OPTIONS

Buena Park Hotel. 7675 Crescent Ave. (at Grand), Buena Park, CA 90620. ☎ **800/422-4444** or 714/995-1111. Fax 714/828-8590. 350 units. A/C TV TEL. $99–$109 double; $175–$250 suite. AE, DC, DISC, MC, V. Free parking; shuttle to Disneyland.

Within easy walking distance of Knott's Berry Farm, the Buena Park Hotel also offers a free shuttle to Disneyland just 7 miles away. The pristine lobby has the look of a business-oriented hotel, and that it is. But vacationers can benefit from the elevated level of service designed for the business traveler. Be sure to inquire about Executive Club rates as well as Knott's or Disneyland package deals. The rooms in the nine-story tower are tastefully decorated, and facilities and services include room service, a charming heated outdoor pool and spa, two restaurants, a 1950s/1960s dance club, and a rental-car desk.

Jolly Roger Hotel. 640 W. Katella Ave. (west of Harbor Blvd.), Anaheim, CA 92802. ☎ **800/446-1555** or 714/772-7621. Fax 714/635-2262. 236 units. A/C TV TEL. $109–$139 double; $250 suite. AE, DC, DISC, MC, V. Free parking; shuttle to Disneyland.

The only thing still sporting a buccaneer theme is the adjoining Jolly Roger Restaurant, and that's just fine. Conveniently across the street from Disneyland, the comfortable but blandly furnished rooms are in either an older two-story L-shaped motel or two newer five-story annexes. I prefer the older units for their quiet and for the palm-shaded heated pool in the center. Across the driveway is the swashbuckling restaurant where dinner will set you back a few doubloons. The all-day coffee shop is more reasonable, and there's nightly entertainment and dancing in the lounge. The Jolly Roger also has meeting and banquet rooms, plus a second pool, a spa, beauty salon, and gift shop.

WORTH A SPLURGE

✪ **Disneyland Hotel.** 1150 W. Cerritos Ave. (west of the Disneyland parking lot), Anaheim, CA 92802. ☎ **714/778-6600.** Fax 714/965-6597. 1,198 units. A/C MINIBAR TV TEL. $175–$270 double; from $425 suite. AE, MC, V. Parking $10.

The Official Hotel of the Magic Kingdom, attached to Disneyland via a monorail system running right to the hotel, is the perfect place to stay if you're doing the park. You'll be able to return to your room anytime you need to during the day, whether it's to take a much-needed nap or to change your soaked shirt and shorts after your Splash Mountain Adventure. Best of all, hotel guests get to enter the park early almost every day and enjoy the major rides before the lines form. The amount of time varies from day to day, but usually you can enter 1½ hours early. Call ahead to check the schedule for your specific day.

The theme hotel is a wild attraction unto itself. The rooms aren't fancy but are comfortably and attractively furnished like a good-quality business hotel. Many rooms feature framed reproductions of rare Disney conceptual art, and the Disney Channel is free on TV, naturally. The beautifully landscaped hotel is an all-inclusive resort, offering six restaurants, five cocktail lounges, every kind of service desk imaginable, a "wharf-side" bazaar, a walk-under waterfall, and even an artificial white-sand beach. The complex also includes the adjoining **Pacific Hotel,** offering a Disney version of Asian tranquillity (including a fine and pricey Japanese restaurant).

When you're planning your trip, inquire about multiday packages that allow you to take on the park at your own pace and usually include free parking for the duration of your stay.

Dining: The best restaurant is Stromboli's, an Italian/American eatery that serves all the pasta staples. Kids love Goofy's Kitchen, where the family can enjoy breakfast and dinner with the Disney characters.

Amenities: Three large heated outdoor pools, complete health club, shuffleboard and croquet courts, concierge, room service, laundry, nightly turndown, special children's programs, baby-sitting, express checkout, shoe-shine, 20 shops.

Sheraton Anaheim Hotel. 1015 W. Ball Rd. (at I-5), Anaheim, CA 92802. ☎ **800/ 325-3535** or 714/778-1700. Fax 714/535-3889. 526 units. A/C MINIBAR TV TEL. $170–$190 double; $290–$360 suite. AE, CB, DC, MC, V. Free parking; shuttle to Disneyland.

This hotel rises to the festive theme-park occasion with its fanciful English Tudor architecture, a castle that lures business conventions, Disney-bound families, and area high-school proms equally successfully. The public areas are quiet and elegant, and you'll find intimate gardens with fountains and koi ponds—a pleasing touch after a frantic day at the park. The rooms are modern and unusually spacious but otherwise not distinctive; a large pool is in the center of the complex, surrounded by attractive landscaping.

Bargain-hunter's tip: Don't be put off by the high rack rates; rooms more commonly go for $100 to $130, even on busy summer weekends.

WHERE TO DINE

Inland Orange County isn't known for its restaurants, most of which are branches of reliable California or national chains. I've listed a few intriguing options, but if you're visiting the area just for the day, you'll probably eat inside the theme parks (see "Disney Tips," above); there are plenty of restaurants to choose from at both Disneyland and Knott's Berry Farm. At Disneyland, in the Creole-themed **Blue Bayou,** you can sit under the stars inside the Pirates of the Caribbean ride—no matter what time of day it is. At Knott's, try the fried chicken dinners and boysenberry pies at Mrs. Knott's historic **Chicken Dinner Restaurant.**

✪ **Belisle's Restaurant.** 12001 Harbor Blvd. (at Chapman), Garden Grove. ☎ **714/ 750-6560.** Main courses $3–$23. MC, V. Sun–Thurs 7am–midnight; Fri–Sat 7am–2am. AMERICAN.

Harvey Belisle's modest pink cottage has been doling out "Texas-size" portions of diner-style food since before Disneyland opened in 1955. This is the place to bring a ravenous football team or just your hollow-legged teenagers. Portions are enormous; I can't say that enough, from the four-egg omelets accompanied by mountains of hash browns to the 12-ounce chicken-fried steak to a chocolate eclair the size of a log—Paul Bunyan would feel right at home. Just say, "Fill 'er up!"

Felix Continental Cafe. 36 Plaza Sq. (at Chapman and Glassell), Orange. ☎ **714/633-5842.** Reservations recommended for dinner. Main courses $6–$14. AE, DC, MC, V. Mon–Thurs 7am–9pm; Fri 7am–10pm; Sat 8am–10pm; Sun 8am–9pm. CUBAN/SPANISH.

If you like the re-created Main Street in the Magic Kingdom, then you'll love the historic 1886 town square in the city of Orange, on view from the cozy sidewalk tables outside this cafe. Dining on traditional Cuban specialties and watching traffic spin around the magnificent fountain and rosebushes of the plaza evokes old Havana or Madrid rather than the cookie-cutter Orange County communities just blocks away. The food receives glowing praise from reviewers and locals alike.

Renata's Caffè Italiano. 227 E. Chapman Ave. (at Grand), Orange. ☎ **714/771-4740.** Reservations recommended for dinner. Main courses $8–$15. AE, DISC, MC, V. Mon–Thurs 11am–9pm; Fri 11am–10pm; Sat 4–10pm. ITALIAN.

Near Felix Cafe in the historic plaza district, owner Renata Cerchiari draws a steady stream of regulars with good if not great contemporary Italian specialties. I found the charming patio dining in this small-town atmosphere a welcome change from Orange County's frantic pace (particularly if you're staying by the amusement parks) and the wide selection of appetizers and pasta dishes more authentic and reasonably priced than anywhere else, though the creamy Caesar salad wins higher marks than the disappointing cannoli.

5 The Orange Coast

Seal Beach is 36 miles S of Los Angeles; Newport Beach, 49 miles; Dana Point, 65 miles

Whatever you do, don't say "Orange County." The mere name evokes images of smoggy industrial parks, cookie-cutter housing developments, and the staunch Republicanism that prevails behind the so-called orange curtain. I'm talking instead about the Orange Coast, one of southern California's best-kept secrets, a string of seaside jewels that have been compared with the Côte d'Azur or the Costa del Sol. Here, 42 miles of beaches offer pristine stretches of sand, tide pools teeming with marine life, ecological preserves, charming secluded coves, quaint pleasure-boat harbors, and legendary surfers atop breaking waves. Whether your bare feet want to stroll a funky wooden boardwalk or your gold card gravitates toward a yacht club, you've come to the right place.

ESSENTIALS

GETTING THERE   See chapter 13 for airport and airline information. By car from Los Angeles, take I-5 or I-405 south. The scenic shore-hugging Pacific Coast Highway (Calif. 1, or just PCH to locals) links the Orange Coast communities from Seal Beach in the north to Capistrano Beach just south of Dana Point, where it merges with I-5. To reach the beach communities directly, take the following freeway exits: **Seal Beach,** Seal Beach Boulevard from I-405; **Huntington Beach,** Beach Boulevard/Calif. 39 from I-405 or I-5; **Newport Beach,** Calif. 55 from I-405 or I-5; **Laguna Beach,** Calif. 133 from I-5; **San Juan Capistrano,** Ortega Highway/Calif. 74 from I-5; and **Dana Point,** Pacific Coast Highway/Calif. 1 from I-5.

VISITOR INFORMATION   The **Seal Beach Chamber of Commerce,** 201 Eighth St., at Central (☎ **562/799-0179**), is open Monday through Friday from 10am to 3pm.

Anaheim Area & Orange Coast Attractions

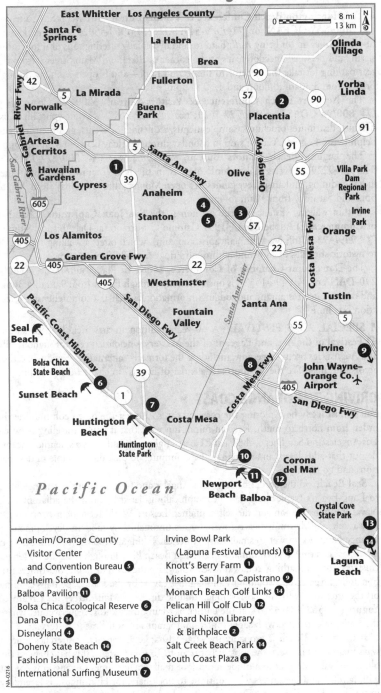

0 ——— 8 mi
13 km
N

Anaheim/Orange County
   Visitor Center
   and Convention Bureau ⑤
Anaheim Stadium ③
Balboa Pavilion ⑪
Bolsa Chica Ecological Reserve ⑥
Dana Point ⑭
Disneyland ④
Doheny State Beach ⑭
Fashion Island Newport Beach ⑩
International Surfing Museum ⑦

Irvine Bowl Park
   (Laguna Festival Grounds) ⑬
Knott's Berry Farm ①
Mission San Juan Capistrano ⑨
Monarch Beach Golf Links ⑭
Pelican Hill Golf Club ⑫
Richard Nixon Library
   & Birthplace ②
Salt Creek Beach Park ⑭
South Coast Plaza ⑧

The **Huntington Beach Conference & Visitors Bureau,** 101 Main St., Suite A-2 (☎ **800/SAY-OCEAN** or 714/969-3492; fax 714/969-5592; www.imark.com/hbcvb), makes up for being *really* hard to find by genially offering tons of info, enthusiasm, and personal anecdotes. It's at the corner of PCH and Main Street—from the rear parking lot take the elevator to the second floor—and is open Monday through Friday from 8:30am to noon and 1:30 to 5pm.

The **Newport Beach Conference & Visitors Bureau,** 3300 W. Coast Hwy. (☎ **800/94-COAST** or 949/722-1611; fax 949/722-1612; www.newport.lib.ca.us/default), distributes brochures, sample menus, a calendar of events, and their free and helpful visitor's guide. Call or stop in Monday through Friday between 8am and 5pm.

The **Laguna Beach Visitors Bureau,** 252 Broadway (☎ **800/877-1115** or 949/497-9229; www.lagunabeachinfo.org), is in the heart of town and distributes lodging, dining, and art-gallery guides. It's open Monday through Friday from 9am to 5pm and Saturday from 10am to 4pm.

Within walking distance of the mission is the **San Juan Capistrano Chamber of Commerce,** El Adobe Plaza, 31931 Camino Capistrano (at Del Abispo), Suite D (☎ **949/493-4700;** www.sanjuancapistrano.com), which offers a walking-tour guide to historic sites. It's open Monday through Friday from 8:30am to 4pm.

The **Dana Point Chamber of Commerce,** 24681 La Plaza, Suite 120 (☎ **800/290-DANA** or 949/496-1555), is open Monday through Friday from 9am to 4:30pm and carries some restaurant and lodging information as well as a comprehensive recreation brochure.

A SPECIAL ARTS FESTIVAL   A 60-year tradition in arts-friendly Laguna, the ✪ **Festival of the Arts and Pageant of the Masters** is held each year throughout July and August. It's pretty large now, including the formerly "alternative" Sawdust Festival across the street. See the "California Calendar of Events" in chapter 2 for details.

DRIVING THE ORANGE COAST

You'll most likely be exploring the coast by car, so I cover the beach communities in order, from north to south. Keep in mind, however, that if you're traveling between Los Angeles and San Diego, the Pacific Coast Highway (Calif. 1) is a splendidly scenic detour that adds less than an hour to the commute. So pick out a couple of destinations and go for it.

Seal Beach, on the border between Los Angeles and Orange counties and neighbor to Long Beach's Naples harbor, is geographically isolated by both the adjacent U.S. Naval Weapons Station and the self-contained Leisure World retirement community. As a result, the charming beach town appears untouched by modern development—Orange County's answer to small-town America. Taking a stroll down Main Street is a walk back in time that culminates in the Seal Beach Pier. Though there are no longer clusters of the sunbathing, squawking seals that gave the town its name, old-timers fish hopefully, lovers stroll swooningly, and families cavort by the seaside, perhaps capping off the afternoon with an old-fashioned double dip from **Main Street Ice Cream & Yogurt** (☎ 562/431-3394), at the corner of Main Street and Ocean Avenue, where the walls are decorated with sepia-toned photographs of Seal Beach's yesteryear.

Huntington Beach is probably the largest Orange Coast city; it stretches quite a ways inland and has seen the most urbanization. To some extent, this has changed the old boardwalk and pier to a modern outdoor mall where cliques of gang kids coexist with families and the surfers who continue to flock here, for Huntington is legendary in surf lore. Hawaiian surfer Duke Kahanamoku brought the sport here in the 1920s, and some say the breaks around the pier and Bolsa Chica are the best in California.

The world's top wave-riders flock to Huntington each August for the rowdy but professional **U.S. Open of Surfing** (call ☎ 310/286-3700 for information). If you'll be around at Christmastime, try to see the gaily decorated marina homes and boats in Huntington Harbour by taking the **Cruise of Lights,** a 45-minute narrated sail through and around the harbor islands. The festivities generally last from mid-December until Christmas; call ☎ 714/840-7542 for schedules and ticket information.

The name **Newport Beach** conjures comparisons to Rhode Island's Newport, where the well-to-do enjoy seaside living with all the creature comforts. That's the way it is here, but on a less grandiose scale. From the million-dollar Cape Cod–style cottages on sunny Balboa Island in the bay, to elegant shopping complexes like Fashion Island and South Coast Plaza (an über-mall with valet parking, car detailing, limo service, and concierge), this is where fashionable socialites, right-wing celebrities, and business mavens can be found. Alternatively, you could explore **Balboa** peninsula's historic Pavilion and old-fashioned pier or board a passenger ferry to Catalina Island.

Laguna Beach, whose breathtaking geography is marked by bold elevated headlands, coastal bluffs, and pocket coves, is known as an artists' enclave, but the truth is that Laguna has became so *in* (read: expensive) that it drove most of the true bohemians *out.* Their legacy remains with the annual **Festival of the Arts and Pageant of the Masters** (see "A Special Arts Festival," above), as well as a proliferation of art galleries intermingling with high-priced boutiques along the town's cozy streets. In warm weather, Laguna Beach has an overwhelming Mediterranean-island ambiance, which makes *everyone* feel beautifully, idly rich.

San Juan Capistrano, nestled in the verdant headlands just inland of Dana Point, is defined by Spanish missions and its loyal flock of swallows. The mission architecture is authentic, and history abounds. Consider San Juan Capistrano a compact life-size diorama illustrating the evolution of a small Western town from Spanish-mission era to secular rancho period, into statehood and the 20th century. Ironically, Mission San Juan Capistrano (see "Seeing the Sights," below) is once again the center of the community, just as the founding friars intended 200 years ago.

Dana Point, the last town south, has been called a "marina development in search of a soul." Overlooking the harbor stands a monument to 19th-century author Richard Henry Dana, who gave his name to the area and described it in *Two Years Before the Mast.* Activities generally center around yachting and Dana Point's jewel of a harbor. Nautical themes are everywhere; particularly charming are the series of streets named for old-fashioned shipboard lights, a rainbow that includes "Street of the Amber Lantern," ". . . the Violet Lantern," ". . . the Golden Lantern," and so on. Bordering the harbor is Doheny State Beach (see "Beaches & Nature Preserves," below), which wrote the book on seaside park and camping facilities.

ENJOYING THE OUTDOORS

BEACHES & NATURE PRESERVES   The **Bolsa Chica Ecological Reserve,** in Huntington Beach (☎ 714/897-7003), is a 300-acre restored urban salt marsh that's a haven to more than 200 bird species, as well as a wide variety of protected plants and animals. Naturalists come to spot herons and egrets as well as California horn snails, jackknife clams, sea sponges, common jellyfish, and shore crabs. An easy 1½-mile loop trail begins from a parking lot on the Pacific Coast Highway (Calif. 1) a mile south of Warner Boulevard; docents lead a narrated walk the 1st Saturday of every month. The trail heads inland, over Inner Bolsa Bay and up Bolsa Chica bluffs. It then loops back toward the ocean over a dike separating the inner and outer Bolsa bays and traversing a coastal sand dune system. This beautiful hike is a terrific afternoon adventure. The

Bolsa Chica Conservancy has been working since 1978 on reclaiming the wetlands from oil companies that began drilling 70 years ago. It's an ongoing process, and you can still see those "seesaw" drills dotting the outer areas of the reserve. Although Bolsa Chica State Beach across the road has superb facilities, fantastic surfing, and well-equipped campsites, you might find that the hulking offshore oil rigs spoil the view.

Huntington City Beach, adjacent to Huntington Pier, is a haven for volleyball players and surfers; dense crowds abound, but at least so do amenities like outdoor showers, beach rentals, and rest rooms. Just south of the city beach is 3-mile-long **Huntington State Beach.** Both popular beaches have lifeguards and concession stands seasonally. The state beach also has rest rooms, showers, barbecue pits, and a waterfront bike path. The main entrance is on Beach Boulevard, and there are access points all along the Pacific Coast Highway (Calif. 1).

Newport Beach runs for about 5 miles and includes both Newport and Balboa piers. There are outdoor showers, rest rooms, volleyball nets, and a vintage boardwalk that may make you feel as though you've stepped 50 years back in time. **Balboa Bike and Beach Stuff** (☎ 949/723-1516), at the corner of Balboa and Palm near the pier, can rent you a variety of items, from pier fishing poles to bikes, beach umbrellas, and body boards. The **Southwind Kayak Center,** 2801 W. Pacific Coast Hwy. (☎ 800/768-8494 or 949/261-0200; www.southwindkayaks.com), rents sea kayaks for use in the bay or open ocean at $10 to $14 per hour; instructional classes are available on weekends, with some midweek classes in summer. They also conduct bird-watching kayak expeditions into the Upper Newport Bay Ecological Reserve for $40 to $65.

Crystal Cove State Park, which covers 3 miles of coastline between Corona del Mar and Laguna Beach and then extends up into the hills around El Moro Canyon, is a good alternative to the more popular beaches for you seekers of solitude. There are, however, lifeguards and rest rooms. The beach is a winding sandy strip, backed with grassy terraces; high tide sometimes sections it into coves. The entire area offshore is an underwater nature preserve. There are four entrances, including Pelican Point and El Moro Canyon. For more information, call ☎ 949/494-3539 or 949/848-1566.

Salt Creek Beach Park lies below the palatial Ritz-Carlton Laguna Niguel; guests who tire of the pristine swimming pool venture down the staircase on Ritz Carlton Drive to wiggle their toes in the sand. The setting is marvelous, with wide white-sand beaches looking out toward Catalina Island (why do you think the Ritz-Carlton was built here?). There are lifeguards, rest rooms, a snack bar, and convenient parking near the hotel.

Doheny State Beach in Dana Point has long been known as a premier surfing spot and camping site. Just south of lovely Dana Point Marina (enter off Del Abispo Street), Doheny has the friendly vibe of beach parties in days gone by: Tree-shaded lawns give way to wide beaches, and picnicking and beach camping are encouraged. There are 121 sites for both tents and RVs, plus a state-run visitor center featuring several small aquariums of sea and tide-pool life. For more information and camping availability, call ☎ 949/492-0802.

BIKING   Bicycling is the most popular beach activity up and down the coast. A slower-paced alternative to driving, it allows you to enjoy the clean fresh air and notice smaller details of these laid-back beach towns and harbors. The Newport Beach Conference & Visitors Bureau (see "Visitor Information," above) offers a free *Bike Ways* map of trails throughout the city and harbor. Bikes and equipment can be rented at **Balboa Bike & Beach Stuff,** 601 Balboa Blvd., Newport Beach (☎ 949/723-1516); **Laguna Beach Cyclery,** 240 Thalia St. (☎ 949/494-1522); and **Dana Point Bicycle,** 34155 Pacific Coast Hwy. (☎ 949/661-8356).

GOLF   Many golf-course architects have used the geography of the Orange Coast to its full advantage, molding challenging and scenic courses from the rolling bluffs. Most courses are private, but two outstanding ones are public. **Monarch Beach Golf Links,** 23841 Stonehill Dr., Dana Point (☎ **949/240-8247**), is particularly impressive, a hilly and challenging course designed by Robert Trent Jones II. Most holes offer great ocean views, but afternoon winds can sneak up, so accuracy is essential. Weekend greens fees are $135; midweek and twilight fees are available.

Another challenge is the **Pelican Hill Golf Club,** 22651 Pelican Hill Rd. S., Newport Beach (☎ **949/760-0707** starter; 949/640-0238 pro shop), with two Tom Fazio–designed courses. The Links course is heavily bunkered, while the Ocean course features canyons and rocky ravines; both have difficult, large, multitier greens. Weekend greens fees are $195; midweek and twilight fees are available. And remember, when putting near the ocean, the break is always toward the water!

SEEING THE SIGHTS

International Surfing Museum. 411 Olive Ave., Huntington Beach. ☎ **714/960-3483.** Admission $2 adults, $1 students, free for kids 5 and under. Mid-June to late Sept daily noon–5pm; the rest of the year Wed–Sun noon–5pm.

Nostalgic Gidgets and Moondoggies shouldn't miss this monument to this laid-back sport that has become synonymous with California beaches. There are gargantuan long-boards from the sport's early days, memorabilia of Duke Kahanamoku and the other surfing greats represented on the "Walk of Fame" near Huntington Pier, and a gift shop where a copy of the *Surfin'ary* can help you bone up on your surfer slang even if you can't hang ten.

Balboa Pavilion. 400 Main St., Balboa, Newport Beach. ☎ **949/673-5245.** From Calif. 1, turn south onto Newport Blvd. (which becomes Balboa Blvd. on the peninsula); turn left at Main St.

This historic cupola-topped structure, a California Historical Landmark, was built in 1905 as a bathhouse for swimmers in ankle-length bathing costumes. During the Big Band era, dancers rocked the Pavilion doing the "Balboa Hop." Now it serves as the terminal for Catalina Island passenger service, harbor and whale-watching cruises, and fishing charters. The surrounding boardwalk is the Balboa Fun Zone, a collection of carnival rides, game arcades, and vendors of hot dogs and cotton candy. For Newport Harbor or Catalina cruise information, call ☎ **949/673-5245;** for sportfishing and whale watching, call ☎ **949/673-1434.**

Laguna Art Museum. 307 Cliff Dr., Laguna Beach. ☎ **949/494-6531.** Admission $5 adults, $4 students and seniors; free for kids under 12. Tues–Sun 11am–5pm.

Reopened in 1997, this beloved local institution is working hard to position itself as the artistic cornerstone of the community. In addition to a small but interesting permanent collection, the museum presents installations of regional works definitely worth a detour. Past examples include a display of surf photography from the coast's 1930s and 1940s golden era and dozens of *plein air* Impressionist paintings (ca. 1900–30) by the founding artists of the colony.

Mission San Juan Capistrano. Ortega Hwy. (Calif. 74), San Juan Capistrano. ☎ **714/248-2048.** Admission $5 adults, $4 children and seniors. Daily 8:30am–5pm.

The seventh of the 21 California coastal missions, Mission San Juan Capistrano is continually being restored. The mix of old ruins and working buildings is home to small museum collections and various adobe rooms as quaint as they are interesting. The intimate mission chapel with its ornate baroque altar is still regularly used for religious services, and the mission complex is the center of the community, hosting performing arts, children's programs, and other cultural events year-round.

This mission is best known for its swallows, which are said to return to nest each year at their favorite sanctuary. According to legend, the birds wing their way back to the mission annually on March 19, St. Joseph's Day, arriving at dawn; they're said to take flight again on October 23, after bidding the mission farewell. In reality, however, you can probably see the well-fed birds here any day, winter or summer.

EXPLORING BALBOA ISLAND

The charm of this pretty little neighborhood isn't diminished by knowing that the island was man-made—and it certainly hasn't affected the price of real estate. Tiny clapboard cottages in the island's center and modern houses with two-story windows and private docks along the perimeter make a colorful and romantic picture. You can drive onto the island on Jamboree Road to the north or take the three-car ferry from Balboa Peninsula (about $1.50 per vehicle). It's generally more fun to park and take the ferry as a pedestrian, since the tiny alleys they call streets are more suitable for strolling, there are usually crowds, and parking spaces are scarce. **Marine Avenue,** the main commercial street, is lined with small shops and cafes that evoke a New England fishing village. Refreshing shaved ices sold by sidewalk vendors will relieve the summer heat.

SHOPPING

Just as the communities along the coast range from casually barefoot summer playgrounds to meticulously groomed yacht-clubby enclaves, so does the shopping scene stretch to both ends of the spectrum. **Seal Beach,** indifferent to tourists, has charming low-tech shops designed to service the year-round residents, while **Huntington Beach** offers a plethora of surf and water-sport shops, reflecting its sporty nature. Both Huntington and Balboa have more than their share of T-shirt and souvenir stands, while tony **Newport Beach** has been called "Beverly Hills south" because of the many European designer boutiques and high-priced shops. **Laguna Beach** is art-gallery intensive; with over 100 at last count, you'll do well to pick up an expanded gallery guide at the Laguna Beach Visitors Bureau (see "Visitor Information," above). Most galleries are clustered along the Pacific Coast Highway, particularly at the northern end of town— a stretch that's historically been known as **Gallery Row.** There's little shopping in **Dana Point** and mostly mission-themed souvenirs in **San Juan Capistrano.**

Shoppers from all over the Southland flock to the two excellent malls below. If that isn't to your taste, a drive along the Pacific Coast Highway will yield many other opportunities for browsing and souvenir purchases.

Fashion Island Newport Beach, 401 Newport Center Dr., Newport Beach (☎ 949/721-2000), isn't actually an island, unless you count the nearly impenetrable sea of parking lots and structures bordering this posh mall, designed to resemble an open-air Mediterranean village. Anchored by Neiman-Marcus and Macy's, the mall is lined with outdoor artwork, upscale shops, and specialized boutiques like the brand-new J. Peterman Company Store.

✪ **South Coast Plaza,** 3333 Bristol St. (at I-405), Costa Mesa (☎ 800/782-8888 or 714/435-2000), is one of the most upscale shopping complexes in the world, so big that it's a day's adventure unto itself. This beautifully designed center is home to some of fashion's most prominent boutiques, including Emporio Armani, Chanel, Alfred Dunhill, and Coach; beautiful branches of the nation's top department stores, such as Saks Fifth Avenue and Nordstrom; and outposts of the best high-end specialty shops, like Williams Sonoma, L.A. Eyeworks, and Rizzoli Booksellers. The multidimensional mall is home to many impressive works of modern art, and snacking and dining options are also a cut above. You won't find Hot-Dog-on-a-Stick among the 40 or so restaurants scattered throughout. Wolfgang Puck Cafe, Morton's of Chicago, Ghirardelli Soda Fountain, Planet Hollywood, and Scott's Seafood Grill lure the hungry away from Del Taco and McDonald's.

WHERE TO STAY

Budget options along the mostly glitzy Orange Coast do exist, they're just few and far between. Some of the national chains have motels near (not on) the beach, but it's not impossible to find a comfortable but small-scale beachfront motel.

Here are some options along the coast: **Harbour Inn,** 16912 Pacific Coast Hwy., Huntington/Sunset Beach (☎ 800/546-4770 or 562/592-4770; fax 562/592-3547); **Best Western Bay Shores Inn,** 1800 W. Balboa Blvd., Newport Beach (☎ 800/222-6675 or 949/675-3463; fax 949/675-4977); **Best Western Laguna Brisas,** 1600 S. Coast Hwy., Laguna Beach (☎ 800/624-4442 or 949/497-7272; fax 949/497-8306); and **Best Western Marina Inn,** 24800 Dana Point Harbor Dr., Dana Point (☎ 800/255-6843 or 949/496-1203; fax 949/248-0360).

MODERATELY PRICED OPTIONS

Blue Lantern Inn. 34343 St. of the Blue Lantern, Dana Point, CA 92629. ☎ **800/950-1236** or 949/661-1304. Fax 949/496-1483. 29 units. A/C TV TEL. $125–$350 double. Rates include full breakfast. AE, DC, MC, V.

A newly constructed New England–style gray clapboard inn, the Blue Lantern is a pleasant cross between a romantic B&B and a sophisticated small hotel. Almost all the rooms, decorated with reproduction traditional furniture and plush bedding, have a balcony or deck overlooking the harbor. All have a fireplace and Jacuzzi tub. Have your breakfast here in private (clad in the fluffy robe provided) or choose to go down to the sunny dining room that also serves complimentary afternoon tea. There's an exercise room and a cozy lounge with menus for many area restaurants. The friendly staff welcomes you with home-baked cookies at the front desk.

Casa Laguna. 2510 S. Coast Hwy., Laguna beach, CA 92651. ☎ **800/233-0449** or 949/494-2996. Fax 949/494-5009. 20 units. TV TEL. $115–$250 double. Rates include breakfast, afternoon wine, and hors d'oeuvres. Off-season and midweek discounts available. AE, DISC, MC, V.

Once you see this romantic terraced complex of Spanish-style cottages amid impossibly lush gardens and secluded patios and find out that it offers all the amenities of a B&B *and* affordable prices, you might wonder, what's the catch? Well, the noise of busy PCH wafts easily into Casa Laguna, a background hum that might prove disturbing to sensitive ears and light sleepers. Still, the Casa has been a favorite hideaway since Laguna's early days. Catalina tile adorns fountains and bougainvillea spills into paths; there's a shaded pool with ocean views, and each room has an individual charm. Request a room in the rear—not only will the noise be less noticeable, but you'll enjoy a better view too.

Doryman's Inn Bed & Breakfast. 2102 W. Ocean Front, Newport Beach, CA 92663. ☎ **800/634-3303** or 949/675-7300. 10 units. A/C TV TEL. $125–$230 double; from $185 suite. Rates include breakfast. AE, MC, V.

The Doryman's rooms are both luxurious and romantic, making this one of the nicest B&Bs anywhere. The rooms are outfitted with French and American antiques, floral textiles, beveled mirrors, and cozy furnishings. Every room has a working fireplace and a sunken marble tub (some have Jacuzzi jets). King- or queen-size beds, lots of plants, and good ocean views round out the decor. The location, directly on the Newport Beach Pier Promenade, is also enviable, though some may find it a bit too close to the action. Breakfast includes fresh pastries and fruit, brown eggs, yogurt, cheeses, and international coffees and teas.

WHERE TO DINE

Options in Seal Beach are limited, but a good choice for seafood is **Walt's Wharf,** 201 Main St. (☎ **562/598-4433**), a bustling, polished restaurant featuring market-fresh selections either plain or with Pacific Rim accents.

SUPER-CHEAP EATS

El Adobe de Capistrano. 31891 Camino Capistrano (near the mission), San Juan Capistrano. ☎ **949/493-1163** or 949/830-8620. Lunch $5–$10; dinner $8–$15. AE, DISC, MC, V. Mon–Thurs 11:30am–10pm; Fri–Sat 11:30am–11pm; Sun 10:30am–2:30pm and 4–10pm. CLASSIC MEXICAN.

This restaurant is housed in a historic landmark 1778 Spanish adobe near San Juan Capistrano's main attraction, the mission. It's understandably touristy, but there's some interesting history inside, like the enclosed lobby that was originally a dirt pathway between two buildings. A former dungeon jail cell makes a fine wine cellar, and El Adobe proudly offers a menu combination named the "President's Choice" after Richard Nixon, who visited often from his Summer White House at the shore nearby. Hot plates overflow with cheesy combinations featuring chiles rellenos, tamales, and enchiladas topped with rich red sauce. Dinner selections also include steak and seafood.

FOR A FEW BUCKS MORE

Las Brisas. 361 Cliff Dr. (off the PCH north of Laguna Canyon), Laguna Beach. ☎ **949/ 497-5434.** Reservations recommended. Main courses $8–$17. AE, MC, V. Mon–Sat 8am–10:30pm; Sun 9am–10:30pm. MEXICAN.

Boasting a breathtaking view of the Pacific, Las Brisas is popular for sunset drinks and alfresco appetizers—so much so that it can get pretty crowded during summer. Affordable during lunch but pricey at dinner, the menu consists mostly of seafood recipes from the Mexican Riviera. Even the standard enchiladas and tacos get a zesty update with crab or lobster meat and fresh herbs. Calamari steak is sautéed with bell peppers, capers, and herbs in garlic-butter sauce, and king salmon is mesquite broiled and served with creamy lime sauce. Though a bit on the touristy side, Las Brisas can be a fun part of the Laguna Beach experience.

Twin Palms. 630 Newport Center Dr., Newport Beach. ☎ **949/721-8288.** Reservations suggested. Main courses $9–$17. AE, CB, DC, MC, V. Sun–Wed 11:30am–10pm; Thurs–Sat 11:30am–1am. MEDITERRANEAN/FRENCH.

When it opened in late 1995, this sibling restaurant to one of Pasadena's most popular eateries quickly headed to the top of the Newport Beach pack. From the famous original started by celebrity investors comes the high-tented, palm-accented circuslike space that's Twin Palms's trademark. Amid this festival atmosphere you can enjoy the French "comfort food" original chef Michael Roberts created as a backlash against pricey haute cuisine. Favorites are juicy roasted sage-infused pork and honey-glazed coriander-scented duck from the rotisserie grill, as well as the popular salt-cod mashed-potato brandade appetizer. Sautéed dishes and salads aren't as successful, but Twin Palms has brought its traditional Sunday "Gospel Brunch" to the new location.

The Orange Coast   543

MODERATELY PRICED OPTIONS

Crab Cooker. 2200 Newport Blvd., Newport Beach. ☎ **949/673-0100.** Reservations not accepted. Main courses $8–$19 at lunch, $10–$25 at dinner. AE, MC, V. Sun–Thurs 11am–9pm; Fri–Sat 11am–10pm. SEAFOOD.

Since 1951, folks in search of well-prepared fresh seafood have headed to this bright-red former bank building. Also a fish market, the Crab Cooker has a casual atmosphere of humble wooden tables, uncomplicated smoked and grilled preparations, and meticulously selected fresh fare. They're especially proud of their Maryland crab cakes and recently added clams and oysters to the repertoire.

5'0" (Five Feet). 328 Glenneyre St., Laguna Beach. ☎ **949/497-4955.** Reservations recommended on weekends. Main courses $14–$24. AE, MC, V. Sun–Thurs 5–10pm; Fri 11:30am–2:30pm and 5–11pm; Sat 5–11pm. CALIFORNIA/ASIAN.

While 5'0" may no longer break culinary ground, chef/proprietor Michael Kang still combines the best in California cuisine with Asian technique and ingredients. The restaurant has a minimalist, almost industrial decor brightened by a friendly staff and splendid cuisine. Menu selections run the gamut from tea-smoked filet mignon topped with Roquefort cheese and candied walnuts to a hot Thai-style mixed grill of veal, beef, lamb, and chicken stir-fried with sweet peppers, onions, and mushrooms in curry-mint sauce.

Harbor Grill. 34499 St. of the Golden Lantern, Dana Point. ☎ **949/240-1416.** Reservations suggested on weekends. Main courses $8–$18. AE, CB, DC, DISC, MC, V. Mon–Sat 11:30am–10pm; Sun 9am–10pm. SEAFOOD.

In a business/commercial mall right in the center of the pretty Dana Point Marina, the Harbor Grill is enthusiastically recommended by locals for mesquite-broiled ocean-fresh seafood. Hawaiian mahimahi with a mango-chutney baste is on the menu, along with Pacific swordfish, crab cakes, and beef steaks.

WORTH A SPLURGE

Splashes Restaurant and Bar. In the Surf and Sand Hotel, 1555 S. Coast Hwy., Laguna Beach. ☎ **949/497-4477.** Reservations recommended. Main courses $16–$26. AE, CB, DC, DISC, MC, V. Mon–Fri 7am–10pm; Sat–Sun 7am–11pm. MEDITERRANEAN.

Splashes is truly stunning. Almost directly on the surf, this light and bright restaurant basks in sun and the calming crash of the waves. At dinner, a basket of fresh-baked crusty bread prefaces a long list of appetizers that may include wild-mushroom ravioli with lobster sauce or sautéed Louisiana shrimp with red chiles and lemon. Gourmet pizzas also make great starters; they come topped with interesting combinations like grilled lamb, roasted fennel, artichokes, mushrooms, and feta cheese. Main courses change daily and might offer baked striped bass and braised duck in cabernet sauce.

15

The Southern California Desert

by Stephanie Avnet Yates

To the casual observer, southern California's desert seems like a desolate place—nothing but vast landscapes baking under a relentless sun. Its splendor is subtle, letting each traveler discover its beauty in his or her own time. For some, it will be the surprising lushness of unique varieties of trees, flowering cacti, fragrant shrubs, and other plants—many of them found only here—that have adapted ingeniously to the harsh climate. The unique Joshua tree, majestic to some and ugly to others, thrives in the upper Mojave Desert. Each spring, the ground throughout the Lancaster area is carpeted with brilliant golds and oranges of the poppy, California's state flower. Like the autumn leaves in New England, the poppies along Calif. 14 draw seasonal tourists in droves.

If it looks like nothing except insects could survive here, look again: You're bound to see the speedy roadrunner or a tiny gecko dart across your path. Close your eyes and listen for the cry of a hawk or an owl. Check the ground for coyote or bobcat tracks. Notice the sparkle of fish in the streams running through flourishing palm oases. Road signs near Barstow warn of desert tortoise crossing. The tortoise is just one of the many endangered species found only here. Fortunately, most of the southern California desert's flora and fauna is protected by the federal government as a wildlife sanctuary.

Or perhaps the beauty you seek is that of personal renewal surrounded by spectacular desert landscape. In the shadow of purple-tinged mountains, amid ancient, otherworldly rock formations, or beside a sparkling swimming pool, you'll find as much or as little to occupy your time as you desire. Destinations range from gloriously untouched national parks to ultra-luxurious resorts. And let's not forget that it's a rare day when the sun doesn't shine out here.

1 En Route to Palm Springs

If you're making the drive from Los Angeles via I-10, your first hour or so will be spent just getting out of the L.A. metropolitan sprawl. Soon you'll leave the Inland Empire auto plazas behind, sail past the last of the bedroom-community shopping malls, and edge ever closer to the snowcapped (if you're lucky) San Bernardino and San Jacinto mountain ranges. (Coming from San Diego via I-15, the area discussed below is east of the junction with I-10.)

T-Rex in the Desert

As the silo-dotted fields give way to pale, dry desert, keep your eyes peeled for the dinosaurs that stand guard over the **Wheel Inn Restaurant** (☎ 909/849-7012), in Cabazon. That's right, a four-story-tall brontosaurus and his Tyrannosaurus rex pal. You can stop and climb up into the belly of the larger one, where you'll find a remarkably spacious gift shop.

For frequent travelers on this stretch of highway, there are certain unmistakable signposts. Perhaps you've stopped, or maybe you haven't, but roadside attractions are part of what helps the frugal traveler enjoy every moment of the vacation. Here are three of my favorites:

Desert Hills Premium Outlets. 48400 Seminole Dr. (off I-10), Cabazon. ☎ **909/849-6641.** Sun–Thurs 10am–8pm; Fri 10am–9pm; Sat 9am–9pm.

Factory-outlet malls are all the rage among bargain hunters, and this one is truly a cut above the rest (or maybe it's just so massive the shlock gets lost in the shuffle). Pick up a map to help navigate this two-part behemoth or you may find yourself browsing Timberland when you'd rather be shopping the Gap. Some of my faves: Kenneth Cole, J. Crew, Eddie Bauer, Coach, Barneys New York, A/X Armani Exchange, Villeroy & Boch, Donna Karan DKNY, Max Studio, Nike, and Quiksilver. The list goes on—there are 15 shoe stores alone.

Hadley's Fruit Orchards. 48190 Seminole Dr. (off I-10), Cabazon. ☎ **800/854-5655** or 909/849-5255. www.hadleys.com. Mon–Thurs 8am–8pm; Fri–Sun 8am–9pm.

This friendly emporium has been a fixture along here since 1931, long before the outlet mall went up down the road. It's always packed with folks shopping for dates, dried fruits, nuts, honey, preserves, and other regional products. A snack bar serves the beloved date shake—there are also plenty of gift-packed treats to carry or ship home. (For more about the date mystique, see the box "Sweet Treat of the Desert: The Coachella Valley Date Gardens," later in this chapter.)

Wind Farm Tours. I-10, Indian Ave. exit, Palm Springs. ☎ **760/251-1997.** $23 adults, $20 seniors and students, $10 kids under 10. Tours daily 9am, 11am, 1pm, 3pm (can vary seasonally).

Travelers through the San Gorgonio Pass have for years been struck by an awesome and otherworldly sight: Never-ending windmill fields that harness the powerful force of the wind gusting through this passage and convert it to electricity to power air conditioners throughout the Coachella Valley. If you really get a charge(!) from them, consider splurging on this unique guided tour offering a look into this alternative energy source. Learn how designers have improved the efficiency of wind turbines (technically they're not windmills, which are used in the production of grain) over the years and measure those long rotors against the average human height (about 10 people could lie along one span).

2 Get Your Kicks—on Historic Route 66

There's a way for nostalgia buffs to take a detour down memory lane on their way to desert destinations: Just eschew the fast-paced, faceless I-10 for a very special interstate highway—Route 66.

Historic Route 66

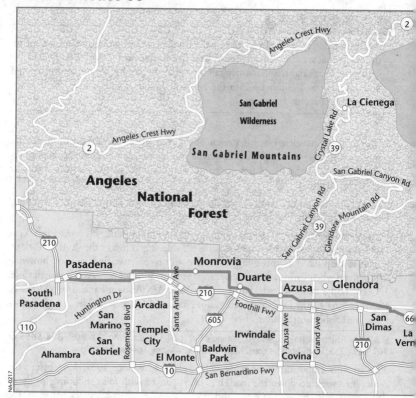

It's been immortalized in film, song, literature, memory, and in the popular imagination, but is anything really left of this great snaking highway, this dependable, comforting spirit John Steinbeck called "the Mother Road"? What of the path to adventure traveled by Tod and Buz in their trademark red Corvette on the namesake 1960s TV series?

The answer is yes, it's still there: You just have to be willing to look for it.

Until the final triumph of the multilane super-slab in the early 1960s, Route 66 was the only automobile route between the windy Chicago shores of Lake Michigan and L.A.'s golden Pacific beaches. "America's Main Street" rambled through eight states, and today, in each one, there are enthusiastic organizations dedicated to preserving its remnants. California is fortunate to have a lengthy stretch of the original highway, many miles of which still proudly wear the designation "California State Highway 66." It's not just weed-split abandoned blacktop, either. These are active streets, often the main commercial drag of the community. Many stretches have become clusters of new home developments, stucco shopping centers, and fast-food chains. Pretty mundane—until you round a curve and unexpectedly see a vintage wood-frame house, perhaps from a predepression ranch. There's poignancy here: That house was probably set way back from the road, amidst a shady grove, before highway workers buried the front yard under asphalt.

Other picturesque relics of that bygone era—single-story motels, friendly two-pump gas stations—exist beside their modern neighbors, inviting nostalgia for a

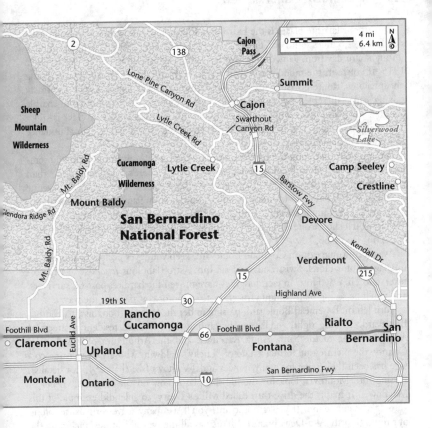

slower, simpler time, a time when the vacation began the moment you backed out of the driveway.

ESSENTIALS

THE ROUTE Our drive begins in Pasadena and ends in downtown San Bernardino, 56 miles west of Palm Springs. In San Bernardino, I-215 intersects Route 66; take it 4 miles south to rejoin I-10 and continue east.

Note: This detour works equally well if your destination is Lake Arrowhead or Big Bear Lake; take I-215 north 3 miles to Calif. 30 and continue into the mountains (see chapter 14). The drive will add anywhere from 30 minutes to 3 hours to your trip, depending on how many relics and photo opportunities you stop to enjoy. We've included some suitably retro meal suggestions in case you want to incorporate lunch into your drive.

INFORMATION For more information, contact the **California Historic Route 66 Association** (☎ 310/997-9817). There's also a quarterly *Route 66 Magazine*, 326 W. Route 66, Williams, AZ 86046 (☎ **520/635-4322**).

LET'S HIT THE ROAD!

Although Route 66 officially ended at the picturesque Pacific, there are very few remainders left in the heart of L.A. Besides, we assume you've already seen the city, so Pasadena is the best point to begin your time-warp experience.

One of our favorite places is the **Fair Oaks Pharmacy,** Fair Oaks Avenue and Mission Street, 1.6 miles south of Colorado Boulevard (☎ **626/799-1414;** open Monday through Saturday from 9am, Sunday from 11am), a fixture on this street corner since 1915. If you're in the mood for a treat, try an authentic ice-cream soda, a sparkling phosphate, a "Route 66" sundae, or an old-fashioned malt (complete with the frosty mixing can), all served by today's fresh-faced soda jerks from behind the marble counter. They also serve soup, sandwiches, and other snacks. The Fair Oaks is still a dispensing pharmacy, and offers a variety of charming gifts, including an abundance of Route 66–themed items.

Perhaps you'd like some appropriate driving music, or a souvenir to help you reminisce about your Route 66 experience later. If so, there's no better place than **Canterbury Records,** 805 E. Colorado Blvd., a block west of Lake Avenue (☎ **626/792-7184;** open Monday through Saturday from 9am, Sunday from 10am). They have L.A.'s finest selection of big-band and pop vocalists on CD and cassette; perhaps you'll choose one of the many renditions of Bobby Troup's homage "(Get Your Kicks on) Route 66."

As you continue east on Colorado Boulevard, keep your eyes peeled for **motels** like the Saga Motor Hotel, Swiss Lodge, Siesta Inn, Astro (fabulous *Jetsons*-style architecture), and Hi-Way Host. In fact, lodgings have proven the hardiest post-66 survivors, and you'll be seeing many unique frozen-in-time motor courts along the way.

Turn left on Rosemead Boulevard, passing under the freeway (boo, hiss) to Foothill Boulevard. Turning right, you'll soon be among the tree-lined residential streets of **Arcadia,** home to the Santa Anita Racetrack and the Arboretum of Los Angeles County, the picturesque former estate of "Lucky" Baldwin, whose Queen Anne cottage has been the setting for many movies and TV shows (see chapter 13 for details). Passing into Monrovia, look for the life-size plastic cow on the southeast corner of Mayflower. It marks the drive-thru called **Mike's Dairy**—a splendid example of this auto-age phenomenon. If you're observant, you'll see many drive-thru dairies along our route (mostly Alta-Dena brand). Mike's has all the typical features, including the refrigerated island display case still bearing a vintage DRIFTWOOD DAIRY PRODUCTS price sign.

Next, look for Magnolia Avenue and the outrageous **Aztec Hotel** on the northwest corner. Opened in 1925, the Aztec was a local showplace, awing guests with its overscale, dark, Native American–themed lobby; garish Mayan murals; and exotic Brass Elephant bar. An arcade of shops once held the city's most prominent barbershop, beauty salon, and pharmacy. Little has changed about the interior, and a glance behind the front desk will reveal the original cord-and-plug telephone switchboard still in use. If you care to wet your whistle, stop into the bar before continuing on.

Leaving the Aztec, you'll pass some splendid Craftsman bungalows and other historic homes. The street dead-ends at Mountain Avenue; turn right to catch up with the 1930s alignment of Route 66. Make a left turn on Huntington Drive, and look out for **The Trails,** a prime example of the "wagon wheel/Wild West" theme restaurants. Its super-tall DINING sign will let you know when you're getting close. Now you're in **Duarte,** where Huntington Drive is lit by graceful and ornate double street lamps on the center median. This stretch also has many fabulous old motor courts; see if you can spot the Filly, Ranch Inn, Evergreen, and the Capri.

Crossing over the wide but nearly dry San Gabriel River, glance right from the bridge to see cars streaming along the Interstate that supplanted Route 66. In Irwindale—which smells just like the industrial area it is, with manufacturing plants ranging from a Miller brewery to Health Valley Foods—the street resumes the Foothill Boulevard name, and you'll pass into Azusa. Look for the elegant 1932 **Azusa City**

Hall and Auditorium, whose vintage lampposts and Moorish fountain enhance a charming courtyard.

Our route swerves right onto Alosta Avenue at the **Foothill Drive-In Theater,** southern California's last single-screen drive-in. As you cruise by, think of the days when our cars were an extension of our living rooms (with the great snacks Mom wouldn't allow at home), and the outdoor theaters were filled every summer evening by dusk.

Continuing on Alosta, you'll enter Glendora, named in 1887 by founder George Whitcomb for his wife, Ledora. Look for the **Palm Tropics,** one of the best-maintained old motels along the route. On the northeast corner of Grand Avenue stands the "world famous" **Derby East** restaurant. It's not affiliated with the legendary Hollywood watering hole, but was clearly built in the 1940s to capitalize on both its famous namesake and the nearby Santa Anita Racetrack. Farther along on the left-hand side is the **Golden Spur,** which began 70 years ago as a ride-up hamburger stand for the equestrian crowd. Unfortunately, the restaurant has been remodeled in boring stucco, leaving only the original sign, with its neon cowboy boot, as a reminder of its colorful past. In a block or two, you'll pass briefly through San Dimas, a ranchlike community where you must pay attention to the HORSE CROSSING street signs. At the corner of Cataract Avenue, a covered wagon announces the **Pinnacle Peak** restaurant, guarded by a giant steer atop the roof.

Don't blink, because almost immediately the street rejoins Foothill Boulevard, passing underneath the ramps to I-210 (boo, hiss); now you're in La Verne, home of **La Paloma** Mexican cafe, a fixture on the route for many years. Continue on to the community of Claremont, known these days for the highly respected group of **Claremont Colleges.** You'll pass several of them along this eucalyptus-lined boulevard. In days gone by, drivers would cruise along this route for mile upon mile, through orchards and open fields, the scenery punctuated only by ambling livestock or a rustic wood fence.

At Benson Avenue in Upland, a classic **1950s-style McDonald's** stands on the southeast corner, its golden arches flanking a low, white, walk-up counter with outdoor stools. The fast-food chain has its roots in this region: Richard and Maurice McDonald opened their first burger joint in San Bernardino in 1939. The successful brothers expanded their business, opening locations throughout southern California, until entrepreneur Ray Kroc purchased the chain in 1955 and franchised McDonald's nationwide. Farther along, look north at the intersection of Euclid Avenue for the regal **monument to pioneer women.**

Pretty soon you'll be cruising through Rancho Cucamonga, whose fertile soil still yields a reliable harvest. You might see impromptu **produce stands** springing up by the side of the road; stop and pick up a fresh snack. If you're blessed with clear weather, gaze north at the gentle slope of the **San Gabriel Mountains** and you'll understand how Foothill Boulevard got its name. The construction codes in this community are among the most stringent in California, designed to respect the region's heritage and restrict runaway development. All new buildings are Spanish/Mediterranean in style and amply landscaped. At the corner of San Bernardino Road, the playful architectural bones of a wonderful old service station can't be obscured by the flashy car-stereo/cellular-phone store which inhabits it now. Across the street is the **Sycamore Inn,** nestled in a grove of trees and looking very much like an old-style stagecoach stop. This reddish-brown wooden house, dating from 1848, has been a private home and gracious inn; today it serves the community of Cucamonga as a restaurant and civic hall.

Rancho Cucamonga has earnestly preserved two historic wineries. First you'll see the **Thomas Vineyards,** at the northeast corner of Vineyard Avenue, established in

1839. Legend holds that the first owner mysteriously disappeared, leaving hidden treasure still undiscovered on the property. The winery's preserved structures now hold two eateries, a country crafts store, and a bookstore housed in the former brandy still. Take a minute to stop into the shopping mall behind the Thomas Winery to tour the Route 66 Territory Museum.

☕ **TAKE A BREAK** If all this driving has made you hungry, consider the **Magic Lamp Inn,** 8189 Foothill Blvd. (☎ **909/981-8659**), open for lunch and dinner Tuesday through Friday and dinner only on Saturday and Sunday. Main courses at lunch run $7.50 to $12; full dinners (including hors d'ouevres, soup or salad, entrée, and side dishes) are $12 to $23. Built in 1957, the Magic Lamp offers excellent continental cuisine (nothing nouvelle about Route 66!) in a setting that's part manor house and part "Aladdin" theme park. Dark, stately dining rooms lurk behind a funky banquette cocktail lounge punctuated by a psychedelic fountain/fire pit and a panoramic view. The genie bottle theme is everywhere, from the restaurant's dinnerware to the plush carpeting, which would be right at home in a Las Vegas casino. Lovers of kitsch and hearty retro fare shouldn't pass this one up.

Continuing on to Hellman Avenue, look for the **New Kansan Motel** (on the northeast corner). With that name, it must have seemed welcoming to Dust Bowl refugees. Near the northwest corner of Archibald Avenue you'll find lonely remnants of a **1920s-era gas station.** Empty now, those service bays have seen many a Ford, Studebaker, or Packard in need of a helping hand. Next you'll pass the **Virginia Dare Winery,** at the northwest corner of Haven Avenue, whose structures now house part of a large business park/shopping mall, but retain the flourish of the original (1830s) winery logo.

Soon you'll pass the I-15 junction and be driving through Fontana, whose name in Italian means "fountain city." There isn't too much worth stopping for along this stretch, but definitely slow down to have a look at the **motor-court hotels** lining both sides of the road. They're of various vintages, all built to cater to the once-vigorous stream of travelers passing through. Although today they're dingy, the melody of their names conjures up those glory days: Ken-Tuck-U-Inn, Rose Motel, Moana, Dragon, Sand & Sage, Sunset, 40 Winks, Redwing.

After entering Rialto, be on the lookout for Meriden Avenue, site of the fanciful **Wigwam Motel.** Built in the 1950s (along with an identical twin motor court in Holbrook, Arizona), the whimsy of these stucco teepees lured many a road-weary traveler in for the night. Their catchy slogan, "Sleep in a wigwam, get more for your wampum," has been supplanted today by the more to-the-point "Do it in a teepee." But as with many of the motor courts we'll pass on this drive, you need only picture a few large, shiny Buicks, T-bird convertibles, and "woodie" station wagons pulling in for the night and your imagination will drift back to days gone by.

Soon Foothill Boulevard will become Fifth Street, a sign that you're nearing **San Bernardino,** which must have been a welcome sight for hot and weary westbound travelers emerging from the Mojave desert. Route 66 wriggled through the steep Cajon Pass into a land fragrant with orange groves, where agricultural prosperity had quickly earned this region a lasting sobriquet: "the Inland Empire."

The year 1928 saw the grand opening of an elegant movie palace, the **California Theater,** 562 W. Fourth St., only 1 block from Route 66. From Fifth Street east, turn right at E Street, then make a right on Fourth Street, where you can pull over to view the theater. Lovingly restored and still popular for nostalgic live entertainment and the rich tones of its original Wurlitzer pipe organ, the California was a frequent site of Hollywood "sneak previews." Here humorist Will Rogers made his last public appearance, in 1935. (Following his death, the highway was renamed the "Will Rogers Memorial Highway" in his honor, but it remained popularly known as Route 66.) Notice the intricate relief of the theater's stone facade, and peek into the lobby to see the red velvet draperies, rich carpeting, and gold banistered double staircase leading up to the balcony.

The theater is the last stop on your time-warp driving tour. Continue west on Fourth Street to the super-slab highway only 2½ blocks away—that's I-215, your entry back into the 1990s (see "Essentials," above).

3 The Palm Springs Desert Resorts

Palm Springs: 120 miles E of Los Angeles, 135 miles NE of San Diego

Palm Springs had been known for years as a golf-course–studded retirement mecca annually invaded by raucous hordes of libidinous college kids at spring break. Well, the city of Palm Springs has been quietly changing its image and attracting a whole new crowd. Former mayor (later U.S. congressman) Sonny Bono's revolutionary "anti-thong" ordinance in 1991 put a lightning-quick halt to the spring migration by eliminating public display of the bare co-ed derrières, and the upscale fairway-condo crowd has decided to congregate in the tony outlying resort cities of Rancho Mirage, Palm Desert, Indian Wells, and La Quinta.

These days, no billboards are allowed in Palm Springs itself, all the palm trees in the center of town are appealingly back-lit at night, and you won't see the word "motel" anywhere. Senior citizens are all over, dressed to the nines in brightly colored leisure suits and keeping alive the retro-kitsch establishments from the days when Elvis, Liberace, and Sinatra made the balmy desert a swingin' place. But they're not alone: Baby boomers and yuppies nostalgic for the kidney-shaped pools and backyard luaus of the Eisenhower/Kennedy glory years are buying ranch-style vacation homes and restoring them to their 1950s splendor. Hollywood's young glitterati are returning too. Today the city fancies itself a European-style resort with a dash of good ol' American small town thrown in for good measure—think *Jetsons* architecture and the crushed-velvet vibe of piano bars with the colors and attitude of a laid-back Aegean island village. One thing hasn't changed: Swimming, sunbathing, golfing, and playing tennis are still the primary pastimes in this convenient little oasis.

Another important presence in Palm Springs has little to do with socialites and Americana. The Agua Caliente band of Cahuilla Indians settled in this area 1,000 years before the first golf ball was ever teed up. Recognizing the beauty and spirituality of this wide-open space, they lived a simple life around the natural mineral springs on the desert floor, migrating into the cool canyons during summer. Under a treaty with the railroad companies and the U.S. government, the tribe owns half the land on which Palm Springs is built and actively works to preserve Native American heritage. It's easy to learn about the American Indians during your visit, and it'll definitely add to your appreciation of this part of California.

ESSENTIALS

GETTING THERE   Several airlines service the Palm Springs **Regional Airport,** 3400 E. Tahquitz Canyon Way (☎ 760/323-8161), including **Alaska Airlines** (☎ 800/426-0333), **America West** (☎ 800/235-9292), **American** (☎ 800/

433-7300), **Delta/Skywest** (☎ 800/453-9417), **United** (☎ 800/241-6522), and **USAirways** (☎ 800/428-4322). Flights from Los Angeles International Airport (see chapter 13) take about 40 minutes.

If you're driving from Los Angeles, take I-10 east to the Calif. 111 turnoff to Palm Springs. You'll breeze into town on North Palm Canyon Drive, the main thoroughfare. The trip from downtown Los Angeles takes about 2 hours. If you're driving from San Diego, take I-15 north to I-10 east; it's a little over a 2-hour drive.

VISITOR INFORMATION   Be sure to pick up *Palm Springs Life* magazine's free monthly **"Desert Guide."** It contains tons of information, including a comprehensive calendar of events. Copies are distributed in hotels and newsstands and by the **Palm Springs Desert Resorts Convention & Visitors Bureau,** in the Atrium Design Centre, 69930 Calif. 111, Suite 201, Rancho Mirage, CA 92270 (☎ **800/41-RELAX** or 760/770-9000). The bureau's office staff can help with maps, brochures, and advice Monday through Friday from 8:30am to 5pm. They also operate a **24-hour information line** at ☎ **760/770-1992** and a Web site at **www.desert-resorts.com**.

The **Palm Springs Visitors Information Center,** 2781 N. Palm Canyon Dr. (☎ **800/34-SPRINGS;** fax 760/323-3021), offers maps, brochures, advice, souvenirs, and a free hotel-reservation service. The office is open Monday through Saturday from 9am to 5pm and Sunday from 8am to 4pm.

ORIENTATION   The commercial downtown area of Palm Springs stretches about half a mile along **North Palm Canyon Drive** between Alejo and Ramon streets. The street is one-way through the heart of town, but its other-way counterpart is **Indian Canyon Drive,** 1 block east. The mountains lie directly west and south, while the rest of Palm Springs is laid out in a grid to the southeast. Palm Canyon forks into **South Palm Canyon** (leading to the Indian Canyons) and **East Palm Canyon** (the continuation of Calif. 111) traversing the resort towns of **Cathedral City, Rancho Mirage, Palm Desert, Indian Wells,** and **La Quinta** before looping up to rejoin I-10 at Indio. **Desert Hot Springs** is north of Palm Springs, straight up Gene Autry Trail. **Tahquitz Canyon Way** creates North Palm Canyon's primary intersection, tracking a straight line between the airport and the heart of town.

ENJOYING THE OUTDOORS

The Coachella Valley desert is truly a playground, and what follows is but a sampling of opportunities to enjoy the abundant sunshine during your vacation. Please keep in mind, however, that the strong sun and dry air that are so appealing can also sneak up in the form of sunburn and heat exhaustion. Especially during summer, but even in milder times, always drink and carry plenty of water. And remember to wear sunscreen and a wide-brimmed hat. A little common sense will ensure hours of outdoor enjoyment.

A FAMILY WATER PARK   Palm Springs Oasis Waterpark, off I-10 south on Gene Autry Trail between Ramon Road and East Palm Canyon Drive (☎ **760/ 325-7873**), is a water playground with 13 water slides, body- and board-surfing, an inner-tube ride, beach volleyball, and more. Dressing rooms, lockers, and private beach cabanas (with food service) are available. Admission is $19 for visitors over 5 feet tall, $12 for kids 3 to 5 feet, and free for kids under 3 feet ($11 for seniors). Mid-March to Labor Day, the park is open daily from 11am to 6pm, plus weekends through all of October.

BIKING   The clean, dry air just cries out to be enjoyed—what could be better than to pedal your way around town or into the desert? **Adventure Bike Tours** (no address; tours meet at local hotels and rentals are available at select hotels or are delivered free

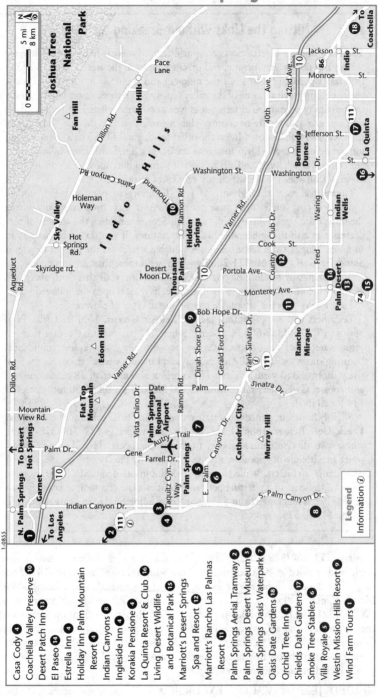

Joshua Tree National Park

N

5 mi
8 km
0

Pace Lane

Indio Hills

To Coachella 18

Jackson St.

42nd Ave.

40th Ave.

Monroe 86

Indio St.

10

Dillon Rd.

Fan Hill

Indio Hills

Palms Canyon Rd.

Holeman Way

Sky Valley

Hot Springs Rd.

Skyridge rd.

Thousand

Washington St.

Bermuda Dunes

Jefferson St.

Washington Dr.

St.

La Quinta 17 111

16

Aqueduct Rd.

Ramon Rd.

Hidden Springs 10

Varner Rd.

Waring

Indian Wells

Desert Moon Dr.

Thousand Palms

10

Portola Ave.

Country Club Dr.

Cook St.

Fred

Palm Desert 14 13 15

12

74

Monterey Ave.

11

Bob Hope Dr. 9

Gerald Ford Dr.

Frank Sinatra Dr.

Rancho Mirage

Dinah Shore Dr.

Dillon Rd.

Edom Hill

Varner Rd.

Date Palm Dr.

111

Sinatra Dr.

Mountain View Rd.

Flat Top Mountain

Vista Chino Dr.

Palm Springs Regional Airport

Ramon Rd.

Cathedral City

Murray Hill

Palm Dr.

Gene Autry Trail

Farrell Dr.

7

To Desert Hot Springs

10

Garnet

N. Palm Springs

Taquitz Cyn. Way

Palm Springs 5 6

E. Palm Canyon Dr.

Indian Canyon Dr.

3

111

4

S. Palm Canyon Dr.

8

To Los Angeles

1

2

Legend

Information (i)

Casa Cody 4
Coachella Valley Preserve 10
Desert Patch Inn 13
El Paseo 14
Estrella Inn 4
Holiday Inn Palm Mountain Resort 4
Indian Canyons 8
Ingleside Inn 4
Korakia Pensione 4
La Quinta Resort & Club 16
Living Desert Wildlife and Botanical Park 15
Marriott's Desert Springs Spa and Resort 12
Marriott's Rancho Las Palmas Resort 11
Palm Springs Aerial Tramway 2
Palm Springs Desert Museum 3
Palm Springs Oasis Waterpark 7
Oasis Date Gardens 18
Orchid Tree Inn 4
Shields Date Gardens 17
Smoke Tree Stables 6
Villa Royale 5
Westin Mission Hills Resort 9
Wind Farm Tours 1

1-0855

Hitting the Links Without Breaking the Bank

The Palm Springs desert resorts are world-famous meccas for golfers. There are almost 100 public, semiprivate, and private courses in the area; if you're the kind who starts polishing your irons the moment you begin planning your vacation, you're best off staying at one of the valley's many golf resorts, where you can enjoy the proximity of your hotel facilities as well as economically smart package deals that can give you a taste of country-club membership (see the box "The Art of the Package Deal," below). If, on the other hand, you'd like to fit a round of golf into an otherwise varied trip and aren't staying at a hotel with its own links, there are courses at all levels and prices open to the public, most of them in Palm Springs. Call ahead to see which will rent clubs or other equipment.

Greens fees vary throughout the year. Contrary to popular belief, not all courses will cost you $100 or more per round. And prices drop drastically during the off-season, usually June or July through September, when the volume of play decreases due to the unbearably high temperatures (if you do choose to play in summer, I suggest you tee up early). A valuable service for the budget traveler is **Stand-By Golf** (☎ 760/321-2665), which helps more than 20 area courses fill their bookings by offering players a healthy discount. Call after 5pm and you'll be told which courses, some of them private, have slots open the following day.

Here are my favorite affordable courses for all types of players:

Beginners will enjoy **Tommy Jacobs' Bel-Air Greens,** 1001 El Cielo, Palm Springs (☎ 760/322-6062), a scenic 9-hole, 32-par executive course that has some water- and sand-trap challenges but also allows for a few confidence-boosting successes. Generally flat fairways and mature trees characterize the relatively short (3,350 yards) course. The complex also offers an 18-hole miniature golf course. Greens fees range from $23 to $27 (off-season $9.50 for 9 holes or $14 for all day).

Slightly more intermediate amateurs will want to check out the **Tahquitz Creek Golf Resort,** 1885 Golf Club Dr., Palm Springs (☎ 760/328-1005), whose two diverse courses appeal to midhandicappers. The "Legend's" wide, water-free holes will appeal to anyone frustrated by the "target" courses popular with many architects, while the new Ted Robinson–designed "Resort" course offers all those accuracy-testing bells and whistles more common to lavish private clubs. Greens fees range from $35 to $85 depending on day and cart rental (off-season $17 to $25).

---

of charge; ☎ 760/328-0282) will outfit you with a bike, helmet, souvenir water bottle, and certified guide; tours start at about $40, and bike rentals are $10 per hour or $28 for the day. If you're just looking to rent some wheels and a helmet, **Mac's Bicycle Rental,** 79953 Calif. 111, between Country Club and Frank Sinatra drives (☎ 760/321-9444), rents bikes for the hour ($7), the day ($19), or the week ($65), and offers children's and mountain models. The **Bighorn Bicycle Rental & Tour Company,** 302 N. Palm Canyon (☎ 760/325-3367) has hourly ($7) and daily ($27) rental rates in addition to guided bike treks (a 4-hour guided ride/hike is $45 per person including all equipment and snacks).

GUIDED JEEP & WAGON EXCURSIONS **Desert Adventures** (☎ 888/440-JEEP or 760/324-JEEP) offers four-wheel-drive ecotours led by experienced naturalist guides. Your off-road adventure may explore the lush palm oases of the

The oldest public-access golf course in the city is the ✪ **Palm Springs Country Club,** 2500 Whitewater Club Dr. (☎ **760/323-8625**), which is especially popular with budget-conscious golfers because its greens fees are only $40 to $50 (off-season $20 to $25), including the required cart. The challenge of bunkers and rough can be amplified by the oft-blowing wind along the 5,885 yards of this unusually laid-out course.

If you're a golf fanatic looking to splurge, the **Westin Mission Hills Resort Course,** at Dinah Shore and Bob Hope drives, Rancho Mirage (☎ **760/ 328-3198**), is worth the extra bucks. It's somewhat more forgiving than most of legendary architect Pete Dye's courses, but don't play the back tees unless you've got a consistent 220-yard drive and won't be fazed by the Dye-trademark giant sand bunkers and elevated greens. Water comes into play on only four holes, and the scenery is an exquisite reward for low-handicappers. Nonguest greens fees are $120 to $130, including the cart (off-season $65 to $75 and $25 after 2pm).

Be aware that many courses close completely for anywhere from 1 week to 1 month during summer and early fall for reseeding. Since most desert facilities have more than one 18-hole course, the process is usually staggered enough so there's always a playable course. But, if you have your heart set on one particular course, call before you go to make sure it'll be open.

For the nonplaying spectator (or anyone longing to see the pros make it look so easy), there are dozens of golf tournaments year-round, including many celebrity and pro-am events and regular PGA, LPGA, and Senior Tour stops. February brings the PGA Tour **Bob Hope Chrysler Classic** at the Bermuda Dunes Country Club and the **Frank Sinatra Celebrity Invitational** at Marriott's Desert Springs Resort and Spa. In March, catch the LPGA Tour **Nabisco Dinah Shore** at Mission Hills Country Club, then in April the Senior PGA **Liberty Mutual Legends of Golf** comes to PGA West. November brings two of the desert's longest-running charity events, the **23rd Annual Frostig Center/Chris Korman Celebrity Tournament** at Westin Mission Hills and the 25-year **Billy Barty/7-Up Celebrity Golf Classic** at Mesquite Country Club in Palm Springs. Also in November, check out the wacky **Palm Desert Golf Cart Parade** along El Paseo.

For more information, you can call the **Palm Springs Desert Resorts Convention and Visitors Bureau** at ☎ **800/41-RELAX** or 760/770-9000. The bureau also maintains an Activities Hot Line at ☎ **760/770-1992.**

ancestral Indian Canyons, the rugged Santa Rosa Mountain roads overlooking the Coachella Valley and the Bighorn Sheep Preserve, or picturesque ravines on the way to the San Andreas Fault. Tours range from 2 to 4 hours and from $69 to $99. Advance reservations are required. The company's trademark red Jeeps depart from the Desert Adventures Ranch on South Palm Canyon near the entrance to the Indian Canyons, but most of the longer excursions include hotel pickup and return.

Covered Wagon Tours (☎ **800/367-2161** or 760/347-2161) embraces the pioneer spirit with a 2-hour ride through the Coachella Valley Nature Preserve followed by an old-fashioned barbecue cookout and live country music. They operate daily from October to mid-May, and the price is $55 for adults, $27.50 for children 7 to 16, and free for kids 6 and under. Without the "grub," the tour is $40 per adult and $20 per child. Advance reservations are required.

HIKING   The most popular spot for hiking is the nearby **Indian Canyons** (☎ 760/325-5673 for information). The Agua Caliente tribe made their home here centuries ago, and remnants of their simple lifestyle can be seen among the streams, waterfalls, and astounding palm groves in Andreas, Murray, and Palm canyons. Striking rock formations and herds of bighorn sheep and wild ponies will probably be more appealing than the "Trading Post" in Palm Canyon, but it does sell detailed trail maps. This is Indian land, and the Tribal Council charges admission of $6 per adult, with discounts for seniors, children, students, and military. The canyons are closed to visitors from late June to early September.

Ten miles east of Palm Springs is the 13,000-acre **Coachella Valley Preserve** (☎ 760/343-1234), open daily from sunrise to sunset. There are springs, mesas, both hiking and riding trails, the Thousand Palms Oasis, a visitor center, and picnic areas.

If you're heading up to Joshua Tree National Park (see the next section), consider stopping at the **Big Morongo Canyon Preserve** (☎ 760/363-7190), which was once an Indian village and later a cattle ranch. It's open for visitors Wednesday through Sunday from 7:30am. The park's high water table makes it a magnet for birds and other wildlife; the lush springs and streams are an unexpected desert treat.

HORSEBACK RIDING   Equestrians from novice to advanced can experience the natural solitude and quiet of the desert on horseback at **Smoke Tree Stables** (☎ 760/327-1372). Located south of downtown and ideal for exploring the nearby Indian Canyon trails, Smoke Tree offers guided rides for $25 per hour. But don't expect your posse leader to be primed with facts on the nature you'll encounter—this is strictly a do-it-yourself experience.

TENNIS   Virtually all the larger hotels and resorts have tennis courts, but if you're staying at a B&B, you might want to play at the **Tennis Center,** 1300 Baristo Rd., Palm Springs (☎ 760/320-0020), which has nine courts and offers day and evening clinics for adults, juniors, and seniors, as well as ball machines for solo practice. USPTA pros are on-hand.

If you'd like to play for free, the night-lighted courts at the **Palm Springs High School,** 2248 E. Ramon Rd., are open to the public on weekends, holidays, and during summer. There are also eight free night-lighted courts in beautiful **Ruth Hardy Park** at Tamarisk and Caballero streets.

MORE TO SEE & DO

Haven't seen any celebrities wandering the streets? You may want to hook up with **Celebrity Tours,** on East Palm Canyon Drive at Gene Autry Trail (☎ 760/ 770-2700). Advance reservations are required for their 1- and 2½-hour tours of Palm Springs, which include some history and lore but mostly the opportunity to gawk at the homes of movie stars and celebrities. The longer tours take in the estates of surrounding Rancho Mirage and Palm Desert, "playground of the international elite." Prices are $12 to $18 for adults, depending on tour length; kids 16 and under are half-price.

Palm Springs Desert Museum. 101 Museum Dr. (just west of the Palm Canyon/Tahquitz intersection), Palm Springs. ☎ **760/325-7186.** Admission $7.50 adults, $6.50 seniors 62 and over, $3.50 military and children 6–17, free for children under 6; free for everyone the 1st Fri of each month. Tues–Sat 10am–5pm; Sun noon–5pm.

Unlikely though it may sound, this well-endowed museum is a must-see. Exhibits include world-class Western and Native American art collections, the natural history of the desert, and an outstanding anthropology department, primarily representing the local Cahuilla tribe. Traditional Indian life as it was lived for centuries before the white presence is illustrated by tools, baskets, and other relics. Check local schedules to find out about (usually excellent) visiting exhibits; plays, lectures, and other events are presented in the museum's Annenberg Theater.

Living Desert Wildlife and Botanical Park. 47900 Portola Ave., Palm Desert. ☎ **760/346-5694.** Admission $7.50 adults, $6.50 seniors 62 and over, $3.50 children 3–12, free for kids under 2. Daily 9am–5pm (last admission 4:30pm); call for summer schedule. Closed Aug and Christmas Day.

This 1,200-acre desert reserve, museum, zoo, and educational center is designed to acquaint visitors with the unique habitats that make up the southern California deserts. You can walk or take a tram tour through sectors re-creating life in several distinctive desert zones. See and learn about a dizzying variety of plants, insects, and wildlife, like bighorn sheep, mountain lions, rattlesnakes, lizards, owls, golden eagles, and the ubiquitous roadrunner.

Palm Springs Aerial Tramway. Tramway Rd. off Calif. 111, Palm Springs. ☎ **760/325-1391.** Tickets $18 adults, $15 seniors, $11 children 5–12, free for kids 4 and under; Ride 'n' Dine combination (available after 2:30pm, dinner served after 4pm) $21 adults, $14 children. Mon–Fri 10am–8pm; Sat–Sun 8am–8pm (closes 1 hr. later Memorial Day to Labor Day). Free parking.

To gain a bird's-eye perspective of the Coachella Valley, take this 14-minute ascent up 2½ miles to the top of Mt. San Jacinto. The whole experience has a fabulous 1960s feel, from the original Swiss funicular equipment to the scratchy recording broadcast during the trip up (often drowned out by the periodic squeals of white-knuckled passengers). There's a whole other world once you arrive: alpine scenery, a ski-lodge-flavored restaurant and gift shop, and temperatures typically 40° cooler than on the desert floor. The most dramatic contrast is during winter, when the mountaintop is a snowy wonderland, irresistible to hikers and bundled-up kids with saucers. The excursion might not be worth the expense during the rest of the year. Guided mule rides and cross-country ski equipment are available at the top.

SHOPPING

Downtown Palm Springs revolves around **North Palm Canyon Drive;** many art galleries, souvenir shops, and restaurants are here, along with a couple of large-scale hotels and shopping centers. This wide one-way boulevard is designed for pedestrians, with many businesses set back from the street itself—don't be shy about poking around the little courtyards you'll encounter. On Thursdays from 6 to 10pm, the blocks between Amado and Baristo roads are transformed into **VillageFest,** a street-fair tradition. Handmade-crafts vendors and aromatic food booths compete for your attention with wacky street performers and even wackier locals shopping at the mouth-watering fresh-produce stalls.

The northern section of Palm Canyon is becoming known for vintage collectibles and being touted as the **"Antique and Heritage Gallery District."** Check out **John's Resale Furnishings,** 891 N. Palm Canyon Dr. (☎ **760/416-8876**), for a glorious collection of midcentury modern furnishings; **Bandini Johnson Gallery,** 895 N. Palm Canyon Dr. (☎ **760/323-7805**), a cramped warren of eclectic treasures; and the **Antiques Center,** 798 N. Palm Canyon Dr. (☎ **760/323-4443**), a discriminating mall-style store whose 35 dealers display wares from vintage linens to handmade African crafts to prized Bakelite jewelry.

Down in Palm Desert lies the delicious excess of **El Paseo,** a glitzy cornucopia of high-rent boutiques, salons, and upscale eateries reminiscent of Rodeo Drive in Beverly Hills, along with a dozen or more major shopping malls just like back home.

Sweet Treat of the Desert: The Coachella Valley Date Gardens

In a splendid display of both wishful thinking and clever engineering, the Coachella Valley has grown into a rich agricultural region, known internationally for grapefruit, figs, and grapes—but mostly for dates. Turn-of-the-century entrepreneurs, fascinated with Arabian lore and fueled by the Sahara-like conditions of the desert around Indio, planted the area's date palm groves in the 1920s. Launched with just a few parent trees imported from the Middle East, the groves now produce 95% of the world's date crop.

Farmers hand-pollinate the trees, and the resulting precious fruit is bundled in wind-protective paper while still on the tree, which makes an odd sight indeed. You'll see them while driving along Calif. 111 through Indio, where the road is sometimes referred to as the "Date Highway."

For decades, **Shields Date Gardens,** 80225 Calif. 111 (☎ 760/347-0996), has been enticing visitors into its splendid 1930s Moderne building with banners proclaiming free admission to the continuously running film *The Romance and Sex Life of the Date* (fair warning: its racy title is the best part). Even if you're not interested in the flick, stop by the lunch counter (date shake anyone?) and store, which sells an endless variety of dates and related goodies, and sample some date ice cream or date crystals, a mysterious sweet product that seems to have many practical uses—until you actually get it home. But the quality and selection of fresh-harvested dates is superb; I guarantee you'll find yourself snacking on them before long. It's open daily from 8am to 6pm.

There's no more picturesque place in the valley to sample dates than **Oasis Date Gardens,** 59111 Calif. 111 (☎ 800/827-8017 or 760/399-5665), started in 1912 with nine Moroccan trees and now one of the largest commercial date groves in the United States. It's a drive—about 40 minutes from downtown Palm Springs—but there's a lot to do there. Picnic tables dot an inviting lawn, videos illustrate the history and art of date cultivation, and there's a cool palm arboretum and cactus exhibit, plus a petting zoo for impatient youngsters. Many varieties of dates are laid out for free tasting; Oasis also sells date shakes, ice cream, chewy date pie by the slice, homemade chili and sandwiches, and gourmet food gifts from all over the Southwest. It's open daily (except Christmas) from 6am to 5:30pm.

Factory-outlet shopping is 20 minutes away in Cabazon (see "En Route to Palm Springs," earlier in this chapter).

One of my favorite local spots is ✪ **Bloomsbury Books,** 555 S. Sunrise Way No. 105, at Ramon Road (☎ 760/325-3862), which is great for browsing. Proprietor Brad Confer is hard at work compiling an impressive array of out-of-print books and signed and rare editions, all reasonably priced and in great condition. Bloomsbury is especially strong in gay/lesbian literature (including rare early magazines and foreign publications) that's meticulously organized by topic. Every section is cleverly decorated with related memorabilia and noteworthy selections. Located in an ugly strip mall several blocks from the center of town, this treasure is well worth the detour. It's open Monday through Saturday from 11am to 9pm.

If it's Palm Springs history or literature you seek, visit the appealingly cluttered **Celebrity Bookstore,** 170 E. Tahquitz Canyon, half a block east of Palm Canyon Drive (☎ 800/320-6575 or 760/320-6575). Owner Darrell Meeks is the resident expert on local publications, and he also sets up tables for VillageFest each week. It's open Monday through Saturday from 9am to 8pm and Sunday from 9am to 4pm.

GAY LIFE IN PALM SPRINGS

Don't think the local chamber of commerce doesn't recognize that the Palm Springs area is one of the current top-three American destinations for gay travelers. After just a short while in town it's easy to tell how the gay tourism dollar is courted as aggressively as straight spending. Real-estate agents cater to gay shoppers for vacation properties, and entire condo communities are marketed toward the gay resident. Ads for these and scores of other proudly gay-owned businesses can be found in *The Bottom Line,* the desert's free biweekly magazine of articles, events, and community guides for the gay reader; it's available at hotels, newsstands, and select merchants.

Throughout the year events are held that transcend the gay community to include everyone. In March the **Desert AIDS Walk** benefits the Desert AIDS Project, while the world's largest organized gathering of lesbians coincides with the **Nabisco Dinah Shore Golf Tournament.**

Be sure to visit **Village Pride,** 214 E. Arenas Rd. (☎ **760/323-9120**), a coffeehouse and local gathering place. Besides offering a selection of gay- and lesbian-oriented reading material, Village Pride serves as the lobby for the **Top Hat Playhouse.** This short block of Arenas is home to a score of gay establishments, including **Streetbar** (☎ **760/320-1266**), a neighborhood gathering spot for tourists and locals alike.

Just a few blocks away is a cozy neighborhood of modest homes and small hotels, concentrated on Warm Sands Drive south of Ramon. Known simply as **Warm Sands,** this area holds the very nicest "private resorts"—mostly discreet and gated B&B-style inns. Locals recommend the co-ed **El Mirasol,** 525 Warm Sands Dr. (☎ **800/327-2985** or 760/326-5913), a charming historic resort; or **Sago Palms,** 595 Thornhill Rd. (☎ **800/626-7246** or 760/323-0224), which is small, quiet, and affordable. Near the center of town lies the **Harlow Club Hotel,** 175 E. El Alameda (☎ **800/223-4073** or 760/320-4333), and **Abbey West,** 772 Prescott Circle (☎ **800/223-4073** or 760/416-2654), two adjacent all-male hotels with the same owner and the same ultra-elegant pampering. **Delilah's Enclave,** 641 San Lorenzo Rd. (☎ **800/621-6973** or 760/325-5269), is one of the few all-women resorts in town.

Gay nightlife is everywhere in the valley, and especially raucous on holiday weekends. Pick up *The Bottom Line* for the latest restaurant, nightclub, theater, and special-events listings.

WHERE TO STAY

The city of Palm Springs offers a wide range of accommodations. I particularly like the inns that've opened as new owners renovate the many fabulous 40- to 60-year-old cottage complexes in the wind-shielded "Tennis Club" area west of Palm Canyon Drive. The other desert resort cities (Rancho Mirage, La Quinta, Palm Desert) have little diversity in lodgings, consisting mostly of luxurious resort complexes, many boasting world-class golf, tennis, or spa facilities and multiple restaurants.

If you're looking for a good base from which to shop or sightsee, Palm Springs, which has the most affordable lodgings in the area, is your best bet. Regardless of your choice, remember that rates given below are high-season (winter, generally Oct through May). During the hotter summer months, it's common to find $300 rooms going for $99 or less as part of off-season packages. Even in season, midweek and golf packages are common, so always ask when making your reservation.

A Desert Accommodations Tip

In desert accommodations parlance, there's more to the year than summer and winter. Spring and fall are known as the "shoulder" season and offer the best of desert weather with the fewest crowds and bargain rates to boot. Though not as dirt cheap as the sweltering summer, the months of October, November, December (except Christmas season), April, and May are the frugal traveler's best bet. Each property defines its own calendar, so check out my listings below for exact details.

If you're planning on staying for a week or more, you may consider renting a privately owned condo or villa. The **Rental Connection** (☎ **800/GO-2-PALM** or 760/320-7336) has a variety of units, all of which require a 3-night minimum stay (1 week for houses).

In addition to the accommodations below, most of the recognized national chains have branches in the Palm Springs area, including the **Quality Inn,** 1269 E. Palm Canyon Dr., Palm Springs (☎ **800/472-4339** or 760/323-2775; $59 to $99); **Travelodge Palm Springs,** 333 E. Palm Canyon Dr. (☎ **800/578-7878** or 760/327-1211; $49 to $75); and **Best Western Las Brisas,** 222 S. Indian Canyon Dr., Palm Springs (☎ **800/346-5714** or 760/325-4372; $56 to $119).

SUPER-CHEAP SLEEPS

✪ **Casa Cody.** 175 S. Cahuilla Rd. (between Tahquitz Way and Arenas Rd.), Palm Springs, CA 92262. ☎ **760/320-9346.** Fax 760/325-8610. 23 units. A/C TV TEL. $69–$79 double; $89–$129 studio; $129–$199 suite. Rates include continental breakfast. Midweek and summer rates available. AE, DC, DISC, MC, V. Pets accepted for $10 per night.

Once owned by "Wild" Bill Cody's niece, this 1920s *casa* with a double courtyard (each with a pool) has been restored to fine condition, sporting a vaguely Southwestern decor and peaceful grounds marked by large lawns and mature blossoming fruit trees. You'll feel more like a house guest than a hotel client at the Casa Cody. It's in the primarily residential "Tennis Club" area of town, a couple of easy blocks from Palm Canyon Drive. Many units have fireplaces and full-size kitchens. Breakfast is served poolside, as is complimentary wine-and-cheese on Saturday afternoon.

Desert Patch Inn. 73758 Shadow Mountain Dr., Palm Desert, CA 92260. ☎ **800/350-9758** or 760/346-9161. Fax 760/776-9661. 14 units. A/C TV TEL. Oct–May $56–$98 double; June–Sept $47–$72 double. Rates include continental breakfast. AE, DISC, MC, V. Free parking. Small pets allowed.

In a quiet residential area near Palm Desert's fancy El Paseo, the Desert Patch offers terrific prices and a friendly setting in a city not known for bargain accommodations. The grounds are well maintained and diverse, with shuffleboard courts and a putting green, plus a pool and whirlpool. The rooms are nicely furnished, many with living rooms and kitchens; all have refrigerators, microwaves, and coffeemakers. Extras like free video rentals (VCRs are available) and local phone calls help make this a nice alternative to impersonal chain hotels.

FOR A FEW BUCKS MORE

Holiday Inn Palm Mountain Resort. 155 S. Belardo Rd., Palm Springs, CA 92262. ☎ **800/622-9451** or 760/325-1301. Fax 760/323-8937. 122 units. A/C TV TEL. High season $79–$169 double. Children under 18 stay free in parents' room. AE, CB, DC, DISC, JCB, MC, V. Free parking.

Within easy walking distance of Palm Springs's main drag, this Holiday Inn (like most in the chain) welcomes kids under 18 free in their parents' room, making it a terrific choice for families. The rooms are in the two- or the three-story wing, and many have a patio or balcony, with a view of the mountains or the heated pool in the large Astro-turf courtyard; all offer the convenience of refrigerators, microwaves, and cof-feemakers. Midweek, summer rates can be as low as $49; there's also a restaurant, lounge, and poolside cabana bar.

Orchid Tree Inn. 261 S. Belardo Rd. (at Baristo Rd.), Palm Springs, CA 92262. ☎ **800/ 733-3435** or 760/325-2791. Fax 760/325-3855. 40 units. A/C TV TEL. $95–$120 double; $130–$295 suite. Extra person $15. Rates include continental breakfast. AE, MC, V. Pets allowed for a $10 fee.

Billed as a "1930s desert garden retreat," the Orchid Tree is a sprawling complex of buildings from the 1920s to 1950s, each with a unique personality, like the individual decor in each room. Dedicated family ownership ensures the place is impeccably maintained, and the rooms are nicer than you'd expect at this price but in keeping with the overall grace and excellence of the entire neighborhood. The room types range from simple hotel-style doubles to charming bungalows to pool-front studios with sliding glass doors. Just a block from Palm Canyon Drive in the historic "Tennis Club" district, the inn nevertheless truly feels like a retreat: Insulated from the sur-rounding streets, the grounds are rich with flowering shrubs, mature citrus trees, and multitudes of twittering hummingbirds, sparrows, and quail drawn by bird feeders and baths. There are three pools, two whirlpools, and an outdoor barbecue area.

MODERATELY PRICED OPTIONS

Ingleside Inn. 200 W. Ramon Rd. (at Belardo Rd.), Palm Springs, CA 92264. ☎ **800/ 772-6655** or 760/325-0046. Fax 760/325-0710. 45 units. A/C TV TEL. $95–$235 double; $205–$285 minisuite; $135–$265 villa; from $295 full suite. Rates include welcome snacks and continental breakfast. AE, CB, DC, DISC, MC, V. Free valet parking.

Once the 1920s estate of the Humphrey Birge family, manufacturers of the Pierce Arrow automobile, this hideaway offers some of the most charming rooms in town. Each guest room and suite is uniquely decorated with antiques—many rooms have wood-burning fireplaces and all have whirlpools and steam baths. There's an old-world charm here that's matched by fine service. The Ingleside is hardly low-key, however, for the management is quick to mention in brochures, on wall plaques, and other places that celebrities like Elizabeth Taylor, Howard Hughes, John Wayne, Bette Davis, Salvador Dali, John Travolta, and Goldie Hawn have stayed here (the celebrity-watching is still first-rate). The Ingleside also has a superlative pool on a sloping hill surrounded by lawn and lounge chairs. Though you can expect indifferent service unless you have a famous face, Ingleside is still tops for experiencing the "Golden Age of the Rat Pack" Palm Springs.

Korakia Pensione. 257 S. Patencio Rd., Palm Springs, CA 92262. ☎ **760/864-6411.** 20 units. $119–$295 double. Rates include breakfast. No credit cards. Free parking.

If you can work within the Korakia's rigid deposit-cancellation policy, you're in for a special stay at this Greek/Moroccan oasis a few blocks from Palm Canyon Drive. The simply furnished rooms and unbelievably spacious suites are peaceful and private, sur-rounded by flagstone courtyards and flowering gardens. The rooms are divided between the main house, a second restored villa across the street, and surrounding guest bungalows. Most have kitchens and many sport fireplaces. This former artist's villa from the 1920s draws a hip international crowd of artists, writers, and musicians.

The Art of the Package Deal

The desert is one of California's best-kept secrets for the budget traveler. No need to book that cheap motel: You can live like royalty here at bargain-basement rates. The caveat, of course, is that you must be willing to be flexible—which usually means heading to the desert when everyone else is fleeing the 100°-plus temperatures. Once their rich-and-famous regulars have gone, many of the area's ritziest resorts offer more-than-generous packages to entice regular folks like you and me. During summer, tariffs literally plummet—it's common to find $300 rooms going for $89 or less as part of off-season packages. If you're willing to brave the heat, you're likely to get quite a deal.

At the ultra-luxurious **La Quinta Resort & Club** in La Quinta (☎ 800/854-1271 or 760/564-4111), *the* place to be if you're serious about your golf or tennis game, midsummer deals can often get you into a *casita* for as little as $99, including a weekend of mariachi music or a round of golf. Many other fine resorts also offer generous golf packages, among them **Marriott's Desert Springs Spa and Resort** in Palm Desert (☎ 800/228-9290 or 760/341-2211), an artificial desert oasis—complete with an indoor "rain forest" and moat, as well as a gaggle of pink flamingos—that's a tourist attraction in its own right. At the other end of the scale are **Marriott's Rancho Las Palmas** in Rancho Mirage (☎ 800/I-LUV-SUN or 760/568-2727), a relaxing Spanish hacienda that's one of the desert's least pretentious luxury resorts; the **Hyatt Grand Champions** in Indian Wells (☎ 800/228-9000 or 760/341-1000); and the **Estrella Inn** in downtown Palm Springs (☎ 800/237-3687 or 760/320-4417), a 1930s property recently restored to its early Hollywood charm. Since the Estrella is the most reasonably priced of the desert resorts—rack rates start at $150—this may be your best bet for a good deal; they often offer attractive golf packages that include play at one of several nearby courses.

If the idea of spending summer in the desert is too much for you, don't despair; there are deals to be had in the more palatable months too. Midweek, family, and golf packages are common year-round, and AAA members can almost always do better than the rack rates. If your timing is right, you may land a great deal even in peak season. Who knows? You may be sunning yourself by the pool before you know it.

All beds are blessed with thick feather duvets, while the windows are shaded by flowing white canvas draperies in the Mediterranean style. Add a sumptuous breakfast served in your room or poolside (*korakia* is Greek for "crow," and a tile mosaic example graces the pool bottom).

✪ **Villa Royale.** 1620 Indian Trail (off East Palm Canyon), Palm Springs, CA 92264. ☎ **800/245-2314** or 760/327-2314. Fax 760/322-3794. www.prinet.com/vroyale. 33 units. A/C TV TEL. $95–$175 double; $150–$250 suite. Rates include continental breakfast. Extra person $25. Substantial off-season discounts. AE, DC, DISC, MC, V. Free parking.

Located 5 minutes from the hustle and bustle of downtown Palm Springs, this charming inn evokes a European cluster of villas, complete with climbing bougainvillea and rooms filled with international antiques and artwork. The main building was once home to Olympic and silver-screen ice-skater Sonya Henie. Villa Royale's reputation had been suffering due to its indifferent management, but 1998 brought new ownership and a renewed dedication to service. The changes were immediate and dramatic, as meticulous perfection replaced shabby maintenance and uniform luxuries (bathrobes, hair dryers, down comforters, and other pampering touches) appeared throughout. The rooms vary widely in size and ambiance; surprisingly, large isn't always better, as some of the most appealing rooms are in the affordable range. Ask for no. 103, 121, 122, 201, 302, or 308—trust me. Many rooms have fireplaces, private patios with whirlpools, full kitchens, or a variety of other amenities.

Breakfast is served in an intimate garden setting around the main pool. The hotel's romantic restaurant, Europa, is a sleeper, offering one of Palm Springs's very best meals (see "Where to Dine," below).

WORTH A SPLURGE

Estrella Inn. 415 S. Belardo Rd. (south of Tahquitz Way), Palm Springs, CA 92262. ☎ **800/ 237-3687** or 760/320-4117. Fax 760/323-3303. 63 units. A/C TV TEL. $150 double; $225–$275 1- or 2-bedroom suite; $250–$350 1- or 2-bedroom bungalow. Rates include continental breakfast. Monthly rates available. AE, CB, DC, MC, V. Free parking. Pets allowed in tile-floored units for a $20 fee.

Once the choice of Hollywood celebrities, this outstanding historic hotel is quiet and secluded yet wonderfully close to the action. Composed of three distinct properties from three different eras, the complex is united by a peachy desert color scheme and uniformly lavish landscaping. The rooms vary widely according to location, but all include pampering touches—some have fireplaces and/or full kitchens, others wet bars or private balconies. The real deals are in the studio bungalows, even though they have tiny 1930s bathrooms. The Estrella has two pools, a children's pool, two whirlpools, an outdoor barbecue, and a lawn with games area. Ask about attractive golf packages that include play at one of several nearby courses.

WHERE TO DINE

Coffee hounds in search of a stylish fix can stop at **Lalajava,** 300 N. Palm Canyon Dr., at the corner of Amado, Palm Springs (☎ **760/325-3494**). The cheerful staff will help you navigate the extensive menu of coffee items, running the gamut from steaming hot cappuccinos to blended iced mochas, including flavored lattes, mochas, and cocoas. Nibble on a fresh muffin or a bagel spread with plain or honey-walnut cream cheese and you'll be well prepared for your day. And for a sweet ice-cream treat, try **Lappert's Hawaiian Ice Cream,** 110B S. Palm Canyon Dr., Palm Springs (☎ **760/778-1855**), a mainland branch of Kauai's local fave. In addition to inventive concoctions of island flavors like chocolate/macadamia nut and coconut/caramel, they serve sweet shave ices and tropical-fruit smoothies.

SUPER-CHEAP EATS

Louise's Pantry. 124 S. Palm Canyon Dr., Palm Springs. ☎ **760/325-5124.** Reservations not accepted. Most items under $10. MC, V. Daily 7am–8:30pm. AMERICAN.

A real old-fashioned diner, Louise's has been a fixture in Palm Springs since it opened as a drugstore lunch counter in 1945. Locals line up for the very few booths (expect a wait during mealtimes) to enjoy premium-quality comfort foods like Cobb salad, Reuben and French-dip sandwiches, chicken and dumplings, hearty breakfasts with biscuits and gravy, and tasty fresh-baked pies.

Mykonos. 139 Andreas (just off Palm Canyon), Palm Springs. ☎ **760/322-0223.** Reservations not accepted. Most items under $10. MC, V. Wed–Mon 11am–10pm. GREEK.

Sit at the simple candlelit tables in this off-street brick courtyard with locals who enjoy the authentic Greek specialties at this family-run spot. Mykonos is super-casual (vinyl tablecloths and so forth) and decorated in white and blue like its Aegean namesake, but it's a pleasant treat in a town of mostly mediocre retro-diner fare. Traditional lamb shanks over rice, dolmades (stuffed grape leaves), salad tangy with crumbled feta cheese, and sweet, sticky baklava are among their best items.

FOR A FEW BUCKS MORE

✪ **Edgardo's Café Veracruz.** 494 N. Palm Canyon Dr. (at W. Alejo Rd.), Palm Springs. ☎ **760/360-3558.** Reservations recommended. Main courses $3.50–$15. DISC, MC, V. Mon–Fri 11am–3pm and 5:30–9:30pm; Sat–Sun 8am–10pm (sometimes later). REGIONAL CENTRAL MEXICAN.

The pleasant but humble ambiance at Edgardo's is a welcome change from touristy Palm Springs and the perfect backdrop for its expert menu of authentic Mayan, Huasteco, and Aztec cuisine. The cheerful interior boasts an array of colorful masks and artwork from Central and South America, but the patio tables (accented by a trickling fountain) are the best place to sample the tangy quesadillas, desert cactus salad, and traditional poblano chile rellenos—perhaps even an oyster/tequila shooter from the oyster bar.

Las Casuelas Terraza. 222 S. Palm Canyon Dr., Palm Springs. ☎ **760/325-2794.** Reservations recommended on weekends. Main courses $7–$13. AE, CB, DC, DISC, MC, V. Mon–Thurs 11am–10pm; Fri–Sat 11am–11pm; Sun 10am–10pm. CLASSIC MEXICAN.

The original Las Casuelas is still open, a tiny storefront several blocks from this popular terraza (terrace) offspring, but the bougainvillea-draped front patio here is a much better place to people-watch over Mexican standards like quesadillas, enchiladas, and mountainous nachos washed down with equally supersize margaritas. Inside, the action heats up with live music and raucous happy-hour crowds. During hot weather, the patio and even sidewalk passersby are cooled by the restaurant's well-placed misters, making this a perfect late-afternoon or early-evening choice.

Livreri's. 350 Indian Canyon Dr. (between Tahquitz and Ramon), Palm Springs. ☎ **760/ 327-1419.** Reservations recommended. Pizza, pasta, and main courses $8–$24. AE, MC, V. Wed–Mon 4:30–10pm. OLD-WORLD ITALIAN.

The Livreri family came to the desert from Long Island, New York, in the mid-1970s and began preparing traditional Italian cuisine served in generous portions: steaming pastas, cheesy pizzas, and garlicky seafood specialties. It's not the glamorous old-money Sinatra spot, but it's conveniently located and satisfying. Separate rooms hold a long leather-upholstered bar and the "Celebrity Room," where a retirement-age crowd gathers to enjoy dinner-theater performances of Broadway show tunes.

MODERATELY PRICED OPTIONS

Doug Arango's. 73520 El Paseo, Palm Desert. ☎ **760/341-4120.** Reservations recommended. Main courses $12–$22. AE, MC, V. Daily 11:30am–2:30pm (Oct–May) and 6–10pm (year-round). ITALIAN.

With so many Italian restaurants either old-world lasagna joints or pricey resort trattorias, it's no wonder Doug's is always packed with locals thankful for an affordable stylish choice offering northern Italian fare without pretension. Expect a friendly, noisy clatter when they're full—and beware, the kitchen can be heavy-handed with the garlic. Crispy, thin-crust individual pizzas are one specialty, and everyone raves about the appetizer of zucchini pancakes with scallion sour cream. The decor is understated, with black and white tiles, glass urns of marinating delicacies, and an open kitchen you can gaze into from the large oval bar.

La Provence. 254 N. Palm Canyon Dr. (upstairs), Palm Springs. ☎ **760/416-4418.** Reservations recommended. Main courses $10–$21. AE, DC, DISC, MC, V. Thurs–Tues 5:30–10:30pm. COUNTRY FRENCH.

A favorite of locals and recommended by knowledgeable innkeepers, the casually elegant La Provence eschews heavy traditional French cream sauces in favor of carefully married herbs and spices. The second-story terrace filled with tables sets a lovely mood on balmy desert evenings, whether or not it "subtly infuses the diner with an elevated sense of tranquillity" as the restaurant gushingly promises. The menu offers some expected items (escargots in mushroom caps, bouillabaisse, steak au poivre) as well as inventive pastas like wild-mushroom raviolis in sun-dried tomato and sweet-onion sauce. Foodies will note with pleasure that executive chef Clay Arkless comes by way of New York City's River Cafe.

La Quinta Cliffhouse. 78250 Calif. 111, La Quinta. ☎ **760/360-5991.** Reservations recommended. Main courses $13–$20. AE, MC, V. Mon 5–9:30pm; Tues–Fri 11:30am–2:30pm; Tues–Sat 5–9:30pm; Sun (fall only) 10am–2pm; closed for lunch in summer. REGIONAL AMERICAN.

King of its own little hill on the east side of Calif. 111, La Quinta Cliffhouse succeeds primarily due to its lovely setting. The stairs leading to the entrance wind through a rocky waterfall, and there's a breathtaking sunset virtually every night. The rustic Southwestern lodge decor is a little tired, but the old-money crowd that packs the valet-only lot doesn't seem to mind. The best dishes come off the grill, like filet mignon with Jack Daniels peppercorn sauce, BBQ pork ribs with chili and jalapeño cornbread, and Pacific ahi in red-bell-pepper sauce with garlic potatoes. In season, they serve an affordable and immensely popular Sunday champagne brunch, and there's a hearty pub menu in the adjacent Cactus Grill.

WORTH A SPLURGE

✪ **Europa Restaurant.** 1620 Indian Trail (at the Villa Royale). ☎ **760/327-2314.** Reservations recommended. Main courses $17–$28. AE, DC, DISC, MC, V. Daily 5:30–10pm. CALIFORNIA/CONTINENTAL.

Long advertised as the "most romantic dining in the desert," Europa is a sentimental favorite of many regulars among an equally gay and straight crowd, all of whom know that through the restaurant's French doors lies a European-style hideaway oozing charm. Whether you sit under the stars on the garden patio or in subdued candlelight indoors, you'll surely savor dinner prepared by one of Palm Springs's most dedicated kitchens and served by a staff who perfectly modulates attention and discretion. Standout dishes are deviled crab fritters on mango-papaya chutney, filet mignon on a bed of crispy onions with garlic butter, and a show-stopping salmon baked in parchment with crème fraîche and dill. For dessert, don't miss their signature chocolate mousse—smooth, grainy, and addictive.

THE DESERT RESORTS AFTER DARK

Every month a different club or disco is the hot spot in the Springs, and the best way to tap into the trend is by consulting *The Desert Guide, The Bottom Line* (see "Gay Life in Palm Springs," above), or one of the many other free newsletters available from area hotels and merchants. **VillageFest** (see "Shopping," above) turns Palm Canyon Drive into an outdoor party every Thursday night. Below I've described a couple of the enduring arts and entertainment attractions around the resorts.

The **Fabulous Palm Springs Follies,** at the historic Plaza Theatre, 128 S. Palm Canyon Dr., Palm Springs (☎ 760/327-0225), is a vaudeville-style show filled with lively production numbers. With a cast of energetic retired showgirls, singers, dancers, and comedians, the revue has been enormously popular around town. Call for show schedule; tickets are $28 to $59.

The **McCallum Theatre for the Performing Arts,** 73000 Fred Waring Dr., Palm Desert (☎ **760/340-ARTS**), offers the only cultural high road around. Frequent symphony performances with visiting virtuosos like conductor Seiji Ozawa or violinist Itzhak Perlman, musicals like Tommy Tune's *Grease* or *A Chorus Line,* and pop performers like the Captain and Tennille or the Ink Spots are among the theater's recent offerings. Call for upcoming-events information.

4 Joshua Tree National Park

The trees themselves are merely a jumping-off point for exploring this seemingly barren desert. Viewed from the roadside, the dry land only hints at hidden vitality, but on closer examination reveals a giant mosaic of intense beauty and complexity. From lush oases teeming with life to rusted-out relics of man's attempts to tame the wilderness, from low plains of tufted cactus to mountains of exposed twisted rock, the park is much more than a tableau of the curious tree for which it's named.

The Joshua tree is said to have been given its name by early Mormon settlers traveling west, for its upraised limbs and bearded appearance reminded them of the prophet Joshua leading them to the promised land.

The hardy desert dweller is really not a tree at all but a variety of yucca, member of the lily family. The relationship is apparent when pale-yellow lilylike flowers festoon the limbs of the Joshuas when they bloom (depending on rainfall) in March, April, or May. When Mother Nature cooperates, the park also puts on quite a wildflower display, and you can get an updated report on prime viewing sites by calling the park ranger (see below).

Joshua Tree National Park's name is fitting, for here the peculiar tree reaches the southernmost boundary of its range. The park straddles two desert environments: The mountainous Joshua tree–studded Mojave Desert forms the northwestern part of the park. Hotter, drier, lower, and characterized by a wide variety of desert flora (including cacti, cottonwood, and native California fan palms), the Colorado Desert comprises the southern and eastern sections. Between them runs the "transition zone," displaying characteristics of each.

The area's geological timeline is fascinating, stretching back 8 million years to when the Mojave landscape was one of rolling hills and flourishing grasslands; horses, camels, and mastodons abounded, preyed on by saber-tooth tigers and wild dogs. Displays at the Oasis Visitor Center (see below) show how resulting climatic, volcanic, and tectonic activity have created the park's signature cliffs and boulders and turned Joshua Tree into the arid desert you see today.

JUST THE FACTS

No restaurants, lodging, gas stations, or stores are found in Joshua Tree National Park. In fact, water is available at only four park locations: Cottonwood Springs, the Black Rock Canyon Campground, the Indian Cove Ranger Station, and the Oasis Visitor Center. Twentynine Palms and Yucca Valley have lots of restaurants, markets, motels, and B&Bs.

Admission to the park costs $5 per car (good for 7 days).

GETTING THERE From metropolitan Los Angeles, the usual route to the Oasis Visitor Center in Joshua Tree National Park is via I-10 to its intersection with Calif. 62 (some 92 miles east of downtown). Calif. 62 (the Twentynine Palms Highway) leads northeast for about 43 miles to the town of Twentynine Palms. Total driving time is around 2½ hours. In town, follow the signs at National Park Drive or Utah Trail to the visitor center and ranger station.

VISITOR CENTERS & INFORMATION   In addition to the main **Oasis Visitor Center** at the Twentynine Palms entrance, there's the **Cottonwood Visitor Center** at the south entrance (along I-10) and the privately operated **Park Center** (☎ **760/ 366-3448**) in the town of Joshua Tree.

The Oasis Visitor Center is open daily (except Christmas) from 8am to 4:30pm. Check here for a detailed map of park roads, plus schedules of ranger-guided walks and interpretive programs. Ask about the weekend tours of the Desert Queen Ranch, once a working homestead and now part of the park.

For information, contact the **Park Superintendent's Office,** 74485 National Park Dr., Twentynine Palms, CA 92277 (☎ **760/367-5500**). A terrific Web site on the park and surrounding communities is **www.desertgold.com**.

SEEING THE HIGHLIGHTS

An excellent first stop, outside the park's north entrance, is the main **Oasis Visitor Center,** alongside the Oasis of Mara, also known as the Twentynine Palms Oasis. For many generations, the native Serrano tribe lived at this "place of little springs and much grass." Get maps, books, and the latest in road, trail, and weather conditions before beginning your tour.

From the Oasis Center, drive south to **Jumbo Rocks,** which captures the complete essence of the park: a vast array of rock formations, a Joshua tree forest, the yucca-dotted desert open and wide. Check out Skull Rock (one of the many rocks in the area that appears to resemble humans, dinosaurs, monsters, cathedrals, and castles) via a 1½-mile-long nature trail that provides an introduction to the park's flora, wildlife, and geology.

At Cap Rock Junction, the main park road swings north toward the **Wonderland of Rocks,** 12 square miles of massive jumbled granite. This curious maze of stone hides groves of Joshua trees, trackless washes, and several small pools of water. To the south is Keys View Road, which dead-ends at mile-high **Keys View.** From the crest of the Little San Bernardino Mountains, enjoy grand desert views encompassing both the highest (Mt. San Gorgonio) and the lowest (Salton Sea) points in southern California.

Don't miss the contrasting Colorado Desert terrain found along Pinto Basin Road—to conserve time, you might plan to exit the park via this route, which ends up at I-10. You'll pass both the **Cholla Cactus Garden** and the spindly **Ocotillo Patch** on your way to vast **Pinto Basin,** a barren lowland surrounded by austere mountains and punctuated by trackless sand dunes. The dunes are an easy hike (2 miles round-trip) from the backcountry camping board, or you can simply continue to **Cottonwood Springs,** near the southern park entrance. Besides a small ranger station and well-developed campground, Cottonwood has a cool palm-shaded oasis that's the trailhead for a tough hike to Lost Palms Oasis.

The museum is open daily from 9am to 5pm, except Thanksgiving and Christmas Day. For more information, call ☎ **760/243-4547.**

ACTIVITIES IN THE PARK

HIKING & NATURE WALKS   The national park holds a variety of nature trails ranging in difficulty from strenuous challenges to kid- (and wimp-) friendly interpretive walks—two of these (**Oasis of Mara** and **Cap Rock**) are even paved and wheelchair accessible. My favorite of the 11 short interpretive trails is **Cholla Cactus Garden,** smack-dab in the middle of the park, where you stroll through dense clusters of the deceptively fluffy-looking "teddy bear cactus."

Joshua Tree National Park

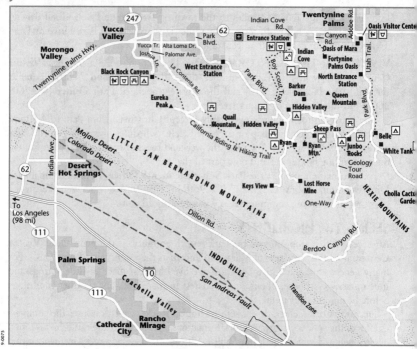

For the more adventurous, **Barker Dam** is an easy 1.1-mile loop accessible by a graded dirt road east of Hidden Valley. A small man-made lake is framed by the majestic Wonderland of Rocks. In addition to scrambling atop the old dam, it's fun to search out Native American petroglyphs carved into the base of cliffs lining your return to the trailhead.

The moderately challenging **Lost Horse Mine** trail near Keys View leads through rolling hills to the ruins of a successful gold-mining operation; once there, a short, steep hike leads uphill behind the ruins for a fine view into the heart of the park.

When you're ready for a strenuous hike, try the **Fortynine Palms Oasis** trail, accessible from Canyon Road in Twentynine Palms. After a steep, harsh ascent to a cactus-fringed ridge, the rocky canyon trail leads to a spectacular oasis, complete with palm-shaded pools of green water and abundant birds and other wildlife. Allow 2 to 3 hours for the 3-mile (round-trip) hike.

Another lush oasis lies at the end of **Lost Palms Oasis** trail at Cottonwood Springs. The first section of the 7.5-mile trail is moderately difficult, climbing slowly to the oasis overlook; from there a treacherous path continues to the canyon bottom, a remote spot attractive to the elusive bighorn sheep.

ROCK CLIMBING   From Hidden Valley to the Wonderland of Rocks, the park has emerged as one of the world's premier rock-climbing destinations. It offers some 4,000 climbing routes, ranging from the easiest of bouldering to some of the sport's most difficult technical climbs. November through May is the prime season to watch these lizardlike humans scale sheer rock faces with impossible grace. Even beginners can get into the act: At **First Ascent** (☎ 800/325-5462), certified guides start the day

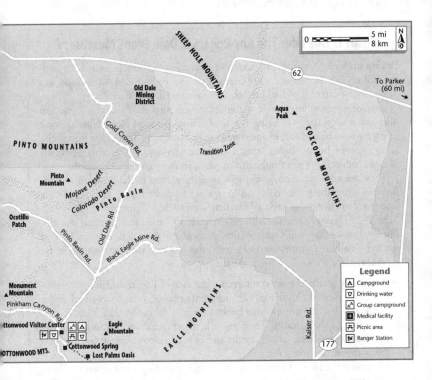

with detailed instruction, then stay with you providing guidance as you learn the ropes. All equipment is provided, and prices start at $75.

MOUNTAIN BIKING   Much of the park is designated wilderness, meaning bicycles are limited to roads; they'll damage the fragile ecosystem if you venture off the beaten track. None of the paved roads has bike lanes, but rugged mountain bikes are a great tool to explore the park via unpaved roads, where distraction from autos is light.

Try the 18-mile **Geology Tour Road,** beginning west of Jumbo Rocks; dry lake beds contrast with towering boulders along this sandy downhill road—you'll also encounter abandoned mines.

A shorter but still rewarding ride begins at the **Covington Flats** picnic area; a steep 4-mile road climbs through Joshua trees, junipers, and pinion pines to Eureka Peak, where you'll be rewarded with a panoramic view.

For other bike-friendly unpaved and four-wheel–drive roads, consult the official park map.

ACCOMMODATIONS & CAMPING

If you're staying in the Palm Springs area, it's entirely possible to make a day trip to the national park. But if you'd like to stay close by and spend more time here, Twentynine Palms, just outside the north boundary of the national park on Calif. 62, offers budget-to-moderate lodging.

Near the Visitor Center in the Oasis of Mara is the rustic **29 Palms Inn** (☎ **760/367-3505;** fax 760/367-4425), a cluster of adobe cottages and old cabins dating from the 1920s; their garden-fresh restaurant is the best in town. Rates are $60 to $95.

This Is Our Life: The Roy Rogers & Dale Evans Museum

Passing through Victorville, it's tough to miss a log fort visible from I-15, with the words "Roy Rogers and Dale Evans Museum" emblazoned on the side, Las Vegas–style—larger than life, brightly lit, embellished with stars.

Fans of cowboy lore, western movies, or country music can tell you the museum is legendary for being the final resting place of Roy's faithful horse Trigger, whom he had stuffed and mounted. For company, Trigger has Buttermilk (Dale's golden horse), Bullet (their canine companion), and a veritable Noah's Ark of taxidermy—Roy's trophies from safaris in every corner of the globe.

These are among the many surprises awaiting visitors to the museum, a glorified attic containing the relics and souvenirs of two lifetimes. The displays are folksy, accented by tags saying "My first cowboy boots" (bronzed, of course), "The 1923 Dodge I came to California in, in 1930," and other personal remarks. But because of Roy and Dale's wealth, years of travel, varied interests, and an apparent inability to throw anything away, this museum truly has something for everyone. Here are some of the highlights:

- Beautifully arranged cases commemorating each of Roy and Dale's three children who died in childhood. On display are photos, toys, letters, and report cards, as well as the inspirational books written in tribute by Dale Evans Rogers after each of their deaths. Their many living children and grandchildren are also well represented; in fact, by the end of your visit you might feel as if you know the whole family personally.

- Gifts from the couple's fans all over the world, including a pair of stitched samplers framed near the entrance, containing poetic tributes both epic and homespun.

- Every piece of Roy Rogers and/or Dale Evans merchandise from over the years: comic books, breakfast-cereal boxes, fan-club items, war-effort promotions, and more. See the 1950s-era "den/playroom" filled with vintage furniture and littered with dozens of Roy and Dale toys, storybooks, dolls, model horses, and board games.

- Roy's personal collection of western memorabilia from his role models—real-life and movie cowboys—including Tom Mix's director's chair, Buck Jones's saddle, Hoot Gibson's piano, and last but not least, an autographed picture of Lee Majors (remember him as Heath in "The Big Valley"?).

The museum is open daily from 9am to 5pm except Thanksgiving and Christmas. For more information, call ☎ **760/243-4547.**

There's also the 100-room **Best Western Gardens Motel** (☎ **760/367-9141;** fax 760/367-2584), a comfortable base from which to maximize your outdoor time. Rates are $65 to $95, with discounts available.

For a complete listing of Twentynine Palms lodgings, contact the **29 Palms Chamber of Commerce,** 5672 Historic Plaza, Twentynine Palms, CA 92277 (☎ **760/367-3445;** fax 760/367-3366; www.cci-29palms.com). Nine **campgrounds** scattered throughout the park offer pleasant though often Spartan accommodations, with just picnic tables and pit toilets for the most part. Only two (**Black Rock Canyon** and **Cottonwood Springs**) have potable water and flush toilets—plus a $10 overnight fee.

5 Mojave National Preserve

Two decades of park politicking finally ended in 1994 when President Clinton signed into law the California Desert Protection Act, which created the new Mojave National Preserve. Thus far, the Mojave's elevated status hasn't attracted hordes of sightseers, and devoted visitors are happy to keep it that way. Unlike a fully protected national park, the "national preserve" designation allows certain commercial land uses, and the continued grazing and mining within the preserve's boundaries are a sore spot for ardent environmentalists.

To most Americans, the East Mojave is that vast, bleak, interminable stretch of desert to be crossed as quickly as possible while leaving California via I-15 or I-40. Few realize that these highways are the boundaries of what desert rats have long considered the crown jewel of the California desert.

This land is a hard one to get to know—unlike more developed desert parks, it has no lodgings or concessions, few campgrounds, and only a handful of roads suitable for the average passenger vehicle. But hidden in this natural fortress are some true gems—the preserve's 1.4 million acres include the world's largest Joshua-tree forest; abundant wildlife, spectacular canyons, caverns, and volcanic formations; nationally honored scenic back roads and footpaths to historic mining sites; tabletop mesas; and a dozen mountain ranges.

JUST THE FACTS

GETTING THERE   I-15, the major route taken between the southern California metropolis and the state line by Las Vegas–bound travelers, extends along the northern boundary of Mojave National Preserve. I-40 is the southern access route to the East Mojave.

WHEN TO GO   Spring is a splendid time (autumn is another) to visit this desert. From March through May, the temperatures are mild, the Joshua trees in bloom, and the lower Kelso Dunes bedecked with yellow and white desert primrose and pink sand verbena.

VISITOR CENTERS & INFORMATION   The best source for up-to-date weather conditions and a free topographical map is the **Mojave Desert Information Center,** 72157 Baker Blvd. (under the "World's Tallest Thermometer"), Baker, CA 92309 (☎ **760/733-4040**), which is open daily and also has a superior selection of books for sale.

Those coming in on I-40 should stop in **Needles,** where an **Information Center,** 707 W. Broadway, Needles, CA 92363 (☎ **760/326-6322**), opened at the end of 1997. It's open daily; call to verify hours.

Additional information and maps are available inside the preserve at the **Hole-in-the-Wall Campground's Visitor Center,** which is open seasonally (as staffing allows).

There's also the **California Desert Information Center,** 831 Barstow Rd., Barstow, CA 92311 (☎ **760/255-8760**), which has a minimuseum and educational displays on the history and characteristics of the desert. It's open daily from 9am to 5pm. And you can visit the preserve on-line at **www.nps.gov/moja.**

SEEING THE HIGHLIGHTS

One of the preserve's spectacular sights is the **Kelso Dunes,** the most extensive dune field in the West. The 45-square-mile formation of magnificently sculpted sand is famous for its "booming": Visitors' footsteps cause mini-avalanches and the dunes to go "sha-boom-sha-boom-sha-boom." Geologists speculate that the extreme dryness of the East Mojave Desert, combined with the wind-polished, rounded nature of the individual sand grains, has something to do with their musicality. Sometimes the low rumbling sound resembles a Tibetan gong; other times it sounds like a 1950s doo-wop musical group.

A 10-mile drive from the Kelso Dunes is **Kelso Depot,** built by the Union Pacific in 1924. The Spanish revival–style structure was designed with a red-tile roof, graceful arches, and a brick platform. The depot continued to be open for freight-train crew use through the mid-1980s, though it ceased to be a railroad stop for passengers after World War II. The National Park Service is considering refurbishing the building for use as the preserve's visitor center.

On and around **Cima Dome,** a rare geological anomaly, grows the world's largest and densest Joshua-tree forest. Botanists say Cima's Joshuas are more symmetrical than their cousins elsewhere in the Mojave. The dramatic colors of the sky at sunset provide a breathtaking backdrop for Cima's Joshua trees, some more than 25 feet tall and several hundred years old.

Tucked into the Providence Mountains, in the southern portion of the preserve, is a treat everyone should try to see. The **Mitchell Caverns,** contained in a state recreation area within the national preserve, are a geological oddity exploited for tourism but still quite fascinating. Regular tours are conducted of these cool rock "rooms"; in addition to showcasing marvelous stalactites, stalagmites, and other limestone formations, the caves have proven to be rich in Native American archaeological finds.

Hole-in-the-Wall and Mid Hills are the centerpieces of Mojave National Preserve. Both locales offer diverse desert scenery, fine campgrounds, and the feeling of being in the middle of nowhere, though in fact they're right in the middle of the preserve.

Linking the two sites is the preserve's best drive. In 1989 **Wildhorse Canyon Road,** looping from Mid Hills Campground to Hole-in-the-Wall Campground, was declared the nation's first official "Back Country Byway," an honor federal agencies bestow on America's most scenic back roads. The 11-mile, horseshoe-shaped road crosses wide-open country dotted with cholla and, in season, delicate purple, yellow, and red wildflowers. Dramatic volcanic slopes and flattop mesas tower over the low desert.

Mile-high **Mid Hills,** so named because of its location halfway between the Providence and New York mountains, recalls the Great Basin Desert topography of Nevada and Utah. Mid Hills Campground offers a grand observation point from which to gaze out at the coffee-with-cream-colored Pinto Mountains to the north and the rolling Kelso Dunes shining on the western horizon.

Hole-in-the-Wall is the kind of place Butch Cassidy and the Sundance Kid would've chosen as a hideout. This twisted maze of rocks called rhyolite is a form of crystallized red lava rock. A series of iron rings aids descent into Hole-in-the-Wall; they're not particularly difficult for those who are reasonably agile and take their time.

Kelso Dunes, Mitchell Caverns, Cima Dome, Hole-in-the-Wall—these highlights of the preserve can be viewed in a weekend. But you'll need a week just to see all the major sights, and maybe a lifetime to really get to know the East Mojave. And right now, without much in the way of services, the traveler to this desert must be well prepared and self-reliant. For many, this is what makes a trip to the East Mojave an adventure.

If Mojave National Preserve attracts you, you'll want to return again and again to see the wonders of this desert, including **Caruthers Canyon,** a "botanical island" of pinion pine and juniper woodland, and **Ivanpah Valley,** which supports the largest desert tortoise population in the California desert.

HIKING & MOUNTAIN BIKING

HIKING   The free-form ambling climb to the top of the **Kelso Dunes** is 3 miles round-trip. A cool, inviting pinion pine/juniper woodland is explored by the **Caruthers Canyon Trail** (3 miles round-trip). The longest pathway is the 8-mile (one-way) **Mid Hills to Hole-in-the-Wall Trail,** a grand tour of basin and range tabletop mesas, large pinion trees, and colorful cactus.

If you're not up for a long day hike, the 1-mile trip from **Hole-in-the-Wall Campground** to **Banshee Canyon** and the 5-mile jaunt to **Wildhorse Canyon** offer some easier alternatives.

Be sure to pick up trail maps at one of the visitor centers.

MOUNTAIN BIKING   Opportunities are as extensive as the preserve's hundreds of miles of lonesome dirt roads. The 140-mile-long historic **Mojave Road,** a rough four-wheel–drive route, visits many of the most scenic areas in the East Mojave; sections of this road make excellent bike tours. Prepare well—the Mojave Road and other dirt roads are rugged routes through desert wilderness.

CAMPING

The **Mid Hills Campground** is in a pinion pine/juniper woodland and offers outstanding views. This mile-high camp is the coolest in the East Mojave. Nearby **Hole-in-the-Wall Campground** is perched above two dramatic canyons. *Warning:* The washboard dirt road between the two might be too jarring for many two-wheel–drive passenger cars.

There are also some sites at **Providence Mountain State Recreation Area** (Mitchell Caverns; see "Seeing the Highlights," above).

One of the highlights of the East Mojave Desert is camping in the open desert all by your lonesome, but certain rules apply. Call the Mojave Desert Information Center for suggestions.

NEARBY TOWNS WITH TOURIST SERVICES

BARSTOW   This sizable town has a great many restaurants and motels and is roughly a 1-hour drive from the center of the preserve. Of the dozen motels in town, the most reliable are **Best Western Desert Villa,** 1984 E. Main St., Barstow, CA 92311 (☎ **760/256-1781**), where doubles go for $69 to $92; and **Holiday Inn,** 1511 E. Main St., Barstow, CA 92311 (☎ **760/256-5673**), where doubles are $89.

BAKER   Accommodations and food are available in this small desert town, a good point to fill up your gas tank and purchase supplies before entering Mojave National Preserve.

Inexpensive lodging ($55 double; midweek discounts available) can be secured at the **Bun Boy Motel,** P.O. Box 130, Baker, CA 92309 (☎ **760/733-4363**). The Bun Boy Coffee Shop is open 24 hours.

For a tasty surprise, stop at the **Mad Greek** (☎ **760/733-4354**). Order a Greek salad, a souvlaki, or baklava and marvel at your good fortune—imagine finding such tasty food and pleasant surroundings in the middle of nowhere.

NIPTON   This charming tiny town boasts a "trading post" that stocks snacks, maps, ice, and native jewelry; and the **Hotel Nipton** (☎ **760/856-2335**), a B&B with a sitting room, two bathrooms down the hall, and four guest rooms, each going for $50 a night. Jerry Freeman, a former hard-rock miner who purchased the entire town in 1984, says hotel occupancy is up 80% since the East Mojave became a national preserve. He and his wife, Roxanne, moved from the famous sands of Malibu to the abandoned ghost town and have gradually brought it back to life. Nipton is located on Nipton Road, a few miles from I-15 near the Nevada state line.

PRIMM (FORMERLY STATELINE) This privately owned town on the California-Nevada border features three hotel/casinos, each as large and garish as an amusement park. **Whiskey Pete's, Buffalo Bill's,** and **Primadonna** are managed by the same company—rooms here are pretty nice, really cheap ($33 to $55 double Friday and Saturday, $18 to $25 double Sunday through Thursday), and (if you have a twisted sense of humor) an ironic counterpoint to the wilderness you came for. With a dozen restaurants, including those low-cost Vegas-style buffets, Primm might also be your best dining bet. For reservations call ☎ **800/FUN-STOP.**

6 Death Valley National Park

Park? Death Valley National *Park?* The forty-niners, whose suffering gave the valley its name, would've howled at the notion. Death Valley National *Park* seems a contradiction in terms, an oxymoron of the great outdoors. To them, other four-letter words would've been more appropriate: *gold, mine, heat, lost, dead.* And the four-letter words shouted by teamsters who drove the 20-mule–team borax wagons need not be repeated.

Americans looking for gold in California's mountains in 1849 were forced to cross the burning sands to avoid severe snowstorms in the nearby Sierra Nevada. Some perished along the way, and the land became known as Death Valley.

Mountains stand naked, unadorned. The bitter waters of saline lakes evaporate into bizarre razor-sharp crystal formations. Jagged canyons jab deep into the earth. Oven-like heat, frigid cold, and the driest air imaginable combine to make this one of the most inhospitable locations in the world.

But, human nature being what it is, it's not surprising that people have long been drawn to challenge the power of Mother Nature, even in this, her home court. Man's first foray into tourism began in 1925, a scant 76 years after the forty-niners' harrowing experiences (which would discourage most sane folks from ever returning). It probably would've begun sooner, but the valley had been consumed with lucrative borax mining since the late 1880s.

Death Valley is raw, bare earth, the way it must've looked before life began. Here forces of the earth are exposed to view with dramatic clarity; just looking out on the landscape, it's impossible to know what year—what century—it is. It's no coincidence that many of Death Valley's topographical features are associated with hellish images—the Funeral Mountains, Furnace Creek, Dante's View, Coffin Peak, and the Devil's Golf Course. But it can be a place of serenity.

In one of his last official acts, President Herbert Hoover signed a proclamation designating Death Valley a national monument on February 11, 1933. With the stroke of a pen he not only authorized the protection of a vast and wondrous land but also helped to transform one of the earth's least hospitable spots into a popular tourist destination.

The naming of Death Valley National Monument came at a time when Americans began to discover the romance of the desert. Land that had previously been considered hideously devoid of life was now celebrated for its spare beauty; places that had once been feared for their harshness were now admired for their uniqueness.

In 1994, when President Clinton signed the California Desert Protection Act, Death Valley National Park became the largest national park outside Alaska, with over 3.3 million acres. Though remote, it's one of the most heavily visited, and you're likely to hear less English spoken than German, French, and Japanese.

Today's visitor to Death Valley drives in air-conditioned comfort, stays in comfortable hotel rooms or well-maintained campgrounds, orders meals and provisions at park concessions, even quaffs a cold beer at the local saloon. You can take a swim in the Olympic-size pool, tour a Moorish castle, shop for souvenirs, and enjoy the desert landscape while hiking along a nature trail with a park ranger.

JUST THE FACTS

GETTING THERE   There are several routes into the park—all involve crossing one of the steep mountain ranges that isolate Death Valley from, well, everything. Perhaps the most scenic entry to the park is via Calif. 190, east of Calif. 178 from Ridgecrest. Another scenic drive to the park is by way of Calif. 127 and Calif. 190 from Baker. You'll be required to pay a $10 per car entrance fee, valid for 7 days' stay.

VISITOR CENTER & INFORMATION   The **Death Valley Visitor Center** at Furnace Creek, 15 miles inside the eastern park boundary on Calif. 190 (☎ **760/786-2331**), offers well-done interpretive exhibits and an hourly slide program. Ask at the desk for ranger-led nature walks and evening naturalist programs. Visitor center hours are daily from 8am to 7pm in winter (to 5pm in summer). For information before you go, contact the **Superintendent, Death Valley National Park,** Death Valley, CA 92328 (☎ **760/786-2331**). The park's Web page is www.nps.gov/deva.

SEEING THE HIGHLIGHTS

A good first stop after checking in at the main park visitor center in Furnace Creek is the **Harmony Borax Works**—a rock-salt landscape as tortured as you'll ever find. Death Valley prospectors called borax "white gold," and though it wasn't exactly a glamorous substance, it was a profitable one. From 1883 to 1888, more than 20 million pounds of borax were transported from the Harmony Borax Works, and borax mining continued in Death Valley until 1928. A short trail with interpretive signs leads past the ruins of the old borax refinery and some outlying buildings.

Transport of the borax was the stuff of legends, too. The famous 20-mule teams hauled the huge loaded wagons 165 miles to the rail station at Mojave. (To learn more about this colorful era, visit the **Borax Museum** at Furnace Creek Ranch and the park visitor center, also in Furnace Creek.)

Badwater, at 282 feet below sea level, the lowest point in the Western Hemisphere, is also one of the hottest places in the world, with regularly recorded summer temperatures of 120°.

Salt Creek is the home of the **Salt Creek pupfish,** found nowhere else. This little fish, which has made some amazing adaptations to survive in this arid land, can be glimpsed from a wooden boardwalk nature trail. In spring, a million pupfish might be wriggling in the creek; but by summer's end only a few thousand remain.

Before sunrise, photographers set up their tripods at **Zabriskie Point** and aim their cameras down at the pale mudstone hills of Golden Canyon and the great valley beyond. This panoramic view is magnificent; another grand park vista is at **Dante's View,** a 5,475-foot viewpoint looking out over the shimmering Death Valley floor backed by the high Panamint Mountains.

Just south of Furnace Creek is the 9-mile loop **Artist Drive,** an easy must-see for visitors (except those in RVs, which can't negotiate the sharp rock-bordered curves in the road). From the highway, you can't see the splendid palette of colors splashed on the rocks behind the foothills; once inside, though, stop and climb a low hill that offers an overhead view, then continue through to aptly named **Artists Palette,** where an interpretive sign explains the source of nature's rainbow.

Scotty's Castle, the Mediterranean hacienda in the northern part of the park, is unabashedly Death Valley's premier tourist attraction. Visitors are wowed by the elaborate Spanish tiles, well-crafted furnishings, and innovative construction that included solar water heating. Even more compelling is the colorful history of this villa in remote Grapevine Canyon, brought to life by park rangers dressed in 1930s clothing. Don't be surprised if the castle cook or a friend of Scotty's gives you a special insight into castle life.

Construction of the "castle"—more officially, Death Valley Ranch—began in 1924. It was to be a winter retreat for eccentric Chicago millionaire Albert Johnson. The insurance tycoon's unlikely friendship with prospector/cowboy/spinner-of-tall-tales Walter Scott put the $2.3-million structure on the map and captured the public's imagination. Scotty greeted visitors and told them fanciful stories from the early hard-rock–mining days of Death Valley.

The 1-hour walking tour of Scotty's Castle is excellent, both for its inside look at the mansion and for what it reveals about the eccentricities of Johnson and Scotty. Tours fill up quickly; arrive early for the first available spots (there's an $8 fee). A snack bar and gift shop make the wait more comfortable. To learn more about the castle grounds, pick up the pamphlet *A Walking Tour of Scotty's Castle,* which leads you on an exploration from stable to swimming pool, from bunkhouse to powerhouse.

Near Scotty's Castle is **Ubehebe Crater,** known as an explosion crater—one look and you'll know why. When hot magma rose from the depths of the earth to meet the groundwater, the resultant steam blasted out a crater and scattered cinders.

HIKING & MOUNTAIN BIKING

HIKING   The trails in Death Valley range from the half-mile **Salt Creek Nature Trail,** an easy boardwalk path suitable for everyone in the family, to the grueling **Telescope Peak Trail** (14 miles round-trip), an all-day challenge. Telescope Peak is a strenuous 3,000-foot climb to the 11,049-foot summit, where you'll be rewarded by the view described this way by one pioneer: "You can see so far, it's just like looking through a telescope." Snow-covered during winter, the peak is best climbed from May through November.

But there are lots of levels in between. I like the trail into **Mosaic Canyon,** near Stovepipe Wells, where water has polished the marble rock into white, gray, and black mosaics. It's a relatively easy 2½-mile scramble through long, narrow walls that seem quite "gallery"-like—and provide welcome shade at every turn.

Romping among the **Sand Dunes** on the way to Stovepipe Wells is also fun, particularly for kids. It's a free-form adventure, and the dunes aren't particularly high—but the sun can be merciless. The sand in the dunes is actually tiny pieces of rock, most of them quartz fragments. As with all desert activities, your water supply is crucial.

Near the park's eastern border, two trails lead from the **Keane Wonder Mill,** site of a successful gold mine. The first is a steep and strenuous 2-mile challenge leading to the mine itself, passing along the way the solid, efficient wooden tramway that carried ore out of the mountain.

If that's beyond your fitness level, try the **Keane Wonder Spring Trail,** leading in another direction. This 2-mile walk is much easier, and the spring that supplied water for the Keane Wonder operation will announce itself with a sulfur smell and piping birdcalls.

If you're visiting **Ubehebe Crater,** there's a steep but plain trail leading from the parking area up to the crater's lip and around some of the contours. Fierce winds can hamper your progress, but you'll get the exhilarating feeling you're truly on another planet.

A Food Tip

Meals and groceries are exceptionally costly here due to the remoteness of the location. If possible, consider bringing a cooler with some snacks, sandwiches, and beverages to last the duration of your visit. Ice is easily obtainable, and you'll also be able to keep water chilled.

Park rangers can provide topographical maps and detailed directions to these and a dozen other hiking trails in the national park.

MOUNTAIN BIKING   Because 94% of the park is federally designated wilderness, cycling is allowed only on roads used by automobiles. Cycling isn't allowed on hiking trails.

Good routes for bikers are **Racetrack** (28 miles, mainly level), **Greenwater Valley** (30 miles, mostly level), **Cottonwood Canyon** (20 miles), and **West Side Road** (40 miles, fairly level with some washboard sections). **Artists Drive** is 8 miles long, paved, with some steep uphills. A favorite is **Titus Canyon** (28 miles on a hilly road)—it's highly recommended you make this a one-way descent.

CAMPING & ACCOMMODATIONS

The park's nine campgrounds are at elevations ranging from below sea level to 8,000 feet. In Furnace Creek, **Sunset** offers 1,000 spaces with water and flush toilets. **Furnace Creek Campground** has 200 similarly appointed spaces. **Stovepipe Wells** has 200 spaces with water and flush toilets. Overnight fees range from $10 to $16.

The **Furnace Creek Ranch** (☎ 760/786-2345) offers 224 no-frills cottage units with air-conditioning and showers. The pool is a popular hangout for tired lodgers. Nearby are a coffee shop, saloon, steak house, and general store. Rates are $85 to $125.

The **Furnace Creek Inn** (☎ 760/786-2345), an elegant resort, boasts 66 deluxe rooms with a formal dining room, a heated pool, golf, and tennis courts. Rates are $140 to $200 June through September and $220 to $300 October through May.

Stove Pipe Wells Village (☎ 760/786-2387) has 74 modest rooms with air-conditioning and showers, plus a casual dining room that closes between meals. Rates are $53 to $76.

The only lodging within the park not operated by the official concessionaire is the **Panamint Springs Resort** (☎ 702/482-7680), a truly charming rustic motel, cafe, and snack shop about an hour east of Furnace Creek. Rates run $50 to $95.

Because accommodations in Death Valley are both limited and expensive, you might consider the money-saving (but inconvenient) option of spending a night at one of the two gateway towns: **Lone Pine** on the west side of the park or **Baker** on the south. **Beatty, Nevada,** which has inexpensive lodging, is an hour's drive from the park's center. The restored **Amargosa Hotel,** P.O. Box 8, Death Valley Junction, CA 92328 (☎ 760/852-4441), offers 14 rooms ($45 to $55 double October through April, $35 to $45 double May through September) in a historic out-of-the-way place, 40 minutes from Furnace Creek.

16 San Diego & Environs

by Stephanie Avnet Yates

San Diego is best known for its benign climate and fabulous beaches, attributes that make the city one big outdoor playground on sunny days. With 70 miles of sandy coastline—plus pretty, sheltered Mission Bay—you can choose from swimming, snorkeling, windsurfing, kayaking, bicycling, skating, and tons of other fun in or near the water. The city is also home to top-notch attractions, including three world-famous animal parks, and splendid Balboa Park, a cultural and recreational jewel that's one of the finest urban parks in the country. Once dismissed as a slow-growth, conservative Navy town, San Diego has been expanding steadily over the past decade or two, and now boasts an almost Los Angeles–like diversity of neighborhoods and residents. A heightened sensitivity to historical preservation means formerly seedy downtown neighborhoods and architecturally rich suburbs are being carefully restored; they draw a stylish young crowd that's updating the face of San Diego dining, shopping, and entertainment. California's first city, San Diego reflects its Spanish/Mexican heritage in every corner—in fact, bustling Tijuana is less than 30 minutes away, just across the border. So, pack a laid-back attitude along with your sandals and swimsuit, and welcome to California's grown-up beach town.

1 Orientation

ARRIVING

BY PLANE **San Diego International Airport,** 3707 N. Harbor Dr. (☎ **619/231-7361**), locally known as Lindbergh Field, is just 3 miles from downtown. Most of the major domestic carriers fly here. Lindbergh Field consists of three adjacent airport terminals, no. 1 (formerly "East Terminal"), no. 2 (formerly "West Terminal"), and the new Terminal 2 Addition. Short local flights use the Commuter Terminal, which is a half-mile away and can be reached from the main airport by the free "red bus" shuttle.

Transportation from the Airport Several major rental-car companies operate at the airport, including **Avis** (☎ 800/331-1212), **Budget** (☎ 800/527-0700), **Dollar** (☎ 800/800-4000), **Hertz** (☎ 800/654-3131), and **National** (☎ 800/CAR-RENT). If you're driving into the city from the airport, take Harbor Drive south to Broadway, the main east-west thoroughfare, and turn left.

Metropolitan Transit System (MTS) bus route 992 provides 10-minute service between the airport and downtown San Diego. Route 992 bus stops are located at each of the three terminals. The one-way fare is $2. Request a transfer if connecting to another bus or San Diego Trolley route downtown. Downtown, Route 992 stops on Broadway. At Broadway and First Avenue is the Transit Store (☎ **619/234-1060**), where the staff can answer your transit questions and provide free route maps to help you get where you're going.

Several **shuttles** run regularly from the airport to downtown hotels. They charge around $5 to $9 per person, and you'll see designated areas outside each terminal. The shuttles are a good deal for single travelers; two or more people traveling together might as well take a taxi.

Taxis line up outside both terminals and charge $7 to $10 to take you to a downtown location.

BY CAR   From Los Angeles, you'll enter San Diego via coastal route I-5. From points northeast of the city, you'll come down on I-15 (link up with I-8 west and Calif. 163 south to drive into downtown). From the east, you'll come in on I-8, connecting with Calif. 163 south (Calif. 163 turns into 10th Avenue). From the south, take I-5. The freeways are well marked, pointing the way to downtown streets.

BY TRAIN   Amtrak (☎ **800/USA-RAIL;** www.amtrak.com) trains connect San Diego to Los Angeles and the rest of the country. Trains pull into San Diego's pretty mission-style **Santa Fe Station,** 1850 Kettner Blvd. (at Broadway), within walking distance of many downtown hotels and 1½ blocks from the Embarcadero. Expect to pay about $20 one-way from Los Angeles.

VISITOR INFORMATION

The official **Visitor Information Center** (☎ **619/236-1212**) is on First Avenue at F Street, street level at Horton Plaza. The multilingual staff offers brochures in six languages. They can provide you with the slick, glossy *San Diego Official Visitors Planning Guide,* as well as the **Visitor Value Pack,** a money-saving coupon book. The center is open Monday through Saturday from 8:30am to 5pm year-round, and Sunday from 11am to 5pm June through August; it is closed Thanksgiving, Christmas, and New Year's Day.

Traveler's Aid (☎ **619/231-7361**) has booths at both airport Terminals 1 and 2, and at the San Diego Cruise Terminal, B Street Pier.

Specialized visitor information outlets include the **Balboa Park Visitors Center,** located in the House of Hospitality at 1549 El Prado (☎ **619/239-0512**); **Coronado Visitors Bureau,** 1047 B Ave., Coronado (☎ **800/622-8300** or 619/437-8788; www.coronado.ca.us); and the **Old Town Information Center,** 4002 Wallace St. (☎ **619/220-5422**). The **Mission Bay Visitors Information Center,** 2688 E. Mission Bay Dr., San Diego (☎ **619/276-8200**), is in a handy location on Mission Bay next to I-5 (exit Clairemont Drive/Mission Bay Drive and head toward the water). The **San Diego North County Convention & Visitors Bureau,** 720 N. Broadway, Escondido (☎ **800/848-3336** or 760/745-4741) can provide information on La Jolla and excursion areas in San Diego County, including Del Mar, Carlsbad, Escondido, Julian, and Anza–Borrego State Park.

To find out what's on at the theater and who's playing in the clubs during your visit, pick up a copy of the *Reader,* a free weekly newspaper available all over the city. There's also a Thursday entertainment supplement called "Night & Day" in the *San Diego Union-Tribune.*

The San Diego Area at a Glance

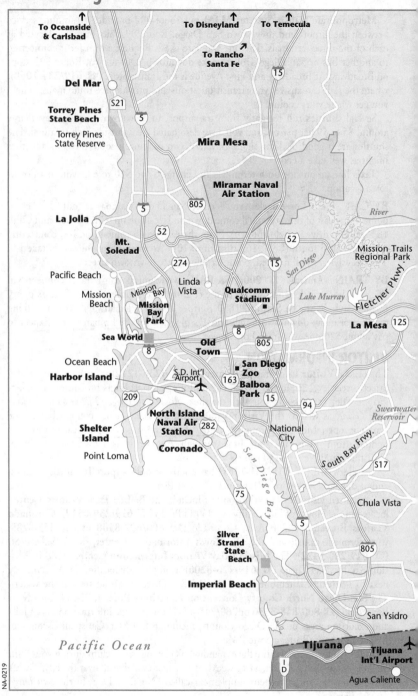

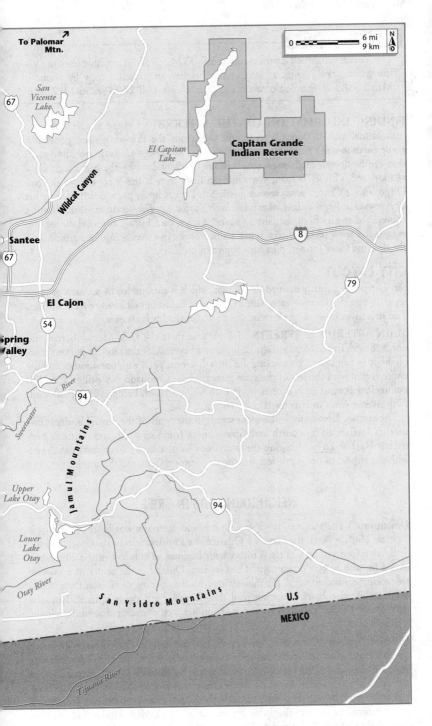

Money-Saving Tip

The Visitor Value Pack is produced annually in March and is available from the Visitor Information Center as long as supplies last, so request a copy by phone in March or April regardless of when you plan to visit. Call ☎ **619/236-1212.**

FINDING INFORMATION ON THE INTERNET   Cyber-travelers interested in a virtual visit to San Diego should check out the following sites: **gocalif.ca.gov/guidebook/SD** has helpful information on San Diego County, including maps that can be downloaded; **www.sandiego.org** is maintained by the San Diego Convention and Visitors Bureau; **www.infosandiego.com** is the Web site for the San Diego Visitor Center; **www.sannet.gov** is San Diego's home page, maintained by the city; **www.sandiego-online.com** is the Web site for *San Diego* magazine, and features abbreviated stories from the current month's issue, plus listings for local dining and events; and **www.sdreader.com** is maintained by the free weekly *Reader,* a great source for club and show listings, plus edgy topical journalism.

CITY LAYOUT

San Diego has a clearly defined downtown, which is surrounded by a dozen or more separate neighborhoods—each with its own personality, but all legally part of the city. The street system is straightforward, so getting around is fairly easy.

MAIN ARTERIES & STREETS   **I-5** runs south to the U.S.–Mexico border and north to Old Town, Mission Bay, La Jolla, and beyond. It's the most important thoroughfare in San Diego, connecting the city's divergent parts with one another and the entire region with the rest of the state. Access to the Coronado Bay Bridge is via I-5. Balboa Park is most easily accessible via 12th Avenue, which becomes Park Boulevard. Fifth Avenue leads to Hillcrest/Uptown area.

   Downtown, **Broadway** is the main street; in the heart of the central business district it's intersected by Fourth and Fifth avenues (running south and north, respectively). **Harbor Drive,** hugging the waterfront (Embarcadero), connects downtown with the airport to the northwest and the Convention Center to the south.

NEIGHBORHOODS IN BRIEF

Downtown   The business, shopping, dining, and entertainment heart of the city, it includes Horton Plaza, the Gaslamp Quarter, the Embarcadero (waterfront), and the distinctive Convention Center. Visitors with business to conduct in the city center would be wise to stay downtown. The Gaslamp Quarter is the center of a massive redevelopment kicked off in the mid-1980s with the opening of Horton Plaza, a colorful multilevel 6-block shopping mall that's a major attraction in itself. Now the once-seedy area is filled with trendy boutiques, chic restaurants, and swingin' nightspots

Hillcrest/Uptown   Despite the cachet of being adjacent to Balboa Park—home to the San Diego Zoo and numerous splendid museums—this once-elite suburban area north of downtown fell into neglect during the 1960s and 1970s. As the turn of the century looms once more, however, Hillcrest's charms have been restored by legions of preservation-minded residents—including a very active and fashionable gay community—and is the local equivalent of L.A.'s West Hollywood or New York's SoHo. Centrally located and packed with the latest in stylish restaurants and avant-garde boutiques, Hillcrest also offers less expensive and more personalized accommodations than anywhere else in the city.

Old Town & Mission Valley   This area encompasses the Old Town State Historic Park, Presidio Park, Heritage Park, and numerous museums harking back to the turn of the century and the city's beginnings. There's shopping and dining here, too, all aimed at tourists. Not far from Old Town lies the vast suburban sprawl of Mission Valley, home to San Diego's gigantic shopping centers. Between them is Hotel Circle, adjacent to I-8, where a string of midprice and budget hotel options offer an alternative to more desirable neighborhoods.

Mission Bay & The Beaches   Mission Bay is a watery playground perfect for water-skiing, sailing, and windsurfing. The adjacent communities of Ocean Beach, Mission Beach, and Pacific Beach are known for their wide stretches of sand fronting the Pacific, active nightlife, and California-casual dining. The boardwalk, which runs from South Mission Beach through North Mission Beach to Pacific Beach, is a popular place for in-line skating, bike riding, and sunset watching.

La Jolla   With an atmosphere that's a cross between Rodeo Drive and a Mediterranean village, this seaside community is home to an inordinate number of wealthy folks who could live anywhere, but choose to live here surrounded by the beach, the University of California at San Diego, outstanding restaurants, pricey and traditional shops, and some of the world's best medical facilities. The name is a compromise between Spanish and American Indian, as is the pronunciation—La-*hoy*-ya—and it has come to mean "the jewel."

Coronado   The "island" of Coronado is actually a peninsula, home to the U.S. Naval Air Station and a town filled with charming cottages, quaint shops along Orange Avenue—the main street—and ritzy hotels and resorts that include the landmark Hotel del Coronado. Coronado has a lovely duned beach; it's also home to more retired admirals than any other community in the country.

2 Getting Around

BY CAR

San Diego has its fair share of traffic, concentrated in the downtown area and also at its height during the morning and evening commuting hours. Aside from that, it's a very car-friendly town and easy to navigate.

Driving downtown, many streets run one-way; the map available from the Visitor Information Center (see "Visitor Information," above) is extremely helpful, since arrows indicate which way each street runs.

You can turn right at a red light after coming to a complete stop, unless an intersection is otherwise posted.

RENTALS   All the large national car-rental firms have counters at the airport, in the major hotels, and at other locations around the city. Several car-rental companies, including **Avis** (☎ **800/331-1212** or 619/231-7171) and **Courtesy Auto Rentals** (☎ **800/252-9756** or 619/497-4800), allow you to take their cars into Mexico. The vehicles may be driven as far as Ensenada, 90 minutes south, providing that you stop before crossing the border and buy Mexican auto insurance. You would also be wise to buy insurance if you drive your own car south of the border.

If the major chains just can't come up with a rental in your price range, consider going to a **discount rental company.** By eliminating some of the service frills of the majors (for example, don't expect a waiting shuttle from baggage claim) and using a fleet of late-model, but not brand-new, cars, these companies are able to shave dollars off your bill. At press time, most were offering deals of $19.95 per day, or $125 per week; some have mileage restrictions, so be sure to get all the details before you take the keys. Remember that most operate only during regular business hours, so if you're arriving late at night, you may have to make other plans until the morning. There are dozens and dozens of these operations around; before using an unfamiliar company, check with the Better Business Bureau—or stick with these agencies we recommend: **Dirt Cheap Car Rental,** 2559 Kettner Blvd. (☎ 619/234-9300); **7 Days Rent-A-Car** (☎ 619/455-1644; fax 619/455-1757), which delivers their cars; **Bargain Auto Rentals,** 3860 Rosecrans St. (☎ 619/299-0009; fax 619/299-9057); **A-1 Rent A Car,** 4250 Pacific Highway (☎ 619/226-4444); or **Rent-A-Wreck,** 19045 Hotel Circle No. (☎ 888/880-7244 or 619/223-3300).

PARKING   Parking meters are plentiful in most San Diego areas: Posted signs indicate operating hours—generally between 8am and 6pm, even on weekends—and most meters accept only quarters. In the popular Gaslamp Quarter, consider parking in Horton Plaza's garage (G Street and Fourth Avenue), which is free to shoppers for the first 3 hours, $1 for every additional hour. It's also free daily after 5pm.

BY PUBLIC TRANSPORTATION
Both city buses and the San Diego Trolley are operated by the **San Diego Metropolitan Transit System (MTS).** The system's Transit Store, 102 Broadway, at First Avenue (☎ **619/234-1060**), is a complete public-transportation information center, supplying travelers with passes, tokens, timetables, maps, and brochures. It's open Monday through Friday from 8:30am to 5:30pm, Saturday and Sunday from noon to 4pm. Request a copy of the useful brochure *Your Open Door to San Diego,* detailing the city's most popular tourist attractions and the buses that take you to them. For bus-route information, you can also call ☎ **619/233-3004** daily between 5:30am and 8:30pm.

BY BUS   Bus stops are marked by rectangular blue signs, every other block or so on local routes. More than 20 bus routes traverse downtown. Most fares range from $1.75 to $2.25, depending on the distance and type of service (local or express). Express buses charge fares that range from $1.75 to $3. Exact change is required ($1 bills are accepted). Most buses run every half hour. Transfers should be obtained from the driver when boarding.

The **Coronado Shuttle,** route no. 904, runs between the Coronado Island Marriott and the Old Ferry Landing along Orange Avenue to the Hotel del Coronado, Glorietta Bay, Loews Coronado Bay Resort, and back again. It costs only 50¢ per person. **Route no. 901** goes to Coronado from downtown San Diego; the fare is $1.75 for adults, 75¢ for seniors and children. Call ☎ 619/233-3004 for information.

BY TROLLEY   The **San Diego Trolley** system runs south to the Mexican border (a 40-minute trip), north to Old Town, and east to the city of Santee. Within the city, trolleys stop at many popular locations, and the fare is only $1; the fare to the Mexican border is $2. Children under 5 ride free; seniors and riders with disabilities pay only 75¢. For recorded trolley information, call ☎ **619/685-4900.** To talk to a live body, you can call ☎ **619/233-3004** daily between 5:30am and 8:30pm.

Trolleys operate on a self-service fare-collection system, where riders purchase tickets from machines in stations before boarding; fare inspectors board trains at random to check tickets. The bright-red trains run every 15 minutes during the day (every half hour at night) and stop for only 30 seconds at each stop. To board, push the lighted green button beside the doors; to exit the car, push the lighted white button.

Money-Saving Transit Passes

The $5 **Day-Tripper pass** allows for 1 day of unlimited rides on the public transit system; you can also get a 4-day pass for $15. Passes are available from the Transit Store.

Trolleys generally operate daily from 5am to about 12:30am, although the Blue Line, which goes to the border, runs around the clock on Saturday.

BY TRAIN   Within the San Diego area, **Amtrak** (☎ 800/USA-RAIL) stops downtown, in Solana Beach, and in Oceanside. A ticket from downtown San Diego to Solana Beach costs $5 one-way; it's $7.50 to Oceanside. You can also get to Disneyland in Anaheim (see chapter 14, "Side Trips from Los Angeles") via the train; call for details.

San Diego's express-rail commuter service, **The Coaster** (☎ 800/COASTER), travels between downtown and Oceanside with stops en route at Old Town, Sorrento Valley, Solana Beach, Encinitas, and Carlsbad.

BY FERRY & WATER TAXI   There's regularly scheduled **ferry service** (☎ 619/234-4111) between San Diego and Coronado. Ferries leave from the Broadway Pier on the hour from 9am to 9pm daily (till 10pm Friday and Saturday), and return from the Old Ferry Landing in Coronado to the Broadway Pier every hour on the 42-minute mark from 9:42am to 9:42pm daily (till 10:42pm Friday and Saturday). Ferries also run from the Fifth Avenue Landing near the Convention Center to the Old Ferry Landing at 1-hour intervals during roughly the same time period. The fare is $2 for each leg of the journey (50¢ extra if you bring your bike). Purchase tickets in advance at the Harbor Excursion kiosk on the Broadway Pier, the Fifth Avenue Landing in San Diego, or at the Old Ferry Landing in Coronado.

Water taxis (☎ 619/235-TAXI) will take you around most of San Diego Bay for $5. If you want to go to the southern part of the bay (to Loews Coronado Bay Resort, for example), you'll be charged a flat fee of $25.

BY TAXI

Cab companies don't have standardized rates, except from the airport into town, which costs about $9 with tip. It's uncommon to find taxis cruising for passengers; phone for a guaranteed pickup. Companies include **Orange Cab** (☎ 619/291-3333), **San Diego Cab** (☎ 619/226-TAXI), and **Yellow Cab** (☎ 619/234-6161). The **Coronado Cab Company** (☎ 619/435-6211) serves Coronado. In La Jolla, use **La Jolla Cab** (☎ 619/453-4222).

BY ORGANIZED TOUR

The **Old Town Trolley** (☎ 619/298-8687) isn't a trolley at all; rather, it's a privately operated open-air tour bus that travels in a continuous loop around the city, stopping at sightseeing highlights. It stops at more than a dozen places around the city, and you can hop on and off as many times as you please during one entire loop (but once you've completed the circuit, you can't go around again). A nonstop tour takes 90 minutes and is accompanied by a fast-moving live commentary on city history and sights. Major stops include Old Town, Presidio Park, Bazaar del Mundo, Balboa Park, the San Diego Zoo, the Embarcadero, Seaport Village, and the Gaslamp Quarter. Tours operate daily from 9am to 5pm; they cost $20 for adults and $8 for children 6 to 12; kids 5 and under ride free.

Gray Line Tours (☎ 619/491-0011) offers a 4-hour escorted bus tour of San Diego that costs $24 for adults (half-price for children). **San Diego Mini Tours** (☎ 619/477-8687) also offers excursions throughout the area.

BY BICYCLE

San Diego is great for bikers; it's relatively flat and many roads have designated bike lanes. If you didn't bring your own wheels, you can rent from **Pennyfarthing's,** 314 G St. in the Gaslamp Quarter (☎ 619/233-7696), or **Hamel's Action Sports Center,** 704 Ventura Place, off Mission Boulevard in Mission Beach (☎ 619/ 488-5050). In Coronado, there's **Bikes & Beyond** at the Old Ferry Landing (☎ 619/435-7180). Bike rentals average about $10 per day. The *San Diego Region Bike Map* is available at visitor centers; to receive a copy in advance, call ☎ 619/ 231-BIKE.

If a bus stop has a bike-route sign attached (not all of them do), you can place your bike on the bus's bike rack for free while you ride. The San Diego Trolley also allows bikes onboard for free. You just need a bike permit, which is available for $4 from the Transit Store, 102 Broadway at First Avenue (☎ 619/234-1060). Bikes can also be brought aboard the San Diego–Coronado ferry.

FAST FACTS: San Diego

American Express   A convenient downtown office is at 258 Broadway (at Third Avenue; ☎ 619/234-4455); it's open Monday through Friday from 9am to 5pm.

Dentists/Doctors   For dental referrals, contact the **San Diego County Dental Society** at ☎ 800/201-0244 or 800/DENTIST. **Hotel Docs** (☎ 800/ 468-3537 or 619/275-2663) is a 24-hour network of physicians, dentists, and chiropractors who claim they'll come to your hotel room within 35 minutes of your call. They accept credit cards, and their services are covered by most insurance policies.

Emergencies   For police, fire, highway patrol, or life-threatening medical emergencies, dial ☎ 911 from any phone. No coins are required.

Hospitals   UCSD Medical Center-Hillcrest, 200 W. Arbor Dr. (☎ 619/ 543-6400), has the best-located emergency room. **Coronado Hospital,** 250 Prospect Place (☎ 619/435-6251), is a good pick in Coronado. In La Jolla, **Thornton Hospital,** 9300 Campus Point Dr. (☎ 619/657-7600), has a good emergency room.

Newspapers/Magazines   The *San Diego Union-Tribune* is published daily, and its informative entertainment section, "Night & Day," is in the Thursday edition. The *Reader,* published weekly (on Thurs), is an alternative source of dining and entertainment information. *San Diego* magazine is filled with entertainment and dining listings for an elite audience. The free *San Diego This Week* has restaurant listings and information about shopping, attractions, nightlife, and the latest goings-on about town.

Police   See "Emergencies," above. For nonemergency matters, contact the downtown precinct, 1401 Broadway (☎ 619/531-2000).

Post Office   The main post office, 2535 Midway Dr., San Diego, CA 92110 (☎ 800/275-8777), is between Barnett Avenue and Rosecrans Street. Counter service is offered from 8am to 5pm Monday through Saturday, but full service is also available at a window in the box area until 1am Monday through Friday. A convenient downtown branch is at 815 E St. (open Mon to Fri from 8:30am to 5pm and Sat from 8:30am to noon).

Safety   As cities go, San Diego is pretty safe. But use particular caution on beaches after dark, and stay on designated walkways and away from secluded areas in Balboa Park—night or day. In the Gaslamp Quarter, stay west of Fifth Avenue. Take particular care to lock your car and park in well-lit areas; San Diego's proximity to the border contributes to its high rate of auto theft.

Smoking   Smoking is prohibited in nearly all indoor public places, including theaters, hotel lobbies, and enclosed shopping malls. In January 1998, California enacted legislation prohibiting smoking in all restaurants and bars, excepting those with outdoor seating.

Taxes   A 7.75% sales tax is added on at the register for all goods and services purchased in San Diego. The city hotel tax is 10.5%.

Time   San Diego is on Pacific time; for the correct time, call ☎ **619/853-1212.**

Weather   For local weather and surf reports call ☎ **619/289-1212.**

3 Accommodations You Can Afford

San Diego offers the cost-conscious traveler a good selection of lodgings. Remember to factor in the city's 10.5% hotel tax and to keep in mind that rates are often higher in summer (especially true of beach hotels). Also keep in mind that hotel rates are usually negotiable. When you call to make a reservation, ask about off-season, AAA, AARP, senior, or military discounts; also ask about the midweek rate and the long-stay rate—whatever is applicable. If you can't wheedle a better price, see if any packages are available. Some motels, for instance, offer a deal that includes passes to the zoo. The Dine-A-Mate coupon book (see ordering instructions in "Great Deals on Dining," below) also offers hotel discounts, as does the Visitor Value Pack (mentioned in "Visitor Information," above).

You might want to compare the price you're quoted with those available through **San Diego Hotel Reservations** (☎ **800/SAVE-CASH** or 619/627-9300; www.save-cash.com). For information on 30 bed-and-breakfasts in the San Diego area, send $3.95 for a 20-page directory to **B&B Resources,** P.O. Box 3292, San Diego, CA 92163 (☎ **800/619-ROOM** or 619/297-3130). You can also get information from the **Bed and Breakfast Guild** of San Diego (☎ **619/523-1300**).

If you like B&Bs, you might want to contact **Eye Openers Bed and Breakfast Reservations,** P.O. Box 694, Altadena, CA 91003-0694 (☎ **213/684-4428** or 818/797-2055; fax 818/798-3640; e-mail: eobb@loop.com). They can find you a bed (and breakfast) in a cozy inn or private home in the San Diego area from $40 a night for two.

If you really want to get away from it all, try one of the properties described in *Guide to Retreat Center Guest Houses* by John and Mary Jensen (CTS Publications, P.O. Box 8355, Newport Beach, CA 92660; $15.95). This 160-page paperback lists restful lodgings in the United States and worldwide that cost $35 to $45 a day including three meals. The retreat centers are abbeys, priories, missions, and sanctuaries that furnish a quiet setting and serene surroundings. The San Diego–area offerings include rooms at the beautiful Mission San Luis Rey near Oceanside.

San Diego Area Accommodations

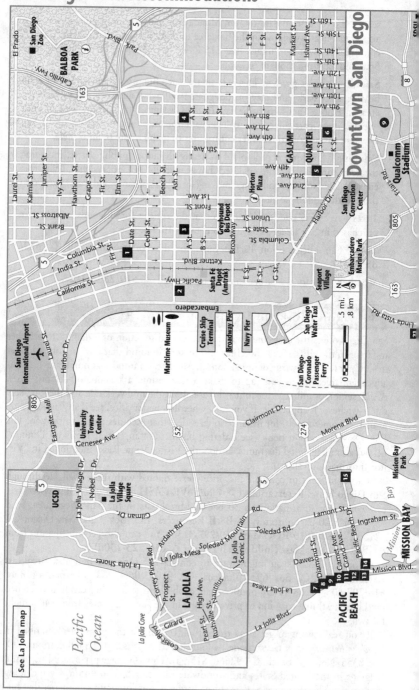

Downtown San Diego

San Diego Zoo
El Prado
BALBOA PARK
Park Blvd.
Cabrillo Fwy.
163

Laurel St.
Kalmia St.
Juniper St.
Ivy St.
Hawthorn St.
Grape St.
Fir St.
Elm St.

Brant St.
Albatross St.

Date St.
Cedar St.

Columbia St.
India St.
California St.

16th St.
13th St.
14th St.
Market St.
Island Ave.
E St.
F St.
G St.
12th Ave.
11th Ave.
10th Ave.
9th Ave.
8th Ave.
7th Ave.
6th Ave.
5th Ave.
4th Ave.

A St.
B St.
C St.
Beech St.
Ash St.
1st Ave.
Front St.

GASLAMP QUARTER
K St.
3rd Ave.
2nd Ave.
1st Ave.

Horton Plaza
Greyhound Bus Depot
Broadway
Columbia St.
State St.
Union St.

San Diego Convention Center
Harbor Dr.

Qualcomm Stadium
Friars Rd.
8
805
163
Linda Vista Rd.
274

Kettner Blvd.
Pacific Hwy.
Santa Fe Depot (Amtrak)

Embarcadero Marina Park

San Diego International Airport
Harbor Dr.
Laurel St.

Embarcadero

Maritime Museum
Cruise Ship Terminal
Broadway Pier
Navy Pier
Seaport Village
San Diego Water Taxi
San Diego–Coronado Passenger Ferry

N
0   .5 mi.
0   .8 km

See La Jolla map

Pacific Ocean

La Jolla Cove
Coast Blvd.
Girard
Prospect
Pearl St.
High Ave.
Rushville St.
Nautilus
LA JOLLA
Torrey Pines Rd.
La Jolla Shores
Ardath Rd.
La Jolla Mesa
La Jolla Scenic Dr.
La Jolla Mountain
Soledad Rd.
La Jolla Blvd.

UCSD
La Jolla Village Dr.
Nobel Dr.
Gilman Dr.
La Jolla Village Square
Eastgate Mall
Genesee Ave.
University Towne Center
805
5
52
Clairmont Dr.
Morena Blvd.

Mission Bay Park
Mission Bay
MISSION BAY
Lamont St.
Ingraham St.
Pacific Beach Dr.
Garnet Ave.
Grand Ave.
Mission Blvd.
Dawes St.
Diamond St.
PACIFIC BEACH

588

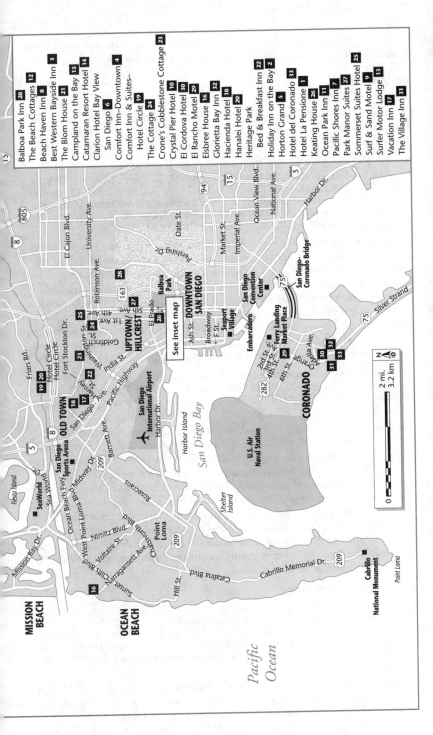

Since we can't give you complete accommodations coverage here, you might want to check out *Frommer's San Diego,* which offers many more options.

DOWNTOWN
SUPER-CHEAP SLEEPS

Inexpensive motels line Pacific Highway between the airport and downtown. The **Days Inn Suites** ($49 to $69), 1919 Pacific Hwy. at Grape Street (☎ **800/325-2525** or 619/232-1077), is within walking distance of the Embarcadero, the Maritime Museum, and the Harbor Excursion.

Comfort Inn-Downtown. 719 Ash St. (at Seventh Ave.), San Diego, CA 92101. ☎ **800/ 228-5150** or 619/232-2525. Fax 619/687-3024. 67 units. A/C TV TEL. $79–$84 double. Extra person $5. Children 17 and under stay free in parents' room. AARP and AAA discounts, weekly rates available. Rates include continental breakfast. AE, DISC, MC, V. Free parking. Free shuttle to train, bus, and airport. Bus: 1, 3, 25, 5, or 105.

Located in the northern corner of downtown, this dollar-wise choice is popular with business travelers *without* expense accounts, and vacationers who just need clean, reliable, and safe accommodations. The hotel is surprisingly quiet, partially because the landmark El Cortez Hotel across the street—once a social mecca—is closed while developers gather funds to transform it into upscale condos and shops. Oddly enough, its distinctive profile is pleasant to gaze upon even boarded up. The Comfort Inn is smartly designed so rooms open onto exterior walkways surrounding the drive-in entry courtyard, lending an insular feel in this less-than-scenic corner of town. There are few frills here, but coffee is always brewing in the lobby and there's also a Jacuzzi.

✪ **Hotel La Pensione.** 606 W. Date St. (at India St.), San Diego, CA 92101. ☎ **800/ 232-4683** or 619/236-8000. Fax 619/236-8088. 80 units. TV TEL. $50–$70 double. Packages available. AE, CB, DC, DISC, MC, V. Limited free underground parking. Bus: 2. Trolley: Little Italy.

This place has a lot going for it: modern amenities, cleanliness, remarkable value, a quiet location within walking distance of the central business district, a friendly staff, and parking, which is a premium for small hotels in San Diego. The three-story La Pensione is built around a courtyard and feels like a small European hotel. The decor throughout is modern and streamlined—plenty of sleek black and chrome surfaces, crisp white walls, and minimal furniture. Guest rooms, while not overly large, make the most of their space and leave you with area to move around in. Each room offers a tub/shower combination, ceiling fan, microwave, and small refrigerator; try to get a bay or city view. La Pensione is located in San Diego's Little Italy neighborhood and within walking distance of eateries (mostly Italian) and nightspots; there are even two restaurants attached to the hotel itself.

FOR A FEW BUCKS MORE

Best Western Bayside Inn. 555 W. Ash St. (at Columbia St.), San Diego, CA 92101. ☎ **800/341-1818** or 619/233-7500. Fax 619/239-8060. 122 units. A/C TV TEL. $90–$110 double. Harbor view $10 extra. Children under 12 stay free in parents' room. All rates include continental breakfast. Weekend rates (except in summer) and packages available. AE, CB, DC, DISC, JCB, MC, V. Free covered parking. Free transportation from airport. Trolley: C St. and Kettner.

Though noisy downtown is just outside, this high-rise representative of reliable Best Western offers quiet lodgings with an accommodating staff and stunning city and harbor views. A mecca for business travelers, it's also close to touristy downtown sites: It's an easy walk to the Embarcadero (it should be called Bayview rather than Bayside), a bit farther to Horton Plaza, 4 blocks to the trolley stop, and 5 blocks to the train station. The comfortable rooms, all remodeled in 1993, have balconies overlooking the bay or downtown.

The hotel's restaurant, the Bayside Bar and Grill, serves breakfast, lunch, and dinner; the bar has a 50-inch TV. Good restaurants and bars are nearby, and meals are available from room service. In-room movies are provided, and you can relax by the outdoor pool or in the Jacuzzi.

MODERATELY PRICED OPTIONS

Clarion Hotel Bay View San Diego. 660 K St. (at Sixth), San Diego, CA 92101. ☎ **800/ 766-0234** or 619/696-0234. Fax 619/231-8199. 312 units. A/C TV TEL. $109–$139 double; $149–$169 suite. Children under 18 stay free in parents' room. Additional person $10. AARP, AAA, and off-season discounts available. AE, DC, DISC, MC, V. Parking $8 per day. Bus: 1. Trolley: Gaslamp/Convention Center.

This relatively new entry on the San Diego hotel scene provides an economical alternative for those attending meetings at the Convention Center—it's almost as close as the Marriott and the Hyatt, but considerably less expensive. Its location near the Gaslamp Quarter makes it a good choice for those who plan to enjoy the nightlife, but until the Quarter's gentrification spreads a couple blocks farther south, the Clarion will remain in a no-man's-land of industrial and commercial neighbors. All quarters are spacious, bright, and modern, and more than half offer views of San Diego Bay and the Coronado Bridge. All rooms have sliding glass doors that provide ample fresh air, coffeemakers, and many have minibars. The carpeted rooftop sundeck offers a great view as well as a Jacuzzi, sauna, workout room, and video arcade. There's a restaurant, bar, and coin-op laundry.

Horton Grand. 311 Island Ave. (at Fourth Ave.), San Diego, CA 92101. ☎ **800/542-1886** or 619/544-1886. Fax 619/544-0058. 132 units. TV TEL. $119–$159 double; $169–$199 minisuite. Weekend and special packages available. Children under 12 stay free in parents' room. AE, DC, DISC, MC, V. Valet parking $8 overnight with unlimited in/out privileges. Bus: 1. Trolley: Convention Center. Pets are accepted with a $100 deposit.

A cross between an elegant hotel and a charming B&B, the Horton Grand combines two hotels dating from 1886. Both were saved from demolition, moved to this spot, and connected by an airy atrium lobby filled with white wicker. The facade, with its graceful bay windows, is original.

Each room is unique and contains antiques and a gas fireplace (on a timer so you can fall asleep in front of it); even the bathrooms, complete with WC and pedestal sink, are genteel. Rooms overlook either the city or the fig-tree-filled courtyard. Suites have a microwave, a minibar, two TVs and telephones, a sofa bed, and computer modem hookup. This is an old hotel, and sounds carry more than they might in a modern one, so if you're a light sleeper, request a room with no neighbors.

Ida Bailey's restaurant, named for the well-loved madam whose establishment used to stand on this spot, is located on the ground floor. Afternoon tea is served in the Palace Bar, and live music is featured Thursday through Saturday evenings and Sunday afternoons.

WORTH A SPLURGE

Holiday Inn on the Bay. 1355 N. Harbor Dr. (at Ash St.), San Diego, CA 92101-3385. ☎ **800/HOLIDAY** or 619/232-3861. Fax 619/232-4924. 580 units. A/C TV TEL. $139–$199 double; from $400 suite. Children under 18 stay free in parents' room. AARP and AAA discounts, packages available. AE, DC, MC, V. Parking $10. Bus: 2, 9, 29, 34, 34A, or 35. Pets accepted at no extra charge.

Renovated in 1992, this Holiday Inn high-rise is basic but well maintained, and located directly on the harbor near the Maritime Museum. It's only 1½ miles from the airport (you can watch the planes landing and taking off) and 2 blocks from the train station and trolley. The rooms are decorated in a California contemporary style; some offer harbor views. In general, the hotel's bathrooms are small, but they have separate sinks with a lot of counter space. There are three restaurants on the premises (including SD's branch of Ruth's Chris steak house), a terrific outdoor pool, and self-service laundry.

Note: Though the Holiday Inn's *official* rack rates place it in our "Worth a Splurge" price category, we know there's *always* a deal to be had. Ask about package plans and other discount rates and you'll be pleasantly surprised.

HILLCREST/UPTOWN
SUPER-CHEAP SLEEPS

✪ **The Cottage.** 3829 Albatross St. (off Robinson), San Diego, CA 92103. ☎ **619/ 299-1564.** Fax 619/299-6213. 2 units. TV TEL. $60–$75 double; $85–$95 cottage. Extra person in cottage $10. Rates include continental breakfast. AE, DISC, MC, V. Free street parking. Bus: 1, 3, 11, or 25.

Built in 1913, the two-room Cottage exists in a secret garden, a private hideaway tucked behind a homestead-style house, at the end of a residential cul-de-sac. There's an herb garden out front, birdbaths, and a flower-lined walkway to the back. Owner Carol Emerick used to run an antique shop, and her house has inherited its treasures. The cottage has a living room with a working wood-burning stove and a queen-size sofa bed, and a charming kitchen with coffeemaker. A guest bedroom in the main house features a king-size bed and a hidden TV. Both accommodations are filled with fresh flowers and antiques put to clever uses, and each features a private entrance and bathroom. Carol serves a scrumptious breakfast, complete with the morning newspaper. Guests are welcome to use the dining room and parlor in the main house, where they sometimes light a fire and rev up the 19th-century player piano. In this haven, expect to wake up to the gentle chirping of birds. The Cottage is very near the cafes of Mission Hills and Hillcrest, and a short drive from Balboa Park.

✪ **Keating House.** 2331 Second Ave. (between Juniper and Kalmia sts.), San Diego, CA 92101. ☎ **800/995-8644** or 619/239-8585. Fax 619/239-5774. www. caliburnus.com/keating. E-mail: ltvkeat@adnc.com. 8 units, 3 with bathroom. $65–$95 double. Rates include lavish breakfast. AE, DISC, MC, V. Free street parking. From the airport, take Harbor Dr. toward downtown; turn left on Laurel St. then right on Second Ave. Bus: 1 or 3.

Gracious owner Larry Vlassoff considers every detail for his guests' comfort. From the meticulous restoration of this grand Bankers Hill mansion—which straddles downtown and stylish Hillcrest and is outfitted with splendid turn-of-the-century furnishings—to the always-inventive breakfast treats, the savvy restaurant recommendations, and a lovingly tended exotic garden, Larry's touch is everywhere. The downstairs entry, parlor, and dining room all have cozy fireplaces, and two of the rooms are secluded in the carriage house (each with private bathroom). In contrast to many B&B's located in Victorian-era homes, this one eschews dollhouse frills for a classy and sophisticated approach.

Park Manor Suites. 525 Spruce St. (between Fifth and Sixth aves.), San Diego, CA 92103. ☎ **800/874-2649** or 619/291-0999. Fax 619/291-8844. 80 units. TV TEL. $69–$89 studio; $89–$119 one-bedroom suite; $109–$169 two-bedroom suite. Children under 12 stay free in parents' room. Extra person $15. Weekly rates available. Rates include continental breakfast. AE, DC, MC, V. Free parking. Bus: 1 or 3.

Popular with actors appearing at the Old Globe Theatre in neighboring Balboa Park, this eight-story Italianate masterpiece was built as a full-service luxury hotel in 1926 on a prime corner overlooking the park. Guest rooms are spacious and comfortable, featuring full kitchens, dining rooms, living rooms, and bedrooms with a separate dressing area. A few have glassed-in terraces; request one when you book. The overall feeling here is that of a prewar East Coast apartment building, complete with steam heating and lavish moldings. Park Manor Suites does have its weaknesses: The bathrooms have mostly original fixtures and could use some renovation; and the rooftop banquet room, where a simple continental breakfast buffet is served each morning, suffers from a bad 1980s re-do with too many mirrors. But prices are quite reasonable for the trendy Hillcrest neighborhood it sits in the heart of; there's a restaurant on the ground floor and laundry service is available.

FOR A FEW BUCKS MORE

Balboa Park Inn. 3402 Park Blvd. (at Upas St.), San Diego, CA 92103. ☎ **800/938-8181** or 619/298-0823. Fax 619/294-8070. www.balboaparkinn.com. 26 units. TV TEL. $80–$95 double; $95–$135 suite; $125–$200 specialty suite. Children under 11 stay free in parents' room. Extra person $8. Rates include continental breakfast. AE, CB, DC, DISC, MC, V. Ample street parking. Bus: 7.

Insiders looking for unusual and well-located accommodations head straight for this pink-hued cluster of four Spanish-colonial-style former apartment buildings converted into a small inn at the northern edge of Balboa Park. Close to the trendy Hillcrest area, the hotel caters to a straight clientele as well as gay travelers drawn to Hillcrest's stylish restaurants and clubs. All the rooms and suites are decorated tastefully but distinctively; the "specialty" suites, however, are over-the-top. There's the "Tara Suite," exhibiting shades of *Gone With the Wind;* the "Nouveau Ritz," which employs every art-deco cliché, including mirrors and Hollywood lighting; and the "Greystoke" suite, a jumbled-up mixture of jungle, safari, and tropical themes climaxing with a completely mirrored bathroom with whirlpool tub. All rooms come with refrigerators, coffeemakers, newspapers Monday through Saturday, and breakfast to start each day. There's ample street parking in this mostly residential neighborhood, and you can walk to Balboa Park attractions.

Crone's Cobblestone Cottage Bed & Breakfast. 1302 Washington Place (2½ blocks west of Washington St. at Ingalls St.), San Diego, CA 92103. ☎ **619/295-4765.** 2 units. $75 double (2-night minimum). Rates include continental breakfast. No credit cards; checks accepted. Free street parking. From I-5, take Washington St. exit east uphill. Make a U-turn at Goldfinch, keeping right at Y-intersection onto Washington Place.

After just 1 night at this magnificently restored Craftsman bungalow, you'll feel like an honored house guest rather than a paying customer. Artist Joan Crone lives in the architectural award-winning addition to her 1913 designated Historic Landmark, so guests have the run of the entire house, including a book-filled wood-paneled den and antique-filled living room. Both bedrooms are cozy and outfitted with antique beds, goose-down pillows and comforters, and eclectic bedside reading. They share a full bathroom; the Eaton Room has a private half-bathroom as well. Book-maker and illustrator Crone lends a calm and literary aesthetic to the surroundings, aided by Sam, the cat with compelling eyes, who peers in from his side of the house. Because the cottage is the antithesis of a hotel, it attracts long-term guests, or those seeking solitude for writing or reflection. The quiet and historic Mission Hills neighborhood, just blocks from Hillcrest and Old Town, is one of San Diego's best-kept secrets.

WORTH A SPLURGE

✪ **Sommerset Suites Hotel.** 606 Washington St. (at Fifth Ave.), San Diego, CA 92103. ☎ **800/962-9665** or 619/692-5200. Fax 619/692-5299. 80 units. A/C TV TEL. $130–$220 double. Discounts available. Children under 12 stay free in parents' room. Rates include large continental breakfast. AE, CB, DC, DISC, MC, V. Free covered parking. Courtesy shuttle to airport, Sea World, the zoo, and other attractions within a 5-mile radius. Take Washington St. exit off I-5. Bus: 16 or 25.

This all-suite hotel on busy Washington Street has the ambiance of a well-kept apartment complex and offers guests a similar independence, with fully equipped kitchens in all rooms (even dishwashers in the executive suites), barbecue facilities poolside, and coin-operated laundry. The staff is friendly and helpful, and in the late afternoon they serve complimentary snacks, soda, beer, and wine in the cozy guest lounge. Accommodations are spacious, attractively furnished, and have in-room safes, large closets, hair dryers, irons and boards, and balconies. Be prepared for noise from the busy thoroughfare below, though. Other amenities include a small outdoor pool, Jacuzzi, rooftop sundeck, concierge, laundry/dry cleaning service, video rentals, and two-line phones and voice mail. Rollaway beds and cribs are available. Several blocks of Hillcrest's chic eateries and shops (plus a movie multiplex) are within easy walking distance.

OLD TOWN & MISSION VALLEY
SUPER-CHEAP SLEEPS

Room rates at properties on Hotel Circle are significantly cheaper than many other parts of the city. There you'll find a cluster of inexpensive chain hotels and motels, including **Best Western Seven Seas** (☎ 800/421-6662 or 619/291-1300), **Mission Valley Center Travelodge** (☎ 800/255-3050 or 619/297-2271), **Ramada Inn** (☎ 800/532-4241 or 619/291-6500), and **Vagabond Inn** (☎ 800/522-1555 or 619/297-1691).

FOR A FEW BUCKS MORE

Comfort Inn & Suites. 2485 Hotel Circle Place, San Diego, CA 92108. ☎ **800/647-1903** or 619/291-7700. Fax 619/297-6179. 200 units. A/C TV TEL. High season $89–$129 double; lower rates off-season. Extra person $10. Children under 18 stay free in parents' room. Rates include continental breakfast. AE, CB, DC, DISC, MC, V. Free parking. Bus: 6. Trolley: Fashion Valley.

This well-priced modern four-story motel at the western (closest to Old Town) end of Hotel Circle underwent a complete refurbishment in 1996 that enlarged rooms by doing away with balconies (many opened onto the noisy freeway side anyway). Bathrooms are small but well equipped, with hair dryers (and coffeemakers) in every room. Rooms and suites are sparingly but adequately furnished with standard hotel-issue. Suites are really the way to go here; all have sleeper sofas in the living room, two TVs, microwave, refrigerator, and separate vanity area. The heated outdoor pool and Jacuzzi adjoin the parking lot; there's a car-rental desk, game room, and washer/dryer. Stay away from the freeway side, and ask instead for a room looking toward the newly refurbished 18-hole public golf course across the street. The hotel doesn't have a restaurant, but offers dinner room service from the steak house next door.

Vacation Inn. 3900 Old Town Ave., San Diego, CA 92110. ☎ **800/451-9846** or 619/299-7400. Fax 619/299-1619. 124 units. A/C TV TEL. June–Aug $110–$115 double; $130–$175 suite. Sept–May $84–$99 double; $114–$165 suite. Extra person $10. Children 17 and under stay free in parents' room. Rates include continental breakfast and afternoon refreshments. AE, CB, DC, DISC, ER, MC, V. Free parking. Bus: 4 or 5/105.

Located just a couple of easy walking blocks from the heart of Old Town, the Vacation Inn has a Spanish-colonial exterior that conforms with the neighborhood's theme. Inside you'll find better-than-they-have-to-be contemporary furnishings and surprising small touches that have made this hotel an affordable option favored by business travelers and families alike. There's nothing scenic on the adjacent streets, so the hotel is smartly oriented toward the inside, around a pleasant courtyard; request a room whose patio or balcony opens directly onto the courtyard. Rooms are thoughtfully and practically appointed, with a coffeemaker, microwave, refrigerator, and a writing table. The lobby features a large fireplace, several sitting areas, and a TV. Dry cleaning and laundry services are offered; the hotel also has an outdoor pool and Jacuzzi. The hotel entrance, on Jefferson Street, is hard to find but definitely worth the search.

MODERATELY PRICED OPTIONS

Hacienda Hotel. 4041 Harney St. (just east of San Diego Ave.), San Diego, CA 92110. ☎ **800/888-1991** or 619/298-4707. Fax 619/298-4771. 170 units. A/C TV TEL. $120–$150 double. Children under 16 stay free in parents' room. AE, CB, DC, DISC, ER, MC, V. Free underground parking. Free shuttle to airport/train. From I-5 take Old Town Ave. exit; turn left onto San Diego Ave. and right onto Harney St.

Perched above Old Town, this Best Western all-suite hotel is spread over several levels overlooking Old Town. Walkways thread through courtyards with bubbling fountains, palm trees, lampposts, and bougainvillea-trimmed balconies, but if you have trouble climbing stairs and hills, you'd be wise to stay elsewhere. Aside from that, the place is tops in its price range; every suite is outfitted with rustic Mexican wood furniture and spacious 20-foot ceilings, and standard equipment includes refrigerators, microwaves, coffeemakers, and VCRs.

The unremarkable Acapulco restaurant (yes, it's Mexican) serves breakfast, lunch, and dinner daily from its perch atop the hotel. Guests also have signing privileges next door at the Brigantine Restaurant and down the street at Cafe Pacifica (see "Great Deals on Dining," below). Other amenities include room service, movie rentals with free popcorn, heated outdoor pool and whirlpool, and fitness center.

Heritage Park Bed & Breakfast Inn. 2470 Heritage Park Row, San Diego, CA 92110. ☎ **800/995-2470** or 619/299-6832. Fax 619/299-9465. www.heritageparkinn.com. E-mail: innkeeper@heritageparkinn.com. 13 units, all with bathroom. $90–$225 double. Extra person $20. Rates include full breakfast and afternoon tea. AE, MC, V. Free parking. Take I-5 to Old Town Ave., turn left onto San Diego Ave., then turn right onto Harney St. to Heritage Park. Bus: 4 or 5/105.

This exquisite 1889 Queen Anne mansion is set in a "Victorian park"—an artfully arranged cobblestone cul-de-sac lined with historic buildings saved from the wrecking ball and assembled here, near Old Town, as a tourist attraction. Once inside, however, that unsettling "fishbowl" feeling subsides as you give yourself in to the pomp and pampering of afternoon tea, candlelight breakfast, and a number of romantic extras (champagne and chocolates, private in-room dinner) available for special celebrations. Like the gracious parlors and porches, each of the rooms are outfitted with meticulous period antiques and luxurious fabrics; the staff provides turndown service. Although the fireplaces are all ornamental, some rooms have whirlpool baths. In the evenings, vintage films are shown in the Victorian parlor. If you long to step back in time, this charming and stately B&B fits the bill perfectly.

WORTH A SPLURGE

Hanalei Hotel. 2270 Hotel Circle N., San Diego, CA 92108. ☎ **800/882-0858** or 619/297-1101. Fax 619/297-6049. www.hanaleihotel.com. E-mail: sales@hanaleihotel.com. 416 units. A/C MINIBAR TV TEL. $130–$150 double; $275–$375 suite. Extra person $10. Midweek and off-season discounts and packages available. AARP and AAA member discounts. AE, CB, DC, DISC, MC, V. Parking $6. Bus: 6. Trolley: Fashion Valley. Pets accepted with $50 cleaning fee.

My favorite hotel on Hotel Circle just emerged from a massive renovation and upgrade with its Polynesian tropics theme splendidly intact—and sporting a level of comfort-conscious sophistication that sets it apart from the rest of the pack. Rooms are split between two high-rise towers, set far away from the freeway and cleverly positioned so that all balconies open either onto the tropically landscaped pool courtyard or the luxurious links of a formerly private golf club meandering along the Mission Valley floor. The heated outdoor pool is large enough for any luau, as is the oversized whirlpool beside it. There's an unmistakable 1960s vibe to the hotel and its Hawaiian ambiance—the restaurant and bar have an over-the-top kitsch featuring dramatically lit rock waterfalls, outrigger canoes, etc.—but guest rooms sport contemporary furnishings and pure 1990s features like coffeemakers, hair dryers, irons and boards, and in-room movies. Some have microwaves and refrigerators; other services include free shuttle to Old Town and other attractions, laundry, and meeting facilities. *Note:* Although their *official* rack rates push the Hanalei into our "Worth a Splurge" price category, you'll find packages and other discounts make this a very affordable option.

MISSION BAY & THE BEACHES
SUPER-CHEAP SLEEPS

Beach Haven Inn. 4740 Mission Blvd. (at Missouri St.), San Diego (Pacific Beach), CA 92109. ☎ **800/831-6323** or 619/272-3812. Fax 619/272-3532. 23 units. A/C TV TEL. $55–$90 double winter. Extra person $5. Higher rates June 15–Sept 15. Children under 12 stay free in parents' room. Rates include continental breakfast. AE, DC, DISC, MC, V. Free parking. Bus: 30 or 34. Small pets allowed with $50 refundable deposit.

A great spot for beach lovers, this motel is about half a block from the sand. Rooms face an inner courtyard, where there is a nice pool and Jacuzzi. On the street side it looks kind of marginal, but once on the property I found all quarters well maintained and sporting modern furnishings—nearly all units have eat-in kitchens. The friendly staff provides free coffee in the lobby and rents VCRs and movies.

Surf & Sand Motel. 4666 Mission Blvd. (at Diamond St.), San Diego, CA 92109. ☎ **619/483-7420.** Fax 619/237-9940. 26 units. TV TEL. High season (Memorial Day to Labor Day) $89–$109 double room; $750–$1,050 (weekly) cottages. Off-season $69–$79 double. Midweek and extended stay discounts. AE, DISC, MC, V. Free parking. Take I-5 to Grand/Garnet exit; go west on Garnet Ave. to Mission Blvd. and turn right. Bus: 34 or 34A.

While I have to admit it's a clean, cheap option just a block from the sands of Pacific Beach, this 1940s-issue motor court feels suspiciously like the site of a film-noir illicit tryst, only with local surfers and beach bums raising a ruckus outside the door. But you can't beat the location, steps from several casual and always-packed eateries, particularly if you just want a room to flop in for several days spent on the beach. *A tip:* Rooms in the back aren't as susceptible to the noise from Mission Boulevard as the ones in the front. Providing only a minimal sense of privacy, rooms have somewhat worn furniture and linens and the small bathrooms are supplied with only the basics, but every room has a minifridge; some even have kitchenettes and air-conditioning (a boon in summer). There's a small, heated pool behind the parking courtyard.

Surfer Motor Lodge. 711 Pacific Beach Dr. (at Mission Blvd.), San Diego, CA 92109. ☎ **800/787-3373** or 619/483-7070. Fax 619/274-1670. 52 units. TV TEL. Summer (June 15–Sept 15) $83–$122; winter $70–$93. Extra person $5. Weekly rates available off-season. AE, DC, MC, V. Free parking. Take I-5 to Grand/Garnet, then Grand Ave. to Mission Blvd.; turn left, then right onto Pacific Beach Dr. Bus: 34 or 34A.

Frankly, this property is looking pretty tired, but it's still often booked solid during the summer because it offers moderately priced digs right on the boardwalk at the beach, as well as a heated pool. Most rooms in this four-story property have balconies and views and are cooled by ocean breezes, and many have kitchenettes. One hopes the management will consider sprucing the place up a bit so it doesn't feel so haggard. On the premises is a coin-operated laundry. A popular restaurant serving three meals a day is adjacent.

FOR A FEW BUCKS MORE

Elsbree House. 5054 Narragansett Ave., San Diego, CA 92107. ☎ **619/226-4133.** Fax 619/223-4133. www.oceanbeach-online.com/elsbree/b&b. E-mail: Ktelsbree@juno.com. 7 units. $95 double; $1,250 (weekly) three-bedroom condo. Room rate includes continental breakfast. MC, V. Free street parking. Driving directions from the airport: take Harbor Dr. west to Nimitz Blvd. to Lowell St., which becomes Narragansett Ave. Buses 35 and 23 stop 1½ blocks away on Narragansett at Cable St.

Katie and Phil Elsbree have turned this recently built, Cape Cod–style four-condo building—located a half block from the beach—into an immaculate and exceedingly comfortable B&B. One of the condos is intact and rents only by the week; another is occupied by the Elsbrees, and the remaining two offer six guest bedrooms with ensuite private bathrooms, plus patio or balcony. A cozy living room with fireplace and TV, a breakfast room, and a kitchen are shared by all guests. Although other buildings on this tightly packed street block any ocean view, sounds of the surf and fresh sea breezes waft in open windows, and there's a beautifully landscaped garden—complete with trickling fountain—running the length of the house. This seaside Ocean Beach neighborhood is eclectic, occupied by ocean-loving couples, dedicated surf bums, and a sometimes disturbing contingent of punk skater kids who congregate near the pier. Its strengths are proximity to the beach, a limited but pleasing selection of places to eat, and some of the best antiquing in the city (along Newport Avenue). No smoking inside.

MODERATELY PRICED OPTIONS

The Beach Cottages. 4255 Ocean Blvd. (a block south of Grand Ave.), San Diego, CA 92109-3995. ☎ **619/483-7440.** Fax 619/273-9365. 61 units, 17 cottages. TV TEL. Summer (July 1–Labor Day) $95–$115 double; $125 studio for up to 4; $145–$190 apt for up to 6; $155–$180 cottage for up to 6; $220–$240 two-bedroom suite for up to 6. Lower rates rest of year. Weekly rates available except in summer. AE, CB, DC, DISC, MC, V. Free parking. Bus: 34 or 34A.

Even though this family-owned establishment has a variety of guest quarters—most geared toward the long-term visitor—it's the cute little detached cottages steps from the sand (look both ways for speeding cyclists before crossing the boardwalk) that give the place its appeal. The other room types are perfectly adequate, especially for budget-minded families who want to log major hours on the beach; stay away, however, from the plain motel rooms—they're just dingy. All rooms except the motel rooms have fully equipped kitchens. The Beach Cottages are within walking distance of shops and restaurants and have barbecue grills, shuffleboard courts, table tennis, and a laundry. The cottages themselves aren't pristine, but have a rustic charm popular with young honeymooners and those nostalgic for the golden age of laid-back California beach culture. With one or two bedrooms, they sleep up to six; each has a patio with tables and chairs.

✪ **Crystal Pier Hotel.** 4500 Ocean Blvd. (at Garnet), San Diego, CA 92109. ☎ **800/ 748-5894** or 619/483-6983. 26 cottages. TV. Cottages for up to 4 people $145–$250 summer; $95–$200 mid-Sept to mid-June. 3-day minimum in summer. Weekly and monthly rates available. DISC, MC, V. Free parking. Take I-5 to Grand/Garnet exit; follow Garnet to the pier. Bus: 34 or 34A.

This historic property, which dates from 1927, offers a unique opportunity to sleep over the water. Built on a pier over the Pacific Ocean, the hotel offers self-contained cottages with breathtaking beach views. While most cottages date from 1936, all have been gutted and completely renovated. Each comes with a private patio, living room, bedroom, and kitchen, and has welcoming blue shutters and window boxes. The around-the-clock sound of waves is soothing, but the boardwalk action is only a few steps (and worlds) away. If you stay here, remember that the quietest quarters are the farthest out on the pier. Guests drive right out and park beside their cottage, a real boon on crowded weekends. There are vending machines and movie rentals. Boogie boards, fishing poles, beach chairs, and umbrellas are also available. The office is open daily from 8am to 8pm. These unique accommodations book up fast. Besides being a restful place to lay your head, the pier is a great place to watch the surfers at sunset.

✪ **Ocean Park Inn.** 710 Grand Ave., San Diego, CA 92109. ☎ **800/231-7735** or 619/483-5858. Fax 619/274-0823. go-explore.com/opinn. 77 units. A/C TV TEL. Summer $104–$154 double; off-season $89–$130 double. $179–$189 suite. Rates include continental breakfast. AE, DC, DISC, MC, V. Free indoor parking. Take Grand/ Garnet exit off of I-5; follow Grand Ave. to ocean. Bus: 34.

This modern oceanfront motor hotel offers attractive, spacious rooms with well-coordinated contemporary furnishings. Although the inn has a level of sophistication uncommon for this casual, surfer-populated area, you won't find solitude and quiet, although the cool marble lobby and plushly carpeted hallways will help you feel a little insulated from the raucous scene outside. You sure can't beat the location (directly on the beach) and the view (ditto), and all rooms are equipped with refrigerators. Rates vary according to view, but all rooms have at least a partial ocean view. The ones in the front, while most desirable, can also get noisy directly above the boardwalk, so try for the second or third floor. The Ocean Park Inn doesn't have its own restaurant, but the casual Firehouse Beach Cafe (see "Great Deals on Dining," below) is right outside the front door.

Pacific Shores Inn. 4802 Mission Blvd. (between Law and Chalcedony), San Diego (Pacific Beach), CA 92109. ☎ **800/826-0715** or 619/483-6300. Fax 619/483-9276. 55 units. TV TEL. Summer (June 15–Sept 15) $103–$108 double; $120 suite. Winter $63–$88 double; $73–$93 suite. Extra person $5. Children under 16 stay free in parents' room. Rates include continental breakfast. AE, DC, DISC, MC, V. Free parking. Bus: 30 or 34. Pets up to 15 lb. accepted for $25 surcharge.

If the beach is going to be a major feature of your San Diego vacation, you couldn't stay in a better location than the one enjoyed by this two-story contemporary motel located at the north end of Pacific Beach. It's several blocks from any of PB's restaurants but enjoys a quiet unheard of down the road—and the beach is still just 100 yards away. They don't advertise "ocean views," but rooms 23, 29, 31, 33, and 35 have them, and there's also a heated pool by the parking area. Half the units have kitchens; the others offer small refrigerators. The furniture is a little ragged, but carpets, drapes, bedspreads, etc., are brand new. Ask for a room away from the street.

A PLACE TO CAMP

Campland on the Bay. 2211 Pacific Beach Dr., San Diego, CA 92109-5699. ☎ **800/ 4-BAY-FUN** or 619/581-4200. Fax 619/581-4206. www.campland.com. E-mail: reservation@ campland.com. 566 sites, most with hookup. Summer $22–$98 for up to 4 people. Off-season $19–$67 for up to 4 people. Senior rates available. Weekly and monthly rates available off-season. Day use of facilities $5. MC, V. Take I-5 to Grand/Garnet exit, follow Grand to Olney and turn left; turn left again onto Pacific Beach Dr. Extra (small) charge for dogs.

This bay-side retreat is popular with a mixed crowd: RVers, campers (with or without van), boaters, and their children and pets. At their fingertips are parks, a beach, a bird

---

ⓗ Affordable Family-Friendly Hotels

The Beach Cottages *(see p. 597)*   Kids enjoy the informality and the terrific location near the beach; parents will enjoy the convenience of kitchens and outdoor BBQs to save a few bucks on family meals.

✪ Crystal Pier Hotel *(see p. 597)*   Where else can you sleep over the surf? Youngsters love the novelty and all the seaside activities just outside the front door.

El Cordova Hotel *(see p. 601)*   El Cordova will welcome the kids—and even the family dog—to comfortable surroundings; there's often a block-party atmosphere in the pool courtyard, and most of Coronado is within walking distance.

Hacienda Hotel *(see p. 595)*   Perched above (but an easy stroll from) Old Town, this better-than-average Best Western boasts all-suite accommodations and free stays for kids. When they get bored sightseeing, you'll be glad each room has a VCR.

---

sanctuary, and a dog walk. Other facilities include pools, a Jacuzzi, catamaran and Windsurfer rentals and lessons, bike and boat rentals, a game room, a cafe that's open for three meals a day, a market, and laundry. Planned activities include games and crafts for children; Sea World is 5 minutes away. Reserve popular spots at least 6 months in advance for spring and summer: The most scenic are the "Bayview" looking into the wildlife reserve. "Beachfront" sites are equally scenic but noisy during the day.

LA JOLLA
SUPER-CHEAP SLEEPS
La Jolla Cove Travelodge. 1141 Silverado St. (at Herschel)., La Jolla, CA 92037. ☎ **800/578-7878** or 619/454-0791. Fax 619/459-8534. 30 units. A/C TV TEL. $59–$98 double. Rates are seasonal and subject to availability; AARP and AAA discounts available. AE, DC, MC, V. Free off-street parking.

While the name is deceptive—the cove is a 10-minute walk away—this corner motel is a good value in tony La Jolla. Fitting in with the village's retro feel, the exterior seems unchanged from the 1940s; though rooms have been diligently updated, no one will thrill to the basic motel decor—including cinder-block walls and small, basic bathrooms. But somehow, the place seems less dreary surrounded by the chic glamour of La Jolla, and rooms come with coffeemakers and daily newspapers; some have kitchenettes and microwaves. There isn't a pool, but there is a modest sundeck on the third floor with a view to the ocean, which is about three-quarters of a mile away.

MODERATELY PRICED OPTIONS
Empress Hotel of La Jolla. 7766 Fay Ave. (at Silverado), La Jolla, CA 92037. ☎ **888/369-9900** or 619/454-3001. Fax 619/454-6387. 73 units. A/C TV TEL. $129–$189 double; $325 suite. Extra person $10. Children under 18 stay free in parents' room. Rates include continental breakfast. Lower rates off-season and for longer stays. AE, DC, DISC, MC, V. Valet parking $5.

The Empress Hotel offers spacious quarters with traditional furnishings a block or two away from La Jolla's "main drag" and the ocean. It's quieter here than at the Prospect Park Inn, and you'll sacrifice little other than direct ocean views—and many rooms on the top floors enjoy a partial view, anyway. If you're planning to explore La Jolla on foot, the Empress is a good base, and exudes a classiness many comparably priced chains lack. Rooms are tastefully decorated (and frequently renovated) and are equipped with refrigerators, hair dryers, coffeemakers, irons and boards, and bathrobes. Bathrooms are of average size but exceptionally well appointed. Four "Empress" rooms have sitting areas with full-size sleeper-sofas. There's room service, valet/laundry service, and a fitness room with spa and sauna. On nice days breakfast is set up on a serene outdoor sundeck.

Prospect Park Inn. 1110 Prospect St. (at Coast Blvd.), La Jolla, CA 92037. ☎ **800/ 433-1609** or 619/454-0133. Fax 619/454-2056. 23 units. A/C TV TEL. $105–$180 double; from $250 suite. Lower rates off-season. Rates include continental breakfast. AE, DC, DISC, MC, V. Free off-site indoor parking. Take the Ardath Rd. exit off I-5 north or the La Jolla Village Dr. west exit off I-5 south. Take Torrey Pines Rd. to Prospect Place and turn right. Prospect Place becomes Prospect St.

This place is a real gem. It's a small property—next door to the swanky La Valencia Hotel—that offers charming rooms, some with narrow ocean views. Built in 1947 as a boarding house for women, this spotless boutique hotel feels more European than Californian—there isn't even an elevator in the three-story building. Fresh fruit and beverages are offered in the library area every afternoon and breakfast is served on the sundeck, which has a great ocean view. Prospect Park Inn enjoys essentially the same location as La Valencia—the beach, park, shops, and myriad restaurants are within steps—at much lower prices. Beach towels and chairs are provided free of charge for guests. This is a nonsmoking establishment.

WORTH A SPLURGE

The Bed & Breakfast Inn at La Jolla. 7753 Draper Ave. (near Prospect), La Jolla, CA 92037. ☎ **800/582-2466** or 619/456-2066. www.InnLaJolla.com. 16 units. $90–$225 double; $250 suite. Rates include full breakfast and afternoon wine and cheese. Extra person $25. AE, MC, V. From I-5 south take La Jolla Village Dr. west. Turn left at Torrey Pines Rd., right on Prospect through the village, then left onto Draper.

A 1913 cubist house designed by prominent local architect Irving Gill—and once occupied by John Philip Sousa and his family—is the setting for La Jolla's genteel and elegant B&B. Reconfigured for this purpose, the house has lost none of its charm, and appropriately unfrilly period furnishings add to the sense of history. The inn also features lovely enclosed gardens and a cozy library/sitting room. Fresh fruit, sherry, fresh-cut flowers, and terry robes await in every room, some of which feature a fireplace or ocean view. The furnishings are tasteful and cottage-style, with plenty of framed historic photos of La Jolla, and a full gourmet breakfast is served each morning wherever you desire—dining room, patio, sundeck, or in your room. They'll also prepare picnic baskets (extra charge) for a picnic or beach outing given a day's notice.

✪ **La Jolla Beach & Tennis Club.** 2000 Spindrift Dr., La Jolla, CA 92037. ☎ **800/624-CLUB** or 619/454-7126. Fax 619/456-3805. www.ljbtc.com. 90 units. TV TEL. High season (mid-June to mid-Sept) $149–$229 double; $329–$559 suite. Off-season $115–$225 double; $269–$469 suite. Children under 12 stay free in parents' room. Additional person $20. AE, DC, MC, V. Located in La Jolla Shores about a mile from the village.

Pack your best tennis whites for a stay at La Jolla's private and historic "B&T" (as it's locally known). Guest rooms are surprisingly plain and frill-free in terms of style—but are equipped with hair dryers, irons and boards, and coffeemakers. Most have well-stocked full kitchens ideal for families or longer stays. Guests have full use of the club's 12 championship tennis courts, as well as a 9-hole pitch-and-putt winding its way around a lagoon along the stately entry drive. Other facilities include a jogging path, children's playground, table tennis, fitness room, and elegant Olympic-size swimming pool. But during the warm months, the beach is most popular, as the staff sets up comfy sand chairs and umbrellas, racing to bring fluffy beach towels, beverages, and snacks. Kayaks and water-sports equipment can be rented; there's even a sand croquet court.

Although there's no room service, the resort has a casual dining room and seasonal beach hut; it's also worth taking a peek into the distinctive Marine Room, where waves literally smash against the windows inches away from well-coiffed diners. The menu is expensive, but the price of a cocktail gets the same astounding view.

CORONADO
SUPER-CHEAP SLEEPS

El Rancho Motel. 370 Orange Ave. (at Fourth St.), Coronado, CA 92118. ☎ **619/ 435-2251.** 6 units. A/C TV. Summer $85–$95 double; winter $65–$75 double. AE, CB, DC, DISC, JCB, MC, V. Free parking. Take I-5 to the Coronado Bridge, and turn right onto Orange Ave. Bus: 901. Ferry: From Broadway Pier.

An alternative to the larger—and more expensive—Coronado hotels, this tiny mom-and-pop motel is a little worn but eager to please. What it lacks in contemporary polish and privacy, it makes up for with comforts like coffeemakers, microwaves, and refrigerators; some rooms even have a whirlpool tub. It can get noisy right here on busy Orange Avenue, but a free island shuttle stops at the corner, and the location is equidistant between the two sides of the peninsula. There's one room with a single twin bed that goes for $45 year-round for single travelers. The motel was listed for sale at press time, so check their status when you book.

The Village Inn. 1017 Park Place (at Orange Ave.), Coronado, CA 92118. ☎ **619/ 435-9318.** 14 units. TEL. Summer $80–$86 double. Winter and weekly rates available. Rates include continental breakfast. AE, MC, V. Free street parking.

Located a block or two from Coronado's main sights—the Hotel del Coronado, the beach, shopping, and cafes—location is the inn's most appealing feature. But historic charm runs a close second, as a charmingly vintage lobby sets the mood in this European-style hostelry; each simple but well-maintained room includes antique dressers and armoires, plus lovely Battenberg lace bedcovers and shams. Front rooms enjoy the best view, and coffee and tea are available all day in the kitchen where breakfast is served. Clean and appealing, the inn's only Achilles heel is tiny, tiny bathrooms, so cramped that you almost have to stand on the toilet to use the small-scale sinks. Surprisingly, though, some have been updated with whirlpool tubs.

MODERATELY PRICED OPTIONS

El Cordova Hotel. 1351 Orange Ave. (at Adella Ave.), Coronado, CA 92118. ☎ **800/ 229-2032** or 619/435-4131. Fax 619/435-0632. 40 units. TV TEL. $95 double; $115–$125 studio with kitchen; $145–$185 one-bedroom suite; $220–$295 two-bedroom suite. Weekly and monthly rates available off-season. Children under 12 stay free in parents' room. AE, DC, DISC, MC, V. No off-street parking.

This Spanish hacienda across the street from the Hotel del Coronado began life as a private mansion in 1902; by the 1930s it had become a hotel, with the original building augmented by a series of retail shops along a ground-floor arcade. Surrounding a courtyard with meandering tiled pathways, flowering shrubs, a swimming pool, and patio seating for Miguel's Cocina Mexican restaurant, El Cordova hums pleasantly with activity. Each room is a little different from the next; some sport a Mexican-colonial ambiance while others evoke a comfy beach cottage. All feature ceiling fans and brightly tiled bathrooms, but lack the frills that command exorbitant rates. El Cordova has a particularly inviting aura, and its prime location makes it a popular option; I advise reserving several months in advance, especially

The Hotel Del

Opened in 1888 and designated a National Historic Landmark in 1977, the **Hotel del Coronado,** or the "Hotel Del," as it's affectionately known, at 1500 Orange Ave. in Coronado, is the last of California's grand old seaside hotels. Here the Duke of Windsor met his duchess, and Marilyn Monroe frolicked in *Some Like It Hot.* This monument to Victorian grandeur boasts tall cupolas, red turrets, gingerbread trim, all spread out on 33 acres. A stay here will put you back some coin (standard rooms start at $210 a night; call ☎ **800/468-3533** or 619/435-8000), but anyone can take a stroll through the grand, wood-paneled lobby or along the Del's pristine wide beach—the Del offers a self-guided walking tour complete with audiocassette.

for summer. Facilities include heated pool, barbecue area with a picnic table, and laundry room.

Glorietta Bay Inn. 1630 Glorietta Blvd. (near Orange Ave.), Coronado, CA 92118. ☎ **800/283-9383** or 619/435-3101. Fax 619/435-6182. www.gloriettabayinn.com. E-mail: rooms@gloriettabayinn.com. 100 units. A/C TV TEL. Annex: $115–$195 double; from $199 suite. Mansion: $155–$165 double; $199–$395 suite. Children 18 and under stay free in parents' room. Extra person $10. Rates include continental breakfast. AE, MC, V. Free parking. Take I-5 to the Coronado Bridge, and turn left on Orange Ave. After 2 miles, turn left onto Glorietta Blvd.; it's across the street from the Hotel del Coronado.

Right across the street and somewhat in the figurative shadow of the Hotel del Coronado, this pretty white hotel is composed of the charmingly historic John D. Spreckels mansion (1908) and two much-later motel-style buildings. Only 11 rooms are in the mansion, which boasts original fixtures, grand staircase, and old-fashioned wicker furniture; the guest rooms are also decked out in antiques and have a romantic and nostalgic ambiance. Rooms in the modern annexes are less expensive but much plainer; both categories are equipped with refrigerators, coffeemakers, and hair dryers. Wherever your room is, you'll gather for breakfast on the main house's sunny veranda. In addition to offering rental bikes and boat rentals on pretty Glorietta Bay across the street, the hotel is within easy walking distance of the beach, golf, tennis, water sports, shopping, and dining. Amenities include a heated swimming pool and coin-op laundry.

4 Great Deals on Dining

San Diego offers a good selection of cheap eats. What follows is only a sampling—for a greater selection, see *Frommer's San Diego.*

Keep in mind that you can stretch your budget with the two-for-one coupons found in the Night & Day section of the *Union-Tribune* and in the *Reader* on Thursdays. If you're going to be in town for more than a few days, you might also profit from Dine-A-Mate, a book of two-for-one and discount coupons to many area eateries. **Dine-A-Mate** costs $25; to order call ☎ **800/248-DINE** or 619/578-4800.

DOWNTOWN
SUPER-CHEAP EATS

✪ **Café Lulu.** 419 F St. (near Fourth Ave.). ☎ **619/238-0114.** Main courses $3–$7. No credit cards. Sun–Thurs 9am–2am; Fri and Sat 9am–4am. Trolley: Gaslamp Quarter. INTERNATIONAL/VEGETARIAN.

Smack dab in the heart of the Gaslamp Quarter, Café Lulu aims to establish a hip, bohemian mood despite its location half a block from bright, commercial Horton Plaza. Ostensibly a coffee bar, the cafe makes a terrific choice for casual dining; if the stylishly metallic interior is too harsh for you, watch the street action from a sidewalk table. The food is health conscious, prepared with organic ingredients and no meat. Soups, salads, cheese melts, and veggie lasagna are on the menu; breads are brought in from the incomparable Bread & Cie uptown (see below). Eggs, granola, and waffles are served in the morning, but anytime is the right time to try one of Café Lulu's inventive coffee drinks, like "cafe Bohème," a mocha with almond syrup, or "cafe L'amour," an iced latte with a hazelnut tinge. Beer and wine are also served.

Filippi's Pizza Grotto. 1747 India St. (between Date and Fir sts. in Little Italy). ☎ **619/232-5095.** Fax 619/695-8591. Main courses $4.75–$12.50. AE, DC, DISC, MC, V. Sun–Thurs 11am–10pm; Fri–Sat 11am–11pm. Free parking. Bus: 5. Trolley: County Center/Little Italy. ITALIAN.

To get to the grottolike dining area decorated with Chianti bottles and red-checked tablecloths, you have to walk through an Italian grocery store/deli strewn with cheeses, pastas, wines, bottles of olive oil, and salamis. You might even end up eating behind shelves of canned olives, but don't feel bad—this has been the tradition since 1950, when the place opened. The intoxicating smell of pizza wafts into the street; Filippi's has more than 15 varieties (including vegetarian) plus old-world Sicilian spaghetti, lasagna, and other pasta. The original of a dozen stores, Filippi's has locations in Pacific Beach, Kearny Mesa, East Mission Valley, and Escondido, among others.

FOR A FEW BUCKS MORE

Kansas City Barbecue. 610 W. Market St. ☎ **619/231-9680.** Reservations taken only for large parties. Main courses $8.75–$11.50. MC, V. Daily 11am–1am. Trolley: Seaport Village. AMERICAN.

Kansas City Barbecue's honky-tonk mystique is fueled by its appearance as the fly-boy hangout in the movie *Top Gun,* and posters from the film share wall space with county-fair memorabilia, old car tags from Kansas, and a photograph of official bar wench Carry Nation. This homey dive is right next to the railroad tracks and across from the tony Hyatt Regency. Their spicy barbecue ribs, chicken, and hot links are slow-cooked over an open fire and served with sliced Wonder bread and your choice of coleslaw, beans, fries, onion rings, potato salad, or corn on the cob. The food is okay, but the atmosphere is the real draw.

Karl Strauss Brewery & Grill. 1157 Columbia St. (between B and C sts.). ☎ **619/234-BREW** (2739). Main courses $7–$15. MC, V. Sun–Wed 11:30am–10pm (beer and wine until 11pm), Thurs–Sat 11:30am–midnight (beer and wine until 1am). Bus: 5. Trolley: America Plaza. AMERICAN.

Brew master Karl Strauss put San Diego on the microbrewery map with this unpretentious factory setting; the smell of hops and malt wafts throughout, and the stainless-steel tanks are visible from the bar. Brews range from pale ale to amber lager, and all are on tap. Five-ounce samplers are 85¢ each; if you like what you taste, 12-oz. glasses, pints, and hefty schooners stand chilled and ready. There's also nonalcoholic beer and wine by the glass. Accompaniments include Cajun fries, hamburgers, German sausage with sauerkraut, fish-and-chips, and other greasy bar food, but it's really secondary to the stylish suds. Beer-related memorabilia and brewery tours are available.

MODERATELY PRICED OPTIONS

Dakota Grill and Spirits. 901 Fifth Ave. (at E St.). ☎ **619/234-5554.** Reservations recommended. Main courses $9–$18. AE, DC, DISC, MC, V. Mon–Fri 11:30am–2:30pm; Mon–Thurs 5–10pm, Fri–Sat 5–11pm, Sun 5–9pm. Valet parking (after 5pm) $5; self-parking in the area $7. Bus: 1, 3, 25, or 945. Trolley: Gaslamp Quarter. AMERICAN/SOUTHWESTERN.

Where to Pack the Perfect Picnic

Because San Diego's benign climate lends itself to dining alfresco, **picnics** have become a popular and relaxing form of portable meals. An excellent spot to pick up sandwiches is **The Cheese Shop,** a gourmet's deli delight located downtown at 401 G St. (☎ **619/232-2303**), or in La Jolla Shores at 2165 Avenida de la Playa (☎ **619/459-3921**). Other places to buy picnic fare include **Girard Gourmet,** in La Jolla at 7837 Girard Ave. (☎ **619/454-3321**); **Boudin Sourdough Bakery and Cafe** (☎ **619/234-1849**) and **The Farmers Market,** both in Horton Plaza; and **Old Town Liquor and Deli,** at 2304 San Diego Ave. (☎ **619/291-4888**). Another spot that's very popular with San Diegans is ✪ **Point Loma Seafoods,** located on the water's edge in front of the Municipal Sportfishing Pier, at 2805 Emerson, near Scott Street, south of Rosecrans and west of Harbor Drive (☎ **619/223-1109**). There's a fish market here, and they sell seafood sandwiches and salads to go. If you decide to make your own sandwiches, the best bread in the county comes from **Bread & Cie,** 350 University Ave., in Hillcrest (☎ **619/683-9322**), or **Primavera Pastry Caffe** on Coronado at 956 Orange Ave. (☎ **619/435-4191**).

This downtown business lunch favorite is always busy and noisy; the Southwestern cowboy kitsch matches the cuisine but can be a little too theme-y for some. The most popular items include shrimp tasso (sautéed with Tasso Cajun ham and sweet peas in an ancho chili cream) and spit-roasted chicken with orange chipotle glaze or Dakota barbecue sauce. When the kitchen is on, Dakota's innovation makes it one of San Diego's best, even though an occasional dud results from the overzealous combination of too many disparate ingredients.

✪ **Fio's.** 801 Fifth Ave. (at F St.). ☎ **619/234-3467.** Reservations recommended for dinner. Main courses $8.95–$21.95. AE, DC, DISC, MC, V. Mon–Fri 11:30am–3pm; Mon–Thurs 5–11pm; Fri–Sat 5pm–midnight; Sun 5–10pm. Valet parking (after 5pm) $6 with validation. Trolley: Gaslamp Quarter. NORTHERN ITALIAN.

Fio's has been *the* spot to see and be seen in the Gaslamp Quarter since opening, and it's the granddaddy of the new wave of trendy Italians. Set in an 1881 Italianate-Victorian that once housed chic Marston's department store, Fio's has a hip, sophisticated ambiance and is *always* crowded. Once cutting-edge, the upscale trattoria menu is now practiced and consistently superior, featuring jet-black linguini tossed with the freshest seafood, delicate angel-hair pasta perfectly balanced with basil and pine nuts, and gourmet pizzas that are also served at the pizza bar. Hurried business folk pack Fio's at lunch, enjoying a lighter menu; the rush is generally over by 1pm, so come later to avoid waiting for a table. At lunch or dinner, you can always sit at the elegant cocktail bar and order from the complete menu.

The Fish Market. 750 N. Harbor Dr. ☎ **619/232-FISH.** Reservations not accepted. Main courses $9–$25. AE, CB, DC, MC, V. Daily 11am–10pm. Valet parking $4. Bus: 7/7B. Trolley: Seaport Village. SEAFOOD.

The red building perched at the end of the G Street Pier houses two of San Diego's most popular seafood restaurants: the Fish Market and its pricier cousin, the Top of the Market. Both offer superb fresh seafood and menus that change daily. The chalkboard out front tells you what's freshest, be it Mississippi catfish, Maine lobster, Canadian salmon, or Mexican yellowtail. At ground level, the Fish Market, a market and casual restaurant, has oyster and sushi bars and a cocktail lounge. There is another Fish Market Restaurant in Del Mar at 640 Via de la Valle (☎ **619/755-2277**).

WORTH A SPLURGE

✪ **Croce's Restaurant & Jazz Bar.** 802 Fifth Ave. (at F St.). ☎ **619/233-4355.** Reservations recommended. Main courses $14–$23. AE, DC, DISC, MC, V. Daily 5pm–midnight. Valet parking $6 with validation. Bus: 1, 3, 25, or 945. Trolley: Gaslamp Quarter. AMERICAN.

Ingrid Croce, widow of singer/songwriter Jim, was instrumental in the resurgence of the once-decayed Gaslamp Quarter. Since first opening in 1979, Ingrid has expanded into every corner of this 1890 Romanesque building; in addition to this primary restaurant, the next-door Top Hat Bar & Grill serves up hip live R&B, and Ingrid's Cantina & Sidewalk Cafe offers casual Southwestern fare. They're all the hottest ticket in town these days, as crowds line up for dinner tables and nightclub shows. Expect a noisy, festive good time any night of the week. Croce's offers a contemporary American menu, featuring dishes like Santa Fe Wellington, a beef fillet with spicy sausage and raisin filling, baked in flaky pastry and served with creamy jalapeño sauce. Diners from either of the full-service restaurants can enter the two adjacent nightspots, the Jazz Bar and the Top Hat, without paying the normal cover charge.

HILLCREST/UPTOWN
SUPER-CHEAP EATS

✪ **Bread & Cie.** 350 University Ave. (between Third and Fourth sts.). ☎ **619/683-9322.** Sandwiches and light meals $3–$6. No credit cards. Mon–Fri 7am–7pm; Sat 7am–6pm; Sun 8am–6pm. BAKERY/MEDITERRANEAN.

Delicious aromas permeate this cavernous Hillcrest bakery where the city's most unusually flavored breads are baked. Honoring the traditions of European artisan bread-making, and attention to the fine points of texture and crust, are the qualities that quickly catapulted Bread & Cie to local stardom. Mouthwatering favorites include anise and fig, black olive, *panella dell'uva* (grape bread), and rye currant (weekends only); even the relatively plain sourdough batard is tart, chewy perfection. Ask for a free sample, or order one of their many sunny Mediterranean-inspired sandwiches on the bread of your choice. They also serve a variety of specialty coffee drinks, the perfect accompaniment to a light breakfast of their fresh scones, muffins, and fruit turnovers. Seating is at bistro-style metal tables in full view of the busy ovens.

Corvette Diner. 3946 Fifth Ave. (between Washington and University). ☎ **619/542-1001.** Reservations not accepted. Main courses $4.50–$9.95. AE, DC, DISC, MC, V. Sun–Thurs 11am–10pm; Fri–Sat 11am–midnight. Free weekday valet parking; evening and weekend valet $4. Bus: 1 or 3. AMERICAN.

Step through a virtual time portal into the rockin' 1950s at this theme diner where the jukebox is loud, the gum-snapping waitresses slide into your booth to take your order, and the decor is vintage Corvette to the highest power. Equal parts *Happy Days* hangout and "Jackrabbit Slim's" (from *Pulp Fiction*), the Corvette Diner is a comfy time-warp in the midst of trendy Hillcrest, and the eats ain't bad, either. Burgers, sandwiches, appetizer munchies (they serve beer and wine only at the large bar in the center of the cavernous dining room), "blue-plate" specials, and salads share the menu with a *very* full page of fountain favorites. The party gets turned up a notch at night, with DJs and even a magician providing more entertainment (on top of the entertaining atmosphere itself).

✪ **The Vegetarian Zone.** 2949 Fifth Ave. (between Palm and Quince). ☎ **619/298-7302** (deli/takeout 619/298-9232). Reservations not accepted. Main courses $5–$9.50. DISC, MC, V. Mon–Thurs 11:30am–9pm; Fri 11:30am–10pm; Sat 8:30am–10pm; Sun 8:30am–9pm. Deli daily 10am–9pm. Bus: 34 or 34A. VEGETARIAN.

San Diego's only strictly vegetarian restaurant is a real treat. Even if you're wary of tempeh, tofu, and meat substitutes, there are plenty of naturally veggie ethnic selections on the menu. Selections include Greek spinach and feta pie, savory Indian curry turnovers, and salads with homemade dressings. Soothing music creates a pleasant ambiance enjoyed by trendy-hip Hillcrest types, business lunchers, and the health-conscious from all walks of life. Just in case you feel deserving of a treat after such a healthful meal, the heavenly Extraordinary Desserts is right next door.

FOR A FEW BUCKS MORE

Celadon. 3628 Fifth Ave. (between Brooks and Pennsylvania). ☎ **619/295-8800.** Reservations recommended on weekends. Main courses $8.50–$14.50. AE, MC, V. Mon–Fri 11:30am–10pm; Sat 5–10pm. Bus: 1 or 3. THAI.

When it opened in the mid-1980s, this sleekly modern Hillcrest restaurant was a pioneer, bringing gourmet Thai to a city unfamiliar with the cuisine. Today they're still known for beautifully prepared and presented dishes, so it seems unfair to grouse about the dated mauve decor. Celadon still fills a niche with moderately priced yet elegant dining. Specialties include shrimp in a spicy, creamy coconut sauce; sautéed scallops in "burnt" sauce with a touch of garlic; *mee krob,* caramelized noodles with chicken and shrimp; and a vegetarian pad Thai with deep-fried tofu. Appetizers range from sweet and savory to hot and spicy; a favorite is Bangkok summer salad, composed of roasted pork with cilantro, mint, and lime juice.

Hob Nob Hill. 2271 First Ave. (at Juniper). ☎ **619/239-8176.** Breakfast and lunch $3.25–$8.25; dinner $8–$14. AE, DC, DISC, MC, V. Daily 7am–9pm. Bus: 1 or 3. AMERICAN.

This homey coffee shop/deli began as a 14-stool lunch counter in 1944 and has grown into one of the most popular neighborhood hangouts in the city. You'll find comfort food at its best, and reasonably priced enough for many regulars to dine here more often than in their own homes. The career waitresses here are also accustomed to plenty of hobnobbing professionals conducting power breakfasts over beef hash, oatmeal with pecans, or fried eggs with thick, hickory-smoked bacon. Stick-to-your-ribs meals appear for lunch and dinner, old favorites like chicken and dumplings, roast turkey, prime rib, or liver grilled with onions. It's a great place to bring the kids, especially on Sunday, when many local families observe a multigeneration dinner tradition.

MODERATELY PRICED OPTIONS

California Cuisine. 1027 University Ave. (east of Tenth St.). ☎ **619/543-0790.** Reservations recommended for dinner. Main courses $13–$20. AE, MC, V. Tues–Fri 11am–10pm; Sat–Sun 5–10pm. CALIFORNIA.

Though the name's no longer as cutting-edge as when this place opened in the early 1980s, California Cuisine's menu keeps creatively up-to-date. The quiet, understated, and romantic ambiance sets the stage for a smoothly professional staff to proffer fine dining at moderate prices to a casual crowd. The seasonally skewed menu changes daily and contains mouth-watering appetizers like sesame-seared ahi with hot-and-sour raspberry sauce, or caramelized onion and Gruyère tart on balsamic baby greens. Main courses are, more often than not, stacked in trendy "towers," but their flavors are composed with equal care. Early-birds and bargain seekers will appreciate the three-course pretheater menu ($20) available nightly from 5 to 7pm. Parking can be scarce along this busy stretch of University; you'll spot the restaurant by its light-strewn bushes out front.

✪ **Laurel.** 505 Laurel St. (at Fifth Ave.). ☎ **619/239-2222.** Reservations recommended. Main courses $14–$19. AE, DISC, MC, V. Sun–Thurs 5–10pm; Fri–Sat 5–11pm. SOUTHERN FRENCH/MEDITERRANEAN.

Given its sophisticated decor, pedigreed chefs, prime Balboa Park location, and well-composed menu of country French dishes with a Mediterranean accent, it's no wonder this relatively new restaurant was an instant success. It's also popular with theatergoers, offering shuttle service to the Old Globe followed by an after-performance dessert. Tantalizing appetizers include eggplant ravioli in a roasted-tomato-and-black-olive jus, house-cured duck-breast prosciutto, follow with pan-roasted veal sweetbreads in black-olive sauce, or grilled salmon with herb-crusted fingerling potatoes. One of the most stylish choices near often-funky Hillcrest, Laurel has an almost New York ambiance coupled with truly modest prices.

Liaison. 2202 Fourth Ave. (at Ivy). ☎ **619/234-5540.** Main courses $10.75–$19.75. AE, CB, DC, DISC, MC, V. Tues–Sun 5–10:30pm. Bus: 1 or 3. FRENCH.

The cuisine and decor evoke a Gallic farmhouse kitchen in this cozy and inviting cafe where copper pots hang from the rafters. Conveniently located for Balboa Park theatergoers, this dinner-only fave has a hearty French country menu including lamb curry, medaillons of pork or beef, coquilles St. Jacques, roast duckling à l'orange, salmon with crayfish butter, and more. A nightly prix-fixe dinner ($46 per couple) is a great deal, since the meal includes pâté, soup and salad, a main course, dessert, and wine for two. The house specialty dessert costs extra: a Grand Marnier chocolate or amaretto soufflé for two, at $5 per person. Ooh la la!

OLD TOWN
SUPER-CHEAP EATS

✪ **Old Town Mexican Cafe.** 2489 San Diego Ave. ☎ **619/297-4330.** Reservations accepted for groups of 10 or more. Main courses $7.50–$11.50. AE, DISC, MC, V. Sun–Thurs 7am–11pm; Fri–Sat 7am–midnight; bar service until 2am. Bus: 4 or 5/105. MEXICAN.

This place is so popular it's become an Old Town tourist attraction in its own right; despite expansion, the wait for a table is still often 30 to 60 minutes. Pass the time gazing in from the sidewalk as tortillas are hand-patted the old-fashioned way, a hot-off-the-grill treat accompanying every meal. Once inside, order what some consider the best margarita in town, followed by one of the cafe's two specialties: *Carnitas*—the traditional Mexican dish of deep-fried pork served with tortillas, guacamole, sour cream, beans and rice; or rotisserie chicken with all the same trimmings. It's loud and crowded and the *cerveza* flows like, well, beer, but this Old Town mainstay is best in the city for traditional Mexican.

FOR A FEW BUCKS MORE

✪ **Berta's Latin American Restaurant.** 3928 Twiggs St. (at Congress St.), Old Town. ☎ **619/295-2343.** Main courses $5–$7 at lunch, $11–$13 at dinner. AE, MC, V. Daily 11am–10pm (lunch menu until 3pm). REGIONAL LATIN AMERICAN.

Tucked away on an Old Town side street, Berta's faithfully re-creates the sundry flavors of Central American regions where chiles and other spices have their heat mellowed by slow cooking. Everyone starts with a basket of fresh flour tortillas and mild *salsa verde;* nibble while you contemplate menu options like Guatemalan *chilimal,* a rich pork/vegetable casserole with chiles, cornmeal *masa,* and spices. Try the lunch-only Salvadoran *pupusas,* dense corn-mash turnovers with melted cheese and black beans. Or settle on a table full of Spanish-style tapas, grazing alternately on crispy *empanadas* (filled turnovers), strong Spanish olives, or *Pincho Moruno,* skewered lamb and onion redolent of spices and red saffron. A welcome change from Old Town's nacho-and-fajita joints, Berta's attracts a large crowd on weekends.

Brigantine Seafood Grill. 2444 San Diego Ave. ☎ **619/298-9840.** Reservations recommended on weekends. Main courses $7.95–29.95; early-bird special $10–$14. AE, CB, DC, MC, V. Mon–Thurs 11am–10:30pm; Fri–Sat 11am–11pm; Sun 10am–10:30pm. Bus: 4 or 5/105. SEAFOOD.

The Brigantine is best known for its oyster-bar happy hour from 4 to 7pm (until 9:30pm on Mon), when beer, margaritas, and food are heavily discounted, and you can expect standing-room only. Early-bird specials are offered Sunday through Thursday from 5 to 7pm; the dinners include seafood, steak, or chicken served with several side dishes and baked bread. The food is good but not great; its above average for a chain, but the congenial atmosphere seems the primary draw. Inside, the decor is upscale and nautical; outside, there's a pleasant patio with a fireplace to take the chill off the night air. At lunch, you can get everything from crab cakes or fish-and-chips to fresh fish or pasta. Lunch specials come with sourdough bread and two side dishes. The bar and oyster bar are open daily until midnight. There's also a Brigantine on Coronado at 1333 Orange Ave. (☎ **619/435-4166**).

Worth a Splurge

Cafe Pacifica. 2414 San Diego Ave. ☎ **619/291-6666.** Reservations recommended. Main courses $12–$22. AE, DC, MC, V. Mon–Sat 5:30–10pm; Sun 5:30–9:30pm. Bus: 4 or 5/105. CALIFORNIA.

Inside this cozy Old Town casita the decor is cleanly contemporary (but still romantic), and the food anything but Mexican. Since its establishment in 1980 by the now-revered duo of Kipp Downing and Deacon Brown, Cafe Pacifica has been serving upscale and imaginative seafood and producing kitchen alumni who've gone on to enjoy their own local fame. Among the temptations on the menu are grilled shrimp cocktail with spicy Chinese mustard; oysters on the half shell; and Dungeness-crab salad with papaya, avocado, and endive—and these are just for starters. Main courses include herb-crusted sea bass, and lamb chops with tomatoes, sweet garlic, and mint pesto. The signature dish is Hawaiian ahi with shiitake mushrooms and ginger butter. Dine early to avoid the crowds.

MISSION BAY & THE BEACHES
Super-Cheap Eats

A noteworthy beach spot is **Kono's Surf Club Cafe,** 704 Garnet Ave. (☎ **619/ 483-1669**), a Hawaiian-themed boardwalk breakfast shack that's cheap and delicious—a plump Kono's breakfast burrito provides enough fuel for a day of surfing or sightseeing.

For a Few Bucks More

Firehouse Beach Cafe. 722 Grand Ave., Pacific Beach. ☎ **619/272-1999.** Reservations recommended on weekends. Main courses $6–$13. AE, DISC, MC, V. Sun–Thurs 7am–9pm; Fri–Sat 7am–10pm. Free parking. Bus: 34 or 34A. AMERICAN.

Ceiling fans stir the air in this cheerful, comfortably crowded place, and there's pleasant rooftop dining with an ocean view if you're lucky enough to snag a seat. Located just off the Pacific Beach boardwalk, the cafe sees a lot of foot traffic and socializing locals. Those in-the-know go for the great breakfasts—including Mexican-style eggs and breakfast burritos, French toast, and omelets—or during the 4-to-6pm

---

🍴 Affordable Family-Friendly Restaurants

If neither of my two selections below grabs you, you could take the clan to **Planet Hollywood,** downtown at 197 Horton Plaza (☎ 619/702-STAR), or that other theme bastion, **Hard Rock Cafe,** in La Jolla at 909 Prospect St. (☎ 619/454-5101).

Corvette Diner *(see p. 605)*   Resembling a 1950s diner, this place appeals to teens and preteens who like the sock-hop surroundings as well as the short-order fare.

Filippi's Pizza Grotto *(see p. 603)*   Children's portions are available, and kids will feel right at home at this red-checked-vinyl-tablecloth kid of joint. The pizza is among the best in town.

Happy Hour for bargain prices on drinks and finger-lickin' appetizers. The rest of the menu is adequate, running the gamut from fish tacos to Tex-Mex fajitas to lasagna and all-American burgers.

⭐ **Sushi Ota.** 4529 Mission Bay Dr. (at Bunker Hill), Mission Bay. ☎ **619/270-5670.** Reservations recommended on weekends. Main courses $8–$15; sushi $2.50–$8. AE, MC, V. Tues–Fri 11:30am–2pm; daily 5:30–10:30pm. JAPANESE.

Chef-owner Yukito Ota's masterful sushi garnered a nearly perfect food rating in the San Diego *Zagat Survey* of restaurant-goers. This sophisticated and traditional restaurant (no Asian fusion here) has a short sushi menu because patrons in-the-know look first to the daily specials posted behind the counter. The city's most experienced chefs, armed with nimble fingers and very sharp knives, turn the day's fresh catch into artful little bundles accented with mounds of wasabi and ginger. The rest of the menu is varied, featuring seafood dishes, teriyaki-glazed meats, feather-light tempura, and a variety of small appetizers perfect to accompany a large sushi order. Located in a nondescript part of Pacific Beach (nearer to I-5 than the ocean), Sushi Ota hides in the rear of a minimall, but don't let this discourage you.

MODERATELY PRICED OPTIONS

The Green Flash. 701 Thomas Ave. (at Mission Blvd.), Pacific Beach. ☎ **619/270-7715.** Reservations recommended. Main courses $10–$20. AE, CB, DC, DISC, MC, V. Mon–Thurs 8am–9:30pm; Fri 8am–10pm; Sat 7:30am–10pm; Sun 7:30am–9:30pm. Bus: 34 or 34A. AMERICAN.

Known throughout Pacific Beach for its location and hip, local clientele, the Green Flash serves reasonably good (and typically beachy) food at decent prices. The menu includes plenty of grilled and deep-fried seafood, straightforward steaks, and giant main-course salads. You'll also find platters of shellfish (oysters, clams, shrimp) and other appetizers. Denizens congregate every evening on the patio to catch a glimpse of the sunset phenomenon for which this boardwalk hangout is named. The decibel level of conversation rises with every round of drinks. They also offer sunset dinner specials (4:30 to 7pm) Sunday through Thursday.

Qwiig's. 5083 Santa Monica Ave. (at Abbott Ave.), Ocean Beach. ☎ **619/222-1101.** Reservations recommended. Main courses $12–$21. AE, MC, V. Mon–Fri 11:30am–9pm; Sat 5–10pm; Sun 5–9pm. CALIFORNIA.

It's taken more than a sunset view overlooking the OB pier to keep this upscale Bar & Grill going since 1985; the restaurant owes its consistent popularity to first-rate food served with lack of pretense. The fresh-fish specials are most popular—choices often include rare ahi with braised spinach and sesame-sherry sauce or Chilean sea bass with lime, tequila, and roasted garlic. Several seafood pastas are offered, plus meat and poultry dishes including prime rib, an outstanding ½-pound burger, and nightly specials that always shine. Wines are well matched to the cuisine, and there are imaginative special cocktails each night. The restaurant got its strange name from a group of OB surfers nicknamed "qwiigs."

WORTH A SPLURGE

Thee Bungalow. 4996 W. Point Loma Blvd. (at Bacon), Ocean Beach. ☎ **619/224-2884.** Reservations recommended. Main courses $14–$23. AE, DC, DISC, MC, V. Sun–Thurs 5:30–9pm; Fri–Sat 5–10pm. FRENCH/CONTINENTAL.

This small cottage stands alone at the edge of Robb Field near the Ocean Beach channel, a romantic hideaway beckoning diners in for consistently good continental cuisine augmented by a well-chosen and well-priced wine list. By far the fanciest restaurant in laid-back Ocean Beach, Thee Bungalow endears itself to the local crowd with early-bird specials ($10 to $13) available 7 days a week. The house specialty is crispy roast duck, served with your choice of sauce (the best are black cherry or spiced pepper rum), ideally followed by one of their decadent, made-to-order dessert soufflés for two (chocolate or Grand Marnier). Another menu standout is osso-buco-style lamb shank adorned with a shallot-and-red-wine purée; first courses are just as appealing, featuring Brie and asparagus baked in puff pastry, warm chicken salad (stuffed with sun-dried tomatoes and basil, then presented with feta cheese and fruit, it also doubles as a light meal), and there's always a pâté sampler plate featuring house-made pâtés with Dijon, cornichons, capers, and little toasts.

LA JOLLA
SUPER-CHEAP EATS

✪ **The Cottage.** 7702 Fay Ave. (at Kline). ☎ **619/454-8409.** Reservations accepted for dinner only. Breakfast and lunch $5–$7; dinner main courses $7–$12. AE, DISC, MC, V. Daily year-round 7:30am–3pm; May 15–Sept 30 only: Tues–Sat 5–9:30pm. CALIFORNIA.

La Jolla's best—and friendliest—breakfast is served at this turn-of-the-century bungalow on a sunny village street corner. Newly modernized, the cottage is light and airy inside, but most diners opt for tables outside, where a charming white picket fence encloses the trellis-shaded brick patio. Omelets and egg dishes feature Mediterranean, Asian, or classic American touches; The Cottage bakes their own muffins, breads, and desserts. While "breakfast" dishes are served all day, toward lunch the kitchen begins turning out freshly made soups, light meals, and sandwiches. Summer dinners are a delight, particularly when seated before dark on a balmy seaside night—the ambiance is charming.

FOR A FEW BUCKS MORE

✪ **Brockton Villa.** 1235 Coast Blvd. (across from La Jolla Cove). ☎ **619/454-7393.** Reservations accepted (call by Thurs for Sun brunch). Breakfast $4–$7.25; dinner main courses $10–$18. AE, DISC, MC, V. Mon–Sun 8am–9pm (later in summer). Validated parking in Coast Walk Center. CALIFORNIA.

Located in a well-restored and much-loved 1894 beach bungalow, this charming cafe has a history as intriguing as its varied, eclectic menu. The biggest buzz is at breakfast time, which features inventive dishes such as soufflélike "Coast Toast" (the house take on French toast), Greek "steamers" (eggs scrambled with an espresso steamer, then mixed with feta cheese, tomato, and basil), and dozens of coffee drinks. Lunch stars homemade soups and salads, plus unusual sandwiches such as turkey meat loaf on toasted sourdough bread with spicy tomato-mint chutney. The dinner menu is constantly expanding, and includes salmon *en croûte* (wrapped with prosciutto, Gruyère, and sage with a grainy mustard sauce) plus pastas, stews, and grilled meats. Steep stairs from the street limit access for wheelchair users.

George's Ocean Terrace and Café. 1250 Prospect St. ☎ **619/454-4244.** Reservations not accepted. Main courses $7.50–$10.75 at lunch; $9.50–$14.95 at dinner. AE, DC, DISC, MC, V. Sun–Thurs 11am–10pm; Fri–Sat 11am–11pm. Valet parking $5. CALIFORNIA.

The main dining room on level one at George's is legendary and has won numerous awards for its haute cuisine. But George's also accommodates those seeking good food and a spectacular setting with a more reasonable price tag—the upstairs Ocean Terrace and Café prepares similar dishes as well as new creations in the same kitchen as the high-priced fare. These two areas offer indoor and outdoor seating overlooking La Jolla Cove and the same great service as the main dining room. For dinner, you can choose from one of several seafood or pasta dishes, or have something out-of-the-ordinary like George's meat loaf served with mushroom-and-corn mashed potatoes. Fans of George's award-winning smoked-chicken, broccoli, and black-bean soup rejoice that it appears on both menus. Valet parking is available, but if you drive around long enough, you'll find a place on the street.

Spice & Rice Thai Kitchen. 7734 Girard Ave. ☎ **619/456-0466.** Main courses $7–$13. AE, MC, V. Mon–Fri 11am–3pm; Sun–Thurs 5–10pm; Fri–Sat 5–11pm. THAI.

This stylish Thai restaurant is a couple of blocks from the village's tourist crush—far enough to ensure effortless parking in front of their romantic patio. The food here is excellent, with a polished presentation and expert renditions of the classics like pad Thai, satay, curry, and glazed duck. The so-called starters listed can often sound as good as the entrees—consider making a grazing meal out of house specialties like "Gold Bags" (minced pork, vegetables, and herbs wrapped in crispy rice paper and served with earthy plum sauce) or minced roast duck spiced with chiles and lime juice; spicy calamari is flavored with ginger, cilantro, lime, and chili sauce. This insider's secret is poised to explode with popularity.

MODERATELY PRICED OPTIONS

Putnam's Restaurant & Bar. In the Colonial Inn, 910 Prospect St. ☎ **619/454-2181.** Reservations recommended. Main courses $18–$23; early-bird specials $12.95 (daily 5–8pm). AE, CB, DC, MC, V. Mon–Fri 7–10am and 11am–2:30pm; Sat–Sun 7am–2:30pm; Sun–Thurs 5–10pm; Fri–Sat 5–11pm. Free valet parking. CALIFORNIA.

When the Colonial Inn was completed in 1928 it housed a drugstore named Putnam's, known in La Jolla as "Putty's." Gregory Peck's father was the pharmacist, and locals flocked there to buy their sundries and enjoy a soda. Today, that corner of the hotel is the site of Putnam's Restaurant, which retains an elegant, old-world atmosphere, complete with polished terrazzo floors, gleaming woodwork, brass fixtures, crisp white tablecloths, and fresh flowers. The dinner menu changes seasonally, but often contains grilled farm-raised chicken with honey-onion marmalade, grilled marinated duck breast with golden tomato-curry sauce, grilled Atlantic salmon fillet, and roasted rack of lamb with mustard herb crust. This is also a popular spot for breakfast and weekend brunch.

✪ **Trattoria Acqua.** 1298 Prospect St., in Coast Walk, La Jolla. ☎ **619/454-0709.** www.trattoriaacqua.com. Reservations recommended. Main courses $13–$22. AE, MC, V. Daily 11:30am–2:30pm; Sun–Thurs 5–9:30pm; Fri–Sat 5–10:30pm. Validated self-parking available. ITALIAN.

Nestled into tiled patio terraces close enough to catch ocean breezes, this excellent northern Italian spot's relaxed ambiance evokes a romantic Tuscan villa. A mixed crowd of suits and well-heeled couples gather to enjoy expertly prepared seasonal dishes; every table starts with bread served with a pungent Mediterranean spread. Acqua's pastas (available as appetizers or main courses) are as good as it gets—rich and heady flavor combinations like spinach, chard, and four-cheese gnocchi, or veal and mortadella tortellini in fennel cream sauce. Other specialties include *saltimboca con funghi* (veal scallopini with sage, prosciutto, and a forest-mushroom sauce), and traditional meat-and-white-bean cassoulet. The well-chosen wine list has received *Wine Spectator* accolades several years in a row.

CORONADO
SUPER-CHEAP EATS

Primavera Pastry Caffé. 956 Orange Ave. ☎ **619/435-4191.** Main courses $4–$6. MC, V. Daily 6:30am–6pm. SANDWICHES/LIGHT FARE.

This fantastic little cafe is the best of it's kind on the island. In addition to fresh-roasted coffee and espresso drinks, they serve up omelets and other breakfast treats (until 1:30pm), burgers and deli sandwiches on their own delicious bread, and a daily fresh soup. It's the kind of spot where half the customers are greeted by name; locals rave about the "Yacht Club" sandwich, a croissant filled with yellowfin tuna, and the breakfast croissant, topped with scrambled ham and eggs and cheddar cheese. See if you can resist Primavera's fat, gooey glazed cinnamon buns.

FOR A FEW BUCKS MORE

Bay Beach Cafe. 1201 First St. (in the Ferry Landing Marketplace). ☎ **619/435-4900.** Reservations recommended for dinner on weekends. Main courses $9–$18; pub menu $6–$10. AE, DISC, MC, V. Mon–Fri 7–10:30am, 11am–4pm, and 5–10:30pm; Sat–Sun 7–11:30am, noon–4pm, and 5–10:30pm. Free parking. AMERICAN/SEAFOOD.

Contrary to its name, this loud and friendly gathering place isn't on the beach at all, but enjoys a prime perch on San Diego Bay. Diners gaze endlessly at the city skyline, which is dramatic by day and breathtaking at night; the cafe is quite popular at happy hour, when the setting sun glimmers on downtown's mirrored high-rises. The ferry docks at a wooden pier a few steps away, discharging passengers into this New England–fishing-village-themed complex of gift shops and restaurants. At the Bay Beach Cafe, the food takes a back seat to the view, but the pub menu of burgers, sandwiches salads, and appetizers is inexpensive and satisfying.

McP's Irish Pub. 1107 Orange Ave. ☎ **619/435-5280.** Main courses $5–$18. AE, DC, MC, V. Daily 11am–9pm; Sun brunch 10am–2pm. IRISH.

Authentic down to the aroma of stale beer, McP's says—or shouts, rather, to be heard over the din—"local." Regulars gather to socialize and enjoy the hearty mulligan stew, corned beef and cabbage, and fish-and-chips. The varied menu also features home-made soups, deli-style sandwiches, burgers, and daily specials. Lunch is served outdoors on the "Paddy-O." Nightly live entertainment—jazz or rock 'n' roll—draws a large blue-jeans-clad crowd, especially on Thursdays.

MODERATELY PRICED OPTIONS

Rhinoceros Cafe & Grill. 1166 Orange Ave. (between 10th and 11th sts.). ☎ **619/435-2121.** Main courses $8.95–$17.95. AE, DISC, MC, V. Mon–Fri 11am–2:45pm; Sat–Sun 8am–2:45pm; daily 5–9pm. AMERICAN.

With its quirky name and something-for-everyone menu, this light, bright bistro is a welcome addition to the Coronado dining scene. It's more casual than it looks from the street, and offers large portions, even if the kitchen is a little heavy-handed with sauces and spices. At lunch the penne à la vodka in a creamy tomato sauce is popular; favorite dinner specials are charbroiled swordfish with citrus glaze, halibut with cucumber dill sauce, and live Maine lobster. The menu is balanced with plenty of crispy fresh salads; breakfast is served on the weekends only. There's a good wine list, or you might decide to try Rhino Chaser's American Ale.

WORTH A SPLURGE

Chez Loma. 1132 Loma (off Orange Ave.). ☎ **619/435-0661.** Reservations recommended. Full dinners (appetizer, main course, side dish) $19–$26. Early-bird specials (daily 5–5:45pm) $13. AE, DC, MC, V. Daily 5–10pm; Sun 10am–2pm. FRENCH.

You'd be hard-pressed to find a more romantic dining spot than this intimate Victorian cottage filled with antiques and subdued candlelight. Tables are scattered throughout the house and on the enclosed garden terrace; an upstairs wine salon, reminiscent of a Victorian parlor, is a cozy spot for coffee or conversation. Among the creative entrees are salmon with smoked-tomato vinaigrette and roasted duckling with green-peppercorn sauce. Follow dinner with a creamy crème caramel or Kahlúa crème brûlée. Chez Loma's service is attentive, and the herb rolls are addictive.

BARGAIN BITES: ONLY IN SAN DIEGO

WOOD-FIRED PIZZA   It all started with Wolfgang Puck, that crafty Austrian chef who dazzled Hollywood restaurant-goers at Spago, and later went on to build a dynasty of California cuisine. By now, everyone is familiar with the building block of that empire; heck, you can even get it in the frozen-food section. We're talking about pizza, of course—and not the marinara-and-pepperoni variety found in other pizza meccas like New York and Chicago. There's now a whole generation of Californians to whom pizza will always mean barbecue chicken, tomato-basil, or goat cheese and sun-dried tomato. **Gourmet pizzas** appear to have overtaken the traditional variety in popularity, and kitchens all over San Diego stoke their wood-fired ovens to keep up with the demand.

Many Italian restaurants in the city feature at least a handful of individual-size pizzas, including **D'Lish** in La Jolla (☎ **619/459-8118**), which has almost 20 eclectic topping variations borrowed from various ethnic cuisines. Always tops in San Diego polls is ✪ **Sammy's California Woodfired Pizza,** with locations in the Gaslamp Quarter at 770 Fourth Ave. at F Street (☎ **619/230-8888**); in La Jolla's village at 702 Pearl St. at Draper Street (☎ **619/456-8018**); and in Del Mar at 12925 El Camino Real at Del Mar Heights Road (☎ **619/259-6600**). Conveniently located and always frustratingly crowded, Sammy's serves up creations like duck sausage, potato garlic, or Jamaican jerk shrimp atop their 10-inch rounds. They also excel at enormous salads, making it easy to share a meal and save a bundle.

A similar menu is available at **Pizza Nova,** a similarly stylish minichain with a similarly vibrant atmosphere. You'll find Pizza Nova in Hillcrest at 3755 Fifth Ave., north of University Street (☎ **619/296-6682**); in Point Loma at 5120 N. Harbor Dr., west of Nimitz Boulevard (☎ **619/226-0268**); and in La Jolla's Golden Triangle at 8650 Genessee Ave., at Noble Drive (☎ **619/458-9525**).

If you're a purist at heart, or are unfamiliar with this trend's granddaddy, head over to Mission Valley and San Diego's new branch of **Wolfgang Puck Café,** 1640 Camino del Rio N., in Mission Valley Center (☎ **619/295-9653**). Like its cousins throughout southern California, the casual cafe has a dizzying decor, loud music, and an army of fresh-faced wait staff ferrying much more than pizza.

✪ **BAJA FISH TACOS**   One of San Diego's culinary ironies is that for a city so conscious of its Hispanic roots—not to mention within visual range of the Mexican border—it's hard to find anything other than gringo-ized combo plates in most of the area's Mexican restaurants. Perhaps the most authentic recipes are those found inside humble **Rubio's Baja Grill.** Actually, it's not so humble anymore, since proprietor Ralph Rubio began branching out into every corner of southern California with his enormously successful yet deceptively simple fare; you can now find Rubio's in Phoenix, Las Vegas, Los Angeles, and even edging out hot dogs in the stands at San Diego's own Qualcomm Stadium. But, back in 1983, it was an achievement for local surfer Rubio to open a tiny walk-up taco stand on busy Mission Bay Drive. After years of scarfing down cheap beers and fish tacos in the Mexican fishing village of San Felipe, Ralph secured the "secret" recipe for this quintessentially Baja treat; batter-dipped, deep-fried fish fillets folded in corn tortillas and garnished with shredded cabbage, salsa, and tangy *crema* sauce. You'll find them dispensed from thatched-roof shacks along Baja's beach roads, and in the past decade they've taken this side of the border by storm. Rubio's has since expanded its menu to include beefy *carne asada,* marinated pork *carnitas,* char-grilled mahimahi, and homemade guacamole, all accented by the distinctively Baja flavors of fresh lime and tangy cilantro. Unlike at your average McDrive-thru, you can wash it all down with an icy cold beer. Because many of the newer locations have a homogenous fast-food look to them, it's fun to stop by the original stand if you're in the neighborhood, 4504 E. Mission Bay Dr., at Bunker Hill Street (☎ 619/272-2801).

Rubio's also has locations in the Gaslamp Quarter, 901 Fourth St., at E Street (☎ 619/231-7731); Hillcrest, 3900 Fifth Ave., at University (☎ 619/299-8873); La Jolla, 8855 Villa La Jolla Dr., at Nobel Drive (☎ 619/546-9377); Pacific Beach, 910 Grand Ave. (☎ 619/270-4800); and Point Loma, 3555 Rosecrans St., at Midway Drive (☎ 619/223-2631).

5 The Main Attractions: The Zoo, the Wild Animal Park & Sea World

✪ **San Diego Zoo.** Park Blvd. and Zoo Place, Balboa Park. ☎ 619/234-3153. TDD 619/233-9639. www.sandiegozoo.org. Admission $16 adults, $7 children 3–11, free for children under 3 and military in uniform. Deluxe package (including admission, guided bus tour, and round-trip Skyfari aerial tram): $22 adults, $19.80 seniors 60 and over, $12 children. Combination Zoo/Wild Animal Park Package $33.55 adults, $19.95 children; includes deluxe package at zoo and admission to the WAP and is valid for 5 days from date of purchase. DISC, MC, V. Open daily year-round 9am–4pm; grounds close at 5pm. Extended summer hours 9am–9pm; grounds close at 10pm. Bus: 7/7B.

More than 4,000 animals reside at this world-famous zoo, founded in 1916 with a handful of animals originally brought here for the 1915–16 Panama-California International Exposition. The zoo's founder was Dr. Harry Wegeforth, a local physician and lifelong animal lover who once braved the fury of an injured tiger in order to toss needed medicine into its mouth while it was roaring.

Today, two giant pandas on loan from China are the big attention-getters, but the zoo has many other rare and exotic species: cuddly koalas from Australia, long-billed kiwis from New Zealand, wild Przewalski's horses from Mongolia, lowland gorillas from Africa, and giant tortoises from the Galapagos. The usual lions, elephants, giraffes, and tigers are present, too, not to mention a great number of tropical birds. Most of the animals are housed in barless, moated enclosures that resemble their natural habitats. The zoo is also an accredited botanical garden, with more than 6,000 species of flora from many climate zones installed to help simulate native environments for the animals who live here.

The **Children's Zoo** is scaled to a youngster's viewpoint. There's a nursery with baby animals and a petting area where kids can cuddle up to sheep, goats, and the like. The resident wombat is a special favorite here.

The zoo offers two types of **bus tours;** both provide a narrated overview and show you about 75% of the park. You can choose the 35-minute guided bus tour, which completes a circuit around the zoo; the cost is $4 for adults and $3 for kids 3 to 11 (there's a daily tour in Spanish at noon). Or you might opt to take the Kangaroo Bus, which for $8 for adults and $5 for children provides unlimited use; you can get on and off the bus as many times as you desire at any of the eight stops and even complete the circuit more than once. Alternatively, you can get an aerial perspective via the **Skyfari,** which costs $1 per person each way. Packages are available which include zoo admission, bus tour, and Skyfari Tramway.

Sea World. 1720 S. Shores Rd., Mission Bay. ☎ **619/226-3901,** 714/939-6212 in L.A., TDD 619/226-3907. Admission $32.95 adults, $29.65 seniors 55 and older, $24.95 children 3–11, free for children 2 and under. Guided 90-min. behind-the-scenes tours $6 adults, $5 children 3–11 and seniors. Ticket sales stop 1½ hr. before closing. DISC, JCB, MC, V. Parking $5 per car, $7 per RV. June–Aug daily 9am–10pm; Sept–May daily 10am–5pm. Bus: 9 or 81. By car, exit I-5 west onto Sea World Dr. or from I-8 onto W. Mission Bay Dr. to Sea World Dr. E.

Sea World is one of the best-promoted attractions in California. The 150-acre, multi-million-dollar aquatic playground is a zoo and showplace for marine mammals, made politically correct with a nominally "educational" atmosphere. At its heart, Sea World is a family entertainment center where the performers are dolphins, otters, sea lions, walruses, and seals. Several successive 4-ton black-and-white killer whales have functioned as the park's mascot, all named Shamu. Shows are presented continuously throughout the day, while visitors rotate to various theaters to watch the performances.

The 2-acre hands-on area called Shamu's Happy Harbor encourages kids to handle everything, including a pretend pirate ship, with plenty of netted towers, tube crawls, slides, and chances to get wet. The newest attraction is Wild Arctic, a virtual-reality trip to the frozen north. Other draws include Baywatch at Sea World, a water-ski show named for the popular TV show, and Shamu Backstage, which makes it possible for visitors to get up close and personal with killer whales.

The **Dolphin Interaction Program** creates an opportunity for people to interact with bottlenose dolphins. Although this program stops short of allowing you to swim with the dolphins, you will wade waist-deep into the water and have plenty of time to stroke the mammals and give commands like the trainers. This 2-hour program (1 hour of education and instruction, 15 min. of wet-suit fitting, and 45 min. in the water with the dolphins) costs $125 per person, which includes a second Sea World admission within a week. Space is limited to eight people per day, so advance reservations are required. Participants must be 13 years old or older.

Although Sea World is best known as Shamu's home, the facility also plays an important role in rescuing and rehabilitating animals found beached along the San Diego coast—more than 300 seals, sea lions, marine birds, and dolphins in a recent year. Following the successful rescue and 1998 release of a young California gray whale, Sea World turned its attention to the tropical manatee, and currently has several on display.

Budget tip: The best deal is the discount for AAA members. The next best is the coupon in the Visitor Value Pack available from the International Visitor Center.

San Diego Attractions

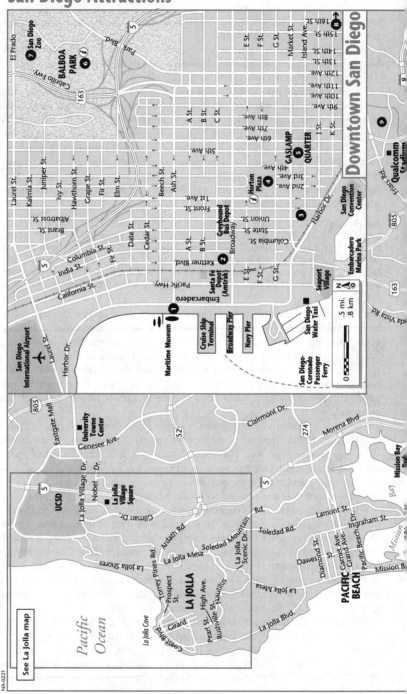

Downtown San Diego

San Diego International Airport

Maritime Museum ①

Cruise Ship Terminal

Broadway Pier

Navy Pier

San Diego Water Taxi

San Diego–Coronado Passenger Ferry

Seaport Village

Embarcadero Marina Park

San Diego Convention Center

Embarcadero

Santa Fe Depot (Amtrak) ②

Greyhound Bus Depot

Kettner Blvd.

Pacific Hwy.

Harbor Dr.

Laurel St.

Harbor Dr.

California St.

Columbia St.

India St.

Fir St.

Date St.

Cedar St.

Beech St.

Ash St.

A St.

B St.

C St.

5th Ave.

4th Ave.

6th Ave.

7th Ave.

8th Ave.

9th Ave.

10th Ave.

11th Ave.

12th Ave.

13th St.

14th St.

15th St.

16th St. ⑧

Market St.

Island Ave.

E St.

F St.

G St.

I St.

K St.

GASLAMP QUARTER ⑤

Horton Plaza ④

Front St.

Union St.

State St.

Columbia St.

Broadway

1st Ave.

2nd Ave.

3rd Ave.

③

Laurel St.

Kalmia St.

Juniper St.

Ivy St.

Hawthorn St.

Grape St.

Fir St.

Elm St.

Brant St.

Albatross St.

Park Blvd.

El Prado

San Diego Zoo ⑦

BALBOA PARK ⑥ ⓘ

Cabrillo Fwy.

163

5

Qualcomm Stadium

Friars Rd.

⑨

805

163

da Vista Rd.

N

.5 mi.

.8 km

0

See La Jolla map

Pacific Ocean

La Jolla Cove

Coast Blvd.

Girard

Pearl St.

High Ave.

Nautilus

Bushville St.

Prospect St.

LA JOLLA

La Jolla Blvd.

Torrey Pines Rd.

La Jolla Shores

Ardath Rd.

La Jolla Mesa

Soledad Mountain

La Jolla Scenic Dr.

Soledad Rd.

La Jolla Mesa

Lamont St.

Diamond St.

Dawes St.

Garnet Ave.

Grand Ave.

Ingraham St.

Pacific Beach

PACIFIC BEACH

Mission B

Mission Bay

Mission

Bay

Clairmont Dr.

Morena Blvd

274

52

5

805

Eastgate Mall

University Towne Center

Genesee Ave.

UCSD

La Jolla Village Dr.

Nobel Dr.

Gilman Dr.

La Jolla Village Square

NA-0221

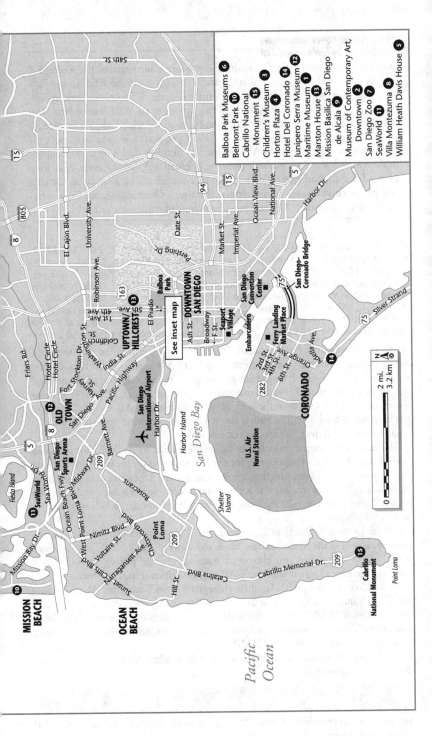

Balboa Park Museums **6**
Belmont Park **10**
Cabrillo National
Monument **15**
Children's Museum **3**
Horton Plaza **4**
Hotel Del Coronado **14**
Junipero Serra Museum **12**
Maritime Museum **1**
Marston House **13**
Mission Basilica San Diego
de Alcala **9**
Museum of Contemporary Art,
Downtown **2**
San Diego Zoo **7**
SeaWorld **11**
Villa Montezuma **8**
William Heath Davis House **5**

Zoo Deals & Discounts

Here's a money-saving tip: Two adults can become members of the Zoological Society for $68; this includes unlimited access to the zoo and the Wild Animal Park for 1 year plus two guest passes to either the zoo or the Wild Animal Park, six discount passes, four twofer bus passes, and free parking at the Wild Animal Park. This is a great deal when you consider that even the combo-package admission price for two adults to these two attractions is $67.10. If you don't buy the annual pass, the best discount is the one for AAA members. The next best deal is using the coupons in the Visitor Value Pack available from the International Visitor Center. Also, keep in mind that the San Diego Zoo is free to everyone on the 1st Monday in October and free to children ages 11 and under all through October. A Koala Club membership for a child costs $15 and provides unlimited entry for a year.

✪ **Wild Animal Park.** 15500 San Pasqual Valley Rd., Escondido. ☎ **760/747-8702.** TDD 760/738-5067. www.sandiegozoo.org. Admission $19.95 adults, $17.95 seniors 60 and over, $12.95 children 3–11, free for children 2 and under and military in uniform. Combination Zoo/Wild Animal Park Package, $33.55 adults, $19.95 children; includes deluxe package at zoo and admission to WAP and is valid for 5 days from date of purchase. DISC, MC, V. Daily 9am–4pm (grounds close at 5pm); extended hours during the summer and the Festival of Lights in December. Parking $3. See "Zoo Deals & Discounts," above. Take I-15 to Via Rancho Pkwy.; follow signs from here for about 3 miles.

Many zoos could learn a lesson from the Wild Animal Park: More than 3,000 animals, many of them endangered species, roam freely over 1,800 acres—it's the humans who are enclosed. This living arrangement encourages breeding colonies, so it's not surprising that more than 75 white rhinoceroses have been born here. Several other species that had vanished from the wilds have been reintroduced to their natural habitats from stocks bred here. The park is also is a botanical preserve with more than two million plants, including 300 species and subspecies.

The best way to see the animals is by riding the 5-mile Wgasa Bush Line monorail (included in the price of admission); for the best views, sit on the right side. During the 50-minute ride, as you pass through areas resembling Africa and Asia, you'll learn interesting tidbits (did you know that rhinos are susceptible to sunburn and mosquito bites?). Trains leave every 20 minutes; you can watch informative videos while you wait in the stations.

On the 1¾-mile Kilimanjaro Safari Walk, you'll see tigers, elephants, and cheetahs close up, as well as the Australian rain forest and views of East Africa. There are three animal shows a day, and you also won't want to miss the petting kraal, Lorikeet Landing, Mombasa Lagoon, and the WAP's newest exhibit, Heart of Africa.

Photo Caravans take place May through September on Wednesday, Thursday, Saturday, and Sunday and cost $60 or $85 (depending on the tour). The most intriguing new program at WAP is the summer-only overnight camp-out program called **Roar and Snore.** To request information by mail, call ☎ **760/738-5049;** reservations can be made by calling ☎ **800/934-CAMP.**

Stroller and wheelchair rentals are available. Take a jacket along—it can get cold in the open-air monorail.

6 San Diego's Best Beaches

San Diego County is blessed with 70 miles of sandy coastline and more than 30 beaches that attract surfers, snorkelers, swimmers, and sunbathers. In summer, the

San Diego & North County Beaches

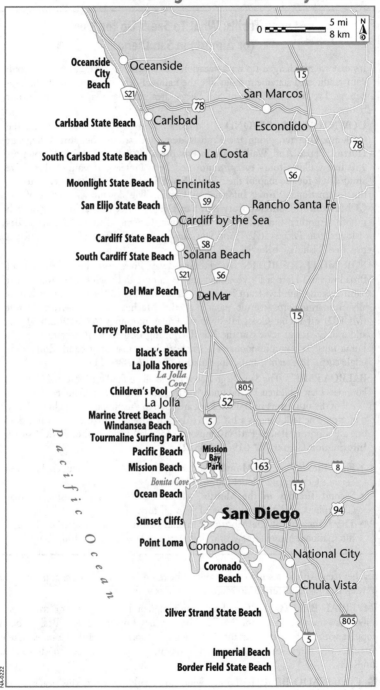

0 — 5 mi
0 — 8 km

N

Oceanside City Beach
Oceanside
S21
San Marcos
Carlsbad State Beach
Carlsbad
78
Escondido
78
South Carlsbad State Beach
5
La Costa
S6
Moonlight State Beach
Encinitas
San Elijo State Beach
S9
Rancho Santa Fe
Cardiff by the Sea
Cardiff State Beach
S8
South Cardiff State Beach
Solana Beach
S21
S6
Del Mar Beach
Del Mar
15
Torrey Pines State Beach
Black's Beach
La Jolla Shores
La Jolla Cove
Children's Pool
805
La Jolla
52
Marine Street Beach
Windansea Beach
5
Tourmaline Surfing Park
Pacific Beach
Mission Bay Park
Mission Beach
163
8
Bonita Cove
Ocean Beach
15
San Diego
94
Sunset Cliffs
Point Loma
Coronado
National City
Coronado Beach
Chula Vista
Silver Strand State Beach
805
5
Imperial Beach
Border Field State Beach

Pacific Ocean

NA-0222

619

Cheap Thrills: What to See & Do for Free (or Almost) in San Diego

It's easy to get charged up on a vacation—$10 here, $5 there, and pretty soon your credit-card statement looks like the national debt. To keep that from happening, I've compiled a list of San Diego–area activities that won't break your budget.

DOWNTOWN & BEYOND   It doesn't cost a penny to stroll around the **Gaslamp Quarter,** along the Embarcadero, and around **Seaport Village** or **Horton Plaza.** And **Walkabout International** (☎ 619/231-7463) sponsors 150 free walking tours every month, led by volunteers. If you'd rather drive around, ask for the map of the 52-mile **San Diego Scenic Drive** when you're at the International Visitor Information Center. The downtown branch of the ✪ **Museum of Contemporary Art, San Diego,** is free the 1st Tuesday of each month. Another fun activity is the Sunset Cinema discussed below under "Movies, San Diego–Style." And you can fish free of charge off any municipal pier (see "Fishing," below).

FOR MILITARY BUFFS   At the **Broadway Pier,** near the intersection of Broadway and Harbor Drive, a navy ship is in port and open for free tours most Saturdays and Sundays from 1 to 4pm (☎ 619/532-1430, ext. 9). There is usually a marine-corps–recruit parade at the **Marine Corps Recruit Depot (MCRD)** off Pacific Coast Highway on Friday mornings (☎ 619/225-3141); and a navy recruit review at the **Naval Training Center** off Rosecrans in Point Loma most Friday afternoons at 1:15, featuring a marching band, drum-and-bugle corps, flag teams, and color guards (☎ 619/225-5311).

BALBOA PARK   The San Diego Zoo is free to all on the 1st Monday of October, Founders Day. Children 11 and under are free every day during October.

   All of the **museums in Balboa Park** are open to the public free of charge 1 day a month. The following is a list of free days; if you can't get there on a free day, buy a Passport to Balboa Park (10 museums for $18) at the **Balboa Park Visitors Information Center** (☎ 619/239-0512).

- **First Tuesday of the Month**   Natural History Museum, Reuben H. Fleet Science Center, and Model Railroad Museum.
- **Second Tuesday of the Month**   Museum of Photographic Arts, Hall of Champions, and Museum of San Diego History.
- **Third Tuesday of the Month**   Museum of Art, Museum of Man, Mingei International Museum of World Folk Art, and Japanese Friendship Garden.

beaches teem with locals and visitors alike. The rest of the year, they are popular places to walk and jog, and surfers don wet suits to pursue their passion.

IMPERIAL BEACH   Half an hour south of San Diego by car or trolley, and only a few minutes from the Mexican border, lies Imperial Beach. Besides being popular with surfers, it hosts the Annual U. S. Open Sandcastle Competition in August, with world-class sand creations ranging from sea scenes to dragons to dinosaurs.

✪ **CORONADO BEACH**   Lovely, wide, and sparkling white, this beach is conducive to strolling and lingering, especially in the late afternoon. It fronts Ocean Boulevard and is especially pretty in front of the Hotel del Coronado. The islands

- **Fourth Tuesday of the Month** San Diego Aerospace Museum and San Diego Automotive Museum.

The following attractions in Balboa Park are **always free:** the Botanical Building and Lily Pond, the House of Pacific Relations International Cottages, and the Timken Museum of Art.

Free 1-hour Sunday **concerts** and free Summer Festival concerts are given at the **Spreckels Organ Pavilion.**

OLD TOWN You can walk around **Heritage Park, Presidio Park,** or **Old Town State Historic Park** without paying a dime, and there's no charge to enjoy the entertainment (mariachis and folk dancers) at the **Bazaar del Mundo** on Saturday and Sunday. There's also no admission charge to **Mission Trails Regional Park,** where there are hiking trails and an interpretive center. Admission to **Mission Basilica San Diego de Alcala** is a suggested $2 donation.

MISSION BAY & PACIFIC BEACH Walk along the beach or around the bay—not only is it free and fun, it's good for you.

LA JOLLA Enjoy the ✪ **free outdoor concerts at Scripps Park** on Sundays from 2 to 4pm, mid-June through mid-September (☎ **619/525-3160**). Anytime is a good time to take a walk around the **La Jolla Cove, Ellen Browning Scripps Park,** and ✪ **Torrey Pines State Reserve.** As you walk along the ocean in La Jolla you're bound to notice the harbor-seal colony at the **Children's Pool** (near the intersection of Coast Boulevard and Jenner). If you're a diver, check out the 6,000-acre **San Diego–La Jolla Underwater Park,** which stretches from La Jolla Cove to the northern end of Torrey Pines State Reserve. It's also fun to meander around the campus of **University of California at San Diego (UCSD)** and view the Stuart Collection of Outdoor Sculpture. The La Jolla branch of the ✪ **Museum of Contemporary Art,** San Diego, is free the 1st Tuesday of each month. For the best vista, follow the SCENIC DRIVE signs to Mt. Soledad and a 360° view of the area.

CORONADO Drive across the **Coronado Bay Bridge** (free for two or more people in a car) and take a self-guided tour of the ✪ **Hotel del Coronado's** grounds and photo gallery. Take a walk on the beach and continue on to the **Coronado Beach Historical Museum.**

visible from here, but 18 miles away, are named "Los Coronados," and they belong to Mexico.

OCEAN BEACH The northern end of Ocean Beach Park is officially known as **Dog Beach,** and is one of only two in San Diego where your pooch can roam freely on the sand (and frolic with several dozen other people's pooches). Surfers generally congregate around the Ocean Beach Pier, where rip currents are strong and discourage most swimmers from venturing out beyond waist-depth. Facilities at the beach include rest rooms, showers, picnic tables, and plenty of metered parking lots.

MISSION BAY PARK In this 4,600-acre aquatic playground, you'll discover 27 miles of bay front, 17 miles of oceanfront beaches, picnic areas, children's

It's a Dog's Beach

If your canine companion is eager to put paw to sand, head to either the northern end of Ocean Beach, a.k.a. "Dog Beach," or Fiesta Island in Mission Bay; these are the only two San Diego beaches where pooches get free reign.

playgrounds, and paths for biking, roller skating, and jogging. The bay lends itself to windsurfing, sailing, jet-skiing, waterskiing, and fishing. There are dozens of access points; one of the most popular is off I-5 at Clairemont Drive, where there's a visitor information center.

MISSION BEACH   While Mission Bay Park is a body of salt water surrounded by land and bridges, Mission Beach is actually a beach on the Pacific Ocean. Surfing is popular year-round here. The long beach and boardwalk extend from Pacific Beach Drive south to Belmont Park and beyond to the jetty.

PACIFIC BEACH   Pacific Beach is the home of **Tourmaline Surfing Park,** where the sport's old guard gather to surf waters where swimmers are prohibited; and there's always some action along Ocean Front Walk, a paved promenade featuring a human parade akin to that at L.A.'s Venice Beach boardwalk. It runs along Ocean Boulevard (just west of Mission Boulevard), north of Pacific Beach Drive.

WINDANSEA   The fabled locale of Tom Wolfe's *Pump House Gang,* Windansea is legendary to this day among California's surf elite. Reached via Bonair Street (at Neptune Place), Windansea has no facilities, and street parking is first-come, first-served. Come to surf, watch surfers, or soak in the camaraderie and party atmosphere of Windansea locals.

CHILDREN'S POOL BEACH   Much of the sand near the point of La Jolla's peninsula is cordoned off for the resident sea-lion population; the rest is inhabited by curious shutterbugs and families taking advantage of the same calm conditions that keep the sea lions around. The beach is located at Coast Boulevard and Jenner Street; there's limited free street parking.

LA JOLLA COVE   The protected, calm waters here—praised as the clearest along the California coast—attract swimmers, snorkelers, scuba divers, and families alike. There's a small sandy beach, and on the cliffs above, the Ellen Browning Scripps Park. The cove's "look but don't touch" policy protects the colorful marine life in this Underwater Park. La Jolla Cove can be accessed from Coast Boulevard.

LA JOLLA SHORES BEACH   The wide, flat mile of sand at La Jolla Shores is popular with joggers, swimmers, and beginning body and board surfers, as well as with families. Weekend crowds can be enormous, though, quickly occupying both the sand and the metered parking spaces in the beach's lot. There are rest rooms, showers, and picnic areas.

BLACK'S BEACH   The area's unofficial (and illegal) nude beach lies north of La Jolla Shores Beach, below some steep cliffs. Black's isn't easy to reach—take North Torrey Pines Road, park at the Glider Port, and walk down from there. *Note:* Although the water is shallow and pleasant for wading, this area is known for its rip currents.

7 Exploring the Area

BALBOA PARK

Balboa Park is one of the nation's largest, loveliest, and most important municipal greenbelts. This is no simple city park; it boasts walkways, gardens, historical

Balboa Park

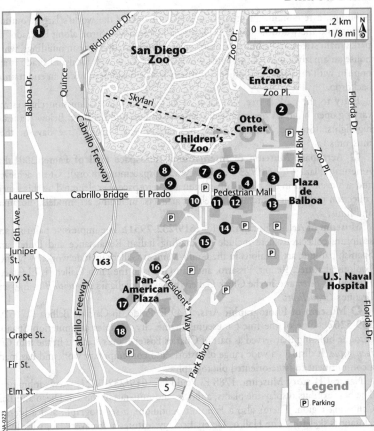

buildings, a restaurant, an ornate pavilion with one of the world's largest outdoor organs, and the world-famous San Diego Zoo (see above). Stroll along El Prado, the park's main street, and admire the distinctive Spanish/Mediterranean buildings, which house an amazing array of museums. Filled on weekends with locals, El Prado is also popular with musicians and other performers whose busking provides an entertaining backdrop.

Entry to the park is free, but most of its museums have admission charges and varying open hours. A free tram will transport you around the park. Below is a list of highlights. (See the "Cheap Thrills" box, above, for a list of free days at these museums.)

✪ **Aerospace Museum & International Aerospace Hall of Fame,** 2001 Pan American Plaza (☎ **619/234-8291;** www.aerospacemuseum.org): Great achievers and achievements in the history of aviation and aerospace are celebrated by this superb collection of historical aircraft and related artifacts, including art, models, dioramas, and films.

Museum of Art, 1450 El Prado (☎ **619/232-7931**): The impressive painting and sculpture collections here include outstanding Italian Renaissance and Dutch and Spanish baroque art. Exhibits in the Grant-Munger Gallery include works by Monet, Toulouse-Lautrec, Renoir, Pissarro, and van Gogh; in the Fitch Gallery is El Greco's *Penitent St. Peter,* and in the Gluck Gallery hangs Modigliani's *Boy with Blue Eyes* and Braque's *Coquelicots.*

✪ **Museum of Photographic Arts,** 1649 El Prado, in Casa de Balboa (☎ **619/ 239-5262**): One of the finest museums in the city occupies an imitation Spanish baroque building that served as part of Charles Foster Kane's Xanadu in the film *Citizen Kane.* It displays a wide range of historic and contemporary work and has made a commitment to issue-oriented photography.

Natural History Museum, 1788 El Prado (☎ **619/232-3821;** www.sdnhm.org): The best exhibits display the plants, animals, and minerals of the San Diego and Baja California region. There's also a Foucault pendulum, a seismograph, and a life-size allosaurus skeleton. The Hall of Desert Ecology features a discovery lab, with living desert denizens.

✪ **Reuben H. Fleet Science Center,** 1875 El Prado (☎ **619/238-1233,** or 619/232-6866 for advance ticket sales; www.rhfleet.org): Easily the park's busiest museum, the Science Center features five galleries with hands-on exhibits as intriguing for grown-ups as for kids. In 1998 they debuted SciTours, a simulator ride that voyages into space and the worlds of science and biology. Equally popular is the OMNIMAX movie theater, surrounding viewers with breathtaking adventure travelogues. You can avoid waiting in line by buying tickets in advance.

Museum of Man, 1350 El Prado (☎ **619/239-2001**): This museum is devoted to the sociology and anthropology of the peoples of North and South America and includes life-size replicas of a dozen varieties of Homo sapiens.

San Diego Automotive Museum, 2080 Pan American Plaza (☎ **619/231-2886**): Check out that classic Bentley and the rare 1948 Tucker, among other gems that appear in a changing array of shows featuring classic, antique, and exotic cars.

Botanical Building (☎ **619/235-1100** for information): More than a thousand varieties of tropical and flowering plants are sheltered within this graceful structure, and the lily pond out front attracts the occasional street performer.

Hall of Champions, 1649 El Prado, in Casa de Balboa (☎ **619/234-2544**): Sports fans will want to check out this museum, which highlights dozens of different professional and amateur sports and athletes.

Japanese Friendship Garden, 2216 Pan America Rd. (☎ **619/232-2780**): Though parts of the garden are still being developed, visitors can sample the tranquillity of traditional elements like a koi-filled stream, pastoral meadow, and ancient *sekitei* (sand-and-stone garden).

Marston House Museum, 3525 Seventh Ave., at Upas Street, in the northwest corner of the park (☎ **619/232-6203**): Designed by local architect Irving Gill, this fine example of Craftsman-style architecture exhibits fine antique and reproduction period furniture.

Model Railroad Museum, 1649 El Prado, in Casa de Balboa (☎ **619/696-0199**): Four scale-model railroads depict southern California's transportation history and terrain. There's a terrific gift shop, plus multimedia exhibits and hands-on Lionel trains for kids.

Museum of San Diego History, 1649 El Prado, in Casa de Balboa (☎ **619/232-6203**): Photographs and other changing exhibits tell the city's story.

Spreckels Organ Pavilion (☎ **619/226-0819**): The ornate pavilion houses a fantastic organ with more than 4,000 individual pipes. Free concerts are given Sunday at 2pm year-round and on summer evenings.

Timken Museum of Art, 1500 El Prado (☎ **619/239-5548**): On display here is the Putnam Foundation's collection of American and European paintings, including works by Boucher, Rembrandt, and Brueghel. The private gallery also exhibits a rare collection of Russian icons and 19th-century American paintings.

Mingei International Museum, 1439 El Prado, in the House of Charm (☎ **619/239-0003**): Its name means "art of the people" in Japanese, and it offers changing exhibitions celebrating human creativity with textiles, costumes, jewelry, toys, pottery, paintings, and sculpture, all employing natural materials. This is one of only two major museums in the United States devoted to crafts on a worldwide scale (the other is in Santa Fe).

Christmas on the Prado takes place in Balboa Park from 5 to 9pm on the 1st Friday and Saturday nights in December. This popular event features free entry to all museums, carol singing in the Spreckels Organ Pavilion, holiday decorations, and various food booths.

MORE ATTRACTIONS IN & AROUND SAN DIEGO

✪ **Cabrillo National Monument.** 1800 Cabrillo Memorial Dr., Point Loma. ☎ **619/557-5450.** Admission $4 per vehicle, $2 for walk-ins; ages 62 and over (with a National Parks Service Golden Age Passport) and 16 and younger free. Daily 9am–5:15pm. Follow I-5 or I-8 to Rosecrans St. (Calif. 209), which leads to Point Loma and the monument via Catalina Blvd.

Enjoy stunning views while you learn about California history at this monument commemorating Juan Rodríguez Cabrillo, the European discoverer of America's west coast. At the restored Old Point Loma Lighthouse, you'll be treated to a sweeping vista of the ocean, bays, islands, mountains, valleys, and plains that make up San Diego. Visit between mid-December and mid-March, and you can see the annual California gray whale migration from a glassed-in observatory; films and other educational exhibits are offered on the whales. A road leads to tide pools that beg for exploration.

Children's Museum of San Diego. 200 W. Island Ave. ☎ **619/233-8792.** Admission $5 for adults and children over 2, $3 for seniors; free for children under 2. Tues–Sun 10am–5pm. Closed most Mon. Trolley: Convention Center stop; the museum is a block away.

This interactive museum encourages hands-on participation and provides ongoing supervised activities, as well as a special celebration and changing exhibits every month. A big draw for kids ages 2 to 10 is the indoor and outdoor art studio. There's also a theater with costumes for budding actors to don.

Maritime Museum. 1306 N. Harbor Dr. ☎ **619/234-9153.** Admission $5 adults, $4 seniors over 62 and teens 13–17, $2 children 6–12, free for children 5 and under. Daily 9am–8pm. Trolley: America Plaza.

This unique museum consists of a trio of fine ships: the full-rigged merchant ship *Star of India* (1863), whose impressive masts are an integral part of the San Diego cityscape; the gleaming white San Francisco–Oakland steam-powered ferryboat *Berkeley* (1898), which worked round-the-clock to carry people to safety following the 1906 San Francisco earthquake; and the sleek steam yacht *Medea* (1904), one of the world's few remaining large steam yachts. You can board and explore each vessel, and from April through October you can watch movies on deck (see "Movies, San Diego–Style" under "San Diego After Dark," below).

Museum of Contemporary Art, Downtown (MCA). 1001 Kettner Blvd. (at Broadway). ☎ **619/234-1001.** Admission $4 adults; $2 students, military with ID, and seniors; free for children 12 and under; free for everyone the 1st Tues of each month. Tues–Sat 10:30am–5pm; Fri 10:30am–8pm; Sun noon–5pm. Parking $2 with validation at America Plaza Complex. Trolley: America Plaza.

MCA Downtown is the second location of the Museum of Contemporary Art—the first is in La Jolla. Two large galleries and two smaller ones present changing exhibitions of distinguished contemporary artists. Lectures and tours for adults and children are offered.

Villa Montezuma. 1925 K St. (at 20th Ave.). ☎ **619/239-2211.** Admission $3 adults, $5 in combination with Marston House, free for children 12 and under. Sat–Sun noon–4:30pm; Dec Thurs–Sun noon–4:30pm. Bus: 3, 3A, 4, 5, 16, or 105 to Market and Imperial sts.

Just east of downtown, this stunning mansion was built in 1887 for then internationally acclaimed musician and author Jesse Shepard. Lush with Victoriana, it features stained-glass windows depicting Mozart, Beethoven, Sappho, Rubens, St. Cecilia (patron saint of musicians), and other notables. The San Diego Historical Society painstakingly restored the house, which is on the National Register of Historic Places, and furnished it with period pieces. If you love Victorian houses, don't miss this one for its quirkiness.

OLD TOWN & BEYOND: A LOOK AT CALIFORNIA'S BEGINNINGS

The birthplace of San Diego is Old Town, the hillside where the Spanish Presidio and Father Junípero Serra's mission (the first in California) were built. By protecting the remaining adobes and historic buildings, the **Old Town State Historic Park** brings to life Mexican California, which existed here until the mid-1800s. Much of the surrounding area, however, has become a mini–Mexican theme park. You can get to Old Town on the trolley or Coaster (see "Getting Around," above), and free walking tours leave daily at 2pm from the park's visitor center, 4002 Wallace St. (☎ **619/ 220-5422**).

Junípero Serra Museum. 2727 Presidio Dr., Presidio Park, Old Town. ☎ **619/297-3258.** Admission $3 adults, free for children 12 and under. Tues–Sat 10am–4:30pm; Sun noon–4:30pm. Take I-8 to Taylor St. exit; turn right on Taylor, then left on Presidio Dr. Or take a bus to the intersection of Taylor and Juan sts. and walk uphill.

Perched on a hill above Old Town, the stately mission-style building overlooks the hillside where California began. Here, in 1769, the first mission and first non-Indian settlement on the west coast of the United States and Canada were founded. Inside, the museum's exhibits introduce visitors to California's origins and to the native American,

Spanish, and Mexican people who first called this place home. On display are their belongings, from cannons to cookware; a Spanish furniture collection; and one of the first paintings brought to California, which survived being damaged in an Indian attack. The mission remained San Diego's only settlement until the 1820s, when families began to move down the hill into what is now known as Old Town. Here, you can also watch an ongoing archaeological dig uncovering more of the items used by early settlers. From the 70-foot tower, visitors can compare the spectacular view with historic photos to see how this land has changed over time.

Mission Basilica San Diego de Alcala. 10818 San Diego Mission Rd., Mission Valley. ☎ **619/281-8449.** Admission $2 adults, $1 seniors and students, 50¢ children 12 and under. Daily 9am–5pm; mass daily 7am and 5:30pm. Bus: 6, 16, 25, 43, or 81. Take I-8 to Mission Gorge Rd. to Twain Ave.

Established in 1769, this was the first link in the chain of 21 missions founded in California by Spanish missionary Junípero Serra. In 1774, the mission was moved to its present site for agricultural reasons and to separate Native American converts from a fortress that included the original building. A few bricks belonging to the original mission can be seen in Presidio Park in Old Town. Mass is held regularly in this still-active Catholic parish.

Whaley House. 2482 San Diego Ave. ☎ **619/298-2482.** Admission $4 adults, $3 seniors 65 and over, $2 children 5–18, free for children under 5. Daily 10am–5pm (until 4:30pm in winter).

In 1856, this striking two-story house (the first one in these parts) just outside Old Town State Historic Park was built for Thomas Whaley and his family. Whaley was a New Yorker who arrived here via San Francisco, where he had been lured by the gold rush. The house is one of only two authenticated haunted houses in California, and 10,000 schoolchildren come here each year to see for themselves. Exhibits include a life mask of Abraham Lincoln, one of only six made; the spinet piano used in the movie *Gone with the Wind;* and the concert piano that accompanied Swedish soprano Jenny Lind on her final U.S. tour in 1852.

MISSION BAY & THE BEACHES
This area is great for walking, jogging, in-line skating, biking, and boating; for details, see "Staying Active," below.

Giant Dipper Roller Coaster. 3146 Mission Blvd. ☎ **619/488-1549.** Sun–Thurs 11am–10pm; Fri–Sat 11am–11pm. Admission to park is free; ride on Giant Dipper is $3. Take I-5 to the Sea World exit, and follow W. Mission Bay Dr. to Belmont Park.

A local landmark for 70 years, the Giant Dipper is one of two surviving fixtures from the original Belmont Amusement Park (the other is The Plunge indoor swimming pool). This vintage wooden roller coaster underwent an extensive restoration and reopened in 1991.

The amusement park contains newer, carnival-style rides; you might also like to participate in the Dive-In Movies shown at The Plunge (☎ 619/488-3110), in which viewers float on rafts in 91°F water and watch water-related movies projected onto the wall. *Jaws* is a perennial favorite. (See "Movies, San Diego–Style" under "San Diego After Dark," below.)

LA JOLLA
Some folks just enjoy driving around La Jolla, taking in the sea views and the 360° vista from the top of Mt. Soledad. However, La Jolla also offers other attractions, including **Torrey Pines State Reserve** (☎ **619/755-2063**), which has an interpretive

center, hiking trails with wonderful ocean views, and a chance to see the rare torrey pine. Admission is free, as are the guided walks on Saturday and Sunday. Access is via North Torrey Pines Road; parking costs $4 per car, $3 for seniors.

✪ **Museum of Contemporary Art, San Diego.** 700 Prospect St. ☎ **619/ 454-3541.** Admission $4 adults; $2 students, military with ID, and seniors; free for children under 12; free for everyone the 1st Tues of each month. Tues–Sat 10am–5pm (Wed till 8pm); Sun noon–5pm.

Museum holdings include works from every major art movement of the past half century, with a strong representation by California artists and particularly noteworthy examples of minimalism, light and space work, conceptualism, installation, and site-specific art (including outdoor sculptures). The museum's facade was redesigned in 1997 to incorporate more of the original Irving Gill architecture, and the rear galleries feature outstanding ocean views.

Birch Aquarium at Scripps. 2300 Expedition Way, La Jolla. ☎ **619/534-FISH** (3474). Fax 619/534-7114. Admission $7.50 adults, $6.50 seniors, $4 youths 3–17, free for children under 3. Parking $3. Daily 9am–5pm. Take I-5 to La Jolla Village Dr. exit, go west 1 mile, and turn left at Expedition Way.

The aquarium-museum offers close-up views of the Pacific Ocean in 33 marine-life tanks. The giant kelp forest is particularly impressive. World-renowned for its oceanic research, Scripps offers visitors a chance to view its marine aquarium and artificial outdoor tide pools. The museum has interpretive exhibits on the current and historical research done at the institution, which has been in existence since 1903.

Stuart Collection. At the University of California San Diego (UCSD). ☎ **619/534-2117.** Free admission. Parking $6 weekdays, $3 weekends at parking meters. From La Jolla, take Torrey Pines Rd. to La Jolla Village Dr., turn right, go 2 blocks to Gilman Dr., and turn left into the campus; in about a block, the information booth will be visible on the right.

This is a work in progress on a large scale. The still-growing collection consists of site-related sculptures by leading contemporary artists placed throughout the 1,200-acre UCSD campus. Among the 12 diverse sculptures on view are Niki de Saint-Phalle's *Sun God,* a jubilant 14-foot fiberglass bird on a 15-foot concrete base, nicknamed "Big Bird" and adopted as an unofficial mascot by the students. Pick up a brochure and map with marked sculpture locations from the information booth at the Northview Drive or Gilman Drive entrance to the campus.

8 Staying Active

For coverage of the San Diego area's best beaches, see "San Diego's Best Beaches," earlier in this chapter.

BIKING & MOUNTAIN BIKING   Mission Bay and Coronado are especially good for leisurely bike rides. The boardwalks in Pacific Beach and Mission Beach can get very crowded, especially on weekends. Most major thoroughfares offer a bike lane. Just remember to wear a helmet; it's the law. For information on bike rentals, see "Getting Around," earlier in this chapter.

Adventure Bike Tours, based at the San Diego Marriott Marina (☎ **619/ 234-1500,** ext. 6514), offers a "Bay to Breakers" bike ride that starts in downtown San Diego and includes Coronado. The cost of $39 covers bikes, helmets, the ferry, and guiding.

BOATING   Club Nautico, at the San Diego Marriott Marina, 333 W. Harbor Dr. (☎ **619/233-9311;** fax 619/689-2363), provides you with an exhilarating way to see

La Jolla

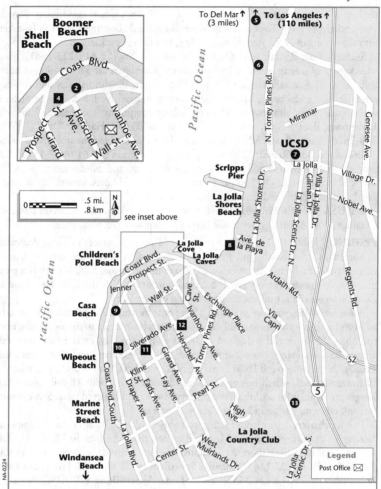

To Del Mar ↑ (3 miles) ⑤
To Los Angeles ↑ (110 miles)

Boomer Beach ❶
Shell Beach
Coast Blvd.
❸
❷
❹
Prospect St.
Girard
Herschel Ave.
Ivanhoe Ave.
Wall St.
⊠

Pacific Ocean

⑥

N. Torrey Pines Rd.

Miramar

UCSD ⑦
La Jolla

Villa La Jolla Dr.
Gilman Dr.
La Jolla Scenic Dr. N.

Village Dr.
Genesee Ave.
Nobel Ave.

Scripps Pier

La Jolla Shores Beach

La Jolla Shores Dr.

Ardath Rd.

Via Capri

Regents Rd.

0 .5 mi. / .8 km N
see inset above

La Jolla Cove
La Jolla Caves
❽

Children's Pool Beach
Coast Blvd.
Prospect St.
Jenner
Wall St.

Ave. de la Playa

Casa Beach
❾

Cave St.
Exchange Place

Ivanhoe Ave.
⑫
Silverado Ave.
Herschel Ave.
Torrey Pines Rd.
⑩
⑪
Girard Ave.
Kline St.
Fay Ave.
Eads Ave.
Draper Ave.
Pearl St.

Wipeout Beach

Marine Street Beach

Coast Blvd. South

La Jolla Blvd.

High Ave.

La Jolla Country Club

⑬

52
5

Windansea Beach ↓

Center St.
West Muirlands Dr.

La Jolla Scenic Dr. S.

Pacific Ocean

Legend
Post Office ⊠

NA-0224

ACCOMMODATIONS:
The Bed & Breakfast Inn at La Jolla ⑩
Empress Hotel of La Jolla ⑪
La Jolla Beach & Tennis Club ❽
La Jolla Cove Travelodge ⑫
Prospect Park Inn ❹

ATTRACTIONS:
Birch Aquarium at Scripps ⑥
Coast Walk ❸
Ellen Browning Scripps Park ❶
La Valencia Hotel ❷
Mount Soledad ⑬
Museum of Contemporary Art ❾
Stuart Collection ⑦
Torrey Pines State Reserve ⑤

the bay by the hour, half day, or full day in 20- to 27-foot offshore powerboats. Rentals start at $89 per hour. They also rent Waverunners and allow their boats to be taken into the ocean, and offer diving, waterskiing, and fishing packages.

Seaforth Boat Rental, 1641 Quivira Rd., Mission Bay (☎ 619/223-1681), has a wide variety of fishing boats for bay and ocean, powerboats for $50 to $90 per hour, and 14- to 27-foot sailboats for $20 to $45 per hour, all with half-day and full-day rates. Canoes, pedal boats, kayaks, and rowboats are available for those who prefer a slower pace. They also rent bicycles and fishing equipment (see "Fishing," below). **Downtown Boat Rental,** at the Marriott Marina, 333 W. Harbour Dr., (☎ 619/239-2628), has sailboats and kayaks for rent. They also offer lessons and guided tours.

Coronado Boat Rental, 1715 Strand Way, in Coronado (☎ 619/437-1514), has powerboats renting from $65 to $90 per hour, with half- and full-day rates; 14- to 30-foot sailboats from $25 to $40 per hour; and jet skis, ski boats, canoes, pedal boats, kayaks, fishing skiffs, and charter boats.

Sail USA (☎ 619/298-6822) offers custom-tailored skippered cruises on a 34-foot Catalina sloop. A half-day bay cruise costs $275 for up to six passengers.

FISHING   Public fishing piers are at Shelter Island (where there's a statue dedicated to anglers), Ocean Beach, and Imperial Beach. Anglers of any age can fish free of charge without a license off any municipal pier in California. Lake Murray is a great place for freshwater fishing (Wed, Sat, and Sun only). Call the **City Fish Line** at ☎ 619/465-3474 for information on fishing on city lakes.

For sportfishing, you can go out on a large boat for about $25 for half a day or $40 to $100 for three-quarters to a full day. To charter a boat for up to six people, the rates run about $550 for half a day and $1,000 for an entire day, more in summer; call around and compare prices. Summer and fall are excellent times for excursions. Locally, the waters around Point Loma are filled with bass, bonito, and barracuda; the Coronado Islands, which belong to Mexico but are only about 18 miles from San Diego, are popular for abalone, yellowtail, yellowfin, and big-eyed tuna. Some outfitters will take you farther into Baja California waters.

Fishing charters depart from Harbor and Shelter islands, Point Loma, the Imperial Beach pier, and Quivira Basin in Mission Bay (near the Hyatt Islandia Hotel). The following outfitters offer short or extended outings with daily departures: **H&M Landing** (☎ 619/222-1144), **Islandia Sportfishing** (☎ 619/222-1164), **Lee Palm Sportfishers** (☎ 619/224-3857), **Point Loma Sportfishing** (☎ 619/223-1627), and **Seaforth Boat Rentals** (☎ 619/223-1681). Participants over the age of 16 need a California fishing license.

GOLF   With nearly 80 courses, 50 of them open to the public, San Diego County has much to offer the golf enthusiast. Courses are diverse, some with vistas of the Pacific, others with views of country hillsides or of desert. **Par-Tee Golf** (☎ 800/PAR-TEE-1) and **M&M Tee Times** (☎ 619/456-8366) can arrange tee times for you at most golf courses. **Greenlink** (☎ 619/456-8346) is also a valuable source of information about golf courses, schools, and equipment.

And where else but San Diego can you practice your golf swing in the middle of the central business district? The **Harborside Golf Center,** on Broadway at Pacific Highway (☎ 619/239-GOLF), is open from 7am to 10pm daily. Here you'll find 80 tees, a USGA putting and chipping area, a pro shop, and golf school. It's lit for after-dark play. Club rental is available at $1 each; a large bucket of balls costs $6; a small bucket, $3.

Space constraints prevent us from listing all of the San Diego area's fine courses; for a more extensive listing, see *Frommer's San Diego.*

✪ **Torrey Pines Golf Course,** 11480 Torrey Pines Rd., La Jolla (☎ **619/ 552-1784** for information, 619/570-1234 for tee times, or 619/452-3226 for the pro shop), is actually two gorgeous 18-hole championship courses located on the coast between La Jolla and Del Mar, only 15 minutes from downtown San Diego. Home of the Buick Invitational Tournament, these municipal courses both overlook the ocean; the north course is more picturesque, the south course more challenging.

Tee times are taken by computer, starting at 5am, up to 7 days in advance by telephone only. Confirmation numbers are issued, and you must have the number and photo identification with you when you check in with the starter a mandatory 15 minutes ahead of time. *Insider's tip:* Single golfers stand a good chance of getting on the course if they just turn up and wait for a threesome.

Golf professionals are available for lessons, and the pro shop rents clubs, if you left yours at home. Greens fees for out-of-towners are $48 during the week and $52 Saturday, Sunday, and holidays for 18 holes (after 4pm Apr through Oct and 3pm Nov through Mar the fee is only $26); $26 for 9 holes. Cart rental is $28.

✪ **Coronado Municipal Golf Course,** 2000 Visalia Row, Coronado (☎ **619/435-3121**), is the first sight that welcomes you as you cross the Coronado Bay Bridge (the course is off to the left). It is an 18-hole, par-72 course overlooking Glorietta Bay, and there's a coffee shop, pro shop, and driving range. Two-day prior reservations are strongly recommended; call anytime after 7am. Greens fees are $20 to walk and $32 to ride for 18 holes; $10 to walk and $17 to ride after 4pm. Club rental is $15, and pull-cart rental is $4.

HIKING/WALKING   The Sierra Club sponsors regular hikes in the San Diego area, and nonmembers are welcome to participate; there are both day and evening hikes, and most are free. For a recorded schedule, call ☎ **619/299-1744,** box no. 4000, or call the office at ☎ **619/299-1743** Monday through Friday between noon and 5pm and on Saturday between 10am and 4pm.

The **Bayside Trail** near Cabrillo National Monument is popular because it affords great views. Drive to the Monument and follow signs to the trail. Parking costs $4 per car. ✪ **Mission Trails Regional Park,** 8 miles northeast of downtown, offers a glimpse of what San Diego looked like before development. Located between Calif. 52 and I-8 and east of I-15, its rugged hills, valleys, and open areas provide a quick escape from urban hustle-bustle. A visitor and interpretive center (☎ **619/668-3275**) is open daily from 9am to 5pm. Access is via Mission Gorge Road from either Calif. 52 or I-8.

There's also a wonderful walkway around **Lake Murray;** take the Lake Murray Boulevard exit off I-8 and follow the signs. **Torrey Pines State Park** in La Jolla is another great spot for hiking; docents lead guided nature walks on weekends. (See also "La Jolla," above.)

The best **beaches** for walking are La Jolla Shores, Mission Beach, and Coronado. You can also walk around Mission Bay on a series of connected foot paths. If a four-legged friend is your walking companion, head for Dog Beach in Ocean Beach or Fiesta Island in Mission Bay, two of the few areas where dogs can legally go unleashed. A little-known scenic path in La Jolla is **Coast Walk,** which starts near the **La Jolla Cave & Shell Shop,** 1325 Coast Blvd. (☎ **619/454-6080**), and affords a fabulous view of beach and beyond.

IN-LINE SKATING   Gliding around San Diego, especially the Mission Bay area, on in-line skates is as much a southern California experience as sailing or surfing. In Mission Beach, rent a pair of regular or in-line skates from **Mike's Bikes & Skates,** 756A Ventura Place (☎ **619/488-1444**), or **Hamel's Action Sports Center,** 704

Castles in the Sand

Sand-castle enthusiasts will want to attend the 2-day **Annual U.S. Open Sand-castle Competition** at the pier in Imperial Beach in July. There's a parade and children's castle contest Saturday at 2pm, but Sunday is the main event. For information, call ☎ **619/424-6663.** A similar event, the **Ocean Beach Sandcastle Event and Family Fun Carnival,** is held in October; for information, call ☎ **619/226-8613.**

Ventura Place, off Mission Boulevard at the roller coaster (☎ **619/488-5050**); and in Pacific Beach at **Pacific Beach Sun & Sea,** 4539 Ocean Blvd. (☎ **619/483-6613**). In Coronado, go to **Bikes & Beyond,** 1201 First St. and at the Ferry Landing (☎ **619/435-7180**).

TENNIS   There are 1,200 public and private tennis courts in San Diego. Public courts are located throughout the city, including the **La Jolla Recreation Center** (☎ **619/459-9950**) and **Morley Field** (☎ **619/295-9278**) in Balboa Park.

9 The Shopping Scene

All-American San Diego has embraced the suburban shopping mall with vigor—several massive complexes in Mission Valley are where many residents do the bulk of their shopping, and every possible need is represented there. Local neighborhoods also offer individualized specialty shopping that meets the needs—and mirrors the personality—of that part of town. For example, hip and trendy Hillcrest is the place to go for cutting-edge boutiques, while conservative La Jolla offers many upscale traditional shops, especially jewelers.

Sales tax in San Diego is 7.75%, and savvy out-of-state shoppers know to have larger items shipped directly home at the point of purchase, thus avoiding the tax.

In addition to the areas described below, remember that it's fun to shop in **Tijuana,** Mexico, just across the border from San Diego. You can also shop on the north side of the international border at the **San Diego Factory Outlet Center.**

DOWNTOWN & GASLAMP QUARTER   The Disneyland of shopping malls, **Horton Plaza,** 324 Horton Plaza (☎ **619/238-1596;** www.hortonplaza.com), is the heart of the revitalized city center, bounded by Broadway, First and Fourth avenues, and G Street. This multilevel shopping center has 140 specialty shops, including art galleries, clothing and shoe stores, several fun shops for kids, bookstores, a 14-screen cinema, three major department stores, and a variety of restaurants and short-order eateries. With a rambling and confusing series of paths and bridges, the complex was supposedly inspired by European shopping districts. Parking is free the first 3 hours with validation (4 hr. at the movie theater and the Lyceum Theatre), $1 per half hour thereafter; parking levels are confusing, and temporarily losing your car is part of the Horton Plaza experience. Take bus 2, 7, 9, 29, 34, or 35; or the Trolley to City Center.

Seaport Village, 849 W. Harbor Dr., at Kettner Boulevard (☎ **619/235-4014,** or 619/235-4013 for events information), a 14-acre ersatz village snuggled alongside San Diego Bay, was built to resemble a small Cape Cod community, but the 75 shops are very much the southern California cutesy variety. Be sure to see the 1890 carousel imported from Coney Island, New York. Take bus 7 or the Trolley to Seaport Village.

HILLCREST/UPTOWN   San Diego's self-proclaimed **Antique Row** is located north of Balboa Park, along Park Boulevard (beginning at University Avenue in

Hillcrest) and Adams Avenue (extending to around 40th Street in Normal Heights). For more information and an area brochure with map, contact the **Adams Avenue Business Association** (☎ **619/282-7329**) or visit them online at www.GoThere.com/AdamsAve.

OLD TOWN & MISSION VALLEY   **Old Town Historic Park** is a restoration of some of San Diego's most historic sites and adobe structures, a number of which now house shops that cater to tourists. Many have a "general store" theme, and carry gourmet treats and inexpensive Mexican crafts alongside the obligatory T-shirts, baseball caps, snow domes, and other San Diego–emblazoned souvenirs. More shops are concentrated in colorful **Bazaar del Mundo,** 2754 Calhoun St. (☎ **619/296-3161**), which is arranged around a fountain courtyard. Book lovers will find the local outpost of **Barnes & Noble** here, at 7610 Hazard Center Dr. (☎ **619/220-0175**).

Mission Valley is home to San Diego's enormous shopping malls: **Fashion Valley Shopping Center,** 352 Fashion Valley Rd. (☎ **619/297-3381**), and **Mission Valley Center,** 1640 Camino del Rio No. (☎ **619/296-6375**).

MISSION BAY & THE BEACHES   The beach communities all offer laid-back shopping in typical California fashion; plenty of surf shops, recreational gear, casual garb, and youth-oriented music stores. Some of San Diego's best **antiquing** can be found in Ocean Beach, along a single block of **Newport Avenue,** the town's main drag.

LA JOLLA   It's clear from the look of La Jolla's village that shopping is a major pastime in this upscale community of moneyed professionals and retirees. Women's-clothing boutiques tend toward conservative and costly, like those lining Girard and Prospect streets (Ann Taylor, Armani Exchange, Polo Ralph Lauren, Talbots, and Sigi's Boutique). Even if you're not in the market for furnishings and accessories, the many home decor boutiques make for great window-shopping, as do La Jolla's ubiquitous jewelers: Swiss watches, tennis bracelets, precious gems, and pearl necklaces sparkle at you from windows along every street. No visit to La Jolla is complete without seeing **John Cole's Bookshop,** 780 Prospect St. (☎ **619/454-4766**), an eclectic, family-run local favorite set in a charming old cottage.

CORONADO   This rather insular, conservative Navy community doesn't have a great many shopping opportunities; what there is lines Orange Avenue at the western end of the island. In addition to some scattered housewares and home-decor boutiques, and several small women's boutiques, there are gift shops at Coronado's major resorts.

The entrance to the **Ferry Landing Marketplace,** 1201 First St., at B Avenue (☎ **619/435-8895;** fax 619/522-6150), is impressive—turreted red rooftops with jaunty blue flags that draw closer as the ferry to Coronado pulls into the slip. As you stroll up the pier, you'll find yourself in the midst of shops filled with gifts, imported and designer fashions, jewelry, and crafts. You can get a quick bite to eat or have a leisurely dinner with a view, wander along landscaped walkways, or laze on a friendly beach or grassy bank. Take I-5 to Coronado Bay Bridge, to B Avenue and turn right; or take bus 901 or the ferry from Broadway Pier.

✪ **FARMERS MARKETS**   Throughout San Diego County, there are no fewer than two dozen regularly occurring street fests featuring the fresh fruits and vegetables from southern California farms as well as crafts, ethnic-food vendors, flower stands, and other surprises. Here's a sampling:

Sunday: In Hillcrest at the corner of Normal Street and Lincoln Avenue, from 9am to noon.

Tuesday: In Coronado at the Old Ferry Landing, corner of First and B streets, from 2:30 to 6pm; and in Escondido at Grand Avenue and Broadway, from 3 to 7pm.

Wednesday: North County Market in Escondido, 3660 Sunset Dr. (across from North County Fair), 9am to noon. In Ocean Beach, in the 4900 block of Newport Avenue (west of Sunset Cliffs Boulevard), from 4 to 8pm. In Carlsbad at Roosevelt Street, between Grand Avenue and Carlsbad Village Drive, from 3 to 6pm.

Thursday: In Mission Valley at Hazard Center, Friars Road at Calif. 163, from 3 to 6:30pm.

Friday: In Rancho Bernardo at Bernardo Winery, 13330 Paseo del Verano Norte, from 9am to noon. In La Mesa at 8500 Allison St. (east of Spring Street), from 3 to 6pm.

Saturday: In Pacific Beach along Mission Boulevard between Reed and Pacific Beach Drive, 8am to noon. In Del Mar at the City Hall parking lot, corner of El Camino Del Mar and 10th Street, from 1 to 4pm. In Carlsbad in the parking lot north of Andersen's Pea Soup, from 2 to 5pm.

10 San Diego After Dark

San Diego is hardly the wild 'n' crazy nightlife capital of America, but pockets of lively after-dark entertainment do exist around the city. On the more sedate side of things, the city offers wonderful and varied live theater experiences—both the Old Globe and La Jolla Playhouse have won Tony awards for Best Regional Theater.

For a rundown of the latest performances, gallery openings, and other events in the city, check the listings in "Night & Day," the Thursday entertainment section of the *San Diego Union-Tribune,* or the *Reader,* San Diego's free alternative newspaper, published every Thursday. For what's happening in the gay scene, get the weekly *San Diego Gay & Lesbian Times.* The *San Diego Performing Arts Guide,* produced every 2 months by the San Diego Theatre Foundation, is also very helpful; you can pick one up at the Times Art Tix booth.

THE PERFORMING ARTS

Half-price tickets to theater, music, and dance events are available at the Times Arts Tix booth, in Horton Plaza Park, at Broadway and Third Avenue (park in the Horton Plaza parking garage and have your parking validated, or pause at the curb nearby). The kiosk is open Tuesday through Saturday from 10am to 7pm. Half-price tickets for Sunday performances are sold on Saturday. Only cash payments are accepted. For a daily listing of half-price offerings, call ☎ **619/497-5000.** Full-price advance tickets are also sold; the kiosk doubles as a Ticketmaster outlet, selling tickets to concerts throughout California.

The **Gaslamp Quarter Theatre Company,** at 444 Fourth Ave. (☎ **619/232-9608** or 619/234-9583), stages contemporary productions in the 250-seat Hahn Cosmopolitan Theatre.

The **San Diego Repertory Theatre** offers professional, culturally diverse productions of contemporary and classic dramas, comedies, and musicals at the Lyceum Theatre, 79 Horton Plaza (☎ **619/235-8025** or 619/231-3586; fax 619/235-0939). Its annual *A Christmas Carol* is a perennial favorite.

Founded in 1948, the **San Diego Junior Theatre,** at Balboa Park's Casa del Prado Theatre (☎ **619/239-8355;** fax 619/239-5048), is the country's oldest continuously producing children's theater, providing training and performance opportunities for children and teenagers 4 to 18. Students act and technically crew five main stage shows each year.

In Coronado, **Lamb's Players Theatre,** at 1142 Orange Ave. (☎ **619/437-0600;** fax 619/437-6053), is a professional repertory company whose season runs from February through December. Shows are staged in their 340-seat theater in Coronado's historic Spreckels building, where no seat is more than seven rows from the stage.

The **San Diego Opera** performs at the Civic Theater, 202 C St. (☎ **619/ 232-7636;** www.sdopera.com), and often showcases international stars. The 1999 season will run from January through May; call for schedule. The box office is located across the plaza from the theater and is open Monday through Friday from 9am to 5pm. Tickets run from $25 to $100. Student and senior discounts and $17 standing-room tickets are available an hour before the performance.

✪ **Old Globe Theatre.** Balboa Park. ☎ **619/239-2255** or 619/23-GLOBE for 24-hr. hot line. www.oldglobe.org. Tickets $28.50–$39 (previews $22); seniors and students $25 matinees, $29 weeknights. Bus: 7 or 25.

Near the entrance to Balboa Park and just behind the Museum of Man is this Tony Award–winning theater, fashioned after Shakespeare's, which has produced the revival of *Damn Yankees* and has billed such notable performers as John Goodman, Marsha Mason, Cliff Robertson, Jon Voight, and Christopher Walken.

The 581-seat Old Globe is part of the Simon Edison Centre for the Performing Arts, which also includes the 245-seat **Cassius Carter Centre Stage** and the 620-seat open-air **Lowell Davies Festival Theatre,** and mounts a dozen plays a year on the three stages between January and October. Tours are offered Saturday and Sunday at 11am and cost $3 ($1 students, seniors, and military). The box office is open Tuesday through Sunday from noon to 8:30pm.

La Jolla Playhouse. 2910 La Jolla Village Dr. (at Torrey Pines Rd.), La Jolla. ☎ **619/ 550-1010.** www.lajollaplayhouse.com.

Winner of the 1993 Tony Award for outstanding American regional theater, the La Jolla Playhouse stages six productions each year in its 500-seat **Mandell Weiss Theater** and 400-seat **Mandell Weiss Forum** on the campus of UCSD. Performances are held May through November. Playhouse audiences cheered *The Who's Tommy* and Matthew Broderick in *How to Succeed in Business Without Really Trying* before they went on to Broadway fame and fortune. The box office is open Monday from noon to 6pm, and Tuesday through Sunday from noon to 8pm. Each show designates one Saturday matinee as a "pay-what-you-can performance." Reduced-price "Public Rush" tickets are available 10 minutes before curtain, subject to availability. Tickets run $19 to $39. Self-parking is $3.

MOVIES, SAN DIEGO–STYLE

In addition to the usual multiplex theaters, San Diegans like to watch movies in some unusual settings. **Movies Before the Mast** are shown on a special "screensail" April through October aboard the *Star of India* (see entry for the Maritime Museum under "Exploring the Area," above). All the films shown are nautical in genre, such as *Black Beard the Pirate* and *Hook.* Call ☎ 619/234-9153 for the schedule.

In August, you can view a mix of classic and current films free of charge from a blanket or chair on the beach during the **Sunset Cinema Film Festival.** Films are projected on screens mounted on a floating barges from San Diego to Imperial Beach. Call ☎ 619/454-7373 for details.

Dive-In Movies are shown at **The Plunge** (☎ 619/488-3110), an indoor swimming pool in Mission Beach. Viewers float on rafts in 91° water and watch water-related movies projected onto the wall. *Jaws* is a perennial favorite.

THE CLUB & MUSIC SCENE

Clubs come and go, so your best bet for finding the latest hot spot is to stroll through the Gaslamp Quarter. The current favorites are **Johnny Loves,** 664 Fifth Ave. (☎ 619/595-0123), which endears itself to an over-30 crowd; **Club 66,** at 901 Fifth Ave. (☎ 619/234-4166), which has a Route 66 motif and caters to those 25 to 45; **E Street Alley,** on the north side of E Street between Fourth and Fifth avenues (☎ 619/231-9200), which is a dressier club; **Blue Tattoo,** 751 Fifth Ave. (☎ 619/557-0146), the destination of choice for Europhiles; **Dick's Last Resort,** 345 Fourth Ave., with entrances on both Fourth and Fifth avenues (☎ 619/231-9100), popular with the college crowd; and **Buffalo Joe's,** 600 Fifth Ave. (☎ 619/236-1616). Cover charges vary from nil to $10, depending on who's playing and what night of the week it is.

Fans of alternative music might enjoy the **Casbah,** 2501 Kettner Blvd. (☎ 619/232-4355), where breakthrough bands are the norm.

From May through October a series of contemporary concerts take place outdoors at **Humphrey's,** 2241 Shelter Island Dr., San Diego (☎ 619/523-1010; www.user.aol.com/humconcert). During a recent season Ray Charles, Willie Nelson, and Wayne Newton were just three of the popular performers who appeared here. For the 1999 schedule, call or check their Web site.

Videos and live bands—sometimes local, sometimes nationally known—take center stage in the **Cannibal Bar,** in the Catamaran Hotel, 3999 Mission Blvd. (☎ 619/539-8650). Open Wednesday through Sunday till about 2am; weekend cover charges range from $3 to $15.

The waterfront location and nautical theme, with a curving wall of windows overlooking the marina, make **The Yacht Club,** in the San Diego Marriott Marina, 333 W. Harbor Dr. (☎ 619/234-1500), a comfortable spot. There's live dance music nightly, with appetizers and light fare available until 11pm, along with a dinner menu served from 5 to 11pm. A band plays 5 nights a week, a DJ 2 nights at 9pm. No cover, no drink minimum.

COMEDY

Top L.A. comics regularly visit the **Comedy Store,** 916 Pearl St., La Jolla (☎ 619/454-9176). Monday and Tuesday are amateur nights; the acts improve as the week progresses. Show time is 8pm Sunday through Thursday, 8 and 10:30pm Friday and Saturday. The cover is $8 to $10, with a two-drink minimum.

JAZZ & BLUES

Croce's. 802 Fifth Ave. (at F St.). ☎ 619/233-4355. No cover at Croce's Jazz Bar or Croce's Top Hat if you have dinner at Croce's Restaurant or Ingrid's Cantina. Otherwise, cover varies.

There's traditional jazz every night in Croce's Jazz Bar and rhythm and blues at Croce's Top Hat, both named after the late musician Jim Croce and owned by his wife, Ingrid. Jim Croce's son, A. J., an accomplished musician in his own right, sometimes performs. Jazz holds sway in the Jazz Bar and drifts easily into the adjoining restaurant (see "Great Deals on Dining," above); it opens nightly at 5pm, and the music starts at 8:30pm. Next door, in Croce's Top Hat, balcony seating overlooks the stage; it's open daily, with music starting at 9pm.

GAY & LESBIAN CLUBS

The Flame. 3780 Park Blvd. ☎ 619/295-4163. Cover Sun–Fri $2, Sat $3.

The Flame has a large dance floor and several bars, including a video bar. Nightly themes vary from Tuesday's "Boy's Night" to Thursday's country-western dancing to Friday's rollicking drag shows. Be sure to call for current schedule.

They Mind Very Much if You Smoke

In January 1998, California enacted controversial legislation banning **smoking** in all restaurants and bars. While opponents immediately began lobbying to repeal the law, it's a good idea to check before you light up in nightclubs, lounges, etc.

Rich's. 1051 University Ave. (between 10th and 11th aves.). ☎ **619/497-4588** for upcoming events. Cover most nights, under $5.

This popular club/dance space welcomes primarily young gay men. Sunday is popular for Tea and Me, when there's no cover between 7 and 9pm, and Thursday for Club Hedonism, with techno tunes and more. On Friday night, go-go dancers and high-energy music set the tone for the night, Saturday it's dance music and erotic dancers. Always check the events hot line, since the schedules can change.

THE BAR & COFFEEHOUSE SCENE
POPULAR BARS

In downtown San Diego, the knowing crowd gravitates to bars such as **Dobson's,** 956 Broadway Circle, between Broadway and Horton Place (☎ 619/231-6711), and **La Gran Tapa,** 611 B St., between Sixth and Seventh (☎ 619/234-8272). For a quieter scene, try the **Palace Bar** in the Horton Grand Hotel, 311 Island Ave., at Fourth Avenue (☎ 619/544-1886). Pub goers head to **The Princess Pub & Grille,** 1675 India St., at Date Street (☎ 619/702-3021). In La Jolla, favorites are the **Whaling Bar** in La Valencia hotel, 1132 Prospect St. (☎ 619/454-0771), and nearby **George's Cafe,** 1250 Prospect St. (☎ 619/454-4244). La Jolla's traditional piano lounge is at **Top o' the Cove,** 1216 Prospect St. (☎ 619/454-7779), where the pianist leans heavily toward Gershwin. Sports fans head out to **Seau's,** 1640 Camino del Rio North, Mission Valley Center (☎ 619/291-7328), named for owner/San Diego Charger Junior Seau.

BREW PUBS

Karl Strauss' Old Columbia Brewery, at 1157 Columbia St. (☎ **619/234-BREW**), opened several years ago and started something of a microbrewery trend in San Diego. The newest Karl Strauss brew pub is located at 1044 Wall St., La Jolla (☎ **619/ 551-BREW**).

The **La Jolla Brewing Company,** 7536 Fay Ave., ☎ **619/456-BREW**), feels like a neighborhood pub, and serves Baja fish tacos and cheeseburgers.

COFFEEHOUSES

Newbreak Coffee Co., 523 University Ave., Hillcrest (☎ **619/295-1600**), is a laid-back place to enjoy your latte or espresso. The desserts are rich, and the art on the wall is the work of local artists. **Upstart Crow,** on the central plaza at Seaport Village (☎ **619/232-4855**), is a coffeehouse/bookstore where tables and chairs fill cozy spaces surrounded by books. The selection of books, coffees, and desserts are scrumptious. And coffee refills are only 25¢. Centrally located in the Gaslamp Quarter and particularly popular with students, **Café Lulu,** 419 F St. near Fourth Avenue (☎ **619/238-0114**), is open late and serves light vegetarian fare, coffee drinks, and beer or wine. In La Jolla, try the **Wall Street Cafe,** at 1044 Wall St., between Girard and Herschel avenues (☎ **619/551-1044**), which was once a bank (the old vault now houses the rest rooms). Live entertainment, such as light jazz or a mellow guitar, makes this a particularly popular place on Friday and Saturday nights.

11 North County Beach Towns

Picturesque beach towns, each poised over their own stretch of sand, dot the coast of San Diego County from Del Mar to Oceanside. These make great day-trip destinations for sun worshippers and surfers.

Getting there is easy: Del Mar is only 18 miles north of downtown San Diego; Carlsbad about 33; Oceanside, 36. If you're driving, follow I-5 north: You'll find freeway exits for Del Mar, Solana Beach, Cardiff by the Sea, Encinitas, Leucadia, Carlsbad, and Oceanside. Check with **Amtrak** (☎ **800/USA-RAIL**), or the **Coaster** (☎ **800/COASTER**), for transit information. **The San Diego North County Convention and Visitors Bureau** (☎ **800/848-3336**) is a good information source.

DEL MAR

Less than 20 miles up the coast lies Del Mar, a small community with just over 5,000 inhabitants in a 2-square-mile municipality. The town has adamantly maintained its independence, eschewing incorporation into the city of San Diego. Sometimes known as "the people's republic of Del Mar," this community was one of the nation's first to ban smoking. Come summer, the town explodes as visitors flock in for the thoroughbred horse racing season and the county's Del Mar Fair. The history and current popularity of Del Mar is, in fact, inextricably linked to the **Del Mar Racetrack & Fairgrounds,** 2260 Jimmy Durante Blvd. (☎ **619/753-5555;** www.delmarfair.com), which, in turn, still glows with the aura of Hollywood celebrity. Established in the 1930s by crooner/actor Bing Crosby, the track still begins each season by playing "Where the Surf Meets the Turf."

Del Mar City Beach is a wide, well-patrolled beach popular for sunbathing, swimming, and body surfing. Get there by taking 15th Street west to Seagrove Park, where college kids can always be found playing volleyball and other lawn games while older folks snooze in the shade. There are **free concerts** in the park during July and August; for information contact the City of Del Mar (☎ **619/755-9313**).

For more information about Del Mar, contact or visit the **Del Mar Chamber of Commerce Visitor Information Center,** 1104 Camino del Mar #101, Del Mar, CA 92014 (☎ **619/755-4844;** www.delmar.ca.us), which also provides a folding, detailed map of the area. Open hours vary according to volunteer staffing, but usually mimic weekday business hours.

A NICE PLACE TO STAY ON THE BEACH

Del Mar Motel on the Beach. 1702 Coast Blvd. (at 17th St.), Del Mar, CA 92014. ☎ **800/223-8449** for reservations, or 619/755-1534. 45 units (some with shower only). TV TEL. $95–$120 double. Lower rates off-season; sometimes higher rates weekends and holidays. Extra person $5. AE, CB, DC, DISC, MC, V. Take I-5 to Via de la Valle exit; go west, then south on U.S. 101 (Pacific Coast Hwy.), veer west onto Coast Blvd.

The only property in Del Mar right on the beach, this little white-stucco motel with blue trim is clean and simply furnished and has been here since 1946. Upstairs rooms have one king-size bed, while those downstairs come with two double beds. All rooms have a refrigerator, coffeemaker, and fan. Half are nonsmoking rooms, and only those rooms with ocean views have bathtubs (the rest have showers only). This is a good choice for beach lovers, because you can walk from here along the beach for miles, and the popular seaside restaurants Poseidon and Jake's are right next door. The motel has a barbecue and picnic table for guests' use.

WHERE TO DINE

Head to the upper level of the centrally located **Del Mar Plaza,** at Camino del Mar and 15th Street, and consider **Il Fornaio Cucina Italiana** (☎ 619/755-8876) for excellent Italian cuisine; **Epazote** (☎ 619/259-9966) for Mexican, Tex-Mex, and Southwestern fare; or **Pacifica Del Mar** (☎ 619/792-0476) for outstanding seafood. Kids like to eat at **Johnny Rockets** (☎ 619/755-1954), an old-fashioned diner on the lower level. Down on the beach, **Jake's Del Mar,** 1660 Coast Blvd. (☎ 619/ 755-2002), and **Poseidon Restaurant on the Beach,** 1670 Coast Blvd. (☎ 619/ 755-9345), are both good for California cuisine and sunset views. If you want to eat at either of these popular spots, reserve early. The racetrack crowd congregates at **Bully's Restaurant,** 1404 Camino del Mar (☎ **619/755-1660**) for burgers, prime rib, and crab legs. And if you're looking for fresh seafood—and lots of it—head to the Del Mar branch of SD's popular **Fish Market,** 640 Via de la Valle (☎ **619/ 755-2277**), located near the racetrack.

CARLSBAD & ENCINITAS

Fifteen miles north of Del Mar and around 30 miles from downtown San Diego (a 45-min. drive), the pretty communities of Carlsbad and Encinitas provide many reasons to linger on the California coast: good swimming and surfing beaches, small-town atmosphere, an abundance of antique and gift shops, and a seasonal display of the region's most beautiful flowers.

   Carlsbad was named for Karlsbad, Czechoslovakia, because of the similar mineral (some say curative) waters they both produced, but the town's once-famous artesian well has long been plugged up. The Danish toy-maker Lego is building a gigantic theme park in Carlsbad; set to open in 1999, it will include children's rides, sculpted gardens, a hands-on building area, and replicas of historical monuments crafted from the familiar interconnecting plastic blocks. Admission is expected to be around $20 to $25 for adults. For an update on the progress of **Legoland,** call their information line (☎ **760/438-5346**).

   Carlsbad is also a noted commercial flower-growing region, along with its neighbor **Encinitas.** A colorful display can be seen each spring at **Carlsbad Ranch** (☎ **760/431-0352**), when 45 acres of solid ranunculus fields bloom into a breath-taking rainbow visible even from the freeway. During December the nurseries are alive with holiday poinsettias. You can also stroll through 30 acres of California native plants, exotic tropicals, palms, cacti, and more at **Quail Botanical Gardens** in Encinitas (☎ **760/436-3036**).

   Carlsbad has two distinct beaches: **Carlsbad State Beach** runs alongside downtown and is a great place to stroll along a wide concrete walkway, surrounded by like-minded outdoors types walking, jogging, and in-line skating, even at night (thanks to good lighting). Enter on Ocean Boulevard at Tamarack Avenue; there's a $4 fee per vehicle.

   Four miles south of town is **South Carlsbad State Beach,** almost 3 miles of cobblestone-strewn sand. A state-run campground at the north end is immensely popular year-round, and the southern portion is favored by area surfers. There's a $4 fee at the beach's entrance, along Carlsbad Boulevard at Poinsettia Lane.

   Down in Encinitas, everyone flocks to **Moonlight Beach,** the city's sandy playground with plenty of facilities, including free parking, volleyball nets, rest rooms, showers, picnic tables and fire grates, and the company of fellow sunbathers. The beach is accessed at the end of "B" Street (Encinitas Boulevard).

The **Carlsbad Visitor Information Center,** 400 Carlsbad Village Dr. (in the old Santa Fe Depot), Carlsbad, CA 92008 (☎ **800/227-5722** or 760/434-6093) has lots of additional information on flower fields and nursery touring.

WHERE TO STAY

Beach Terrace Inn. 2775 Ocean St., Carlsbad, CA 92003. ☎ **800/433-5415** outside Calif., 800/622-3224 in Calif., or 760/729-5951. Fax 760/729-1078. 49 units. A/C TV TEL. Summer $119–$229 double; from $149 suite. Winter $109–$189 double; from $129 suite. Extra person $15. Rates include continental breakfast. AE, CB, DC, DISC, ER, MC, V. Free parking.

Carlsbad's only beachside hostelry (others are across the road or a little farther away), this downtown Best Western property has a helpful staff, and rooms and an outdoor pool with ocean views. Rooms, although not elegant, are extra-large, and some have balconies, fireplaces, and kitchenettes; suites have separate living rooms and bedrooms. VCRs and films are available at the front desk. It's good for families. You can walk everywhere from here, and there is street parking.

Pelican Cove Inn. 320 Walnut Ave., Carlsbad, CA 92008. ☎ **800/PEL-COVE** or 760/434-5995. www.pelican-cove.com/pelican. E-mail: PelicanCoveInn@sandcastleweb.com. 8 units. $85–$175 double. Rates include full breakfast. Extra person $15. AE, MC, V. From downtown Carlsbad, follow Carlsbad Blvd. south to Walnut Ave.; turn left and drive 2½ blocks.

Located 2 blocks from the beach, this Cape Cod–style hideaway combines romance with luxury. Hosts Kris and Nancy Nayudu see to your every need, from furnishing guest rooms with soft feather beds and down comforters, to providing beach chairs and towels or preparing a picnic basket (with 24 hr. notice). Each of the inn's eight rooms features a fireplace and private entrance; some have private spa tubs. The airy, spacious "La Jolla" room is loveliest, with bay windows and cupola ceiling. A full breakfast is included in your stay, and can be enjoyed in the garden if weather permits. Courtesy transportation from Oceanside train station is available.

Tamarack Beach Resort. 3200 Carlsbad Blvd., Carlsbad, CA 92008. ☎ **800/334-2199** or 760/729-3500. Fax 760/434-5942. E-mail: tamarack@pacbell.net. 23 units, 54 vacation rentals. A/C TV TEL. $125–$200 double; $220–$330 vacation rental. Children under 12 stay free in parents' room. AE, MC, V. Free underground parking.

This resort property's rooms, in the village and across the street from the beach, are restfully decorated in tropical colors and wicker furniture, with small refrigerators, coffee-making facilities, and VCRs (movies are complimentary). The fully equipped vacation rentals (including washer and dryer) are available on a daily or weekly basis. The pretty Tamarack also has a pleasant lobby, a heated pool in a sunny courtyard setting, two Jacuzzis, exercise facilities, valet services, barbecue grills, and a good restaurant, Dini's by the Sea, that is popular with locals.

WHERE TO DINE

Local favorites include **Neiman's,** 2978 Carlsbad Blvd., Carlsbad (☎ 760/729-4131), serving American fare in a restored Victorian mansion; and the **Potato Shack,** 120 West I St., Encinitas (☎ 760/436-1282), a spuds-intensive diner open for breakfast and lunch only.

OCEANSIDE

The most northerly town in San Diego County, Oceanside claims almost 4 miles of beaches and one of the West Coast's longest over-the-water wooden piers. A tram transports people from the street to the end of the 1,954-foot-long pier and back for 25¢ each way. The wide, sandy beach; the pier; and a well-tended recreational area

North County Beach Towns

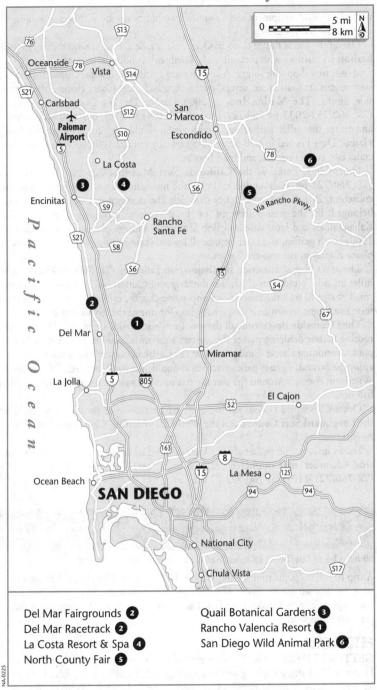

0 — 5 mi
0 — 8 km

N

Pacific Ocean

S13
76
Oceanside
78
Vista
S14
S21
Carlsbad
S12
San Marcos
15
✈ Palomar Airport
S10
Escondido
5
La Costa
❸
❹
S6
78
❻
Encinitas
S9
❺
Via Rancho Pkwy.
S21
Rancho Santa Fe
S8
S6
15
S4
❷
67
Del Mar
Miramar
La Jolla
5
805
El Cajon
52
163
Ocean Beach
8
La Mesa
125
15
SAN DIEGO
94
94
National City
Chula Vista
S17

Del Mar Fairgrounds ❷
Del Mar Racetrack ❷
La Costa Resort & Spa ❹
North County Fair ❺

Quail Botanical Gardens ❸
Rancho Valencia Resort ❶
San Diego Wild Animal Park ❻

NA-0225

with playground equipment and an outdoor amphitheater are within easy walking distance of the train station.

One of the nicest things to do in Oceanside is take a stroll around the city's upscale **harbor;** it's bustling with pleasure craft, lined with condominiums, and boasts a Cape Cod–inspired shopping village. A launch ramp, visitor-boat slips, charter fishing, and boat rentals are found here; several restaurants, including **Chart House,** offer harborside dining. **The Marina Inn,** at 2008 Harbor Dr. N., Oceanside, CA 92054 (☎ **800/252-2033** or 760/722-1561; fax 760/439-9758), has comfortable rooms and suites that offer harbor and ocean views; doubles go for $100 to $175. The Harbor Days Festival in mid-September typically attracts 100,000 visitors to enjoy a crafts fair, entertainment, and food booths.

Oceanside is home to the **California Surf Museum,** 223 N. Coast Highway (☎ **760/721-6876**); founded in 1985, the museum has an unbelievably extensive collection. Boards and other relics chronicle the development of the sport—many belonged to the names revered by local surfers, including Hawaiian Duke Kahanamoku and local daredevil Bob Simmons. Vintage photographs, beach attire, 1960s beach graffiti, and "surf" music all lovingly bring surfing to life—there's even a photo display of the real-life Gidget.

The area's biggest attraction is **Mission San Luis Rey** (☎ **760/757-3651**), a few miles inland. Founded in 1798, it is the largest of California's 21 missions. There is a small charge to tour the mission, its impressive church, exhibits, grounds, and cemetery. You might recognize it as the backdrop for one of the Zorro movies.

The **Oceanside Beach** runs all the way from just outside Oceanside Harbor, where routine harbor dredging makes for a pretty substantial amount of fluffy, clean white sand, continuing almost 4 miles south at the Carlsbad border. Along the way you can enjoy the **Strand,** a grassy park stretching alongside the beach between Fifth Street and Wisconsin Avenue. Around the pier are rest rooms, showers, picnic areas, and volleyball nets.

Oceanside's world-famous surfing spots attract numerous competitions, including the **Longboard Surf Contest** and the **World Bodysurfing Championships,** both in August.

For an information packet about Oceanside and its attractions, contact the **Oceanside Chamber of Commerce,** 928 North Coast Hwy., Oceanside, CA 92054 (☎ **760/721-1101;** fax 760/722-8336).

12 Julian: Apples, Pies & a Slice of Small-Town California

60 miles NE of San Diego; 35 miles W of Anza-Borrego Desert State Park

A trip to Julian (population 1,500) is a trip back in time. The old gold-mining town, now best known for its apples, has some good eateries and a handful of cute B&Bs, but its popularity is based on the fact that it provides a chance for city-weary folks to get away from it all.

ESSENTIALS

GETTING THERE The 90-minute drive can be made via Highway 78 or I-8 to Highway 79. I suggest taking one route going and the other coming back. Highway 79 winds through scenic Rancho Cuyamaca State Park, while Highway 78 traverses open country and farmland.

VISITOR INFORMATION   Town maps and flyers for accommodations are available from the **Town Hall** on Main Street at Washington Street. The town has a **24-hour hot line** (☎ 760/765-0707) that provides information on lodging, dining, shopping, activities, upcoming events, weather, and road conditions. For a brochure on what to see and do, contact the **Julian Chamber of Commerce** (☎ 760/765-1857; www.icsol.com/west/julian). The **Julian Arts Guild** (☎ 760/765-0560) can answer questions about the Spring Fine Arts Show (see below).

SPECIAL EVENTS   Special events here have special appeal, especially Julian's popular **fall apple harvest** starting in mid-September and continuing for an entire month. The annual **wildflower show** lasts for a week in early May; there's also a **Spring Fine Arts Show** in May. And the annual **weed show,** a tradition since 1961, is usually held the last few weeks in August or the beginning of September. Contact the Julian Chamber of Commerce (see above) for details on all of these events.

EXPLORING THE TOWN

This 1880s gold-mining town has managed to retain a rustic, woodsy sense of its historic origins. Radiating the dusty aura of the Old West, Julian offers an abundance of early California history, quaint Victorian streets filled with apple-pie shops and antique stores, crisp fresh air, and friendly people. Be forewarned, however, Julian's charming downtown can become exceedingly crowded during the fall harvest season, so consider making your trip another time to enjoy this unspoiled relic with a little privacy (rest assured, apple pies are baking around town year-round.) At around 4,500 feet elevation, the autumn air is crisp and bracing, and Julian sees a dusting (and often more) of snow during the winter months.

The best way to experience tiny Julian is on foot. After stopping in at the Chamber of Commerce in the old Town Hall—check out the vintage photos of Julian's yesteryear—cross the street to the **Julian Drug Store,** 2134 Main St. (☎ 760/765-0332), an old-style soda fountain serving sparkling sarsaparilla. The circa-1870 **Eagle and High Peak Mines,** at the end of C Street (☎ 760/765-0036), although seeming to be a tourist trap, offers an interesting and educational look at the town's one-time economic mainstay. While in Julian, consider a ride in a horse-drawn carriage with **Country Carriages** (☎ 760/765-1471). A rambling drive down country roads and through town is $20 per couple, or choose an abbreviated spin around town for $5 per adult, $2 per child. The town's **Pioneer Cemetery** is a must-see for graveyard buffs; contemporary graves belie the haphazard, overgrown look of this hilly burial ground, and eroded older tombstones tell the intriguing story of Julian's rough pioneer history. You can drive in via the A Street entrance, or climb the steep stairway leading up from Main Street; until 1924 this ascent was the only point of entry, even for processionals.

Apple pie is the town's mainstay, and the **Julian Pie Company,** 2225 Main St. (☎ 760/765-2449), is the most charming pie shop of them all. They serve original, Dutch, apple/mountain berry, and no-sugar-added pies as well as other baked goodies. Another great bakery is the aptly-named **Mom's Pies,** 2119 Main St. (☎ 760/765-2472), whose special attraction is a sidewalk plate-glass window through which you can observe the Mom-on-duty rolling crust, filling pies, and crimping edges. Nearby is the **Julian Cider Mill,** 2103 Main St. (☎ 760/765-1430), where you can see cider presses at work from October through March; they offer free tastes of the fresh nectar, and jugs to take home.

A short and scenic drive from town leads to the **Menghini Winery,** a family business 2 miles out on Farmer's Road (follow it west out of town until you see the winery sign, then bear to the left down the hill). The winery is usually open Monday, Friday, Saturday, and Sunday from 10am to 4pm, daily in October and December, or call for an appointment (☎ 760/765-2072). The grapes come from Ramona and Temecula, and the local favorite wine is Julian Blossom. The tanks are right in the tasting room, and the wines are sold only locally, for $7 to $10 per bottle. You may enjoy your purchase right away in the picnic area in the apple orchard.

Ask any of the San Diegans who regularly make excursions to Julian; no trip would be complete without a stop at **Dudley's Bakery,** Highway 78, Santa Ysabel (☎ 800/225-3348 or 760/765-0488), for a loaf or three of their popular bread. Loaves are stacked high, and folks are often three-deep at the counter clamoring for the 20(!) varieties of bread baked fresh daily—varieties range from raisin-date-nut to jalapeño, with some garden-variety sourdough and multigrain in between. They're open Wednesday through Sunday from 8am to 5pm (subject to early closure on Sun).

OUTDOOR PURSUITS

Within 10 miles of Julian are numerous **hiking trails** traversing rolling meadows, high chaparral, and thick pine forests. The most spectacular hike is at **Volcan Mountain Preserve,** north of town along Farmers Road; the trail to the top is a moderately challenging hike of around 3½ miles round-trip, with a 1,400-foot elevation gain. From the top, hikers have a panoramic view of the desert, mountains, and sea. Docent-led hikes are offered, at no charge, year-round (on Saturdays only, about one per month). For a hike schedule, call ☎ 760/765-0650.

In **William Heise County Park,** off Frisius Drive outside of Pine Hills, the whole family can enjoy hikes ranging from a self-guided nature trail and a cedar-scented forest trail to moderate-to-vigorous trails into the mountains. A ranger kiosk at the entrance can provide trail maps.

Along Highway 79 southeast of Julian, **Cuyamaca Rancho State Park** covers 30,000 acres, the centerpiece of which is Cuyamaca Lake. In addition to lake recreation (for boat rental and fishing information call ☎ 760/765-0515 or 760/447-8123), there are several sylvan picnic areas, three campgrounds, and 110 miles of hiking trails through the Cleveland National Forest. Activities at the lake include fishing (trout, bass, catfish, bluegill, and crappie) and boating; there's a general store and restaurant at lake's edge. Fishing fee (license required) is $4.75 per day for adults and $2.50 per day for kids 8 to 15; rowboats are $12 per day, and outboard motors an additional $13. Canoes and paddleboats can be rented by the hour for $4 to $7. For a trail map and further information about park recreation, stop in at **park headquarters,** on Hwy. 79 (☎ 760/765-0755), Monday through Friday from 8am to 5pm. An adjacent park museum is open Monday through Friday from 10am to 5pm and Saturday and Sunday from 10am to 4pm.

For a different way to tour, try **Llama Trek,** P.O. Box 2363, Julian, CA 92036 (☎ 800/LAMAPAK or 760/765-1890; fax 760/765-1512; www.llamatreks.com). Trips include rural neighborhoods, a historic gold mine, mountain and lake views, and apple orchards. They even conduct a trek to the local winery. Rates for the 4- to 5-hour trips vary from $65 to $85 per person and include lunch (the winery trek also includes wine tasting).

WHERE TO STAY

For a list and description of more than 20 B&Bs, contact the **Julian Bed & Breakfast Guild** (☎ 760/765-1555; www.julianbnbguild.com). Noteworthy member inns worth a splurge are the **Artists' Loft** (☎ 760/765-0765), a peaceful hilltop retreat offering two artistically decorated rooms and a cozy cabin with a wood-burning stove

($110 to $120 double); the **Julian White House** (☎ 800/WHT-HOUS or 760/765-1764), a lovely faux-antebellum mansion 4 miles from Julian in Pine Hills with four frilly Victorian-style guest rooms ($90 to $145 double); and the romantic **Random Oaks Ranch** (☎ 800/BNB-4344 or 760/765-1094), which features two themed cottages, each with its own wood-burning fireplace and outdoor Jacuzzi ($125 to $165 double). *A word of caution:* Reservations for the fall harvest season must be made several months in advance.

Julian Hotel. Main St. and B St. (P.O. Box 1856), Julian, CA 92036. ☎ **760/765-0201.** Fax 760/765-0327. 14 units. $72–$105 double with detached private bathroom; $82–$125 double with ensuite bathroom; $125–$175 cottage. Rates include full breakfast and afternoon tea. AE, MC, V.

Built in 1897 by freed slave Albert Robinson, this frontier-style hotel is a living monument to the area's gold boom days. Centrally located at the crossroads of downtown, the Julian Hotel isn't as secluded or plush as the many B&B's in town, but if you seek historically accurate lodgings to complete your weekend time-warp, this is the place. The 14 rooms, with private bathrooms, have been authentically restored and boast antique furnishings; the inviting private lobby is stocked with a wood-burning stove, books, games, and literature on local activities.

WORTH A SPLURGE

Orchard Hill Country Inn. 2502 Washington St. at Second St. (P.O. Box 425), Julian, CA 92036-0425. ☎ **800/71-ORCHARD** or 760/765-1700. Fax 760/765-0290. 22 units. A/C MINIBAR TV TEL. $140–$195 double. Extra person $25. 2-night minimum stay if including Fri or Sat. Midweek discounts and seasonal packages available. Rates include breakfast and hors d'oeuvres. AE, MC, V.

Hosts Darrell and Pat Straube offer the most upscale lodging in Julian, a two-story lodge and four Craftsman cottages situated on a hill overlooking the town. Ten guest rooms, a guests-only dining room, and a "great room" with a massive stone fireplace are located in the lodge. Twelve suites are in cottages spread over 3 acres of grounds. All quarters feature contemporary and unfrilly country furnishings, private bathrooms, TV/VCRs, and snacks. While rooms in the main lodge are rather hotel-ish in feel, the cottage suites are secluded and luxurious, featuring private porches, fireplaces, whirlpool tubs, and bathrobes. Rates include full breakfast and afternoon hors d'oeuvres. Several hiking trails lead from the lodge into adjacent woods.

WHERE TO DINE

Julian Grille. 2224 Main St. (at A St.). ☎ **760/765-0173.** Reservations required Fri–Sun. Main courses $13–$21. AE, MC, V. Daily 11am–3pm; Tues–Sun 5–9pm. AMERICAN.

Set in a cozy cottage festooned with lacy draperies, flickering candles, and a warm hearth, the Grille is the nicest eatery in town. Lunch here is an anything-goes affair, ranging from soups, sandwiches, and large salads to charbroiled burgers, chicken sandwiches, and hearty omelets. Dinner features grilled and broiled meats, seafood, and prime rib. Dinners are complete, with soup or salad, hot rolls, potatoes, and vegetables. The Grille is popular, and dining options are limited, so reservations are a necessity on weekends year-round.

Romano's Dodge House. 2718 B St. (just south of Main). ☎ **760/765-1003.** Main courses $8–$14. No credit cards. Fri–Sat 11am–10pm (to 9pm in winter); Sun–Mon and Thurs 11am–9pm. ITALIAN.

Occupying a historic home (vintage photos illustrate the little farmhouse's past) just off Main Street, Romano's is proudly the only restaurant in town *not* serving apple pie.

A home-style Italian joint with red-checked tablecloths and straw-clad Chianti bottles, Romano's serves individual lunch pizzas, pastas bathed in a rich marinara sauce, veal parmigiana, chicken cacciatore, and their signature dish, pork Juliana (loin chops in a whisky-apple cider sauce). There's seating on a narrow shaded porch in addition to the wood-plank dining room.

13 Anza-Borrego Desert State Park

90 miles NE of San Diego; 35 miles E of Julian

The sweeping 600,000-acre Anza-Borrego Desert State Park is home to fossils and rocks dating from 540 million years ago; human beings arrived only 10,000 years ago. The terrain ranges in elevation from 15 feet above sea level to more than 6,000 feet and incorporates dry lake beds, sandstone canyons, granite mountains, palm groves fed by year-round springs, and more than 600 kinds of desert plants. After the spring rains, thousands of wildflowers burst into bloom, transforming the desert into a brilliant palette of pink, lavender, red, orange, and yellow. The rare bighorn sheep can often be spotted navigating rocky hillsides, and an occasional migratory bird stops off on the way to the Salton Sea. When planning a trip here, keep in mind that temperatures rise to as high as 115° in summer.

JUST THE FACTS

The **Anza-Borrego Desert State Park Visitor Center** lies just west of the town of Borrego Springs. You can contact park headquarters at ☎ **760/767-4205;** the Visitor Center is open October through May daily from 9am to 5pm and June through September weekends from 10am to 5pm. For other local information, contact **the Borrego Springs Chamber of Commerce,** 622 Palm Canyon Dr., Borrego Springs, CA 92004 (☎ **760/767-5555;** www.borregosprings.com).

From mid-March to the beginning of April, the desert wildflowers and cacti are usually in bloom, a hands-down, all-out natural special event that's not to be missed. The **wildflower hot line** is ☎ **760/767-4684.**

EXPLORING THE DESERT

You can explore the desert's stark terrain on one of the hiking trails or on a self-guided driving tour; the Visitor Center can supply maps. The **Borrego Palm Canyon** self-guided hike (1½ miles each way), which starts at the campgrounds near the Visitor Center, is beautiful, easy to get to, and easy to do and leads in about half an hour to a waterfall and massive fan palms. You can also take one of the organized tours of the desert offered by **Desert Jeep Tours** (☎ **888/BY-JEEPS** or 619/528-2241; www.desertjeeptours.com; e-mail: paul@desertjeeptours.com). Led by Paul Ford ("Borrego Paul"), these tours go to the awesome viewpoint at Font's Point, where you can look out on the Badlands, so named by the early settlers because it was an impossible area for moving or grazing cattle. While enjoying the view, Paul tells his passengers about the history and geology of the area.

If you want to explore the desert on two wheels instead of four, call **Carrizo Bikes** at ☎ **760/767-3872.** For a thrilling 12-mile bicycle ride down Montezuma Valley Grade, try the Desert Descent offered by **Gravity Activated Sports,** P.O. Box 683, Pauma Valley, CA 92061 (☎ **800/985-4427** or 760/742-2294; fax 760/742-2293; www.gasports.com).

WHERE TO STAY

The park has two developed campgrounds. **Borrego Palm Canyon,** with 117 sites, is 2½ miles west of Borrego Springs and near the Visitor Center. Full hookups are

Safety Tip

Remember when you're touring in this area, hydration is of paramount importance. Whether you're walking, cycling, or driving, always have a bottle of water at your side.

---

available, and there's an easy hiking trail. **Tamarisk Grove,** at Highway 78 and county road S3, has 27 sites. Both have rest rooms with showers and a campfire program; reservations are a good idea. The park allows open camping along all of the trail routes. For more information check with the Visitor Center (☎ 760/767-4205).

La Casa del Zorro Desert Resort. 3845 Yaqui Pass Rd., Borrego Springs, CA 92004. ☎ **800/824-1884** or 760/767-5323. Fax 760/767-5963. www.lacasadelzorro.com. 77 units. A/C TV TEL. Winter $115 double; from $235 suite or casita. Lower rates midweek and off-season. Extra person $10. Special packages available. AE, CB, DC, DISC, MC, V.

This pocket of heaven on earth was built back in 1937, and the tamarind trees that were planted back then have grown up around it. Accommodations are scattered around La Casa's lushly landscaped grounds; guests can choose from standard hotel rooms, suites, or one-, two-, or three-bedroom adobe casitas with tile roofs. All the casitas have a minifridge and microwave, some have a fireplace or pool, and each bedroom has a separate bathroom. Facilities include two dining rooms, three swimming pools, tennis courts, bicycle rentals, massage, child care, and plenty of recreational choices. If you come to this desert oasis during the week, you'll benefit from lowered room rates.

WHERE TO DINE

The Coffee & Book Store. 590 Palm Canyon Dr. (in the Center shopping mall). ☎ **760/767-5080.** Most items under $6. MC, V. Daily 6am–4pm. LIGHT FARE.

Rely upon this small but well-stocked shop for books, postcards, maps, and a freshly ground espresso or cup o' joe. It also has a nice selection of sandwiches, salads, muffins, and desserts, making it a reliable choice for a quick breakfast or lunch. You can also pack up a pretty good picnic if you're off to explore the desert.

Krazy Coyote Saloon & Grille. 2220 Hoberg Rd. (in the Palms at Indian Head). ☎ **760/767-7788.** Main courses $7–$12. AE, MC, V. Open daily; call for seasonal hours. ECLECTIC MENU.

The same stylish touch and perfectionism that pervades the attached bed-and-breakfast is evident in this casual restaurant overlooking the inn's swimming pool and the vast desert beyond. An eclectic menu brings together quesadillas, club sandwiches, burgers, grilled meats and fish, and individual gourmet pizzas; they also offer breakfast (rich and hearty for an active day, or light and healthy for diet-watchers).

Appendix: Useful Toll-Free Numbers & Web Sites

AIRLINES

Aeromexico
☎ 800/237-6639

Air Canada
☎ 800/776-3000
www.aircanada.ca

Alaska Airlines/Alaska Commuter
☎ 800/426-0333
www.alaskaair.com

American Airlines/ American Eagle
☎ 800/433-7300
☎ 800/543-1586 TDD
www.americanair.com

America West Airlines
☎ 800/235-9292
www.americawest.com

British Airways
☎ 800/247-9297
☎ 0345/222-111 in Britain
www.british-airways.com

Canadian Airlines
☎ 800/426-7000
www.cdnair.ca

Continental Airlines
☎ 800/525-0280
☎ 800/343-9195 TDD
www.flycontinental.com

Delta Air Lines
☎ 800/221-1212
☎ 800/831-4488 TDD
www.delta-air.com

Hawaiian Airlines
☎ 800/367-5320
www.hawaiianair.com

Kiwi International Air Lines
☎ 800/538-5494
www.jetkiwi.com

Midway Airlines
☎ 800/446-4392

Midwest Express
☎ 800/452-2022

Northwest Airlines/ Northwest Airlink
☎ 800/225-2525
www.nwa.com

Reno Air
☎ 800/RENO-AIR
www.renoair.com

Skywest Airlines
☎ 800/453-9417
www.skywest.com

Southwest Airlines
☎ 800/435-9792
www.iflyswa.com

Tower Air
☎ 800/34-TOWER outside New York
☎ 718/553-8500 in New York
www.towerair.com

Trans World Airlines (TWA)
☎ 800/221-2000
www.twa.com

United Airlines/United Express
☎ 800/241-6522
www.ual.com

USAirways/USAir Express
☎ 800/428-4322
www.usairways.com

Virgin Atlantic Airways
☎ 800/862-8621 in the continental U.S.
☎ 0293/747-747 in Britain
www.fly.virgin.com

CAR-RENTAL AGENCIES

Advantage
☎ 800/777-5500
www.arac.com

Alamo
☎ 800/327-9633
www.goalamo.com

Auto Europe
☎ 800/223-5555
www.autoeurope.com

Avis
☎ 800/331-1212 in the continental U.S.
☎ 800/TRY-AVIS in Canada
☎ 800/331-2323 TDD
www.avis.com

Budget
☎ 800/527-0700
☎ 800/826-5510 TDD
www.budgetrentacar.com

Dollar
☎ 800/800-4000
www.dollarcar.com

Enterprise
☎ 800/325-8007
www.pickenterprise.com

Hertz
☎ 800/654-3131
☎ 800/654-2280 TDD
www.hertz.com

Kemwel Holiday Auto (KHA)
☎ 800/678-0678
www.kemwel.com

National Car Rental
☎ 800/CAR-RENT
☎ 800/328-6323 TDD
www.nationalcar.com

Payless
☎ 800/PAYLESS
www.paylesscar.com

Rent-A-Wreck
☎ 800/535-1391
www.rent-a-wreck.com

Sears
☎ 800/527-0770

Thrifty
☎ 800/367-2277
☎ 800/358-5856 TDD
www.thrifty.com

Value
☎ 800/327-2501
www.go-value.com

MAJOR HOTEL & MOTEL CHAINS

Best Western International
☎ 800/528-1234
☎ 800/528-2222 TDD
www.bestwestern.com

Clarion Hotels
☎ 800/CLARION
☎ 800/228-3323 TDD
www.hotelchoice.com

Comfort Inns
☎ 800/228-5150
☎ 800/228-3323 TDD
www.hotelchoice.com

Courtyard by Marriott
☎ 800/321-2211
☎ 800/228-7014 TDD
www.courtyard.com

Days Inn
☎ 800/325-2525
☎ 800/325-3297 TDD
www.daysinn.com

Doubletree/Red Lion Hotels
☎ 800/222-TREE
☎ 800/528-9898 TDD
www.doubletreehotels.com

Econo Lodges
☎ 800/55-ECONO
☎ 800/228-3323 TDD
www.hotelchoice.com

Embassy Suites
☎ 800/EMBASSY
☎ 800/458-4708 TDD
www.embassy-suites.com

Fairfield Inns by Marriott
☎ 800/228-2800
☎ 800/228-7014 TDD
www.fairfieldinn.com

Hampton Inn
☎ 800/HAMPTON
☎ 800/451-HTDD TDD
www.hampton-inn.com

Hilton Hotels
☎ 800/HILTONS
☎ 800/368-1133 TDD
www.hilton.com

Holiday Inn
☎ 800/HOLIDAY
☎ 800/238-5544 TDD
www.holiday-inn.com

Howard Johnson
☎ 800/654-2000
☎ 800/654-8442 TDD
www.hojo.com

Hyatt Hotels & Resorts
☎ 800/228-9000
www.hyatt.com

ITT Sheraton
☎ 800/325-3535
☎ 800/325-1717 TDD
www.sheraton.com

La Quinta Motor Inns
☎ 800/531-5900
☎ 800/426-3101 TDD
www.laquinta.com

Marriott Hotels
☎ 800/228-9290
☎ 800/228-7014 TDD
www.marriott.com

Motel 6
☎ 800/4-MOTEL6 (800/466-8536)

Omni Hotels
☎ 800/843-6664

Quality Inns
☎ 800/228-5151
☎ 800/228-3323 TDD
www.hotelchoice.com

Radisson Hotels
☎ 800/333-3333
www.radisson.com

Ramada Inns
☎ 800/2-RAMADA
☎ 800/228-3232 TDD
www.ramada.com

Red Carpet Inns
☎ 800/251-1962

Red Roof Inns
☎ 800/843-7663
☎ 800/843-9999 TDD
www.redroof.com

Residence Inn by Marriott
☎ 800/331-3131
☎ 800/228-7014 TDD
www.residenceinn.com

Rodeway Inns
☎ 800/228-2000
☎ 800/228-3323 TDD
www.hotelchoice.com

Super 8 Motels
☎ 800/800-8000
☎ 800/533-6634 TDD
www.super8motels.com

Travelodge
☎ 800/255-3050
www.travelodge.com

Vagabond Hotels
☎ 800/522-1555
www.vagabondinns.com

Wyndham Hotels & Resorts
☎ 800/822-4200 in the continental
  U.S. and Canada
www.wyndham.com

Index

Page numbers in italics refer to maps.

Present this coupon at any Knott's ticket booth and receive $5 off full-priced admission, or $3 off full-priced child admission (ages 3-11). Limit six discounts per coupon. Not valid for special-ticket events. Cannot be combined with any other offer or discount. Offer expires 3/31/2000.

Promo #1112

SAVE UP TO $12

at the

World Famous SAN DIEGO ZOO

Present this coupon at any ticket booth to SAVE $2 off the Deluxe Package, which includes a 35 minute double-deck bus tour, round trip Skyfari aerial tram ride, all animal shows & exhibits.

Gates open 9:00 A.M. daily. For more information and directions to the San Diego Zoo, call (619) 234-3153. Not valid with any other offer or membership. Prices subject to change. Good for up to six (6) persons per coupon.

FROMMER'S® NATIONAL PARK GUIDES

Family Vacations in the
National Parks
Grand Canyon

National Parks of the
American West
Yellowstone & Grand Teton

Yosemite & Sequoia/
Kings Canyon
Zion & Bryce Canyon

FROMMER'S® GREAT OUTDOOR GUIDES

New England
Northern California

Southern California & Baja
Pacific Northwest

FROMMER'S® MEMORABLE WALKS

Chicago
London

New York
Paris

San Francisco
Washington D.C.

FROMMER'S® IRREVERENT GUIDES

Amsterdam
Boston
Chicago

London
Manhattan

New Orleans
Paris

San Francisco
Walt Disney World
Washington, D.C.

FROMMER'S® BEST-LOVED DRIVING TOURS

America
Britain
California

Florida
France
Germany

Ireland
Italy
New England

Scotland
Spain
Western Europe

THE COMPLETE IDIOT'S TRAVEL GUIDES

Boston
Cruise Vacations
Planning Your Trip to Europe
Hawaii

Las Vegas
London
Mexico's Beach Resorts
New Orleans

New York City
San Francisco
Walt Disney World
Washington D.C.

THE UNOFFICIAL GUIDES®

Branson, Missouri
California with Kids
Chicago
Cruises
Disney Companion

Florida with Kids
The Great Smoky &
Blue Ridge
Mountains

Las Vegas
Miami & the Keys
Mini-Mickey
New Orleans

New York City
San Francisco
Skiing in the West
Walt Disney World
Washington, D.C.

SPECIAL-INTEREST TITLES

Born to Shop: Caribbean Ports of Call
Born to Shop: France
Born to Shop: Hong Kong
Born to Shop: Italy
Born to Shop: New York
Born to Shop: Paris
Frommer's Britain's Best Bike Rides
The Civil War Trust's Official Guide
to the Civil War Discovery Trail
Frommer's Caribbean Hideaways
Frommer's Europe's Greatest Driving Tours
Frommer's Food Lover's Companion to France
Frommer's Food Lover's Companion to Italy
Frommer's Gay & Lesbian Europe

Israel Past & Present
Monks' Guide to California
Monks' Guide to New York City
New York City with Kids
New York Times Weekends
Outside Magazine's Guide
to Family Vacations
Places Rated Almanac
Retirement Places Rated
Washington, D.C., with Kids
Wonderful Weekends from Boston
Wonderful Weekends from New York City
Wonderful Weekends from San Francisco
Wonderful Weekends from Los Angeles

www.frommers.com

Arthur Frommer's   OUTSPOKEN ENCYCLOPEDIA OF TRAVEL

You've Read our Books, Now Visit our Website...

With more than 6,000 pages of the most up-to-date travel bargains and information from the name you trust the most, Arthur Frommer's Outspoken Encyclopedia of Travel brings you all the information you need to plan your next trip.

Register to Win free tickets, accommodations and more!

Arthur Frommer's Daily Newsletter

Bookmark the daily newsletter to read about the hottest travel news and bargains in the industry or subscribe and receive it daily on your own desktop.

Hot Spot of the Month

Check out the Hot Spot each month to get the best information and hottest deals for your favorite vacation destinations.

200 Foreign & Domestic Destinations

Choose from more than 200 destinations and get the latest information on accommodations, airfare, restaurants, and more.

Frommer's Travel Guides

Shop our online bookstore and choose from more than 200 current Frommer's travel guides. Secure transactions guaranteed!

Bookmark www.frommers.com for the most up-to-date travel bargains and information—updated daily!

Finally,

Vacations for <u>Real</u> People.

You've read the guides, now check out the magazine...
Arthur Frommer's **BUDGET TRAVEL** magazine is your top source for hardhitting, practical info you can really use to plan your next affordable getaway. Each issue is crammed with hot tips, cool prices, and useful facts. After reading your very first issue, you'll undoubtedly save many times the cost of the subscription on your next vacation.
